SCIENCE MUSEUM / NATIONAL RAILWAY MUSEUM

A BIBLIOGRAPHY OF BRITISH RAILWAY HISTORY

SUPPLEMENT: 7951 – 12956

Books, parts of books, pamphlets and academic theses on the history and description of public rail transport in the British Isles published up to the end of 1980, with an Addenda to the entries in the original work of 1966 (reprinted with corrections, 1983)

COMPILED BY

GEORGE OTTLEY

FOREWORD BY PROFESSOR JACK SIMMONS

LONDON: HER MAJESTY'S STATIONERY OFFICE

330777

Printed in the United Kingdom for Her Majesty's Stationery Office
Dd 236258 C20 10/88

To Mandy and Merry
with love

CONTENTS

FOREWORD

We owe an immense debt to the compilers of good works of reference. They are a small band in every generation: private, self-devoted, endlessly tenacious. As a rule they are not much rewarded, except in the gratitude of those who constantly turn to their works—and that gratitude is apt to remain silent. But anyone who wishes to understand his own world or to look at its past, anyone who writes, must value the works of reference, at home or in his public library, very highly: the great dictionaries of languages and biography, and the bibliographies that survey and analyse, record and recall the literature of the subjects that interest him.

Especially perhaps the pioneers, those who were the first to compile such works in the fields they had chosen. George Ottley is one of them. His original work, published in 1966, established itself immediately as the first comprehensive bibliography of British railway history. "Ottley 7712" soon became a familiar note to an entry in booksellers' catalogues. (The variant "Not in Ottley" was also to be found, but seldom. The discoverer of such a rarity was well entitled to plume himself on spotting it.) For most bibliographers this achievement would have been gratifying, and final. But it was not final for this one. He never laid down his pen, continuing quietly and steadily to note particulars of fresh works published, year by year, after his book had gone to press and, where necessary, to correct printers' errors and other mistakes, in the hope of being able to record them later in a supplement.

That hope was a brave one, very far from certainty. The original book went out of print in 1974. Second-hand copies soon became sought after. There was then a clear and steady demand for a reprint, and for a continuation of the work. However financed, both these things would be costly, and it was a slow business to find the means of funding the project. It was managed however by the Science Museum and Her Majesty's Stationery Office, and managed in full. In 1983 a reprint of the first book appeared, with some corrections. Now we have the long-desired second, which records additions to the original volume and then lists and describes another 5000 works, issued down to the end of the year 1980.

Some bibliographies are records, no more. Their compilers hold their cards close to their chests, revealing nothing at all of themselves. One wonders what impulses took them to the subjects they chose. George Ottley is not one of them. He gave his attention to railways because he had always liked them, and he makes that quite clear. His affection shines through the book. It appears plainly in his introduction, which includes a useful survey of the changes in the writing of railway history and its publication since the first volume was compiled; in the notes, terse and informative, that he often appends to his entries, telling the student what he may expect to find in the work recorded, sometimes disguised under a misleading or fanciful title; and in the attention he pays to pseudonyms (see for example 6678 in the first book, and 10440 in this one). The organisation of the work itself provides an anatomy of much of the history of British railways, and access is given to it by a laborious and well-considered index.

Twenty years ago I was honoured by being asked to introduce the original book. I am honoured no less by the invitation to introduce its successor and delighted to salute George Ottley, who has helped many students of the history of railways, and of transport in general, not only in Britain but across the world.

23 July 1986   JACK SIMMONS

COMPILER'S INTRODUCTION

Summary

1. The subject range of the constituent material

2. The assimilation of railways into transport development generally since 1900

3. Diversification in railway literature since the 1950s, a: The literature of Enthusiasm; the effects of the rise of the railway preservation movement upon the proportional representation of railway subjects; the ascendency of illustrations over text in popular railway books

4. Diversification in railway literature since the 1950s, b: The literature of Railway History

5. The main work as a Second Edition, and its Supplement

6. Bibliographical detail supplied to entries in the Supplement broadened in order to identify more readily the wide diversity of content, depth and treatment to be found in modern railway literature, particularly with regard to the use of illustrations

7. The Proceedings of the Great Western Railway (London) Lecture and Debating Society and its successor under British Railways, and rail tour itineraries

8. Modern developments in documentation and in library expertise generally

9. The quest for completeness; the British National Bibliography and the problem of copyright deposit evasion by individuals and amateur groups as publishers

10. Notes on changes in the Classification Scheme, and on the style of bibliographical description used, both in the main work and its Supplement

1. The subject range of the constituent material

The range of material described in the Supplement corresponds to that of the main volume, published in 1966: books, parts of books, pamphlets, theses, and relevant papers from the *Journal of Transport History*[1]. No fundamental departure from structure and style has been required—both the Classification Scheme and the way items are described are essentially unchanged. Some alteration here and there in the Classification Scheme has been called for, however: two thirds of the entries are for works published since 1963, the cut-off date for the main volume, and the Bibliography has had to take on the shape prescribed for it by modern railway books by providing adequate accommodation for subjects which have come to the fore since then—principally locomotives, and locomotive and railway preservation—without disturbing its established structure. The circumstance can be likened to that of a school which without departing from its established pattern of teaching must adapt itself to the educational needs of a changing world by introducing more specialization into its curriculum and adding new facilities—a computer centre, perhaps, or a wild-life garden. The Bibliography has been able to embrace its required modifications quite easily by introducing more subdivision where this was called for[2]. Its overall subject coverage is, however, unchanged: the history and description of all forms of rail transport in the British Isles from their introduction[3] down to the present, including all aspects of the Railway's economic and social environment.

2. The assimilation of railways into transport development generally since 1900

A problem which had only begun to make itself known when compiling the main volume in the 1950s has become a matter to be dealt with quite frequently in the Supplement. It is not, in essence, a bibliographical problem, but rather an inherent characteristic of railway development itself, of little concern until the latter half of the nineteenth century, but one which today dominates the whole transport scene and commands the very future of railways as a viable means of transport—that of changing inter-modal relationships. In *The Railway in England and Wales*, by Jack Simmons, (vol 1, Leicester University Press, 1978), the author, discussing the growth of urban railway transport networks during the period 1876–1914, describes, on page 102, the mounting competition which railways had to face from buses and trams as 'not negligible even when they were horse-drawn, serious when they went over to steam or cable traction, formidable when they turned to electricity'. When peace-time conditions returned in 1919, bus and tram services resumed their already well-established hold, but road/rail rivalry was to increase dramatically during the 1920s as advances in motor technology and mass-production methods made private car ownership, road haulage, buses and 'charabancs', increasingly popular. Sixty years on, the process is still with us, with air travel an additional competitor to be faced by the railways. So, whenever serious studies into British railway development since 1900—and more especially since 1920—are ventured into, it will generally be found impossible, and unwise, even, to consider the subject in isolation; the researcher will not get far before finding himself caught up in a developing complex of inter-modal rivalry. Railway history of the twentieth century is, inherently, part of transport history, and the lesson for bibliographers is clear: for an adequate representation of sources for the study of British railway development since 1900, books on transport development must be taken into account whenever the railway element—which will not necessarily be always prominently featured—is clearly a significant one.

3. Diversification in railway literature since the 1950s, a: the literature of Enthusiasm; the effects of the rise of the railway preservation movement upon the proportional representation of railway subjects; the ascendency of illustrations over text in popular railway books

Since the 1960s the representation of the subjects has changed, both in the choosing of topics and in the way those topics have been portrayed. The middle-depth writings of C. J. Allen, Hamilton Ellis, O. S. Nock[4] and others from the late 1940s to the end of the 1970s—well-illustrated company or locomotive histories—no longer constitute the main body of railway history publishing. Several hundred had been produced during that period, but even then a generation was in being which had grown up after the 1923 amalgamation of 120 companies into the 'Big Four'—LMS, LNER, GWR (new company) and the Southern—and there were others whose early association with the railway scene was after 1948, the year in which what remained of colour and variety was virtually washed away by the nationalization of those four companies into British Railways.

The popular railway-book publisher had always relied upon his ability to recall to the reader/purchaser the railway scenes of his boyhood, and although increasing road/rail competition had called forth some notable and exciting developments in locomotive design and performance since 1920, and although there was electrification on the Southern, and important advances in architecture and design on London's expanding underground railway system, the period in general was one of increasing financial difficulty and outwardly, one of growing shabbiness. By 1960 it was becoming increasingly difficult to write for the average railway book reader in a satisfyingly interesting way about the railway scene of the recent past and by 1970 the first phase of what can be called the Railway Book Mania was on the wane.

The colourful past was not to fade away completely, however. When the commercially defunct Talyllyn Railway was re-opened by a group of enthusiasts in 1950, the event unleashed a latent desire to rescue and revive our steam-age past. The Festiniog was the next, in 1954, and in 1960, three more: the Welshpool & Llanfair, and the first standard-gauge lines to be revived: the Middleton Railway in Leeds, and in Sussex, a five-mile stretch of the old London Brighton & South Coast Railway—the 'Bluebell Line'. Today, the railway preservation movement is active in all areas of the British Isles, with over 500 societies and amateur groups occupied in the rescue, renovation and preservation of up to 1000 locomotives, an unknown quantity of rolling stock of every kind, and over 100 tramcars[5]. Most of these are at work on one or other of fifty re-opened lengths of line, while others are to be seen in numerous museums and disused locomotive depots or 'steam centres'. Above them all stands the crowning achievement of the National Railway Museum in York, where the whole course of railway development is so splendidly portrayed and described for all to see.

Evidently, this nation-wide determination to re-present and re-enact our railway past is here to stay[6], along with a body of equally fervent and well-ordered activity on behalf of all other modes of transport[7]. The preserved railway scene, piecemeal and somehow over-zealous though it may sometimes appear to be when visited on isolated stretches of line, has provided publishers of railway books with endless possibilities for capturing and portraying the process and its achievements, and railway bookshops are stocked to capacity with a seemingly never-ending supply of books, booklets, 'society publications', and commercially-motivated 'albums' depicting locomotives and trains of the latter years of the railway steam age and their successors, the diesels and electrics. One's first impression upon entering a railway bookshop is that nobody *reads* books today, for so much of what is on sale consists of albums of illustrations with captions and a brief introduction the only textual support. Furthermore, there is, all too often, no evidence that a balanced presentation of a subject has been attempted. 'Put in what you have managed to find and just leave out the rest' seems to be the general rule.

4. Diversification in railway literature since the 1950s, b: The literature of Railway History

The situation confronting all who look for railway history in books is all too apparent. The subject, in recent years, has been practically overwhelmed by the demand for, and the supply of, illustrations of locomotives of the recent past and the preserved present, and of railway scenes of that part of our railway past which is still within recall. Railway history has indeed been largely displaced by this shop-windowing of its surviving artefacts, with the term 'Our Railway Heritage' freely used to describe them.

But our actual railway heritage is of a different order, and is only to be discovered in the fulness of all its aspects, woven into the weft and warp of social and economic development. It cannot be adequately presented by illustrations, however glossy, of its functional and aesthetic features.

Within the railway bookshop's great array of popular publications, however, a work of more substance is occasionally to be found—one designed to be *read*, and further browsing will reveal that among railway books of today there runs, even yet, an upper stratum of well-formulated studies based upon the authors' own research, with a bibliography which is more than a list of works consulted, an uninhibited provision of notes, tables, a chronology, a list of Acts, perhaps, and more maps than the publisher had said 'would do'[8]. But new work at this level, costly to produce and costly to buy, can be held back from publication because the publisher feels, understandably, that he may not be able to break even, let alone make a profit. If fully-worked-out writing of serious intent continues to be debarred from commercial publishing unless the author is willing to allow his work to be crippled by cost-saving deletions, a cottage industry may then spring up, with finished work, unabbreviated by the dictates of accountants, being run off to order on hired photocopiers, including the copy required to be deposited by law with the British Library. If that should come about, and if there is ever a second supplement to this present work, bibliographical descriptions of these uncompromised works will, let us hope, more than redress the imbalance of the 'glossies' which characterise certain areas of this present Supplement.

Contrariety of presentation has been a feature of railway book publishing at least since the 1920s, but in those days popular reading on this subject—and on many other subjects (natural history for instance)—had been directed mainly towards boys and girls. It was not until the late 1940s that, for reasons already discussed, a steady stream of popularised railway history began to appear, and ten years later the Railway Book Mania was in full career. It was Michael Robbins who first placed on record the question then beginning to be asked by historians, 'What kind of railway history do we want?', in a paper under that title in the *Journal of Transport History*, in 1957, later revised and enlarged to become chapter 2 of his *Points and Signals: a railway historian at work* (Ottley 7890 and 12917 respectively).

Michael Robbins's theme—'Let us get railway history writing into true perspective'—was taken up again twelve years later by J. R. Kellett. Reviewing the situation at the end of the 1960s he says 'It is not surprising that a great deal of the so-called railway history written in recent years has a restricted readership and is often rejected by economic and social historians . . .', and 'The imbalance and inadequacy of existing published treatment is obvious, and will be rectified only when the extraordinary spell which has been cast over the subject is broken, and contributions are made to railway history by writers whose main interests extend beyond railways themselves, and to whom the sights and sounds of the steam locomotive are not so overwhelmingly personal a memory' ('Writing on Victorian Railways: an essay in nostalgia', *Victorian Studies*, 1969, (Ottley 12920).

Three years later, J. H. Cleary, commenting upon Kellett's words, and incidentally those of Robbins, adds further emphasis to the nature of the quandary in an essay entitled 'Criticism and the writing of railway history: the significance of a review by Dr J. R. Kellett' in the Oxford University

Railway Society's *Commemorative Journal, 1931–72* (1972), pp. 4–5, when he says '. . . There would seem to be a tragic situation today, where instead of there being an acknowledged place for writing aimed simply at the railway enthusiast, and a clear distinction between it and that writing which is the result of serious and disciplined research, there is in fact a vast body of work which lies *between* these two classes—writing on railway history which is too important to be ignored, in that the railways are of great significance in nineteenth century history and yet which is not researched in such a way as to make it valuable in the study of history. For this kind of work to become of general significance there must be a shift of emphasis towards placing the railway in its widest context—social, political and economic . . . Such an approach is vital to any real understanding of the railway's importance in nineteenth century Britain and, more immediately, of the problems facing the railways now and over the past two decades'.[9]

5. The main work as a Second Edition, and its Supplement

The Second Edition of the main work was published in 1983 as a photo-litho reprint with about 200 minor typographical corrections incorporated into its text. Additions and corrections requiring more space—for the describing, for instance, of a subsequent (i.e., post-1963) edition of a work, or to provide an explanatory note, are carried forward to become Part One of the present volume. These are coupled to the entries to which they refer by means of an asterisk (*) being placed alongside relevant entries in the 1983 Reprint. This always means 'See the Supplement'.

A second list of additions and corrections, too late to be marked with asterisks in the Reprint, precedes the main listing.

The Supplement proper, which constitutes the major part of the present volume, consists of a classified presentation of an additional 5000 works (7951–12956). Two-thirds of the entries are for books and pamphlets published after 1963 (the cut-off date for the original volume) and before January 1981. The remaining one-third is for works of an earlier date discovered since the first Bibliography was compiled, and of this one-third, one-sixth (about 300) are for works published before 1901.

It has already been noted that the Supplement contains a larger percentage of books on locomotives and on preservation than did the original work. In terms of that compilation its Supplement is, therefore, disproportionate. This is unavoidable. The shape of the present work has not been determined by the compiler, but by changes in the way the subject has been presented in the books themselves, two-thirds of which are post-1963 publications. Consequently, some Classes are seemingly over-subscribed while others are disappointingly thin. It is only by consulting both volumes that something approaching a complete and proportionate documentation may be obtained of the available book sources for any aspect of the development of rail transport in the British Isles.

6. Bibliographical detail supplied to entries in the Supplement broadened in order to identify more readily the wide diversity of content, depth and treatment to be found in modern railway literature, particularly with regard to the use of illustrations

Although the Supplement, as a continuation, has been happy to follow the lines laid down for the original volume, it has had to adapt itself to a different terrain. In the introduction to the main work the structure and style of the Bibliography was discussed at some length (pp.11–18, 19 of the Second Edition) and it is necessary now only to explain what steps have been taken to reflect bibliographically, changes in the nature and content of railway literature over the past twenty years or so, and to explain how the Classification Scheme has been adapted to accommodate those changes.

After 500 years of book printing it has fallen to the popular railway book to reverse the traditional relationship between text and illustration. Whereas illustrations had always been brought in to throw light upon the text, now, a book with a title such as *The Locomotives of the Schools Class of the Southern Railway* might, on examination, be found to be an informative treatise on that excellent breed, but it is more likely that it would turn out to be an album of illustrations with no text at all apart from accompanying captions and a brief Introduction. The general increase in the proportion of illustrations carried by railway books of today calls for greater precision in the describing of them bibliographically. No longer will it suffice to say 'with illus'; one needs to know how many, on plates and in the text, and of those on plates, how many are coloured. It is important also to ensure that depth of treatment can be recognised when describing highly illustrated railway books, for this class of publication has its own upper stratum of high-quality productions, notably those of the Oxford Publishing Company, and more recently, of Wild Swan Publications, under the editorship of Paul Karau, invariably in large octavo or Quarto format and consisting of original photographs on a clearly defined subject, well supported by annotations and often with generous supporting text and tabular data—potentially valuable visual records of railway development 'on the ground'. As books of illustrations have now become so common a feature of railway literature they can no longer be regarded as a special class of material, and for this reason **Q4** is not used in this Supplement. (It can be brought in again, of course, if in the event of a second supplement being compiled it is found that the terrain has changed back again.) Books of illustrations are now classified normally, according to the subject of the illustrations, and will be found mostly, but not exclusively, within the range of classes for Mechanical Engineering, E6–E15, where, individually, their pictorial content is described.

7. The Proceedings of the Great Western Railway (London) Lecture and Debating Society and its successor under British Railways, and rail tour itineraries

Two sources of historical value which had only occasional representation in the main volume are introduced into the Supplement in quantity, if not in full measure: the *Proceedings of the Great Western Railway (London) Lecture and Debating Society* and its successor, *British Railways (Western Region) London Lecture and Debating Society*, and a number of rail tour itineraries.

The Great Western Railway set up its lecture and debating society in 1905, as a forum for its staff. Speakers were from within the Company and from the world outside—industrialists, economists, politicians, specialists, and other non-railway persons, including some well-known public figures. Mostly, the topics lectured upon and discussed were related to railway administration and operation. The papers reveal much of interest on practical aspects, thus supplementing the more formal and theoretical approach of textbooks. Of quite unique value are the discussions which follow the lectures, usually reported verbatim, for within them lies a great scattering of detail, not to be found in any other sources, about the handling of problems and circumstances at first hand, in an often spirited exchange of opinions, comments, anecdotes, explanations, agreement and disagreement, between Great Western railwaymen. The series—and there are over 500 papers in all, from 1905 to 1970—could be regarded as a 65-year-long oral history record of the GWR. But allowance must be made for opportunism on the part of some who stood up to say their piece in these discussions, for the Society, from the outset, had the support of the Board, its president was always the General Manager, and directors and senior officers were regular attenders. Indeed, it is known that 'more than one young man has attracted attention to his abilities by displaying shrewd sense and capable exposition in debate' at the fortnightly meetings[10].

There were other lecture and debating societies, run by the GWR in Bristol and in Cardiff, and by other railway companies, but this one, in London, with its successor under British Railways was by far the most well-established and well-supported, with an estimated membership of 3000 in 1935. It was also the only one to have printed its proceedings from the start, distributing copies to all members.

The papers contribute significantly to some Classes, accounting for no less than two-thirds of the entries in **F, G, G1,** and **G2**. Sets are to be found in Leicester University Library's Transport History Collection, in the Clinker Collection in Brunel University Library, and in the British Library of Political and Economic Science (London School of Economics and Political Science).

The other class of publication introduced in quantity into this Supplement is the rail tour itinerary; but whereas the *Lecture & Debating Society Proceedings* were members of one series, and therefore easy to locate in libraries[11], itineraries of rail tours are individual monographs produced by a number of amateur societies and in consequence are not brought together under a common title. Each one relates to a single occasion—a pre-arranged train journey after which it would expect to be thrown away, as out-of-date timetables are, or at best, stuffed away into a cupboard to be, perhaps, forgotten. What is not generally recognised is that like the albums of illustrations discussed in section 6, above, ephemera is also possessed of its own aristocracy—in our subject, timetables, railway company prospectuses and rail tour itineraries. All three, if saved instead of being discarded are thereby elevated from their erstwhile transient status to one of lasting usefulness. They will have become documents, offering information not available from any other source. Scholars working in transport history know this, but librarians, as a rule, do not. They have not yet come to regard such items as source material and rail tour itineraries are therefore not commonly to be found in libraries[12]. All those described in this Supplement, are, however, in Leicester University Library's Transport History Collection (LU(THC)), and it is to be hoped that others will be added as and when they become available[13].

Each tour has a name, and for convenient reference it is required to be short—the 'Southern Rambler' or the 'South Yorkshire Rail Tour', but for the describing of itineraries for the Bibliography it has been thought desirable to provide each entry with a summary outline of the actual route taken. As these items are hard to come by it was decided that a concise delineation of the route taken would help to avoid the frustration of repeatedly not finding what was wanted, for in order to make each trip historically interesting, the routeings, especially those around London, sometimes were made to take on the complexity of a tangled skein of wool. As running commentaries, the depth of detail varies, of course, but there is usually a route map and a timetable. At its best, when the writer's historical perception is keen, and when enough space is available, rail tour itineraries can be valuable aids to the understanding of local railway development 'on the ground'.

8. Modern developments in documentation and in library expertise generally

The compiling of the Supplement has been much helped by three modern developments: 1, Leicester University's Transport History Collection, founded in 1953 by a gift of 250 books from Professor Jack Simmons, and now a collection of national importance well over one hundred times its original size[14]. As its Librarian from 1967 to 1982, the compiler was able to make full use of the THC as a centre of activity for the Supplement; 2, Progress with the compiling has benefited from advances made over the past twenty years or so in information-retrieval techniques in libraries, particularly in regard to Inter-Library Loan. As most wanted publications can now be obtained by applying to virtually any library, the location symbols which in the first volume were appended to entries have in this Supplement generally been omitted; 3, Works of depth and detail are better-endowed with bibliographies, notes, tables, and other accessories than was customary twenty years ago. Undoubtedly this is accountable, in the main, to improving standards generally, but may there not also be, in the preparing of transport history studies for publication, a sharpened awareness of the need to establish clearly, the level of presentation?

9. The quest for completeness; the British National Bibliography and the problem of copyright deposit evasion by individuals and amateur groups as publishers

Finally, there is the question of completeness to consider. Is this Bibliography—the main work and its Supplement—a documentation[15] of *all* books and pamphlets relating to the development of rail transport in the British Isles?

The short answer to this question is—it has tried to be that. The overall aim has been to provide a complete documentation of the subject in the form of detailed descriptions presented in a classified order with a full index, but this was found to be an objective impossible to achieve. Under Section 15 of the Copyright Act of 1911 (modified by the 1932 Act) the publisher of every book[16] is required to deliver a copy to the Copyright Receipt Office of the British Library, 2 Sheraton Street, London, W1V 4BH, within one month of its publication. It is evident however, that many publications issued by groups of enthusiasts and preservationists are not sent in, either because of ignorance of this legal obligation, or of wilful non-compliance, or simply because modesty has dissuaded the author/publisher from doing so. A work which is not deposited is not likely to become known, and may quite easily escape into oblivion, unless some errant bibliographer or devoted researcher should chance upon a copy sometime, somewhere. It will have by-passed the British National Bibliography ('BNB').

BNB is issued weekly, then monthly, and in progressively larger cumulations, and is circulated to virtually all libraries in the British Isles apart from small branches, and to a great many abroad. It does not claim to be a complete record of British publishing since 1950, its first year of publication, but it is, nevertheless, a primary source of reference. Its coverage is clearly stated on the title page of all issues:

'A Subject Catalogue of new British books received by the Copyright Receipt Office of the British Library, arranged according to the Dewey

Decimal Classification and catalogued according to the Anglo–American Cataloguing Rules, with a full author & title index and a subject index.'

Immense practical problems would be created if the British Library were to attempt to make certain that the letter of the law was to be observed to the extent of ensuring that a copy of every publication liable for deposit must be tracked down and secured. Should every parish magazine be sought out, for example, and regularity of supply insisted upon, involving the sending out of hundreds of reminders every month? Clearly, this would not be practicable.

When all reasonable non-compliance is allowed for, however, the fact remains that BNB is no more than a record of received copyright deposit material, and that a systematic discovery of delinquencies is not, apparently, possible.

Evasion of the obligation to deposit is not only an offence in law; it is, for a publisher, sheer folly. BNB assures world-wide publicity to every work described in its pages, at no cost to the publisher other than that of the supplied copy and its delivery to the British Library. A work not in BNB is a work committed to oblivion by its publisher and a work not in our national library—the British Library—is one that has not taken its rightful place. Until it does so it must remain, virtually, a 'missing book'.

Copyright deposit evasion is more common in subjects which have a lively amateur following, producing printed matter as a regular activity. Transport enthusiasts are one such group, but non-deposit is also very common in Local History, and the 'recent books' section of the periodical *The Local Historian* provides ample evidence of this.

Surely there can be nothing more desirable in the world of learning than that a national library and its national bibliography should try to be definitive[17].

10. Notes on changes in the Classification Scheme, and on the style of bibliographical description used, both in the main work and its Supplement

Entries within each Class are arranged chronologically by date of publication, then alphabetically by author, except for **O**, Railways in Literature, where they are arranged alphabetically by author within each subdivision of literary form.

Works of reference precede other works. Historical (i.e., retrospective) works precede contemporaneous works (i.e., publications on contemporary events or developments).

The Classification Scheme has been adapted by some libraries to provide an arrangement of actual books on their shelves and for this reason some Classes with only a few entries which might arguably have been allocated to contiguous areas have been left in where they belong. Several subdivisions of Classes have only one or two entries and one has no entry at all! A supplement to a classification scheme should ensure that whatever changes are introduced, the coverage of the scheme must not be weakened in the process (but see the note about **Q4** below).

Adjustments made to the Classification Scheme for the Supplement, mostly to accommodate changes in the pattern of subject representation of railway history over the past twenty years .

Location symbols are generally abandoned (See section 8 of this Introduction)

B   The optional grouping of contiguous periods in **B1–B10** allows historical works to be placed more accurately

B 10   Subdivision is introduced to separate the large number of modern books on locomotives and rolling stock from other **B10** subjects

C   Rearranged to conform to the Standard Regions of England and Wales, with finer subdivisions for Greater London. The order is from South to North working successively from West to East, except for **C1c** South East Region, which allows Greater London to precede Hampshire. Local railways not incorporated into British Railways are classed here

C1–C2   C1 and C2 are bridged by **C1–C2**, for England to Scotland routes

C 5   Now includes the Southern Railway and British Railways (Southern Region) on the Isle of Wight

E   Now includes Industrial Archaeology

E8   Now subdivided to present four distinctive approaches found in modern books on locomotives: general, construction, running and maintenance, and preservation

E9–10   For collective works on electric and diesel traction

F & G   are redefined: **F** for Administration, with Management its executive function; **G** for Operation, with Railway Air Services, now at **G6**, displacing Public Relations & Publicity, now **G9**

H   Now 'Railway Life and Labour'

K 6   Now 'Parliament, Government and the Railways'

L   For the main-stream development of the railway system of Britain: the network of 120 companies (the 'old companies' or 'pre-Grouping companies') which were amalgamated to form the LMS, LNER, GWR (new company) and the Southern Railway in 1923 (see main work, pp. 472–3), and their subsequent history as the 'Big Four' up to their nationalization in 1948 when, together with fifty-five smaller companies not included in the 1923 Grouping, 'British Railways' was formed (see main work, p. 474)

O   Subdivided by form of literary expression

Q 1   Includes general works on restoration and preservation

Q 4   No longer useful, profuse illustrating having become so common a feature of railway book production (see p. 13)

R   Includes works on railway historians, railway-book authors and publishers; also dictionaries and glossaries previously classed in **T**, and guides to sources of railway history

S   Includes actual statistics (general)

T   For atlases and gazetteers only

In describing the works which comprise the Bibliography (both main volume and Supplement), a 'humanised' collation[18] and note are used. The work is intended to be a practical guide to sources and the aim has been to make each one come to life in the mind's eye of the user. A formalised collation can sometimes confuse and obstruct, I believe, and in order to be helpful to the generality of consultants it is important to avoid over-abbreviation and to try instead to convey the make-up of a book's content in a manner which is at once intelligible. To do this, a free-flowing, expansive, style is used, in which the accepted principles of bibliographical description are followed, but not allowed to hide, the individuality of books.

Three other features of the Supplement should be noted:

In recent years some publishers have re-issued a single edition of a work which originally appeared serially—a timetable, for example. These are regarded as 'separates' and are included.

In giving the number of sources in a book's bibliography, it is impossible to provide the exact figure when authors refer to lesser sources in a general way: '. . . and various issues of the Railway Magazine'. In such cases a way round the difficulty has been sought by describing the number of sources as, for example, '100+ sources'.

The use of capitals in the transcribing of book titles is explained on p. 16 (Second edition) of the main work, with a note on p. 18.

Fairlight, East Sussex   G.O.
February 1987

NOTES

(1) Academic theses are the property of the university which accepted them for a degree. Brief details only are given, for in order to publish full descriptions in this Bibliography it would have been necessary to obtain permission in every case from the university and from the author. This was seen to be impracticable, but all those represented in this Supplement have been seen by the compiler.

At the time of compiling the original work (1953–1965), the *Journal of Transport History* (University of Leicester) was the only academic journal exclusively devoted to that subject. Although the Bibliography is for monographs, papers from the *JTH* relating to British railway history were included exceptionally. For consistency this practice is continued in the Supplement.

(2) A summary of adjustments to the Classification Scheme is appended to this Introduction.

(3) In the 1560s. See *Early Wooden Railways*, by M. J. T. Lewis (Routledge & Kegan Paul, 1970), pp. 15–17.

(4) O. S. Nock has written over 120 books and at least 500 periodical articles on railways. See his *Line Clear Ahead: 75 years of ups and downs* (Patrick Stephens, 1982), pp. 212–15, 'A Bibliography of Works by O. S. Nock'. This lists 111, but several books by this author have been published since.

(5) See *Steam '82: the complete enthusiasts' handbook to railway preservation activities and minor railways in the British Isles*, edited by Roger Crombleholme and Terry Kirtland (Allen & Unwin, 1982). This work provides, under one cover, all essential information about 512 centres of railway and tramway preservation and operation. Each entry has as much detail as could be obtained, including stock listings.

In view of the present difficulty in locating guides and stocklists of individual preservation societies (see Section 9 of this Introduction), the usefulness of this annual publication is beyond doubt.

A more selective work of the same kind, with abbreviated information, is *Railways Restored: guide to preserved railways* (Ian Allan, 1982), an annual publication produced with the co-operation of the Association of Railway Preservation Societies. The 1982 edition describes 87 major preserved railways, railway museums, and preservation centres in the British Isles. The information is set out in tabular form, with complete stock listings and timetables.

(6) The furtherance of railway preservation and the maintenance of standards, including safety standards, are the aims of the Association of Railway Preservation Societies, founded in 1959. Advice and information is communicated to over 500 individual and 120 organisational members by means of its *Newsletter* and *Yearbook*.

(7) The Transport Trust is actively concerned with the rescue, restoration and preservation of transport relics of all kinds, including water and air transport, and is not solely concerned with locomotion as such. Its library is now incorporated into that of Brunel University. Membership: 1,160 individuals and 300 corporate bodies. Special travel facilities on member railway lines are conferred upon T T members, and its quarterly journal *Yesteryear Transport* is circulated to them via Ian Allan Ltd.

(8) *The Golden Valley Railway: railway enterprise on the Welsh Border in late Victorian times*, by C. L. Mowat (University of Wales Press, 1964) is described by Professor Jack Simmons as 'probably the most perfect history of a British railway company yet written' in his *The Railway in England and Wales* (Leicester University Press, 1978), p. 110, note 38.

(9) A guide to sources, research method and presentation, written to encourage young readers (ages 11–18) who want to know more about railway history is *A History of the Railway*, by John Ray (Heinemann Educational, 1969) (Ottley 12921).

(10) *Great Western Progress, 1835–1935* (GWR, 1935, repr., David & Charles, 1972), pp. 176–7.

(11) It has never been practicable to produce and publish a union catalogue of all books in all libraries in the British Isles. The British Library is the main depository library for the nation's books. Under the law of Copyright, publishers must deliver to it a copy of every book, pamphlet, periodical part and newspaper, within one month of publication.

The BL's *General Catalogue of Printed Books* and its supplements are published, and will be found in many of the larger libraries throughout the country and abroad. More commonly available is the *British National Bibliography* ('*BNB*'), a serial publication describing books published in Britain from 1950 down to the present (but see note 17 below).

For locations of periodicals in British libraries, see the *British Union Catalogue of Periodicals* ('*BUCOP*'), also to be found in many reference libraries.

(12) For some known locations of collections of timetables and prospectuses see *Railway History: a guide to sixty-one collections in libraries and archives in Great Britain*, by George Ottley (Library Association, Reference, Special and Information Section, 1973) (Ottley 12926).

(13) The decision to include rail tour itineraries came too late in the process of compiling to allow for a prolonged search to be made for copies to describe. With hindsight, a direct approach to the various railway societies in the early stage of compiling would no doubt have provided the Bibliography with more, and the compiler regrets that it was not possible to make an eleventh hour effort of this kind. The ones included were purchased together from The Smokebox, railway-book shop, Kingston-on-Thames.

(14) Described in *Guide to the Transport History Collection in Leicester*

University Library, by George Ottley (Leicester University Library, 1981).
(15) Documentation: 'The art of collecting, classifying and making accessible the records of all kinds of intellectual activity' (*The Librarians' Glossary*, by L. M. Harrod, 4th edn, A. Deutsch, 1977).
(16) 'Book': an ambiguous term: widely, an independent bibliographical unit which is not a periodical and for which a main entry can be made in a library catalogue; and in its narrower sense, a non-periodical printed publication of at least forty-nine pages, exclusive of covers.

'Pamphlet': a non-periodical printed publication of at least five but not more than forty-eight pages, exclusive of the cover pages.

'Leaflet': a once-folded sheet printed to produce up to four pages of text. (These three definitions are also from *The Librarians' Glossary*).
(17) It would seem to be impracticable to devise some means of ensuring that everyone who publishes a book will automatically comply with this obligation, short of the setting up of some kind of 'check-out point' through which a book must pass before it is, in legal terms, published.

Meanwhile it might well be possible to detect, quite simply, many instances of non-compliance. A pre-paid postcard included with every copy of the British Library's widely circulated *British National Bibliography*, would enable librarians everywhere to supply details of the known existence of any published work which, after a three-month check in BNB, had apparently escaped documentation.
(18) Collation: 'That part of a description of a book, apart from the contents, which describes the book as a physical object by specifying the number of volumes, pages, columns, leaves, illustrations, photographs, maps, format, size, etc.' (*The Librarians' Glossary*, by L. M. Harrod, 4th edn, 1977).

ACKNOWLEDGEMENTS

This Supplement is a continuation of the original work of 1966 (reprinted as a Second Edition with corrections, HMSO 1983) and as such it has not had to resolve the problems of form, scope and style that confront the compiler of an entirely new work of reference. Nor has there had to be a repeat of the shelf-by-shelf search for railway history sources in the many libraries and private collections that provided material for the main volume. In consequence, it has not needed to be so dependent as was the parent work on a generality of co-operation by other librarians. But a supplement has its own problems, of correcting, gap-filling and extending, and the compiler invites users of the present work to join him in thanking those who have taken time and trouble to free the main work of errors and to help this, its successor, to get as near as was practicable to a complete coverage of the subject.

The Addenda and Corrigenda which comprise the first part of the work are largely attributable to the goodwill of three learned historians who, having noted mistakes and omissions in the course of their use of 'Ottley I' sent lists of their findings to the compiler: Michael Robbins, whose 'Reflections on Ottley' in the July 1967 issue of the *Journal of the Railway and Canal Historical Society* and his subsequent discoveries, established the need for corrections to be made and omissions to be incorporated, and for these to appear in published form whenever this were possible. For the pre-history of public railways within the text of the present work, Professor Michael J. T. Lewis, author of one of the railway history 'greats', *Early Wooden Railways* (1970), also by means of submitting lists, has brought to light in the following pages many remote references to our subject in early topographical works; some, no more than passing references by travellers, qualify for inclusion by reason of their early date. Thirdly, Professor Jack Simmons, author of many scholarly books and papers on railway history subjects, including the nascent *The Railway in England and Wales*, for his listings and for his friendly counsel at all times on matters arising from our shared interest in the literature of the subject.

In the Supplement proper which constitutes the main body of this volume, two factors have made the harvesting of wanted items a far more rewarding and satisfying task than was the compiling of the original bibliography (ca. 1953–1965). Since the 1950s writers of studious works have become increasingly aware of the need to provide good bibliographical support to their text; and secondly, as a happy corollary to this growing interdependence among scholars, the world of libraries has shown what can be achieved by means of planned co-operation; for over this same period, and especially since the setting up of the British Library's Lending Division at Boston Spa, Yorkshire, in 1973, and the absorption into it the following year of the National Central Library, the retrieving of requested books and periodicals via Inter-Library Loan has been made to become a well-organised, prompt and efficient service.

For these two developments all bibliographers and users of libraries will be grateful, but there is still one area of retrieval which awaits the introduction of an efficient means of control: the main problem in compiling a bibliography on railways or on any transport mode, on local history, or on any other subject with an active and enthusiastic following that includes publishing as one of its on-going activities is, where to find copies to describe of the publications issued by amateur societies. In our subject there are well over 500, each concerned with the restoration and preservation of railways, locomotives and tramcars. Some of their publications find their way into the bookshops of preservation societies, others are kept by members, but copies of this class of publication are not generally to be found where they are required to be by law—on the shelves of the British Library.

Three collectors of railway books who have allowed their interest to extend to the acquiring of 'society publications' have helped to overcome this difficulty: William J. Skillern, of Stockport, whose help with the original volume was generous and prolonged, is responsible for the inclusion in this present work of several locally-produced 19th century publications relating to railways and tramways in the Manchester area (9156 and 9162 being singularly important finds); Peter Johnson of Leicester provided copies from his collection from which no less than 300 entries in this Supplement have been made—an indication of the extent of recalcitrance among non-professional publishers today; David Garnett of Little Somerford, Wiltshire, who died recently, is the third. He made a special study of multi-edition works, including maps, relating to railways and it is due to his supplied detail (David was *by nature* a bibliographer!) that it has now been possible to provide several entries of this kind with more detail than would otherwise have been possible without prolonged searching; in particular, what would appear to be a near-complete record (one dares not assume that there are no gaps whatever!) of a forty-six year run of *Railway Facts and Figures* (Ottley 7953).

Railways in Literature (Class **O**) has benefited significantly from the work of two scholars: D. A. Peart, whose M.A. thesis, *Literature and the Railway in the Nineteenth and Twentieth Centuries* (1964) (Ottley 12592) has been used selectively as a source, with his kind permission, and Philip L. Scowcroft, whose series 'Railways in Detective Fiction' (*Journal of the Railway and Canal Historical Society*) (Ottley 12593) has also been used to select items for inclusion.

Work on the Supplement was carried out during the period of the compiler's semi-retirement (1977–1982) and was centred upon Leicester University Library's Transport History Collection. Whilst the venture was in no way an officially-supported one, support there always was, in the generous understanding by his library colleagues of the needs and the problems of compiling a large bibliography. No headway could have been made without that kind of help and the compiler is grateful to them for this kindness to him all the way through. Those of them with responsibilities for the administration of the Library and its departments during this five year period of compiling were: Douglas G. Walker (Librarian), Brian Burch (Deputy Librarian, now Librarian after Mr Walker's retirement in 1982), and the three Sub-Librarians, David L. Allen, Leszek M. Beldowski and Michael W. Grose. Colleagues who kindly helped with specific problems which arose in the course of the work were: Michael W. Grose (some awkward orthographic and bibliographic queries), Stephen Rawlinson (urgent postal enquiries relating to individual works in the Library's Transport History Collection), A. Rashid Siddiqui (some remote and inadequately-cited official publications of the inter-war years were quickly identified by Rashid), Sue Smith (useful preparatory work with BNB, The National Union Catalogue and other general sources, and the typing of several thousand index entries), J. David Welding (urgent queries by letter relating to books in the Transport History Collection—a task shared with Steve, above), and Christopher West, who checked the Welsh language entries, and who, with his staff of the library's Inter-Library Loans Department, through much painstaking effort over a long period, ever cheerfully given, procured the loan of many scarce books from other libraries.

W. H. Brock, Ph.D, Director, Victorian Studies Centre, University of Leicester, kindly provided details of some socio-historical bibliographical sources not known to the compiler.

Ian Paterson, of the Central Photographic Unit, University of Leicester, is responsible for the Frontispiece, taken in the Library one morning in the Summer vacation, 1983, with happy result.

Help is also thankfully acknowledged from the following persons: Philip S. Bagwell, Ph.D, railway historian (social and economic), for information on some lesser-known sources of trade union history

The late Teddy Boston (Rev. Edwin Boston) and his wife, Audrey, of Cadeby, Leicestershire, for the cheery hospitality which made visits to their home with its large collection of books, models and railway films, so enjoyable

Graham A. Boyes, professional railwayman (a BR manager), for sending details of works for inclusion in this Supplement

Roger Bristow, librarian, of East Sussex County Libraries, for his ready response to urgent bibliographical queries

C. R. Clinker, railway historian of Padstow, Cornwall (deceased), who sent lists of some scarce and unusual items to be considered for inclusion

C. P. Corney, Deputy Librarian, London School of Economics Library, for his kind words—a quite unexpected and heart-warming offering sent to me in 1966 and reproduced on page 544 of this Supplement

John Culley, librarian and railway-book seller of Leicester (Murrays Books), for valued information on current publications and on railway and steam locomotive matters, on many occasions

J. Diandas, chartered accountant, of Colombo, Sri Lanka, for sending a carefully-produced and annotated list of errata and desiderata—alas, too late to be incorporated into this present Supplement (some had already been done)

Victor A. Hatley, Campus Librarian, Nene College, Northampton, for help with Northamptonshire items

Shelagh R. Head, librarian, of Hertfordshire County Libraries, for a valued list of main volume lacunae

Ken Hoole, railway historian, of Scarborough, for details of works on railways of the North East

Norman Kerr, railway-book seller (antiquarian), of Cartmel, Cumbria, for details of forty items for inclusion in the Supplement

Harry Paar, railway historian, of Chigwell, Essex, for sending details of uncommon sources of railway history whenever he discovered them

John E. C. Palmer, librarian, of Rare Book Collections, British Library, for help with queries relating to some early works

Vivian Ramsbottom, J.P., lecturer, of Cambridge University and friend of the compiler, for valued opinion on the presentation of the prelims to the Supplement

Joyce Randon, typist, of Leicester, for her careful typing of a selection of unusually long and complicated entries

John B. Snell, Managing Director, Romney, Hythe & Dymchurch Rly, for his co-operation in allowing access to the railway's bookshops at Hythe and at New Romney stations

Donald S. Steggles, librarian, of Devon County Libraries, for a valuable list of non-transport books (non-fiction), each with a significant railway element

Some members of the compiler's family have played a part in helping the work along:

Doris Kemsley Ottley, loving and lovable wife of the compiler, who helped in the alphabetizing of the work's 20,000 index entries (see Dedication to the main work). This activity, extending over many weeks, was visible to passers-by, giving the impression, she feared, that we were running an insurance agency. But no one ever came to the door with money; Irene Lane, her sister, of Caversham, Berkshire; Meredith Wilson, younger daughter, of Leicester (see Dedication) and her eldest son, Joe, and William and Michael Summers of Teddington, Middlesex, sons of our elder daughter, Marian E. Summers (see Dedication).

At the Science Museum, I would like to thank Dr Derek Robinson, Keeper of the Department of Museum Services and, in particular, Pippa Richardson, Publications Manager. Thanks are also due to Dr John Coiley, Keeper of the National Railway Museum, York.

Finally, it is to Professor Jack Simmons of Leicester that all who use this work should be grateful. He has been closely involved in the progress of the whole venture from the time in the mid-1970s when the compiler decided to begin work on a Supplement to the 1966 volume. When compiling had got well under way it was Professor Simmons who took up the possibility of publication by HMSO, and his encouragement and interest has been maintained throughout the course of the work.

Compiling a large, detailed bibliography from actual examination of the works to be described can be a lonely and frustrating task. This Supplement could never have been brought to what I hope will be found to be an acceptable degree of coverage, accuracy and detail without the goodwill and active support of others, and the compiler is profoundly grateful to all who have helped to bring it to fruition.

ABBREVIATIONS
(Locations and Sources)

BLACK   *A Catalogue of Pamphlets on Economic Subjects published between 1750 and 1900*, compiled by R. D. C. Black (The Queen's University, Belfast, 1969)

BLACKWELL   B. H. Blackwell Ltd, booksellers, Oxford

G   Guildhall Library, London

LU(THC)   Leicester University Library, Transport History Collection

MCL   Manchester Central Library

N.KERR   Norman Kerr, railway-book seller, Cartmel, Cumbria

NUC   *National Union Catalog*

UL(GL)   University of London (Goldsmiths' Library)

PART ONE

ADDENDA AND CORRIGENDA TO THE MAIN WORK

The original printing of the main volume ran to 2000 copies and when in the mid-1970s all had been sold, the question arose of the possibility of compiling a new edition. The now out-of-print work was still in demand but a factor of more pressing concern was the ever-increasing number of railway books that had been published since the cut-off date, 1963. By 1975 this was running into thousands. The Railway Book Mania, which had its beginnings in the 1950s, was now, twenty-five years later, just showing signs of being on the wane, indicating that a start should be made on a new edition. By the time the work was ready for publication—if indeed this was found to be practicable—the phenomenon would surely have run itself out of steam.

Professor Jack Simmons of the University of Leicester—who may fairly be described as the Edward Pease of railway bibliography—discussed the feasibility of a new edition with interested publishers but it soon became clear that a re-setting of the work as a revised and enlarged edition would be impracticable. Thousands of new entries would have to be inserted into as many places within the existing text. This, and the consequent re-numbering and re-indexing, would add thousands of pages to an already bulky volume. No one would be able to afford to buy it! It was therefore decided to compile a Supplement and to seek to publish also a photo-litho reprint of the original work into which corrections would be incorporated.

A photo-litho reprint of the original work (1966) was published as a Second Edition by HMSO in 1983 (ISBN 0 11 290334 7*). Into it was incorporated all minor corrections—those not requiring any movement of type.

Additions and corrections requiring more than the altering of a single letter or numeral, such as the supplying of details of subsequent (i.e., post-1963) editions of a work, or an explanatory note, are here listed in numerical order and are linked to the entries to which they refer by means of an asterisk (*) being placed against the relevant entry number in the 1983 Reprint.

Some asterisks were omitted, by mischance. They should now be marked into that volume:

93	1760	3406	7100
168	1894	3684	7514
177	2018	3761	7517
180	2057	4259	7518
181	2251	4295	7546
182	2437	5216	7556
253	2516	5265	7672
306	2762	5622	7682
368	2787 (2786 marked in error)	5699	7691
549	2790	5749	7698
565	2923	6045	7832
1660	2940	6264	7926
1694	3379	6923	

3 Reprint of the 1st edn, 1831, with a new introduction by Charles Hadfield. *Newton Abbot: David & Charles*, 1969. pp. xiv, 702, viii; folded map. A facsimile reprint.

Reprint of the [2nd] edn, 1831, with an introductory note on the compiler by W. H. Chaloner. *London: Frank Cass*, 1967. pp. [6], xii, 776, [2], x, with folded plan. A facsimile reprint.

4 The title-page of the BL copy gives the author as James Gilbert. The publisher is E. Grattan.

16 Reprint. *David & Charles*, [1968]. 2 vols. in 1 (pp. xii, 308; viii, 282). A facsimile reprint of the original edition of 1851, with a new introduction by C. R. Clinker.

42 2nd edn (1883). Reprint [with an introduction by Charles E. Lee]. *London: Frank Cass*, 1968. (Cass Library of Railway Classics, 1). pp. viii, iii–xvi, 514.

48 [Baker's Handbook]. Reprint. *Newton Abbot: David & Charles*, 1969. pp. 128, [1], 7–36. Cover title, *A Handbook to Various Publications* . . . , 1893. Spine title, *Catalogue of Early Railway Books*. The title-page title, however, is that of the much smaller publication of the same year, *A Bibliography and Priced Catalogue of Early Railway Books* (Ottley 45). The Index to the Handbook was published with the Supplement of 1895 and in the reprint this is made to follow p. 128.

This combined Handbook and Index was offered free by David & Charles to subscribers to volumes 1 and 2 of their periodical *Transport History* and was also available for purchase as a bound volume.

'A facsimile reproduction of the first major catalogue of second-hand railwaybooks [containing] nearly 500 items, many of them described in great detail' [from publisher's note on back cover].

52 5th edn reprint. *London: Ian Allan*, [1964]. A straight reprint, the only addition being the Ian Allan imprint and colophon.

61 Reprint, with an introductory note by C. R. Clinker. *Newton Abbot: David & Charles*, 1970. pp. vi, xii, 532.

68 Dr. Chaloner's bibliographical introduction supplements that of the original edition. He includes works published since 1916 and some earlier ones that Jackman had missed.

69 *See* 7954.

93 'Mercury' is C. J. Allen.

96 Reprint. *London: Frank Cass*, 1969, pp. 376.

101 Revised edn. *David & Charles*, 1968. pp. xxii, 526, with a new introduction by C. R. Clinker.

108 *See* 7991.

120 3rd edn. *John Murray*, 1968. (Changing Shape of Things series). pp. 47.

145 Revised edn. Inland transport in Britain. 1971. (Reference Pamphlet, 138). pp. 16.
—— rev. edn. 1976. (Reference Pamphlet, 138). pp. 19.
—— 2nd edn. 1977. (Reference Pamphlet, 138). pp. 20.
—— 3rd edn. 1979. (Reference Pamphlet, 138). pp. 20.

150 2nd edn, revised. *London: Macmillan*, 1968. pp. xi, 276, with frontis, 25 illus on 13 plates, & in text, 12 contemporaneous engravings, 8 maps; 219 footnotes. Appendix A, 'The Railways Act, 1921' [schedules]; Appendix B (pp. 244–63), 'Literature, maps, museums' an evaluative bibliography and commentary; Appendix C (pp. 264–7), 'List of locomotives preserved'.

168 vol. 1, pp. 242 & 268, wagonways underground at Whitehaven and Carron; vol. 2, p. 542, wagonways underground at Allendale.

172 Reprint ['*2nd edn*'], with a new introduction by Charles Lee. *London: Frank Cass*, 1970. (Cass Library of Railway Classics, 4). pp. 4, 96, with 5 folded plates.
Facsimile reprint of 1st edn, 1797.

177 'The manner of the carriage [of coals] is by laying rails of timber from the colliery down to the river, exactly streight and parallel; and bulky carts are made with four rowlets fitting these rails, whereby the carriage is so easy that one horse will draw down four or five chaldron of coals, and is an immense benefit to the coal merchants.'
—— 3rd edn. *London: W. Clarke*, 1819. 2 vols. (vol. 1, p. 265).

180 vol. 2, p. 279, proposed wagonway at Coalisland in Tyrone, Ireland; vol. 3, p. 142, Yorkshire railways.

181 Another edn. Two excursions to the ports of England, Scotland, and Ireland, in 1816, 1817, and 1818; with a description of the breakwater at Plymouth, and of the Caledonian Canal. Translated from the French . . . with notes, critical and explanatory, by the translator, 1819. pp. 108.   UL(GL)

182 p. 42, Railways in Liverpool docks.

208 *See* 68.

253 French edn. Force commerciale de la Grande Bretagne. *Paris*, 1824. 2 vols.
vol. 1, pp. 148 ff, wood and iron railways in Great Britain; p. 187, Llanmynech railway.
vol. 2, p. 26, railways in London docks; pp. 77, 80, railways in Hull docks; pp. 86, 91, at Hetton; pp. 209 ff, in Liverpool docks.
—— 2nd edn. *Paris: Bachelier*, 1826. 2 vols.

262 Reprint, by *E & W Books* via *Robert Hale & Co., London*, 1970. pp. 39, with 2 tables. A facsimile reprint with panelled front cover.

268 The complete work translated into English: Railways in England, 1826 and 1827. Ueber Schienenwege in England: Bemerkungen gesammelt auf einer Reise in den Jahren 1826 und 1827. Concerning railways in England: observations collected during a journey in the years 1826 and 1827; translated from the German text by E. A. Forward, edited by Charles E. Lee, in collaboration with K. R. Gilbert. *Cambridge: W. Heffer & Sons for the Newcomen Society*, 1971. (Extra Publication, 7). pp. x, 83, with 30 diagrams on 5 plates, a folded map of proposed lines for a railway between Liverpool and Manchester, and 73 notes by C. E. Lee.

The first translation into English of the original work excluding only some lengthy extracts translated from English works into German (see fn. on p. 79). The work is not a comprehensive survey of all railways and wagonways in England, but a selective and representative one, describing four of the more important lines in detail: the Stockton & Darlington (28 pages), the Hetton Colliery Rly (10 pages), the Liverpool & Manchester under construction (4 pages), and the Bolton & Leigh (4 pages). A selection of 23 shorter descriptions of some other lines occupies a further 27 pages. C. E. Lee's Foreword is an historical account of the background to the survey and its two authors.

273 Introduction: seven reprinted articles from Liverpool newspapers, 1826–1829, the 6th & 7th (pp. 7–16) from the *Liverpool Mercury*, October 9th & 17th [1829] being day-by-day reports on the Rainhill Trials. Then follows a 2 pp. 'Memorial of the President and directors of the Baltimore and Ohio Railway to the Senate and House of Representatives of the United States in Congress assembled' on their progress in constructing the line and appealing for support from Congress; then follows 'Extracts of a letter from a respectable gentleman in Liverpool to his friend in this city [Baltimore], dated 19 November 1829' relating to the increasing confidence in railways evident in England since the Rainhill Trials of the previous month.

293 Traité pratique sur les chemins en fer et sur les voitures destinées à les parcourir: principes d'après lesquels on peut évaluer leur force, leurs proportions et la dépense annuelle qu'ils nécessitent . . . traduit de l'anglais par T. Duverne. *Paris: Bachelier*, 1826. pp. xxiv, 263, with 4 plates.

Bibl. Nat. cat.

306 Originally published as: Note sur la comparaison des avantages respectifs de diverses lignes de chemins de fer, et sur l'emploi des machines locomotives. *Paris: Carilian-Gœury*, 1835. pp. 51. (Extrait des *Annales des Ponts et Chaussées*).

—— Addition à la Note sur la Comparaison des Avantages Respectifs . . . *Carilian-Gœury*, 1835, pp. 7. (Extrait des *Annales des Ponts et Chaussées*).

324 2nd edn, 1842. pp. 26.

361 2nd edn. *Paris: Langlois et Leclercq*, 1858–60. 2 vols.

—— 3rd edn, revue, corrigée et considérablement augmentée. *Paris: Garnier Frères*, 1865. 4 vols. (pp. 583, 695, 688, 868), with tables & many fine engravings & maps.

A detailed analysis of railway progress in all countries, including the British Isles.

366 Addendum: 'with descriptive chapters on some of his most important works, by William Pole'.

368 2nd edn. *Newcastle-upon-Tyne: J. M. Carr*, 1882. pp. 73, with 4 plates (1 folded), & a map & diagram in text.

Blackwells cat. A1051 (1976) 46

377 *See* 68.

378 Reprint, with a foreword by Reginald Hackworth Young. *Shildon: Shildon Stockton & Darlington Railway Jubilee Committee*, 1975. pp. 406, xxxii & [36] leaves of plates. A facsimile reprint in a slip case.

384 For vols 2 & 3 *see* 8078.

388 Reprint. *Oxford University Press*, 1971. pp. xvii, 246, with 48 plates, 100 illus. 'Reprinted with a new introduction from corrected sheets of the first edition'. New introduction by W. H. Chaloner.

401 [3rd edn]. *David & Charles*, 1966. pp. 291, with 20 plates, & in text, 42 illus & 12 maps; 145 notes & a bibliography (70+ sources); index (pp. 280–91) with 60 page refs under 'Railways' and 'Tramroads' and others under the names of individual railways. On the title page: 'The third impression of the second edition', but on p. 14 identified as the third edition.

—— 4th edn. *David & Charles*, 1969. pp. 291, with 28 illus on 20 plates, & in text, 42 illus, 17 maps; 145 notes & a bibliography (80+ sources); index (pp. 280–91) with 60 page refs under 'Railways' and 'Tramroads' and others under the names of individual railways.

—— 5th edn. *David & Charles*, 1974. pp. 356, with 38 illus on 20 plates, & in text, 45 illus, 17 maps, 146 notes & a bibliography (158 sources); index (pp. 345–56) with many entries relating to railways and tramroads generally and individually. This edition also has a Series Index (pp. 338–44) which identifies the volume in the *Canals of the British Isles* series containing the principal historical account for any given canal, river navigation, branch or project.

B

—— 6th edn. *David & Charles*, 1979. pp. 362, with 38 illus on 20 plates, & in text, 45 illus, 17 maps, 146 notes & a bibliography (161 sources); index (pp. 351–62); series index (see note to 5th edn above) (pp. 344–50).

420 2nd edn, reprinted as: Whishaw's Railways of Great Britain & Ireland (1842): a reprint, with a new Introduction by C. R. Clinker. *Newton Abbot: David & Charles*, 1969. pp. xxvi, 500, with 18 plates (2 folded), illus, maps & plans. A facsimile reprint.

440 Reprint of the 2nd American printing (1855) of the 1st edn (1850). *David & Charles*, 1968. pp. 442.
    Also published in New York, by A. M. Kelley, 1968.

476 By C. A. Harmsworth, later Lord Northcliffe. See *Northcliffe*, by Reginald Pound and Geoffrey Harmsworth (1959), p. 68.

549 'Mercury' is C. J. Allen.

565 An earlier edn: The main-line railways of Great Britain, 1923–1933. *Westminster*, December 1934, pp. 40.

575 For editions of this work published under variant titles between 1924 and 1980 *see* 7953.

596 Republished as: London Transport at War, 1939–1945. *New Malden: Almark*, in association with *London Transport*, 1974, pp. 97, with frontis (2 illus on 3 pp.) & 100 illus in text.

636 American edn. *Washington: Traffic Service Corporation*, 1949. pp. 24.

667 *See* 8168.

676 *See* 145.

718 Reprint. *Ian Allan*, 1976.

726 4th edn. *Ian Allan*, 1968. pp. vii, 272, with 102 illus on 40 plates, 4 maps & 4 track occupation diagrams.
    —— 5th edn. Southern Electric, 1909–1979 . . . *Ian Allan*, 1979. pp. 280; 78 illus on 40 plates, 4 maps, 4 diagrams.

754 Paperback edn, revised. *Allen & Unwin*, 1975, pp. xxxii, 414.
    For vol. 2 *see* 8603.

756 *See also* 8604 or 12583.

757 2nd edn. *David & Charles*, 1971. (Regional History of the Railways of Great Britain, 3). pp. xii, 227, with frontis, 43 illus on 16 plates, 18 in text (maps, diagrams, graphs & tables), a bibliography (90+ sources) & a folded col. map at end.

784 An earlier edn [between 1905 and 1911]. pp. 16, with portrait & 2 illus.   LU(THC)

810 *See* 596.

817 2nd edn. rev. & enlarged. *London: Barnet London Borough Council, Libraries & Arts Committee*, 1973. pp. 70, with frontis, and 4 illus & 2 maps on 4 plates.

830 2nd, rev. edn. The London tramcar, 1861–1952, with rolling stock notes by D. W. K. Jones. *South Godstone: Oakwood Press*, [ca. 1959]. (Locomotion Papers, 7). sm. 8°. pp. 46, with 46 illus.
    —— 3rd, rev. edn. *Oakwood Press*, 1965. (Locomotion Papers, 7). pp. 50, with 55 illus.
    —— [4th edn]. *Oakwood Press*, [1975]. (Locomotion Papers, 7). pp. 45, with 54 illus on 20 plates.

837 2nd edn. *C. S. Smeeton for the Tramway & Light Railway Society*, 1962. pp. 24, with 14 illus, map, chronology & 2 tables.

838 Another edn. *L.R.T.L.*, [1975]. pp. 27, with 28 illus, a map & a plan.
    Originally published in the periodical *Modern Tramway* as three separate essays: 'London's tramway subway', by C. S. Dunbar (pp. 3–14); 'Subway memories', by J. H. Price (pp. 15–25); 'Unfulfilled Subway proposals', by B. G. Wilson (pp. 26–7).

890 Reprint. *London: Light Railway Transport League, with the co-operation of London Transport*, 1973. pp. 17, with 14 illus. A facsimile reprint with added cover.

892 Reprint. *Light Railway Transport League*, 1976. A facsimile reprint.

899 Inserted in end pocket: 1, 'Map of extension lines into Metro-land' (on reverse, a map of the Metropolitan Rly in Central London); 2, 'Map of London' (Metropolitan Railway and connections), a folded pocket map with 4 inset maps and descriptions of places in 'Metro-land', with 4 illus; 3, 'Metro-land', an 8-page publicity leaflet with 4 illus; 4, 'Country homes in Metro-land', a 4-page leaflet with 3 illus; 5, Four colour plates (a) River Chess, Chesham, (b) Trout farm, Chorley Wood, (c) Hartwell Park, near Aylesbury, (d) near Northwood.

918 Revised edn. Sixty years of the Northern. *London Transport*, 1967. pp. 28, with frontis, map of the Northern Line, 25 illus on 12 plates.
    —— new edn. The Northern Line. *London Transport*, 1973. pp. 31, with frontis, map & 25 illus on 12 plates. Cover title: The Northern Line: a brief history.

924 4th edn. *Ian Allan*, 1967. pp. 142, with 89 illus on 36 plates, chronology (pp. 123–7), Victoria Line maps & plans (pp. 129–39).

927 [2nd edn]. *London Transport*, 1966. pp. v, 156; 30 illus on 16 plates; col. folded map.
    —— [3rd edn]. *London Transport*, 1971. pp. 189; 46 illus on 24 plates, 3 maps in text & col. folded map.

—— [4th edn]. *London Transport*, 1972. pp. vii, 160; col. frontis, 62 illus on 32 plates, 3 maps, col. folded map.

—— [5th edn]. *London Transport*, 1974. pp. 200; col. frontis, 46 illus on 24 plates, 3 maps, col. folded map.

—— [6th edn]. *London Transport*, 1978. pp. 168; col. frontis, 62 illus on 32 plates, 3 maps, col. folded map.

1048a Revised edn. [2nd edn]. *London Transport*, 1966. sm. 8°. pp. viii, 117, with 28 illus on 16 plates, 23 maps & diagrams, col. folded map.
—— 2nd rev. edn. [3rd edn]. *L.T.*, 1966. sm. 8°. pp. viii, 117; 28 illus on 16 plates, 23 maps & diagrams, col. folded map.

1061 4th edn. *London Transport*, [1961]. pp. 27, with frontis, 21 illus on 7 plates, map, a folded map of welfare facilities, & list in pocket.

1142 2nd edn. *David & Charles*, 1968. pp. 173, with 35 illus on 20 plates, & in text, 14 maps, 3 facsimiles & a drawing, a bibliography & 202 notes.

1165 *See* 8441 or 8577.

1166 2nd edn. *David & Charles; Macdonald*, 1964. (Regional History of the Railways of Great Britain, 2). pp. ix, 218, with frontis, 36 illus on 16 plates, & in text, maps, diagrams, table & an evaluative bibliography (pp. 209–11); col. folded map at end.
—— 3rd edn. *David & Charles*, 1969. (Regional History of the Railways of Britain, 2). pp. ix, 218, with frontis, 36 illus on 16 plates, 9 layout plans & maps; evaluative bibliography (pp. 209–11) & col. folded map.

1175 2nd edn. *David & Charles*, 1963. (Regional History series, 1). pp. x, 214; 56 illus on 21 plates, 8 illus & 4 maps in text; folded map.
—— 3rd edn. *David & Charles*, 1966. (Regional History series, 1). 56 illus on 21 plates, 8 illus & 4 maps in text; folded map.
—— 4th edn, completely reset. *David & Charles*, 1973. (Regional History series, 1). pp. 274; 56 illus on 21 plates, 8 illus, 4 maps, folded map.

1186 Reprint. *Oleander Press*, 1976. (Cambridge Town, Gown & County series, 4). pp. 40, with frontis & 26 illus. A facsimile reprint.

1187 Reprint. *Oleander Press*, 1976. (Cambridge Town, Gown & County series, 2). pp. 28, with 4 plates. A facsimile reprint.

1195 [2nd edn]. *R. & C.H.S.*, 1973, pp. 16 with map.
Dates of incorporation, opening & amalgamation, etc. A corrected and extended version of the 1955 edition.

1209 Reprint, with some alterations. *The author*, 1978. pp. 52, with 18 illus & a map. The main text is unaltered but the Foreword by H. H.

Merchant and the Frontispiece are omitted and there is a different cover illustration.

1242 2nd edn. *Forest of Dean Local History Society*, [1977]. (Occasional Papers, 2). pp. 11 & 2 maps. Reproduced typescript, printed cover.

1319 *See* 9211.

1339 [LEICESTER]. CITY OF LEICESTER TRAM-WAYS AND MOTOR OMNIBUS DEPART-MENT. Traffic rules and regulations for motormen, omnibus drivers and conductors . . . *Leicester: Alfred Tacey*, [*for the Tramway Dept.*, 1929]. sm. 8°. pp. 31. Text dated 'February 1929'.
                                                    LU(THC)

1349 REPRINT. *Avon-Anglia*, 1978. pp. 27, with 4 illus, 2 maps, tonnage & revenue table, 1806–1906, & 107 notes.

1411 2nd edn, revised. *Macmillan*, 1968. pp. xi, 276, with frontis, 25 illus on 13 plates, & in text, 12 contemporaneous engravings, 8 maps; 219 footnotes. Appendix A, 'The Railways Act, 1921' (Schedules); Appendix B (pp. 244–63), 'Literature, maps, museums', an evaluative bibliography and commentary; Appendix C (pp. 264–7), 'List of locomotives preserved'.

1420 Revised edn. Volk's Electric Railway, Brighton. *Eltham: Light Railway Transport League*, [1979]. pp. 20, with 22 illus & a plan.
Includes (pp. 16–20) 'The Brighton & Rottingdean Seashore Electric Tramroad', with 5 illus.

1449 Revised edn, with a new introduction & notes by Kenneth Hoole. *Nidd Valley Narrow Gauge Rly*, 1970. pp. x, 165. A facsimile reprint of the original edition of 1879 with marginal references in the text to notes on pp. vi & vii of Ken Hoole's Introduction.

1470 [Revised edn]. Revised by Baron F. Duckham. *East Yorkshire Local History Society*, 1974. (East Yorkshire Local History series, 3). pp. 38, with map, chronology & bibliography (29+ sources).

1474 3rd edn, edited by Richard V. Proctor. *Sheffield City Libraries*, 1975. (Local Study Leaflets). pp. [12], with a la. map & a list of closed stations. Title from cover. Text & illus extend onto covers.

1495 Reprint of the 1st edn. *Ian Allan*, 1976. pp. 168, with 61 illus on plates. There are slight alterations to the plates and this edition has no col. frontis.

1522 2nd edn. *David & Charles*, 1974. pp. 260, with 45 illus on 20 plates, & in text, 8 illus, facsimiles & a map.
Steam locomotive production in the four manufactories at Springburn, Glasgow: St. Rollox works (Caledonian Rly), Hyde Park works (Neilson, Reid & Co.), Atlas works (Sharp, Stewart & Co.), and the Cowlairs works of the North British Rly.

1523 vol. 2, p. 270: railway at Newton upon Ayr
vol. 10, p. 507: railway at Halbeath
vol. 13, p. 467: railway at Charlestown; p.
471: Earl of Elgin's railway
vol. 15, p. 270: railway at Fordell
vol. 16, p. 519: railway at Wemyss

1584 Reprint. *Light Railway Transport League
(London Region)*, 1970. pp. 48. No illus.

1597 [2nd edn]. *Scottish Tramway Museum Society*, [1965]. pp. 24, with 18 illus & a fleet list.
—— [3rd edn]. 'Second reprint'. *S.T.M.S.*,
[1977]. pp. 20, with 19 illus & a 2-page
drawing; fleet list inside cover.

1620 [2nd edn], with drawings by J. M. Lloyd.
Oakwood Press, 1965. pp. 298, with 169 illus
on 84 plates, & in text, many drawings, maps,
tables, layout plans, gradient profiles; bibliography (26+ sources). Maps on end papers.
—— 2nd edn. rev. & enl. [3rd edn]. *Oakwood Press*, 1970. pp. 300, with 200 illus,
maps & drawings on 92 plates, & in text,
many illus, line drawings, gradient profiles,
maps, layout plans & tables; bibliography (43
sources).
A source book of outstanding depth and detail for
the Corris Rly, Talyllyn Rly, Glyn Valley Tramway,
Fairbourne Miniature Rly, Vale of Rheidol Light
Rly, Welshpool & Llanfair Light Rly, miscellaneous
tramways and the Narrow Gauge Railway Museum.

1630 2nd edn. *David & Charles, in conjunction
with University of Wales Press*, 1967. (Canals
of the British Isles series). pp. 272, with 9 illus
on 8 plates, & in text, 9 maps, 774 notes, a
'note on sources' and a 10-part tabular summary as appendices. Index, pp. 259–72, with
249 page refs under 'Tramways'. Railways are
entered under their individual names.

1660 1st edn. *Dublin: R. Milliken*, 1836. pp. 42.
Black 4743

1694 1st edn. *Dublin: J. Falconer, McGlashan &
Gill*, 1858. pp. 16. Black 7805

1760 2nd edn, with variant title. *Dublin: A. Thom*,
1846. pp. 40. Black 6002

1776 Reprint, with a new introduction by K.
Mellor. *Wakefield: S.R. Publishers*, 1970. pp.
v, 204. In this facsimile reprint the illustrations are made to follow the text.

1777 5th edn. *Oakwood Press*, 1971. (Light Railway Handbooks, no. 4). pp. 28, with 16
plates.

1804 2nd edn. *New York: A. M. Kelley*, 1969. (A
History of the Narrow Gauge Railways of
North-West Ireland, part 1). pp. 208, with
col. frontis, 49 illus on 20 plates & 28 illus in
text (maps, layout plans, facsimiles, timetables, gradient profiles); a bibliography (48
sources), 5 appendices & a la. folded 2-page
table of locomotives & rolling stock.

Both editions include the histories of the constituent companies: the Finn Valley Rly, 1860–1892;
the West Donegal Rly, 1879–1892; the Donegal Rly,
1892–1906; the County Donegal Railways Joint
Committee, 1906–1960.

2nd edn. *David & Charles*, 1969. (A History
of the Narrow-Gauge Railways of North-West Ireland, 1). pp. 208, with 22 plates (1
folded).
—— Amer. edn. *New York: A. M. Kelley*,
1969. pp. 208.
—— Reprint. *Pan Books*, 1972. (David &
Charles series). pp. [8], 229, [16]. Re-set as a
paperback.

1822 Reprint. *Blackrock: Carraig Books*, 1971. pp.
16, with 14 line illus & 6 pp. of text. A
facsimile reprint.

1846 Reprint, with some textual revision & an
addendum. *Oakwood Press*, 1980. (Oakwood
Library of Railway History, 60). pp. 48, with
18 illus on 8 plates, 3 layout plans, & a map.
p. 45: 'Note to 1980 edition', by C.
McAteer.

1894 See 'A Curiosity in Isle of Wight Railway
Literature', by Michael Robbins, *Journal of
the Railway & Canal Historical Society*, vol.
20, no. 2 (July 1974), pp. 46–8.

1903 New, rev. edn. *Ian Allan*, 1968, pp. 111, with
38 illus, 18 line drawings (map, diagrams,
lists, layout plans, tables, gradient profiles).
Cover title: The Isle of Man Railway.
This edition has a new Introduction and an
additional chapter, 'The railway since 1945', by
James Joyce.

1906 [2nd edn]. Snaefell Mountain Railway, 1895–
1970. *Light Railway Transport League; Douglas: Manx Electric Railway Board*, [1971]. pp.
16, with 17 illus & 2 maps.

1910 2dn edn. *Oakwood Press*, 1967. pp. 215, with
90 illus on 48 plates, 4 maps, 4 drawings, 31
layout plans (21 on end papers), gradient
profile and 9 appendices, incl. 4 specimen
timetables, 11 dimensioned drawings, & 3
tables; bibliography (17+ sources).
—— 3rd edn, incorporating additional research by Brian E. Crompton, with drawings
by J. M. Lloyd. *Oakwood Press*, 1973. pp.
244, with 96 illus on 48 plates, map, & many
small diagrams & layout plans; bibliography
(17+ sources); 10 appendices.

2018 The sub-title of the 1928 edn is: London and
Paris in 2hrs 45mins.

2057 Other editions appeared in 1878, 1880, 1887
and 1887/8. These are all described in the
NUC as [Rev. ed. with appendix]. All have
230 pages and were published in New York,
or New York & London, by G. P. Putnam.

2100 2nd edn. *Hassocks: Harvester Press*, 1974. pp.
188, with frontis, & 65 illus on 32 plates.

2102 2nd edn. *B.T.C.*, 1962. pp. 36, with 17 illus & 4 lists of vehicles (road & rail) preserved in the Museum of British Transport, Clapham, The Railway Museum in York, and elsewhere.

2110 2nd edn. *Branch Line Society*, 1971. pp. 43.
About 3500 articles are indexed in this edition, from the *Railway Magazine*, *Trains Illustrated* and the *Railway World*, with an addendum for 1970.
—— Cumulative Supplements, 1972 to 1980. These are in typescripts, published annually by the Society.

2113 2nd edn. *David & Charles*, 1974. pp. xiv, 327, with 47 illus on 32 plates, 14 line drawings, maps & layout plans & 3 appendices; bibliography (72+ sources).

2115 Subsequently published in parts. *See* Index.

2228 3rd edn. *London: H. Alabaster, Gatehouse & Co.*, 1905, sm. 8°. pp. vii, 117, with 71 illus & diagrams.

2251 Reprint. *Portmadoc: Festiniog Rly*, 1969. pp. 36. A facsimile reprint.

2258 Reprint. North British Locomotive: a catalogue of narrow gauge locomotives . . . introduced by John Thomas; with additional notes compiled by Alan Dunbar. *Newton Abbot: David & Charles*, 1970. obl. format. pp. [8], 79, with 215 illus & tabulated details.
A reproduction of the North British Locomotive Company's catalogue of narrow gauge locomotives, 1912.

2261 Reprint, with a new introduction by K. Mellor. *Wakefield: S.R. Publications*, 1970. pp. v, 204.
In this facsimile reprint the illustrations are made to follow the text.

2266 [2nd edn], with drawings by J. M. Lloyd. *Oakwood Press*, 1965. pp. 298, with 169 illus on 84 plates, & in text, many drawings, maps, tables, layout plans, gradient profiles; bibliography (26+ sources). Maps on end papers.
—— 2nd edn. rev. & enl. [3rd edn]. *Oakwood Press*, 1970. pp. 300, with 200 illus, maps & drawings on 92 plates, & in text, many illus, line drawings, gradient profiles, maps, layout plans & tables; bibliography (43 sources).
A source book of outstanding depth and detail for the Corris Rly, Talyllyn Rly, Glyn Valley Tramway, Fairbourne Miniature Rly, Vale of Rheidol Light Rly, Welshpool & Llanfair Light Rly, miscellaneous tramways and The Narrow Gauge Railway Museum.
The Fairbourne Miniature Railway (pp. 178–91), with 16 illus on 8 plates & a table of rolling stock) reprinted as a monograph. *Fairbourne: Fairbourne Rly*, ca. 1955), with an Introduction by J. C. Wilkins, director.

2279 Reprint. *Burton-on-Trent: Bass Museum*, 1977.

2286 Pocket Book B. *See* 8449.
—— D Industrial locomotives of Eastern England. 1960. pp. 102.
—— E. Industrial locomotives of the East Midlands. 1963. pp. 148.
—— F. *See* 9670.
—— G. *See* 9636.
—— H. *See* 8449.
—— K. Industrial locomotives of the North Riding of Yorkshire. 1964. pp. 60.
—— L. Industrial locomotives of Durham. 1962. pp. 124.

2300 Another edn. Townsend Hook and the railways of the Dorking Greystone Lime Co. Ltd. *Betchworth: Brockham Museum*, 1980. pp. 36, with 20 illus, 2 maps, 2 drawings & 10 other illus.

2376 An earlier edn [between 1905 and 1911]. pp. 16, with portrait & 2 illus. Imprint on back cover.
LU(THC)

2377 Another edn. The Kearney High-Speed Railway: a paper read before the Society of Engineers, 17 Dec., 1917 [by E. W. C. Kearney]. *Westminster: Society of Engineers*, 1917. pp. 37, with 15 diagrams & illus; 5 appendices.
This description is of a copy, in LU(THC) marked 'Advanced Proof'.

2395 3rd edn reprint. *Turntable Publications*, 1974. pp. 59, with 17 illus & 6 diagrams on 23 plates. A facsimile reprint.

2405 [Revised edn]. [1966 or 7]. pp. [4], with 11 illus & a plan.
—— another edn. [*Worfield*, 197–]. obl. format. pp. [20], with 16 illus, a plan & 2 stocklists.

2406 2nd edn. *East Budleigh: Rolle Estate Office*, 1967. pp. 32, with 10 illus, plan (double spread) & 2 diagrams; map & col. illus on covers.
—— Souvenir Guide to Bicton Gardens. *East Budleigh*, [between 1976 & 1981]. pp. [24], with 15 col. illus, & plan (double spread); map & 2 col. illus on covers.
pp. [14] – [17], 'The Bicton Woodland Railway', with 3 illus on pp. [22] & [23]. The course of the railway is shown on the plan (centre pages).

2437 This entry should be in the section for George and Robert Stephenson, 2446–2492.

2449 Addendum: 'with descriptive chapters on some of his most important works, by William Pole'.

2454 Reprint. *Frank Graham*, 1975. pp. xii, [2], 118. A straight facsimile reprint with added title-page.

2471 Dutch edn. George Stephenson, uit het Engelsch van Samuel Smiles door A. Winkler Prins. *Amsterdam: C. L. Brinkman*, 1864. pp. viii, 373, with vignettes.

2472 New & rev. edn, 1874, republished: The lives of George and Robert Stephenson . . . , introduction by Eric de Mare. *London: The Folio Society*, 1975, pp. 305, with col. frontis, 7 plates (5 col.), col. illus & 22 woodcuts in text; panelled front cover.
From the 'new & revised' edition of 1874, with illustrations from that of 1862.

2492 American reprint. *Westport (Conn.): Greenwood Press*, 1977.
—— Reprint in paperback. *Harmondsworth: Penguin*, 1978. (Pelican Biographies.)

2503 1st edn reprint, with added introduction by Jack Simmons. *London: Evelyn, Adams & Mackay*, 1969. pp. xxix, 386, with frontis (port.), 7 plates. 4 maps & 2 engravings. A facsimile reprint. The new introduction, pp. v–xvii.

2515 *See* 10256.

2516 The text is by A. S. Quartermaine.

2564 3rd edn reprint. *Bath: Kingsmead Reprints*, 1969. pp. 240, with 13 folded plates, illus, maps, plans. A facsimile reprint of the 3rd edition of 1891 'excluding 4 portraits'.

2582 2nd edn, rev. by A. C. O'Dell and P. S. Richards. *Hutchinson*, 1971. pp. 248, with 10 maps & diagrams, 6 tables, 242 notes & an evaluative bibliography (pp. 231–41).

2598 Reprint ['2nd edn'], with a new introduction by Charles Lee. *London: Frank Cass*, 1970. (Cass Library of Railway Classics, 4). pp. 4, 96, with 5 folded plates.
Facsimile reprint of 1st edn, 1797.

2620 *See* 10290.

2652 3rd edn, edited by R. A. Hamnett. *Permanent Way Institution*, 1964. pp. 507, [8].
—— 4th edn, edited by D. H. Coombs. *Permanent Way Institution*, 1971. pp. 607. In pocket at end: 'Cant, speed and transition graphs and lead diagrams'. ['Lead' — points, turn-outs or junctions.]

2691 Note: Individual architectural features of particular railways are only findable from the index, and must be sought under the names of individual towns or companies. Ireland is included.

2707 2nd edn [*Virtue Bros.*, 1864] reprint. *Bath: Kingsmead Reprints*, 1970. A facsimile reprint.
—— 4th edn. *London: Lockwood*, [1877]. pp. 136.   NUC

2738 Reprint. *Secker & Warburg*, 1966. pp. ix, 221, with 12 illus on 8 plates.
—— reprinted with a new Foreword by the author. *Secker & Warburg*, 1975. pp. xii, 220; 12 illus on 8 plates.

—— Large print edn. *Leicester: Ulverscroft*, 1980. pp. [12], 365.

2741 Another edn. 1948. 2 parts.

Part 2 reprinted, with a list of subsequent additions to the collection, 1948.

2743 Reprint. *Pan Books*, 1971. pp. 110, with 40 illus (8 full-page col.) on 24 plates, & 2 appendices.
Reset in smaller format but with text unabridged.

2762 An earlier edn. *Glasgow: Collins*, 1864. pp. xiv, 320, with plates & diagrams.   NUC
—— American edn. *New York: Wiley*, 1864–5. 2 pts.   NUC

2778 5th edn. *Ian Allan*, 1967. pp. 220, with 66 illus on 32 plates.

2787 Later issued both in successive combined editions and in a series of editions for particular types of locomotion: steam, electric and diesel, and for locomotive headcodes, and for locomotive sheds and codes.

2790 The 4th and subsequent editions are revised by W. J. Bell.

2804 5th edn, revised and edited by H. C. Casserley. *F. Warne*, 1966. (Observer's Pocket Series, 23). pp. 256, with 8 col. plates & 217 illus.

2830 Supplement: HACKWORTH, J. W. Replies to letters which appeared in The Times, the Royal Cornwall Gazette and the Railway Herald. [*Leamington*]: *printed by Hamblen of Leamington*, [no date].
Three letters by J. W. Hackworth with dates in 1876, 1879 and 1889, concerning the invention of the blast pipe and the identity of the originator of the steam locomotive. Information supplied by M. J. T. Lewis.

2847 Reprint, with a new Introduction by W. A. Tuplin. *Newton Abbot: David & Charles*, 1970. la. 8°. pp. xiii, 461, with many illus.

2848 Reprint, with a Foreword by Reginald Hackworth Young. *Shildon: Shildon Stockton & Darlington Railway Jubilee Committee*, 1975. pp. 406, xxxii, & [36] leaves of plates. A facsimile reprint in a slip case.

2849 *See* 10434.

2850 Reprint, with new introduction. The Chronicles of Boulton's Siding: a new impression, introduced by John Marshall and with an index added. *Newton Abbot: David & Charles*, 1971. pp. [ix], 11–276. A facsimile reprint.

2859 Reprint, with a new introduction and epilogue by R. A. Le Masena. *Milwaukee: Kalmbach Publ. Co.*, 1971. pp. 650.

[38]

—— Les Locomotives articulées. *Brussels: Imprimerie F. van Buggenhoudt*, 1926. la. 8°. pp. 327.

2876 *See* 9839.

2890 New edn. *British Railways Board*, 1958. pp. 39, with 34 illus.

2895 2nd edn. *Allen & Unwin*, 1968. pp. 273, with col. frontis & 105 illus on 32 plates.

2897 Revised edn. *H. Evelyn*, 1964. la. obl. format. Preface & 10 col. plates, each interleaved with commentary & details.

2908 Revised edn. *Spring Books*, 1965. pp. 482, with 690 illus on 345 plates. All classes of steam locomotive owned by BR since 1 January 1948, with historical notes on each class.
—— 3rd edn. Steam locomotives of British Railways. *Hamlyn*, 1973. pp. 484, with 710 illus on 355 plates; (pp. 9–113, historical notes).

2911 Re-issue. *Ian Allan*, 1974.

2914 Revised edn. *Ian Allan*, 1967. pp. 178, with 161 illus on 40 plates.

2917 Reprint. *E & W Books* [via] *Robert Hale*, 1970. pp. 39, with 2 tables. A facsimile reprint with panelled front cover.

2923 Another edn. *London*, 1837. pp. 863.

2929 [1st edn]. *London: printed for J. Taylor*, 1827. pp. xix, 370.   NUC
Illustrations of steam machinery and steam naval architecture: atlas to the enlarged edition, re-issued in an improved form, of Tredgold's work on the steam engine . . . [*London*]: *J. Weale*, 1843. pp. 1 & 125 plates.
—— [2nd] edn Appendices. *London: J. Weale*, 1844. 5 pts in 1 vol. & an atlas of 124 plates.
Appendices A, B, C, D, E, F, G, to the new edition of Tredgold on the Steam Engine and on steam navigation, comprising the works of the following eminent engineers and naval architects: 1, William Fairbairn; 2, George Forrester; 3, John Hague; 4, Oliver Lang; 5, John Laird; 6, John Miller; 7, G. Pitcher; 8, William Pole; 9, Messrs Scott, Sinclair & Co.; 10, John Seward; 11, Sir William Symonds . . .
—— [3rd] edn. *J. Weale*, 1850–3. 3 vols. in 4. No general title-page: each volume has its own.
vol. 1: The principles and practice and explanation of the machinery of locomotive engines in operation on the several lines of railway. 1850. pp. 8, [376].
vol. 2 is on marine engines and vol. 3 is on one-locomotive steam engines.

2933 Reprint. *Kingsmead Reprints*, 1969. Limited

edition of 750 copies. A facsimile reprint. Cover title: Rules for the management of a locomotive engine.

2936 2nd edn reprinted as: Whishaw's Railways of Great Britain & Ireland (1842); a reprint with a new introduction by C. R. Clinker. *Newton Abbot: David & Charles*, 1969. pp. xxvi, 500, with 18 plates (2 folded), illus, maps & plans. A facsimile reprint.

2940 *See* 'The North Midland Railway and its enginemen, 1842–3', by Michael Robbins (6928).

2943 Note: on pp. 56–9 of 1841 edn, 'Statistical data of the principal railways in Great Britain': a 10-column table giving engineering and financial details of all railways in 1841. In the 2nd edn (1848) this is on pp. 50–55.

2965 3rd edn re-issued. *London: Crosby, Lockwood & Son*, 1888. pp. 240.   NUC
—— 4th edn. *London: Crosby Lockwood*, 1904. pp. 204.   NUC

2969 The work ran into many editions from 1847 to 1885, published in London and in New York, and there was also an Introduction to it, separately published as *Recent Improvements in the Steam Engine* in various editions from 1865 to 1880.
The best generally-available guide to this work is to be found in the *National Union Catalog: Pre-1956 Imprints*, but this is a far from complete record, being no more than a set-out reprinting of entries sent in by various American libraries, with consequent variation in depth of detail; some full, others too brief to identify as particular editions.
The present Bibliography does not normally include technical works on railway engineering after 1850 (see 'Exclusions', p. 13 of vol. 1). The NUC has a good description of the 3rd edition, of 1850 (published in London by Longman, Brown, Green & Longmans; pp. vi, 284), and in the British Library there is a 12th edition in Chinese, dated 1873, with a letter in English from the author enclosed.

2977 4th edn. 1897. pp. 96.
—— 5th edn. 1897. pp. 102, [32].
—— 8th edn. 1900. pp. 102, [32].
—— 10th edn. 1902. pp. 102, [32].
—— 14th edn. 1908. pp. 102, [32].

2986 2nd edn. *Locomotive Publishing Co.*, 1907. pp. 99.

3023 2nd edn. *London: Locomotive Publishing Co.*, 1900. pp. 180, with 16 plates, 37 text illus & 3 folded working drawings of H. A. Ivatt's 4–4–0 locomotive, GNR.
—— Reprinted, 1903.
—— 7th edn. *Locomotive Publishing Co.*, 1920. pp. 184, 4, with 24 plates.

3031 Reprint as a combined edn. *Wakefield: E. P.*

Publishing, 1974. pp. 84, with 65 illus, 12 diagrams; pp. 48, with 41 illus.

A reprint of *Sentinel Patent Locomotives* (1931) and *Concrete Cases* (ca. 1928).

Steam locomotives for industrial railways, for light passenger and goods haulage and for shunting in marshalling yards; pp. 82–3, 'Some users of Sentinel locomotives' (83 corporate bodies).

3035 [Locomotive Stock Books.] The locomotive stock of the main line companies of Great Britain as at 31 December 1935, including alterations to stock during 1935; compiled by D. R. Pollock, C. Smith and D. E. White. *Anerley (London): R.C. & T.S.*, 1936. (Railway Observer Supplement, 2). pp. xxiv, with 27 illus.

—— as at 31 December 1936, compiled by D. R. Pollock, C. Smith, D. E. White & K. R. Prentice. *R.C. & T.S.*, 1937. (Railway Observer Supplement, 3). pp. 28, 18, with 48 illus.

—— Appendix: alterations to stock during 1937 . . . compiled by D. R. Pollock, C. Smith, D. E. White and K. R. Prentice. *R.C. & T.S.*, 1938. (Railway Observer Supplement, 3). pp. 20, with 20 illus on 6 plates. 7 in text.

Lists of locomotives of all British and Irish railways.

pp. 4–6, British locomotives: a review.

—— 1939, compiled by D. R. Pollock, C. Smith, D. E. White & K. R. Prentice. *R.C. & T.S.*, 1939, (R.O. Suppl., 2). pp. 54, with 56 illus.

All British and Irish railways. pp. 5–8, British locomotives, 1938: a review.

—— 1946.

—— Appendix, 1947 . . . compiled by D. R. Pollock, P. Proud, C. Smith and D. E. White. *R.C. & T.S.*, 1947 (R.O. (1947) Supplement, 5). pp. 28, with 21 illus on 6 plates, 1 in text.

Issued as a Supplement to the *Locomotive Stock book*, 1946.

All British & Irish railways, incl. narrow gauge lines.

pp. 5–8, British locomotives, 1946: a review.

—— 1948: complete classified lists, with names of all locomotive stock of railways vested in the Railway Executive and London Transport Executive on 1st January 1948; British Railways locomotive re-numbering scheme; alterations to locomotive stock, 1947; locomotives on loan. Compiled by D. R. Pollock, P. Proud, C. Smith and D. E. White. *R.C. & T.S.*, 1948. (Railway Observer (1948) Supplement, 4). pp. 52, with 26 illus on 8 plates.

pp. 5–6, British locomotives, 1947: a review, and a tabular analysis of locomotives, 1922–1947 and of the locomotives of the constituent companies of the main line railways, 1922–1947.

—— 1950.

—— 1952 . . . compiled by R. F. Kemball, D. R. Pollock, P. Proud, C. Smith and D. E. White. *R.C. & T.S.*, 1952. (Railway Observer (1952) Supplement, 4). pp. 54, with 90 illus on plates & 1 in text.

Lists of locomotives of all British and Irish railways.

pp. 4–6, British locomotives, 1950–1951: a review.

—— 1960, compiled by W. T. Stubbs & M. G. Boddy. *R.C. & T.S.*, [1960]. pp. 84, with 186 illus.

Lists of locomotives of all British & Irish railways, with alterations to stock, 1955–59.

pp. 4–10, British locomotives, 1955–1959: a review.

—— 1963, compiled by W. T. Stubbs and M. G. Boddy; edited by J. W. Knowles and R. A. Lissenden. *R.C. & T.S.*, [1963].

pp. 67, with frontis & 165 illus on 49 plates.

Locomotives of all railways in Britain and Ireland, with (pp. 4–11), 'A review of motive power changes, British Railways, 1960–1962', by D. F. Tee.

—— 1966, compiled by W. T. Stubbs, J. W. Knowles & R. A. Lissenden. *R.C. & T.S.*, [1966]. pp. 55, with frontis & 123 illus on 42 plates.

Lists of locomotives on all British & Irish railways, with (pp. 4–11), 'A review of motive power changes, British Railways, 1963–1965', by Don Rowland.

—— 1969, compiled by D. A. Hope, P. Mallaband, G. Belton, R. A. Lissenden. *R.C. & T.S.*, 1969. pp. 90, xx, with frontis, & 105 illus on 37 plates & in text.

Lists of locomotives on all British and Irish railways, and preserved locomotives, with (pp. 8–14), 'A review of motive power changes, British Railways, 1966–1968', by Don Rowland.

—— 1977 edn. Locomotive stock of British Railways: including detail differences, compiled by Roger B. Wood and P. Mallaband. *R.C. & T.S.*, [1977]. pp. 49, with an addenda page tipped in at end.

3089 Re-published by *Ian Allan*, 1977.

3094 13th edn. *Ian Allan*, 1965. pp. 96.

3139 3rd edn. *G. H. Lake*, 1960. pp. 168, with 117 illus & diagrams (some col.).

—— 4th edn. *Ian Allan*, 1963. pp. 210, with 143 illus & diagrams (some col.).

3189 2nd edn. *B.T.C.*, 1962. pp. 36, with 17 illus & 4 lists of vehicles (road & rail) preserved in the Museum of British Transport, Clapham, and in the Railway Museum, York, and elsewhere.

3191 3rd edn. ABC British Railways coaches: standard locomotive-hauled stock. *Ian Allan*, [1962]. pp. 64, with illus & diagrams.

3357 The Signalman's Pocket Book. new edn. *London: J. Aitken*, [1938]. pp. 112.

3373 2nd edn. *Ian Allan*, 1968. pp. 104, with many illus & diagrams (some col.).

—— 3rd edn. *Ian Allan*, 1975. pp. 120, with 59 illus, 47 diagrams & (pp. 49–56) col. diagrams of semaphore & colour-light signals.

Appendix 1: signalbox bell codes; Appendix 2, signalbox lever colours.

—— 4th edn. *Ian Allan*, 1978. pp. 136, with 64 illus, 55 diagrams & (pp. 49–56), col. diagrams of semaphore & colour-light signals.

Appendix 1: signalbox bell codes; Appendix 2, signalbox lever colours.

3379 A photocopy of this work is in LU(THC).

3400 Also in *Railways in the Victorian Economy*, edited by M. C. Reed (1969), pp. 138–61, with 125 notes.

3402 Also in *Railways in the Victorian Economy*, edited by M. C. Reed (1969), pp. 212–8, with 85 notes.

3406 2nd edn. *London: Smith, Elder & Co.*, 1845. pp. 84. BLACK 5869

3510 3rd edn. *London: Butterworth*, 1968. pp. 211, with 26 diagrams & graphs.

3609 Another edn. Railway rates: how they affect the cost of living. *R.C.H.*, April 1923. pp. 19.

3661 [Gauge Evidence]. Extracts from 'Gauge Evidence: the history and prospects of the railway system', reprinted, with a new introduction by K. Miller. *Wakefield: S.R. Publishers; Leeds: Turntable Enterprises*, [1971]. pp. various.
    A selective reprinting of the first edition, 1846.
    Contents: New introduction by K. Miller; title-page of *Gauge Evidence*; Railways sanctioned by Parliament in the session 1845, narrow gauge lines [a list]; Map of the districts occupied by broad and narrow-gauge railways respectively, showing all the breaks of gauge; A brief history of the gauge question; The railway system illustrated: narrow-gauge evidence; Intermediate gauge evidence of C. B. Vignolles, cross-examined on his preference for a 6ft gauge; Broad gauge evidence. Bibliographical note on reverse of title-page, each chosen section being given in full.

3662 *See* 3661.

3684 Another edn. for 'January 1864'. *London: Truscott, Son & Simmons*, 1864. pp. 180, with tables, index & appendix. TCD

3687 Revised edn. The Railway Clearing House: its origin, object, work and results, with a brief description of the clubs and societies in operation amongst the officers. *London: McCorquodale* [printer], 1884. pp. 37.

3704 Re-issued in 1927: vol. 1 dated 1927; vol. 2 undated.

3727 6th edn, edited, revised and enlarged, with an appendix on recent progress in working and management, by S. M. Phillp. *London, New York; Whittaker*, 1899. pp. 412.
    pp. 1–36, 'Biography' [of George Findlay]; pp. 377–94, 'Recent progress in working and management'.
    —— Reprinted, with a new introduction by Jack Simmons. *Wakefield: E P Publishing*, 1976. pp. xiv, 412.

3761 A war-time reprint was issued (ca. 1941 or 1942), on inferior paper. pp. 162.

3767 1936 edn. The Railway Trainman's Manual. *Glasgow: the author*, 1936. pp. 130.

—— 15th edn. The Railway Trainman, incorporating the Trainman's Manual. [ca. 1946]. pp. 136.
—— another edn. The Railway Trainman. *Glasgow: The Railwayman's Annual* (S. B. Aitken), [ca. 1948]. pp. 136.

3788 3rd edn. *Butterworth*, 1968. pp. 211, with 26 diagrams & graphs.

3790 2nd edn. rev. by A. C. O'Dell and P. S. Richards. *Hutchinson*, 1971. pp. 248, with 10 maps & diagrams, 6 tables, 242 notes & an evaluative bibliography (pp. 231–41).

3798 [2nd] edn. *Ian Allan*, [1961]. pp. 72.
—— 3rd edn. *Ian Allan*, [1963]. pp. 105.
—— 5th edn. *Ian Allan*, [1968]. pp. 88.

3860 *See* 10911.

3864 [3rd, much enlarged, edn; 1st printed edn]. *Ian Allan*, [1964]. pp. 96, with 63 illus on 32 plates. Period: 1919 to 1963.
    Includes narrow-gauge railways.
—— 2nd edn. *Ian Allan*, 1973. pp. 110, with 99 illus on 40 plates. Period: 1919 to 1973.
—— 3rd edn. *Ian Allan*, 1980. pp. 144, with frontis & 107 illus on 47 plates. Period: 1919 to 1979.
    The 1964 edition was the first to appear as a printed book and is virtually a new work, with much enlarged text and with illustrations on plates.

3865 *See* 10861.

3866 *See* 10911.

3872 Reprint. *Ian Allan*, [1964]. (Classics of Railway Literature). A facsimile reprint of the original edition of 1889.

3908 Another edn. *H. Blacklock*, 1918. pp. 478.

3923 2nd edn. *Prescot: T. Stephenson*, 1967. pp. xii, 355, with 87 illus on plates. Index, pp. 335–55.

3937 BRITISH TRANSPORT FILM LIBRARY. [Catalogues of films and filmstrips available for loan]. *London: B.T.C. (British Transport Films; British Transport Film Library)*, 1952– . In progress.
    A catalogue in successive editions describing sound films (16mm.) and filmstrips produced by BR, London Transport, the Post Office and by various other corporate bodies and railway preservation societies for educational, instructional and publicity purposes. Available on loan for showing to lecture audiences, societies, institutions, clubs and schools. The stock is continually being revised and augmented.
—— 1952, pp. 32; 1954, pp. 40; 1957, pp. 59; 1960, pp. 75; 1963, pp. 78; 1966, pp. 66; 1968/9, pp. 76; 1970/71, pp. 96; 1973/4, pp. 37; 1975, pp. 70; 1976/7, pp. 64; 1978, pp. 84.

3960 Reprint. *[Derby]: the author*, 1963.

3976 Reprint, with a foreword by Reginald Hackworth Young. *Shildon: Shildon Stockton & Darlington Railway Jubilee Committee*, 1975. pp. 406, xxxii, & [36] leaves of plates. A facsimile reprint in a slip case.

3979 Another edn, edited and revised by Arthur Elton. *Chatham: Evelyn, Adam & Mackay*, 1968. la. 8°. pp. xvii, 222, with 117 illus on 72 plates & 8 col. plates in text; notes & bibliography, pp. 185–99.
ch. 7 (pp. 134–65 & col. plate II, opp. p. 46) 'The Railway Age'. 38 of the 117 illustrations are of railway subjects.

3991 *See* 11019.

4024 Reprint of vol. 1 as: Memoirs of a Station Master, 1879, by Ernest J. Simmons [i.e. Hubert A. Simmons], edited by Jack Simmons. *Bath: Adams & Dart*, 1974. pp. xv, 165, with 90 footnotes.
Editor's introduction, pp. v–x; Key to places and characters, p. xi.

4032 4th edn. *London: Crosby Lockwood*, 1880. pp. xiii, 258, with illus & tables. NUC
—— 12th edn. *Crosby Lockwood*, 1904. pp. xiii, 258, with illus & tables. NUC

4042 Reprint. *London: Hugh Evelyn*, 1968. obl. format. pp. 72, with 26 illus (engravings), vignettes & diagrams.
An abridged edition without the author's Preface re-set into double-column and with contemporary illustrations introduced into the text.

4109 Reprint, with a new introduction by Leonard Clark. *Newton Abbot: David & Charles*, 1969. pp. xiii, 315.
'The most daring and comprehensive condemnation of factory life to have appeared in Europe for thirty years' (Leonard Clark in his biography, *Alfred Williams: his life and work*, 1945, p. 9).

4112 1920 edn. *London: Co-operative Printing Society (for the N.U.R.)*, 1920. pp. 96. Text dated January 1st, 1920.

4251 MINISTRY OF LABOUR and the CENTRAL OFFICE OF INFORMATION. Railways. *London: H.M.S.O.*, 1960. (Choice of Careers series, 88). pp. 48, with illus.

4259 *See* 68.

4264 Reprint. *London: Frank Cass*, 1969. pp. 376.

4275 *See* 8441.

4279 [3rd edn]. *David & Charles*, 1966. pp. 291, with 20 plates, & in text, 42 illus & 12 maps, 145 notes & a bibliography (70+ sources); index (pp. 280–91) with 60 page refs under 'Railways' and 'Tramroads' and others under the names of individual railways. On the title page: 'The third impression of the second edition', but on p.14 identified as the third edition.
—— 4th edn. *David & Charles*, 1969. pp.

291, with 28 illus on 20 plates, & in text, 42 illus, 17 maps, 145 notes & a bibliography (80+ sources); index (pp. 280–91) with 60 page refs under 'Railways' and 'Tramroads' and others under the names of individual railways.
—— 5th edn. *David & Charles*, 1974. pp. 356, with 38 illus on 20 plates, & in text, 45 illus, 17 maps, 146 notes & a bibliography (158 sources); index (pp. 345–56) with many entries relating to railways and tramroads generally and individually.
This edition has also a Series Index (pp. 338–44) which identifies the volume in the *Canals of the British Isles* series containing the principal historical account for any given canal, river navigation, branch or project.
—— 6th edn. *David & Charles*, 1979. pp. 362, with 38 illus on 20 plates, & in text, 45 illus, 17 maps, 146 notes & a bibliography (161 sources); index (pp. 351–62); series index (see note to 5th edn above), pp. 344–50.

4281 2nd edn, revised. *Hutchinson*, 1966. pp. 222, with 10 tables, 307 notes & a bibliography (92 sources).
Road & rail transport in Britain up to 1964.
—— 3rd edn, by T. C. Barker and C. I. Savage. *Hutchinson*, 1974. pp. 280, with 377 notes; index, pp. 267–80.
Railways mainly in chaps 3, 4, 5 & 6, with 175 notes & refs.
Of the nine chapters, the first five have been rewritten by Professor Barker and chapter 9 is substantially revised by him, bringing the history up to 1973.

4295 3rd edn. *London: H. Renshaw*, 1836. pp. 16.
BLACK 4839

4345 Reprint of the 2nd American printing (1855) of the 1st edn (1850). *David & Charles*, 1968. pp. 442.
Also published in New York, by A. M. Kelley. 1968.

4443 *See* 11185.

4488 Re-issue with an extended prefatory note. *London: Railway Gazette*, 1911. pp. xii, 455.

4585 Another edn. *G.W.R.*, 1925. (Great Western Pamphlets, 15). pp. 8.

4733 Reprinted in: *Sources and Nature of the Statistics of the United Kingdom*, edited by Maurice G. Kendall, vol. 1 (1952), pp. 279–302, including a bibliography (43 sources).

4749 *See* 11153.

4774 Reprint. *David & Charles*, [1968]. 2 vols in 1. (pp. xii, 308, viii, 282.) A facsimile reprint of the original edition of 1851, with a new introduction by C. R. Clinker.

4776 2nd edn. (1883) reprinted [with an introduction by Charles E. Lee]. *London: Frank Cass*,

1968. (Cass Library of Railway Classics, 1). pp. viii, iii–xvi, 514.

4782 Another edn, edited & revised by Arthur Elton. *Chatham: Evelyn, Adams & Mackay*, 1968. la. 8°. pp. xvii, 222, with 117 illus on 72 plates & 8 col. plates in text; notes & bibliography (pp. 185–99).
ch. 7 (pp. 134–65 & col. plate II), 'The Railway Age'. 38 of the 117 illustrations are of railway subjects.

4815 AGNEW, A. The Sabbath and the railway trains: a letter on the responsibilities of railway directors and all shareholders members of Christian churches; addressed to . . . the Marquis of Breadalbane, chairman of the Scottish Central Railway Company. 4th edn. *Edinburgh: Johnstone*, 1848. pp. 12.

4904 2nd edn by A. C. O'Dell and P. S. Richards. *Hutchinson*, 1971. pp. 248, with 10 maps & diagrams, 6 tables, 242 notes & an evaluative bibliography (pp. 231–41).

4914 2nd edn. *Newton Abbot: David & Charles*, 1969. pp. 288. A reprint with minor corrections.

4926 Reprint, edited, and with a new Introduction, by Jack Simmons. *Bath: Adams & Dart*, 1971. pp. 116, with 12 line drawings in text.
A re-setting of the original sm. 8° edition of 1862 into crown octavo format, with notes and added contemporary illustrations. The new Introduction, pp. 7–13.

4944 Reprint. *Ian Allan*, [1964]. (Classics of Railway Literature series). A facsimile reprint of the original edition of 1889.

4974 2nd 'extended' edn. *David & Charles*, 1966. pp. 287, with 22 illus on 12 plates & a bibliography (13 sources).
Appendix 1, Copy of a letter from George Stephenson to the President of the Board of Trade, March 31st, 1841, urging Government supervision over design in railway engineering, the speed of trains, signalling and braking.
Appendix 2, The first requirements of the Inspecting Officers of Railways, 1858.
Chronological Index of the accidents mentioned in the text (pp. 285–7).
In this edition the survey is updated to the St Johns (Lewisham) accident of 4 December 1957.
—— 3rd edn, revised and with chapters 11 and 12 by Geoffrey Kichenside. *David & Charles*, 1976. pp. 297, with 22 illus on 12 plates; bibliography (14 sources) & chronology, but without the appendices of the 2nd edition. Published with an errata slip for p. 296.
In this edition the coverage is extended to the Moorgate tube disaster of 28 February and the Nuneaton derailment of 6 June 1975.

5052 For vols 2 & 3 *see* 11507.

5189 *See* 11535.

5211 Reprint. *Allen & Unwin*, 1964.

5213 Revised edn. *David & Charles*, 1968. pp. xxii, 526, with a new introduction by C. R. Clinker.

5216 Reproduced in *Railways in the Victorian Economy*, edited by M. C. Reed, 1969.

5265 'Crowquill' is a *nom de plume* used by the brothers Charles Robert Forrester (1803–50) and Alfred Henry Forrester (1804–72), Charles Robert being the writer and Alfred Henry the illustrator. See *Dictionary of National Biography*.

5351 Revised edn. *David & Charles*, 1968. pp. xxii, 526, with a new introduction by C. R. Clinker.

5372 *See also* 11602.

5428 MINISTRY OF TRANSPORT. Requirements for passenger lines and recommendations for goods lines of the Ministry of Transport in regard to railway construction and operation. *London: H.M.S.O.*, 1925. pp. 22, with folded diagram of clearances.
—— another edn. 1928. pp. 22, with folded diagram.
—— another edn. 1950. pp. 38, with 3 appendices.
Appendix 2, Variations from and relaxations of the Requirements in the case of light railways or lines of local interest; Appendix 3, coloured folded diagram of lateral and overhead clearances.
—— 1977 edn. Railway construction and operation requirements: structural and electrical clearances. pp. 12 & 3 folded diagrams.

5457 *See* 11619.

5477 *See* 8077.

5488 *See also* 11630.

5491 [12th edn.] Supplement to 12th edn. '1867–1871'. 1872. pp. 136.

5510 Supplementary Index to the Local and Personal Acts, 1948–1966: classified lists of the Local and Personal Acts, together with alphabetical and chronological lists, for the years 1948–1966 inclusive. *London: H.M.S.O.*, 1967. pp. liii, 167.
pp. 13–17, Class II, Transport: 1, Railways.
pp. 18–21, Class II, Transport: 2b, Tramway and trolley vehicles.
Subsequent indexes published annually.
'Contains a considerable number of errors, numerous chapter numbers are wrong, several whole companies are left out, 'street tramways' and 'tramroads' are inter-mingled and some light railways are not included. A list of corrections was submitted [to the publisher] but although this was acknowledged the required amendments were not made in the Supplementary Index, 1967.'
C.R. Clinker.

5512 4th edn, 'with the assistance of John Hucker'. *Stevens & Sons*, 1965. pp. xlvii, 815.
There is no index entry under 'Railways'. For railway subjects see 'Contents' and in the Index,

entries such as 'British Railways Board', 'Common Carrier' and 'Passengers' luggage'.

5515 Reprint. *David & Charles*, 1968. pp. viii, 727.

5526 Reprint. *London: Frank Cass*, 1969. pp. 376.

5553 POST OFFICE. Post Office Railway. *London: The Post Office*, [1970]. la. 8°. pp. 12, with 7 illus, 2 diagrams & a col. map.

5563 6th edn, edited, revised and enlarged, with an appendix on recent progress in working and management, by S. M. Phillp. *London, New York: Whittaker*, 1899. pp. 412.
   pp. 1–36, 'Biography' [of George Findlay]; pp. 377–94, 'Recent progress in working and management'.
   —— Reprinted, with a new introduction by Jack Simmons. *Wakefield: E P Publishing*, 1976. pp. xiv, 412.

5584 2nd edn, reprinted as: Whishaw's Railways of Great Britain & Ireland (1842): a reprint with a new introduction by C. R. Clinker. *Newton Abbot: David & Charles*, 1969. pp. xxvi, 500, with 18 plates (2 folded), illus, maps & plans. A facsimile reprint.

5591 5th edn reprinted. *London: Ian Allan*, [1964]. A straight reprint with added Ian Allan imprint and colophon.

5601 3rd edn, rev. & enl. *Allen & Unwin*, 1970. (re-issued, 1976). pp. 234, with col. frontis, 7 col. plates, & 128 illus in text; bibliography (40 sources).
   Includes notes on liveries and steamer funnel identification and a table of data on locomotives, rolling stock and ships at the time of the Grouping. This edition has a new introduction by the author but excludes the la. folded map of the 2nd edition. The eight coloured plates are of paintings by J. D. Goffey.

5619a Reprint, with addenda and amendments. *Oakwood Press*, 1978. (Oakwood Library of Railway History, 57). pp. 149–215 with addenda, and amendments on pp. 214–5.

5622 [2nd edn. Much enlarged.] *E. Griffith*, 1970. pp. 64, with 67 illus, 3 facsimiles, map, gradient profile, & a timetable.
   pp. 30–40: 'The Wrecker', an account, with illustrations, of the making of the film of 1928, involving the actual wrecking of a train by collision with a steam lorry at Salter's Ash crossing, near Lasham; pp. 50–55, 'Oh, Mr Porter', an account, with illustrations, of the making of the comedy film of 1937 centred upon Cliddesden station.

5625 2nd edn. *Bracknell: West Country Publications*, 1965. (West Country Handbooks, 1.) pp. 19, with 8 illus on 4 plates, 2 diagrams, 2 plans & a map on covers.
   —— reprinted, 1968, and by *Forge Books*, 1976.

5627 2nd edn. *E. C. Griffith*, 1969. pp. 80, with 80 illus & 2 maps.

5670 Reprint. *Llandybie: C. Davis*, 1973. pp. xiv, 157, with frontis. 45 illus (incl. many ports.) on 28 plates; folded map. A facsimile reprint with a new introduction by F. Llewellyn-Jones.

5674 *See 9117.*

5677 Rev. 2nd edn [of 1958], with additional notes by C. T. Goode. *Oakwood Press*, [1978]. (Oakwood Library of Railway History, 5). pp. 78, with 25 illus on 12 plates, 4 maps, 5 layout plans & 5 appendices.
   pp. 55 to end are by C. T. Goode, bringing the history up to 1978.

5681 Extended edn. *Oakwood Press*, [1977]. (Locomotion Papers, 21). pp. 32, with 16 illus on 8 plates, map, 5 layout plans & a bibliography (7 sources). The 1963 edition with a 'Postscript' (pp. 26–31).

5684 Reprint. *Corris Railway Society*, 1972. A facsimile reprint with minor corrections and notes by the Society. Published with a second (outer) cover.

5699 A print-out from a microfilm copy of this work is in LU(THC).

5706 another edn. [*Portmadoc*, 1962]. pp. 36.
   another edn. [*Portmadoc*, 1967]. pp. 56.
   another edn. [*Portmadoc*, 1969]. pp. 60.
   another edn. [*Portmadoc*, 1970]. pp. 60.
   another edn. [*Portmadoc*, 1971]. pp. 60.
   another edn. [*Portmadoc*, 1972]. pp. 60.
   After 1972 the *Festiniog Railway Guide* and the *Festiniog Pictorial* were brought together and published as the *Traveller's Guide to the Festiniog Railway. See 9734.*

5707 2nd edn. *Portmadoc*, September 1958.
   —— 3rd edn. *Portmadoc*, June 1959. pp. 25; 58 illus, map & 2 timetables.
   Continued as: *The Festiniog Railway in Pictures. See 5712.*

5708 [3rd edn] (vol. 1 only). *Oakwood Press*, 1965. pp. [viii], 194, with 148 drawings on 6 folded plates, & over 100 illus, maps, diagrams & tables.
   —— 4th edn, completely revised & much enlarged. The Festiniog Railway: a history of the narrow gauge railway linking the slate quarries of Blaenau Ffestiniog with Portmadoc, North Wales; together with outline histories of quarry undertakings connected to the railway, 1800–1974, by James I. C. Boyd, with drawings by J. M. Lloyd. [*Tarrant Hinton*]: *Oakwood Press*.
   vol. 1: History and route, 1800–1953. 1975. pp. 297, with 60 illus on 40 plates, 25 layout plans, gradient profile; general map, symbols & abbreviations on end papers.
   vol. 2: Locomotives, rolling stock and quarry feeders. 1975. pp. 320–626, with 98 illus on 52 plates & ca. 100 drawings in text; 21 appendices, incl. a bibliography (148 sources); maps on end papers.

5709 Rev. & enl. edn. Editor, Roy Cunningham.

Portmadoc: F.R. Society, 1965. pp. 32, with 9 illus, 2 diagrams & a folded map. Printed.
—— 3rd edn. *Porthmadog: F.R. Company*, 1975. pp. 48, with folded map.

5712 The Festiniog Railway in pictures, 1951–1963: the story in pictures. *Portmadoc: F.R.*, 1964. pp. 24, with 68 illus & a map.
—— The Festiniog Railway: 130 years in pictures, 1836–1966. *Portmadoc: F.R.*, 1966. pp. 24, with 66 illus, a map & a plan.
—— The Festiniog Railway in pictures. *Portmadoc: F.R.*, 1969. pp. 24, with 48 illus & facsimile of the Ministry of Transport Blaenau Extension Amendment Order.
—— Festiniog Pictorial. *Portmadoc: F.R.*, 1970. pp. 32. Intro (inside front cover) & 51 illus (4 col.), with descrs.
—— series two. *Portmadoc: F.R.*, 1971. pp. 32. Intro & illus (4 col.) with descrs.
—— series three. *Porthmadog: F.R.*, 1972. pp. 32. Intro & 50 illus (5 col.) with descrs.
   After 1972 the *Festiniog Pictorial* and the *Festiniog Railway Guide* were brought together and published as the *Traveller's Guide to the Festiniog Railway. See* 9734.

5749 vol. 3. *See* 11717.

5751 2nd edn. The last main line: an illustrated history of the building of the Great Central Railway. *Leicester Museums*, 1968. pp. 20, with 36 illus & a map. Title from cover.

5752 Reprint. *Leicester Museums*, 1974. pp. 36, with 24 illus & 12 dimensioned drawings. A reprint with a different cover.

5776 Reprint. *Allen & Unwin*, 1964.

5784 5th edn. Great Eastern locomotives, past and present, 1862–1948. *Brightlingsea: the author*, 1949. pp. 122, with 62 illus & many tables & lists.
—— 7th edn: The locomotives of the Great Eastern Railway, 1862–1962: a brief descriptive illustrated souvenir of types and LNER rebuilds, with detailed stock list. *Wickford: the author*, October 1969. (Langloco Series, 1). pp. 148, with frontis & 68 illus, many lists, & a table, 'Census & analysis of G.E.R. locomotive stock, 1st January 1923', and (pp. 123–48), 'G.E.R. locomotive stock list, 1922, with subsequent years of withdrawal'.

5788 4th edn, with a foreword by H. C. Johnson. *Ian Allan*, 1967. pp. viii, 242, with 93 illus on 32 plates, chronology (pp. 234–9) & a folded map.
—— 5th edn, with a foreword by Sir Henry Johnson. *Ian Allan*, 1968. pp. x, 242, with 94 illus on 32 plates, 10 tables & a chronology (6 pp).
—— Re-issued as a paperback, *Ian Allan*, 1975.

5856 Another edn. Memoranda connected with the Locomotive, Carriage and Wagon Departments, Stratford Works. *Stratford: G.E.R.*, June, 1900. pp. 28, with 9 dimensioned drawings of locomotives, 2 plans, of Stratford Works and of Temple Mills Wagon Works.
—— Reproduced in photostat and published by the Great Eastern Railway Society, December 1979. (Information Sheet no. M115, Guide to Stratford Works, June 1900).

5877 [3rd, extended, edn]. History of the Great Northern Railway, 1845–1922, with supplementary chapters by H. V. Borley and C. Hamilton Ellis. *Allen & Unwin*, 1966. pp. xix, 490, with frontis, 17 illus on 8 plates; illus & maps in text.
   The history is extended from 1902 to the end of the GNR's separate existence, 1922 (pp. 454–480).

5883 Reprint. *London: Allen & Unwin*, 1964.

5884 2nd edn. *Nottingham: Gresley Society*, 1970. pp. 79, with 35 illus on 16 plates, 20 line illus & 5 tables.
   A reprint of the original edition of 1947 with some minor corrections.

5930 An earlier issue. *London: Tilt*, 1843. pp. 76.
   Apparently only a few copies were published, the work being re-issued fully in 1846 by Bogue (The Tilt & Bogue partnership ended in 1843). A copy with the earlier imprint & date was sold by Phillips on 12 June 1980 (Sale no. 22823, lot 272).
—— Reprinted with a new title: Bourne's Great Western Railway: a reproduction of the history and description of the Great Western Railway. *David & Charles Reprints*, [1969]. Folio. pp. iv, 13, 13–58, with 33 drawings, a map and gradient profiles on 32 plates.
   A facsimile reprint of all but the non-railway parts of the text and plates of the original work of 1846 (1843). (See 'Bibliographical note' at foot of title-page).
   Dictionary of National Biography attributes authorship to George Thomas Clark.

5932 Reprint, with an introduction by L. T. C. Rolt. *David & Charles*, 1971. pp. xxviii, 568.

5935 *See* 11830.

5937 2nd edn. *London: Digby Long & Co.*, 1895. pp. xvi, 373. A reprint with 'Second edition' on the title page.   Leicester City Library (Stretton Collection)

5942 Revised and annotated edn. The birth of the Great Western Railway: extracts from the diary and correspondence of George Henry Gibbs, edited by Jack Simmons. *Bath: Adams & Dart*, 1971. pp. viii, 96, with 4 plates & 223 notes.
   A substantially revised and annotated edition with a new preface and introduction by Professor Simmons (pp. vii–viii, 1–14), 223 notes arising from his editing, and an index. The work, in consequence, is re-set from the small-sized pamphlet of 1910 into a bound volume. The text of the Correspondence section in the present volume is that of the original MS in Guildhall Library, London. The existence or location of the original Diary is not known.

5945 Reprint, with a new introduction by Leonard Clark. *Newton Abbot: David & Charles*, 1969. pp. xiii, 315.
'The most daring and comprehensive condemnation of factory life to have appeared in Europe for thirty years' (Leonard Clark in his biography, *Alfred Williams: his life and work*, 1945, p. 9).

5948 Reprint. *Cambridge: P. Stephens*, 1970. pp. [vi], 131. A facsimile reprint of the original edition (*GWR*, 1923).

5949 Reprint. [*Cambridge: P. Stephens*, 1970.] pp. 199. A facsimile reprint of the original edition (*GWR*, 1924).

5953 Reprint, with an introduction by Sue Fletcher. *Cambridge: P. Stephens*, 1972. pp. 205, with folded map.

5958 Revised edn of vol. 2, 1863–1921, by C. R. Clinker. *London: Ian Allan*, 1964. pp. 362, with 60 illus on 32 plates, 12 tables, 8 illus & diagrams, 5 maps (1 folded), 4 gradient profiles, many foot-notes, 4 appendices, including a chronology (pp. 307–51).
A continuation as vol. 3, by O. S. Nock, brings the history of the GWR up to its end in 1947. *See* 11795.

5959 Reprint in a combined edition, with an introduction by Jack Simmons. *Bath: Adams & Dart*, 1970. pp. xiv, 120, 120, 112, with a map.
A facsimile reprint of the three series in one volume (no. 1 of 1918, no. 2 of 1921, and no. 3 of 1923) omitting the plates from series 1 and 3 but with the map which appeared in the abridged edition of 1926.
The Introduction by Professor Simmons (pp. v–xiv) is a detailed biographical essay on Cecil Torr, his character and surroundings, with 12 notes.

5960 Reprint. *Cambridge: P. Stephens*, 1971. pp. [10], 232. A facsimile reprint of the original edition (*GWR*, 1934).

5962 Reprint. *David & Charles*, 1972. pp. 180, with frontis, 44 illus, & map on end papers.
Originally published in the Great Western Railway Centenary issue of *The Times*, 31 August 1935 and reprinted in book form by the GWR in that year.

5968 Reprint. *Cambridge: P. Stephens*, 1971, with a new introduction by Norman Simmons. A facsimile reprint of the original edition (*GWR*, 1936).

5971 Reprint. *Cambridge: P. Stephens*, 1971. pp. 260. A facsimile reprint of the original edition (*GWR*, 1935).

5976 New edn, rev. & enl., with altered title: Great Western London suburban services. *Oakwood Press*, 1978. (Locomotion Papers, 48). pp. 102, with 26 illus on 12 plates, 4 tables, 2 layout plans & a map.

5981 Another edn. BRITISH RAIL ENGINEERING LTD. Swindon Works and its place in British railway history. *Swindon: B.R. Engineering*, [1975]. obl. format. pp. 40, with 75 illus & a plan.

5988 Rev edn. Sixty years of Western express running. [*Shepperton*]: Ian Allan, 1973. pp. viii, 408, with 95 illus (4 col) on 52 plates, 130 tables (logs of runs), drawings & 5 gradient profiles. Period, 1904–1964.
Previously published as *Fifty years of Western express running* (1954).

5990 Reprint. *Bracknell: Town & Country Press*, 1968. pp. xii, 233, with portrait (mounted) & 17 illus on 12 plates, & in text, 20 line drawings & facsimiles.
A facsimile reprint of the original edition (1954) with a new Foreword by Felix Pole junr, a publisher's note and some added illustrations.

5992 Reprinted in: *Railways in the Victorian Economy*, edited by M. C. Reed (1969), pp. 111–37, with 58 notes & 3 detailed tables.

5996 2nd edn. *Allen & Unwin*, 1965. pp. xiv, 194, with frontis, 44 illus on 16 plates, & in text, 5 drawings & 6 detailed tables.

6005 10: Absorbed engines, 1922–1947. 1966. pp. 280, with col. frontis, 469 illus on 126 plates & 4 maps.
925 locomotives of constituent and subsidiary companies absorbed into the GWR on 1st January 1923.
12: A chronological and statistical survey. 1974. pp. 188, with 133 illus & 3 folded tables (stock totals).
Includes a Foreword (single sheet insert) and an Index to the 12 parts as a whole.

6015 *See* 8564.

6045 6th edn. *London*, 1846. pp. 57.

6096 Reprint of 2nd edn, 1861. *Oxford Illustrated Press*, 1973. pp. [8], 800, [8], 280.
A facsimile reprint with no added imprint except for the publisher's monogram on the spine. Bound with *The Official Illustrated Guide to the Bristol & Exeter, North and South Devon, Cornwall, and West Cornwall, and South Wales railways . . .* 2nd edn, (Griffin, Bohn & Co., 1861).

6098 Reprint. *Shrewsbury: Shropshire County Library*, [1971]. pp. 50. Spiral binding. A facsimile reprint in a limited edition.

6110 Reprint with a new introduction by K. Millar. *Wakefield: E.P. Publishing*, 1972. pp. xii, 3–88, with 3 maps, 3 folded gradient profiles; tables & logs of journeys. A facsimile reprint.

6113 *See* 6150.

6129 Reprint. *Cambridge: P. Stephens*, 1971. pp. 148. A facsimile reprint of the original work, with a new introduction by Norman Simmons. (*N. N. Appleby & the GWR*, 1927).

6132 Reprint. *Cambridge: P. Stephens*, 1971. pp. [vi], 149. A facsimile reprint of the original edition (*GWR*, 1928).

6145 Another edn. *G.W.R.*, 1939. pp. 44, with 38 illus on 31 plates.
General arrangements and tarriffs of each GWR hotel and of restaurant cars and steamboats. Includes a list of stations where breakfast, luncheon and tea baskets may be had, and a list of stations and refreshment rooms. Printed on cover 'Gratuitous'.

6150 Title varies: Names of engines. 1911. pp. 22 (*see* 6113); Great Western Railway engines, by J. A. L. White (1914), pp. 22; 1917, pp. 47; 1919, pp. 47; 1921, pp. 48; 1922, pp. 47; 1923, pp. 47; 1925, pp. 47; 1926, pp. 51; 1928, pp. 64; 1929, pp. 64; The G.W.R. Engine Book. (anon). 1932, pp. 72; The Engine Book. (anon). 1935, pp. 80; G.W.R engines, by W. G. Chapman, 1938, pp. 112; 1939 (not seen); 1946, pp. 108; 2nd 1946 edn, pp. 124.
For an historical note on this series see Preface of the 1938 edition. This mentions 13 editions up to 1935.
GREAT WESTERN RAILWAY. GWR engines: names, numbers, types & classes . . . *David & Charles*, 1971. pp. 23, 64, 18, 108, with 96 illus & many lists. A composite reprint of the *Engine Books* of 1911, 1928 and 1946, with some pages from that of 1938.

6152 [Next Station]. The Great Western Railway's last look forward, being a reprint of 'Next Station'. *Newton Abbot: David & Charles*, 1972. pp. [9], 113, with frontis, 14 illus (drawings) & 5 diagrams. Originally published as *Next Station* (1947).

6154 2nd edn. *Ian Allan*, 1969. sm. 8°. pp. 96, with 36 illus on 16 plates, lists, logs of runs & 3 appendices.

6167 *See* 9601.

6171 3rd edn. *David & Charles*, 1969. pp. 185, with col. frontis, 46 illus on 16 plates, 6 maps, 3 layout plans, facsimiles, line drawings, 5 appendices & a postscript by C. R. Clinker (p. 181).
—— [4th edn], revised & brought up to date by C. R. Clinker. *London: Pan Books*, 1972. sm. 8°. pp. xii, 219, with 44 illus on 16 plates, maps, line illus, chronology, tables & 7 appendices.

6177 Rev. & enl. edn. *E. C. Griffith*, 1968. pp. 63, with 66 illus, 2 maps & 2 layout plans.

6191 2nd edn. *Ian Allan*, 1975. pp. 236, with 96 illus on 32 plates, 7 gradient profiles, 10 maps (1 folded), 2 plans, 9 diagrams, 11 line drawings & 33 tables.

6197 Reprint with a new introduction by C. R. Clinker. *Newcastle upon Tyne: Frank Graham*, 1971. la 4°. A facsimile reprint.

6220 New edn. *Bradford Barton*, 1965. pp. 68, with

21 illus on 12 plates, 7 layout plans, gradient profile & a folded map.
The pseudonym 'Manifold' used for the authorship of this work is a corporate name for J. R. Hollick, C. A. Moreton, G. N. Nowell-Gossling, F. M. Page and W. J. Stubbs.

6237 3rd edn. *L.N.E.R.*, 1929. pp. 128, with frontis, 88 illus & a map.

6250 [New edn]. *Ian Allan*, 1972. pp. [v], 154, with 40 illus on 16 plates. Apparently a reprint with plates matt on text paper.
Memoirs of 40 years with steam locomotives (cleaner, fireman, driver) based on Haymarket loco depot, Edinburgh, 1910–1949, latterly with Gresley Pacifics on the East Coast route to London.

6256 part 2 A: Tender engines, classes A1 to A10. 1973. pp. 231, with col. frontis, 275 illus on 118 plates, 26 diagrams, & detailed lists (2 folded).
part 2 B: Tender engines, classes B1 to B19. 1975. pp. 167, with 260 illus incl. frontis & 3 dimensioned drawings on 115 plates, & detailed lists.
part 3 A: Tender engines, classes C1 to C11. 1979. pp. 148, with 146 illus on 61 plates, incl. frontis, & many detailed lists.
part 3 B: Tender engines, classes D1 to D12. 1980. pp. 108, with 126 illus on 48 plates, incl. frontis, & many detailed lists.
part 4: Tender engines, classes D25 to E7. 1968. pp. 157, with col. frontis, 222 illus on 87 plates, diagrams & many detailed lists.
part 5: Tender engines, classes J1 to J37. 1966. pp. 231, with frontis & 328 illus on 120 plates, & many detailed lists.
part 6: (published too late for inclusion).
part 7: Tank engines, classes A5 to H2. 1964. pp. 118, with frontis & 208 illus on 72 plates, & many detailed lists.
part 8 A: Tank engines: classes J50 to J70. 1970. pp. 102, with frontis & 111 illus on 32 plates, 2 charts & many detailed lists.
part 8 B: Tank engines, J71 to J94. 1971. pp. 95, with frontis & 93 illus on 31 plates, & many detailed lists.
part 9 A: Tank engines, classes L1 to N19. 1977. pp. 170, with 181 illus on 66 plates & frontis, & many detailed lists.
part 9 B: Tank engines, classes Q1 to Z5. 1977. pp. 116, with 138 illus on 44 plates & frontis, diagrams & many detailed lists.

6264 'Voyageur' is C. J. Allen.

6269 Another edn. Doncaster Locomotive and Carriage Works. *London: British Railways (Eastern Region)*, 1960. pp. 15 (incl. covers), with 7 illus & a plan.

6286 3rd edn. *Brown, Son & Ferguson*, 1972. pp. xi, 257, with frontis, 77 illus on 40 plates, fleet lists (pp. 153–237), & a bibliography (36 sources).
Includes steamer services of the Glasgow & South Western Rly, North British Rly, LMS, LNER and BR(Sc.R).

6309 Reprint of '2nd edition, 1849', with an added Introduction by C. R. Clinker. *Newton Abbot: David & Charles*, 1968. pp. vii, 208.
—— 5th edn. *London: J. Murray*, 1851. pp. 224.

6310 Addendum: 'with descriptive chapters on some of his most important works, by William Pole'.

6348 Reprint, with a new introduction by Jack Simmons. *Wakefield: E.P. Publishing*, 1974. pp. xv, 544.
A facsimile reprint of the 1904 edition with an added introduction.

6369 Another edn. *Oakwood Press*, [1969]. (Oakwood Library of Railway History, 25). pp. 68, with map, 14 illus on 8 plates, 18 gradient profiles, 15 track plans, 5 appendices, including a chronology. The 1948 edition reprinted with (pp. 66–7) additional notes for the period 1948–1968.

6376 Reprinted as: The first public railway in Lancashire: the history of the Bolton & Leigh Railway, based on the Hulton Papers, 1824–1828. *Manchester: printed by H. Rawson & Co. for the Society*, 1963.

6380 2nd edn. *Railway & Canal Historical Society*, 1965. pp. 30, with map & gradient profile.

6381 [3rd edn]. *Oakwood Press*, 1971. (Locomotion Papers, 10). pp. 42, with 14 illus, map & a gradient profile.

6398 Reprint. *E & W Books via Robert Hale & Co.*, 1970. pp. 39, with 2 tables. A facsimile reprint with panelled front cover.

6404 New impression, with new introduction by Charles E. Lee. *Frank Cass*, 1969. pp. vii, 104, with frontis, folded map and 'observations' (additional notes).

6419 Reprint, with an added introduction by C. R. Clinker. *Newcastle upon Tyne: Frank Graham*, 1970. pp. [32], including the 4 plates in monochrome.
A facsimile reprint with C. R. Clinker's introduction and an added title-page carrying an abbreviated form of the title: 'Views of the most interesting scenery on the Liverpool and Manchester Railway'.
The original work was issued in two parts, and the title page of part 2 is reproduced; also a page announcing that part 3 'will be published the first of May'. This was to contain plates 9 to 12, but part 3 was never published.
At the end of the work a footnote by Arnold Hyde is added. This relates to the Shaws, father and son, and the original edition of the work. Plate IV reproduced on the cover which also carries an abbreviated title: Views on the Liverpool and Manchester Railway.

6420 [Reprint]. Coloured views on the Liverpool and Manchester Railway . . . : a facsimile of the original edition published in 1831 by R. Ackermann, with an historical introduction to the railway by George Ottley. *Oldham: Hugh Broadbent*, 1976. 4°. pp. xi, 8, 16 col. plates (3 folded), map, and an evaluative bibliography by J. M. Lloyd (p. iv). General introduction by H. A. Broadbent. Includes 'three large extra plates which were issued as optional supplements to the original publication, 1831'.
—— De Luxe edition, bound by Zaehnsdorf in Lavana calf and with gilt edges. Limited to 250 numbered copies. *H. Broadbent*, 1977. pp. xviii, 8, 16 col. plates followed by a facsimile reproduction of the wrappers of the original edition, parts 1 & 2, 1831. This edition also has a 'Catalogue Raisonné', compiled by J. M. Lloyd (pp. xi–xviii).

6423 *See* 12134.

6426 1st edn reprint. *Lancashire & Cheshire Antiquarian Society*, 1968. pp. 46, with folded map & diagram. A facsimile reprint of the 1st edition, 1830, with an Introduction by W. H. Chaloner on inside of outer cover.

6431 Reprinted by Deanprint Ltd. of Stockport for the *Liverpool Road Station Society, Manchester*, 1980. pp. 46, with 3 folded plates.
The original title-page is reproduced, with 'Reprinted by Deanprint Ltd. 1980' added at the foot and on the reverse of the title-page, 'Reprinted 1980 by Deanprint Ltd . . . and published on their behalf by Liverpool Road Station Society . . . This edition copyright, Deanprint Ltd. 1980'. Two of the five plates of the original edition are printed back-to-back.

6451 [2nd] edn reprint. *London: E & W Books*, 1970. pp. 180.

6452 Reprint. *Frank Graham*, 1969. pp. 110, [i]. A facsimile reprint.

6453 Reprint of [2nd] edn, 1838. *Buxton: Moorland Publishing Co.*, 1974 (Moorland Reprints). pp. 147, 44, with folded map, folded table of fares & distances, illus & vignettes. A facsimile reprint.

6465 Reprint, with an historical and descriptive account by John Britton. *David & Charles*, 1970. Folio. pp. 26, with 31 plates, & maps. A complete facsimile reprint of the original edition of 1839.

6536 Reprint of 2nd edn, 1849. *E & W Books*, 1970. pp. 158, with folded map.

6545 Reprint, with a new introduction by Barrie S. Trinder. *Chichester: Phillimore*, 1973. pp. [x], 254, with 24 engravings, but without the map and some publisher's advertisements of the original edition.
Primarily a guide book for travellers but includes observations, some quite lengthy, on railway matters, mostly LNWR. The added Introduction by B. S. Trinder is about the author and the book and the social environment of mid-nineteenth-century England.

6557 2nd edn, [1861]. pp. 344, with 150 engravings.

[Bound with *Measom's Guide to the North-Western Railway and all its branches*. 2nd edn, [1861]].   STOCKPORT PL

6558 2nd edn, [1861]. pp. 536, with 360 engravings. [Bound with *Measom's Guide to the Lancaster & Carlisle, Edinburgh & Glasgow, and Caledonian railways*. 2nd edn, [1861]].
STOCKPORT PL

6583 6th edn, edited, revised and enlarged, with an appendix on recent progress in working and management, by S. M. Phillp. *London, New York: Whittaker*, 1899. pp. 412.
pp. 1–36. 'Biography' [of George Findlay]; pp. 377–94. 'Recent progress in working and management'.
—— Reprinted, with a new introduction by Jack Simmons. *Wakefield: E.P. Publishing*, 1976. pp. xiv, 412.

6595 [Another edn]. *Crewe: C. Williams*, 1922. pp. 90, [6].
Includes a list of engines in use on the Dundalk, Newry & Greenore Rly.
—— Supplement to the Register, 1922 edn, showing corrections to 30th June, 1924. *Crewe: C. Williams*, [1924]. pp. 12.

6608 Reprint. *E.P. Publishing*, 1973. pp. viii, 139, with frontis & 3 plates. A facsimile reprint of the 1882 edition with a new introduction by Richard A. Powell.

6616 *See* 12241.

6668 Reprint. *Sidcup: Electric Railway Society*, 1964. pp. 19. A facsimile reprint.

6670 3rd (rev.) edn. *Oakwood Press*, 1978. (Oakwood Library of Railway History, 6). pp. 51, with 44 illus & a map on 16 plates, gradient profile & a brief bibliography.

6678 2nd edn [i.e. 1st edn reprinted], with a new Introduction by W. O. Skeat. *Hassocks: Branch Line (Harvester Press)*, 1975. pp. xiii, 245. A facsimile reprint of the 1st edition (1903).

6693 [New edn]. *Ian Allan*, 1971. pp. 271, with 79 illus on 32 plates, map & 2 appendices.

6777 Reprint. *Oxford Publishing Co.*, [1975]. A facsimile reprint.

6796 Re-issued in paperback. *Ian Allan*, 1975. pp. 190.

6819 Reprint. *Bressingham Steam Museum*, 1977. A facsimile reprint.

6827 3rd edn. *Brown, Son & Ferguson*, 1972. pp. xi, 257, with frontis, 77 illus on 4 plates, fleet lists (pp. 153–237), bibliography (36 sources).
Includes steamer services of the Glasgow & South Western Rly, North British Rly, LMS, LNER and BR(Sc.R).

6887 *See* 9673.

6895 3rd edn, rev. & ed. by M. D. Crew. *Middleton Railway Trust*, 1965. pp. 24, with table & map. Reproduced typescript.
—— 3rd impression of 3rd edn. 1967. pp. 14, [8].
—— 4th edn. rev. by J. Bushell and M. D. Crew. *Middleton Railway Trust*, 1968. pp. 24.

6896 [WRIGHT, W.] T' history o' t' Haworth Railway [by] Bill o' th' Hoylus. *printed by Hainsworth Press, Keighley*, no date. pp. [20], with a portrait [the author?] on front cover. Text extends onto inside of back cover.
LU(THC)
—— Reprint. Th' history o' Haworth Railway fra' th' beginning to th' end, by William Wright (Bill o' th' Hoylus End); Foreword and glossary of dialect terms by Smith Midgley. *Haworth Station: Keighley & Worth Valley Railway Preservation Society*, 1972. pp. 28, with portrait.
A contemporary account in Yorkshire dialect of the building of the Keighley & Worth Valley Railway in 1862.

6900 Reprinted as: Williams's Midland Railway: its rise and progress; a narrative of modern enterprise. 5th edn, 1888, with a new introduction, notes and corrections, by C. R. Clinker. *Newton Abbot: David & Charles*, 1968. pp. [vi, xvi,] 510, with 172 engravings & 7 maps. A facsimile reprint, but without the engraved title-page of the original edition.

6919 Reprint. *Allen & Unwin*, 1964.

6920 2nd edn. *Advertiser Press*, 1965. pp. 151, with frontis, 40 illus on 32 plates, 2 appendices, folded map & folded gradient profile at end.

6922 Reprint. *Avon–Anglia*, 1977. pp. 72, with addenda and postscript. Originally published, 1954.

6923 The Midland Railway in pictures. *Hampton Court: Ian Allan*, 1957. 32 plates (87 illustrations with descriptions). No text.
Reprinted from *The Midland Railway*, by C. Hamilton Ellis (1953, 2nd edn 1955). 'The number of copies of the picture section thus reprinted is strictly limited.'

6929 2nd edn, by R. O. T. Povey. *Keighley & Worth Valley Light Rly*, 1968. pp. [40], with 13 illus, map, plan & chronology.
—— 3rd edn, by R. O. T. Povey. *K & W.V.L. Rly*, 1970. pp. [40], with 14 illus, map, plan & chronology.
—— 4th edn, by R. O. T. Povey. *K & W.V. Rly Preservation Society*, 1976. pp. [44], with 16 illus, map, layout plan, gradient profile & chronology.
—— 5th edn, by R. O. T. Povey. *K & W.V. Rly Preservation Society*, 1977. pp. [44], with 16 illus, map, plan & chronology.

6934 Reprint: The Nottingham and Derby Railway

Companion, 1839, with a new introduction by J. B. Radford. *Chesterfield: Derbyshire Record Society*, 1979. (Occasional Paper, 3, 1979). pp. xvi, 50, 72. The new introduction is headed 'The Midland Counties Railway'.

7009 [2nd edn], 1895. Reprinted with a new Introduction by John Thomas. *David & Charles*, 1972. pp. [ix], 179, 'with 230 illustrations from original drawings made on the spot'.

7011 New edn [2nd edn]. The North Devon & Cornwall Junction Light Railway (Torrington–Halwill). *Bracknell: Forge Books*, 1980. pp. 48, with 18 illus, 6 layout plans, 3 timetables & 2 maps. Text extends onto back cover.

7018 Reprint. *Frank Graham*, 1974. pp. xix, 315, with 5 plates. A facsimile reprint of the 1875 edition.

7025 2nd edn reprint, with a new Introduction by K. Hoole . . . , and a postscript by G. D. Calvert, Archivist, North Yorkshire Moors Railway Preservation Society. *S.R. Publishers*, 1969. pp. v–viii, 81, v, ix–x, with frontis, 42 illus on plates & in text, incl. a folded map & a folded gradient profile.

7028 New edn, with title: Tomlinson's North Eastern Railway: its rise and development; new edition with introduction by K. Hoole. *Newton Abbot: David & Charles*, 1967. pp. xx, 820, with 240 illus on plates and in text, incl. maps & plans; 6 appendices. Index, pp. 781–820.
    The Introduction by Kenneth Hoole (pp. v–viii) includes errata.

7029 Reprint, with a foreword by Reginald Hackworth Young. *Shildon: Shildon Stockton & Darlington Railway Jubilee Committee*, 1975. pp. 406, xxxii, [36] leaves of plates. A facsimile reprint in a slip case.

7033 *See* 8030.

7035 Reprint. *Allen & Unwin*, 1964.

7050 [2nd] edn. *Ian Allan*, 1974. pp. 240, with 125 illus on 48 plates, & in text, maps, plans & diagrams.

7079 *See* 12405.

7085 [New edn, with altered title]: A tour of the Whitby & Pickering Railway in 1836, by Henry Belcher, with notes and Introduction by John Cranfield. *London: Cranfield & Bonfiel Books*, 1977. pp. vi, 44, with 'Pictorial section, taken from drawings by G. Dodgson' (20 engravings on 10 plates).
    An unabridged re-setting in smaller format of the original work, referred to in the Introduction as 'Belcher's Scenery of the Whitby & Pickering Railway' — an adaptation of the wording of the half-title of 1836. The editing by John Cranfield has, in his own words, been 'kept to a minimum'.

7096 Reprint. Views on the Newcastle & Carlisle Railway, from drawings by J. W. Carmichael; text by John Blackmore, with an introduction by Frank Graham. *Newcastle upon Tyne: F. Graham*, 1969. pp. 53, with 23 engravings; decorated cover. The original edition of 1836 reprinted, with the engravings rearranged.
    'Carmichael's Views were published in parts from 1836 to 1838 as the various sections [of the line] were completed. In 1839 they were re-issued in what was really a second edition. Our facsimile reproduction is based on the first issue of the plates. We have not however kept them in chronological order but have arranged them topographically, starting at Newcastle and ending at Carlisle'. (F. Graham in his Introduction).

7100 Another edn. *Scarborough*, 1844. pp. 9, with Supplement.   G. A. BOYES

7117 Reprint. *Newcastle upon Tyne: Frank Graham*, [197–?]. A straight reprint, including covers.

7156 Another edn. Trade and commerce of the North Eastern district. [*York: L.N.E.R.*, 1923]. pp. 80. 'Private: for use of the Company's servants only'.
    A re-issue of the 1921 edn, with a la. folded col. map of the LNER, a key map of the NER also in colour and 10 maps in text.

7162 5th edn ('5th impression'). *Oakwood Press*, 1959. pp. 29, with 11 illus & 2 maps on 8 plates; bibliography (20+ sources).
    —— 6th edn. *Oakwood Press*, 1967. pp. 30, with 14 illus & 2 maps on 8 plates; bibliography (20+ sources).
    —— 7th edn, with addenda. *Oakwood Press*, 1974. (Oakwood Library of Railway History, 1). pp. 31, with 14 illus & 2 maps on 8 plates & a bibliography.

7182 2nd edn. 1965. pp. 36.
    —— 3rd edn, rev. by W. J. K. Davies, 1970. pp. 36.
    —— 4th edn, rev. by W. J. K. Davies, 1973. pp. 36.
    —— 5th edn. Text by W. J. K. Davies and D. M. E. Ferriera, 1978. pp. 32.

7183 Revised & extended edn. *Bradford Barton*, 1966. pp. 102, with 15 illus on 8 plates, 4 maps, gradient profile, 2 detailed tables, rules & regulations, & 18 notes.

7186 'Golden Jubilee Commemorative Reprint of the 1927 Official Guide', with a new introduction consisting of a brief historical survey. [*R.H. & D. Rly Association*, 1977]. pp. 34, with 13 illus & a map.

7187 5th edn, by P. Ransome-Wallis. *Ian Allan*, 1968. pp. 56, with 54 illus, 6 layout plans, lists & map.

7189 Earlier editions: October 1936. [*Hythe: R.H. & D. Rly*], 1936. sm. obl. format. pp. 16, with 4 illus, map, timetable, 2 fare tables.

—— September 1937. [*R.H. & D. Rly*], 1937. sm. obl. format. pp. 16, with 5 illus, 2 timetables (Summer & Winter), 2 fare tables. No map.

—— Winter 1937. [*R.H. & D. Rly*], 1937. sm. obl. pp. 16, with 7 illus, timetable, 2 fare tables. No map.

—— April 1938. [*R.H. & D. Rly*], 1938. sm. 8°. pp. 16, with 8 illus, 2 timetables, 2 fare tables. No map.

—— Another 1946 edn. *Ian Allan*, 1946. pp. 23, with 12 illus, stock list & 2 timetables; map inside front cover.

—— 1974 edn, compiled by C. R. J. Hawkins, 1974. pp. 24, with 17 col. illus; map inside back cover.

—— Golden Jubilee edn. Official Guidebook: Golden Jubilee edition. *Hythe: Romney, Hythe & Dymchurch Rly*, [1977]. obl. 8°. pp. 22, with 25 col. illus (incl. cover illus); map inside front cover.

7190 Another edn. *Ian Allan*, [1969]. pp. [24]. 40 illus with descrs.

7191 5th edn, by P. Ransome-Wallis. *Ian Allan*, 1968. pp. 56, with 54 illus, 6 layout plans, lists & a map.
—— 6th edn. *Ian Allan*, 1970. pp. 48, with 47 illus, 6 layout plans & a map.

7195 Reprint of the earlier of the two editions [ca. 1920–5]. *Shrewsbury: Shropshire County Library*, 1977. pp. 37, [5], with 7 illus & a map.
Six of the illustrations are of stations and bridges on the line.

7196 Rev. & enl. edn. *Industrial Railway Society*, 1972. pp. 102, with 70 illus, 3 layout plans, 8 lists & a map.
Period, 1861–1960.

7197 Rev. & enl. edn. *Industrial Railway Society*, 1974. pp. 52, with 34 illus, 9 diagrams, 4 plans & a map.

7198 4th edn, by Patrick Ransome-Wallis. *Ian Allan*, 1967. pp. 48, with 36 illus, 5 diagrams, 2 facsimiles, a map & a bibliography (7 sources); gradient profile on end papers.
—— 5th edn, by P. Ransome-Wallis. *Ian Allan*, 1969. pp. 48.

7206 Reprint. *Conway Maritime Press*, 1971.

7217 *See* 7219.

7219 2nd edn. *Oakwood Press*, 1963. (Oakwood Library of Railway History, 53). pp. 98, with 67 illus on 28 plates, 8 maps & plans, & 2 bibliographies.
An enlarged edition of this author's *The South Eastern Railway and the S.E. & C.R.* (1953) combined with his *The London, Chatham & Dover Railway* (1952).
—— Reprint with amendments & additional material [1978].

7226 New, rev. edn, with altered title: The locomo-

tive history of the London Chatham and Dover Railway. *London: Railway Correspondence & Travel Society*, 1979. pp. [vi], 127, with 93 illus, 2 maps & many tables. A much enlarged edition.

7230 [Paperback edn]. *Ian Allan*, 1971. pp. 198, with 71 illus on 32 plates.

7244 [Another edn]. *London: Printed by Brown & Syrett*, 1839. pp. 32.

7284 Reprint of 1858 edn. *E & W Books, distributed by R. Hale*, 1970. A facsimile reprint.

7320 2nd enl. edn (2 vols), reprinted in 1 vol. *Ian Allan*, 1968. pp. 553.
After p. 278 the pagination differs from that of the 1963 two-volume edition, there being no intervening subsidiary papers.

7337 Locomotive adventure, vol. 2: Running experiences. *Ian Allan*, 1965. pp. 316, with frontis, 36 illus on 16 plates, & many tables & diagrams.
A detailed class-by-class record of locomotive performance on the Southern Rly in the inter-war years, with logs of particular runs. Includes an account of the filming of 'The Wrecker' at Lasham in 1928, and of the introduction of the Sentinel rail bus service on the Southern, 1932–5.

7338 2nd edn, revised. *Allen & Unwin*, 1968. pp. 303, & 70 illus on 34 plates.
—— Reprint. *Allen & Unwin*, 1977.

7343 2nd edn. Locomotives of the Southern. *Locomotive Publishing Co. for the Southern Rly*, [ca. 1927]. obl. format. pp. 72, with col. frontis & 26 illus with details on facing pages. Front cover has a window to the frontispiece. Title from cover.

7376 Originally published with the date 'August 1946' on reverse of title-page. In the reprints of 'September 1946' and '1947' the two illustrations on p. 35 are replaced by an advertisement.

7377 *See* 12515.

7379 *See* 12515.

7382 2nd edn, by Alan R. Taylor and Eric S. Tonks. *London: Ian Allan*, [1965]. pp. 64, with frontis, 32 illus on 16 plates, 11 layout plans, 5 composite dimensioned drawings of locomotives & rolling stock (pp. 56–60) & a map. No title-page. Title on cover.
—— 3rd edn, by Alan R. Taylor and Eric S. Tonks. *Ian Allan*, 1979. pp. 64, etc.

7385 Rev. & enl. edn. *Oakwood Press*, [1977]. (Oakwood Library of Railway History, 10). pp. 72, with 28 illus on 12 plates, plans, gradient profiles, map, detailed chronology, lists, timetables & a bibliography (12 sources). 'Entirely new edition, revised and enlarged by J. W. P. Rowledge and others.'

7402 2nd edn. *Oakwood Press*, 1970. (Locomotion Papers, 50). pp. 52, with 16 illus on plates, & in text, 3 maps, plan, facsimiles, diagrams & timetable.
The 1954 edition reprinted, with additions. First published as *The First Passenger Railway* (1942) (Ottley 7401).

7412 Official Guide. [*Towyn*]: *Talyllyn Rly*, [1952]. pp. 16, with illus, map & timetable.
Subsequent editions: [1953], pp. 16; [1954], pp. 16 (the 1952 edn re-issued with the 1954 timetable pasted over the one for 1952 on p. 14); 1955, pp. 24; [1957], pp. 40; [Centenary edn, 1965], pp. 64.

7415 *See* 9749.

7419 Another edn. *Ian Allan*, 1970. pp. 56, with 46 illus, map, 12 layout plans, gradient profile, 2 tables & a bibliography (10 sources).
—— Another edn. *Ian Allan*, 1978. pp. 56, with 42 illus, map, 12 layout plans, gradient profile, 2 tables & a bibliography (10 sources).

7420 *See* 9763.

7422 Reprinted October 1962, September 1963, May 1964, October 1965, March 1968, April 1970.

7425 2nd edn. 1964. pp. [28], with 17 illus, 2 maps (1 in sections), a plan & a gradient profile.
—— 3rd edn. 1968. pp. [32], with 18 illus, 2 maps, plan & g.p.
—— 4th edn. 1970. pp. [32], with 22 illus, 2 maps, plan & g.p.
—— 5th edn. 1973. pp. [32], with 22 illus, 2 maps, plan & g.p.
—— 6th edn. 1977. pp. [16], with 14 illus (8 col)., map & plan.
Editions 1 to 5 are in obl. format; the 6th is in normal 8°.

7427 2nd edn. *David & Charles*, 1970. pp. 128, with 25 illus on 12 plates, 18 drawings, maps & facsimiles, 4 appendices, 2 folded maps, 170 notes & a bibliography (7 sources).

7434 Paperback edn. *Pan Books*, 1971. pp. 110, with 40 illus (8 col). on 24 plates & 2 appendices.
Re-set in smaller format but with text apparently unaltered.

7443 Another edn, ed. & rev. by Arthur Elton. *Chatham: Evelyn, Adams & Mackay*, 1968. la. 8°. pp. xvii, 222, with 117 illus on 72 plates & 8 col. plates in text; notes and bibliography, pp. 185–99.
ch. 7 (pp. 143–65 & col. plate II), 'The Railway Age'. 38 of the 117 illus relate to railways.

7457 *See* 8804 or 12583.

7459 2nd edn. *Newton Abbot: David & Charles*, 1969. pp. 288. A reprint with minor corrections.

7514 The venue is the Metropolitan District Railway (Circle Line), not the Metropolitan Railway.
For a commentary on railways in the Sherlock Holmes stories see 'Railways in English fiction', by Neil Caplan, *Railway Magazine* (May 1957), pp. 347–50.

7517 The original title of this play was *Still Life* (7518).

7518 Widely known by its later name, *Brief Encounter* (7517).

7519 First published as: *Beware of the Trains: sixteen stories* (Gollancz, 1953). pp. 192.

7520 Reprinted in: *Crime on the Lines*, edited by Bryan Morgan (1975), pp. 130–6.

7546 John Chester Craven, Locomotive Superintendent of the LBSCR, 1847–1870, is also featured in this story.

7551 First published by Chatto & Windus, 1909.

7552 First published by Hodder & Stoughton, 1912. Republished in *Crime on the Lines*, edited by Bryan Morgan, (1975).

7556 Virtually the whole of this story is set in Cornwall, the viaduct being Calstock (called 'Caradon' in the book), and the period is shortly after 1900.

7658 Reprinted in *Crime on the Lines*, edited by Bryan Morgan (1975), pp. 97–108.

7663 Reprinted in *Crime on the Lines*, edited by Bryan Morgan (1975), pp. 85–96.

7664 Reprinted as: Stories of the Railway, with a Foreword by Bryan Morgan. *London & Henley: Routledge & Kegan Paul*, 1977. pp. 248. A facsimile reprint with altered title.
A collection of 15 of his short stories, originally published in *Pearson's Magazine* and *Harmsworth's Magazine* and issued as a collection in 1912 entitled *Thrilling Stories of the Railway*. Contents:
Peter Crane's Cigars
The Tragedy on the London and Mid-Northern
The Affair of the Corridor Express
Sir Gilbert Murrell's Picture
How the Bank was saved
The Affair of the German Dispatch-Box
How the Bishop kept his Appointment
The Adventure of the Pilot Engine
The Stolen Necklace
The Mystery of the Boat Express
How the Express was saved
A Case of Signalling
Winning the Race
The Strikers
The Ruse that succeeded

7672 First published in [Mozley's] *Magazine for the Young*, 1849.
First published in book form, June 1855.

7682 Series two, compiled by S. Evelyn Thomas.

Whetstone: Good Humour Publications, [1947–9?]. pp. 64.

Stories, jokes & drawings.

7691 This is in fact a burlesque on F. Fanshawe's prize poem (7692).

Blackwell's cat. 865/625

7698 Said to have been written by a Reading railwayman named Godfrey. See *Seen from the Railway Platform*, by W. Vincent (1919), p. 106.

7740 Reprint. *Ian Allan*, [1968]. pp. 96. A facsimile reprint.

—— Reprint. *Duckworth*, 1974. pp. 96. A facsimile reprint, slightly enlarged. A new Foreword replaces the original.

7786 Reprint. *Pan Books*, 1971. pp. 110, with 40 illus (8 full-page col.) on 24 plates, & 2 appendices. Reset in smaller format but with text unabridged. Paperback.

7801 *See* 10201.

7821 Part 2, reprinted, with a list of subsequent additions to the collection, 1948.

7825 Another edn. *B.R.*, 1954. pp. 10, with 8 illus & a track plan. A portable publicity exhibit.

7832 2nd rev. edn. [*York*], 1950. pp. 49.

7846 [Shop, Shed and Road]. L.B.S.C.'s Shop, Shed and Road, edited by Martin Evans. [1st edn], revised and reprinted under the original title. *Hemel Hempstead: Model & Allied Publications*, 1969. pp. 192, with 30 illus on 16 plates & over 100 groups of drawings.

Originally published as *Shop, Shed & Road* (1929). Reprinted as *The Live Steam Book* (1950, 2nd edn 1954). This edition completely revised and with new drawings and plates and additional chapters.

7848 Reprint. *Model & Allied Publications*, 1977. pp. [6], 170, with 165 dimensioned drawings (external features only) by F. C. Hambleton.

7855 *See* 7846.

7858 [2nd] edn. *P. Marshall*, 1962. pp. x, 172, with 96 illus on 36 plates & 132 dimensioned drawings.

Small-scale steam locomotives.

7882 Reprinted in: *Sources and Nature of the Statistics of the United Kingdom*, edited by Maurice G. Kendall, vol. 1 (1952), pp. 279–302, including a bibliography (43 sources).

7894 *See* 12919.

7896 *See* 12927.

7900 Still in MS. An enlarged coverage is planned and publication in 1988 is at least a possibility.

7901 *See* 12926.

7914 Another set: RAILWAY Chronicle Travelling Charts. *London: Railway Chronicle*, [1845–46 or 47].

A series of multi-fold pictorial route charts of varying lengths for rail journeys to places within 100 miles of London. The railway is represented by 4 end-to-end parallel lines (2 for the up line, 2 for the down) with tunnels, bridges and junctions. The mileage, gradient, and notes about physical features of the railway and the immediate area are arranged on either side of this continuous diagram.

Each chart has an introductory paragraph or two, and a full-width drawing as a head-piece—more often than not the London terminus. The central diagrammatic section with its notes is flanked on either side by a running historical & topographical commentary on features of interest which can be seen from the train, with numerous small pen drawings of particular structures or picturesque scenes, including an occasional one of the railway itself. Some of the charts have a map and some have a tailpiece drawing, similar to that at the head, which may depict the provincial terminus of the line.

The engravings are by 'Messrs Thompson' from drawings by 'David Cox, jnr'. There is considerable repetition on charts which share the same terminus and route out of London.

Additional notes: copies, now scarce, are weak at the folds. To preserve, charts should be strengthened by backing or lamination and kept rolled, not folded.

The following descriptions are of the set in LU(THC) which is in the form of a guard book, each chart being in its original folded form and tipped in at the head. The order of publication is not certain but might be arrived at by referring to the *Railway Chronicle* itself. The order given here is simply that of the bound up set in LU(THC).

—— 2nd edn. *Brighton Public Libraries*, 1972.

[1], London and Brighton. [1845]. Length, 6ft. 72 border sketches incl. 8 railway scenes, & a map.

A facsimile reprint. Bound into the same volume is the related series *Felix Summerly's Pleasure Excursions*, also published by the Railway Chronicle in the same period.

[2], Great Western: London to Hanwell and Southall. Length, 1ft 5ins. 11 border sketches (4 of the railway).

[3], London to Kingston and Hampton Court. Length, 1ft 6ins. 16 border sketches (2 of the railway).

[4], London to Basingstoke, Winchester and Southampton on the South Western. Length, 7ft 8ins. 123 border sketches (7 of the railway).

[5], London to Wolverton. Length, 4ft 10ins. 66 border sketches (8 of the railway).

[6], London to Ashford, Folkestone and Dover. Length, 8ft 6ins. 95 border sketches (5 of the railway); map.

[7], London to Bishops Stortford and Cambridge on the Eastern Counties. Length, 6ft 6ins. 44 border sketches (4 of the railway); map.

[8], Great Western: London to Reading, Didcot and Oxford. Length, 6ft 9ins. 72 border sketches (13 of the railway); map.

7919 Reprint. *Sidgwick & Jackson*, 1973. pp.

xxxiv, 318. A reprint of part of the original work published by E. Churton in 1851 which had 590 pages. In the reprint the original text is reproduced as far as the middle of pp. 260 & 261, and the complete index to the original edition is then made to follow, with page numbering altered to follow on from p. 260, as pp. 261–318. A note under the heading 'Publisher's Announcement' and dated 'April, 1973' indicates that the re-publication of vol. 2, for provincial routes, is imminent. Apparently, this has so far not appeared.

7926 A revised entry: Handbook of Stations. *London: R.C.H.*, 1862–1956. 17 editions, with supplementary appendices and leaflets. (See *Railway History Sources*, by C. R. Clinker, 1976, pp. 12–13).
—— Reprint of 1904 edn. The Railway Clearing House Handbook of Railway Stations, 1904: a reprint, with an introduction by C. R. Clinker. *Newton Abbot: David & Charles*, 1970. pp. [iv], 600.

7947 [4th edn]. British Rail Atlas and Gazetteer. *Ian Allan*, 1965. pp. 45, 49–84.
A modified form of the Pre-Grouping Atlas & Gazetteer (edns 1, 2 & 3). In the Atlas section the six regions are in distinctive colours but the lines are still identified by the initials of their pre-Grouping companies.
—— 5th edn. British Railways Pre-Grouping Atlas and Gazetteer. *Ian Allan*, 1972. pp. 84 (no p. 46).
In this edition the colouring and naming of the lines revert to 'pre-Grouping', as in editions 1, 2 & 3.

7949 1869 edn reprinted, with enlarged type and an introduction by C. R. Clinker. *David & Charles*, 1969. pp. [4], xxiv, 118, with la. folded map at end.

7950 no. 1, 19 October 1839. 'Bradshaw's Railway Companion'. *Turntable Enterprises*, 1971. A reprint in enlarged format, with an introductory note.
no. 649, August 1887: a new edition . . . , with enlarged type and Introduction by David St John Thomas. *David & Charles*, 1968. pp. [3], xxxvi, 596.
no. 921, April 1910: a new edition . . . , with enlarged type and Introduction by David St John Thomas. *David & Charles*, 1968. pp. [iv], lxxiii, 1190.
no. 1260, July 1938: a new edition . . . , with enlarged type and Introduction by David St John Thomas. *David & Charles*, 1969. pp. [iv], liii, 9, 135, 1138.

p.588 MARSH, D'Arcy. The tragedy of Henry Thornton (1935).
Henry Thornton was General Manager of the Great Eastern Rly, 1914–1922. This biography, however, is almost wholly concerned with his career from 1922 to 1933, in Canada.
See 'Desperation at Liverpool Street, 1922' by Michael Robbins, *Journal of the Railway & Canal Historical Society*, vol. 25, no. 3 (September 1979), pp. 89–94.

PART TWO
SUPPLEMENTARY ENTRIES
7951–12956

Two-thirds of these entries are for works published after 1963 (the cut-off date for the main work) and before January 1981. The remaining one-third are for works of an earlier date discovered since the original Bibliography was compiled, and of this one-third, one-sixth (about 300) are for works published before 1900.

CLASSIFICATION SCHEME
Summary Table

For greater detail see these headings within the text of the Bibliography

*For changes made in the Classification Scheme for this Supplement,
see page 19 or at the head of affected Classes*

A GENERAL HISTORY AND DESCRIPTION OF RAIL TRANSPORT IN THE BRITISH ISLES

B RAIL TRANSPORT AT PARTICULAR PERIODS:

B 1 ORIGIN, ANTIQUITY AND EARLY USE OF RAIL TRANSPORT
Prepared stone trackways of ancient times—Wagonways in mines and quarries in mediaeval Europe and their evolution in Britain during the 16th, 17th and 18th centuries as feeders from mines and quarries to rivers, canals and the sea

B 2 THE TRANSITIONAL PERIOD, FROM MINERAL WAGONWAY TO PUBLIC PASSENGER RAILWAY, 1800–1830 . . . 1850

B 3 1830–1914   THE RAILWAY AGE

B 4 – B 10   1914–1980

B 4 1914–1918   RAILWAYS DURING THE FIRST WORLD WAR

B 5 1918–1923   POST-WAR RECOVERY AND THE PERIOD ENDING WITH THE 'BIG FOUR' AMALGAMATIONS OF 1923

B 6 – B 10   1921–1980

B 6 1921–1939   THE 'BIG FOUR' AMALGAMATIONS OF 1923 (Railways Act, 1921) AND RAILWAYS DURING THE 1920s AND 1930s

B 7 – B 10   1939–1980

B 7 1939–1945   RAILWAYS DURING THE SECOND WORLD WAR

B 8 1945–1947   POST-WAR RECOVERY, AND RAILWAYS DURING THEIR FINAL YEARS OF PRIVATE OWNERSHIP

B 9 NATIONALIZATION, 1948. THE ESTABLISHMENT OF THE BRITISH TRANSPORT COMMISSION AND 'BRITISH RAILWAYS'

B 10 1948–   RAILWAYS OF THE BRITISH ISLES IN GENERAL AND 'BRITISH RAILWAYS'

B 10 (ER) Eastern Region
B 10 (LMR) London Midland Region
B 10 (NER) North Eastern Region
B 10 (Sc.R) Scottish Region
B 10 (SR) Southern Region
B 10 (WR) Western Region

C RAIL TRANSPORT IN THE REGIONS AND COUNTIES OF THE BRITISH ISLES:

C 1 ENGLAND

C 1 a   SOUTHERN ENGLAND (South West Region, South East Region, West Midlands Region, East Midlands Region, East Anglia)

C 1 b   SOUTH WEST REGION (Cornwall, Devon, Somerset, Dorset, Avon, Wiltshire, Gloucestershire)

C 1 c   SOUTH EAST REGION (Greater London, Hampshire, Isle of Wight, West Sussex, East Sussex, Surrey, Kent, Berkshire, Oxfordshire, Buckinghamshire, Bedfordshire, Hertfordshire, Essex)

C 1 d   WEST MIDLANDS REGION (Herefordshire and Worcestershire, Warwickshire, Shropshire, West Midlands, Staffordshire)

C 1 e   EAST MIDLANDS REGION (Northamptonshire, Leicestershire [with Rutland], Derbyshire, Nottinghamshire, Lincolnshire)

C 1 f   EAST ANGLIA (Cambridgeshire, Suffolk, Norfolk)

C 1 g   NORTHERN ENGLAND (North West Region, Yorkshire & Humberside, North Region)

C 1 h   NORTH WEST REGION (Cheshire, Merseyside, Greater Manchester, Lancashire)

C 1 i   YORKSHIRE & HUMBERSIDE REGION (South Yorkshire, West Yorkshire, North Yorkshire, Humberside)

C 1 j   NORTH REGION (Cumbria, Durham, Cleveland, Northumberland, Tyne & Wear)

C 1 – C 2   ENGLAND TO SCOTLAND—The East Coast and West Coast routes

C 2   SCOTLAND

C 2 a   DUMFRIES & GALLOWAY REGION

C 2 b   STRATHCLYDE REGION, including Glasgow

C 2 c   BORDERS REGION

C 2 d   LOTHIAN REGION, including Edinburgh

C 2 e   CENTRAL REGION

C 2 f   FIFE REGION

C 2 g   TAYSIDE REGION

C 2 h   HIGHLAND REGION

C 2 i   GRAMPIAN REGION

C 2 D 1   LIGHT RAILWAYS AND TRAMWAYS IN SCOTLAND (generally)

C 2 E   RAILWAY ENGINEERING (Civil and Mechanical)

C 2 G 3   PASSENGER TRAIN SERVICES IN SCOTLAND

C 2 K   SOCIAL ASPECTS

C 2 L   SCOTTISH RAILWAY COMPANIES

C 3   WALES

C 3 a   SOUTH WALES (The Glamorgans and Gwent)

C 3 b   West Glamorgan, Mid Glamorgan, South Glamorgan

C 3 c   Gwent

C 3 d   NORTH, WEST AND MID WALES (Dyfed, Powys, Gwynedd and Clwyd)

C 3 e   Dyfed

C 3 f   Powys

C 3 g   Gwynedd (with Anglesey)

C 3 h   Clwyd

C 3 D   WELSH NARROW GAUGE MINERAL/PASSENGER LINES

C 3 L   STANDARD GAUGE WELSH RAILWAYS

C 4   IRELAND—The Republic of Ireland and Northern Ireland

C 4 A   GENERAL HISTORY AND DESCRIPTION OF RAIL TRANSPORT IN IRELAND

C 4 B   CONTEMPORANEOUS WORKS

C 4 C   RAIL TRANSPORT IN THE COUNTIES OF IRELAND

C 4 D   LIGHT AND NARROW GAUGE RAILWAYS AND TRAMWAYS IN IRELAND

C 4 E   RAILWAY ENGINEERING (Civil and Mechanical)

C 4 K   SOCIAL ASPECTS

C 4 L   IRISH RAILWAY COMPANIES

C 4 Q   PRESERVATION AND APPRECIATION

C 5   ISLE OF WIGHT

C 6   ISLE OF MAN

C 7   CHANNEL ISLANDS

C 8   CHANNEL TUNNEL

C 9   SCOTLAND TO IRELAND TUNNEL SCHEME

C 10   BRITISH RAIL TRANSPORT COMPARED WITH THAT OF OTHER COUNTRIES

C 11   INTERNATIONAL CO-OPERATION

D   SPECIAL TYPES OF RAILWAY AND LOCOMOTION:

D 1   LIGHT RAILWAYS AND TRAMWAYS

D 2   NARROW GAUGE RAILWAYS

D 3 INDUSTRIAL, MINERAL, DOCK, HARBOUR, AND PUBLIC UTILITIES SYSTEMS

D 4 ELECTRIC AND UNDERGROUND RAILWAYS

D 5 UNUSUAL FORMS OF RAILWAY AND LOCOMOTION

D 6 MINIATURE RAILWAYS

E RAILWAY ENGINEERING (Civil and Mechanical)   Archaeology of railways

E 1 BIOGRAPHIES OF RAILWAY CIVIL AND CIVIL/MECHANICAL ENGINEERS

E 2 RAILWAY CIVIL ENGINEERING (General)

E 3 PERMANENT WAY

E 4 ELECTRIC RAILWAY ENGINEERING Electrification—Underground electric railways

E 5 ARCHITECTURE AND DESIGN   Bridges, viaducts, stations, tunnel entrances, etc—Archaeology of railway structures

E 6 RAILWAY MECHANICAL ENGINEERING (General)

E 7 LOCOMOTIVES

E 8 STEAM LOCOMOTIVES

E 9 – 10 ELECTRIC AND DIESEL LOCOMOTIVES

E 9 ELECTRIC LOCOMOTIVES AND TRAINS

E 10 DIESEL, DIESEL-ELECTRIC, AND OTHER SELF-GENERATING TYPES OF LOCOMOTIVE AND TRAIN

E 11 ROLLING STOCK (Carriages and wagons)

E 12 CARRIAGES

E 13 WAGONS

E 14 BRAKES

E 15 SAFETY ENGINEERING   Signals and signalling

E 16 OTHER RAILWAY EQUIPMENT

F RAILWAY ADMINISTRATION Organization, finance and management, commercial aspects

F 1 RATES, CHARGES, FARES, TOLLS AND TICKETS

F 2 INTER-RAILWAY RELATIONS   Competition—Co-operation and amalgamation— Gauge controversy

F 3 CLEARING HOUSE SYSTEM

G RAILWAY OPERATION

G 1 OPERATION OF RAILWAY SERVICES   Train control—Station and goods depot management—Closures

G 2 FREIGHT TRAFFIC   Marshalling—Cartage

G 3 PASSENGER TRAIN SERVICES

G 4 RAILWAY ROAD SERVICES   Omnibus and freight

G 5 RAILWAY WATER SERVICES   Docks and harbours—Train ferries and boat trains

G 6 RAILWAY AIR SERVICES

G 7 ANCILLARY SERVICES   Hotels and catering—Station kiosks and bookstalls— Camping coaches

G 8 RESEARCH (operational and maintenance)

G 9 PUBLIC RELATIONS AND PUBLICITY

H RAILWAY LIFE AND LABOUR   Work and working conditions—Trade unions— Strikes—Staff welfare—Memoirs of railway life

K RAILWAYS AND THE NATION Railways within the framework of national life—Railway policy—Integration of transport modes—Planning—Railways and politics

K 1 RAILWAYS AND SOCIETY Railways and the life of the people—Urban and suburban development—Commuting—Increased facilities for travel—Holidays and tourism—Objections to Sunday trains (19th century)—Social aspects of rail closures

K 2 RAILWAYS AND THE PASSENGER Travelling conditions—Accounts of train journeys

K 3 SAFETY IN TRANSIT Accidents and their prevention

K 4 RAILWAYS AND INDUSTRY, TRADE AND AGRICULTURE Consignor aspects

K 5 RAILWAYS AND THE MONEY MARKET Investment—The 'Railway Mania'

K 6 PARLIAMENT, GOVERNMENT AND THE RAILWAYS Government control and inspection—The Railway Interest—Acts—Railway Passenger Duty

K 7 RAILWAY LAW

K 8 RAILWAYS AND CRIME Railway police

K 9 RAILWAYS AND THE POST OFFICE Travelling post offices—Post Office (London) Underground Rly—Railway philately

K 10 RAILWAYS AND NATIONAL DEFENCE The use of public railways for movements of military personnel and their equipment—Ambulance trains

K 11 MILITARY RAILWAYS Systems owned, operated and maintained by military or naval authorities

L INDIVIDUAL RAILWAYS The history and description of railway companies up to their nationalization into British Railways in 1948

M HERALDRY AND LIVERY

N THE RAILWAY IN ART

O THE RAILWAY IN LITERATURE Autobiography, memoirs, novels and verse

P HUMOUR, HUMOROUS DRAWING AND SATIRE

Q APPRECIATION OF RAILWAYS

Q 1 PRESERVATION, MUSEUMS, RESTORED AND RE-OPENED LINES

Q 2 MODEL RAILWAY ENGINEERING

Q 3 RAILWAY PHOTOGRAPHY, CINEMATOGRAPHY AND FILMS

R RESEARCH AND STUDY OF RAILWAYS AND RAILWAY HISTORY Bibliography and guides to sources—Railway historians—Railway-book publishing—Glossaries and dictionaries

S STATISTICS, STATISTICAL SOURCES AND METHOD

T ATLASES AND GAZETTEERS

A GENERAL HISTORY AND DESCRIPTION OF RAIL TRANSPORT IN THE BRITISH ISLES

7951–8048

Reference sources (bibliographies, catalogues, encyclopaedias, chronologies) 7951–84

For collective histories of individual railways see L (Collective Works)
For railways in general at particular periods see B
For railways in particular localities see C

7951 TUCK, H. Railway Compendium to Tuck's Map of the Railways of England and Wales, showing by reference to the figures on the map the length and termini of all railways in England and Wales for which Acts have been obtained. *London: E. Wilson*, January 1847. la. folded s. sh, 28in × 16in.

> Bound in with the LU(THC) copy is a map (28in × 22in). This shows lines 'open for traffick, in course of construction, and projected'.   LU(THC)

7952 BAKER, E. Railroadiana; consisting of books, pamphlets, maps, guides, timetables, etc., connected with the origin, rise and development of railways . . . *Birmingham: E. Baker*, [1904]. (Catalogue, 232). pp. 84.

> 1483 items, with notes, sometimes lengthy.

7953 FACTS and figures about British railways. [Title varies]. Published by the British Railways Press Office, 1927 to 1947, and thereafter by British Railways.
1924. Some facts about British railways.
[ca. 1927]. Some facts about British railways. pp. 14.
1930, November. Facts about British railways. pp. 28.
1932, February. Facts about British railways, 1932. pp. 32.
1933, February. Facts about British railways, 1933. pp. 20.
1934, February. Facts about British railways, 1934. pp. 28.
1935, February. Facts about British railways, 1935. pp. 32, with map.
1936, February. Facts about British railways, 1936. pp. 32, with map.
1937, February. Facts about British railways, 1937. pp. 32, with map.
1938, February. Facts about British railways, 1938. pp. 32, with map.
1939, February. Facts about British railways, 1939. pp. 32, with map.
1940, April. Facts about British railways, 1940. pp. 32.
1941, April. Facts about British railways in wartime. 1941. pp. 44.
1942, May. Facts about British railways in wartime. 1942. pp. 40.
1943. Facts about British railways in wartime. 1943. pp. 64.
1944. British railways in peace and war. 1944. pp. 72.
1944, September. British railways: facts and figures. pp. 16.

1945. It can now be revealed: more about British railways in peace and war. 1945. pp. 64.
1946. British railways: facts and figures.
1947. British railways: facts and figures. pp. 28.
1952. Facts and figures about British Railways. pp. 32.
1953. Facts and figures about British Railways. pp. 38.
1954. Facts and figures about British Railways.
1955. Facts and figures about British Railways. pp. 40.
1956. Facts and figures about British Railways. pp. 48.
1957. Facts and figures about British Railways. pp. 48.
1958. Facts and figures about British Railways. pp. 44.
1959. Facts and figures about British Railways. pp. 44.
1962. British Railways Yearbook. pp. 40.
1963. British Railways Yearbook. pp. 40.
1965. British Railways Yearbook. pp. 44.
1966. Facts and figures about British Rail. pp. 44.
1967. Facts and figures about British Rail. pp. 44.
1978. Facts and figures. 1978. pp. 64 & a 2p. addendum to replace pp. 48–52.
1980. Facts and Figures. 2nd edn, 1980. pp. 67.

> Tables, diagrams and maps relating to the present and recent past of railway activity, including, latterly, data on other transport modes and related topics such as tourism, commuting, environmental factors and international comparisons.
> The 1924 edition was produced for the British Empire Exhibition at Wembley in 1924. For a note about it by D. S. M. Barrie, See *Journal of the Railway & Canal Historical Society*, vol. 6, no. 3 (May 1960) p. 57.

7954 WILLIAMS, J. B. A Guide to the Printed Materials for English Social and Economic History, 1750–1850. *New York: Columbia University Press.* 2 vols.
vol. 1. 1926. pp. xxiii, 535; pp. 467–91, 'Railways:' a bibliography with annotations.

7955 KERR, N. Some Notes towards a Bibliographical History of the Stockton & Darlington and other railways, 1770–1926: a priced catalogue of the collection of . . . John Creswell Brigham of Darlington . . . [and other items once the property of] R. Stephenson, Francis Mewburn, J. Pease, John Graham, John Dixon . . . *Cartmel: N. Kerr, Bookseller*, 1935. (Catalogue no. 18, Nov. 1935). pp. 16.

317 items, of which the first 56 relate to the Stockton & Darlington Rly.

7956 LEICESTER CITY LIBRARIES. Catalogue of the Stretton Collection, November 1953. pp. 6. Reproduced typescript.

An alphabetical listing of about 220 books, pamphlets and periodicals on railways. The Collection has been added to continuously since this list was made. Not published but available to readers and enquirers, Leicester City Libraries.

7957 TRANSPORT history in current periodicals, *in* Journal of Transport History, 1953 to 1979.

An annual bibliography published in alternate issues, for papers in journals not specifically devoted to Transport. From 1953 to 1965 compiled by Professor Jack Simmons, and from 1966 to 1979 by George Ottley. From 1953 to 1974 the work was entitled 'Transport Bibliography'.

7958 RECENT literature, *in* Journal of the Railway & Canal Historical Society.

A bibliography published regularly in each issue of the J.R.C.H.S. (now thrice yearly). From October 1955 to November 1978 the compiler is William J. Skillern; from March 1979 it is Donald R. Steggles. The number of works listed (books, pamphlets and—exceptionally—essays in periodicals) in recent issues has been about 75.

Although the entries are required to be brief, this is the best available guide to the whole range of current railway literature. The compiling is not restricted to works sent in for review in the *Journal* but includes many publications by individuals and provincial societies or groups. The work provides a most useful four-monthly supplement to the present *Bibliography of British Railway History*.

7959 SIMMONS, J. The railways of Britain: an historical introduction. *London: Routledge & Kegan Paul*, 1961. pp. xii, 264, with 25 illus on 17 plates, & 14 illus & 6 maps in text.

pp. 233–50, 'Literature and maps'; a classified & annotated select bibliography.

—— 2nd edn. revised. *London: Macmillan*, 1968. pp. xi, 276.

pp. 244–63, 'Literature, maps, museums'.

7960 CARTER, E. F. The Railway Encyclopaedia. *London: H. Starke*, 1963. pp. 365. Nearly 5,000 entries.

A collection of facts and information on the railways of the United Kingdom: their history, construction, engineering, personnel and operation.

7961 PEART, D. A. Literature and the Railway in the nineteenth and twentieth centuries: a thesis for the degree of Master of Arts in the School of English Language and Literature, University of Liverpool, 1964. pp. 306.

Section A (pp. 2–65), 'Books on railways as such': a commentary on 125 works:

ch. 1, The railway guide book

ch. 2, General books relating to the early days of railways

ch. 3, Some of the biographical material relating to the early days of railways

ch. 4, Later general books about railways

ch. 5, Locomotive books

ch. 6, Some important railway histories

ch. 7, Allen, Nock and Ellis: the most influential modern writers on railways proper

Section B (pp. 66–294), 'The Railway in English Literature': an analytical survey of 224 books and poems:

ch. 8, Dickens and the Railway

ch. 9, Railways in the nineteenth century novel and short story

ch.10, Railways in the twentieth century novel and short story

ch.11, Railways in the detective story

ch.12, Carlyle and Ruskin

ch.13, Some railway essayists

ch.14, Nineteenth century magazines

ch.15, Poems celebrating or deploring the coming of the Railway

ch.16, Poems about the Train

ch.17, The railway scene in poetry

ch.18, Railway love poems

ch.19, Poems on underground railways

ch.20, John Betjeman's railway poems

ch.21, Railwaymen's verse

The Index entries are under author and title arranged chronologically within a framework of subject headings.

7962 DYOS, H. J. Transport history in university theses, 1959–63, *in* Journal of Transport History, vol. 7 (1965–6), pp. 54–6.

30 sources, 5 of which are on railways. A continuation of Professor Dyos's first listing, in vol. 4 (1959–60) (Ottley 7896). *See also* 7974.

7963 OTTLEY, G. Bibliography of British Railway History [vol. 1], compiled by George Ottley, with the co-operation of William J. Skillern, C. R. Clinker, J. E. C. Palmer and C. E. Lee; foreword by Jack Simmons. *London: Allen & Unwin*, 1965 [1966]. pp. 683, in double column.

Thesis, F.L.A., Library Association, 1967.

7950 entries, for books, parts of books and pamphlets, on railways, wagonways and tramways and other forms of laterally-controlled transport in the British Isles from the earliest times to the present (1963). Arranged by subject with author, title & subject index (pp. 477–683): classification scheme (pp. 27–30) duplicated on end papers. Appendix I, First Schedule of the Railways Act, 1921, with alphabetical list of railways; Appendix II, List of railways nationalised under the Transport Act, 1947; Appendix III, Genealogical tables of the GWR, LNWR, Midland Rly and London Transport, devised by Charles E. Lee.

The date of publication on reverse of the title-page was wrongly printed as 1965.

7964 BRYANT, E. T. Railways: a reader's guide. *London: C. Bingley*, 1968. pp. 249.

An evaluative select bibliography of about 700 books & pamphlets published from 1945 to 1967, arranged under broad subject headings. Excluded are highly technical works and brief generalised introductory writing. A number of American and other overseas publications are included.

7965 ELLIS, C. H. The Pictorial Encyclopedia of Railways. *Feltham: Paul Hamlyn*, 1968. pp. 591, with 43 col. illus on plates, & 830 illus in text; index, pp. 581–91.

An illustrated commentary on the world's railways, past and present, arranged not under countries but by railway subjects.

7966 BLACK, R. D. C. A Catalogue of Pamphlets on Economic Subjects published between 1750 and 1900 and now housed in Irish libraries. *Belfast: The Queen's University*, 1969. pp. ix, 632 (in double column).

Arranged alphabetically by author under year of publication, with locations added. Author index but no index of subjects. Although the subject matter represented is for the whole of the British Isles, a high proportion of the entries relates to Ireland, a factor which adds particular value to the general usefulness of the work. The railway items not in the original volume of 'Ottley' have been incorporated into the present Supplement.

7967 [BLACKWELL]. B. H. BLACKWELL LTD. Rare and interesting books on science, mainly related to transport and technology, (compiled by Peter Fenemore). *Oxford: Blackwells*, 1969. (Catalogue 865). pp. 203.

1158 entries, of which 354 are for railway items. The railway section is in two parts, 'General' and 'British Companies'. In the latter each railway is introduced with an historical note. Full bibliographical descriptions are given, with annotations often containing highly informative detail. The work is most generously produced both in content and format and constitutes a valuable reference aid.

7968 DYOS, H. J. and ALDCROFT, D. H. British transport: an economic survey from the seventeenth century to the twentieth. *Leicester: Leicester University Press*, 1969. pp. 473, with 25 maps, 8 tables and an extensive bibliographical commentary with its own index (pp. 401–44); general index (pp. 445–73). —— reprint. *Penguin Books*, 1974. (Pelican Books). pp. 511. A re-setting in smaller format.

7969 ALTHOLZ, J. L. Victorian England, 1837–1901. *Cambridge: for the Conference on British Studies at the University Press*, 1970. pp. xi, 100.

A bibliography (2500 sources). ch. 8 (pp. 40–51): 'Economic history'; 332 sources, including railways.

7970 TAMES, R. The transport revolution in the 19th century: a documentary approach. *London: Oxford University Press*.

vol. 1, Railways, 1970. pp. 64, with 18 illus.

The text consists of 65 extracts from railway history literature covering the period 1750–1850, with a summary, chronology & bibliography at the end. Each section has an introduction. Presentation is at senior-school level.

7971 GUINNESS Book of Rail Facts and Feats. *Enfield: Guinness Superlatives*.

1st edn, compiled by John Marshall. 1971. pp. 255, with ca. 300 illus (some col.), maps & tables.

—— 2nd edn, compiled by J. Marshall. 1975. pp. 253, with over 400 illus (some col.), maps & tables.

—— 3rd edn, compiled by J. Marshall. 1979. pp. 252, with ca. 240 illus (some col.), maps & tables.

7972 COOPER, B. S. Decennial Index, no.1: Journal of the Railway & Canal Historical Society, vols 1–10 (1955–1964). *Caterham: R. & C.H.S.*, 1973. pp. 27.

—— Decennial Index no.2: vols 11–20, 1965–1974. *R. & C.H.S.*, 1975. pp. 31.

7973 ROUNDHOUSE [bookshop & publisher]. A Catalogue of Material Relating to Railways, 1973 [compiled by Iris Doyle]. *Harrow-on-the-Hill: The Roundhouse*, [1973]. pp. 125.

2447 items: books, pamphlets, maps, Acts & other parliamentary publications, deposited plans & sections, railway company documents & publications, guide books, brochures & timetables.

7974 OTTLEY, G. Transport history in British university theses, 1964–72, *in* Journal of Transport History, new series, vol. 2 (1973–4), pp. 234–8.

Bibliographical descriptions of 84 theses, of which 23 are on subjects within the field of railway humanities. A continuation of two previous listings, both by Professor H. J. Dyos, in the *J.T.H.*, vol. 4, no. 3 (May 1960) and vol. 7, no. 1 (May 1965). *See* 7896.

7975 BAGWELL, P. S. The Transport Revolution from 1770. *London: Batsford*, 1974. pp. 460, with 21 maps, 21 tables, 33 diagrams, 964 notes & an evaluative bibliography (pp. 419–46). Index, pp. 447–60.

7976 CORNWELL, E. L. Pictorial Story of Railways, edited by E. L. Cornwell. *London: Hamlyn*, [1974]. la. 8°. pp. 256, with col. frontis & many illus (mostly col.), & maps.

World coverage. Includes British Isles.

7977 ROBERTSON, P. The Shell Book of Firsts. *London: Ebury Press; Michael Joseph*, 1974. pp. 256.

Railways, pp. 151–4 & in the chronology; ca. 100 entries in index under 'Railways', 'Train Ferry' and 'Tram'.

7978 FERNEYHOUGH, F. The history of railways in Britain. *Reading: Osprey*, 1975. pp. 228, with col. frontis; 144 illus (13 col.), 3 maps, many tables & lists, & a bibliography (60+ sources).

A comprehensive companion of reference essays, with three detailed indexes.

ch. 1: Chronology; chs. 2–9: General developments; ch. 10: Classic locomotives; ch. 11: Biographies. Appendix A: Accidents; Appendix B: London Underground railways; Appendix C: Directory of Railway Enthusiasts' and Preservation societies.

7979 KERR, N. Railroadiana: a souvenir catalogue of books, documents, manuscripts, prints and pictures, issued to commemorate 150 years of the Stockton & Darlington Railway, 1825–1975, and 42 years of railway bookselling, 1933–1975. *Cartmel: N. Kerr*, 1975. (Catalogue no. 224). pp. 55, with 4 folded plates & many illus. Title from cover.

A generously produced catalogue with many detailed historical notes on 317 items, mostly relating to early 19th century railways, and a bibliographical essay on Richard Trevithick.

7980 ROUNDHOUSE [bookshop & publisher]. A Catalogue of Material Relating to Railways, 1974–5 [compiled by Iris Doyle]. *Harrow-on-the-Hill: The Roundhouse*, [1975]. pp. 235.

3745 items: books, pamphlets, maps, Acts & other parliamentary publications, deposited plans & sections, railway company documents & publications, guide books, brochures & timetables.

7981 UNIVERSITY OF LONDON LIBRARY. Catalogue of the Goldsmiths' Library of Economic Literature. *London: Cambridge University Press*. 2 vols.

vol. 1: Printed books to 1800, compiled by Margaret Canney and David Knott, with an introduction by J. H. P. Pafford, Goldsmiths' Librarian, 1945–67. 1970. pp. xxiii, 838. Introduction includes biographical details of Professor H. S. Foxwell and the development of the Goldsmiths' Library.

vol. 2: Printed books, 1801–1850, compiled by Margaret Canney, David Knott and Joan M. Gibbs. 1975. pp. vii, 772.

Arranged by year of publication divided by subject, Railways being under 'Transport' in vol. 2.

7982 HANHAM, H. J. Bibliography of British History, 1851–1914 . . . , compiled and edited by H. J. Hanham. *Oxford: Clarendon Press*, 1976. pp. xxvii, 1606. (Index, pp. 1239–1606).

'Issued under the direction of the American Historical Association and the Royal Historical Society of Great Britain.'

A monumental work with annotations to entries and a very fine index. Provides a select bibliography on any historical/social/economic subject. For Railways see Section F, sub-section 4 (pp. 697–713, entries 6193–6326).

7983 KIRBY, H. R. Doctoral theses in transport from Great Britain: first series, 1960–1975; edited by Howard R. Kirby. *London: Universities Transport Study Group, University College London*, 1977. (U.T.S.G. Occasional Publication, 1). la. 8°. pp. 24. Reproduced typescript.

A single-sequence alphabetical listing of 264 theses: 'Planning; Operations, management & control; History; Way engineering; Vehicle design and engineering'. Not limited to transport in the British Isles. The comparatively few theses on British railway history subjects are incorporated into the present Bibliography.

The aims and scope of the work, the sources used, and the difficulty of attempting to classify material which is characterised not by subject so often as by subject relationships, are explained in detail in the editor's Introduction.

7984 NOCK, O. S. Encyclopaedia of Railways; general editor, O. S. Nock; foreword by John Coiley. *London: Octopus Books*, 1977. la. 8°. pp. 480, with many hundreds of illustrations (some col.), col. maps, tables; pp. 398–427, Biography; pp. 442–7, Chronology; pp. 454–65, Glossary.

7985 MAYHEW, A. Railway enterprise of the United Kingdom. *London: Eyre & Spottiswoode*, 1893. pp. 8.   BLACK 9820

7986 CAMPLING, F. K. and NICHOLLS, J. T. The story of the railway. *London: Cassell*, [1920]. (Cassell's Continuous Readers; general series, 11). pp. 96, with col. frontis, 3 plates, 2 line drawings & a diagram.

A general introductory account for school use.

7987 ADAMS, J. G. and ELLIOTT, C. A. Our railways. *London: Blackie*, 1922. (Rambles among our Industries series). pp. 80, with 15 illus & 26 line drawings.

An introductory history for school use.

7988 RAILWAY Centenary procession and exhibition. *London: Railway Publishing Co.*, [1925]. pp. 55, with frontis, 62 illus & a map.

Revised and re-set from an essay in the *Railway Gazette*, 10 July 1925.

7989 [STOCKTON-ON-TEES]. BOROUGH OF STOCKTON-ON-TEES. Railway Centenary Celebrations, 2nd and 3rd July 1925. *Stockton: The Borough Council*, 1925. pp. 64.

7990 TIMES [newspaper]. Public steam railways: British enterprise and achievement: evolution of the railway services. *London: The Times*, 1925. (Times Trade & Engineering Supplement, July 4, 1925: Railway Centenary Section, pp. ix–xxiv).

pp. xvi–xviii, reports on the International Railway Congress, London, July 1–3, 1925.

7991 CLAPHAM, J. H. An Economic History of Modern Britain. *Cambridge: Cambridge University Press*.

—— vol. 2: Free Trade and steel, 1850–1886. 1932. pp. xiii, 554, with 9 diagrams & maps, & many notes. Railways, pp. 180–98 *et passim*.

—— vol. 3: Machines and national rivalries, 1887–1914, with an epilogue, 1914–1929. 1938. pp. xiv, 577, with 11 diagrams & many notes. Railways, pp. 347–62 *et passim*.

7992 ROLT, L. T. C. Look at railways; illustrated by Thomas Godfrey. *London: H. Hamilton*, 1959. (A School Look Book). pp. 96, with vignettes (drawings).

An introduction to railway history and operation, for young readers (8–12).

—— School edn. *H. Hamilton*, 1963. (Look Books). pp. 96.

—— rev. edn, illustrated by John Young. *Panther Books*, 1969. pp. 96, with illus.

7993 HALSON, G. R. Discovering railways, with illustrations by J. Martin Gregory. *London: University of London Press*, 1961. (Discovery Reference Books series). pp. 128, with frontis, 18 illus on 10 plates, & in text, line drawings, maps & an evaluative bibliography (40+ sources).

7994 JOHNS, C. The Picture Story of World Railways. *London: World Distributors*, 1963. Quarto. pp. 157, with frontis & 153 illus.

Concise accounts of railways, country by country.

7995 SNELLGROVE, L. E. From 'Rocket' to railcar: an outline of rail development since 1804 . . . , illustrated by Harry Toothill. *London: Longmans*, 1963. pp. 123, with 15 illus on 8 plates, and line illus & maps in text.

7996 WALKER, C. Progress on rails . . . , illustrated by John Lathey. *London: Edward Arnold*, 1964, pp. 64, with 44 illus (drawings, photos & maps), & a glossary.
For young readers (10–14 years).

7997 SNELL, J. B. Britain's railways under steam. *London: A Barker*, 1965. 4°. pp. 224, with 206 illus (26 col)., 7 maps, tables, diagram & a bibliography (31 sources).
—— 2nd edn. *London: Ian Allan*, 1977. 4°. pp. 224, with 206 illus (26 col)., 7 maps, tables, a diagram & a bibliography (31 sources).

7998 WHITEHOUSE, P. B. Railway Anthology, compiled by P. B. Whitehouse. *London: Ian Allan*, 1965. pp. ix, 223.
A bedside book of 54 essays on a variety of railway subjects by various authors taken from periodicals produced or absorbed by Ian Allan Ltd. They date from 1896 to 1964, but most are post-1950.

7999 ELLIS, C. H. Railway history. *London: Studio Vista*, 1966. pp. 160, with frontis, 161 illus, & a chronology.
The subject presented pictorially with captions and accompanying text.

8000 HENNESSEY, R. A. S. Transport. *London: Batsford*, 1966. (Past into Present series). pp. 96, with many illus.
pp. 28–52: 'The Railway Revolution', with 19 illus, map & diagram. Introductory, with generous notes and descriptions to illustrations.

8001 NOCK, O. S. Steam railways in retrospect. *London. A. & C. Black*, 1966. pp. xvii, 268, with frontis & 7 col. plates (artist, K. Welch), 97 illus on 48 plates, 3 maps & 2 diagrams.
Essays on various elements of British railway history.

8002 VALLANCE, H. A. The Railway Enthusiast's Bedside Book. *London: Batsford*, 1966. pp. 264, with 43 illus on 32 plates, 3 facsimiles, & frequent vignettes.
27 original essays of which 21 relate to railways in the British Isles, interspersed with anecdotes from a variety of published sources:
Thoughts on the Bull [i.e. O. V. S. Bulleid], by Elmer T. Rudd
Scotland's mountain barriers, by Robert M. Hogg
Timetable science, by G. E. Williams
Unusual mishaps, by G. O. Holt
Ghosts Underground, by Alan A. Jackson [Closed stations on London Underground railways]
Exposure!, by A. W. V. Mace. [Railway photography]
By train to Bantry, by C. L. Mowat
Private stations, by J. Horsley Denton
Three faces of independence, by R. K. Kirkland [Railways which escaped the Groupings of 1923]
'There's a lot of old stuff!', by L. C. Johnson,

Archivist, British Transport Historical Records
The Great Locomotive Row, by C. Hamilton Ellis. [The L.N.W.R. and the formation of the Locomotive Builders' Association]
Modern monorails, by John R. Day
Backward look, by M. D. Greville
By any other name, by William J. Skillern [The naming of railways]
Early letters of the Stockton & Darlington Rly, by E. H. Fowkes
Southern occasions, by J. N. Faulkner
Railway circles round London, by C. E. Lee [Routes made obsolete by the advent of tube, tram and bus]
The Waverley Route, by 'Lammermoor'
Railway rarebits, by R. C. H. Ives
Railways in law, by A. J. F. Wrottesley
From London to Inverness by day, by H. A. Vallance [A journey by the *Flying Scotsman*, June, 1962]

8003 JOYCE, J. The story of passenger transport in Britain. *London: Ian Allan*, 1967. pp. 208, with 68 illus on 30 plates.
ch. 3 (pp. 59–85), Early railways; ch. 4 (pp. 86–113), The Railway Era; ch. 5 (pp. 114–141), Town transport. Appendices: speed tables (modal comparisons, historical), notable dates, books (53 sources).
An informative introductory work.

8004 ROBBINS, M. Points and Signals: a railway historian at work. *London: Allen & Unwin*, 1967. pp. 256, with 8 illus on 4 plates, & 10 maps.
Reprinted essays by M. Robbins on various aspects of British railway history; also (pp. 18–31) 'The railway historian's craft', on elements regarded as essential to the study and presentation of the subject.

8005 DAY, J. R. Trains . . . , illustrated by David A. Warner & Nigel W. Hearn. *London: Hamlyn*, 1969. sm. 8°. pp. 159.
An introductory general history of railways, with many coloured illustrations.

8006 DYOS, H. J. and ALDCROFT, D. H. British transport: an economic survey from the seventeenth century to the twentieth. *Leicester: Leicester University Press*, 1969. pp. 473, with 25 maps, 8 tables and an extensive bibliographical commentary with its own index (pp. 401–44); general index (pp. 445–73).
—— Reprint. *Penguin Books*, 1974. (Pelican Books). pp. 511. A resetting in smaller format.

8007 GREGORY, S. Railways and life in Britain. *London: Ginn & Co.*, 1969. (Aspects of Social & Economic History series). obl. 8°. pp. 80, with 8 col. plates, & in text, 30 illus & 2 tables.
An informative introductory survey.

8008 RAY, J. A history of the railways. *London: Heinemann Educational*, 1969. pp. [8], 77, with 66 illus, incl. 2 maps; bibliography (97 sources).
Written to encourage young readers (ages 11–18) who want to know more about railway history. A guide to sources, research method, and presentation.

8009 FERNEYHOUGH, F. Railways. *London:*
Wayland, 1970. (Wayland Picture Histories
series). la. 8°. pp. 128, with frontis, 136 illus,
3 maps, chronology, & a bibliography (35
sources).
Introductory.

8010 TAMES, R. The transport revolution in the
19th century: a documentary approach. *Lon-*
don: Oxford University Press.
vol. 1: Railways. 1970. pp. 64, with 18 illus.
The text consists of 65 extracts from railway
history literature covering the period 1750–1850,
with a summary, chronology & bibliography at the
end. Each section has an introduction. Presentation
is at senior-school level.

8011 HAMMERSLEY, A. and PERRY, G. A. Railways and rail transport. *London: Blandford*
Press, 1972. (Approaches to Environmental
Studies, 10). pp. 96, with 101 illus (22 col)., &
2 col. maps.
Introductory and general. For class work in
conjunction with *Teachers' Guide Book*, no. 2.

8012 HASTINGS, P. Railroads: an international
history. *London: Benn*, 1972. (Industries &
Inventions: International Histories). pp. 144,
with 79 illus, 7 maps & a bibliography (27
sources).
Introductory.

8013 HISTORY of railways: a journey of romance,
invention and powerful splendour. *London:*
New English Library, [1972]. la. 8°. pp. 960,
with a great many illus (mostly col).. Issued in
48 weekly parts. No title-page; title on the
two binders only (separately supplied). Index, pp. 954–60.
Essays on a great variety of railway subjects, with
world-wide coverage. Includes tramways.
—— [Book edn]. *Hamlyn: New English Lib-*
rary, 1976. (New English Library Edition). la.
8°. pp. 512. Introduction by J. T. Shackleton.
Index pp. 510–12.

8014 WHITING, J. R. S. The coming of the railways, 1808–1892. *London: Evans Bros*, 1972.
la. 8°. pp. 54, with 55 illus.
For school use. A selection of illustrations with
descriptions and an introductory essay.

8015 AYERST, D. The Guardian Omnibus, 1821–
1971: an anthology of 150 years of Guardian
writing, chosen and edited by David Ayerst.
London: Collins, 1973. pp. 768.
'The Railway Age: a tragic beginning', pp. 48–52.
The fatal accident to W. Huskisson, M.P., from the
Guardian 18 September, 1830.
'A strike the Guardian saved', pp. 284–6. A strike
on the Midland Rly in March 1913 averted by the
reporting by Walter Meakin of the *Guardian* of an
interview with guard Richardson.
'London Underground', from an A.R.P. corres-
pondent, *Guardian*, 19 November, 1940. pp. 587–8.
Social life of air raid shelterers in underground
(tube) stations.

8016 GREAT trains: sequel to History of Railways.
London: New English Library, 1973. Issued
in 48 weekly parts. Title from cover.

A wide selection of essays supported by a great
number of coloured illustrations. World wide coverage. Includes tramways.

8017 HENNESSEY, R. A. S. Railways. *London:*
Batsford, 1973. la. 8°. (Past-into-Present
series). pp. 96, with 64 illus, map, an evaluative bibliography (pp. 92–4) & a list of
principal Acts relating to railways generally.
An introduction to British railway history.

8018 INNES, B. The saga of the railways; foreword
by Henry Sampson. *London: Purnell*, 1973.
tall 8°. pp. 94, with 80 illus (40 col)..
Introductory.

8019 ALDCROFT, D. H. Studies in British transport history, 1870–1970. *Newton Abbot:*
David & Charles, 1974. pp. vi, 309. Index,
pp. 303–9.
Chapters in which railways have particular emphasis:
  1. Railways and economic growth (pp. 12–30; 28
     notes).
  2. The efficiency and enterprise of British railways,
     1870–1914 (pp. 31–52; 37 notes).
  5. The decontrol of shipping and railways after the
     First World War (pp. 117–43; 115 notes).
  10. The railways and air transport, 1933–9 (pp.
     226–42; 39 notes).
  11. Innovation on the railways (pp. 243–62; 44
     notes).
  12. The changing pattern of demand for passenger
     transport in post-war Britain, by D. H. Aldcroft
     and P. J. Bemand (pp. 263–74; 15 notes & 2
     statistical tables in appendix).

8020 BAGWELL, P. S. The Transport Revolution
from 1770. *London: Batsford*, 1974. pp. 460,
with 21 maps, 21 tables, 33 diagrams, 964
notes & an evaluative bibliography (pp.
419–46). Index, pp. 447–60.

8021 HIRST, C. The British railways system,
prepared by Chris Hirst for the [Systems
Management] Course Team. *Milton Keynes:*
Open University Press, 1974. tall 8°. (Systems
Management; unit 2). pp. 86, with illus,
maps, facsims & a bibliography (32 sources).
Period, 1870–1973.

8022 BRITISH RAILWAYS. Yesterday, today &
tomorrow: passenger railways 150th anniversary, including calendar of events to mark
the occasion. [*London*]: *B.R.*, 1975. pp. 16,
with 18 illus (14 col)..

8023 BRITISH RAILWAYS. Your Easy Inter-City
Travel Guide to Rail 150. *London: B.R.*,
1975. pp. 16 (incl. covers), with 3 illus, 2
maps, a plan, & 6 timetables of principal
Inter-City services to North East England,
and local services, May to September.

8024 BRITISH RAILWAYS. EASTERN REGION.
Cavalcade reflections: official British Rail
Eastern Region souvenir. *York: B.R. (ER)*,
1975. pp. 48, mostly of illus, with some
facsimiles.
A photographic record by staff of British Transport Films of the Grand Steam Cavalcade 1975,

marking the 150th anniversary of the opening of the Stockton & Darlington Rly.

8025 BRITISH RAILWAYS. EASTERN REGION. Cavalcade retrospect: official British Rail Eastern Region souvenir. *York: B.R. (ER)*, 1975. pp. 48, chiefly illus.

A photographic record by staff of British Transport Films of the Grand Steam Cavalcade, 1975, marking the 150th anniversary of the opening of the Stockton & Darlington Rly.

8026 DARLINGTON S & D 150 COMMITTEE. S & D 150 Rail Anniversary. Darlington Souvenir Programme, 1975. *Darlington: the Committee*, 1975. pp. 52, with 15 illus.

8027 ELLIS, C. H. Steam railways. *London: Eyre Methuen*, 1975. pp. [64], with 150 illus.

8028 FERNEYHOUGH, F. The history of railways in Britain. *Reading: Osprey*, 1975. pp. 228, with col. frontis, 144 illus (13 col)., 3 maps, many tables & lists, & a bibliography (60+ sources).

A comprehensive companion of reference essays, with three detailed indexes.

ch. 1: Chronology; chs. 2–9: General developments; ch. 10: Classic locomotives; ch. 11: Biographies. Appendix A: accidents; Appendix B: London Underground railways; Appendix C: Directory of railway enthusiasts' and preservation societies.

8029 NOCK, O. S. Railways then and now: a world history. *London: Paul Elek*, 1975. 4°. pp. 215, with 202 illus (40 col). on plates, 8 maps, facsims & a diagram.

8030 NORTHERN ECHO [newspaper]. [Railway Centenary Celebrations in Darlington, 1925]. *Darlington: Northern Echo*, 1975. pp. [8].

A reprint, with no added imprint, of a selected 8 pages from issue no. 17255, Friday 2 July 1925, carrying news items relating to the Railway Centenary Celebrations held in Darlington. Printed on simulated (yellowed) faded paper. *See* Ottley 7033.

8031 RAIL 150 EXHIBITION. Stockton & Darlington Railway, 1825–1975: souvenir guide (Grand Steam Cavalcade); editor, A. M. Bowman. *Darlington: Exhibition Administration*, 1975. pp. 80, with 96 illus (48 col). & a map.

8032 RAILWAY Special, 1825–1975. *London: Historical Times*, 1975. pp. 64, with many illus (6 col).. Magazine format. One of the *British History Illustrated* series.

pp. 2–13, Railway builders to the world, by Alan Wykes; pp. 14–25, Brunel, giant of the broad gauge, by Peter Hay; pp. 26–32, Royal trains (anonymous); pp. 33–41, Engineers and navigators, by Terry Coleman; pp. 42–55, Rivalry on rail, by Derek Barrie; pp. 56–64, Stockton & Darlington Railway, by Robert A. Whitehead.

8033 RUSSELL, P. Salute to the Stockton & Darlington Railway and Special Centenary Memoir (1825 to 1875). *Bexleyheath: Locomotive Club of Great Britain*, 1975. (Bulletin Supplement). pp. xii, with 12 illus.

An account of the Railway Centenary Celebrations at Darlington, July 1925, with a descriptive list of the 54 locomotives in the Procession, 2nd July.

8034 SEMMENS, P. W. B. Stockton & Darlington: one hundred and fifty years of British railways. (Editors, P. B. Whitehouse and J. H. L. Adams). *London: New English Library*, 1975. pp. 160, with 199 illus (31 col). & a map.

8035 SIMMONS, J. Rail 150: the Stockton & Darlington Railway and what followed, by Ken Hoole, Jack Simmons, Michael Bonavia and Ian Waller; edited by Jack Simmons. *London: Eyre Methuen*, 1975. pp. 198, with 4 col. plates, 78 monochrome plates, 17 text illus & 5 maps & an evaluative select bibliography (pp. 193–4).

The Stockton & Darlington Railway, by Ken Hoole, pp. 13–46; The railway in Britain, 1825–1947, by Jack Simmons, pp. 47–117; The nationalised railways, 1948–75, by Michael Bonavia, pp. 119–64; Today and tomorrow, by Ian Waller, pp. 165–90; A note on books, by Jack Simmons, pp. 193–4.

8036 BRITISH RAILWAYS. EASTERN REGION. Cavalcade remembered, 1925. *York: B.R. (E.R.)*, 1976. pp. 84, Intro. 65 illus with descrs, & a facsimile of the pages relating to the procession of locomotives on 2nd July 1925 taken from the L.N.E.R.'s *Programme of Arrangements*.

The illustrations are from official photographs.

8037 COOK, C. A history of the great trains. *London: Weidenfeld & Nicolson*, 1977. la. 8°. pp. 144, with 107 illus (30 col.).

A popular illustrated history, world coverage; pp. 7–45, Britain.

8038 OLDHAM, M. The British Book of Railways, *London: New English Library*, 1978. la. 8°. pp. 96, with many illus, mostly coloured.

Short introductory essays on a variety of railway topics, largely extracted from his publisher's *History of Railways* (1972) and its sequel, *The Great Trains* (1973).

8039 ALLEN, G. F. The Illustrated History of Railways in Britain. *London: Marshall Cavendish Books*, 1979. la. 8°. pp. 272, with 300 illus (22 col.).

Contributors: Peter Semmens, Basil Cooper, John Clay, G. F. Allen; photographs selected by Phil Soar.

8040 FRENCH, O. and ROBERT-BLUNN, J. The Iron Road: the Liverpool–Manchester Railway, 1830–1980. *Manchester: Manchester Evening News*, [1979]. newspaper format. pp. 32, with 49 illus (2 col.), 10 facsimiles, a plan & a col. map.

8041 BODY, G. and BLENKINSOP, R. J. Liverpool and Manchester: a photographic essay: the official British Rail photographic record of the 1980 Rainhill cavalcade of rail transport, based on the photographs of R. J.

Blenkinsop and compiled by Geoffrey Body; Foreword by Peter Manisty. *Weston-super-Mare: Avon-Anglia*, 1980. pp. 48, with 100 illus.

Includes a table of locomotives & rolling stock of the Grand Cavalcade, Rainhill, 24, 25, 26 May, 1980.

8042 MANCHESTER EVENING NEWS. The Iron Horses: a picture record of the 1980 Rainhill Celebrations. *Manchester*, [1980]. newspaper format. pp. 31, with many illus.

'Compiled by Owen French, with special articles by John Robert-Blunn and Fred Hackworth.'

8043 NOCK, O. S. 150 years of main line railways. *Newton Abbot: David & Charles*, 1980. pp. 191, with 32 illus on 16 plates & a bibliography (26 sources).

8044 RAIL Mail: The Liverpool and Manchester Railway 150th anniversary. *Manchester: produced for the North Western Museum of Science and Industry by courtesy of the Daily Mail*, [1980]. newspaper format. pp. 12, with 37 illus & a map.

8045 RAILWAY Pictorial: the Iron Road, ancient and modern, with the Giants of Steam. *Plymouth: West of England Newspapers*, 1980. newspaper format. pp. 39, with 93 illus (3 col.), 8 portraits, & 2 maps.

8046 ROBERTS, D. The Wonder Book of Railways. *London: Ward Lock*, 1980. (Wonder Book series). pp. 45, with 80 col. illus.

A general introductory work for older children. Not to be confused with the popular work of the same name published in twenty-one editions, 1911–1950 (Ottley 7869).

8047 SIMMONS, J. Rail 150: 1975 or 1980? *in* Journal of Transport History, 3rd series, vol. 1, no. 1, September 1980. pp. 1–8, with 22 notes.

8048 WRATE, C. H. Into the eighties, with Stephenson. *Walsall: Ray*, [1980]. pp. 13, with 22 illus. Title from cover.

Brief commentaries on recent railway history celebrations and railway history in the making today.

B RAIL TRANSPORT AT PARTICULAR PERIODS
8049–8436
For this subject related to localities see **C**

B 1 ORIGIN, ANTIQUITY AND EARLY USE OF RAIL TRANSPORT

Prepared stone trackways of ancient times—Wagonways in mines and quarries in mediaeval Europe and their evolution in Britain during the 16th, 17th and 18th centuries as feeders from mines and quarries to rivers, canals and the coast

8049–60

Reference source 8049

8049 BAXTER, B. Stone blocks and iron rails. *Newton Abbot: David & Charles*, 1966. (Industrial Archaeology of the British Isles series). pp. 272, with 41 illus on 17 plates, 4 line drawings in text, & 203 bibliogr. notes.
Gazetteer of wagonways & tramroads. pp. 143–236; Bibliography (384 sources). pp. 237–55; Index, pp. 264–72; Addenda, pp. 259–60.

8050 AFFIDAVITS, certificates and presentments, proving the facts mentioned in the case of Sir Humphry Mackworth and the Mine-Adventurers, with respect to the irregular proceedings of several justices of the peace for the County of Glamorgan and of their agents and dependents. *London*, 1705.

8051 The Compleat Collier; or, the whole art of sinking, getting and working coal-mines, etc., as is now used in the northern parts, especially about Sunderland and Newcastle, by J. C. *London: printed for G. Gonyers at the Ring in Little Brittain*, 1708. pp. 55.
—— Reprinted by *M. A. Richardson, Newcastle*, 1845. (Reprints of Rare Tracts, etc. miscellaneous, VI). pp. 55.
—— Republished by *Frank Graham: Newcastle upon Tyne*, 1968. pp. 55.
pp. 36–40, transport below ground: sledges and trams.

8052 DEFOE, D. The complete English tradesman, in familiar letters . . . 2nd edn. 1727. [Reprint, *New York: Augustus M. Kelley*, 1969]. 2 vols. pp. xv, 447; xvi, 298, 176.
vol. 2, pt. 2, pp. 28–30 has a short description of Tyneside wagonways and comments upon the high cost of successive loadings and unloadings in the course of the journey from pit to consumer.

8053 POCOCKE, R. Northern journeys of Bishop Richard Pococke, *in* Publications of the Surtees Society, vol. 124 (1915), pp. 199–252.
A transcript of British Library Additional MS. 14256.
On pp. 240–1, Tyneside wagonways briefly described, in 1760.

8054 PENNANT, T. A tour in Scotland and voyage to the Hebrides, 1772. *Chester: J. Monk; London: B. White*, 1774, 76. 2 parts.

pt. 1, p. 48, wagonway & staith at Whitehaven (briefly mentioned).
pt. 2, p. 217, mention of 'a variety of rail roads' at lime-kilns near Dunfermline; p. 311, 'the coal is brought down in waggons along rail roads' along the Tyne.

8055 MORAND, J. F. C. L'Art d'exploiter les mines de charbon de terre. *Paris: Saillant et Nyon*, 1776–8. (Description des Arts et Métjers, Académie des Sciences). 3 vols.
vol. 2, pt. 2, section 3 (pp. 698–9), & plate 34.3 in vol. 4, pt. 2, section 5 describe & illustrate in detail a Tyneside wagon.
vol. 3, pt. 2, section 4 (p. 865) corrects this account and adds a description of a wagon at Workington (plate 34).

8056 CHAPMAN, W. Observations on the various systems of canal navigation, with inferences practical and mathematical, in which Mr Fulton's plan of wheel-boats and the utility of subterraneous and of small canals are particularly investigated, including an account of the canals and inclined planes of China. *London: J. Taylor*, 1797. 4°. pp. 104, with 2 folded maps & 3 diagrams on plates.
Much of the work is taken up with describing methods of overcoming differences of level in canal courses, including the use of inclined planes.

8057 FAUJAS DE SAINT-FOND, B. A journey through England and Scotland to the Hebrides in 1784 . . . , a revised edition of the English translation, edited, with notes and a memoir of the author, by Sir Archibald Geikie. *Glasgow: Hugh Hopkins*, 1907, 2 vols.
Translated from *Voyage en Angleterre, en Écosse et aux Iles Hébrides* (Paris, 1797). Edition limited to 450 copies.
vol. 1 (pp. 139–42), an account of the construction and use of Tyneside wagonways.

8058 NEMNICH, P. A. Neueste Reise durch England, Schottland und Ireland . . . *Tübingen*, 1807.
pp. 64–6: Iron railways in the Midlands and on Tyneside (in German).

8059 DUNN, M. A treatise on the winning and working of collieries . . . *Newcastle: M. Dunn*, 1848. pp. 372 & 27 plates, incl. folded frontis.

pp. 25–30, 129–55: surface & underground wagon-ways, past and present.

—— 2nd edn. *M. Dunn*, 1852. pp. xii, 391. (pp. 13–18, 122–30).

8060 LEWIS, M. J. T.   Early wooden railways.

London: Routledge & Kegan Paul, 1970. pp. xxiii, 436, with 74 illus on 32 plates, 56 maps & diagrams, 9 tables, a glossary & 1157 notes. Index, pp. 413–36.

    A comprehensive & detailed work on the evolution of lateral control for wheeled transport. In Britain, from the 1560s to the early 19th century.

B 2   THE TRANSITIONAL PERIOD, FROM MINERAL WAGONWAY TO PUBLIC PASSENGER RAILWAY, 1800–1830 . . . 1850

8061–73

The experimental and formative period during which developments in the design of locomotives and the construction of track following the success of Richard Trevithick's engine at Penydarren in 1804 resulted in the establishment of the first public passenger railway, between Liverpool and Manchester in 1830.

Included here are works on the comparative merits of railways, canals and roads during this period and works analysing theories and practices associated with the development of the idea of rail transport as a new means of communication between towns.

For the later, developed, relationship between railways as an established feature of national life and other forms of transport (canals, roads, coastwise shipping and air) and for railways within the general pattern of national life, see **K, K 1,** *etc.*

This period of transition is not easy to define by dates. The general superiority of the steam locomotive over other forms of traction was established by the success of George Stephenson's *Rocket* during the trials at Rainhill on the nascent Liverpool & Manchester Railway in October 1829, and the general form which public passenger railways were to take was settled when this line was opened in September 1830. The Liverpool & Manchester was the first railway to provide safe travel at fixed rates by a regular service of steam-hauled trains owned by the railway. While 1830 may be regarded as a convenient date for marking the end of the experimental and formative period and the beginning of the Railway Age, it must be borne in mind that there was no sudden end to the quest for improvement and innovation. This section, however, is concerned with the efforts made to resolve the *primary* problems presented by the challenging concept of an extended use of wagonways and a more efficient steam locomotive. The two were brought together in 1830.

It was not until 1845 that differences regarding choice of gauge for new railways was settled by the recommendations of the Gauge Commission, and experiments with atmospheric propulsion as an alternative to steam locomotion continued until 1848. Contemporary writings on these matters were, however, part of the general process of ideas which preceded the advent of the Liverpool & Manchester and are included in this section.

Safety problems came under the surveillance of the Board of Trade, via Parliament, in the early 1840s and by 1850 the increasing speed, weight and frequency of trains and growing public anxiety had obliged the railway companies, often somewhat reluctantly, to devise better protection for travellers. Consequent developments in signalling, brakes, interlocking of points, and emergency passenger/driver communication are subjects resulting from the process of transition from mineral wagonway to public passenger railway and are not included here.

For problems of safety in transit see **K 3**
For safety engineering and operation see **E 15**

8061 LITTLE, J. Practical observations on the improvement and management of mountain sheep and sheep farms; also, remarks on stock of various kinds. *Edinburgh: Macredie, Skelly & Muckersy; London: Longman, Hurst, Rees, Orme & Brown*, 1815. pp. iii, 198.

ch. 7 (pp. 128–47), Observations on the improvement of the country by means of railways. 'Were rail-ways formed throughout the country all the different classes of the community would derive as much benefit from them as either merchants or manufacturers'.

Advocates feuing the land adjacent to railways.

8062 SIMOND, L. Journal of a Tour and Residence in Great Britain during the years 1810 and 1811. *Edinburgh: A. Constable.*

2nd edn, vol. 1, 1817. pp. 276–7, wagonways near Swansea described (1 para.).

2nd edn, vol. 2, 1817. pp. 76–7, wagonways in Newcastle area described (1 para.); pp. 79–80, from mines to ships (1 para.).

—— Reprinted in an abridged edition as: An American in Regency England: the journal of a tour in 1810–1811, edited, with an introduction and notes, by Christopher Hibbert, *London: Robert Maxwell*, 1968. pp. 176.

p. 107, description of wagonways from mines to the waterfront in the Newcastle area (1 para.).

8063 BAADER, J. [R]. von. Neues System der fortschaffenden Mechanik. *[München]: the author?*, 1822. obl. folio. pp. viii, [4], 220.

—— Atlas, 1822. obl. folio. 16 plates.

2. Abschnitt (paras 17–41, pp. 23–61), Geschichte und Beschreibung der englischen Eisenbahnen, ihre Kosten, ihre Wirkung, ihre Vorzüge vor den gewöhnlichen Strassen und vor den schiffbaren Kanälen, ihre Mängel und Unbequemlichkeiten.

3. Abschnitt (paras 42–60, pp. 62–88), Beschreibung einer neu-erfundenen Construction von Eisenbahnen und dazu gehörigen Wagen, welche den Mängeln der englischen Vorrichtungen nicht unterworfen ist . . .

There is a List of Contents but no Index. The 16 plates comprise 113 mechanical drawings illustrating current practice in the lateral control of wagons and include diagrams of Shropshire-type cast-iron rail and plate-rail not to be found elsewhere in published sources. The work is believed by Dr. M J. T. Lewis to be the best available source for general and detailed illustrations of early 19th century wagonways and wagons and their various modifications for particular classes of haulage by horse and man-power.

8064 DEHANY, W. K. The General Turnpike Acts, 3 Geo. IV, c. 126 & 4 Geo. IV, c. 95, with the reasons for passing the explanatory Act . . . and with notes and observations on the law. *London: J. Butterworth*, 1823. pp. xxxix, 227.

Contains two passing references to railways: p. 78, Railway and canal companies empowered to reduce tolls on road materials; and, p. 139, Carriages used on tram roads not to be drawn on turnpike roads for more than 100 yards.

8065 GREGORY, O. Mathematics for practical men, being a common-place book . . . *London: Baldwin, Cradock & Joy*, 1825.

pp. 362–8 & plate 2, Comparative tables and remarks on steam engines, rail-roads, canals, and turnpike-roads (Extracted from *Tredgold on Railways*.).

—— 2nd edn. *Baldwin & Cradock*, 1833. pp. xii, 427, ch. 14 (pp. 373–83).

—— 3rd edn, rev. & enl. by Henry Law. *London: J. Weale*, 1848, pp. xix, 392, 118, with 11 very detailed tables & 13 folded plates.

8066 MACLAREN, C. Railroads and locomotive steamcarriages, *in his* Select Writings . . . (1869), vol. 2, pp. 59–62.

Reprinted from *The Scotsman*, 26 January 1830.

8067 HANN, J. and DODDS, I. Mechanics for practical men . . . , with a short dissertation on rail-roads, etc. *Newcastle upon Tyne: printed for the authors by Mackenzie & Dent*, 1833, pp. vii, 208.

pp. 169–84, 'On rail-roads'; pp. 184–92, 'On locomotive engines'. Largely a record of the Rainhill Trials, Liverpool & Manchester Rly, October 1829.

8068 GERSTNER, F. J. von. Handbuch der Mechanik. *Prag: Johann Spurny*, 1831–4. 3 vols.

vol. 1, 1833, pp. 663, with tables & mathematical calculations. In ch. 7 (paras 552–79, pp. 601–42), 'Eisenbahnen in England und Schottland'.

8069 GERSTNER, F. J. von. Kupfertafeln zum Handbuche der Mechanik . . . , aufgesetzt, mit Beiträgen von neuern englischen Konstruktionen vermehrt und herausgegeben von Franz Anton Ritter von Gerstner. *Prag*, 1831, 1832 (*Wien*, 1834). 3 vols. la. obl. format.

vol. 1, plate 30, Eisenbahnen. Achsenlager bei den Wägen der Manchester und Liverpoolbahn. (19 engineering drawings); plate 31, Ausweichplatze und Wegübersetzungen bei Eisenbahnen. (14 drawings); plate 32, Englische Eisenbahnen, railroads genannt. (14 drawings); plate 33, Wagen auf den englischen railroads. (9 drawings); plate 34, Englische Eisenbahnen, tramroads genannt, und Wägen. (18 drawings); plate 35, Eisenbahnen *auf schiefen Flächen*; plate 36, Eisenbahn von Hetton nach Sunderland. (2 drawings – a landscape and a train).

vols. 2 & 3 contain no drawings relating to railways in the British Isles.

8070 TELFORD, T. Life of Thomas Telford, civil engineer, written by himself, containing a descriptive narrative of his professional labours, with a folio atlas of copper plates; edited by John Rickman . . . *London: Payne & Foss*, 1838. la 8°. pp. xxiv, 719, with tables.

pp. xxi–xxii, & p. 688, his opinions on railroads (horse-powered trains) compared with canals.

p. 864, wooden and cast-iron rails; wrought-iron rails tried at Walbottle [1805].

p. 689, two Scottish wagonways: at Pixie, near Musselburgh ('Hope's railway') [1814], and at Hinton.

—— Atlas. *Payne & Foss*, 1838. Folio. Frontis (portrait), contents list, map of Great Britain showing particularly the places referred to in Mr. Telford's narrative, & 82 plates of the Caledonian Canal; pl. XXV, map of the new Harecastle Tunnel, with temporary railway; pl. XXXVII, temporary railway used in constructing Aberdeen Harbour.

8071 RAISTRICK, A. Quakers in science and industry: being an account of the Quaker contributions to science and industry during the 17th and 18th centuries. *London: Bannisdale Press*, 1950.

p. 137, Richard Reynolds at Coalbrookdale, 1750s, with portrait; pp. 216–7, Friends and transport (Edward Pease and the Stockton & Darlington Rly, 1820s).

8072 BOUCHER, C. T. G. John Rennie, 1761–1821: the life and work of a great engineer. *Manchester: Manchester University Press*, 1963. pp. x, 149, with 14 plates & 20 illus in text.

Includes Rennie's work on canal wagonways and early railways.

8073 NOCK, O. S. The dawn of world railways, 1800–1850; illustrated by Clifford and Wendy Meadway. *London: Blandford Press*, 1972. (Railways of the World in Colour series). pp. 179. 184 col. illus (pp. 9–104) with individual commentaries by O. S. Nock.

B 3   1830–1914   THE RAILWAY AGE

8074–84

8074 RAILWAYS, *in* The Parliamentary Gazetteer of England and Wales (1843), pp. 4–12, with table of weekly traffic and other returns.

8075 RICHARDSON, B. W. Thomas Sopwith, M.A., C.E., F.R.S., with excerpts from his diary of fifty-seven years. *London: Longmans, Green*, 1891. pp. xii, 400.

Index has page refs to early rail travel, the opening of the Newcastle & Carlisle Rly, the Atmospheric Rly, and to George Stephenson, Robert Stephenson, I. K. Brunel and T. Brassey.

8076 MacINNES, A. G. Recollections of the life of Miles MacInnes, compiled by his sister, Anna Grace MacInnes. *London: Longmans, Green*, 1911. pp. ix, 276, with frontis and 8 plates.

ch. 5 (pp. 49–65), 'Our railways: contrast between past and present;' a lecture delivered by Miles MacInnes, who had been a director of the LNWR since 1876, at Carlisle, ca. 1897.

8077 RAPER, C. L. Railway transportation: a history of its economics and of its relation to the state. *New York, London: Putnam*, 1912. pp. xi, 331.

Based on *Railroad Transportation: its history and its laws*, by A. T. Hadley, 1885. pp. 14–60, 'Railway transportation in Great Britain'.

8078 CLAPHAM, J. H. An Economic History of Modern Britain. *Cambridge: Cambridge University Press*.

vol. 2: Free Trade and steel, 1850–1886. 1932. pp. xii, 554, with 9 diagrams & maps & many notes. Railways, pp. 180–98 *et passim*.

vol. 3: Machines and national rivalries, 1887–1914, with an epilogue, 1914–1929. 1938. pp. xiv, 577, with 11 diagrams & many notes. Railways, pp. 347–62 *et passim*.

8079 REED, M C. Railways in the Victorian economy: studies in finance and economic growth, edited by M. C. Reed. *Newton Abbot: David & Charles*, 1969. pp. 231. Introduction by M. C. Reed.

Eight studies based upon source material in British Transport Historical Records, with a general index.

1, The coming of the railway and United Kingdom economic growth, by B. R. Mitchell, pp. 13–32, with 58 notes & a table showing capital formation by railway companies, 1831–1919.

2, The railways and the iron industry: a study of their relationship in Scotland, by Wray Vamplew, pp. 33–75, with 173 notes & sources, & 5 tables.

3, Pricing policy of railways in England and Wales before 1881, by G. R. Hawke, pp. 76–110, with 152 notes & 5 diagrams.

4, The Great Western Railway and the Swindon Works in the Great Depression, by D. E. C. Eversley, pp. 111–37, with 58 notes & 3 detailed tables.

5, Aspects of railway accounting before 1868, by Harold Pollins, pp. 138–61, with 125 notes.

6, Railways and the growth of the capital market, by M. C. Reed, pp. 162–83, with 96 notes & 4 tables.

7, The sources of railway share capital, by S. A. Broadbridge, pp. 184–211, with 116 notes & 5 tables.

8, Railway contractors and the finance of railway development in Britain, by Harold Pollins, pp. 212–28, with 85 notes.

8080 POLLINS, T. H. Britain's railways: an industrial history. *Newton Abbot: David & Charles*, 1971. (Industrial Histories of Britain series). pp. 223, with 22 tables, 4 maps, 2 graphs, 111 notes & an evaluative bibliography of ca. 80 selected sources (pp. 213–8).

Railways as a developing industry in the 19th century. The book has four main themes: Sources and patterns of investment, operating practices, management and organisation, and labour relations, but the presentation of the work as a whole is arranged within broad chronological periods. 'An examination of the [railway] industry's activities in relation to the various pressures and constraints that it faced.'

8081 MOWAT, C. L. The heyday of the British railway system: vanishing evidence and the historian's task, *in* Journal of Transport History, new series vol. 1 (1971–2), pp. 1–17, with 36 notes.

8082 The GOLDEN years of trains, 1830–1920, [edited by Peter Kalla-Bishop, illustrated by

J. W. Wood & Associates, written by Harry Weaver]. *London: Hamlyn; Phoebus*, 1977. la. 8°. pp. 128, with over 200 illus (some col.), facsims, col. maps.
  World coverage.

8083 COWIE, L. W. The Railway Age. *London: Macdonald Educational, for Marks & Spencer Ltd*, 1978. la. 8°. pp. 61, with over 150 illus (mostly col.).
  Popular introductory essays on various aspects of railway history, in Britain and abroad.

8084 SIMMONS, J. The railway in England and Wales, 1830–1914. *Leicester: Leicester University Press.*
  —— vol. 1, The system and its working. 1978. pp. 295, with 12 detailed tables, 5 line illus, 663 notes, a la. col. folded map and a more detailed one for London. The colouring of the general map indicates by period the development of the railway system. Appendix I, A note on train services (with tables 10, 11 & 12); Appendix II, Statistical summary of the growth of the system, 1860–1914.

B 4–B 10   1914–1980   RAILWAYS SINCE 1914

8085–88

8085 PARLIAMENT. HOUSE OF COMMONS. LIBRARY. The railways of Great Britain: pre-war, during the war, and now. *Westminster: H. of C. Library*, 2nd July 1951. (Statistical Memorandum, 21). obl. format. pp. 17. Reproduced typescript.
  15 tables for varying periods between 1913 and 1951.

8086 ALDCROFT, D. H. British railways in transition: the economic problems of Britain's railways since 1914. *London: Macmillan*, 1968. pp. xvi, 252, with 25 tables & 6 maps. Bibliography, pp. 226–39 (274 sources).

8087 ALDCROFT, D. H. British transport since 1914: and economic history. *Newton Abbot: David & Charles*, 1975. pp. 336, with 16 illus, 26 tables & 413 bibliogr. notes; Select bibliography, pp. 296–307.
  ch. 5, pp. 127–63: The railways (with 39 bibliogr. notes).

8088 ALDCROFT, D. H. A new chapter in transport history: the twentieth century revolution, *in* Journal of Transport History, new series, vol. 3 (1975–6), pp. 217–39, with 73 bibliogr. notes.

B 4   1914–1918   RAILWAYS DURING THE FIRST WORLD WAR

8089–92

8089 METROPOLITAN RAILWAY WAR SERVICE CORPS. [Programmes of sports meetings, president's addresses and reports of sections, 1916–19].
  Contents: Programme of sports meeting, 16 September, 1916. pp. 15.
  President's address and reports of sections, 8th February 1917. pp. 32.
  Programme of sports meeting, 28th July 1917. pp. 15.
  President's address and reports of sections, 14th February 1918. pp. 40.
  Programme of sports meeting, 27th July 1918. pp. 34.
  2 specimen letters sent with parcels to employees on war service, and 3 Christmas greeting cards.
  A group photograph is mounted as a frontispiece.
                                                    LU(THC)

8090 FAIRLIE, J. A. British war administration.

New York: Oxford University Press, 1919. (Preliminary Economic Studies of the War, 8). pp. x, 302.
  ch. 9 (pp. 165–96): 'Trade and transportation', with 79 notes.

8091 BAKER, C. W. Government control and operation of industry in Great Britain and the United States during the World War. *New York: Oxford University Press*, 1921. (Preliminary Economic Studies of the war, 18). pp. vii, 138.
  ch. 4 (pp. 34–42): 'Railways in Great Britain.'

8092 HAMILTON, J. A. B. Britain's railways in World War I. *London: Allen & Unwin*, 1967. pp. 220, with 19 illus on 16 plates, & in text, 5 illus, 4 maps, 7 lists & a bibliography (13 sources). Index, pp. 209–20.

B 5   1918–1923   POST-WAR RECOVERY AND THE PERIOD ENDING WITH THE 'BIG FOUR' AMALGAMATIONS OF 1923

8093–96

8093 RAILWAY Officials Directory for 1922, with a new introduction by K. Miller. *Wakefield: S. R. Publishers*, 1971. pp. VI, [2], 187.

A facsimile reprint. Some pages have been omitted from the original edition—the diary section, some calculation tables, blank pages for the noting of memoranda, etc.

8094 MORRIS, A. A. Making the most of existing traffic facilities by special attention to working details. Great Western Railway (London) Lecture & Debating Society, meeting on November 11th, 1920 [no. 125]. pp. 16, with discussion & 15 diagrams & illus.

8095 JOHNSON, P. B. Land fit for heroes. *Chicago & London: University of Chicago Press*, 1968. pp. viii, 540, with 12 illus on 8 plates, many notes & a bibliography.

Railways during the period 1916–19, (*passim*: 15 page refs in index).

8096 ARMITAGE, S. The politics of decontrol of industry: Britain and the United States, with a preface by C. L. Mowat. *London: London School of Economics & Political Science*, 1969. (L.S.E. Research Monograph, 4). pp. vii, 213.

Decontrol of shipping, mining and railways after the First World War. ch. 3, 'Railways', pp. 46–100, with 204 notes.

FACTS and figures about British railways. [Title varies]. Published annually by the British Railways Press Office from 1927 to 1947 and thereafter by British Railways. *See* 7953.

B 6–B 10   1921–1980   RAILWAYS SINCE 1921

8097–8106
Locomotives 8100–6

8097 PARLIAMENT. HOUSE OF COMMONS. LIBRARY. The railways of Great Britain: prewar, during the war, and now. *Westminster: H of C Library*, 2nd July 1951. (Statistical Memorandum, 21). obl. format. pp. 17, Reproduced typescript.

15 tables for varying periods between 1913 and 1951.

8098 PEARSON, A. J. Men of the Rail, with a Foreword by Sir John Elliot. *London: Allen & Unwin*, 1967. pp. 203, with 42 illus on 23 plates, incl. frontis.

An autobiographical survey of railways and railway management by a senior railway officer in close contact with many leading railwaymen, 1934–1963, with particular reference to the LMS and BR (LMR).

8099 BONAVIA, M. R. The four great railways. *Newton Abbot: David & Charles*, 1980. pp. 223, with 30 illus on 16 plates, 4 maps & 4 appendices: The Scottish Experience; The Irish Enclaves; The Joint Lines; Bibliography (evaluative) pp. 217–8.

The Great Western, The London & North Eastern, The London Midland & Scottish and the Southern, 1923–1947.

Locomotives

8100 FLOWERS, A. W. Forty years of Steam, 1926–1966. *London: Ian Allan*, 1969. pp. 144, with 334 illus.

An album of photographs with captions, arranged under LNER, LMS, GWR and Southern.

8101 NOCK, O. S. Railways at the zenith of Steam, 1920–40; illustrated by Clifford and Wendy Meadway. *London: Blandford Press*, 1970. (Railways of the World in Colour). pp. 184, with 184 col. illus (pp. 9–104) individually described (pp. 105–84).

8102 NOCK, O. S. The Golden Age of Steam: a critical and nostalgic memory of the last twenty years before Grouping on the railways of Great Britain. *London: A & C Black*, 1973. la. 8°. pp. 235, with 7 col. plates by Jack Hill, 45 illus & 5 maps.

8103 BLENKINSOP, R. J. Shadows of the Big Four. *Oxford: Oxford Publishing*, 1975. la. 8°. pp. [96]. Intro & 94 illus with descrs.

Photographed 1951–6.

8104 BLENKINSOP, R. J. Echoes of The Big Four. *Oxford: Oxford Publishing*, 1976. la. 8°. pp. [96]. Intro & 94 illus with descrs.

Photographed 1956–8.

8105 BLENKINSOP, R. J. Reflections of the Big Four. *Oxford: Oxford Publishing Co.*, 1978. la. 8°. pp. [96]. Intro & 96 illus with descrs.

Photographed 1969–72.

8106 RANSOME-WALLIS, P. Locomotives & trains of the Big Four. *London: Ian Allan*, 1978. pp. 128. Intro & 268 illus with descrs.

B 6   1921–1939   THE 'BIG FOUR' AMALGAMATIONS OF 1923 (Railways Act, 1921) AND RAILWAYS DURING THE 1920s AND 1930s

8107–15

Reference sources 8107–9

For the Schedule of the Railways Act (1921) and a list of the companies amalgamated to form the LMS, LNER, GWR (new company) and the Southern, see Appendix I of the main work, pp. 469–73

8107 [MATHIESON], F. C. MATHIESON & SONS. Railway Groups completed: amalgamation and absorption schemes, final dividends, tables, etc. *London: F. C. Mathieson & Sons*, August 1923, pp. 35.

8108 RAILWAY GAZETTE. Financial results of the British Group railway companies in 1924. *London: Railway Gazette*, [1925]. la. 8°. pp. 34. Intro (pp. 3–6) & 30 tables. (pp. 6–34).
Reprinted from the *Railway Gazette*, April 24, 1925. An analysis of the accounts and statistics as shown in the published reports of the LMS, LNER, GWR and Southern for the past year.
—— Financial results of the British Group railway companies in 1926. *London: Railway Gazette*, [1927]. la. 8°. pp. 32. Intro (pp. 1–4) & 30 tables (pp. 4–32).
Reprinted from the *Railway Gazette*, March 18, 1927.

8109 LONDON, MIDLAND & SCOTTISH RLY. Handbook of Statistics, years 1929, and 1933 to 1936. *London: LMS*, October 1937. pp. 288.
Trade statistics (pp. 24–35); financial & statistical tables for the LMS (pp. 36–205); and for all British railways (pp. 207–76); Index (pp. 277–88).
—— Handbook of Statistics, 1930–31: years 1913 and 1923 to 1929. [*LMS*, 1923?].

8110 PATON, A. Will British railways grouping bring about American operating conditions? Great Western Railway (London) Lecture & Debating Society, meeting on December 22nd 1921 (no. 143). pp. 24, with discussion, 7 illus & diagrams.

8111 GODFREY, E. The Railways Act, 1921: is it a failure? Great Western Railway (London) Lecture & Debating Society, meeting on December 4th, 1924 (no. 176). pp. 17, with discussion.

8112 CHURCHILL, [Viscount]. Annual dinner of Plymouth Chamber of Commerce, January 23rd 1925: speech by Viscount Churchill. *Paddington Station [London]: Great Western Rly*, [1925]. (Great Western Pamphlets, 13). pp. 7.
The GWR and Plymouth, and current general problems confronting railways.

8113 REVIEW of the Railways Act, 1921. pp. 60. Reproduced typescript. Text dated 'April 3rd, 1925'. Possibly not published. Author not known.
Detailed explanatory notes on each section of the Act.   LU(THC)

8114 CASSERLEY, H. C. Railways between the wars. *Newton Abbot: David & Charles*, 1971. pp. 127, with col. frontis & 163 illus.
pp. 27–30, '1921 Railways Act: constituents of newly formed groups', with route mileages & notes; also a list of joint lines not affected by the Act.
pp. 30–32, a chronology, 1918–1939.

8115 NOCK, O. S. O. S. Nock's railway reminiscences of the interwar years. *London: Ian Allan*, 1980. pp. 176, with 180 illus.
A series of informal observations on some noteworthy aspects of the railway scene of the 1920s and 1930s, illustrated by the author's own photography.

B 7–B 10   1939–1980   RAILWAYS SINCE 1939

8116–17

8116 CASSERLEY, H. C. Railways since 1939. *Newton Abbot: David & Charles*, 1972, pp. 128, with 143 illus, map of railways in 1954, chronology, & a bibliography (23 sources).

8117 NOCK, O. S. Railways in the transition from steam, 1940–1965; illustrated by Clifford and Wendy Meadway. *London: Blandford Press*, 1974. (Railways of the World in Colour). pp. 162, with 153 col. illus (pp. 13–92) individually described (pp. 93–155).

B 7   1939–1945   RAILWAYS DURING THE SECOND WORLD WAR

8118–29

8118 LONDON TRANSPORT. Air Raid Precautions Manual. *London: London Passenger Transport Board*, 1938. pp. 38, with a separate pamphlet bound in as an appendix entitled: Air Raid Precautions. First Aid, June 1940. pp. viii.

8119 WEBSTER, J. L. Air raid precautions and the Great Western Railway. G.W.R. (London) Lecture & Debating Society, meeting on 27th January 1938, no. 320. pp. 9.
Author, 'Office of Supt of the Line'.

8120 HOME from Dunkirk: a photographic record in aid of the British Red Cross; Introduction by J. B. Priestley. *London: John Murray*, 1940. pp. 32. Intro & 46 illus with descrs, 20 of which are scenes on the Southern Rly.

8121 BRITISH RAILWAYS PRESS OFFICE. Railway finance and statistics. [*London*]: *British Railways (GWR-LMS-LNER-SR-LT)*, [1944].
A printed folder with text & tables for the period 1938 to 1943.   LU(THC)

8122 BEYER, PEACOCK & CO. The Second World War. [*London*]: *the Company*, [1945]. la. 8°. pp. [64], with 7 col. plates, incl. map, & many illus, incl. portraits, in text.
'The story of the wide variety of the problems and achievements of the Company, 1939–1945, in producing locomotives, weaponry and machine tools'.

8123 BRITISH COUNCIL. They carry the goods. *London: British Council*, [1945]. (The British People: How They Live and Work series, 5). pp. 32, with 38 illus.
Illustrations, with running commentary, on the wartime transport of freight by rail, road and canal.

8124 BONSOR, N. R. P. The Jersey Eastern Railway and the German occupation lines in Jersey. *Lingfield: Oakwood Press*, 1964. (Oakwood Library of Railway History, 58A).

(Railways of the Channel Islands, 2). pp. 9–142, with 27 illus, 2 maps & a layout plan on 12 plates, and in text, map, layout plan & tables.
—— rev. edn. *Oakwood Press*, 1977. pp. 91–142, with 24 illus, & a plan on 8 plates, & in text, map, plan, 5 tables; 2 maps & 1 illus on inside covers.

8125 F., I. N. Gordon Highlander: 4th L.N.E.R. Battalion H.Q. Company Home Guard, [by] I.N.F. *Privately printed*, 1966. pp. 4.
Light-hearted recollections of locomotive maintenance at 'a well-known locomotive works' and the running of an armoured train, Scotland, 1940–45.

8126 BONSOR, N. R. P. The Guernsey Railway: the German occupation lines in Guernsey, and the Alderney Railway. *Lingfield: Oakwood Press*, 1967. (Oakwood Library of Railway History, 58B). (Railways of the Channel Islands, 3). pp. 143–198, with 32 illus on 12 plates, 3 maps & 15 detailed lists of locomotives and tramcars.
Includes (pp. 194–5), 'Railways of the Island of Herm'.

8127 CALDER, A. The People's War: Britain, 1939–45. *London: Jonathan Cape*, 1969. pp. 656, with many notes, a detailed evaluative bibliography, and an Index of 17 pp.
Social aspects of war-time Britain. Includes the evacuation of school children and the use of London Underground tube stations as shelters from air raids.

8128 NOCK, O. S. Britain's railways at war, 1939–1945. *London: Ian Allan*, 1971. pp. 224, with frontis, 97 illus on 48 plates, tables, maps, plans & poster reproductions.

8129 KINGDOM, A. The Newton Abbot 'blitz'. *Oxford: Oxford Publishing Co.*, 1979. pp. 32, with 22 illus & 2 station layout plans.
The air bombing of Newton Abbot station, 20 August 1940.

B 8   1945–1947   POST-WAR RECOVERY, AND RAILWAYS DURING THEIR FINAL YEARS OF PRIVATE OWNERSHIP

[No entries]

B 9   NATIONALIZATION, 1948. THE ESTABLISHMENT OF THE BRITISH TRANSPORT COMMISSION AND 'BRITISH RAILWAYS'

8130–31

For a list of undertakings nationalized under the Transport Act (1947) see Appendix II of the main work (p. 474)

8130 BEEVOR, M. The work of the British Transport Commission. (Proceedings of the British Railways (W.R.) London Lecture & Debating Society, 1948–9, no. 361). pp. 15, with discussion.
Author, 'Chief Secretary & Adviser, B.T.C.'

8131 CALLAGHAN, L. J. Problems of nationalised industries. (Proceedings of the British Railways (W.R.) London Lecture & Debating Society, 1948–49, no. 352). pp. 12, with discussion.

Author, 'Parliamentary Secretary to the Ministry of Transport', later Prime Minister.

B 10   1948— RAILWAYS OF THE BRITISH ISLES IN GENERAL AND 'BRITISH RAILWAYS'

8132–8436

For London Transport see **C 1 c** (London)

British Railways generally and railways in Britain generally
8132–8265

Reference sources 8132–37
Historical 8138–60
Contemporaneous 8161–81 (Reference 8161–3)

Locomotives and trains generally 8182–83
Steam locomotives 8184–8201
Electric locomotives and trains 8202–5
Diesel locomotives 8206–61
Rolling stock 8262–64
Signalling 8265

Reference sources

FACTS and figures about British railways. [Title varies]. Published annually by the British Railways Press Office from 1927 to 1947 and thereafter by British Railways. *See* 7953.

8132 PARLIAMENT. HOUSE OF COMMONS. LIBRARY. British Railways. [*Westminster*]: *H of C Library*, July 1964. (Statistical Memorandum, 39). obl. format. pp. 20, consisting of 11 tables. Reproduced typescript.

8133 BRITISH RAILWAYS. The development of the major railway trunk routes. *London: B.R.*, February 1965. la. 8°. pp. 100, with 27 col. maps, contemporary and projected (1984), 13 tables and additional tables & diagrams in Appendices A, B, C & D.

8134 PASSENGER transport in Great Britain. *London: HMSO*, 1963 (for 1962)—1975 (for 1973). (Ministry of Transport Statistical Papers series, 1).
A summary of public transport information, including statistics, issued in successive annual editions of between 32 pp. & 66 pp. Includes a section 'Railways since Nationalisation'.

8135 CENTRAL OFFICE OF INFORMATION. REFERENCE DIVISION. Freight transport. *London: HMSO*, 1971. (Reference Pamphlet, 101). pp. 28 & 9 plates. Includes railways.
—— 2nd edn, 1975. pp. 28, with 8 illus on 4

plates, 7 tables & a bibliography (22 sources).
—— 3rd edn, 1978. pp. 36, with 8 illus on 4 plates, 9 tables & a bibliography (25 sources).
—— 4th edn, 1979. pp. 34, with 9 tables & a bibliography (22 sources). No illus.

8136 BODY, I. G. Modern rail facts and information. [*Bristol*]: *Avon-Anglia Publications*, 1978. pp. 28.
A concise guide (tables, statistics, locations, etc.) to a wide range of features of BR.

8137 RAIL Data Book: a modern railway companion. *Weston-super-Mare: Avon-Anglia*, 1980. sm. 8°. pp. 32.
A concise book of reference: 23 classified sections, including locomotives, rolling stock, depots, electrified routes, 100 mph sections, tunnels, summits, bridges, gradients, addresses, etc., etc.

Historical

8138 MUNBY, D. L. The nationalised industries, *in* The British Economy in the Nineteen-Fifties, ed. by G. D. N. Worswick and P. H. Ady (1952), ch. 11 (pp. 378–428), with 87 notes, 3 tables & a bibliography (13 sources).
Includes transport.

8139 BRITISH Rail in the fifties. *London: Ian Allan*, sm. obl. format.
A series of booklets each consisting of 32 pages of illustrations, originally published as *Trains Album*, nos. 1–15 (1953–9).
no. 1, Western Region. [1975]; no. 2, London Midland Region. [1975]; no. 3, Southern Region.

[1975]; no. 4, Eastern and North Eastern Regions. [1975]; no. 5, Scottish Region. [1977]; no. 6, Western Region. [1977]; no. 7, London Midland Region. [1977]; no. 8, Southern Region. [1977]; no. 9, Eastern and North Eastern Regions. [1977].

8140 ROBSON, W. A. Nationalised industry and public ownership. *London: Allen & Unwin*, 1960. pp. 544.

Railways and the British Transport Commission are important elements in the work. The index and bibliography are both detailed and together occupy pp. 499–544.

—— 2nd edn. *Allen & Unwin*, 1962. pp. xxxiii, [11], 544.

This 2nd edition is substantially unchanged, apart from the correction of a few literal inaccuracies, but in the new Introduction the author discusses a number of important matters of policy which had arisen since the publication of the first edition.

8141 LEE, N. Factors responsible for the financial results of British Railways, 1948–58. Thesis, Ph. D., University of London (L.S.E.), 1962–3.

8142 HANSON, A. H. Nationalisation: a book of readings, edited by A. H. Hanson. *London: Allen & Unwin, for the Royal Institute of Public Administration*, 1963. pp. 475.

Extracts from periodicals, pamphlets and reports, introduced and presented as a guide for students. Includes the B.T.C.

8143 GILBERT, P. J. The changes in the administration of British Railways since the appointment of Dr. Beeching. Thesis, Diploma in Public Administration, University of London, 1964. Typescript.

8144 ALLEN, G. F. British Rail after Beeching. *London: Ian Allan*, 1966. pp. viii, 384, with frontis, 102 illus on 32 plates, & a map.

8145 POLANYI, G. Contrasts in nationalised transport since 1947: a study of the conflict between co-ordination and competition as criteria for transport policy in Britain. *London: Institute of Economic Affairs*, 1968. (Background Memorandum, 2). la. 8°. pp. 54, with 4 tables.

A comparison between the policies of BR and the Transport Holding Co. (road haulage and buses).

8146 GIBSON, P. D. Railways in retrospect. (British Rail Western London Lecture & Debating Society, Proceedings, 1969–70, no. 505). pp. 9, with discussion.

Author, General Manager (Group Personnel), Shell Mex & B.P. Ltd. Reminiscences of his service with BR in the Beeching re-organization period, 1962–65.

8147 BONAVIA, M. R. The organisation of British Railways. *London: Ian Allan*, 1971. pp. 192, with 4 maps, 9 tables, 60 notes & a bibliography (119 sources). Foreword by Lord Beeching.

Based on the author's thesis (Ph.D., University of London, 1968). Includes a review of railway organization from the earliest days of public railways.

8148 PRYKE, R. Public enterprise in practice: the British experience of nationalization over two decades. *London: MacGibbon & Kee*, 1971. pp. xiii, 530, with 1259 notes (pp. 475–515).

Contains much detail on British Railways, especially in ch. 4, '1958–68: the productivity decade'; ch. 10, 'British Rail's loss of traffic'; and ch. 11, 'The rail deficit'. Index has 93 page refs under 'Railway' headings, 15 under 'London Transport' and 169 under 'British Rail'.

8149 JOY, S. The train that ran away: a business history of British Railways, 1948–1968. *London: Ian Allan*, 1973. pp. 160, with 283 notes.

Alleged mismanagement.

8150 THOMSON, A. W. J. The nationalized transport industries. *London: Heinemann Educational*, 1973. pp. viii, 356.

ch. 3 (pp. 124–213), The railways, with 14 tables & 109 notes.

8151 The BRITISH railways system, prepared by Chris Hirst for the Course Team. *Milton Keynes: Open University Press*, 1974. (Systems Management; unit 2 (T242; 2)) tall 8°. pp. 86, with illus, facsimiles, maps & a bibliography (32 sources).

Period, 1870–1973. A study of the organization and management structure of British railways before and after nationalization.

—— 2nd edn, prepared by Roger Spear. *Open University*, 1975. pp. 72, with illus, etc. & a bibliography (45 sources).

8152 SMITH, R. G. Ad hoc governments: special purpose transportation authorities in Britain and the United States. *Beverly Hills; London: Sage Publications*, 1974. (Sage Library of Social Research, 10). pp. 256, with a bibliography (161 sources).

pp. 143–55, the conflict of autonomy and accountability in British Railways and in London Transport before and after the Transport Act, 1962.

8153 PRYKE, R. W. S. and DODGSON, J. S. The rail problem . . . *London: Robertson*, 1975. pp. x, 294, with 41 tables and 63 notes.

An analysis of the financial career of BR since the Transport Act of 1968.

8154 ADAMS, J. and WHITEHOUSE, P. British Rail Scrapbook, 1948. *London: Ian Allan*, 1976. pp. 64. Intro & 99 illus wtih descrs.

pp. 3–14, 'The railway enthusiast's year, 1948'. An illustrated record of railway events.

8155 ADAMS, J. and WHITEHOUSE, P. British Rail Scrapbook, 1955. *London: Ian Allan*, 1976. pp. 64. Intro & 99 illus with descrs.

pp. 3–16, 'The railway enthusiast's year, 1955'. An illustrated record of railway events.

8156 ADAMS, J. and WHITEHOUSE, P. British Rail Scrapbook, 1950. *London: Ian Allan*, 1978. pp. 64. Intro & 112 illus with descrs.

pp. 5–18, 'The railway enthusiast's year, 1950'. An illustrated record of railway events.

8157 ADAMS, J. and WHITEHOUSE, P. British Rail Scrapbook, 1953. *London: Ian Allan*,

1978. pp. [64]. Intro & 114 illus with descrs.
pp. 3–21, 'The railway enthusiast's year, 1953'.
An illustrated record of railway events.

8158 MARSH, R. Off the Rails: an autobiography.
London: Weidenfeld & Nicolson, 1978. pp.
214, with 16 illus on 8 plates.
pp. 158–83, 'Rail and de-rail'; Richard Marsh's
chairmanship of BR (also pp. 185–204); pp. 122–6,
his earlier work with the Ministry of Transport.

8159 PARKER. P. A way to run a railway, by Peter
Parker, Chairman, British Rail. *London:
Birkbeck College, University of London*,
1978. (Haldane Memorial Lecture, 41). pp.
19.
Management objectives: a review of past and
present difficulties and the challenge to improve
efficiency and productivity.

8160 BONAVIA, M. R. The birth of British Rail.
London: Allen & Unwin, 1979. pp. 110, with
62 illus & a bibliography.
The period of the Railway Executive, 1948–1953.

Contemporaneous

8161 BRITISH TRANSPORT COMMISSION. Transport Directory, no. 2, January 1950. *Westminster: B.T.C.*, 1950, pp. 51.
Officials of the B.T.C., the Railway Executive
and all other B.T.C. executive bodies.
—— no. 3, March 1951. 1951. pp. 58.
Inserted in the LU(THC) copy are five amendment lists.

8162 BRITISH RAILWAYS. British Rail national
networks and regional boundaries as at 31
July 1966. *London: B.R.*, November 1966. A
folded col. map.

8163 MINISTRY OF TRANSPORT and BRITISH
RAILWAYS BOARD. British Railways net-
work for development. *London: H.M.S.O.*,
March 1967. la. folded map.
Foreword by the Minister of Transport (Barbara
Castle) and the Chairman of the British Railways
Board (Stanley Raymond).
The basic network to be retained and developed;
post-Beeching stabilization. Shows lines which it is
proposed not to include in the scheme.

8164 CHESTER, D. N. The nationalised industries: a statutory analysis. *London: Institute of
Public Administration*, 1948. pp. 48.
The constitution, powers, finance, etc. of a
number of large public corporations, including the
British Transport Commission (1948) and the London Passenger Transport Board (1933).

8165 DADGE, F. A. Control of expenditure on
the British Railways. (Proceedings of the
British Railways (W.R.) London Lecture &
Debating Society, 1953–54, no. 412). pp. 15,
with discussion.
Author, 'Assistant Accountant, Western Region'.

8166 MINISTRY OF TRANSPORT AND CIVIL AVI-
ATION. Railways Re-organisation Scheme.
(The submission of the British Transport

Commission to the . . . Minister of Transport
and Civil Aviation: Reorganisation of Railways). *London: HMSO*, 1954. (Cmd 9191).
pp. 22.
Introduction by the Minister of Transport followed by the full text of the B.T.C. scheme: pt 1,·
Explanatory statement; pt 2, The British Transport
Commission (Organisation) Scheme, 1954.

8167 BRITISH ELECTRICAL POWER CONVENTION
[Torquay, May 1956]. British Electrical Power Convention. *London: Railway Gazette*,
1956. pp. 38, with 23 illus & a map.
Principally concerned with railway electrification
and electric traction, and the implementation of
B.T.C.'s Modernisation Plan (January 1955).

8168 BRITISH TRANSPORT COMMISSION. Financial situation and prospects of British Transport: summary of the Commission's report to
the Minister of Transport and Civil Aviation.
London: B.T.C., October, 1956. pp. 20.
The report referred to is *Proposals for the
Railways*, H.M.S.O., 1956 (Cmd 9880) (Ottley 667).

8169 TRAIN, J. C. L. The Modernisation Plan.
Proceedings of the British Railways (W.R.)
London Lecture & Debating Society, 1955–
56, no. 422. pp. 15, with discussion & 6 illus.
Author, Member of the B.T.C.

8170 BRITISH RAILWAYS. British Railways Modernisation Plan: 1957–8 programme. *London:
B.T.C.*, 1957. tall pocket-book format. pp.
[12].
A publicity pamphlet.

8171 WATKINSON, H. The implications of the
Railway Modernisation Plan. Proceedings of
the British Railways (W.R.) London Lecture
& Debating Society, 1956–57, no. 434. pp. 10,
with discussion.
Author, Minister of Transport & Civil Aviation.

8172 BRITISH TRANSPORT COMMISSION. All
along the line. *London: B.T.C.*, 1959. la. 8°.
pp. 32, with 26 illus & a further 6 inserted in
end pocket together with a la. folded map.
On back cover, 'Facts & figures' (statistics).
A general account of the activities and plans of
BR.

8173 MINISTRY OF TRANSPORT AND CIVIL
AVIATION. Re-appraisal of the plan for the
modernisation and re-equipment of British
Railways. *London: H.M.S.O.*, 1959. (Cmnd
813). pp. 52.

8174 MINISTRY OF TRANSPORT. Re-organisation
of the nationalised transport undertakings.
London: H.M.S.O., [1961]. (Cmnd 1248).
pp. 14.

8175 BRITISH TRANSPORT COMMISSION. British
Railways progress. *London: B.T.C.*, May
1962. pp. 48, with 31 illus.

8176 NOCK, O. S. British Railways in transition.
London: T. Nelson, 1963. pp. xiii, 193, with

col. frontis, 3 col. plates & 48 monochrome illus on 48 plates, & 5 maps in text.
Engineering and operational aspects of BR's modernisation plan.

8177 ROLT, L. T. C. Alec's Adventures in Railwayland. *London: Ian Allan*, 1964. pp. 46, with 13 drawings.
A satire on current railway policy. The Prime Minister at this time was Sir Alec Douglas Home.

8178 BRITISH RAILWAYS BOARD. Report on organization, presented to Parliament, December 1969. *London: H.M.S.O.*, 1969. (H.C. Paper, 50). pp. 35, with 4 organisational structure charts on 2 folded sheets.
—— 2nd report, presented April 1972. *H.M.S.O.*, 1972. (H.C. Paper, 223). pp. 15, with map & folded chart of 'proposed territory organisation structure'.
—— 3rd report [of B.R.'s Shipping and International Services Division]. *H.M.S.O.*, 1978. (H.C. Paper, 2). pp. 6.

8179 WILSON, G. The task ahead. Proceedings of the British Railways (W.R.) London Lecture & Debating Society, 1969–70, no. 502. pp. 20, with discussion, 13 charts & a table.
Author, Member of the BR Board. The financial position of British Railways.

8180 MARSH, R. The future of British Railways. *London: Royal Society of Arts*, 1973. (Journal of the R.S.A., vol. 120, Dec. 1971–Nov. 1972; Paper no. 5190 May 1972), pp. 370–81. (Discussion, pp. 378–81).
Richard William Marsh, Chairman of British Railways Board, 1971–6.

8181 BRITISH RAILWAYS. British Rail today and tommorrow. *London: B.R.*, 1974. la. 8°. pp. [48], with 89 col. illus & a col. folded map 'British Rail Passenger Network. 1974'. In pocket at end of single-sheet insert, 'British Rail 1973: financial & statistical summary'.

Locomotives and trains generally

8182 NOCK, O. S. Railways of the modern age since 1963 . . . illustrated by Clifford and Wendy Meadway. *Poole: Blandford Press*, 1975. (Railways of the World in Colour). pp. 155, with 152 col. illus (pp. 9–88) individually described (pp. 89–150).
Mostly locomotives, world coverage, with supporting maps, diagrams and insignia.

8183 FRITH, J. M. Railway Pictorial Jubilee Album: a photographic survey of British Railways, 1952 to 1977. *Dorking: Railway Pictorial Publications*, [1977], sm. obl. format. pp. [48]. Intro & 53 illus with descrs.

Steam locomotives

8184 COX, E. S. British Railways standard steam locomotives. *London: Ian Allan*, 1966. pp. 218, with 68 illus on 40 plates, & in text, 42 tables & 26 diagrams.

8185 RANSOME-WALLIS, P. The last steam locomotives of British Railways. *London: Ian Allan*, 1966. la. 8°. pp. 191. Intro, frontis, & 316 illus with descrs; lists & tables at end.
Photographs of locomotives at work, 1955–60, with historical notes; arranged under Whyte classes.
—— 2nd edn. *Ian Allan*, 1973. la. 8°. pp. 191.
318 illus with detailed descrs & 10 introductions to each Whyte class of locomotive. Period, 1955–1960.

8186 KRAUSE, I. S. Steam. *Hatch End: Roundhouse Books; [Shepperton]: Ian Allan*, 1967. pp. [112]. Intro & 107 illus with descrs.
Period, 1950s & 1960s.

8187 WOLSTENCROFT, J. A. The 'Britannia' Pacifics: an appreciation. *Stockport: Stockport (Bahamas) Locomotive Society*, [1968]. pp. [28] incl. covers, with 14 illus, 2 logs of runs & a list.

8188 CROSS, D. B.R. Standard Steam in action. *Truro: Bradford Barton*, 1974. pp. 96. Intro & 94 illus with descrs.

8189 WEEKES, G. BR Standard Britannia Pacifics: a study of British Railways Standard class 7P express passenger locomotive, edited by G. Weekes. *Truro: Bradford Barton*, 1975. pp. 96. Intro, frontis, & 93 illus with descrs.

8190 WEEKES, G. BR Standard class 9F: a study of British Railways Standard class 9F 2-10-0 heavy freight locomotive, edited by G. Weekes. *Truro: Bradford Barton*, 1975. pp. 96. Intro & 106 illus with descrs.

8191 BURTON, E. D. British Steam, 1948–1955. *London: Ian Allan*, 1976. la. 8°. pp. 128. Intro, frontis & 188 illus with descrs.

8192 HARESNAPE, B. Ivatt and Riddles locomotives: a pictorial history. *London: Ian Allan*, 1977. pp. 112, with 154 illus & a bibliography (11 sources).

8193 MONTAGUE, K. British Railways Standard Steam. *Oxford: Oxford Publishing Co.*, 1977. (Pocket Railway Books, 3). pp. [64]. Intro, frontis & 112 illus with descrs. Spiral binding.

8194 PIRT, K. R. and PENNEY, D. E. British Steam around the Regions. *Truro: Bradford Barton*, [1977]. pp. 96. Intro & 89 illus with descrs.
Period, mid 1950s.

8195 NOCK, O. S. The last years of British Railways steam: reflections ten years after. *Newton Abbot: David & Charles*, 1978. pp. 143, with 32 illus on 16 plates.

8196 BLOOM, A. Locomotives of British Railways, written by Alan Bloom; compiled by David Williams. *Norwich: Jarrold*, 1980. (Jarrold Railway Series, 5). pp. [32], with 59 illus (53 col.) & a map. Text & illus extend onto covers.
Steam locomotives.

8197 COCKMAN, F. G. British Railways' steam locomotives. *Princes Risborough: Shire Publications*, 1980. (History in Camera series). pp. 80, with 95 illus, a 4p list of preserved locomotives, a gazetteer (museums & preserved lines) & a bibliography (12 sources).

8198 FAIRCLOUGH, T. and WILLS, A. BR Standard Steam in close-up. *Truro: Bradford Barton*. 2 vols.
vol. 1, [1980]. pp. 96. Intro (pp. 5–7) & 95 illus with descrs & 3 diagrams.
vol. 2, [1980 or 81]. pp. 96. Intro (pp. 5–7) & 93 illus with descrs & 3 diagrams.

8199 SEMMENS, P. W. B. Steam on British main lines: text and photographs by Peter Semmens. *Norwich: Jarrold Colour Publications*, 1980. (Jarrold Nostalgia Series). pp. [34] incl. covers, with 38 illus (20 col.) incl 4 on covers.
Period, since 1947.

8200 WHITELEY, J. S. and MORRISON, G. W. The power of the BR Standard Pacifics. *Oxford: Oxford Publishing Co.*, 1980. la. 8°. pp. [112]. Intro, & 220 illus (10 col.), with descrs.

8201 WILLIAMS, A. BR Standard Steam Album. *London: Ian Allan*, 1980. pp. 86. Intro (pp. 3–7) & 133 illus with full descrs.

Electric locomotives and trains

8202 MALLABAND, P. The electric multiple-units of British Railways. *Sutton Coldfield: Electric Railway Society*, [1972]. pp. iii, 80.
A detailed survey of stock at the end of 1971, with many lists.

8203 WEBB, B. and DUNCAN, J. AC electric locomotives of British Rail. *Newton Abbot: David & Charles*, 1979. pp. 96, with 75 illus, drawings, diagrams & lists.

8204 BRITISH Rail electric locomotives & multiple-units. *London: Ian Allan*, 1980. (abc series). sm. 8°. pp. 64. Classified lists & 43 illus.

8205 HARDY, B. BR electric multiple-units. *Truro: Bradford Barton*, 1980. pp. 64. Intro & 123 illus with descrs.

Diesel locomotives

8206 SMEDDLE, R. A. Dieselisation: problems, prospects and progress. Proceedings of the British Railways (W.R.) London Lecture & Debating Society, 1958–59, no. 455. pp. 15, with discussion, 6 illus & 4 diagrams.
Author, 'Chief Mechanical & Electrical Engineer, W.R.'

8207 PATTISON, F. D. Dieselisation: planning and progress. (Proceedings of the British Railways (W.R.) London Lecture & Debating Society. 1960–61, no. 469). pp. 17, with discussion & 6 illus.
Author, 'Head of Operating Officer's Research Section, W.R.'

8208 SHIRLEY, J. British Railways' diesel multiple-unit allocations. 1st edn. [*Newport*]: *Monmouthshire Railway Society*, Spring 1961. pp. 18. Reproduced typescript.
A two-column listing of units 50,000 to 79,999.

8209 MATTHEWSON-DICK, T. From steam to diesel. (Proceedings of the British Railways (W.R.) London Lecture & Debating Society, 1969–70, no. 503). pp. 16, with discussion, 7 illus & 3 charts.
Author, 'Assistant General Manager, W.R.'

8210 The DELTICS: a symposium, [by] Cecil J. Allen . . . [and others]. [*Shepperton*]: *Ian Allan*, 1972. pp. 64, with 38 illus on 24 plates, 8 tables (logs of 14 runs), & 2 diagrams.
Essays by: C. J. Allen, G. F. Fiennes, Roger Ford, B. A. Haresnape, Brian Perren.
—— 2nd edn. *Ian Allan*, 1977. pp. 79.

8211 CARTER, R. S. British railways main-line diesels. *London: Ian Allan*, 1963. la. obl. format. pp. 47.
A set of scale drawings, each with photo, description and specification.
—— British Rail main-line diesels, compiled by S. W. Stevens-Stratten; drawings by R. S. Carter. [rev]. & enl. edn of the earlier work by R. S. Carter. *Ian Allan*, 1975. obl. format. pp. 63.
Dimensioned drawings of 32 locomotive classes for modellers, with accompanying photographs & livery notes.

8212 DOBSON, P. A. Diesels in London and the Home Counties. *Truro: Bradford Barton*, 1974. pp. 96. Intro & 89 illus with descrs.

8213 MONTAGUE, K. Diesels. *Oxford: Oxford Publishing Co.*, 1974. (Pocket Railway Books, 1). pp. [64]. Intro & 117 illus with descrs. Spiral binding.

8214 PREEDY, N. E. and FORD, H. L. BR diesels in close-up. *Truro: Bradford Barton*, 1974. pp. 96. Intro & 110 illus with descrs.

8215 WEEKES, G. BR diesels in action. *Truro: Bradford Barton*.
[vol. 1], 1974. pp. 96. Intro, frontis, & 115 illus with descrs.
vol. 2, 1975. pp. 96. Intro & 117 illus with descrs.
vol. 3, 1976. pp. 96. Intro & 105 illus with descrs.
no. 4, 1977. pp. 96. Intro & 112 with descrs.
no. 5, 1980. pp. 96. Intro & 107 illus with descrs.

8216 CROSS, D. BR diesels in the landscape. *Truro: Bradford Barton*, 1975. pp. 96. Intro & 86 illus with descrs.

8217 MONTAGUE, K. Westerns, Hymeks and Warships. *Oxford: Oxford Publishing Co.*, 1975. la. 8°. pp. [80]. Intro & 116 illus with descrs.
Diesel-hydraulic locomotive classes, Western Region of BR, from 1958: a sequel to this author's *Diesels, Western style* (1974).

8218 VAUGHAN, J. A. M. Branch lines round Britain in the diesel era. *Truro: Bradford Barton*, 1975. 4°. pp. 96. Intro, frontis & 105 illus with descrs.

8219 FOWLER, P. J. DMU's countrywide. *Truro: Bradford Barton*, 1976. pp. 96. Intro, frontis & 103 illus with descrs.
Diesel trains on secondary lines.

8220 PREEDY, N. E. BR diesels on shed. *Truro: Bradford Barton*, 1976. pp. 96. Intro & 104 illus with descrs & an index of depots.

8221 WALKER, J. A. BR Sulzer class 44, 45, 46, diesel-electric locomotives. *Truro: Bradford Barton for the Diesel & Electric Group*, 1976. pp. 32, with 22 illus, 3 diagrams, tables.

8222 WEBB, B. The English Electric main line diesels of British Rail. *Newton Abbot: David & Charles*, 1976. pp. 96, with 49 illus, 23 tables & 15 diagrams.

8223 DIESEL AND ELECTRIC GROUP. Preserved class 35, Hymek D7017 . . . *Potters Bar: the Group*, 1977. pp. 15, with 8 illus & 8 diagrams.
Research by Clive Burrows, John Hembry; edited by John M. Crane.

8224 DIESELS nationwide. *Oxford: Oxford Publishing Co.* [vol.1], by Keith Montague. 1977. 4°. pp. [136]. Intro & 268 illus with descrs. & a map.
—— vol. 2, by Colin Judge. 1979. 4°. pp. 64. Intro & 242 illus with descrs, & a map.

8225 KICHENSIDE, G. British Rail in action. *Newton Abbot: David & Charles*, 1977. pp. 96. Intro, frontis & 129 illus with descrs.
Period, 1970–76.

8226 PREEDY, N. E. The English Electric type 4s (BR class 40s): a picture study; principal photographs by Norman E. Preedy; edited & published by Peter Watts . . . *Gloucester: P. Watts*, 1977. obl. format. pp. 20. 25 illus with descrs. No text.

8227 WEEKES, G. BR diesels doubleheaded. *Truro: Bradford Barton*, 1977. pp. 96. Intro & 102 illus with descrs.

8228 WHITELEY, J. S. and MORRISON, G. W. The power of the Deltics. *Oxford: Oxford Publishing Co.*, 1977. 4°. pp. [102]. Intro & 191 illus (20 col.) with descrs.

8229 BRITISH Rail's class 24s: a picture study. *Gloucester: Peter Watts*, 1978. obl. format. pp. [20]. Intro & 19 illus with descrs & 2 on covers.
Photographs by Norman Preedy, Grenville R. Hounsell, John Chalcroft & G. Scott-Lowe.

8230 COOPER-SMITH, J. Deltic Pictorial: a photographic tribute by the author to the most powerful diesels on British Rail . . . *Dorking: Railway Pictorial Publications*, [1978?]. pp. [48]. Intro & 46 illus with descrs.

8231 HEMMING, R. British Rail DMU/EMU Allocation Book. 1st edn, compiled by R. Hemming. *National Railway Enthusiasts Association*, August 1978. sm. 8°. pp. [36].
—— 6th edn. Spring, 1979. pp. 36.

8232 OAKLEY, M. Class 24: The unsung performers. *Sutton Coldfield: Diesel & Electric Group, in association with Mercian Railtours*, 1978. la. 8°. pp. 24 incl. covers, with 21 illus, 5 logs of runs, 2 maps, list, graph & a dimensioned drawing.

8233 OAKLEY, M. Class Forty: the great survivors. *Sutton Coldfield: Diesel & Electric Group*, [1977 or 78]. la. 8°. pp. 24 incl. covers, with 22 illus, tables, 3 logs of runs, 2 dimensioned drawings, performance graph & a map.
—— another edn. *D & E Group*, 1978. pp. 24, with illus, etc.

8234 WEBB, B. Sulzer diesel locomotives of British Rail. *Newton Abbot: David & Charles*, 1978. la. 8°. pp. 96, with 65 illus, 21 tables, 9 logs of runs & 8 graphs.

8235 WHITELEY, J. S. and MORRISON, G. W. The power of the 40s, compiled by J. S. Whiteley and G. W. Morrison. *Oxford: Oxford Publishing Co.*, 1978. la. 8°. pp. [116]. Intro, & 246 illus (12 col.) with descrs.
The class 40 diesel-electric locomotives.

8236 BRITISH Rail class 37's: a picture study. *Gloucester: Peter Watts*, 1979. sm. obl. format. pp. [20]. Intro & 22 illus & 2 on covers.

8237 CROSS, D. B.R. diesels departed. *Truro: Bradford Barton*, 1979. pp. 32. Intro & 36 illus with descrs.
A photographic record of the more important classes of diesel locomotives withdrawn from regular service up to June 1978.

8238 FORD, H. L. and PREEDY, N. E. Warships: B.R. class 42/43 diesel-hydraulics. *Truro: Bradford Barton*, 1979. pp. 96. Intro & 96 illus with descrs.

8239 JUDGE, C. W. BR shunters. *Oxford: Oxford Publishing Co*, 1979. (Transport Topic series, 4). pp. [32]. Intro, & 47 illus with descrs, & 7 diagrams.

8240 MORRISON, B. BR diesel cavalcade. *Truro: Bradford Barton*, [1979]. pp. [32]. 41 illus with descrs. No text.

8241 OAKLEY, M. BR diesel shunting locos: a pictorial history . . . *Sutton Coldfield: Diesel & Electric Group*, [1979?]. pp. 40. 47 illus & 8 lists.

8242 OAKLEY, M. BR-EE class 37 diesel electrics, by Michael Oakley, with additional material by . . . [others]. *Truro: Bradford Barton; Sutton Coldfield: Diesel & Electric Group*, [1979]. pp. [32], with 28 illus, 5 tables (logs of runs), a dimensioned drawing & a map.

8243 OAKLEY, M. The Fifty-fifties: EE class 50 diesel-electrics . . . with additional material by Robert Tiller. *Truro: Bradford Barton*, [1979]. pp. 32, with 23 illus, 3 tables, 2 diagrams & a map.

8244 RINGER, B. Brush-Sulzer class 47 diesel-electrics. *Truro: Bradford Barton*, [1979]. pp. 48, with 29 illus, 2 dimensioned drawings & a 'statistical appendix'.

8245 TAYLER, A. T. H., THORLEY, W. G. F., and HILL, T. J. Class 47 diesels. *London: Ian Allan*, 1979. pp. 96. Text, with 67 illus, 23 graphs & diagrams, 5 tables, a list, & a dimensioned drawing on end papers.

8246 TUFNELL, R. M. The diesel impact on British Rail, with a Foreword by T. C. B. Miller. *London: Mechanical Engineering Publications*, 1979. pp. ix, 184, with 92 illus, drawings & diagrams, & 25 tables; 10 appendices.
The change-over from steam to diesel on BR, 1957–1968: a detailed narrative of this period of experimentation with an appraisal of the strength and weaknesses of every type of diesel locomotive used on main line haulage during this period.

8247 VAUGHAN, J. A. M. The power of the 50s. *Oxford: Oxford Publishing Co.*, 1979. la. 8°. pp. [128]. Intro & 240 illus (10 col.), with descrs.

8248 WEEKES, G. BR diesel miscellany: no. 1. *Truro: Bradford Barton*, 1979. pp. 96. 102 illus with descrs. No text.

8249 WILLIAMS, A. BR Diesel Locomotive Album. *London: Ian Allan*, 1979. pp. 91, with 126 illus.

8250 GOSLING, J. B. Depot and Stabling Directory: guide book of British Rail establishments. 3rd edn. *Leamington Spa: J. B. Gosling*, [197–?]. pp. [36].

8251 BRITISH Rail diesel locomotives. *London: Ian Allan*, 1980. (abc series). sm. 8°. pp. 48. Classified lists & 29 illus.

8252 BRITISH Rail diesel multiple-units. *London: Ian Allan*, 1980. (abc series). sm. 8°. pp. 64. Classified lists & 29 illus.

8253 CRANE, J. M. Preserved class 35s: Hymeks D7017, D7018. *Potters Bar: Diesel & Electric Group*, [1980]. pp. 13, with 9 illus (4 on covers), & 7 diagrams.

8254 HEMBRY, P. J. Class 14: the cinderellas of the diesel-hydraulic era. *Potters Bar: Diesel & Electric Group*, 1980. la. 8°. pp. 24, with 25 illus.

8255 MORRISON, B. The power of the 47s. *Oxford: Oxford Publishing Co.*, 1980. la. 8°. Intro & 242 illus with descrs.

8256 NICHOLAS, D. and MONTGOMERY, S. Profile of the Westerns: *Oxford: Oxford Publishing Co.*, 1980. la. 8°. pp. [80]. Intro, 163 illus with descrs & a 6-column table of the locomotives of the 'Western' class 52.

8257 NICOLLE, B. Spotters' Guide to Diesel Recognition. *Oxford: Oxford Publishing Co.*, 1980. (Transport Topic series, 10). pp. 32. Intro, & 26 illus with 26 diagrams.

8258 OAKLEY, M. BR diesel freight in the traditional era. *Truro: Bradford Barton; Sutton Coldfield: Diesel & Electric Group*, [1980]. pp. [48], with 45 illus, each with a full description.
—— BR diesel freight in the era of specialisation. *Truro: Bradford Barton; Sutton Coldfield: Diesel & Electric Group*, [1980]. pp. [48], with 45 illus, each with a full description.
The two works illustrate the evolution both of the diesel locomotive and its usage, from shunting to long-distance haulage. The esoteric presentation may challenge the wits of steam-propelled readers.

8259 OAKLEY, M. and MORRISON, B. BR diesels in detail. *Truro: Bradford Barton*, [1980]. pp. 96. Intro (pp. 5–7) & 99 illus with descrs.

8260 VAUGHAN, J. Double-headed diesels nationwide. *Oxford: Oxford Publishing Co.*, 1980. la. 8°. pp. [128]. Intro & 242 illus with descrs, & 2 appendices.

8261 WHITELEY, J. S. and MORRISON, G. W. Profile of the Deltics. *Oxford:Oxford Publishing Co.*, 1980. la. 8°. Intro & 152 & [6] illus with descrs.
Diesel-electric locomotives, 1970s.

Rolling stock

8262 LARKIN, D. BR standard freight wagons: a pictorial survey. *Truro: Bradford Barton*, 1975. pp. 64. Intro, list, & 120 illus with descrs.

8263 LARKIN, D. BR general parcels rolling stock: a pictorial survey. *Truro: Bradford Barton*, 1978. pp. 64. Intro & 120 illus with detailed descrs.
Non-passenger vehicles for carrying parcels, luggage, mail, motor vehicles, livestock, & perishables.

8264 LARKIN, D. BR departmental rolling stock: a pictorial survey. *Truro: Bradford Barton*, 1979. pp. 64. Intro & 120 illus with descrs.
Special duty freight vehicles and converted passenger stock, snow-ploughs, breakdown trains, tampers, cranes, etc.

Signalling

8265 BRITISH RAILWAYS. Automatic Train Control: the British Railways standard system. [*London*]: B.R., [1975]. obl. format. pp. [16], with 7 illus (2 inside covers), & 8 col. diagrams.

B 10 (ER) EASTERN REGION

8266–89

General, and administration 8266–70
Locomotives and trains 8271–89

General, and administration

8266 BRITISH RAILWAYS. EASTERN REGION. Description of automatic train control on the Fenchurch St–Shoeburyness section. *Kings Cross Stn. (London): B.R.(ER)*, February 1950. pp. 12 & 2 folded diagrams.

8267 BRITISH TRANSPORT COMMISSION. RAILWAY EXECUTIVE HEADQUARTERS COMMITTEE ON THE ELECTRIFICATION OF THE LONDON, TILBURY AND SOUTHEND LINE. Report. *London: the Committee*, 1950. pp. 44, with 4 la. folded addenda (map, specimen timetables of proposed electric services; plan of proposed re-arrangement of track layout at Barking, diagrams of proposed multi-unit rolling stock). Chairman: C. M. Cock.

8268 FIENNES, G. F. I tried to run a railway. *London: Ian Allan*, 1967. pp. vii, 139, with 63 illus (incl. portraits & map) on 32 plates.
   Author was in railway service from 1928 to 1967, mostly with the LNER and BR(ER), but with BR(WR) as Chairman of the Western Railway board, 1963–65. From 1965–67, he was Chairman, Eastern Railway Board and Gen. Manager, Eastern Region of BR.

8269 BRITISH RAILWAYS. EASTERN REGION. Your new electric railway: the Great Northern suburban electrification. *London: B.R.(ER)*, May 1973. la. 8°. pp. 18, with 25 illus, map & a diagram.

8270 RANKIN, S. A huge palace of business. *York: B.R.(ER)*, [1979]. obl. format. pp. 20, with 13 illus & 3 plans.
   The history, from 1836, of the buildings in the Eastern Region Headquarters complex (station, hotel and administrative centre) in York.

Locomotives and trains

8271 BRITISH RAILWAYS. Doncaster Locomotive, Carriage and Wagon Works Centenary, 1953: short account of 100 years' progress. *London: B.R.*, [1953]. pp. 24, incl. covers, with 8 illus, plan, & 2 lists.
   Compiled from material collected ·by Messrs Day and Slingsby, members of the Works staff·.

8272 SHAW, W. King's Cross to York: a journey in pictures, with an essay by W. A. Tuplin. *Hemel Hempstead: Model & Allied Publications*, 1969. (Days of Steam series, 1). sm. obl. format. pp. [36], with 26 illus.
   Period, 1949–61.

8273 HARDY, R. H. N. Steam in the Blood. *London: Ian Allan*, 1971. pp. 200, with 72 illus on 32 plates.
   The first 21 years of a career in locomotive running and maintenance, LNER and BR(ER), 1941–1962.

8274 WALKER, C. Kings Cross. *Oxford: Oxford Illustrators*, 1971. (Steam Railway series, 3). obl. 8°. pp. [64]. Intro & 59 illus with descrs.
   1950s–1960s.

8275 LYNCH, P. J. North Eastern Steam from lineside. *Truro: Bradford Barton*, 1974. pp. 96. Intro & 111 illus with descrs.
   Locomotives & trains in the Eastern Region, 1950s–1960s.

8276 MORRISON, B. North Eastern Steam in action. *Truro: Bradford Barton*, 1974. pp. 96. Intro & 100 illus with descrs.
   BR(ER) 'from Darlington to Kings Cross and Liverpool St'. Period, 1950s–1970s.

8277 MANN, J. D. Great Eastern railways: a pictorial collection. *Frinton: South Anglia Productions*, [1975]. pp. [20]. Historical intro & 44 illus with descrs. Period, 1948–1973.

8278 PREEDY, N. E. Diesels on Eastern Region. *Truro: Bradford Barton*, 1975. pp. 96. Intro & 108 illus with descrs.

8279 TOWNEND, P. N. Top shed: a pictorial history of Kings Cross locomotive depot. *London: Ian Allan*, 1975. pp. 175, with 169 illus, 3 plans & 2 diagrams.
   Period, 1850–1963, but principally 1956–1963 when the author was in charge of the depot.

8280 WALKER, C. Trails through Peterborough. *Oxford: Oxford Publishing Co.*, [1975]. (Trails of Steam series, 2). obl. format. pp. [64]. Intro & 60 illus with descrs.
   Period, 1960s.

8281 ALLEN, I. C. East Anglian Album. *Oxford: Oxford Publishing Co.*, 1976. 4°. pp. [96]. Intro & 130 illus with descrs, & 6 maps.
   Period, 1950s & 1960s.

8282 BRITISH RAILWAYS. EASTERN REGION. The 'Deltics': facts and figures. *York: B.R.(ER)*, 1976. pp. 10, with 7 illus & technical diagrams. Reproduced typescript.
   A brief outline of the design features of this class of diesel-electric locomotive.

8283 BRITISH RAILWAYS. EASTERN REGION. Eastern Region diesel locomotive classes. *York: B.R.(ER)*, 1976. tall 8°. pp. [26], with 22 diagrams. Reproduced typescript.

8284 MANN, J. D. The Eastern Region in pictures. *Frinton: South Anglia Productions*, [1976]. la. 8°. pp. [20]. Intro & 42 illus with descrs.

8285 OAKLEY, M. Deltic: a profile of the East Coast class 55s. *Sutton Coldfield: Diesel & Electric Group*, 1976. la. 8°. pp. 24, with 19 illus, 4 logs of runs, 6 line drawings, 2 lists & a map.
   —— another edn. *D & E Group*, 1978. pp. 24; 23 illus, 4 logs of runs, 3 diagrams & a map.

8286 ALLEN, I. C.   East Anglian Branch Line Album. *Oxford: Oxford Publishing Co.*, 1977. 4°. pp. [80]. Frontis, intro & 127 illus with descrs.

8287 PREEDY, N.   Book of the Deltics: British Rail class 55s . . . , with additional material by Ray Hinton and John Augustson. *Gloucester: Peter Watts*, 1978. pp. [28]. Intro & 45 illus with captions.
'Deltic' locomotives on the East Coast main line, 1961–1977.

8288 WALKER, C.   Trails through Grantham. *Oxford: Oxford Publishing Co.*, 1979. (Trails of Steam series, 6). obl. format. pp. [64]. Intro & 60 illus with descrs.
1950s–1960s.

8289 ALLEN, I. C.   Diesels in East Anglia. *Oxford: Oxford Publishing Co.*, [1980]. pp. [80]. Intro & 130 illus with detailed descrs.

B 10 (LMR)   LONDON MIDLAND REGION

8290–8334

General, and administration 8290–6
Steam locomotives and trains 8297–8322
Electric locomotives and trains 8323–25
Diesel locomotives 8326–33
Rolling stock 8334

General, and administration

8290 BRITISH RAILWAYS. LONDON MIDLAND REGION.   Freight Handbook: facilities and principal express freight train services. *London: B.R.(LMR)*, 1964. pp. 60, with 35 illus.

8291 BRITISH RAILWAYS.   Your new railway; Foreword by S. E. Raymond, Chairman, B.R. *London: B.R.*, 1966. pp. 36, with 38 illus, and illus & map on covers.
Electrification plans for the London Midland Region, London to Manchester & Liverpool.

8292 NOCK, O. S.   Britain's new railway: electrification of the London-Midland main lines from Euston to Birmingham, Stoke-on-Trent, Crewe, Liverpool and Manchester. *London: Ian Allan*, 1966. pp. 224, with col. frontis, 97 illus on 48 plates, 29 figures in text (layout plans, gradient profiles, drawings, diagrams & maps) 6 logs of runs & some additional tables at end.

8293 TIMES [newspaper].   Supplement. Railway electrification, London–Manchester–Liverpool. *London: The Times*, 18 April 1966. pp. iv, with 13 illus.

8294 BRITISH RAILWAYS. LONDON MIDLAND REGION.   Traveller's Guide to the new London–Birmingham rail speed-link. *London: B.R.(LMR)*, [1967]. pp. 88, with illus.
A guide for visitors to the towns *en route*, with a rail travel information section, pp. 81–8.

8295 RAILWAY CORRESPONDENCE & TRAVEL SOCIETY.   Itinerary of the End of Steam Commemorative Rail Tour, Sunday, 4th August, 1968. *R.C. & T.S.*, [1968]. pp. [24], with 4 illus, 2 line drawings, 4 maps & a timetable (route schedule). Detailed historical notes by G. H. Brown, H. C. Casserley and D. Murphy; maps by A. G. Coffin and schedule by E. N. T. Platt. Red covers.
Euston—Rugby—Stoke-on-Trent—Stockport—Edgley—Manchester—Oldham—Rochdale—Bury—Bolton—Blackburn—Hellifield—Skipton—Rose Grove—Lostock Hall—Aintree—Tue Brook—Broad Green—Manchester—Edgley—Crewe—Rugby—Euston.

8296 NOCK, O. S.   Electric Euston to Glasgow. *London: Ian Allan*, 1974. pp. 186, wih 91 illus on 48 plates, maps, layout plans, diagrams & line drawings.

Steam locomotives and trains

8297 HIGSON, M.   LM Pacific: a pictorial tribute. *Hatch End: Roundhouse Books*, 1967. pp. [120]. Frontis & 135 illus.

8298 DOHERTY, D.   Camden. *Seaton: Peco*, [1968]. (Railscene, 1). sm. obl. format. pp. [32]. Intro & 28 illus with descrs.
Trains in the approach to Euston Station, London, 1960s.

8299 SHAW, W.   Euston to Carlisle: a journey in pictures, with an essay by W. A. Tuplin. *Hemel Hempstead: Model & Allied Publications*, 1969. (Days of Steam series, 3). sm. obl. format. pp. [36], with 26 illus.
Period 1956 to 1961, but mostly 1959.

8300 MERCHANT NAVY LOCOMOTIVE PRESERVATION SOCIETY.   The Midlands Enterprise Rail Tour, Saturday, 11th April 1970. [*London: the Society*, 1970]. pp. 12, with 5 illus; loose map inserted.
Itinerary: Waterloo—Willesden—Stockport—Sheffield—Crewe—Stafford—Wolverhampton for Bridgnorth—Birmingham—Coventry—Rugby—Euston.

8301 HIGSON, M. F.   London Midland fireman. *London: Ian Allan*, 1972. pp. 144, with 44 illus on 20 plates, 2 diagrams, & 2 tables showing rates of firing.

8302 WALKER, C.   Over the Pennine Fells: the Settle and Carlisle line. *Oxford: Oxford Illustrators*, 1972. (Steam Railway series, 4). obl. 8°. pp. [64]. Intro & 59 illus with descrs.

8303 CARTER, J. R.   London Midland Steam in the North-West. *Truro: Bradford Barton*, 1973. pp. 96. Intro & 100 illus with descrs.

8304 BLAKE, W. A.   London Midland Steam in action. *Truro: Bradford Barton*.
LMS steam trains in BR(LMR) days, 1948–1960s.
[no. 1]: 1974. pp. 96. 105 illus with descrs.
no. 2: 1975. pp. 96. 103 illus with descrs.
no. 3: 1975. pp. 96. 98 illus with descrs.
no. 4: [1979]. pp. 96. 118 illus with descrs.

8305 HILLIER, J. R. London Midland Steam in the Peak District. *Truro: Bradford Barton*, 1974. pp. 96. Intro & 107 illus with descrs.

8306 MENSING, M. London Midland Steam in the Midlands. *Truro: Bradford Barton*, 1974. pp. 96. Intro, frontis & 103 illus with descrs.

8307 COOKSON, P. London Midland Steam in Yorkshire. *Truro: Bradford Barton*, 1975. pp. 96. Intro & 95 illus with descrs.

8308 DYCKHOFF, N. F. W. More London Midland Steam in the North-West. *Truro: Bradford Barton*, 1975. pp. 96. Intro & 110 illus with descrs.

8309 GREENWOOD, R. S. London Midland Steam on the ex L & Y. *Truro: Bradford Barton*, 1975. pp. 96. Intro & 106 illus with descrs.

8310 HIGHET, C. All steamed up! *Oxford: Oxford Publishing Co.*, 1975. pp. [iv], 106, with 97 illus.
> Recollections of a career in motive power management, Midland Rly, LMS Rly and BR, 1920–1964.

8311 LESLIE, R. H. London Midland Steam around Carlisle. *Truro: Bradford Barton*, 1975. pp. 96. Intro & 108 illus with descrs.

8312 MORRISON, B. London Midland Steam from lineside. *Truro: Bradford Barton*, 1975. pp. 96. Intro & 95 illus with descrs.

8313 LESLIE, R. H. and SHORT, R. H. London Midland Steam, Skipton–Carlisle. *Truro: Bradford Barton*, 1976. pp. 96. Intro & 99 illus with descrs.

8314 WALKER, C. Trails through Rugby. *Oxford: Oxford Publishing Co.*, [1976]. (Trails of Steam series, 3). obl. format. pp. [64]. Intro & 60 illus with descrs.
> 1950s–1960s.

8315 POWELL. A. J. Living with London Midland locomotives. *London: Ian Allan*, 1977. pp. 156, with 48 illus on 24 plates & 18 dimensioned drawings.
> Based on a series of essays written by the author in *Trains Illustrated* between November 1957 and March 1959 under the pseudonym '45671' on the subject of steam locomotives on the LMS and BR(LMR), 1936–1960s.

8316 WALKER, C. Midland trails through Leicestershire & Rutland. *Oxford: Oxford Publishing Co.*, 1977. (Trails of Steam series, 4). obl. format. pp. [60]. Intro & 60 illus with descrs.

8317 BLAKE, W. A. London Midland Steam double-headed. *Truro: Bradford Barton*, 1978. pp. 80, 82 illus with descrs.

8318 HORNBY, F. and BROWNE, N. London

Midland Region Steam. *London: Almark*, 1978. pp. 72. Intro & 124 illus with descrs.

8319 REAR, W. G. London Midland Steam in North Wales. *Truro: Bradford Barton*, 1979. pp. 96. Intro & 112 illus with descrs.

8320 CROSS, D. Roaming the West Coast rails. *London: Ian Allan*, 1980. la. 8°. pp. 128. Preface, intro, & 221 illus with descrs; map on end papers.
> London to Carlisle in five sections, each with introductory text. The ex-LNWR line, 1950–1978.

8321 ESSERY, T. Firing days at Saltley. *Truro: Bradford Barton*, [1980]. pp. 174, with frontis (portrait), & 13 illus on 8 plates (pp. 81–88).
> Locomotive work centred upon Saltley motive-power depot, Birmingham, 1950–59.

—— More firing days at Saltley. *Truro: Bradford Barton*, [1980 or 1981]. pp. 163, with frontis (portrait), & 14 illus on 7 plates.

8322 HEYES, A. London Midland Steam: the closing years. *London: Ian Allan*, 1980. pp. 80. Intro & 167 illus with descrs.
> Mostly in Lancashire in the 1960s.

Electric locomotives and trains

8323 OAKLEY, M. The Pennine electrics. *Sutton Coldfield: Diesel & Electric Group and the Electric Railway Society*, 1978. la. 8°. pp. 24, incl. covers, with 17 illus, 4 logs of runs, map, gradient profile & dimensioned drawing.
> Electric locomotives on the Manchester–Sheffield line.

8324 LONGHURST, R. Electric locomotives on the West Coast main line . . . , with additional material by Michael Oakley. *Truro: Bradford Barton*. [1979]. pp. [32], with 26 illus, 7 dimensioned drawings, lists & a map.

8325 NICOLLE, B. BR (Midland Region) electrics. *Oxford: Oxford Publishing Co.*, 1979. (Transport Topic series, 3). pp. 32. Intro & 52 illus with descrs.

Diesel locomotives

8326 BRITISH RAILWAYS. LONDON MIDLAND REGION. MANCHESTER DIVISION. Reddish diesel-electric maintenance depot: open day, Sunday 9th September, 1973. *Manchester: B.R.(LMR), Manchester Division*, 1973. pp. 36, with many illus.
> A companion guide to the depot, the exhibits and brief information on current technical developments on BR generally.

8327 WEEKES, G. Diesels on Midland Region. *Truro: Bradford Barton*, 1974. pp. 96. Intro & 112 illus with descrs.

8328 WALKER, J. A. Toton's 'top ten': a perspective on the first true 'Peaks'. [*Sutton Coldfield*]: *Diesel & Electric Group*, 1977. pp. 16, with 7 illus, 3 tables & a diagram.

8329 MONTAGUE, K. The power of the Peaks.

Oxford: Oxford Publishing Co., 1978. la. 8°.
pp. [112]. Intro, frontis, & 208 illus (12 col.)
with descrs.
    Diesel locomotives, classes 44, 45 & 46.

8330 OAKLEY, M. The Midland double-headers:
classes 20 & 25; railtour souvenir booklet.
Sutton Coldfield: Diesel & Electric Group.
1978. pp. [24] incl. covers, with 13 illus, map
& lists.

8331 CHALCRAFT, J. and TURNER, S. Class 40s
in and around Manchester. *Midsomer Norton: Rail Photoprints*, 1979. obl. format. pp.
[32]. Intro & 34 illus with descrs, incl. 4 on
covers.

8332 NICOLLE, B. J. Diesels under the wires
around Crewe. *Gloucester: Peter Watts*, 1979.
obl. format. pp. [48]. Map, intro, & 43 illus
with descrs.
    Photographs of diesel-hauled trains on the West
coast main line, 1977–9.

8333 PREEDY, N. Book of the Peaks: British Rail
class 46s, with additional material by Ray
Hinton, John Augustson, Michael Jacob and
Derek Hawkins. *Gloucester: Peter Watts*,
1980. pp. [36]. Intro & 59 illus with captions.

Rolling stock

8334 RADFORD, J. B. A century of progress:
centenary brochure of the Derby Carriage
and Wagon Works; Introduction by P. Gray,
Works Manager. *Derby: British Rail Engineering*, [1976]. pp. 56, with 87 illus & plan.

B 10 (NER)   NORTH EASTERN REGION
8335–38

8335 BRITISH RAILWAYS. NORTH EASTERN RE-
GION. Named trains on the East Coast main
line, 11th Sept 1961 to 16th June 1962.
[*York*]: *B.R.(NER)*, 1961.
    A 16pp folder with timetables of eight named
trains, and on the reverse, a route map with notes.

8336 DOHERTY, D. Sheffield. *Seaton: Peco*, 1968.
(Railscene series, 5). sm. obl. format. pp.
[32]. Intro & 27 illus with descrs.
    Trains in and around Sheffield, 1960s.

8337 DOHERTY, D. York. *Seaton: Peco*, 1968.
(Railscene series, 3). sm. obl. format. pp.
[32]. Intro & 27 illus with descrs.
    Trains in and about York station, 1960s.

8338 DUNNETT, M. North Eastern Steam in
Northumbria. *Truro: Bradford Barton*, 1973.
pp. 96. Intro & 93 illus with descrs.
    Area, BR North Eastern Region in Northumber-
land and Durham; period, 1960s.

B 10 (Sc.R)   SCOTTISH REGION
8339–43

8339 BRITISH RAILWAYS. SCOTTISH REGION.
Queen Street, station of the 70s. [*Glasgow*]:

B.R.(ScR), [1970]. pp. [12], with 16 illus & a
plan.
    Issued to publicise the recent modernisation of the
station. Historical introduction.

8340 WEIR, T. The Oban line: an illustrated
history and guide. *Gartocharn: Famedram
Publishers*, 1973. pp. [18], with 13 illus on 8
plates & a map.
    From Glasgow to Oban via Helensburgh &
Crianlarich.

8341 RICKARD, S. Diesels on Scottish Region.
Truro: Bradford Barton, 1975. pp. 96. Intro
& 106 illus, with descrs.
    Period. 1960–1974.

8342 WEEKES, G. BR diesels in the Highlands.
Truro: Bradford Barton, 1976. pp. 96. Intro
& 119 illus with descrs.

8343 MEACHER, C. Living with locos. *Truro:
Bradford Barton*, [1980]. pp. 108, with 9 illus
& a map.
    A sequel to his *LNER Footplate Memories* (1978).
Memoirs based on Thornton motive power depot.
Fife; steam locomotives. LNER & BR (ScR).

B 10 (SR)   SOUTHERN REGION
8344–75

Reference sources 8344–46
General, and administration 8347–54
Locomotives and trains (steam and
    electric) 8355–67
Electric locomotives and trains 8368–74
Diesel locomotives 8375

*For British Railways (Southern Region) on
the Isle of Wight see* **C 5**

Reference sources

8344 CLARK, R. H. A Southern Region Record,
compiled by R. H. Clark. *Lingfield: Oakwood Press*, 1964. pp. vii, 164, with 18 illus &
23 specimen pages from timetables.
    A detailed chronology and historical record,
including Acts, for the period 1803 to 1964.

8345 YONGE, J. BR Southern Region Country
Track Map . . . , drawn by John Yonge.
Exeter: Quail Map Co., 1979. Folded map
printed on both sides, measuring 22½ × 16½
inches.
    The Southern Region network outside the Great-
er London and outer suburban area as far west as
Weymouth and including the Isle of Wight. There
are 3 insets for places where the detail of complicated trackwork requires an enlarged scale
(Ashford, Brighton, Dover, Eastleigh, Southampton, etc.).

8346 YONGE, J. BR Southern Region Suburban
Track Map, drawn by John Yonge. *Exeter:
Quail Map Co.*, 1979. Folded map, 22½ ×
16½ inches, printed on both sides.
    The track layout of the Southern Region network
within a radius of about 25 miles from the London
termini, as in September 1978. On the reverse are 13
detailed plans on a larger scale of areas of complicated trackwork: Waterloo, Clapham Junction,

Stewart's Lane area, Selhurst & Norwood, Hither Green, Wimbledon, Bricklayer's Arms, New Cross Gate, Redhill, Slade Green, Angerstein Wharf, Streatham Hill and Strawberry Hill.

General, and administration

8347 RAILWAY CORRESPONDENCE & TRAVEL SOCIETY. Itinerary of the Southampton Docks and Fawley branch rail tour, Sunday, 17th May, 1953. *R.C. & T.S.*, [1953]. pp. [4], with map, 2 illus & notes.

8348 BRITISH RAILWAYS. SOUTHERN REGION. Extension of electrification from Gillingham to Sheerness-on-Sea, Ramsgate and Dover . . . *London: B.R.(SR)*, May 1959. la. 8°. pp. [40], with 28 illus & other drawings & diagrams, plan of Chislehurst Junction & a folded map at end. Cover title: Kent Coast electrification: first phase.

8349 BRITISH RAILWAYS. SOUTHERN REGION. Want to run a railway? *London: B.R.(SR)*, October 1962. pp. 43, with 21 illus, 4 map diagrams & a train occupation graph.
    Published for the enlightenment of commuters and issued free as a spirited response to current criticisms about train delays. 'Perhaps you could run the Southern better than we do!'. The complex nature of running a high-capacity network of services revealed in a counter-challenge of facts, statistics and comparisons.

8350 BRITISH RAILWAYS. SOUTHERN REGION. Southern Travellers Handbook, 1965–66. *London: B.R.(SR)*, 1965. pp. 320, with topographical illus in colour & a sectional map (pp. 297–312).

8351 BRITISH RAILWAYS. SOUTHERN REGION. Weekday census at London termini, Oct.–Nov. 1971. *Waterloo (London): B.R.(SR), Economic Survey Office*, March 1972. pp. 148, with many tables & diagrs. Reproduced typescript.

8352 SWANAGE Railway Album, edited by Robin Brasher, George Moon, Michael Stollery. *Swanage: Southern Steam Trust*, 1977. obl. 8°. pp. [72]. Intro & 83 illus with descrs, & a map.
    Scenes on the 10-mile branch from Wareham to Swanage during the 1950s & 1960s.

8353 BRITISH RAILWAYS. SOUTHERN REGION. Weekday census at London termini, Oct.–Nov. 1978. *Waterloo (London): B.R.(SR), Economic Survey Office*, May 1979. pp. 133, consisting of 26 detailed tables. Reproduced typescript.

8354 RAYNER, B. W. and CHAPTER, J. F. Southern Region unusual train services, 1979. [1st edn]. *Purley: Southern Electric Group*, June 1979. pp. 24, incl. covers.
    Details of train workings 'difficult or impossible to identify from the public timetables'; variations in multiple-unit rolling stock; locomotive-hauled trains.

—— 2nd edn. Southern Region unusual train services, 1979. *Southern Electric Group*, October 1979. pp. 24, incl. covers.
    —— 3rd edn. Southern Region unusual train services. 1980–81. *Southern Electric Group*, 1980. pp. 24, incl. covers.

Locomotives and trains (steam and electric)

8355 RAILWAY CORRESPONDENCE & TRAVEL SOCIETY. Itinerary of the Brighton Works Centenary Special, 5th October, 1952. *R.C. & T.S.*, [1952]. pp. 8, with gradient profile, route diagram & schedule.
    London (Victoria) to Brighton and back.

8356 DOHERTY, D. Bournemouth. *Seaton: Peco*, 1968. (Railscene series, 4). sm. obl. format. pp. [32]. Intro & 27 illus with descrs.
    Trains in and around Bournemouth, 1960s.

8357 SHAW, W. Waterloo to Bournemouth: a journey in pictures, with an essay by W.A. Tuplin. *Hemel Hempstead: Model & Allied Publications*, 1969. (Days of Steam series, 2). sm. obl. format. pp. [38], with 26 illus.
    Period 1949–66, but mostly 1961.

8358 WALKER, C. Southern to the South West. *Oxford: Oxford Illustrators*, 1972. (Steam Railway series, 6). obl. 8°. pp. [64]. Intro & 59 illus with descrs.

8359 KELLAWAY, J. Steam into Swanage, by John Kellaway, with photographs by Chris Phillips and Colin Caddy. *Swanage: Purbeck Mail*, [1973 or later]. pp. 79. Intro & 79 illus with captions; col. illus on cover.
    Photographs taken during the 1950s & 1960s.

8360 BEAVOR, E. S. Steam was my calling. *London: Ian Allan*, 1974. pp. 184, with 76 illus on 48 plates.
    Locomotive running & maintenance, LNER and BR(SR).

8361 NASH, S. C. Southern Region Steam Album, 1948–1967. *London: Ian Allan*, 1974. pp. 111. Frontis & 175 illus with descrs.

8362 FAIRCLOUGH, T. and WILLS, A. More Southern Steam in the West Country . . . *Truro: Bradford Barton*, 1975. pp. 96. Intro & 138 illus with descrs.
    BR(SR) in South West England, 1946–1960s.

8363 FAIRCLOUGH, T. and WILLS, A. More Southern Steam, south and west. *Truro: Bradford Barton*, 1975. pp. 96. Intro & 111 illus with descrs.
    The old LSWR lines of BR(SR) out of Waterloo, 1950s & 1960s.

8364 HORNBY, F. and BROWNE, N. Southern Region Steam, Western section. *London: Almark*, 1977. pp. [72]. Intro & 23 illus with descrs.

8365 PETERS, I. Southern Steam Album. *London: Ian Allan*, 1979. la. 8°. pp. 112. Intro &

211 illus with descrs; map & gradient profiles on end papers.

Scenes on the Salisbury to Exeter line and its branches, and the Bournemouth to Weymouth line, 1950s & 1960s.

8366 AYNSLEY, B. W. Nothing like Steam!: footplate work on Southern Region. *Truro: Bradford Barton*, [1980]. pp. 112, with 12 illus.

8367 EVANS, J. Man of the Southern: Jim Evans looks back; edited by Peter Grafton. *London: Allen & Unwin*, 1980. pp. 102, with 59 illus & commentaries.

Memoirs of a locomotiveman, 1944 to his driving of the last steam-hauled train out of Waterloo Station, 6 July 1967.

Electric locomotives and trains

8368 BEECROFT, G. D. and RAYNER, B. W. Southern Region two-character headcodes. *Purley: Southern Electric Group*, November 1973. pp. 14. Intro & two listings: numerical codes and letter codes. Text extends onto covers. Reproduced typescript. Paper covers.

—— 2nd edn. *Southern Electric Group*, June 1974. A5 format. pp. 28.

—— 3rd edn. *Southern Electric Group*, June 1976. pp. 28.

—— 4th edn. *Southern Electric Group*, May 1978. pp. 28.

8369 RAYNER, B. Southern electrics: a pictorial survey, edited by Brian Rayner for the Southern Electric Group. *Truro: Bradford Barton*, 1975. pp. 96. Intro & 149 illus with descrs & a 5-column list of rolling stock (pp. 6–9).

Period, 1950s–1970s.

8370 BEECROFT, G. D. 3142, Portsmouth to Peterborough. *Purley: Southern Electric Group*, 1977. pp. 12, with 4 illus diagram & map.

A BR(SR) 4-car electric multiple-unit, to 1972, and subsequent preservation.

8371 WILLIAMS, A. Southern Electric Album. *London: Ian Allan*, 1977. pp. 96. Intro & 133 illus with descrs.

The first and last pages of the text are pasted down as endpapers.

The Southern Rly, and BR(SR) to 1970.

8372 OAKLEY, M. Southern diesel and electric locomotives. *Purley: Diesel & Electric Group and the Southern Electric Group*, [1978?]. la. 8°. pp. 24 incl. covers, with 22 illus, 7 logs of runs, 5 dimensioned drawings & a map.

8373 BEECROFT, G. D. Southern Region multiple-unit trains. *Purley: Southern Electric Group*, 1979. pp. 67. Title on cover only. Contents on p. [2]. Text extends to p. 67 (p. [3] of cover).

8374 MARSDEN, C. J. SR electric multiple-units. *Oxford: Oxford Publishing Co.*, 1980. (Transport Topic series, 7). pp. [32]. Intro & 49 illus with descrs.

Diesel locomotives

8375 VAUGHAN, J. A. M. Diesels on the Southern. *Shepperton: Ian Allan*, 1980. pp. 112. Intro & 222 illus with descrs.
BR(SR).

B 10 (WR) WESTERN REGION

8376–8436

Reference source 8376
General, and administration 8377–85
Locomotives and trains generally 8386–88
Steam locomotives 8389–8402
Diesel locomotives 8403–31
Signalling 8432–35
Other subjects 8436

Reference source

8376 BRITISH RAILWAYS. WESTERN REGION. General statistics. *London: B.R.(WR), General Manager's Office*, May 1956, pp. 48.

37 tables of W.R. operational statistics, preceded by 3 tables for receipts, salaries & wages, and numbers of staff employed. Most of the tables are for each calendar month, 1953 to 1956, but annual figures are also sometimes given for 1938 to 1956. For Milford Haven fish traffic the table is for every fifth year from 1890 to 1956, and for traffic dealt with at London depots (Paddington, Smithfield, Brentford, Poplar, Victoria & Albert Dock, South Lambeth), there are figures for every fifth year from 1865 to 1955.

The tables relate to the Western Region and, before 1948, to the Great Western Rly.   LU(THC)

General, and administration

8377 HENBEST, R. G. Town planning as it affects the Western Region. (Proceedings of the British Railways (W.R.) London Lecture & Debating Society, 1951–52, no. 387). pp. 15, with discussion.

Author, 'Estate & Rating Surveyor, W.R.'

8378 CLARK, R. H. A survey of any selected area served by the Western Region, with special reference to Transport and its adequacy to modern requirements. (Proceedings of the British Railways (W.R.) London Lecture & Debating Society, 1952–53, no. 404). pp. 14, with discussion.

Prize essay in the competition with the above title. Area surveyed, the London Operational District of the Western Region. Author, 'Office of the Chief Regional Officer, Paddington'.

8379 SWIFT, H. H. The importance of the South Wales area to the Western Region. Proceedings of the British Railways (W.R.) London Lecture & Debating Society, 1953–54, no. 409. pp. 12, with discussion.

Author, 'South Wales Area Officer, W.R.'

8380 BRITISH RAILWAYS. WESTERN REGION. Margam marshalling yard, Port Talbot, South Wales. [*London*]: *B.R.(WR)*, 1960. pp. 24, with 10 illus & a folded map.

8381 FLYNN, J. R. G. Organisation planning and

its application on the Western Region. (Proceedings of the British Railways (W.R.) London Lecture & Debating Society, 1963–64, no. 483). pp. 16, with discussion & 8 diagrams.
Author, Assistant General Manager, BR(WR).

8382 IBBOTSON, L. W. Western Region looks forward. (Proceedings of the British Railways (W.R.) London Lecture & Debating Society, 1966–67, no. 494). pp. 10, with 20 maps, & tables & diagrams.

8383 THOMAS, D. St. J. and SMITH, S. R. Summer Saturdays in the West . . . , with illustrations by Peter Gray & Kenneth Leech. *Newton Abbott: David & Charles*, 1973. pp. 173, with 22 illus (pp. 52–73) & a map.
Western Region train workings in general during the 1950s, and on 27 July 1957. Appendix is a table showing the pattern of train travel to & from the West of England on that day (pp. 139–72).

8384 ANTELL, R. Southern's South Western memories. *London: Ian Allan*, 1977. pp. 112. Intro, map, & 164 illus with descrs.
The L & SWR main line to the West of England in Western Region days, and the Lynton & Barnstaple Rly.

8385 ALLEN, G. F. The Western since 1948. *London: Ian Allan*, 1979. la. 8°. pp. 160, with 208 illus & layout plans on end papers.
A survey of administrative, operational and technical development on the Western Region.

Locomotives and trains generally

8386 CORNICK, M. J. The Railway News Stock Book of ex-GWR and B.R.(WR) push/pull auto coaches. 5th edn. [*Newport*]: *Railway Publishing Society*, Summer 1959. sm. 8°. pp. 11.
The 'Railway News' was a duplicated news sheet first published by the R.P.S. (later Monmouthshire Railway Society) in Spring 1958.

8387 CORNICK, M. J. The Railway News Stock Book of the ex-GWR and B.R.(WR) restaurant cars, including buffet, cafeteria and kitchen & dining cars. 1st ed. [*Newport*]: *Railway Publishing Society* [*later Monmouthshire Railway Society*], Spring 1960. sm. 8°. pp. 11. Title on cover page only.

8388 JONES, J. R. Western Region restaurant car survey, 9th July, 1960. [*Newport*]: *Monmouthshire Railway Society*, Summer 1961. pp. 10. Reproduced typescript.
151 trains observed at Paddington, Newport, Bristol, Birmingham and Exeter on the first Summer saturday of 1960 on which day the maximum number of restaurant car workings was scheduled.

Steam locomotives

8389 DOHERTY, D. W.R. Midlands. *Seaton: Peco*, 1968. (Railscene series, 2). sm. obl. format. pp. [32]. Intro & 27 illus with descrs.
Trains in the West Midlands, 1960s.

8390 SHAW, W. Paddington to Wolverhampton: a journey in pictures, with an essay by W. A. Tuplin. *Hemel Hempstead: Model & Allied Publications*, 1969. (Days of Steam series, 4). sm. obl. format. pp. [36], with 26 illus.
Period 1957–62.

8391 WALKER, C. Oxfordshire remembered. *Oxford: Oxford Illustrators*, 1970. (Steam Railway series, 1). obl. 8°. pp. [64]. Intro & 59 illus with descrs.
Mostly GWR and BR(WR) scenes.

8392 WALKER, C. Shrewsbury. *Oxford: Oxford Illustrators*, 1971. (Steam Railway series, 2). obl. 8°. pp. [64]. Intro & 59 illus with descrs.
Locomotives & trains in the Shrewsbury area during the 1960s.

8393 WALKER, C. Birmingham to Wolverhampton, Western Region. *Oxford: Oxford Illustrators*, 1972. (Steam Railway series). obl. 8°. pp. [46]. Intro & 59 illus with descrs.
Mostly Kings and Castles of the GWR, in BR(WR) days, 1960s.

8394 WALKER, C. North West from Paddington: a main line trail. *Oxford: Oxford Publishing Co.*, 1974. (Trails of Steam series, 1). obl. format. pp. [64]. Intro & 60 illus with descrs.
Scenes on the old GWR line from Paddington to Chester, 1950s–1960s.

8395 WILLIAMS, C. L. Great Western Steam around Bristol, edited by C. L. Williams. *Truro: Bradford Barton*, 1975. pp. 96. Intro & 107 illus with descrs.
ex-GWR locomotives in BR(WR) days, 1950s–60s.

8396 ADAMS, J. and WHITEHOUSE, P. Western Steam in camera. *London: Ian Allan*, 1976. pp. 64. Intro & 78 illus with descrs.
Period, 1948 to 1970.

8397 BARFIELD, T. When there was steam: memories of a Western Region fireman. *Truro: Bradford Barton*, 1976. pp. 116, with 20 illus on 16 plates, map & plan.
Locomotive working centred upon Kidderminster depôt, 1950s.

8398 HORNBY, F. and BROWNE, N. Western Region Steam. *London: Almark*, 1977. pp. [72]. Intro & 129 illus with descrs.

8399 HEIRON, G. Trains to the West. *London: Ian Allan*, 1978. la. 8°. pp. 112. Intro & 176 illus (172 photos & 4 col. paintings) by George Heiron, with descrs.
Western Region locomotives & trains, 1950–1977.

8400 GWILLAM, R. A locomotive fireman looks back: Western Region recollections, Laira & Swindon. *Truro: Bradford Barton*, [1979]. pp. 151, with 10 illus.
Period, from 1951.

8401 FLEMING, D. J. St Philips Marsh: memories of an engine shed. *Truro: Bradford Barton*,

[1980]. pp. 114, with 30 illus on 16 plates.
Period, 1956 until closure in 1964. (In 1976 a new depot was erected in preparation for the introduction of the High Speed Trains).

8402 HEIRON, G. F. Roaming the Western rails. *London: Ian Allan*, 1980. la. 8°. pp. 128. Intro & 200 illus.
Photographs by George Heiron of locomotives and trains on the Western Region of BR west of Reading.

Diesel locomotives

8403 BRITISH RAILWAYS. WESTERN REGION. The first British-built gas turbine locomotive, no. 18100: a description of the 3,000 h.p. gas turbine electric locomotive built for British Railways by Metropolitan-Vickers Electrical Co. Ltd. *London: B.R.(WR)*, [1952]. pp. 24, with 6 illus on plates & 5 diagrams (2 folded) in text.
Reproduced typescript.

8404 METROPOLITAN-VICKERS ELECTRICAL COMPANY. The first British-built gas turbine locomotive, no. 18100: a description of the 3,000 h.p. gas turbine electric locomotive built for British Railways by Metropolitan-Vickers Electrical Co. Ltd. *Paddington (London): The Railway Executive, Western Region.* [1952]. pp. 3, with 1 plate.

8405 BRITISH RAILWAYS. WESTERN REGION. Laira diesel depot, Plymouth. [*Plymouth*]: *B.R.(WR)*, [1973?]. pp. [8], with 2 illus & a plan.
A guide to the depot and to the exhibits assembled there for an 'open day'.

8406 FORD, H. L. Diesels on Cornwall's main line. *Truro: Bradford Barton*, 1973. pp. 96. Intro & 94 illus with descrs.

8407 FORD, H. L. Diesels on the Devon main line. *Truro: Bradford Barton*, 1974. pp. 96. Intro & 121 illus with descrs.

8408 FORD, H. L. Diesels on Western Region. *Truro: Bradford Barton*, 1974. pp. 96. Intro & 115 illus with descrs.

8409 MONTAGUE, K. Diesels, Western Style. *Oxford: Oxford Publishing Co.*, 1974. la. 8°. pp. [72]. Intro & 105 illus (15 col.), with descrs.

8410 PREEDY, N. E. and GILLHAM, G. F. WR diesel-hydraulics. *Truro: Bradford Barton*, 1974. pp. 96. Intro & 105 illus.

8411 BANNISTER, G. F. Diesels in the West Midlands and Central Wales. *Truro: Bradford Barton*, 1975. pp. 96. Intro & 130 illus with descrs.

8412 BRITISH RAILWAYS. WESTERN REGION. LONDON DIVISION. Deltics. *Reading: the Division*, [1975]. pp. [16], chiefly illus & plans.

'Published . . . to commemorate the first Deltic-hauled passenger train from Paddington, Sunday 12 October 1975.'

8413 BRITISH RAILWAYS. WESTERN REGION. LONDON DIVISION. 'Western Enterprise': a celebration in pictures and words of the Western class 2,700 h.p. diesel-hydraulic locomotives, designed and developed at Swindon, built at Swindon and Crewe, 1961–1964. *Reading: the Division*, 1975. pp. 16, with 28 illus, incl. 8 on covers.

8414 KICHENSIDE, G. Farewell to the Westerns: a pictorial tribute to the B.R.'s class 52 diesels. *Newton Abbot: David & Charles*, 1975. 4°. pp. [72]. Text & list (2 pp.), & 71 illus with descrs.

8415 REED, B. Diesel-hydraulic locomotives of the Western Region. *Newton Abbot: David & Charles*, 1975. pp. 112, with 82 illus, 26 tables, diagrams & line drawings.

8416 FORD, H. L. and PREEDY, N. E. The Westerns: B.R. class 52 diesel-hydraulics. *Truro: Bradford Barton*, 1976. pp. 96. Intro & 105 illus with descrs.

8417 WESTERN: The Western Region class 52s. *Bolton: Western Locomotive Association*; *Sutton Coldfield: Diesel & Electric Group*, 1976. pp. 24, with 16 illus, 5 tables, diagram, map & chronology. 'Written by Michael Oakley'; research, graphics, photographs, typing, design & printing by 19 others (named).

8418 JUDGE, C. The power of the Westerns. *Oxford: Oxford Publishing Co.*, 1977. 4°. pp. [112]. Intro & 224 illus (29 col.) with descrs.

8419 PREEDY, N. Book of the Westerns: British Rail class 52s. *Gloucester: Peter Watts*, 1977. pp. [40]. Intro & 74 illus with captions.

8420 PREEDY, N. Western memories: a pictorial reminiscence of the class 52 'Western' railtours, 1971–1977; principal photographs by Norman E. Preedy. *Gloucester: Peter Watts*, 1977. pp. [76]. Intro, dedicatory verse, 117 illus with captions, & a valedictory essay from *The Guardian*, 28 February 1977 by Rick Sanders. Text extends onto p. [3] of cover.

8421 PREEDY, N. Western Pictorial: photographs by Norman Preedy. *Dorking Railway Pictorial Publications*, 1977. pp. [40]. Intro & 74 illus with captions.
A photographic record of every one of the seventy-four class 52 locomotives – the 'Western' diesel-hydraulics of BR.

8422 VAUGHAN, J. A. M. The last year of the Westerns. *Dorking: Railway Pictorial Publications*, [1977]. obl. format. pp. [48]. Intro & 56 illus with descrs, & a list (4 column) of the locomotives of BR's class 52 (diesel-hydraulics).

8423 VAUGHAN, J. A. M. and SAWYER, M. G. 'Western' diesels in camera. *London: Ian Allan*, 1977. pp. 96. Intro, text (including 'The class 52 in retrospect' by M. G. Sawyer, pp. 7–11), & 160 illus (8 col.), with descrs.

8424 WATTS, P. The Western finale, Saturday 12th February 1977: Exeter to York and return: a farewell railtour in tribute to the class 52 Western diesel-hydraulic locomotives. *Bristol: Western Locomotive Association*, 1977. pp. [8], with 11 illus (photographs by Norman E. Preedy) and a list.

8425 WESTERN Stock List. [*Camberley: Steam & Diesel Publications*, 1977]. pp. 34, with 28 illus (7 on covers).
Diesel trains on BR(WR).

8426 CURTIS, A. Western Anthology . . . , with additional material by Ian Norledge. *Gloucester: the author*, 1978. pp. 52, with 18 illus & col. illus on cover.
An appreciation of BR's class 52 Western diesel-hydraulic locomotives.

8427 PREEDY, N. and HINTON, R. Book of the Peaks: British Rail class 44s. *Gloucester: Peter Watts*, 1978. pp. [16]. Intro & 21 illus with captions. On cover: 'part 1'.

8428 VAUGHAN, J. A. M. Western Region Diesel Pictorial. *Dorking: Railway Pictorial Publications*, [1978]. obl. format. pp. [48]. Intro & 59 illus with descrs.

8429 'WARSHIP' Stock List [*Camberley: Steam and Diesel Publications*, 1978]. pp. 34, with 34 illus (10 on covers).
Diesel-hydraulic locomotives of BR(WR).

8430 GILLHAM, G. F. Diesels West. *Truro: Bradford Barton*, 1979. pp. 96. Intro & 107 illus with descrs.

8431 BRITISH Rail class 20s: a picture study. *Gloucester: Peter Watts*, 1980. obl. format. pp. [20]. Intro & 27 illus with descrs.

Signalling

8432 CARDANI, A. A. Modernisation and developments in the Signal Engineering Department. (Proceedings of the British Railways (W.R.) London Lecture & Debating Society, 1960–61, no. 464). pp. 16, with discussion, 4 illus, a map & a chart.
Author, Chief Signal Engineer, BR(WR). The activities of the Department in response to BR's Modernisation Plan.

8433 CARDANI, A. A. The Newport multiple-aspect signalling scheme. (Proceedings of the British Railways (W.R.) London Lecture & Debating Society, 1961–62, no. 476). pp. 18, with discussion, 3 diagrams & 2 illus.
Author, Chief Signal & Telecommunications Engineer, BR(WR).

8434 A REVIEW of signalling and telecommunications development in the Western Region of British Railways. *Bristol: Avon Anglia Publications*, [1977]. (Specialist Monographs & Reprints, 2). pp. 24, with 11 illus. Reproduced typescript. Cover title, Signalling: from mechanics to modules. No title page. Title at head of text only.
First published in *Western Management News*.

8435 VAUGHAN, A. BR(WR) signalling. *Oxford: Oxford Publishing Co.*, 1979. (Transport Topic series, 5). pp. 32. Intro, & 45 illus of semaphore signals with descrs & a signalling diagram, with key.

Other subjects

8436 BRITISH RAILWAYS. WESTERN REGION HEADQUARTERS STAFF DINING CLUB. Rules. [*London: B.R.(WR)*, 1949]. pp. 10.
Established by the GWR in 1859.

C RAIL TRANSPORT IN THE REGIONS AND COUNTIES OF THE BRITISH ISLES

The arrangement of entries in **C 1**, **C 2** and **C 3** conforms to the Standard Regions and Counties established in 1974–5. The order is from South to North working successively West to East except for **C 1 c SOUTH EAST REGION** which allows Greater London to precede Hampshire

Local railways not incorporated into British Railways are classed here, at **C 1 – C 7**

For the Regions of British Railways see **B 10 (ER)**, **(LMR)**, *etc.*

C 1   ENGLAND

8437–9431

For England as a whole see **A** *for general historical and descriptive works and* **B** *for particular periods. For British Railways see* **B 10**

C 1 a   SOUTHERN ENGLAND (South West Region, South East Region, West Midlands Region, East Midlands Region, East Anglia)

8437–9105

SOUTHERN ENGLAND GENERALLY

8437–39

8437 COOKE, D. N. Industrial steam locomotives of Southern England and South Wales. *Knowle: Warwickshire Railway Society*, [1967 or 8]. pp. 36.

8438 BRANCH LINE RE-INVIGORATION SOCIETY. Unprofitable lines?: a financial study of certain railway passenger services in Somerset, Dorset and Hampshire. *London: the Society*, October 1963. pp. 26, with diagrams & a map. Reproduced typescript.
The case against threatened closures by BR. The validity of revenue and cost figures supplied by BR to objectors is questioned.

8439 HUDSON, K. The industrial archaeology of Southern England: Hampshire, Wiltshire, Dorset, Somerset, and Gloucestershire east of the Severn. *Dawlish: David & Charles; London-Macdonald*, 1965. (Industrial Archaeology of the British Isles series), pp. 218, with 59 illus on 31 plates, 14 maps & facsims, & (pp. 175–80), an evaluative bibliography & notes.
The index has 90 page refs to railway development in the area.

C 1 b   SOUTH WEST REGION (Cornwall, Devon, Somerset, Dorset, Avon, Wiltshire, Gloucestershire)

8440–8573

South West Region Generally 8440–52

8440 BOOKER, F. The industrial archaeology of the Tamar Valley. *Newton Abbot: David & Charles*, 1967. (Industrial Archaeology of the British Isles series). pp. 303, with 52 illus on 33 plates; maps & diagrams in text.
Index has ca. 50 refs to railways of the area.
—— 2nd impr., rev. *David & Charles*, 1971.

(Industrial Archaeology of the British Isles series). pp. 303, with 52 illus on 33 plates, etc.

8441 HADFIELD, C. The canals of south-west England. *Newton Abbot: David & Charles*, 1967. (Canals of the British Isles series). pp. 206, with 32 illus on 16 plates, 11 facsims &

map, 234 notes & 2 appendices (tabular summaries).
An extended version of part of this author's *The Canals of Southern England* (1955). Index has 28 page refs to tramroads in text.

8442 CLEW, K. R. The Kennet & Avon Canal: an illustrated history, with . . . a foreword by Charles Hadfield. *Newton Abbot: David & Charles*, 1968. (Inland Waterways Histories). pp. 206, with col. frontis, 29 illus on 16 plates, & in text, 16 illus, 4 maps, 182 notes, 5 appendices & a bibliography (60 sources).
Railways, *passim*, and ch. 7 (pp. 102–6) 'The Avon & Gloucestershire Railway', and ch. 8 (pp. 107–25), 'Under new management, 1852–99' [the GWR].

8443 CLEW, K. R. The Dorset & Somerset Canal: an illustrated history . . . with a foreword by Peter Pagan. *Newton Abbot: David & Charles*, 1971. (Inland Waterways Histories). pp. 116, with col. frontis, 7 illus on 4 plates, & in text, 7 illus, 3 maps, 149 notes, & 5 appendices, incl. a bibliography (21 sources).
Railways (The Western Rly and the Radstock, Shaftesbury & Poole Rly), pp. 64–79 *et passim*.

8444 ESAU, M. Steam into Wessex. *Shepperton: Ian Allan*, 1971. pp. 128. Intro, frontis, & 225 illus with descrs.

8445 RILEY, R. C. The West Country. *Newton Abbot: David & Charles*, 1972. (Railway History in Pictures series). pp. 112, with col. frontis, 162 illus & a map.

8446 APPLEBY, J. B. West Country electric trams. *Glossop: Transport Publishing Co.*, 1975. obl. format. pp. 38. Intro (pp. 2–4), & 68 illus with descrs.

8447 CASSERLEY, H. C. Wessex. *Newton Abbot: David & Charles*, 1975. (Railway History in Pictures series). pp. 96. Intro & 112 illus with commentaries; map.
Area, Central Southern England and the Isle of Wight.

8448 FAIRCLOUGH, T. and SHEPHERD, E. Mineral railways of the West Country. *Truro: Bradford Barton*, 1975. pp. 96. Intro & 175 illus, incl. maps & facsimiles, with descrs.

8449 HATELEY, R. Industrial locomotives of South Western England. *Greenford: Industrial Railway Society*, 1977. (Handbook series, H). pp. xxx, 135, with 48 illus on 24 plates, 41 maps & plans.
A revised and up-dated edition of the South Western portion (Cornwall, Devon, Somerset, Avon & Dorset) of Handbook B, *Industrial Locomotives of Southern England* (1958).

8450 RAILWAY CORRESPONDENCE & TRAVEL SOCIETY. Itinerary of the R.C.T.S. 25th Anniversary Special: Waterloo—Exeter—Paddington, and the Lyme Regis branch, Sunday, 28th June, 1953. *R.C. & T.S.*,

[1953]. pp. 8, with 3 gradient profiles & 3 illus.
Loosely inserted in the LU(THC) copy are one of the gradient profiles and two typescript route modifications.

8451 RAILWAY CORRESPONDENCE & TRAVEL SOCIETY. Itinerary of the Wessex rail tour 'The Wessex Wyvern' . . . , Sunday, 8th July, 1956. *R.C. & T.S.*, [1956]. pp. 4, with map & schedule; text by E. A. Course.
Waterloo—Southampton—Brockenhurst—Ringwood—Wareham—Dorchester—Weymouth—Portland—Easton—Yeovil—Frome—Westbury—Trowbridge—Devizes—Pewsey—Severnake—Ludgershall—Andover—Whitchurch—Basingstoke—Woking—Waterloo.

8452 RAILWAY CORRESPONDENCE & TRAVEL SOCIETY. Itinerary of the Somerset and Dorset Farewell Rail Tour . . . , Sunday, 6th March, 1966. *R.C. & T.S.*, [1966]. pp. [8], with 1 illus, map & schedule. Text by M. Warburton.
Waterloo—Southampton—Bournemouth—Evercreech—Highbridge—Bristol—Bath—Evercreech—Templecombe—Salisbury—Waterloo.

Cornwall 8453–73

8453 COMMITTEE OF THE PROPOSED LINE OF RAILWAY FROM PERRANPORTH BY PERRAN ALMS-HOUSE TO TRURO. An answer to remarks on the proposed railway, from Perran Porth to Truro [with a letter from Richard Thomas to the Committee]. *Truro: printed by J. Brokenshir*, [1831]. pp. 15.
A rebuff to criticisms by an opposing venture planning a route via Zeala.

8454 LIDDELL, T. Observations on the proposed railway between St Minver and Camelford, delivered at a public meeting held at St Teath Church-Town on Monday the 19th of January, 1835. *Bodmin: Liddell & Son*, [1835]. pp. 16.
Blackwell's cat. A 1051 (1976), 296

8455 HENDERSON, C. The names of Cornish railway stations. *Long Compton: The King's Stone Press*, [192–?]. pp. 22.
'. . . the strange and musical names that adorn the boards of her 79 stations and halts.'

8456 BARTON, R. M. A history of the Cornish china-clay industry. *Truro: Bradford Barton*, 1966. pp. 212, with 35 illus on 20 plates; in text, 17 maps, facsimiles & diagrams, & many footnotes.
Index has 64 page refs to railways & wagonways.

8457 CROMBLEHOLME, R., STUCKEY, D., and WHETMATH, C. F. D. Callington railways: Bere Alston—Calstock—Callington. *Teddington: Branch Line Handbooks; Bracknell: West Country Handbooks, in association with the Narrow Gauge & Light Railway Society*, 1967. pp. 56, with 23 illus, 3 maps, 7 line drawings & 4 timetables.

The East Cornwall Mineral Rly and the Southern Rly's branch from Bere Alston to Callington.

8458 ANTHONY, G. H. The Hayle, West Cornwall and Helston railways. *Lingfield: Oakwood Press*, 1968. (Oakwood Library of Railway History, 21). pp. 71, with 25 illus on 10 plates, map, & a bibliography (25 sources).

8459 HIBBS, J. Report on the provision of public passenger transport at the town of Lostwithiel. *Saffron Walden: Consultancy in Transport*, 1968. pp. 16, with 5 maps & 6 tables.
Available modes of transport compared.

8460 TANGYE, M. Portreath: some chapters in its history. *Redruth: John Olson*, May 1968. pp. 40.
pp. 19–20, 'The Portreath-Poldice tram-road, 1809–1866'; pp. 20–3, 'The incline: the Portreath branch of the Hayle Railway, 1838–1932,' with an illus & a map. Page 40 is wrongly printed '30'.

8461 FAIRCLOUGH, T. The story of Cornwall's railways. *Truro: Tor Mark Press*, 1970. pp. 47, with 20 illus, map & 2 line drawings.

8462 BARTON, R. M. Life in Cornwall in the mid nineteenth century: being extracts from the West Briton newspaper in the two decades from 1835 to 1854, selected and edited by R. M. Barton. *Truro: Bradford Barton*, [1971]. pp. 244, with illus.
In index, 16 page refs under 'Railways & tramroads' and additional refs under names of individual lines.

8463 CARTER, C. The blizzard of '91. *Newton Abbot: David & Charles*, 1971. pp. 204, with illus on plates & in text, line drawings, weather charts & a bibliography.
The storm which swept the West Country, 8–9 March, 1891. Index has 13 refs to railways in the text. Railway damage is depicted in 4 of the illustrations.

8464 BARHAM, L. F. Cornwall's electric tramcars: the history of the Camborne and Redruth system. *Penryn: Glasney Press*, [1972]. la. 8°. pp. 84, with 80 illus, 3 col. plates, 2 drawings & a map.
The Camborne & Redruth Light Railway of the Urban Electric Supply Co., 1902–1934.

8465 BARTON, R. M. Life in Cornwall in the late nineteenth century, being extracts from the West Briton newspaper in the two decades from 1855 to 1875, selected and edited by Rita M. Barton. *Truro: Bradford Barton*, 1972. pp. 280, with 12 illus.
About 800 extracts. In index, 58 page refs under 'Railways' and 'Railway Time'.

8466 FAIRCLOUGH, T. Cornwall's railways: a pictorial survey. *Truro: Bradford Barton*, 1972. pp. 96. Intro & 143 illus with descrs.
An historical selection.

8467 TODD, A. C. and LAWS, P. The industrial archaeology of Cornwall. *Newton Abbot: David & Charles*, 1972. pp. 288, with 27 illus on 16 plates, & 6 maps.
pp. 207–67, Gazetteer; pp. 268–75, Biographical notes.
In the index, railways are entered only under their individual names, but stations are to be found under 'Railway stations'.

8468 SOUTHERN, J. The Forest Railway. *Dobwalls (Liskeard): the author*, [1973]. pp. [16], with 15 illus (9 col.); text & 4 illus (2 col.) on covers.
The Forest Railroad Park: Two 1 mile lines, 7¼ in. gauge; spectacular civil engineering features, automatic signalling; steam locomotives of North American design.
—— Forest Railroad Park. [1979 or 80]. pp. 16, with 18 col. illus & col. map (double spread); 3 col. illus & plan on covers.

8469 BARTON, R. M. Life in Cornwall at the end of the nineteenth century: being extracts from the West Briton newspaper in the years from 1876 to 1899, selected and edited by Rita M. Barton. *Truro: Bradford Barton*, 1974. pp. 174.
In index, 41 page refs under 'Railways' and 'Railway viaducts'.

8470 TOLSON, J. M. Railways of Looe and Caradon, by J. M. Tolson, G. F. Roose and C. F. D. Whetmath. *Bracknell: Forge Books*, 1974, pp. 90, with 30 illus, map, gradient profile, 5 layout plans, diagram & timetables.
The Liskeard & Caradon Rly and the Liskeard & Looe Rly, to 1974.

8471 POPPLEWELL, L. The railways, canals and mines of Looe and Liskeard. *Blandford: Oakwood Press*, 1977. (Oakwood Library of Railway History, 42). pp. 72, with 39 illus on 16 plates, 7 plans, & 2 maps.
Includes the Liskeard & Looe and the Liskeard & Caradon railways.

8472 MESSENGER, M. J. Caradon and Looe: the canals, railways and mines; a history of the Liskeard & Looe Union Canal, the Liskeard & Caradon Railway, the Liskeard & Looe Railway, and the mines and industries they served. *Truro: Twelveheads Press*, 1978. pp. 128, with frontis (map), 36 illus, 17 maps & plans, & 6 appendices, incl. a chronology.

8473 LAPPA VALLEY RLY. A Souvenir of your visit to LVR (Lappa Valley Railway). *Newquay: L.V. Rly*, [1979]. sm 8°. pp. 16 incl. covers, with 12 col. illus & a map.
A passenger carrying line; 1 mile in 15 in. gauge.

Devon 8474–8506

General and local

8474 RENNIE, J. An historical, practical and theoretical account of the breakwater in Plymouth Sound. *London: H. G. Bohn; J. Weale*, 1848. Folio. pp. vii, 21, 43, 72, with 26 plates incl. frontis.
 pp. 19–21, & plates x & xii: a wagonway laid in 1812 for carrying stone.

8475 HUNT, W. Then and now; or, fifty years of newspaper work. *Hull: 42 Whitefriargate; London: Hamilton Adams & Co.*, 1887. pp. vii, 255.
 pp. 52–5 *et passim*, observations on railways in South Devon, 1840s.

8476 CLAMP, A. L. Motoring and seeing old railways in Devon. *Plymouth: Westway Publications*, [1967]. pp. [32], with 18 illus & 11 maps.
 The history, course and features of eleven defunct lines.

8477 HARRIS, H. The industrial archaeology of Dartmoor. *Newton Abbot: David & Charles*, 1968. (Industrial Archaeology of the British Isles series). pp. 239, with 45 illus on 24 plates, & in the text, 17 maps, diagrams & line drawings.
 Railways & mineral wagonways: 26 page refs in the index.

8478 FARQUHARSON-COE, A. Devon's railways. *St. Ives (Cornwall): J. Pike*, 1974. (Viewing Devon series). pp. 32, with 10 illus.
 —— rev. edn. *J. Pike*, 1975. (Viewing Devon series). pp. 32, with 8 illus & map.

8479 KINGDOM, A. R. The railways of Devon: a pictorial survey. *Truro: Bradford Barton*, 1974. pp. 96. Intro & 101 illus, including facsimiles, drawings & maps.
 An historical selection.

8480 HEAL, M. The story of the Beer Heights Light Railway. *Beer: Peco Patent Product Co.*, [1976]. pp. 12, with 12 illus & a plan. Text extends onto covers.
 A 7¼ inch gauge railway, ½ mile in length.

8481 MAGGS, C. G. Railways to Exmouth. *Tarrant Hinton: Oakwood Press*, 1980. (Locomotion Papers, 122). pp. 64, with 26 illus on 12 plates, 6 station plans, map & a bibliography (20+ sources).
 GWR and LSWR.

Tramways

8482 DEVONPORT AND DISTRICT TRAMWAYS COMPANY. Speeds and stops regulations, 1915; duplicated reproduction, with a new introduction by Brian Bishop. *Plymouth: B. S. Moseley*, 1971. pp. 10.

8483 PRICE, J. H. The Seaton Tramway. *Hanwell (London): Light Railway Transport League*, [1974]. pp. 16, incl. covers, with 14 illus, map, stocklist & a humorous drawing (double-spread).

Reprinted from *Modern Tramway*.
The Seaton & District Electric Tramway; 2½ miles in 2ft 9ins. gauge.

8484 SAMBOURNE, R. C. Plymouth: 100 years of street travel. *Falmouth: Glasney Press*, [1974]. la. 8°. pp. 104, with 166 illus (8 col.), 2 maps, 2 fleet lists (tramcars and buses).

8485 SAMBOURNE, R. C. Exeter: a century of public transport. *Falmouth: Glasney Press*, 1976. la. 8°. pp. 104, with 154 illus, 4 maps, 2 fleet lists (tramcars and buses).
 pp. 9–51, 'Tramways'.

8486 BARHAM, F. Torbay transport: an illustrated study of road passenger vehicles in Torquay and Paignton during the early years of the 20th century. *Falmouth: Glasney Press*, 1979. la. 8°. pp. 112, with 116 illus, 2 maps & 12 appendices.
 The Torquay Tramways Company 1900–1934, and the Babbacombe Cliff Rly.

Mineral and industrial railways

8487 MOORE, T. The history of Devonshire from the earliest period to the present. *London: R. Jennings*, 1829, 31. 2 vols. & a vol. of plates (vol. 1, pp. 574; vol. 2, pp. 908).
 The index (3 pp. only) has no entries for railways or wagonways, but see 'An index of transport references in T. Moore's *History of Devonshire*, 1829–31', [by H. Compton] in *Journal of the Railway & Canal Historical Society*, vol. 21, no. 2 (July 1975), p. 35, and an important supplementary note by Walter E. Minchinton in vol. 25, no. 2 (July 1979), pp. 69–70.
 The railways referred to are the Plymouth & Dartmoor and the Hay Tor.

8488 EWANS, M. C. The Haytor granite tramway and Stover Canal. *Dawlish: David & Charles*, 1964. pp. 63, with 25 illus on 12 plates, 3 maps, 54 notes & a bibliographical note (6 sources).
 'L' section granite blocks laid to form a track of 4ft 3in gauge. Opened 1820.

8489 STABB, I. and DOWNING, T. The Redlake tramway and the china clay industry. [*Bittaford*]: *I. Stabb*; [*Ivybridge*]: *T. Downing*, 1977. pp. 8, with 9 illus; map on covers.

8490 GILLHAM, J. C. A Map to show the Plymouth and Dartmoor Tramway (1823–1916), the Lee Moor Tramway (1854–1960) and adjacent parts of the South Devon, Great Western, and London and South Western railways in the area to the north-east of Plymouth. *Plymouth: Plymouth Railway Circle and the Lee Moor Tramway Preservation Society*, [197–]. 4 printed maps & a sheet of historical notes (reproduced typescript).
 'Based upon the 25 inch Ordnance Survey and reduced to about one quarter of the original size. Research by R. C. Sambourne, maps drawn by J.C. Gillham'. The historical notes are by J. C. Gillham and B. Mills.

Lynton & Barnstaple Rly

8491 BROWN, G. A., PRIDEAUX, J. D. C. A., and RADCLIFFE, H. G. The Lynton & Barnstaple Railway. *Dawlish: David & Charles; London: Macdonald*, 1964. pp. 134, with col. frontis, 58 illus on 24 plates, & in text, map, 7 layout plans, 5 line drawings, gradient profile, 6 diagrams, facsimile, & tables; 7 appendices, incl. chronology & 6 station building diagrams; bibliography (12 sources).
—— another edn. *David & Charles*, 1971. pp. 134, with col. frontis & 58 illus on 24 plates.
Described on jacket as a 'new and revised edition'.

8492 PRIDEAUX, J. D. C. A. Lynton & Barnstaple Railway Album. *Newton Abbot: David & Charles*, 1974. pp. 96, with intro, map & 120 illus with descrs.

8493 YEOMANS, J. R. The Lynton & Barnstaple Railway. *Truro: Bradford Barton*, 1979. pp. 80. Intro, frontis, 96 illus & a map.

Dart Valley and Torbay Steam Rlys

8494 The DART Valley Railway. *London: Ian Allan*, 1967. sm. 8°. pp. 38, with 28 illus & 3 plans.
—— 1968 edn. *Ian Allan*, 1968. pp. 38, with 26 illus & 2 plans.
—— 1969 edn. *Ian Allan*, 1969. pp. 38, with 26 illus & 3 plans. Price on cover '3/-' (3 shillings).
—— 1969 edn (variant). *Ian Allan*, [1971]. pp. 38, with 29 illus & 3 plans. Price on cover, '20p'.
This is perhaps a re-issue of the 1969 edition in 1971 when metric coinage was introduced. The illustrations are different on pages 16, 22, 29, 31, 35 & 36.

8495 DART VALLEY RAILWAY ASSOCIATION. Dart Valley Railway Stock Book. *Buckfastleigh: the Association.* [1st edn], compiled by C. G. Woodford; drawings by C. J. Freezer; goods stock drawings by F. J. Roche. [1971]. pp. 55, with 27 illus, 13 dimensioned drawings & a map.
—— [2nd edn], compiled by C. G. Woodford, with drawings by C. J. Freezer and F. J. Roche. 1972. pp. 64, with 42 illus, 19 dimensioned drawings, a gradient profile & a map.
—— [3rd edn], compiled by C. G. Woodford, with drawings by C. J. Freezer and F. J. Roche. 1974. pp. 72 incl. covers, with 54 illus, 28 dimensioned drawings, 2 gradient profiles & 2 maps.
Includes the Torbay Steam Railway.
—— 4th edn, compiled by John Brodribb. 1978. pp. 72, with 40 illus, 40 dimensioned drawings, 3 maps, 2 gradient profiles, 4 layout plans & 4 lists of stock.

8496 TOURS, H. The Dart Valley Railway story. *Buckfastleigh: Dart Valley Light Rly Co.*, [1972]. pp. 23, with 11 illus, & timetables for 1879, 1902 & 1972.

8497 BESLEY, J. R. Dart Valley Railway Pictorial, edited by Tony Fairclough and Alan Wills; photographs by J. R. Besley. *Truro: Bradford Barton*, [1976]. pp. 32. Intro & 38 illus with descrs.

8498 FAIRCLOUGH, T. and WILLS, A. Torbay Steam Railway Pictorial. *Truro: Bradford Barton*, [1976]. pp. 32. Intro & 47 illus with descrs.

8499 DART VALLEY LIGHT RLY. Portrait of the Dart Valley Railway: a pictorial souvenir of the Buckfastleigh and Torbay & Dartmouth tourist steam railways. *Buckfastleigh: the Railway*, 1978. pp. 96, with 148 illus & 3 maps.

8500 DART VALLEY RLY. A Visitor's Guide to the Dart Valley & Torbay Steam Railways. *Buckfastleigh: the Railway*, [after 1972]. pp. 24, with 13 col. illus, map, stock list & 2 additional col. illus on covers.
—— another edn. 1979. pp. 32; 14 col. illus (photos by Peter Zabek), map.

Social aspects

8501 DEVON flood story. *Dawlish: David & Charles*, 1960. pp. 32, with 33 illus. Title on cover only.
Includes an account of the dislocation of railway services, Sept. 28th to Oct. 8th.

8502 MINISTRY OF TRANSPORT. Rural transport surveys: report of preliminary results. *London: H.M.S.O.*, 1963. pp. 14, wih 7 tables.
Of six of the areas surveyed, in England, Wales and Scotland, only one, in Devon, West of Crediton, still had a rail service in March/April 1963.

8503 THOMAS, D. St J. North Devon Railway Report: the findings of the North Devon Railway Enquiry. *Dawlish: David & Charles*, 1963. pp. 32, with map.
A report of the enquiry sponsored by Dartington Hall, addressed to the North Devon Railway Action Committee.

8504 HIBBS, J. Travelling in the country: a report on transport problems in the rural district of South Molton, North Devon. *Saffron Walden: Consultancy in Transport*, 1968. pp. 41, with 2 maps & 12 tables.
Local transport alternatives.

8505 DEPARTMENT OF THE ENVIRONMENT. Study of rural transport in Devon: report by the Steering Group. (Chairman T. L. Beagley). *London: D.o.E.*, 1971. pp. 25.
'Railways no longer play any significant part in the rural transport scene in Devon.'

8506 POLYTECHNIC OF CENTRAL LONDON. TRANSPORT STUDIES GROUP. A survey and review of the Exeter–Barnstaple railway service, [by] S. R. Williams, P. R. White [and] P. Heels. *London: P.C.L.*, February 1976. tall 8°. pp. 62, with maps, tables & diagrams.

A survey carried out in June 1975. 'It is shown clearly that revenue generated over the inter-city network as a result of the Barnstaple line's existence is well in excess of the operating loss assigned to the route. this confirms views generally held since the time of the 'Beeching' period cuts, that the role of feeder traffic is often under-stated.'

Somerset 8507–23

General and local 8507–13
East Somerset Rly 8514–17
West Somerset Rly 8518–20
Mineral railways 8521–23

General and local

8507 ATTHILL, R. Old Mendip. *Dawlish: David & Charles*; *London: Macdonald*, 1964. pp. 204, with 43 illus on 24 plates, & in text, 7 line drawings & maps; 100 notes & additional refs to 'main sources' or 'further sources' consulted.
'An interpretation of the palimpsest of the countryside from the author's long acquaintance with the area'. pp. 158–64, 'The little railways', with map & 4 illus. (Branches and mineral lines in north-east Somerset).
—— rev. edn. *David & Charles*, 1971. pp. 204.

8508 CLEW, K. R. The Somersetshire Coal Canal and railways . . . *Newton Abbot: David & Charles*, 1970. pp. 176, with col. frontis & 29 illus on 16 plates; 12 illus & 3 maps in text, 269 notes, bibliography (42 sources).
Includes chapters on the Radstock tramway, 1805–1815, and the Camerton & Limpley Stoke Rly, 1907–1951.

8509 DOWN, C. G. and WARRINGTON, A. J. The history of the Somerset coalfield. *Newton Abbot: David & Charles*, [1971]. pp. 283, with 28 illus, & 58 diagrams, maps and plans; bibliography & notes (pp. 262–72).
In index, numerous page refs under 'Railways', 'Inclines', 'Locomotives', 'Tramways', and under the names of individual railways.

8510 MADGE, R. Railways round Exmoor. *Dulverton: Exmoor Press*, 1971. pp. 72, with 22 illus on 16 pp., 12 line drawings, 3 maps (1 folded), 18 notes & a bibliography (16 sources).

8511 HAYES, R. Railways in the Wells area; edited by Patricia Haywood-Hicks. *[Wells]: Wells Education Centre*, 1977. pp. iii, 24, incl. covers, with 10 illus, a map & a plan. Reproduced typescript.
The GWR and the SDJR. Introductory. Author was the last stationmaster at Wells, 1957–64. A more extensive edition of this work was published in 1982 as *Railways in Wells*, by R. Hayes and M. Shaw.

8512 HANDLEY, C. The railways and tramways of Radstock. *Bristol: Somerset & Dorset Railway Museum Trust*, 1979. tall 8°. spiral binding. pp. 70, with 12 illus, 8 maps & 6 plans.
The GWR, the SDJR and colliery wagonways.

8513 RAILWAY CORRESPONDENCE & TRAVEL SOCIETY. Itinerary of the North Somerset Rail Tour . . . , Sunday, 28th April, 1957. *R.C. & T.S.*, [1957]. pp. 4, with map & schedule. Text by P. Proud.
Waterloo—Reading—Trowbridge—Bath—Bristol—Burnham—Bristol—Radstock—Reading—Paddington.

East Somerset Rly

8514 SHEPHERD, D. The East Somerset Railway: an illustrated guide (The Cranmore story). *Cranmore: E.S. Rly* (1973), 1975. obl. format. pp. 20, with 17 illus (incl. 2 col. reproductions of David Shepherd's paintings of locomotives).
—— Re-issued, 1976, with an addenda & errata slip inside front cover.

8515 EAST SOMERSET RLY (1973). [Prospectus]. *Bath: E.S. Rly*, [1976]. pp. 12, with 3 illus & an application form for loan stock and deed of covenant (pp. 11 & 12, detachable).
The prospectus includes a history of the venture by the founder, David Shepherd, with an outline of plans for future progress, and financial details. Text extends onto covers.

8516 EAST SOMERSET RLY (1973). Stock Book. 1st edn, photographed & compiled by R. P. Weisham. *Cranmore: E.S. Rly*, [1976]. pp. 24, with 27 illus & 4 dimensioned drawings of locomotives.

8517 SHEPHERD, D. Sketches of the East Somerset Railway at Cranmore. [*Cranmore: East Somerset Rly*, 1976]. pp. 18, of illus.

West Somerset Rly

8518 WEST SOMERSET RLY (1971). Stock List, 1977 (compiled by T. J. King). *Minehead Station: the Railway*, 1977. pp. 16, incl. covers, with 9 illus.
—— [2nd] edn, much enlarged, by M. K. Smith, 1980. pp. 48, with 58 illus (1 col.) & 5 dimensioned drawings.

8519 WEST SOMERSET RLY (1971). Official Guide, written by Allan Stanistreet. *Oxford: Oxford Publishing Co. for the West Somerset Railway*, [1978]. pp. 20, with 22 illus (19 col.); map & additional 2 illus (1 col.) on covers.
—— rev. edn, by A. Stanistreet. [1979]. pp. 24, with 22 illus (17 col.); map & 1 col. illus on covers.

8520 CLINKER, C. R. The West Somerset Railway: a history in pictures, with an account by C. R. Clinker. *Dulverton: Exmoor Press*, 1980. (Microstudies series). pp. 64, with 84 illus, 15 notes, & a map & gradient profile inside covers.
The line was closed by BR in 1971 but a 20 mile stretch, from Minehead to Bishops Lydeard, was restored and re-opened by the West Somerset Rly Co. (1971) between 1976 & 1979, to provide a year-round daily passenger service (Sundays excepted).

Mineral railways

8521 SELLICK, R. J. The old mineral line: an illustrated survey of the West Somerset Mineral Railway from Watchet to the Brendon Hills as it was, and is today. *Dulverton: Exmoor Press*, 1976. pp. 64. Text, pp. 5–12, & 87 illus on 75 plates (pp. 13–64); 2 illus in text & 2 maps inside covers.

8522 The WRINGTON Vale Light Railway, [by] Michael Farr, Robert Lovell, Colin G. Maggs, Charles Whetmath. *Bristol: Avon Anglia*, 1978. pp. 28, with 10 illus, 5 layout plans, 3 timetables, a gradient profile, a map & a bibliography (16 sources).
Period, 1901–1931 . . . 1963. An independent line.

8523 DOWN, C. G. and WARRINGTON, A. J. The Newbury Railway. Industrial Railway Record no. 82, June–September 1979. (Special Monograph Issue). pp. 48, with 27 illus, map, 10 layout plans, lists, 19 notes & 5 appendices, incl. chronology.
A colliery railway from Mells Road Station, Somerset (GWR) to Vobster and Newbury collieries, ca. 1870–mid 1960s.

Dorset 8524–31

General and local 8524–27
Bournemouth 8528–31

General and local

8524 STEVENSON, W. General view of the agriculture of the county of Dorset, with observations on the means of its improvement; drawn up for the consideration of the Board of Agriculture and Internal Improvement. *London: printed by B. McMillan*, 1812. [Reprinted by EP Microfilm Ltd, East Ardsley, 1978].
p. 440, description (2 paragraphs) of a wagonway for conveying potters' clay from Norden, near Corfe Castle, to Poole harbour (3 miles) – the 'Middlebere plateway'.

8525 LUCKING, J. H. Railways of Dorset: an outline of their establishment, development and progress from 1825. *London: Railway Correspondence & Travel Society, by arrangement with the Dorset Natural History & Archaeological Society*, 1968. pp. 67, with 84 illus on 42 plates, 32 maps, & tables of Acts, openings & closures (chronology), & a bibliography (25 sources).
The Mansel-Pleydell Prize Essay of the Dorset Natural History & Archaeological Society, 1965.

8526 KIDNER, R. W. The railways of Purbeck. *Lingfield: Oakwood Press*, 1973. (Locomotion Papers, 68). pp. 47, with 39 illus on 16 plates, 2 maps & 10 diagrams.
Includes mineral railways.

8527 JARMAN, R. The railways of Dorset: their relevance to wildlife conservation. Thesis, M.Sc., University of London (UCL), 1974.

Bournemouth

8528 MAWSON, J. W. Bournemouth Corporation Transport. *Huddersfield: Advertiser Press*, 1967. pp. 276, with illus. & 6 folded maps inserted at end.
ch. 2 (pp. 40–79), 'General history, 1899–1932': railways and tramways, with 16 illus on 8 plates.

8529 ROBERTS, C. G. Bournemouth trams and buses. *Lingfield: Oakwood Press*, 1972. (Locomotion Papers, 59). pp. 82, with 22 illus on 8 plates & a map.

8530 POPPLEWELL, L. Bournemouth railway history: an exposure of Victorian engineering fraud. *Sherborne: Dorset Publishing Co.*, 1973. pp. 224, with 38 illus on 36 plates, a map & 4 appendices.
A general survey of railway development in the Bournemouth area, with the machinations of Charles and William Waring, contractors, revealed as an important element in the story.
—— 2nd edn. *Dorset Publishing Co.*, 1974. pp. 224, etc.

8531 YOUNG, J. A. The 19th century railways of Bournemouth and Christchurch. *Bournemouth: Bournemouth Local Studies Publications*, 1979. pp. 36, with 6 maps, chronology, list & bibliography (11 sources).
The LSWR and the SDJR.

Avon 8532–49

Bristol 8532–42
Bath 8543–48
Weston-super-Mare 8549

Bristol

8532 MCADAMS, W. The tramways: some reasons against purchase. How municipalities make 'profits'. *Bristol: St Stephen's Printing Works*, [1914]. pp. 15.
Reprinted from the *Bristol Times & Mirror*, 9th June 1914. The author, vice-chairman of the Bristol Ratepayers' Association, is opposed to the taking over of Bristol Tramways Co. by the Corporation.

8533 ARNEY, F. D. The Port of Bristol and railways. (Proceedings of the British Railways (W.R.) London Lecture & Debating Society, 1959–60, no. 462.) pp. 11, with 3 illus & discussion.
Author, General Manager, Port of Bristol Authority.

8534 APPLEBY, J. B. Bristol's trams remembered. *Bristol: J. B. Appleby*, 1969. pp.70, with 58 illus & 3 maps.

8535 BUCHANAN, R. A. and COSSONS, N. The industrial archaeology of the Bristol region. *Newton Abbot: David & Charles*, 1969. (Industrial Archaeology of the British Isles series). pp. 335, with 32 illus on 16 plates, & in text, 20 maps, diagrams & line drawings.
pp. 201–23, Railways, with 12 notes & a bibliography (15 sources). pp. 259–62, Railway sites. pp. 283–97, Railway chronology of the Bristol region.

8536 BUCHANAN, R. A. and COSSONS, N. Industrial history in pictures: Bristol. *Newton Abbot: David & Charles*, 1970. pp. 112, with 163 illus & maps; bibliographical note.
Railways, pp. 70–77 *et passim*.

8537 COFFIN, R. O. Steam around Bristol. *Oxford: Oxford Publishing Co.*, 1974. obl. format. pp. [64]. Intro & 83 illus with descrs.

8538 WINSTONE, R. Bristol's trams . . . *Bristol: the author*, 1974. pp. 84, with 264 illus (pp. 63–80, adverts).

8539 MAGGS, C. G. The Bristol Port Railway & Pier and the Clifton Extension Railway. [*Tarrant Hinton*]: *Oakwood Press*, 1975. (Oakwood Library of Railway History, 37). pp. 59, with 24 illus on 12 plates, map, 4 layout plans, 2 line drawings, a revenue table (1875–1893), & a bibliography (25+ sources).

8540 BRISTOL SUBURBAN RLY. Bitton Railway Centre: guide book and stock list. *Bristol: the Railway*, 1977. pp. 16, with 2 illus, map, plan & 4 additional illus on covers.

8541 VINCENT, M. Lines to Avonmouth: a story of railways in the Bristol area. *Oxford: Oxford Publishing Co.*, 1979. pp. [vi], 149, with 75 illus, 2 layout plans, 2 maps, a timetable & a bibliography (18 sources).
GWR, Midland Rly, dock and industrial railways.

8542 BRISTOL SUBURBAN RAILWAY SOCIETY. Bristol Avon Railway and the Bitton Railway Centre. *Weston-super-Mare: Avon Anglia*, 1980. pp. 24, with 17 illus, 2 maps & 4 plans.
A description of the early railways to the north of Bristol, the Midland Rly's lines in the area and the establishment of the Bristol Suburban Railway Society in 1973.

Bath

8543 WOOD, J. An essay towards a description of Bath. 2nd edn. *London: C. Hitch*, 1749. 2 vols (pp. 456).
vol. 2, (pp. 424–5), an account of Ralph Allen's wagonway (2 paras). '. . . such a road between the summit of the hill and the River Avon as the gentlemen of the north of England had made between their collieries and the River Tyne . . .'

8544 OWEN, E. Observations on the earth, rocks, stones and minerals for some miles about Bristol, and on the nature of the Hot-Well and the virtues of its water, by Mr Owen. *London: W. Johnston*, 1754. sm. 8°.
p. 240, Ralph Allen's quarry and wagonway. 'The method in which they carry this stone down the hill is also very singular and the contrivance very ingenious . . .' (2 paragraphs).

8545 JONES, R. [Autobiography] *in* Ralph Allen and Prior Park, by William Gregory (*Bath*, 1886), pp. 36–45.
Richard Jones (b. 1703) was superintendent of Ralph Allen's quarries on Combe Down for 30 years. He mentions the wagonway at various points in his story, but only briefly.

8546 KIELMANSEGGE, F. Diary of a journey to England in the years 1761–1762. *London: Longmans, Green*, 1902, pp. vi, 287.
pp. 132–3. Brief description (1 para.) of Ralph Allen's quarry near Bath, and its wagonway.

8547 EVELYN, H. The history of the Evelyn family, with a special memoir of William John Evelyn. *London: E. Nash*, 1915. pp. 568.
p. 179 quotes from a letter of John Evelyn, describing (briefly) Ralph Allen's wagonway at Bath, dated Nov. 19th, 1738.

8548 MAGGS, C. G. Bath tramways. *Lingfield: Oakwood Press*, 1971. (Locomotion Papers, 52). pp. 47, with 16 illus on 8 plates, & 2 maps.

Weston-super-Mare

8549 MAGGS, C. The Weston-super-Mare tramways, *Lingfield: Oakwood Press*, 1974. (Locomotion Papers, 78). pp. 38, with 15 illus on plates (pp. 17–24), & a map.

Wiltshire 8550–54

8550 RAILWAY CORRESPONDENCE & TRAVEL SOCIETY. Itinerary of the Swindon & Highworth Special . . . , Sunday, 25th April, 1954. [*London*]: *the Society*, 1954. pp. 4, with map, 1 illus, schedule, & notes by A. E. Hurst, J. R. Fairman & R. K. McKenny.
Victoria—Kensington Olympia—Didcot—Swindon—Highworth Branch—Reading—Virginia Water—Weybridge—East Putney—Victoria.

8551 LEE, C. J. The Salisbury Railway and Market House Company: the first hundred years: a short survey of the work of the Company, written by C. J. Lee from the company minutes . . . [*Swindon: Wiltshire Libraries & Museums Service*, 1956]. pp. 31. Reproduced typescript.

8552 RAILWAY CORRESPONDENCE & TRAVEL SOCIETY. Itinerary of the 'Moonraker' Special, Sunday, 18th August, 1957. *R.C. & T.S.*, [1957]. pp. [2], with schedule. Written by P. Proud.
Paddington—Malmesbury—Swindon—Paddington.

8553 DALBY, L. J. The Swindon tramways and electricity undertaking. *Lingfield: Oakwood Press*, 1973. (Locomotion Papers, 65). pp. 44, with 8 illus on 4 plates, map, plan & 3 tables.

8554 BACKINSELL, W. G. C. The Salisbury Railway & Market House Company. *Salisbury: South Wilts Industrial Archaeology Society*, October 1977. (S.W.I.A.S. Historical Monograph, 1). pp. [8] with plan & 3 line drawings.
A ¼ mile branch from the Basingstoke & Salisbury line, 1856–1964. 'The shortest standard gauge line in the country'. Worked by the LSWR & successors, but in fact an independent company.

Gloucestershire 8555–73

Reference source 8555
General and local 8556–63
Cheltenham 8564–67
Forest of Dean 8568–73

Reference source

8555 AUSTIN, R. Catalogue of the Gloucestershire Collection: books, pamphlets and documents in the Gloucester Public Library relating to the County, cities, towns and villages of Gloucestershire, compiled by Roland Austin. *Gloucester: Gloucester Public Library*, 1928. pp. xii, 1236.
Railways, (nos. 2290–446) pp. 206–18.
Tramways, (nos. 4378–90) pp. 370–1.

General and local

8556 GLOUCESTER & BRISTOL RLY. Railways from Gloucester to Bristol. *Gloucester: J. E. Lea, printer, Westgate St.*, [1837]. Folio. pp. 4.
Comparative statements as to distances & gradients, etc., of the Bristol & Gloucester and Gloucester & Bristol railways; issued by Chadborn & Weedon, solicitors for the latter, dated 31 Dec., 1836.

8557 GLOUCESTERSHIRE COUNTY COUNCIL. Gloucester and District Light Railway; Stroud and District Light Railway; railway from Gloucester to Brockworth. [A printed circular letter from the Clerk of the County Council, dated 8th May, 1902]. pp. 13.
An exchange of correspondence between the County Council and Gloucester Town Council printed to remind local councils that under the terms of the Light Railways Act, 1896, they are required to consult with and agree with the County Council before constructing any tramway across town boundaries into the County.

8558 BICK, D. E. The Gloucester & Cheltenham Railway and the Leckhampton Quarry tramroads. *Lingfield: Oakwood Press*, 1968. (Locomotion Papers, 43). pp. 62, with 17 illus on 8 plates, 2 maps, 4 layout plans & lists.

8559 HOUSEHOLD, H. The Thames & Severn Canal, with . . . a foreword by Charles Hadfield. *Newton Abbot: David & Charles*, 1969. (Inland Waterways Histories). pp. 237, with col. frontis, 32 illus on 16 plates, 15 illus & maps in text, 486 notes, 7 appendices.
Railways, pp. 158–83 *et passim*.

8560 BICK, D. E. Old Leckhampton: its quarries, railways, riots and the Devil's Chimney. *Cheltenham: the author*, 1971. pp. 52, with frontis, 20 illus, map, 3 plans & a facsimile inside cover.

8561 AWDRY, W. Industrial archaeology in Gloucestershire, edited by W. Awdry. 2nd edn. *Gloucester: Gloucestershire Society for Industrial Archaeology*, 1975. pp. 32, with illus, maps & a bibliography.
pp. 11–13, 20, 'Tramroads and railways'.

8562 DAVIES, R. and GRANT, M. D. Forgotten railways: Chilterns and Cotswolds. *Newton Abbot: David & Charles*, 1975. pp. 256, with 31 illus on 16 plates, 26 maps, diagrams & drawings in text; folded map at end; bibliography (110 sources).

8563 DAVIES, R. and GRANT, M. D. Chilterns and Cotswolds, [compiled by] R. Davies and M. D. Grant. *Newton Abbot: David & Charles*, 1977. (Railway History in Pictures series). pp. 96, with 126 illus & maps.
Another work with the same title and written by the same authors was published, also in 1977, by David & Charles in their *Forgotten Railways* series.

Cheltenham

8564 CHELTENHAM & GREAT WESTERN UNION RLY. Refutation of the statements set forth in a pamphlet purporting to be an address from the directors of the Cheltenham and Great Western Union Railway Company to the shareholders, from the Cheltenham Journal. *Cheltenham: Williams, Lee, Davies, Lovesy & Wight*, 1836. pp. 49.
A detailed rebuttal of forty statements alleged to have been made by the Stroud & Swindon Rly Co. in its pamphlet entitled *'An Address from the directors of the Cheltenham & Great Western Union Railway to the shareholders* [Ottley 6015] and now denounced as 'either a barefaced and iniquitous forgery or as an impudent attempt by officials to deceive their employers'.
The Cheltenham, Oxford & Tring Rly was in opposition to the C. & G.W.U. at this time.

8565 CHELTENHAM, OXFORD AND TRING RLY [proposed]. Direct line of railway connecting South Wales, Gloucester, Cheltenham, Oxford, Tring and London. *Cheltenham: G. A. Williams, J. Lee . . .*, 1836. pp. 23.
Arguments in favour of a line via Oxford to London, joining the London & Birmingham Rly at Tring, rather than via the GWR at Didcot.

8566 GWINNETT, W. H. The Cheltenham railways: which is the best?: a letter from W. H. Gwinnett. *Cheltenham: J. J. Hadley, printer, Journal Office*, [1845]. pp. 10.
Support for a proposed London & Cheltenham direct line rather than the Cheltenham & Oxford line planned by the GWR. Text headed 'The Cheltenham railways: to the inhabitants of Cheltenham'.

8567 APPLEBY, J. B. and LLOYD, F. Cheltenham's trams and buses, 1890–1963. *Cheltenham: 21 Tram Group*, 1964. pp. 86, with 68 illus, 3 maps, 2 lists.
—— 2nd edn. Cheltenham's trams and buses remembered. *Glossop: Transport Publishing Co.*, 1973. pp. 72, with 60 illus, 2 maps, 3 lists.

Forest of Dean

8568 SOPWITH, T. Index Map to the series of sixteen engraved plans of coal and iron mines in Her Majesty's Forest of Dean, surveyed . . . by T. Sopwith. *London: J. Weale*, 1835.

[Republished as a facsimile reprint as] Sop-with's map of the Forest of Dean, 1835; showing the enclosures, roads, railways, coal and iron mines. 2¼ inches to the mile. *Newent: Pound House*, [197–]. A folded map with introductory notes by David Blick on back cover.

8569 RAILWAY CORRESPONDENCE & TRAVEL SOCIETY. Itinerary of the Bristol and South Gloucestershire Rail Tour . . . , Saturday, 26th September, 1959. *R.C. & T.S.*, [1959]. pp. 4, with map & schedule.
Written by M. B. Warburton.

8570 RAILWAY CORRESPONDENCE & TRAVEL SOCIETY. Itinerary of the Gloucestershire Rail Tour . . . , Sunday, 21st July, 1963. *R.C. & T.S.*, [1963]. pp. 4, with map & schedule. Notes by M. B. Warburton.
Paddington—Swindon—Port of Bristol Authority—Sharpness—Dursley—Nailsworth—Stroud—Gloucester—Paddington.

8571 PAAR, H. W. A history of the railways of the Forest of Dean. *Dawlish, Newton Abbot: David & Charles*.
part 1, The Severn & Wye Railway. 2nd edn. 1973. pp. 174, with col. frontis, 39 illus on 16 plates, 16 maps, plans, gradient profiles & diagrams & a folded map at end, 98 notes.
part 2, The Great Western Railway in Dean. [1965]. pp. 168, with col. frontis, 41 illus on 16 plates, 17 maps, plans, diagrams, gradient profiles; folded map at end; 209 notes.
—— 2nd edn. *David & Charles*, 1971. pp. 171, with col. frontis, 41 illus on 16 plates, 17 maps, plans, diagrams, gradient profiles; folded map at end; 221 notes.

8572 BODY, G. Guide to the Dean Forest Railway Preservation Society. *Bristol: Avon Anglia*, 1975. pp. 16, with 8 illus & map.

8573 DEAN FOREST RAILWAY SOCIETY. Guide & Stockbook, including Forest railway history. *Norchard: the Society*, 1979. pp. 32, with 25 illus, a map & a plan; 2 col. illus on covers.

C 1 c   SOUTH EAST REGION (London, Greater London, Middlesex and London suburban areas of the Home Counties, Hampshire, West Sussex, East Sussex, Surrey, Kent, Berkshire, Oxfordshire, Buckinghamshire, Bedfordshire, Hertfordshire, Essex)

8574–8911

For the Isle of Wight see C 5

South East Region generally 8574–91

Rail tour itineraries 8588–91

8574 BRANCH LINE RE-INVIGORATION SOCIETY. Uprofitable lines?: a financial study of certain railway passenger services in Somerset, Dorset and Hampshire. *London: the Society*, October 1963. pp. 26, with diagrams & a map. Reproduced typescript.
The case against threatened closures by BR questions the revenue and cost figures supplied by BR to objectors.

8575 MINISTRY OF HOUSING & LOCAL GOVERNMENT. The South East Study, 1961–1981. *London: H.M.S.O.*, 1964. pp. xii, 145, with many maps & tables & a col. folded map.
ch. 8, pp. 41–8, 'Travel to work in London'; pp. 58–63, 'Communications in the South East'; & in Summary, pp. 98–101.

8576 VINE, P. A. L. London's lost route to the sea: an historical account of the inland navigations which linked the Thames to the English Channel. *Dawlish: David & Charles; London: Macdonald*, 1965. pp. xx, 267, with col. frontis, 65 illus on 32 plates, & in text, 26 illus & 16 maps, a chronology, 134 notes & 9 appendices incl. a bibliography (70 sources).
Index has 26 page refs under 'Railways'.
—— 2nd edn. *Newton Abbot: David & Charles*, 1966. pp. xix, 267, etc.

—— 3rd edn. *David & Charles*, 1973. pp. xxiv, 267, with col. frontis, 65 illus on 32 plates, & in text, 26 illus, 16 maps, a chronology, 138 notes, & 9 appendices incl. a bibliography (102 sources).
Index has 40+ page refs under 'Railways'.

8577 HADFIELD, C. The canals of South and South-East England. *Newton Abbot: David & Charles*, 1969. (Canals of the British Isles series). pp. 393, with 32 illus on 16 plates, & in text, 45 illus & maps, 552 notes, a 10-part tabulated summary as appendices; index, pp. 381–93, with 47 page refs under 'Tramroads'.
A considerably extended version of part of this author's *The Canals of Southern England* (1955).

8578 FOOT, D. H. S. and STARKIE, D. N. M. Ashford-Hastings railway line: cost benefit appraisal. *Reading: [University of Reading]*, 1970. pp. 39, with map, tables, questionnaire and interviewing roster.

8579 ESAU, M. Steam into Wessex. *Shepperton: Ian Allan*, 1971. pp. 128. Intro, frontis, & 225 illus with descrs.

8580 WIKELEY, N. and MIDDLETON, J. Railway

stations, Southern Region. *Seaton: Peco*, 1971. pp. vii, 181. Intro & 443 illus in 12 sections, each with an introduction & map.

The architecture of stations in the south-eastern counties of England, photographed between 1968 and 1970.

8581 FAULKNER, A. H. The Grand Junction Canal. *Newton Abbot: David & Charles*, 1972. (Inland Waterways Histories). pp. 240, with 32 illus on 16 plates, 18 maps & illus, 213 notes.

Railways: 'The Railway Age', pp. 152–82 *et passim*.

8582 SYMES, R. and COLE, D. Railway architecture of the South East. *Reading: Osprey*, 1972. (Railway Architecture Series). pp. 128. Intro (pp. 7–15) & 42 drawings with commentaries.

Pen drawings of a selected 42 stations and other railway structures and detail on the Southern Rly in Kent, Surrey, Sussex & Hampshire, each with an historical & descriptive note. The Introduction provides a general historical commentary and the work is a factual, not imaginative, encapsulation of what is judged to be noteworthy (significant, striking or characteristic) in 19th century railway architecture in this area.

8583 COURSE, E. The railways of Southern England. *London: Batsford*. 3 vols.

A detailed and systematic description of the evolution of all railways east of the London–Southampton main line (which is included), presented as an historical companion to the interested traveller in 1971.

[vol. 1]: The main lines. 1973. pp. x, 318, with 48 illus on 29 plates, & in text, 24 diagrams & maps, a note on sources (pp. 5–7), 80 notes & 5 detailed appendices.

[vol. 2]: Secondary and branch lines. 1974. pp. 289, with 29 illus on 16 plates, & in text, 21 diagrams & maps, 3 drawings, 71 notes & 5 detailed appendices.

[vol. 3]: Independent and light railways. 1976. pp. ix, 189, with 46 illus on 24 plates, & in text, 4 diagrams, 3 maps, 88 notes & 6 detailed appendices.

Includes narrow-gauge and minor-gauge lines, cliff railways and industrial lines.

8584 CASSERLEY, H. C. Wessex. *Newton Abbot: David & Charles*, 1975. (Railway History in Pictures series). pp. 96. Intro & 112 illus with commentaries; map.

Area, Central Southern England and the Isle of Wight.

8585 STANDING CONFERENCE ON LONDON AND SOUTH EAST REGIONAL PLANNING. TECHNICAL PANEL. Transport Policy: Government consultation; report. *London: the Conference*, 1976. (Agenda item, 8; SC 618). pp. 18.

8586 WHITE, H. P. Forgotten railways: South East England. *Newton Abbot: David & Charles*, 1976. pp. 192, with 32 illus on 16 plates, gazetteer (pp. 153–90) & a folded map at end.

8587 HASELFOOT, A. J. The Batsford Guide to the Industrial Archaeology of South East England: Kent, Surrey, East Sussex, West Sussex. *London: Batsford*, 1978. pp. 153, with 68 illus.

Railways: 68 page refs to railways in the index.

Rail tour itineraries

8588 RAILWAY CORRESPONDENCE & TRAVEL SOCIETY. Itinerary of the Invicta Special . . ., Sunday, 12th September, 1954. [*London*]: *the Society*, 1954. pp. 4, with map, schedule, & notes by A. E. Hurst & J. R. Fairman.

Liverpool St—Gravesend—Chatham—Sheerness—Canterbury—Minster—Dover—Oxted—Nunhead—Blackfriars.

8589 RAILWAY CORRESPONDENCE & TRAVEL SOCIETY. Itinerary of the Kent and East Sussex Rail Tour, 'The Wealden Limited' . . ., Sunday, 14th August, 1955. *R.C. & T.S.*, [1955]. pp. 4, with map, schedule (pasted onto p. 4) & notes.

A slip bearing the date 'Sunday, 14th August, 1955' is pasted over the original date, 12th June, 1955.

Victoria—Lewisham—Oxford—Tonbridge—Paddock Wood—Hawkhurst—Tunbridge Wells—Robertsbridge—Hastings—Polegate—Lewes—Horsted Keynes—East Grinstead—Oxted—East Croydon—Sydenham—New Cross Gate—Victoria.

8590 LOCOMOTIVE CLUB OF GREAT BRITAIN. The 'Rother Valley Limited', Sunday, 19th October, 1958. *L.C.G.B.*, [1958]. pp. 12, with map, schedule and route history (opening dates). Reproduced typescript.

Paddington—Tenterden—Bexhill West—Hastings—Newhaven—Victoria.

8591 RAILWAY CORRESPONDENCE & TRAVEL SOCIETY. Itinerary of the Sussex Coast Limited . . ., Sunday, 13th April, 1958. *R.C. & T.S.*, [1958]. pp. 4, with 1 illus, map & schedule. Notes by J. R. Fairman.

Victoria—Clapham Junction—East Croydon—Purley—Coulsdon North—Horley—Three Bridges—Haywards Heath—Lewes—Newhaven—Lewes—Brighton—Hassocks—Wivelsfield—Gatwick Airport—Earlswood—Victoria.

London, Greater London, Middlesex and London suburban areas of the Home Counties

8592–8806

Reference sources 8592–95

A Historical 8596–8613
B Contemporaneous 8614–26
C Rail transport generally in specific areas 8627–60

  North London 8627–31
  North East London 8632–35
  East London 8636–41
  South London 8642–44
  South East London 8645–48

Reference sources

8592 MULTUM in Parvo. London & Suburban Omnibus & Tramway Guide, and Metropolitan and District Railways Time Tables . . . , no. 3 [February 1879]. *London: Guest*, 1879. pp. [14], 124, 20.

Tramway services on 6 pages and Met. Rly and Met. District Rly timetables on 2 folded leaves at end. G

8593 [PHILIP]. GEORGE PHILIP AND SONS LIMITED. Map of the Railway System of London and its suburbs . . . *London: G. Philip & Son, for the Railway Executive, B.T.C.*, 1951. A folded col. map (4ft × 3ft) in 36 foldings, scale ca. 1 mile to ¾ inches. Title on map: London and suburbs: main line railways and connecting railways of the London Transport Executive.

8594 LONDON TRANSPORT. Chronology, 1836–1962. *London: L.T.*, 1973. pp. 14. Reproduced typescript.

8595 [SWAN]. JOHN SWAN & COMPANY. Commuter's Map of 60 miles around London. *London: John Swan & Co.*, [1977]. La. folded col. map ¼ inch to 1 mile, with inset diagram map showing passenger traffic density into London termini, 7.00 to 9.00 a.m.

Concentric circles at radii of 10 miles, 20 miles, etc. to 60 miles are superimposed upon the map. On the reverse is an index to ca. 750 stations, including underground stations. This gives terminus, journey time, current season ticket rate and map reference.

A　Historical

8596 HAWKINS, L. C. Passenger transport in London. (Proceedings of the British Railways

(W.R.) London Lecture & Debating Society, 1953–54, no. 411). pp. 12, with discussion.

Author, member of the London Transport Executive. Problems, past and present.

8597 BARKER, T. C. Passenger transport in nineteenth century London, *in* Journal of Transport History, vol. 6, 1963–4. (Sources of Transport History series). pp. 166–74.

8598 COPPOCK, J. T. and PRINCE, H. C. [*editors*]. Greater London. *London: Faber*, 1964. pp. 405, with 31 plates, 78 maps & diagrams, & 22 tables.

ch. 3 (pp. 52–79), 'The development of communications' by Peter Hall, with 4 maps, 3 tables & 87 notes. The index has over 300 page refs to railways and underground railways.

8599 COURSE, E. Transport and communications in London, *in* The Geography of Greater London, edited by R. Clayton (*G. Philip*, 1964). pp. 74–110, with 5 maps, 5 illus, 4 railway gradient profiles & a chart; bibliography (13 sources).

8600 BOWIE-MENZLER, M. F. A. A. Menzler . . . born October 18th 1888, died November 1st 1968. *Privately printed by G Berridge*, [1969]. pp. 13. Facsimile signature of F. A. A. Menzler printed on cover. Written 'in memory of my husband'.

F. A. A. Menzler was the author of 'London and its Passenger Transport System' (*Jnl. Royal Statistical Society, series A (General)*, vol. 113, pt 3 (1950), pp. 298–345); he was Actuary to the Underground Group of Companies and in 1939, Chief Financial Officer to the London Passenger Transport Board, and to London Transport until 1966.

8601 LONDON TRANSPORT. What is London Transport? *London: L.T.*, 1973. obl. format. pp. [32], incl. cover, with many illus & diagrams, & a map.

A concise guide containing much detail and statistical information. Issued free to school parties visiting the London Transport Collection at Syon Park.

8602 LAY, R. W. Crosstown Railtour [no. 1], Saturday, 2nd November. *Wimbledon: B.R.(SR), South Western Division*, 1974. pp. 20, with area map on covers.

Itinerary, with timings and route chart alongside text. Compiled and drawn by Ron W. Lay. Copies distributed only to those taking part in the tour.

Wimbledon—Merton Park—Wimbledon—Twickenham—Cricklewood—Upper Holloway—South Tottenham—Stratford—Dalston—Willesden—Kensington Olympia—Southall—Brentford—Southall—Greenford—Kensington Olympia—Clapham Junction—Wimbledon.

8603 BARKER, T. C. and ROBBINS, M. A History of London Transport: passenger travel and the development of the Metropolis; volume 2, the twentieth century to 1970. *London: Allen & Unwin for the London Transport Executive*, 1974. pp. x, 554, with col. frontis, 159 illus on 88 plates, 11 maps, 1337 notes. The 6 Appendices (pp. 417–521)

contain: much detail on bus operators, traffic statistics, a bibliography of published articles and speeches of Lord Ashfield and Frank Pick, a list of Board members and principal officers of constituent bodies of railway, bus and tramway undertakings and of L.P.T.B., L.T.E. and L.T.B. Appendix 6 is a corrigenda list for vol. 1 and the Index (pp. 523–54) is for both volumes. Vol. 1 was published in 1963. (Ottley 754).
—— vol. 2 reprinted in paperback, with minor revision. *Allen & Unwin*, 1976. pp. xx, 550.

8604 SMITH, R. G. Ad hoc governments: special purpose transportation authorities in Britain and the United States. *Beverley Hills; London: Sage Publications*, 1974. (Sage Library of Social Research, 10). pp. 256, with a bibliography (161 sources).
pp. 143–55, the conflict of autonomy and accountability in British Railways and in London Transport before and after the Transport Act, 1962.

8605 LAY, R. W. Crosstown Railtour [no. 2]. *Wimbledon: B.R.(SR), South Western Division*, [1975]. pp. 20, with area map on covers.
Itinerary, with route chart alongside text. Compiled and drawn by Ron W. Lay. Copies distributed only to those taking part in the railtour:
Wimbledon—Clapham Junction—Victoria—Latchmere Junction—Kensington Olympia—Willesden Low Level Sidings—Sudbury Sidings—Wembley Central—Watford Junction—Croxley Green—Watford Junction—Wembley Central—Willesden High Level Sidings—Kensal Green Junction—Camden Road—Dalston Junction—Broad Street—Canonbury Junction—Finsbury Park—Wood Green—Palmers Green—Gordon Hill—Dalston—Western Junction—Victoria Park—Lea Junction—Liverpool Street—Forest Gate Junction—Barking—West Ham—Fenchurch Street—Gas Factory Junction—Bow Junction—Stratford High Level—South Tottenham—Kentish Town—Cricklewood—Brent Junction No. 2—Acton Central—Kew—Clapham Junction—Waterloo.

8606 KLAPPER, C. London's lost railways. *London: Routledge & Kegan Paul*, 1976. pp. xiv, 139, with 43 illus on 32 plates, 2 maps & 2 timetables.
The changing pattern of railway routes and services.

8607 KLAPPER, C. F. Roads and rails of London, 1900–1933. *London: Ian Allan*, 1976. pp. 191, with 179 illus (8 col.).
A confident and penetrating narrative founded upon the author's recorded observations over this period, supported by a selection of noteworthy photographs.

8608 LAY, R. W. Crosstown 3 [Railtour], Saturday, 16th October. *Wimbledon: B.R.(SR), South Western Division*, [1976]. pp. 18.
Itinerary, with route chart alongside text, by Ron W. Lay. Distributed only to those taking part in the tour:
Clapham Junction—Kensington Olympia—Willesden Junction—Acton Wells Junction—Ealing—West Drayton—Staines West—West Drayton—Reading—Didcot—Radley—Abingdon—Kennington Junction—Morris Cowley—Cholsey—Wallingford Branch—Reading—Frimley—Guildford—Shalford—Guildford—Leatherhead—Epsom—Sutton—West Croydon—Clapham Junction—Loughborough Junction—Nunhead—Hither Green—Bromley North—Grove Park—New Cross—London Bridge.

8609 OLSEN, D. J. The growth of Victorian London. *London: Batsford*, 1976. 4°. pp. 384, with 98 illus & Stanford's Library Map of London & its Suburbs (ca. 1863) reproduced in 24 page sections; 899 notes.
The index has 41 refs to railways and tramways in the text.

8610 JACKSON, A. A. London's local railways. *Newton Abbot: David & Charles*, 1978. pp. 384, with 64 illus on 32 plates, 4 line illus & 14 maps; sources used, pp. 377–9 (ca. 80 refs).

8611 LAY, R. W. Crosstown 4 [Railtour], Saturday 11 March 1978. *Wimbledon: B.R.(SR), South Western Division*, [1978]. pp. 24.
A detailed itinerary (an informative historical commentary) with route chart alongside the text, compiled and drawn by Ron Lay. Distributed only to those taking part in the railtour:
Waterloo—Clapham Junction—Chessington South Goods—Clapham Junction—Herne Hill—Crystal Palace—Sydenham—Bricklayers Arms—Greenwich—North Kent Line—Slade Green—Bexley—Lee Spur—Grove Park—Chislehurst—Orpington—Bickley—Catford Loop—Factory Junction—Clapham Junction—New Kew Junction—Cricklewood—Upper Holloway—Harringay—Hornsey—Finsbury Park—Canonbury Junction—Dalston—Stratford Low Level—North Woolwich—Stratford Southern Junction—Bow Junction—Liverpool Street—Hackney Downs—Seven Sisters—Enfield Town—Seven Sisters—South Tottenham—Stratford High Level—Victoria Park—Dalston—Camden Road—Gospel Oak—Willesden Junction—Kensington Olympia—North Pole Junction—Old Oak Common—Ealing—Southall—Greenford Loop—Old Oak Common—Kensington Olympia—Willesden Low Level Goods—Acton Canal Wharf—Kew East Junction—Clapham Junction—Waterloo.

8612 BARMAN, C. The man who built London Transport: a biography of Frank Pick. *Newton Abbot: David & Charles*, 1979. pp. 287, with 54 illus on 32 plates.
Planning, improved efficiency in management and operation, and with the co-operation of the architect Charles Holden, the introduction of new standards of architectural design that became at once a distinctive feature of the fabric of London during the inter-war years.

8613 BARKER, T. Towards an historical classification of urban transport development since the late eighteenth century, *in* Journal of Transport History, 3rd series, vol. 1, no. 1, September 1980, pp. 75–90, with table & 44 notes.
A statistical survey of the growth and decline of road & rail transport in London, 1825 to 1977, from which a framework of constants is derived and formulated into a table (p. 77) that may be applied to other urban areas.

B   Contemporaneous

8614 [HEMMING, J.] London Grand Junction Railway Bill. *London: Spottiswoode*, 1838. pp. 15.
Observations on the origin and prospects of the scheme to have a branch from the London & Birmingham Rly at Camden Town to Snow Hill and the Thames.

8615 PEARSON, C. City central terminus: address to the citizens from Charles Pearson preparatory to the public meeting at the London Tavern, Bishopsgate Street on Monday the 1st of November, at one o'clock. [*London*, 1852]. pp. 12.

8616 LEANING, H. J. London railway reconstruction. Great Western Railway (London) Lecture & Debating Society, meeting on October 19th, 1922 (no. 150). pp. 18, with discussion & 4 maps.
Author, *London Society*. The London railway network: present problems, and plans for improving mobility and access.

8617 MINISTRY OF TRANSPORT. LONDON AND HOME COUNTIES TRAFFIC ADVISORY COMMITTEE. Report . . . to the Minister of Transport in regard to Parliamentary Private Bills promoted by the London County Council and the London Electric Railway Companies in the 1928–29 Sessions of Parliament. *London: H.M.S.O., 1929*.
The need to adhere to the principle and unified control over transport planning.

8618 RASMUSSEN, S. E. London: the unique city; with an introduction by James Bone. *London: Jonathan Cape*, 1937. pp. 404.
Originally published in Copenhagen, 1934.
ch. 14 (pp. 339–64), 'London Transport', with 19 illus, 4 facsimiles, 2 diagrams & a plan.
—— 2nd edn. *J. Cape*, 1948. pp. 440.
ch. 14 (pp. 339–64), 'London Transport'.

8619 MINISTRY OF TRANSPORT AND CIVIL AVIATION. COMMITTEE OF INQUIRY INTO LONDON TRANSPORT. Report. *London: H.M.S.O.* (Chairman, S. P. Chambers).
part 1: 1955, pp. viii, 121, with 9 appendices, incl. 2 folded maps, folded L.T. admin. chart, detailed financial tables, 1948–63, & tables of hours of attendance of the staff of 16 Government departments in Central London.
A slip pasted onto the title-page states: 'Part II is of considerable length and is not being printed at present'.
Terms of reference: 'To inquire into the conduct of the undertaking carried on by the London Transport Executive with a view to ascertaining what practical measures can be taken by the British Transport Commission and the Executive in order to secure greater efficiency or economy'.

8620 MINISTRY OF TRANSPORT. Transport in London. *London: H.M.S.O.*, 1968. (Cmnd 3686). pp. iii, 85, with 1 illus.
The disbandment of the London Transport Board and the setting up of the London Transport Executive.

8621 GREATER LONDON COUNCIL. The future of London Transport: a paper for discussion. *London: G.L.C.*, October 1970. pp. 52, with 8 financial & statistical graphs & tables.

8622 GREATER LONDON COUNCIL. Transport in London: a balanced policy. [*London*]: *G.L.C.*, March 1970. pp. 19, with 10 illus & 2 maps.
'The elements of the G.L.C.'s overall coordinated transportation policy.'

8623 GREATER LONDON COUNCIL. Transport Policy Consultation Document: Greater London Council's comments. *London: G.L.C.*, June 1976. pp. 7.

8624 GREATER LONDON COUNCIL. Transport policies and programme, 1978–83. *London: G.L.C.*, [1977]. pp. 108, with 34 tables, 7 maps & diagrams.
—— 1979–84. *G.L.C.*, 1978. pp. 113, with 28 tables, 5 maps.

8625 GREATER LONDON COUNCIL. LONDON TRANSPORT COMMITTEE. London Transport: a new look. *London: G.L.C.*, [1977]. tall 8°. pp. 28, [vii], with 4 tables & 2 graphs. Reproduced typescript.
The need to integrate railway, bus and underground services.

8626 BRITISH RAILWAYS. A cross-London rail link: a British Railways Board discussion paper. *London: B.R.*, [1980]. pp. 33, with 4 diagrams, 3 tables, 2 maps & 2 illus. Intro by Peter Parker, Chairman, B.R.
The need for a through-train link to relieve congestion and delay caused by outward spread of a population having to make multi-mode cross-London journeys.

C   Rail transport in specific areas

North London

8627 SHERRINGTON, R. O. The story of Hornsey. *London: F. E. Robinson*, 1904. pp. 134.
ch. 4 (pp. 32–9), 'The Railway Revolution': the effect of railways (the GNR & the Tottenham & Hampstead Joint Rly) on the growth & development of Hornsey (Middlesex).

8628 CRESSWELL, H. Winchmore Hill: memories of a lost village . . . , by H. C. 2nd edn. *Dumfries: T. Hunter, Watson & Co.*, 1912. pp. 110–15, 'The coming of the railway.' The Wood Green–Enfield branch ('Hertford Loop') of the Great Northern Rly, in 1869.

8629 MINISTRY OF TRANSPORT. LONDON AND HOME COUNTIES TRAFFIC ADVISORY COMMITTEE. Report upon the public inquiry held in October 1925 with respect to the travelling facilities to and from North and North-East London. *London: H.M.S.O.*, 1926. pp. 15, with 2 maps. (Chairman: Sir Henry P. Maybury).

8630 RAILWAY CORRESPONDENCE & TRAVEL SOCIETY. Itinerary of the London Area Rail

Tour, 10th October, 1953. *R.C. & T.S.*, [1953]. pp. 4, with 2 maps & a schedule. No text.
Marylebone—Acton—Kensington—Battersea—Blackfriars—Kings Cross—South Tottenham—Victoria Park—Broad Street.

8631 LOCOMOTIVE CLUB OF GREAT BRITAIN. Itinerary of the Poplar and Edgware Rail Tour, Saturday, 5th May, 1956. *Isleworth: L.C.G.B.*, 1956. pp. 8, with schedule & map. Notes by E. A. Course.
North London Rly to Finsbury Park, then onto the GNR's branch to Edgware.

North East London

8632 RAILWAY CORRESPONDENCE & TRAVEL SOCIETY. Itinerary of the North East London Rail Tour, 29th March, 1952. *R.C. & T.S.*, [1952]. pp. 4, with map, & notes by Peter Proud.
London Bridge—New Cross Gate—East London Line to Liverpool Street—Stratford—South Tottenham—Palace Gates—Bounds Green—Wood Green—Kings Cross—Blackfriars Junction—Cannon Street.

8633 ASHWORTH, W. Types of social and economic development in suburban Essex, *in* London: aspects of change (Centre for Urban Studies Report no. 3, 1964) pp. 62–87, with area population table, 1851–1961, and a table showing local employment movements, 1921 and 1951, & 58 notes.
Includes railways as a factor of change.

8634 LINE 112 GROUP. The railway to Walthamstow & Chingford. *London: Walthamstow Antiquarian Society*, 1970. (Monographs, new series, 9). pp. 78, with frontis, 27 illus, 2 maps, 5 layout plans, notes on maps & illus, a chronology, 10 tables & a bibliography (60+ sources).
Suburban lines of the Great Eastern Rly, and the Tottenham & Forest Gate line of the Midland Rly. Published to mark the centenary of the opening of the Great Eastern line to Walthamstow in 1870, in LNER days (1923–47) designated 'branch line 112'.

8635 POND, C. C. The Chingford line and the suburban development of Walthamstow and Chingford. *London: Walthamstow Antiquarian Society*, 1975. (Monographs, new series, 17). pp. 20, with 28 illus & map on 16 plates.

East London

8636 MINISTRY OF TRANSPORT. LONDON AND HOME COUNTIES TRAFFIC ADVISORY COMMITTEE. Public inquiry with regard to the alleged inadequacy of travelling facilities to, from, and within, certain areas in the East of London. Minutes of Evidence and Report. *London: H.M.S.O.*, 1926. pp. 26, 54, appendices & map. (Chairman: Sir Henry P. Maybury).

8637 RAILWAY CORRESPONDENCE & TRAVEL SOCIETY. Itinerary of the East London Rail Tour, 14th April, 1951. *R.C. & T.S.*, [1951]. pp. 4, with map & notes by Peter Proud.

8638 RAILWAY CORRESPONDENCE & TRAVEL SOCIETY. Itinerary of the East London Rail Tour no. 2, Saturday, 24th March, 1956. *R.C. & T.S.*, [1956]. pp. 4, with map & schedule. Notes by P. Proud.
Fenchurch Street—Upminster—Romford—Beckton—Stratford Market—Millwall Junction—Poplar Central—Broad Street.

8639 RAILWAY CORRESPONDENCE & TRAVEL SOCIETY. Itinerary of the East London no. 3 Rail Tour . . . , Saturday, 6th October, 1962. *R.C. & T.S.*, [1962]. pp. 4, with map, plan & schedule. Text by A. E. Bennett.
Liverpool Street—Custom House—North Woolwich—Beckton—Canning Town—Temple Mills—Broxbourne—Buntingford—Liverpool Street.

8640 ASHWORTH, W. Metropolitan Essex since 1850, *in* Victoria History of the County of Essex, vol. 5, 1966, pp. 1–92, with 571 notes. Railways, pp. 12–13, 23–7, 71–3.

8641 DOCKLANDS DEVELOPMENT TEAM. The docklands spine: tube, bus or tram? *London: the Team*, April 1975. (Docklands Joint Committee. Working Papers for Consultation, 3); (Docks, 56). pp. 32, with 4 maps & 4 tables.
A consultation paper. Considers the proposal for a new underground railway to link Central London (Fenchurch St.) to Thamesmead.

South London

8642 SIMMONDS, H. All about Battersea. *London: Ashfield, printer*, 1882. pp. vii, 181.
pp. 85–91, describes the engine-shed of the LBSCR and the Longhedge Works of the LCDR.

8643 BINFORD, H. C. Residential displacement by railway construction in North Lambeth. Thesis, M.A., University of Sussex, 1968.

8644 BINFORD, H. C. Land tenure, social structure, and railway impact in North Lambeth, 1830–61, *in* Journal of Transport History, new series vol. 2, 1973–4, pp. 129–54, with 5 tables, 3 maps & 66 notes.

South East London

8645 MINISTRY OF TRANSPORT. LONDON AND HOME COUNTIES TRAFFIC ADVISORY COMMITTEE. Public inquiry with regard to the alleged inadequacy of travelling facilities to, from, and within, certain areas in the South-East of London. *London: H.M.S.O.*, 1926. pp. 247. (Chairman: Sir Henry P. Maybury).
Report and Minutes of Evidence.

8646 MINISTRY OF TRANSPORT. LONDON AND HOME COUNTIES TRAFFIC ADVISORY COMMITTEE. Report upon the public enquiry held in October 1926 with respect to the travelling facilities to and from South-East London. *London: H.M.S.O.*, 1927. pp. 15, with map.
Includes a statistical table for Southern Rly traffic and London County Council Tramways services.

8647 RAILWAY CORRESPONDENCE & TRAVEL SOCIETY. Itinerary of the London River Rail Tour . . . , Saturday, 29th March, 1958. *R.C. & T.S.*, [1958]. pp. 4, with map, schedule & notes by E. A. Course.
London Bridge—Deptford Wharf—Bricklayers Arms—New Cross—Angerstein Wharf—St Johns—Surrey Docks—Liverpool Street.

8648 ROLFE, E. M. The growth of South-East London, 1836–1914, with special reference to the development of communications. Thesis, Ph.D., University of London (Q.M.C.), 1968.
chaps. 4 & 5 (pp. 57–78). 'Railways, omnibuses and trams', with 36 & 31 notes.

South West London

8649 RAILWAY CORRESPONDENCE & TRAVEL SOCIETY and STEPHENSON LOCOMOTIVE SOCIETY. Itinerary of the South Western Suburban Rail Tour . . . , Sunday, 2nd December, 1962. *R.C. & T.S., & S.L.S.*, [1962]. pp. 4, with illus, map & schedule. Notes by J. R. Fairman on the Beattie 2–4–0 locomotives which worked these lines for many years.
Waterloo—East Putney—Hampton Court—Chessington South—Kingston—Shepperton—Twickenham—Waterloo.

8650 MINISTRY OF TRANSPORT. Report of a study of rail links with Heathrow Airport . . . *London: H.M.S.O.*
pt 1, Summary and conclusions. 1970. pp. v, 10.
pt 2, Details of the study. 1970. pp. iii, 64, with tables.
Favours an extension of the Piccadilly Line from Hounslow West to the Airport.

West London

8651 POTTER, S. The story of Willesden. *London: Pitman*, 1926. pp. 247.
ch. 29 (pp. 149–57), 'The coming of the railways', with 31 illus.

8652 RAILWAY CORRESPONDENCE & TRAVEL SOCIETY. Itinerary of the West London Rail Tour . . . , Saturday, 13th October, 1956. *R.C. & T.S.*, [1956]. pp. 4, with map & schedule. Text by E. A. Course.

8653 WAGER, D. and FRISCHMANN, W. West End Minirail: a preliminary study for a fine-mesh transport system in central areas; with particular reference to the West End of London. *London: Construction Publications*, 1967. obl. format. pp. 13, with numerous maps, diagrams, & a sketch drawing.

8654 REEDER, D. A. A theatre of suburbs: some patterns of development in West London, 1801–1911, *in* The Study of Urban History, edited by H. J. Dyos (1968), pp. 253–71, with 2 maps (1847 and 1904) and 64 notes.
The development of Paddington and Hammersmith, and factors, including railways, contributing to changes in the settlement pattern of social groups.

8655 JAHN, M. A. Railways and suburban development: outer West London, 1850–1900. Thesis, M. Phil, University of London, 1971.
Acton, Chiswick, Ealing & Hanwell.

8656 TRANSPORT 2000. Airport links: Heathrow fourth terminal: rail links to Heathrow Airport. *London: Transport 2000*, 1978. pp. 8 & contents page. Reproduced typescript; no covers.

8657 SHEPHERDS BUSH LIBRARY. ARCHIVES DEPARTMENT. How we used to travel. *London: Hammersmith & Fulham Libraries*, 1979. pp. 36, incl. covers, with 10 illus & a map of local railways.
Includes railways and tramways.

North West London

8658 BALINT, M. L.M.R. Survey, Watford Line: report of method. *London: Greater London Council, Dept of Highways & Transportation, Transportation Branch*, Oct. 1968. (Research Memoranda, 119). Reproduced typescript.
The strategic planning and data processing of the Survey, and the distribution, collection, sampling and coding of the questionnaires.

8659 MAY, T. Road passenger transport in Harrow in the nineteenth and early twentieth centuries, *in* Journal of Transport History, new series vol. 1 (1971–2), pp. 18–38, with map & 103 notes.
Includes railway development and schemes for tramway extensions to Harrow.

8660 THOMPSON, F. M. L. Hampstead: building a borough, 1650–1964. *London: Routledge & Kegan Paul*, 1974. pp. xi, 459, with 14 plates, 18 drawings, 7 maps, 5 tables & many notes.
In the Index of Subjects, 101 page refs under 'Railway stations,' & 'Railways . . . ,' and for tramways, 6 refs under 'Transport: road'.

D 1   Tramways

Historical

8661 A FEW remarks on the proposed street railways as they will affect the ordinary users of the roads and householders. *London: Waterlow & Sons, printers*, 1868. pp. 6.
'By a ratepayer and large property-holder in the Metropolis.'   MCL

8662 HALL, F. L.C.C. tramways. *London: London Municipal Society*, [1912]. (Municipal Reform Pamphlets, 51). pp. 16.
Lecture at Caxton Hall, Thursday June 13th, 1912. In the chair, W. J. Squires. A review of the L.C.C.'s tramway development & operation, with financial tables (pp. 14–16).

8663 GARDINER, A. G. John Benn and the Progressive Movement. *London: Benn*, 1925, pp. xiii, 522, with frontis & 19 illus & maps on 15 plates.
ch. 13, 'London traffic', & ch. 14, 'The Tramway Victory' (pp. 214–48) *et passim*.

8664 HAWARD, [Sir] H. The London County Council from within: forty years official recollections. *London: Chapman & Hall*, 1932. pp. xii, 437.
ch. 30 (pp. 288–313), Tramways (mainly).

8665 GIBBON, [Sir] G. and BELL, R. W. History of the London County Council, 1889–1939. *London: Macmillan*, 1939. pp. xxi, 696, with plates and text illus.
Tramways, pp. 615–21 *et passim*.

8666 LONDON COUNTY COUNCIL. [Collection of 515 L.C.C. documents relating to transport in London, 1889–1945.]
Acts, reports, memoranda, statements and estimates, chronologically arranged within each of the 15 boxes which house the material, with a typescript index of 26 pp., in a binder.
Of the 515 items, 3 relate to main-line railways, 27 to workmen's trains, 20 to underground railways and 230 to tramways. LU(THC)

8667 McBRIAR, A. M. Fabian Socialism and English politics, 1884–1918. *Cambridge: Cambridge University Press*, 1962. pp. x, 387.
ch. 8, Municipalization of tramways; the influence of the Fabians in the London County Council.
pp. 26, 191–2, 222–5 *et passim*, nationalization of railways.

8668 DARLING, V. H. London Bus and Tram Album. *London: Ian Allan*, [1963]. pp. 128.
pp. 74–93, 'The evolution of the London tramcar' (39 illus with descrs.).
— 2nd series. *Ian Allan*, [1967]. pp. 128.
pp. 76–90, 'The London tramcar' (37 illus with descrs.) and 6 in the two end chapters.

8669 DUNBAR, C. S. Idealism and competition: the fares policy of the London County Council Tramways. [*Luton: Transport Ticket Society*, 1967]. pp. 15, with 10 illus.
Reprinted from *Modern Tramways*, May & June 1967. The presidential address of the T.T.S., 1967.

8670 THOMPSON, J. London trams in camera: an illustrated survey of the last years of the London tramways. *London: Ian Allan*, 1971. pp. 127, with frontis (general map), 214 illus, a map (Embankment to Wimbledon) & a plan.

8671 MARSHALL, P. Wheels of London: the story of London's street transport; text by Prince Marshall; edited by George Perry; designed by Gilvrie Misstear and Michael Rand. *London: Sunday Times Magazine*, 1972. obl. format. pp. 144, with illus, 5 folded route maps, 40 reproductions of tickets & 30 cigarette cards, the whole encased.
Limited and numbered edition of 3000 volumes.

8672 WILLOUGHBY, D. W. and OAKLEY, E. R. London Tramway Pictorial. *Hartley: the authors*, 1972. Foreword & 83 illus with captions.

8673 WILLOUGHBY, D. W. and OAKLEY, E. R. London Transport Tramways Handbook. *Hartley: the authors*, 1972. pp. 120, with frontis, 24 illus, 3 diagrams (1 col.), 3 plans, lists of openings and routes. Inserted are 2 folded fare tables (1 la. folded); map at end.

8674 ELLIS, H. London tramway memories: New Cross and Holloway depots, 1946–1952. *Farnborough (Hants): Light Railway Transport League*, 1975. pp. 16.

8675 COLLINS, S. G. and COOPER, T. The wheels used to talk to us, [by Stanley G. Collins]; edited by Terence Cooper. *Sheffield: Sheaf Publishing*, 1977. pp. [iv], 172, with 185 illus & diagrams, line drawings, maps, layout plans & tables; map on front end papers, plans on back end papers; bibliography (16 sources).
S. G. Collins was a London tramwayman from 1913 to 1951. The work is a transcription of recorded interviews with him by T. Cooper, rearranged chronologically, and augmented with chapter introductions by T. Cooper consisting of historical & operational data. The five appendices (pp. 137–70), also by T. Cooper, supply further detail on tramway working in South London and on working conditions and management labour relations.
A detailed first-hand account of London tramway working and the life and working conditions of tramwaymen, with substantial background information supplied by the editor.

8676 DAY, J. R. London's trams and trolleybuses. *London: London Transport*, 1977. pp. 113, with 160 illus, 4 maps & a bibliography (10 sources).
— 1979 edn. *L.T.*, 1979. Apparently a reprint of the 1977 edition, but with a pictorial cover.

8677 'KENNINGTON'. London County Council Tramways Handbook, by 'Kennington' [i.e. E. R. Oakley, A. D. Packer, C. S. Smeeton, D. W. Willoughby]. *London: Tramway & Light Railway Society*, 1970. pp. 96, with frontis, 58 illus, 2 maps (1 la. folded), 2 depot plans, 2 diagrams, chronology, lists of services, stock & other details.
— 2nd edn. *C. S. Smeeton for the T. & L.R.S.*, 1974. pp. 98, with frontis, 55 illus, 2 maps (1 la. folded), 2 depot plans, 2 diagrams, chronology, lists of services, stock & other details.
— 3rd edn. *T. & L.R.S.*, 1977. pp. 98, with frontis, 55 illus, 2 maps (1 la. folded), 2 depot plans, 2 diagrams, chronology, lists of services, stock & other details.

8678 OAKLEY, E. R. The British horse tram era, with special reference to the Metropolis. *Tramway & Light Railway Society*, 1979. (Walter Gratwicke Memorial Lecture, 1978). pp. 44, with 18 illus, 6 diagrams & a layout plan.

Contemporaneous

8679 LONDON COUNTY COUNCIL. HIGHWAYS COMMITTEE. London Tramways Guide.

London, 1908. pp. xx, 32, with illus. Cover title: Official Tramways Guide.
The first L.C.C. Tramways guide. 32 routes, with maps and details of services.   LU(THC)

London north of the Thames

8680 LONDON COUNTY COUNCIL TRAMWAYS. A Guide to Kingsway Subway. *London: L.C.C. Tramways*, [1931]. pp. 32, with 9 illus, map, time & fare tables.

8681 HATLEY, A. R. Across the years: Walthamstow memories, edited by Annie R. Hatley. *Walthamstow: Walthamstow Antiquarian Society*, 1953. pp. 112, with illus.
pp. 75–82, The tramway systems (Walthamstow U.D.C. Light Railways).

8682 ROBBINS, G. J. Historical and Current Notes in connection with the tour of the last London trolleybus routes, 601, 602, 603, 604, 605, 607 & 667, 6th May 1962. *Omnibus Society*, 1962. (Publication L & SC, 6/62). pp. 11. Reproduced typescript.
'The whole of the tour comprises roads formerly covered by the London United Tramways'. The notes are mostly about the tramway services of the L.U.T., with additional data on both the L.U.T. and London County Council Tramways periods, by J. C. Gillham, F. Merton Atkins and H. E. Murrell.

8683 TONKIN, W. G. S. Public transport in Walthamstow before the Council tramways. *Walthamstow: Walthamstow Antiquarian Society*, 1962. pp. 12, with 3 illus & a map on 1 plate.
The Lea Bridge, Leyton & Walthamstow Tramways Company, 1889–1906; horse-hauled cars.

8684 BURROWS, V. E. Tramways in Metropolitan Essex. *Huddersfield: Advertiser Press*.
vol. 1, The North Metropolitan Tramways Co., the Lea Bridge, Leyton & Walthamstow Tramways Co., the London County Council Tramways. 1967. pp. 163, with 39 illus; folded map at end.
vol. 2, comprising the systems of East Ham Corporation, Ilford Council, Barking Town Urban District Council, West Ham Corporation. 1976. pp. 220, with 56 illus on 28 plates; folded map, list of rolling stock (folded sheet), both as loose inserts in end pocket.

8685 'RODINGLEA'. The tramways of East London. *London: Tramway & Light Railway Society; Light Railway Transport League*, 1967. pp. 252, with frontis, 124 illus, 13 maps, many detailed tables, a chronology, and diagrams on end papers. A correction slip is inserted.
'Rodinglea': F. Merton Atkins, Wingate H. Bett, Richard Elliott, Tony A. Gibbs, Leonard A. Thomson.

8686 BARRIE, J. North London's tramways, 1938–1952. *London: Light Railway Transport League*, 1969. pp. 28, with 12 illus on 4 plates, map & illus on cover.

8687 THOMSON, L. A. By bus, tram and coach in Walthamstow. *London: Walthamstow Anti-* *quarian Society*, 1971. (Monographs, new series, 11). pp. 40, with 43 illus & 2 maps on 24 plates.
pp. 5–22, Tramways.

8688 WILSON, G. London United Tramways: a history, 1894 to 1933. *London: Allen & Unwin*, 1971. pp. 240, with 136 illus on 48 plates, 4 appendices (pp. 181–232), & a bibliography (40 sources). Map on end papers. Appendix 1, Routes & service numbers, by A. W. McCall; appendix 2, Fares and tickets, by A. W. McCall; appendix 3, The fleet; appendix 4, Rules and regulations.
Integral to this history is its detail of the life and career of Sir James Clifton Robinson, pioneer of London's electric tramways and Managing Director & Engineer of the L.U.T. until 1910.

8689 WILLOUGHBY, D. W. and OAKLEY, E. R. Trams in West London: a pictorial souvenir. *Hartley: the authors*, 1978. pp. 44. Foreword & 78 illus with descrs.

8690 THOMSON, L. A. Trams and trolleybuses in Ilford. *Ilford: Ilford & District Historical Society*, 1979. (Ilford & District History Transactions, 2). pp. 52, with 16 illus, 3 drawings, 2 facsimiles, map, depot plan & a table.

8691 WILLOUGHBY, D. W. and OAKLEY, E. R. Trams in East London: a pictorial souvenir. *Hartley: the authors*, 1979. pp. 44. Intro & 82 illus with descrs & a folded map.

8692 WILLOUGHBY, D. W. and OAKLEY, E. R. Trams in inner North London. *Hartley: the authors*, 1980. pp. 40. Intro & 81 illus with descrs.

8693 WILLOUGHBY, D. W., OAKLEY, E. R. and JONES, D. W. K. Trams in outer North London: a pictorial souvenir. *Hartley: the authors*, 1981. pp. 44. Intro & 82 illus with descrs.

London south of the Thames

8694 JEFFERSON, E. F. E. Woolwich and the trams. *Woolwich: Woolwich & District Antiquarian Society*, 1954. pp. 15, with 1 illus.
Reprinted from the Society's *Proceedings*, vol. 30 (1954).

8695 HARVIE, K. G. The tramways of South London & Croydon, 1899–1949. 4th edn. *Lee: the author*, [1969]. pp. [A]–D, 122, with 136 illus, 4 plans, 3 maps & 2 pp. illustrating 27 tickets. Reproduced typescript. Edition limited to 500 copies.
—— 5th edn. *London: London Borough of Lewisham Council*, 1975. pp. iv, 160, with 18 illus on 32 plates, 3 maps, 9 plans & 2 pp. illustrating tickets. Printed.
—— Picture Supplement A. [1975]. 17 illus.
—— Text & Picture Supplement B. [1975]. 16 illus.
—— List of Additions and Amendments to the 5th edition, 1978. pp.[9].

The work was originally published as a series of essays in local newspapers of the Lewisham area and reprinted ca. 1954 as a 16-page reproduced typescript booklet with 6 illus, 2 maps & 2 diagrams. Two further revised & enlarged editions had appeared by 1958. The 5th edition has much detail, including two chronologies of air raid incidents, 1940–5, with notes. The two supplements to this edition were made available by the author to offset the limitation set by the publisher on the number of illustrations which could be incorporated into the 5th edition (from information kindly supplied by the author).

The historical value of the work is enhanced by the recording of reminiscences and anecdotes by several tramwaymen.

8696 DUNBAR, C. S. Tramways in Wandsworth and Battersea, with some notes on 'the Western system' of the L.C.C. (with additional notes and reminiscences by Frank E. Wilson). *London: Light Railway Transport League*, 1971. pp. 80, with 52 illus, 3 maps & 7 plans.
'Originally published in 1945, revised and republished in 1950. Reprinted with revisions and additions in the *Tramway Review* under the title 'The South London Tramways Co. and its successors . . .'

8697 WILLOUGHBY, D. W. and OAKLEY, E. R. Trams in South East London: a pictorial souvenir looking back 25 years. *Hartley: the authors*, 1977. pp. 48. Intro & 90 illus with descrs.

8698 WILLOUGHBY, D. W. and OAKLEY, E. R. Trams in South West London: a pictorial souvenir. *Hartley: the authors*, 1978. pp. 40. Intro & 74 illus with descrs.

D 4   Underground railways

Reference sources

8699 LINDSEY, C. F. Underground railways in London: a select bibliography. *London: C. F. Lindsey*, 1973. pp. 14. Reproduced typescript. Title from cover.
83 sources (books, annual reports and periodicals).

8700 GUILDHALL LIBRARY, [LONDON]. Handlist of Books in Guildhall Library relating to underground railways in London [compiled by Richard Alan Martin Harvey], *in* Guildhall Studies in London History, vol. 1, no. 3, October 1974, pp. 192–209, with plate. 206 sources (printed books, reports and extracts from periodical literature), with notes.

8701 YONGE, J. London Transport Railway Track Map, drawn by and compiled from the researches of John Yonge aided by . . . Trevor Haynes. 2nd edn, incorporating revisions by courtesy [of the] London Underground Railway Society. *Exeter: Quail Map Co.*, April 1979. Folded map, 23 inches × 16 inches.
The scale is enlarged where details of complex trackwork need to be shown, and some of the

outlying branches are reduced in scale. 18 plans of the larger depots are shown as insets. The Post Office Railway is added but not the Waterloo & City Line, BR(SR).

General history and description

8702 HAWARD, [Sir] H. The London County Council from within: forty years official recollections. *London: Chapman & Hall*, 1932. pp. xii, 437.
ch. 38 (pp. 377–81), Tube railway amalgamations. The formation of the Underground Electric Railways Company of London, 1902.

8703 DAY, J. R. Railways under the ground. *London: A. Barker*, 1964. (Age of Science series). pp. 135, with illus, maps & diagrams.
pp. 9–33: London railways, with 4 illus & 2 maps. Introductory.

8704 SIMMONS, J. The pattern of tube railways in London: a note on the Joint Select Committee of 1892, *in* Journal of Transport History, vol. 7 (1965–6). pp. 234–40, with 33 notes.
A commentary on the report from the Joint Committee on the Electric and Cable Railways (Metropolis), with the proceedings, Evidence, Appendix, and Index, Parl. Papers, 1892, XII, 1–172.

8705 HAVERS, H. C. P. Underground railways of the world: their history and development. *London: Temple Press*, 1966. pp. x, 197, with 56 illus on 36 plates & 30 maps in text.
Includes London Underground railways

8706 LEE, C. E. Sixty years of the Bakerloo. [*London*]: *London Transport*, 1966. pp. 24, with frontis, map of Bakerloo Line & 23 illus on 12 plates.
—— new edn. The Bakerloo Line. *London Transport*, 1973. pp. 23 with frontis, map & 23 illus on 12 plates. Cover title: the Bakerloo Line: a brief history.

8707 LEE, C. E. Sixty years of the Piccadilly. [*London*]: *London Transport*, 1966. pp. 25, with frontis, map of Piccadilly Line, & 24 illus on 12 plates.
—— [2nd edn]. The Piccadilly Line. *London Transport*, 1973. pp. 26, with frontis, map, & 24 illus on 12 plates. Cover title: The Piccadilly Line: a brief history.

8708 LEE, C. E. 100 years of the District. *Westminster: London Transport*, [1968]. pp. 32, with 30 illus on 12 plates & a map.
The Metropolitan District Rly.
—— [2nd edn]. The District Line. *London Transport*, 1973. pp. 35, with 30 illus on 12 plates & a map.

8709 BRIXTON SCHOOL OF BUILDING. Victoria Line underground railway, 1965–1970. *London: Construction Industry Information Group*, 1970. (Bibliography, no. 20.) s.sh.
31 periodical sources 'compiled by Brixton School of Building, October 1970'.

8710 LEE, C. E. Seventy years of the Central.

London: London Transport, [1970]. pp. 32, with frontis, 25 illus on 12 plates, 2 maps & a plan.
—— [2nd edn]. The Central Line. London Transport, [1974]. pp. 33, with frontis, 25 illus on 12 plates, 2 maps & a plan.

8711 LEE, C. E. The Tower Subway: the first tube tunnel in the world. London: Institution of Mechanical Engineers, 1970. pp. 24, with 55 notes. Reproduced typescript in printed covers.
A paper read at a joint meeting of the Newcomen Society and the I.M.E., Wednesday 18th November 1970.

8712 DAY, J. R. and FENTON, W. The last drop: the steam age on the Underground, from 1863 to 1971. London: London Transport, 1971. pp. [24], with frontis, 40 illus (10 col.) & lists.

8713 NOCK, O. S. Underground railways of the world. London: A. & C. Black, 1973. pp. 288, with 155 illus, 21 maps & plans, 12 diagrams & line drawings.
Of the 22 chapters, 13 are about underground railways in London, and one is on the Glasgow District Subway.

8714 FOLLENFANT, H. G. Reconstructing London's Underground. London: London Transport, 1974. pp. xi, 184, with 43 illus on 24 plates, 17 diagrams & 74 bibliogr. notes & a la. historical folded map by F. H. Stingemore, showing opening dates of lines, extensions and stations, with 10 insets.
Period, 1922–1972.

8715 BRUCE, J. G. The Big Tube: a short illustrated history of London's Great Northern & City Railway. London: London Transport, 1976. pp. 56, with 37 illus & 6 maps.

8716 LEE, C. E. The East London Line & the Thames Tunnel. Westminster: London Transport, 1976. pp. 24, with 25 illus on 12 plates, map & 2 illus in text. Cover title: The East London Line and the Thames Tunnel: a brief history.

8717 HARRIS, C. M. What's in a name?: the origins of station names on the London Underground. Tunbridge Wells: Midas Books, in association with London Transport, 1977. pp. 96.
Historical details and opening dates.

8718 PENNICK, N. Tunnels under London. Cambridge: Fenris-Wolf Publications, 1980. la. 8°. pp. 27, with 15 maps, plans & drawings & a bibliography (50+ sources). Text extends onto p. [3] of covers.
—— 2nd edn. Fenris-Wolf, March 1981. la. 8°. pp. 24; 16 maps, plans & drawings; bibliography (47+ sources).
—— 3rd edn. Cambridge: Electric Traction Publications, August 1981. 8°. pp. 28, with 5 illus, 17 drawings, 5 maps, 2 plans & a gradient profile.
Includes information on war-time Tube shelters and abandoned tube tunnels.

Contemporaneous

8719 LONDON MAIN TRUNK UNDERGROUND RLY. Statement for the promoters. [London]: printed by Butler for the solicitors handling the Bill, Martin & Leslie, 1864. pp. [3]. On reverse: Statement in support of Mr. Ayton's motion for Friday the 15th of April, 1864.
A proposed underground line for the East End of London.

8720 LUIGGI, L. La nuova ferrovia elettrica sotterranea di Londra. Roma: Typografia del Genio Civile, 1891. pp. 20 & folded plate with 12 engineering diagrams, incl. map, plan & section of the borings and of the locomotive. Extract from Giornale del Genio Civile, 1891.
The City & South London Rly.

8721 WEBB, S. The London programme. London: Swan Sonnenschein, 1891. pp. viii, 218.
pp. 73–85, 'London's tramways', with 2 tables. The plight of grossly under-paid and over-worked tramwaymen in London.
Urges the adoption of the eleven tramway companies by the London County Council.

8722 CHARING Cross, Euston and Hampstead Railway no.1 & no.3 Bills: Edgware and Hampstead Railway Bill. Memorandum prepared on behalf of the committee representing a large body of inhabitants of Hampstead and the neighbourhood. Signed on behalf of the committee, 'Samuel Figgis, chairman, Montagu Grove, Hampstead, 20th December, 1901'. pp. [4]. Printed. No imprint, but 'Session 1902' printed in the top l.h. corner of the first page indicates that the memorandum was directed to Members of Parliament.
LU (THC)

8723 CENTRAL LONDON RLY. East to West: London's new connecting link. [London: C.L.R. 1912]. 4 leaves with folded plan at end. Title on cover only.
A publicity brochure. The extension from the Bank to Liverpool Street station.

8724 MACKENZIE, HOLLAND AND WESTINGHOUSE POWER SIGNAL COMPANY. The re-signalling of the Central London Railway. London: the Company, [1914]. pp. 20, with illus.
Reprinted from the Railway Gazette, 12 June 1914.

8725 UNDERGROUND ELECTRIC RAILWAYS COMPANY OF LONDON. Typical examination papers for operating staff. London: the Company, [1920]. pp. [44]. Separate papers bound into a single volume with the above title printed on a label on the cover. Certificates of proficiency, to be signed by trainer and trainee, are inserted.

The papers are for motormen, conductors (these vary for individual lines), gatemen, liftmen, ticket collectors, porters and booking clerks.   LU (THC)

8726 LONDON TRANSPORT. Signal aspects. *London: L.T.*, June 1954. obl. format. pp. 31, with col. diagrams.
A manual for motormen.

8727 LONDON TRANSPORT. The Victoria Line (London's new tube). [*London*]: *Bayard Press, for London Transport*, [1965?]. sm. 8°. pp. [16], with 9 illus, 2 maps & 2 diagrams.
An advance publicity brochure.

8728 FOLLENFANT, H. G. Underground railway construction. [*London*]: *London Transport*, 1968. pp. 26, with 23 illus on 12 plates, 4 diagrams & a table of engineering standards for railway construction in London.
Author writes as Chief Civil Engineer, London Transport.

8729 FOSTER, C. D. and BEESLEY, M. E. The Victoria Line, *in* Transport: selected readings, edited by Denys Munby (1968). pp. 223–44, with 2 tables & 25 notes.
The findings of a study to estimate the gains and losses to be expected from the proposed tube railway.

8730 DAY, J. R. The story of the Victoria Line. *London: London Transport*, 1969. sm. 8°. pp. 121, with map (frontis), 34 illus on 16 plates, 3 layout plans & a diagram.
—— 2nd edn. *London Transport*, 1972. sm. 8°. pp. 127; map, 35 illus on 16 plates, 3 l.p.s. & a diagram.

8731 LONDON TRANSPORT. The Victoria Line: a pictorial guide; published on the occasion of the opening of the line by Her Majesty the Queen. [*London*]: *L.T.*, March 1969. la. obl. format. pp. 47 with ca. 120 illus (20 col.), incl. maps & facsimiles, & dimensioned drawings of rolling stock on end papers.
The planning, design, construction and opening of the Victoria Line.

8732 LONDON TRANSPORT. Victoria Line: tile motifs. *London: L.T.*, [1969]. sm. 8° format. A printed folder opening to 16 concertina pages.
'Twelve motifs, one from each of the twelve Victoria Line stations now open, in full colour'. A brief description with the artist's name accompanies each illustration.

8733 LONDON TRANSPORT. The Brixton extension of the Victoria Line . . . *London: London Transport*, July 1971. pp. 43, with 20 illus (10 col.), & 3 maps (1 on end paper).

8734 LONDON TRANSPORT. Victoria Line Traffic Study: a report on the traffic implications of the Victoria Line north of Victoria. *London: London Transport Executive*, 1973. tall 8°. pp. 44, with tables & notes as Appendices A to Q and 2 la. folded maps; one general, and the other showing the effects of the Victoria

Line on the traffic density of other railways in the vicinity.

8735 BROOKS, D. Race and Labour in London Transport. *London: Oxford University Press, for the Institute of Race Relations and the Acton Society Trust*, 1975. pp. xxii, 389, with 87 tables, 5 diagrams, a questionnaire and a bibliography (ca. 140 sources). Index, pp. 381–9.
Chaps. 7–10 (pp. 123–237), The Railway Operating Department.

8736 WHITING, J. London Transport Scrapbook for 1975. *Stanmore: Capital Transport*, 1976. pp. 56, with 131 illus (4 col.).
Includes underground railways.
—— London Transport Scrapbook for 1976. *Capital Transport*, 1977. pp. 68, with 233 illus.
—— London Transport Scrapbook for 1978. *Capital Transport*, 1979. pp. 95, with 224 illus.

8737 LONDON TRANSPORT. The Jubilee Line . . . *London: L.T. Executive*, 1979. obl. 8°. pp. [30], with 24 illus (22 col.), 2 maps (1 col. & 1 on both covers), & a plan.
'Published by London Transport on the occasion of the opening of the Jubilee Line by HRH The Prince of Wales, 30 April, 1979.' A commemorative brochure issued on the opening of stage one of the new line, from Baker St to Charing Cross (operationally, from Stanmore to Charing Cross).

Rolling stock

8738 BAKER, W. S. G. Modern electric rolling stock for urban operation. Great Western Railway (London) Lecture & Debating Society, meeting on 14th October 1937, no. 313. pp. 8, with discussion.
Author, Chief Mechanical Engineer, London Transport.

8739 LONDON TRANSPORT. Underground Centenary; display of rolling stock at Neasden depot, Saturday May 25 and Sunday May 26, 1963. [*London: Bayard Press, for London Transport*, 1963.] pp. [8], with 11 illus. Title on cover.
Illustrations of the 11 exhibits, with notes.

8740 BRUCE, J. G. Tube trains under London: a short illustrated history of London Transport tube rolling stock. *London: London Transport*, 1968. obl. format. pp. [8], 114, with 109 illus.
—— rev. edn. *London Transport*, January 1972. pp. 116, with 111 illus, incl. 2 maps at end.
—— [3rd edn]. . . . including Heathrow Airport and Fleet Line trains. enl. & completely rev. edn. *London Transport*, 1977. pp. [viii], 133, with 122 illus, incl. 2 maps; 4 tables.

8741 BRUCE, J. G. Steam to silver: an illustrated history of London Transport railway surface rolling stock. *Westminster: London Transport*, 1970. obl. format. pp. 169, with 147 illus.

8742 HARDY, B. London Underground rolling stock. *Stanmore: Capital Transport*, 1976. pp. 76, with 56 illus & many stock lists.
Cars and unit formations in current use.
—— 2nd edn. *Capital Transport*, 1977. pp. 88, with 79 illus & many lists.
—— 3rd edn. *Capital Transport*, 1978. pp. 95, with 88 illus & many lists.
—— 4th edn. *Capital Transport*, 1979. pp. 96, with 210 illus & many lists.
—— 5th edn. *Capital Transport*, 1980. pp. 112, with 94 illus & many lists.

8743 HEAPS, C. S. London Transport Railways Album. *London: Ian Allan*, 1978. pp. 96. Intro (pp. 5–7) & 166 illus with detailed accompanying notes.
Past and present railway scenes.

8744 LONDON Transport rolling stock & locomotives. *London: Ian Allan*, 1978. (ABC Series). pp. 64, with 42 illus & many lists.
Tube, surface and service stock, historical, contemporary and preserved.

D 5   Minitrams (proposed)

8745 WESTMINSTER CITY COUNCIL. An aid to pedestrian movement. *London: the Council*, 1971. la. 8°. pp. x, 62, with 31 illus, maps & diagrams.
Report by a working party on the introduction of a new mode of transport in Central London, published as a consultation document prior to consideration by the authorities concerned. An elevated trackway from Waterloo Station to Oxford Circus and to the Covent Garden area, with 'mini-tram' vehicles.

8746 WAGER, D. and FRISCHMANN, W. West End minirail: a preliminary study for a fine-mesh transport system in central areas; with particular reference to the West End of London. *London: Construction Publications*, 1967. obl. format. pp. 13, with numerous maps, diagrams, & a sketch drawing.

E 5   Station architecture

8747 RESEARCH INSTITUTE FOR CONSUMER AFFAIRS. London stations: a user's assessment. *London: the Institute*, 1963. (Essays & Enquiries, 3). pp. 40, with 2 tables, 2 sketch maps & a plan.
Compiled with the co-operation of Michael Owen, with sections by Christopher Martin and Brian Richards.

8748 BRITISH RAILWAYS. LONDON MIDLAND REGION. The new Euston Station, 1968. *London: B.R.(LMR)*, 1968. la. 8°. pp. [30], with 30 illus (5 col.), map, col. plans. Inside front cover is inserted a four-page programme of the official opening by H.M. The Queen, 14th October 1968.

8749 EUSTON Station: a special report to mark today's opening by the Queen. *London: The Times*, October 14, 1968. pp. iv, with 9 illus.

8750 SIMMONS, J. St Pancras Station. *London: Allen & Unwin*, 1968. la. 8°. pp. 120, with 51 illus on 24 plates, 359 notes & (pp. 114–5), 'Passenger traffic and working expenses, 1872–1922', a table of annual figures in 5 columns.
A detailed study of the conception, building and subsequent career of the station as a great London railway terminus and its significance now as an established feature of London's architectural heritage.

8751 SMITHSON, A. and SMITHSON, P. The Euston Arch and the growth of the London Midland & Scottish Railway; foreword by Nikolaus Pevsner. *London: Thames and Hudson*, 1968. la. obl. format. pp. [72], with many illus, facsimiles & maps relating to the construction of Euston Station, its history, and its destruction in the 1960s.
A memorial to the 'Old' Euston: a vigorous outcry against the senseless destruction of an outstanding monument to 19th century achievement and a protest also against the obduracy of an official decision made in the face of widespread contrary opinion. (See *Architectural Review*, April 1962, pp. 234–8).

8752 CAMP, J. Discovering London railway stations, being a brief history of London's more important railway stations, together with details of passenger traffic and usage at the present day. *Tring: Shire Publications*, 1969. sm. 8°. pp. 55, with 16 illus on 8 plates (pp. 33–40) & a 6-column table of traffic statistics (pp. 54–5).

8753 JACKSON, A. A. London's termini. *Newton Abbot: David & Charles*, 1969. pp. 368, with col. frontis, 43 illus on 24 plates, 28 plans & a map; list of opening dates, 4 tables of traffic statistics, 68 detailed notes & a bibliography (66 sources). Index, pp. 363–8.

8754 SUMMERSON, J. Victorian architecture: four studies in evaluation. *New York & London: Columbia University Press*, 1970. pp. 131.
ch. 2 (pp. 19–46), 'Two Victorian stations': Kings Cross and St Pancras Station & Hotel, with 26 illus + 30 notes (on pp. 121–2).

8755 BETJEMAN, J. and GAY, J. London's historic railway stations, [by] John Betjeman, photographed by John Gay. *London: J. Murray*, 1972. la. 8°. pp. 126, with frontis & 150 illus.
—— re-issued, 1978.

8756 CONNOR, J. and HALFORD, B. L. Forgotten stations of Greater London. *Bracknell: Town & Country Press*, 1972. pp. 48. Lists (station, company, dates of opening and closure), and 32 illus.
—— new edn. *Forge Books*, 1978. pp. 54, with 38 illus on 16 plates, & 6 maps.

8757 SYMES, R. and COLE, D. Railway architecture of Greater London. *Reading: Osprey*, 1973. pp. 128. Intro (pp. 7–15) & 120 drawings of 62 stations and other structures, with commentaries.

A companion work to *Railway Architecture of the South East* (1972) by the same author/artists. The Introduction, like that of the former work, is an historical commentary. Both works achieve more than is usually attainable by photography in conveying style and character.

8758 THORNE, R. Liverpool Street Station [by Robert Thorne]. *London: Academy Editions, for the Greater London Council*, 1978. la. 8°. (London Architectural Monographs). pp. 88, with 56 illus, 16 line drawings, maps & plans & 221 notes.

The station and its Great Eastern Hotel, past and present: its architecture and its operational features and problems.

8759 CLINKER, C. R. Paddington. 1854–1979: an official history of Brunel's famous London railway station in its 125th year. *London: British Railways (W.R.); Bristol: Avon–Anglia*, 1979. pp. 28, with 33 illus, incl. map & plan.

E 6 Locomotives and trains

8760 LONDON Transport locomotives and rolling stock. *London: Ian Allan*, 1966. pp. 72. Text, lists, & illus on 24 plates.
—— *Ian Allan*, [1969]. pp. 64; 30 illus on 16 plates.
—— London Transport rolling stock and locomotives. *Ian Allan*, [1978]. pp. 64; 42 illus.

8761 ALLEN, G. F. London Steam in the 1930s, edited by G. Freeman Allen. *London: Ian Allan*, 1979. pp. 112. Intro & 208 illus with descrs; map on end papers.

Photographs from the Wethersett Collection.

8762 MORRISON, B. London Steam in the fifties. *London: Ian Allan*, 1975. pp. 128. 238 illus with descriptive notes.

G Train services and operation

8763 LONDON TRANSPORT. Silver Jubilee services: a record of train services operated on the occasion of the Silver Jubilee of His Majesty King George V, 6 May 1935. *Westminster: L.T.*, *1935*. la. 8°. pp. [14] incl. covers, with 5 illus, graph, map & train recording dials showing density of trains for each of the six underground lines.

Produced for L.T. staff by the Office of the General Manager (Railways) as a message of appreciation of their 'cheerful and efficient' handling of a record number of 36 million passengers carried on the Underground on the Saturday, Sunday & Monday.

8764 HUTCHINGS, H. T. Railway traffic operation on the London Passenger Transport Board. (Proceedings of the Great Western Railway (London) Lecture & Debating Society, 1946–47, no. 340). pp. 12, with discussion.

8765 LATHAM, C. [Lord Latham]. Efficiency in London Transport. *London: Institute of Public Administration*, 1952. pp. 14.

A lecture by the chairman of London Transport.

8766 BRITISH RAILWAYS. CROSS-LONDON FREIGHT WORKING PARTY. Final report. *London: B.R.*, July 1953. pp. 140, with folded diagrams, gradient profiles & maps. Not published.   LU(THC)

8767 BETT, W. H. The evolution of the all-day facilities and tickets in the London Area. *London: Ticket & Fare Collection Society*, [1955]. pp. 27. Reproduced typescript.

Tram & trolley bus services; period, 3 January 1925 to 12 October 1942.

8768 MINISTRY OF TRANSPORT AND CIVIL AVIATION. COMMITTEE OF INQUIRY INTO LONDON TRANSPORT. Report. *London: H.M.S.O.* Chairman, S. P. Chambers.

part 1, 1955. pp. viii, 121, with 9 appendices, incl. 2 folded maps, folded L.T. admin. chart, financial tables (detailed) for 1948–53, and a table of hours of attendance for sixteen government departments in Central London.

A slip tipped in to face the title-page states: 'Part 2 is of considerable length and is not being printed at present.'

Terms of reference: To inquire into the conduct of the undertaking carried on by the London Transport Executive, with a view to ascertaining what practical measures can be taken by the British Transport Commission and the Executive in order to secure greater efficiency or economy.

8769 McCALL, A. W. London in 1947: the fare and ticket systems of London Transport's buses, trams, trollybuses and coaches. *Luton: Transport Ticket Society*, 1974. pp. 29, with tables. Reproduced typescript.

8770 LEONARD, A. A Chronology of Passenger Stations in the Greater London Area. *Croydon: A. Leonard*, 1980. pp. [70]. Intro, 3-column chronological and 6-column alphabetical listings for over 600 stations, with additional sections on London termini, and BR Regions in the GLC area; a bibliography (44 sources). Cover title. A Chronology of Railway Stations in Greater London.

K Social aspects
Historical

8771 MACASSEY, L. The evolution of the London traffic problem. Great Western Railway (London) Lecture & Debating Society, meeting on 7th February 1924 (no. 168). pp. 19, with discussion.

8772 MOORE, M. L. A century's extension of passenger transport facilities (1830–1930) within the present London Transport Board's area, and its relation to population spread. Thesis, Ph.D., University of London, 1948.

8773 POLLINS, H. Transport lines and social divisions, *in* London: aspects of change (Centre for Urban Studies, Report no. 3, 1964), pp. 29–61, with 65 bibliogr. notes.

The history of transport in London and the developing pattern of class and area in relation to the provision of routes (trains, underground, tram & bus). Social ecology and planning.

8774 JACKSON, A. A. Semi-detached London: suburban development, life and transport, 1900–39. *London: Allen & Unwin*, 1973. pp. 381, with 53 illus on 24 plates, 8 maps, 2 graphs, numerous footnotes, 6 appendices (including chronologies of railway and tramway development) and an evaluative bibliography (pp. 361–9).

8775 HEPBURN, D. R. C. Analysis of changes in rail commuting to Central London, 1966–71. *Crowthorne: Transport & Road Research Laboratory*, 1977. (Supplementary Report SR 268). tall format. pp. 12, with 6 tables & a bibliography (7 sources).

Contemporaneous

8776 COMMUNIST PARTY OF GREAT BRITAIN. LONDON DISTRICT TRAMWAYMEN'S COMMITTEE. The London County trams and the traffic combine: the coming struggle: report on the financial position and the tramworkers' claims. *London: C.P.G.B.*, [1925]. pp. 8.
Text headed: 'Report on the financial position of the London County tramways.'
The case for nationalisation and municipalisation of the tramways expressed by tramwaymen as distinct from 'Labour movement theorists'.

8777 MORTON, H. V. From Bow to Ealing *in his* The Heart of London (*Methuen*, 1925), pp. 133–6.
A journey in the motorman's cab of an underground train on the District Line.

8778 MINISTRY OF TRANSPORT. LONDON AND HOME COUNTIES TRAFFIC ADVISORY COMMITTEE. Omnibus competition with tramways. *London: H.M.S.O.*, 1926. pp. 16. (Chairman: Sir Henry P. Maybury).

8779 MORTON, H. V. The Last Tube, *in his* The Spell of London (*Methuen*, 1926), pp. 209–13.
Observations on home-going passengers, Northern Line, London Underground.

8780 MORTON, H. V. When the 'Tubes' stop, *in his* The Nights of London (*Methuen*, 1926), pp. 11–15.
Night life on London Underground: the maintenance workers.

8781 MINISTRY OF TRANSPORT. LONDON AND HOME COUNTIES TRAFFIC ADVISORY COMMITTEE. Report . . . to the Minister of Transport giving particulars of a scheme for the co-ordination of passenger transport facilities in the London Traffic Area. *London: H.M.S.O.*, 1927. pp. 12. (Chairman: Sir Henry P. Maybury).

8782 DOWNTON, A. The London Transport scandal. *London: Communist Party, London District Committee*, June 1936. pp. 30.
Alleged discontent of the people of London with passenger transport services, and also among the Board's employees; suggestions for improvement.

8783 MINISTRY OF TRANSPORT. RAILWAY (LONDON PLAN) COMMITTEE, 1944. [Future of railway terminals in London north of the Thames]. *London: H.M.S.O.* (Chairman: Sir Charles Inglis).
Interim report, 1946. pp. 26, with 3 la. folded maps in pocket.
Final report, 1948. pp. iv, 8.
Recommendations on the future of the Railway terminals in London north of the Thames, except those of the Southern Rly (BR(SR)), and of freight traffic and distribution within the context of the City of London Plan, 1943.

8784 TABER, T. T. Some information, observations and conclusions concerning the handling of London's half-million daily commuters by railroad in 1961: a study . . . *Morristown (New Jersey): Board of Public Transportation of Morris County*, 1962. pp. 57, with 33 illus & line drawings, 3 tables & 2 maps.

8785 LONDON AND HOME COUNTIES ELECTRIC TRACTION SOCIETY. Greater London Railway Guide. *London: the Society*, March 1963. pp. 52, with 1 illus & 2 folded maps.
A guide to passenger rail facilities in the area.

8786 SAVE THE BROAD STREET—RICHMOND LINE HAMPSTEAD COMMITTEE. Hampstead and the Broad Street line: a report. *London: the Committee*, [1964]. pp. 51, with 9 tables, 7 illus, 2 diagrams & 2 maps inside covers.

8787 HUTCHINGS, K. Urban transport: public or private? *London: Fabian Society*, 1967. (Fabian Research Series, 261). pp. 24.
The problem in London, primarily.

8788 LAZARUS, D. Freeing London's gluepot. *London: Conservative Political Centre*, May 1967. (C.P.C., no. 366). pp. 32, with map.
Includes railways.

8789 THOMAS, R. Journeys to work. *London: Political & Economic Planning*, 1968. (P.E.P. Broadsheet, no. 504) (Planning, vol. xxxiv). pp. 419–535, with ca. 100 notes & 20 tables. Title from cover.
Much of the work relates to commuting in London.

8790 BALINT, M. Railheading Study: phase 1. *London: Greater London Council, Dept of Highways & Transportation, Transportation Branch*, June 1969. (Research Memoranda, 162). pp. [28]. Reproduced typescript.
Road–rail (park & ride) usage simulated to discover the best journey-to-work routes.

8791 OPSTAD, C. T. The journey to work in the London region. Thesis, Ph.D., University of London (U.C.L.), 1970.
Transport and transport planning in Greater London during the 1960s. Includes surface and underground railways.

8792 SAFAVI, H. A. and STANNARD, R. B. Rail commuting to Central London. *London: Greater London Council, Dept. of Planning & Transportation, Research & Intelligence*

Unit, February, 1970. (Research Memoranda, 225). pp. 14, iii. Reproduced typescript.
Work trips to Central London by rail from places beyond Greater London.

8793 PHILLIPS, J. Travel facilities for the disabled. [Caption title]. [*London: London Transport Passengers Committee*, 1971]. pp. 3, & 5 pp. tables. Reproduced typescript.
A memorandum for wheel-chair passengers on London Underground.

8794 CROWTHER, G. L., VICKERS, P. H. and PILLING, A. D. A new Ring Rail for London: the key to an integrated public transport system. *London: Just & Co.*, March 1973, obl. 8°. pp. xii, 67, with frontis, 5 photographs, 29 drawings, diagrams & maps, with 21 additional diagrams of proposed layouts of interchange points.
—— Supplement, 1974. pp. [2] (text & revised map).

8795 A GUIDE to London's Underground Stations for the handicapped person . . . , produced by a group of physically-handicapped children from Cloudesley School in London . . . *London: Central Council for the Disabled*, [1973]. pp. 32, with map.
An alphabetical table in 6 columns, and notes to facilitate interchanging.

8796 LLEWELYN-DAVIES, WEEKS, FORESTIER-WALKER and BOR. S.E. London and the Fleet Line: a study of land use potential carried out for London Transport Executive. [*London: the firm*], 1973. pp. xiv, 172, with many illus, plans, maps & diagrams. Spiral binding.
Transport and land use planning based on the location of stations on the proposed line to New Cross Gate and to Lewisham, in South East London.

8797 SARICKS, C. L. Commuter choice and station catchment areas in metropolitan rail transport, with special reference to the London region. Thesis, M.Phil., University of London, 1973.

8798 TRANSPORT 2000. LONDON & HOME COUNTIES COMMITTEE. A transport strategy for London. *Transport 2000*, [1973?]. pp. 20, with 4 maps & 3 diagrams.
Includes a proposal for a 'Ring-Rail' around London.

8799 COLLINS, M. F. and PHAROAH, T. M. Transport organisation in a big city: the case of London; foreword by W. A. Robson. *London: Allen & Unwin for the London School of Economics*, 1974. pp. 660, with 45 tables, 24 diagrams, maps & plans and many notes.
The effects of economic, social & political change over the past 40 years upon passenger transport operation in London. Includes a series of 15 case studies by sociologists of the Greater London Group of the L.S.E. An historical survey (pp. 23–44) precedes the main work.

8800 LONDON Rail Study. [*London]: Greater London Council; Department of the Environment*. (Chairman, Sir David Barran). 2 vols.
'The Study Team was drawn from the four bodies concerned with London's railways: the British Railways Board, Department of the Environment, the Greater London Council and the London Transport Executive.'
pt. 1: 1974. pp. 44, with 8 folded col. maps, 4 tables, & col. plans. An abridged version containing the essential arguments and data, and the Study Team's conclusions.
pt. 2: 1974. pp. 118, [24] folded leaves, col. illus, col. plans. The full report.

8801 ROBERTS, J. R. S. Ringrail reviewed: a new outer circle for London. [*London]: Just & Co.*, March 1974. (Ringrail Publication, 3). tall 8°. pp. 79, with 19 maps & diagrams, & a bibliography (19 sources).

8802 STURT, A. R. Spatial aspects of commuting to Central London, 1951–66. Thesis, Ph.D., University of London (L.S.E.), 1974.
ch. 7 (pp. 242–308), 'Rail accessibility and commuting to Central London', with 60 notes, tables & a map.

8803 SAVE PUBLIC TRANSPORT CAMPAIGN COMMITTEE. Save our public transport services: background briefing material. *London: the Committee*, December 1976. pp. 14.
pp. 4–9, London Transport; pp. 10–12, British Rail [in London].

N Posters

8804 LONDON TRANSPORT. London Transport posters [presented, with an historical commentary and notes] by Michael F. Levey, with an introduction by Roy Strong. *London: Phaidon Press*; *London Transport*, 1976. la. 8°. pp. [16], 80.
80 illustrations (64 in col.) being reproductions of L.T. and earlier (i.e. pre-1933) posters. A different work with the same title was published by London Transport in 1963 (*See* 756 or 7457).

Q Preservation

8805 LONDON TRANSPORT. The London Transport Collection of Historical Relics at Syon Park. 1973. pp. 8. Reproduced typescript.
A descriptive list of the exhibits, for visitors.

8806 LONDON TRANSPORT. The London Transport Collection, Syon Park, Brentford, Middlesex. [*London: L.T.*, 1976]. obl. format. pp. [24], with 64 illus (62 col.) & a diagram.
Includes tramcars and locomotives.

Hampshire 8807–18

8807 HAMPSHIRE ARCHIVISTS GROUP. Transport in Hampshire and the Isle of Wight: a guide to the records. *Winchester: the Group*, 1973. la. 8°. pp. 126.
Includes railways and tramways.

8808 RAILWAY CORRESPONDENCE & TRAVEL SOCIETY. Itinerary of the Hampshire and

West Sussex Rail Tour, 'The Hampshireman'
. . ., Sunday, 6th February, 1955. *R.C. &
T.S.*, [1955]. pp. 4, with map, schedule &
notes by A. E. Hurst & J. R. Fairman.
   Waterloo—Hounslow—Chertsey—Woking—
Guildford—Cranleigh—Horsham—Pulborough—
Midhurst—Petersfield—Havant—Fareham—West
Meon—Alton—Aldershot—Frimley—
Farnborough—Waterloo.

8809 VINE, P. A. L. London's lost route to
Basingstoke: the story of the Basingstoke
Canal. *Newton Abbot: David & Charles*,
1968. (Canal History Series). pp. 212, with
col. frontis, 41 illus on 20 plates, & in text, 16
illus, 11 maps, a chronology, 167 notes & 5
appendices, incl. a bibliography (44 sources).
   Index has 14 page refs under 'Railways' incl. (pp.
108–16), the London & Southampton Rly.

8810 COURSE, E. Portsmouth railways. *Portsmouth: Portsmouth City Council*, 1969.
(Portsmouth Papers, 6). pp. 26, with 14 illus,
incl. 3 maps, 2 plans, & 2 facsimiles.

8811 COOPER, F. W. The AGWI Refinery railway: an account of the narrow gauge railway
at the Fawley (Hants) refinery of the AGWI
Petroleum Corporation Ltd. *Surbiton: Narrotrack Ltd*, 1973. pp. 24, with 20 illus, lists, & a
detailed plan.

8812 ALLCOCK, G. A. Gosport's railway era.
*Gosport: Gosport Historical Records &
Museum Society*, 1975. la. 8°. pp. 60, with 25
illus (incl. 2 maps), & a bibliography (35
sources).

8813 ELLIS, M. Hampshire industrial archaeology: a guide, edited by Monica Ellis. [*Southampton*]: *Southampton University Industrial
Archaeology Group*, 1975. pp. 52, with illus.
   pp. 27–33, Bridges, electric tramways, and railways, including military and industrial systems.

8814 LEWIS, C. The Mid-Hants 'Watercress'
Line: a brief history. [*Alresford*]: *Mid-Hants
Railway Preservation Society*, [1975]. pp. 20,
with 10 illus & 2 on covers, & a map.
   The revived Winchester & Alton line of the
former L & SWR.
—— [3rd edn]. 1977. pp. 20; 10 & 2 illus,
map.
—— [5th edn]. September 1978. pp. 20; 10 &
2 illus (1 col.), map.
—— enlarged edn [7th]. August 1980. pp. 32;
22 illus (1 col.), map.

8815 LAY, R. W. The Docks Explorer [Railtour],
Saturday 13th March, 1976. *Wimbledon: B.R.
(SR), South West Division*, [1976]. pp. 20.
   Itinerary with 2 plans, & a route chart alongside
the text. Compiled & drawn by Ron W. Lay. Copies
distributed only to those taking part in the tour.
   Waterloo—Richmond—Reading Central
Goods—Basingstoke—Winchester—Southampton
Docks—Millbrook—Eastleigh—Romsey—
Salisbury—Wilton—Andover—Ludgershall—
Andover—Basingstoke—Weybridge—Surbiton—
Wimbledon—Waterloo.

8816 LAY, R. W. The Anniversaries Rail Tour,
Sunday 10 July, 1977. *Wimbledon: B.R. (SR),
South Western Division*, [1977]. pp. 20.
   Itinerary, with route chart alongside text, & (pp.
13–20), historical notes. Compiled & drawn by Ron
W. Lay. Copies distributed only to those taking part
in the tour.
   Waterloo—Wimbledon—Guildford New Line—
Petersfield—Havant—Fareham—Southampton—
Romsey—Salisbury—Romsey—Eastleigh—
Southampton—Bournemouth—Weymouth—
Bournemouth—Southampton—Winchester—
Basingstoke—Weybridge—Wimbledon—Waterloo.

8817 MID-HANTS RAILWAY PRESERVATION
SOCIETY. The Mid-Hants 'Watercress Line':
stock list (July 1977 issue). *Alresford: the
Society*, [1977]. pp. [7].
—— 1979 [i.e. 5th] edn. 1979. pp. [28], with
21 illus & cover illus. An errata slip mounted
inside cover.
—— 1979 [5th] edn reprinted with minor
corrections, with a slip pasted onto cover: '5th
edition revised, 1979'.

8818 POPPLEWELL. L. Railway competition in
Central Southern England, 1830–1914. *Fern-
down: Melledgen Press*, 1978. tall 8°. pp. 29,
with map on cover. Reproduced typescript.
   A study of the territorial tactics of the LSWR and
the LBSCR, and to some extent the GWR, in the
battle for the approach routes to Southampton and
Portsmouth.

Sussex (East Sussex and West Sussex) 8819–41

8819 NEWTON, S. C. Rails across the Weald, by
S. C. Newton, County Archivist. *Lewes: East
Sussex County Council*, 1972. (East Sussex
Record Office Handbooks, 4). pp. 26, with 1
illus & a map.
   Archive material available for local railway his-
tory research; pp. 12–26, a chronological list of
deposited plans.

8820 BISHOP, J. G. A Peep into the Past:
Brighton in the olden time, with glances at
the present. *Brighton: the author*, 1880. la. 8°.
pp. 390, with 28 illus.
   pp. 251–67, 'The railway and its growth', with a
detailed chronological table of the LBSCR network,
1835–79, & 4 other tables.

8821 VOLK, M. Volk's Electric Railway and how
it is worked: particulars of the Brighton
electric railway, by Magnus Volk. [Facsimile
of 7th edn, ca. 1894]. *Farnborough* [*Hants*]:
*Light Railway Transport League (London
Area) & Conrad Volk*, 1972. pp. 8, with 3
illus.

8822 CHAMBERS, G. F. East Bourne memories
of the Victorian period, 1895 to 1901 . . .
Eastbourne: V. T. Sumfield, 1910. pp. xv,
304, with 98 illus.
   ch. 11 (pp. 122–43), 'Railways and travelling',
including references to various proposed railways in
Sussex.

8823 MAIDSTONE AND DISTRICT MOTOR SER-
VICES. Hail & Farewell! . . . *Maidstone:*

M. & D.M.S., [1959]. pp. 24, with 16 illus.
pp. 4–11, The tramway era, 1905–1928, with 7 illus. The Hastings Tramway Co's line from Hastings to Bexhill, worked by the Dolter system of current collection until 1921.

8824 RAILWAY CORRESPONDENCE & TRAVEL SOCIETY. Itinerary of the Sussex Special Rail Tour . . . , Sunday, 7th October, 1962. *R.C. & T.S.*, [1962]. pp. 4, with map & schedule. Text by J. Pulford and R. Kirkby.
London Bridge—Brighton—Seaford—Brighton—Horsham—Sutton—Peckham Rye—London Bridge.

8825 POORE, G. The railways of East Grinstead. *East Grinstead: The Imberhorne Advertiser*, [the magazine of Imberhorne County Secondary School], [1964]. pp. 10, with 7 illus., diagrams, map & plan. Reproduced typescript.
Written by a school-boy, with help from another, Anthony Shonfeld, and from Roger Norgate who did the illustrations. The text ends with 'An open letter to Dr. Beeching' by J. Diffey, about the threatened closure of the East Grinstead to Three Bridges line. The work is introduced by J. Whittle of the teaching staff.

8826 BLUEBELL RLY. Guidebook to the Bluebell Railway (written and compiled by T. C. Cole). [*Sheffield Park*]: *Bluebell Rly*, [1966]. pp. 22, with 16 illus. Title on cover only. Text extends onto covers.
—— Guidebook, 1969, by Terry Cole. 1969. pp. 22, incl. covers, with 18 illus, stock list & timetable.
—— Guide to the Bluebell Railway, by T. Cole. 197–?. pp. 16, with 11 col. illus & stock list; map, additional text & 2 more col. illus on covers.
—— A Guide to the Bluebell Railway. 1980. pp. 16, incl. covers, with 12 col. illus & a stock list.

8827 BUCKMAN, J. C. The locational effects of a railway closure: a case study of the withdrawal of passenger services from the Steyning line in March, 1966. Thesis, M.Sc., University of Bristol, 1972–3.
The Horsham to Shoreham line.

8828 BEAUVAIS, A. J. and MARX, K. A journey through the Weald of Sussex on the Bluebell Railway, and stock list. 2nd edn, revised by H. May and J. I. Hatch. [*Sheffield Park*]: *Bluebell Rly*, [1969?]. pp. 8, with 4 illus.

8829 RYA. The Rye and Camber tram, by 'Rya'. *Rye: Rye's Own*, [1969]. pp. [6], with 10 illus.
The Rye & Camber Tramways Co., 1895–1939: a reprint of an essay first published in the September 1967 issue of *Rye's Own*.

8830 COLE, T. C. Bluebell Railway: steaming on! [*Sheffield Park: Bluebell Rly Preservation Society*], May 1970. pp. 32, incl. covers, with 24 illus, map & gradient profile.
A history and description of the line and its rejuvenation by the B.R.P.S., with a detailed description of the stock.

—— 2nd edn, May 1971. pp. 36, incl. covers; 30 illus, map & gradient profile.

8831 MUSGRAVE, C. Life in Brighton from the earliest times to the present. *London: Faber*, 1970. pp. 503, with illus.
part IV, ch. 5 (pp. 258–72), 'The railway, 1820 to 1960'; *et passim*.
—— rev. edn. *Rochester: Rochester Press*, 1981. pp. 522. (pp. 258–72).

8832 VOLK, C. Magnus Volk of Brighton. *London & Chichester: Phillimore*, 1971. pp. xi, 240, with 23 illus on 16 plates & a bibliography (82 sources).

8833 MARX, K. Famous Fenchurch, 1872–1972. *Sheffield Park Station: Bluebell Railway Preservation Society*, [1972]. pp. 34, with 30 illus & a map.
A detailed history of the ex-L.B.S.C.R. 'Terrier' class 0–6–0 tank locomotive no. 72, now in service on the Bluebell Rly.

8834 MARX, K. The Adams radial tank no. 488. [*Sheffield Park*]: *Bluebell Railway Preservation Society*, [1973]. pp. 19, with 14 illus, 1 sectional drawing. Text & illustrations extend onto covers.

8835 ESAU, M. The Bluebell Railway: a pictorial impression; introduction by Johnny Morris. *Ipswich: Boydell Press*, 1975. pp. 16, with 153 illus (26 col.) on 80 plates, list of locos & rolling stock, map inside cover.
pp. 6–12, 'From the footplate' by David White.

8836 CLARK, P. The railways of Devil's Dyke. *Sheffield: Turntable Publications*, 1976. (Minor Railways of Britain series). pp. 69, with folded plate (diagrams), 29 illus, 2 maps, & 5 appendices.
The Brighton & Dyke Rly, also the Aerial Cableway, and the Brighton Dyke Steep Grade Railway.

8837 COLE, T. The Bluebell Railway's historic collection of locomotives, coaches and goods vehicles. *Oxford: Oxford Publishing Co.*, [1976]. pp. 51, with 43 illus. Title & Contents on p. [2] of cover; stock list on p. [3] of cover.
Detailed descriptions with historical commentaries.

8838 ESAU, M. Bluebell Steam in action. *Sheffield Park Station: Bluebell Rly*, [1978]. sm. obl. format. pp. [32]. Intro & 32 illus with descrs. Cover has additional text & 1 illus. Title from cover.

8839 MARX, K. Bluebell Line Historical Album, 1879–1965, by Klaus Marx, archivist to the Bluebell Railway Preservation Society. *Sheffield Park: Bluebell Rly*, 1978. pp. 64, with 52 illus.

8840 HOARE, J. Sussex railway architecture: an historical survey. *Hassocks: Branch Line (Harvester Press)*, 1979. pp. 109, with frontis, 99 illus, a map & a bibliography (8 sources).

8841 BLUEBELL RLY. Bluebell Steam in retrospect. *Sheffield Park Station: Bluebell Rly Preservation Society*, 1980. la. 8°. pp. [112]. Intro & 217 & 10 illus with descrs.
Photographs to commemorate 20 years of operation.

Surrey 8842–48

For the outer London suburban areas of the Home Counties see also the subdivision of C 1 c for London and Greater London, 8592–8806

8842 STEVENSON, W. General view of the agriculture of the county of Surrey; drawn up for the consideration of the Board of Agriculture and Internal Improvement. *London: Sherwood, Neely & Jones*, 1813. [Reproduced on microfiche by EP Microform Ltd, East Ardsley, 1978].
p. 252 (2 paragraphs) & p. 556 (1 paragraph), descriptions of the Surrey Iron Railway.

8843 RAILWAY CORRESPONDENCE & TRAVEL SOCIETY. Itinerary of the Bisley Tramway and North West Surrey Rail Tour, 23rd November 1952, with notes by J. R. Fairman. *R.C. & T.S.*, [1952]. pp. 4, with map, 2 illus & a schedule.
Bisley Tramway—a short branch railway from Brookwood to Bisley Camp.

8844 RAILWAY CORRESPONDENCE & TRAVEL SOCIETY. Itinerary of the Sapper Rail Tour . . . , Saturday, 4th October, 1958. *R.C. & T.S.*, [1958]. pp. 4, with 1 illus, map & schedule. Notes by R. C. Riley.
London (Waterloo)—Guildford—Haslemere—Liss—Longmoor Military Rly—Bentley—Aldershot—Brookwood—Woking—London (Waterloo).

8845 LATHAM, J. B. The locomotives of Croydon Gas & Electricity Works. *Woking: J. B. Latham via Lens of Sutton*, 1970. pp. 24, with 21 illus & 2 plans.

8846 HESELTON, K. Y. Sunbury and the Thames Valley Railway. *Sunbury: Sunbury & Shepperton Local History Society*, 1975. (Periodical Publication, 1). pp. 24, with map, plan & a bibliography (26 sources).

8847 HESELTON, K. Y. The Metropolitan Water Board Light Railway. *Sunbury-on-Thames: Sunbury & Shepperton Local History Society*, 1976. (Occasional Publication, 1). pp. [4], with map. Reproduced typescript. Cover title: Sunbury and the Metropolitan Water Board Light Railway.

8848 TOWNSEND, J. L. Townsend Hook and the railways of the Dorking Greystone Lime Co. Ltd. *Bletchworth: Brockham Museum*, 1980. pp. 36, with 20 illus, 2 maps, 2 dimensioned drawings (composite) & 10 other line illus & facsimiles.
The Fletcher-Jennings 0–4–0 industrial locomotive (1880) that became the foundation exhibit of the Brockham Museum in 1962.

Kent 8849–71

For the outer London suburban areas of the Home Counties see also the subdivision of C 1 for London and Greater London, 8592–8806

8849 CARLEY, J. Public transport timetables, 1838. *Gravesend: Fourteen Pelham Road Ltd.* part 1, Kent and East Sussex. 1971. pp. [24], with folded map at end. Historical introduction and 58 time tables.
Stage coach, mail coach, Thames steamer, carriers' cart and vans, the London & Greenwich Rly and the Canterbury & Whitstable Rly.

8850 ROMNEY, HYTHE & DYMCHURCH RLY. World's smallest railway: Romney, Hythe, Dymchurch & Dungeness. Southern Budget Letter Card; 6 art pictures. [1928 or after].
6 sepia-toned views of the railway folded into a printed wallet with tuck-in flap.

8851 KENT & EAST SUSSEX RLY (1961). Stockbook. 2nd edn, compiled by Roger Crombleholme. 1965. pp. 16, with 11 illus.
—— 1970 edn, compiled by Alan G. Dixon and Arthur E. Loosley. [1970]. pp. 48, with 42 illus. Cover title: Locomotives and stock on the Farmers' Line.
—— another edn. Stockbook . . . , compiled by Alan Dixon and Donald Wilson. [1975 or after]. pp. 48, with 47 illus.

8852 KIDNER, R. W. The Romney, Hythe & Dymchurch Railway. *Lingfield: Oakwood Press*, 1967. (Locomotion Papers, 35). pp. 34, with 37 illus, map, 5 layout plans & 4 appendices.
—— 2nd edn. *Oakwood Press*, 1978. (Locomotion Papers, 35). pp. 36, with 44 illus on 16 plates, map, 9 layout plans & 4 appendices.

8853 SMITH, J. L. Rails to Tenterden: being a pictorial record of the Kent and East Sussex Railway . . . *Sutton: Lens of Sutton*, 1967. pp. [80], with 136 illus, 8 tables, & a map.

8854 BAKER, R. F. Transport in the urban development of Kentish Thames-side since the late eighteenth century. Thesis, M.A., University of London, 1968.
Gravesend, Northfleet and Swanscombe.

8855 BODY, G. and EASTLEIGH, R. L. The Ramsgate Tunnel Railway. *London: Trans-Rail Publications*, [1968]. (Trans–Hist series, 2). tall 8°. pp. [16], with 9 illus & 2 maps.

8856 TAYLOR, M. M. The Davington Light Railway. *Lingfield: Oakwood Press*, 1968. (Locomotion Papers, 40). pp. 19, with 10 illus & 2 drawings on 6 plates (incl. frontis), a map & a plan.
A line from Davington, near Faversham, to Uplees, operated by the Admiralty during the Great War to serve four munitions factories in the area.

8857 RATCLIFFE, R. L. The Bowater Railway, 1906–1969. *Rochester: Locomotive Club of*

Great Britain, [1969]. pp. [20], with 21 illus & a map.

The industrial railway system of Messrs Bowaters United Kingdom Paper Co. of Sittingbourne, Kent, and the adoption of part of the line by the L.C.G.B. (the Sittingbourne & Kemsley Light Rly).

8858 CATT, A. R. The East Kent Railway. *Lingfield: Oakwood Press*, 1970. (Locomotion Papers, 47). pp. 35, with 17 illus on 8 plates, 4 maps, 3 drawings, a gradient profile, 2 appendices and a specimen timetable.

8859 'INVICTA'. The tramways of Kent, by 'Invicta', edited by G. E. Baddeley. *London: Light Railway Transport League, in association with the Tramway & Light Railway Society*. 2 vols.

vol. 1, West Kent. 1971. pp. 176, with frontis, 60 illus, 4 diagrams, 7 maps; bibliography (35 sources); plans & drawings on end papers.

vol. 2, East Kent. 1975. pp. 179–360, with frontis, 95 illus, 7 maps, 4 detailed tables & a bibliography (33 sources); diagrams on end papers.

8860 RATCLIFFE, R. L. The Bowater Railway in pictures, 1906–1970. *Rochester: Locomotive Club of Great Britain*, [1971 or 72]. pp. 16, with 28 illus, map & plan. Text extends onto inside covers.

'Compiled by the Sittingbourne & Kemsley Light Rly and produced by R. L. Ratcliffe.'

8861 GARRETT, S. R. The Kent & East Sussex Railway. *Lingfield: Oakwood Press*, 1972. pp. 44, with 26 illus, 2 maps, 4 station plans, lists & timetables.

8862 STOYEL, B. D. and KIDNER, R. W. Cement railways of Kent. *Lingfield: Oakwood Press*, 1973. (Locomotion Papers, 70). pp. 83, with 85 illus on 24 plates, 13 layout plans & many lists of locomotives.

8863 GRAY, A. Isle of Grain railways. *Lingfield: Oakwood Press*, 1974. (Locomotion Papers, 77). pp. 65, with 25 illus on 12 plates, map & 12 layout plans of stations, junctions and cement works systems.

The North Kent line of the S.E.R., the Hundred of Hoo Rly, the Chattenden & Upnor Rly, the Chattenden Naval Tramway, Francis & Co's cement works and other industrial lines in the area.

8864 DAVIES, W. J. K. The Romney, Hythe & Dymchurch Railway. *Newton Abbot: David & Charles*, 1975. pp. 208, with 35 illus on 16 plates, 15 line drawings, diagrams, gradient profile, timetables, & (pp. 192–203, Appendix 5), 'Atlas of the line', and 26 additional layout plans; bibliography (11 sources).

8865 SITTINGBOURNE & KEMSLEY LIGHT RLY. S.K.L.R. Stockbook and Guide, 1975. *Sittingbourne: S.K.L.R.*, 1975. pp. 32, with 27 illus, map & plan.

8866 WOLFE, C. S. Historical Guide to the Romney, Hythe & Dymchurch Light Railway. *New Romney: R.H. & D.R. Associa-*

tion, 1976. pp. 60, with 45 illus, 6 layout plans, 3 maps, a chronology (pp. 48–53), stock lists & a bibliography (17 sources).

8867 DYER, B. R. Kent railways. *St. Ives (Cornwall): James Pike*, 1977. pp. 32, with 6 illus & 2 maps.

An introductory historical and descriptive account of all railways in the county: public, industrial, preserved, and the R.H. & D. Rly.

8868 TRANSPORT 2000. Passenger trains on the Hoo Peninsular: a feasibility study; summary report produced for Medway Borough Council . . . , statistical tables. *London: Transport 2000*, [1978]. pp. [11]. 10 tables. Title from cover. Text headed: Tables of statistics . . . the restoration of passenger train services on the Hundred of Hoo Peninsular.

8869 CARLEY, J. The Tunbridge Wells, Snodland & Edenbridge Suspension Railway: an abortive scheme of 1825–26, with notes on two more. *Meopham: Meopham Publications*, 1979. pp. 20, with 5 maps, a drawing & a bibliography (6 sources).

Includes as addenda, notes on the Kentish Railway (1825) scheme, and the Penshurst & Tunbridge Wells Tramway scheme of 1832.

8870 KENT & EAST SUSSEX RLY (1961). The Kent & East Sussex Railway Guide, by Simon B. Green. *Tenterden: Tenterden Rly Co.*, 1974. pp. 16, with 21 illus (incl. 6 col. illus on covers), & 2 maps.

—— another edn, by Simon B. Green. *Tenterden: K. & E.S. Rly*, [ca. 1980]. pp. 24, incl. covers, with 16 illus (2 col.), 2 maps, 5 layout plans & a gradient profile.

8871 TENTERDEN ROLLING STOCK GROUP. Carriage and wagon stock on the Kent and East Sussex Railway: a description and history of the 48 carriages and wagons on the railway. *Tenterden: the Group*, 1980. pp. [12]. Reproduced typescript.

Berkshire 8872–75

8872 RAILWAY CORRESPONDENCE & TRAVEL SOCIETY. Itinerary of the Berks & Wilts Rail Tour . . . , Sunday, 9th April, 1961. *R.C. & T.S.*, [1961]. pp. 4, with schedule. Text by M. B. Warburton.

Paddington—Windsor—Reading—Swindon Works —Malmesbury—Highworth—Faringdon— Wallingford—Didcot—Paddington.

8873 HEPPLE, J. R. Abingdon and the G.W.R., or: why the Oxford line missed the town, *in* Journal of Transport History, new series vol 2 (1973–4), pp. 155–66, with 3 maps & 70 notes.

8874 WILKINSON, R. Wantage Tramway: a concise history, illustrated by the author. *Carlisle: the author*, 1974. pp. 40, with 12 illus (drawings) & facsimiles, a map, stocklist, & a bibliography (14 sources).

—— another edn. *Tarrant Hinton: Oakwood Press*, 1976. (Locomotion Papers, 92). pp. 39, with 18 illus on 8 plates, 6 facsimiles, 5 drawings, a map & a bibliography (14 sources).

8875 SOUTH, R. Crown, college and railways: how the railways came to Windsor. *Buckingham: Barracuda Books*, 1978. pp. 136, with frontis, 34 illus, incl. portraits, 8 maps, 7 facsimiles, a chronology & a bibliography (190 sources).

Oxfordshire 8876–81

8876 OXFORDSHIRE COUNTY COUNCIL. A Handlist of Plans, Sections and Books of Reference for the proposed railways in Oxfordshire, 1825–1936. *Oxford: Clerk of the County Council*, 1964. (Record Publication, 3). pp. i, 23.
Compiled by S. G. Baker.

8877 CLARK, G. N. and COLE, G. D. H. The tram strike: a letter to City and University. [*Oxford*, 1913]. pp. 4.
The strike of Oxford tramwaymen, March–April 1913.

8878 GREAT WESTERN SOCIETY. Locomotives and rolling stock of the Great Western Society. *Didcot: G.W.S.*, 1971. obl. format. pp. 17, with 46 illus; text extends onto covers.

8879 COMPTON, H. J. The Oxford Canal. *Newton Abbot: David & Charles*, 1976. (Inland Waterways Histories). pp. 171, with 30 illus on 16 plates, & in text, 16 illus & maps, 155 notes, 2 appendices, & a bibliography (31 sources).
In index, 6 page refs under the names of railway companies.

8880 OXFORDSHIRE Rambler: Morris Cowley, Abingdon, Wallingford, Bicester branches, on Sunday 30th April 1978: a souvenir booklet of photographs depicting local scenes. *Oxford: Oxford Publishing Co.*, [1978]. (Railtour, 3). pp. [15], with 26 illus, map & 4 timetables. Text (pp. 1–2) by Colin Judge.

8881 GREAT WESTERN SOCIETY. Vintage Train. *Didcot: the Society*, 1980. pp. 32, with 52 illus (5 col.)
An illustrated record of the Society's Vintage Train trips (restored carriages) from 1972 to the final one on 26 January 1980.

Buckinghamshire 8882–86

For the outer London suburban areas of the Home Counties see also the subdivision of C 1 c *for London and Greater London, 8592–8806*

8882 HOSKINS, P. J. An Illustrated Guide to the Quainton Railway Centre at Quainton Road Station, nr. Aylesbury, Bucks. *Quainton: the Society*, [1973?]. pp. 26 (incl. covers), with 14 illus & a map.
—— another edn. [1976?]. obl. format. pp. 36 (incl. covers), with 31 illus (1 col.) & 3 maps.

—— another edn. [1979?]. obl. format. pp. 44 (incl. covers), with 24 illus (1 col.) & 3 maps & a layout plan.

8883 QUAINTON RAILWAY SOCIETY. [Stockbooks.] 2nd edn, compiled by P. J. Hoskins & A. A. Harland. *Quainton: the Society*, [1973]. pp. 44, with 41 illus.
—— 3rd edn, by P. J. H. and A. A. H. [1975]. pp. 48; 45 illus.
—— 4th edn, by A. A. H. and P. J. H. [1978]. pp. 52; 53 illus (3 col.).

8884 DAVIES, R. and GRANT, M. D. Forgotten railways: Chilterns and Cotswolds. *Newton Abbot: David & Charles*, 1975. pp. 256, with 31 illus on 16 plates, 26 maps, diagrams & drawings in text; folded map at end; bibliography (110 sources).

8885 DAVIES, R. and GRANT, M. D. Chilterns and Cotswolds, [compiled by] R. Davies and M. D. Grant. *Newton Abbot: David & Charles*, 1977. (Railway History in Pictures series). pp. 96, with 126 illus, & maps.
Another work with the same title and written by the same authors was published, also in 1977, by David & Charles in their *Forgotten Railways* series.

8886 COLES, C. R. L. Railways through the Chilterns. *London: Ian Allan*, 1980. pp. 126. Intro (pp. 5–7) & 218 illus with descrs, and essays describing the three routes; bibliography (16 printed sources & 2 l.p. records); map on end papers.

Bedfordshire 8887–92

8887 BLYTH, T. A. The History of Bedford and Visitor's Guide. *London: Longman, Green, Reader & Dyer*, [1873]. pp. 318.
Index has 7 page refs to railways, 2 of which (the Leicester & Hitchin Rly and the Bedford & Cambridge Rly) are to passages of useful length and detail.

8888 HAMSON, J. Bedford town and townsmen: a record of the local history of Bedford during the last half century. *Bedford: Bedfordshire Times Office*, 1896. sm. 8°. pp. 20, 168, 37–41.
'A sketch of the principal events and movements recorded in the *Bedfordshire Times & Independent* since 1845.' Index has 19 page refs to railways in Bedford.

8889 LELEUX, S. A. The Leighton Buzzard Light Railway and associated quarry lines. *Lingfield: Oakwood Press*, 1969. pp. 126, with 30 illus on 12 plates, map, 9 layout plans, 6 working drawings, & lists.

8890 LEIGHTON BUZZARD NARROW GAUGE RAILWAY SOCIETY. Guide . . . *Leighton Buzzard: the Society*, [1972]. pp. 17, with 12 illus; map on cover.
pp. 10–17, 'Motive power'.
—— 2nd edn, 1974. pp. 40, with 25 illus; map on cover.
—— another edn, [1979]. pp. [16], with 14

illus (11 col.); motive power list, map & col. illus on covers.

8891 COCKMAN, F. G. The Railway Age in Bedfordshire. *Bedfordshire Historical Record Society*, 1974. (Publications, no. 53). pp. viii, 143, with 15 illus & 2 maps on 10 plates, & timetables.

8892 WHIPSNADE & UMFOLOZI RLY. [Guide]. *Dunstable: Whipsnade Zoo Park*, [197–]. pp. 12, with 15 illus; text, 2 maps & 2 col. illus on covers. Compiled by Robin Butterell and Trevor Barber.
   2 miles; 2ft 6in gauge.

Hertfordshire 8893–96

For the outer London suburban areas of the Home Counties see also the subdivision of C 1 c *for London and Greater London,* 8592–8806

8893 RAILWAY CORRESPONDENCE & TRAVEL SOCIETY. Itinerary of the Hertfordshire Rail Tour, Saturday, 30th April, 1955. *R.C. & T.S.*, [1955]. pp. [4], with 2 maps, schedule & notes.
   St Pancras—Kentish Town—Tottenham South Junction—Hertford—Welwyn Garden City—St Albans—Watford—Rickmansworth—Watford—Willesden Junction—St Pancras Junction—Copenhagen Junction—Finsbury Park.

8894 JOHNSON, W. B. Industrial archaeology of Hertfordshire. *Newton Abbot: David & Charles*, 1970. (Industrial Archaeology of the British Isles series). pp. 206, with 32 illus on 16 plates, 12 maps, plans & diagrams in text; bibliography (48 sources).
   pp. 122–33 *et passim*, Railways.

8895 STEVENAGE DEVELOPMENT CORPORATION. A survey of rail commuting in Stevenage. [*Stevenage: the Corporation*, 1977]. tall 8°. pp. [83], with maps, diagrams, tables & graphs. Cover title: The effects of opening the new Stevenage railway station: survey of rail commuters in Stevenage during 1975.

8896 COCKMAN, F. G. The railways of Hertfordshire. *Hertford: Hertfordshire Library Service; Hertfordshire Local History Council*, 1978. (Hertfordshire Local Studies, 1). pp. vi, 86, with 16 plates, 14 outline maps, 10 specimen timetables, & a bibliography (19 sources). Text extends onto p. [3] of cover.

Essex 8897–8911

For the outer London suburban areas of the Home Counties see also the subdivision of C 1 c *for London and Greater London,* 8592–8806

8897 YOUNG, A. General view of the agriculture of the county of Essex . . . *London: R. Phillips*, 1807. 2 vols. (pp. xv, 400; vii, 450).
   vol. 2, pp. 224–5, mentions iron railways in Mr Whitbread's lime-kiln establishment at Purfleet, 1806. 'Since these ways have been made, four horses do the work [instead of the previous 25]', with a

folded plate depicting the wagonway, another of a wagon, and a third showing wagon details in 4 drawings (Plates L, LI & LII).

8898 RAILWAY CORRESPONDENCE & TRAVEL SOCIETY. Itinerary of the Southend Centenary Special, Sunday 11th March 1956, *the Society*, [1956]. pp. 4, with map & rail tour schedule.
   From Bishopsgate (GER) to Southend, and back on the LTSR line to Fenchurch St.

8899 RAILWAY CORRESPONDENCE & TRAVEL SOCIETY. Itinerary of the Northern & Eastern Rail Tour . . . , Sunday, 10th August, 1958. *R.C. & T.S.*, [1958]. pp. [4], with map & schedule. Notes by P. Proud.
   London (Liverpool St)—Stratford—Broxbourne—Bishop's Stortford—Dunmow—Braintree—Witham—Marks Tey—Halstead—Haverhill—Cambridge—Potton—Sandy—Bedford—London (St Pancras).

8900 GRIEVE, H. E. P. The Great Tide: the story of the 1953 flood disaster in Essex, with maps drawn by P. A. Sparke. *Chelmsford: Essex County Council*, 1959. pp. 883.
   Arranged chronologically, passages relating to railways being therefore scattered. In the index are 59 page refs under 'Railways' but this index entry is not sub-divided.

8901 BURROWS, V. E. The tramways of Southend-on-Sea. *Huddersfield: Advertiser Press*, 1965. pp. 189, with 50 illus, 2 detailed lists of rolling stock, & in pocket at end, 1 folded map, 2 folded drawings of cars. Includes Southend Pier Tramway.

8902 FROST, K. A. The Southend Pier Railway. *London: P. R. Davis*, 1965. (Signal Transport Papers, 3). pp. 24, with 17 illus, layout plan & bibliography (15 sources).

8903 GAYLER, H. J. The coastal resorts of Essex; their growth and present-day functions. Thesis, M.A., University of London, October 1965.
   Southend, Canvey Island, Clacton and other coastal areas of Essex. Ch. 4, pp. 43–76, The impact of the railway on the Essex resorts.

8904 STAPLETON, N. J. The Kelvedon and Tollesbury Light Railway. 2nd edn. *Bracknell: Town & Country Press*, 1968. pp. 32, with 19 illus, 3 layout plans & a map.
   —— Reprint, *Bracknell: Forge Books*; *Colchester: Stour Valley Railway Preservation Society*, 1975.
   Worked successively by the GER, LNER & BR(ER), 1904–1962.

8905 STOUR VALLEY RAILWAY PRESERVATION SOCIETY. Stock List. *Chappel & Wakes Colne Station: the Society*.
   1st edn, compiled by R. M. Coe, March 1973; 2nd, December 1973; 3rd, May 1975, (amended reprint, September 1975); 4th edn, May 1976.

8906 BOOKER, J. Essex and the Industrial Revolution. *Chelmsford: Essex County Council*,

1974. (Essex Record Office Publications, 66).
pp. 134–62, Water and rail, with 220 notes. Index
has 65 page refs to Railways and 9 to Tramways.

8907 COLNE VALLEY RAILWAY PRESERVATION
SOCIETY. The Colne Valley Railway: a
pictorial survey. *the Society*, 1977. pp. [40]. 5
pp. of text, 66 illus and 10 layout plans; map
inside cover.

8908 STOUR VALLEY RAILWAY PRESERVATION
SOCIETY. A Guide to Chappel & Wakes
Colne Steam Centre. [*Chappel*]: *Stour Valley
Railway Preservation Society*, 1977. pp. 48,
with 10 illus, 13 drawings & diagrams, site
plan & map; 2 illus on covers.
—— Reprint, with minor amendments, 1977.
—— 2nd edn. A Guide to Chappel Steam

Centre, by C. M. Wright. *the Society*, 1979.
pp. 48; 9 illus, plan & 15 drawings.

8909 WOOD, R. G. E. Railways in Essex, until
1923. *Chelmsford: Essex County Council*,
1978. (Essex Record Office Publications, 72).
(Seax Series of Teaching Portfolios, 10).
A plastic wallet containing an 8-page introductory
leaflet with 2 maps, a chronology, a bibliography, &
a list of 40 separate items (illustrations, facsimiles,
maps, plans, letters, newspaper extracts, etc.).

8910 [Entry deleted]

8911 COLNE VALLEY RLY (1972). A Guide to
the Colne Valley Railway. *Castle Hedingham:
C.V. Rly*, [197–?]. pp. 8, incl. covers, with 3
illus, map & stock list.

C 1 d   WEST MIDLANDS REGION (Herefordshire & Worcestershire, Warwickshire, Shropshire, West Midlands (County), Staffordshire)

8912–8987

West Midlands Region generally 8912–25

8912 LONDON, Worcester and South Staffordshire
railways, and Oxford and Rugby, and
Oxford, Worcester and Wolverhampton railways. Digest of the evidence taken before the
Select Committee of the House of Commons
on the above Bills. *London: printed by C.
Roworth*, 1845. pp. 52.   MCL

8913 EVANS, R. C. Industrial steam locomotives
of central England: a review of the remaining
steam locomotives on industrial systems in
the Midlands, compiled by R. C. Evans;
photographs by R. Hickman. *Knowle: Warwickshire Railway Society*, 1966. pp. 36. Lists,
with 10 illus.

8914 HADFIELD, C. The canals of the West
Midlands. *Newton Abbot: David & Charles*,
1966. (Canals of the British Isles series). pp.
352, with 27 illus on 16 plates, & in text, 20
illus & maps, 726 notes, & a 10-part tabular
summary as appendices.
Index, pp. 337–52, has 51 page refs under
'Tramroads'. Railways are entered under their
individual names.
—— 2nd edn. *David & Charles*, 1969. pp.
352, with 27 illus on 16 plates, & in text, 20
illus & maps, 726 notes & a 10-part tabular
summary as appendices.

8915 RAILWAY CORRESPONDENCE & TRAVEL
SOCIETY. Itinerary of the East Midlander
no. 9 Railtour, Saturday, 21st May, 1966:
Nottingham to Crewe Works. *R.C. & T.S.*,
[1966]. pp. [4], with 1 illus, map & schedule.
Written by F. A. Quayle.
Nottingham—Burton on Trent—Tamworth—
Wolverhampton—Stafford—Wellington—Crewe—
Warrington—Stockport—Millers Dale—Nottingham.

8916 CASSERLEY, H. C. and DORMAN. C. C.

The Midlands. *Newton Abbot: David &
Charles*, 1969. (Railway History in Pictures
series). pp. 111, with col. frontis; map. Intro
& 201 illus with descrs.

8917 HALE, M. Steam in the Black Country
(1948–1967), photographed by Michael Hale.
Dudley: M. Hale, [1971]. sm. obl. format. pp.
[36]. Intro, & 58 illus with descrs.

8918 CHRISTIANSEN, R. The West Midlands.
Newton Abbot: David & Charles, 1973. (A
Regional History of the Railways of Great
Britain, 7). pp. 292, with frontis & 31 illus on
16 plates, 13 in text, with 7 maps & a folded
col. map at end; chronology (pp. 257–78);
bibliography (50 sources).

8919 HALE, M. Railways of the Severn Valley:
photographed by Michael Hale. *Dudley: M.
Hale*, 1973. obl. format. pp. [36]. Intro, map
& 58 illus with descrs.

8920 ASHWORTH, B. J. Steam in the West Midlands and Wales. *London: Ian Allan*, 1975.
pp. 120. Intro (pp. 5–7) & 195 illus (8 col.)
with descrs.
Period, 1959–1974.

8921 NOYES, K. J. Some aspects of route selection for canals, railways and roads in the West
Midlands. Thesis, Ph.D., University of Manchester, 1976.

8922 BRIDGES, A. J. Industrial locomotives of
Cheshire, Shropshire and Herefordshire.
*Market Harborough: Industrial Railway Soci-
ety*, 1977. (Industrial Railway Society Handbook, G). pp. xli, 116, with 64 illus on 32
plates, maps & plans.

8923 BROOK, F. The West Midlands: Hereford,

Worcester, Shropshire, Staffordshire, Warwickshire, [County of] West Midlands. *London: Batsford*, 1977. (Industrial Archaeology of the British Isles series). pp. 223, with 67 illus.

In index, over 100 page refs to railways in the area.

8924 HALE, M. More Steam in the Black Country: photographed by Michael Hale. [*Dudley*]: *M. Hale*, [1978]. obl. format. pp. 36. Intro & 58 illus with descrs.

8925 LAMBERT, A. J. West Midlands Branch Line Album. *London: Ian Allan*, 1978. pp. 112. Intro & 208 illus with descrs; map on end papers.

Herefordshire & Worcestershire 8926–28

8926 WORCESTERSHIRE RECORD OFFICE. Handlist of Plans, Sections, Books of Reference and other documents deposited with the Clerk of the Peace before 1 April 1889, pertaining to public schemes. [*Worcester: Worcestershire Record Office*], 1955. pp. 70 (70 single-side reproduced typescript leaves), with a supplementary 39 leaves for the period commencing with the institution of the County Council in November 1889, to November 1952.

8927 FIELD, G. J. A look back at Norchard. *Broadstairs: G. J. Field*, 1978. pp. 31, with 36 illus, 10 maps & plans, 3 diagrams.

Coal mining at Norchard Colliery in the Forest of Dean up to its closure in 1965, including its wagonways and railways, train workings and rolling stock.

8928 MORGAN, D. R. The Redditch railways, 1859–1979; edited by David R. Morgan. *Redditch: Redditch College, Department of Adult Education*, 1980. la. 8°. pp. 48, with col. map, facsimiles, & line drawings by David G. Budgen. 'Contents' & text extend onto covers. Reproduced typescript.

Warwickshire 8929–31

8929 ELRINGTON, C. R. Communications, *in* Victoria History of the Counties of England: a history of Warwickshire, vol. 7, 1964, pp. 26–42 (railways, pp. 37–42), with 3 maps, 6 illus on plates & 355 notes.

8930 SIMMONS, J. Rugby Junction. *Oxford: Dugdale Society*, 1969. (Dugdale Society Occasional Papers, 19). pp. 25, with map & 62 notes.

An historical study of developments resulting from the confluence of the LNWR (London & Birmingham Rly until 1846) and the Midland Rly (Midland Counties Rly until 1844), and later, the routeing of the Great Central Rly through the town.

8931 SWINGLE, S. L. and TURNER, K. The Leamington & Warwick Tramways. *Tarrant*

Hinton: *Oakwood Press*, 1978. (Locomotion Papers, 112). pp. 39, with 8 illus on 4 plates & a map.

Shropshire 8932–46

8932 SHROPSHIRE RECORD OFFICE. Canals and railways: a list of plans and related documents deposited at the Shirehall, Abbey Foregate, Shrewsbury. rev. edn [compiled by J. Horsley Denton]. *Shrewsbury: Shropshire Record Office*, 1969. pp. [100].

Previous edition, 1902.

8933 RANDALL, J. Broseley and its surroundings. *Madeley: Salopian & West Midland Journal Office*, 1879. pp. 328.

pp. 57–9, 74, 77, 96–7, railways in this area since the 17th century.

8934 DENTON, J. H. Railways and canals in West Shropshire. *Codsall: Cottage Press*, June 1963. pp. 18, with maps. Reproduced typescript.

A guide to a tour by the Railway & Canal Historical Society, compiled principally from notes by E. A. Wilson.

8935 GRIGGS, M. Shrewsbury in steam days. *Wolverhampton: the author*, [1967]. pp. 20, with map & 2 plans. Reproduced typescript.

8936 SEVERN VALLEY RLY (1965). [Stockbooks]. [1st edn]. Severn Valley Railway locomotives and rolling stock, Summer 1968. *Bridgnorth: S.V. Rly*, [1968]. pp. 16. Intro, 14 illus with descrs, & a stock list.

—— [2nd edn]. Locomotives and rolling stock of the Severn Valley Railway, Summer 1970. [1970]. pp. 28. Intro, 26 illus with descrs, & a stock list.

—— 5th edn. Severn Valley Railway Stock Book, compiled by D. C. Williams. 1974. pp. 84, with 127 illus & 4 detailed lists.

—— 6th edn, by D. C. Williams. [1977]. pp. 84, with 127 illus & 4 detailed lists.

—— 7th edn, by D. C. Williams. [1980]. pp. 85, with 139 illus & 4 detailed lists.

8937 RAILWAY DEVELOPMENT ASSOCIATION. MIDLAND AREA. The Shrewsbury modules: an exercise in timetabling converging regular-internal train services. *Birmingham: R.D.A., Midland Area*, [1970]. (Development Survey, 10). pp. 12, with 2 tables.

Reproduced typescript (single sided), printed cover.

8938 NABARRO, G. Severn Valley Steam. *London: Routledge & Kegan Paul*, 1971. pp. 108, with 96 illus on 48 plates, map (frontis), 3 detailed tables, & a timetable.

pp. 79–99, 'Steam nostalgia': a review of preservation achievements of societies other than the Severn Valley Rly Co., with stock lists.

8939 SEVERN VALLEY RLY (1965). [Guides]. *Bridgnorth: S.V. Rly*.

—— 1st edn. 1971/2. [1971]. pp. 32, with 17

illus, map & plan. Text by D. N. Cooke & D. C. Williams; maps by D. W. Frewin.
—— 2nd edn. 1972/3. [1972]. pp. 36, with 23 illus, map & plan.
—— 3rd edn. 1974. pp. 48, with 36 illus, map & 2 plans.

8940 TRINDER, B. The Industrial Revolution in Shropshire. *Chichester: Phillimore*, 1973. pp. xi, 455, with frontis, 32 illus on 28 plates, 13 maps & drawings, & 805 notes.
Index has 118 page refs under 'Railways'.

8941 WILLIAMS, D. C. Severn Valley Railway Album: 140 photographs of Severn Valley Railway locomotives and trains. *Bridgnorth: S.V. Rly*, [1974]. obl. format. pp. 140. Intro, a summary account of the S.V. Rly (1965) & its stock, & 140 photos with descrs, taken since 1967.

8942 SEVERN VALLEY RLY (1965). [Colour Guides] Severn Valley Railway Colour Guide; text by D. C. Williams. *Bewdley: S.V. Rly*, 1976. pp. [16], with 20 col. illus (2 on covers); map & stocklist inside covers.
—— another edn. 1978. pp. [16], with 21 col. illus (3 on covers); map & stocklist inside covers.

8943 WILLIAMS, D. The Severn Valley Limited, Saturday 23rd April, 1977: illustrated itinerary. *[Bewdley]: Severn Valley Rly (1965)*, 1977. pp. [8].
Produced to accompany a tour of the West Midlands from Bridgnorth via Bewdley, Kidderminster, Hereford & Chester, and back.

8944 WILLIAMS, D. C. Steam focus on the Severn Valley Railway, by David Williams. *Bridgnorth: S.V. Rly (1965)*, [1977]. pp. 8 incl. paper covers, with 14 illus (6 col.).
Published as a supplement with *Railway Forum: Steam*, Spring/Summer edition, 1977.

8945 WALKER, C. Trails from Shrewsbury. *Oxford: Oxford Publishing Co.*, 1978. (Trails of Steam series, 5). obl. format. pp. 64. Intro & 59 illus with descrs.
Locomotives & trains of the GWR, LMS & BR.

8946 SMITH, W. and BEDDOES, K. The Cleobury Mortimer and Ditton Priors Light Railway. *Oxford: Oxford Publishing Co.*, 1980. la. 8°. pp. 122, with ca. 200 illus, maps, plans, dimensioned drawings, facsimiles & a bibliography (11 sources).

West Midlands (County), including Birmingham 8947–71

8947 YONGE, J. West Midlands Railway Track Map, drawn by John Yonge. *Exeter: Quail Map Co.*, 1979. Folded map, 21in. × 16in.
From West to East: Wolverhampton to Nuneaton and from North to South, Walsall to Barnt Green, as in October 1978, with three insets in larger scale for areas of complex trackwork.

8948 To the inhabitants of Birmingham; a protest against diverting London to Lancashire railway traffic from Birmingham by means of the South Union Railway and the Tamworth & Rugby branch of the Birmingham and Derby Railway, and in support of a plan to bring railway traffic to the town by the Grand Junction Railway and the Manchester, Cheshire & Staffordshire Railway. [Signed] An Inhabitant, and dated Jan 17, 1837. pp. [4]. Folio. (One page of text and one coloured map). UL(GL)

8949 GILL, C. and BRIGGS, A. History of Birmingham. *London: Oxford University Press*. 2 vols.
vol. 1, Manor and borough to 1865, by Conrad Gill. 1952. pp. xv, 454.
pp. 283–318, 'The Railway Age' with 5 illus on 4 plates & a bibliography (23 sources), *et passim*.
vol. 2, Borough and City, 1865–1938, by Asa Briggs. 1952. pp. xi, 384.
Railways to a lesser degree than in vol. 1, but Tramways, pp. 91–4, 143–8, 248–56 *et passim*.

8950 WEST BROMWICH TRANSPORT DEPARTMENT. Golden Jubilee, 1964. *West Bromwich: the Department*, 1964. pp. 14.
A souvenir brochure, with a brief account of the tramways period.

8951 GILBERT, C. Memories of Birmingham's steam trams. *Hanwell (London): Light Railway Transport League*, [1965]. pp. 22, with 16 illus, map, plan, diagram, stock lists.
Reprinted from *Modern Tramway*, April & May 1965.

8952 DOHERTY, D. Birmingham. *Seaton: Peco*, 1969. (Railscene series, 7). sm. obl. format. pp. [32]. Intro & 27 illus with descrs.
Trains in the Birmingham area.

8953 LIGHT RAILWAY TRANSPORT LEAGUE. Time to go: a rapid transit system for Birmingham. *Cardiff: L.R.T.L.*, [1970?]. pp. 12 (incl. covers), with 13 illus, map & table.
Reprinted from *Modern Tramway*.

8954 LIGHT RAILWAY TRANSPORT LEAGUE. The way ahead with Speedrail. *London: L.R.T.L.*, [1970?]. pp. 12 (incl. covers), with 11 illus, a map & 5 tables.
A proposed rapid transit system for Birmingham.

8955 RAILWAY DEVELOPMENT ASSOCIATION. MIDLAND AREA. Speed-Rail: a low-cost rapid transit system. *Birmingham: R.D.A.; Solihull: Light Railway Transport League*, [1970?]. pp. 7, with map & diagram. Reproduced typescript.
A proposed rapid-transit network for Birmingham.

8956 BARKER, T. The tramways of Halesowen. *Birmingham: Birmingham Transport Historical Group*, 1971. (Paper, 4). pp. 26.
The story of unsuccessful negotiations to build a line, 1900–1922.

8957 DORMAN, C. C. Birmingham railway scene. *Bracknell: Town & Country Press*, 1971. pp. 100. Frontis, intro, 2 maps, & 164 illus with descrs.

8958 HARDY, P. L. and JAQUES, P. A short review of Birmingham Corporation Tramways. *Reading: H.J. Publications*, 1971. pp. 52, with 48 illus on 24 plates, 3 lists & a folded map.

8959 HALE, M. Through Birmingham (Snow Hill), photographed by Michael Hale. *Dudley: M. Hale*, 1972. sm. obl. format. pp. [36]. Intro, map, & 58 illus with descrs.

8960 WISEMAN, R. J. S. Birmingham. *Huddersfield: Advertiser Press*, 1972. (British Tramways in Pictures, 3). pp. 40, with 56 illus.
—— 2nd edn. *Advertiser Press*, 1977. (British Tramways in Pictures, 3). pp. 40, with 56 illus.

8961 RAYBOULD, T. J. The economic emergence of the Black Country: a study of the Dudley estate. *Newton Abbot: David & Charles*, 1973. pp. 272.
pp. 70–88, Railways, & 35 notes.

8962 BROADBRIDGE, S. R. The Birmingham Canal Navigations. *Newton Abbot: David & Charles*. (Inland Waterways Histories).
vol. 1: 1768–1846. 1974. pp. 205, with 16 illus on 8 plates, & in text, 8 maps & illus & 3 tables; 343 notes.
ch. 8 (pp. 169–86), The coming of the railways.

8963 CHATHAM, G. L. Steam at Round Oak. *Kinver: Halmar Publications*, 1974. pp. 36, with 51 illus, map, & list of locomotives.
The Pensnett Railway and the Round Oak Steel Works, Brierley Hill, Staffordshire.

8964 [COVENTRY]. CITY OF COVENTRY. PUBLIC TRANSPORT COMMITTEE. Coventry transport, 1912–1974: a brochure . . . *Coventry: the Committee*, [1974]. tall 8°. pp. 43.
Includes tramways, with 13 illus & map.

8965 HALE, M. and WILLIAMS, N. By rail to Halesowen: a history of the GWR branch from Dudley to Halesowen via Old Hill and the Halesowen Railway to Northfield. *Dudley: M. Hale with Uralia Press*, 1974. pp. 92, with 42 illus on 20 plates, & in text, 4 illus, map, 8 layout plans, 4 facsimile notices, & a chronology (1852–1973).

8966 MAYOU, C. A. Electric tramcars in Birmingham: depots and allocations. *Cheltenham: Birmingham Transport Historical Group*, 1974. (B.T.H.G. Paper, 5). pp. ii, 44, 54. Reproduced typescript.
A comprehensive history with detailed lists occupying the second half of the work.

8967 GALE, W. K. V. A history of the Pensnett Railway. *Cambridge: Goose*, 1975. pp. 111, with 14 illus on 8 plates, map, & a detailed table of locomotive data.

A mineral line in the Brierley Hill area of the Black Country, 1829 to the present day.

8968 WEBB, J. S. Black Country tramways: company-worked tramways and light railways of the West Midlands industrial area. *Walsall: the author*. 2 vols.
A large, detailed work based on his *Tramways of the Black Country* (1954).
vol. 1: 1872–1912. 1974. pp. vii, 279, with frontis, 73 illus, a bibliography (59 sources), chronology (pp. 273–8) & 2 maps on folded sheet in end pocket.
vol. 2: 1913–1939, including the Kidderminster & Stourport Tramways. 1976. pp. vii, 273, with frontis, 75 illus, combined bibliography for vols. 1 & 2 (59 sources), chronologies & 6 appendices (pp. 213–73) & a map on folded sheet in end pocket.

8969 DEWEY, S. and WILLIAMS, N. Wolverhampton Railway Album. *Wolverhampton: Uralia Press*.
vol. 1: 1978. pp. [56]. Intro & 170 illus with descrs. Text & illus extend onto covers.

8970 LAY, R. W. Brummegem Belle Railtour, Saturday, 14 October 1978. *Wimbledon: B.R. (SR), South Western Division*, 1978. pp. 40.
Itinerary with map, a route chart alongside text, and (pp. 22–40), historical notes. Compiled & drawn by Ron W. Lay. Copies distributed only to those taking part in the tour.
Clapham Junction—North Pole Junction—Old Oak Common—Northolt—High Wycombe—Banbury—Leamington Spa—Coventry—Stretford—Perry Bar—Bescot—Wolverhampton—Dudley Port—Soho Loop—Perry Bar—Birmingham New Street—Old Hill—Stourbridge Junction—Dudley—Walsall—Aldridge—Castle Bromwich—Camp Hill—Lifford East & West Junctions—Selly Oak—Birmingham New Street—Water Orton—Nuneaton—Wigston South Junction—Bedford—Hendon—Brent Junction No 2—Neasden—New Kew Junction—Clapham Junction.

8971 COXON, R. J. Roads and rails of Birmingham, 1900–1939. *London: Ian Allan*, 1979. pp. 192, with 151 illus.
Railways, tramways and buses.

Staffordshire 8972–87

8972 TURNER, K. and TURNER, S. L. The Kinver Light Railway. *Lingfield: Oakwood Press*, 1964. (Locomotion Papers, 73). pp. 30, with 10 illus on 4 plates, a map & a plan.

8973 CLARK, P. L. Railways, *in* A History of the County of Stafford. *Oxford University Press, for the Institute of Historical Research*, 1967. (Victoria History of the Counties of England: Staffordshire, vol. 2). pp. 304–34, with 4 maps, 6 tables, & 235 notes.

8974 LEWIS, R. A. Railways in Staffordshire, [edited, and with an introduction and notes by R. A. Lewis, with the co-operation of S. C. Newton]. *Stafford: Staffordshire Education Dept*, 1971. (Local History Source Book, 9). tall 8°. pp. [2], 36, with reproductions of 28 sources (documents, extracts from books, periodicals, reports, letters & maps).

8975 THOMAS, J. The rise of the Staffordshire potteries, with a preface by G. D. H. Cole. *Bath: Adams & Dart*, 1971. la. 8°. pp. xi, 228.
ch. 9 (pp. 95–102), 'Railways'.

8976 KEYS, R. and PORTER, L. The Manifold Valley and its light railway. *Buxton: Moorland Publishing Co.*, 1972. pp. 58, with frontis (map), 2 layout plans, & 84 illus with descrs.

8977 RAYBOULD, R. The economic emergence of the Black Country: a study of the Dudley estate. *Newton Abbot: David & Charles*, 1973. pp. 272.
pp. 52–88, 'Transport developments', with 3 maps & 35 notes (railways, pp. 70–88).

8978 CHATHAM, G. L. Steam at Round Oak. *Kinver: Halmar Publications*, 1974. pp. 36, with 51 illus, map, & list of locomotives.
The Pensnett Railway and the Round Oak Steel Works, Brierley Hill, Staffordshire.

8979 THOMPSON, W. J. Industrial archaeology of North Staffordshire. *Buxton: Moorland Publishing Co.*, [1974]. pp. 168, with 79 illus on 40 plates, & in text, 33 maps & a diagram.
ch. 4 (pp. 26–30), Railways.

8980 SHERLOCK, R. The industrial archaeology of Staffordshire. *Newton Abbot: David & Charles*, 1976. (Industrial Archaeology of the British Isles series). pp. 216, with 27 illus on 16 plates, 24 diagrams, maps and line drawings.
Index has 24 page refs to railways.

8981 WILLIAMS, J. K. A Foxfield Album. *Blurton: the author*, 1978. pp. [48], with 81 illus & a map.
An illustrated chronology of the Foxfield Light Railway Society's progress since its inception in 1965.

8982 LEAD, P. The Caldon Canal and tramroads, including the Uttoxeter and Leek canals and North Stafford Railway. *Tarrant Hinton: Oakwood Press*, 1979. (Locomotion Papers, 116). pp. 56, with 24 illus on 12 plates, 11 maps & a bibliography (44 sources).
Includes the Woodhead tramroad and the Caldon Low tramways (1778).

8983 BAKER, A. C. Birchenwood and its locomotives. *Industrial Locomotive Society*, [197–]. pp. 42, with 12 illus & a map.
Coke production at the National Coal Carbonising Ltd, Kidsgrove, North Staffordshire.

8984 FOXFIELD LIGHT RAILWAY SOCIETY. The Foxfield Colliery Railway: a short account of the railway to Foxfield and the locomotives used on it. *Longton: the Society*, [197–]. pp. [8], with 7 illus; 2 stocklists & 2 additional illus on covers.

8985 BILLS, D. M., GRIFFITHS, E. and GRIFFITHS, W. R. By tram to Kinver, 1901–1930; edited and produced by Harold Parsons. *Kinver: Elda Publications*, 1980. pp. 24, with 16 illus (incl. cover illus), folded map & 3 plans.
The Kinver Light Railway.

8986 TURNER, K. The Leek & Manifold Valley Light Railway. *Newton Abbot: David & Charles*, 1980. pp. [48], with 60 illus, 7 station layouts, 4 dimensioned drawings, a map & a bibliography (5 sources).

8987 WILLIAMS, N. By road and rail to Tettenhall. *Wolverhampton: Uralia Press*, 1980. pp. [75], with 49 illus (incl. 5 on covers, 2 col.), 9 facsimiles (incl. timetables) & 2 maps & a plan on inside cover.
On cover: 'Trams, trolleys, buses, trains: Wolverhampton, Chapel Ash, Newbridge, Tettenhall and Compton'.

C 1 e   EAST MIDLANDS REGION (Northamptonshire, Leicestershire (with Rutland), Derbyshire, Nottinghamshire, Lincolnshire)

8988–9068

East Midlands Region generally 8988–9002

8988 BELL, G. E. The railway as a factor in the location of manufacturing industry in the East Midlands. Thesis, Ph.D., University of Nottingham, 1958–9.

8989 RAILWAY CORRESPONDENCE & TRAVEL SOCIETY. Itinerary of the Fernie Rail Tour . . . , Saturday, 25th August, 1962. *R.C. & T.S.*, [1962]. pp. 4. Written by T. E. Rounthwaite. No map.
Northampton—Market Harborough—Seaton—Uppingham—Peterborough—Stamford Town—Luffenham—Oakham—Kettering—Thrapston—Wellingborough—High Ferrers—Bedford—Northampton.

8990 LOCOMOTIVE CLUB OF GREAT BRITAIN [and the] RAILWAY CORRESPONDENCE & TRAVEL SOCIETY. Itinerary, the North Midlands Rail Tour, Saturday, 11th May, 1963. *L.C.G.B. & R.C. & T.S.*, 1963. pp. 11, with 2 illus, map with 4 insets, & schedule. Text by T. Rounthwaite and P. Armstrong.
St Pancras—Derby—Trent—Ambergate—Buxton—Ashbourne—Burton—Coalville—St Pancras.

8991 SMITH, D. M. Industrial archaeology of the East Midlands: Nottinghamshire, Leicestershire, and the adjoining parts of Derbyshire. *Dawlish: David & Charles; London: Macdonald*, 1965. pp. 304, with 68 illus on 32 plates & 31 in text; gazetteer (pp. 227–86), notes (pp. 287–90).

Railways, pp. 166–75 and, via Index, at 39 other places in the text.

8992 HADFIELD, C. The canals of the East Midlands, including part of London. *Newton Abbot: David & Charles*, 1966. (Canals of the British Isles series). pp. 294, with 32 illus on 16 plates, & in text, 15 illus & maps, 492 notes & 2 appendices (Appendix I, pp. 266–78, a 12-column table, 'Summary of facts about the canals & navigations of the East Midlands').
    Index has over 200 page refs to rail transport in the area, under Railways, Wagonways, Coal, and under the names of individual lines.
    —— 2nd edn. *David & Charles*, 1970. (Canals of the British Isles series). pp. 294; 32 illus on 16 plates, 15 text illus & maps, 492 notes & 2 appendices, etc.

8993 COSSONS, N. A Railway Geography of the East Midlands, 1830–1905. Thesis, M.A., University of Liverpool, 1969.

8994 ANDERSON, P. H. Forgotten railways: the East Midlands. *Newton Abbot: David & Charles*, 1973. pp. 224, with 32 illus on 16 plates, 21 maps & line drawings, folded col. map in pocket & a bibliography (67 sources).

8995 BETT, W. H. and GILLHAM, J. C. The tramways of the North Midlands, edited by J. H. Price. *London: Light Railway Transport League*, 1974. pp. 51, with 64 illus, 5 maps, 10 fleet lists, bibliography & a map on cover.
    Reprinted from *Great British Tramway Networks*, 4th edn., 1962.

8996 FRANKS, D. L. The Ashby & Nuneaton Joint Railway, together with the Charnwood Forest Railway. *Sheffield: Turntable Publications*, 1975. (Minor Railways of Britain series). pp. 63, with 20 illus & folded map.

8997 LELEUX, R. The East Midlands. *Newton Abbot: David & Charles*, 1976. (A Regional History of the Railways of Great Britain, 9). pp. 240, with 31 illus on 16 plates; 7 maps, 2 plans, graph, table & facs in text; bibliogr. (71 sources), fold. map at end.

8998 HINCHLIFFE, B. Steam in the North Midlands. *Sheffield: Turntable Publications*, 1976. pp. 96. Intro & 103 illus with descrs; map.
    Photographs by Ken Boulter, Pete Hughes, John Naylor and Fred Ravenhill.

8999 SIVIOUR, G. R. Post-war changes in the railway geography of the East Midlands. Thesis, Ph.D., University of Nottingham, 1976–7.

9000 LAMBERT, A. J. East Midlands Branch Line Album. *London: Ian Allan*, 1978. pp. 128. Intro & 263 illus with descrs.

9001 BETT, W. H. and GILLHAM, J. C. Tramways of the East Midlands, edited by J. H. Price. *Light Railway Transport League*, [1979]. pp. 66, with 79 illus, 10 maps & a bibliography (pp. 64–6); map on cover.

Previously published as *Tramways of the North Midlands* (1974).

9002 DENTON, A. S. North Midlands trains in the thirties. *Trowbridge: Oakwood Press*, [1980]. (Locomotion papers, 127). pp. 64, with 26 illus.

Northamptonshire 9003–9

9003 ADDRESS to the land owners . . . who have signed a petition to the House of Commons against the proposed line of railroad from Leicester through Harborough and Northampton to Blisworth. *Market Harborough: Thomas Abbott (printer)*, 1836. pp. 19.
                                                    NORTHAMPTON PL

9004 BIRMINGHAM LOCOMOTIVE CLUB. INDUSTRIAL LOCOMOTIVE INFORMATION SECTION. Staveley Minerals Limited: Scaldwell tramway. *Birmingham: B.L.C.*, [1963]. pp. 8, with folded map. Reproduced typescript.
    —— Re-issued as The Scaldwell ironstone tramway, by the Brockham Museum Association, 1966. pp. ii, 8. With an added introduction.

9005 HATLEY, V. A. The Blisworth Hill Railway, 1800–1805: Northamptonshire's first railway. *Northampton: Northamptonshire Antiquarian Society*, [1964]. (Northampton Historical Series, 2). pp. 13, with 3 illus, map & 33 notes.
    —— Reprinted from the *Reports & Papers of the Northamptonshire Antiquarian Society*, 1962 and 1963.
    —— Reprinted with a few minor alterations, 1965. pp. 13.
    —— Reprinted with addenda, 1967. pp. 14.
    —— 2nd edn. Rails over Blisworth Hill: the story of Northamptonshire's first railway. *Northampton: Northamptonshire Antiquarian Society*, 1970. (Northampton Historical Series, 2). pp. 10, with 3 illus, map, & 35 notes. Appended to this work, on pp. 11–12: 'Quarry line at Blisworth: notes on Northamptonshire's third railway,' by George Freeston, with a map.
    —— 3rd edn, in preparation.

9006 HATLEY, V. A. Northampton hoodwinked?: how a main line of railway missed the town a second time, *in* Journal of Transport History, vol. 7 (1965–6), pp. 160–72, with map & 61 notes.
    Northampton, having been by-passed by the London & Birmingham Rly when constructing its line through the county in 1836–8 (see 1364 & 1366, and ch. 3 of *The East Midlands*, by R. Leleux) was again avoided by the Midland Counties Rly's decision to join the L & B at Rugby, a route proposed by a Northampton promotion, the South Midland Railway, instead of via Market Harborough and Northampton to join it at Roade or Blisworth.

9007 FAREWELL to the narrow gauge: tour of the metre-gauge ironstone tramway of Stewarts & Lloyds Minerals Ltd at Wellingborough, Saturday 1st October 1966. *Birmingham*

Locomotive Club, and Narrow Gauge Railway Society, [1966]. pp. [10], with 2 illus, a map & 2 locomotive lists.

Record of a visit to the quarries at Finedon to see the last mineral railway in Britain, closed during that month.

9008   MARKHAM, C. A.   The Iron Roads of Northamptonshire: an early history of the railway systems. [Facsimile reprint by *Pilgrim Publications, Wilbarston*, 1970]. pp. 32, with frontis, 5 plates & a map.

A straight reprint, with added illustrations, of a work originally published in the *Journal of the Northamptonshire Natural History Society & Field Club*, vol. 12, no. 99 (September 1904), pp. 239–70. This had one illustration, of Blisworth station, and a map. In the monograph reprint the illustration is the frontispiece and five are added, 3 contemporaneous and 2 modern.

9009   STARMER, G. H.   Preserved steam locomotives from Northamptonshire ironstone quarries. *Northampton: Northamptonshire Ironstone Railway Trust*, 1975. pp. 16, with 8 illus.

A tabulated record of the careers and present locations of 50 locomotives.

Leicestershire (with Rutland) 9010–27

9010   PITT, W.   General view of the agriculture of the county of Leicester . . . *London: printed for Richard Philips*. 1809.

p. 313, a description (1 para). of the twelve-mile wagonway from the Ashby Canal to Ashby, Cole-Orton and Ticknall.

—— Reprinted on microfiche. *East Ardsley: EP Microfilm*, 1978. 7 fiches.

9011   [LEICESTER.] CITY OF LEICESTER TRAMWAYS DEPARTMENT.   Instructions to men engaged on car cleaning, overhauling, etc. *Leicester: the Department*, July 1924, pp. 16.

9012   [LEICESTER.] CITY OF LEICESTER TRAMWAYS & MOTOR OMNIBUS DEPARTMENT. City of Leicester tramways. (Souvenir of the coming-of-age celebrations of the electric tramways system, 18th May 1925). [*Leicester*, 1925]. la. 8°. pp. 10, with 21 illus (16 portraits), 2 tables, 1 chart; 1 illus mounted on cover.

9013   PATTERSON, A.T.   Radical Leicester: a history of Leicester, 1780–1850. *Leicester: University College of Leicester*, 1954. pp. x, 405.

ch. 14 (pp. 260–74) *et passim*, 'The coming of the railways', with 96 notes. The Midland Rly, its constituents, and other railways of the East Midlands, both actual and proposed, up to 1850.

9014   STAPLEFORD MINIATURE RLY.   The Stapleford Miniature Railway: a story in pictures . . . *London: Ian Allan*, [1964]. pp. 24, with 42 illus (incl. cover illus), map & gradient profile.

A passenger-carrying line of 1½ miles on 10¼ in gauge, with 2 model liners operating a marine service on the lake.

9015   PEARSON, M. S. W.   Leicester's trams in retrospect. *Crich: Tramway Publications, Tramway Museum Society*, [1970]. pp. 70, with 67 illus, 2 maps (1 folded), & 3 lists.

9016   STEVENS, P. A.   The Leicester line: a history of the Old Union and Grand Union canals. *Newton Abbot: David & Charles*, 1972. (Inland Waterways Histories). pp. 216, with col. frontis, 31 illus on 16 plates, 6 maps & illus, 218 notes, a bibliography (7 sources) & 5 appendices.

Railways: in index, 26 page refs under 'Midland Rly', 'L & N W Rly' and 5 other railways.

9017   BOSTON, E. R.   Rails around the rectory: the story of the Cadeby Light Railway, by the Rev. E. R. Boston, General Manager, published in the year of the line's tenth anniversary, 1973. *Loughborough: Book House*, 1973. pp. 18, with 22 illus & diagrams, map, plan, & timetable.

A 2ft gauge line with a steam-hauled passenger train.

9018   SIMMONS, J.   Communications and transport, *in* Leicester and its region, edited by N. Pye. *Leicester: Leicester University Press for the Local Committee of the British Association*, 1972. ch. 13, pp. 311–24, with 28 notes.

Railways are included in some of the maps but there is no railway map as such. Disused lines are shown in the map (fig. 33) on p. 161.

9019   BILLINGTON, M. H.   Cliffe Hill mineral railway, Leicestershire. *Leeds: Turntable Enterprises*, 1974. (Minor Railways of Britain series). pp. 48, with 17 illus, a diagram & a map.

9020   GREAT CENTRAL RLY (1976). Stockbook, Guide and Passenger Timetable, 1975. *Loughborough: G.C. Rly*, 1975. pp. 12, incl. covers, with 14 illus & map.

—— 1977 edn. 1977. pp. 16, incl. covers, with 23 illus.

—— Stockbook. 4th edn, 1978. sm. obl. 8°. pp. 28, incl. covers, with 14 illus.

9021   GREAT CENTRAL RLY (1976). [Prospectus]. Invitation to subscribe . . . *Loughborough: G.C.R. (1976)*, 1976. pp. 14, with 3 illus, map & illus on covers and a share application form.

9022   BOSTON, E. R.   Rails around the rectory: the Cadeby Light Railway information brochure. Commemorative 1st edition. *Cadeby: C.L. Rly* 1978. pp. 4, with illus & line drawings and a scenic cut-out model of Cadeby Church and the railway.

This edition, part printed in gold-colour ink and signed, is limited to 500 copies, consecutively numbered.

9023   GREAT CENTRAL RLY (1976). Main Line Steam: a guide to the Great Central Railway. *Loughborough: G.C.R. (1976)*, 1978, obl. format. pp. [24], with 22 illus, 2 maps, 2 plans, 2 diagrams, & 2 additional maps & 3 illus (1 col.) on covers. Title from cover.

9024 SHACKERSTONE RAILWAY SOCIETY. Shackerstone: guide to Leicestershire's steam branch line. *Burbage: the Society*, [1976–80]. pp. 28, with 21 illus & a map inside cover.
At least three variants were published during this period. These have minor alterations on p. 27 of the text, and different covers.
The Market Bosworth Light Railway, with (pp. 6–9), 'The Ashby & Nuneaton Joint Railway', by Philip A. Stevens and another.

9025 MARKET OVERTON INDUSTRIAL RAILWAY ASSOCIATION. Handbook & Guide. *Grantham: the Association*, 1978. pp. 8, with 2 plans; map inside cover.
These are at least four other editions or variants before 1980, all undated.

9026 HEWLETT, H. B. The quarries; ironstone, limestone, sand, of the Stanton Ironstone Company Limited. *Cottesmore: Market Overton Industrial Railway Association*, 1979. pp. 46, with 35 illus, 9 maps & a drawing.
A reprint of the original publication of 1935.

9027 RAILWAYS in Rutland; compiled by A. R. Traylen. *Oakham: Rutland Local History Society*, 1980. (Rutland Series, 3). pp. 100, with 131 illus, incl. cover illus, 15 facsimiles & 2 maps.
Period, 1820s to 1895 (mainly). Text by John Clay (on public railways) and Eric S. Tonks (on ironstone railways), augmented by extracts from the *Stamford Mercury* and by anecdotes from local inhabitants.

Derbyshire 9028–54

9028 DERBYSHIRE COUNTY LIBRARY. Derbyshire: books and other material available in the County Library. *Matlock: Derbyshire County Library*, 1971. pp. 107. Title from cover. No introduction.
pp. 30–32: 'Railways and tramways'; 40 sources (books, periodical articles, Acts and official publications).

9029 GOULD, R. Derbyshire railway history: a bibliography. [*Derby*]: *Derbyshire Library Service*, 1979. la. 8°. pp. 34, with map. Reproduced typescript. Title from cover.
The 304 sources, arranged into 19 sections, are books and periodical essays in the three main local studies collections at Derby, Matlock and Chesterfield.

9030 FAREY, J. General view of the agriculture of Derbyshire . . . drawn up for the consideration of the Board of Agriculture and Internal Improvement. *London: Sherwood, Nelly & Jones*, 1817. 3 vols.
vol. 3, pp. 286–90: 'Iron rail-ways' (as feeders to canals) and beyond this section to p. 454 where there are countless references to canal feeder railways in Derbyshire and elsewhere (M. J. T. Lewis). Map showing wagonways facing p. 193.

9031 FRYAR, M. Some chapters in the history of

Denby. *Denby: Bemrose*, 1934. pp. xii, 291.
pp. 113–23, 'corf roads, waggon ways and railways' with 11 illus (photographs of plateways, 1908).

9032 PLANT, K. P. The Ashover Light Railway. *Lingfield: Oakwood Press*, 1965. (Locomotion Papers, 30). pp. 88, with 27 illus on 12 plates, 5 diagrams, 4 layout plans, gradient profiles, 9 appendices & a chronology.
On the title page the work is wrongly described as 'Locomotion Papers, number twenty-nine'. Period, 1918–1951.

9033 LAMB, B. Visit to, and tour of, the Bugsworth complex of the Peak Forest Canal and tramway, Saturday, 20 May 1967; leader, Brian Lamb. *Railway & Canal Historical Society, North-West Group*, 1967. pp. 3 & folded map. Reproduced from MS.

9034 CLAYTON, H. The Duffield Bank and Eaton railways. [*Lingfield*]: *Oakwood Press*, 1968. pp. 92, with 36 illus & 5 diagrams on 24 plates; 4 maps & diagrams and 3 lists in text.
15-inch gauge lines built by Arthur Heywood: for his own estate near Derby, 1874, and for the Duke of Westminster's estate at Eaton, near Chester, 1896.

9035 LAMB, B. The Peak Forest Canal and tramway: the canal, Bugsworth complex; tramway; a discourse in maps. *Stretford: B. Lamb*, 1968. pp. [12], with 9 maps, plans & diagrams (some folded), drawn by the author. Paper cover. Reproduced from MS.
—— [rev. edn].. [*Sheffield?*]: *Inland Waterways Protection Society*, 1976. pp. 13. Reproduced typescript.
The Derbyshire Hamlet of Bugsworth changed its name to Buxworth in 1930.

9036 RIPLEY, D. The Peak Forest tramway, 1794–1936. *Lingfield: Oakwood Press*, [1968]. (Locomotion Papers, 38). pp. 27, with 9 illus, 11 layout plans, map, diagram & gradient profile.

9037 NIXON, F. The industrial archaeology of Derbyshire. *Newton Abbot: David & Charles*, 1969. (Industrial Archaeology of the British Isles series). pp. 307, with frontis & 32 illus on 16 plates, 30 maps, diagrams & line drawings.
pp. 151–7, 'Tramroads'; pp. 157–68, 'Railways'; pp. 168–70, 'Street tramways'; (16 notes, pp. 289–90).

9038 STEVENSON, P. The Nutbrook Canal, Derbyshire, with . . . foreword by Charles Hadfield. *Newton Abbot: David & Charles*, 1970. (Inland Waterways Histories). pp. 159, with col. frontis & 15 illus on 8 plates, 13 maps & illus, 167 notes & 4 appendices.
Railways: 78 page refs in index.

9039 'DOWIE'. The Crich mineral railways, by 'Dowie'. *Crich: Tramway Publications, the Tramway Museum*, [1971]. pp. 40, with 28 illus, 2 diagrams, facsimile & map inside covers, & a bibliography (32 sources).
—— [2nd edn., 1976]. pp. 40, with 34 illus, 2

diagrams, facsimile, map & a bibliography (35 sources).

'Dowie' is a composite name for A. R. Cowlishaw, J. H. Price and R. G. P. Tebb.

9040 HARRIS, H. The industrial archaeology of the Peak District. *Newton Abbot: David & Charles*, 1971. (Industrial Archaeology of the British Isles series). pp. 256, with 32 illus on 16 plates, & in the text, 14 maps & line drawings.

Railways & wagonways: 52 page refs in the index.

9041 NICHOLSON, C. P. and BARNES, P. Railways in the Peak District. *Clapham (Yorks): Dalesman Books*, 1971. pp. 96, with 20 illus, map, & layout plan of Miller's Dale Station.
—— 2nd edn. *Dalesman Books*, 1975. pp. 96; 20 illus, map & layout plan.
—— 3rd edn. *Dalesman Books*, 1978. pp. 96; 20 illus, map & layout plan.

9042 The CABLE tramway from Matlock Bridge to Matlock Bank: report of the inaugural ceremony, with views and portraits. *Matlock: Arkwright Society*, 1972. pp. 46, with 13 illus, incl. portraits.

Reprint of the original souvenir booklet of 1893, with a new introduction by S. V. Fay. Cover title: The Matlock Steep-Gradient Tramway.

9043 BRISTOW, M. R. and RODRIGUEZ, F. A cost-benefit study of the Manchester to Buxton railway . . . commissioned by the Local Authorities' Joint Committee for Railway Services (Manchester–Stockport–Buxton). [*Manchester*]: *University of Manchester Centre for Urban & Regional Research*, 1973. pp. [iv], 117, [9], with 14 tables, 10 diagrams, 9 maps (1 folded) & a facsimile. Reproduced typescript.

The study was conducted under the direction of Professor T. Parry Lewis.

9044 RIPLEY, D. The Little Eaton gangway, 1793–1908: one of the earliest mineral tramways in the Midlands. *Lingfield: Oakwood Press*, 1973. (Locomotion papers, 71). pp. 27, with 10 illus on 4 plates, 6 maps, 2 layout plans, a gradient profile & a bibliography (26 sources).

9045 PEARSON, R. E. and KNIBBS, R. D. Towns and transport. *Derby: Derby Lonsdale College of Higher Education*, 1974. tall format, spiral binding on top edge.

pp. 13–15, Tramways, & 13 illus & 2 maps of Derby tramways.
—— 2nd edn. *Bishop Lonsdale College*, 1977. obl. format. pp. 65. (Tramways, with illus & maps, pp. 14–19 *et passim*).

9046 ROWSLEY railway nostalgia. [*Matlock*]: *Arkwright Society*, 1975. pp. 6, with 3 illus, a map & a plan.

The Midland Rly—LMS—BR(LMR) in Rowsley: an historical account by Lawrence Knighton and supporting essays by Glyn Waite, Jess Bradshaw and Chris Charlton.

9047 TRANSPORT 2000. PEAK DISTRICT WORKING GROUP. Re-opening the railway from Derby to Manchester. *Belper: the Group*, January 1975. pp. 24, with 3 maps, 4 layout plans (composite), 2 line drawings & a proposed timetable.

9048 BOWTELL, H. D. Reservoir railways of Manchester and the Peak, with maps specially drawn by Arthur Chambers. *Tarrant Hinton: Oakwood Press*, 1977. pp. 130, with 40 illus & 10 maps.

The railways used in building dams and reservoirs.

9049 BROOMHEAD, N. Steam trails in the Peak District. *Bakewell: Peak National Park*, 1977. pp. 16, with 13 illus & a map.

Brief histories of three redundant lines which traversed the Peak National Park: the Cromford & High Peak Rly, the Buxton & Ashbourne line of the LNWR, and the Leek & Manifold Valley Light Rly.

9050 NICHOLSON, C. P. Branch lines in the Peak District. *Clapham (Yorks): Dalesman Books*, 1977. pp. 80. Map, intro, & 111 illus with descrs in 4 sections, each with a short introduction.

9051 NICHOLSON, C. P. Main lines in the Peak District: a pictorial history. *Clapham (Yorks): Dalesman Books*, 1977. pp. 80. Intro & 108 illus with descrs.

9052 GOTHERIDGE, I. The Ashover Light Railway and the Clay Cross Company. *London: Gemini*, 1978. obl. format. pp. 48, with col. frontis, 60 illus & facsimiles, diagrams, timetable, map & 3 plans.

9053 HEANOR AND DISTRICT LOCAL HISTORY SOCIETY. Two centuries of transport in the Heanor area. *Ilkeston: Morley's Bible Bookshop, for the Society*, 1978. pp. 65, with illus.

Includes colliery wagonways, railways and tramways. pp. 29–47: 'The Railway Age', by Brian Key, with 7 illus & 2 maps.

9054 BROOMHEAD, N. The High Peak & Tissington railways: a pictorial guide; text and photographic research by Nic Broomhead. *Bakewell: Peak Park Joint Planning Board; Matlock: Derbyshire County Council*, 1980. obl. format. pp. 42. Historical intro (2pp)., 42 illus (2 col.), 6 facsimiles & a map. Title from cover.

Part of the Cromford & High Peak Rly and part of the LNWR Buxton to Ashbourne line, before closure. The photographs are of the lines before closure and include some 19th century railway scenes.

Nottinghamshire 9055–61

9055 RAILWAY CORRESPONDENCE & TRAVEL SOCIETY. Nottingham Rail Tour, Saturday, 16th June, 1951. *R.C. & T.S.*, [1951]. pp. [4], with map & schedule. Itinerary compiled by A. G. Cramp.

9056 CHURCH, R. A. Economic and social change in a Midland town: Victorian Nottingham, 1815–1900. *London: Frank Cass*, 1966. pp. xxiv, 409.
   Includes railways and tramways, with illus & map.

9057 NOTTINGHAM and its Region; edited by K. C. Edwards. *Nottingham: British Association (Nottingham Local Executive Committee)*, 1966. la. 8°. pp. xxiii, 538.
   ch. 19 (pp. 315–40), 'Communications', by K. C. Edwards; (pp. 321–30, 'Railways', with map).

9058 RAILWAYS of Nottingham. *Railway Correspondence & Travel Society, East Midlands Branch*, [1969]. pp. 48, with 12 illus, 4 maps, 3 station plans, a list of 479 exhibited photographs & 2 timetables.
   An exhibition at Wollaton Hall, Nottingham, 17th May–22nd June, 1969, covering 130 years of railway history in Nottingham, 1839–1969.

9059 GROVES, F. P. Nottingham City Transport, by F. P. Groves, General Manager, City of Nottingham Transport. *Glossop: Transport Publishing Co.*, 1978. obl. format. pp. 96, with 227 illus (some col.).
   Includes tramways.

9060 GROVES, F. P. Nottingham's tramways; text by Philip Groves, General Manager, City of Nottingham Transport, from notes compiled by the late Bob Parr. *Crich: Tramway Museum Society*, 1978. pp. 32, with 47 illus, 4 lists & 2 maps.

9061 ILIFFE, R. and BAGULEY, W. Old Nottingham transport: a story in pictures. *Nottingham: Nottingham Historical Film Unit.* 3 parts (of a proposed 6). magazine format.
   vol. 1: Broughams & hansoms, horse buses, horse trams, steam trams, electric trams. 1978. pp. 48, with 78 illus, facsimile & plan.
   vol. 2: Victoria Station and its approaches. 1978. pp. 48, with 77 illus, incl. a plan of the station.
   vol. 3: The railway comes to Nottingham; electric trams (part two). 1979. pp. 48, with 70 illus, incl. facsimiles, 2 plans & 2 timetables.

Lincolnshire 9062–68

9062 RAILWAY CORRESPONDENCE & TRAVEL SOCIETY. Itinerary of the Lincolnshire Rail Tour, 16th May 1954. *R.C. & T.S.*, [1954]. pp. [8]. Scheduled itinerary by D. R. Dalton, 3 illus & 3 maps.
   From Nottingham to Lincoln, then over various lines of the former GNR in Lincolnshire.

9063 RAILWAY CORRESPONDENCE & TRAVEL SOCIETY. Itinerary of 'The Fensman' no. 2 [Rail Tour] . . . , Sunday, 9th September, 1956. *R.C. & T.S.*, [1956]. pp. 4, with map & schedule.
   London (King's Cross) or Nottingham—on to Peterborough—Benwick branch—March West Curve—Wisbech & Upwell Tramway—Sleaford & Bourne—Spalding—London, or Nottingham.

9064 HARTLEY, K. E. The Lincolnshire Coast Light Railway. *Selby: the Railway*, 1970. sm. 8°. pp. 28, with 7 illus & a map on 4 plates.
   1 mile, gauge 1ft 11½in., for holiday-makers at Humberston, near Cleethorpes.

9065 BECKWITH, I. The history of transport and travel in Gainsborough. *Gainsborough: Gainsborough Urban District Council*, 1971. (Making of Modern Gainsborough series, 9). pp. 38, with frontis, 7 illus & a map.
   pp. 33–7: the railways.

9066 LINDSEY COUNTY COUNCIL. Disused railways in Lindsey: policy for after use. *Lincoln*, 1971. obl. 8°. pp. 44, with 73 illus, 8 maps & a col. route map, spiral binding.
   Includes recommendations for certain lengths of line to be re-utilised by the Council.

9067 LUCAS, W. H. Memories of Grimsby and Cleethorpes transport. *Sheffield: Turntable Publications*, [1974]. pp. 46, with 35 illus & map.
   Includes tramways.

9068 RUDDOCK, J. G. and PEARSON, R. E. The railway history of Lincoln. *Lincoln: J. G. Ruddock & Partners*, 1974. pp. 272, with frontis, 46 illus, 30 line drawings, 22 maps & plans & a bibliography (25 sources); 4 facsimile adverts on end papers.

C 1 f   EAST ANGLIA (Cambridgeshire, Suffolk, Norfolk)

9069–9105

East Anglia generally 9069–81

9069 RAILWAY CORRESPONDENCE & TRAVEL SOCIETY. Itinerary of East Anglian Special . . . , Sunday, 6th September, 1953. *R.C. & T.S.*, [1953]. pp. 8, with 4 illus, map & schedule. Written by P. Proud.
   Bishopsgate—Marks Tey—Bury—Newmarket—Cambridge—Hitchin—Liverpool Street.

9070 NORFOLK RAILWAY SOCIETY. Report of a traffic census held on 20th July 1957. *Norwich: the Society*, December 1957. pp. 16, with 10 detailed analysis tables. Reproduced typescript.
   A 'First Summer Saturday' traffic census report taken at 7 points in East Anglia covering all major train movements (372 in all) over the ex-GER and ex-MGNR systems.

9071 NORFOLK RAILWAY SOCIETY. Report of a traffic census held on 19th July 1958. *Norwich: the Society*, December 1958. pp. 13, with 9 detailed analysis tables. Reproduced typescript.

The second census by the N.R.S., covering 366 trains in movement across East Anglia using the same census points as in the first, with Liverpool Street Stn (London) added. Includes the MGNR system.

9072 NORFOLK RAILWAY SOCIETY. Report of a traffic census held on 18th July 1959. *Norwich: the Society*, [1959]. pp. 13, with 7 detailed analysis tables. Reproduced typescript.

The third census by the N.R.S., covering the movements of 312 trains across East Anglia at 6 census points and at Liverpool Street Stn (London). The MGNR system had closed since the previous census in 1958.

9073 NORFOLK RAILWAY SOCIETY. Report of a traffic census held on 16th July 1960. *Norwich: the Society*, [1960]. pp. 12, with 6 detailed analysis tables. Reproduced typescript.

The fourth 'First Summer Saturday' census by the N.R.S., taken at 7 census points in East Anglia and at Bethnal Green Station in preference to Liverpool Street Stn as in the previous censuses.

9074 GORDON, D. I. The Eastern Counties. *Newton Abbot: David & Charles*, 1968. (A Regional History of the Railways of Great Britain, 5). pp. 252, with frontis & 39 illus on 16 plates, 8 illus & 8 maps in text, folding map & an evaluative bibliography (pp. 234–8, ca. 90 sources).
—— 2nd edn. *David & Charles*, 1977. (Regional History of the Railways of Great Britain, 5). pp. 256, with frontis, 39 illus on 16 plates, 8 timetables, facsims & 8 maps in text, evaluative bibliography & folding map.

9075 ANDERSON, R. C. The tramways of East Anglia. *London: Light Railway Transport League*, 1969. pp. 196, with frontis, 99 illus, 8 maps, lists & tables.

Includes light railways (steam) and pier tramways.

9076 SUMMERS, D. The Great Ouse: the history of river navigation. *Newton Abbot: David & Charles*, 1973. (Inland Waterways Histories). pp. 247, with col. frontis, 31 illus on 16 plates, 10 maps & illus, 442 notes & 6 appendices.

pp. 167–78 *et passim* & Appendix 4, 'Railway competition'.

9077 MANN, J. D. Branch line metamorphosis: former railways of Essex and Suffolk. *Frinton: South Anglia Productions*, [1974]. pp. 20, with 14 illus & a map.

9078 BOYES, J. and RUSSELL, R. The canals of Eastern England. *Newton Abbot: David & Charles*, 1977. (Canals of the British Isles series). pp. 368, with 32 illus on 16 plates, & in text, 18 illus & maps, 586 notes & 2 appendices.

Canals in the Eastern Counties, from Lincolnshire to Essex and east of the area already covered in other volumes in the series. Mostly canalised river navigations. Railways, *passim* (55 page refs in index).

9079 JOBY, R. S. Forgotten railways: East Anglia. *Newton Abbot: David & Charles*, 1977. pp. 175, with 32 illus on 16 plates, folded map & a bibliography (63 sources).

9080 OKAYAY, T. Railway development and population change in nineteenth century East Anglia. Thesis, Ph.D., University of Bristol, 1979.

9081 SHEWRING, C. Steam in East Anglia. *Norwich & King's Lynn: Becknell Books*, 1980. pp. 96. Intro & 149 illus with descrs.

Presented in four county sections, each with an introduction and a map.

Cambridgeshire 9082–90

9082 DARBY, H. C. Note on railway construction [in Cambridgeshire] *in* Victoria History of the Counties of England: Cambridgeshire, vol. 2, 1948. pp. 1–3, with 6 notes & a chronology.

9083 RAILWAY CORRESPONDENCE & TRAVEL SOCIETY. Itinerary of the Cambridgeshire Rail Tour 'The Fensman' . . . , Sunday, 24th July, 1955. *R.C. & T.S.*, [1955]. pp. 4, with map & schedule.

Liverpool St—Audley End—Saffron Walden— Bartlow—Cambridge—Quy—Fordham— Mildenhall—Ely—Denver—Stoke Ferry—Sutton— St Ives—Somersham—Ramsey East—Histon— Cambridge—Broxbourne—Liverpool St.

9084 GADSDEN, E. J. S., WHETMATH, C. F. D. and STAFFORD-BAKER, J. The Wisbech & Upwell Tramway. *Teddington: Branch Line Handbooks*, 1966. pp. 51, with frontis, 20 illus, 2 col. maps, 6 col. layout plans, a page of tickets (col.), 4 timetables, 7 diagrams, 3 tables. Preface and postscript 'Tales of the Tramway', by Rev. W. Awdry.

9085 SWINGLE, S. L. The Cambridge Street Tramways. *Lingfield: Oakwood Press*, 1972. (Locomotion Papers, 61). pp. 32, with 9 illus on 4 plates, & a map.

The Cambridge Street Tramways Company, 1880–1914, with horse-hauled cars throughout its career.

9086 AUSTIN, G. D. Peterborough tramways. *Peterborough: Peterborough Arts Council*, 1975. (Peterborough Papers, 1). obl. format. pp. 55, with 28 illus, 3 diagrams & 2 maps.

9087 NENE VALLEY RLY. Mini Guide. *Wansford Station: Peterborough Railway Society*, 1976. pp. 12, with 4 illus, a map & a stock list.

9088 PETERBOROUGH RAILWAY SOCIETY. Nene Valley Railway: a visitor's guide, compiled by Peter Waszak [& others]; written by Clive Brown, designed by Peterborough Development Corporation. *Peterborough: the Society*,

1977. pp. 34, with 34 illus (9 col.), 2 maps, 2 plans & a gradient profile.

—— another edn, compiled by members of the Peterborough Railway Society, 1980. pp. 24, with 18 col. illus, 2 maps & 2 layout plans.

9089 DANE, R. A. Railways of Peterborough. *Peterborough: Greater Peterborough Arts Council*, 1978. (Peterborough Papers, 2). obl. 8°. pp. 47, with 43 illus. incl. maps & portraits, and a chronology.

9090 FINCHAM, A. V. Steam near the Nene: further memories from the last days of steam; edited, and photographs, by A. V. Fincham. *Peterborough: The Model Shop*, [1978]. obl. format. pp. 66. 64 illus with descrs. Title & imprint from cover.

Suffolk 9091–98

9091 JENKINS, A. B. Memories of the Southwold Railway. *Southwold: F. Jenkins*, 1964. pp. 30, with 9 illus & a map.

—— 3rd edn. *F. Jenkins*, 1966. pp. 31, with 6 illus on 4 plates, map on reverse of title-page, drawing inside back cover.

—— 5th edn. Jenkins of Southwold, 1973. pp. 33, with 6 illus; no map.

9092 LONG, P. D. Bus or train?: a commentary on the 1965 proposal to close the East Suffolk Railway passenger services. [*London*]: *B. H. Wintle, for & on behalf of, the Omnibus Society*, 1968. pp. 23, with 4 maps, & time-tables.

The proposal to close the line from Ipswich to Yarmouth.

9093 IPSWICH INFORMATION OFFICE. Public transport, 1880–1884. *Ipswich: the Office*, 1969. (Ipswich Information, no. 29, May–June 1969). pp. 4, with 5 illus & a map.

Horse tramways in Ipswich.

9094 MARKHAM, R. Public transport in Ipswich, 1880–1970. *Ipswich: Ipswich Information Office*, [1970]. pp. [28], with 37 illus & 5 maps.

Includes tramways.

9095 TRANSPORT topics, edited by Gladys Driver. *Ipswich: Ipswich & District Historical Transport Society*, [1971]. (Ipswich & District H.T.S., Handbooks, 2). pp. 34, with 14 illus on 8 plates.

Includes three essays on railways and tramways in the area.

9096 CHRISTIE, V. G. Problems of passenger transport provision in East Suffolk. Thesis, M.Phil, University of London, 1974.

Railways and buses: historical development and present state, with a detailed study of the situation in the mid-1960s.

9097 BRANDON, R. Songs of the Southwold Railway: a potted history in rhyme, written

and illustrated by Robert Brandon. *Southwold: printed at the Southwold Press*, 1978. pp. 18.

'Limited edition of 200 numbered copies, signed by the author.' Verses with 10 line drawings on covers and as vignettes.

9098 SOUTHWOLD Railway Centenary, 24th September 1979: the only 3 foot gauge public railway in England, opened 24th September, 1879; closed 11th April, 1929. [*Southwold*]: [*Southwold Archaeological Museum?*], [1979]. pp. [16], with cover illus & a route map on 4 pages.

Published as a companion to the centenary exhibition held at the Museum, 2–7 August, 1979.

Norfolk 9099–9105

9099 BECKETT, M. D. and DAVISON, A. P. Locomotives in Norfolk, 1953. *Cambridge: Midland & Great Northern Joint Railway Society*, 1973. pp. 9, with lists of steam locomotives extant, and their shed allocations. Reproduced typescript. Title on cover only.

9100 NORFOLK RAILWAY SOCIETY. Norfolk Railway Society, 1955–1965 (Tenth anniversary souvenir booklet), compiled and written by K. A. Creighton and A. W. E. Hoskins. *Norwich: the Society*, 1965. pp. [32], with 8 illus & 2 operational tables.

9101 BECKETT, M. D. and DAVISON, A. P. North Norfolk Railway Stocklist . . . [*Cambridge*]: *Midland & Great Northern Joint Railway Society*, 1972. pp. 11. Reproduced typescript. Title from cover.

9102 NORTH NORFOLK RLY. North Norfolk Railway: official guide and map, edited by Andrew Darwin; designed and produced by David Perrott. *Sheringham: the Railway*, [after 1974]. pp. 2, with col. frontis, 11 illus (7 col., incl. frontis), col. map, 8 line drawings & a gradient profile. Foreword by John Betjeman.

—— another edn. Text by Gordon Perry. [1978]. obl. format. pp. 32, with 25 illus (9 col.), map & gradient profile.

9103 JOBY, R. S. Norfolk's railways: 1, Pictures, timetables & maps. *Norwich: Klofron*, 1976. obl. format. pp. 24, with 25 illus, 2 maps & timetables.

Title on cover only.

9104 WARREN, A. Rebirth of an engine: the story of our J 15. *Sheringham: Midland & Great Northern Joint Railway Society*, 1978. (Publication, 3). pp. [32], with 35 illus.

The renovation and re-employment of a GER class Y14 0–6–0 locomotive (LNER class J 15).

9105 NORTH NORFOLK RLY. A Short Guide to

the Museum, signal box, locomotives and rolling stock at Sheringham Station. *Sheringham: the Railway*, [1979]. pp. 19, with 17 illus

(drawings), 2 diagrams & a bibliography (15 sources from juvenile literature).
Designed for use by parties of school-children.

C 1 g   NORTHERN ENGLAND (North West Region, Yorkshire & Humberside Region, North Region)

9106–9431

Northern England generally 9106–16

9106 PARRIS, H. W. Railways in the northern Pennines to 1880. Thesis, M.A., University of Leeds, 1953–4.

9107 RAILWAY CORRESPONDENCE & TRAVEL SOCIETY. Itinerary of the Roses Rail Tour . . . , Sunday 8th June, 1958. *R.C. & T.S.*, [1958]. pp. [4], with map & a schedule.
Manchester Victoria—Bury—Ramsbottom—Accrington—Skipton—Ilkley—Harrogate—Thorpe Arch—Doncaster—Barnsley—Dewsbury—Rochdale—Radcliffe Central—Manchester Victoria.

9108 McCUTCHEON, W. A. The development and subsequent decline of the chief inland waterways and standard gauge railways of the North of England. Thesis, Ph.D., Queen's University, Belfast, 1962–3.

9109 TONKS, E. S. Industrial locomotives of Northern England, edited by Eric S. Tonks. *Birmingham: Birmingham Locomotive Club*, 1966. sm. 8°. pp. 105, with 24 illus on 12 plates.

9110 COOKE, D. N. Industrial steam locomotives of North East and North West England: a review of the remaining steam locomotives on industrial systems in the North, compiled by D. N. Cooke; photographs by D. Alexander, R. P. Hickman & R. Monk. *Knowle: Warwickshire Railway Society*, 1968. pp. 32. Lists, with 14 illus.

9111 DOHERTY, D. Capital approaches: northern. *Seaton: Peco*, 1969. (Railscene series, 6). sm. obl. format. pp. [32]. Intro & 27 illus with descrs.
Trains in the North of England, 1960s.

9112 JOY, D. Railways in the North: a pictorial introduction. *Clapham (North Yorks): Dalesman*, 1970. pp. 96, with 84 illus, a map & an evaluative bibliography (pp. 86–94).
—— 2nd edn. *Dalesman*, 1972. pp. 96, with 84 illus, map, bibliography (pp. 85–94).
—— 3rd edn, *Dalesman*, 1975. pp. 96, with 84 illus, map, bibliography (pp. 85–94).

9113 TREACY, E. Roaming the Northern rails. *London: Ian Allan*, 1976. la. 8°. pp. 208. Intro: 'Photographic Autobiography' (pp. 7–13), with an introduction to each of the 13 sections, & 255 illus (5 col.) with descrs.

9114 BETT, W. H. and GILLHAM, J. C. Tramways of North-East England, edited by J. H. Price. *London: Light Railway Transport League*, [1977]. pp. 67, with 77 illus, 29 maps & plans, & a bibliography (48 sources).
A revised edition of part of *Great British Tramway Networks*, 4th edn, 1962. Darlington, Gateshead, Hartlepools, Middlesbrough, Newcastle, Scarborough, South Shields, Stockton, Sunderland and Tynemouth.

9115 FEARNLEY, A. and TREACY, E. Steam in the North: an enthusiast's guide, featuring the paintings of Alan Fearnley and the photographs of Eric Treacy. *Clapham (N. Yorks): Dalesman*, 1978. sm. obl. pp. 40, with 12 paintings (2 on covers) & 9 photographs. Text on facing pages; introduction by David Joy.

9116 HOOLE, K. Branch line trains in the North East: a pictorial survey compiled by K. Hoole. *Clapham (North Yorkshire): Dalesman Publishing Co.*, 1979. obl. format. pp. 80. Intro & 105 illus with descrs.

C 1 h   NORTH WEST REGION (Cheshire, Merseyside, Greater Manchester, Lancashire)

9117–9237

North West Region generally 9117–27

9117 EXTRACTS from the Minutes of Evidence given in support of the Cheshire Junction Railway Bill before the Committee of the House of Lords in the Session of 1836. *Manchester: G. Wheeler*, 1836. pp. 56.
A proposed line from Manchester to Birmingham but by-passing Stockport, Macclesfield, Congleton and Leek. *See* 5674.

9118 RAILWAY CORRESPONDENCE & TRAVEL SOCIETY. Itinerary of the Four Counties Rail Tour . . . , Saturday, 23rd September, 1961. *R.C. & T.S.*, [1961]. pp. 4, with map & schedule.
Manchester—Waterside branch—Stockport—Higher Buxton—Ashbourne—Uttoxeter—Leek—Stoke-on-Trent—Crewe—Wilmslow—Manchester.

9119 PATMORE, J. A. and CLARKE, J. Railway

history in pictures: North-West England. *Newton Abbot: David & Charles*, 1968. pp. 112, with col. frontis, 172 illus, 16 maps & a gradient profile.

Text by J. A. Patmore, and photographs from the collection of John Clarke.

The railway scene north of Crewe and west of the Pennine watershed.

9120 YOUNG, I. D. Register of Industrial Locomotives: South Lancashire and North Cheshire. *Liverpool: Liverpool University Public Transport Society, via B. J. Towey*, [1968]. pp. 14, incl. covers. Reproduced typescript.

9121 COOKE, D. N. Industrial steam locomotives of Lancashire, Yorkshire and Cheshire: a review of the remaining steam locomotives on both sides of the Pennines, compiled by D. N. Cooke; photographs by R. Monk. *Knowle: Warwickshire Railway Society*, 1969. pp. 36, with 16 illus.

9122 HADFIELD, C. and BIDDLE, G. The canals of North West England. *Newton Abbot: David & Charles*. (Canals of the British Isles series).

vol. 1, [to 1845]. 1970. pp. 236, with 16 illus on 8 plates, & in text, 15 illus & maps, 500 notes. Index, pp. 226–36, with 30 refs under 'Tramroads'. Railways are entered under their individual names.

vol. 2, 1790–1845 contd, & 1845–1969. 1970. pp. 237–496, with 15 illus on 8 plates, & in text, 18 illus & maps, 448 notes & a 10-part tabular summary as appendices. Index to both volumes, pp. 475–96, with 46 page refs to Tramroads. Railways are entered under their individual names.

9123 HARDWICK, P. A. Geographical aspects of inter-urban passenger transport in North-West England. Thesis, M.Sc., University of Salford, 1971.

9124 CARTER, J. R. London Midland Steam in the North-West. *Truro: Bradford Barton*, 1973. pp. 96. Intro & 100 illus with descrs.

9125 CROSS, D. London Midland Steam over Shap. *Truro: Bradford Barton*, 1973. pp. 96. Intro & 96 illus with descrs.

9126 CROSS, D. London Midland Steam in the northern fells. *Truro: Bradford Barton*, 1974. pp. 96. Intro & 98 illus with descrs.

9127 HOLT, G. O. The North West. *Newton Abbot: David & Charles*, 1978. (Regional History of the Railways of Great Britain, 10). pp. 256, with 32 illus on 16 plates, 10 maps, plan, a la. folded map at end & an evaluative bibliography (pp. 251–2).

Cheshire 9128–38

9128 CHESHIRE COUNTY COUNCIL. Alphabetical List of Deposited Plans . . . regarding railways. [*Chester*]: *Cheshire County Record Office*, [ca. 1938]. pp. [12].

9129 RAILWAY CORRESPONDENCE & TRAVEL SOCIETY. Itinerary of the Warrington and District Rail Tour, Saturday, 17th October, 1953. *R.C. & T.S.*, [1953]. pp. [4]. Scheduled itinerary by R. Dyson, & a map.

A tour of Cheshire branch lines now (1953) closed.

9130 DEAN, R. J. Ellesmere Canal Packet; or, Historical notes to accompany a cruise on the Shropshire Union Canal and tour of places of interest between Ellesmere Port and Chester . . . September 9th, 1967. [*Chester*]: *Railway & Canal Historical Society, North Western Group*, 1967. pp. 8, with 3 maps, & 6 plans (3 of Chester railway stations), & a cover illus. Reproduced typescript.

pp. 6–8, 'Chester Station and its railways'.

9131 CLAYTON, H. The Duffield Bank and Eaton railways. [*Lingfield*] *Oakwood Press*, 1968. pp. 92, with 36 illus & 5 diagrams on 24 plates; 4 maps & diagrams and 3 lists in text.

Two 15-inch gauge lines built by Arthur Heywood: for his own estate at Duffield Bank near Derby, 1874, and for the Duke of Westminster's estate at Eaton, near Chester, 1896.

9132 MAUND, T. B. Local transport in Wallasey. [*London*]: *B. H. Wimpole for the Omnibus Society*, 1969. pp. 35, with 15 illus, fleet lists & inserted folded map.

Includes tramways.

9133 BRACKENBURY, A. Railways and canals in the Macclesfield area: itinerary and historical notes for a visit on 13th June 1970. *Railway & Canal Historical Society, N.W. Group*, 1970. pp. 22, with 3 maps. Reproduced typescript.

9134 HEWITT, H. J. The building of railways in Cheshire, down to 1860. *Manchester: E. J. Morten*, 1972. pp. 66, with 21 illus & folded map.

9135 NORTON, P. Waterways and railways to Warrington. *Caterham: Railway & Canal Historical Society*, 1974. pp. 70, with 5 maps & a bibliography (25 sources).

9136 WILSON, E. A. The Ellesmere and Llangollen Canal: an historical background. *Chichester: Phillimore*, 1975. pp. [x], 148, with 32 illus on 16 plates, 21 maps, plans & drawings (incl. 1 in sections, pp. 117–28), 3 appendices & a bibliography (42+ sources).

Glyn Valley Tramway and Pontcysyllte Tramway and other quarry lines are indexed under 'Tramways'.

9137 ROCHESTER, M. Salt in Cheshire. *Winsford: Cheshire Libraries & Museums*.

pt. 3, Transport in the salt industry. [1977]. A portfolio (la. obl. format) containing section 3, 'Railways' (pp. 44–56), incl. illus.

Public railways as well as industrial systems serving the salt industry.

9138 CLARK, W. D. and DIBDIN, H. G. Trams and buses of the City of Chester. *Rochdale:*

Manchester Transport Museum Society, August 1979. pp. 80, with 60 illus & folded map at end.

pp. 5–36, 'The tramways' (30 illus); map.
pp. 65–70, 'Fares and tickets', with illus.

Merseyside 9139–55

9139 BASS, RATCLIFFE & GRETTON LIMITED. Excursion to Liverpool and New Brighton by the Midland and Cheshire Lines railways via the Peak of Derbyshire, on Friday July 15th, 1904. (Produced by William Walters, Traffic Manager). [*Burton-on-Trent*]: *the firm*, [1904]. Reprinted in facsimile by the *Bass Museum*, 1977. pp. 96, with 117 illus, 3 maps & 2 plans.

pp. 54–60, 'The Liverpool Overhead Railway';
pp. 61–4, 'The Mersey Railway', with map.

Inserted is a folded memo, 'Train arrangements', with an illustrated plan of the docks at Liverpool.

9140 FORWOOD, W. B. Recollections of a busy life, 1840–1910. *Liverpool: Lee & Nightingale*, 1910. pp. iii, 204.

pp. 124–6, 'The Overhead Railway' (Liverpool Overhead Railway).

9141 LIVERPOOL OVERHEAD RLY. Descriptive Map and Guide of the railway and docks. *Liverpool: the Railway*, [ca. 1937]. A printed folder.

9142 LIVERPOOL OVERHEAD RLY. Notes of historical interest. rev. edn. *Liverpool: the Railway*, 1953. pp. 4. Reproduced typescript.

9143 ROWE, K. Geographical aspects of the journey to work in Liverpool. Thesis, M.A., University of Liverpool. 1957. 2 vols.

9144 PATMORE, J. A. The railway network of Merseyside.

Reprinted from *Transactions and Papers of the Institute of British Geographers* as *Publication* 29, 1961. pp. 231–44, with 9 maps & diagrams, 4 notes & 10 refs.

9145 LIVERPOOL CITY COUNCIL. PLANNING DEPT. Outer Rail Loop feasibility study, [by] Walter G. Bor, City Planning Officer. *Liverpool: City Planning Dept*, May 1965. pp. 28, with 7 col. maps, 2 tables, 10 diagrams (1 col.).

9146 MUNRO, S. A. Tramway companies in Liverpool, 1859–1897.

Reprinted from *Transactions of the Historic Society of Lancashire & Cheshire*, vol. 119 (1967), pp. 181–212, with 2 illus, 10 diagrams, map & 70 notes.

9147 BLACKBURN, R. E. Liverpool tramways, 1943 to 1957. *London: Light Railway Transport League*, 1968. pp. 59, with 58 illus, 6 maps. Text extends onto covers.

Reprinted from the 1967 and 1968 issues of *Modern Tramway*.

9148 STRETCH, E. K. St Helens tramways. *St Helens: the author*, for St Helens Corporation Transport, 1968. tall format (foolscap). pp. 58, with 12 illus on 4 plates, 2 fleet lists (tramcars & trolleybuses), a chronology (7 columns) & 4 statistical tables (6, 7 & 8 columns). Foreword by A. C. Barlow, General Manager & Engineer, St Helens Corporation Transport. Reproduced typescript in printed cover.

A book-length work produced in single-spaced typescript on foolscap.

9149 LIVERPOOL CORPORATION TRAMWAYS. The building and repair works of the Liverpool Corporation Tramways and Motor Bus Undertaking at Edge Lane, Liverpool. *Merseyside Tramway Preservation Society*, 1971. pp. 24, with 19 illus (1 folded), & a folded plan of Edge Lane tram works and car depot at end.

A facsimile of the 1928 souvenir brochure, published to aid the restoration of Liverpool tramcar no. 869.

9150 DIBDIN, H. E. Liverpool Tramway Album. *Broxton: the author*, 1972. pp. 7. Intro & 71 illus with descrs.

9151 MARTIN, T. J. Liverpool Corporation Tramways. [*Liverpool*]: *Merseyside Tramway Preservation Society*.

[part 1], 1897–1937. [1973]. pp. [40]. Intro (pp. 5–10) & 69 illus with descrs.

part 2, 1937–1957. [1980]. pp. [40]. Intro (a tribute to Jerome McWatt and a brief foreword, pp. 2–3), 75 illus with descrs, & a list of route closures, 1948–1957.

9152 HORNE, J. B. and MAUND, T. B. Liverpool transport. *London: Light Railway Transport League*.

vol. 1, 1830–1900. 1975. la. 8°. pp. 153, with frontis, 60 illus, 11 maps & many facsims, diagrams & drawings, & a bibliography.

Includes tramways, but not the Liverpool Overhead Rly.

9153 MALTBY, D., LAWLER, K. A. and MONTEATH, I. G. A monitoring study of rail commuting on Merseyside, with particular reference to the effects of increases in the price of petrol; prepared for the Science Research Council by D. Maltby, K. A. Lawler and I. G. Monteath. *Salford: University of Salford, Centre for Transport Studies*, 1976. (Working Papers, 4). pp. [7], ix, 169, with 4 leaves & 2 pp. of plates, illus & map.

Period, 1974–76.

9154 MARTIN, T. J. Liverpool Tramways Fleet List: details of all Liverpool's electric trams from 1898 to 1957. [*Liverpool*]: *Merseyside Tramway Preservation Society*, 1978. obl. format. pp. 72, with 62 illus.

1,398 cars described in a 10-column listing, with general notes on each class or group.

9155 LISTER, M. D. The industrial railways of Port Sunlight and Bromborough Port. *Tarrant Hinton: Oakwood Press*, 1980. (Locomotion Papers, 121). pp. 64, with 36 illus on 16 plates, 9 layout plans & a map.

Greater Manchester 9156–9206

General and historical 9156–91
Contemporaneous 9192–9206

General and historical

9156 A HISTORY of the Manchester railways. [*Collection of press cuttings*]. 5 vols.
STOCKPORT PL
vol. 1, April 1882–July 1887; vol. 2, August 1887–May 1895; vol. 3, March 1899–February 1903; vol. 4, February 1903–November 1906; vol. 5, December 1906–August 1911.
vol. 1, 72 pp., vols. 2–5, 80 pp., each with a MS index.
The volume for the period June 1895 to February 1899 is wanting.
A collection of local newspaper cuttings on railways and street tramways in and around Manchester. A visiting card bearing the name 'W. Harrison' is mounted on the inside cover of vol. 1. In view of the publication by William Harrison in 1882 of a work entitled *A History of the Manchester Railways* (*See* 9162) (the original articles of which begin vol. 1 of this set) it would seem reasonable to suppose that he was the compiler, but there is no real evidence such as a signature or a statement to support this. The visiting card could be merely evidence of ownership. (Note by W. J. Skillern).

9157 RAILWAY CORRESPONDENCE & TRAVEL SOCIETY. Itinerary of the Manchester and District Rail Tour, 26th July, 1953. *R.C. & T.S.*, [1953]. pp. [4]. Scheduled itinerary by R. Dyson, & a map.

9158 RAILWAY CORRESPONDENCE & TRAVEL SOCIETY. Itinerary of the South Lancashire Coalfield Rail Tour . . . , Saturday, 29th September, 1956. *R.C. & T.S.*, [1956]. pp. [4], with map & schedule. Notes by C. H. A. Townley.
Manchester (Ancoat Goods)—Glazebrook—Lowton St Mary's—St Helens (Central)—Wigan area—Haigh Junction—Pennington—Eccles—Manchester (Oxford Road).

9159 BEACROFT, B. W. The streets and street traffic of Manchester, 1890–1914: a case study of the traffic problem. Thesis, M.A., University of Leicester, 1963.
Includes tramways and discusses also the need for an underground railway system.

9160 GRAY, E. Trafford Park tramways, 1897 to 1946: an account of gas, electric and steam traction on the Trafford Park Estate, Manchester, covering the Estate Company's own undertaking together with those of the Manchester and Salford tramways. *Lingfield: Oakwood Press*, 1964. (Locomotion papers, 26). pp. 66, with 29 illus on 12 plates, 3 maps, 2 plans & 4 appendices.

9161 GRAY, E. The tramways of Salford. 2nd edn, rev. & enlarged. *Rochdale: Manchester Transport Museum Society* 1967. pp. 88, with

66 illus, 16 line drawings & diagrams, 5 maps (1 folded), lists & tables.

9162 HARRISON, W. A history of the Manchester railways. *Manchester: City News Office*, 1882. (Supplement to the *Manchester City News Notes and Queries* for July–December 1882, which formed the last part of vol. 4 for 1881–82) pp. 33, with table.
—— Reprinted as 2nd edn. *Manchester: Lancashire & Cheshire Antiquarian Society*, 1967. pp. 34, with map & table.
A facsimile of the first edition with (p. 34) a 'note to the second edition' by W. H. Chaloner, and a map on verso of title page.
The text of this reprint originally appeared as a series of anonymous contributions to the weekly *Manchester City News*, between 15th April and 26th August 1882. The collected pieces were then issued as a supplement (still anonymously) to vol. 4 of *City News Notes & Queries* (1881–2). In his note to the 1967 reprint authorship is assigned by Dr. Chaloner to William Harrison, an attribution first made by Charles Sutton, Manchester's Chief Librarian in 1902 in a *Handbook and Guide to Manchester*, prepared for the annual meeting of the British Medical Association. Sutton states that 'A History of the Manchester Railways was the title of a little book by Mr. William Harrison published anonymously twenty years ago'. This publication followed an announcement in the *City News* of 26th August that in addition to the reprinting of the work as a supplement, a limited number of separate pamphlets would be issued at one shilling in a few days. The issue of 16th September reported that only 80 of these pamphlets had been printed and a week later it was stated 'all copies . . . are now sold'. None is known to have survived and the present reprint is of the Supplement to the *City News Notes & Queries* of July–December 1882. (From information supplied by Harry Horton, Sub-Librarian, Social Services Library, Manchester Central Library).

9163 JOHNSTON, F. R. Eccles: the growth of a Lancashire town. *Eccles: Eccles & District History Society*, [1967]. pp. viii, 147.
pp. 77–83, Liverpool & Manchester Rly, with 35 notes.

9164 CLARKE, J. Railways. *London: University of London Press*, 1968. (It Happened Round Manchester series). sm. 8°. pp. 64, with frontis, 29 illus, 2 maps & a bibliography (30 sources); map on end papers.
—— 2nd edn., revised by C. W. Heaps. *Manchester: Greater Manchester Council*, 1976. (It Happened Round Greater Manchester series). sm. 8°. pp. 64, with frontis, 32 illus, 2 maps; bibliography (16 sources).

9165 HYDE, W. G. S. The Manchester Album: a pictorial survey of Manchester's tramways (prepared and edited by W. G. S. Hyde, with the assistance of A. K. Kirby and Clifford Taylor). *Castleton: Manchester Transport Museum Society*, 1969. la. obl. format. pp. [76], with 100 illus.

9166 RAILWAY AND CANAL HISTORICAL SOCIETY. The railway termini and canals of Manchester: historical notes (by Allan Brack-

enbury, C. J. Nettleship & I. P. Moss). *Chester: the Society, N.W. Group*, 1969. pp. 15, with map & 2 plans. Reproduced typescript.
'Written for a visit to the area on May 3rd 1969 to mark the closure of Central and Exchange stations.'
—— [2nd edn]., revised, and with a foreword, by H. P. White. [*Stockport*]: *R. & C.H.S., North Western Group*, 1979. pp. 19, with map & 2 plans. Reproduced typescript in a printed cover.

9167 [STOCKPORT]. COUNTY BOROUGH OF STOCKPORT. Transport Department, 1901–1969. [*Stockport: Transport Committee*, 1969]. pp. [13], with 16 illus. Title from cover.
Includes tramways.

9168 MATHER, F. C. After the Canal Duke: a study of the industrial estates administered by the trustees of the Third Earl of Bridgewater in the age of railway building, 1825–1872. *Oxford: Clarendon Press*, 1970. pp. xx, 392, with 3 plates, 6 maps & plans, many notes & a bibliography (pp. 367–73).
The index contains many page refs under 'Railways' (in the Manchester and Liverpool area).

9169 STRETCH, E. K. The South Lancashire Tramways Company, 1900–1958. *Castleton: Manchester Transport Museum Society*, 1972. pp. 139, with 68 illus, 16 maps & plans (1 folded), 6 tables & a chronology.

9170 GILBERT, A. C. and KNIGHT, N. R. Railways around Manchester: a pictorial review of the nineteen-fifties. *Rochdale: Manchester Transport Museum Society*, 1973. obl. format. pp. [50]. Intro & 103 illus with descrs, chronology & folded map.

9171 GILL, D. Transport treasures of Trafford Park. *Glossop: Transport Publishing Co.*, 1973. obl. format. pp. 98. Intro (pp. 1–6), & 170 illus with descrs.
Trafford Park industrial estate, 1890s to the present.

9172 MOSS, I. P. and COLE, J. H. S. The railways of Stockport [by Ian P. Moss and J. H. S. Cole]. [*Stockport: Teachers' Centre*, 1973]. pp. [ii], 3, 18, 1, 12, 18, 4, 5, 9, 12, with 13 illus & 18 facsimiles, 7 maps (4 col.) & a bibliography (1p).. Reproduced typescript. Title from cover.
A teachers' information pack. Includes also (printed), A Summary of a Report on the Future of Public Transport for Greater Manchester. *Manchester: South East Lancashire & North East Cheshire Public Transport Authority*, 1972. pp. 5, with 2 col. maps.   STOCKPORT PL

9173 ELLIS, D. N. Land, railways, and Manchester's transport problem: a critical analysis of the development of a public transport executive and its influence upon use and final disposal of railway land. Thesis, B.Sc. in Urban Estate Surveying, Trent Polytechnic, 1974.

9174 KIRBY, A. K. Dan Doyle's railway: a record of Manchester Corporation Tramways, 1901–1906. *Castleton: Manchester Transport Museum Society*, 1974. obl. format. pp. 100, with 77 illus, 2 maps, chronology & 4 statistical tables.
Councillor Daniel Boyle was chairman of Manchester Corporation Tramways Committee, 1898–1906.

9175 ANDERSON, D. The Orrell coalfield, Lancashire, 1704–1850. *Ashbourne: Moorland Publishing Co.*, 1975. pp. 208.
pp. 108–21, 'Surface transport' (colliery wagonways), with 9 illus & a map.

9176 ASHMORE, O. The industrial archaeology of Stockport. *Manchester: University of Manchester, Dept of Extra-Mural Studies*, 1975. pp. 100, with illus.
Railways, pp. 63–70 *et passim*.

9177 MARSHALL, M. Stockport Corporation Tramways. *Rochdale: Manchester Transport Museum Society*, 1975. pp. 160, with 139 illus, 3 maps, a la. folded track plan at end, facsimiles & 4 appendices.

9178 THOMAS, K. H. J. Economic change and the journey to work in the Leigh area of South Lancashire since 1951. Thesis, M.Sc., University of Salford, 1975.

9179 TODD, A. A. The development of railway passenger traffic in late Victorian and Edwardian Manchester. Thesis, M.A., University of Manchester, 1975.

9180 BETT, W. H. and GILLHAM, J. C. The tramways of South-East Lancashire, edited by J. H. Price. *Light Railway Transport League*, [1976]. pp. 74, with 84 illus, 13 maps & 16 fleet lists. Map on cover.
Adapted from *Great British Tramway Networks*, 4th edn, 1962.

9181 ASHMORE, O. Historic industries of Marple and Mellor. *Stockport: Metropolitan Borough of Stockport Recreation & Culture Division*, 1977. pp. [iv], 131. Compiled by members of the Marple branch of the Workers' Educational Association.
pp. 113–20. Tramroad and railways with 2 illus & map.

9182 BOWTELL, H. D. Reservoir railways of Manchester and the Peak, with maps specially drawn by Arthur Chambers. *Tarrant Hinton: Oakwood Press*, 1977. pp. 130, with 40 illus & 10 maps.
The railways used in building dams and reservoirs.

9183 GRAY, E. The Manchester Carriage and Tramways Company: a history to mark the centenary of the first Manchester tramway. *Castleton: Manchester Tramway Museum Society*, 1977. pp. 128, with 100 illus (incl. cover), numerous tables (financial statistics, fleet lists, timetables, fare tables, chronologies), diagrams, plans & 2 maps (1 la. folded with depots as insets).

Horse trams in Manchester, 1877 to 1903.

9184 ABELL, P. H. Transport and industry in Greater Manchester. *Barnsley: P. H. Abell*, 1978. pp. 85, with 40 illus, 3 maps, list of local railways & a bibliography (pp. 79–81).

9185 HYDE, W. G. S. Greater Manchester Review, edited by W. G. S. Hyde; consultant editors, Edward Gray, Eric Ogden, Clifford Taylor. *Glossop: Transport Publishing Co.*, 1978. tall 8°. pp. 128, with many illus, incl. 9 of railways & 21 of tramways, 1 railway map & 2 tramway maps; bibliography (14 sources).

pp. 111–19, 'Railways in Greater Manchester'. Tramways are described in chapters on individual areas.

9186 MERSEYSIDE PASSENGER TRANSPORT EXECUTIVE and BRITISH RAILWAYS. The story of Merseyrail. [*Liverpool*]: *M.P.T.E. and B.R.*, December 1978. pp. [18], with 30 illus (21 col.) & map. Text extends onto covers.

Period, 1830–1978.

9187 STRETCH, E. K. The tramways of Wigan. *Castleton: Manchester Transport Museum Society*, 1978. pp. 216, with 102 illus, tables, maps, & track plans in text and on folded s.sh at end; 7 appendices. A 4 pp. corrections supplement is loosely inserted.

9188 KIRBY, A. K. Manchester's little tram. 2nd edn. *Rochdale: Manchester · Transport Museum Society*, 1979. pp. 40, with 25 illus (1 col.) & folded map of route 53.

An historical account of the service and rolling stock of no. 53 route (the 'Circular'), 1904–1939.

9189 HYDE, W. G. S. A history of public transport in Ashton-under-Lyne. *Castleton: Manchester Tramway Museum Society*, 1980. pp. 120, with 140 illus (incl. 9 col. on pp. 104–5, & 25 tickets on pp. 108–9), numerous detailed tables, including fleet lists, & a summary of legislation (pp. 95–119).

pp. 9–60, The Oldham, Ashton & Hyde Tramway and the Ashton-under-Lyne Corporation Tramways, with 65 supporting illus.

9190 HYDE, W. G. S. The Manchester, Bury, Rochdale and Oldham steam tramway. *Glossop: Transport Publishing Co.*, [1979 or 1980]. pp. 104, with 78 illus (4 col.), 5 lists, 3 plans & 2 maps (1 la. folded with 3 insets).

9191 NETTLESHIP, C. J. and MOSS, I. P. The railway termini and canals of Manchester: historical notes. [*Stockport: Railway & Canal Historical Society, North Western Group*, 1980]. tall 8°. pp. 20, with 3 maps. Reproduced typescript.

A revised version of notes originally made for a visit to mark the closure of Central and Exchange stations, 3 May 1969.

Contemporaneous

9192 HOGREWE, J. L. Beschreibung der in England seit 1759 angelegten und jetzt grösstentheils vollendeten schiffbaren Kanäle . . . *Hannover: M. Pockwitz* (printer), 1780. pp. [12], iv, [2], 164, & 10 col. folded plates.

p. 146 describes a limekiln wagonway near Manchester and p. 150 an underground line at Worsley on the Bridgewater Canal, with trains of 4 to 6 wagons.

9193 HOLT, J. General view of the agriculture of the county of Lancaster with observations on the means of its improvement, drawn up for the consideration of the Board of Agriculture and Internal Improvement. *London: G. Nicol*, 1795. pp. 241.

pp. 97–8, description and dimensioned drawing of the iron plateway used in draining operations on Chat Moss and Trafford Moss peat lands, 1793.

9194 STATEMENT in support of the system of tramways for the suburbs of Manchester and Salford, proposed by the Manchester Suburban Tramways Company Limited. *Manchester: Slater & Poole*, 1872. pp. 6.　　MCL

9195 [GRUNDY, C. S]. Considerations against the adoption of penny fares by the Manchester Carriage and Tramways Company, by the Deputy-Chairman [C.S. Grundy]. *Manchester: Charles Sever, printer*, 1884. pp. 16.

9196 MANCHESTER CORPORATION TRAMWAYS. Parcels express, for the conveyance of parcels by tramway for delivery or further despatch: rates & arrangements. *Manchester*, 1905. (Reprinted by *Manchester Transport Museum Society*, 1972). pp. 48, with folded map.

9197 LONDON & NORTH WESTERN RLY. List of Caterers, railway fares, places of interest for Sunday school parties, within easy access from Manchester. *Euston Stn (London)*: *L.N.W.R.*, 1907. pp. 16, with 18 illus.

9198 MANCHESTER CORPORATION TRAMWAYS. Instructions to drivers and guards. [*Manchester: M.C.T.*, 1914]. [Republished as a facsimile reprint with added material by] *Manchester Transport Museum Society, Rochdale*, 1970. pp. 159 & a folded diagram showing the general power circuit (overhead supply) on tramways.

Inserted into the reprint are: a 2-page Introduction preceding the title-page, 16 plates (photos of Manchester tramway scenes), a col. folded map & a list of M.T.M.S. publications.

9199 BOILEAU, I. E. A study of traffic conditions in the central area of Manchester and of the relationship between traffic circulation and building accommodation. Thesis, Ph.D., University of Manchester, 1957.

9200 SELNEC PASSENGER TRANSPORT EXECUTIVE. SELNEC Picc-Vic Line: Manchester's underground rail link; a vital need for the whole region NOW; speedy, easy travel to

and through the heart of the city. [*Manchester*]: *SELNEC P.T.E.*, October 1971.
A printed folder (10 pp). with col. illus (drawings), a map & a col. route chart.

9201 SOUTH EAST LANCASHIRE AND NORTH EAST CHESHIRE PASSENGER TRANSPORT EXECUTIVE. Public transport plan for the future. *Manchester: SELNEC P.T.E.*, January 1973. la. 8°. pp. [x], 107, with many illus, maps, diagrams, graphs & tables.
Based on the SELNEC Transportation Study carried out between 1966 & 1971, but with planning extended beyond 1984 to the end of the century.

9202 FOSTER, C. D. Report on a social cost-benefit study of the Manchester (Piccadilly)—Hadfield/Glossop and Manchester (Piccadilly)—Marple/New Mills suburban railway services. *London: British Railways, London Midland Region.*
pt. 1, Main report, 1974. pp. viii, 46, with maps & tables.
pt. 2, Methodology, 1974. pp. viii, 162, with many tables & graphs.

9203 The PICC-VIC Project. *Manchester: Greater Manchester Council; Greater Manchester Transport*, April 1975. la. obl. format. pp. [24], with 4 plates (2 maps, a plan & a col. diagram of the Picc-Vic network), an illus & 3 appendices (financial tables) & col. pictorial cover.
Issued to publicise plans for improving the public transport of Manchester and its services, including a two-mile tunnel beneath central Manchester linking Piccadilly and Victoria stations.

9204 GREATER MANCHESTER TRANSPORT. Yes to Picc-Vic now! [*Manchester: G.M.T.*, 1977].
A 10-page col. pictorial folder-pamphlet with a col. diagram map on reverse.

9205 BURY Interchange, 1980. [*Manchester: Greater Manchester Transport; British Rail*, 1980]. la. 8°. pp. [12], with 29 col. illus & a col. plan.
An illustrated brochure issued to commemorate the opening of the Bury (bus/train) Interchange complex by Princess Alexandra, 9th July 1980.

9206 FITZGERALD, R. S. Liverpool Road Station, Manchester: an historical and architectural survey. *Manchester: Manchester University Press in association with the Royal Commission on Historical Monuments and the Greater Manchester Council*, 1980. (R.C.H.M. Supplementary Series, 1). la. 8°. pp. 64, with 51 illus, 16 architectural drawings, 2 plans, and 177 notes.
A detailed, informative work, the result of a special survey undertaken by R. S. Fitzgerald, under the sponsorship of the R.C.H.M. and the G.M.C. The drawings are by students of the School of Architecture, Manchester University.

Reference source

9207 GREVILLE, M. D. Chronology of the railways of Lancashire: dates of incorporation, opening and amalgamation, etc., of all lines in the county. *Caterham: Railway & Canal Historical Society*, 1973. pp. [19].

General and historical

9208 MOSS, I. P. Farewell to the Summit: historical notes to accompany a visit to the Walton Summit branch of the Leeds and Liverpool Canal and the Lancaster Canal tramway, made by members and friends of the North Western Group on May 4th, 1968. *Chester: Railway & Canal Historical Society*, 1968. pp. [10], with 2 maps, & 2 plans by W. J. Dean on folded plates at end, & a drawing on cover by Norman Wilkinson.

9209 PALMER, G. S. and TURNER, B. R. Blackpool by tram. *Blackpool: the authors*, [1968]. la. 8°. pp. 100, with ca. 100 illus, line drawings, maps, plans, facsimiles, fleet lists & a chronology.
83 years of tramways and light railways in Blackpool.

9210 ASHMORE, O. The industrial archaeology of Lancashire. *Newton Abbot: David & Charles*, 1969. pp. 352.
ch. 8 (pp. 181–208), Railways, with 2 maps, 3 plans, & an evaluative bibliography (pp. 334–5).

9211 [BURY]. COUNTY BOROUGH OF BURY TRANSPORT DEPARTMENT. 66 years of municipal passenger transport organisation, 1903–1969: commemorative brochure. *Bury*, [1969]. pp. 32, with 8 illus, 1 facsimile & a statistical table.

9212 WARNES, A. M. The increase of 'journey to work' and its consequences for the residential structure of towns, with special reference to Chorley, Lancashire. Thesis, Ph.D., University of Salford, 1969.

9213 GIBBS, W. M. Walton Summit and branch canal. *Preston: the author*, 1970. pp. 32, with 20 illus.
A tour of the course of the Preston & Walton Summit Plateway, with detailed observations of its flora.

9214 MACKENZIE, J. Always a tram in sight: Blackpool, 1885 to 1972 (a picture history of Blackpool's trams). *Croydon: Light Railway Transport League*, [1972]. pp. iii, 60, with 93 illus & a map.

9215 ROBERTS, B. Railways and mineral tramways of Rossendale. *Lingfield: Oakwood Press*, 1974. (Locomotion Papers, 76). pp. 27, with 18 illus, a map & a plan.

9216 BLACKPOOL'S tramways: 90 years of progress. *Glossop: Transport Publishing Co. for the Blackpool Civic Trust*, [1975]. An illustrated folder.

9217 DAWSON, T. Tramway Treasury: a pictorial history of Accrington & District Tramways, 1886–1932. [*Accrington*]: *T. Dawson*, 1975. pp. 64, with 84 illus & a chronology (pp. 8–11, 20–22).

9218 EDWARDS, M. The Garstang–Knott End Railway. *Lancaster: Lancaster Museum*, 1975. pp. [v], 10, with map. Reproduced typescript. 'A Lancaster Museum Monograph.'

9219 GILBERT, A. C. and KNIGHT, N. R. Railways around Lancashire: a pictorial survey. *Rochdale: Manchester Transport Museum Society*, 1975. obl. format. pp. [100]. Intro & 135 illus with descrs, table of openings & a la. folded map.

9220 JOY, D. Railways in Lancashire: a pictorial history. *Clapham (North Yorks): Dalesman Books*, 1975. pp. 96, with 151 illus, 2 maps & a bibliography (19 sources).
—— 2nd edn. *Dalesman*, 1976. pp. 96; 150 illus, 2 maps, bibliography (19 sources).

9221 ROBERTS, J. E. History of Preston–Kendal Canal, railways in the North West, iron and steel works, and the changing face of Carnforth. [*Carnforth: the author*, 1975]. pp. 61, with 24 illus on 8 plates.
pp. 15–34, Railway development north from Lancaster and in the Carnforth area. Includes railway trade union development in this area and an account of the 'Steamtown' Railway Museum.

9222 GARNHAM, J. A. Blackpool: a tradition of trams. *Guildford: J. A. Garnham*, 1976. pp. 48, with 50 illus, 1 map, & 2 illus on cover.

9223 KIRBY, A. K. Middleton tramways. *Castleton: Manchester Transport Museum Society*, 1976. pp. 88, with 66 illus, tables, 6 maps & a plan (4 on folded sheet at end), & 3 appendices.

9224 SHUTTLEWORTH, S. The Lancaster and Morecambe tramways. *Tarrant Hinton: Oakwood Press*, 1976. (Locomotion Papers, 95). pp. 42, with 16 illus on 8 plates (pp. 19–26), 3 maps & a plan.

9225 TURNER, B. Blackpool to Fleetwood. *London: Light Railway Transport League*, [1977]. pp. 99, with 72 illus, 10 line drawings, 3 maps & a table. The text and illustrations extend onto covers.
Reprinted, with additions, from the 1975 and 1976 issues of *Modern Tramway* (periodical).

9226 WEST LANCASHIRE LIGHT RLY. West Lancashire Light Railway, 1967–1977. *Hesketh Bank: W.L.L.R.*, [1977]. pp. 5, incl. a stock list. Reproduced typescript.
A new 2ft gauge line, 440 yards long.

9227 CATLOW, R. and COLLINGE, T. Over the setts: East Lancashire trams & buses. *Chorley: Countryside Publications*, 1978. pp. 48, with 43 illus (21 of tramcars).
pp. 3–28, Tramways.

9228 MEREDITH, C. P. Transport developments in East Lancashire, 1780–1860. Thesis, M.A., University of Manchester, 1978.

9229 BLACKPOOL & FLEETWOOD TRAMWAY. Blackpool and Fleetwood Tramway, 1979. *Blackpool: Blackpool Transport*, 1979. pp. 12. Brief history, timetables, fare tables & fleet list. 2 illus on covers.

9230 FIELDS, N., GILBERT, A. C. and KNIGHT, N. R. Liverpool to Manchester. *Castleton (Rochdale): Manchester Transport Museum Society*, 1980. pp. [110], with illus.
265 photographs (2 in col.) of scenes on the four routes between the two cities, taken between 1930 and 1980.

9231 NUTTALL, K. and RAWLINGS, T. Railways around Lancaster. *Clapham (N. Yorks): Dalesman*, 1980. pp. 79, with 47 illus, map, plan & a bibliography (15 sources).

9232 PALMER, S. and TURNER, B. Picture postcards from Blackpool & Fylde coast, 1898–1939, collected by Steve Palmer and Brian Turner. *Cleveleys (Blackpool): Palmer & Turner*, [1980]. pp. [40], with 95 illus (incl. 7 in col. on covers), 34 of which depict: tramways (31), two of railway interest, and one of 'the Switchback', a straight-track scenic railway along the beach.

Contemporaneous

9233 BOARD OF AGRICULTURE. General view of the agriculture of the County of Lancaster . . . *London: G. Nicol*, 1795. (Board of Agriculture. Agriculture Surveys).
pp. 94–8, Mosses, drainage of Trafford Moss and the method of transporting marl and sand by horse wagonways, with illustrations showing detail of wagon and portable iron track.

9234 DICKSON, R. W. General view of the agriculture of Lancashire . . . drawn up for the consideration of the Board of Agriculture and Internal Improvement; revised and prepared for the press by W. Stevenson. *London: Sherwood, Neely & Jones*, 1815.
p. 459, Peat transport over a wagonway on Chat Moss; pp. 613–4, Iron railways.

9235 The MEMORIAL of the undersigned merchants, manufacturers and others resident in the town and neighbourhood of Warrington in the County of Lancaster. [no imprint, no date]. [1845?]. s.sh., with a la. folded col. map on reverse.
Fears that the proposed bridging of the Mersey at Runcorn by the Grand Junction Rly would interfere with river commerce. Addressed 'To the Right Honourable the Commissioners of the Conservancy of the River Mersey'.

9236 LINGARD, J. Where to go by car [i.e. tramcar], with routes and interesting walks,

giving fares and distances: Lancashire. 5th edn. *Manchester: the author*, [ca. 1920?]. pp. 32. Intro & text extends onto covers.
—— a later edn. Where to go by tram. *Manchester: the author*, [1924?]. Republished by *Manchester Transport Historical Collection*, [196–?]. pp. 32 with map & 10 illus added.
—— 13th edn. *Didsbury: J. Lingard*, [ca. 1930?]. pp. 32.

9237 BANKES, J. H. M.   A nineteenth-century colliery railway. Reprinted from Transactions of the Historic Society of Lancashire & Cheshire, vol. 114 (1962), pp. 155–88, with 8 illus, 2 drawings, a map & 26 notes (some lengthy).
An industrial line from Winstanley Colliery to Wigan Pier, created & owned by Meyrick Bankes, coal merchant.

C 1 i   YORKSHIRE AND HUMBERSIDE REGION (South Yorkshire, West Yorkshire, North Yorkshire, Humberside)

9238–9337

Yorkshire & Humberside Region generally 9238–52

9238 APPLETON, J. H.   The historical geography of railways in Yorkshire. Thesis, M.Sc., King's College, Durham, 1955–6.

9239 DUCKHAM, B. F.   The Yorkshire Ouse: the history of a river navigation. *Newton Abbot: David & Charles*, 1967. pp. 226, with 31 illus on 16 plates, 10 maps & plans, 410 notes, & 7 appendices.
Includes much on railways in the area (a list on p. 206).

9240 WHEELER, R. M.   Yorkshire Steam. *Burley-in-Wharfedale: North Eastern Locomotive Preservation Group*, October 1968. pp. 18. Reproduced typescript.
A directory of steam locomotives still at work in collieries and other industrial sites in Yorkshire.

9241 SPEAKMAN, C.   Transport in Yorkshire. *Clapham (N. Yorks): Dalesman*, 1969. pp. 96, with illus.
ch. 8 (pp. 51–67), 'The Railway Age', with 5 illus & maps.

9242 KEAVEY, J.   Rails at random: a North Country railway miscellany. *[Embsay]: Yorkshire Dales Railway Society*, [1970]. pp. 21, with 6 illus.
Short essays on railways, mostly in Yorkshire.

9243 YORKSHIRE railways. *Leeds: Yorkshire Post Newspapers*, 1971. newspaper format. pp. 24, with many illus (some col.).
Railway preservation in Yorkshire.

9244 HADFIELD, C.   The canals of Yorkshire and North East England. *Newton Abbot: David & Charles*. (Canals of the British Isles series). 2 vols.
vol. 1, [to 1845]. 1972. pp. 254, with 16 illus on 8 plates, & in text, 22 illus & maps, 623 notes. Index, pp. 243–54, has 44 page refs under 'Tramroads'. Railways are entered under their individual names.
vol. 2, 1790–1845 contd, & 1845–1972. 1973. pp. 255–506, with 15 illus on 8 plates, & in text, 17 illus & maps, 542 notes, & a 10-part tabular summary as appendices. Index to both volumes, pp. 487–506, with 64 page refs under 'Tramroads'. Railways are entered under their individual names.

9245 FRANKS, D. L.   East & West Yorkshire Union Railways. *Leeds: Turntable Enterprises*, 1973. (Minor Railways of Britain series). pp. 44, with 9 illus, 2 diagrams, gradient profile, map & a folded diagram of track layouts.

9246 JOY, D.   South and West Yorkshire: the industrial West Riding. *Newton Abbot: David & Charles*, 1975. (A Regional History of the Railways of Great Britain, 8). pp. 304, with frontis, 32 illus on 16 plates, 7 illus & 9 maps in text & a folded map at end; bibliography (over 150 sources) & a 'Reference Section' (pp. 238–86) giving the basic details of all railways in the region arranged to accord with the chapter order.

9247 ROWLEY, A. and McLEAN, A. P.   Yorkshire Steam . . . originated and edited by Allen Rowley; research by Allan P. McLean. vol. 1. *[Leeds]: Yorkshire Post Newspapers*, [1977?]. sm. obl. format. pp. [72].
71 photographs from Yorkshire Post Newspaper Studios, with captions.

9248 BAIRSTOW, J. M.   Railways of Keighley. *Clapham (N. Yorks): Dalesman*, 1979. pp. 80, with 32 illus, map, 8 plans, tables, & a bibliography (15 sources).
Includes tramways.

9249 BOWTELL, H. D.   Reservoir railways of the Yorkshire Pennines, with maps specially drawn by Arthur Chambers. *Tarrant Hinton: Oakwood Press*, 1979. pp. 128, with 47 illus & 12 maps.

9250 HAIGH, A. and JOY, D.   Yorkshire railways, including Cleveland and Humberside. *Clapham (N. Yorks): Dalesman*, 1979. pp. 96, with 50 illus, 6 general maps, gradient profile, 25 smaller maps & plans, & a reference section consisting of tabulated details in 10 sections (pp. 77–94).

9251 REDMAN, R. N.   Railway byways in Yorkshire. *Clapham (N. Yorks): Dalesman Publishing Co.*, 1979. pp. 80, with 57 illus.
Light railways, narrow-gauge, industrial and miniature railways, extant and extinct.

9252 BETT, W. H. and GILLHAM, J. C. Tramways of South Yorkshire & Humberside, edited by J. H. Price. *Light Railway Transport League*, [197–]. pp. 75, with 98 illus, 11 maps, lists & a bibliography (pp. 72–5).
A revised edition of part of *Great British Tramway Networks*, 4th edn., 1962.

South Yorkshire 9253–66

9253 LEADER, R. E. Sheffield in the eighteenth century. *Sheffield: Sheffield Independent Press, and Pawson & Brailsford*, 1901. pp. 362.
pp. 84–5, 341 n: the building of a two-mile wagonway with wooden rails for coal transport in 1774, its destruction by objectors and its [alleged] reconstruction with iron rails. (See *Early Wooden Railways*, by M. J. T. Lewis (1970), p. 132. for evidence refuting this allegation).
—— 2nd edn *W. C. Leng*, 1905. (same pages).

9254 POOL, A. G. A survey of transport in Sheffield, prepared for the committee by A. G. Pool. *Sheffield: Sheffield Social Survey Committee*, January 1933. (Survey Pamphlet, 8). pp. 48.
pp. 5–17, 'Development of tramways in Sheffield'; pp. 18–28, 'The Sheffield tramways'; pp. 41–5, 'Railway transport'.

9255 RAILWAY CORRESPONDENCE & TRAVEL SOCIETY. Itinerary of the South Yorkshire Rail Tour, 11th May, 1952. *R.C. & T.S.*, [1952]. (Railway Observer Supplement no. 3, March 1952). pp. 5, with map, & itinerary notes by A. L. Barnett.
Sheffield (Wicker) Station—Grimesthorpe Junction—Masborough North Junction—Mexborough Junction—Lowfield Junction—Wrangbrook Junction—Brierley Junction—St Catherine's Junction—Shireoaks—and back to Sheffield Victoria via Woodhouse.

9256 RAILWAY CORRESPONDENCE & TRAVEL SOCIETY. Itinerary of the South Yorkshire Rail Tour no. 2, 7th June, 1953. *R.C. & T.S.*, [1953]. pp. [4], with map, & notes by A. L. Barnett.
Sheffield (Midland)—Shireoaks—Mexborough—Stairfoot Junction—Cudworth Junction—Nostell South Junction—Staincross—Stairfoot Junction—Blackburn Valley Junction—Sheffield (Midland).

9257 RAILWAY CORRESPONDENCE & TRAVEL SOCIETY. Itinerary of the South Yorkshire Rail Tour no. 3, Sunday, 20th June, 1954. *R.C. & T.S.*, [1954]. pp. 4, with map & schedule. Notes by A. L. Barnett.
Sheffield—Scunthorpe—Stainforth—Selby—York—Knottingley—Shaftholme Junction—Doncaster—Sheffield.

9258 GOODFELLOW, A. W. The development of communications, *in* Sheffield and its Region: a scientific and historical survey, edited by David L. Linton. *Sheffield: British Association*, 1956. (pp. 161–7), with map.

9259 RAILWAY CORRESPONDENCE & TRAVEL SOCIETY. Itinerary of the South Yorkshire Rail Tour no. 4 . . . , Sunday, 21st September, 1958. *R.C. & T.S.*, [1958]. pp. 4, with map & schedule. Text by A. L. Barnett.
Sheffield (Victoria)—Chapletown (Central)—Stairfoot—Staincross—Wakefield (Kirkgate)—Rotherwell—Stanley—Garforth—Dearne Valley—Carcroft—Stainforth—Low Ellers—Shireoaks—Sheffield (Victoria).

9260 WISEMAN, R. J. S. Sheffield. *Huddersfield: Advertiser Press*, 1964. (British Tramways in Pictures, 1). pp. 32, with 56 illus.
—— enlarged edn. *Advertiser Press*, 1976. (British Tramways in pictures, 1). pp. 44, with 69 illus.

9261 ELLIOTT, B. J. The South Yorkshire Joint Railway. *Lingfield: Oakwood Press*, 1972. (Oakwood Library of Railway History, 33). pp. 68, with 10 illus on 4 plates, & in text, map, plan, gradient profile, lists and timetables.
Opened in 1909 to serve the new coalfield south of Doncaster and controlled by five main-line railway companies in the area.

9262 ELLIOTT, B. J. Transport in South Yorkshire, 1830–1970, edited by B. J. Elliott. *Sheffield: University of Sheffield Institute of Education*, 1972. (Local History Pamphlets, 6). pp. 36, with drawings, map & a bibliography (15 sources).
The text consists of 22 extracts from local newspapers, 1830–1968.
—— 2nd edn. 1973. pp. 36. (Revised bibliography, 15 sources).

9263 GOODE, C. T. Railways in South Yorkshire. *Clapham (North Yorks): Dalesman Publishing Co.*, 1975. pp. 96, with 14 illus, 9 maps, 5 layout plans & 5 tables.

9264 ABELL, P. H. Transport and industry in South Yorkshire, by P. H. Abell; maps by S. A. Harper. *Barnsley: P. H. Abell*, 1977. pp. 84, with 25 illus, 9 maps & a bibliography (87 sources).
ch. 6, 'The Railway Age' (pp. 51–64); ch. 7, 'The Twentieth Century' (pp. 65–75).

9265 HALL, C. C. Sheffield transport. *Glossop: Transport Publishing Co.*, [1977]. pp. 332, with 444 illus (some col.) & 4 maps (1 la. folded).
A very detailed work with information on the development of the tramway system occupying seven-tenths of the volume. No index. Tramways mainly on pp. 30–153, 185–270, 289–300, 317–27.

9266 DENTON, A. S. The Dearne District Light Railways. *Bromley Common: Omnibus Society*, 1980. pp. 24, with 11 illus & a map. Cover title: D.D.L.R.: the story of the Dearne District Light Railways and competitors.
Period, July 1924–September 1933.

West Yorkshire 9267–9303

9267 LETTERS from Scotland, by an English commercial traveller, written during a journey to Scotland in the summer of 1815. *London: Longman, Hurst, Rees, Orme & Brown*, 1817. pp. xii, 224, & errata page [235].
pp. 13–15, At Leeds, a locomotive and train on the Middleton Railway is seen and described.

9268 SCHINKEL, C. F. Aus Schinkel's Nachlass: Reisetagebücher, Briefe und Aphorismen; mitgetheilt . . . von A. von Wolzogen. *Berlin*, 1863.
vol. 3, pp. 86–7, description in German by Carl Friedrich Schinkel of the Middleton Rly, Leeds, on 30 June 1826.

9269 HOLLIS AND WEBB [chartered surveyors & auctioneers]. Plans, illustrated particulars and special conditions of sale of the Tramway Depot at Guiseley . . . 24th September 1947. A folder containing 5 pp. text with 4 mounted photos (1 on cover) & 2 folded plans in end pocket.

9270 MIDDLETON RAILWAY PRESERVATION SOCIETY. The two oldest railways united, 1758 & 1804. [*Leeds*]: *the Society*, 1962. pp. 4, with 5 illus on 2 plates. Reproduced typescript.
Commemorates the donation of the Swansea & Mumbles Rly locomotive 'Swansea' to the Middleton Colliery Rly.

9271 KING, J. S. Keighley Corporation transport. *Huddersfield: Advertiser Press*, 1964. pp. 159, with 38 illus, 2 maps, & 7 appendices (detailed tables).
Period, from 1886. Includes tramways.

9272 KEIGHLEY & WORTH VALLEY RLY (1962). Worth Valley Railway Stockbook. 1968 edn. December 1967. pp. [32] with illus, descrs & lists.
—— Summer 1968 edn. (2nd edn.). July 1968. pp. [32].
—— 3rd edn. May 1969. pp. [32].
—— another edn. March 1970. pp. 56. Compiled by J. A. Cox.
—— 4th edn. December 1973. pp. 72. Compiled by Robin Lush & others from the original by J. A. Cox.
—— 5th edn. March 1976. pp. 64. Compiled by Robin Lush and Ian Holt.

9273 BROOK, R. The story of Huddersfield, with a foreword by Harold Wilson. *London: McGibbon & Kee*, 1968. pp. xvii, [3], 394.
ch. 10 (pp. 146–59), 'The Huddersfield Improvement Commissioners and the coming of the railways' *et passim*.

9274 HIRD, H. Bradford in history: twenty-four essays . . . *Bradford: the author*, 1968. pp. xvi, 232.
pp. 161–77, 'Bradford's vanished railway stations', with 7 illus; pp. 178–89, 'Nidd Valley Light Railway', with 4 illus.

9275 SCRAFTON, D. An analysis of public passenger transport services in West Yorkshire, 1896–1963. Thesis, Ph.D., University of London, 1967/68.
Changes in the pattern of modal choice, from railways to buses, influenced by economic, social and political factors.

9276 MIDDLETON RLY (1960). [Stockbooks]. [*Leeds*], 1968. sm. obl. format. pp. 16, incl. covers, with 9 illus. *Leeds*, 1974. pp. [12], with 10 illus. Text extends onto cover. Title on cover only.

9277 BERRY, J. G. Worth Valley week-end: 20 photographs of the Keighley and Worth Valley Light Railway. *West Kirby: the author*, [1969]. obl. format. pp. 20. Preface, & 20 illus with captions. Title from cover.
Photographs taken 19th–20th April 1969.

9278 KEIGHLEY & WORTH VALLEY RLY (1962). [Guides, with illus. (some col.) & maps]. [1st edn]., 1969. pp. [36]. By J. A. Cox.
—— 2nd edn. 1972. pp. [48]. By M. Goodall.
—— 3rd edn. 1975. pp. [36]. By M. Goodall.
—— 4th edn. 1978. pp. [40]. By M. Goodall.

9279 KEIGHLEY & WORTH VALLEY RAILWAY. Steam in the Worth Valley: a pictorial record. *Keighley: K. & W.V. Rly*. 2 vols.
[vol. 1], by G. R. Cryer and R. S. Greenwood. 1970. pp. [32], Intro & 36 illus with descrs.
vol. 2, by G. R. Cryer. 1972. pp. [32], Intro & 38 illus with descrs, map.
Includes scenes of the filming of 'The Railway Children' and other television films.
vol. 3, by I. G. Holt and J. M. Bairstow. 1980. pp. [32]. 54 illus with descrs.

9280 YOUNG, A. D. One hundred years of Leeds tramways. *Leeds: Turntable Enterprises*, 1970. pp. 102, with 74 illus, chronologies, lists & a map.

9281 HUDSON, G. S. The Aberford Railway and the history of the Garforth collieries. *Newton Abbot: David & Charles*, 1971. pp. 184, with col. frontis & 34 illus on 16 plates, 27 maps, plans, drawings & diagrams; a gazetteer, 85 notes & a bibliography (45 sources).
An independent colliery railway with a public passenger service.

9282 LEIGH, C. M. The journey to work in Leeds: its influence upon the spatial structure of a city. Thesis, Ph.D., University of Leeds, 1971/2.

9283 KEIGHLEY & WORTH VALLEY RLY (1962). Worth a second glance: a photographic record of the Worth Valley Railway. *Haworth Station: K. & W.V. Rly*, 1972. pp. 82, 120 illus with descrs; textual summary, pp. 78–82. Written by John W. Holroyd and others; foreword by Eric Treacy.
—— vol. 2, compiled by D. Whitehead. *K. & W.V. Rly*, 1981. pp. 116. Intro & 175 illus (10 col., incl. cover) with descrs & commentaries.

9284 MACK, R. F. Leeds City Tramways: a pictorial souvenir. *Leeds: Turntable Enterprises*, 1972. pp. [32], with 57 illus.

9285 WILLIAMS, P. Rails in the Worth Valley. *Clapham (N. Yorks): Dalesman*, 1973. pp. 96. Intro & 155 illus with descrs.
The Keighley & Worth Valley Rly [1968].

9286 WHOMSLEY, D. A landed estate and the railway: Huddersfield, 1844–54, *in* Journal of Transport History, new series, vol. 2 (1973–74), pp. 189–213, with 3 maps & 174 notes.
The Ramsden estate and the Manchester & Leeds Rly and the Huddersfield & Manchester Rly, 1843–9.

9287 HAIGH, A. Railways in West Yorkshire. *Clapham (N. Yorks): Dalesman Books*, 1974. pp. 96, with 48 illus, 6 maps, 3 plans, 2 appendices, a table & a bibliography (11 sources).
—— 2nd edn. *Dalesman*, 1978. pp. 88, with 46 illus on 24 plates, 13 maps, plans & diagrams, & 4 tables.

9288 HARTLEY, F. A brief history of Bradford's horse and steam tramways, 1882–1903. [*Bradford: Bradford Art Galleries & Museums*, 1974]. pp. 16, with 12 illus & 3 on covers.
A tabulated record. The work has no imprint and no date but a small, adhesive slip with this information printed on it was affixed to copies before publication.

9289 YOUNG, A. D. Leeds trams, 1932–1959. *London: Light Railway Transport League*, [1974?]. pp. 115, with frontis, 125 illus, 6 diagrams & 4 maps. Title from cover.

9290 BUSHELL, J. The world's oldest railway: a history of the Middleton Railway. *Sheffield: Turntable Publications*, 1975. pp. 36, with 17 illus & diagrams, lists, tables, folded diagrams as frontis & folded map at end; bibliography (22 sources). Foreword and postscript by the Middleton Railway Trust.

9291 NORTH EASTERN LOCOMOTIVE PRESERVATION GROUP. North Eastern revival. *Keighley: the Group*, 1975. pp. 44, with 56 illus. Text extends onto covers.
The restoration to full working order of three ex-NER locomotives for work on the North Yorkshire Moors Rly.
—— 2nd edn. *N.E.L.P.G.*, 1979. pp. 64; 88 illus & 5 dimensioned drawings.

9292 WHITELEY, J. S. and MORRISON, G. W. Steam in the West Riding, with an introduction by David Joy. *Newton Abbot: David & Charles*, 1975. 4°. pp. [72]. Intro (pp. 5–8), frontis, map, & 80 illus with descrs.

9293 CROFT, D. J. Bradford tramways. *Tarrant Hinton: Oakwood Press*, 1976. (Locomotion Papers, 90). pp. 70, with 16 illus on 8 plates, 8 diagrams, 2 maps, & chronologies of each route.

9294 JOY, D. West Riding (a picture history). *Clapham (North Yorks): Dalesman Books*, 1976. (Railways in Yorkshire series). pp. 80. Intro, map & 108 illus with descrs.
—— 2nd edn. *Dalesman*, 1976. pp. 80; map & 109 illus.

9295 GOODCHILD, J. The Lake Lock Rail Road. *Wakefield: Wakefield Metropolitan District Libraries*, 1977. (Archives Publication, 4). tall 8°. pp. 18, with a map & 118 notes. Reproduced typescript.
One of a number of coal wagonways in the Stanley-cum-Wrenthorpe area of Yorkshire leading down to the north bank of the River Calder at Lake Lock, ca. 1798–ca. 1854. A brief survey of other 18th century wagonways of the area, with 9 notes, is given on p. [18].

9296 PRIESTLEY, H. B. Halifax in the Tramway Era. *Sheffield: Turntable Enterprises*, 1977. pp. 44, with 67 illus & 3 maps.

9297 HINCHLIFFE, B. Huddersfield in the tramway era. *Sheffield: Turntable Publications*, 1978. pp. 48, with 73 illus, 2 maps & a plan.

9298 KEIGHLEY & WORTH VALLEY RLY. Worth Valley in colour: ten years of achievement (compiled by R. Higgins). *Haworth: K. & W.V. Rly*, 1978. pp. [32], with 25 col. illus.

9299 KIRKLEES METROPOLITAN COUNCIL LIBRARIES AND MUSEUMS SERVICE. Local transport, 1870–1940. *Huddersfield*, 1978. (Kirklees Camera, 1). obl. format. pp. 60. 60 illus, incl. 7 on railways, 11 on tramways, and 1 depicting both.
Selected from the Library's collection of photographs of local scenes.

9300 MIDDLETON RLY. The Middleton Railway Resource Pack. *Leeds: Middleton Rly Trust*, [1979?].
A selection of 18 study materials for historical studies on the Middleton Rly, issued in a plain folder.

9301 THORNTON, D. Middleton Railway. *Leeds: the author*, [1979]. sm. 8°. pp. 16, of illus.
The story told in a series of over 100 line drawings, each with an historical note.

9302 POVEY, R. O. T. and HOLROYD, J. W. Worth Valley Railway Route Guide, compiled and drawn by R. O. T. Povey and John W. Holroyd. *Haworth Station: Keighley & Worth Valley Railway Preservation Society*, [197–]. sm. obl. 8°. pp. [12] incl. covers, with 1 col. illus.
A large scale route map (7 inches to 1 mile) in paged sections with a running description on facing pages.

9303 PICKLES, W. The tramways of Dewsbury and Wakefield. *Broxbourne: Light Rail Transit Association*, 1980. pp. 192, with 150 illus & 8 maps (2 on end papers).

North Yorkshire 9304–31

9304 THOUGHTS on a railway from Whitby into the interior, by A Townsman. *Whitby: printed at the office of R. Rodgers*, 1831. pp. 8.
Advocating a line to Pickering with a branch to Lealholm Bridge.   LU(THC)

9305 RAILWAY CORRESPONDENCE & TRAVEL SOCIETY. Itinerary of the Pennine Diesel Rail Tour ('The Little North Western') . . . , Saturday, 15th September, 1956. *R.C. & T.S.*, [1956]. pp. 4, with map & schedule. Text by A. L. Barnett.
Leeds—Ilkley—Skipton—Settle Junction—Penrith—Hellifield—Skipton—Leeds.

9306 HARTLEY, K. E. The Sand Hutton Light Railway. *Huddersfield: Narrow Gauge Railway Society*, 1964. pp. 68, with 12 illus, 2 maps, 3 plans, 4 gradient profiles, 3 diagrams, 6 tables & a bibliography (12 sources).
7½ miles: 1912–1922, 15-inch gauge; 1922–1932, 18-inch gauge.

9307 READING, S. J. The Derwent Valley Light Railway. *Lingfield: Oakwood Press*, 1967. (Locomotion Papers, 37). pp. 55, with 14 illus & map on 8 plates, 10 station plans, 5 statistical tables & a map.
—— 2nd edn. The Derwent Valley Railway, revised by D. S. M. Barrie. *Blandford: Oakwood Press*, 1976. pp. 55.
—— 3rd edn. [abridged]. The Derwent Valley Railway, rev. by D. S. M. Barrie. *Tarrant Hinton: Oakwood Press*, 1978. pp. 24, with 16 illus on 8 plates, 5 tables & a map, with the second map transferred to the back cover.
The author was General Manager of the D.V.L.R., 1926–63. D. S. M. Barrie was formerly General Manager B.R. (ER) and a director of the D.V.R. (The D.V.L.R. became the D.V.R. in March 1963).
The line, originally from York to Cliff Common, near Selby (16 miles) was opened in 1913 but only one quarter of its original route is now used. The company runs the railway, pays its staff as BR, and in recent years the maximum allowed dividend has been paid to shareholders.

9308 BAUGHAN, P. E. The railways of Wharfedale. *Newton Abbot: David & Charles*, 1969. pp. 272, with col. frontis, 48 illus on 24 plates, & in text, 10 maps, facsimiles & layout plans.

9309 KNARESBOROUGH RAILWAY COMMITTEE. [Report of the Knaresborough Railway Committee, 1819]. The Knaresborough Railway Report, 1819: a lithographic reprint with notes on the background to the scheme. *Knaresborough: Nidd Valley Narrow Gauge Railways*, [1969]. pp. [3], 36.
A facsimile of the original report on Thomas Telford's survey, published in March 1820, but without the map, for want of finding a copy in a reproducible condition.

9310 HARTLEY, K. E. The Easingwold Railway. *Lingfield: Oakwood Press*, 1970. (Locomotion Papers, 46). pp. 55, with 14 illus on 7 plates, map, 2 station plans, 2 groups of drawings, financial tables & a bibliography (22 sources).

9311 NORTH YORKSHIRE MOORS HISTORICAL RAILWAY TRUST. Stock Book. *Pickering: the Trust*, [1971]. pp. [23], with illus, map & plan.
—— 1974 edn, pp. 48, with 56 illus.

9312 CROFT, D. J. The Nidd Valley Railway. *Lingfield: Oakwood Press*, 1972. (Locomotion Papers, 55). pp. 27, with 9 illus on 4 plates, map & 4 station layouts; timetables. Period, 1907–1936.

9313 NORTH YORKSHIRE MOORS RLY. Illustrated Guide. *Lichfield: Harraton, for the N.Y.M. Rly*, [1972]. pp. [8], with 8 illus. Title & additional text & illus on covers.
—— rev. & enl. edn. Around the railway, by Harry Mead. *[Pickering]: the Railway*, 1974. pp. 16 & card covers, with 21 col. illus & 2 maps.

9314 BOYES, G. The Heck Bridge and Wentbridge Railway. *Leeds: Turntable Enterprises*, 1973. (Minor Railways of Britain series). pp. 35, with 9 illus, map, 2 diagrams, and 45 notes.
A proposed line to carry limestone from Kirk Smeaton to the Knottingley & Goole Canal at Heck Bridge. An abortive venture. Not opened.

9315 MOORE, R. F. Paddy Waddell's railway. *Whitby: Whitby Literary & Philosophical Society, in conjunction with North York Moors Rly*, 1973. pp. 56, with line illus & folded map.
The Cleveland Extension Mineral Railway: an abortive project (1872–96) intended to link two branches of the N.E. Rly in North Yorkshire.

9316 NORTH YORKSHIRE MOORS RLY. Official opening by H.R.H. the Duchess of Kent, May 1st, 1973. *Pickering: the Railway*, 1973. obl. format. pp. [36], with 14 illus.
A commemorative brochure recording the history of the line from 1833 and its renaissance and subsequent development by the North York Moors Historical Railway Trust.

9317 BINNS, D. The railways of Craven. *Nelson: Hendon Publishing Co.*, 1974. obl. format. pp. [40], with 65 illus & 2 sketch maps.
The Skipton area of Yorkshire.

9318 GRIGG, A. O. and SMITH, P. G. An opinion survey of the Yorkshire Dales rail service in 1975. *Crowthorne: Transport & Road Research Laboratory*, 1977. (T.R.R.L. Report, LR 769). tall 8°. pp. 25, with 12 tables & 5 maps.
A monitoring of the 'Dales Rail' transport and recreation experiment.

9319 HOOLE, K. Railways in the Yorkshire Dales. *Clapham (North Yorkshire): Dalesman*, 1975. pp. 96, with 58 illus & a map.

9320 HOOLE, K. The railways of York. *Clapham*

(North Yorkshire): Dalesman Publishing Co., 1976. pp. 95, with 48 illus on 24 plates, map, 4 layout plans, & tables.

9321 YORKSHIRE DALES RAILWAY SOCIETY. Embsay Steam Centre: stockbook & guide. 1st edn, compiled by J. R. Ellis. *Embsay (Skipton): the Society*, 1976. pp. [24] incl. covers, with 20 illus, map & plan.
—— 2nd edn. ed. by J. R. Ellis, 1978. pp. [24], with 22 illus & plan.

9322 HOOLE, K. North Riding (a pictorial history). *Clapham (North Yorks): Dalesman*, 1977. (Railways in Yorkshire series). pp. 80. Intro, map, & 100 illus with descrs.

9323 RANKIN, S. and THOMPSON, D. York 100: 1877–1977; the story of a station, with a foreword by Kenneth Appleby, Area Manager, York. *York: C. W. F. Cook*, 1977. pp. 36, with 13 illus & 2 plans.

9324 WILLIAMS, P. and JOY, D. North Yorkshire Moors Railway: a pictorial survey. *Clapham (North Yorks): Dalesman*, 1977. pp. 80, with 90 illus with descrs, a map & a gradient profile.

9325 GRIGG, A. O. and HUDDART, L. An opinion survey of the Yorkshire Dales rail service in 1977. *Crowthorne: Transport & Road Research Laboratory*, 1979. (T.R.R.L. Report, LR 906). tall 8°. pp. 35.
   The 'Dales Rail' transport and recreation experiment.

9326 JOY, D. Steam on the North York moors: a guide to the Grosmont-Pickering Railway. *Clapham (North Yorks): Dalesman*, 1978. sm. 8°. pp. 48, with 16 illus on plates (pp. 17–20, 29–32), 4 drawings, a map, a gradient profile & an evaluative bibliography (pp. 47–8).
   —— 2nd edn. *Dalesman*, 1980. pp. 48; 16 illus, etc.; bibliography.

9327 COUNTRYSIDE COMMISSION. Dales Rail: a report of an experimental project in the Yorkshire Dales National Park. *Cheltenham: the Commission*, 1979. pp. iv, 33, with 13 illus, map, chart & 4 appendices.
   An integrated train and bus service utilising the Settle–Carlisle line to facilitate access to the countryside from Leeds.

9328 KEAVEY, J. Ten years hard: a brief history and an account of the re-opening for passenger traffic of the Yorkshire Dales Railway, 'The Station in the Dales'. *Embsay (Skipton): Yorkshire Dales Rly*, [1979]. pp. [24], with 25 illus.

9329 NORTH YORKSHIRE MOORS RLY. North Yorkshire Moors Railway Stock as at 1 April, 1979. [*Pickering: the Railway*, 1979]. pp. [4]. Reproduced typescript.
   A six-column list of 99 locomotives, carriages, wagons and service vehicles.

9330 NORTH YORKSHIRE MOORS RLY. Guideline to the North York Moors Railway. [*Pickering: the Railway*, 1977]. A 12-page printed folder.
   A route map companion, with notes on features to be seen from the train, and a gradient profile.
   —— another edn. *Pickering: the Railway*, 1980. pp. 15. A booklet, with 29 illus, gradient profile, & a route map on pp. 4–9.

9331 MURRAY, H. The horse tramways of York, 1880–1909: the birth, life and death of a transport system. *Broxbourne: Light Rail Transit Association*, 1980. pp. 112, with 28 illus, 8 maps, 6 facsimiles, 4 diagrams, 4 gradient profiles, tables & extracts from documents, & a bibliography (20+ sources).

Humberside 9332–37

9332 LEE, G. A. The tramways of Kingston-upon-Hull, 1871–1945. Thesis, Ph.D., University of Sheffield, 1968.

9333 INGRAM, M. E. Railways, *in* A History of the County of York, East Riding, vol. 1, The City of Kingston-upon-Hull. *London: Oxford University Press*, 1969. (Victoria History of the Counties of England). pp. 392–7, with 109 notes.

9334 SHARP, J. An investigation into the effects of the closure of the Hull–Hornsea and Hull–Withernsea railway. Thesis, M.A., University of Hull, 1975.

9335 CHARLESWORTH, M. and ROBINSON, S. F. C. The Kingston-upon-Hull street tramways: a history of enterprise in Hull tramway operation, 1870 to 1899. *Kingston-upon-Hull: the authors*, 1976. pp. 22. Reproduced typescript.   LU(THC)

9336 HARTLEY, K. E. The Spurn Head Railway. *Industrial Railway Record*, no. 67, August 1976. Special monograph issue. pp. 249–92, with 30 illus, 2 diagrams & 3 maps.
   A coastal defence railway, 3¾ miles long; period 1915–1959.

9337 HOOLE, K. East Riding (a pictorial history). *Clapham (North Yorks): Dalesman*, 1976. (Railways in Yorkshire series). pp. 80. Intro, map, & 112 illus with descrs.

C 1 j   NORTH REGION (Cumbria, Durham, Cleveland, Northumberland, Tyne & Wear)

9338–9420

**North Region generally (including
'North East England')
9338–45**

9338 BRITISH TOURIST AUTHORITY and BRITISH RAILWAYS. Northumbria. *B.T.A. & B.R.*, [1975]. pp. [6]. A printed publicity folder with 12 illus & a map.
An introduction to Northumbria as the cradle of railway history.

9339 TAYLOR, T. J. The archaeology of the coal trade, *in* Memoirs Chiefly Illustrative of the History and Antiquities of Northumberland, communicated to the annual meeting of the Archaeological Institute of Great Britain and Ireland held at Newcastle on Tyne in August 1852, vol. 1: Miscellaneous Papers. *London: Bell & Daldy*, 1858. pp. 150–223, with 17 illus, col. map of the Durham & Northumberland coal field showing railways & wagonways; footnotes & 9 appendices.
—— Reprint. *Newcastle on Tyne: Frank Graham*, 1971. pp. 76.
A facsimile reprint omitting the map of the Northern coal field.

9340 HOOLE, K. North East England. *Newton Abbot: David & Charles*, 1965. (A Regional History of the Railways of Great Britain, 4). pp. 237, with frontis, 44 illus on 20 plates, 8 maps & col. folded map at end.
—— [2nd edn]. The North East. *David & Charles*, 1974. (Regional History series, 4). pp. 237, etc.

9341 GARD, R. M. and HARTLEY, J. R. Railways in the making: an archive teaching unit for the study of waggon ways in the North East and the evolution of the steam locomotive prior to 1825. *Newcastle upon Tyne: University of Newcastle upon Tyne, Department of Education; distributed by Hill*, 1969. (Archive Teaching Units, 3). Introduction (s.sh.) & 26 reproduced documents (facsims), a 4-page glossary and a 31-page handbook, all in a portfolio.

9342 HOOLE, K. North East England. *Newton Abbot: David & Charles*, 1969. (Railway History in Pictures series). pp. 112. Intro, col. frontis & 206 illus with commentaries.

9343 HOOLE, K. Forgotten railways: North East England. *Newton Abbot: David & Charles*, 1973. pp. 212, with 32 illus on 16 plates, 13 maps in text & a col. folded map at end.

9344 ATKINSON, F. The industrial archaeology of North East England: the counties of Northumberland and Durham and the Cleveland district of Yorkshire: *Newton Abbot: David & Charles*. (Industrial Archaeology of the British Isles series).
vol. 1, [Geological background and the development of industries]. 1974. pp. 215, with 32 illus on 16

plates, & in text, 33 maps, diagrams & line drawings.
ch. 6 (pp. 117–49), 'Transport', with 13 bibliogr. notes & a bibliography (22 sources).
vol. 2, The sites. 1974. pp. [ix], 225–368, with 6 illus (drawings & diagrams).
pp. 225–336, 'Gazetteer' & 57 notes; appendix 1 (pp. 337–43), 'Preservation in the region', including railway sites); appendix 2 (pp. 344–7), 'An outline of railway development in the Northumberland and Durham coalfield' by H. A. Townley; appendix 3 (pp. 348–51), 'Stockton & Darlington Railway house plaques'; appendix 4 (pp. 352–8), 'Railway inclines in County Durham; pp. 359–60, 'The Plessey Waggon Way', a song [18th century].

9345 ALLANSON, E. W. The historical geography of the railway network of South Durham and Teesside. Thesis, Ph.D., University of Hull, 1975.

Cumbria 9346–76

9346 HUTCHINSON, W. The history of the County of Cumberland. *Carlisle: F. Jollie*, 1794–7. (re-published by *EP Publishing* in co-operation with Cumberland County Libraries, 1974).
vol. 2, pp. 47, 66–8, Wagonways at Whitehaven (brief descriptions only).

9347 DIXON, J. The literary life of William Brownrigg, with an account of the coal mines near Whitehaven . . . *Whitehaven*, 1801. pp. xiii, 239.
pp. 98–112, underground wagonways in Whitehaven mines; pp. 108–12, surface lines.

9348 LYSONS, D. and LYSONS, S. Magna Britannia. *London: T. Cadell & W. Davies*, [1806]–1822. 4°. 6 vols.
vol. 4, 1816. pp. cxii–cxxiii, wagonways at Whitehaven, ca. 1720.

9349 REMARKS on the utility and practicability of the formation of a rail road between Whitehaven and Carlisle. *Workington*, 1830. pp. 30.
Predicts the carriage of mail by railways.
N. Kerr cat. 224/47 (xi).

9350 The PROJECTED railway extensions to Silloth Bay from Wigton or Drumburgh. *Wigton: printed by William Robertson*, 1853. pp. 10.
A protest against the making of a railway from Drumburgh to Silloth Canal, and preference for a line from Wigton or Leegate.

9351 LAKE DISTRICT DEFENCE SOCIETY. [Prospectus]. *Ambleside: the Society*, 1885. pp. 7, with 2 maps of proposed lines and a list of members (pp. 2–7).
'Formed to offer . . . opposition to the introduction of unnecessary railways into the Lake District'.
—— Balance sheets [of the Derwentwater and Borrowdale Defence Fund and of the Lake District Defence Society], 1883–1885. pp. [4].   LU(THC)

9352 THOMAS, D. St J. Lake District Transport Report: the findings of the Lake District Transport Enquiry, by David St John Thomas: sponsored by Dartington Hall Trustees, Totnes, Devon. *Dawlish: David & Charles*, 1961. pp. 64, with map.
Foreword by Sir Patrick Hamilton, promoter of the enquiry.
pp. 35–48 *et passim*, Railways.

9353 STADDON, S. A. The tramways of Sunderland. *Huddersfield: Advertiser Press*, 1964. pp. 164, with frontis & 70 illus.

9354 DAVIES, W. J. K. The Ravenglass & Eskdale Railway. *Newton Abbot: David & Charles*, 1968. pp. 204, with 51 illus on 24 plates, 18 drawings, diagrams, 2 maps, 26 layout plans, gradient profile, lists & tables; bibliography (23 sources).

9355 JOY, D. Cumbrian Coast railways. *Clapham (North Yorks): Dalesman Publishing Co.*, 1968. pp. 96, with 58 illus, 3 maps & a bibliography (ca. 50 sources).

9356 BUTLER, P. E. B. and LYNE, J. D. The Ravenglass and Eskdale Railway. *Lingfield: Oakwood Press*, 1969. (Locomotion Papers, 44). pp. 20, with 20 illus on frontis & 8 plates, 2 maps, 2 composite layout diagrams, gradient profile & timetables.

9357 MARSHALL, J. D. and DAVIES-SHIEL, M. The industrial archaeology of the Lake Counties. *Newton Abbot: David & Charles*, 1969. (Industrial Archaeology of the British Isles series). pp. 287, with 27 illus on 16 plates, 25 maps & diagrams.
ch. 7 (pp. 180–200), Transport.

9358 NATIONAL COUNCIL ON INLAND TRANSPORT. Carlisle–Keswick passenger rail service: written submission to the Minister. *London: N.C.I.T.*, [Oct. 1970]. pp. 4. Reproduced typescript.
Closure would suggest a callous indifference to the welfare of large sections of the community already threatened by withdrawal of bus services.

9359 RAVENGLASS & ESKDALE RLY. Handbook. 3rd edn, 1970. pp. 36, with illus, map & gradient profile. Text & tables revised by W. J. K. Davies.
—— 4th edn, 1973. pp. 36.
—— 5th edn, 1978. pp. 32.

9360 RAVENGLASS & ESKDALE RLY. The story of the 'River Mite'. *Ravenglass: R & E. Rly*, 1971. pp. 20, with 16 illus, incl. cover illus.
The construction of a 15-inch gauge 2-8-0 steam locomotive for passenger train work on the railway; pp. 3–7 by Patrick G. Satow, and an account of its delivery by traction engine haulage from York to Ravenglass, by Douglas Ferreira (pp. 8–20).

9361 CHARTERS, J. N. The Brampton Railway, 1798–1953. *Lingfield: Oakwood Press*, [1972]. (Oakwood Library of Railway History, 31).

pp. 96, with 28 illus & map on 12 plates, 19 layout plans & diagrams in text.
A colliery railway on Tindale Fell, Cumberland, owned by Lord Carlisle, leased to James Thompson and his descendants, 1837–1908 and to the Naworth Coal Co., 1908–1924. Ownership thereafter was by Naworth Collieries Ltd, 1924–47, and the National Coal Board from 1947 to closure in 1953.

9362 DORMAN, C. C. Carlisle (Citadel) railway scene. *London: Allen & Unwin*, 1972. pp. 143, with 118 illus, incl. frontis, list of signal boxes, 3 maps & a chronology.
A pictorial history of the station, host to seven pre-Grouping railways, and after 1922, to the LMSR and LNER.

9363 WEBB, D. R. The Cumbrian Explorer, Saturday May 13th 1972. *Ravenglass: Ravenglass & Eskdale Rly*, 1972. pp. 12, with 4 illus & a map.
A guide to a tour from Leicester to Ravenglass and to Keighley, consisting principally of an historical essay by D. R. Webb (pp. 3–8) entitled 'The railways of Furness and West Cumberland'. Itinerary (pp. 9–10); timetable (p. 11).

9364 WILLIAMS, P. Rails from Ravenglass: a pictorial study of 'La'al Ratty'. *Lancaster: Dalesman*, 1972. pp. 96, with 113 illus.
The Ravenglass & Eskdale Rly.

9365 JOY, D. Railways of the Lake counties. *Clapham (North Yorks): Dalesman*, 1973. (Dalesman Pictorial Histories). la. 8°. pp. 80, with 125 illus, 3 maps, chronology & a bibliography (32 sources).

9366 WALKER, C. Carlisle. *Oxford: Oxford Illustrators*, 1973. (Steam Railway series). obl. 8°. pp. [64]. Intro & 58 illus with descrs.
Railways in the Carlisle area, 1960–63.

9367 CORMACK, I. L. Transport of Barrow-in-Furness: ninety years on wheels. *Glasgow: Scottish Tramway Historical Studies*, [1974]. pp. 12, with 19 illus; folded map as insert.
Includes tramways.

9368 DAVIES, W. J. K. The Bedside 'Ratty', compiled by W. J. K. Davies. [*Ravenglass: Ravenglass & Eskdale Rly Co.*, 1974]. tall 8°. pp. 65, with 57 illus & facsimile extracts & documents, including the prospectus, Act of Incorporation and the Board of Trade Inspecting Officer's Report (1876), timetables, and verses. Text extends on to covers.

9369 LAKESIDE & HAVERTHWAITE RLY. Official Stock List and Guide, compiled by Bill Ballard. [3rd edn.] *Haverthwaite Station: the Railway*, 1974. pp. [40], with 31 illus, map & gradient profile; 2 illus (1 col.) on cover.
A re-opened 3½ mile section of the Plumpton Junction to Lakeside branch of the Furness Rly.

9370 FERRIERA, D. Ratty's 100: the story of 100 years of the Ravenglass & Eskdale Railway in over 100 pictures. *Ravenglass: R. & E. Rly*, 1976. la. 8°. pp. 71, with 133 illus. Intro on inside cover.

9371 WALTON, J. K. The Windermere tourist trade in the age of the railway, 1847–1912, in Windermere in the Nineteenth Century, ed. by Oliver M. Westall, 1976. (University of Lancaster, Centre for North-West Regional Studies, Occasional Paper, 1), pp. 19–38, with 48 notes.

9372 QUAYLE, H. L. and JENKINS, S. C. Lakeside and Haverthwaite Railway. *Clapham (N. Yorks): Dalesman*, 1977. pp. 72, with 15 illus on plates, 5 layout plans, 2 lists, a gradient profile, a drawing & a bibliography (21 sources).
A preserved section of the Ulverston to Lakeside branch of the Furness Rly.

9373 WEBB, B. and GORDON, D. A. Lord Carlisle's railways. *Railway Correspondence & Travel Society*, 1978. (Industrial Railway Record, no. 79, October 1978). pp. 127, [13], with 57 illus on 65 pp. 25 maps, plans & layout plans, 6 line drawings of rolling stock, 4 ink sketches & 2 gradient profiles.
A detailed account of the wagonway and later railways on land owned by Frederick Howard (5th Earl of Carlisle, 1748–1825) in the Naworth colliery area of Cumberland between Brampton and Lambsley, 1798–1953, often referred to as the Brampton Railway.

9374 ROBERTS, J. E. Thrilling runs on 'Cumbrian Coast Express' and 'North Yorkshireman'. *Carnforth: Steamtown Museum*, [1979]. sm. 8°. pp. [56], with 8 col. illus on 4 plates, & 36 illus & 2 maps in text.

9375 LAKESIDE & HAVERTHWAITE RLY. The Lakeside & Haverthwaite Railway: a short history; a driver's view of the line; stock list. *Haverthwaite Station: the Railway*, [1980 or 81]. pp. [24], with 35 col. illus, incl. 4 on covers.

9376 ROBINSON, P. W. Railways of Cumbria. *Clapham (N. Yorks): Dalesman*, 1980. obl. format. pp. 96, with 177 illus, incl. 5 on covers (1 col.), 2 plans & a bibliography (14 sources).

Durham 9377–91

9377 TURNER, R. M. Maps of Durham, 1576–1872, in the University Library, Durham, including some other maps of local interest: a catalogue by Ruth M. Turner. *Durham: Durham University Library*, 1954. pp. 40.
The importance of railway development in the county is well noted by the compiler and of the 153 maps described at least 16 are of wagonways or railways, or include them. Maps within printed books are included for works published before 1851.
LU(THC)

9378 SANDERSON, P. The antiquities of the Abbey, or cathedral church, of Durham; also, a particular description of the County Palatine of Durham. *Newcastle: printed by J.*

White & T. Saint for P. Sanderson, 1767. 2 pts (pp. 141; pp. 147).
pt 2, pp. 77–8, Tyneside wagonways and staithes.

9379 HUTCHINSON, W. History and antiquities of the County Palatine of Durham. *Newcastle: printed for S. Hodgson*, 1785–94. 3 vols.
vol. 2 (1787), p. 423, an early mention of the Causey Arch (1 para.).
vol. 3 (1794), pp. 497–8, Tyneside wagonways, in a section on coal working, from the foot of p. 493 to p. 504, with 2 plates. This includes an account of the formation of the 'Grand Alliance' of coal mine owners, and has details of wagonways, of wagon construction, and of staithes (2 long paragraphs in all).
—— another edn. *Durham: G. Walker*, 1823. 3 vols.

9380 SOPWITH, T. A treatise on isometrical drawing. *London: J. Weale*, 1834. pp. xxvi, 239 & 32 plates.
pp. xxiv, 232 & pl. XXVII, details, plans & elevation of the Causey Arch, built in 1727 for conveying coal from pits over Tanfield Moor to the River Tyne.

9381 LOVEDAY, J. Diary of a Tour in 1732 through parts of England, Wales, Ireland and Scotland. *Edinburgh: privately printed*, 1890.
p. 172, a visit to the Tanfield wagonway and Causey Arch in County Durham.

9382 HARLEY, Edward [Lord, 2nd Earl of Oxford]. Journal, in Report on the MSS of the Duke of Portland (Royal Commission on Historical Manuscripts, 1901), vol. 6.
On p. 104 is a brief description of Allan's and Hedworth's colliery wagonways (5 miles together) at Chester-le-Street, Co. Durham, on 6 May 1725.

9383 HEARSE, G. S. The tramways of Gateshead. *Corbridge: the author*, 1965. pp. viii, 123, with frontis, 59 illus & 2 folded maps.

9384 HEARSE, G. S. The tramways of Jarrow and South Shields. *Corbridge: the author*, 1971. pp. 147, with frontis, 44 illus & 3 maps.

9385 WHITTLE, G. The railways of Consett and north-west Durham. *Newton Abbot: David & Charles*, 1971. pp. 248, with col. frontis, 32 illus on 16 plates, & in text, 27 illus, maps & diagrams; chronology, tables of mileage, receipts & expenditure, and of traffic.
The development of the network of railways of this area, some of which were incorporated into the NER (1854) and others which remained as independent colliery lines.

9386 HOWE, R. Darlington municipal transport. *Darlington: Darlington Corporation*, 1972. la. 8°. (Darlington Public Library, Local History Publications, 4). pp. 27, with 9 illus, a map & a bibliography (33 sources).
Includes tramways.

9387 BRITISH RAILWAYS. Rail 150 Tour: a journey into yesterday. *[London]: B.R.*, [1975]. A printed folder with 9 illus & 4 maps.
A special tour from Darlington along the routes of

early railways in Durham county, arranged for Saturdays in July, August and September, 1975.

9388 CORKIN, R. Shildon, cradle of the railways: story, Robert Corkin; photographs, Ken Beetham. *Newcastle upon Tyne: Frank Graham*, 1977. (Northern History Booklets, 76). pp. 40, with 21 illus.

9389 MOUNTFORD, C. E. and CHARLTON, L. G. Industrial locomotives of Durham. *Market Harborough: Industrial Railway Society*, 1977. (Handbook Series, L). pp. [5], vii, 403, with frontis, 144 illus on 72 plates, 25 maps, & 15 plans of colliery railway systems.
This very detailed work, both in text & index, is a much revised & extended version of the 1962 edition of Handbook L.

9390 TANFIELD RLY (1971). The Tanfield Railway: an illustrated guide & history. *Newcastle [upon Tyne]: Tanfield Rly*, 1977. sm. obl. format. pp. 16 & covers, with 23 illus, 3 maps & a stock list.
The revival of what is believed to be the oldest existing railway in the world (Tanfield wagonway, 1725).

9391 WILCOCK, D. The Durham coalfield. *Durham: Durham County Library*.
part 1, 'The Sea Coal Age'. 1979. (Local History Publications, 14). pp. viii, 89, with 18 drawings, 11 maps & plans & a bibliography (20 sources).
ch. 9 (pp. 46–59), 'Transporting the coal'. Includes wagonways and the Causey Arch.

Cleveland 9392–94

9392 CHAPMAN, S. K. Gazetteer of Mines of the Cleveland ironstone industry. *Guisborough: Langbaurgh Museum Service*, 1967. (Dorman Museum Research Report, 1). pp. 11, with folded map.
72 mines described. Includes railway & wagonway connections.
—— 2nd edn. *Langbaurgh Museum Service*, 1976. pp. 32.
83 mines and their railways & wagonways.

9393 HOOLE, K. Railways in Cleveland. *Clapham (North Yorkshire): Dalesman Books*, 1971. la. 8°. pp. 96, with 33 illus, 3 maps & tables.

9394 TRANSIT for Cleveland: a transport study prepared by E. Relton, P. J. Walker, J. D. Wiggins. *Croydon: Light Railway Transport League*, [1973]. pp. 24, with 10 illus, a map & a diagram.
Proposals for a light rapid-transit system.

Northumberland 9395–9407

9395 NORTHUMBERLAND RECORD OFFICE. Northumberland railways, from 1700. (Exhibition of original documents, maps, pictures and relics . . . held at the Northumberland Record Office . . . May 1969–December 1970), compiled, with introduction, by R. M.

Gard. *Newcastle upon Tyne: Northumberland Record Office*, 1969. pp. 57, with 5 illus.
181 exhibits listed, some with notes and longer descriptions; historical introductions to each group of exhibits; a list of deposited plans (pp. 52–6); a book list (15 works) and two poems on pp. [3 & 4] of cover.

9396 HUTCHINSON, W. A view of Northumberland . . . *Newcastle: W. Charnley & Messrs Vesey & Whitfield*, 1778. 2 vols. with plates.
vol. 2, p. 416 (note): 'Waggonways were first used in this neighbourhood soon after the Revolution, by Mr Allan of Flatts, in the County of Durham, and on the Tyne by Charles Montague, Esq., at Stella.'

9397 The PICTURE of Newcastle upon Tyne, containing a guide to the town & neighbourhood, an account of the Roman Wall, and a description of the coal mines. *Newcastle: D. Akenhead*, 1807. [Republished as a facsimile reprint by *E & W Books*, 1969].
pp. 178–9, Tyneside wagonways; pp. 181–6, a long, detailed and graphic account of a ride on the underground wagonway at Kitty's Drift near Newcastle.

9398 MACKENZIE, E. An historical, topographical and descriptive view of the county of Northumberland and of those parts of the county of Durham situated north of the River Tyne, with Berwick-upon-Tweed. 2nd edn. *Newcastle upon Tyne: Mackenzie & Dent*, 1825. 2 vols.
vol. 1, p. 126, the underground wagonway at Kitty's Drift; pp. 194–5, general description of Tyneside wagonways.
vol. 2, p. 285, Wylam wagonway mentioned (1 para.).
—— 2nd edn. *Mackenzie & Dent*, 1825. 2 vols.
vol. 1, pp. 146–9, Wagonways.
vol. 2, p. 372, Wylam wagonway (1 para.).

9399 POCOCKE, R. Northern journey, 1760, *in* Publications of the Surtees Society, vol. 124, 1915.
pp. 240–1, Tyneside wagonways briefly described.

9400 BERGEN, C. History of the Bedlington ironworks, 1736–1867. *Bedlington: privately issued*, n.d. [ca. 1925]. pp. 28.
Includes reference to George Stephenson and to early railway history in the area.

9401 A HISTORY of Northumberland, issued under the direction of the Northumberland County History Committee. *Newcastle upon Tyne: Andrew Reid; London: Simpkin, Marshall, Hamilton, Kent & Co.*, 1893–1940. 15 vols.
vol. 8, The parish of Tynemouth, by H. H. E. Craster. 1907. pp. xiv, map, 457. Index has 13 page refs under 'Railways'. *See also* pp. 17–34, 'Collieries and the Coal Trade', and for wagonways, pp. 20–1, 27–8.
vol. 9, The parochial chapelries of Earsdon and Horton, by H. H. E. Craster. 1909. pp. xii, map, 410. Index has 7 page refs under 'Railways'.
vol. 12, The parishes of Ovingham, Stamfordham and Ponteland, by Madeleine Hope Dodds. 1926.

pp. xviii, map, 611. Index has 8 page refs under 'Railways'.

vol. 13, The parishes of Heddon-on-the-Wall, Newburn, Long Benton and Wallsend; the chapelries of Gosforth and Cramlington; the townships of Benwell, Elswick, Heaton, Byker, Fenham and Jesmond, by Madeleine Hope Dodds. 1930. pp. xvi, map, 593. Index has 16 page refs under 'Railways' and one is led to the same passages in the text from index entries under, e.g., Hackworth, Hedley, Stephenson, and Wylam.

Considering the massive scale of this work—occupying a whole library shelf—and the importance of Northumberland as the cradle of railway history, the work is disappointing as a study source.

9402 WRIGHT, A. The North Sunderland Railway. *Lingfield: Oakwood Press*, 1967. (Locomotion Papers, 36). pp. 48, with 15 illus on 6 plates, 9 composite drawings, 5 layout plans, 3 tables & 2 maps.

An independent light railway branch from the North Eastern Rly at Chathill via North Sunderland to Seahouses, Northumberland; opened 1898, closed 1952.

9403 NORTHUMBERLAND RECORD OFFICE. Northumberland railways, from 1700. (Exhibition of original documents, maps, pictures and relics . . . held at the Northumberland Record Office . . . May 1969–December 1970, compiled, with introduction, by R. M. Gard). *Newcastle upon Tyne: Northumberland Record Office*, 1969. pp. 57, with 5 illus.

181 exhibits listed, some with notes and longer descriptions; historical introductions to each group of exhibits; a list of deposited plans (pp. 52–6); a book list (15 works) and 2 poems on pp. [3 & 4] of cover.

9404 BROOKS, P. R. B. A walk around Wylam. *Wylam: Wylam Local History Society*, 1975. pp. [12], with 5 illus & a map.

The birthplace of George Stephenson, Timothy Hackworth and Nicholas Wood.

9405 BROOKS, P. R. B. Wylam and its railway pioneers . . . *Wylam: Wylam Parish Council*, October 1975. pp. 41, with 28 illus.

The August 1975 edition reprinted with minor amendments.

—— [2nd edn]. Where railways were born . . . *Wylam Parish Council*, 1979. pp. 48, with 36 illus & facsimiles.

9406 WARN, C. R. Rails across Northumberland. *Newcastle upon Tyne: Frank Graham.*

part 1, Wagonways and early railways of Northumberland, 1605–1840. 1976. (Northern History Booklets, 70). pp. 56, with 26 illus & a map section (pp. 35–45) showing the evolution of railways in the area.

part 2, Main line railways of Northumberland. 1976. (Northern History Booklets, 70). pp. 63, with 29 illus on 16 plates, 13 maps, 7 facsimiles & line drawings.

part 3, Rural branch lines of Northumberland. 1975. (Northern History Booklets, 70). pp. 56, with 24 illus, 16 maps, 2 facsimiles & 2 tables.

part 4, Railways of the Northumberland coalfield. 1976. (Northern History Booklets, 70). pp. 60, with 29 illus on 16 plates, 20 maps & plans.

Includes public railways as well as mineral lines.

9407 JOHN SINCLAIR RAILWAY MUSEUM. Handbook and Guide. *Blyth: the Museum*, 1977. pp. [24], with 19 illus & a chronology of local railway events, 1618–1978. Written by J. A. Wells. Reproduced typescript.

Exhibits: photographs, maps, charts, diagrams, documents, railway relics and a simulated booking office.

Tyne & Wear 9408–20

9408 C., J. The Compleat Collier; or, the whole art of sinking, getting and working coal-mines, etc. as is now, used in the northern parts, especially about Sunderland and Newcastle, by J. C. *London: printed for G. Conyers at the Ring in Little Britain*, 1708. pp. 55.

—— reprinted by M. A. Richardson, *Newcastle*, 1845.

—— republished by Frank Graham, *Newcastle upon Tyne*, 1968.

pp. 36–40, underground transport: sledges and 'trams'.

9409 SANDERSON, P. The antiquities of the Abbey, or cathedral church, of Durham; also, a particular description of the County Palatine of Durham. *Newcastle: printed by J. White & T. Saint for P. Sanderson*, 1767. 2 pts (pp. 141; pp. 147).

pt. 2, pp. 27–8, Tyneside wagonways and staithes.

9410 BAILLIE, J. An Impartial History of the Town and County of Newcastle upon Tyne and its Vicinity. *Newcastle: Vint & Anderson*, 1801. pp. 612.

pp. 483–4, list of the number of persons employed and dependent on the coal trade on the rivers Tyne and Wear in the year 1792. Includes waggon-smiths, waggon and waggon-way wrights, engine-men, brake-men, waggon-men, creasers, staithmen, and off-putters.

9411 AKENHEAD, D. The picture of Newcastle upon Tyne, containing a guide to the town & neighbourhood, an account of the Roman Wall, and a description of the coal mines, illustrated by a map of the coal district and a plan of Newcastle. *Newcastle: printed by and for D. Akenhead & Sons*, [1807]. [E & W Books, 1969]. pp. 190. A facsimile reprint.

The colliery wagonways are shown on the map.

9412 RICHARDSON, W. History of the parish of Wallsend . . . *Newcastle upon Tyne: Northumberland Press*, 1923.

pp. 213–6, 472–6, the Wallsend and Willington wagonways.

9413 ROUNTHWAITE, T. E. The railways of Weardale. [*Gillingham*]: *Railway Correspondence & Travel Society*, 1965. pp. 37, with 48 illus on 12 plates, & 4 maps.

Includes industrial railways.

9414 MOUNTFORD, C. E. The Bowes Railway, formerly the Pontop & Jarrow Railway. *Sheffield: Birmingham Locomotive Club,*

1966. pp. 141, with 80 illus, 2 maps, 5 plans, a gradient profile & a bibliography (2 pp.).

—— 2nd edn, rev. & enl. *London: Industrial Railway Society and the Tyne & Wear Industrial Monuments Trust*, 1976. pp. 188, with 176 illus, 17 maps, layout plans, 6 detailed tables, a gradient profile & a bibliography (21 sources).

A detailed account of an important 15 mile colliery railway (1826–1974) owned & operated by John Bowes & Partners Ltd from 1886 to 1947 when the system and its collieries were vested in the National Coal Board. In 1982 the northern section, from Monkton to Jarrow was still in use by the NCB, and 1½ miles of the main line is now a scheduled Ancient Monument, currently operated as a public passenger line by the Tyne & Wear Industrial Monuments Trust.

9415 WHEELER, R. M. Tyneside Steam. 2nd edn. *Burley-in Wharfedale: North Eastern Locomotive Preservation Group*, August 1968. pp. 19. Reproduced typescript.

A directory of steam locomotives still at work in collieries and other industrial sites in Northumberland and Durham.

—— [3rd edn]. *N.E.L.P.G.*, June 1969. pp. 20, with 1 illus & a map on covers. An errata slip is inserted.

9416 SLATER, J. Newcastle upon Tyne City Transport undertaking, 1901–1969. *Newcastle: Newcastle Corporation*, 1969. obl. 8°. pp. 24, with 17 illus (1 col.) & 3 maps.

Includes tramways.

9417 HEARSE, G. S. Remember the trams?: Tyneside. *Ramsey: the author*, 1972. pp. 64, with frontis & 63 illus.

9418 HEARSE, G. S. Remember the trams?: Newcastle upon Tyne: *Ramsey: the author*, 1978. pp. 40. Intro (3 pp). & 37 illus, map & lists.

9419 TYNE AND WEAR PASSENGER TRANSPORT EXECUTIVE. Horse tram to Metro: one hundred years of local public transport in Tyne and Wear. [*Newcastle upon Tyne*]: *Tyne & Wear P.T.E.*, 1978. obl. format. pp. 44, with 106 illus, & 4 on covers.

Includes railways and tramways and the first phase of the Tyne and Wear Metro.

9420 RANKIN, S. and WOODS, M. Newcastle 900 railways: a celebration of the 900th anniversary of Newcastle upon Tyne. [*York*]: *British Rail, Eastern Region*, 1980. pp. [32], with 25 illus, a map & a bibliography (13 sources).

C 1 – C 2   ENGLAND TO SCOTLAND (SCOTLAND TO ENGLAND)

The East Coast and West Coast routes

9421–31

9421 ROBINSON, S. E. A geographical analysis of the development of transport in selected areas of the Anglo–Scottish borderlands. Thesis, Ph.D., University of Durham, 1962/63.

9422 HIBBS. J. Report on the intended closure of the Waverley line between Edinburgh and Carlisle, including the impact of closure on the Borders and the feasibility of retaining a railway between Hawick and Edinburgh. *Saffron Walden: Consultancy in Transport*, December 1968. pp. 33, with 10 tables & a map. Reproduced typescript. Introduction by David Steel, M.P. for Roxburgh, Selkirk & Peebles. Cover title: Transport in the Borders.

9423 DAVID BLOCK ASSOCIATES. Border Union Railway Co. Ltd: feasibility study. *London: David Block Associates*, [1969]. pp. 37. Reproduced typescript.

A detailed report in support of a proposed re-opening of the Waverley Route (Carlisle–Edinburgh).

9424 McLAGAN, W. and SHIELDS, T. Glasgow–London: a travellers' guide, with a short digression to the Lake District. *Gartocharn: Famedram*, 1974. pp. [32], with 11 illus & a chart.

The West Coast route. Two-thirds of the text describes features north of Carlisle.

9425 COOPER-SMITH, J. H. The North and East. *London: Ian Allan*, 1975. (British Rail Album, 1). pp. 80. Intro, & 154 illus (12 col.), with descrs.

Trains in their environment on the East Coast Route from London to Edinburgh and from there to Mallaig, from Derby to Manchester and Sheffield to Glasgow, with smaller sections for East Anglia and on the line from Liverpool via Leeds to Hull. Period, 1969–1973.

9426 KICHENSIDE, G. The West Coast route to Scotland: the history and romance of the railway between Euston and Glasgow. *Newton Abbot: David & Charles*, 1976. pp. 96, with 136 illus, route map (pp. 10–13), 4 timetables, chronology, gradient profile & a bibliography (27 sources).

9427 BRITISH RAILWAYS. EASTERN REGION. Quest for speed: the official story of East Coast enterprise. *York: B.R. (ER)*, 1977. pp. 96, with many varied illus (some col.) & a map. Cover title only.

The past, present and future of the East Coast route to Scotland. Includes a log of the record-breaking run of 12 June 1973, from York to Darlington by BR's prototype High Speed Train.

9428 HOOLE, K. The East Coast main line since 1925. *London: Ian Allan*, 1977. pp. 128, with 142 illus.

9429 ROBINSON, P. J. West Coast border Steam. *London: Ian Allan*, 1977. pp. 64. Intro & 107 illus with descrs.

9430 TREACY, E. Roaming the East Coast route. *London: Ian Allan*, 1977. la 8°. pp. 112. Foreword & Intro (pp. 3–7), col. frontis, & 152 illus with descrs.

9431 BROCK, P. Border Steam: with a camera on the footplate. *Truro: Bradford Barton*, 1978. pp. 80. Intro & 81 illus with descrs.
Period, 1960s.

C 2   SCOTLAND

Scotland generally—Dumfries & Galloway—Strathclyde—Borders—Lothian—
Central—Fife—Tayside—Highland—Grampian

9432–9617

Subdivided by a modified version of the main Classification Scheme

Scotland generally 9432–47

Reference sources 9432–33

9432 SCOTTISH RECORD OFFICE. List of Scottish Railway Archives. *Edinburgh: Scottish Record Office*, [1970?]. pp. 9. Reproduced typescript; no covers.
The Scottish railway records transferred from British Transport Historical Records' Scottish Archive, Waterloo Place, in January 1969.

9433 PAISLEY COLLEGE OF TECHNOLOGY. LIBRARY. A Calendar of Scottish Railway Documents held by Paisley College of Technology Library (compiled by H. C. MacLachlan, College Librarian). *Paisley: [the Library]*, 1978. la. 8°. pp. 131. Limited edition of 60 copies.
297 documents arranged alphabetically within 24 headings of Scottish railway companies, and one 'miscellaneous' section.

9434 BALD, R. General view of the coal trade of Scotland: Edinburgh, chiefly that of the River Forth and Mid-Lothian . . . *Edinburgh: Oliphant Waugh & Innes*, 1812. pp. xvi, 203.
p. 90, Scottish wagonways in the 18th century (1 para)., and on p. 10 is a brief mention that at that time (1709) wagonways were in use at Newcastle, but were not introduced into Scotland 'till a considerable time afterwards'.

9435 The NEW Statistical Account of Scotland, by the ministers of the respective parishes, under the superintendence of a committee of the Society for the Benefit of the Sons and Daughters of the Clergy. *Edinburgh & London: W. Blackwood & Sons*, 1845. 15 vols.
Incidental references to railways:
vol. 1, p. 512, Edinburgh & Dalkeith.
vol. 5, p. 554, Kilmarnock & Troon.
vol. 6, pp. 205, 411, Garnkirk & Glasgow; p. 411, Monkland & Kirkintilloch; pp. 467, 798, Wishaw & Coltness; p. 700, Glasgow, Paisley, Kilmarnock & Ayr, and the Glasgow, Paisley & Greenock.

vol. 8, pp. 30–31, Alloa Rly; pp. 202–3, Monkland & Kirkintilloch.
vol. 9, p. 186, Fordell Rly; p. 245, Habeach wagonways.
vol. 10, p. 246, Dundee & Newtyle (very briefly).

9436 BREMNER, D. The industries of Scotland: their rise, progress and present condition. *Edinburgh: A. & C. Black*, 1869. pp. viii, 535.
pp. 80–105, 'Railways'. The history of railway development in Scotland and the manufacture of locomotives and rolling stock at the North British Railway's work at Cowlairs, and the work and wages of railway servants.
—— Reprint, with a new introduction by John Butt and Ian L. Donnachie. *David & Charles*, 1969. pp. [15], viii, 535.
A facsimile reprint.

9437 POCOCKE, R. Tours in Scotland, 1747, 1750, 1760 . . . *Reprinted in* Scottish Historic Society Publications, vol. 1. *Edinburgh*, 1887.
On p. 276, a brief mention of 'a waggon road' seen at Leven in 1760.

9438 BUTT, J. The industrial archaeology of Scotland, by John Butt; research associates, John R. Hume, Ian L. Donnachie. *Newton Abbot: David & Charles*, 1967. (Industrial Archaeology of the British Isles series). pp. 344, with 60 illus on 44 plates; gazetteer (pp. 193–320); notes (pp. 321–6).
Index has ca. 180 page refs to railways, tramways and wagonways.

9439 THOMAS, J. Scottish railway history in pictures. *Newton Abbot: David & Charles*, 1967. pp. 112. Brief intro, col. frontis, 4 col. illus on 2 plates, & 176 illus with descrs.

9440 CAMPBELL, R. H. and DOW, J. B. A. Source Book of Scottish Economic and Social History. *Oxford: Blackwell*, 1968. pp. xxiii, 280.

pp. 269–80: 'Railways': reprints of extracts from 12 contemporaneous sources, 1845 to 1963.

9441 LINDSAY, J. The canals of Scotland. *Newton Abbot: David & Charles*, 1968. (Canals of the British Isles series). pp. 238, with 20 plates, & in text, 15 maps, 313 notes & 4 appendices.
Railways, *passim*; in index under individual names.

9442 SMITH, D. L. The little railways of South-West Scotland. *Newton Abbot: David & Charles*, 1969. pp. 228, with col. frontis, 32 illus on 16 plates, 19 maps, gradient profiles & plans.
The Portpatrick Rly, Wigtownshire Rly, Girvan & Portpatrick Junction Rly, Glasgow & South Western Rly and the Cairnryan Military Rly.

9443 THOMAS, D. St J. Scotland: the Lowlands and the Borders. *Newton Abbot: David & Charles*, 1971. (Regional History of the Railways of Great Britain, 6). pp. 288, with frontis, 28 illus on 15 plates, 10 illus in text, 8 maps & plans, chronology (pp. 257–75), bibliography (46 sources), index (pp. 279–88).

9444 MAGNER, G. Cornwall to Caithness, 1972. (Great Western Railtour, May 19, 20, 21, 1972; Orcadian Railtour [Crewe to Wick & Thurso & back], October 6, 7, 8, 1972). *Bromborough: Wirral Railway Circle*, 1973. pp. 48, with 10 illus & 4 lists.
A commemorative booklet of the two tours.

9445 SIMMONDS, J. Scottish railways. *St Ives (Cornwall): J. Pike*, 1975. (Viewing Scotland series). pp. 32, with 12 illus of locos & a map.
An introductory history, and lists of preserved lines, societies, & museums.

9446 THOMAS, J. Forgotten railways: Scotland. *Newton Abbot: David & Charles*, 1976. pp. 224, with 33 illus on 16 plates, 11 maps & 8 timetables, gazetteer (pp. 211–9); bibliography (46 sources).

9447 THOMAS, J. The Scottish Railway Book. *Newton Abbot: David & Charles*, 1977. pp. 96, with 135 illus, facsimiles & plans; chronology & tables.
A development of the author's *Scottish Railway History in Pictures* (1967), with the addition of substantial text, new illustrations, facsimiles of documents, 6 appendices, & biographies of 50 Scottish railway personalities.

C 2 a   Dumfries & Galloway Region 9448–50

9448 DONNACHIE, I. L. The industrial archaeology of Galloway: South-West Scotland, including Wigtown, Kirkcudbright and adjoining parts of Dumfries. *Newton Abbot: David & Charles*, 1971. (Industrial Archaeology of the British Isles series). pp. 271, with 32 illus on 16 plates, 39 maps & diagrams, inventory (pp. 199–242), notes & refs (pp. 243–54), & a bibliography (pp. 255–63).

In the Index, ca. 60 page refs to railways & wagonways.

9449 THORNE, H. D. Rails to Portpatrick. *Prescot: T. Stephenson*, 1976. pp. xvi, 261, with frontis, 27 illus on 14 plates, & in text, 15 detailed tables, incl. timetables & gradient profiles, 3 appendices & a bibliography (21 sources); map inside covers.
The Portpatrick Railway, the Wigtownshire Railway, the Portpatrick & Wigtownshire Joint Railway; period, 1856–1923.

9450 SCOTTISH ASSOCIATION FOR PUBLIC TRANSPORT. The Stranraer–Dumfries railway: a case for re-opening. *Glasgow: the Association*, 1977. (Study papers, 8). pp. ii, 18, with 2 maps inside back cover.

C 2 b   Strathclyde Region 9451–92

(Glasgow, 9461–92)

9451 CORMACK, I. L. Tramways of the Monklands: the history of tramways in Airdrie and Coatbridge. [*Glasgow*]: *Scottish Tramway Museum Society*, [1964]. pp. 76, with 39 illus, 3 maps & a fleet list.

9452 SMITH, D. L. The Dalmellington Iron Company: its engines and men. *Newton Abbot: David & Charles*, 1967. pp. 256, with frontis, 42 illus on 20 plates, 19 maps, plans & line drawings.
ch. 8 (pp. 100–121), 'Dalmellington Iron Company transport'.
ch. 9 (pp. 122–236), 'The engines and the men'.
A 'man & boy' narrative—'the product of 60 years of listening, memorising and note-taking'. The author's family connections with the Company go back to 1849 and the work is exceptional for the penetrating detail which the author is able to place on record, both of the history of the firm generally, and, from p. 100 onwards, of the working of its several feeder lines to the Ayr & Dalmellington Railway.

9453 FARR, A. D. The Campbeltown & Machrihanish Light Railway. *Lingfield: Oakwood Press*, 1969. (Locomotion Papers, 45). pp. 48, with 21 illus on 8 plates, map, layout plan, 2 facsimiles, 2 tables & a bibliography (14 sources).

9454 CORMACK, I. L. Lanarkshire tramways . . . *Cambuslang (Glasgow): Scottish Tramway Museum Society*, [1970]. pp. 64, with 39 illus, map, fleet list, & timetables.

9455 MACMILLAN, N. S. C. The Campbeltown & Machrihanish Light Railway . . . , illustrated by Fraser Cameron. *Newton Abbot: David & Charles*, 1970. pp. 164, with col. frontis, 34 illus on 16 plates, 18 maps, plans, drawings, gradient profiles, diagrams, 6 appendices & a bibliography (35 sources).
Scotland's only narrow gauge railway (2ft. 3ins), 1906–1931.

9456 MACMILLAN, N. S. C. Coal mining and associated transport in Kintyre, 1750–1967.

Thesis, M.Sc., University of Strathclyde, 1972.

Includes a detailed study of the Argyll Coal & Cannel Co., subsequently the Campbeltown & Machrihanish Light Rly, with mounted photographs, diagrams, tables, plans & a bibliography (56 sources).

9457 SCOTTISH RAILWAY DEVELOPMENT ASSOCIATION. Proposals for the improvement of the Kilmarnock–Stewarton–Glasgow rail service. *Clarkston: the Association*, 1972. pp. 7, with 2 appendices.

p. 6 (appx 1), Present & proposed timetables.
p. 7 (appx 2), Social grants to certain Scottish commuter routes, 1971.

9458 CORMACK, I. L. Tramways of Greenock, Gourock and Port Glasgow. *Cambuslang (Glasgow): Scottish Tramway Museum Society*, 1975. pp. 48, with 40 illus, map & a diagram.

The Vale of Clyde, and the Greenock & Port Glasgow tramway companies.

9459 SCOTTISH ASSOCIATION FOR PUBLIC TRANSPORT. Strathclyde's transport tomorrow: a submission to the Strathclyde Region. *Glasgow: the Association*, 1975. (Memorandum, 75/5). pp. 8.

Includes railways.

9460 PRITCHETT, C. Greenock tramways, 1871–1929: teaching materials. *Jordanhill: Jordanhill College*, 1979. pp. 24. Reproduced typescript.

20 extracts from books and newspapers and 4 statistical tables, for tramways in the U.K., and for Scotland, 1878–1914, and for the Greenock & Port Glasgow Co., 1890–1925; and a tramway chronology. Produced as a Local History teaching aid.

Glasgow 9461–92

General and miscellaneous

9461 BLAKE, G. Glasgow Electric: the story of Scotland's new electric railway. *[Glasgow]: B.R. (Scotland)*, 1960. la. obl. format. pp. [40], with 38 illus (15 col.) & 2 maps.

A commemorative brochure issued to celebrate the opening of phase 1 (Airdrie—Glasgow—Helensburgh) of Glasgow's suburban line electrification.

9462 SIMPSON, M. Urban transport and the development of Glasgow's West End, 1830–1914, *in* Journal of Transport History, new series, vol. 1 (1971–2), pp. 146–60, with 29 notes.

Includes railways, tramways and the Glasgow District Subway.

9463 HUME, J. R. Industrial archaeology of Glasgow. *Glasgow & London: Blackie*, 1974. pp. xviii, 327, with 96 illus on 48 plates & 19 illus in text; gazetteer (pp. [145]–285), extensive & detailed, in 13 sections, each with a key map;

indexes, pp. 291–327, locating 1154 sites; evaluative bibliography, pp. 287–90.

Includes railways and tramways.

9464 OCHOJNA, A. P. Lines of class distinction: an economic and social history of the British tramcar, with special reference to Edinburgh and Glasgow. Thesis, Ph.D., University of Glasgow, 1974.

9465 SCOTTISH ASSOCIATION FOR PUBLIC TRANSPORT. Transport & environment: a better Glasgow; a statement issued jointly by [the] Scottish Association for Public Transport [and others]. *Glasgow: the Association*, 1974. pp. 3.

9466 JOHNSTON, C. and HUME, J. R. Glasgow stations. *Newton Abbot: David & Charles*, 1979. pp. 175, with 30 illus on 16 plates, 2 maps, 31 plans & line drawings, & a bibliography (47 sources).

9467 SMITH, W. A. C. Rails around Glasgow, compiled by W. A. C. Smith; introduction by John Thomas. *[Glasgow]: Scottish Steam Railtours Group* [1980?]. pp. 56. Historical intro (pp. 3–4), & 97 illus with descrs.

Tramways

9468 GLASGOW CORPORATION TRANSPORT. Coplawhill Car Works and Larkfield Garage. *[Glasgow: G.C.T.*, 1936]. sm. obl. format. pp. 20, with 8 illus (6 of the tramway depot). Title from cover.

9469 GLASGOW CORPORATION TRANSPORT. Experimental four-wheel tramcars: official inspection, 16th January 1940. *Glasgow: the Corporation*, 1940. pp. 17, with 4 illus.

9470 MILLER, B., LANGMUIR, G. E. and McKIM, R. B. Glasgow Corporation Tramways rolling stock. *Cricklewood (London): Light Railway Transport League*, 1946. Magazine format. pp. [8], with 14 illus.

Reprinted from *Modern Tramway*. Past & present tramcars, including auxiliary vehicles with lists of the rolling stock of the Paisley & District Tramway Co., the Airdrie & Coatbridge Tramway Co., and Glasgow Corporation Tramways.

9471 OAKLEY, C. A. The last tram. *[Glasgow]: Corporation of the City of Glasgow Transport Department*, [1962]. pp. 124, with 86 illus & drawings, 6 maps & a chronology of closures.

Published to commemorate the closing of the tramway system in Glasgow, 4 September 1962.

9472 THOMSON, D. L. A Handbook of Glasgow Tramways. *Glasgow: Scottish Tramway Museum Society*, [1962]. pp. 108, with 37 illus & 2 maps.

A revised and extended presentation of the information contained in the Society's *Glasgow Tramway and Railway Rolling Stock*, by John A. N. Emslie (1958).

Includes the Glasgow District Subway.

9473 GLASGOW MUSEUM OF TRANSPORT. Glasgow's trams: their history, and a descriptive guide to the various types which have been used. *Glasgow: Transport Museum*, 1964. obl. format. pp. 42, with frontis & 11 illus (2 col.) & a map on plates.

9474 WISEMAN, R. J. S. Glasgow. *Huddersfield: Advertiser Press*, 1965. (British Tramways in Pictures, 2). pp. 36, with 60 illus.
—— 2nd edn. *Advertiser Press*, 1971.
—— 3rd edn. *Advertiser Press*, 1977. (British Tramways in Pictures, 2). pp. 48, with 59 illus.

9475 CORMACK, I. L. Rutherglen tramways. *[Glasgow]: Scottish Tramway Museum Society*, 1966. pp. 12, with 11 illus, & a map loosely inserted.

9476 CORMACK, I. L. Glasgow trams beyond the boundary. *[Glasgow]: Scottish Tramway Museum Society*, [1967]. pp. 12, with 14 illus, & a map loosely inserted. Title on cover only.

9477 CORMACK, I. L. 1894 and all that. *Glasgow: Scottish Tramway Museum Society*, 1968. pp. 8, with 3 illus.
The take-over of the Glasgow Tramway Co. by Glasgow Corporation, 1st July 1894.

9478 BARRIE, J. Memories of Glasgow's tramways, 1927–1962. *Farnborough (Hants): Light Railway Transport League*, 1971. pp. 24, with 15 illus on 8 plates.

9479 BRASH, R. W. Glasgow in the tramway age . . . , illustrated from contemporary sources. *London: Longman*, 1971. (Then & There series). pp. 96, with 47 illus & 3 maps.
An informative introductory work for school use.

9480 CORMACK, I. L. A century of Glasgow tramways. *Glasgow: Scottish Tramway Museum Society*, [1972]. pp. 24, with 38 illus & 4 line drawings; map inside cover.

9481 CORMACK, I. L. Glasgow tramways. *Glasgow: Scottish Tramway Museum Society*, [1973]. pp. 16, with 28 illus (1 col.); map.

9482 STEWART, I. G. McM. Glasgow by tram. *[Glasgow]: Scottish Tramway Museum Society*, May 1977. pp. 48, with 81 illus & a chronology, 1872–1964.
A selection of Glasgow Corporation Tramways promotional posters are reproduced as a centre double-spread illustration.

9483 STEWART, I. G. McM. More Glasgow by tram. *Glasgow: Scottish Tramway Museum Society*, 1978. pp. 48. Intro, 82 illus with descrs, & a map.

9484 COONIE, I. M. The Glasgow 'Coronations'. *London: Light Railway Transport League*, [1979] pp. 20, with 25 illus & a dimensioned drawing.
Glasgow Corporation's new tramcars, 1937.

9485 STEWART, I. G. McM. Round Glasgow by tram. *Glasgow: Scottish Tramway Museum Society*, 1979. pp. 48. Intro & 84 illus with descrs, a drawing (inside front cover) & a 5-column table of routes.

Glasgow District Subway

9486 THOMPSON, D. L. and SINCLAIR, D. E. The Glasgow Subway. *Glasgow: the authors, for the Scottish Tramway Museum Society*, 1964. pp. 78, with 57 illus, 3 maps, 3 diagrams, a gradient profile & 5 appendices.

9487 BOWNES, J. S. Glasgow Underground: a study in urban transport planning. Thesis, M.Sc., University of Strathclyde, [1974–5?].

9488 CASELEY, G. and HAMILTON, BILL. I belong to Glasgow: the human story of the Glasgow Underground. 2nd edn. *Glasgow: Nexus Press*, 1976. pp. 96, with frontis & 24 illus (4 col.).
A photographic souvenir.

9489 BARZILAY, D. H. Glasgow Underground: the end of an era. *Belfast: Century Books*, 1977. pp. 47, with 45 illus & 2 maps.
The Glasgow District Subway before modernisation in the 1970s.

9490 GREATER GLASGOW PASSENGER TRANSPORT EXECUTIVE. Glasgow Underground modernisation. *Glasgow: the Executive*, [1977]. pp. [4].
A printed folder with 3 col. illus & a col. map, depicting the prototype of the 33 vehicles being produced for the line by Metro-Cammell Ltd.

9491 KELLY, P. J. and WILLSHER, M. J. D. Glasgow Subway, 1896–1977. *London: Light Railway Transport League*, [1977]. pp. 27, with 20 illus, fare & time tables & 3 maps (one inside cover).
Reprinted from *Modern Tramway*.

9492 STIRLING, A. and LEECH, S. Glasgow Subway scenes, photographed by Alastair Stirling and Stanley Leech. *Glasgow: A. Stirling*, [1977]. pp. 32, 68 illus with captions. Introduction on inside of front cover.

C 2 c   Borders Region
[No entries]

C 2 d   Lothian Region, including Edinburgh
[9493–9504]

9493 MINISTRY OF TRANSPORT. Edinburgh Corporation Tramways. Report of an inquiry held with regard to the application of the Corporation for permission to use centre-poles, etc. in connection with the equipment of the tramways in Princes Street for electrical working. *London: H.M.S.O.*, 1922. pp. 5.

9494 BOOTH, G. A. Edinburgh experimental vehicles. *Omnibus Society*, 1963. pp. 6, with 8 illus.
Tramcars and buses.

9495 HUNTER, D. L. G. Edinburgh's transport. *Huddersfield: Advertiser Press*, 1964. pp. 398, with 78 illus, many lists & 5 maps on 2 sheets inserted in end pocket.
Includes tramways.

9496 KEIR, D. The City of Edinburgh. *Glasgow: Collins*, 1966. (Third Statistical Account of Scotland, vol. 15). pp. xvi, 1044, with plates & illus.
pp. 423–8, 'Railways'; pp. 405–10, 'Tramways', with 2 illus facing p. 14.

9497 HUNTER, D. L. G. Edinburgh Tramways Album. *Leeds: Turntable Enterprises*, 1972. pp. [32], with 54 illus.

9498 PAGE, P. J. The influence of public transport on the growth of Edinburgh in the nineteenth and twentieth centuries. Thesis, M.Sc., University of Edinburgh, 1972.

9499 HENDRY, A. W. Road & rail: an alternative transport strategy for Edinburgh. *Edinburgh: Edinburgh Amenity & Transport Association*, [1973]. pp. 35, with 8 maps & diagrams. Reproduced typescript.
A plan for integrated transport, with increased provision for railways.

9500 OCHOJNA, A. P. Lines of class distinction: an economic and social history of the British tramcar, with special reference to Edinburgh and Glasgow. Thesis, Ph.D., University of Edinburgh, 1974.

9501 SCOTTISH ASSOCIATION FOR PUBLIC TRANSPORT. Development of British Rail short-distance passenger services in the Edinburgh area of the Lothian region. *Glasgow: the Association*, July 1977. (Study Papers, 9). pp. 12, with map.

9502 JORDANHILL COLLEGE. Early transport in the Monklands. *Glasgow: Jordanhill College*, June 1978. pp. 43. Extracts from newspapers. Reproduced typescript.
ch. 2 (pp. 17–36), Railways of the Monklands.

9503 BROTCHIE, A. W. Edinburgh: the tramway years. *Dundee: N.B. Traction Group*, [1979]. pp. 40. Intro & 80 illus with descrs.

9504 The LAST trains. *Edinburgh: Moorfoot Publishing*.
vol. 1, Edinburgh & S.E. Scotland. 1979. pp. [24], with 44 illus & descrs.
Photographs of the last trains (but not always the *very* last) on lines now closed.

C 2 e   Central Region 9505–6

9505 BROTCHIE, A. W. The tramways of Falkirk. *Dundee: N.B. Traction Group*, 1975. (Tram-

ways of Fife and the Forth Valley, 1). pp. 35, with 26 illus & 1 folded map.

9506 BROTCHIE, A. W. The tramways of Stirling. [Dundee]: *N.B. Traction Group*, 1976. (Tramways of Fife and the Forth Valley, 2). pp. 32, with 22 illus & 3 maps at end.

C 2 f   Fife Region 9507–10

9507 STEVENSON, R. An account of the Bell Rock Lighthouse . . . *Edinburgh: A. Constable*, 1824. la. 8°. pp. xix, 533.
pp. 189–90, wagonways built on the site by John Baird of Shotts Iron Works for the transport of stone, 1808; also plate X, figures 13–16. The Bell Rock, or Inchcape, lighthouse lies about 16 miles off the coast of Fife.

9508 BROTCHIE, A. W. Wemyss and District Tramways Company Ltd. *Dundee: N.B. Traction Group*, 1976. (Tramways of Fife and the Forth Valley, 3). pp. 71, with col. frontis (crest), 46 illus, 5 maps, 3 layout plans, & 2 diagrams.

9509 BROTCHIE, A. W. The Dunfermline & District Tramways Company. *Dundee: N.B. Traction Group*, 1978. (Tramways of Fife & the Forth Valley, 5). pp. 63, with 53 illus, & a folded map at end.

9510 BROTCHIE, A. W. The tramways of Kirkcaldy. *Dundee: N.B. Traction Group*, 1978. (Tramways of Fife and the Forth Valley, 4). pp. 60, with 40 illus, & a folded map at end.

C 2 g   Tayside Region 9511–13

9511 BROTCHIE, A. W. Tramways of the Tay Valley . . . *Dundee: Dundee Museum & Art Gallery*, 1965. pp. 104, with 52 illus & 2 folded maps.
'A history of the tramways of Perth, Dundee and Monifieth, with notes on the light railways of the Tay Valley region.'

9512 BROTCHIE, A. W. and HERD, J. J. Old Dundee from the tram cars. *Dundee: N.B. Traction Group*, 1974. pp. 48. Intro, 73 illus with captions, & a chronology.

9513 PERKINS, J. Steam trains to Dundee, 1831–1863. *Dundee: City of Dundee District Council, Museums & Art Galleries Dept*, 1975. pp. 36, with 19 illus & 4 maps.

C 2 h   Highland Region 9514–21

9514 MINISTRY OF TRANSPORT. Transport services in the Highlands and Islands. *London: H.M.S.O.*, 1963. pp. 55, with 8 appendices & a folding map.
Report of the Highland Transport Enquiry (1959–63) to the Minister of Transport, the Secretary of State for Scotland and the Minister of Aviation. Includes railways.
'Existing transport services; trends of traffic;

financial aspects; the future of transport in the Highlands.'

9515 HIGHLAND TRANSPORT BOARD. Highland transport services: report. *Edinburgh: H.M.S.O.*, May 1967. pp. xi, 111, with 5 illus on 3 plates, 16 maps (some folded), 2 tables & 19 appendices, incl. further detailed tables. Chairman: R. H. W. Bruce.

9516 SCOTTISH RAILWAY DEVELOPMENT ASSO-CIATION. The Kyle railway and the future pattern of transport to Wester Ross and the Isles. [*Glasgow*]: *the Association*, 1971. tall 8°. pp. 18, with 5 appendices.
A potential future for the former Highland Rly west of Dingwall.

9517 CAMERON, A. D. The Caledonian Canal. *Lavenham: T. Dalton*, 1972. pp. 164, with 85 illus & a bibliography (36 sources); map on end papers.
In index, 33 page refs. under 'Rails', 'Railways', 'Tramways' (wagonways), and 'Waggon'.

9518 SCOTTISH ASSOCIATION FOR PUBLIC TRANSPORT. Communications to the Moray Firth: expenditure priorities, 1974–79. *Glasgow: the Association*, November 1973. (Memorandum 73/4). pp. 7.
The feasibility of improved rail and water transport should be examined before deciding to proceed with improvements to the A9 (road).

9519 HIGHLANDS AND ISLANDS DEVELOPMENT BOARD. Highlands and Islands transport review, 1975. *Inverness: the Board*, [1975]. (Occasional Bulletin, 6). pp. 93, with 20 illus & 6 maps; bibliography (pp. 77–9).
Includes railways.

9520 STRATHSPEY RLY (1971). Strathspey Railway Guide Book, [by] Neil T. Sinclair. [*Aviemore*]: *the Railway*, 1975. obl. 8°. pp. 28, with 20 illus, map, & 2 plans; bibliography (11 sources), map & col. illus on covers.
A passenger-carrying steam railway, Aviemore to Boat of Garten (5½ miles) on the former Highland Rly.

9521 BRITISH RAILWAYS. Inverness to Kyle of Lochalsh. [*London: B.R.*, 1977?]. pp. 8.
A coloured brochure for travellers and tourists.

C 2 i   Grampian Region 9522–26

9522 MacKENZIE, H. R. Aberdeen's trams, 1874–1914: the first forty years in photographs; 30 photographs with notes by H. R. MacKenzie. *Broughty Ferry: N.B. Traction*, 1967. pp. 24.

9523 PARHAM, E. T. The Deeside Railway line: its potential use, especially for recreation; a report to the Countryside Commission for Scotland, by E. T. Parham, with assistance from Elizabeth Bacon. *Perth: the Commission*, October 1971. pp. 30, with 6 illus & 4 appendices; 3 la. folded maps in end pocket.

Reproduced typescript with photocopied illus; spiral binding.
The possible development of parts of the 43-mile-long trackbed.

9524 MacKENZIE, H. R. and BROTCHIE, A. W. Aberdeen's trams, 1874–1958. *Glasgow: Scottish Tramway Museum Society*; *Dundee: N.B. Traction Group*, 1974. pp. 32. Intro & 45 illus with descrs.

9525 WATERMAN, J. J. The coming of the railway to Aberdeen in the 1840s. *Old Aberdeen: University of Aberdeen, Centre for Scottish Studies*, [1979]. (Local History Pamphlet series, 1). pp. 38, with 1 illus on back cover & 148 precise bibliogr. refs. to Scottish newspapers and *The Times*, 1844–1850.
pp. 1–26, The Aberdeen Railway; pp. 27–35, The Great North of Scotland Railway.

9526 MITCHELL, M. J. and SOUTER, I. A. The Aberdeen Suburban Tramways. *Dundee: N.B. Traction*, 1980. pp. 64, with 44 illus & a folded map loosely inserted.

C 2 D1   **Tramways and light railways in Scotland, generally**
9527–31

9527 SCOTTISH TRAMWAY MUSEUM SOCIETY. Tramway Track maps.
Aberdeen: (a) Aberdeen District Tramways Co. (horse tramway, 1874–1898), (b) Aberdeen Corporation Tramways (electric), (c) Aberdeen Corporation Tramways and Aberdeen Suburban Tramways Co. as in 1926.
Edinburgh Corporation Tramways (electric, 1922–1956).
Glasgow Corporation Transport: electric tramways and subway.
Greenock & Port Glasgow Tramways Co. as in 1914, and Dumbarton Burgh & County Tramways Co. as in 1919.
Kilmarnock Corporation Tramways: route map, 1923, with fares & stages table on reverse.
Lanarkshire Tramways Co. as in 1912.
All except Kilmarnock are carbon copies of re-drawn maps measuring ca. 36 in. × 24 in. and all except Glasgow are on a scale of 3 in. to 1 mile. Kilmarnock is printed, and measures only 10 in. × 8 in.
Glasgow is 2.5 in. to 1 mile. The maps have larger scale insets for depot layouts, and historical notes.

9528 BROTCHIE, A. W. Scottish tramway fleets. *Dundee: N.B. Traction*, 1968. pp. 60, with 22 illus. Lists, with historical notes.

9529 CORMACK, I. L. Tramways of Scotland, *Glasgow: Scottish Tramway Museum Society*, [1974]. pp. 16. 32 illus with descrs. Title on cover only. No text.

9530 HUNTER, D. L. G. Scottish electric tramways. *Leeds: Turntable Publications*, 1974. pp. [36]. Intro & 52 illus with descrs.

9531 GAMMELL, C. J. Scottish branch lines, 1955–1965. *Oxford: Oxford Publishing Co.*,

1978. 4°. pp. [96]. Intro, frontis & 163 illus with descrs arranged into areas, each with a map. Appendix: Scottish branch lines closed to passengers since Grouping, 1923, compiled by R. Hamilton.

C 2 E   Engineering (Civil and Mechanical)
9532–52

9532 ARROL, W. How the Forth Bridge was built: a lecture to accompany a set of photographic transparencies by William Arrol. n.pl., n.d. [ca. 1890]. pp. 15, with a line drawing of the author on cover.   LU(THC)

9533 DOUGLAS, E. Crossing the Forth. *London: R. Hale*, 1964. pp. 191, with 18 illus on 16 plates, 2 maps, & a bibliography (56 sources).
Includes the Forth railway bridge.

9534 HAMMOND, R. The Forth Bridge and its builders. [*London*]: *Eyre & Spottiswoode*, 1964. pp. 226, with frontis, 40 illus, 31 diagrams & a bibliography (28 sources).

9535 STEAM in Scotland. [2 vols].
vol. 1, edited by W. J. V. Anderson and D. Cross. *Harrow-on-the-Hill: Roundhouse*, 1968. pp. 159, with col. frontis & 23 illus; maps.
vol. 2, edited by Brian Stephenson. *London: Ian Allan*, 1972. pp. 114, with col. frontis & 141 illus.

9536 HIGHET, C. Scottish locomotive history, 1831–1923. *London: Allen & Unwin*, 1970. pp. 240, with col. frontis & 37 illus on 32 plates. Foreword by Rowland C. Bond.

9537 MITCHELL LIBRARY [Glasgow]. Scotland's Locomotive Builders: an exhibition illustrative of the development of the locomotive industry in Scotland, 11th–23rd October 1971. *Glasgow: Mitchell Library*, 1971. pp. 14, with a bibliography (23 sources).
Brief histories of 15 manufactories, 1830s to 1960s.

9538 GLASGOW MUSEUM OF TRANSPORT. Scottish railway locomotives: a history of the railways of Scotland and a descriptive guide to Scottish locomotives in the Museum of Transport, Glasgow. rev. edn. *Glasgow: Transport Museum*, 1972. obl. format. pp. 50, with frontis, 9 illus & 4 maps on 8 plates; col. illus on cover.
pp. 32–48, 'List of railway companies in Scotland prior to 1923' (5 columns); p. 49, 'List of Scottish locomotive builders'.

9539 CROSS, D. London Midland Steam north of the Border. *Truro: Bradford Barton*, 1973. pp. 96. Intro & 99 illus with descrs.

9540 MIDDLEMASS, T. Mainly Scottish Steam. *Newton Abbot: David & Charles*, 1973. pp. 157, with 24 illus on 16 plates, & a map.
Boyhood recollections of the railway scene in the Falkirk area, 1920s–1930s.

9541 STEPHEN, R. D. Scottish Steam in the 1920s. *Truro: Bradford Barton*, 1975. pp. 96. Intro & 117 illus (photos by R. D. Stephen).

9542 ATKINS, C. P. The Scottish 4–6–0 classes. *London: Ian Allan*, 1976. pp. 123, with 128 illus on 48 plates, & in text, 34 locomotive drawings with dimensions & constructional details; bibliography (26 sources).

9543 BRIDGES, A. J. Industrial locomotives of Scotland, edited by Alan Bridges. *Market Harborough: Industrial Railway Society*, 1976. (Pocket Book series, N). pp. vi, 296, with 112 illus on 56 plates.

9544 KERNAHAN, J. Scottish branch line Steam, edited by Jack Kernahan for the Scottish Railway Preservation Society. *Truro: Bradford Barton*, 1977. pp. 96. Intro, frontis & 105 illus with descrs.

9545 STEPHEN, R. D. Scottish Steam Miscellany. *Truro: Bradford Barton*, 1977. pp. 96. Intro & 105 illus with descrs.
Period, 1920s.

9546 CROSS, D. Roaming the Scottish rails. *London: Ian Allan*, 1978. la. 8°. pp. 208. Intro. (pp. 8–12) & 255 illus with descrs; maps on end papers. Foreword by Eric Treacy.
Period, 1960s with a few before and after.

9547 KERNAHAN, J. Steam in the Western Highlands . . . , edited by Jack Kernahan for the Scottish Railway Preservation Society. *Truro: Bradford Barton*, 1978. Intro & 120 illus with descrs.

9548 MORRISON, B. Scottish Steam Album. *Oxford: Oxford Publishing Co.*, 1978. la. 8°. pp. [144]. Intro & 273 illus with descrs.
Period, 1950s.

9549 CASSERLEY, H. C. Scottish railways in the heyday of Steam. *Truro: Bradford Barton*, [1979]. pp. 96. Intro & 115 illus with descrs.

9550 CROSS, D. The last decade of Scottish Steam. *Truro: Bradford Barton*, 1979. pp. 96. Intro & 105 illus with descrs.

9551 KERNAHAN, J. Scottish main line Steam, edited by Jack Kernahan for the Scottish Railway Preservation Society. *Truro: Bradford Barton*, 1979. pp. 96. Intro, & 120 illus with descrs.

9552 STEPHEN, R. D. Steam supreme: recollections of Scottish railways in the 1920s. *Truro: Bradford Barton*, [1980]. pp. 151, with 48 illus on 24 plates.

C 2 G3   Passenger train services 9553

9553 SCOTTISH RAILFANS. Scottish steam passenger services. *Edinburgh: Scottish Railfans*, [1965]. obl. format. pp. 22. Reproduced typescript in printed covers.

Tables of all advertised steam-hauled passenger services, with details of locomotives and depots.

C 2 K   Social aspects 9554–66

9554 SCOTTISH RAILWAY DEVELOPMENT ASSO-CIATION. Scottish railways: the next five years. *Galashiels: the Association*, 1964. pp. 11, with a diagram as insert.
'The Beeching Report (1963) closure proposals were derived from narrowly-based criteria, in many respects contrary to Scotland's present and future needs.' Alternative proposals are made, based on Scotland's real needs, generally, and for the continued use of specified stretches of line.

9555 HONDELINK, E. R. Transport plan for Scotland. *Transport Conference of Scotland*, 1965. pp. 23, with a forecast balance sheet of proposed Scottish Transport Board the first year after one transition year. Reproduced typescript.

9556 CAMPBELL, R. H. and DOW, J. B. A. Source Book of Scottish economic and social history. *Oxford: Blackwell*, 1968. pp. xxiii, 280.
pp. 269–80: 'Railways': reprints of extracts from a selection of 12 sources.

9557 SCOTTISH RAILWAY DEVELOPMENT ASSO-CIATION. Scottish railways in the 1970s. *Glasgow: the Association*, 1969. pp. 31, with 2 maps showing 1, minimum, and 2, desirable, networks.

9558 VAMPLEW, W. Railways and the transformation of the Scottish economy. Thesis, Ph.D., University of Edinburgh, 1969.
Railways and the rise of heavy industries in 19th century Scotland; the source and productivity of railway capital; the railways as employers; their influence on Scottish agriculture and their effect on other forms of transport.

9559 CRAIG, A. D. Co-ordination of road and rail in the '70s: an analysis on the use of road–rail vehicles in Scotland. *Glasgow: the author*, 1970. pp. 15, with 6 illus & 13 refs.
Advocating wide use of rail-buses in rural Scotland.

9560 PARHAM, E. T. Disused railway lines in Scotland: a strategic appraisal; a report to the Countryside Commission for Scotland. *Perth: the Commission*, 1972 [1973]. (Occasional Papers, 4). pp. 44, with 10 illus, 2 maps & a bibliography.

9561 SCOTTISH ASSOCIATION FOR PUBLIC TRANSPORT. The Far North line: a plan for the future. *Glasgow: the Association*, 1972. (Study Papers, 1). pp. 18, with map & 5 appendices.
The Highland Rly north of Inverness.

9562 VAMPLEW, W. Railways and the Scottish transport system in the nineteenth century, *in* Journal of Transport History, new series, vol. 1 (1971–2), pp. 133–45, with 38 notes.

9563 SCOTTISH ASSOCIATION FOR PUBLIC TRANSPORT. Transport policy in Scotland, 1974–80: a submission to Government. *Glasgow: the Association*, April 1974. pp. 8.
Scotland's vital need to maintain and improve its railway services.

9564 SCOTTISH ASSOCIATION FOR PUBLIC TRANSPORT. Scottish transport policy: a statement of principles. *Glasgow: the Association*, March 1975. pp. [8].

9565 SCOTTISH ASSOCIATION FOR PUBLIC TRANSPORT. The Transport White Paper implications for Scotland. *Glasgow: the Association*, 1977. pp. 14.
A commentary on *Transport Policy: a consultation document* (Cmnd 6836).

9566 SCOTTISH ASSOCIATION FOR PUBLIC TRANSPORT. Scottish transport: a new era; policies and programmes, 1980–2000. *Glasgow: the Association*, 1979. 3 parts.
pt 1, Transport policies. November 1979. pp. 19.
pt 2, Transport programmes. November 1979. pp. 18.
pt 3, Selected statistics on Scottish transport, with some English comparisons. January 1980. pp. 16.
Railways are specifically considered in part 2.

C 2 L   Individual Scottish railways 9567–9617

Caledonian Rly 9567–76

9567 ABERDEEN RLY. Statement by the board of directors of the Aberdeen Railway Company in reply to the charges of Col. Fraser contained in his letters to the chairman published in the Aberdeen Herald . . ., 16th & 30th March 1850. *Aberdeen: printed by Geo. Cornwall*, 1850. pp. 26, including, as appendix, 9 letters & board minutes.
'The Board feel called upon to vindicate themselves from the accusations . . .'

9568 HISTORICAL MODEL RAILWAY SOCIETY. The Caledonian Railway: locomotives, 1883–1923; with an introduction by George Dow. *Reading: the Society*, [1966]. (Livery Register, 1). pp. 17, with 4pp. of diagrams (2 in col.).

9569 THOMAS, J. The Callander & Oban Railway. *Newton Abbot: David & Charles*, 1966. pp. 200, with col. frontis, 42 illus on 20 plates, & 26 illus in text (map, layout plans, gradient profiles, facsimiles, timetables, drawings); 10 appendices, incl. a chronology & a bibliography (41 sources).

9570 THOMAS, J. The story of 828: the working life, threatened extinction and restoration of a locomotive of the McIntosh '812' class. *Newton Abbot: David & Charles*, [1967]. pp. 32, with 11 illus, & tables. Title on cover.
A Caledonian Rly locomotive of 1899 preserved in Glasgow Museum of Transport.

9571 NOCK, O. S. The Caledonian Dunalastairs and associated classes. *Newton Abbot: David*

& Charles, 1968. pp. 159, with col. frontis & ca. 150 illus, drawings & diagrams; lists, numerous tables, incl. logs of runs, & 6 appendices.

9572 KENNEDY, D. The birth and death of a Highland railway. *London: J. Murray*, 1971. pp. x, 171, with 16 illus on 8 plates & a map.
The Ballachulish branch from Connel Ferry on the Callander & Oban Rly.

9573 CORNWELL, H. J. C. Forty years of Caledonian locomotives, 1882–1922. *Newton Abbot: David & Charles*, 1974. pp. 221, with 32 illus on 16 plates, 9 appendices (detailed lists); bibliography (73+ sources).

9574 SLOAN, J. and MUIR, M. The Glasgow, Paisley and Greenock Railway Company. [*Glasgow: Jordanhill College*, 1978]. tall 8°. pp. 59.
A collection of 76 facsimiles of documents, presented as basic source material for historical study: Acts, minute-book extracts, newspaper extracts, mostly 1835–1849, but some much later; also a map, 2 drawings and a table.

9575 BRITISH RAILWAYS. SCOTTISH REGION. 100 years of the 'Central'. *Glasgow: B.R. (Sc.R)*, 1979. pp. [20], with 38 illus, incl. cover illus.
An illustrated booklet commemorating the centenary of the Central Station (Caledonian Rly). Foreword by Leslie Soane, General Manager, B.R. Scotland; Introduction by John Calder.

9576 GLEN, A. E. and GLEN, I. A. Caledonian Cavalcade, [by] A. E. Glen, I. A. Glen, with A. G. Dunbar. *London: Ian Allan*, 1979. pp. 96. Intro & 183 illus with descrs; maps on end papers.

Glasgow & South Western Rly
9577–80

9577 SCOTT, STEPHEN AND GALE [engineers & architects]. An examination of Mr. G. Stephenson's report on the two lines of railway projected between Glasgow and Ayrshire, wherein the principle upon which his decision is founded is proved to be entirely fallacious; also, an exposure of the misstatements contained in his report, as well as those formerly published by Messrs Grainger & Miller, with a general view of the whole question involved. *Glasgow: R. McPhun*, 1837. pp. 40.
A criticism of G. Stephenson's preference for the line proposed by Grainger and Miller rather than the route recommended by Scott, Stephen & Gale. Appendix (pp. 35–40), 'Mr. Stephenson's report to the directors of the Glasgow, Paisley, Kilmarnock & Ayr Rly, dated 16 October, 1836'.

9578 HIGHET, C. The Glasgow & South Western Railway. *Lingfield: Oakwood Press*, 1965. (Oakwood Library of Railway History, 59). pp. 92, with frontis, 37 illus on 16 plates, 5 maps, 1 layout plan, 3 appendices & a bibliography (ca. 40 sources).

9579 GLASGOW AND SOUTH WESTERN RAILWAY ASSOCIATION. Centenary Souvenir Booklet, issued in connection with the centenary exhibition held at the McLean Art Gallery, Greenock . . . 1969. *Glasgow: the Association*, [1969]. pp. [6], with 7 illus.

9580 SMITH, D. L. Locomotives of the Glasgow and South Western Railway. *Newton Abbot: David & Charles*, 1976. pp. 192, with 36 illus, 19 line drawings & a map; 6 appendices, incl. (pp. 151–80) a complete listing in 7 columns.

Great North of Scotland Rly
9581–90

9581 HENDERSON, J. What does the present mode of conveyance to the north cost the public?: and what would be the saving by railway? *Aberdeen: Lewis Smith*, 1852. pp. 27, with folded map showing the Great North of Scotland Rly & connections south from Aberdeen.
A detailed argument in favour of the proposed railway.

9582 GREAT NORTH OF SCOTLAND RAILWAY. Timetables from 2nd October 1922 and until further notice. *Aberdeen: G.N. of S. Rly*, 1922. Reprint by the G.N. of S.R. Association, 1969. pp. 40.
A facsimile reprint, including a 4-page yellow insert giving details of new (1922) through services. This was the last timetable to be issued by the GNSR before its amalgamation into the LNER.

9583 GREAT NORTH OF SCOTLAND RAILWAY. Working time tables, main line and branches . . . 2nd October, 1922 and until further notice. *Aberdeen: G.N. of S. Rly*, 1922. Reprint by the G.N. of S.R. Association, 1969. pp. 39.
A facsimile reprint of the last working timetable to be used by the GNSR before its amalgamation into the LNER.

9584 VALLANCE, H. A. The Great North of Scotland Railway. *Dawlish: David & Charles; London: Macdonald*, 1965. pp. 192, with col. frontis, 58 illus on 20 plates, 13 maps, layout plans, facsimiles, timetables & 4 appendices.
The history of the line up to 1964.

9585 FARR, A. D. The Royal Deeside line. *Newton Abbot: David & Charles*, 1968. pp. 158, with col. frontis, 46 illus on 16 plates, 21 line drawings, facsimiles, timetables, map, gradient profile, 10 appendices, incl. 14 layout plans, and lists: bibliography (23 sources).
Aberdeen to Ballater on the Great North of Scotland Rly, originally (1852 to 1875) the Deeside Rly.

9586 FARR, A. D. Stories of Royal Deeside's railway. *Knaresborough: Kestrel Books*, 1971. pp. 77, with 32 illus on 16 plates, map, diagram, & 2 tables.

9587 STEPHENSON LOCOMOTIVE SOCIETY. 'Little and Good': the Great North of Scotland

Railway. *Durham: S.L.S.*, 1972. pp. 112, with frontis, 16 illus on 8 plates, chronology, 1844–1922, diagrams & lists, but no map.

9588 COOK, R. A. Great North of Scotland Railway and Highland Railway historical maps. *Caterham: Railway & Canal Historical Society*, 1977. tall 8°. pp. 15, & 8 maps on 8 pp.
The text consists mainly of a concise history of the two lines but also includes a list of all their Acts and those of their constituent companies.

9589 GREAT NORTH OF SCOTLAND RAILWAY ASSOCIATION. Great North memories: scenes of the North East's own railway. *Aberdeen: the Association*, July 1978. pp. 30. Intro & 50 illus with descrs. Title from cover. Map inside front cover; imprint inside back cover.
Period covered, 1880–1930.

9590 GLEN, A. E. and GLEN, I. A. Great North of Scotland Railway Album, [compiled by] A. E. Glen, I. A. Glen with A. G. Dunbar. *London: Ian Allan*, 1980. pp. 96. Intro & 199 illus with descrs; map on end papers.

Highland Rly
9591–9601

9591 MITCHELL, J. On the construction and works of the Highland Railway, *in* Report of the Thirty-Seventh meeting of the British Association for the Advancement of Science held at Dundee in September 1867. *London: John Murray*, 1868. (pp. 151–61, with a table).

9592 BEATON, A. J. Illustrated Guide to the Black Isle Railway . . . *Dingwall: A. M. Ross*, 1894. sm. 8°. pp. 44, & 12 pp. of adverts.
Mainly historical & topographical accounts of places served by the railway.

9593 CAMERON, J. E. The Iron Track through the Highlands: glimpses of it in the past, by J. E. C. [i.e., J. E. Cameron]. *Inverness: Highland News*, [1914?]. pp. 134, with frontis & 7 plates.
A revised presentation of pieces originally published in the *Highland News, Highland Times* and *Football Times*. A collection of anecdotes, mostly on personalities of the Inverness & Nairn Rly and the later Highland Rly.

9594 NOCK, O. S. The Highland Railway. *London: Ian Allan*, 1965. pp. viii, 177, with col. frontis, 66 illus on 32 plates, map, 4 layout plans, tables.

9595 HUNTER, D. L. G. Carriages and wagons of the Highland Railway. *Leeds: Turntable Enterprises*, 1971. pp. 99, with 50 illus, 107 dimensioned drawings, & lists.

9596 WEIR, T. The Kyle line: an illustrated history and guide. *Gartocharn: Famedram Publishers*, 1971. pp. 28, with 3 illus.

The former Highland Rly line from Dingwall to Kyle.

9597 LAMBERT, A. J. Highland Railway Album [no. 1]. *London: Ian Allan*, 1974. pp. 112. Intro, col. frontis & 235 illus with descrs.
Highland Rly and LMS Rly.
—— Highland Railway Album, no. 2. *Ian Allan*, 1978. pp. 128. Intro, col. frontis & 249 illus with descrs.

9598 WEIR, T. The Highland line: Perth, Pitlochry, Aviemore, Inverness, Wick, Thurso; a pictorial guide. *Gartocharn: Famedram Publishers*, [1975]. pp. [111], with 60 illus, a map & a bibliography (11 sources).

9599 COOK, R. A. Great North of Scotland Railway and Highland Railway Historical Maps. *Caterham: Railway & Canal Historical Society*, 1977. tall 8°. pp. 15 & 8 maps on 8 pp.
The text consists mainly of a concise history of the two lines but also includes a list of all their Acts and those of their constituent companies.

9600 THOMAS, J. The Skye Railway. *Newton Abbot: David & Charles*, 1977. pp. 168, with 18 illus on 8 plates, 2 maps, a route map, gradient profile, facsimiles, chronology & a bibliography (30 sources).

9601 TATLOW, P. A history of Highland locomotives. *Oxford: Oxford Publishing Co.*, 1979. la. 8°. pp. viii, 120, with frontis, 158 illus & many dimensioned drawings, a bibliography (19 sources) & 15 appendices (detailed lists, pp. 108–17).
A revision and extension of M. C. V. Allchin's work of the same name (1947).

North British Rly
9602–16

9602 An AUTHENTIC statement of the affairs of the Edinburgh, Leith and Newhaven Railway Company, from the period of its projection in 1835 to the close of the year 1840, by an original proprietor. *Bristol: Lavars & Ackland*, 1840. pp. 28.

9603 CARLISLE AND SILLOTH BAY DOCK AND RAILWAY. Carlisle & Silloth Bay Dock and Railway Bill: minutes of evidence and proceedings, session 1854, with charts and plans by Thomas Webster, barrister-at-law. *Westminster: J. Bigg*, 1854. pp. 114, with 1 folded & 2 la. folded charts at end. Chairman, Viscount Jocelyn.
Minutes of evidence and proceedings of parliamentary select committees appointed to examine Private Bills were not usually published. Thomas Webster was one of the three counsel for the Bill. There is no introduction or commentary by him and the words 'by Thomas Webster' on the title-page can only mean that he was responsible for promoting the publication of this work. LU(THC)

9604 NORTH British Railway (Carlisle deviation): opposed on third reading; statement of promoters. *London: Sherwood*, 1867. pp. 2. MCL

9605 LOMAX, E. S. The Edinburgh and Dalkeith Railway: a brief historical outline. [*Glasgow: Stephenson Locomotive Society*, 1962]. pp. 6. Reproduced typescript.
Issued to participants in the Edinburgh & Dalkeith Rail Tour, 25th August 1962.   LU(THC)

9606 THOMAS, J. The West Highland Railway. *Dawlish: David & Charles*; *London: Macdonald*, 1965. pp. 172, with col. frontis, 52 illus on 24 plates, & 16 in text; map, gradient profile, bibliography (39 sources), 10 appendices & 'author's notes'.
Period, 1889–1964.
—— Paperback reprint, *Pan Books*, 1970. pp. x, 197, with 28 illus on 16 plates.
—— 2nd edn, with a new introduction. *David & Charles*, 1976. pp. 172, with 52 illus on 24 plates, etc.

9607 GOSFORTH ROUND TABLE. The Wansbeck Piper: the end of the Wansbeck Valley Railway—the Heatherbell Line: the last train, the Wansbeck Piper, Sunday afternoon, October 2nd, 1966. [*Newcastle: Gosforth Round Table*, 1966]. pp. 16, with 'Eyewitness Supplement' as pp. i–viii stitched in between pp. 4 & 5, 15 illus, 3 facsimiles (1865), 2 maps & a gradient profile.
A detailed souvenir booklet of the closing day activities of the 21½ mile branch of the former North British Railway from Woodburn to Morpeth. Includes a list of the professions and occupations of the 574 passengers who signed the visitors' book.

9608 THOMAS, J. The North British Railway. *Newton Abbot: David & Charles*.
vol. 1, [1842–1879]. 1969. pp. 256, with col. frontis, 29 illus on 16 plates, & in text, 31 (maps, gradient profiles, timetables, diagrams, facsimiles, line drawings); 5 appendices, chronology, 1842–79 (pp. 239–42), & a bibliography (12+ sources).
vol. 2, [1880–1923]. 1975. pp. 224, with col. frontis, 30 illus. on 16 plates, & in text, 19 (diagrams, facsimiles, tables, & a map); chronology, 1880–1923 (pp. 204–16), & a bibliography (23+ sources).

9609 STEPHENSON LOCOMOTIVE SOCIETY. Locomotives of the North British Railway, 1846–1882. *S.L.S.*, 1970. pp. 106, with frontis & 13 illus on 8 plates, & many lists.

9610 THOMAS, J. The North British Atlantics. *Newton Abbot: David & Charles*, 1972. pp. 188, with col. frontis, 29 illus on 16 plates, & in text, 14 diagrams, facsimiles & tables; 11 appendices.

9611 WEIR, T. The Mallaig line: an illustrated history and guide. *Gartocharn: Famedram Publishers*, [1972]. pp. [24], with 8 illus & a map.
The Fort William to Mallaig section of the West Highland, later North British, Rly.

9612 BRITISH RAILWAYS. SCOTTISH REGION. A line for all seasons: the West Highland line. [*Glasgow*]: *B.R. (Sc.R)*, [1973]. pp. [12].
A sectioned coloured map of the line from Glasgow to Oban & Mallaig, overprinted with an historical and descriptive commentary.

9613 MACLEAN, A. A. North British Album. *London: Ian Allan*, 1975. pp. 144. Intro (pp. 6–13), col. frontis & 170 illus with descrs.
NBR—LNER—BR(ScR).

9614 BRODIE, I. Steamers of the Forth. *Newton Abbot: David & Charles*, 1976. pp. 168, with illus & fleet lists.
ch. 4 (pp. 47–59), the railway ferries, with 4 illus on 2 plates. The North British Rly, the LNER, and BR.

9615 MARTIN, D. The Monkland & Kirkintilloch Railway. [*Glasgow*]: *Strathkelvin District Libraries & Museums*, 1976. (Auld Kirk Museum Publications, 2). pp. 16, with 4 illus & a map.

9616 LESLIE, R. H. Steam on the Waverley route. *Truro: Bradford Barton*, 1978. pp. 96. Intro & 95 illus with descrs & a map.

Portpatrick & Wigtownshire Joint Rly
9617

9617 MacHAFFIE, F. G. The short sea route . . . *Prescot: T. Stephenson*, 1975. pp. xvi, 286, with 106 illus, 189 notes & a bibliography (ca. 150 sources).
ch. 4 (pp. 41–8), A railway for Portpatrick. (The Portpatrick & Wigtownshire Joint Railway). There are many references in the Index to other railways with steamboat connections, in Scotland and Ireland.

C 3   WALES

Wales generally—West Glamorgan—Mid-Glamorgan—
South Glamorgan—Gwent—Dyfed—Powys—Gwynedd
(with Anglesey)—Clwyd

9618–9782
Subdivided by a modified version of the main Classification Scheme

Wales generally 9618–29

9618 JONES, T. I. J. Acts of Parliament concerning Wales, 1714–1901; compiled and edited by T. I. Jeffreys Jones. *Cardiff: University of*

Wales Press, 1966. (Board of Celtic Studies, University of Wales History of Law series, 17). pp. xiii, 343.
pp. 81–167, 'Railways and early tramways' (726 Local & Personal Acts, 3 Public General Acts); pp.

168–70, 'Urban tramways' (23 Local & Personal Acts).

9619 JONES, R. E. Rheilffyrdd Cymru. The railways of Wales. *Caernarfon: Cymdeithas Llyfrgelloedd Cymru; Welsh Library Association*, 1979. pp. 154, with 4 illus.
A detailed chronology with 5 lists and an index of 182 railways; pp. 7–68 in Welsh, pp. 73–138 in English.

9620 BLOCK, G. D. M. Transport in Wales. *London: Conservative Political Centre*, July 1964. (Publication no. 304). pp. 42, with 3 maps showing traffic density, railways and roads.

9621 CASSERLEY, H. C. Wales and the Welsh border counties. *Newton Abbot: David & Charles*, 1970. (Railway History in Pictures series). pp. 111, with col. frontis, 144 illus with descrs, 2 maps, & 2 diagrams.

9622 WALES TRANSPORT 2000. (TRAFNIDIAETH CYMRU DWY FIL). A short review of transport policy in Wales. *Treherbert: Wales Transport 2000*, September 1973. pp. 6. Reproduced typescript.
Concern over rail closures. Urges the setting up of a Passenger Transport Authority for Wales. A shortened version of *Transport Policy in Wales* (Wales Transport 2000, 1973).

9623 WALES TRANSPORT 2000. (TRAFNIDIAETH CYMRU DWY FIL). Transport policy in Wales. *Treherbert: Wales Transport 2000*, September 1973. pp. 25, with 2 maps. Reproduced typescript in printed cover.
An historical introduction followed by a detailed statement of the present situation with regard to rail services and the closing of lines. Recommends an integrated transport system and the setting up of a Passenger Transport Authority for Wales.

9624 ASHWORTH, B. J. Steam in the West Midlands and Wales. *London: Ian Allan*, 1975. pp. 120. Intro (pp. 5–7) & 195 illus (8 col) with descrs.
Period, 1959–1974.

9625 REES, D. M. The industrial archaeology of Wales. *Newton Abbot: David & Charles*, 1975. (Industrial Archaeology of the British Isles series). pp. 302, with 32 illus on 16 plates, 30 maps, drawings, diagrams, 110 notes & a bibliography (118 sources).
The index has ca. 160 page refs to railways and tramroads (wagonways).

9626 REES, G. L. and WRAGG, R. A study of the passenger transport needs of rural Wales. [*Cardiff*]: *Welsh Council*, 1975. pp. [8], 139, with many tables & maps.
Loosely inserted: 'The transport research project: note by the Welsh Council' (pp. 3).
Includes railways, and proposals for an alternative rail network.

9627 REES, G. L. and WRAGG, R. A study of the passenger transport needs of urban Wales, prepared for the Welsh Council by Richard Wragg. *Cardiff: Cyngor Cymru; Welsh Council*, 1977. pp. xii, 283, with many tables & maps.
A discussion document. ch. 3 (pp. 41–53), 'The rail system of South Wales'.

9628 WELSH OFFICE. TRANSPORT AND HIGHWAYS GROUP. [Rural transport: a symposium 1977]. Papers presented at a symposium on rural transport held at the Old Hall, University College of Wales, Aberystwyth, on Saturday 18 June 1977. *Cardiff: Welsh Office*, Summer 1977. tall 8°. pp. 137, with tables, diagrams & maps. Cover title: Rural transport: a symposium, 1977. spiral binding.
Paper no. 4 (pp. 27–29), The problems and challenges of operating rail services in rural areas, by D. Ashton.

9629 CASSERLEY, H. C. Welsh railways in the heyday of Steam. *Truro: Bradford Barton* [1979]. pp. 96, Intro & 142 illus with descrs.

C 3 a   South Wales
(Gwent and the Glamorgans)
9630–64

South Wales generally 9630–43

9630 DONOVAN, E. Descriptive excursions through South Wales and Monmouthshire in the year 1804 and the four preceding summers. *London: printed for the author*, 1805. 2 vols.
vol. 1, pp. xxii, & pl. XXIII (col. engraving) in vol. 2: Neath Abbey railway for conveying coal from pits to smelting houses 'drawn with the greatest ease by a single horse upon the rail roads . . .' The engraving depicts 3 cross-overs.

9631 SVEDENSTIERNA, E. T. [Resa igenom en del af England och Skottland, åren 1802 och 1803]. Svedenstierna's tour, Great Britain, 1802–3: the travel diary of an industrial spy; translated from the German by E. L. Dellow, with a new introduction by M. W. Flinn. *Newton Abbot: David & Charles*, 1973. pp. xx, 192.
pp. 45, 48–51, 55, wagonways seen in South Wales.
[German edn.: *Reise durch einen Teil von England und Schottland in den Jahren 1802 und 1803 . . .* (1811)].

9632 DAVIES, W. General view of the agriculture and domestic economy of South Wales . . . drawn up for the consideration of the Board of Agriculture and Internal Improvement. *London: W. Nicol & others*, 1814.
vol. 2, pp. 383–9, 398–9: 'Rail-Roads'. An account of wagonways in South Wales, including a lengthy quotation from B. Outram's report to Brecon Canal proprietors in 1799 recommending a change-over from edge-rail to plate-rail.

9633 JOHN, A. H. The industrial development of South Wales, 1750–1850. *Cardiff: University of Wales Press*, 1950. pp. x, [2], 201.
pp. 103–5, production of rails for English and foreign railways, with 12 notes.

9634 BROOKS, E. Regional functions of the mineral transport system in the South Wales coalfield, 1830–1951. Thesis, Ph.D., St John's College, Cambridge, 1957–8.

9635 RAILWAY CORRESPONDENCE & TRAVEL SOCIETY. Itinerary of the Central Wales Scenic Rail Tour . . . , Saturday, 14th May, 1966. *R.C. & T.S.*, [1966]. pp. 6 (printed folder), with map, schedule, & notes by M. B. Warburton.
Worcester—Cheltenham—Gloucester—Cardiff—Llanelly—Craven Arms—Hereford—Newport—Bristol.

9636 COOKE, D. N. Industrial steam locomotives of Southern England and South Wales. *Knowle: Warwickshire Railway Society*, [1967 or 8]. pp. 36.

9637 GREEN, A. C. O. The Alexandra (Newport & South Wales) Docks & Railway Company. *Newport (Gwent): the author*, 1973. pp. [30], with 2 illus on 1 plate, 3 maps (1 loosely inserted), 7 plans (1 on cover & 1 loosely inserted).

9638 GLADWIN, D. D. and GLADWIN, J. M. The canals of the Welsh valleys and their tramroads. Camlasau'r cymoedd a'u dramffyrdd; with engravings by J. K. Ebblewhite. [*Lingfield*]: *Oakwood Press*, 1974. pp. 91, with 32 illus on 16 plates, 17 maps & plans, & 25 bibliogr. notes.
pp. 41–56, 'Canal tramroads'; pp. 57–63, 'Tramroad relics'.

9639 WILLIAMS, S. Vintage buses & trams in South Wales, edited by Stewart Williams; consultants, John F. Andrews, Viv Corbin, Chris Taylor, E. A. Thomas. *Barry: S. Williams*, 1975. pp. [128]. Intro, frontis & 203 illus with descrs.
The photographs are introduced by six essays on particular areas and undertakings.

9640 RAILWAY CORRESPONDENCE & TRAVEL SOCIETY. [Itinerary]. Golden Jubilee Limited, Saturday, 1st April, 1978. *Arundel: D. A. Murphy, for the R.C. & T.S.*, [1978]. pp. 12, with 4 illus, map, & schedule of the tour. Golden yellow cover. Text by A. C. MacLeod.
Cheltenham—Gloucester—Cardiff—Port Talbot—Llandeilo—Llandrindod Wells—Craven Arms—Ludlow—Hereford—Worcester—Cheltenham.

9641 CAVALIER, P. and SILCOCK, G. Visions of Steam: the four seasons of Steam in industrial South Wales. *Oxford: Oxford Publishing Co.*, 1979. obl. format. pp. [120]. Intro, map & 138 illus, with captions in English & Welsh.
Environment photographs by Peter Cavalier and Geoff Silcock, 1960s & 1970s.

9642 PAGE, J. Forgotten railways: South Wales. *Newton Abbot: David & Charles*, 1979. pp. 192, with 32 illus on 16 plates, 12 maps, gazetteer (pp. 140–86) & a bibliography (52 sources).

9643 BARRIE, D. S. South Wales. *Newton Abbot: David & Charles*, 1980. (A Regional History of the Railways of Great Britain, 12). pp. [288], with 34 illus on 16 plates, 11 maps & a folded map at end; bibliography (75+ sources).

C 3 b The Glamorgans 9644–57

9644 BRUSH ELECTRICAL ENGINEERING COMPANY. Brush cars for the Mumbles Railway. *Loughborough: the Company*, [1928]. pp. [4], with 3 illus & diagram.
Reprinted from the *Electric Railway & Tramway Journal*, 7 September, 1928.

9645 LLOYD, W. L. Trade and transport: an account of the trade of the Port of Swansea and the transport facilities and industry in the district. *Swansea: University of Wales Press Board*, 1940. (Social & Economic Survey of Swansea & District, pamphlet no. 6). p. 108, with maps, tables & graphs.
Includes railways.

9646 BEVAN, T. The Green: terminus of the Bridgend Railway, in Official Brochure, Bridgend Urban District Council Festival of Britain, 1951 and Centenary of Local Government in Britain [celebrations]. *Bridgend: the Council*, 1951. pp. 39–43.

9647 RANDALL, H. J. Bridgend: the story of a market town. *Newport (Mon).: R. H. Johns*, 1955. pp. xv, 156.
ch. 15 (pp. 80–85), 'The Bridgend Railway', with 1 illus & 10 notes.
Incorporated ca. 1825 as a horse tramroad, into Llynfi Rly in 1854, & into GWR in 1883.

9648 BOWEN, D. G. City of Cardiff: 68 years of electric transport. *Guildford: National Trolleybus Association*, [1970]. sm. obl. 8°. pp. [8], with 4 illus, chronology & map.
'Published to commemorate 68 years of electric passenger transport . . . , 2nd May 1902 to 11th January 1970'. Includes tramways.

9649 GOULD, D. Cardiff's electric tramways. *Tarrant Hinton: Oakwood Press*, 1974. (Locomotion Papers, 81). pp. 87, with 30 illus, 2 line drawings & 4 maps on 16 plates, & a timetable for 1903.

9650 TRANSPORTATION PLANNING ASSOCIATES. Vale of Glamorgan rail passenger line: feasibility study report. [*Cardiff: County of South Glamorgan, Dept of Environment & Planning*, 1974]. pp. [ix], 158, [xii], with many tables, maps & graphs.
Produced for the South Glamorgan County Planning Officer by Transportation Planning Associates in association with Research & Marketing Wales & the West, Ltd.
Object: to try to assess the advantages to be gained by re-opening the line from Bridgend down the Vale of Glamorgan to Barry and up to Cardiff. Concludes with a qualified prediction that this would be a social and economic benefit.

9651 LEWIS, M. J. T. Steam on the Penydarren. *Industrial Railway Society*, 1975. (Industrial Railway Record, 59 (April 1975)). pp. 36, with 12 illus, 12 groups of dimensioned drawings (9 of early locomotives), & a map.

Early history (from 1791) of the Penydarren tramroad (also known as the Merthyr tramroad), South Glamorgan, its locomotives and its track. The locomotives described and illustrated are: of the Penydarren Co., R. Trevithick's locomotives of 1802–3, and 1804, *Eclipse* (1832); and of the Dowlais Iron Co., *Perseverance* (1829), *Yn Barod Etto* (1832), *Mountaineer* (1833?), *Dowlais* (1834 or 5), *Charles Jordan* (1838) and *John Watt* (1838).

9652 ANDREWS, J. F. Keep moving!: the story of Solomon Andrews and his family. *Barry: Stewart Williams*, 1976. obl. format. pp. 144, with ca. 200 illus (photos, some col. drawings, facsimiles). Limited edition of 1000 copies.

Solomon Andrews, 1835–1908, coachbuilder, bus proprietor and tramway operator, Cardiff, Pontypridd, Newport and Pwllheli.

9653 ILES, T. Transport in South Glamorgan. *Treherbert: Wales Transport 2000*, 1976. (Transport Study, 2). pp. 19, with 5 maps. Reproduced typescript.

9654 THOMAS, R. 'Communications' *in* Neath: a symposium, by Elis Jenkins (1976), ch. 12, pp. 36–51, with 7 illus on 4 plates & 12 bibliogr. notes.

pp. 244–8, 'Railways'. For tramways of the area there are 14 page refs in the index.

9655 LARGE, R. Passenger tramways of Pontypridd. *Tarrant Hinton: Oakwood Press*, 1977. (Locomotion Papers, 106). pp. 52, with 12 illus & a map.

9656 OWEN, J. A. The Dowlais Iron Works, 1759–1970. *Newport (Gwent): Starling Press*, 1977. pp. 164, with many illus, a bibliography (56 sources), a calendar of the Dowlais Iron Co. papers at the County Record Office, Cardiff (pp. 146–52) and a chronology (pp. 153–61).

There is no index, but the sections of the work dealing with the Penydarran tramroad, the manufacturing of rails and of locomotives, and the joint lines in the Taff Bargoed Valley are fairly easy to locate from the List of Contents (pp. 5–7).

9657 THOMAS, N. L. The Mumbles, past and present. *Llandysul: Gomer Press*, 1978. pp. xi, 253, with illus & a bibliography (59 sources).

ch. 3 (pp. 72–116), 'The Mumbles Railway', with 11 illus.

C 3 c   Gwent 9658–64

9658 HASSALL, C. General view of the agriculture of the county of Monmouth . . . drawn up for the consideration of the Board of Agriculture and Internal Improvement. *London: G. & W. Nicol & others*, 1812. pp. xi, 142.

Section 2 (pp. 105–22), 'Iron rail-ways', with 1 illus of a plateway.

9659 FINCH, E. Description of the wrought-iron suspension bridge on the South Wales Railway over the River Wye at Chepstow; from the designs of I.K. Brunel, constructed by Edward Finch, Bridge Works, Chepstow. *London: printed by Robson, Levey & Franklyn*, 1856. pp. 11.

—— Reprinted, with an introduction and additional notes as: Brunel's tubular suspension bridge over the River Wye. *Chepstow Society*, 1970. pp. [iv], 11, [v], with 5 illus [1 folded and 2 depicting the new substructure).

—— 2nd reprint edn, edited by Ivor Walters. *Chepstow Society*, 1976. (Chepstow Society, Pamphlet Series, 8). pp. iii-x, 20, with 9 illus, folded map & folded plate. Limited edition of 500 copies.

9660 TASKER, W. W. The Sirhowy Tramroad and Railway in Monmouthshire. *Shrewsbury: the author*, [1972]. pp. 17, with 2 drawings & a timetable & map inside front cover. Reproduced typescript. Title on cover and at head of text.

9661 TIPPER, D. A. Stone and steam in the Black Mountains. *[Rochdale]: the author*, 1975. pp. 73, with frontis, 16 illus on 8 plates, & in text, 12 illus, 8 maps & a bibliography (28 sources).

Includes an account of the Abertillery & District Water Board's narrow-gauge line from Lower Cwmyoy to Blaen-y-Cwm, and from 1919 on to Llanfihangel, 1912–1930.

9662 MAGGS, C. Newport trams. *Tarrant Hinton: Oakwood Press*, 1977. (Locomotion Papers, 105). pp. 60, with 16 illus & 3 maps.

9663 TASKER, W. W. Railways in the Sirhowy Valley. *Tarrant Hinton: Oakwood Press*, 1978. (Locomotion Papers, 113). pp. 44, with 13 illus on 6 plates, 4 diagrams, 3 maps & a bibliography (14 sources).

The Sirhowy Valley Tramroad Co., the Sirhowy Rly Co., the LNWR, LMSR, and BR.

9664 VAN LAUN, J. The Clydach Gorge: industrial archaeology trials in a north Gwent valley. (Drawings by Michael Blackmore). *Brecon: Brecon Beacons National Park Committee*, 1979. pp. 24, with 20 drawings, 7 photos, 2 maps & a bibliography.

A detailed guide, with historical notes, to the sites of an 18th & 19th century iron-making industry in the Valley. The courses of three wagonways are followed: the Clydach railroad (1794), the Llammarch railroad (1794), Bailey's tramroad (1821), and that of the Merthyr, Tredegar & Abergavenny Railway (1859, into LNWR 1866).

A noteworthy feature is the table on p. 24 which links passages in the text to particular sources in the bibliography.

C 3 d   North Wales, West Wales and Mid-Wales
(Dyfed, Powys, Gwynedd (with Anglesey), Clwyd)
9665–9782

North, West, and Mid-Wales generally
9665–84

9665 BINGLEY, W. North Wales, including its scenery, antiquities, customs . . . *London: T. N. Longman & O. Rees*, 1804. 2 vols.
vol. 1, pp. 230–4, a trip on an underground wagonway in Llanberis copper mine in 1801.

9666 CUBITT, W. [and others]. London and Dublin direct communication: opinions of William Cubitt, George Stephenson and George Roskell respecting the St. George's Harbour and Chester Railway. *London: Baily*, 1838. pp. 3.
A printed report by W. Cubitt with supporting letters from G. Stephenson and G. Roskell. A proposed line from Chester to the coast near Llandudno.

9667 ST GEORGE'S harbour and railway project. *Chester: Fletcher*, [1839]. pp. 4. Text dated Chester, January 12th 1839.
An attack on the proposed scheme (1836) for a railway from Chester to Ormeshead (Llandudno).

9668 RAILWAY CORRESPONDENCE & TRAVEL SOCIETY. Itinerary of the North Wales Rail Tour . . . , Sunday, 2nd October 1955. *R.C. & T.S.*, [1955]. pp. [4]. Scheduled itinerary & map.
Chester—Flint—Prestatyn—Dyserth—Rhyl—Denbigh—Ruthin—Corwen—Caerwys—Mold—Coed Talon—Llong—Penyffordd—Caergwrle—Gwersyllt—Wrexham—Hawarden—Saughall—Chester.

9669 CLAYTON, G. and REES, J. H. The economic problems of rural transport in Wales. *Cardiff: University of Wales Press*, 1966. (Welsh Economic Studies, 5). pp. 44, with notes & 21 tables.
Mid and West Wales, with a special study of the Central Wales line (Shrewsbury to Swansea).

9670 BIRMINGHAM LOCOMOTIVE CLUB. Industrial and independent locomotives and railways of North Wales; edited by V. J. Bradley and P. Hindley; cartographer, R. E. West. *Great Sutton (Wirral): the Club*, [1968]. (Pocket Books, F). pp. xxi, 97.
Originally published 1950.

9671 JONES, G. W. The development and decline of public transport services in mid-Wales, 1861–1966, and the effects thereof. Thesis, M.A., University of London, 1968.

9672 DENTON, J. H. Railways and waterways in North Wales; notes for a tour. *Chester: Railway & Canal Historical Society*, 1969. pp. 16, with 11 sketch maps of track layouts.

9673 COZENS, L. The Mawddwy, Van and Kerry railways and the Hendre-Ddu and Kerry tramways. [*Lingfield*]: *Oakwood Press*, 1972. (Oakwood Library of Railway History, 32). pp. 68, with 32 illus on 16 plates, 5 maps & 5 layout plans.

Originally published separately as *The Van & Kerry Railways with the Kerry Tramway* (1953) and *The Mawddwy Railway with the Hendre-Ddu Tramway* (1954).

9674 WRIGHT, H. E. Welsh railways, Rheilffyrdd Cymru. *St Ives (Cornwall): J. Pike*, 1975. (Viewing Wales series). pp. 40, with 9 illus & a map. Text in English.
Narrow-gauge railways.

9675 CHRISTIANSEN, R. Forgotten railways: North and Mid Wales. *Newton Abbot: David & Charles*, 1976. pp. 160, with 32 illus on 16 plates, 20 in text (maps, diagrams & drawings), la. folded map at end; pp. 117–50, gazetteer, with historical details of lines; pp. 151–55, bibliography (63 sources).

9676 PRIDEAUX, J. D. C. A. The Welsh narrow gauge railway: a pictorial history. *Newton Abbot: David & Charles*, 1976. pp. 96, with 123 illus, map, a tabular summary (pp. 92–6) & a bibliography (27 sources).

9677 WIRRAL RAILWAY CIRCLE. North Wales land cruise: a guide to the railways of North and Mid Wales along with the main connecting routes from England. [*Wirral*]: *the Circle*, [1976]. pp. 56. Reproduced typescript; 6 illus on covers.
Crewe—Chester—Shrewsbury—Machynlleth—Aberystwyth—Barmouth—Pwllheli—Blaenau Ffestiniog—Betws-y-Coed—Llandudno, and the 'great little trains of Wales'.

9678 CAMPBELL, J. E. Railway preservation in North and Mid Wales, edited by J. E. Campbell. [Published by] *Cambrian Railways, Corris Railway Society, Foxcote Manor Society, Glyn Valley Tramway Group, and Rheilffordd Llyn Tegid Cyf (Bala Lake Rly, Ltd)*, 1977. pp. 32, with 14 illus; map on cover.

9679 BICK, D. E. The old metal mines of mid-Wales [cumulative edition]. *Newent: the author*, 1978. pp. 309, with illus, maps, diagrams & bibliographies.
A limited edition of 250 numbered copies signed by the author. Previously published in separate parts:
1, Cardiganshire, south of Devil's Bridge. [1974]. pp. 52.
2, Cardiganshire, the Rheidol to Goginan. [1974]. pp. 52.
3, Cardiganshire, north of Goginan. 1976. pp. 72.
4, West Montgomeryshire. 1977. pp. 64.
5, Aberdovey, Dinas Mawddwy and Llangynog. 1978. pp. 52.

9680 PERKINS, D. Great little trains of Wales, by Derek Perkins, new edn. *Swansea: Celtic Educational (Services) Ltd*, 1978. sm. obl. 8°. pp. 79, with 20 illus (13 col.), a general map, 9 route maps & 12 line drawings.

9681 WAINWRIGHT, S. D. Rails to North Wales. *London: Ian Allan*, 1978. pp. 80. Intro (pp. 5–7) & 124 illus with descrs; map on front end papers.
Steam trains and locomotives on routes from Chester and Shrewsbury, 1950s & 1960s.

9682 BAUGHAN, P. E. North and Mid Wales. *Newton Abbot: David & Charles*, 1980. (Regional History of the Railways of Great Britain, 11). pp. 248, incl. 48 illus on 16 plates, 2 illus in text, 12 maps & a la. folded map at end; bibliography (55 sources).

9683 GREAT little trains of Wales. *St. Ives (Cambs): Photo Precision*, [1980]. pp. 32, with 48 col. illus & maps. 'A Colourmaster Publication'.
A guide to Welsh narrow gauge passenger railways now in operation.

9684 KNEALE, E. N. North Wales Steam, 1927–1968. *Oxford: Oxford Publishing Co.*, 1980. la. 8°. pp. [104]. Intro (English and Welsh) & 178 illus with descrs (in English); map on end papers.

C 3 e Dyfed
(including the Vale of Rheidol Light Rly)

9685–93

9685 PRICE, M. R. C. The Saundersfoot Railway. *Lingfield: Oakwood Press*, 1964. pp. 21, with 12 illus & 4 maps.
—— re-issued with an addendum, 'Postscript' (p. 22), [1976].

9686 STICKINGS, T. G. The story of Saundersfoot. *Tenby: H. G. Walters*, 1970. pp. 169, with 36 illus, incl. maps, & a bibliography (21 sources).
Contains many illustrations and much information on the Saundersfoot Rly, especially pp. 110–18, 'The Saundersfoot Railway & Harbour'.

9687 WEST WALES NATURALISTS TRUST. What you will see in the Vale of Rheidol: Britain's first railway nature trail; Norman R. Young, editor. *Haverfordwest: the Trust*, 1971. pp. 27, with drawings & folded map.
Describes what can be seen by passengers on the Vale of Rheidol Rly, 'port out, starboard home' being the required orientation.

9688 REEVES, J. Vale of Rheidol Railway Pictorial. *Truro: Bradford Barton*, [1975]. Intro & 84 illus with descrs.

9689 WADE, E. A. The Plynlimon & Hafan Tramway. *London: Gemini Publishing Co.*, 1976. la. obl. format. pp. 64, with 12 illus, 9 diagrams (8 of which are composite), 4 layout plans, 3 maps, a gradient profile & a bibliography (16 sources). Title from cover.

9690 HOWELLS, R. Old Saundersfoot, from Monkstone to Marros. *Llandysul (Dyfed): Gomer Press*, 1977. pp. 133, with 225 illus, of which 27 are of the Saundersfoot Railway.

9691 BRITISH RAILWAYS. LONDON MIDLAND REGION. Facts and figures about the Vale of Rheidol Railway. [*London: B.R. (LMR)*,

1978]. 3 separate fact sheets in a folder.
1, A brief history of the railway and historical calendar.
2, Engine nos. 7, *Owain Glyndŵr*, and 8, *Llywelyn*, with 2 illus.
3, Conversion to oil firing; with schematic diagram & a dimensioned drawing.

9692 BROOKS, J. Vale of Rheidol Railway. [*London*]: *British Railways, London Midland Region*, [1978]. pp. [16], with 14 illus (12 col.) & a map.

9693 GWILI RLY. Stock Book. 2nd edn. *Neath: Gwili Rly*, 1979. pp. [16], with 7 illus.
A re-opened 1¼ mile length of the GWR's Teifi Valley line in Dyfed.

C 3 f Powys
(including the Welshpool & Llanfair Light Rly)

9694–9702

9694 SMITH, D. J. The Welshpool & Llanfair Railway. *Teddington: Branch Line Handbooks; Bracknell: West Country Handbooks*, 1966. pp. 68, with 23 illus, 4 maps, 3 dimensioned drawings, 2 plans, a gradient profile & a stocklist.
—— 2nd edn. *Bracknell: Town & Country Press*, 1969. pp. 68, with 24 illus, 4 maps, 3 diagrams, 2 line drawings, a gradient profile, timetable & stocklists.

9695 LLANFAIR Railway Companion, number one. *Llanfair Caereinion: Welshpool & Llanfair Light Rly Preservation Co.*, 1969. pp. 24 incl. covers, with 17 illus.
Composed of material previously published in literature distributed free to members.

9696 CARTWRIGHT, R. and RUSSELL, R. T. The Welshpool & Llanfair Light Railway . . . with drawings by Michael Christiansen. *Newton Abbot: David & Charles*, 1972. pp. 207, with col. frontis, 35 illus on 16 plates, & in text, 44 maps, plans, diagrams & layout plans, timetables & a bibliography (30+ sources).

9697 FAIRS, G. L. A history of the Hay: the story of Hay-on-Wye. *London & Chichester: Phillimore*, 1972. pp. xi, 356, with 32 illus on 16 plates.
pp. 267–75. 'Rail transport' (wagonways & railways) *et passim*. The Hay Rly, the Hereford, Hay & Brecon Rly and the Golden Valley Rly, with 8 bibliogr. notes.

9698 CARTWRIGHT, R. Welshpool & Llanfair Railway Pictorial [edited by Ralph Cartwright]. *Truro: Bradford Barton*, 1975. pp. 48. Intro & 60 illus with descrs.

9699 WELSHPOOL & LLANFAIR LIGHT RLY (1956). The Welshpool & Llanfair Light Railway in pictures. *Llanfair Caereinion: the Railway*, 1975. pp. 20. Intro & 45 illus with descrs; plan & gradient profile.

9700 ELLIS, D. M. Transport in Powys. *Treherbert: Wales Transport 2000*, [1976?]. (Transport Study, 1). pp. 27 & 3 maps. Reproduced typescript.
A detailed analysis of the current overall situation, including rail services, with recommendations for future needs.

9701 WELSHPOOL & LLANFAIR LIGHT RLY (1956). The Welshpool extension project. *Llanfair Caereinion: the Company*, [1977]. pp. 20, incl. covers, with 8 illus (1 col.) & a map & drawing of the proposed new terminus.
The planned re-instatement of the line from its present terminating point at Sylfaen station, to Raven Square, Welshpool.

9702 RATTENBURY, G. Tramroads of the Brecknock & Abergavenny Canal. *Oakham: Railway & Canal Historical Society*, 1980. pp. 136, with 20 illus, 11 maps & plans (incl. frontis) & 379 notes.
A detailed study. The photographs are by P. G. Rattenbury and R. Derek Sach and the maps and plans are the work of M. J. Messenger, from tracings by the author.

C 3 g   Gwynedd, with Anglesey
(including the Cambrian Coast line)

9703–8

9703 WILLIAMS, G. J. Hanes plwyf Ffestiniog, o'r cyfnod boreuaf. *Wrexham: Hughes & Son*, [1882]. pp. 240.
pp. 128–33, 'Y Rheilffyrdd'. An account of the Festiniog, Festiniog & Blaenau, the LNWR and the GWR, at Ffestiniog.

9704 WILLIAMS, G. H. Rheilffyrdd yng Ngwynedd, (Railways in Gwynedd). [*Caernarfon*]: *Gwynedd Archives Service*, 1979. sm. 4°. pp. [32], with 90 illus, col. map & col. illus of tickets inside covers. In Welsh and English.
Standard gauge railways (LNWR, GWR & Cambrian Rlys) in north west Wales.

9705 MINISTRY OF TRANSPORT. The Cambrian Coast line: a cost/benefit analysis of the retention of railway services on the Cambrian Coast line (Machynlleth—Pwllheli). *London: H.M.S.O.*, 1969. pp. 45, with 16 tables, 4 appendices & 5 folded maps in end pocket.

9706 NATIONAL COUNCIL ON INLAND TRANSPORT. Memorandum to the Minister of Transport on the Cambrian Coast line. *London: N.C.I.T.*, July 1970. pp. 4, with 2-page financial notes loosely inserted. Reproduced typescript.
Strongly advocating the retention of the line.

9707 ROGERS, J. D. Rheilffordd y Cambrian. The Cambrian line: an illustrated history and guide. *Gartocharn: Famedram Publishers*, 1974. pp. [72], with 12 illus & a map.
Text in English and Welsh. Concern for the future of the coastal section of the line, from Machynlleth

to Pwllheli, and the combined efforts of BR, the Department of the Environment and the Cambrian Coast Line Action Group to encourage an increase in fare-paying support.

9708 BRITISH RAILWAYS. British Rail's beautiful Cambrian Coast line. [*London: B.R.*, 1979 or 1980]. pp. [8], with 12 illus (5 col.), 2 facsimiles & a map.
The line from Pwllheli to Aberystwyth along the coast of Cardigan Bay (70 miles).

C 3 h   Clwyd
(including the Conwy Valley line)

9709–15

9709 WILLETT, R. A Memoir of Hawarden parish, Flintshire . . . *Chester: printed by J. Fletcher*, 1822.
pp. 103–5, early coal railways in the area.

9710 VEYSEY, A. G. Guide to the Flintshire Record Office; edited for the County Records Committee by A. G. Veysey, County Archivist. [*Mold*]: *Flintshire County Council*, 1974. pp. xvii, 188.
Index has 59 page refs under 'Railway . . .', 'Railways', 'Tramroads & tramways'.

9711 BRITISH RAILWAYS. British Rail's beautiful Conwy Valley line. [*London: B.R.*, 1979].
An 8pp publicity folder with 15 illus (8 col.) & a col. map. Includes historical details.

9712 BRITISH RAILWAYS. LONDON MIDLAND REGION: STOKE ON TRENT DIVISION. Conwy Valley Centenary Celebrations, Sunday, 22nd July 1979. *Stoke-on-Trent: B.R. (LMR)*, July 1979. pp. 12 & a plan of Blaenau Ffestiniog station (BR). Reproduced typescript. Produced with the co-operation of the North Wales Railway Circle.
A detailed programme of BR activity planned for the 22nd July, for staff involved in the working of the special train from Crewe to Blaenau Ffestiniog and the ancillary arrangements on the Conwy Valley branch and on the North Wales Coast line.

9713 NORTH WALES RAILWAY CIRCLE. Conwy Valley Railway Centenary, July 1979. [*n.p.*]: *the Circle*, [1979]. pp. [16], with 8 illus on 4 plates, 2 drawings by Alastair Bainbridge & a double-spread plan of Llandudno Junction.

9714 ANDERSON, R. C. A history of the Llandudno & Colwyn Bay Electric Railway Limited. *Exeter: Quail Map Co.*, 1968. (Transport Series, 2). pp. [28], with 19 illus, 2 maps & a table (of bus fleet).
—— reprinted, with minor corrections, 1970.

9715 ANDERSON, R. C. Great Orme Tramway. *Battersea (London): Light Railway Transport League*, [1970]. pp. 20, with 21 illus & a map.
Reprinted from *Modern Tramway*.
—— Great Orme Tramway: the first 75 years. *London: L.R.T.L.*, [1977]. pp. 20, with 21 illus & a map.

Reprinted from *Modern Tramway*, January–April 1967.

—— new edn. *L.R.T.L.*, [1979]. pp. 20, with 21 illus & a map.

C 3 D   Narrow gauge mineral/passenger railways
9716–69

Generally 9716–24

9716 LINDSAY, J. A history of the North Wales slate industry. *Newton Abbot: David & Charles*, 1974. pp. 376, with 31 illus on 16 plates & a map, a gazetteer (pp. 308–33), 708 notes & a bibliography (over 100 sources).
Accounts of mineral railways in the area are scattered throughout the text but the work provides material on the setting within which each line was constructed and worked. The detailed index and the generous notes and bibliography facilitate reference and further reading on particular lines.

9717 WHITEHOUSE, P. B. Welsh Narrow Gauge Album, by P. B. Whitehouse in association with John Adams. *London: Ian Allan*, 1969. pp. 88. Intro & 19 illus with descrs.

9718 BOYD, J. I. C. Narrow gauge railways in south Caernarvonshire . . ., with drawings by J. M. Lloyd. *Lingfield: Oakwood Press*, 1972. pp. 381, with 109 illus on 56 plates, & in text, numerous diagrams of station & junction layouts, & of rolling stock; bibliography (24+ sources).

9719 ROOKSBY, D. A. Narrow gauge railways of Wales. *Norwich: Jarrold*, 1973. pp. [32], with col. title-page, 32 illus (19 col.) & 8 maps.

9720 WRIGHT, H. E. Welsh railways. Rheilffyrdd Cymru. *St. Ives (Cornwall): J. Pike*, 1975. (Viewing Wales series). pp. 40, with 9 illus & a map. Text in English.
Narrow-gauge railways.

9721 PRIDEAUX, J. D. C. A. The Welsh narrow gauge railway: a pictorial history. *Newton Abbot: David & Charles*, 1976. pp. 96, with 123 illus, map, a tabular summary (pp. 92–6) & a bibliography (27 sources).

9722 BOYD, J. I. C. On the Welsh narrow gauge. *Truro: Bradford Barton*, [1978]. pp. 96. Intro & 125 illus with descrs.

9723 PERKINS, D. Great little trains of Wales, by Derek Perkins. new edn. *Swansea: Celtic Educational (Services) Ltd*, 1978. sm. obl. 8°. pp. 79, with 20 illus (13 col.), a general map, 9 route maps & 12 line drawings.

9724 GREAT little trains of Wales. *St Ives (Cambs): Photo Precision*, [1980]. pp. 32, with 48 illus & maps. 'A Colourmaster Publication'.
A guide to Welsh narrow gauge passenger railways now in operation.

Corris Rly 9725–28

9725 CORRIS RAILWAY SOCIETY. The Corris Railway and the Dulas Valley: a short survey of the railway and the neighbourhood which it served. *Corris: the Society*, 1970. obl. 8°. pp. 28, with 4 illus & a map.

9726 CORRIS RLY. Corris Railway. *Corris: Corris Rly*, 1895. [*Corris: Corris Railway Society*, 1976]. sm. 8°. pp. 16, with 5 illus & 3 timetables.
A facsimile reprint in a newly designed cover with the title 'Reproduction of the Corris Railway Guide of 1895'. Map inside covers.

9727 MORGAN, J. S. The Corris Railway Company. *London: Gemini Publishing*, 1977. obl. 8°. pp. 63, with 59 illus, 2 maps, gradient profile, diagrams & timetables. Title from cover.

9728 CORRIS RAILWAY SOCIETY. Track Plans. *Corris: the Society*, 1979. sm. obl. 8°. pp. 16. Intro. & on pp. 3–13, paged sections of the Ordnance Survey map of 1901 with line diagrams of ca. 1930, followed by text. General map inside front cover.

Festiniog Rly 9729–42

9729 TYLER, H. W. On the Festiniog Railway for passengers as a 2-feet gauge with sharp curves, and worked by locomotive engines . . ., with an abstract of the discussion upon the paper; edited by James Forrest. *London: printed by W. Clowes*, 1865. pp. 34, with diagram (C. H. Gregory in the chair).
Reprinted by permission of the Council, from *Minutes of Proceedings of the Institution of Civil Engineers*, vol. 24, Session 1864–65. (Paper 1130, read April 11, 1865).
'During the past Autumn the Company carried passengers experimentally, without taking fares, and at the commencement of the present year the line was regularly opened for passenger traffic' (p. 5).
In the Discussion on the Paper (pp. 11–34) contributions were made by W. Bridges Adams, J. J. Allport, Peter Barlow, G. P. Bidder, Peter Bruff, James Brunlees, Zerah Colburn, George England, Charles Fox, W. R. Galbraith, Alfred Giles, C. H. Gregory, T. E. Harrison, C. W. Hemans, Robert Mallett, [Mr.] Phipps, Thomas Savin and E. Woods.
At the following meeting, on 25th April, the discussion was continued 'to the exclusion of any other subject' (note at end).

9730 The RAILWAY problem and the railways of the future. *London: printed by Waterlow & Son*, 1870. pp. 53.
'Reprinted from *The Times*, 19th, 20th, 21st October 1869, and 18th February & 1st March 1870'.
The advantages of narrow gauge over standard gauge railways. R. F. Fairlie's bogie-carriages and his double-bogie locomotive 'Little Wonder' of the Festiniog Railway.

9731 HOLLAND, S. Memoirs of Samuel Holland, one of the pioneers of the North Wales slate

industry. *Dolgelley: Merioneth Historical & Record Society*, [1953]. (Extra Publications, series 1, no. 1). pp. vii, 32. Transcribed and edited, and with a preface, by Sir William Llewellyn Davies.
Records of the pioneer work of Samuel Holland in developing quarries in the Festiniog area from 1821, and (pp. 17–27), his meeting with Henry Archer and James Spooner in 1829 and the subsequent construction of the Festiniog Railway.

9732 LEWIS, M. J. T. How Ffestiniog got its railway. *Caterham: Railway & Canal Historical Society*, 1965. pp. viii, 48, with frontis, 2 folded plates (maps) & 143 notes.
—— 2nd edn. *R. & C. H.S.*, 1968. pp. viii, 48.

9733 FESTINIOG RLY (1954). The Tan-y-Bwlch decade in pictures. *Portmadoc: F.R.*, 1968. pp. 24. 62 illus with descrs. Intro headed 'The Festiniog Railway: ten years development'.

9734 FESTINIOG RLY (1954). Building back to Blaenau. *Manchester: Holliday & Edwards*, 1973. pp. 12, with 19 illus, 4 maps & 3 illus on covers.
The planned Llyn Ystradau deviation from Dduallt to join the original line at Tan-y-Grisiau.

9735 FESTINIOG RLY (1954). Festiniog Railway Companion: history of locomotives, rolling stock, equipment. *Porthmadog: F.R.*, [1973]. pp. 40, with 75 illus (2 col. on covers) & a stock list.
—— 2nd edn. *F.R.*, [1975]. pp. 40, 75 illus (2 col. on covers) & stock list. Only the cover differs from the 1973 edition.

9736 FESTINIOG RAILWAY (1954). A Traveller's Guide to the Festiniog Railway: its history, scenery and rolling stock described. *Portmadoc: F.R.*, [1973]. la. 8°. pp. 32, with 29 col. illus, & 3 maps (1 in sections).
—— another edn. *F.R.*, [1977]. la. 8°. pp. 32, with 29 col. illus & 3 maps (1 in 8 sections).
—— another edn. *F.R.*, [1978]. pp. 20, with 25 illus (24 in col.) & 3 maps.
The *Traveller's Guide* was preceded by two separate publications: 1; the *Festiniog Railway Guide* (1956–1972), and 2; the *Festiniog Pictorial* (1958–1972), the first three editions appearing as *A Pictorial History of the Festiniog Railway* (1958 (2) & 1959). *See* 5706 and 5712.

9737 WINTON, J. The 'Little Wonder': the story of the Festiniog Railway. *Portmadoc: Festiniog Rly; London: M. Joseph*, 1975. pp. xi, 205, with 31 illus on 16 plates, a bibliography (50+ sources) & a map on lining papers.

9738 FESTINIOG RAILWAY SOCIETY. An introduction to the Festiniog Railway Society Limited. *Porthmadog: F.R. Society*, [1976]. pp. 8, with 1 illus & 1 map.

9739 SCHOFIELD, R. and MARTIN, J. The Story of Merddin Emrys and the Festiniog Railway. *Cheam: Travel About Books*, 1977. sm. 8°. pp. [16], with 20 col. drawings.

An exquisite presentation of the history of the Festiniog Rly: pictures by Roy Schofield, story by Joe Martin.

9740 FESTINIOG RLY (1954). Blaenau Ffestiniog, here we come! . . . [*Porthmadog: F.R.*, 1978]. 4°. pp. 12, with 30 illus (22 photos & 8 drawings) & a folded map.
Issued to celebrate the completion of the spiral deviation between Dduallt and Tan-y-Grisiau.

9741 FESTINIOG RLY (1954). Boston Lodge works: souvenir brochure, by P. A. Dukes, works manager. 1st edn. *Portmadoc: F.R.*, June 1980. pp. 10, with 2 drawings & a plan.

9742 GURLEY, N. F. Narrow gauge Steam out of Portmadoc: twenty-five years of the Festiniog Railway. *Truro: Bradford Barton*, 1980. pp. 96. Intro, 104 illus with descrs & a map.
Photographs by the author and other members of the F.R.

Snowdon Mountain Rly 9743–44

9743 CREW, P. Snowdon Mountain Railway Travelogue: a description of the ascent of Snowdon by the Mountain Railway. *Snowdon: Snowdon Mountain Rly*, 1971. pp. 16, with 12 col. illus (2 in covers) & map inside cover. Title on cover only.
The scenery, not the railway, is described.
—— 3rd edn. *S.M. Rly*, 1977. pp. 16, with 1 col. illus & map.
—— 4th edn. *S.M. Rly*, 1979. pp. 16, with 12 col. illus. & map.

9744 TURNER, K. The Snowdon Mountain Railway. *Newton Abbot: David & Charles*, 1973. pp. 165, with col. frontis, 32 illus on 16 plates, & in text, 3 layout plans, map, gradient profile, facsimile & diagram; 4 appendices (incl. a chronology) & a bibliography (27 sources).

Talyllyn Rly 9745–56

9745 TALYLLYN RAILWAY (1951). Rules and regulations. *Towyn: T.R.*, 1953. pp. 8.
—— Amendment no. 1, Jan. 1955.
—— Rules for observance by employees and members of the Talyllyn Railway Preservation Society when they are working on the Railway. *Towyn: T.R.*, February 1962. pp. 27. Cover title: Operating Rule Book.
—— Amendments and alterations (Amendment Notice A), July 1969. pp. [2].

9746 ROLT, L. T. C. The Talyllyn Railway. *London: Newcomen Society*, 1960. pp. 14.
Paper, read 2 November 1960.

9747 ROLT, L. T. C. Talyllyn century: the Talyllyn Railway, 1865–1965, edited by L. T. C. Rolt. *Dawlish: David & Charles; London: Macdonald*, 1965. pp. 126, with 47 illus on 24 plates, & 2 maps.

9748 TALYLLYN RAILWAY (1951). Talyllyn Railway Centenary Magazine. *Dawlish: David &*

Charles; London: Macdonald, for the Talyllyn Railway Preservation Society, 1965. magazine format. pp. 36, with many illus (some col.) & a map.

A collection of essays and lesser pieces, supported by photographs and other illustrative material, all relating to the Talyllyn, presented in the form of a magazine, to commemorate the railway's centenary.

9749 TOWYN URBAN DISTRICT COUNCIL. TALYLLYN RAILWAY CENTENARY COMMITTEE. [Brochure]. [*Towyn: the Committee*, 1965]. obl. format. pp. [44], with 45 illus (22 of the Talyllyn Rly). No title. Cover reads: Centenary year, Talyllyn Railway Company, 1865–1965, Towyn, Merioneth.

9750 TALYLLYN RAILWAY PRESERVATION SOCIETY. Talyllyn Handbook. *Newton Abbot: David & Charles*, 1968. sm. obl. format. pp. 64, with 21 illus, 4 layout plans, 2 tables, gradient profile & a map inside covers. Text extends onto p. [3] of cover.
—— another edn. *Towyn: Talyllyn Rly.*, [ca. 1979]. normal 8° format. pp. 36, with 25 illus, map, plan of Towyn & a route map in sections.

9751 ROLT, L. T. C. Talyllyn adventure, introduced by L. T. C. Rolt. *Newton Abbot: David & Charles*, 1971. pp. xx, 289, with 46 illus on 24 plates, 2 maps & a timetable.
Contents: *Railway Adventure*, by L. T. C. Rolt, originally published 1953; *Talyllyn Century*, ed. by L. T. C. Rolt, originally published 1965.
The 1961 edn was re-set and published as a paperback by *Pan Books*, 1971. pp. xx, 152 with 19 illus on 12 plates.

9752 RHEILFFORDD Talyllyn: seremoni agor yr estaniad o Abergynolwyn i Nant Gwernol, Dydd Sadwrn, Mai 22 ain, 1976. Talyllyn Railway: ceremonial opening of the extension from Abergynolwyn to Nant Gwernol, Saturday, May 22nd, 1976. *Towyn*, [1976]. pp. [4], with plan. *Biblioteca Celtica*, 1980

9753 TALYLLYN RAILWAY (1951). Talyllyn Railway. *Towyn: T.R. Preservation Society*, [197–]. By J. I. C. Boyd.
A booklet with coloured illustrations and map issued in successive undated editions from ca. 1976: a brief, inexpensive, but attractive guide. One of the later editions has 24 pp, with 25 illus (24 col.) & 2 maps.

9754 HOLMES, A. and THOMAS, D. Quarry tracks, village ways: a descriptive history of Bryneglwys slate quarry and Abergynolwyn village. *Towyn: Talyllyn Railway Co.*, 1977. pp. 24, with 3 maps, a plan & 10 illus; 3 col. illus on covers.
The Talyllyn Railway's catchment area.

9755 WHITE, C. Talyllyn Railway extension. Abergynolwyn to Nant Gwernol. *Towyn: Talyllyn Rly*, 1978. la. 8°. pp. [40], with 83 illus & a map.
Published to celebrate the opening of the extension, 22 May, 1976.

9756 BOYD, J. I. C. Talyllyn Railway: the background to your journey. [*Towyn*]: *Talyllyn Railway Preservation Society*, [197–]. pp. 24, with 23 illus (13 col.), plan, & map inside cover.

Welsh Highland Rly 9757–60

9757 WELSH HIGHLAND LIGHT RAILWAY (1964). More about the Welsh Highland Railway. *Newton Abbot: David & Charles, with the W.H.L.R. and the Raleigh Press*, 1966. pp. 49–109, with 26 illus, 10 plans, 3 maps, gradient profile, timetables & (pp. 96–109), facsimiles.
A sequel to *The Welsh Highland Railway*, by Charles E. Lee (1962).
—— rev. edn. *David & Charles*, 1972. pp. 49–109, with 26 illus, etc.

9758 BOYD, J. I. C. and WHITEHOUSE, P. B. Meet the Welsh Highland. *Worcester: West Highland Light Railway (1964)*, 1969. pp. 28, with 22 illus & a map. Reprinted in 1970 with '1970' on cover and title-page. Reprinted, 1973.
Republished essays by J. I. C. Boyd and P. B. Whitehouse.

9759 DEEGAN, P. Introducing 'Russell'. *Cleveleys: Russell Restoration Fund*, 1969. pp. 36, with 16 illus on 8 plates.
A narrow gauge locomotive built for the North Wales Narrow Gauge Rly, used on the Welsh Highland Rly and now restored for continued use on the W. H. Rly (1964).

9760 TURNER, S. D. The Welsh Highland Railway today, 1975. *Porthmadog: Welsh Highland Rly*, 1975. pp. 22, with 4 illus, a map & a plan.

Other lines 9761–69

9761 LEE, C. E. The Penrhyn Railway. [*Rochdale*]: *C. E. Lee and the Welsh Highland Rly (1964)*, 1972. pp. 38, with 30 illus, map, 2 diagrams & 2 lists.

9762 CARRINGTON, D. C. and RUSHWORTH, T. F. Slates to Velinheli: the railways and tramways of Dinorwic slate quarries, Llanberis. *Bury: Maid Marian Locomotive Fund*, [1973?]. pp. 60, with 50 illus, plans, diagrams & maps, & a bibliography (35 sources).
—— 2nd edn. [1977?]. pp. 64, with 56 illus.
A reprint of the 1st edn with a supplementary section (pp. 60–64).

9763 LLANBERIS LAKE RLY. RHEILFFORDD LLYN LLANBERIS. Guide Book. Llawlyfr. *Llanberis: the Railway*, [1973?] pp. 16, with 13 illus (11 col.), 2 maps & 3 col. illus on covers.
—— another edn. [1976?] p. 16, with 14 illus (12 col.), 2 maps & 2 col. illus on covers.

9764 LEWIS, M. J. T. and DENTON, J. H. Rhosydd slate quarry. *Shrewsbury: Cottage Press*, 1974. pp. 100, with 16 illus, 28 maps,

plans, diagrams & 23 sketch drawings.
ch. 5 (pp. 72–88): 'Transport': the Rhosydd and the Croesor tramroads.

9765 TURNER, S. L. The Padarn and Penrhyn railways and their associated systems. *Newton Abbot: David & Charles*, 1975. pp. 192, with 35 illus on 16 plates, & in text, 19 maps, plans, diagrams, facsimiles & drawings; 10 appendices (incl. a chronology) & a bibliography (35 sources).

9766 HUNT, J. Arriving at Dinas Mawddwy. *Dinas Mawddwy: Meirion Publications*, 1976. obl. format. pp. 24, with 11 illus & a plan.
An account of the economic & social history of the village, including the coming and going of the Mawddwy Railway, the subsequent restoration of the station premises by Meirion Mill Ltd (Welsh woollen wear) and the creation of the Meirion Mill Light Railway on the original trackbed.

9767 FAIRBOURNE Railway. [*Fairbourne: Fairbourne Rly*, ca. 1977]. pp. 24, with 12 illus (11 col.), map, & 2 illus & map on covers. Introduction by J. C. Wilkins, Chairman & Managing Director.

9768 JONES, I. W. and HATHERILL, G. Llechwedd and other Ffestiniog railways. *Blaenau Ffestiniog: Quarry Tours*, 1977. pp. 24, with 16 illus, 6 diagrams & a map.

9769 BALA LAKE RAILWAY. RHEILFFORDD LLYN TEGID. A Visitor's Guide to Bala Lake Railway. Arweiniad Ymwelwyr i Rheilffordd Llyn Tegid; main text written by Christopher M. A. Jackson; edited by James E. Campbell. *Llanuwchllyn Station: the Railway*, 1980. pp. 32, with 15 illus & map, incl. covers.

C 3 E   Britannia and Conway bridges 9770–73

9770 An ACCOUNT of the grand flotation of one of the monster tubes over the Menai Straits, Britannia Bridge, June 20th 1849, with an engraving. The stupendous tubular bridge was projected by R. Stephenson, M.P. *Carnavon: printed by James Rees, High Street and sold by the booksellers, Carnavon and Bangor and by Mrs. Fisher, Menai Bridge*, 1849. pp. 18.
At head of title page: 'The Triumph of Science'.

9771 RICHARDS, R. Two bridges over Menai. *Cardiff: ap Dafydd Publications*, 1975. pp. 40, with 18 illus.
pp. 21–36, 39, 'The Britannia'.

9772 ROSENBERG, N. and VINCENTI, W. G. The Britannia Bridge: the generation and diffusion of technological knowledge. *Cambridge (Mass.); London: M.I.T. Press*, 1978. pp. viii, 107, with 16 illus, 194 notes & a folded map in end pocket: Chapman's Map of Railways in Great Britain (1851).
The significance of the Britannia (and the Conway) tubular bridges in the evolution of technology.

9773 GWASANAETH ARCHIFAU GWYNEDD. GWYNEDD ARCHIVES SERVICE. Pontydd Menai. Menai bridges. *Caernarfon: Gwasanaeth Archifau Gwynedd; Cardiff: Welsh Arts Council*, 1980. sm. 4°. pp. [72], with 31 illus (9 col.) incl. 2 cover illus.
The Menai Bridge (Telford, 1826) and the Britannia Bridge (R. Stephenson, 1850): design & construction. Their significance as symbols of human enterprise.

C 3 L   Cambrian Rlys 9774–82

9774 CAMBRIAN RAILWAYS. Timetables, July, Aug. & Sept. 1904, including working timetables. [Reprint]. *Oxford: Oxford Publishing Co*, 1969. pp. 98, 32, with la. folded sh. of 2 maps & 6 illus.
—— Reprinted, 1977.

9775 STEPHENSON LOCOMOTIVE SOCIETY. Photographic souvenir in connection with the last passenger train on the Moat Lane to Brecon and Brecon to Hereford lines, Sunday 30th December, 1962, organised by the Stephenson Locomotive Society, Midland Area. *Handsworth: S.L.S.*, [1963]. pp. 16, incl. covers, with 25 illus & 2 maps.
Cambrian Rlys and the Midland Rly.

9776 CHRISTIANSEN, R. and MILLER, R. W. The Cambrian Railways. *Newton Abbot: David & Charles*.
vol. 1, 1852–1888. 1967. pp. 178, with col. frontis, 37 illus on 16 plates, 20 in text (maps, layout plans, gradient profiles, diagrams, timetables); 4 appendices.
vol. 2, 1889–1968. [1968]. pp. 218, with col. frontis, 46 illus on 20 plates, 28 in text (maps, layout plans, gradient profiles, drawings); 11 appendices and a chronology.
—— new edn. *David & Charles*, 1971.
vol. 1, 1852–1888. 1971. pp. 179, with col. frontis, 37 illus on 16 plates, 22 in text; 5 appendices.

9777 WREN, W. J. The Tanat Valley: its railways and industrial archaeology. *Newton Abbot: David & Charles*, 1968. pp. 92, with 48 illus on 16 plates, 33 maps, layout plans, a gradient profile & a bibliography (28 sources).
Index has 174 page refs to railways.
The Cambrian Rlys and (pp. 27–107) 'The Tanat Valley Light Railway'. *See* 9782.

9778 JONES, E. V. Mishaps on the Cambrian Railways, 1864–1922. *Newtown (Montgomeryshire): Severn Press*, June 1972. pp. 40, with 11 illus, 11 time & fare tables, map, detailed chronology.

9779 RYAN, J. Cambrian Coast Express: an illustrated route description and history of the Cambrian rail routes and associated lines. *Bebington: Wirral Railway Circle*, 1973. pp. [48], with 27 illus & a loose map.
The 4th CCE rail tour, 8th December 1973: Crewe—Chester—Shrewsbury—Machynlleth—Towyn—Pwllheli, then back to Dovey Junction & Aberystwyth. Return via Machynlleth to Shrewsbury and Crewe.

The generously-detailed historical commentary (pp. [4]–[43]) may be used as a companion to travel by normal service trains on the Cambrian Coast line. It includes the narrow gauge railways of the area.

9780 GREEN, C. C. Cambrian Railways Album. *London: Ian Allan*, 1977. pp. 112, with col. frontis, 244 illus (incl. facsims, ports & a map) with descrs.
The descriptive notes are often extended to provide historical perspective, with anecdotes.

9781 OWEN, I. J. Codi Stêm. [*y Bontnewydd (Caernarfon)*]: *Tŷar y Graig*, 1979. pp. 130, with 16 plates.

'Getting up steam': a history of the Cambrian Rlys down to the present. Text in Welsh.

9782 WREN, W. J. The Tanat Valley Railway. *Tarrant Hinton: Oakwood Press*, 1979. (Oakwood Library of Railway History, 48). pp. 80, with 18 illus, 20 layout plans, 2 graphs, timetables, a gradient profile and a bibliography (28 sources). Cover title: The Tanat Valley Light Railway.
'Comprising the railway history included in *The Tanat Valley*, by Dr Wren, published by David & Charles in 1968. Most of the early industrial history has been omitted; the railway portion has been edited and updated' (note, rev. t.p.).

C 4   IRELAND

The Republic of Ireland and Northern Ireland

9783–9893

Subdivided by a modified version of the main Classification Scheme

C 4 A   General history and description of rail transport in Ireland
9783–9800 (Reference sources 9783–88)

9783 BLACK, R. D. C. A Catalogue of Pamphlets on Economic Subjects published between 1750 and 1900 and now housed in Irish libraries. *Belfast: The Queen's University*, 1969. pp. ix, 632 (in double column).
Arranged alphabetically by author under year of publication, with locations added. Author index but no index of subjects. Although the work embraces the whole of the British Isles, a high proportion of the entries relates to Ireland, a factor which adds particular value to the general usefulness of the work. The railway items not in the original volume of 'Ottley' have been incorporated into the present Supplement.

9784 LECKEY, J. J. A List of Irish Railways, with a classification of railway maerial. *Dublin: Irish Railway Record Society*, 1973. (Occasional Publications, 2). pp. iii, 32.
pt. 1, 'A list of Irish railways': 733 lines, including wagonways, tramways, contractors' lines, industrial lines, inclined planes and aerial ropeways, from 1740 to the present day.
pt. 2, 'A classification of Irish railway material': a guide to the resources of seven national repositories in the form of a detailed classification of classes of documents within three main groups: administration records, capital structure records, and engineering records.

9785 WALL, T. F. An Index to the Journal of the Irish Railway Record Society, volumes 1–9 [June 1947–October 1970]. *Dublin: the Society*, 1973. (Occasional Publications, 1). tall 8°. pp. viii, 115. Foreword by Kevin A. Murray, Editor, I.R.R.S. Reproduced typescript.
A detailed work, providing a key to the thousands of historical facts, opinions and observations contained in these first nine volumes.
part 1, Main articles, pp. 2–7: headings used in list of main articles, p. 2; list of main articles (under broad subject headings), pp. 3–7.
part 2, Index, pp. 9–115: headings used in index, p. 10; railways and topics in index, pp. 11–17; index, pp. 19–115.
—— An Index to the Journal of the Irish Railway Record Society, volumes 10–12 [February 1971 to October 1976]. *Dublin: the Society*, 1976. (Occasional Publications, 5). tall 8°. pp. vii, 81. Reproduced typescript.
part 1 (pp. 1–11), List of main articles; part 2 (pp. 13–81), Index.
—— Appendix 1, Publications of the I.R.R.S.
—— Appendix 2, Ephemera preserved in the I.R.R.S. archives (mostly itineraries and souvenir accounts of rail tours organised by the Society).
p. 81, Corrections and omissions relating to vol. 1.
Much of Irish railway history is opened up by the generous indexing of this work, enabling inroads to be planned into studies of the subject covered by the Journal. The work is strong on company, C.I.E. and locomotive history, for which minute guidance is given. Not so, however, on social, economic and geographical aspects. Tramways are indexed only under the names of undertakings and there are also no general headings for Biography or Personalities either collectively or under individual names. William Dargan, for example, being indexed under 'Contractors and Engineering Firms'.

9786 HAJDUCKI, S. M. A Railway Atlas of Ireland. *Newton Abbot: David & Charles*, 1974. pp. x, [39], xi–xxxii.
Irish railways immediately before 1925, with later lines and stations added; 37 sectional maps and 2 showing closures and present network. The sea and inland waterways are printed in red.
pp. vii–x, Introduction & historical survey; pp. xi–xvii, Table of companies with brief historical data; pp. xix–xxvii, Index & gazetteer; pp. xxix–xxxi, Bibliography (46 sources).

9787 ANDREWS, J. H. A paper landscape: the

Ordnance Survey in nineteenth-century Ireland. *Oxford: Clarendon Press*, 1975. pp. xxiv, 350, with plates, & in text, figures.
    T. A. Larcom's ¼ inch railway map of 1839, pp. 183–5 & plate X; railways generally, *passim*.

9788 LECKEY, J. J. and RIGNEY, P. I.R.R.S. archival collections, D1–D10. *Dublin: Irish Railway Record Society*, 1976. pp. xii, 33.
    Reproduced typescript.

9789 McCUTCHEON, W. A. The canals of the north of Ireland. *Dawlish: David & Charles; London: Macdonald*, 1965. (Canals of the British Isles series). pp. 180, with 40 illus on 20 plates, 17 illus & maps, 230 notes & a 7-part tabular summary. Index, pp. 175–180, with 27 page refs to railways.

9790 DELANY, V. T. H. and DELANY, D. R. The canals of the south of Ireland. *Newton Abbot: David & Charles*, 1966. (Canals of the British Isles series). pp. 260, with 36 illus on 20 plates, 21 illus & maps, 394 notes & a series of tabular summaries as appendices (pp. 228–51).
    Railways, pp. 64–74, 204–15 *et passim*.

9791 GRAY, T. The Irish answer: an anatomy of modern Ireland. *London: Heinemann*, 1966. pp. 411.
    pp. 198–213, 'Trains and boats and planes', since 1922.

9792 FLANAGAN, P. J. Transport in Ireland, 1880–1910; text by Patrick Flanagan, pictures from the Lawrence Collection of the National Library of Ireland. *Dublin: Transport Research Associates*, 1969. pp. 184.
    Section 3 (pp. 57–83), Tramways, with 27 illus.
    Section 5 (pp. 119–79), Railways, with 52 illus.

9793 McCUTCHEON, A. Railway history in pictures: Ireland. *Newton Abbot: David & Charles*.
    vol. 1, 1969. pp. 112, with col. frontis & 141 illus with descrs.
    vol. 2, 1970. pp. 112, with col. frontis & 147 illus with descrs & a bibliography (144 sources).

9794 BAKER, M. H. C. Irish railways since 1916. *London: Ian Allan*, 1972. pp. 224, with 65 illus on 32 plates, 3 line drawings, 4 maps & a bibliography (33 sources).

9795 DELANY, R. The Grand Canal of Ireland. *Newton Abbot: David & Charles*, 1973. (Inland Waterways Histories). pp. 255, with col. frontis, 32 illus on 16 plates, 24 maps & illus, 167 notes & 7 appendices.
    ch. 8 (pp. 163–84), 'Famine and the coming of the railways' (1840s).

9796 NOWLAN, K. B. Travel and transport in Ireland, edited by Kevin B. Nowlan. *Dublin: Gill & Macmillan*, 1973.
    ch. 7 (pp. 96–109), 'The Transport Revolution: the coming of the railways', by Kevin B. Nowlan, with 9 illus, notes & a bibliography.

ch. 8 (pp. 110–19), 'The Golden Age of Irish Railways', by Joseph Lee, with 5 illus, notes & a bibliography.
    ch. 11 (pp. 150–69), 'The latest phase in Irish transport', by Gerard Quinn and Patrick Lynch, with 11 illus, notes & a bibliography.

9797 CASSERLEY, H. C. Outline of Irish railway history. *Newton Abbot: David & Charles*, 1974. pp. 303, with 68 illus on 32 plates, & in text, 39 illus, 10 maps & la. folded map at end; bibliography (32 sources).
    A brief but substantial general survey followed by histories of individual companies, including details of locomotives and rolling stock.

9798 DONALDSON, D., McDONNELL, B., O'NEILL, J. A decade of Steam on C.I.E. in the 1950s. *[Belfast]: Railway Preservation Society of Ireland*, 1974. pp. 42, with 58 illus & 3 tables on 32 plates & a bibliography (10 sources); folded map at end.
    A class-by-class survey of locomotive characteristics and performance.

9799 BAKER, M. H. C. The railways of the Republic of Ireland: a pictorial survey of the G.S.R. and C.I.E., 1925–75. *Truro: Bradford Barton*, 1975. pp. 96. Intro & 125 illus with descrs.

9800 MURRAY, K. Irish railways: text, Kevin Murray; illustrations, Peter Jay. *[Tallaght]: Folens*, [1978]. (Irish Environmental Library series, 44). pp. 97–128, with 34 col. illus.
    An informative introductory work.

C 4 B Contemporaneous publications 9801–21

9801 A LETTER to a Commissioner of the Inland Navigation concerning the Tyrone collieries. *Dublin: R. Main*, 1752. pp. 9.
    Financial support needed to build a wagonway from Drumglass colliery to Coalisland on the Tyrone Navigation.

9802 WHITE, W. and BARRINGTON, M. On a Western packet station at Limerick and a railroad between that city and Dublin. pp. 10. [Printed, but with no title-page & no imprint]. [1836].
    The text consists of two letters from William White, President of the Chamber of Commerce in Limerick to Matthew Barrington, Crown Solicitor for the Province of Munster, dated 13th April 1836, and the reply from London dated 2nd May.
                                                            LU(THC)

9803 DIRECT communication between London & Dublin. *n.p.: n. pub.*, 1838. pp. 32. A series of accounts and reports of meetings, 1836–38 relating to the choice of route from London to Porth Dynllaen on the North Wales Coast. Includes (pp. 8–28) a report by Charles B. Vignoles, civil engineer, 29th Nov. 1837.

9804 A LETTER to the Marquis of Lansdowne on the report of the Irish Railway Commissioners, by a shareholder in the Kilkenny Railway. *London: P. Richardson*, 1838. pp. 38, with appendix, incl. tables.

9805 STEPHENSON, G. Report of George Stephenson upon the proposed railway communications with Ireland. *Chester: Spence*, 1838. pp. 4 (2 la. sheets).   BLACK 5076

9806 LOYAL NATIONAL REPEAL ASSOCIATION. Report of the Parliamentary Committee of the Loyal National Repeal Association on the subject of having the enquiries connected with Irish railway legislation transacted in Dublin. *Dublin: J. Browne*, 1845. pp. 93–103, with 2 tables.   MCL

9807 PORTER, J. G. V. Irish railways: a few observations upon our present railway system in Ireland. *Dublin: Hodges & Smith*, 1847. pp. 31.
   Calling for a parliamentary standing committee 'to look into the internal faults of our present railway companies, and of our whole railway system'.

9808 PORTER, J. G. V. A letter to shareholders in Irish railway companies. *Dublin: Hodges & Smith*, 1848. pp. 16, with tables.

9809 KENNEDY, J. P. A railway caution!!; or, exposition of changes required in the law and practice of the British Empire to enable the poorer districts to provide for themselves the benefits of railway intercourse . . . , illustrated in reports addressed to the proprietors and directors of the Waterford and Limerick Railway Company. *Calcutta: R. C. Lepage*, 1849. pp. iii, 66, with plate, 3 folded tables & a diagram.

9810 LEVY, J. Summer rambles to the West: employment for the people; harbours of refuge; tramways. *Dublin: Hodges, Smith*, 1863. pp. 32.
   Reprints of letters to various newspapers, Letter 3 (pp. 16–25), the need for a tramway (light railway) between Clifden and Galway.

9811 BUTT, I. Irish government and Irish railways: an argument for Home Rule: a speech delivered at the meeting of the Home Government Association on Monday May 27th, 1872. *Dublin: Home Government Association*, 1872. pp. 20.

9812 The IRISH Parliament and Irish property: railways. *Dublin: E. Ponsonby*, 1886. pp. 14.
          BLACK 9493

9813 SMITH, J. C. On the practicability of reducing railway rates in Ireland. *Dublin: printed for the author by John Falconer*, 1886. pp. 69, with 2 folded graphs at end.

9814 EIRE. COMMITTEE OF INQUIRY INTO INTERNAL TRANSPORT. Report. *Dublin: Stationery Office*, 1957. pp. 259, with 66 tables, 3 charts, 2 maps (1 folded).

part 3 (pp. 170–3, paras, 353–8), Conclusions and recommendations on the question of the abandonment of railways.

9815 REYNOLDS, D. J. Inland transport in Ireland: a factual survey. *Dublin: Economic Research Institute*, 1962. (Papers, 10). pp. 17, with 33 tables.
   pp. 7–10, Rail transport.

9816 CÓRAS IOMPAIR ÉIREANN. Córas Iompair Éireann, 1958–1963. *Dublin: C.I.E.*, 1963. pp. [24].
   Addressed to the Minister for Transport & Power. Text signed 'C. S. Andrews, chairman of C.I.E.'.

9817 PENDER, B. and RICHARDS, H. Irish railways today. *Dublin: Transport Research Associates*, 1967. pp. 168, with 39 illus & 11 line drawings (small area maps), lists & a folded map inside back cover.
   A companion for railway travellers, describing routes, locomotives & rolling stock, signals and other lineside features.

9818 CÓRAS Iompair Éireann: special issue of Administration: Journal of the Institute of Public Administration of Ireland, vol. 16, no. 4, Winter 1968. pp. 331–440.
   Contents:
   The philosophy of public transport in Ireland, by F. Lemass. pp. 331–5.
   The integration of transport resources in Western Europe, by Eric Upmark. pp. 336–43.
   The operations of C.I.E., by Michael Viney. pp. 344–9.
   Productivity in C.I.E., by Lucas Collins. pp. 350–65.
   Marketing, by Edmond O'Flaherty. pp. 366–79, with 2 tables.
   The financial background, by B. M. O'Farrell. pp. 380–91, with 5 tables.
   Personnel management, by Patrick Murphy. pp. 392–9.
   The legal background, by Brendan A. McGrath. pp. 400–14.
   Tourism and transport, by T. J. O'Driscoll. pp. 415–20.
   School transport, by Sean MacGearailt. pp. 421–6.
   Transport balance in large cities, by D. H. Crompton. pp 427–31.
   The future of C.I.E., by Daniel Herlihy. pp. 432–9.
   Industrial surveys: a comment, by C. K. McGrath. p. 440.
   The C.I.E. was the subject of a series of four consecutive essays in vol. 10, no. 3 of *Administration* (Autumn 1962) entitled 'The Future of C.I.E.'. The authors were C. S. Andrews (pp. 292–301), P. J. Beddy (pp. 301–4), G. B. Howden (pp. 304–6) and D. Reynolds (pp. 306–9).

9819 CÓRAS IOMPAIR ÉIREANN. Córas Iompair Éireann in brief. *Dublin: C.I.E.*, 1970. pp. 24, with 16 illus & map.

9820 McKINSEY & Co. Defining the role of public transport in a changing environment. *Dublin: Stationery Office*, 1971. pp. xxii, 122, with 53 diagrams, graphs, maps, & tables.
   A report prepared for the Department of Trans-

port & Power, Department of Finance, and Córas
Iompair Éireann.
'The railway is the main current cause for con-
cern.'

9821 LEYDON, K. A. Irish railway policy in the
context of the common transport policy of the
E.E.C. Thesis, M.A., University of Ireland,
Dublin, 1972–3.

C 4 C   Railways in particular areas of Ireland
9822–36

Republic of Ireland 9822–27

9822 BARRINGTON, W. L. Tramways in Dublin:
a letter addressed to the citizens. *Dublin:
R. D. Webb*, 1871. pp. 16.
Objections dispelled; advantages made clear.

9823 NEWHAM, A. T. The Dublin and Lucan
Tramway. *Lingfield: Oakwood Press*, [1965].
(Locomotion Papers, 29). pp. 40, with 20 illus
& 2 maps.

9824 FLEWITT, R. C. The Hill of Howth Tramway. *Dublin: Transport Research Associates*,
1968. pp. 64, with 16 illus, chronology, 2
diagrams, a drawing & a map (in pocket).

9825 QUANEY, J. A penny to Nelson's Pillar.
Portlaw (Co. Waterford): Volturna Press,
1971. pp. vii, 223, with frontis (mounted
portrait) & 13 illus on 8 plates. No map.
A biography of Kerr ('Kyran') Quaney, electrical
engineer who with William M. Murphy created the
first electric tramway in Dublin.

9826 DUN LAOGHAIRE BOROUGH COUNCIL.
Guide and Directory (written by M. Tierney).
Dublin: F.C. Publications, 1978. pp. 190.
pp. 76–90, Railways.
—— Centennial Year edn. *F.C. Publications*,
[1980]. pp. 240.
pp. 149–57, Railways.

9827 KENNELLY, P. J. Some aspects of my Connemara. *Ballyconneely*, 1976. pp. 69.
pp. 6–9, 'The "Connemara Railway".' The 2 mile
narrow gauge line built by the Marconi Wireless
Telegraph Co. to convey peat (for fuel) and other
supplies over the Connemara bog from Ballyconneely to its transmitting station at Clifden on the
coast of Galway Bay, 1906–1922.

Northern Ireland 9828–36 (General 9828–31)

9828 POPE, F. A. Integration of transport in
Northern Ireland. (Proceedings of the British
Railways (W.R.) London Lecture & Debat-
ing Society, 1951–52, no. 385). pp. 11, with
discussion & chart.
Author, 'Member, B.T.C.'

9829 MINISTRY OF COMMERCE [Northern Ire-
land]. Report of an inquiry dated 11th
September, 1956. Great Northern Railway
Board: termination of certain services. *Bel-
fast: the Ministry*, 1956. tall 8°. pp. 71.
Reproduced typescript.
Closures: Omagh—Enniskillen—Newtownbutler;
Portadown—Armagh—Tynan; Bundoran Junction
—Belleek.

9830 BENSON, H. Northern Ireland railways. *Belfast: Ministry of Home Affairs*, 1963. (Cmd.
458). pp. 99, with 26 tables & 3 folded maps
in end pocket.
Recommendations for the future of railways in
Northern Ireland. The 'Benson Report'.

9831 TRANSPORT TRIBUNAL FOR NORTHERN
IRELAND. Ulster Transport Authority *versus*
Tyrone County Council and others: judge-
ments of the Transport Tribunal dated 30th
October 1964 and 15th January 1965 on the
proposals to terminate certain railway transport services, etc. *Belfast: H.M.S.O.*, 1965.
pp. 34 & folded map.
The U.T.A. seeking to reduce its railway losses in
order to avoid financial collapse.

9832 NEWHAM, A. T. The Bessbrook & Newry
Tramway. *Tarrant Hinton: Oakwood Press*,
1979. (Locomotion Papers, 115). pp. 34, with
16 illus on 8 plates, a combined map & 4
plans.

9833 TRANSPORT TRIBUNAL FOR NORTHERN
IRELAND. Ulster Transport Authority *v.*
Down County Council and others: judgement
of the Transport Tribunal on the proposal to
terminate certain railway transport services in
the County of Down, 15th December 1949.
Belfast: H.M.S.O., 1950. pp. 48.
The main line of the Belfast & County Down Rly
in County Down.

9834 CURRIE, J. R. L. The Portstewart Tramway. *Lingfield: Oakwood Press*, 1968.
(Locomotion Papers, 41). pp. 31, with 4 illus
on 2 plates, & a map.

9835 ARNOLD, R. M. Steam over Belfast Lough:
a look at the railways to Bangor and Larne,
and especially the work of locomotives. *Lingfield: Oakwood Press*, 1969. pp. 89, with 20
illus on 10 plates, map, 12 detailed tables on
train workings & an appendix of locomotive
data.

9836 HUNTER, R. A. Gone but not forgotten:
Belfast trams, 1872–1954, compiled by R. A.
Hunter, R. C. Ludgate and J. Richardson.
*Whitehead (Co. Antrim): Railway Preserva-
tion Society of Ireland, and the Irish Transport
Board*, [1979]. pp. 47, with illus.
Detailed observations and records of train work-
ings on the County Down line and the Larne Line
from the 1930s.

C 4 D   Light and narrow-gauge railways and tramways
9837

9837 MACDEVITT, E. O. A Manual of the Acts for the construction of Tramways and Light Railways in Ireland, being a reprint of those Acts, with a concise and popular exposition of their provisions; explanatory notes and practical forms. *Dublin: Alex Thom*, 1883. pp. 92.
LU(THC)

C 4 E   Engineering (Civil and Mechanical)
9838–45

9838 LIDDLE, L. H. Steam finale: a review of present-day steam traction on Irish railways. [*Harrow*]: *Irish Railway Record Society, London Area*, 1964. pp. 66, with 16 illus on 8 plates, map, line drawing & lists.
—— Supplement, March 1965. pp. 4.

9839 SHEPHERD, W. E. Twentieth century Irish locomotives. [*London*]: *Union Publications*, 1966. sm. 8°. pp. 61, with 24 illus on frontis & 11 plates.
Lists (7, 8 or 9 columns) of locomotives which have worked on Irish railways since 1925, arranged under companies.
The work is offered as a successor to *The ABC of Irish Locomotives*, by R. N. Clements & J. M. Robbins (1949) (Ottley 2876).

9840 BOOCOCK, C. P. Irish Railway Album. *London: Ian Allan*, 1968. pp. 128, with frontis, map, & 200 illus with descrs.

9841 ROWLEDGE, J. W. P. The turf burner: Ireland's last steam locomotive design. *Billericay: Irish Railway Record Society*, [1972]. pp. 24, with 12 illus & 7 diagrams (3 col.).
O. V. S. Bulleid's 0-6-6-0 locomotive no. CC1 of Córas Iompair Éireann.

9842 SHEEHY, J. Kingsbridge Station. *Ballycotton: Gifford & Craven*, 1973. (Gatherum series, 1). pp. 12, with illus & a bibliography (pp. 9–11).
Kingsbridge station, Dublin; architect, Sancton Wood, 1815–1886.
NUC

9843 COX, R. C. Engineering Ireland, 1778–1878: exhibition catalogue. *Dublin: Trinity College*, 1978. obl. 8°. pp. 68. Reproduced typescript.
A bio-bibliographical companion to the exhibition, held to celebrate the centenary of the incorporation of the Institution of Engineers of Ireland. Bibliographical entries by M. Melvin of Trinity College Library.

9844 CASSERLEY, H. C. Irish railways in the heyday of Steam. *Truro: Bradford Barton*, [1979]. pp. 96. Intro & 119 illus with descrs.

9845 DOYLE, O. and HIRSCH, S. Locomotives and rolling stock of Córas Iompair Éireann and Northern Ireland Railways. *Malahide (Co. Dublin): Signal Press*, 1979. sm. 8°. pp. 96, with 107 illus.
Tabulated details of current stock.

C 4 K   Social aspects 9846–49

9846 CÓRAS IOMPAIR ÉIREANN. The C.I.E. Report on Internal Public Transport, prepared by the staff of Córas Iompair Éireann. *Dublin: C.I.E.*, October 1963. 2 vols in 1 (ca. 350 pp.), with many detailed tables, graphs & maps.
The future of public transport in the Irish Republic, including the consideration of alternative modes. Prepared by C.I.E. at the request of the Secretary of the Department of Transport & Power in October 1962, to assist in making a basic assessment of requirements and appropriate policies. Conclusions on pp. 4–12 of part 1.
BLPES

9847 LEE, J. The railways in the Irish economy, *in* The Formation of the Irish Economy, ed. by L. M. Cullen. *Cork: Mercier Press*, 1969. (Thomas Davis Lectures). ch. 6, pp. 77–87.
The impact of railway development upon social and economic life in Ireland since 1850. Includes analyses of parallel developments in Britain and offers cautionary comment on some established opinions.

9848 McKINSEY & COMPANY. Defining the role of public transport in a changing environment: a report prepared for Department of Transport and Power, Department of Finance, Córas Iompair Éireann, July 1971. *Dublin: Government of Ireland Stationery Office*, 1971. pp. xvii, 122, with many tables, graphs & maps.
An analysis of the factors responsible for CIE's increasing deficit. The views of many experts are included besides those of the study team.
pp. v–xi, Summary of the conclusions and recommendations: the railway is the main current cause for concern. Commuter services, from a strictly commercial viewpoint, should be terminated immediately.

9849 LECKEY, J. J. Nineteenth century railway politics in the Belfast—Dublin—Enniskillen triangle, with a note on sources. *Dublin: Irish Railway Record Society*, 1973. (Occasional Publications, 3). pp. iii, 33, with 70 notes, 3 maps, 2 facsimiles (prospectus & 3 lists of directors), & guide to classes of material (primary and secondary) including locations, & a select bibliography (12 sources).
A lecture prepared for the staff and post-graduate seminar in the Institute of Irish Studies, The Queens University of Belfast, 20th November 1973.

C 4 L   Individual railways (including narrow gauge railways) 9850–90

Collective histories 9850
Individual companies (arranged alphabetically)
9851–90

Collective histories

9850 CASSERLEY, H. C. Outline of Irish railway history. *Newton Abbot: David & Charles*, 1974. pp. 303, with 68 illus on 32 plates, & in text, 39 illus, 10 maps & la. folded map at end; bibliography (32 sources).
A brief but substantial general survey followed by

histories of individual companies, including details of locomotives and rolling stock.

Individual companies
(arranged alphabetically)

9851 TWENTY-five years gone, [compiled by] R. J. A. Pue. *Millside (Co. Down): Belfast & County Down Railway Museum Trust*, 1975. pp. 75, with 52 illus, 8 layout plans, 4 gradient plans & a map; bibliography (36 sources).
'Published to commemorate the 25th anniversary of the closing of the major portion of the B & C D Rly.'
Reprints of essays, by H. Fayle & others, selected and presented by R. J. A. Pue.

9852 FLANAGAN, P. J. The Cavan & Leitrim Railway. *Newton Abbot: David & Charles*, 1966. pp. 192, with col. frontis, 61 illus on 24 plates, 24 maps, layout plans, facsimiles, gradient profiles, timetables; 13 appendices & a bibliography (12 sources).
—— Reprinted as a paperback, *Pan Books* 1972. pp. [12], 211, with 34 illus on 16 plates, plans, etc. & 13 appendices.

9853 PATTERSON, E. M. The Clogher Valley Railway. *Newton Abbot: David & Charles*, 1972. pp. 271, with col. frontis & 36 illus on 16 plates, 14 maps, layout plans, facsimiles & drawings, a bibliography (42 sources) & 8 appendices.

9854 NEWHAM, A. T. The Cork and Muskerry Light Railway. *Lingfield: Oakwood Press*, 1968. (Locomotion Papers, 39). pp. 36, with 14 illus & map on 8 plates, map, 6 layout plans, gradient profile & list of rolling stock.

9855 CORK, BANDON AND SOUTH COAST RAILWAY. 'Prince of Wales' route to Glengarriff & Killarney. *Dublin: Irish Tourist Development Publishing Co.*, 1896. pp. 52, with 47 illus, map & timetable.

9856 NEWHAM, A. T. The Cork, Blackrock & Passage Railway. *Lingfield: Oakwood Press*, 1970. (Locomotion Papers, 49). pp. 40, with 17 illus & a map on 8 plates, map on rev. t.p., 9 layout plans & a descriptive list of the steamships operated by the railway company (pp. 38–40).

9857 DOUGHERTY, H. The bus services of the County Donegal Railways, 1960–1971. *Dublin: Transport Research Associates*, 1973. pp. 36, with 7 illus; bibliography (14 sources).

9858 LECKEY, J. The records of the County Donegal Railways Joint Committee. *Belfast: Irish Railway Record Society; Dublin: Irish Economic Press*, 1980. (Occasional Publications of the I.R.R.S., no. 6). pp. vi, 31. Reproduced typescript.

9859 CUBITT, W. and PIM J. [Letters to Joseph Kincaid, chairman of the Dublin & Kings-town Railway on the subject of the proposed atmospheric railway. *Dublin*, 1841]. pp. 3. la. 8°. printed.   BLACK 5379

9860 SHEPHERD, W. E. The Dublin & South Eastern Railway. *Newton Abbot: David & Charles*, 1974. pp. 231, with 32 illus on 16 plates, 25 maps, station plans, diagrams, timetables, facsimiles & a gradient profile; Appendices 1–8, detailed stock lists (pp. 191–224), & a bibliography (32 sources).

9861 DUNDALK WESTERN RAILWAY. Prospectus of the Dundalk Western Railway to connect the western and north western counties of Ireland with the port of Dundalk. *London: Roake & Varty, printers*, 1837. pp. 16, with 3 tables & map.
A proposed line from Dundalk to Ballybay, using horse-power as well as locomotives.

9862 NIMMO, A. Report of Alexander Nimmo, Esq. to the directors of the Great Central Irish Railway (Oct. 12, 1836). *Dublin: printed by John Chambers*, 1836. pp. 9, with a gradient table & a supporting letter from Charles Vignoles.
His survey of the proposed route.

9863 CLONTARF & HILL OF HOWTH TRAMROAD COMPANY. Fare and Time Tables. (Electric cars between Dublin (Nelson's Pillar) and Raheny, Baldoyle, Sutton, Howth. Timetable, August 1905). *Howth: the Company*, 1905. pp. 40, with folded map.

9864 GAMBLE, N. E. The Dublin & Drogheda Railway project, 1835–1844. Dissertation, B.A., Trinity College Dublin, Dept of History, 1972.

9865 LECKEY, J. J. The organisation and capital structure of the Irish North Western Railway. Thesis, M.Sc(Econ), The Queens University of Belfast, 1973–4.

9866 The GREAT Northern. *Billericay: Irish Railway Record Society, London Area*, 1976. (Irish Railways in Pictures series). pp. 32, with 65 illus. Text extends onto inside covers.
The Great Northern Railway (Ireland), since 1930.

9867 ARNOLD, R. M. The golden years of the Great Northern Railway. *Belfast: Blackstaff Press*.
A detailed narrative of the daily organisation and working of the GNR(I) during the 1920s and 1930s.
vol. 1, [Northern section of the GNR(I)]. 1976. pp. xii, 148, with 102 illus, map, many station & junction layout plans and gradient profiles. Detailed lists, pp. 130–48.
—— vol. 1, new edn, 1979. pp. [viii], 158, with 122 illus, 2 maps, many station & junction layout plans and gradient profiles. Detailed lists, pp. 130–48.
vol. 2, Newry, Armagh and Clones areas. 1980. pp. viii, 186, with frontis, 163 illus, 30 layout plans & 4 gradient profiles, lists & 3 specimen timetables (1 on endpaper).

9868 PIM, J. A letter to George Carr, Esq., chairman of the Great Southern and Western Railway of Ireland, by James Pim, Jun. *Dublin: Webb & Chapman*, 1846. pp. 23. At head of title-page: 'For private circulation only'.

An invitation to the GSWR to amalgamate with the Grand Canal Co. with the object of building a line westwards to Galway, using the banks of the Canal as far as the Shannon.

9869 LE FANU, W. R. Report to the directors of the Great Southern & Western Railway on the port of Cork as a packet station for communication with America; *Dublin: printed by Edward Bull*, 1851. pp. 16, with folded map. BLACK 7033

9870 FLANAGAN, P. J. The 101 class locomotives of the G.S. & W.R., 1866–1966, edited by P. J. Flanagan. [*Blackrock*]: *Irish Railway Record Society*, 1966. pp. 44, with 12 illus.

9871 MURRAY, K. A. and McNEILL, D. B. The Great Southern & Western Railway. *Dublin: Irish Railway Record Society*, 1976. pp. 206, with 56 illus on 24 plates (pp. 81–104), 9 maps & diagrams (1 folded), 7 appendices (incl. chronology), & a bibliography (pp. 199–200).

9872 IRISH Eastern & Western, or Great Central Railroad, from Dublin by Athlone to Galway. *London: Blades & East*, 1836. pp. 32, with tables. Includes an engineer's report from W. Bald and D. J. Henry.

9873 LISTOWEL & BALLYBUNION RLY. Opening of the Listowel & Ballybunion Railway: Lartigue single rail system, 29th February 1888. [*London*]: *Metchim & Son*, 1888. pp. 7.

9874 NEWHAM, A. T. The Listowel & Ballybunion Railway. *Lingfield: Oakwood Press* [1967]. (Locomotion Papers, 33). pp. 27, with 15 illus on 8 plates, map, & 2 station plans.

A monorail line (Lartigue system): length 10 miles, 20 chains.

9875 ORCHARD, C. J. D. Londonderry and Lough Swilly Railway. *P.S.V. Circle*, 1966. (Publication R13). pp. 12. Reproduced typescript.

A fleet list of the buses operated by this erstwhile railway.

9876 THOMSON, K. M. Lough Swilly's 50 years: a tribute to 50 years' motor-bus operation by the Londonderry & Lough Swilly Railway Co., 1929–1979. *Londonderry: Irish Transport Trust*, [1979]. pp. 63, with 25 illus, map, fleet list (pp. 50–62), timetables & fascimiles.

9877 BERMINGHAM T. A letter from Thomas Bermingham, Esq., to the people of Ireland, particularly to the inhabitants of the provinces of Leinster & Connaught, on the subject of the Irish Great Western Railway from Dublin to Galway, with 3 maps . . . April 26, 1845. [*London*, 1845]. pp. [6].

9878 A LETTER to the shareholders of the Irish Great Western Dublin to Galway Railway on the present crisis in their affairs. *London: printed by H. G. Smith*, 1846. pp. 18. Text dated April 1846.

9879 MIDLAND GREAT WESTERN RLY. Handbook of the Midland Great Western Railway and guide to Connemara and the west of Ireland. *Edinburgh: R. M. Cameron*, [ca. May 1877]. pp. ii, 160, ii, with numerous illus (engravings) in text & 8 lithograph maps (tinted). BLACKWELLS CAT. A1051 (1976), 54

9880 O'CUIMIN, P. The baronial lines of the Midland Great Western Railway: the Loughrea & Attymon Light Railway: the Ballinrobe & Claremorris Light Railway. *Dublin: Transport Research Associates*, 1972. pp. 88, with 19 illus, 5 line drawings, 2 gradient profiles, 2 chronologies & a map.

9881 PATTERSON, E. M. The Ballycastle Railway. *Dawlish: David & Charles*, 1965. (A History of the Narrow-Gauge Railways of North East Ireland, 1). pp. 154, with col. frontis, 40 illus on 20 plates, & in text, 20 illus (tables, line drawings, layout plans, gradient profiles, timetables & a map); bibliography (39 sources).

9882 PATTERSON, E. M. The Ballymena lines. *Newton Abbot: David & Charles*, 1968. (A History of the Narrow-Gauge Railways of North East Ireland, 2). pp. 200, with col. frontis, 39 illus on 16 plates, 24 illus in text (maps, layout plans, gradient profiles, diagrams, facsimiles & timetables), lists, & a bibliography (39 sources).

The Ballymena, Cushendall & Red Bay Rly, the Ballymena & Larne Rly and the Glengariff Rly.

9883 ARNOLD, R. M. N.C.C. Saga: being a story of the LMS (Northern Counties Committee) where the enginemen were the heroes and the villain the diesel engine. *Newton Abbot: David & Charles*, 1973. pp. 231, with frontis, 32 illus & a map.

9884 CURRIE, J. R. L. The Northern Counties Railway. *Newton Abbot: David & Charles*. 3 vols.

vol. 1, Beginnings and development, 1845–1903. 1973. pp. 294, with col. frontis, 34 illus on 16 plates, 13 maps & 2 pp. seals, 6 appendices, incl. a list (4 pp.) of Acts.

vol. 2, Heyday and decline, 1903–1972. 1974. pp. 248, with 34 illus on 16 plates, 5 maps & plans, 2 pp. of seals & crests, 7 appendices, incl. Acts, omnibus services (6 pp.), and rail closure dates.

vol. 3, 'for locomotives, rolling stock, signalling, operation and other more technical aspects, and a full bibliography and acknowledgements' (Foreword, vol. 1). Not yet published (1980).

9885 SPRINKS, N. W. Sligo, Leitrim and Northern Counties Railway. *Billericay: Irish Railway Record Society, London Area*, 1970. pp. 154, with 63 illus, 8 layout diagrams, 4 timetables & a map.

9886 ROWLANDS, D. G. The Tralee & Dingle Railway. *Truro: Bradford Barton*, 1977. pp. 96. Intro, map & gradient profile, & 134 illus with descrs, 14 line drawings, facsimile of pp. 7–12 of Rule Book & a bibliography (31 sources).

9887 WATERFORD and Kilkenny Railway. *Dublin*, 1853. pp. 20, with tables.
A letter from a shareholder, dated 5 December 1853, addressed to William Slade Parker, Secretary to the W & K Rly urging the abandonment of the proposed Kilkenny and Great Southern & Western Rly scheme.
                         LU(THC)

9888 FAYLE, H. and NEWHAM, A. T. The Waterford & Tramore Railway. *Dawlish: David & Charles*, 1964. pp. 48. with 33 illus on 12 plates, 3 layout plans, 3 facsimiles, map & gradient profile.
Period, 1853–1925.
—— 2nd edn. *David & Charles*, 1972. pp. 63, with 33 illus on 12 plates, 3 layout plans, 3 facsimiles, map & gradient profile.

9889 WATERFORD and Limerick Railway connecting the two important rivers of the Shannon and Suir, and passing through one of the richest districts of Ireland. *Waterford: printed by Harvey*, 1844. pp. 4.   LU(THC)

9890 WATERFORD, LIMERICK & WESTERN RLY. Programme of Waterford, Limerick and Western Railway [tourist, seaside and] excursion arrangements, from 1st May to 31st October, 1898; second issue i.e. 1st edn reprinted; with an introduction by C. B. Mac an tSaoir. *Dublin: Transport Research Associates*, 1969. pp. [2], 39, with map. tall 8°. Facsimile reprint of 1st edn, 1898.

C 4 Q   Preservation 9891–93

9891 SHANE'S CASTLE RAILWAY AND NATURE RESERVE. Official Guide, compiled and edited by David Barzilay; foreword by Lord O'Neill. *Shane's Castle (Antrim): Lord O'Neill*, 1975. pp. 48, with 42 illus & 2 plans.
A 3ft gauge line, 1½ miles long.

9892 RAILWAY PRESERVATION SOCIETY OF IRELAND. Steam Brochure, 1976. *Bangor (Co. Down): the Society*, 1976. pp. 28, with 5 illus.
A handbook recording the progress and activities of the R.P.S.I.
—— 1978 edn. pp. 24.
—— 1979 edn. pp. 28.

9893 LLOYD, D. J. The Foyle Valley Railway and Museum: a short history. *Londonderry: North West of Ireland Railway Society*, [1978]. obl. 8°. pp. 12, with 7 illus, map & plan.
The history of Victoria Road Station, County Donegal Rly, and its restoration as a live museum with adjacent rail approach roads in operation as the first stage of a planned service to Prehen.

C 5   ISLE OF WIGHT

including the Southern Rly and British Railways (Southern Region)
on the Island

9894–9907

Reference sources 9894–96

9894 WIGHT LOCOMOTIVE SOCIETY. Isle of Wight Track Diagram. 2nd edn. [*Newport*]: *the Society*, 1967. A folded railway map, 40 inch × 27 inch (drawn by I.E.W.?) with enlarged scale for junctions, termini, & stations. The Isle of Wight railway network as in 1948–49.

9895 ISLE OF WIGHT CENTRAL RLY. Working Time Table for October 1909 and until further notice. *Newport (I.o.W.): I.W.C. Rly*, 1909. Reprint, *Isle of Wight Railway Company (1972)*. [197–?] s. sh. A tall 8°. card printed on both sides.

9896 SOUTHERN RLY. ISLE OF WIGHT SECTION. Working timetables of passenger & freight trains from 18th June 1932 . . . [*Oxford: Oxford Publishing Co.*, 1978]. pp. 32.
Facsimile reprint of the original publication, Southern Rly, 1932.

9897 WHETMATH, C. F. D. The Isle of Wight Central Railway. *Teddington: Branch Line Handbooks*, 1962. (Branch Line Handbook, 12). pp. 34, with 6 illus on 2 plates & a folded map. Reproduced typescript in paper covers.

9898 BLACKBURN, A. and MACKETT, J. The Freshwater, Yarmouth & Newport Railway, with a section on tickets by D. G. Geldard. *Teddington: Branch Line Handbooks; Bracknell: West Country Handbooks*, 1966. pp. 66, with 22 illus, 14 layout plans, 6 tables, & at end, 2 maps & gradient profile on one folded sheet. Bibliography (42 sources), 4 appendices.

9899 ALLEN, P. C. and MacCLEOD, A. B. Rails in the Isle of Wight. *London: Allen & Unwin*, 1967. pp. 68, with col. frontis, 1 col. plate & 135 monochrome illus on 30 plates, map & 6 gradient profiles.

9900 KICHENSIDE, G. M. Isle of Wight Album.

London: Ian Allan, [1967]. la. 8°. pp. [96]. Text (pp. 5–17) & 190 illus with descrs.

9901 BURROUGHS, R. E. The great Isle of Wight train robbery: the story of the Isle of Wight railway closures, with a foreword by E. R. Hondelink. *London: Railway Invigoration Society*, [1968]. pp. 47, with 14 illus & a map.

9902 BLACKBURN, A. and MACKETT, J. The railways and tramways of Ryde. *Bracknell: Town & Country Press*, 1971. pp. 163, with 70 illus (incl. maps, plans, & track diagrams), 6 tables, stock lists & a bibliography (32 sources).

9903 ISLE OF WIGHT RLY (1972). The Isle of Wight Steam Railway Company Limited: a descriptive brochure. *Haven Street (I.W.): the Company*, 1972. obl. format. pp. 20 with detachable 2 pp. application form at end, & 8 plates.
Includes a stock list.

9904 ISLE OF WIGHT RLY (1972) [Guides]. [1st edn]. *Haven Street Stn: the Railway*, 1972. pp. [30], with 19 illus; map inside cover.
—— 2nd edn. 1973. pp. 40; 26 illus & map.
—— 3rd edn. (abridged). 1975. pp. 16; 6 illus, 2 maps & a plan.
—— 4th edn. (enlarged). 1978. pp. 48; 37 illus (4 col.) & 2 maps.

9905 WHITTINGTON, C. J. Railways in the Wight. 2nd edn. *Shanklin: G. G. Saunders*, [1972]. pp. 30, with 7 illus.

9906 FAIRCLOUGH, T. and WILLS, A. Southern Steam on the Isle of Wight . . . *Truro: Bradford Barton*, 1975. pp. 96. Intro, map, & 132 illus with descrs.
Period, 1950s & 1960s.

9907 PAYE, P. and PAYE, K. Steam on the Isle of Wight, 1956–1966. *Oxford: Oxford Publishing Co.*, 1979. la. 8°. pp. 96. Intro, frontis & 174 illus with descrs, layout plan, map, historical notes & a sectioned working timetable.

C 6   ISLE OF MAN

9908–34

9908 JUBILEE of the Isle of Man Railway, July 1873 to July 1923. *Douglas: Brown & Sons, printers*, [1923]. pp. 7.
Reprinted from the *Isle of Man Weekly Times*, June 30th, 1923.

9909 PUBLIC service vehicles in the Isle of Man. *P.S.V. Circle*, July 1961. (Publication RC6). pp. 28. Reproduced typescript.
A revised edition of P52 (1963). Includes tramcars, electric trains and road vehicles of the Isle of Man Rly Co.

9910 PRICE, J. H. Manx Electric, 1957–1962: a Modern Tramway report on the first five years' work of the Manx Electric Railway Board. *London: Light Railway Transport League*, [in conjunction with the] Manx Electric Railway Board, [1962]. pp. 12, with 10 illus & a map.

9911 LAMBDEN, W. Manx transport systems: road, rail, tram, sea and air. *London: Omnibus Society*, 1964. pp. 64, with 43 illus, 4 maps, 8 detailed lists (2 on separate folded sheet).

9912 ISLE of Man Tramways Album: a historical souvenir of the Manx tramways. *Isle of Man: Douglas Cable Car Group*, [1968]. obl. format. pp. 52. Intro, 3 pp. of text and 75 illus with descrs, 2 dimensioned drawings, 2 maps & a plan.

9913 WYSE, W. J. and JOYCE, J. Isle of Man Album. *London: Ian Allan*, 1968. pp. 108, Intro (pp. 9–16), & 215 illus with descrs.
Railways (steam and electric) and tramways.

9914 PEARSON, F. K. The Isle of Man tramways. *Newton Abbot: David & Charles*, 1970. pp. 379, with 69 illus on 32 plates, & in text, 136 (maps, layout plans, diagrams, drawings, gradient profiles, & route maps).
Includes cliff lifts and (pp. 349–57), 'Manx tramway tickets', by W. H. Bett.

9915 PEARSON, F. K. Snaefell Mountain Railway, 1895–1970. *London: Light Railway Transport League* [in conjunction with the] Manx Electric Railways Board, [1970]. pp. 16, with 17 illus, a map & a dimensioned drawing.

9916 RAILWAYS in the Isle of Man. *Douglas: Isle of Man Tourist Board*, [1970]. sm. 8°. pp. 32, with 19 illus.

9917 MANX ELECTRIC RLY. Manx Electric Railway; Snaefell Mountain Railway. *Douglas: M.E. Rly*, [1974 or 5]. pp. 16, with 4 illus & a map; stock list, illus & map on covers.
—— another edn, [1976 or 7]. pp. 16, with 5 illus & a map; stock list, illus & map on covers.

9918 CONSTANTINE, H. Douglas Corporation horse trams: the first 100 years; written and photographed by Harry Constantine; illustrated by Sandra Constantine. *Douglas: Douglas Corporation Transport Dept*, 1975.

la. 8°. pp. 24, with 22 photos (7 col.) & 15 drawings. Cover has 3 illus (1 col.), 2 plans & a drawing.
pp. 1–8, a chronology; pp 8–24, 'The system today'.

9919 CONSTANTINE, H. Isle of Man tramway travels, written and illustrated by Harry Constantine: an illustrated guide to the island's scenery as seen from the trams, with suggested visits. *Douglas: Manx Electric Railways Board*, [1975]. la. 8°. pp. [16], with 15 photos (13 col.) & 14 drawings. Intro, 3 col. illus & a map on covers.

9920 ISLE OF MAN STEAM RAILWAY SUPPORTERS ASSOCIATION. Isle of Man Railway: a report on the 1975 season and suggestions for the future. *Douglas: the Association*, October 1975. pp. 16.

9921 BOYD, J. I. C. The Isle of Man Railway: an illustrated guide. [*Douglas: Isle of Man Rly*, ca. 1976]. pp. 16, with 10 col. illus, & 2 maps.

9922 GOODWYN, A. M. Is this any way to run a railway? [*Douglas*]: *Manx Electric Railway Society*, 1976. sm. obl. format. pp. 23, with 5 illus (2 inside covers).
'The story of the Manx Electric Railway since its nationalisation in 1957 to the present unhappy time . . .'

9923 HENDRY, R. Preston, and HENDRY, R. Powell. Isle of Man Railway Album. *Newton Abbot: David & Charles*, 1976. (British Light Railway Albums series). pp. 112.
pp. 5–23, Preface, map & outline history of the Isle of Man Railways, with 10 illus; pp. 24–95, Photographic section (105 illus with descrs); pp. 96–112, 4 appendices, with reproduced timetables & tickets.

9924 ISLE OF MAN STEAM RAILWAY SUPPORTERS ASSOCIATION. The Isle of Man Railway: an analysis of the present situation, including proposals for 1977 and beyond. *Douglas: the Association*, September 1976. pp. [32], with plan of proposed modifications to Douglas station.

9925 DOWN, C. G. and SMITH, D. H. 'Polar Bear' and the Groudle Glen Railway. *Haywards Heath: Brockham Museum Association*, 1977. pp. 40, with 18 illus, 2 maps, 2 plans, 7 line drawings & a chronology.
The G.G. Rly, 1893–1962 and the subsequent transfer and restoration of the locomotive 'Polar Bear' in Brockham Museum, near Dorking.

9926 PEARSON, F. K. Cable tram days. [*Doug-las?*]: *Douglas Cable Car Group*, 1977. pp. 8, with 26 illus on 24 plates & a chronology , pp. 6–8.
The Upper Douglas Cable Tramway, 1896–1929.

9927 RYAN, J. M. Technical Report on the Manx Electric Railway's Northern Line. [*Douglas*]: *Manx Electric Railway Society*, 1977. pp. 14. 'Reproduced typescript.
'The Manx Electric Railway Northern Line Report, 1977', dated January 12, 1977.
The cost and practicability of rehabilitating the line between Laxey and Ramsey (closed by Tynwald Resolution but not abandoned) in time for the 1977 season. The report of an examination by John M. Ryan, C.E. and a team of other civil engineers.

9928 BOYD, J. I. C. On the Isle of Man narrow gauge. *Truro: Bradford Barton*, 1978. pp. 96. Map, intro, & 137 illus with descrs.

9929 GOODWYN, A. M. Douglas Head Marine Drive & Electric Tramway, by A. M. Goodwin. *Isle of Man: Manx Electric Railway Society*, 1978. pp. [32], with 23 illus (3 on covers), 7 drawings & a map.

9930 HENDRY, R. Preston, and HENDRY, R. Powell. Manx Electric Railway Album. *Rugby: Hillside Publishing Co.*, 1978. la. 8°. pp. 112, with 172 illus, facsims, maps & plans.

9931 ISLE OF MAN STEAM RAILWAY SUPPORTERS ASSOCIATION. The Isle of Man Railway: a report of the seasons of 1977 and 1978. *Douglas: the Association*, 1978. pp. 42.

9932 GOODWYN, A. M. Manx Transport Kaleidoscope, by A. M. Goodwin. *Douglas: Manx Electric Railway Society & the Isle of Man Steam Railway Supporters Association*, [1979]. pp. [36], with 55 illus, map & stock lists, 5 additional illus, (2 col.) & a bibliography (4 sources) on covers.
The Isle of Man Rly, Manx Electric Rly, Douglas Corporation Tramways (horse-drawn cars) and the Snaefell Mountain Rly.

9933 GOODWYN, A. M. and TOWNSEND, A. The Unofficial Guide to the Isle of Man railways: an incredible compendium of Manx railway cartoons. *Douglas: Manx Electric Rly*, 1980. obl. format. pp. [64]. Intro & 68 humorous drawings with captions, & 3 pages of verse.

9934 HENDRY, R. Preston, and HENDRY, R. Powell. The Manx Northern Railway. *Rugby: Hillside Publishing Co.*, 1980. la. 8°. pp. 136 with ca. 150 illus, maps, plans, facsimiles & dimensioned drawings.

C 7   CHANNEL ISLANDS 9935–38

9935 BONSOR, N. R. P. The Jersey Eastern Railway and the German occupation lines in Jersey. *Lingfield: Oakwood Press*, 1964. (Oakwood Library of Railway History, 58A). (Railways of the Channel Islands, 2). pp. 91–142, with 27 illus, 2 maps & a layout plan

on 12 plates, and in text, map, layout plan & tables.
—— rev. edn. *Oakwood Press*, 1977. pp. 91–142, with 24 illus & a plan on 8 plates, & in text, map, plan & 5 tables; 2 maps & 1 illus on inside covers.

9936 BONSOR, N. R. P. The Guernsey Railway: the German occupation lines in Guernsey, and the Alderney Railway. *Lingfield: Oakwood Press*, 1967. (Oakwood Library of Railway History, 58B). (Railways of the Channel Islands, 3). pp. 143–198, with 32 illus on 12 plates, 3 maps & 15 detailed lists of locomotives and tramcars.

Includes (pp. 194–5) 'Railways of the Island of Herm'.

9937 BONSOR, N. R. P. The Jersey Railway, *in* One Hundred Years of Public Transport in Jersey. *Gloucester: British Publishing Co.*, [1970]. pp. 7–27, with 9 illus & 2 maps.

9938 WILSON, F. E. Railways in Guernsey; with special reference to the German steam railways. *St Peter Port: Paramount-Lithoprint*, [1972]. pp. 56, with 47 illus, diagrams & maps & a sectional map (pp. 38–47); general map & diagram on insides of covers.

C 8   ENGLISH CHANNEL TUNNEL and other Channel rail crossing schemes
9939–80

Reference sources 9939–41
For Channel train ferry services see **G 5**

9939 BROWN, A. G. Channel Tunnel Bibliography, compiled by A. G. Brown. *London: Channel Tunnel Association*, 1969. pp. 42.
603 sources: books, reports, pamphlets, government publications, lectures, letters, articles in periodicals and newspapers.

9940 DAVIES, G. A. The Channel Tunnel: a bibliography of the fixed link. *Coventry: Cadig Liaison Centre*, 1973. tall 8°. pp. 36, 323 sources.
Arrangement: chronological by date of publication within each subject class. Material: books, reports, official publications (parliamentary and departmental), & periodical articles.

9941 PUGH, H. A. The Channel Tunnel: a select list of references. 2nd edn. *London: Department of the Environment Library*, January 1973. (Bibliography, 15). Reproduced typescript. pp. 23.
187 works described. Includes (a) publications of government departments, British and French, (b) Channel Tunnel organisations, (c) background works, (d) periodical articles, (e) periodicals, (f) addresses of organisations. Modern (i.e. post-1950) works, with a few earlier ones. No introduction, no index. Entries arranged chronologically within each section.

9942 LEY, W. Engineers' dreams. *London: Phoenix House*, 1955. pp. 192, with plates & illus.
pp. 11–36, 'Forbidden tunnel'. The Channel Tunnel, with 2 illus on 1 plate, & in text, 2 maps & 3 diagrams.

9943 WHITESIDE, T. The Tunnel under the Channel. *London: Rupert Harte-Davis*, 1962. pp. 133, with 21 illus (3 photos & 18 drawings).

9944 TRAVIS, A. S. Channel Tunnel, 1802–1967. *London: P. R. Davis*, 1967. (Signal Transport Papers, 2). pp. 84, with 38 illus, maps &

diagrams on 20 plates & 1 map in text; bibliography (24 sources).

9945 LE ROI, D. The Channel Tunnel. *Brighton: Clifton Books*, 1969. pp. 120, with 7 illus on 4 plates, 2 maps, & a diagram.

9946 GIBBONS, G. Trains under the Channel. *Huddersfield: Advertiser Press*, [1970]. pp. 149, with 13 plates; bibliography by Antony G. Brown (pp. 124–45) consisting of 247 brief refs, including many to periodical articles and lecture papers.
An historical introduction followed by a general discussion of contemporary schemes and prospects.

9947 GARRETT, R. Cross Channel. *London: Hutchinson*, 1972. pp. xii, 228, with 35 illus on 20 plates.
Crossing by all means, including swimming. Includes railway ferry services and the Channel Tunnel schemes.

9948 HAINING, P. Eurotunnel: an illustrated history of the Channel Tunnel scheme. *London: New English Library*, 1973. la. 8°. pp. 144, with 152 illus (some col.), incl. facsimiles, maps, plans & portraits.

9949 THOMÉ DE GAMOND, A. Mémoire sur les plans du projet nouveau d'un tunnel sous-marin entre l'Angleterre et la France, produits a l'Exposition Universelle de 1867, et sur les différents systèmes projetés pour la jonction des deux territoires depuis l'origine de ces études en 1833: tunnel immergé, pont sur le détroit, bac flottant; Isthme de Douvres, tunnel sous-marin. 2 éd *Paris: Dunod*, 1869. pp. xxiv, 134.   NUC

9950 FIGUIER, L. G. Les nouvelles conquêtes de la science [tome 2]: Grands tunnels et rail-

ways métropolitains. *Paris: E. Girard & A. Boitte*, [1884]. pp. 644, with 214 engravings, incl. portraits.
   pp. 401–502, Le tunnel sous-marin du Pas-de-Calais;
   pp. 503–640, Les railways métropolitains: les trois systèmes; les tunnels, les voies de niveau, et les chemins de fer sur arcades. (pp. 511–33, Le railway métropolitain de Londres).

9951 BUNAU-VARILLA, P. Varilla mixed passage: a system of communication by rail between England and France avoiding any military and naval objections . . . *Paris: May et Motteroz*, [1890 or 1891]. 4°. pp. 52, with coloured plans.   NUC
—— another edn, Varilla mixed passage: proposed new system of railway communication between England and France, by P. Bunau-Varilla, C.E. [*n.p.*]: *the author*, 1891. tall 8°. pp. 52, with 7 la. folded col. plans and 28 diagrams in text.
   Produced in the style of a British Parliamentary Paper. Printed on the cover: 'Presented by the author', suggesting that this version was not published but distributed only to persons likely to be interested in supporting the author's extraordinary proposal, summarised thus by him (p. 7): 'The solution called 'mixed passage' consists in prolonging the English and French railways into the sea to a certain distance from the coasts on raised viaducts, then to lower the entire trains by special water-excluding apparatus (inclined planes or lifts) down to the level of the submarine tunnel and lastly, by a tunnel passing under the central portion of the Straits, to connect the extremities of the descents'.
            LU(THC)

9952 GODFREY, E. A Channel Tunnel? Great Western Railway (London) Lecture & Debating Society, meeting on the 16th January 1930 (no. 238). pp. 14, with discussion & 1 illus.

9953 ECONOMIST INTELLIGENCE UNIT. Channel Tunnel: traffic and revenue study, prepared by the Economist Intelligence Unit Limited, London [and the] Société d'Études Techniques et Économiques, Paris [and] De Leuw, Cather & Co., Chicago. *London: Channel Tunnel Study Group*, November 1959. 3 vols. Reproduced typescript.
   part A, General. pp. 81.
   part B, Passengers and accompanied vehicles. pp. 87 & 23 tables, 45 graphs, 21 maps.
   part C, Goods traffic. pp. 428, with 15 maps & diagrams.

9954 CHANNEL TUNNEL STUDY GROUP. Report, 28th March, 1960. *London: the Group*, 1960. pp. 33.
   Proposes a road and rail tunnel under Franco-British ownership and operation, with capital to be raised from private sources for the bare tunnel, portal to portal.

9955 MINISTRY OF TRANSPORT. The Channel Tunnel: excerpt from Proposals for a Fixed Channel Link (Cmnd 2137, *H.M.S.O.*, 1963, pp. 3–4, 16–19, 24–33, 53–9), *in* Transport: selected readings, edited by Denys Munby, pp. 245–75, with 16 notes & 7 appendices.

9956 MINISTRY OF TRANSPORT. Proposals for a fixed Channel link. *London: H.M.S.O.*, 1963. (Cmnd 2137). pp. iv, 60.
   A joint report by British and French officials on a proposed tunnel (Channel Tunnel Study Group, March 1960), and a proposed bridge (Channel Bridge Study Group, October 1961).

9957 CHANNEL TUNNEL STUDY GROUP. The Channel Tunnel:? the facts. *London: Whittaker, Hunt & Co., for the Channel Tunnel Study Group*, 1964. pp. 36.

9958 PEQUIGNOT, C. A. Chunnel: everyman's guide to the technicalities of building a Channel Tunnel. *London: C.R. Books*, 1965. pp. 206, with 74 illus on plates & in text.

9959 KENT COUNTY COUNCIL. PLANNING DEPARTMENT. The Channel Tunnel: a discussion of terminal requirements on the British side and possible locations for terminal facilities in Kent. [*Maidstone*]: *K.C.C.*, December 1968. tall 8°. pp. 13, with 6 folded col. maps & 3 perspective drawings.

9960 BRITISH TRANSPORT COMMISSION. Channel Tunnel model. Modèle du Tunnel sous la Manche. [*London*]: *B.T.C.*, [196–?]. pp. 4, with 2 illus.
   Text in French and English.

9961 CUNDILL, M. A. Channel Tunnel: pedestrian movements in proposed ferry trains. *Crowthorne: Transport & Road Research Laboratory, Transport Operation Dept*, 1972. (TRRL Report LR 436). tall 8°. pp. 13, with 10 plates, 11 diagrams & graphs.

9962 DEPARTMENT OF THE ENVIRONMENT. The Channel Tunnel: agreement no. 1, dated 20 October 1972 (made between the Secretary of State for the Environment, the British Channel Tunnel Company Ltd., Société Française du Tunnel sous la Manche, and members of the Group). [*London: the Dept*, 1972]. tall 8°. pp. ii, 76.
   A working document. The Group is defined on p.1 as the British Sub-Group and the French Sub-Group (21 corporate bodies in all).

9963 ELLSON, P. B. and LAYFIELD, R. E. Channel Tunnel: vehicular movements in proposed ferry trains. *Crowthorne: Transport & Road Research Laboratory, Transport Operations Dept*, 1972. (TRRL Report, LR 435). tall 8°. pp. 50, with 27 plates, & 11 diagrams & graphs.

9964 GREATER LONDON COUNCIL. Channel Tunnel: London passenger terminal: a document for consultation. *London: G.L.C.*, 1972. tall 8°. pp. 24, with 10 col. maps & diagrams (7 folded).
   Prepared with the co-operation of British Railways. The problem of siting a terminal in London.

9965 AFCO ASSOCIATES. The Channel Tunnel project: an answer: a report prepared by Afco Associates for the Channel Tunnel Opposition Association. *London: C.T.O.A.*, June 1973. la. 8°. pp. vii, 60, [30], with illus & map. Reproduced typescript. Title on cover only.

9966 AFCO ASSOCIATES. The Channel Tunnel project: key issues: a dialogue of dissent published in the interests of the British tax-payer: a report prepared for the Channel Tunnel Opposition Association. *London: [C.T.O.A.]*, Oct. 1973. la. 8°. pp. ii, 33, with illus & facsims. Reproduced typescript. Title on cover only.

9967 BRITISH RAILWAYS. Express link with Europe: British Rail and the Channel Tunnel. *London: B.R.*, 1973. pp. 13, with 4 maps & 1 diagram.

9968 CHANNEL TUNNEL: A PUBLIC DISCUSSION [Conference, London, 1973]. Supplement to the Society's Journal containing the proceedings of a conference entitled 'The Channel Tunnel: a public discussion' held in the Society's house in John Adam Street, Adelphi, London on 5th June, 1973. *London: Royal Society of Arts*, [1973]. pp. [3], 62.

9969 CHANNEL TUNNEL OPPOSITION ASSOCIATION. The Channel Tunnel project: an independent appraisal. *Folkestone: the Association*, July 1973. pp. 7.
—— inserted, a folder: The Channel Tunnel: the reasons why it should not be built. pp. 6.

9970 COOPERS AND LYBRAND ASSOCIATES LIMITED. Channel Tunnel: a United Kingdom transport cost-benefit study presented to the Secretary of State for the Environment, 31st May 1973. *London: H.M.S.O.*, 1973. tall 8°. pp. 48, with 42 tables.

9971 DEPARTMENT OF THE ENVIRONMENT. The Channel Tunnel: presented to Parliament by the Secretary of State for the Environment. *London: H.M.S.O.*, 1973. pp. iv, 75, [8], with illus & plan. (Cmnd 5430).

9972 DEPARTMENT OF THE ENVIRONMENT. The Channel Tunnel project, presented to Parliament . . . *London: H.M.S.O.*, 1973. pp. vi, 33, [4], with 5 illus on 4 plates, 3 maps & a diagram. (Cmnd 5256).

9973 ECONOMIC CONSULTANTS LIMITED. The Channel Tunnel: its economic and social impact on Kent: report presented to the Secretary of State for the Environment, 24th April 1973 ([by] Economic Consultants Ltd in association with the Shankland-Cox Partnership). *London: H.M.S.O.*, 1973. tall format. pp. [8], 259, with 2 maps, tables & 7 appendices.

9974 EUROPEAN FERRIES LIMITED. The Channel Tunnel project: an objective appraisal. *London: the firm*, April 1973. pp. 14.
Relating to Cmnd 5256.

9975 BRITISH RAILWAYS. Channel Tunnel: London-Tunnel new rail link: a document for consultation. *[London]: B.R.*, 1974. tall 8°. pp. 7, with 12 folded plates (1–3 of the proposed rail link and terminal, and 4–10, a map of the route from the White City (London) through Surrey to Saltwood, the Cheriton terminal in Kent and the Channel Tunnel approach).

9976 CHANNEL TUNNEL OPPOSITION ASSOCIATION. The White Paper on the Channel Tunnel (Cmnd 5430): a reply by the Channel Tunnel Opposition Association. *Folkestone: the Association*, [1974]. pp. 16.

9977 CALVERT, R. Chunnel replanned. *London: the author*, 1975. pp. 14.
The current position and its problems considered.

9978 CHANNEL TUNNEL ADVISORY GROUP. The Channel Tunnel and alternative cross-Channel services: a report presented to the Secretary of State for the Environment. *London: H.M.S.O., for the Department of the Environment*, 1975. la. 8°. pp. v, 54, with tables.

9979 NATIONAL COUNCIL ON INLAND TRANSPORT. A report on cross-Channel rail link, published by the British Railways Board, April 1979. *London: N.C.I.T.*, May, 1979. pp. 4. Reproduced typescript.
Welcoming the scheme, with some reservations, and commenting upon various aspects.

9980 RAILWAY DEVELOPMENT SOCIETY. Channel Tunnel: why we need it NOW. *London: R.D.S.*, [1979 or 80]. pp. [4].

C 9   SCOTLAND TO IRELAND TUNNEL SCHEME
9981

9981 BARTON, J. The proposed tunnel between Scotland and Ireland, *in* Proceedings of Section 1, Railways, International Engineering Congress, Glasgow, 1901. *London: William Clowes*, 1902. pp. 62–77, with 2 folded sheets (map & section). Discussion, pp. 68–77.
From Stranraer to Belfast.

C 10   BRITISH RAIL TRANSPORT COMPARED WITH THAT OF OTHER COUNTRIES

9982–91

9982 RENDELL, T. H. The International Railway Congress in America, 1905. Great Western Railway (London) Lecture & Debating Society, meeting on March 29th, 1906 [no. 26]. pp. 12, with 4 illus.

9983 RAPER, C. L. Railway transportation: a history of its economics and of its relation to the state. *New York, London: Putnam*, 1912. pp. xi, 331.
    Based on *Railroad Transportation: its history and its laws*, by A. T. Hadley, 1885, pp. 14–60, 'Railway transportation in Great Britain'. International comparisons, with statistics, are frequently made throughout the text.

9984 MANCE, [Sir] H. O. Recent developments in international railway questions. Great Western Railway (London) Lecture & Debating Society, meeting on the 5th December 1929 (no. 236). pp. 13, with discussion.

9985 MIDDLETON, P. H. Railways of thirty nations: governments *versus* private ownership. *New York: Prentice-Hall*, 1937. pp. xix, 328, with frontis & 63 illus. Summary, pp. 291–305; bibliography, pp. 309–12.
    pp. 37–55, 'Great Britain'. Government ownership examined, country by country, in order to determine whether or not the U.S.A. should also nationalise its railways.

9986 ASSOCIATION OF AMERICAN RAILROADS. British and European railroads: report on inspection by the Association of American Railroads delegation to British and European railroads during July 1960. *Chicago: the Association*, [1960]. pp. iv, 157, with 53 illus, 9 tables, 2 diagrams.
    Management, general administration, train operation, equipment (motive power, rolling stock, signalling, electric traction), research and education.

9987 ROBBINS, M. and POSTGATE, R. Passenger fares: a consideration of the economic aspects of alternative fares structures. *Brussels: International Union of Public Transport*, 1961. (34th International Congress, Copenhagen, 1961, paper no.7). pp. 19, with 4 folded tables.
    The very detailed tables enable comparisons to be made on a world-wide scale, of fares by road transport and by rail in particular towns.

9988 HABAKKUK, H. J. American and British technology in the nineteenth century: the search for labour-saving inventions. *Cambridge: Cambridge University Press*, 1962. pp. [x], 222.
    pp. 86–9 *et passim*, Objectives and methods in the U.S.A. and in Britain. In Britain, permanence, achieved at great cost; in the U.S.A., speed, itself an economy but also a factor in competition between rival lines.

9989 ALLEN, C. J. The future of railways, *in* Journal of the Royal Society of Arts, vol. 113 (no. 5015, April 1965), pp. 334–51, with 6 illus & discussion.
    A paper read to the Society on 3rd February 1965. Chairman, G. F. Fiennes, General Manager BR(WR).
    Modern developments in railway operation and technology in France, Germany, Italy, Japan and the U.S.A. and their value as indicators for planning on the railways of Britain.

9990 VUILLET, G. Railway reminiscences of three continents. *London: T. Nelson*, 1968. pp. x, 357, with frontis, 91 illus on 48 plates, & 7 tables.
    Detailed studies of locomotive performance in Great Britain, Europe, North America and Africa, 1903 to 1960.

9991 GWILLIAM, K. M. and PRIDEAUX, J. D. C. A. A comparative study of European rail performance. *London: British Railways Board*, 1979. tall 8°. sp.b. pp. 150, with many tables.

C 11   INTERNATIONAL CO-OPERATION

9992

9992 DESPICHT, N. S. Policies for transport in the Common Market . . . , maps and diagrams by Margaret M. Despicht . . . *Sidcup: Lambarde Press*, 1964. pp. xii, 308, with 20 maps & diagrams.
    A survey on the national transport policies of the six member states of the E.E.C. and of the implementation of the transport provisions of the Treaty of Rome.

D   SPECIAL TYPES OF RAILWAY AND LOCOMOTION

9993–10170

For local railways and tramways see C

D 1   LIGHT RAILWAYS AND TRAMWAYS
including their locomotives and rolling stock

9993–10078

Reference sources

9993   [DUNCAN'S Tramway Manual]. Manual of the Tramway Companies in the United Kingdom, together with traffic tables of the principal companies, and a map of those in London. *London: Effingham Wilson*, 1877.
Continued as:
Duncan's Manual of British and Foreign Tramway (and Omnibus) Companies (Duncan's Manual of Tramways, Omnibuses & Electric Railways). 1878–1905.
The work is scarce, but a near complete set is available in the British Library. The 1888 volume, in LU(THC), has 407 pages and its contents may be briefly described as follows:
Tables of individual tramways, British, then foreign, with directors, officers, financial & statistical records (mileage, rolling stock, number of horses or locomotives, number of passengers carried, receipts per mile, total expenses per mile, profits, etc.).
This is followed by some detailed general tables and a 'Tramway Directory: directors, officials, engineers, auditors and other firms and individuals connected with tramway enterprise'. The end section consists of advertisements (some illustrated).

9994   CLINKER, C. R. Light Railway Orders: introductory notes on, and schedule of, Light Railway Orders confirmed by the Board of Trade and its successors under the terms of the Light Railways Acts of 1896, 1901, 1906 and 1912. *Bristol: Avon Anglia Publications*, 1977. (Reference Aid Series, 2). pp. 31.
561 confirmed L.R.O.s are listed, from the first on 9 December 1897 to the last to be authorised in 1976.

General and historical

9995   [MILNES]. GEORGE F. MILNES & CO. Tramway cars: electric, steam, cable & horse . . . , also . . . light railway and electric rolling stock manufactured by Milnes & Co. Ltd. [ca. 1899]. pp. 45, with 52 illus.
A brief history of the firm and its works and a detailed description of the numerous specialized processes.   BLACKWELL'S CAT. A1051 (1976), 63

9996   ROCHFORD, J. The Lorain surface contact system of electric traction. *Dublin: printed for the author by John Falconer*, 1907. pp. 27, with 7 illus & 6 diagrams on 10 plates.
Read before the Institution of Civil Engineers of Ireland, 2nd November, 1904.

9997   PILCHER, R. S. Road passenger transport: survey and development. *London: Pitman*, 1937. pp. xii, 393, with 33 illus.
Includes tramways, and the effect of suburban railway electrification on road passenger transport services.

9998   SLEEMAN, J. F. An economic study of the British tramway industry. Thesis, M.A.(Com.), University of London, 1939.

9999   CORNWELL, E. L. Commercial road vehicles. *London: Batsford*, 1960. pp. 288, with 82 illus on plates & in text.
Tramways, pp. 129–148.

10000   TRAMWAY CENTENARY EXHIBITION, London, 1960. Tramway Centenary Exhibition, 1860–1960, Bishopsgate Institute, August 25th–27th 1960: catalogue & guide. *London: Tramway & Light Railway Society*, 1960. pp. 8.
81 models, 28 relics, 23 photographs, tickets, drawings.

10001   JOYCE, J. Tramway twilight: the story of British tramways from 1945 to 1962. *London: Ian Allan*, 1962. pp. vii, 112, with 124 illus & 5 appendices.

10002   WHITEHOUSE, P. B. Branch Line Album [first series]. *London: Ian Allan*, 1962. pp.

124. pp. 5–32 (text with illus), & pp. 33–124 (pictorial section). 210 illus in all, with descrs.
Period, 1930s–1950s.

10003 WHITEHOUSE, P. B. Branch Line Album: second series. *London: Ian Allan*, [1965]. pp. 115. 231 illus with descrs.

10004 GILL, D. Tramcar Treasury. *London: Allen & Unwin*, 1963. pp. xv, 147, with 160 illus.

10005 JOYCE, J. Tramway heyday. *London: Ian Allan*, [1964]. pp. viii, 128, with frontis & 108 illus.

10006 NATIONAL TRAMWAY MUSEUM. The Crich Tramway Museum: official handbook of the Tramway Museum Society . . . , compiled by Dennis Gill. *Birmingham: Tramway Museum Society*, 1964. pp. [56], with 42 illus, a map & a plan.
General information about the Tramway Museum, its foundation and progress, followed by illustrated descriptions of each of the 36 tramcars and a fleet list.
—— rev. edn, revised by J. A. Senior. *T.M.S.*, 1967. pp. 56, 42 exhibits described & illustrated.
The Crich Tramway Museum: official guide. *Birmingham: T.M.S.*, 1968. pp. 32, with 29 illus (5 col.) & map. Prepared by W. G. S. Hyde.
—— 1970 edn. 1970. pp. 40, with 40 illus (12 col.) & map.
—— 1972 edn. 1972. pp. 28 incl. covers, with 36 illus (23 col.) & map.
—— 1975 edn. 1975. pp. 28 incl. covers, with 37 illus (26 col.) & map.
—— 1977 edn. 1977. pp. [20] incl. covers, with 27 illus (25 col.) & map.
—— 1979 edn. 1979. pp. [20] incl. covers, with 27 illus (25 col.); no map.
—— 1981 edn. 1981. pp. [32] incl. covers, with 70 illus (41 col.) & map.

10007 TRUSSLER, D. J. Early buses and trams. *London: Hugh Evelyn*, 1964. la. obl. format. pp. [48]. Preface & 10 col. plates, each interleaved with a commentary and details.
Five buses and five tramcars are depicted and described; three of the tramcars are British, two foreign.

10008 VALLANCE, H. A. British branch lines. *London: Batsford*, 1965. pp. 216, with 87 illus on 48 plates & (pp. 200–07). Summary table of authorisation and opening dates and ownership of branches (5 columns). Index, pp. 209–16.

10009 JOYCE, J. Tramway memories. *London: Ian Allan*, 1967. pp. x, 134, with 74 illus on 32 plates.

10010 ABELL, P. H. British tramways & preserved tramcars. [*Stockport: the author*, 1968]. pp. 40, with 55 illus on 28 plates.
—— 2nd edn. British Tramway Guide.

Sheffield: the author, 1975. pp. 48, with 60 illus on 30 plates & a bibliography.
Working tramways, The National Tramway Museum (Crich) and other museum collections and preserved tramcars.

10011 EDWARDIAN tramcars. *Lingfield: Oakwood Press*, [1968]. pp. [24]. Intro & 44 illus with descrs.
Reproduced from a collection of pictorial postcards owned by A. Wood, with captions by J. H. Price and H. Brearley.

10012 JOWITT, R. E. A Desire of Tramcars. *London: Ian Allan*, 1969. pp. 200, with 242 illus.
Intro, pp. 9–29; 'Trams', p. 31; illustrations of a variety of aspects of the tramway environment in towns in Western Europe, including Britain, with brief captions, pp. 32–200.

10013 SENIOR, D. J. H. Ten years at Crich: the Tramway Museum. *Crich: The Tramway Museum*, 1969. pp. 21, with 55 illus.
Introduction inside front cover.

10014 JOYCE, J. Trams in colour since 1945: illustrations from the collections of W. J. Wyse, J. H. Price, Martin Rickitt and others. *London: Blandford Press*, 1970. pp. 160, 145 col. illus with brief descriptions on pp. 17–96, fully described on pp. 97–150. A list of tramcars in museums, p. 151.

10015 WOODCOCK, G. Minor railways of England and their locomotives, 1900–1939. *Norwich: Goose & Son*, 1970. pp. 192, with 54 illus & 23 line drawings.

10016 JACKSON-STEVENS, E. British electric tramways. *Newton Abbot: David & Charles*, 1971. pp. 112, with col. frontis, 125 illus & (pp. 108–9), a list of towns with tramways, giving dates of opening & closing of lines, and their gauges.

10017 LEE, C. E. Some tramway pioneers, known and unknown. *London: Tramway and Light Railway Society*, 1971. (Walter Gratwicke Memorial Lecture, 1971). pp. 14.
This description is from a proof copy, with typographical corrections made by the author, in Leicester University Library. Regrettably, the work has not yet been published.

10018 [FOWLER]. JOHN FOWLER AND COMPANY (LEEDS). Light railway machinery: locomotives. [Reprint]. *Greenford: Industrial Railway Society*, 1972. obl. format. pp. iii, 36, [ii], with 37 illus.
A facsimile reprint of a catalogue originally published in 1926. The new Introduction by the I.R.S. is an outline history of Fowler steam locomotive manufacture.

10019 HYDE, W. G. S. and PEARSON, F. K. The Dick Kerr Album . . . , designed and produced by W. G. S. Hyde and F. K. Pearson. *Ashton-under-Lyne: the authors*, 1972.

la. obl. format. pp. 51. Intro & 67 illus on 44 plates, of tramcars and of Preston works, with notes.

'A selection from the builders' photographs of the United Electric Car Co. of Preston and its successor, the English Electric Co.' On cover: 'A souvenir of Preston Guild, 1972'.

—— 2nd edn, 1975. pp. 51, with 67 illus on 44 plates.

10020 TURNER, K. Pier railways. *Lingfield: Oakwood Press*, 1972. (Locomotion Papers, 60). pp. 45, with 22 illus on 8 plates & a bibliography (21 sources).

10021 TRAMWAY MUSEUM, [Crich]. Grand Transport Extravaganza: official programme. *Crich: the Tramway Museum*, [1973]. pp. 14, incl. covers, with 9 illus (2 col).

The Tramway Museum's 6th annual 'Extravaganza'. The text consists of six short historical essays, and inserted is a 12-page printed list of the 464 exhibits.

10022 OCHOJNA, A. P. Lines of class distinction: an economic and social history of the British tramcar, with special reference to Edinburgh and Glasgow. Thesis, Ph.D., University of Edinburgh, 1974.

10023 BADDELEY, G. E. and OAKLEY, E. R. Current collection for tramway and trolleybus systems. *Hartley: the authors*, 1975. pp. 112, with 30 illus & over 70 illus (single and multiple).

10024 BUCKLEY, R. J. History of tramways, from horse to rapid transit. *Newton Abbot: David & Charles*, 1975. pp. 184, with 30 illus, 11 diagrams & a bibliography (40 sources).

World coverage.

10025 GAMMELL, C. J. The branch line age: the minor railways of the British Isles in memoriam and retrospect. *Buxton: Moorland Publishing Co.*, 1976. pp. [96], with frontis & 124 illus with commentaries. pp. 88–96, Appendix of closed lines.

10026 McKAY, J. P. Tramways and trolleys: the rise of urban mass transport in Europe. *Princeton (N.J.): Princeton University Press*, 1976. pp. xvi, 266, with 16 illus, 12 tables & an extensive evaluative bibliography (pp. 247–55).

Includes Great Britain.

10027 PRICE, J. H. The Brush Electrical Engineering Company Limited & its tramcars. *[London]: Tramway & Light Railway Society*, 1976. (Walter Gratwicke Memorial Lecture, 1975). pp. 32, with 8 illus & cover illus. Title from cover.

10028 RUSH, R. W. British electric tramcar design, 1885–1950. *Oxford: Oxford Publishing Co.*, 1976. la. 8°. pp. 122, with 70 illus supported by a large number of composite line drawings & a 22-column table of dimensions.

51 classes of provincial tramcar are described. London cars are excluded.

10029 BADDELEY, G. E. Tramway and light railway liveries. *Tramway & Light Railway Society*, 1977. (Walter Gratwicke Memorial Lecture, 1977). pp. 32, with 8 illus & 11 diagrams; bibliography (50 sources).

10030 CORMACK, I. L. and KAYE, D. Trams and trolleybuses: an illustrated history. *Bourne End: Spur Books*, [1977]. pp. 160, with 78 illus, 2 chronologies (pp. 150–6), opening & closing dates of tram and trolleybus systems, & a bibliography (79 sources).

10031 GOODWYN, A. M. The evolution of the British electric tramcar truck, by A. M. Goodwin. *Tramway & Light Railway Society*, 1977. (Walter Gratwicke Memorial Lecture, 1976). pp. 42, with 18 illus & diagrams, & (pp. 38–41) a detailed 5-column table of the manufacturer, type, date, dimensions and allocation of all known varieties.

10032 HENDRY, R. P. Railway documents illustrated; editor, R. Powell Hendry. *Rugby: Isle of Man Railway Society*.

Vol. 1, The minor lines. 1977. pp. [16]. 27 miscellaneous photocopies.

10033 PRICE, J. H. Hurst Nelson tramcars. *Hartley: Nemo Productions*, 1977. pp. 44, with 22 illus & a six-column list (pp. 40–43).

10034 TURNER, K. Discovering trams and tramways. *Aylesbury: Shire Publications*, 1977. (Discovering Series, 231). pp. 64, with 28 illus on 16 plates, & a brief evaluative bibliography (10+ sources).

A stock guide to tramcar preservation in Britain, on working tramways and in museums.

10035 FOLKARD, L. F. British trams: a pictorial survey. *Truro: Bradford Barton*, 1978. pp. 96. Intro, frontis & 114 illus with descrs.

10036 KIDNER, R. W. The carriage stock of minor standard gauge railways. *Tarrant Hinton: Oakwood Press*, 1978. (Locomotion Papers, 109). pp. 50, with 58 illus on 24 plates & many tables & line illus in text.

Accounts of the stock of 130 railways, alphabetically arranged.

10037 MARTIN, B. P. Tramways in Britain. *Sale: Brennan Publications*, 1978. pp. 32, with 23 illus.

Descriptions of tramways currently in operation, tramcars preserved, closures of tramway systems, and societies for tramway history, preservation, and operation.

10038 MORGAN, J. S. The Colonel Stephens railways: a pictorial survey. *Newton Abbot:*

G

David & Charles, 1978. pp. 96, with 132 illus, 17 maps & a bibliography (19 sources).
pp. 92–5, 'Tabular Summary': a 9-column table presenting details of the 16 lines and their locomotives.

10039　PRICE, J. H. The British Electric Car Company . . . , with car design notes by Roy Brook. *Hartley: Nemo Productions*, 1978. pp. 48, with 25 illus & facsimiles, 3 plans, some line drawings and a list of all tramcars built by the company.

10040　THOMPSON, J. British trams in camera. *London: Ian Allan*, 1978. pp. 128, with 218 illus.
Historical accounts of 18 tramway systems in the British Isles, with accompanying illustrations.

10041　CASSERLEY, H. C. Light railways of Britain: standard gauge and narrow gauge. *Truro: Bradford Barton*, 1979. pp. 96. 4°. Frontis, intro & 110 illus with descrs.

10042　JOYCE, J. Trams of the past: photographs from the Whitcombe Collection, edited by J. Joyce. *London: Ian Allan*, 1979. pp. 96. Intro & 205 illus with descrs.
In two parts: a selection from the Whitcombe collection in the Science Museum, London, followed by photographs taken by Dr Whitcombe in the late 1920's.

10043　PRESCOTT-PICKUP & CO. Tramcyclopaedia: tramcars, tramways and trackless trams. *Bridgnorth: the Company*, 1979. (Railed Transport, 3). pp. 60. Text & illus, with descrs.
An album with many illustrations, some coloured, and with blank panels for mounting a set of 60 coloured postcards of tramcars, issued separately.

10044　BURROWS, V. E. The Southerden tramway scene: historic photographs of tramcars, 1925–1935, taken by the late Geoffrey Nevey Southerden. *Falmouth: Glasney Press*, 1980. pp. 112. Foreword by V. E. Burrows, contents list & 101 illus, with descrs.
The contents list is a 4-column table of the tramways represented in the text (name, gauge, mileage, and number of cars).

10045　JARRAM, A. P. The restoration of a Brush-built lower tramcar saloon, Nottingham no. 101; edited by A. P. Jarram [*Burton-on-the-Wolds*]: *British Transport Enthusiasts Club*, 1980. pp. [8]. Reproduced typescript. Title from cover. No illus.
The discovery, acquisition and removal to Loughborough of a derelict Nottingham Corporation tramcar body from a farm in Lincolnshire.

10046　PRICE, J. H. Mountain & Gibson: history of Mountain & Gibson Ltd, 1905–10; the M & G Truck & Engineering Co. Ltd, 1910–1915 . . . *Hartley: Nemo Publications and E. R. Oakley with J. H. Price*, 1980. pp. 60, with 39 illus, drawings and facsimiles.

The history and development of the McGuire family of tramcar truck manufacturers in America and Britain.

10047　PRICE, J. H. A Source Book of Trams. *London: Ward Lock*, 1980. sm. obl. format. pp. 151, with 118 illus & lists of 22 tramways and 16 tramway museums in the British Isles (including 12 cliff railways, and transport museums with tramway exhibits).

10048　QUAYLE, H. I. and JENKINS, S. C. Branch lines into the eighties. *Newton Abbot: David & Charles*, 1980. pp. 96, with 56 illus, 33 maps, 3 plans & a bibliography (73 sources).
Thirty-nine branches; their history and prospects.

10049　SCOTT-MORGAN, J. British independent light railways. *Newton Abbot: David & Charles*, 1980. pp. 96, with 123 illus, 6 drawings, a location map, a 7-column table (pp. 90–95) & a bibliography (21 sources).

10050　VAUGHAN, J. A. M. Modern Branch Line Album. *London: Ian Allan*, 1980. pp. 128. Intro & 246 illus with descrs.
Period, 1960s–1970s.

Contemporaneous

10051　[NOBLE]. JOHN NOBLE & COMPANY. Street railways. Messrs John Noble & Company invite particular attention to the following: official reports on the street railways of several cities in the United States and Canada; also, to the report of Mr Isaacs, the surveyor to the Holborn District Board of Works, on the Metropolitan Tramway Bill; and the opinions of the Liverpool daily papers on the crescent rail as now laid down by permission of the Corporation in Castle Street, Liverpool. *Westminster: printed by G. Phipps*, 1866. pp. 31.　　MCL

10052　OBSERVATIONS on tramways, by a resident. Manchester: *Cave & Sever, printers*, 1870. pp. 22.
Objections outweighed by advantages.　MCL

10053　LIGHT railways: reprints from Liverpool papers, etc. *Widnes: Richard White & Sons*, [1894]. pp. 2.
Three letters from Liverpool newspapers of 23 & 24 November 1894 following a public address by J. Walwyn White to the Liverpool Chamber of Commerce, 22nd November, on the subject of light railways, and a letter from *The Times* of 20 November by Mr. White describing his own narrow gauge railway at Widnes.

10054　LIGHT Railways: conference held at the Westminster Palace Hotel, London . . . 28th November 1895, Sir Albert K. Rollitt in the chair. [*London: Eyre & Spottiswoode, printers, 1895*]. pp. 28.
A privately printed report of the proceedings, with a list of delegates. Held to discuss the need for legislation designed for light railways.

10055 [KOPPEL]. ARTHUR KOPPEL [Light railway engineers]. Locomotive catalogue no. 786. *London: A. Koppel*, [ca. 1905]. la. 8°. [Republished by Barnicotts of Taunton, 1979]. pp. 76, with numerous illustrations & tables.
Locomotives, locomotive parts, and rolling stock.

10056 HOLT, R. B. Tramway track construction and maintenance. *London: Tramway & Railway World Offices*, [1915]. pp. xv, 249, with 160 illus, diagrams and geometrical drawings, with 16 additional geometrical drawings in a chapter (Appendix A) entitled 'Special trackwork calculations' by Ernest Larmuth.
Based on material published in the *Tramway & Railway World*.

10057 ENGLISH ELECTRIC COMPANY. Illustrations of typical tramcars, etc. *London: the Company*, Dec. 1922. (Publication, no. 443). pp. 6, with 10 illus.

10058 MINISTRY OF TRANSPORT. TRAMWAYS COMMITTEE. Tramways and trackless trolley undertakings: report of the committee appointed to consider the form of the return. *London: H.M.S.O.*, 1923. pp. 32. Chairman, A. E. Kirkus.

10059 BRITISH ALUMINIUM COMPANY. Railway and tramway rolling stock. *London: the Company*, 1928. pp. D76–D130. sm. 8°. Intro & 27 illus with captions.
A trade brochure.

10060 BURTON, J. L. The tramcar: present and future . . . , assisted by H. H. Andrews. *London: English Electric Co.*, 1930. pp. 25, with 12 illus.

10061 ENGLISH ELECTRIC COMPANY. New tramcars for Calcutta. *London: the Company*, [1931]. (Tramway Contracts Series, 1001). pp. 11, with 7 illus, 2 diagrams, & a graph.
Reprinted from *Tramway & Railway World*, 4 July 1931.

10062 ENGLISH ELECTRIC COMPANY. 86-seater tramcar for Bombay. *London: the Company*, [1932]. (Tramway Contract Series, no. 1002). pp. 7, with 7 illus & a folded diagram.
Reprinted from *Tramway & Railway World*, 9 June 1932.

10063 ENGLISH ELECTRIC COMPANY. English Electric tramcars & equipments throughout the world. *London: the Company*, June 1932. (Publication, N.76). pp. 7, with world map & 3 illus.

10064 ENGLISH ELECTRIC COMPANY. Modern tramcars for Huddersfield. *London: the Company*, July 1932. (Tramway Contracts Series, 1003). pp. 4, with 4 illus & a diagram.

10065 MINISTRY OF TRANSPORT. Tramways & trolley vehicle undertakings, 1948–49: return of statistics and financial information of tramways, including light railways operated as tramways, and trolley vehicle undertakings, in Great Britain, for financial years ended between 1 April 1948 and 31 March 1949. *London: H.M.S.O.*, 1950. pp. 8, with tables.
—— for 1949–50. 1950. pp. 8, with 15 tables.
Returns from 1880 to 1914 were published as Parliamentary Papers, and from 1918 to 1937 by the Ministry of Transport. No returns were published between 1938 and 1950.

10066 DRUCE, G. Modern tramcar types. *London: Light Railway Transport League*, 1951. obl. format. pp. 16. 15 illus with descrs. No text.

10067 JOYCE, J. Round Britain by tram. *London: Light Railway Transport League*, 1964. pp. 32. Intro & 69 illus with descrs.

10068 PRICE, J. H. Britain's new tramway. [*London*]: *Light Railway Transport League, in conjunction with Crich Tramway Company*, [1965]. pp. 12, with 15 illus & a map.
The National Tramway Museum, Crich, Derbyshire.
First published as an essay in *Modern Tramway*.

10069 TRAMWAY MUSEUM SOCIETY. Crich Tramway Museum bye-laws. *Crich: the Society*, 1965. pp. 10. Reproduced typescript in printed cover.

10070 WALKER, P. J. The new tramway: the case for light railway rapid transit. *Cardiff: Light Railway Transport League*, [1968]. tall 8°. pp. 37, with 4 diagrams & a bibliography (25 sources). Reproduced typescript in printed cover.
A comprehensive but non-technical account of the characteristics and potentialities of modern tramway engineering (civil & mechanical) and operation, with chapters on costs and on comparisons with other modes of urban public passenger transport.

10071 HOWSON, H. F. The rapid transit railways of the world. *London: Allen & Unwin*, 1971. pp. 183, with 83 illus on 40 plates.
Includes Glasgow, London, Manchester, and Liverpool.

10072 DE LEUW, CHADWICK, O HEOCHA. A study of intermediate-capacity rapid transit systems: a report prepared for the Department of the Environment. *London: the Department*, 1972. pp. iv, [125].

10073 GRANT, B. E. and RUSSELL, W. J. Opportunities in automated urban transport. *Crowthorne: Transport Research Assessment Group*, 1973. tall 8°. pp. 46, with many illus, diagrams, maps, tables & graphs.

Produced for TRAG by Robert Matthew, Johnson-Marshall & Partners to illustrate the possibilities presented by new automated tracked vehicle systems for urban public transport (Minitram and Cabtrack).

10074   WATERS, M. H. L. Minitram: the TRRL programme. *Crowthorne: Transport & Road Research Laboratory*, 1973. pp. 7 with 2 tables & 5 bibliogr. notes.
Paper read at the Moving People in Cities Conference at the TRRL, 5 & 6 April 1973.

10075   FOWLER, P. J. DMU's countrywide. *Truro: Bradford Barton*, 1976. pp. 96. Intro, frontis & 103 illus with descrs.
Diesel trains on secondary lines.

10076   TRAMWAY MUSEUM SOCIETY. Opera-tions Handbook. *Crich: T.M.S.*, 1976. pp. 14 (1 folded).

10077   LIGHT RAILWAY TRANSPORT LEAGUE. Light rapid transit: the city system. [*London: L.R.T.L.*], [1979?]. pp. [12] incl. covers, with 10 illus.
A brief statement of the main advantages, with illustrations of European systems in operation.

10078   PENNELL, H. Light rail systems and London: a select bibliography. *London: Greater London Council*, August 1980. (Research Documents Guide, 6). la. 8°. pp. 4. Reproduced typescript.
20 sources (books, periodicals & reports, 1967–1980), with annotations.

D 2   NARROW GAUGE RAILWAYS

Railways with gauges less than 4ft 8½in. (standard gauge) down to 12¼in.

10079–98

For narrow gauge industrial and mineral railways see **D 3**

For miniature railways see **D 6**

Note: Narrow gauge railways are generally distinguishable from miniature railways by the degree to which the locomotives, rolling stock and rail gauge are scaled down; this being less severe in narrow gauge practice than is customary with miniature railways. But at least one narrow gauge line – the Fairbourne Rly – has a gauge of 12¼in., *less* than that of the Romney, Hythe & Dymchurch Rly, a 15 in. miniature railway.

The essential difference centres upon the design of the locomotives. Narrow gauge locomotives allow the driver to sit, if not to stand, in his cab, and traditionally, to have space enough for a fireman. On miniature railways this practical, indeed, humane, requirement, has to take second place to the over-riding principle that the locomotives must be standard gauge prototypes in miniature. This means that the driver must *squat* in his cab and look ahead over the roof.

10079   The RAILWAY problem and the railways of the future. *London: printed by Waterlow & Son*, 1870. pp. 53.
'Reprinted from *The Times*, 19th, 20th, 21st October 1869 and 18th February and 1st March 1870.'
The advantages of narrow gauge over standard gauge railways, R. F. Fairlie's bogie-carriages and his double-bogie locomotive 'Little Wonder' of the Festiniog Rly.

10080   [WHITE]. RICHARD WHITE & SONS. Light railways: reprints from Liverpool papers, etc. *Widnes: R White & Sons, railway engineers*, [1894]. pp. 2.
Reports of three addresses by J. Walwyn White and a letter to *The Times* advocating narrow gauge railways for agriculture and industry.   LU(THC)

10081   MAWSON, E. O. Pioneer irrigation: a manual of information for farmers in the colonies, by E. O. Mawson, with additional chapters on light railways by E. R. Calthrop. *London: Crosby Lockwood*, 1904. pp. xvi, 260, iv, 16, with 39 illus, 91 drawings & diagrams, & 8 appendices with tables.
ch. 9 (pp. 172–91), 'Light railways in relation to irrigated lands', by E. R. Calthrop; ch. 10 (pp. 192–215), 'The choice of gauge and rolling stock for light railways', by E. R. Calthrop.
The two chapters by E. R. Calthrop contain much that is applicable to light railways wherever constructed, including hilly & mountainous terrain such as that in North Wales. Gauges of 2ft. 6 inches or 2ft. are recommended, according to expected weight of train loads.

10082   DEWHURST, P. C. The 'Fairlie' locomotive: part 1, The formative period. Paper,

Newcomen Society, 4th April, 1962. pp. 18 & lists (2pp). of locomotives. Reproduced typescript.

10083 INDUSTRIAL LOCOMOTIVE SOCIETY. Steam on the narrow gauge: a collection . . . *Dawlish: David & Charles,* 1965. obl. format. pp. 48. Intro & 45 illus with descrs.

10084 DAVIES, W. J. K. Light railways of the First World War: a history of tactical rail communications on the British fronts, 1914–18. *Newton Abbot: David & Charles,* 1967. pp. 196, with frontis, 58 illus on 24 plates, 35 maps & diagrams, 14 tables & a bibliography (22 sources).
Railways laid down and operated by the Royal Engineers Railway Operating Division.

10085 NARROW GAUGE RAILWAY MUSEUM. A Description of The Narrow Gauge Railway Museum. *Towyn: the Museum,* [ca. 1968]. sm. obl. format. pp. [7], with 6 illus.

10086 ABBOTT, R. A. S. The Fairlie locomotive. *Newton Abbot: David & Charles,* 1970. pp. 103, with frontis, 70 illus, 13 diagrams & working drawings, detailed tables (pp. 85–88) & a bibliography.

10087 BOYD, J. I. C. The Narrow Gauge Railway Museum, Towyn, Merioneth, Wales. *Lingfield: Oakwood Press, on behalf of the Museum,* 1972. pp. 27, with 24 illus and a list of exhibits.

10088 BUCK, J. Discovering narrow gauge railways. *Aylesbury: Shire Publications,* 1972. sm. 8°. pp. 80, with 23 illus on 16 plates; map.
An introduction to 29 railways including minor gauge lines.

10089 MESSENGER, M. J. British narrow gauge Steam. *Truro: Bradford Barton,* 1973. pp. 95. Intro & 111 illus with descrs.

10090 MESSENGER, M. J. More British narrow gauge Steam. *Truro: Bradford Barton,* 1974. pp. 96. Intro & 110 illus with descrs.

10091 PETERS, I. The narrow gauge charm of yesterday. *Oxford: Oxford Publishing,* 1976. la. 8°. pp. [128]. Intro & 250 illus with descrs, 7 maps & a gradient profile.
Passenger railways and industrial lines in the British Isles.

10092 PRIDEAUX, J. D. C.A. The Welsh narrow gauge railway: a pictorial history. *Newton Abbot: David & Charles,* 1976. pp. 96, with 123 illus, map, a tabular summary (pp. 92–6) & a bibliography (27 sources).

10093 PRIDEAUX, J. D. C.A. The English narrow gauge railway: a pictorial history. *Newton Abbot: David & Charles,* 1978. pp. 96. Intro (pp. 5–9), map, & 125 illus with detailed notes; tables (pp. 92–5).

10094 BROCKHAM MUSEUM. Museum Guide. 1st edn, compiled by C. G. Down, revised by D. H. Smith. *Haywards Heath: Brockham Museum Association,* 1979. pp. 24, with 22 illus, map, 8 diagrams & plans.
A ½ mile line of 2ft gauge is used to demonstrate the adaptabilities of narrow gauge rail traction.

10095 CASSERLEY, H. C. Light railways of Britain: standard gauge and narrow gauge. *Truro: Bradford Barton,* 1979. 4°. pp. 96. Frontis, intro & 110 illus with descrs.

10096 HENDRY, R. P. Narrow gauge story. *Rugby: Hillside Publishing Co.,* 1979. la. 8°. pp. 128, with 214 illus, facsims, tables.
A diverse selection of lines in Britain & Ireland: steam, electric, pleasure ground systems and some industrial lines.

10097 HARRIS, M. On the British narrow gauge. *London: Ian Allan,* 1980. pp. 128. 198 illus with descrs & 4 introductory essays.

10098 HEAVYSIDE, G. T. Narrow gauge into the eighties. *Newton Abbot: David & Charles,* 1980. pp. 96. Intro (pp. 5–11), 147 illus with descrs, & 3 location maps.
Within the text are seven regional essays, and accounts of the Romney, Hythe & Dymchurch Rly and the Talyllyn Rly. In all, 34 railways are described & illustrated.

D 3   INDUSTRIAL, MINERAL, DOCK, HARBOUR, AND PUBLIC UTILITIES SYSTEMS

10099–10128

For dock and harbour railways owned and operated by railway undertakings see **G 5** *for general works,* **L** *for individual companies and* **B 10** *for British Railways*

10099 INDUSTRIAL RAILWAY SOCIETY. Industrial locomotives of Great Britain. *Crewe: the Society.*
3rd edn, 1973. pp. 320; 32 illus on 16 plates.
4th edn, 1976. pp. 318; 32 illus on 16 plates.

5th edn, 1979. pp. 339; no illus. Includes miniature locomotives.

10100 PECKETT & SONS. Some views in the workshops and a few examples of the locomotives built therein . . . *Bristol: the firm,* [ca. 1910]. obl. format. pp. 78, with frontis, map, 69 illus & an embossed illus on covers.

Tank locomotives for industrial use.   LU(THC)

10101 BRITISH IRON AND STEEL RESEARCH ASSOCIATION. Conference on Works Transport held at Ashorne Hill . . . , July 6th & 7th, 1954. Chairman, W. F. Cartwright. *London: the Association*, [1954]. pp. 44.

Ten papers with discussions, concluding remarks and three appendices.

10102 INDUSTRIAL LOCOMOTIVE SOCIETY. Steam on the narrow gauge: a collection . . . *Dawlish: David & Charles*, 1965. obl. format. pp. 48. Intro & 45 illus with descrs.

10103 EVANS, R. C. Industrial steam locomotives of central England: a review of the remaining steam locomotives on industrial systems in the Midlands, compiled by R. C. Evans; photographs by R. Hickman. *Knowle (Warks).: Warwickshire Railway Society*, 1966. pp. 36. Lists, with 10 illus.

10104 INDUSTRIAL LOCOMOTIVE SOCIETY. Steam locomotives in industry. *Newton Abbot: David & Charles*, 1967. la. 8°. pp. 127, with intro (pp. 9–18), frontis & 152 illus with descrs.

10105 COOKE, D. N. Industrial steam locomotives of North East and North West England: a review of the remaining steam locomotives on industrial systems in the North, compiled by D. N. Cooke; photographs by D. Alexander, R. P. Hickman & R. Monk. *Knowle: Warwickshire Railway Society*, 1968. pp. 32. Lists, with 14 illus.

10106 COOKE, D. N. Industrial steam locomotives of Southern England and South Wales. *Knowle: Warwickshire Railway Society*, [1967–8]. pp. 36.

10107 YOUNG, I. D. Register of Industrial Locomotives: South Lancashire and North Cheshire. *Liverpool: Liverpool University Public Transport Society, via B. J. Towey*, [1968]. pp. 14, incl. covers. Reproduced typescript.

10108 COOKE, D. N. Industrial steam locomotives of Lancashire, Yorkshire and Cheshire: a review of the remaining steam locomotives on industrial systems on both sides of the Pennines, compiled by D. N. Cooke; photographs by R. Monk. *Knowle: Warwickshire Railway Society*, 1969. pp. 36, with 16 illus.

10109 CROMBLEHOLME, R. Sir Berkeley: the story of a Manning Wardle [locomotive]. *Bracknell: Town and Country Press*, 1969. pp. 36, with 12 illus & a genealogical table of Manning Wardle & Co.

An 0-6-0 industrial locomotive adopted by the Keighley & Worth Valley Rly Preservation Society.

10110 INDUSTRIAL RAILWAY SOCIETY. British industrial locomotives; edited by A. Roy Etherington, Peter S. Excell and Eric S. Tonks. *Great Sutton: Industrial Railway Society*. (Pocket Book EL). 2 parts.

part 1, [Anglesey to Rutland]. 1969. pp. v, 139, with 16 illus on 8 plates.

part 2, [Shropshire to Yorkshire, Scotland, Ministry of Defence Army Dept, National Coal Board, Ireland]. 1969. pp. v, 140–248, with 16 illus on 8 plates.

10111 PENRHYN CASTLE INDUSTRIAL RAILWAY MUSEUM. Handbook. *National Trust*, [1969?]. pp. 24, with 24 illus.

—— Supplement, 1970. pp. viii.

—— 2nd edn compiled by K. A. Jaggers and I. W. Jones. 1974. pp. 32, with 42 illus.

10112 ETHERINGTON, A. R. National Coal Board surface systems, 1967–1969; edited by A. R. Etherington. *Crewe: Industrial Railway Society*, 1970. (British Industrial Locomotives: Pocket Book N.C.B).. pp. 90, with 24 illus on 12 plates.

Detailed lists.

10113 FOX, M. J. and KING, G. D. Industrial Steam Album [no.1]. *London: Ian Allan*, 1970. pp. 144. Intro & 234 illus with descrs.

—— no. 2, *Ian Allan*, 1976. pp. 136. Intro & 212 illus (10 col.).

10114 INDUSTRIAL RAILWAY SOCIETY. Industrial preserved and minor railway locomotives in Great Britain. *Great Sutton: the Society*. (Pocket Book EL).

pt. 1, England & Wales. vol. 1, Anglesey to Rutland. 2nd edn 1970. pp. viii, 138, with 16 illus on 8 plates. Lists.

pt. 2, Shropshire to Yorkshire, Scotland, Ministry of Defence, National Coal Board, Ireland. 2nd edn, 1970. pp. vii, 139–269, with 12 illus on 6 plates. Lists.

10115 YOUNG, I. D. The locomotives of Peckett and Sons. *Liverpool: Liverpool University Public Transport Society*, [1970]. pp. 21. Reproduced typescript with illus on cover.

All Fox Walker and Peckett locomotives known or believed to exist on 1st August 1969: pp. 2–5, general survey; pp. 5–21, lists.

10116 LELEUX, S. A. Brooke's industrial railway. *Lingfield: Oakwood Press*, 1972. (Locomotion Papers, 63). pp. 41, with 21 illus on 8 plates, 6 layout plans & a diagram.

The quarry railways of Joseph Brooke & Sons, pioneer manufacturers of concrete paving and suppliers of road surface material, at Lightcliffe, near Halifax (pp. 5–28), and in Alderney (Channel Islands Granite Co)., Frodingham (Lincs), Penmaenbach (North Wales Granite Co)., Tan-y-Grisiau (Moel Ystradau Quarries), Tunstall, (Staffs. Tarbitumac, Ltd) and two lines in Scandinavia.

10117 TONKS, E. S. Former British Rail diesel locomotives in industrial service. *Wistanston: Industrial Railway Society*, 1972. pp. 24, with 13 illus.

A listing in 10 columns.

10118 GARRATT, C. D. Masterpieces in Steam. *London: Blandford*, 1973. pp. 204, with 61 col. illus on 80 plates (i.e. pp. 13–92).

European locomotives (Gt. Britain, Finland, France, Italy, Austria, West Germany, Yugoslavia), including 22 from British industrial railway systems.

10119 TONKS, E. S. Ruston & Hornsby locomotives. *Greenford: Industrial Railway Society*, 1974. pp. 92, with 79 illus & a layout plan.

Diesel locomotives, with detailed listings on pp. 77–92.

10120 HALL, V. F. Industrial steam locomotives. *Moorland Publishing Co*, [1975]. pp. 96. Intro (pp. 7–10), frontis, & 127 illus with commentaries and a list of preserved locomotives.

10121 NICHOLSON, P. D. Industrial narrow gauge railways in Britain. *Truro: Bradford Barton*, 1975. pp. 96. Intro & 129 illus with descrs.

Period, 1950s–1970s.

10122 BOOTH, A. J. Industrial Steam. *Truro: Bradford Barton*, 1976. pp. 96. Intro & 113 illus with descrs.

10123 BRIDGES, A. J. Industrial locomotives of Scotland, edited by Alan Bridges. *Market Harborough: Industrial Railway Society*, 1976. (Pocket Book Series, N). pp. vi, 296, with 112 illus on 56 plates.

10124 GIFFORD, C. T. and GAMBLE, H. Steam railways in industry. *London: Batsford*, 1976. pp. 96, with 141 illus & descrs.

10125 BOOTH, A. J. A Pictorial Survey of industrial diesels around Britain. *Truro: Bradford Barton*, 1977. pp. 64. Intro, list, & 126 illus with detailed descrs.

10126 HEAVYSIDE, G. T. Steam in the coalfields. *Newton Abbot: David & Charles*, 1977. pp. 16, [17–96], with 114 illus with descrs, a map & 5 layout plans.

Arranged under National Coal Board coalfield areas.

10127 CAVALIER, P. and SILCOCK, G. Visions of Steam: the four seasons of steam in industrial South Wales. *Oxford: Oxford Publishing Co*, 1979. obl. format. pp. [120]. Intro, map, & 138 illus, with captions in English and Welsh.

Environment photographs by Peter Cavalier and Geoff Silcock, 1960s & 70s.

10128 LANE, K. Industrial railways of the British Isles. *Oxford: Oxford Publishing Co*. la. 8°. vol. 1, Steam. 1979. pp. [96]. 130 illus with descrs.

D 4   ELECTRIC AND UNDERGROUND RAILWAYS

10129–34

For electric tramways see **D 1** *for general works and* **C** *for tramways in particular localities*
For individual underground railway systems see **C**
For the Post Office (London) Railway see **K 9**
For electric railway engineering and the electrification of railways see **E 4**

10129 PARSHALL, H. F. and HOBART, H. M. Electric railway engineering. *London: A. Constable*, 1907. la. 8°. pp. xxiv, 475, with 437 illus (some folded) & 123 tables.

10130 BRITISH ELECTRICAL POWER CONVENTION [Torquay, May 1956]. British Electrical Power Convention. *London: Railway Gazette*, 1956. pp. 38, with 23 illus & a map.

Principally concerned with railway electrification and electric traction, and the implementation of B.T.C.'s Modernisation Plan (January 1955).

10131 JACKSON, A. A. Inside underground railways . . . , drawings by John W. Wood. *London: Ian Allan*, 1964. (Inside Stories series). pp. 64, with 43 line drawings & a bibliography (12 sources).

The modern underground railway described; ch. 1, historical. An informative introductory work.

10132 COOPER, B. K. Electric railways. *London:* *Ian Allan*, 1965. sm. 8°. pp. 67, with 29 illus on 16 plates, & in text, 12 drawings & diagrams.

10133 HOPE, R. and YEARSLEY, I. Urban railways and rapid transit. *London: I.P.C. Business Press*, 1972. (Railway Gazette Management Study Manual, 1). la. 8°. pp. 95, with many illus, drawings, maps, diagrams & tables. Foreword by John Hibbs.

A selection of articles from the *Railway Gazette* on the salient features of urban rail planning and operation, with a new introduction to each of the six sections.

10134 DAY, J. R. A Source Book of Underground Railways. *London: Ward Lock*, 1980. sm. obl. format. pp. 128, with 126 illus.

World coverage, historical, from London's Metropolitan Rly (1863) to the present automated Rapid Transit. No bibliography.

D 5 UNUSUAL FORMS OF RAILWAY AND LOCOMOTION

General, monorail, atmospheric, pneumatic, elevated, suspension, cable,
cliff (funiculars), lifts (elevators), escalators, travolators, minirail, minitram,
rack railways, hovertrains, linear induction, etc.

10135–63

Historical 10135–41
Contemporaneous 10142–63

Historical

10135 WALKER, H. C. Reminiscences of 70 years
in the lift industry. *Printed for the author,*
[1934]. pp. 100, with 88 illus.
Reminiscences of 68 years (1865–1933) in the
service of Waygood Otis, lift manufacturers,
latterly as Chairman.
For a history of the Otis Elevator Co., the
parent company in the U.S.A., see *The First
Hundred Years*, a 44 page booklet, with illustrations published by the firm in New York, 1953.
Copies of both works in LU(THC)

10136 HARRODS OF KNIGHTSBRIDGE. A story
of British achievement, 1849–1949. [*London: Harrods Ltd.*, 1949]. 4°. pp. 58, with 31
illus (11 col. & double spread).
A history of Harrods, including (pp. 34–5) the
installation of Britain's first escalator (1898).

10137 BODY, G. and EASTLEIGH, R. L. Cliff
railways of the British Isles, including inclined cliff lifts and passenger cableways.
*Dawlish: David & Charles; Enfield: Trans-
rail Publications*, 1964. pp. 48, with 27 illus.

10138 CLAYTON, H. The atmospheric railways.
Lichfield: the author, 1966. pp. 142, with 39
illus (4 folded).

10139 HADFIELD, C. Atmospheric railways: a
Victorian venture in silent speed. *Newton
Abbot: David & Charles*, 1967. pp. 240,
with 24 plates, & in text, 15 drawings, maps,
facsimiles & diagrams, & a bibliography (68
sources).

10140 PRIGMORE, B. J. Lifts and escalators, by
members of a final year group project
supervised by B. J. Prigmore. *London:
Imperial College of Science & Technology*,
May 1968. tall 8°. pp. 60, with 20 diagrams
& over 150 bibliographical notes (mostly
technical, & patent specifications). Reproduced typescript.
pt. 1, Lifts from earliest times until 1920, by
R. E. Allen.
pt. 2, Lifts from 1920 to 1960, by R. E.
Peckham.
pt. 3, Modern lifts from 1960, by J. S. Butler.
pt. 4, Passenger traffic control, by R. B. Kemp.
pt. 5, Lift safety, by R. B. Kemp.
pt. 6, Escalators, by K. N. Pragnell.

10141 WILKES, R. E. Louis Brennan, C.B.:
gyroscopic monorail. *Gillingham: Gillingham Public Libraries*, 1973. (Local History
Series, 5). Reproduced typescript in printed
covers.

part 1, Dirigible torpedo. [1973]. pp. 23, with 1
illus; bibliography (pp. 20–22).
part 2, Gyroscopic monorail. [1973]. pp. 30,
with 1 illus; bibliography (pp. 29–30).

Contemporaneous

10142 FARRELL, I. The Archimedean Railway: a
letter to Peter Purcell, Esq., chairman of
the Great Southern and Western Railway,
etc., etc., etc. *Dublin*, 1845. la. 8°. pp. 9,
with 2 folded diagrams.
Motion derived from a continuous longitudinal
screw laid between the rails, a system used 79
years later for the 'Never-Stop Railway' at the
British Empire Exhibition, Wembley.

10143 PNEUMATIC COMPANY. Proposed
pneumatic tube, Euston Square to Gresham
Street, London. *London: Pneumatic Co.*,
1872. pp. 9, with map & illus.
The report of William Henry Barlow, consulting
engineer to the Midland Rly Co., as to experiments concerning the practicability of adapting the
tube for the conveyance of parcels and goods from
the Midland Rly goods station at Agar Town (St.
Pancras) into the City.

10144 KEARNEY HIGH SPEED TUBE RAILWAY
COMPANY. The Kearney High Speed Tube
Railway. [*London: the Company*, 1925].
A printed folder with 7 illus, plan of a proposed
suspension line in a tunnel under the Tyne
between North Shields and South Shields (½ mile
in length), and an excerpt from *The Times* of 8
January 1925 by Col. Moore Brabazon headed
'More tubes needed'.

10145 BLYTH, H. Modern telpherage and ropeways, with a section on cableways and cable
cranes. *London: E. Benn*, 1926. la. 8°. pp.
xvi, 156, with 64 illus on plates, & in text, 63
diagrams & 6 tables.

10146 ANNETT, F. A. Electric elevators: their
design, construction, operation and
maintenance. 1st edn. *New York, London:
McGraw-Hill Book Co.*, 1927. pp. xii, 447,
with 351 illus & diagrams.
Electric and electro-hydraulic elevators, escalators, moving sidewalks and ramps.
—— 2nd edn, 1935. pp. xiv, 495, with 346
illus & diagrams.
—— 3rd edn, 1960. pp. xi, 388, with 290
illus & diagrams.

10147 BOOT, C. A scheme for the abolition of
large slum areas. [*London?: the author?*],
printed by McCorquodale, [ca. 1931?] pp.
46, with 19 mounted illus & a folded col.
map.

A scheme for a 'rail-plane' route from Waltham Abbey via Tottenham, Walthamstow, Leyton, West Ham & Dagenham. Illustrations include the experimental rail-plane mono-rail system (of George Bennie) erected over the LNER near Milngavie, Strathclyde, in July 1930.

10148 PHILLIPS, R. S. Electric lifts: a manual on the current practice in the installation, working and maintenance of lifts. *London: Sir Isaac Pitman*, 1939. pp. x, 293, with 191 illus & 4 appendices (relevant sections of the Factories Act, 1937) & tables.
—— 2nd edn. *Pitman*, 1947. pp. x, 340, with 209 illus & diagrams, 6 appendices & a bibliography (21 sources).
—— 3rd edn. *Pitman*, 1951. pp. xii, 377, with 211 illus & diagrams, bibliography (27 sources), & 6 appendices.
—— 4th edn. *Pitman*, 1958. pp. x, 411, with 235 illus & diagrams (5 folded), bibliography (35 sources) & 5 appendices.
—— 5th edn. *Pitman*, 1966. pp. x, 485, with ca. 150 illus & numerous diagrams (some folded) & graphs; bibliography (54 sources).
Includes lifts for multi-storey buildings.
—— 6th edn. *Pitman*, 1973. pp. xi, 515, with over 150 illus, etc.; bibliography (66 sources).
Includes a chapter on 'paternosters'.

10149 HONEY, L. W. Lifts: a collation of British legislation and authoritative publications together with recommendations for lift design and installation. *London: Marryat & Scott*, 1946. pp. 223, with 19 illus, numerous diagrams & tables, & a list (pp. 155–85) of electricity supply undertakings in the British Isles, with their respective voltages.

10150 BRITISH RAILWAYS. SOUTHERN REGION. Britain's first travolator, at the Bank Station, Waterloo & City Line: the facts . . . [*London: B.R. (SR)*, 1959]. pp. [9], with illus, diagrams & a folded plan. Title on cover only.
A publicity booklet with a 6-fold plan of the travolator.

10151 TAYLOR WOODROW CONSTRUCTION. Taylor Woodrow/Safege monorail. *Southall: the firm*, [1965]. obl. format. pp. 30, with 22 diagrams & 3 illus.

10152 GREATER LONDON COUNCIL. DEPARTMENT OF HIGHWAYS & TRANSPORTATION. Monorails in London: a preliminary assessment of the feasibility of monorails, and some possible alternatives, for passenger distribution in Central London. *London: G.L.C.*, 1967. la. 8°. pp. [vi], 40, with 10 illus, diagrams (1 folded), maps, & a bibliography (9 sources).

10153 STRAKOSCH, G. R. Vertical transportation: elevators and escalators. *New York, London & Sydney: John Wiley*, 1967. pp. xii, 365, with illus & many diagrams & tables.

10154 WAGER, D. and FRISCHMANN, W. West End Minirail: a preliminary study for a fine-mesh transport system in central areas; with particular reference to the West End of London. *London: Construction Publications*, 1967. obl. format. pp. 13, with numerous maps, diagrams & a sketch drawing.

10155 SMITH, J. E. R. Automatic taxi studies. *London: Greater London Council*, 1969. (Research Memoranda, 156). pp. 5.
Report of a feasibility study on an automated elevated cabtrack system for urban areas. Route prescribed by ticket selected.

10156 WRIXON, T. Britain's hovertrain plans. *London & Cambridge: Tracked Hovercraft Ltd*, [1969]. A printed folder, with 5 illus & diagrams.
Reprinted from *Air Cushion Vehicles* [periodical], November 1969.

10157 TOUGH, J. M. and O'FLAHERTY, C. A. Passenger conveyors: an innovatory form of communal transport. *London: Ian Allan*, 1971. pp. 176, with 23 illus on 16 plates, 36 diagrams, drawings & charts; pp. 147–62, Directory of the main passenger conveyor installations throughout the world; pp. 163–8, bibliography (157 sources).

10158 TRACKED HOVERCRAFT LTD. The Hovertrain. *London: the firm*, 1971. publicity folder with 2 illus, 2 diagrams & a graph.
Includes an illustrated account of the evolution of Hovertrain track design from 1961 to 1971.

10159 TRANSPORT AND ROAD RESEARCH LABORATORY. Comparative assessment of new forms of inter-city transport. *Crowthorne: T.R.R.L.*
vol. 1, 1970. (Supplementary Report, 1).
vol. 2, Appendices. 1971. (Supplementary Report, 2).
vol. 3, Final Report. 1971. (Supplementary Report, 3).

10160 TRACKED HOVERCRAFT LTD. Technology in transport: application of new developments. *London & Cambridge: the firm*, [1972]. tall 8°. pp. [16], with 28 illus & diagrams.
Hovertrains: air cushion, magnetic, & suspension systems; linear induction motors; monorail 'guideway' track design.

10161 [MATTHEW]. ROBERT MATTHEW, JOHNSON-MARSHALL AND PARTNERS. Minitram in Sheffield: a report of civil engineering, planning and operational studies to examine the feasibility of a Minitram system in the centre of Sheffield. *London: the firm*, 1974. la. 8°. pp. 87, with many illus, maps, plans & diagrams (some col.).
A project commissioned by the Transport & Road Research Laboratory of the Department of the Environment.
—— Appendix: Minitram guideway in inner city and suburban settings. January

1975. pp. 65, with many illus, plans & diagrams related to 13 site studies.
—— Appendix: Minitram in Castle Square. January 1975. pp. [10], with illus & diagrams.

10162 [MATTHEW]. ROBERT MATTHEW, JOHNSON-MARSHALL AND PARTNERS. Transport for countryside recreation: a report prepared for the Countryside Commission. *Cheltenham: Countryside Commission*, May 1974. tall 8°. pp. [ii], iii, 114.
Discusses (pp. 25–38) a wide variety of tracked systems for conveying visitors in recreational areas, with 8 illus & 5 tables.

10163 MURRAY, J. The Dingwall and Ben Wyvis Railway: a prospectus to build Scotland's first mountain line, by John Murray. *Bridge of Allan: the author*, 1979. sm. obl. format. pp. 42, with 37 illus (12 col)., 5 drawings, 5 maps, 2 diagrams, gradient profile, timetable, & train frequency planning graph.
A detailed draft scheme for a standard-gauge rack railway of 5.8 miles from BR's Kyle line.
Not a prospectus in the business sense of the term—there is no appeal for investment, no share application form to detach and no address to which to write for further information. The LU(THC) copy has two single-sheet inserts; 1, a summary of the scheme, and 2, a twelve-point outline of the advantages of rack railways. This is headed 'SLM' and is dated 25/9/78.

D 6   MINIATURE RAILWAYS

Passenger-carrying railways of 2ft gauge or less with locomotives, rolling stock and track scaled down to conform as far as possible to the relative proportions on full-size railways
10164–70

For the difference between miniature railways and narrow gauge railways see the note at the head of **D 2**

For garden railways and for model engineering see **Q 2**

10164 LEITHEAD, R. H. Miniature Railways Stockbook and Guide. *Surbiton: Narrotrack*, 1975. pp. 32, with 18 illus.
A directory of 124 locations with brief descriptions (details of gauge, locomotives, length of track, & notes). A further 84 locations are appended, of lines run by model engineering societies, or at holiday centres, and of museums exhibiting model steam locomotives of 7¼ inch gauge and over.

10165 BASSETT-LOWKE LTD. The Bassett-Lowke Catalogue of 15in. gauge miniature railways and equipment. *Northampton: Bassett-Lowke*, April 1914. pp. 22, with 30 illus & diagrams. Cover title: Scale Models.

10166 BUTTERELL, R. Miniature railways. *London: Ian Allan*, [1966]. sm. 8°. pp. 72, with 65 illus.
63 lines described (7¼in to 2ft gauges), with tabulated details of locomotives, rolling stock, track, and length of line.

10167 CLAYTON, H., JACOT, M. and BUTTERELL, R. Miniature railways. [*Lingfield*]: *Oakwood Press*.
vol. 1, 15 inch [gauge]. [1971]. pp. 129, with 51 illus on 24 plates; bibliography (12 sources).

10168 STEEL, E. A. and STEEL, E. H. The miniature world of Henry Greenly. *Kings Langley: Model & Allied Publications*, 1973. pp. 251, with frontis (portrait) & 105 illus & diagrams, & a bibliography (58

sources), including Henry Greenly's published works.
Henry Greenly was the leading figure in the development of minor-gauge passenger-carrying railways pioneered by Sir Arthur Heywood in the 1870s and was consultant and designer of twenty-two lines constructed from 1904 to 1938 and of twenty-eight 15-inch gauge steam locomotives, the author of nineteen books on small-scale locomotive engineering and of numerous essays in thirty periodicals.
This biography, compiled from research into documentary material accumulated by Mr. Greenly and from the author's close acquaintance with him (Elenora H. Steel being his daughter) reveals H. G. as the J. S. Bach of the world of miniature railways. This being so, the story of his life is to a large extent the story of the development of that branch of railway engineering in which he played so prominent a part. The main elements in H.G.'s career, apart from his prodigious literary work, were associated with Wenman Joseph Bassett-Lowke, the Ravenglass & Eskdale Railway and most important of all, the Romney, Hythe & Dymchurch Railway which he designed throughout, locomotives, bridges, buildings and all!

10169 ADAMS, J. H. L. and WHITEHOUSE, P. B. Model and miniature railways. *London: Hamlyn; New English Library*, 1976. magazine format. pp. 512. Profusely illustrated. Issued serially.

10170 BUTTERELL, R. Steam on Britain's miniature railways, 7¼ inch to 15 inch gauge. *Truro: Bradford Barton*, 1976. pp. 96, with frontis & 115 illus with notes.

E RAILWAY ENGINEERING (Civil and Mechanical)

The physical features of railways (generally)—The railway scene—
The visual impact of railways—Archaeology of railways (in general)

10171–10210

For mechanical engineering see **E 6 – E 16**
For structural engineering see **E 5**
For museums and preservation see **Q 1**

Reference sources   10171–73
Historical   10174–92
Contemporaneous   10193–10210

Reference sources

10171 WEXLER, P. J. La formation du vocabu-
laire des chemins de fer en France, 1778–
1842. *Genève et Lille: Société du Publications Romanes et Françaises*, 1955. (Publication, 48). pp. 160, with many notes & an
extensive bibliography of MS & printed
sources (pp. 138–59).
Includes many references to railways in Britain
and their terminology.

10172 NOCK, O. S. The Railway Enthusiast's
Encyclopaedia. *London: Hutchinson*, 1968.
pp. 341, with illus, chronology (pp. 13–20),
biographies of 93 personalities (pp. 311–33)
& a bibliography (pp. 223–41) of 106
sources.
British railway development, largely in mechanical engineering.
—— [Paperback edn]. *London: Arrow
Books*, 1970. pp. 316.

10173 COSSONS, N. The BP Book of Industrial
Archaeology. *Newton Abbot: David &
Charles*, 1975. pp. 496, with 103 illus. & 31
line drawings, a gazetteer of sites (pp.
428–50), list of museums (pp. 451–7), list of
organisations (pp. 458–75), & a bibliography (pp. 476–88). Index (pp. 489–96).
Railways: pp. 366–99 *et passim*.

Historical

10174 LOXTON, H. Railways. *London: Hamlyn*,
1963. la. 8°. pp. 152, with frontis, ca. 300
illus (some col.).
A picture history of railway technology. 36
essays on various aspects of railways 'on the
ground'. Worldwide coverage.
—— rev. edn, *Hamlyn*, 1968. pp. 152.
—— rev. edn, *Hamlyn*, 1970. pp. 152.

10175 MURPHY, J. S. and KEEPING, C. Railways. *London: Oxford University Press*,
1964. (How They were Built series). pp. 32,
with illus.
An informative introductory work. Text by J. S.
Murphy; illustrations by C. Keeping.

10176 SIMMONS, T. M. Railways. *London:
H.M.S.O.* (Science Museum Booklets).
vol. 1, To the end of the nineteenth century.
1964. pp. [48]. Intro & 20 col. plates with descrs.

vol. 2, The twentieth century. 1969. pp. [48].
Intro & 20 col. plates with descrs.

10177 SNELL, J. B. Early railways. *London:
Weidenfeld & Nicolson*, 1964. (Pleasures &
Treasures series). 4°. pp. 128, with 132 illus
(38 col.).
Technological development on railways up to
1914.
—— *Octopus Books*, 1972. pp. 97, with 132
illus (38 col.).

10178 LELEUX, S. A. Brotherhoods, engineers.
Dawlish: David & Charles, 1965. pp. 85,
with 14 illus on 8 plates.
Manufacturers of railway equipment, incl.
points & crossings, wagons, bridges, signals and
locomotives; established 1842.

10179 HARESNAPE, B. Railway ·design since
1830. *London: Ian Allan*. 2 vols. la. 8°.
vol. 1, 1830–1914. 1968. pp. 130, with frontis &
239 illus.
vol. 2, 1914–1969. 1969. pp. 128, with 249 illus.

10180 ROLT, L. T. C. Railway engineering. *London: Macmillan*, 1968. (Quantum Books,
9). pp. 112, with frontis & 37 illus.
Past, present and future.

10181 HORSFIELD, B. Steam Horse, Iron Road;
edited by Brendan Horsfield. *London: British Broadcasting Corporation*, 1972. pp.
112, [12], with over 100 illus (27 col.), maps
& diagrams. Introduction by Brenda
Horsfield (pp. 7–14).
An anthology, based upon the B.B.C.'s television series of the same name.

10182 SNELL, J. B. Land transportation by rail,
in A History of Transport, edited by G. N.
Georgano (1972), pp. 71–118, with 10 col.
illus on 5 plates & 63 illus in text.
British and foreign railways.

10183 FARNWORTH, W. Railways: photographs
by Alec Davis, the author, and from contemporary sources; drawings by Tony
Matthews. *London: Mills & Boon*, 1973.
(Mills & Boon on Location series, 3). pp.
94, with 55 illus, & over 80 drawings &
maps.
Introductory. A visual approach, with commentary.

10184 LEE, C. E. Railways, *in* The Archaeology of the Industrial Revolution, ed. by Brian Bracegirdle (1973). pp. 41–58, with 14 col. illus on 4 plates & 17 illus in text.

10185 SPENCE, J. Victorian and Edwardian railways from old photographs; introduction and commentaries by Jeoffry Spence. *London; Sydney; Batsford*, 1975. pp. [124]. Intro (pp. [7–13]) & 155 illus with descrs.

10186 UPTON, N. An Illustrated History of Civil Engineering. *London: Heinemann*, 1975. pp. 192, with illus.
pp. 82–130, 'Railway engineering', with 38 illus.

10187 WHITEHOUSE, P. B. World of trains . . . ; picture research, Patricia E. Hornsey. *London: Hamlyn; New English Library*, 1976. la. 8°. pp. 144, with many illus (mostly col.).
A wide-ranging coverage, including railways in Britain.

10188 SPENCE, J. Victorian and Edwardian railway travel; introduction and commentaries by Jeoffry Spence. *London: Batsford*, 1977. pp. [116]. Intro (pp [5–10]) & 144 illus with descrs.
The passenger's scene: period 1870s to ca. 1911.

10189 WHITEHOUSE, P. B. Britain's main-line railways; edited by P. B. Whitehouse. *London: New English Library*, 1977. la. 8°. pp. 224, with 509 illus, incl. coats of arms, facsimiles, & maps (mostly in colour).

10190 COURSE, E. Railways then and now. *London: Batsford*, 1979. pp. 168, with 272 illus.
Photographic comparisons of 130 railway scenes, mostly stations, each supported by a general introduction and a detailed historical commentary.

10191 HARESNAPE, B. British Rail, 1948–78: a journey by design. *Shepperton: Ian Allan*, 1979. la. 8°. pp. 176, with 334 illus (31 col.). Foreword by Sir Peter Parker, chairman, BR.
The importance of good design. Visual, aesthetic and amenity aspects, past, present & future, in locomotives, carriages, livery, graphics and uniforms.

10192 UNWIN, P. Travelling by train in the Edwardian Age. *London: Allen & Unwin*, 1979. pp. 106, with 59 illus.
The Edwardian railway scene recalled.

Contemporaneous

10193 BLUNT, C. J. Blunt's Civil Engineer and Practical Machinist . . . by C. J. Blunt and R. M. Stephenson. *London: Ackerman*, [1834–7]. la. obl. format. 10 folding plates of composite drawings in full mechanical detail.
Division B, 'Bridges and viaducts, with the original specifications of the London and Birmingham Railway, the locomotive and bogie engines in detail, the goods waggons, tenders and divers specifications of works, etc., etc., by Robert Stephenson; Locomotive engine on the Newcastle and Carlisle Railway, by George Stephenson; Great Western Railway bridge by J.[*sic*] K. Brunel. Lawley Street Viaduct; the London & Birmingham Railway bogie locomotive engine; the Hercules locomotive engine on the Newcastle & Carlisle Railway: London & Birmingham Rly goods waggon; goods waggon wheels, carriages, etc from the manufactory at Newcastle; Great Western Railway bridge, and detail of the goods wagon and tender; Great Western Railway bridge with River Thames at Maidenhead'.

10194 NICHOLSON, J. Le mécanicien anglais; ou, description pratique des arts mécaniques de la Grande Bretagne . . . nouv. éd. . . . , revue, corr. et augm. d'un appendice sur les chemins de fer et les machines à vapeur, par Félix et Prosper Tourneux. *Paris: Ledentu*, 1824. 2 vols, with diagrams (some folded).
Kress Cat. C.5894

10195 DEMPSEY, G. D. Railways, *in* Papers on Subjects connected with the duties of the Corps of Royal Engineers, vols. 7, 8 & 9. *London: J. Weale.*
'A condensed account of the engineering and mechanical operations and structures which are combined in the making and equipment of a railway' (p. 96).
vol. 7, 1845. Paper 14, pp. 96–159, with plates 24–42 (composite drawings of earthworks).
vol. 8, 1845. Paper 14, pp. 85–155, with plates 25–42 (composite drawings of walls, bridges, tunnels and permanent way).
vol. 9, 1847. Paper 14, pp. 156–76, with plates 33–55 (composite drawings of stations & their fittings: locomotives & carriages). Examples are drawn from the London & Blackwall Rly.

10196 GARDNER, E. V. The Practical Contractors' & Builders' Pocket Guide, comprising numerous rules and tables. 2nd edn. *London: Trelawney W. Saunders*, 1848. sm. 8°, pp. [36], (52 tables). Cover title: Contractors' & Builders' Pocket Guide.
Tables of quantities, weights, lengths etc., and of prices of materials, for constructing railways, roads and buildings.

10197 The WORLD's railways and how they work, illustrated with numerous photographs and specially-drawn maps and pictures. *London: Odhams Press*, 1947. pp. 320, with 250 illus, including maps & many sectional drawings.
An introductory but highly informative work with numerous 'cut-away' drawings of machinery and structures.
pp. 5–115 are about railways in Britain.

10198 INTERNATIONAL RAILWAY CONGRESS [London, 1954]. Willesden Exhibition. *London: the Congress*, 1954. pp. [48], with 87 illus & diagrams, & a folded plan of the exhibition site.
A guide to 78 exhibits representing a wide range of modern railway equipment in use on BR.

10199 SUMMERSON, T. H. Design and transport. Proceedings of the British Railways (W.R.)

Lecture & Debating Society, 1960–61, no. 467. pp. 14, with discussion & 7 illus.
Author: Chairman, Design Panel, B.T.C.

10200 ANDERSON, J. F. The Railway Book: a handbook for spotters and others interested in railways. *London: Museum Press*, 1963. pp. 124, with 50+ line drawings (some composite).
An introduction to the form, purpose and function of track and lineside features, and of trains, with a chapter on train working; bibliography (25 sources).

10201 SPARK, R. Railways: a special issue [of the periodical publication Design]. *London: Design*, no. 171, March 1963. pp. 92, with many illus.
The work and aims of BR's Design Panel (1956) and its application of design principles to locomotives, ships, carriages, uniforms, stations and (pp. 72–7, by Alec Davis) to graphics.

10202 RANSOME-WALLIS, P. British railways today. *London: A. & C. Black*, 1964. (Black's Junior Reference Books). 4°. pp. 64, with 96 illus.
Introductory. A brief history, and description of the physical features of railways and their operation.

10203 GIFFORD, C. T. Each a glimpse. *Shepperton: Ian Allan*, 1970. la. 4°. pp. [180]. 273 'railway environment' photographs, with captions.

10204 JONES, K. W. Steam in the landscape; photographs by A. J. Hudson. *London: Blandford Press*, 1971. pp. 187, with 187 col. illus on pp. [35] to [130] of which nos. 1–137 are scenes on railways of the British Isles; period, 1960s.

10205 HOBSON, A. W. Modern Rail Album, edited by A. W. Hobson for the Phoenix Railway Photographic Circle. *Truro: Bradford Barton*, 1974. pp. 96. Intro & 85 illus with descrs.
A widely varied selection of photographs, 1960s & 1970s.

10206 BRITAIN's railways in the seventies: North, South, East, & West. *Shepperton: Ian Allan*, 1975. pp. 80. Intro & 129 illus of trains in the railway environment.

10207 GIFFORD, C. T. Steam finale north. *London: Ian Allan*, 1976. la. 4°. pp. 96. Intro & 158 illus with descrs.
Steam trains in their North of England environment, 1958–68.

10208 HUNT, J. and KRAUSE, I. On and off the beaten track. *London: New English Library*, 1976. obl. format. pp. [128], with 145 illus.
An evocation in words & photographs of railways and locomotives ca. 1965–1975, in Britain, Turkey and South Africa.

10209 STEENEKEN, H. All trains to stop! *London: Ian Allan*, 1979. obl. format. pp. 137. Intro & 187 illus with captions, amplified on pp. 134–7.
A photographic 'requiem'. The closing years of steam-hauled trains, mostly in Britain, France and Germany.

10210 ALLEN, G. F. Modern railways. *London: Hamlyn*, [1980]. la. 8°. pp. 256, with many illus (some col.), & 12 maps.
World coverage. Gt. Britain, pp. 11–41, with 42 illus (12 col.) & a map.

E 1   BIOGRAPHIES OF RAILWAY CIVIL ENGINEERS

(including the civil/mechanical engineers) 10211–55

For civil/mechanical engineers such as I. K. Brunel whose work is strongly associated with a particular railway, see L
For locomotive engineers see E 7 – E 10

Reference sources   10211–12
Collective biographies   10213–14
Individual biographies (alphabetically arranged under the subject)   10215–55

Reference sources

10211 BELL, S. P. A Biographical Index of British Engineers in the 19th Century. *New York & London: Garland*, 1975. pp. x, 246.
3,500 British engineers who died before 1901. Citations of obituary notices in 40 contemporaneous engineering periodicals. Includes classes of persons related to engineering (inventors, some entrepreneurs, company directors, architects, patent agents). The specialist field of each one is given. Some 500 or so are associated with railways or tramways in the British Isles.

10212 MARSHALL, J. A Biographical Dictionary of Railway Engineers. *Newton Abbot: David & Charles*, 1978. pp. 252.
About 750 entries, each giving date & place of birth & death, a brief biography, and sources for further information. The work includes some railway personalities other than engineers (promoters and managers like Edward Pease, Henry Booth, Josiah Stamp, and many others), also North American and European engineers whose influence was international.

Collective biographies

10213 ROLT, L. T. C. Great engineers. *London: G. Bell*, 1962. pp. xii, 244, with 20 illus on 16 plates, & a bibliography (31 sources).
Includes William Jessop, builder of canals and railways, pp. 43–65; Matthew Murray, pioneer mechanical engineer, pp. 66–87; Joseph Locke, railway engineer, pp. 106–28; Benjamin Baker, designer of the Forth Bridge, pp. 154–75.

10214 BARRIE, A. The railway builders. *London: Wayland*, 1973. (An Eyewitness Book). pp. 96, with frontis & 80 illus, incl. map, & a bibliography (6 sources).
Introductory. For young readers.

Individual biographies (arranged alphabetically by subject)

10215 BLOUNT, E. Memoirs of Sir Edward Blount; edited by Stuart J. Reid. *London: Longmans, Green & Co.*, 1902. pp. vi, [2], 308, with 3 plates (portraits).
ch. 4 (pp. 51–68), The beginnings of French railways.
ch. 5 (pp. 69–91), My railway career in France.
The building and operation by British engineers and workmen of the Paris & Rouen and other early railways in France in the 1840s. The author was, for a four month period, a locomotive driver in the early days of the P & R and later became its chairman, a position he held from 1864 to 1894, in which latter year, at the age of 94, he set down these memoirs. He was a life-long friend of the contractor Thomas Brassey, and frequently refers to his work and his benevolence.

10216 MIDDLEMAS, R. K. The master builders: Thomas Brassey, Sir John Aird, Lord Cowdray, Sir John Norton-Griffiths; foreword by Asa Briggs. *London: Hutchinson*, 1963. pp. 328, with 6 illus on 3 plates, 3 maps & a bibliography.
pp. 29–118, 'Thomas Brassey', with 6 plates, 3 maps & 69 notes.

10217 WALKER, C. Thomas Brassey: railway builder. *London: F. Muller*, 1969. pp. viii, 183, with 20 illus on 12 plates, 3 maps & a plan, & a bibliography (18 sources).
pp. 169–73, 'Brassey's contracts, 1834–1870': a list, with notes.

10218 GOULD, J. Thomas Brassey: an illustrated life of Thomas Brassey, 1805–1870. *Aylesbury: Shire Publications*, 1975. (Lifelines, 36). pp. 48, with 20 illus, 2 maps, chronology, & a bibliography (11 sources).

10219 HADFIELD, C. and SKEMPTON, A. W. William Jessop, engineer. *Newton Abbot: David & Charles*, 1979. pp. 315, with 22 illus on 12 plates; in text, 24 maps, facsimiles, plans, diagrams & 691 notes.
pp. 168–83 *et passim*: iron railways, early iron plate railways, the Charnwood Forest Rly, Leicester & Nanpantan Rly, Surrey Iron Rly, and other lines in England, Scotland & Wales (listed in index on p. 310).

10220 WEBSTER, N. W. Joseph Locke: railway revolutionary. *London: Allen & Unwin*,

1970. pp. 218, with 33 illus on 16 plates & 3 line illus.

10221 WALKER, C. Joseph Locke, 1805–1860: an illustrated life of Joseph Locke. *Aylesbury: Shire Publications*, 1975. (Lifelines series, 35). pp. 48, with 18 illus, 2 maps & a bibliography (11 sources).

10222 MITCHELL, J. Reminiscences of my life in the Highlands; printed for the author at the Gresham Press, Unwin Bros, Chilworth & London 1883,' 84. Republished as a reprint with a new introduction, corrigenda and index by Ian Robertson. *Newton Abbot: David & Charles*, 1971. 2 vols. (vol. 1, pp. xvi, 362; vol. 2, pp. viii, 268).
vol. 2, chapters 17–19, 22–24: Joseph Mitchell's work in surveying various proposed railways in Scotland and in England between 1837 and ca. 1870, notably the Highland Rly.
Appendix I (pp. 229–51) is an appraisal of George Hudson based on personal acquaintance and observation and some modest investment in Hudson lines, with some examples of share value variations in the 1840s. Twenty-two years after Hudson's downfall Mitchell met him again and was instrumental in persuading the North Eastern Rly to end its 20-year-long litigation against Hudson, on grounds of humanity. Nine letters between Mitchell and Hudson and H. S. Thompson, chairman of the N.E. Rly July–November 1871, are reproduced.

10223 The LATE Sir Morton Peto; reprinted from the Kent and Sussex Courier, November 22nd 1889. 3 columns.   LU(THC)

10224 PETO, H. Sir Morton Peto: a memorial sketch (by H.P.) [i.e., Henry Peto]. *London: printed for private circulation by Elliot Stock*, 1893. pp. 119, with 2 portraits & a folded genealogical table of the Grissell and Peto families and (pp. 116–9), 'Railway and other works executed by Sir Morton Peto', a three-column list.

10225 STORY about George Stephenson, the great railway engineer. *London: Richardson & Son*, 1858. sm. 8°. pp. 6.
A biography for boys.

10226 NEWTON, W. A letter on the Stephenson Monument and the education of the district; addressed to the Right Hon. Lord Ravensworth. *Newcastle upon Tyne: R. Fisher*, 1859. pp. 8.
Instead of a statue to Robert Stephenson, like that of Earl Grey, a Stephenson Scholarship to a proposed new high school for the sons of clerks, merchants and artisans.

10227 JANIN, A. Fulton, Georges et Robert Stephenson; ou, les bateaux à vapeur et les chemins de fer. *Paris: Grassart*, 1861. sm. 8°. pp. 448.
pp. 145–434: 'Georges et Robert Stephenson; ou, la locomotive et les chemins de fer'.

10228 HELLFELD, K. George Stephenson der Gründer des Eisenbahnwesens und Erbauer der ersten Locomotive; ein Werkmeister von seltener Einsicht, Genialität und Ausdauer, der deutschen Jugend als Vorbild dargestellt. *Frankfurt am Main: Joh. Ehr. Hermann'sche Verlagsbuchhandlung*, 1863. pp. 155.

10229 'Z'. Georg Stephenson, lefnadsteckning, af Z. *Norrköping: Foreningens Boktryckeri*, 1863. (Historiskt Bildergalleri, 2). pp. 16, with 6 illus.

10230 JONVEAUX, E. Histoire de quatre ouvriers anglais: Henry Maudslay, George Stephenson, William Fairbairn, James Nasmyth. *Paris: Hachette*, 1868. sm. 8°. pp. vii, 227.
Based on the biographies of Samuel Smiles. pp. 67–151, George Stephenson; pp. 153–95, William Fairbairn.

10231 STOKOE, J. The Father of Railways; or, a hero from humble life: a lecture, enlarged and revised, by Rev. John Stokoe. *London: E. Stock*, [1870]. sm. 8°. pp. 46.
A tract, based on the character of George Stephenson.

10232 MAASLIEB, W. George Stephenson, der Vater der Eisenbahnen: ein Kultur- und Lebensbild für die reisere Jugend und das Volk. *Leipzig: A. Oehmigke*, [1873?]. pp. iv, 177, with 4 col. illus.

10233 HORN, W. O. von. George Stephenson, der Mann der Eisenbahnen und Lokomotiven: ein Lebensbild für die deutsche Jugend u. das Volk. 2nd edn. *Wiesbaden: Ebend*, 1876. pp. 96, with 4 illus.

10234 The STEPHENSON Centenary at Chesterfield, June 9, 1881. *Chesterfield*, 1881. pp. 71, with 1 illus.
Reprinted from the *Derbyshire Courier* of June 11th.

10235 BOLTON, C. E. The life of G. Stephenson, founder of the railway system, constructor of the first passenger railway in England. How the poor colliery boy by perseverance became famous. *Cleveland (Ohio): Cleveland Educational Bureau*, 1882. (Twelve Books for the People, 4). sm. 8°. pp. 24, with portrait.
Introductory.

10236 CLARKE, F. L. George Stephenson: his life and career. *London: W. S. Sonnenschien*, 1884. pp. 140, with 4 engravings.

10237 LAYSON, J. F. Famous engineers of the nineteenth century. *London: W. Scott*, 1885. pp. 304, with frontis & 5 illus.
George & Robert Stephenson, R. Trevithick, W. Hedley, T. Hackworth, & I. K. Brunel.

10238 MATEAUX, C. L. George and Robert Stephenson. *London: Cassell*, 1885. (The World's Workers series). pp. 128, with frontis (portrait).

A popular biography enlivened with supposed conversations.

10239 LAYSON, J. F. Robert Stephenson and the extension of the railway system. *London: Tyne Publishing Co.*, [188–?]. pp. 128, with portrait.

10240 STEBBING, G. Beating the record: a story of the life and times of George Stephenson. *London: J. F. Shaw*, [1896]. pp. 383, with 8 illus (drawings).
An imaginative biography.

10241 DEANE, D. J. George Stephenson, father and founder of the railway system. *London: S. W. Partridge*, [1899]. pp. 176, with frontis & illus (mostly vignettes).

10242 BIEDENKAPP, G. George Stephenson und die Vorgeschichte der Eisenbahnen: eine biographische Skizze, mit 31 Abbildungen. *Stuttgart: Verlag der Technischen Montashefte*, [1913]. pp. 52, with illus.

10243 BARRETT, A. L. George Stephenson, father of railways. *New York: Paebar Co.*, 1948. pp. [6], iv, [2], 7–287, v–vii, with 15 plates & a bibliography (50 sources).
'Written for the average reader.'

10244 CHALONER, W. H. The Stephensons, father and son, *in his* People and industries, *Frank Cass*, 1963, pp. 64–73, with 2 portraits.

10245 TAYLOR, B. George Stephenson and the railways. *London: University of London Press*, [1964]. pp. 63, with 24 illus on 24 plates, & in text, 3 illus & a chronology.
An informative introductory work.

10246 VIRGINSKII, V. S. Dzhordzh Stefenson, 1781–1848. *Moskva: Nauka*, 1964. pp. 213.

10247 ROBBINS, M. George and Robert Stephenson. *London: Oxford University Press*, 1966. (Clarendon Biographies). pp. 64, with 14 illus, drawings & maps on 8 plates, 2 maps on end papers & 2 portraits on cover.
—— Reprint. *Westport (Connecticut): Greenwood Press*, 1977.

10248 JAMIESON, M. The railway Stephensons. *Newcastle upon Tyne: Oriel Press*, 1970. pp. 32, with 15 illus & a bibliography (7 sources).
Introductory.

10249 ROWLAND, J. Railway pioneer: the story of George Stephenson; illustrated by Peter North. *Woking: Lutterworth Press*, 1971. pp. 121, with frontis & 10 illus (line drawings).
Introductory; for young readers, with imaginary conversations.
—— [2nd edn.] Rocket to fame . . . *London: Target Publishing Co.*, 1974. pp. 121.

10250 SELLMAN, R. R. George and Robert Stephenson. *London: Methuen Educational*, 1971. (Methuen's Brief Lives series). pp. 31, with 6 illus, 2 portraits & 4 maps.
An informative introductory work.

10251 SIMMONS, J. A holograph letter from George Stephenson, *in* Journal of Transport History, new series, vol. 1 (1971–2), pp. 108–15, with plate & 17 notes.
To his son Robert in Colombia, dated February 23rd 1827. One of the few surviving examples of a letter written by George Stephenson in his own hand. It is printed here as a straight transcript of the original, no change in word or letter being made. Instead, Professor Simmons has supplied notes where explanation or postulation is called for.
Much of the text relates to the writer's work on the Liverpool & Manchester Rly then under construction, and there are references to other projects in which he is involved, but the letter is also valuable for the insight it provides into the extent of G.S.'s resources with pen and paper and the testimony it bears to an underlying affinity between father and son—a matter on which some doubt has been expressed in the past.
The original is in Liverpool Record Office (385 MD 12). It runs to about 1200 words.

10252 SKEAT, W. O. George Stephenson: the engineer and his letters. *London: Institution of Mechanical Engineers*, 1973. la. 8°. pp. 268, with frontis & 77 illus, incl. maps, portraits, diagrams & facsimiles; bibliography (13 sources).

10253 SMITH, D. J. Robert Stephenson: an illustrated life of Robert Stephenson, 1803–1859. *Aylesbury: Shire Publications*, 1973. (Lifelines series), 8). pp. 48, with 28 illus, facsimiles & maps, a chronology & a bibliography (10 sources).

10254 DAVIES, H. A biographical study of the Father of Railways, George Stephenson . . . *London: Weidenfeld & Nicolson*, 1975. pp. xiii, 337, with 35 illus on 16 plates & a bibliography (46 sources).

10255 DORMAN, C. C. The Stephensons and steam railways. *London: Priory Press*, 1975. (Pioneers of Science & Industry). 4°. pp. 95, with 65 illus, chronology & a short bibliography.
Introductory.

E 2   CIVIL ENGINEERING

Construction and maintenance—Problems of terrain
(gradients, cuttings, tunnels, embankments)

10256–89

Reference sources 10256–58
Historical 10259–70
Contemporaneous 10271–89

Reference sources

10256 BRITISH Rail Main Line Gradient Profiles. *London: Ian Allan, in co-operation with Tothill Press*, [1966]. pp. [74], with 6 maps. 156 lengths in profile.
—— another edn. *Ian Allan*, [1970]. pp. 78, with 6 maps. 156 lengths in profile.

10257 SKEMPTON, A. W. Early printed reports and maps, 1665–1850, in the library of the Institution of Civil Engineers. *London: the Institution*, 1977. pp. xv, 84, with 14 plates.
A listing of ca. 1000 reports by civil engineers, of which ca. 125 are on railways.

10258 BENNETT, A. E. Cumulative Index to the Railway Junction Diagrams published by John Airey and the Railway Clearing House, compiled by A. E. Bennett. *Caterham: Railway & Canal Historical Society*, 1971. obl. format. pp. 64, with Foreword by David Garnett, including additional historical information.
A single alphabetical listing of all the junctions shown in the official indices of the complete series of 12 editions from 1867 to 1928 & the 1939 supplement.

—— Supplement, by David Garnett. *R. & C.H.S.*, 1979. pp. 4.
This includes details from the 3rd edn (1872) not in the main work.

Historical

10259 GIBBONS, T. H. My experiences as a Divisional Engineer. Great Western Railway (London) Lecture & Debating Society, meeting on November 7th 1907 [no. 42]. pp. 11.
The Plymouth Division, GWR. Includes the gauge conversion of 1892.

10260 KERR, I. The Caffin story: the first fifty years.' *London: Caffin & Co.*, 1958. pp. 28, with 18 illus.
Railway contractors & civil engineers.

10261 SANDSTRÖM, G. E. The history of tunnelling: underground workings through the ages. *London: Barrie & Rockliff*, 1963. pp. xii, 427, with 152 illus & diagrams, a glossary & a bibliography.
pp. 84–101, 'Early railway tunnels'.
pp. 340–58, 'The Channel comedy'.

10262 BLOWER, A. British Railway tunnels. *London: Ian Allan*, 1964. pp. 108, with 53 illus on 32 plates, 3 tables & a bibliography (20 sources).
75 of the longer tunnels described.

10263 PANNELL, J. P. M. An Illustrated History of Civil Engineering. *London: Thames & Hudson*, 1964. pp. 376, with 228 illus.
pp. 91–128, 'Railways', with 20 illus.

10264 APPLETON, J. H. A morphological approach to the geography of transport. *Hull: University of Hull*, 1965. (Occasional Papers in Geography, 3). pp. 44, with 8 maps, 87 notes & refs.

10265 APPLETON, J. H. Transport and the landscape of northern England, *in* Northern geographical essays in honour of G. H. J. Daysh, ed. by J. W. House, 1966. pp. 178–95, with map & a bibliography (29 sources).
A socio/geographical commentary. Includes railways.

10266 APPLETON, J. H. Railways and the morphology of British towns, *in* Urbanization and its problems, ed. by R. P. Beckinsale and J. M. Houston, 1968. pp. 92–118, with 6 illus on 4 plates, 31 town maps & a table of steepest gradients on selected main lines.
The place of railways within towns.

10267 ROBINSON, C. D. Pennine Power Tunnel: a short history of the three railway tunnels between Dunford Bridge and Woodhead in the Southern Pennines and an account of the installation of high voltage cables by the Central Electricity Generating Board in the disused north bore. *London: C.E.G.B.*, March 1970. (News Letter, 82). pp. [12], with 4 illus, a plan, 2 diagrams & a bibliography (10 sources).
The railway history of the tunnels, pp. [1–5].

10268 MORGAN, B. Civil engineering: railways. *London: Longman*, 1971. (Industrial Archaeology, 5). pp. xvi, 176, with 44 illus on 16 plates, 11 line drawings & maps, & a select evaluative bibliography, pp. 166–8.
A companion volume to *Mechanical Engineering: Railways*, by J. B. Snell (1971). Both works republished as paperbacks by Arrow Books, 1973. but with titles: *Railways: civil engineering*, and *Railways: mechanical engineering*.

10269 WHITE, H. P. Terrain technology and transport history: a tour of the Harecastle area of North Staffordshire. *Railway & Canal Historical Society, North West Group*, 1971. pp. 8. Reproduced typescript.
Notes prepared for a visit of the Group on 1st May 1971 to learn the relationship between the physiography of the area and the routeing of turnpike, canal, railway (North Staffordshire Rly) and motorway construction.

10270 BEAVER, P. A history of tunnels. *London: Peter Davies*, 1972. pp. xii, 155, with 24 illus on 12 plates, 27 diagrams in text & a bibliography (28 sources).
British and foreign examples and techniques. Includes Channel Tunnel proposals.

Contemporaneous

10271 SOPWITH, T. On the preservation of railway sections and of accounts of borings, sinkings, etc. in elucidation of the measures recently taken by the British Association; a paper read before the Geological & Polytechnic Society of the West Riding of Yorkshire, September 23rd, 1841. *Leeds: printed by Edward Baines & Sons*, 1842. pp. 16.
Aim, to record the geological features unearthed in railway building excavation, on charts, 40 ft. to 1 inch scale.

10272 HUGHES, J. Concise tables to facilitate the calculation of earthwork and land required in the construction of railways, canals and other public works; adapted to the practice of the engineer, architect and surveyor. *London: Effingham Wilson*, 1846. sm. 8°. pp. 26. Cover title: Hughes' tables.

10273 MULLINS, B. and MULLINS, M. B. The origin and reclamation of peat bog, with some observations on the construction of roads, railways, and canals, in bog. *Dublin: S. B. Oldham*, 1846. pp. 48, & 5 col. plates (map, plans & section).
'Extracted from the *Transactions of the Institution of Civil Engineers of Ireland.*'
pp. 33–4: 'Railways in bog: trenching, draining, ballasting and boxing with gravel & sand, and the laying-in of 'fascines' of brushwood.

10274 SIMMS, F. W. A Treatise on the Principles and Practice of Levelling, shewing its application to purposes of railway engineering and the construction of roads; together with a practical mode of setting out the widths of ground for a railway or canal . . . 3rd edn rev., with additions, with Mr. Law's practical examples for setting out railway curves. *London: J. Weale*, 1846. pp. vii, 150, with illus, tables, diagrams & plates.
Previous editions were concerned primarily with road works.
—— 4th edn. *J. Weale*, 1856. pp. vii, 215.
—— 5th edn. *London: Lockwood*, 1866. pp. vii, 215.
—— 5th edn. with corrections. *New York: D. Van Nostrand*, 1870. pp. 157.
—— 6th edn. *London: Lockwood*, 1875. pp. vii, 215.
—— 7th edn. *Lockwood*, 1884. pp. vii, 215.

10275 WILME, B. P. A Hand-Book for Mapping, Engineering and Architectural Drawing, in which maps of all descriptions are analyzed . . . , illustrated with forty-three large plates and thirty-nine woodcuts . . . *London: published for the author by J. Weale*, 1846. pp. 8, iii–viii, 69, [8].
Most of the examples relate to railway mapping.
NUC

10276 DEMPSEY, G. D. Brick bridges, sewers and culverts: a series of examples adapted for application in the construction of roads and railways . . . *London: Atchley*, 1850. Folio. pp. 28.
—— Plates. Folio. no t.p. Britannia Bridge over the Menai Straits: general view (a drawing and 55 drawings on 10 plates).

10277 APPLEBY BROTHERS. Illustrated Hand-Book of Machinery and Iron Work. 2nd ed. *London*, 1869. pp. xvi, 442, with numerous illus.
Manufacturer's catalogue including many items of railway contractors' equipment (cranes, wagons, locomotives, etc).

10278 COOKSON, A. C. The construction of a new railway. Great Western Railway (London) Lecture & Debating Society, meeting on Thursday, March 8th 1906 (no. 10) [no. 24]. pp. 10, with 8 illus.
The process of construction of a conceptual length of line is described.

10279 SMITH, A. G. A day's work in the Engineering Department. Great Western Railway (London) Lecture & Debating Society, meeting on January 27th, 1910 [no. 66]. pp. 22, with 20 illus & diagrams.

10280 QUARTERMAINE, A. S. The work of an Engineering Division. Great Western Railway (London) Lecture & Debating Society, meeting on February 28th, 1924 (no. 170). pp. 24, with discussion & 13 illus.

10281 QUARTERMAINE, A. S. The relation of civil engineering to transport problems. Great Western Railway (London) Lecture & Debating Society, meeting on 21st February, 1929 (no. 229). pp. 20, with discussion, 13 illus & a diagram.
Author, Asst. Chief Engineer (P.W. and Docks).

10282 MATHESON, E. G. The work of the Engineering Department. Great Western Railway (London) Lecture & Debating Society, meeting on the 30th January, 1930 (no. 239). pp. 31, with 21 illus & 4 tables & discussion. Author, 'Assistant Chief Engineer (Works & Structures)'.

10283 QUARTERMAINE, A. S. Some present-day methods of construction and maintenance. Great Western Railway (London) Lecture & Debating Society, meeting on 19th October, 1933 (no. 274). pp. 24, with discussion & 25 illus.
Author, 'Assistant Chief Engineer, G.W.R.'.

10284 WAR OFFICE. Notes on military railway engineering. *London: War Office.* 2 vols.
pt 1, Survey. 1940. pp. vi, 126, with 20 tables & 25 diagrams (7 folded).
pt 2, Engineering. 1940. pp. 195, with 23 tables & 97 diagrams (64 folded).

10285 TICEHURST, A. G. What mechanisation means to the Civil Engineer's Department. Proceedings of the British Railways (W.R.) Lecture & Debating Society, 1952–53, no. 397. pp. 14, with discussion & 10 illus.
Author, Plant Assistant to the Civil Engineer, Western Region.

10286 STEVENS, S. The work of an Engineering District. Proceedings of the British Railways (W.R.) London Lecture & Debating Society, 1953–54, no. 407. pp. 20, with discussion, 9 illus & a chart.
Author, District Engineer, London District, W.R.

10287 STEPHENS, T. C. The Severn Tunnel and its pumping engines. Proceedings of the British Railways (W.R.) London Lecture & Debating Society, 1954–55, no. 421. pp. 15, with discussion & 8 illus.
Author, Manager, Severn Tunnel Pumping Station, Sudbrook.

10288 BRITISH RAILWAYS. WESTERN REGION. Western Area Board plant demonstration at Glebe sidings, Hayes, 17 April 1957. [*London*]: *B.R. (WR)*, 1957. pp. 14, interleaved with 14 plates.
Track maintenance equipment: a guide to the exhibits with explanatory notes on the working of each appliance.

10289 BRITISH RAILWAYS. WESTERN REGION. The Soil Mechanics Laboratory. *London: B.R. (WR)*, [195–], tall 8°. pp. 30, with 17 illus & 2 diagrams.
Investigating soil behaviour related to track bed, embankments, cuttings and structures.

E 3   PERMANENT WAY

10290–9

For special forms of track see **D 1 – D 5**

10290 'METALLUM'. Comments on a pamphlet entitled Observations by the Permanent Way Company upon opinions expressed at a meeting of the members of the Institution of Civil Engineers on Tuesday, February 17, 1857, by 'Metallum'. *London: Great Northern Printing Office*, 1857. pp. 15.
The pamphlet referred to is Ottley 2620.
BLACKWELL CAT. A1051 (1976), 72

10291 WOOD, L. R. The construction and maintenance of the permanent way. Great

Western Railway (London) Lecture & Debating Society, meeting on January 25th, 1912 [no. 87]. pp. 19, with 16 illus.
With special reference to the GWR.

10292 LONDON, MIDLAND & SCOTTISH RLY. The Hallade track recorder, and hints on the maintenance of curves. *London: L.M.S. Rly*, 1934. sm. 8°. pp. 70, with 7 illus & diagrams & 2 specimen Hallade charts (1 folded).

10293 BUTLAND, A. N. Modern permanent way maintenance. (Proceedings of the British Railways (W.R.) London Lecture & Debating Society, 1948–49, no. 357). pp. 15, with discussion & 7 illus.
Author, 'Divisional Engineer, Taunton'.

10294 COOKSON, E. C. History of the permanent way. (Proceedings of the British Railways (W.R.) London Lecture & Debating Society, 1949–50, no. 367). pp. 16, with discussion, 7 illus & 7 diagrams.
Author, 'Assistant Engineer, Permanent Way'.

10295 HANCOCK, R. M. and REES, J. The running of the track testing car on the Western Region. (Proceedings of the British Railways (W.R.) London Lecture & Debating Society, 1957–58, no. 441). pp. 23, with discussion, 7 illus & 5 diagrams.

10296 BRITISH RAILWAYS. Permanent way mechanised equipment. *London: B.R.*, [195–]. pp. [32], with 33 illus. Title from cover.

10297 BARNWELL, F. R. L. Modern track maintenance. (Proceedings of the British Railways (W.R.) London Lecture & Debating Society, 1965–66, no. 492). pp. 11, with discussion & 7 illus.
Author, Chief Engineer, Western Region.

10298 RIDEN, P. J. The Butterley Company, 1790–1830: a Derbyshire iron-works in the Industrial Revolution. *Chesterfield: P. J. Riden*, 1973. la. 8°. pp. 63, with an extensive bibliography (pp. 56–8) & 433 notes.
A detailed study based on the Company's records, being a revised version of an essay submitted in the Final Honour School of Modern History, University of Oxford, June 1973.
pp. 44–6, The work of Benjamin Outram and of William & Josias Jessop; rail manufacture for the Cromford & High Peak Rly and other railways.

10299 MILLIGAN, J. The resilient pioneers: a history of the Elastic Rail Spike Company and its associates. *Aberdeen, Edinburgh: Paul Harris Publishing*, 1975. pp. xi, 143, with 31 illus (8 col.) on 12 plates, & 7 line drawings.
The history of the development of the elastic rail spike, the Pantrol chip and the Lockspike.

E 4   ELECTRIC RAILWAY ENGINEERING

Electrification—Underground electric railways (tube and subway)

10300–10331

For electric locomotives and trains see **E 9**
For electrical safety engineering see **E 15**

10300 CARUS-WILSON, C. A. The economy of electricity as a motive power on railways at present driven by steam, *in* Proceedings of Section 1, Railways, International Engineering Congress, Glasgow, 1901. *London: William Clowes*, 1902. pp. 12–21, with 4 tables & (pp. 18–21), 'Discussion'.

10301 SMITH, R. T. The electrification of the Hammersmith and City Railway. Great Western Railway (London) Lecture & Debating Society, meeting on March 22nd, 1906 [no. 25]. pp. 19, with 24 illus.

10302 DICK, KERR AND COMPANY. Electric traction on a main line railway (Lancashire & Yorkshire Railway): contractors, Dick, Kerr & Co. *London: the Company*, [1911]. (Pamphlet 205). pp. 53, with frontis (col. map), 28 illus, 15 diagrams & 4 tables.

10303 SCOTT, W. J. Should we electrify? Great Western Railway (London) Lecture & Debating Society, meeting on December 4th, 1913 [no. 105]. pp. 23–7, with discussion.

The main-line railways flanking the GWR (the LNWR and the LSWR) are both engaged in electrifying their suburban lines. To match this enterprise, and to meet growing competition from tramways, the GWR should build an electric line into suburban areas within its region which are not yet served by rail.

10304 MASLIN, A. R. Is the day far distant when electricity will supersede the use of steam for locomotion? Great Western Railway (London) Lecture & Debating Society, meeting on January 15th 1920 [no. 118]. pp. 53–9.

10305 MINISTRY OF TRANSPORT. Electrification of railways: interim report. *London: H.M.S.O.*, 1920.
—— Final report. *H.M.S.O.*, 1921.

10306 RAVEN, V. L. Advantages of electrification. Great Western Railway (London) Lecture & Debating Society, meeting on January 4th, 1923 (no. 155). pp. 28, with discussion, diagrams, tables & illus.
Steam and electric locomotives compared.

10307　RUSSELL, F. V. A comparative review of heavy suburban passenger train operation by steam and electric traction. Great Western Railway (London) Lecture & Debating Society, meeting on February 1st, 1923 (no. 157). pp. 20, with discussion.
Author, 'Assistant to General Manager, G.E. Rly'.

10308　MINISTRY OF TRANSPORT. RAILWAY ELECTRIFICATION COMMITTEE. Report. *London: H.M.S.O.*, 1928. pp. 14, with 5 plates & 3 la. folded maps, for London & its environs, England & Wales, and Scotland.

10309　MINISTRY OF TRANSPORT. COMMITTEE ON MAIN LINE ELECTRIFICATION. Report. *London: H.M.S.O.*, 1931. pp. 57, with 2 maps & 2 diagrams.

10310　MARSH, H. and TAYLOR, S. B. Debate: That electrification of main line railways should be undertaken without delay. (Proceedings of the Great Western Railway (London) Lecture & Debating Society, 1931–32, no. 261). pp. 18, with discussion.

10311　'THAT an increased use of electric traction for main line working is desirable:' a joint debate introduced by H. C. L. Trickett & J. M. Leighton-Bailey and R. H. Whittington & F. T. Barwell. Great Western Railway (London) Lecture & Debating Society, 3rd March 1938, no. 321. pp. 14, with discussion.

10312　BRITISH ELECTRICAL POWER CONVENTION [Torquay, May 1956]. British Electrical Power Convention. *London: Railway Gazette*, 1956. pp. 38, with 23 illus & a map.
Principally concerned with railway electrification and electric traction, and the implementation of the BTC's Modernisation Plan (Jan. 1955).

10313　BRITISH RAILWAYS. EASTERN REGION. Modernisation, Eastern Region. *London: B.R. (ER)*, [1959]. la. 8°. pp. 48, with 83 illus. Cover title: Eastern Region modernisation.

10314　BRITISH RAILWAYS. SOUTHERN REGION. Extension of electrification from Gillingham to Sheerness-on-Sea, Ramsgate and Dover. . . . *London: B.R. (SR)*, May 1959. la. 8°. pp. [40], with 28 illus & other drawings & diagrams, plan of Chislehurst Junction & a folded map at end. Cover title: Kent Coast electrification: first phase.

10315　BRITISH ELECTRICAL & ALLIED MANUFACTURERS' ASSOCIATION. Railway electrification. *London: the Association*, [1960]. (Publication no. 176). pp. 28, incl. covers, with 41 illus (1 col.).
Issued to publicise the products of 13 British manufacturers of railway electrical equipment, including locomotives.

10316　BRITISH RAILWAYS. EASTERN REGION. Electrification opening: Bishop's Stortford, Hertford East, Enfield Town, Chingford, Liverpool St; Wednesday 16th November 1960. *London: B.R. (ER)*, 1960. pp. [20]. with 25 illus & a map.

10317　RAILWAY electrification progress: issued on the occasion of the British Railways Electrification Conference, London, October 3–7, 1960. *London: Railway Gazette*, 1960. pp. 48, with many illus, ports & maps. (120 pp. of adverts fore & aft).

10318　BRITISH RAILWAYS. Your new railway; foreword by S. E. Raymond, Chairman, B.R. *London: B.R.*, 1966. pp. 36, with 38 illus, and illus & map on covers.
Electrification plans for the London Midland Region, London to Manchester & Liverpool.

10319　BRITISH RAILWAYS. LONDON MIDLAND REGION. Crewe—Manchester electrification: British Railways modernisation. *London: B.R. (LMR)*, [1966?]. pp. 24, with 12 illus, map, route chart, layout plan, glossary of terms & a folded sheet of diagrams at end.

10320　BRITISH RAILWAYS. LONDON MIDLAND REGION. The main line electrification: London—Manchester—Liverpool. *London: B.R. (LMR)*, [1966]. sm 8°. pp. 16, with 8 illus on 4 plates.
A concise but detailed account of progress from the proposal in 1954 until completion in 1965.

10321　MINISTRY OF TRANSPORT. Railway electrification on the overhead system: requirements for clearances. *London: H.M.S.O.*, 1966. pp. 4, with 2 folded diagrams.

10322　TIMES [newspaper]. Railway electrification, London—Manchester—Liverpool. *London: The Times*, 18 April, 1966. Supplement, pp.iv, with 13 illus.

10323　CONFERENCE ON PERFORMANCE OF ELECTRIFIED RAILWAYS, [Institution of Electrical Engineers, London, 1968]. A survey of main line and rapid transit systems in many countries. *London: the Institution*, 1968. (I.E.E. Conference Publication, 50).
Part 1, Contributions. 1968. pp. vii, 571, with 22 plates (19 folded), illus, maps & a bibliography.

10324　FOLLENFANT, H. G. Underground railway construction. [*London*]: *London Transport*, 1968. pp. 26, with 23 illus on 12 plates, 4 diagrams & a table of engineering standards for railway construction in London.
Author writes as Chief Civil Engineer, London Transport.

10325　BRITISH RAILWAYS. EASTERN REGION. Your new electric railway: The Great Northern suburban electrification. *London: B.R.(ER)*, May 1973. la. 8°. pp. 18, with 25 illus, map & diagram.

10326 SCOTTISH ASSOCIATION FOR PUBLIC TRANSPORT. The case for a Scottish railway electrification programme. *Glasgow: the Association*, June 1973. (Memorandum, 73/3). pp. 5.

10327 FOLLENFANT, H. G. Reconstructing London's Underground. *London: London Transport*, 1974. pp. xi, 184, with 43 illus on 24 plates, 17 diagrams & 74 bibliogr. notes; index, pp. 179–84; large historical map by F. H. Stingemore.

10328 BRITISH RAILWAYS. Railway electrification. *London: B.R.*, 1978. pp. 20, with diagrams & tables.
'A British Railways Board discussion paper', with a foreword by Peter Parker, Chairman. A policy document submitted to the Minister of Transport.

10329 RAILWAY INDUSTRY ASSOCIATION OF GREAT BRITAIN. Railway electrification in Britain: the railway industry view. *London: the Association*, 1978. pp. 16.
A spirited response from the railway manufacturers to proposals for main-line electrification plans.

10330 DEPARTMENT OF TRANSPORT. Review of main line electrification: interim report [of a joint steering group, Dept. of Transport and British Railways Board]. *London: H.M.S.O.*, 1979. pp. iii, 42, with 18 tables & 3 appendices.
—— Final report. *H.M.S.O.*, 1981. pp. iv, 92, with 50 tables, 10 diagrams & graphs & 7 appendices, incl. 4 maps (network options).

10331 BRITISH Isles railway electrification. [Maps]. *Exeter: Quail Map Co.*, 1980. a folded s. sh. printed on both sides.
A general map with an inset for Tyneside, and on reverse, maps for South-East England and six smaller maps for London, Clydeside, Manchester, Merseyside, West Midlands, & Glasgow. The present network.

E 5   ARCHITECTURE AND DESIGN

Stations, bridges, viaducts, tunnel entrances, etc.—Archaeology of railway structures

10332–56

10332 DEMPSEY, G. D. Iron roofs: a series of examples, illustrating various combinations of iron, both malleable and cast, in the construction of roofs for warehouses, factories, railway stations and other buildings . . . *London: Atchley*, 1850. la 8°. pp. 17.
—— Atlas. (10 plates). 1850.

10333 DEMPSEY, G. D. Engineering examples: working drawings of stations, enginehouses, manufactories, warehouses, workshops, etc, etc. . . . *London: Atchley*, 1856. Folio. pp. 28, & 146 architectural drawings on 16 plates.
—— Atlas.

10334 FAIRBAIRN, W. Life of Sir William Fairbairn, partly written by himself; edited and completed by William Pole. *London: Longmans, Green*, 1877. (Reprinted by David & Charles, 1970. pp. xxiii, xvi, 473, with illus).
The reprint has a new introduction by A. E. Musson, with 58 bibliogr. notes and includes Fairbairn's work on railway bridges.

10335 COX, H. Architectural engineering of railway companies. Great Western Railway (London) Lecture & Debating Society, meeting on March 31st, 1910 [no.70]. pp. 36, with discussion & 47 illus.

10336 GLEADOW, F. Reconstruction of bridges. Great Western Railway (London) Lecture & Debating Society, meeting on February 19th 1914 [no. 110]. pp.17, with 20 illus.

10337 DESIGN AND INDUSTRIES ASSOCIATION. The Face of the Land: the year book of the Design & Industries Association, 1929–30; edited by H.H.P. [Harry Hardy Peach] and N.L.C. [Noel Carrington], with an introduction by Clough Williams-Ellis. *London: Allen & Unwin*, 1930.
ch. 8 (pp. 123–32), 'The Railway', with 15 illustrations of past and present design features, mostly in station architecture.

10338 BERRIDGE, P. S. A. The erection and construction of large railway bridges. (Proceedings of the British Railways (W.R.) London Lecture & Debating Society, 1950–51, no. 380). pp. 16, with discussion & 7 illus & diagrams.

10339 CAVANAGH, H. E. B. Architecture and the railways. (Proceedings, British Railways (W.R.) London Lecture & Debating Society, 1951–52, no. 392). pp. 19, with discussion & 9 illus.
Author, 'Architect, Western Region'.

10340 DE MARÉ, E. The bridges of Britain. *London: Batsford*, 1954. pp. 226, with col. frontis, 156 illus on plates, line drawings in text.
In index, 11 page refs to railway bridges.

10341 LEWIS, B. B. The architectural aspects of railway planning in England. Thesis, Ph.D., University of London (U.C.L.), 1954–5.

10342 DENTON, J. H. British railway stations.

London: Ian Allan, 1965. pp. 63, with 67 illus on 32 plates & 16 plans in text.

10343 MINETT, M. J. The railway stations of George Townsend Andrews, *in* Journal of Transport History, vol. 7 (1965–6), pp. 44–53, with 5 drawings & 19 notes.
York, Normanton, Hull, and other Yorkshire stations.

10344 LLOYD, D. and INSALL, D. Railway station architecture. *Newton Abbot: David & Charles*, [1967]. pp. 60, with 16 illus on 8 plates.
Reprinted from *Industrial Archaeology* (August 1967), with corrections.
—— [Reprint]. *David & Charles*, 1978. pp. [ii], 60, with 16 illus on 8 plates.
A reprint with a new introduction and a few corrections.

10345 BERRIDGE, P. S. A. The girder bridge: after Brunel and others. *London: R. Maxwell*, 1969. pp. xviii, 172, with frontis & 47 illus on 37 plates, & in text, 18 line drawings & diagrams.

10346 KUBINSKY, M. Bahnhofe europas: ihre Geschichte, Kunst und Technik für Eisenbahnfreunde, Architekten und kulturgeschichtlich Interessierte; mit 375 Abbildungen. *Stuttgart: Franck'sche Verlagshandlung*, 1969. la. 8°. pp. 320, with 375 illus.
pp. 180–98 *et passim*, 'Grossbritannien'.
Each station is indexed under the name of its town or city.

10347 GOSLING, F. A. A Register of Closed Signal Boxes. *Edinburgh: D.E.D. Blades*, [1971]. pp. [52]. Reproduced typescript.
Scotland only, arranged alphabetically under pre-Grouping company names. Period, 1887 to 1967.

10348 HOLLAND, H. Travellers' architecture. *London: Harrap*, 1971. la. 8°. pp. 223, with numerous illus.
ch. 4 (pp. 35–135), 'Travel on the railways', with 150 illus (photos, sketches, architectural drawings, maps & plans), & a bibliography (17 sources).
Coverage, British Isles and other countries. 'Derived from personal experience over a period of 76 years based at Euston, LMSR and BR (LMR), and on journeys in connection with the design, construction and supervision of stations and ancillary buildings.'

10349 TURTON, F. Railway bridge maintenance. *London: Hutchinson Educational*, 1972. pp. 152, with illus & diagrams.
A technical non-historical work for engineers, but in ch. 1 (pp. 15–18) 'Historical records' provides a useful summary account of historical aspects such as ageing and weight-load increases now far in excess of original estimates.

10350 BIDDLE, G. Victorian stations: railway stations in England and Wales, 1830–1923. *Newton Abbot: David & Charles*, 1973. pp. 256, with 48 illus on 24 plates, & 46 line drawings in text. Glossary of architectural terms (pp. 231–5).

10351 BOWERS, M. Railway styles in building, with photographs by Patrick Watters. *London: Almark*, 1975. pp. 95, with frontis & 148 illus (47 col.).

10352 COCKMAN, F. G. Railway architecture. *Princes Risborough: Shire Publications*, 1976. pp. 32, with 58 illus, & notes & illus on covers.

10353 BIDDLE, G. and SPENCE, J. The British railway station; drawings by Peter Fells. *Newton Abbot: David & Charles*, 1977. (Railway History in Pictures series). pp. 96. Intro (pp. 7–15) & 128 illus with descrs.

10354 SAVE BRITAIN'S HERITAGE. Off the rails: saving railway architecture; a companion to the exhibition at the RIBA Heinz Gallery, 19 January to March, 1977; edited by David Pearce and Marcus Binney of Save Britain's Heritage. *London: Save Britain's Heritage*, 1977. pp. 68, with 60 illus & 2 inside covers.
pp. 54–57, 'Selected station architects': a list of the more notable British architects with their chief works, by Matthew Saunders.
pp. 58–62, 'Listed buildings': stations, viaducts, houses and bridges, of special architectural or historic interest (England & Scotland).
pp. 63–66, 'Demolished and maltreated stations', by Alan Young.
'This book is more than a guide to an exhibition; it is a unique study of railway architecture, its history, legacy and maltreatment . . . [published] to arouse concern about the continuing destruction of historic buildings'. Coverage, England, Scotland and Wales.

10355 COLTAS, J. A. G. H. Railway stations of Britain: just a glimpse. *Crete (Nebraska): J-B Publishing Co*, 1979. (Railway History Monograph, vol.8). pp. ii, 56, with frontis & 56 illus.
Photographs, with brief commentaries on the buildings, station facilities, and the nature of the traffic served.

10356 SAVE BRITAIN'S HERITAGE. Railway architecture, written by members and associates of Save Britain's Heritage; edited by Marcus Binney and David Pearce. *London: Orbis*, 1979. la. 8°. pp. 256, with frontis, 208 illus (mostly col.), & maps.
Introduction, by Marcus Binney
Major city stations, by David Atwell
Large town stations, by David Lloyd
Small town stations, by Peter Burman
Country and suburban stations, by Alan Young
Railway hotels, by Christopher Monkhouse
Bridges & viaducts, by Richard Hughes
Engine sheds, by Chris Hawkins & George Reeve
Railway towns, by Sophie Andreae
Half steam ahead: British Rail's attitude today, by David Pearce.
Re-using railway buildings, by Marcus Binney
Appendix [notes on selected stations and associated buildings], by Marcus Binney
Bibliography (27+ sources).

E 6   MECHANICAL ENGINEERING
(Locomotives, carriages and wagons, generally)
10357–82

For the operation of trains, and train services, see **G 1, G 2** *and* **G 3**

10357 NOCK, O. S. Steam railways of Britain in colour; illustrated by Clifford and Wendy Meadway. *London: Blandford Press*, 1967. pp. 195, with 194 col. illus (pp. 13–108), individually described (pp. 109–95).

Locomotives, carriages, signals, insignia: a companion volume to *The Pocket Encyclopaedia of British Steam Locomotives*, by O. S. Nock (1964).

10358 NOCK, O. S. The Railway Enthusiast's Encyclopaedia. *London: Hutchinson*, 1968. pp. 341, with illus, chronology (pp. 13–20), biographies of 93 personalities (pp. 311–33), & a bibliography (pp. 335–41) of 106 sources.

British railway development, largely in mechanical engineering.

—— [Paperback edn]. *London: Arrow Books*, 1970. pp. 316.

10359 LARDNER, D. Letter to Peter Barlow . . . respecting some parts of his reports addressed to the directors and proprietors of the London and Birmingham Railway Company. *London: printed by Rich and Taylor*, 1835. pp. 51–6. No title-page. 'Reprinted from the London and Edinburgh Philosophical Magazine and Journal of Science for January 1836.'

The effects of gradients (rising and falling) upon the speed of trains. The writer challenges Peter Barlow to 'show how these views of mine are at variance with the established principles of mechanics'.

10360 EXTRACTS from Proceedings before the Judicial Committee of Her Majesty's Most Honourable Privy Council, February 12, 1849, on the petition of Mr. Hardy and others for the extension of letters patent for making railway axles. Present, Lord Brougham, Lord Langdale, Dr. Lushington, Mr. Pemberton Leigh. *Birmingham: Josiah Allen & Son, printers*, 1849. pp. 14.

10361 DREDGE, J. A record of the transportation exhibits at the World's Columbian Exposition of 1893 . . . *New York: J. Wiley; London: Engineering*, 1894. la. 8°. pp. lii, 779, with 192 plates, 404 illus & 108 tables. 'Partly printed from Engineering.'

Sections 4, 5 & 6 (pp. 103–504, & plates 22–136) have a great many descriptions of British exhibits, including historical drawings of older locomotives. The LNWR is particularly well represented.

10362 TRITTON, J. S. The Inspecting Engineer's contribution to railway economy. [*privately printed?*]. pp. 35, with 18 illus (diagrams, specimen forms, tables of procedure, photos).

'Reprint of presidential address delivered before the Institution of Locomotive Engineers on 17th October 1951.'

The inspection of locomotives, rolling stock and permanent-way material after manufacture and before release for service. Based upon the author's 'long personal experience' in this area of activity.

10363 RAILWAY CORRESPONDENCE & TRAVEL SOCIETY. In memory of a great royal railway traveller: H.M. King George VI, 1936–1952. *R.C. & T.S.*, 1952. pp. 4. 8 illus of royal trains. No text.

10364 WHITEHOUSE, P. B. Main Line Album. *London: Ian Allan*, 1964. pp. 33 (text, with 22 illus), & 174 illus on 94 plates, with descrs.

From the late 1920s to 1963.

pp. 6–15, A generation in railway photography, by M. W. Earley; pp. 16–33, Locomotive reflections, by Norman Harvey.

10365 RAILWAY Colour Album. *London: Ian Allan*, [1967]. pp. 37. Intro (pp. 3–7), & 44 illus (28 col.), with descrs.

Locomotives and trains.

10366 ROLT, L. T. C. The Mechanicals: progress of a profession. *London: Heinemann, for the Institution of Mechanical Engineers*, 1967. pp. xii, 163, with 76 illus on 36 plates.

10367 NOCK, O. S. Railways at the turn of the century, 1895–1905; illustrated by Clifford and Wendy Meadway. *London: Blandford Press*, 1969. (Railways of the World in Colour). pp.v, 186, with 192 col. illus (pp. 7–102) individually described (pp. 103–86).

10368 HISTORICAL MODEL RAILWAY SOCIETY. A Portfolio of Railway Drawings. *Bromley: the Society*.

Vol. 1, 1970. obl. format. pp. 32, 47 groups of dimensioned drawings of locomotives, rolling stock, signals, buildings and miscellaneous lineside features.

10369 NOCK, O. S. Railways in the years of pre-eminence, 1905–1919; illustrated by Clifford and Wendy Meadway. *London: Blandford Press*, 1971. (Railways of the World in Colour). pp. 194, with 188 col. illus (pp. 11–106) individually described (pp. 107–88).

10370 SNELL, J. B. Mechanical engineering: railways. *London: Longman*, 1971. (Industrial Archaeology series). pp. xi, 177, with 33 illus on 16 plates, 7 line drawings, bibliographical notes (pp. 162–6) & a bibliography (40 sources).

A companion volume to *Civil Engineering: railways*, by B. Morgan (1971). Both works were republished as paperbacks by Arrow Books, 1973, but with titles: *Railways: mechanical engineering*, and *Railways: civil engineering*.

10371 ELLIS, C. H. The Lore of the Train. *New York: Crescent Books*, 1973. 4°. pp. 240, with 9 reproduced paintings (col.) & over 300 line drawings (44 col.) & other illus; bibliography (71 sources).
A *de luxe* edition designed and produced by Tre Tryckare AB, Sweden, and based on the ideas of Ewert Cagner; supervising editor, Turlough Johnston. The main illustrations (line drawings) are by Åke Gustavsson.
A detailed and profusely illustrated survey of the development of railway locomotion, in seven chapters, the first two covering the period before 1830. An appendix entitled 'The future of the Train' is written by P. M. Kalla-Bishop.

10372 MORGAN, B. The great trains; editor, Bryan Morgan; assistant editor, Alan A. Jackson, with contributions by John Snell . . . [and others]; foreword by Sir John Elliott. *Cambridge: P. Stephens, 'created & produced by Edita Lausanne', Switzerland*, 1973. 4°. pp. 259, with over 200 illus (26 col.) & maps (some col.).

10373 NOCK, O. S. Railways in the formative years, 1851–1895; illustrated by Clifford and Wendy Meadway. *London: Blandford Press*, 1973. (Railways of the World in Colour). pp. 156, with 151 col. illus (pp. 13–92) individually described (pp. 93–156).

10374 ELLIS, C. H. The royal trains. *London: Routledge & Kegan Paul*, 1975. pp. [viii], 183, with 105 illus.

10375 WHITEHOUSE, P. B. Great trains of the world, edited by Patrick B. Whitehouse; picture research, Patricia E. Hornsey. *London: New English Library; Hamlyn Books*, 1975. la. 8°. pp. 256, with 375 illus (mostly col.), & 6 maps.

10376 RUSSELL, P. A Silver Jubilee tribute to British royal trains. *Locomotive Club of Great Britain*, [1977]. (Bulletin Supplement). pp. xvi, with 22 illus. Title from cover.
Photographs from the Ken Nunn Collection, with text and historical notes by Patrick Russell.

10377 CROSS, D. Double-headed trains. *London: Ian Allan*.
vol. 1, South. 1979. pp. 96. Intro & 165 illus with descrs.

10378 WALLACE, M. Engine drivers of the great steam trains; illustrated by Michael Turner. *London: Macdonald Educational*, 1979. (Macdonald Living History series). pp. 61, with ca. 85 col. illus (drawings).
Brief accounts of trains and travel in various countries. Not a biographical work or one of collected memoirs.

10379 WESTWOOD, J. N. Trains. *London: Galley Press; Cathay Books*, 1979. pp. 64, with 70 col. illus. Cover title, 'Trains in colour'.
A world-wide selection of modern locomotives and trains.

10380 DUNN, J. Modern trains. *London: New English Library*, 1980. Large print. pp. 155. 245 col. illus with accompanying descriptions.
World-wide selective coverage. Includes rapid transit and mountain railways.

10381 ROGERS, H. C. B. Transition from steam. *London: Ian Allan*, 1980. pp. 128, with 175 illus.

10382 TILLER, R. BR125, High Speed Train; edited with additional material by Michael Oakley; graphics by Bob Morriss. *Truro: Bradford Barton; Sutton Coldfield; Diesel & Electric Group*, [1980]. pp. [32], with 22 illus, 3 tables (logs of runs), a dimensioned drawing, & a map of 'High Speed' routes.

E 7   LOCOMOTIVES

General works on steam, electric and diesel locomotives

10383–94

10383 YARWOOD, J. K. The Dumpy Pocket Book of Locomotives. *London: Sampson Low*, 1961. sm. obl. 8°. pp. 191, with many illus, lists, diagrams, & a supplementary section on railway signalling (pp. 179–89).
'Most of the principal types and classes of locomotives, multiple-units and railcars on BR and in six neighbouring countries of Europe.'

10384 BURRIDGE, F. H. A. Nameplates of the Big Four, including British Railways. *Oxford: Oxford Publishing*, 1975. pp. 160, with over 600 illus & diagrs, with notes and lists.

10385 URIE S15 PRESERVATION GROUP. The Barry List. 2nd edn. [*n.p.*]: *the Group*, 1975. pp. [5], with 16 illus (6 on covers).
Lists, with details, of 150 locomotives stored at Woodham Brothers' scrapyard, Barry Docks.
—— 3rd edn. *Isleworth: the Group*, [1978]. pp. [24], with 14 illus (5 on covers).
130 locomotives.

10386 CADE'S Locomotive Guide, written by Dennis Lovett and Leslie Wood; edited by Reg Cade. *Bletchley: Marwain*, [1980]. pp. 168, with many illus.

A handbook of historical & technical data on locomotives currently available as commercially-produced models in OO and HO scales.

10387　BRUSH ELECTRICAL ENGINEERING COMPANY. Locomotives. *Loughborough: the Company*, January 1904. (Brush Bulletin, 5). [A reprint]. *Market Harborough: Industrial Railway Society*, 1974. pp. 28.
An illustrated publicity brochure with detailed descriptions and additional notes by the I.R.S. Cover title: Steam & electric locomotives.

10388　PELLOW, W. N. The work of the Motive Power Department. (Proceedings of the British Railways (W.R.) London Lecture & Debating Society, session 1951–52, no. 390). pp. 23, with discussion, 5 illus, 4 charts & a plan.
Author, 'Motive Power Supt, W.R.'

10389　ROLT, L. T. C. A Hunslet hundred: one hundred years of locomotive building by the Hunslet Engine Company. *Dawlish: David & Charles; London: Macdonald*, 1964. pp. 177, with frontis, 48 illus on 28 plates, 11 plans (5 folded) of the works from 1847 to 1963. Index, pp. 169–77.
Steam and diesel locomotives.

10390　SIMMONS, J. Four locomotives. *Leicester: Leicester Museums*, 1968. pp. 9, with 5 illus.
Two Midland Rly locomotives, a North Eastern Rly electric locomotive of 1904, and an industrial

tank locomotive of 1905, principal exhibits housed in a temporary museum, formerly the Stoneygate terminus tramway depot.

10391　BOND, R. C. A lifetime with locomotives. *Cambridge: Goose & Son*, 1975. pp. 329, with 84 illus on 40 plates & a bibliography (34 sources).
An autobiography from apprenticeship, Derby Works, Midland Rly, 1920, to Chief Mechanical Engineer, BR Central Staff, 1953–58 and later appointments.

10392　WEAVER, R. Baguley locomotives, 1914–1931 . . . *Sheffield: Industrial Railway Society*, 1975. pp. 96, with 68 illus on 34 pp., 9 diagrams & 7 tables.
Steam, internal combustion, and electric locomotives.

10393　ANTELL, R. Rail scene in colour. *London: Ian Allan*, 1978. pp. 64. Intro [by B. K. Cooper], pp. 5–17, & 77 illus (all col.) with descrs.
Locomotives, 1960s–1970s.

10394　NELSON, R. I. Locomotive performance: a footplate survey. *London: Ian Allan*, 1979. pp. 231, with 55 illus on 24 plates & 63 tables (logs of runs).
Records of journeys made on steam, diesel, & electric locomotives over a period of 30 years, on British and Irish railways. The logs include degrees of boiler pressure, regulator use, and valve cut-off.

E 8　STEAM LOCOMOTIVES

10395–10601

General works 10395–10509

E 8 a Steam locomotive construction　10510–48
E 8 b Steam locomotive performance　10549–72
E 8 c Steam locomotive preservation　10573–601

For locomotives of a particular railway see **L**; *for those of railways in a specific area see* **C 1–C 7**, *and for those of British Railways see* **B 10**

For steam locomotives on light railways and tramways see **D 1**; *narrow gauge railways,* **D 2**; *industrial railways,* **D 3**; *miniature railways,* **D 6**

For biographies of steam locomotive engineers associated with a particular railway, such as Nigel Gresley, see **L, C 1–C 7,** *or* **B 10**

For model locomotive engineering see **Q 2**

Steam locomotives generally
10395–10509

Reference sources 10395–401
Biographies and memoirs 10402–7
(Collective, 10402–3)
Historical and contemporaneous in one chronological sequence by date of publication 10408–10509

Reference sources

10395　NOCK, O. S. The Pocket Encyclopedia of

British Steam Locomotives in Colour . . . illustrated by Clifford and Wendy Meadway. *London: Blandford Press*, 1964. pp. 192, with historical intro (pp. 7–13), 6 maps & 192 col. illus (pp. 17–112) individually described (pp. 113–86).
A companion volume to *Steam Railways of Britain in Colour*, by O. S. Nock (1967).

10396　WILLIAMS, A. and PERCIVAL, D. B.R. steam locomotives from nationalisation to modernisation: a complete list . . . *London: Ian Allan.*

part 1, Ex-GWR locomotives 1–9799: also ex-War Department and BR standard locomotives 70000–92250. 1967. pp. 79. Intro, tables, & 128 illus on 32 plates.

part 2, Ex-SR locomotives 1–2699, C1–40, 21C1–170, W1–34, BR 30001–36001, W1–36. 1967. pp. 64. Intro, table & 128 illus on 32 plates.

part 3, Ex-LMS locomotives 1–28622, BR 40001–58937. 1967. pp. 72. Intro, tables & 127 illus on 32 plates.

part 4, Ex-LNER locomotives 1–10000 (BR 60001–69999). 1967. pp. 80. Intro, tables & 128 illus on 32 plates.

10397 JONES, K. P. Steam locomotive development: an analytical guide to the literature on British steam locomotive development, 1923–1962. *London: Library Association,* 1969. pp. 413.

A comprehensive & detailed bibliography based on a thesis accepted by the L.A. for Fellowship, 1968. Sources: books, periodical essays, reports, publications of professional bodies and of amateur societies.

10398 REED, B. Locomotives in profile; general editor, Brian Reed, with illustrations by David Warner, Peter Warner, Arthur Wolstenholme. *Windsor: Profile Publications.* 4 vols.

vol. 1, 1971. pp. 292, with 428 illus (54 col.), 60 drawings, 117 tables, diagrams, maps & graphs.
Contents:

LNER non-streamlined Pacifics	Brian Reed
New York Central Hudsons	Brian Reed
Great Western 4-cylinder 4-6-0s	Brian Reed
American Type 4-4-0	Brian Reed
British Single-Drivers	Brian Reed
The Mallets	Brian Reed
The Rocket	Brian Reed
Royal Scots	Brian Reed
Camels and Camelbacks	Brian Reed
The Met Tanks	Brian Reed
Norris Locomotives	Brian Reed
BR Britannias	Brian Haresnape

vol. 2, 1972. pp. 288, with 434 illus (42 col.), 120 tables, diagrams, maps & graphs.
Contents:

Nord Pacifics	Brian Reed
Pennsylvania Pacifics	Brian Reed
The Crewe Type	D. H. Stuart & Brian Reed
Union Pacific 4-12-2s	Brian Reed
Jones Goods & Indian L	Brian Reed
German Austerity 2-10-0	Brian Reed
Gresley A4s	Ron Scott & Brian Reed
The American 4-8-4	Brian Reed
R.O.D. 2-8-0s	Brian Reed
Merchant Navy Pacifics	Brian Reed
Darjeeling Tanks	Brian Reed
Pennsylvania Duplexii	Brian Reed

vol. 3, 1974. pp. 148, with frontis & 106 illus (22 col.), 44 tables, drawings, maps, graphs & gradient profiles.
Contents:

Locomotion	Brian Reed
The Hiawathas	Brian Reed
Tilbury Tanks	Kenneth H. Leech
S.P. Cab-in-Fronts	Brian Reed
Austrian 2-8-4s Dr.-Ing.Fr. Altmann & B. Reed
G.N. Large Atlantics	Ron Scott

vol. 4, 1974. pp. 288, with triple frontis, 221 illus (24 col.), 46 tables, diagrams, maps & graphs.
Contents:

Lima Super-Power	C. P. Atkins & Brian Reed
The Brighton Gladstones	Brian Reed
B.R. Class 9F 2-10-0	Brian Reed
Caledonian 4-4-0s	
	Alan G. Dunbar & Brian Reed
Canadian Pacific Selkirks	C. P. Atkins
South African 4-8-2s	Brian Reed

10399 CASSERLEY, H. C. The Observer's Book of British Steam Locomotives. *London: F. Warne,* 1974. (Observer's Pocket Series, 23). sm. 8°. pp. 190, with 140 illus.

10400 BAXTER, B. British Locomotive Catalogue, 1825–1923, compiled by the late Bertram Baxter; edited by David Baxter. *Hartington: Moorland Publishing Co.*

An intended 8-volume work recording the known data of every locomotive built during this period, including steam miniature railways up to 1939. (Approximately 44,000 locomotives and 370 owning companies).

vol. 1, General summary. Index of locomotive-owning companies. 1977. pp. 88.

vol. 2A, London & North Western Railway and its constituent companies. 1978. pp. 180.

vol. 2B, London & North Western Railway and its constituent companies [cont.]. 1979. pp. [4], 185–395.

10401 CASSERLEY, H. C. The Observer's Directory of British Steam Locomotives. *London: F. Warne,* 1980. sm. obl. format. pp. 239, with 565 illus.

565 locomotive types described and illustrated.

Biographies and memoirs

10402 CHARLTON, L. G. The first locomotive engineers: their work in the North East of England. *Newcastle upon Tyne: Frank Graham,* 1974. (Northern History Booklet, 55). pp. 72, with 9 illus & map on 8 plates, 16 diagrams & 3 facsims in text.

10403 WESTWOOD, J. N. Locomotive designers in the age of steam. *London: Sidgwick & Jackson,* 1977. pp. 285, with 57 illus on 32 plates, & 40 diagrams.

A world-wide survey: part 1, 'Outstanding men'; part 2, 'A biographical encyclopaedia which includes both the big names and the more interesting of the lesser men.'

10404 BROOKS, P. R. B. William Hedley: locomotive pioneer. *Newcastle upon Tyne: Tyne & Wear Industrial Monuments Trust,* 1980. pp. 16, with 14 illus (drawings, facsimiles, portrait), & 3 illus & a map on covers; bibliography (9 sources).

10405 HOWE, W. L. A short biography of William Howe, 1814–1879, inventor of the 'Stephenson' reversing link motion. [*Liverpool: the author,* 1963]. pp. 7, with 2 diagrams.

10406 ROGERS, H. C. B. The last steam locomotive engineer: R. A. Riddles. *London: Allen & Unwin*, 1970. pp. 215, with frontis & 59 illus on 30 plates & a bibliography (55 sources).

10407 HODGE, J. Richard Trevithick, 1771–1833. *Princes Risborough: Shire Publications* 1973. (Lifelines series, 6). pp. 48, with 25 illus, a chronology, and a brief bibliography.

Historical and contemporaneous

(arranged into one chronological sequence by date of publication)

10408 MILLINGTON, J. An epitome of the elementary principles of natural and experimental philosophy; part the first, comprehending the general properties of matter, mechanics, . . . and a copious account of the invention, progress and present state of the steam engine . . . *London: the author*, 1823. pp. vii, 358, with col. frontis & 13 folded plates.

pp. 323–31 have refs to R. Trevithick's 'steam engine' (locomotive) and fig. 137 of plate 13 depicts the stationary version.

—— 2nd edn. *London: Simpkin & Marshall*, 1830. pp. xiv, 542, with frontis but no plates, the illus from the 1st edn. having been brought into the text and re-engraved. The frontispiece of the BL copy is not coloured.

pp. 493–8 & fig. 165, Trevithick's engine.

10409 GUYONNEAU DE PAMBOUR, F. M. A new theory of the steam engine and the mode of calculation by means of it of the effective power, etc., of every kind of steam engine, stationary or locomotive. *London: J. Weale*, 1838. pp. 58.

10410 DIXON, J. Traction on railways and the alleged loss of power at high speeds practically considered, by John Dixon, Engineer in Chief of the Stockton and Darlington Railway. *Darlington: the author*, 1864. pp. 45, with 3 tables. 'For private distribution only'.

Calculations based on experimental runs with locomotives on the S. & D. Rly in 1862 and 1863.

10411 GREENER, T. Timothy Hackworth, one of the greatest inventors of the 19th century. [no date: ca. 1895]. pp. 16.

N. KERR CAT. 224/115.

10412 STACKHOUSE, J. F. Our locomotives, by 'J.F.S.'. *London: Headley Bros.*, 1895. obl. format. pp. [66], with 16 illus.

Drawings by J. F. Stackhouse with descriptions on facing pages. Preface: 'Recognising the demand . . . for sketches and particulars of the chief express engines of the great railway companies it is our aim in the following pages, to meet this'. The first 'locomotive album'?

The drawings are made from photographs and drawings supplied by various railway companies.

10413 LOCOMOTIVE Magazine Special Series, nos. 1 to 6. *London: Locomotive Publishing Co.*, 1900. la. 8°. pp. [92]. No title-page or Introduction. Title on cover: 'British expresses . . .'

Six supplements originally issued with the *Locomotive Magazine*, 1898–1900, re-issued as a bound collection with the title of each printed on the cover.

[1], British expresses, 1898; Christmas number of the Locomotive Magazine. *London: F. Moore*, December 1898. pp. [16]. Col. folded frontis, contents page & 15 illus.

[2], The World's famous railway trains, 1899: the Summer number of the Locomotive Magazine. *London: Locomotive Publishing Co.*, July 1899. pp. [16]. Col. frontis, intro & 17 illus.

[3], The British express locomotive during the Victorian era. *London: Locomotive Publishing Co.*, [Christmas, 1899]. pp. [16], intro & 12 illus.

[4], Locomotives of 1900: Summer number of the Locomotive Magazine. *London: Locomotive Publishing Co.*, [1900]. pp. [16]. Text, col. frontis & 14 illus.

5, Locomotives at work: Xmas Supplement to the Locomotive Magazine, 1900; no. 5 of Special Series. *London: Locomotive Publishing Co.*, 1900. pp. [12]. Intro & 25 illus.

6, Cars of 1900: Supplement to the Locomotive Magazine, no. 6 of Special Series. *London: Locomotive Publishing Co.*, [1900]. pp. 16. Text, 14 illus & 17 dimensioned drawings.

10414 JOHNSON, H. G. Some features of the steam locomotive. Great Western Railway (London) Lecture & Debating Society, meeting on 6th February 1936, no. 300. pp. 20, with discussion, 12 illus & 7 diagrams.

10415 CHAPELON, A. La locomotive à vapeur. *Paris: J. B. Baillière*, 1938. pp. 914, with 14 folded plates & many illus.

'A scientific analysis of every function of the locomotive, from the firegrate to the driving wheels . . . : a summary of existing knowledge' (Review by E. L. Diamond in the *Railway Magazine*, June 1938, p. 451). Includes British locomotive development.

10416 KIDNER, R. W. The early history of the railway locomotive, 1804–1879. *Chislehurst: Oakwood Press*, 1946. (A Short History of Mechanical Traction & Travel, 3). pp. 38, with 18 illus on 8 plates, & 71 drawings by the author.

10417 COOK, A. F. Locomotion. *London: Ian Allan*, 1948. sm. obl. 8°. Intro & 25 illus with descrs.

10418 ROBERTS, G. P. British War Department locomotives, 1952–1960; edited by Eric S. Tonks. *Birmingham: Birmingham Locomotive Club*, 1960. (Pocket Book, WD). sm. 8°. pp. 20.

Lists (6-column), with notes.

10419 FAMOUS railway engines of the world. *London: Percival Marshall*, [1961]. obl. format. pp. 32, with 20 illus.

Of the seventeen steam locomotives described, eight are British.

10420 LEEDS CITY MUSEUM. 150 years of steam locomotives, 1812–1962: exhibition, Leeds City Museum, September 15th–22nd 1962. [*Leeds: the Museum*, 1962]. pp. 8, incl. cover. Reproduced typescript, printed cover.
Date on cover altered in MS from '22nd' to '29th'.

10421 LIVSEY, J. The development of the Fairlie double engine. [*Newport*]: *Monmouthshire Railway Society*, June 1962. pp. 8.

10422 WESTERN, B. and ORCHARD, R. Locomotive Library. *Percival Marshall*, 1962. sm. obl. format. pp. 60. Brief intro, & 61 illus with descrs.
Photographs of steam locomotives in service in early 1960 taken for the *Model Engineer* by Brian Western, with descriptions by Robin Orchard.

10423 COLE, D. Contractors' locomotives. *London: Union Publications*.
part 1, Brassey, Firbank, Walker. 1964. pp. 15. Three 6-column chronological listings.

10424 FENTON, E. W. Nineteenth century locomotive engravings. *London: Hugh Evelyn*, 1964. la. obl. format. pp. [24].
20 engravings originally published in the *Railway Engineer*, and the *Engineer*, prefaced by an introduction & notes.

10425 KIDNER, R. W. Contractors' locomotives. *Lingfield: Oakwood Press*, [1964]. pp. [22]. Intro & 35 illus with captions.

10426 NOCK, O. S. British steam locomotives in colour, with 192 locomotives illustrated by Clifford and Wendy Meadway. *London: Blandford Press*, 1964. pp. 192. 192 col. illus on 86 plates, with individual commentaries by O. S. Nock.

10427 ROCHE, F. J. Historic locomotive drawings in 4mm. scale, drawn by F. J. Roche. *London: Ian Allan*, [1964]. obl. format. pp. 104.
A representative selection of 100 composite dimensioned drawings of locomotives, mostly from all four Group companies; front, side & end elevations.
—— 1971, *Ian Allan*. pp. 104.
—— 1976, *Ian Allan*. pp. 104.

10428 ROLT, L. T. C. Patrick Stirling's locomotives. *London: Hamish Hamilton*, 1964. pp. 64, with 70 illus & 7 mechanical drawings.

10429 WILLIAMS, A. and PERCIVAL, D. Steam locomotives. *London: Ian Allan*, 1964. (Veteran & Vintage Series). pp. 64, with 60 illus.
60 locomotive classes described & illustrated.

10430 ELLIS, C. H. The splendour of Steam; with a foreword by Peter Allen. *London: Allen & Unwin*, 1965. obl. 8°. pp. 132, with col. frontis, 15 col. plates & 43 drawings.
Mostly British locomotives & trains.

10431 GIFFORD, C. T. Decline of Steam. *London: Ian Allan*, [1965]. la. obl. format. pp. [171]. Preface, pictorial t.p. & 291 illus.

10432 LOCOMOTIVE drawings; comprising a selection of work by F. C. Hambleton, L. Ward, J. N. Maskelyne, J. C. Cosgrave, G. F. Bird, R. C. Menzies, etc. (Compiled by W. Beckerlegge & W. J. Reynolds). *London: Stephenson Locomotive Society*, [1965]. obl. format. pp. [vi], 61 (verso pages blank) composed of 200 drawings. No text. Title from cover.
'Published in response to a demand for an issue in permanent form of the numerous drawings by F. C. Hambleton and L. Ward which have appeared in the *Journal of the S.L.S.*, with additional drawings from *The Locomotive*. The index relates each illustration to its source in one or other of these periodicals, where particulars and dimensions may readily be found.'

10433 KITE, J. E. 1850–1925 Vintage Album. *Hatch End: Roundhouse Books*, 1966. pp. [102], with 199 illus.
Photographs of locomotives with commentaries, selected 'for rarity of subject matter rather than for excellence of photography'.

10434 NOCK, O. S. The British steam railway locomotive, 1925–65, [vol. 2], by O. S. Nock. *London: Ian Allan*, 1966. pp. 276, with frontis, 415 illus, including diagrams & working drawings (some folded).
A sequel to *The British Steam Railway Locomotive, 1825 to 1925* by E. L. Ahrons (1927) & in this sense 'vol. 2' (on spine only).

10435 TREACY, E. Lure of Steam. *London: Ian Allan*, 1966. pp. 208, with intro, frontis, & 440 illus with descrs.
A 'personal selection' by Canon Treacy of photographs taken by him over the past 35 years. His autobiographical Introduction (pp. 7–10) is noteworthy.

10436 GLOVER, G. British locomotive design, 1825–1960, with photographs selected and supplied by J. H. Court. *London: Allan & Unwin*, 1967. pp. 113, with 52 illus on 24 plates, & 12 drawings in text.

10437 LAST years of British Steam. *London: Ian Allan*.
1st series, compiled by G. Freeman Allen. 1967. pp. [128]. Intro & 189 illus, with descrs.
2nd series, 1973. pp. [194]. 344 illus with descrs.
The second series was originally published as the four 1972 issues of the Ian Allan quarterly *Trains Illustrated*.

10438 TREACY, E. Portrait of Steam. *London: Ian Allan*, 1967. pp 200. 4°. Frontis & 383 photographs by E. Treacy, with descrs.
A second selection.

10439 ALLEN, C. J. British Atlantic locomotives. *London: Ian Allan*, 1968. pp. 164, with 70 illus on 32 plates; 53 tables.
—— [another edn.], rev. & enl. by G.

Freeman Allen. *Ian Allan*, 1976. pp. 143, with 111 illus on 48 plates; 53 tables.

10440 'FENMAN' [i.e. John L. Boyd & others]. Images of Steam, [by] 'Fenman'. *Shepperton: Ian Allan*, 1968. 4°. pp. 192. Intro & 276 photographs with captions and with details listed at end (pp. 187–92).

Introduced with essays by the five photographers who produced the work under the joint pseudonym of 'Fenman'—John Boyd, John Coiley, Stephen Crook, David Hepburne-Scott, 'Atque Quintus'—all of Cambridge University Railway Club in the 1950s.

10441 JACKSON, B. H. Photo-rail: the Bryan H. Jackson Collection. *Harrow-on-the-Hill: B. H. Jackson*, 1968. pp. 44, with 11 illus.

A sales catalogue of ca. 500 photographs of steam locomotives, 1950s–1960s, arranged by classes under BR Regions, with technical data, and date & place of the photography.

10442 KICHENSIDE, G. M. Steam Portfolio, edited by G. M. Kichenside; photographed by Malcolm Dunnett, Paul Hocquard, Roderic Hoyle, Ian Krause, Leslie Nixon, John Vaughan. *London: Ian Allan*, 1968. 4°. pp. 238. 373 illus with captions, each photographer's section being introduced with brief details on technique.

10443 LEECH, J. Farewell to Steam: a photographic impression. *Manchester: Bahamas Locomotive Society*, 1968. obl. format. pp. [32]. 54 illus.

—— 2nd impression (with some alterations), pp. [32]. 54 illus.

10444 COX, E. S. World Steam in the twentieth century. *London: Ian Allan*, 1969. pp. 191, with 111 illus on 56 plates, & 34 tables.

10445 DURRANT, A. E. The Garratt locomotive. *Newton Abbot: David & Charles*, 1969. pp. 144, with illus, diagrams & a bibliography (19 sources).

Includes examples on British railways: the Great Central, LMS, LNER, and on the Surrey Border & Camberley Rly, a private line in 10½in. gauge.

10446 KITE, J. E. Vintage Steam. *London: Ian Allan*, 1969. pp. 104. Preface & 223 illus with descrs.

10447 TREACY, E. Glory of Steam. *London: Ian Allan*, 1969. la. 8°. Intro (pp. 5–7) & 154 illus with descrs.

Photographs made by Canon Treacy since the 1930s.

10448 TUPLIN, W. A. British Steam since 1900. *Newton Abbot: David & Charles*, 1969. pp. 200, with frontis & 63 illus on 16 plates, & 14 line drawings in text; 6 appendices, no. 2 (pp. 169–86) being a detailed reference list in 15 columns of the dimensions of 208 locomotives, with an introduction. Appendix 6 is a bibliography (39 sources).

—— Reprint, *Pan Books*, 1971.

10449 WHITEHOUSE, P. B. Steam on the shed. *London: Ian Allan*, 1969. la. 8°. pp. 192. Intro & 303 illus with descrs.

Locomotives photographed in, or outside their depots. Arranged into 34 sections, each with an introduction. Period, early 1930s to late 1960s.

10450 CLAY, J. F. Essays in Steam: an anthology of articles from the Journal of the Stephenson Locomotive Society. *London: Ian Allan*, 1970. pp. viii, 216, with 60 illus on 32 plates.

23 essays, with an added 3-part general index.

10451 GARRATT, C. D. Symphony in Steam, written and photographed by Colin D. Garratt; with a foreword by O. S. Nock. *London: Blandford Press*, 1970. pp. 193, with 147 col. illus on 96 plates (i.e. pp. [17] to [112]).

Mostly British locomotives.

10452 HIGHET, C. Scottish locomotive history, 1831–1923. *London: Allen & Unwin*, 1970. pp. 240, with col. frontis & 37 illus on 32 plates. Foreword by Rowland C. Bond.

10453 NOCK, O. S. Rail, steam and speed. *London: Allen & Unwin*, 1970. pp. 163, with 62 illus on 32 plates.

Speed in British locomotive history.

10454 REED, B. A Source Book of Locomotives. *London: Ward Lock*, 1970. sm. obl. format. pp. 160, with 145 illus. Index.

World-wide coverage. Notes & summary data accompany each illustration.

10455 COX, E. S. Speaking of Steam. *London: Ian Allan*, 1971. pp. 128, with 76 illus on 32 plates.

An appraisal of opinions on locomotive developments expressed in past speeches to the Institution of Mechanical Engineers and the Institution of Civil Engineers by F. W. Webb, G. Hughes, G. J. Churchward, C. J. Bowen Cooke, H. Fowler, H. N. Gresley, W. A. Stanier, and O. V. S. Bulleid, accompanied by informative commentaries by the author with, at the end (pp. 114–22), his own 'Conclusion' in which the views of these eight prominent Chief Mechanical Engineers are placed 'in the broad stream of design practice right up to the end of steam traction on our railways'.

10456 DOHERTY, D. 'Model Railways' Locomotive Album, edited by Douglas Doherty. *Hemel Hempstead: Model & Allied Publications*, 1971. pp. 111, with 165 illus, and dimensioned drawings.

32 essays on a variety of railway subjects, mostly on steam locomotives.

10457 REED, B. Locomotives: a picture history. *London: Pan Books*, 1971. (A Piccolo Book). sm. obl. format. pp. 160. 145 illus, with descrs. & technical details. Of these, 80 are British and Irish locomotives.

Originally published as *A Source Book of Locomotives* (1970).

10458   RUSH, R. W. British steam railcars. *Tarrant Hinton: Oakwood Press*, [1971]. (Locomotion Papers, 53). pp. 144, with 29 illus on 12 plates, 64 dimensioned drawings, lists, and a bibliography (20 sources). pp. [143–4], corrigenda & addenda.
A detailed survey, arranged by companies.

10459   UNDERWOOD, H. Locos I have loved. *Huddersfield: Advertiser Press*, 1971. pp. 180, with frontis & 58 illus on 31 plates. Foreword by Eric Treacy.

10460   [CASSERLEY, H. C.]. Famous railway photographers: H. C. Casserley. *Newton Abbot: David & Charles*, 1972. pp. 96. Intros (pp. 5–10, 93–5) & 84 photographs with descriptive commentaries.
Period, pre-1939.

10461   CAWSTON, A. C. A Railway Photographer's Diary. *Bracknell: Town & Country Press*, 1972. pp. 91, with frontis, & 111 illus on plates & in text.
Steam locomotives and trains.

10462   GARRATT, C. D. Twilight of Steam; written and photographed by Colin D. Garratt. *London: Blandford Press*, 1972. (Last Steam Locomotives of the World series). sm. 8°. pp. 185, with 100 col. illus on 96 pp. (plates).
Steam locomotives currently at work in Western Europe: sixteen in Britain.

10463   NOCK, O. S. British steam locomotives. [*St. Ives: Photo Precision*, 1972]. 'A Colour-master publication'. pp. 39. 30 col. illus by Clifford and Wendy Meadway, individually described by O. S. Nock.
A selection from the two Blandford Press publications: *British Steam Locomotives in Colour* (1964) and *Steam Railways of Britain in Colour* (1967).

10464   ROGERS, H. C. B. Chapelon: genius of French Steam. *London: Ian Allan*, 1972. pp. 175, with 65 illus on 32 plates.
'In Great Britain, every Chief Mechanical Engineer from the 1930s onwards incorporated André Chapelon's ideas into his new construction or rebuilding' (p. 150).

10465   STEAM in camera, 1898–1959; edited by Patrick Russell for the Locomotive Club of Great Britain; photographs from the Ken Nunn Collection; graphics by Brian Stephenson. *London: Ian Allan*, 1972. pp. 128, with frontis & 217 illus with descrs, and a biographical introduction on Kenneth A. C. R. Nunn.

10466   VAUGHAN, A. The Kenning Collection, compiled by A. Vaughan. *Oxford: Oxford Publishing Co.*, 1972. obl. format. pp. 59. Intro & 59 illus of locomotives, with descrs.
A selection of photographs taken by W. L. Kenning between 1913 and the 1920s with an introduction and detailed notes to each illustration by A. Vaughan.

10467   TREACY, E. Spell of Steam. *London: Ian Allan*, 1973. la. 8°. pp. 208. Intro & 273 illus with descrs.
Including 'the best of my work over the last 40 years'.

10468   KAY, F. G. Steam locomotives. *London: Hamlyn*, 1974. la. 8°. pp. 128, with 141 illus (32 col.).
A general introductory history.

10469   KEELEY, R., PREEDY, N. and WAINWRIGHT, S. Breath of Steam. *Oxford: Oxford Publishing Co.*, 1974. la. 8°. pp. [64]. Intro & 114 illus with descrs.
A selection from the work of these three photographers.

10470   TUPLIN, W. A. The steam locomotive: its form and function. *Bath: Adams & Dart*, 1974. (Jupiter Books series). pp. 158, with frontis, 61 illus on 16 plates, 21 drawings, 3 tables & 2 appendices.
Technicalities made clear: a lucid exposition of the design, function and working of the steam locomotive and its parts.
—— Reprint, *Bradford-on-Avon: Moonraker Press*, 1980.

10471   BRITISH Railways Steam. *Great Barr: M. R. York*, [1974 or 5]. pp. 48. 85 illus with descrs. Introduction on inside cover.
'Produced jointly by the preservation funds responsible for the purchase and renovation of locomotives 75069 and 80079 on the Severn Valley Railway.'
Photographs of steam-hauled trains on BR, 1948–1968, mostly reproduced from blocks used for illustrations in the Stephenson Locomotive Society's *Journal*.

10472   ADAMS, J. and WHITEHOUSE, P. Vintage engines; edited by John Adams and Patrick Whitehouse. *London: New English Library*, 1975. obl. 8° format. pp. 160. Frontis & 217 illus with descrs.
Locomotives at work, 1880–1955: a collection from the work of various photographers.

10473   KICHENSIDE, G. Steam: portraits of the great days of the British steam locomotive, edited by Geoffrey Kichenside. *Newton Abbot: David & Charles*, 1975. 4°. pp. [72]. Intro, frontis, & 68 illus with descrs.
A selection of photographs, ca. 1900–1970s.

10474   LYNCH, P. J. Memories of Steam around Britain. *Truro: Bradford Barton*, 1975. pp. 96. Intro & 111 illus with descrs.

10475   NOCK, O. S. Locomotion: a world survey of railway traction. *London: Routledge & Kegan Paul*, 1975. obl. format. pp. viii, 280, with 207 illus (photos & line drawings), tables & a bibliography (28 sources).
Historical, world coverage. Mostly steam locomotives.

10476   REDER, G. The world of steam locomotives . . . [translated from the German by

Michael Reynolds]. *London: Blandford Press*, 1975. la. 4°. pp. 339, with 423 illus (some col.), plans, tables & a bibliography (pp. 315–7). Index.

10477   REED, B. 150 years of British steam locomotives. *Newton Abbot: David & Charles*, 1975. pp. 128, with frontis, 51 illus, 23 working drawings, 9 tables & 59 notes.

10478   TRIBUTE to British Steam. *Shepperton: Ian Allan*, [1975]. la. 8°. pp. [60]. 85 col. illus (paintings & photographs).

Paintings, chiefly by George Heiron; photographs, chiefly by Peter Williams.

10479   ZIEL, R. and EAGLESON, M. The twilight of World Steam. *London: Hamlyn*, 1975. la. 8°. pp. 304, with over 350 illus.

A pictorial record of the last years of steam locomotive working in 55 countries.

10480   CARTER, J. R. Working Steam, by J. R. Carter, footplate cameraman. *Douglas: Viking Publications*, 1976. 4°. pp. [109], with frontis, intro & 143 illus with descrs.

Period, 1952–1973.

10481   CIVIL, A. and BAKER, A. C. Fireless locomotives: being a history of all British-built examples with notes on the general history of the type and its principles of operation. *Tarrant Hinton: Oakwood Press*, 1976. (Locomotion Papers, 97). pp. 94, with 43 illus on 20 plates; 7 diagrams & 5 detailed lists.

Locomotives charged with high-pressure steam from lineside boilers, in gas works, paper mills, chemical plants, oil refineries and munitions factories. The index includes a list of builders, Andrew Barclay Ltd. producing the largest number, and a list of users: industrial railways under 'Locomotive Owners', and public passenger railways and tramways under 'Railways & Tramways'.

10482   GARRATT, C. D. The last of Steam: steam locomotives of today with colour photographs. *London: Sidgwick & Jackson*, 1976. la. 8°. pp. 128, with 19 illus (46 col.).

World-wide coverage.

—— re-published, 1978.

10483   GORDON, S. P. Trains: an illustrated history of locomotive development. *London: [Cathay Books] for W. H. Smith & Son*, 1976. la. 8°. pp. 192, with 243 illus (101 col.) & a map.

10484   NOCK, O. S. Great steam locomotives of all time . . . , illustrated by Clifford and Wendy Meadway. *Poole: Blandford Press*, 1976. pp. 145, incl. 64 col. plates, individually described (pp. 101–45).

10485   PETERS, I. Somewhere along the line: fifty years love of trains. *Oxford: Oxford Publishing [Co.]*, 1976. la. 8°. pp. [208]. Intro & 480 illus with descrs.

Locomotives and trains, mostly steam, and the railway environment, including industrial lines.

10486   POPE, M. Steam ramble. *London: Ian Allan*. la. 8°.

no. 1, South and West. 1976. pp. 96. Intro & 154 illus, with descrs.

no. 2, North and West. 1976. pp. 96. Intro & 143 illus, with descrs.

From Euston (Camden shed) via the West Coast route to Scotland.

10487   SIMMONS, J. Great British locomotives. *London: John Pinches Ltd*, 1976. pp. xxii, 114, with 12 line drawings & (pp. 112–4) 'Literature': a select bibliography.

The 50 locomotives described are those depicted on a set of 50 ingots offered for sale by John Pinches Ltd. The book was not published, copies being reserved for presentation to purchasers of the ingots as an historical companion. A unique feature of the work is the essay as Appendix 2 (pp. 109–11), 'The price of locomotives'.

10488   TOURRET, R. War Department locomotives. *[Abingdon]: Tourret Publishing*, 1976. (Allied Military Locomotives of the Second World War, 2). la. 8°. pp. 82, with 93 illus, 13 maps & a plan; lists & diagrams.

Includes chapters on the Longmoor and the Melbourne (Derbyshire) military railways, the Shropshire & Montgomeryshire Rly and the War Department's light railway at Shoeburyness.

10489   WHITEHOUSE, P. B. The splendour of British Steam, edited by P. B. Whitehouse; picture research, Patricia E. Hornsey. *London: New English Library*, [1976]. la. 8°. pp. 142, with over 200 illus (112 col.).

10490   CLAY, J. F. The British 4-6-0. *London: New English Library*, 1977. la. 8°. pp. 96, with 140 illus (27 col.).

10491   ROWLEDGE, J. W. P. Heavy goods engines of the War Department. *Poole: Springmead Railway Books*.

vol. 1, The R.O.D. 2-8-0. 1977. pp. 72, with 67 illus on 20 plates, 7 dimensioned drawings & 11 detailed tables.

vol. 2, Stanier 8F 2-8-0. 1977. pp. 64, with 65 illus on 24 plates, dimensioned drawings & detailed lists.

vol. 3, Austerity 2-8-0 and 2-10-0. 1978. pp. 64, with 72 illus (1 col.) on 24 plates, dimensioned drawings & detailed lists.

10492   TOURRET, R. United States Transportation Corps locomotives. *Abingdon: Tourret Publishing*, 1977. (Allied Military Locomotives of the Second World War, 2). la. 8°. pp. 101, with 224 illus & many dimensioned drawings; lists.

Includes their work in Great Britain.

10493   BAXTER, D. Victorian locomotives. *Buxton: Moorland Publishing Co.*, 1978. pp. [112]. Intro & 129 illus with detailed descrs.

Most of the illustrations are from photographs made by R. F. Bleasdale during the period 1870s to 1890s. Arranged under companies.

10494   GAMMELL, C. J. The Steam Age. *Buxton: Moorland Publishing Co.*, 1978. pp. 96. Frontis & 120 illus.

10495 GREAT locomotives, selected from Ian Allan magazines 'Trains Illustrated' & 'Locomotives Illustrated'. *London: Ian Allan*, 1978. la. 8°. pp. 128. Intro & 202 illus with descrs.

10496 MIDDLEMASS, T. Locomotive nicknames. *Theydon Bois: Steamchest Publications*, [1978]. pp. 64, with 21 illus on 12 plates. Title from cover.
'Aberdares' to 'Yorkies', with historical notes.

10497 WHITEHOUSE, P. B. The wonderful world of steam locomotives. *London: Hamlyn*, 1978. la. 8°. pp. 96, with 108 col. illus (22 of locomotives & trains in the British Isles).

10498 ADLEY, R. British steam in Camera-colour, 1962–68. *London: Ian Allan*, 1979. la. 8°. pp. 104. Intro & 75 col. illus with descrs.

10499 CREER, S. Cross-country Steam. *London: Ian Allan*, 1979. pp. 80. Intro, frontis & 151 illus with descrs.

10500 GARRATT, C. D. Veterans in Steam. *Poole: Blandford Press*, 1979. la. 8°. pp. 160, with col. frontis & 52 col. illus.
Locomotives of various countries; 14 on British industrial railway systems.

10501 HEIRON, G. and TREACY, E. Steam's 'Indian Summer'. *London: Allen & Unwin*, 1979. pp. [124]. Intro & 147 illus (photos by George Heiron and Eric Treacy), with descrs.
Period, 1950s & 1960s.

10502 SIMPSON, C. R. H. The Rainhill Locomotive Trials: the story of a contest, the outcome of which was to revolutionize transport in every continent. [*Rainhill*]: *Rainhill Trials Celebration Committee*, 1979. obl. format. pp. 44, with 35 illus (6 col.), facsimiles, drawings, & 2 maps. Foreword by Alastair Pilkington; editor, A. A. H. Scott; production, R. B. Williamson; illustrator, J. W. Petrie.

10503 CAWTHORN, D. My Railway Album: a collection of original photographs by David Cawthorn. *Blackburn: D. Cawthorn*, [ca. 1980]. obl. format. pp. [72]. 71 illus of locomotives, mostly steam, with captions. No text. Title from cover.

10504 GREGGIO, L. The steam locomotive, [by] Luciano Greggio; translated and adapted by Peter Kalla-Bishop; artwork by Guido Canestrari. *London: Hamlyn*, 1980. pp. 263, with ca. 550 illus (ca. 250 col.).
From the beginning to the end of railway steam locomotion; world-wide coverage. On pp. 228–53, a detailed 5-column table of wheel arrangements (French, British, American & German classifications) and a table of leading dimensions, index, & a bibliography (125 sources).

10505 HAGAN, D. R. Indian Summer of Steam. *London: Ian Allan*, 1980. pp. 80. Intro & 160 illus (photos by D. R. Hagan).

10506 HIGGINS, R. N. Over here: the story of the United States Army Transportation Corps class S160 locomotives; Foreword by F. J. Bellwood. [*Barnoldswick: the author*, 1980. pp. 80, with 55 illus (3 col.).

10507 MORRISON, B. The Steam Cameramen, compiled by Brian Morrison for the Railway Photographic Society. *Oxford: Oxford Publishing Co.*, 1980. la. 8°. pp. [240], with 412 illus. Foreword by Maurice W. Earley, introduction by Brian Morrison. A limited edition of 2,000 copies. Issued in a slip case.
A record of the work of 58 members of the Society, 1922–1976, consisting of a selected 6 photographs from each, with a portrait and brief biographical note.

10508 SIVITER, R. Tempo of Steam. *London: Ian Allan*, 1980. la. 8°. Intro & 168 illus with descrs.
Photographs by Roger Siviter of steam locomotives in Britain and abroad, 1966 to 1979.

10509 WHITEHOUSE, P. B. Classic Steam; general editor, Patrick B. Whitehouse. *London: Hamlyn*, 1980. la. 8°. pp. 192, with many illus (some col.).
World coverage. Gt. Britain, pp. 6–51, with 66 illus (13 col.). Period, 1930s–1960s.

E 8 a Steam locomotive construction
10510–48

10510 LOWE, J. W. British steam locomotive builders. *Cambridge: Goose & Son*, 1975. pp. 705, with 585 illus (photos & line drawings), & many lists; bibliography (48 sources), index (pp. 683–704).
A comprehensive work embodying great detail.

10511 ROUNDHOUSE [bookshop & publisher]. A List of Locomotive Manufacturers' Catalogues, with some relevant items [compiled by Iris Doyle]. *Harrow-on-the-Hill: The Roundhouse*, June 1980. pp. 8. Reproduced typescript.
150 catalogues and histories of firms, British and foreign.

10512 DODD, G. British manufactures . . . *London: C. Knight*, 1844–51. 6 vols.
vol. 6 (1846) includes a section (pp. 247–56) on locomotives.

10513 ELORDI, J. J. and ESTEVES, F. Comparison of English and American locomotives in the Argentine Republic . . . , with the reply thereto of Mr. R. Gould, locomotive engineer to the Buenos Ayres Great Southern Railway. [*La Plata*]: *Department of Provincial Engineers of Argentina*, 1892. pp. 51 & 3 folded plates (5 Baldwin locomotives, U.S.A., and 4 Beyer Peacock locomotives, Gt. Britain).

Concern over the unsuitability (not the quality) of the British engines in use on the Great Southern Rly of Argentina compared with the American engines on the Western Rly.

10514 HUGHES, G. The construction of the modern locomotive. *London: E. & F.N. Spon*, 1894. pp. xiii, 261, with many diagrams (3 folded) & tables.

10515 McDONNELL, R. W. Through locomotive works, being advice to young mechanical engineers. *Dublin: Wm McGee*, 1894. pp. 66.
Paternal guidance, based on the author's own experience.

10516 REYNOLDS, M. First principles of the locomotive. *London: Biggs*, [1895]. pp. 152 & 4 pp. of index.
A textbook on the construction and function of the steam locomotive, in simplified terms.

10517 [KOPPEL.] ARTHUR KOPPEL [light railway engineers]. Locomotive Catalogue no. 786. *London: A. Koppel*, [1905]. Reproduced as a facsimile reprint by *Gotton Engineering, Cheddon Fitzpaine, Taunton*, 1979. la. 8°. pp. 76, with 22 illus on pp. 66–75 and numerous illus & tables in text.
Standard and narrow gauge steam locomotives for special classes of work, including fireless locomotives and tramway locomotives.

10518 STANIER, W. A. The construction of a modern locomotive. Great Western Railway (London) Lecture & Debating Society, meeting on January 31st, 1907 [no. 35]. pp. 10, with 6 illus.
Swindon locomotive works, GWR.

10519 PECKETT & SONS. Some view in the workshops and a few examples of the locomotives built therein . . . *Bristol: the firm*, [ca. 1910]. obl. format. pp. 78, with frontis, map, 69 illus, & an embossed illus on covers.
Tank locomotives for industrial use.   LU(THC)

10520 NASH, A. H. A day's work in the Swindon foundry. Great Western Railway (London) Lecture & Debating Society, meeting on January 12th, 1911 [no. 75]. pp. 11, with 14 illus & diagrams.

10521 NORTH BRITISH LOCOMOTIVE CO. An account of the manufactures of the North British Locomotive Co. Ltd. during the period of the War, 1914–1919, with a short history of the firms which constituted the Company when formed in 1903. *Glasgow: the Company*, [1920?]. la. obl. format. pp. 123, with route map from Glasgow station & 150 illus, incl. portraits. Cover title: The manufacture of locomotives and other munitions of war during the period 1914–1919.
The illustrations include some of patients (soldiers) in Springburn Hospital, part of the Company's administration building placed at the disposal of the British Red Cross Society.

10522 HALL, F. C. The why and wherefore of locomotive design. Great Western Railway (London) Lecture & Debating Society, meeting on March 1st, 1923 (no. 159). pp. 18, with discussion & 16 illus.

10523 STANIER, W. A. Recent developments in locomotive design: presidential address delivered before the Institution by W. A. Stanier on the 30th September 1936 in London. *London & Lewes: The Lewes Press*, [1936]. pp. 44, with 24 illus, diagrams, tables & graphs & 15 appendices.
Reprinted from the *Journal of the Institution of Locomotive Engineers*, vol. 26, 1936, no. 133, pp. 549–94 (but not in the index to this volume).
The 'Discussion' (pp. 42–4 in the reprint) includes comments on the address made by Sir Nigel Gresley and, briefly, by R. E. L. Maunsell.

10524 BEYER PEACOCK & CO. Beyer-Garratt articulated locomotives. *Manchester: the Company*, 1947. 4°. pp. xvi, 164, with many illus.
pp. 118–23, on British railways (LNER and LMS), with 7 illus.

10525 [STEPHENSON.] ROBERT STEPHENSON AND HAWTHORNS LIMITED. Locomotives by Robert Stephenson and Hawthorns Ltd, Darlington and Newcastle. *Darlington: the Firm*, [1948]. la. 8°. pp. 80, with 110 illus of locomotives, with specifications. Text in English, French & Spanish.
The foreword is a concise history of the firm, founded in 1817 as R. & W. Hawthorn.

10526 COLE, D. Fletcher, Jennings. *London: Union Publications*, 1965. (British Locomotive Builders Works Lists, 1). pp. 2. Tables.
Steam locomotives, 1840–1912.

10527 EVANS, M. Inverness to Crewe: the British 4-6-0 locomotive. *Hemel Hempstead: Model Aeronautical Press*, 1966. pp. 164, with frontis, 122 illus & 15 tables.
4-6-0 steam locomotives built at works located between these two towns, with performance data.

10528 MITCHELL LIBRARY [Glasgow]. Scotland's Locomotive Builders: an exhibition illustrative of the development of the locomotive industry in Scotland, 11th–23rd October 1971. *Glasgow: Mitchell Library*, 1971. pp. 14, with a bibliography (23 sources).
Brief histories of 15 manufactories, 1830s to 1960s.

10529 RADFORD, J. B. Derby Works and Midland locomotives: the story of the works, its men, and the locomotives they built. *London: Ian Allan*, 1971. pp. 239, with 105 illus on 48 plates, plan of works, 6 line drawings of locomotives, 4 appendices, 3 of which are very detailed lists of locomotives & boiler construction; brief bibliography.
Period, 1839–1967.

10530 ROLT, L. T. C. Landscape with machines:

H

an autobiography. *London: Longman*, 1971. pp. xi, 230, with 32 illus on 16 plates.

pp. 85–104, 'Stoke-on-Trent': apprenticeship with Kerr Stuart & Co., locomotive manufacturers; also, pp. 105–19, 'Shropshire railways and canals'; week-end visits to the Shropshire & Montgomeryshire Light Railway's workshop at Kinnerley Junction.

10531 PERRYMAN, A. C. Life at Brighton locomotive works, 1928–1936. *Lingfield: Oakwood Press*, [1972]. (Locomotion Papers, 54). pp. 67, with 20 illus on 8 plates, & a plan.

10532 REDMAN, R. N. The Railway Foundry, Leeds, 1839–1969: E. B. Wilson–Hudswell Clarke & Co. Ltd. *Norwich: Goose & Son*, 1972. 4°. pp. [x], 206, with 150 illus & 20 drawings, plans & diagrams; 5 appendices containing supplementary illustrations & a detailed 10-column list of the locomotives produced by the original foundry prior to 1868 (pp. 144–81); bibliography (27 sources).

10533 HILLS, R. L. 'Motive power engineering' *in* The Great Human Exploit, edited by J. H. Smith (1973), pp. 62–9.

Steam locomotive manufacture in the Manchester area, from 1830.

10534 KYLE, I. Steam from Lowca: a history of the rise and fall of locomotive building at Lowca Foundry, 1840 to 1921. *Moresby: the author*, 1974. pp. 40, with 30 illus & a map.

The Lowca Engineering Co., near Whitehaven, Cumberland.

10535 LOWE, J. W. British steam locomotive builders. *Cambridge: Goose & Son*, 1975. pp. 704, with 585 illus (photos & line drawings) & many lists; bibliography (48 sources), index (pp. 683–704).

A comprehensive work embodying great detail.

10536 GUDGIN, D. S. E. Vulcan Foundry locomotives, 1832–1956. *Truro: Bradford Barton*, 1976. pp. 96, with 119 illus, incl. 2 plans of the works.

10537 SATOW, F., SATOW, M. G., and WILSON, L. S. Locomotion: concept to creation: the story of the reproduction, 1973–1975. *Beamish: The Locomotive Trust*, 1976. pp. 48, with 20 illus (8 col.), & a map.

The replica of the Stockton & Darlington Rly locomotive, *Locomotion*.

10538 MOSS, M. S. and HUME, J. R. Workshop of the British Empire: engineering and shipbuilding in the West of Scotland. *London & Edinburgh: Heinemann*, 1977. pp. xv, 192, with 177 illus.

Includes locomotive building and in particular that of Andrew Barclay, Sons & Co. of Kilmarnock.

10539 PURDOM, D. S. British Steam on the pampas: the locomotives of the Buenos Aires Great Southern Railway . . . ; foreword by Andrew B. Henderson. *London: Mechanical Engineering Publications*, 1977. pp. [viii], 118, with 33 illus on 16 plates, 50 line drawings, 3 maps & a 15-column table of locomotives, 1924–1967 (pp. 112–13).

British-built locomotives in Argentina.

10540 WEAR, R. The locomotive builders of Kilmarnock. *London: Industrial Railway Society Publications*, 1977. (Industrial Railway Record, no. 69, January 1977). pp. 325–408, with 91 illus, facsimiles & diagrams, 4 works plans & 10 lists of locomotives.

The lists are of locomotives built by Barclays & Co., Allan Andrews & Co., Andrews, Barr & Co., Barr, Morrison & Co., Dick, Kerr & Co., Kilmarnock Engineering Co., Thomas McCulloch & Sons, McCulloch Sons & Kennedy, and Grant Ritchie & Co.

10541 WESTWOOD, J. N. British-built steam locos overseas. *Truro: Bradford Barton*, 1977. pp. 96. Intro & 102 illus with descrs.

Photographs by John N. Westwood and others. Period, 1940–1975.

10542 COURT, J. H. North British steam locomotives built 1857–1956 for railways overseas. *Truro: Bradford Barton*, [1978]. pp. 112. Intro & 114 illus with descrs.

10543 TORRENS, H. The evolution of a family firm: Stothert & Pitt of Bath. *Bath: Stothert & Pitt*, 1978. pp. 86, with 24 illus & many notes.

pp. 35–42 *et passim*, railway locomotive manufacture from 1838.

10544 WEAR, R. and LEES, E. Stephen Lewin and Poole Foundry. [*Wellingborough*?]: *Industrial Railway Society*; [*Woking*?]: *Industrial Locomotive Society*, 1978. pp. 101, with 60 illus, plans & line drawings, & 119 notes.

The manufacture of small industrial steam railway locomotives.

10545 COURT, J. H. North British steam locomotives built 1833 to 1948 for railways in Britain. *Truro: Bradford Barton*, [1979]. pp. 112. Intro & 113 illus with descrs.

An illustrated record of the manufacture of steam locomotives by the North British Locomotive Company.

10546 HILLS, R. L. Beyer Peacock: locomotive builders of Gorton. *Manchester: North Western Museum of Science & Industry*, 1979. pp. 19, incl. covers, with 7 illus.

10547 LARKIN, E. J. Memoirs of a railway engineer. *Bury St Edmunds: Mechanical Engineering Publications*, 1979. pp. [x], 212, with over 200 illus, working drawings, maps, diagrams & tables.

52 years in railway service (1914–1965), with the Midland, the LMS and BR(LMR). Steam locomotive design, building & maintenance; workshop training of apprentices and engineers.

10548 LOWE, J. W. Building Britain's locomotives. *Ashbourne: Moorland Publishing Co.*, 1979. la. 8°. pp. [112]. General intro, & brief intros to each of the 8 chapters, with frontis & 150 illus with descrs.
The 150 photographs are of scenes in the workshops of 26 manufactories.

E 8 b   Steam locomotive performance
Running and maintenance—Memoirs of locomotivemen   10549–72

For memoirs of locomotivemen of a particular railway see **L**, *or of British Railways,* **B 10**; *or of a railway in a particular area of the British Isles,* **C 1 – C 7**

10549 BIRD, W. R. Water softening for locomotive purposes, etc. Great Western Railway (London) Lecture & Debating Society, meeting on January 25th, 1906 [no. 22]. pp. 6, with 8 illus.

10550 SMITH, R. H. The practical working of locomotives. Great Western Railway (London) Lecture & Debating Society, meeting on November 22nd, 1906 [no. 30]. pp. 7.
The duties of locomotivemen, GWR.

10551 PRICE-WILLIAMS, R. On the serviceable life and average annual cost of locomotives in Great Britain. *London: Institution of Civil Engineers*, 1909. pp. 27, with 2 folded charts at end.

10552 LELEAN, W. A. The Locomotive Inspector's Record Book. *London: Institution of Locomotive Engineers*, [1915]. pp. 32.
'Issued as a supplement to a paper read before the Institution.'

10553 HALY, G. Fuel oil for locomotives. Great Western Railway (London) Lecture & Debating Society, meeting on January 29th, 1920 [no. 119]. pp. 60–77, with 15 illus & diagrams.

10554 'SOCRATES'. The propulsive principles of the steam locomotive, by 'Socrates' [i.e. Alfred Oliver]. *London: Co-operative Printing Society for the National Union of Railwaymen*, 1923. sm. 8°. pp. viii, 133, with 26 diagrams (4 folded).
A handbook for enginemen.

10555 PEPPERCORN, A. H. Use of coal, water and steam in the locomotive. *London: L.N.E. Rly*, [1938]. pp. 48, with 19 diagrams.
Reprint of a series of essays in the *LNER Magazine*, 1937. Addressed to 'readers in general and to locomotive footplate staff in particular'.

10556 CUNNINGHAM, J. Mutual improvement classswork: 300 examination questions with answers arranged for locomotivemen, by James Cunningham. *London: T. Nelson*, [1941]. pp. 96.

10557 BRITISH RAILWAYS. Motive power depots: code nos. and letters. *London: Railway Executive, Chief Officer (Motive Power)*, February 1950. (Circular, M.P.8).
A printed folder.

10558 ELL, S. O. Locomotive testing in the fields of design and economic operation. (Proceedings of the British Railways (W.R.) London Lecture & Debating Society, 1952–53, no. 403). pp. 16, with discussion, 5 charts & 4 illus.
Author, 'Technical Assistant (Locomotive Testing) to the Mechanical & Electrical Engineer, Swindon'.

10559 BRITISH RAILWAYS. EASTERN REGION. Stratford Locomotive and Carriage Works. *London: B.R.(ER)*, July 1955. pp. 8, with 4 illus & a folded plan.

10560 BRITISH RAILWAYS. Good firemanship. *London: B.T.C., Railways Division*, 1956. sm. 8°. pp. 32, with 10 col. diagrams.
A practical guide to efficient yet economical locomotive firing.

10561 COX, E. S. Locomotive Panorama. *London: Ian Allan*.
vol. 1, [1917–1947]. 1965. pp. xi, 164, with 53 illus on 30 plates, 25 diagrams & 13 tables.
vol. 2, [1948–1965]. 1966. pp. viii, 158, with 80 illus on 32 plates, 15 tables & 4 diagrams.
Steam locomotive development: a biographical account based on a career in locomotive design and testing (Lancashire & Yorkshire Railway, LMS, BR), and in vol. 2, the BR period and the change from steam to diesel, and (pp. 81–113) 'Steam in retrospect'.

10562 COX, E. S. Chronicles of Steam. *London: Ian Allan*, 1967. pp. x, 182, with 66 illus on 40 plates, & in text, 19 tables & 21 diagrams.
Memoirs of steam locomotive development and operation, 1917–1947: a sequel to his *Locomotive Panorama* (1965, 66).

10563 NOCK, O. S. British steam locomotives at work. *London: Allen & Unwin*, 1967. pp. 276, with 94 illus on 48 plates.
Accounts of runs on a variety of locomotives.

10564 VUILLET, G. Railway reminiscences of three continents. *London: T. Nelson*, 1968. pp. x, 357, with frontis, 91 illus on 48 plates, & 7 tables.
Detailed studies of locomotive performances in Great Britain, Europe, North America and Africa, 1903 to 1960.

10565 McKENNA, F. A. Glossary of Railwaymen's Talk: a compendium of slang terms, old and new, used by railwaymen, together with anecdotes of footplate life at Carlisle (Kingmoor), Willesden Junction and Kentish Town; brief recollections of the railwaymen's hostel in Somers Town and the footplate strike of 1955; and a young man's experience of night life in Leicester Square and the Strand, collected and arranged by

Frank McKenna. *Oxford (Ruskin College): History Workshop*, 1970. (History Workshop Pamphlets, 1). pp. x, 44. Title from cover.

The glossary occupies pp. 31–44. The autobiographical section of the work (pp. 1–27) is noteworthy as a lively account of the off-duty life of young steam-locomotivemen on the LMSR, 1946–1966.

10566   ELLIOT, G. C. N.   Raised in Steam: the story of an association. *Newcastle upon Tyne: Oriel Press*, 1972. pp. [6], 138, with ca. 80 illus, incl. line drawings & facsims; 4 appendices.

An affectionate memoir of the L.N.E.R. Pupils Association. The lighter side of locomotive maintenance work and the social life of enginemen.

10567   MORGAN, B. and MEYRICK, B.   Behind the steam. *London: Hutchinson*, 1973. pp. 222, with 19 illus on 12 plates.

Autobiography of a locomotiveman (GWR & BR (WR), 1916–1964) centred upon Neyland depot, Dyfed.

10568   NOCK, O. S.   'Out the line'. *London: Paul Elek*, 1976. pp. x, 163, with 35 illus on 16 plates, 4 maps & a drawing, & a bibliography of 82 works by O. S. Nock (books only).

Reminiscences of adventures and occasions experienced in the course of collecting data for writing his long succession of books and essays on railway subjects, and on his professional duties in railway safety engineering. Many footplate runs are recalled and the period covered is 1907–1976. The title chosen for the book is the Scottish railwayman's vernacular for being 'out on the line', i.e. engaged on railway activity away from the depot.

10569   LONDON Midland Steam on shed, compiled by '45562'. *Truro: Bradford Barton*, 1978. 4°. pp. 96. 59 illus of locomotives at 43 depots, and 39 locomotive depot plans, with a list of depots, with page refs.

10570   HOLLINGSWORTH, B.   How to drive a steam locomotive. *London: Astragal Books*, 1979. pp. vi, 152, with many halftone & line illus, diagrams, maps, a list of 'live steam clubs' & a bibliography (18 sources).

A detailed description of technicalities, addressed to aspiring steam locomotive drivers of today. Includes 'miniature railway' locomotives.

10571   HILTON, J.   The steam locomotive and its operation. *Hadlow: the author*, 1980. pp. 53, with 26 diagrams.

Based on a series of notes for trainee drivers and firemen on an unspecified preserved line.

10572   NOCK, O. S.   Rocket 150: a century and a half of locomotive trials. *London: Ian Allan*, 1980. pp. 128, with 114+ illus.

A survey of the more interesting and important locomotive trials held in Britain, South Africa, Australia and the USA, commencing with that at Rainhill in 1829.

E 8 c   Steam locomotive restoration and preservation (generally)   10573–10601

Reference sources 10573–77

See also **Q 1** *for this subject in museums and on re-opened lines*

10573   SCOTTISH RAILFANS. [Stored locomotives in Scotland]. 3rd edn. List of stored locomotives. *Edinburgh: Scottish Railfans*, June 1962. pp. 4. Reproduced typescript.

—— 4th edn. List of stored locomotives in Scotland. April 1963. pp. 4.

—— 5th edn. May 1964. pp. 12.

—— 6th edn. Stored locomotives in Scotland. April 1965. pp. 12.

A listing of steam locomotives awaiting scrapping, arranged under depots.

10574   CASSERLEY, H. C.   Preserved locomotives. *London: Ian Allan*, 1968. pp. 256, with 235 illus.

All preserved locomotives in Britain (mostly steam), individually described.

—— 2nd edn. *Ian Allan*, 1969. pp. 312, with 280 illus.

—— 3rd edn. *Ian Allan*, 1973. pp. 341, with 7 col. illus on 8 plates & ca. 300 illus in text.

—— 4th edn. *Ian Allan*, 1976. pp. 368, with 314 illus.

—— 5th edn. *Ian Allan*, 1980. pp. 192, with 313 illus.

part 1, Locomotives built between 1813 and the 1850s (pp. 7–16).

part 2, Locomotives built for public and passenger-carrying railways from the 1860s (pp. 17–128).

part 3, Industrial locomotives from the 1860s (pp. 129–65).

part 4, Foreign or British-exported locomotives (pp. 166–9).

Index of industrial and light railway locomotives (pp. 170–87); principal centres of preserved locomotives (pp. 187–8).

The arrangement is chronological within each section.

10575   SWIFT, M.   Preserved locomotives in the British Isles, 1970; edited by M. Swift. *Industrial Railway Society and the Narrow Gauge Railway Society*, 1970. pp. 114, with 64 illus on 32 plates.

Details of locomotives listed under their owners and operators. Index, pp. 95–114.

—— Additions & amendments, March to September 1970. [1970]. pp. iv. Reproduced typescript.

10576   WILDISH, G.   Preserved locomotives of the world. 2nd edn. *Cambridge: Railway Preservation Society*, 1971. la. 8°. pp. [vi], 42, with 7 illus & a drawing.

Lists arranged under countries with an index of railway companies and owners of locomotives.

The 'first edition' (1969) was in reproduced typescript and was not published.

10577   HANDS, P. B.   What happened to Steam. *Solihull: the author*, 1980–81. 20 parts.

14-column listings of allocations and reallocations of BR steam locomotives during their latter years of general service, from January 1957 to August 1968, with details of their withdrawal, storage, scrapping, or adoption for preservation.

vol. 1, The Great Western 2-8-0s. pp. 24.

vol. 2, The Great Western Castles and Kings, 4-6-0s. pp. 29.

vol. 3, The London Midland 'Jubilees', 4-6-0s. pp. 30.

vol. 4, The London [&] North Eastern A4, A3, A1 & A2 Pacific locomotives. pp. 30.

vol. 5, The Southern West Country, Battle of Britain, Merchant Navy & Schools classes. pp. 30.

vol. 6, Ex-G.W.R. Halls, 4-6-0s. pp. 34.

vol. 7, The London Midland Patriot, Royal Scot, Princess & Coronation classes. pp. 30.

vol. 8, The London [&] North Eastern V2s, 2-6-2s. pp. 26.

vol. 9, The B.R. Britannias, Clans, Dukes & Class 5s, 4-6-0s. pp. 34.

vol. 10, The Great Western Counties, Granges, modified Halls, & Manors, 4-6-0s. pp. 34.

vol. 11, The Southern H15 & N15, King Arthurs, S15 & Lord Nelson 4-6-0s, G16 4-8-0 tanks; H16 4-6-2 tanks. pp. 26.

vol. 12, The B.R. Standard 95 2-10-0s. pp. 34.

vol. 13, The L.N.E.R. B1 4-6-0s. pp. 54.

vol. 14, The Great Western 43XX 2-6-0s, & Dukedog 4-4-0s. pp. 30.

vol. 15, The L.M.S. Ivatt 2-6-0s nos. 43000–161, & 46400–527. pp. 42.

vol. 16, The Southern K, N, N1, U, & U1 2-6-0s, & W 2-6-4 tanks. pp. 20.

vol. 17, The B.R. class 4 4-6-0s nos. 75000–79 and class 4 2-6-0s nos. 76000–114. pp. 40.

vol. 18, The L.N.E.R. B16, B12, B2 & B17 4-6-0s. pp. 26.

vol. 19, the L.M.S. 'Crabs' & Stanier 'Crabs' nos. 42700–944, & 42945–84. pp. 42.

vol. 20, The Great Western 14XX 0-4-2 tanks, & 45XX 2-6-2 tanks. pp. 30.

10578 FENTON, E. W. Locomotives in retirement: second series. *London: Hugh Evelyn,* 1967. la. obl. format. pp. [23]. Intro & 10 col. plates of preserved engines, each interleaved with a full-page description.

The author's note about colour reproduction, in his preface, is noteworthy.

10579 The BRITANNIA Pacifics: an appreciation. *Stockport (Bahamas) Locomotive Society,* [1968]. pp. [28], with 14 illus & 2 logs of runs.

10580 BLOOM, A. Steam engines at Bressingham: the story of a live steam museum. *London: Faber,* 1970. pp. 233, with 37 illus on 28 plates (8 col.).

Exhibits include 13 railway locomotives.

10581 HOLLINGSWORTH, J. B. Blue Peter: the story of Britain's most powerful steam locomotive. *[York]: Blue Peter Locomotive Society,* [1970]. pp. [28] incl. cover, with 17 illus & 4 tables.

The restoration of a Gresley Pacific locomotive of 1948.

10582 STEAM Alive; editor, P. B. Whitehouse. *Shepperton: Ian Allan,* [1969–71]. 12 parts.

A series of 12 issues on steam locomotive preservation produced in small magazine format.

Each has 48–52 pp., with many illus (some col.). Binder supplied.

1, Preserved express Steam

2, Preserved narrow gauge Steam

3, Preserved standard gauge railways

4, Standard gauge preservation miscellany

5, 20th anniversary Special

6, Live museum Steam; Industrial Steam

7, The Talyllyn story: a unique venture

8, Live Steam in Europe & the U.S.A.

9, Main line steam engines in aspic

10, Standard gauge steam railways

11, Narrow gauge steam railways

12, A look back over 21 years: back to steam on the main line?

10583 STEAMTOWN RAILWAY MUSEUM. Steamtown: the Carnforth Line Steam Museum: a visitor's guide, by David Joy. *Clapham (North Yorks): Dalesman,* 1972. pp. 40, with 24 illus, & illus & map on covers.

10584 BULMER'S Railway Centre, Hereford. *Oxford: Oxford Publishing Co. for the 6000 Locomotive Association,* [1973]. pp. 16, with 12 illus (8 col., incl. covers) & a plan.

—— 1976 edn. *O.P.C.,* [1976]. pp. 16, with 14 illus (incl 9 col.), dimensioned drawing & a plan.

10585 COFFIN, R. O. Mainline Steam in the seventies: a pictorial story of preserved locomotives at work. *Hereford: 6000 Locomotive Association; Oxford: Oxford Publishing Co.,* 1974. 4°. pp. [80]. Intro & 117 illus with descrs.

10586 CLARE, A. C. 'Clan Line': the first ten years. *Basingstoke: Merchant Navy Locomotive Preservation Society,* [1975]. pp. 32, with 28 illus & cover illus.

The adoption and restoration of the ex-Southern Rly 4-6-2 locomotive no. 35028 (O. V. Bulleid's Merchant Navy class, 1948).

10587 LATHAM, J. B. Railways and preservation. *Woking: the author,* 1975. obl. 8°. pp. 70, with 46 illus & a diagram.

Technical, practical and administrative problems of locomotive preservation.

10588 PRINCESS ELIZABETH LOCOMOTIVE SOCIETY. The rebirth of a giant. *Haraton Ltd, for the Society,* [1976]. pp. [8], with 40 illus.

The adoption and restoration of the ex-LMS Pacific locomotive 6201, *Princess Elizabeth.*

10589 WHITEHOUSE, P. B. British steam: a profile . . . ; picture research, Patricia E. Hornsey. *[London]: New English Library,* 1976. la. 8°. pp. 112, with 140 illus (mostly col.).

Essays on a variety of locomotives of the past, and on contemporary preserved lines.

10590 MIDDLEMASS, T. The road to preservation. *Theydon Bois: Steamchest Publications,* [1977]. pp. 56, with 61 illus.

Details of the history and restoration of 57 steam locomotives.

10591 NUTTY, E. J. G.W.R. two-cylinder piston-valve locomotives. 2nd edn. *Swindon: the author*, 1948. pp. 36, with 12 diagrams & a table.

—— [3rd edn, greatly enlarged]. *Swindon: E. J. Nutty & Sons*, [1977]. pp. 107, with 19 illus & 39 diagrams & tables.

A detailed exposition on the construction, characteristics and working of this type of locomotive, produced as a workshop guide for those engaged in their restoration, running and maintenance. Based on the author's life-long acquaintance with GWR locomotives at Swindon works.

10592 STOUR VALLEY RAILWAY PRESERVATION SOCIETY. 80151: the design, construction, service and restoration of a British Railways class 4MT locomotive. *Chappel: Anglian Locomotive Group, for the S.V.R.P.S.*, 1977. pp. 24, with 19 illus, & a dimensioned drawing of the locomotive; 2 illus on covers. Title from cover.

pp. 1–7, Design & construction, by E. S. Cox.
pp. 8–13, Service, by W. R. Allen.
pp. 14–22, Restoration, by the Anglian Locomotive Group.

10593 WHITEHOUSE, P. B. The Last Parade: an authorised tribute to British Steam preservation, compiled and edited by P. B. Whitehouse. Contributors: The Viscount Downe, P. W. B. Semmens, J. A. Coiley, P. B. Whitehouse, M. G. Satow, L. S. Wilson, M. Williams, M. Dean, J. F. Clay. *London: New Cavendish Books*, 1977. (Grand Format series). la. obl. format. pp. 192, with col. frontis, 320 illus (100 col.). Issued in a slipcase.

Produced to commemorate the Stockton & Darlington 150 Celebrations in 1975 and also as a tribute to the achievements of railway preservationists over the past 30 years, culminating in the establishment of the National Railway Museum, opened September 1975. A high quality production, limited to 3000 copies.

10594 CORNWELL, E. L. Still in steam. new edn. *London: Ian Allan*, 1978. pp. 80, with 109 illus.

Contents: How a steam locomotive works, by B. K. Cooper; Great locomotives still at work, by W. L. Cornwell; Focus on preserved coaches, by G. M. Kichenside; Running a preserved railway, by G. M. Kichenside; Where live steam can be seen, by B. K. Cooper.

10595 LEANDER LOCOMOTIVE LTD. The Leander Guide. [*Leander Locomotive Ltd*, 1978]. sm. obl. 8°. pp. [8], incl. covers, with 7 illus (1 col.) & a dimensioned drawing (double spread).

The restoration of the ex-LMS 4-6-0 locomotive 5690, 'Leander' (W. Stanier's Jubilee class, 1936).

10596 BLENCOWE, S. V. Life begins at forty: the rescue and resurrection of Great Western locomotive no. 7812, 'Earlstoke Manor'. *Bewdley: Earlstoke Manor Fund*, 1979. pp. 52, with 62 illus & a table.

Built at Swindon workshops, January 1939.

10597 HANDLEY, B. Graveyard of Steam; with a foreword by Wynford Vaughan Thomas. *London: Allen & Unwin*, 1979. pp. [76], with 100 illus & a list of preservation societies that have salvaged locomotives from Woodham Brothers' railway dismantling yard on Barry Island, Glamorgan.

10598 TREVENA, N. Steam exposure: photography on Britain's preserved railways. *Penryn: Atlantic Books*, 1979. obl. format. pp. [88], with text [pp. 4–14], & 142 illus with descrs.

10599 WHITEHOUSE, P. B. Preserved Steam in Britain. *London: Allen & Unwin*, 1979. pp. 168, with frontis (map) & 170 illus.

10600 HARVEY, D. W. A Manual of Steam Locomotive Restoration and Preservation. *Newton Abbot: David & Charles*, 1980. pp. 96, with 52 illus, & 10 drawings by the author. Appendices: 1, Random data and rules of thumb; 2, Glossary in six languages; 3, Bibliography (15 sources).

Based on 50 years practical experience with locomotives.

10601 NICHOLSON, P. Rising Steam. *Beaconsfield: Barry Steam Locomotive Action Group*.

vol. 1, A Pictorial Record of the first 25 steam railway locomotives to be rescued from Barry Scrapyard in South Wales, and restored to working order by railway enthusiasts. 1980. obl. format. pp. [28]. Intro & 26 illus with descrs & commentaries, & an 8-column summary inside back cover.

E 9 – E 10   ELECTRIC AND DIESEL LOCOMOTIVES [as one subject]

10602–14

10602 HINDE, D. W. and HINDE, M. Electric and diesel-electric locomotives. *London: Macmillan*, 1948. pp. x, 366, with 167 illus (many composite & some folded), & 3 appendices.

The third appendix (pp. 265–359) consists of four sets of tables of great detail, drawn up from information gathered from many countries: (a) d.c. locomotives from 1925, (b) a.c. locomotives from 1925, (c) convertor-type locomotives from

1925, (d) 'three-power' locomotives, (e) diesel-electric locomotives from 1930.

10603 PRITCHARD, R. and SMITH, A. Railcar Checklist: a numerical list of British Railways internal combustion and electric railcars, with allocations. *Worcester: Worcester Locomotive Society*, 1974. pp. 32, with 4 illus.

10604 BRITISH Rail Traction Depot Directory. *Watford: Termini Enthusiasts; Railway Enthusiasts Society*, [1980]. sm. 8°. pp. 75.
BR maintenance depots and stabling points.

10605 NATIONAL RAILWAY ENTHUSIASTS ASSOCIATION. British Railways Spotters Companion. 2nd edn. *Oxford: Oxford Publishing Co.*, 1980. sm. 8°. pp. 80. Lists, with 19 illus.

10606 OAKLEY, M. Named locomotives of British Rail: diesel and electric. *Truro: Bradford Barton*, [1980]. 51 illus, some with insets (nameplates), & an appendix (pp. 49–54), 'Official names carried by locomotives on BR to 24 March, 1980'.

10607 TARREY, M. and OAKLEY, M. A history of British Railways diesel & electric locomotive numberings. *Sutton Coldfield: Diesel & Electric Groups*, 1980. la. 8°. pp. 16, with 18 illus & 20+ lists.

10608 CAREY, D. The locomotive: diesel and electric; with illustrations by B. H. Robinson. *Loughborough: Wills & Hepworth*, 1968. (Ladybird 'How it Works' Books, 5). sm. 8°. pp. 52, with 50 col. illus.
Introductory.

10609 HOBSON, A. W. B.R. diesels and electrics around Britain, edited by A. W. Hobson for the Phoenix Railway Photographic Circle. *Truro: Bradford Barton*, 1976. pp. 96. Intro & 91 illus with descrs.

10610 KICHENSIDE, G. M. Diesels and electrics in action. *Newton Abbot: David & Charles*, 1976. (Railway History in Pictures series).

pp. 96. Map, intro (pp. 5–10), & 127 illus with descrs.

10611 OAKLEY, M. Southern diesel and electric locomotives. *Purley: Diesel & Electric Group and the Southern Electric Group*, [1978?]. la. 8°. pp. 24 incl. covers, with 22 illus, 7 logs of runs, 5 dimensioned drawings & a map.

10612 DYER, M. A History of British Railway Diesel and Electric Locomotive Liveries; edited by Michael Oakley: photographed by C. Bush . . . [*et al.*]. *Sutton Coldfield: Diesel & Electric Group*, 1979. magazine format. pp. 32, with 55 illus (13 col., incl. 5 on covers).
—— rev. edn., with photos supplied by John C. Baker & 21 others. *D. & E. Group*, 1980. pp. 24 incl. covers, with 55 illus (13 col.).

10613 KENNEDY, R. Diesels and electrics on shed. *Oxford: Oxford Publishing Co.*
vol. 1, London Midland Region. 1979. la. 8°. pp. [80]. Intro, map, list, & 155 illus with descrs.
vol. 2, Eastern Region. 1980. la. 8°. pp. 96. Intro, map, & 83 illus with descrs.

10614 SCOTT-LOWE, G. Diesels and electrics on tour, 1977. *Gloucester: Peter Watts*, 1980. pp. [48]. Intro & 48 illus with descrs & a list of rail tour organisations.
—— Diesels and electrics on tour, 1978. *Peter Watts*, 1980 (1981). pp. [56]. Intro & 70 illus with descrs.
—— Diesels and electrics on tour, 1979. *Peter Watts*, 1981. pp. [60]. Intro & 72 illus with descrs.

E 9   ELECTRIC LOCOMOTIVES AND TRAINS
10615–22

For those of particular railways see **L** *and* **B 10,** *and for those of railways in specific areas see* **C 1 – C 7**

10615 CALISCH, L. Electric traction. *London: Locomotive Publishing Co.*, [1914]. pp. [v], 116, with 19 illus, 19 diagrams & graphs, & 12+ tables.
A revised and up-dated edition of a series of essays first published in the *Great Eastern Railway Magazine*.

10616 'SOCRATES'. Elementary principles of the electric locomotive, by 'Socrates' [i.e. Alfred Oliver]. *London: Co-operative Printing Society*, 1924. sm. 8°. pp. xvi, 171, with 112 illus & diagrams (some folded).

10617 BRITISH ELECTRICAL POWER CONVENTION [Torquay, May 1956]. British Electric Power Convention. *London: Railway Gazette*, 1956. pp. 38, with 23 illus & a map.

Principally concerned with railway electrification and electric traction, and the implementation of B.T.C.'s Modernisation Plan, 1955.

10618 CALVERLEY, H. B. Developments in 50-cycle traction. *London: English Electric Co.*, [1961]. pp. 39. Text headed: 'English Electric developments in 50 c/s traction'.

10619 HAUT, F. J. G. The history of the electric locomotive. *London: Allen & Unwin*, 1969. pp. 147, with col. frontis, 12 col. illus on 5 plates, & 258 monochrome illus on 68 plates and in text, 4 folded diagrams; bibliography (55 sources).

10620 LAITHWAITE, E. R. The linear motor and its application to tracked hovercraft. *Lon-*

don: Institution of Civil Engineers, 1971. (Parsons Memorial Lecture, 1971). pp. 12, with 14 illus, & line drawings & diagrams.

An introduction to the author's adaptation of the principle of direct linear motion to laterally-guided vehicles, fully expounded in his *Transport without Wheels* (1977).

10621 COOPER, B. K. Electric trains in Britain. *London: Ian Allan*, 1979. pp. 128, with

95 illus, 15 line drawings, graphs and diagrams.

10622 MARSDEN, C. J. The power of the electro-diesels. *Oxford: Oxford Publishing Co.*, 1980. la. 8°. Intro & 215 illus with descrs, & 5 tables of technical data.

BR electro-diesel locomotive classes 73 & 74, constructed to work on electrified or non-electrified lines.

E 10   DIESEL, DIESEL-ELECTRIC, AND OTHER SELF-GENERATING TYPES OF LOCOMOTIVE AND TRAIN

10623–48

For light railways, narrow gauge and other special forms of railway
see **D 1 – D 6**

10623 NICHOLSON, P. Diesel locomotives in preservation. *Cheltenham: P. Nicholson*.

no. 1, Standard gauge industrial locomotives. 1980. pp. 24 & an 8 pp. list of all known diesel locomotives in preservation in the British Isles, including industrial railways; 41 illus with descrs.

no. 2, Former British Rail and L.M.S.R. locomotives. 1980. pp. [28]. Intro, 38 illus with descrs, 4 dimensioned drawings & a list.

10624 DREWRY CAR COMPANY. Internal combustion railway motor cars and locomotives. *London: Drewry Car Co.*, 1925. pp. 48, with 41 illus, 2 diagrams, & a table.

A publicity booklet. Includes a section on rolling stock.

10625 HOBSON, J. W. The internal combustion locomotive. *Newcastle upon Tyne: North East Coast Institution of Engineers & Shipbuilders*, 1925. pp. 100, with 33 illus & diagrams; graphs, 6 tables.

A paper read before the Institution on 13 February, 1925. Discussion and Correspondence, pp. 50–88; author's reply, 88–100. The paper opens (pp. 1–12) with an examination of the comparative efficiencies, advantages and disadvantages of steam, electric and internal combustion (i.e. diesel) locomotives.

10626 ARMSTRONG   WHITWORTH   &   CO. Armstrong-Sulzer diesel-electric locomotives, rail-cars and multiple-unit trains with mobile power houses. *London: the Company*, [1930]. (Brochure 444). pp. 36, with 22 illus, diagrams & graphs.

10627 TRUTCH, C. J. H. Armstrong Whitworth diesel traction progress. *London: Armstrong-Whitworth & Co.*, 1932. pp. 8, with 8 illus.

Reprinted from the *Armstrong Whitworth Record*, Autumn [1932].

10628 ARMSTRONG WHITWORTH & CO. The Armstrong Whitworth diesel railbus: trial results and recorder diagrams. *Newcastle upon Tyne: the Company*, August 1933. pp. [8], with 3 illus & 3 diagrams.

Reprinted from the periodical *Transport*, July 1st 1933. An account of the diesel-electric railbus demonstration on the LNER, July 30 and August 2 & 3.

10629 TRUTCH, C. J. H. and BECKETT, C. M. Modern methods of railway locomotion. *London: Institute of Fuel*, [1933]. pp. 19, with 21 illus & diagrams.

Diesel traction: its advantages over steam.

10630 ARMSTRONG WHITWORTH & CO. The selection of a diesel shunting locomotive. *London: the Company*, 1934. pp. 23, with 6 illus, 10 diagrams & tables.

10631 COVENTRY PNEUMATIC RAILCAR COMPANY. Coventry pneumatic railcar. *Coventry: the Company*, [193–?]. pp. 8, with illus & diagrams. Title on cover only.

A sales brochure, with performance tables on the use of the pneumatic-tyred car on French railways.

10632 DYMOND, A. W. J. Gas jets and gas turbines for railway traction. (Proceedings of the British Railways (W.R.) London Lecture & Debating Society, 1948–9, no. 360). pp. 20, with discussion.

Author, 'Assistant to the C.M.E.'.

10633 DIESEL locomotives: photographs from the Times Weekly Review. *London: The Times Publishing Co.*, [1953]. obl. format. pp. 20, incl. covers, with 10 illus.

British diesel and gas-turbine locomotives and diesel railcars, in pictures from *The Times Weekly Review*.

10634 ROLE of the railcar. *Coventry: Self-Changing Gears Ltd*, 1955. obl. format. pp. 24, with 16 illus (3 on covers) & a diagram.

'A short survey of the advantages and scope of railcar operation.'

10635 BRITISH UNITED TRACTION. Diesel rail power: a review of activities by one of the world's largest suppliers of diesel train

units. *London: B.U.T.*, [1960?]. pp. 20, with 27 illus.
A publicity booklet presenting past and present achievements.

10636 BRITISH RAILWAYS. Diesel traction for enginemen. *London: B.R.*, 1962. pp. 271, with 186 diagrams (some col.).

10637 DOHERTY, D. Diesel locomotive practice: the design, construction, operation and maintenance of locomotives and railcars. *London: Odhams Press*, 1962. pp. 256, with over 200 illus & diagrams.

10638 MANN, R. H. Diesel rail-cars: an introduction. *Richmond: Draughtsmen's & Allied Technicians' Association*, 1963. pp. 78, [4], with 14 diagrams, 13 tables, 13 illus, 3 graphs & a bibliography (25 sources).

10639 ENGLISH ELECTRIC COMPANY. The conversion of a railway from steam to diesel operation. *London: the Company*, [n.d.]. (Rail Traction Bulletin, 2). pp. 13, with 3 diagrams.

10640 ENGLISH ELECTRIC COMPANY. Diesel locomotive characteristics, with particular reference to tractive effort and adhesion. *London: the Company*, [n.d.]. (Rail Traction Bulletin, 1). pp. 8.

10641 ENGLISH ELECTRIC COMPANY. Protective devices on diesel-electric locomotives. *London: E.E.C.*, [196–?]. (Rail Traction Bulletin, no. 3). pp. 10.
The need for simple but reliable automatic devices to protect and warn against potential and imminent technical failures.

10642 METROPOLITAN CAMMELL CARRIAGE & WAGON CO. Diesel-electric Pullman trains. *Birmingham: Metro Cammell*, [196–?]. la. 8°. pp. 8, with col. folded illus.
A publicity brochure.

10643 DAVY, V. Diesel and diesel-electric locomotives, illustrated by Norman Murphy. *London: Macdonald*, 1969. (NOW Books series). pp. 59, with 58 explanatory diagrams.
Introductory.

10644 DAVIES, W. J. K. Diesel rail traction: an illustrated history of diesel locomotives, rail-cars and trains. *London: Almark*, 1973. pp. 104, with 171 illus (13 col.), & dimensioned drawings.

10645 WEBB, B. The British internal-combustion locomotive, 1894–1940. *Newton Abbot: David & Charles*, 1973. la. 8°. pp. 120, with 100 illus.

10646 TOMS, G. Brush diesel locomotives, 1940–78. *Sheffield: Turntable Publications*; *Glossop: Transport Publishing Co.*, 1978. la. 8°. pp. 112, with 165 illus (12 col.) & a 6-column table of locomotives of BR class 31 (type 2).

10647 NICOLLE, B. J. Modern diesels in focus. *London: Ian Allan*, 1979. pp. 112. Intro, 203 illus with descrs, & 3 in the preliminary pages undescribed.
All but a few of the photographs are by B. J. Nicolle.

10648 TUFNELL, R. M. The diesel impact on British Rail, with a foreword by T. C. B. Miller. *London: Mechanical Engineering Publications*, 1979. pp. ix, 184, with 92 illus, drawings & diagrams, & 25 tables; 10 appendices.
The change-over from steam to diesel on BR, 1957–1968: a detailed narrative of this period of experimentation with an appraisal of the strength and weaknesses of every type of diesel locomotive used on main line haulage during this period.

E 11   ROLLING STOCK (Carriages and wagons)

10649–54

For travelling post offices see **K 9**

10649 BERGIN, T. F. Observations on the thorough buffing apparatus in use on the Dublin & Kingstown Railway. *Dublin: printed by R. D. Webb*, 1836. pp. 15.
The author's patent spring buffers described.

10650 MARILLIER, F. W. Carriage and wagon construction in regard to traffic requirements. Great Western Railway (London) Lecture & Debating Society, meeting on November 8th, 1906 [no. 29]. pp. 17, with 29 drawings & 1 illus.

10651 RANDLE, H. The design and construction of rolling stock. (Proceedings of the British Railways (W.R.) London Lecture & Debating Society, 1950–51, no. 382). pp. 18, with discussion & 8 illus.
Author, 'Carriage & Wagon Engineer, W.R.'.

10652 CHARLES ROBERTS AND COMPANY. Charles Roberts and Company Limited, 1856–1956. [*Wakefield: the Company*, 1956]. pp. 53, with 55 illus.
Manufacture of railway wagons & carriages, and tramcars: a centenary history of the firm.

10653　WILKES, E. G. M. Appearance and amenity design of rolling stock. *London: Institution of Locomotive Engineers*, 1965. pp. 21, with 14 illus & 3 diagrams.
A paper to be read 18 January 1965.

10654　CASSERLEY, R. M. and MILLARD, P. A. A Register of West Coast Joint Stock: being a description of the London and North Western and Caledonian railway companies' joint rolling stock, with particular reference to the distinctive features of mechanical design, an account of train working between England and Scotland, including particulars of noteworthy accidents and notes on other relevant topics of importance to the historian and the model maker. *Frome: Historical Model Railway Society*, 1980. pp. viii, 316, with frontis, 299 illus (photos & dimensioned drawings), & many tables, incl. timetables.
Passenger rolling stock, with ch. 13 on 'Post Office carriages', and ch. 14, 'Fish vans and goods rolling stock'.

E12　CARRIAGES
10655–69

For restaurant cars see also **G 3** *and* **G 7**

10655　MALLABAND, P. and BOWLES, L. J. The coaching stock of British Railways: classifications, allocations, formations, detail variations, multiple units, hauled stocks. *Kenilworth: Railway Correspondence & Travel Society*, [1972]. pp. iii, 128.
Lists of the 24497 vehicles in stock at the end of 1971.
—— [2nd edn.], 1974. pp. iii, 132.
23331 vehicles in stock at end of 1973, with added notes.
—— [3rd edn.], 1976. pp. 138, with 18 illus on 6 plates.
22907 vehicles in stock at end of 1975, with added notes.
—— [4th edn.], 1978. pp. 92, with 78 illus on 36 plates.
21907 vehicles in stock at end of 1977.
Addenda and corrigenda are noted in all editions including the first which has two lists loosely inserted as well as having an addenda page inside the front cover as p.iii. The contents page is inside the back cover and is p.ii.

10656　PULLMAN CAR COMPANY. The story of Pullman. 2nd edn. [*Chicago: the Company*, 1904]. pp. 30, with frontis (portrait), 12 plates & a col. drawing in 15 foldings at end. No title page. Title on cover only.
A re-issue of a booklet first issued for the Columbian Exposition, 1893, with a statistical addenda (pp. 29–30) up to July 1904. The work does not include any account of Pullman cars on British railways.

10657　TWEEDIE, M. G. Train lighting by electricity. Great Western Railway (London) Lecture & Debating Society, meeting on February 9th, 1911 [no. 78]. pp. 12, with discussion & 17 illus.

10658　BRITISH ALUMINIUM COMPANY. Railway and tramway rolling stock. *London: the Company*, 1928. sm. 8°. pp. D76–D130. Intro & 27 illus with captions.
A trade brochure.

10659　COOPER, R. A. British Pullman cars. [*Newport*]: *Monmouthshire Railway Society*, Summer 1961. pp. 23. Reproduced typescript.
A fleet list of the cars currently in service, with an historical introduction.

10660　KICHENSIDE, G. M. Railway carriages, 1839–1939. *London: Ian Allan*, [1964]. (Veteran & Vintage series). pp. 64, with 106 illus & a list of preserved carriages.

10661　ELLIS, C. H. Railway carriages in the British Isles, from 1830 to 1914. *London: Allen & Unwin*, 1965. pp. 279, with 111 illus (2 col.) on 40 plates, & 49 line illus.

10662　KICHENSIDE, G. M. Railway Carriage Album. *London: Ian Allan*, 1966. obl. format. pp. 228, with 398 illus (9 col.).
—— [2nd] edn. *Ian Allan*, 1980. obl. format. pp. 244; 419 illus (6 col.).
pp. 7–53, Historical survey.

10663　JENKINSON, D. and CAMPLING, N. Historic carriage drawings in 4mm. scale. *Shepperton: Ian Allan*.
vol. 1, L.M.S. and L.N.E.R. 1969. la. obl. format. pp. xii, 100.
100 groups of dimensioned drawings with detailed notes. The work is introduced with notes on livery and numbering.

10664　PASSENGER ENVIRONMENT: a conference arranged by the Railway Division of the Institution of Mechanical Engineers, 23rd–24th March 1972. *London: I.M.E.*, 1972. la. 8°. pp. x, 119, with illus & diagrams.
Nine papers, with discussions, on design, interior furnishing, vibration, air-conditioning, passenger ergonomics, urban BR stock, the Advanced Passenger Train, and Underground cars.

10665　BRITISH RAILWAYS. A hundred years of the sleeping car. (Sleeping Car Centenary, 1873–1973). [*London*]: *B.R.*, 1973. A printed folder, with 15 illus.

10666　HARRIS, M. Preserved railway coaches. *London: Ian Allan*, 1976. pp. 208, with 188 illus.

A chronological record of over 600 carriages, each with a detailed description of up to one page and in most cases supported by a photograph. Great Britain & Northern Ireland, 1834 to 1958.

10667 KICHENSIDE, G. Orion and the Golden Arrow: the story of a Pullman car. *Seaton: Peco*, 1978. pp. 27, with 30 illus & 3 diagrams (incl. a double-spread dimensioned drawing).
The adoption of the Pullman Kitchen car *Orion* and its restoration and revival as a restaurant car at Beer (Devon) Victoria Station.

10668 KIDNER, R. W. The carriage stock of minor standard gauge railways. *Tarrant Hinton: Oakwood Press*, 1978. (Locomotion Papers, 109). pp. 50, with 58 illus on 24 plates & many tables & line illus in text.

Accounts of the stock of 130 railways, alphabetically arranged.

10669 NATIONAL RAILWAY MUSEUM. Centenary Express: a guide to the National Railway Museum Catering Centenary Train. *London: H.M.S.O.; York: N.R.M.*, 1979. sm. obl. format. pp. 16, with 26 illus (19 col.). Intro by J. A. Coiley, Keeper, N.R.M.
Published to mark the centenary of on-train catering in Britain. The booklet describes and illustrates each of the nine vintage carriages (average age ca. 60 years) restored for main-line running by British Rail Engineering Ltd with the collaboration of BR, and the modern kitchen car for the supply of meals on the series of journeys prescribed for the train.

E 13   WAGONS and other non-passenger vehicles for special classes of work
10670–9

10670 ESSERY, R. J., ROWLAND, D. P. and STEEL, W. O. British goods wagons, from 1887 to the present day. *Newton Abbot: David & Charles*, 1970. pp. 144, with 110 illus & 32 line drawings; bibliography (18 sources); appendices 1–9, detailed tabulated reference data.

10671 LLOYD & PLAISTER LTD. Rail motor trolley constructed under White's patent. *Wood Green (London): the firm*, [ca. 1905?]. sm. obl. format. pp. [20], with 4 illus & 1 in window of cover. Cover title: 'The last word in rail trolleys'.
A sales brochure.   LU(THC)

10672 WAGON REPAIRS LTD. List of works, depots and repairing stations. *Birmingham: Wagon Repairs Ltd*, [1920]. pp. 32. LU(THC)

10673 ROCHE, F. J. Historic wagon drawings in 4mm. scale, drawn by F. J. Roche. *London: Ian Allan*, 1965. obl. format. pp. 38.
68 wagon types of the Big Four companies with a few from pre-Grouping days; front, side & end elevations.

10674 ABBOTT, R. A. S. Crane locomotives: a survey of British practice. [*Norwich*]: *Goose & Sons*, 1973. pp. 80, with 50 illus on 24 plates.

10675 BROWNLIE, J. S. Railway steam cranes: a survey of progress since 1875, with notes on

geographical spread of the British crane trade and biography of leading member firms. *Glasgow: J. S. Brownlie*, 1973. pp. xxvi, 369, with 130 illus & 17 diagrams, 11 detailed tables, glossary, bibliography (49 sources) & a full index.
A comprehensive and detailed work.

10676 HUDSON, B. Private owner wagons. *Oxford: Oxford Publishing Co.* 4°.
vol. 1, 1976. pp. x, 118, with 109 & [5] illus described in detail; brief bibliography.
vol. 2, 1978. pp. viii, 136, with 109 illus described in detail, 14 dimensioned drawings & a brief bibliography. Includes an errata list for vol. 1.
Most of the illustrations in the two volumes are from the records of Charles Roberts & Co., railway wagon manufacturers.

10677 LARKIN, D. Private owner freight wagons on British Railways: a pictorial survey. *Truro: Bradford Barton*, 1976. pp. 64. Intro & 120 illus with descrs.

10678 ESSERY, R. J. and MORGAN, K. R. The L.M.S. wagon. *Newton Abbot: David & Charles*, 1977. pp. 128, with 101 illus, 37 dimensioned drawings, many detailed lists, & specimens of lettering.

10679 LARKIN, D. Pre-nationalisation freight wagons on British Railways: a pictorial survey. *Truro: Bradford Barton*, 1977. pp. 64. Intro, list, & 120 illus with descrs.

E 14   BRAKES and passenger/driver communication
10680–1

10680 WESTINGHOUSE AIR BRAKE COMPANY. Air brake tests. *Wilmerding (Pa.): the Company*, 1904. pp. 323, with frontis, 130 illus (photos, diagrams & graphs) & 50 tables.

'Compiled & published in connection with the Company's braking appliances exhibit at the Louisiana Purchase Exhibition, 1904.'

The Railway Regulation Act of 1889 compelled railway companies to fit automatic brakes to all passenger vehicles. Some chose the Vacuum Brake, others the Westinghouse Air Brake. Uniformity came only when British Railways decided on the Vacuum Brake, in the 1950s. (See *The Railways of Britain*, 2nd edn, 1968, by Jack ' Simmons, pp. 164–5).

10681 PRIGMORE, B. J. Background to brakes. *Hornchurch: P. R. Davies; New Malden: Eltrac Publications*, [1967]. (Signal Transport Papers, 4). pp. 29, with 12 diagrams (i.e. 17 figures in 12 groups) by R. B. Owen.

An introduction to the principles, design and operation of brakes.

E 15   SAFETY ENGINEERING

Signals and signalling methods—Interlocking of points and signals

10682–10706

For social aspects of safety in transit by rail see **K 3**

10682 BRUNEL, M. I. and DANIELL, J. F. As the electric telegraph has recently attracted a considerable share of public attention . . . [1841]. Folio, s. sh.

A printed statement supporting the claims of Wm. F. Cooke and C. Wheatstone to have invented the electric telegraph. Dated 27 April, 1841. Appended to the University of London (Goldsmiths' Library) copy of *Telegraphic railways*, by William F. Cooke (1842).   UL(GL)

10683 TIMMIS, I. A. Modern practice in railway signalling, *in* Proceedings of Section 1, Railways, International Engineering Congress, Glasgow, 1901. *London: William Clowes*, 1902, pp. 22–32, with 6 folded composite diagrams; 'Discussion', pp. 29–32.

10684 INSELL, R. J. Manual versus power systems of locking and signalling. Great Western Railway (London) Lecture & Debating Society, meeting on Friday, February 17th, 1905 (no. 11). pp. 4.

10685 JACOBS, C. M. Some recent improvements in electric signalling and electric signalling apparatus. Great Western Railway (London) Lecture & Debating Society, meeting on January 6th, 1905 [no. 7]. pp. 9, with 10 illus.

10686 BOWDEN, E. A. The safe working of a railway: its ideals and limitations. Great Western Railway (London) Lecture & Debating Society, meeting on Thursday, January 16th, 1908 [no. 46]. pp. 13, with discussion & 4 diagrams.

10687 JACOBS, C. M. Should cab-signalling be generally adopted, and should it supersede the semaphore distant signal? Great Western Railway (London) Lecture & Debating Society, meeting on March 10th, 1910 [no. 69]. pp. 8, with discussion & 6 illus.

10688 MINISTRY OF TRANSPORT. AUTOMATIC TRAIN CONTROL COMMITTEE. Report. *London: HMSO*, 1922. pp. 33. (Chairman: Col. J. W. Pringle).

10689 [STEELE, A.] Questions and answers upon the rules and regulations affecting signalmen, by A Stationmaster (A. Steele). *Glasgow: Civic Press*, 1924. sm. 8°. pp. 76.

370 questions and answers; a practical interpretation with the relevant rule or regulation cited in every case. In the LU(THC) copy a small printed label affixed to the inside of the back cover bears the words: 'Supplied by A. Steele, Station Master, Oakley, Fifeshire.'

10690 LONDON, MIDLAND & SCOTTISH RLY. Signalling model, British Empire Exhibition, Wembley, 1925. [*London*]: L.M.S.R., [1925]. pp. 20, with 3 plates, 3 diagrams, 5 mounted illus & 2 col. folded charts.

A model railway transferred from one of the LMS schools of signalling to demonstrate to visitors the process of controlling train movements from five inter-related signal boxes.

10691 CROOK. G. H. Signalling in relation to railway operation. Great Western Railway (London) Lecture & Debating Society, meeting on 3rd February 1927 (no. 203). pp. 28, with discussion & 20 diagrams.

Author, 'Signal Engineer's Office, W.R.'.

10692 MINISTRY OF TRANSPORT. AUTOMATIC TRAIN CONTROL COMMITTEE, 1927. Report, November 3, 1930. *London: H.M.S.O.*, 1930. pp. 27. (Chairman, Sir John W. Pringle).

10693 GREAT WESTERN RAILWAY. Description and notes on the G.W.R. system of automatic train control. *London: G.W.R.*, July 1931. pp. 15, with 14 diagrams & illus (some folded). Cover title: Automatic train control.

10694 CROOK, G. H. Automatic train control.

(Proceedings of the Great Western Railway (London) Lecture and Debating Society, 1931–32, no. 259). pp. 27, with discussion, 17 diagrams & illus.
Author, 'Assistant to the Signal Engineer'.

10695 RAILWAY SIGNAL COMPANY. Signalling of single lines: arrangements for trolley working. *London: Railway Signal Co.*, [1932]. (Bulletin, 14). pp. 7.
Reprint from *Modern Transport*, Feb 27th, 1932.

10696 HONEYBONE, F. The work of a main line signalman. Great Western Railway (London) Lecture & Debating Society, meeting on 1st December 1938, no. 327. pp. 14, with discussion & 9 illus.
Author, 'Divisional Supt's Office, Paddington'.

10697 CARR, T. H. Train signalling. [*London: L.M.S. Magazine*], 1939. pp. 24.
Revised essays from the *LMS Magazine*, 1937–38.

10698 TYLER, J. F. H. Modern power signalling. Proceedings of the Great Western Railway (London) Lecture and Debating Society, 1947–8, no. 347. pp. 22, with discussion & 8 diagrams.
Author, Assistant to the Signal & Telegraph Engineer (Electrical).

10699 MINISTRY OF TRANSPORT AND CIVIL AVIATION. Report on level crossing protection based on a visit to the Netherlands, Belgian and French railways by officers of the Ministry of Transport & Civil Aviation and of the British Transport Commission. *London: H.M.S.O.*, 1957. pp. 14, with 2 diagrams & 2 appendices. Cover title, Level crossing protection.

10700 LE SEUR, C. M. deV. A history of railway signalling. (Proceedings of the British Railways (W.R.) London Lecture & Debating Society, 1957–58, no. 442). pp. 27, with discussion & 18 illus.
Author, Signal Engineer's Office, Reading (W.R.). Includes frequent references to developments and practice on the GWR.

10701 CHALLIS, W. H. Principles of the layout of signals, British practice. 3rd edn. *Reading: Institution of Railway Signal Engineers*, 1960. (Booklet, no. 1). pp. 35.
One of a series of 14 technical introductions for students.

10702 HUBBARD, G. Cooke & Wheatstone and the invention of the electric telegraph. *London: Routledge & Kegan Paul*, 1965. pp. ix, 158, with 19 illus on 1 plate & 17 diagrams.

10703 NOCK, O. S. British railway signalling: a survey of fifty years' progress. *London: Allen & Unwin*, 1969. pp. 180, with 58 illus on 20 plates.

10704 KIEVE, J. The electric telegraph: a social and economic history. *Newton Abbot: David & Charles*, 1973. pp. 310, with 16 illus on 8 plates, 2 maps, 7 line illus & charts, & a bibliography (75 sources).
The index has ca. 100 page refs from 'Railways' and from the names of individual lines.

10705 DEPARTMENT OF TRANSPORT. Report on level crossing protection, including visits to the Netherlands, French, West German and Swiss railways, by officers of the Department of Transport and of the British Railways Board. *London: H.M.S.O.*, 1978. pp. vii, 68, with 27 illus on 16 plates, & appendices A to O (diagrams & other addenda). Cover title: Level crossing protection.

10706 NOCK, O. S. Railway signalling; a treatise on the recent practice of British Railways . . . *London: A. & C. Black*, 1980. obl. 8°. pp. viii, 312, with 187 diagrams & graphs. (Foreword by K. E. Hodgson, President, Institution of Railway Signal Engineers).
'Prepared under the direction of a committee of the Institution of Railway Signal Engineers under the general editorship of O. S. Nock, Honorary Fellow and Past President of the Institution.'

E 16   OTHER RAILWAY EQUIPMENT

10707–9

10707 RILEY, E. C. and CLIFTON, G. B. Gas or acetylene lighting *v.* electric lighting for railways. Great Western Railway (London) Debating Society, meeting on Friday, February 3rd, 1905 [no. 9]. pp. 11.
For trains and railway premises.

10708 BABCOCK & WILCOX LTD. Silent gravity bucket & tray conveyors, automatic railways, etc. *London: the firm*, 1921. (Publication no 367, June, 1921). pp. 58, with 59 illus & 24 folded plates.

The mechanical handling of coal & quarry material, railway truck tippers, and industrial automatic railways.

10709 BRITISH RAILWAYS. Mechanical aids for railway goods stations. [*London*]: *B.R.*, [1954]. pp. 27, with 25 illus.
A practical guide to lifting and shifting equipment currently in use: elevating trucks, pallet trucks, fork-lift trucks, mobile cranes, conveyors and portable lighting: how they are used and how much they cost to install and to run.

F RAILWAY ADMINISTRATION

The organisation, finance and management of railway
undertakings—Commercial aspects

10710–67

Historical 10710–17
Contemporaneous 10718–67 (Reference source 10718)

Historical

10710 CARTWRIGHT, F. A. Some aspects of the commercial development of British railways. Great Western Railway (London) Lecture & Debating Society, meeting on 9th March, 1933 (no. 272). pp. 22, with discussion.

Author, 'District Goods Manager's Office, Shrewsbury'.

The historical development of goods rates & charges, cheap travel facilities, and general improvements in rail travel. The present problems of declining revenue in the face of growing road competition, inequitable legislation, and trade recession. Discussion, pp. 18–22.

10711 FEINSTEIN, C. H. Domestic capital formation in the U.K., 1920–1938. *London: Cambridge University Press*, 1965. la. 8°. (Studies in the National Income & Expenditure of the United Kingdom, 4). pp. xii, 270, with tables & diagrams.

Includes railways. The measurement of flows in gross investment, depreciation and net investment, and estimates of the accumulated stock of fixed assets.

10712 GOURVISH, T. R. British railway management in the nineteenth century, with special reference to the career of Captain Mark Huish, 1808–1867. Thesis, Ph.D., University of London, 1968.

10713 MITCHELL, B. R. The coming of the railway and United Kingdom economic growth, *in* Railways in the Victorian Economy, ed. by M. C. Reed (1969). pp. 13–32, with 58 notes & a table showing capital formation by railway companies, 1831–1919.

10714 GOURVISH, T. R. Mark Huish and the London & North Western Railway: a study of management. *Leicester: Leicester University Press*, 1972. pp. 319, with 8 plates (portraits), 6 maps, 3 line illus., 63 tables (nos. 44–63 in appendix 1), 819 notes & a select bibliography (pp. 301–9) of ca. 170 sources.

10715 JOY, S. The train that ran away: a business history of British Railways, 1948–1968. *London: Ian Allan*, 1973. pp. 160, with 283 notes.

Alleged mismanagement.

10716 PARKER, P. A way to run a railway, by Peter Parker, Chairman, British Rail. *London: Birkbeck College, University of London*, 1978. (Haldane Memorial Lecture, 41). pp. 19.

Management objectives: a review of past and present difficulties and the challenge to improve efficiency and productivity.

10717 CAIN, P. J. Private enterprise or public utility?; output, pricing and investment on English and Welsh railways, 1870–1914, *in* Journal of Transport History, 3rd series, vol. 1, no. 1, September 1980. pp. 9–28, with 8 tables, a graph & 46 notes.

A study of the decline of profitability in British railway history.

Contemporaneous

10718 SOUTHGATE, J. F. O. Rail transport. *London: Chartered Institute of Transport*, April 1977. (Transport Bibliography no. 6, Rail Transport). pp. 89. Reproduced typescript.

About 1300 sources (books, pamphlets & periodical essays), including *see also* references appended to some entries, arranged under 30 subject headings.

Historical works are not included. Produced by the Librarian of the C.I.T. to facilitate research into rail transport technology and administration of the recent past, the present, and the future.

The compiler's notes are an important feature of the work.

10719 [ABBOTT.] JOHN ABBOTT & CO. John Abbott's analysis of British railways [1879]. *London: the Company*, 1880. pp. 65. Tables (capital & revenue) of individual companies for 1879.

10720 LAW, H. C. and NICOLE, R. C. Wholesale versus retail trade from a railway point of view. Great Western Railway (London) Lecture & Debating Society, meeting on November 16th, 1905 [no. 18]. pp. 8.

10721 GRIFFITHS, H. R. Some aspects of railway economics. Great Western Railway (London) Lecture & Debating Society, meeting on January 3rd, 1907 [no. 33]. pp. 7.

10722 NICHOLLS, R. H. The work of a Divisional Superintendent's office. Great Western Railway (London) Lecture & Debating Society, meeting on April 5th, 1907 [no. 39]. pp. 18.

The London Division of the GWR.

10723 PLANT, A. The published accounts as a

basis for railway working comparisons. Great Western Railway (London) Lecture & Debating Society, meeting on March 14th 1907 [no. 38]. pp. 7, with 2 tables.

10724 LARKING, F. P. The business value of departmental co-operation on railways. Great Western Railway (London) Lecture & Debating Society, meeting on December 14th, 1910 [no. 74]. pp. 11, with discussion.

10725 PRICE, D. W. B. The Audit Office and its functions. Great Western Railway (London) Lecture & Debating Society, meeting on November 17th, 1910 [no. 72]. pp. 12, with discussion.

10726 HADLEY, E. S. Is a profit-sharing or co-partnership scheme applicable to railway companies? Great Western Railway (London) Lecture & Debating Society, meeting on January 30th, 1913 [no. 97]. pp. 11, with discussion.

10727 NEWTON, C. H. The Railway Companies (Accounts and Returns) Act, 1911. Great Western Railway (London) Lecture & Debating Society, meeting on February 13th, 1913 [no. 98]. pp. 11, with discussion.

10728 POTTER, F. Presidential address. Great Western Railway (London) Lecture & Debating Society, meeting on October 15th, 1913 [no. 102]. pp. 4.
Criticisms sometimes made against railways, with added comments by Lord Churchill, Chairman of the GWR.

10729 SMITH, R. J. How British railways strike a new recruit: are they well organised? Great Western Railway (London) Lecture & Debating Society, meeting on January 16th, 1913 [no. 96]. pp. 13, with discussion.

10730 SCOTT, W. J. Some possible ways of railway organization. Great Western Railway (London) Lecture & Debating Society, meeting on October 30th, 1919 [no. 113]. pp. 11.
A reprint of the author's series 'Railway management in Utopia', G.W.R. Magazine, January 1914. pp. 3–4; November 1915, pp. 289–90; February 1916, p. 42, and a letter from the author on p. 24.

10731 COLLIER, R. A. H. [Lord Monkswell]. How restricting output and living on capital lead to famine. Great Western Railway (London) Lecture & Debating Society, meeting on March 3rd, 1921 [no. 135]. pp. 11, with discussion.
The imminent threat of national bankruptcy. Various points relating to railway administration arise out of the discussion.

10732 BENNETT, J. R. and TWEEDIE, M. G. Is 'Divisional' better than 'Departmental' organisation on railways? Great Western Railway (London) Lecture & Debating Society, meeting on November 30th, 1922 (no. 153). pp. 14, with 2 charts.
A debate, with discussion and vote.

10733 TRAVIS, C. Railway organization. Great Western Railway (London) Lecture & Debating Society, meeting on January 12th, 1922 (no. 144). pp. 32, with discussion, 20 illus & maps.
Divisional as opposed to Departmental structure.

10734 The SCIENTIFIC spirit in transport: is it lacking? Great Western Railway (London) Lecture & Debating Society, meeting on March 15th, 1923 (no. 160). pp. 20, with discussion.
A debate between F. C. Warren, E. A. Lyons, J. Davies and H. F. Kelley.

10735 The BEST way of obtaining and retaining traffic on the railways, by J. F. Anstey, L. J. L. Lean, Percy H. Liddington, W. H. Victory. Great Western Railway (London) Lecture & Debating Society, meeting on 18th February, 1926 (no. 192). pp. 31, with discussion.

10736 PARNELL, W. P. Detail and its place in an efficient railway organisation. Great Western Railway (London) Lecture & Debating Society, meeting on 18th March, 1926 (no. 194). pp. 12, with discussion.

10737 HOWARD, H. W. The Staff Department: its work and opportunities. Great Western Railway (London) Lecture & Debating Society, meeting on 16th February, 1928 (no. 217). pp. 17, with discussion.
The GWR Staff Department.

10738 NEWTON, C. H. Railway accounting and finance. Great Western Railway (London) Lecture & Debating Society, meeting on 15th March 1928 (no. 219). pp. 22.
Author, 'Assistant Accountant, LNER, King's Cross'.

10739 PICK, F. A survey of railways. Great Western Railway (London) Lecture & Debating Society, meeting on 2nd February 1928 (no. 215). pp. 18, with discussion.
Problems of efficiency and economy in face of the growth of road transport. Author, 'Assistant Managing Director, London Underground Rlys'.

10740 GIBB, R. The rationalisation of industry. Great Western Railway (London) Lecture & Debating Society, meeting on the 27th February, 1930 (no. 241). pp. 14, with discussion.
Considers its application to modern railway problems. Author, 'Chief Goods Manager's Office'.

10741 NEWTON, C. A. Railway accounts: their statutory form and the practice of the railway companies to give effect thereto. London: Pitman, 1930. pp. ix, 245, with many specimen tabulations.
Author, 'Chief Accountant, LNER'.

10742 PAYNE, H. W. Getting and keeping business (Goods Department). Great Western Railway (London) Lecture & Debating Society, meeting on 6th November 1930 (no. 244). pp. 23, with discussion.
Author, 'District Goods Manager, Newport'.

10743 LAMPITT, F. W. Goods station accounts: are present methods too costly? Great Western Railway (London) Lecture & Debating Society, meeting on 26th February, 1931 (no. 251). pp. 18, with discussion.

10744 WESTCOTT, L. F. What adjustments or developments are desirable in British railway charges, services, publicity and administrative costs? Proceedings of the Great Western Railway (London) Lecture & Debating Society, 1931–32, no. 260. pp. 13, with discussion.
Author, 'Chief Goods Manager's Office'.

10745 BRISTOW, B. H. By what means can the individual and co-operative efficiency of railway staff be enhanced? Great Western Railway (London) Lecture & Debating Society, meeting on 9th February 1933, no. 271. pp. 12, with discussion.

10746 'THAT an increase in the scale of railway transport is to be sought more in quality than in price': introduced by P. Hogbin & L. F. Westcott and J. Adshead & G. E. Boden. Great Western Railway (London) Lecture & Debating Society, meeting on 28th October 1937, no. 314. pp. 11, with discussion.

10747 'THAT railway facilities are not sufficiently flexible to meet the requirements of the public': introduced by D. R. Reese & F. W. Jones and R. D. H. Jones & B. Seymour. Great Western Railway (London) Lecture & Debating Society, meeting on 10th November 1938, no. 326. pp. 13, with discussion.

10748 COLEMAN, C. J. and COOPER, N. J. The criteria of an efficient railway system. Great Western Railway (London) Lecture & Debating Society, meeting on 9th February, 1939, no. 331. pp. 12, with discussion.

10749 BRITISH RAILWAYS. WESTERN REGION. The Powellson pay-slip: the story behind a pay packet. *London: B.R. (WR)*, [ca. 1950]. obl. format. pp. 22.
Produced to show how the processing of the pay slip of an imaginary railwayman—'Dai Powellson'—can be facilitated by means of the British Tabulating Machine Company's Hollerith electronic computer.

10750 SMALLPIECE, B. The use of statistics in the measurement of efficiency in transport. Proceedings of the British Railways (W.R.) London Lecture & Debating Society, 1949–50, no. 367. pp. 15, with discussion.
Author, 'Director of Costs & Statistics, B.T.C.'.

10751 LLOYD, J. E. By what means can the net revenue of the British Railways be improved in present circumstances? (Proceedings of the British Railways (W.R.) London Lecture & Debating Society, 1950–51, no. 384). pp. 14, with discussion.

10752 HOOPER, F. C. Management today and tomorrow. (Proceedings of the British Railways (W.R.) Lecture & Debating Society, 1952–53, no. 398). pp. 12, with discussion, in which the subject is related to railways.
Author, Managing Director of Schweppes Ltd and Kia-Ora Ltd.

10753 SARGENT, W. H. Electronics in the office and elsewhere. Proceedings of the British Railways (W.R.) London Lecture & Debating Society, 1955–56, no. 425. pp. 15, with discussion & 3 diagrams.
Author, Assistant to Accountant (Paybills), Swindon, WR.

10754 BRITISH RAILWAYS. WESTERN REGION. Electronic accounting. *Swindon: B.R. (WR)*, 1957. pp. 14, with 26 illus, 2 punched cards, pay slip & folded diagram in pocket at end.
The system in use at Swindon Works.

10755 JOY, S. C. The variability of railway track costs and their implications for policy, with special reference to Great Britain. Thesis, Ph.D., University of London, 1964.
Investment and recovery (rates & fares) decisions should be related to constructional and maintenance costs.

10756 FIENNES, G. F. Meeting the challenge of safety, convenience, speed, reliability, comfort and economy on the Western Region. Presidential address. British Railways (W.R.) London Lecture & Debating Society, 1964–65 (no. 486). pp. 20, with discussion, 9 diagrams, & 5 maps.
Author, 'General Manager, BR (WR)'.

10757 FAULKS, R. W. Elements of transport. *London: Ian Allan*, 1965. pp. xi, 200, with 40 illus on 18 plates, 20 diagrams & a list of Acts.
A textbook: definitions and commentaries.
—— 2nd edn. *Ian Allan*, 1969. pp. 244; 40 illus on 24 plates, 17 diagrams, Acts.
—— [3rd edn]. Principles of transport. *Ian Allan*, 1973. pp. 220; 47 illus on 24 plates, 12 diagrams, Acts.

10758 FIENNES, G. F. I tried to run a railway. *London: Ian Allan*, 1967. pp. vii, 139, with 63 illus (incl. portraits & map) on 32 plates.
The author was in railway service from 1928 until 1967, mostly with the LNER and BR(ER), but with BR(WR) as Chairman of the Western Railway Board, 1963–65. From 1965–67, Chairman, Eastern Railway Board and General Manager, Eastern Region of BR.

10759 JOY, S. Railway track costs, *in* Transport: selected readings, edited by Denys Munby (1968), pp. 130–49, with 4 tables, 25 notes & 12 bibliographical sources.

10760 HAWKE, G. R. Pricing policy of railways in England and Wales before 1881, *in* Railways in the Victorian Economy, edited by M. C. Reed (1969), pp. 76–110, with 152 notes & 5 diagrams.

Based on the author's thesis (Ph.D., University of London, 1968). Includes a review of railway organisation from the earliest days of public railways.

10761 HIBBS, J. Transport studies: an introduction. *London: John Baker*, 1970. pp. 120, with 24 illus on 16 plates, 2 maps, 2 diagrams, 8 tables, & a bibliography (30 sources).
The pattern of modern transport: its problems in face of advancing technology and with changes in its own modal relationships. A plea for an understanding of the realities of the contemporary transport industry, addressed mainly to students of transport administration and management.

10762 BOSWORTH, J. M. W. Corporate planning. Proceedings of the British Rail Western London Lecture & Debating Society, Session 1970/71, no. 507, 20 October 1970. pp. 15, with 8 diagrams.
Author, Vice-Chairman, BR.

10763 BONAVIA, M. R. The organisation of British Railways. *London: Ian Allan*, 1971. pp. 172, with 4 maps, 9 tables, 60 notes & a bibliography (119 sources). Foreword by Lord Beeching.

10764 KAY, F. G. How to run a railway. *London: J. Baker*, 1971. (How to Run series). pp. 62, with 40 illus on 24 plates.
Railway activities described in outline: a career guide. Includes a glossary of railway terms.

10765 WREN, A. Computers in transport planning and operation. *Shepperton: Ian Allan*, 1971. pp. 152, with illus & a bibliography.
ch. 8 (pp. 97–109), 'Railway operations'. Includes a number of programs developed by BR.

10766 SCOTTISH ASSOCIATION FOR PUBLIC TRANSPORT. The finance and organisation of transport: proposals for reforms. *Glasgow: the Association*, November 1972. (Study Papers, 2). pp. 14.
p. 13, 'The railway infrastructure, freight, and passenger service accounts'.

10767 BRITISH RAILWAYS. Measuring cost and profitability in British Rail. [*London: B.R.*, 1978]. pp. 30, with 2 illus & 5 diagrams.
Problems associated with financial analyses of railway operations. An outline of the ways in which these problems are being tackled.

F 1   RATES, CHARGES, FARES, TOLLS AND TICKETS
10768–97

For passenger aspects see **K 2**
For consignor aspects see **K 4**

10768 BOARD OF TRADE. Railway and Canal Traffic Act, 1888 . . . Copy of letter to the Railway Companies' Association; copy of letter to [railway companies] with draft classification of merchandise traffic, applicable to the [several railways]. *London: printed for H.M. Stationery Office by Harrison & Sons*, [1890].   NUC

10769 BOARD OF TRADE. Railway rates and charges. Correspondence between the Board of Trade and the Railway Companies Association and various railway companies with regard to the revised rates charged for the conveyance of merchandise traffic, January 2nd to May 10th, 1893. *London: printed for H.M. Stationery Office by Eyre & Spottiswoode*, 1893.

10770 BELL, H. Cheaper railway fares. [Paper read at a meeting of the International Engineering Congress held at the University, Glasgow, September 1901]. *London: Wm. Clowes*, 1902. pp. 89. (Proceedings of Section 1, Railways, pp. 78–84).

10771 EDMONDSON, J. B. John B. Edmondson's Railway Ticket and Apparatus Catalogue, including the latest improvements in railway ticket printing, backing, counting, dating, issuing, and destroying machines, invented by the late Mr. Thomas Edmondson, originator and inventor of the railway ticket system. *Cheetham (Manchester): J. B. Edmondson*, [1905?]. (reprinted by the Lancashire & Cheshire Antiquarian Society, 1966). pp. 20, with 15 illus in text. A facsimile reprint with an added note by W. H. Chaloner. Cover title: The early history of the railway ticket: a documentary reprint.
pp. 3–6, 'To whom are we indebted for the railway ticket system?: an account of the life and work of Thomas Edmondson, by John B. Edmondson.

10772 BOARD OF TRADE. Correspondence between the Board of Trade and the Railway Companies Association with regard to certain arrangements entered into by railway companies with regard to rebates on traffic, etc. Presented to both Houses of Parliament by command of His Majesty. *London: printed for H.M. Stationery Office by Darling & Son, Ltd*, 1907.

10773 PHILLIPS, F. E. Railway companies' obligations and liabilities: rates and fares. Great Western Railway (London) Lecture & Debating Society, meeting on November 4th, 1909 [no. 62]. pp. 8.

10774 GIBB, R. Should British railways adopt a system of wagon-load and less-than-wagon-load rates? Great Western Railway (London) Lecture & Debating Society, meeting on February 17th, 1910 [no. 67]. pp. 9, with discussion.

10775 JONES, G. G. Railway Rates Tribunal: jurisdiction and practice. *London: Palethorpe & Cond*, [1922]. pp. 120.
A guide to the powers of the Tribunal under the Railways Act 1921 in determining merchandise rates, passenger fares and conditions of carriage.

10776 MINISTRY OF TRANSPORT. Classification of merchandise for conveyance by railway, determined by Rates Advisory Committee. *London: H.M.S.O.*, 1923. pp. 265.

10777 HAWKESWOOD, D. H. Railway rates and food prices: a comparison and a contrast. *Paddington Station (London): Great Western Rly*, 1925. (Great Western Pamphlets, 17). pp. 15, with a 7-column table.
Reprint from the *GWR Magazine*, June, 1925. Railway rates not responsible for recent increases in food prices.

10778 PAYNE, H. W. Keeping abreast of the times in the Goods Department. Great Western Railway (London) Lecture & Debating Society, meeting on 11th January 1934, no. 279. pp. 27, with 15 illus & 8 diagrams.

10779 HOWARD, H. W. Claims and their prevention. (Proceedings of the British Railways (W.R.) London Lecture & Debating Society, 1949–50, no. 370). pp. 19, with discussion, 8 illus & a diagram.
Author, 'Claims & Salvage Agent, W.R.'.

10780 POOLE, H. D. Railway rates and charges as affected by the Transport Act, 1953. (Proceedings of the British Railways (W.R.) London Lecture & Debating Society, 1953–54, no. 410). pp. 14, with discussion.
Author, 'Assistant to Commercial Supt. (Rates & Charges), W.R.'.

10781 DETERMINING pattern of railway charges structure. *London: The Times Publishing Co.*, 1957. pp. [3].
Reprinted from *The Times*, June 26, 1957.

10782 ROBBINS, M. and POSTGATE, R. Passenger fares: a consideration of the economic aspects of alternative fares structures. *Brussels: International Union of Public Transport*, 1961. (34th International Congress, Copenhagen, 1961, paper no. 7). pp. 19, with 4 folded tables.

The very detailed tables enable comparisons to be made on a world-wide scale, of fares by road transport and by rail in particular towns.

10783 DICKINSON, G. Traffic costing today: a critical appraisal. (Proceedings of the British Railways (W.R.) London Lecture & Debating Society, 1961–62, no. 474.). pp. 16, with discussion.
Author, Principal Traffic Costing Officer, Paddington.

10784 GELDARD, D. G. Cab toll tickets. *Luton: Transport Ticket Society*, February 1966. (Special Publication, 2). tall 8°. Reproduced typescript. pp. 9, with 7 facsimiles of tickets & a bibliography (7 sources).
Used by main line railway companies in London 1908–1917, to control the flow of cabs calling to set down and pick up passengers.

10785 STEWART, M. G. British Platform Ticket Check List. *Luton: Transport Ticket Society*, 1967. la. 8°. pp. 46. Reproduced typescript in printed covers. Title on cover and at head of text.
Two alphabetical lists of stations: 1, Charged platform tickets, stations only; & 2, Free platform tickets, all known issues; with introductory notes to both sections. *See* 10790.

10786 CAIN, P. J. The railways rates problem and combination amongst the railway companies of Great Britain, 1893–1913. Thesis, B. Litt., University of Oxford, 1968.

10787 PASK, B. P. Tickets of the Glasgow Underground. *Luton: Transport Ticket Society*, 1971. pp. iv, 28, with 31 facsimiles of tickets. Reproduced typescript in printed covers.

10788 FAIRCHILD, G. H. I. A world of tickets . . . *Brighton: the author*, 1972. pp. 43, with facsimiles of 102 railway tickets (17 British), with descrs; 3 indexes and 3 appendices. Reproduced typescript in card covers.
'Derived from tickets in the author's collection.'

10789 JENSON, A. G. A nostalgic journey to the days of geographical and other early tickets. *Luton: Transport Ticket Society*, 1974. pp. 12, with 61 illus (55 of tickets) on 7 plates. Reproduced typescript.
Presidential address to a meeting of the Society at Caxton Hall, London, 2 November 1974.

10790 STEWART, M. G. Platform Ticket Check List: issuing stations in the British Isles. *Luton: Transport Ticket Society*, 1975. la. 8°. pp. 34. Reproduced typescript in printed covers. Title on cover and at head of text.
An up-dated version of the first part (Charged platform tickets) of this author's, *British Platform Ticket Check List* (1967). (10785)

10791 WYSE, W. J. A computer man looks at ticket and fare systems: presidential address. *Luton: Transport Ticket Society*, [1975]. pp. 17.

10792 LE GUILLOU, M. Freight rates and their influence on the Black Country iron trade in a period of growing domestic and foreign competition, 1850–1914, *in* Journal of Transport History, new series, vol. 3 (1975–6), pp. 108–18, with 32 notes.

10793 PAGE, G. H. Tickets please: some design aspects of tickets. *Luton: Transport Ticket Society*, 1976. pp. 16, with facsimiles of 66 bus, tram & railway tickets. Reproduced typescript.
Presidential address, 1976.

10794 PASK, B. P. Tickets: the road-rail link. *Luton: Transport Ticket Society*, 1977. pp. 15, with facsimiles of 98 tickets on 5 plates.
Presidential address, 1977. The development of interchange facilities between road & rail (pp. 1–2, pre-1918; pp. 2–15, post 1918).

10795 KIDD, C. Ashton, S.H.M.D. and Stock-port: the tickets of Ashton-under-Lyne Corporation; Stalybridge, Hyde, Mossley & Dukinfield Joint Board; Stockport Corporation and their forerunners and neighbours. *Luton: Transport Ticket Society*, 1978. pp. 48, with 34 facsimiles of tickets and 2 maps.
Tramway tickets.

10796 FARR, M. Thomas Edmondson, 1792–1851: transport ticket pioneer. [*Lancaster*]: Lancaster Museum, 1979. pp. 14, incl. covers, with a bibliography (9 sources). Title from cover. 'A Lancaster Museum Monograph'.

10797 WYSE, W. J. Fare and ticket systems: the key to success or failure in rail transport. *Tramway & Light Railway Society*, 1980. (Walter Gratwicke Memorial Lecture, 1980). pp. 36, with 12 illus (facsimiles of tickets, maps & posters).

F 2   INTER-RAILWAY RELATIONS

Competition—Co-operation and amalgamation

10798–10805

For the gauge controversy of the 1840s see **K**
For the amalgamations of 1923 see **B 6**
For the unification of British railways in 1948 see **B 9**

10798 ARTHURTON, A. W. Railway co-operation and combination: epoch-making agreements. Great Western Railway (London) Lecture & Debating Society, meeting on December 19th, 1907 [no. 45]. pp. 12, with discussion.

10799 SCOTT, W. J. Competition or development? Great Western Railway (London) Lecture & Debating Society, meeting on October 8th, 1908 [no. 50]. pp. 8.
'The substitution of healthy development for mere competition on the railways.' Some historical examples cited.

10800 BOARD OF TRADE. DEPARTMENTAL COMMITTEE ON RAILWAY AGREEMENTS AND AMALGAMATIONS, 1911. Report, Appendices & Minutes of Evidence. (Chairman, Russell Rea). *London: H.M.S.O.*, 1911. (Cd 5631). pp. 49, 1023.
On the nature and terms of agreements between Government and railway companies, and between railway companies.

10801 MINISTRY OF TRANSPORT. DEPARTMENTAL COMMITTEE ON RAILWAY AGREEMENTS. Report & Appendices. *London: H.M.S.O.*, 1921. pp. [various] & 257. (Cmd 1132). (Chairman, Lord Colwyn).
—— Minutes of Evidence. *H.M.S.O.*, 1921.
The nature and terms of agreements made between Government and the railway companies relating to the possession by the Government of the undertakings of the companies.

10802 MINISTRY OF TRANSPORT. RAILWAY POOL COMMITTEE. Report. *H.M.S.O.*, 1932.

10803 CAIN, P. J. The railway rates problem and combination amongst the railway companies of Great Britain, 1893–1913. Thesis, B. Litt., University of Oxford, 1968.

10804 CASSERLEY, H. C. Britain's joint lines. *London: Ian Allan*, 1968. pp. 224, with 220 illus.
A survey of the inter-relationships of 64 railway companies. Examples of 79 tickets are depicted and the appendix consists of detailed lists, illus & notes on locomotives and rolling stock.

10805 CHANNON, G. Pooling arrangements between railway companies involved in Anglo-Scottish traffic, 1851–1869. Thesis, Ph.D., University of London, 1975.

10806 BENNETT, A. E. Cumulative Index to the Railway Junction Diagrams published by John Airey and the Railway Clearing House, compiled by A. E. Bennett. *Caterham: Railway & Canal Historical Society*, 1971. obl. format. pp. 64, with foreword by David Garnett, including added historical information.

A single alphabetical listing of all junctions shown in the official indices in the complete series of 12 editions from 1867 to 1928 & the 1939 supplement.

—— Supplement, by David Garnett. *R. & C.H.S.*. 1979. pp. 4. This includes details from the 3rd edn (1872) not in the main work.

10807 RAILWAY CLEARING HOUSE. Extracts from the Regulations of the Railway Clearing House, 1882. *London: printed by Jas. Truscott*, 1882. pp. 180.

In classified sections for ease of reference. pp. 118–39, 'Ticket nippers: a list of stations at which ticket nippers are now in use'.

10808 McDERMOTT, E. The Railway Clearing House: its place in relation to the working and management of English railways. *London: Railway News*, 1890. pp. 64.

'Reprinted from the *Railway News & Joint Stock Journal*.'

10809 RAILWAY CLEARING HOUSE. Regulations, 1895. *London: J. Truscott*, 1895. pp. ix, 216.

10810 RAILWAY CLEARING HOUSE. Official Railway Junction Diagrams. *London: R.C.H.*, 1915. [Republished as a facsimile reprint by *David & Charles*, 1969]. pp. 7, xxix, 158, with an 'Introduction to the 1969 reprint' by David St John Thomas.

Over 300 coloured diagrams. A reprint of the 1915 edition of a volume of junction diagrams published at intervals from 1867. *See* 10798.

10811 FOWKES, E. H. The records of the Railway Clearing House, *in* Journal of Transport History, vol. 7, 1965–6. (Sources of Transport History). pp. 141–8, with 30 notes.

10812 BAGWELL, P. S. The Railway Clearing House in the British economy, 1842–1922. *London: Allen & Unwin*, 1968. pp. 320, with 11 illus on plates, 3 maps, over 600 bibliogr. notes & a bibliogr. essay (pp. 307–13) with refs to over 60 primary & secondary sources relating to the R.C.H. and related subject areas.

G RAILWAY OPERATION

(Excluding the working of trains)

10813–36

For the working of trains see **G 1**, **G 2**, *and* **G 3**

10813 PITMAN, I. The Phonographic Railway Phrase Book: an adaptation of phonography to the requirements of railway business and correspondence. *London: F. Pitman, Phonetic Dept; Bath: Isaac Pitman, Phonetic Institute*, 1884. sm. 8°. pp. 20.
In the introduction, Isaac Pitman includes a summary history of the teaching of shorthand to railway clerks from 1860 when classes were arranged by the Manchester Sheffield & Lincolnshire Rly.
—— 8th edn. Pitman's Shorthand Railway Phrase Book. *London: Sir Isaac Pitman*, [1899]. pp. 27, with the historical preamble on pp. 3–4.

10814 STANIER, W. H. The stores department of a railway. Great Western Railway (London) Lecture & Debating Society, meeting on Thursday, December 14th, 1905 [no. 20] (no. 6). pp. 10.

10815 HUMPHREY, B. Diagrammatic representation of railway business. Great Western Railway (London) Lecture & Debating Society, meeting on December 5th, 1907 [no. 44]. pp. 12, with discussion & 9 diagrams.
'Graphical and mechanical methods of collecting, recording and calculating ordinary railway results'.

10816 LONDON & NORTH WESTERN RLY. The Accounts Instruction Book for the guidance of station masters, goods agents and others in the preparation of their accounts, etc: approved by the Board of Directors on the 15th November, 1907. *London: McCorquodale & Co.*, 1908. pp. liv, 283.
—— Audit supplementary instructions, nos. 1–9 (1908–1915).

10817 GIBBS, C. Railway telegraphs and telephones. Great Western Railway (London) Lecture & Debating Society, meeting on January 28th, 1909 [no. 56]. pp. 9, with 9 statistical charts.

10818 BIRAM, R. S. Interior daylight illumination of railway offices. Great Western Railway (London) Lecture & Debating Society, meeting on November 2nd 1911 [no. 82]. pp. 9, with discussion.
Author, 'North Eastern Rly'.

10819 ROWBOTTOM, R. Simplification of railway methods. Great Western Railway (London) Lecture & Debating Society, meeting on November 7th, 1912 [no. 92]. pp. 4, with discussion.
Author, 'Great Central Rly'.

10820 GIBBS, C. Is the telephone the best medium for train-working and general railway communication? Great Western Railway (London) Lecture & Debating Society, meeting on January 2nd, 1913 [no. 95]. pp. 11, with discussion, 11 diagrams & illus.

10821 [PITMAN.] SIR ISAAC PITMAN AND SONS. Railway: an adaptation of Pitman's Shorthand to the requirements of railway correspondence, together with specimens of the forms used and a description of the duties of short-hand typists engaged in such business. (Centenary edition). *London: Pitman*, [1913]. sm. 8°. pp. 96.

10822 STANIER, W. H. The purchase and distribution of railway materials, with notes on American practice. Great Western Railway (London) Lecture & Debating Society, meeting on November 13th, 1913 [no. 104]. pp. 15–22, with discussion.
GWR Stores Department methods in the light of a recent visit to railways in the U.S.A.

10823 WILLIS, W. C. The supply of railway stores at home and with H.M. Forces in the field. Great Western Railway (London) Lecture & Debating Society, meeting on October 28th, 1920 [no. 125]. pp. 21, with discussion.

10824 MACDONALD, M. The future of electricity as applied to railways. Great Western Railway (London) Lecture & Debating Society, meeting on 3rd March 1927 (no. 205). pp. 22, with discussion.
Author, 'Electrical Section, C.M.E.'s Dept., Swindon'. The present and potential use of electricity for lighting, heating of premises, operation of lifts, trollies, workshop appliances, and for traction.

10825 PLAISTER, C. A. The scope and organisation of the Stores Department. Great Western Railway (London) Lecture & Debating Society, meeting on 13th December 1928 (no. 225). pp. 23, with discussion & 29 illus.
Author, 'Principal Assistant to Stores Supt.'.

10826 SPITTLE, G. H. Lighting, particularly on the Great Western Railway. Great Western Railway (London) Lecture & Debating Society, meeting on 1st November 1928 (no. 222). pp. 23, with discussion, 11 illus & diagrams.
Author, Chief Engineer's Office, Paddington. The use of natural and artificial light on railway premises.

10827 MATTHEWS, S. N. The storing and season-
ing of timber used by a railway company.
(Great Western Railway (London) Lecture
& Debating Society, meeting on 3rd
November 1932. Proceedings, no. 265). pp.
16, with discussion, 16 illus & diagrams.
Author, 'Timber Storekeeper, Swindon'.

10828 LONDON & NORTH EASTERN RLY. Let's
send a message by the single-needle (let's
take a message by the single-needle). *London: L.N.E.R.*, 1943. sm. 8°. pp. 28, with 2
cover illus & 5 line illus in text. Title from
front & back covers.
The use of the Morse Code in railway operations: a booklet issued for use at LNER training
centres.

10829 AITKEN, J. The Railwayman's Handbook.
1934 3rd ed. *Glasgow: J. Aitken*, [1934]. pp.
128.
Information on all aspects of railway working.
—— 7th edn, [1936]. pp. 153, xxiv, with
diagrams & tables.
—— 13th edn, [1947]. pp. 176.

10830 LONDON, MIDLAND & SCOTTISH RLY.
Instructions to district goods & passenger
managers, goods agents, station masters,
passenger and parcels agents, and others
concerned, in England, Wales and Scotland, relative to procedure in dealing with
claims. rev. edn. *London: L.M.S. Rly*,
1938. (Circular C 200). pp. 64.

10831 LONDON & NORTH EASTERN RLY. Sending messages by teleprinter. [*London:
L.N.E.R.*, 1947]. pp. 32, with 5 illus, 6
diagrams, 3 tables of contracted signals and
codes.
An introductory guide for LNER teleprinter
trainees.

10832 BROWNE, C. A. Railway telecommunications. (Proceedings of the British Railways
(W.R.) London Lecture & Debating Society, 1949–50, no. 369). pp. 24, with discussion and 13 illus & diagrams. Errata slip.
Author, 'Head of Telecommunications, W.R.'.

10833 WEBB, H. R. Modern methods of
storekeeping. Proceedings of the British
Railways (W.R.) London Lecture & Debating Society, 1951–52, no. 389. pp. 17, with
discussion & 10 illus.
Author, 'Stores Supt, Western Region'.

10834 FLAXMAN, A. E. Mechanisation in the
Commercial Department. (Proceedings of
the British Railways (W.R.) London Lecture & Debating Society, 1956–57, no. 438).
pp. 20, with discussion & 13 illus.
Author, 'Assistant to Chief Commercial Manager (Terminals & Charges), Western Region of
BR'.

10835 SINGH, J. Statistical aids to railway operation. *London: Asia Publishing House*, 1965.
pp. 195, with tables, maps and mathematical workings.
A revised edition of the Indian Ministry of
Information's Technical Paper, no. 330 (same
title).
Statistical mathematics based on Indian railway
working, but applicable to railway operation in
any country.

10836 NICHOLSON, G. L. Decimal money. (Proceedings of the British Railways (W.R.)
London Lecture & Debating Society, 1968–
69, no. 500). pp. 12, with discussion.
Particular problems which may arise in applying
decimalisation to railway working.

G 1   OPERATION OF RAILWAY SERVICES

Train control—Station and goods depot management—Closures of services
and abandonment of lines (generally)

10837–69

For passenger station management see also **G 3**

For curtailment of passenger train services see also **G 3**

For social aspects of rail closures, **K 1**

10837 ALDINGTON, C. Light railways or motor
cars as feeders to main lines. Great Western
Railway (London) Lecture & Debating
Society, meeting on Friday November 18th,
1904 (no. 4). pp. 7.

10838 GRIFFITHS, H. R. A day's work at a
roadside station. Great Western Railway
(London) Lecture & Debating Society,
meeting on Friday November 4th, 1904 (no.
3). pp. 10.
The round of duties at a hypothetical country

station with nine or ten staff, including two
signalmen.

10839 HADLEY, E. S. The train control system:
what are its advantages? Great Western
Railway (London) Lecture & Debating
Society, meeting on February 23rd, 1911
[no. 79]. pp. 12, with discussion.

10840 LOCOMOTIVE office work: a brochure on
the clerical routine of the Locomotive,
Carriage & Wagon Departments, by 'A

Loco Clerk'. *London: Locomotive Publishing Co.*, 1911. pp. 60.

10841 STANIER, W. A. The arrangement of engine power for train working. Great Western Railway (London) Lecture & Debating Society, meeting on March 7th, 1912 [no. 90]. pp. 16, with discussion & 12 diagrams (3 folded).
GWR practice. W. A. Stanier was at this time Assistant to the Locomotive Works Manager, succeeding him in 1920.

10842 WARREN, F. C. The load gauge, and some exceptional loads. Great Western Railway (London) Lecture & Debating Society, meeting on February 27th 1913 [no. 99]. pp. 15, with 14 diagrams & illus.

10843 ROBERTS, T. The control of engine power. Great Western Railway (London) Lecture & Debating Society, meeting on March 5th, 1914 [no. 111]. pp. 83–95, with discussion.
The economical use of manpower, locomotives and train working.

10844 SEDDON, G. The advantages of a train-control system embracing all stations. Great Western Railway (London) Lecture & Debating Society, meeting on December 9th, 1920 [no. 128]. pp. 18, with discussion & 15 illus.
The system in use on the Lancashire & Yorkshire Rly.

10845 A SHORT Course of Instruction in Railway Signalmen's Duties: double lines of railway. [*London?*]: *printed by Press Printers*, [early 1920s]. pp. 29, with 18 illus & 7 diagrams.
Based on the Railway Clearing House standard regulations for train signalling. The LU(THC) copy is bound with four similar works and on the upper cover is engraved a hand-tooled supplied title: 'Emergency Instructions in Railwaymen's Duties'. The other four works are:
Railway shunting. pp. 12, with 12 illus & 2 diagrams.
· Passenger guards' duties. pp. 7, with 6 illus.
Goods guards' duties. pp. 8, with 9 illus.
The duties of railway enginemen and firemen. pp. 8, with 3 illus.
There is no general title-page to this collection of five pamphlets but at the foot of the Preface to the first pamphlet is a monogram composed of the letters 'SI' in a broken circle.

10846 DAVIES, A. Some important aspects of railway traffic operation. Great Western Railway (London) Lecture & Debating Society, meeting on November 6th, 1924 (no. 174). pp. 20, with discussion.
Author, 'L.M. & S. Rly, Derby'.

10847 WHAT statistics and/or other data should a station master or goods agent have at his disposal, and why? Great Western Railway (London) Lecture & Debating Society, meeting on 20th January, 1927 (no. 202). pp. 17, with discussion.
Four short papers by H. E. Banks, B. H. Bristow, H. S. Fish and V. G. A. Pottow.

10848 BARRINGTON-WARD, V. M. Modern train operating requirements and organisations: a paper read at a meeting of the London & North Eastern Railway (London) Lecture & Debating Society, 14th November, 1928. pp. 10.
Author, 'Supt, Western Section, L & N E Rly'.

10849 POTTER, F. R. Features of railway operation. Great Western Railway (London) Lecture & Debating Society, meeting on the 2nd January 1930 (no. 237). pp. 28, with discussion, 14 illus, 4 tables, a diagram & a map.
Author, 'Operating Assistant to Supt of the Line'.

10850 MATTHEWS, G. Recent developments in railway operation. Great Western Railway (London) Lecture & Debating Society, meeting on 12th January, 1933, no. 269. pp. 18, with discussion & 11 illus.
Author, 'Assistant to Superintendent of the Line'.

10851 HAWKESWOOD, D. H. and DEAN, F. G. The working of special traffics. Great Western Railway (London) Lecture & Debating Society, meeting on 2nd December, 1937, no. 316. pp. 22, with 12 illus.

10852 RAILWAY CORRESPONDENCE & TRAVEL SOCIETY. The possibilities of regular interval train services on the British railways. [*London*]: *the Society*, 1944. (Railway Observer Supplement, no. 1 of 1944). pp. 12, with map & 10 timetables (conjectural).
A report by a committee of RCTS members.

10853 KERRY, H. G. The working of a locomotive shed. (Proceedings of the Great Western Railway (London) Lecture & Debating Society, 1946–47, no. 338). pp. 20, with discussion, an illus & a diagram.

10854 PELLOW, W. N. The work of the Motive Power Department. (Proceedings of the British Railways (W.R.) London Lecture & Debating Society, session 1951–52, no. 390). pp. 23, with discussion, 5 illus, 4 charts & a plan.
Author, 'Motive Power Supt, W.R.'.

10855 IBBOTSON, L. W. Some principles and practices of railway operation. (Proceedings of the British Railways (W.R.) London Lecture & Debating Society, 1952–53, no. 400). pp. 15, with discussion & 3 charts.
Author, 'Assistant to Operating Supt, W.R.'.

10856 PENNEY, G. E. R. Modernisation and its effects on the Operating Department. (Proceedings of the British Railways (W.R.) London Lecture & Debating Society, 1958–59, no. 453). pp. 15, with discussion.
Author, 'Assistant to Operating Officer (Research)'.

10857 BRITISH RAILWAYS. WESTERN REGION. General guide to the four-character train identification system. *Paddington (London): B.R. (WR)*, June 1960. pp. 10.

10858 FLAXMAN, A. E. Traffic problems and progress. (Proceedings of the British Railways (W.R.) London Lecture & Debating Society, 1959–60, no. 461). pp. 14, with discussion, 4 illus, map, & a diagram.
Author, 'Chief Freight Officer, B.T.C.'.

10859 BAILEY, M. R. [British Railways headcodes]. The ABC of British Railways Headcodes: a complete list of all British Railways and London Transport head-lamp, disc and two- and four-character codes. *London: Ian Allan*, [1961]. pp. 72, with illus, tables & diagrams.
—— [2nd edn]. *Ian Allan*, [1962]. pp. 96.
—— [3rd edn]. *Ian Allan*, [1963]. pp. 105.
—— [4th edn]. British Railways headcodes. *Ian Allan*, [1965]. pp. 104.

10860 RAILWAY CORRESPONDENCE & TRAVEL SOCIETY. Sheffield Traffic Survey. *R.C. & T.S.*, [1962]. pp. 61, with 10 tables & 9 detailed folded tables. Title from cover. Reproduced typescript.
A record by 20 observers of individual train movements on the principal lines of the former LMSR in the Sheffield area on Saturday, 11th August 1962.

10861 CLINKER, C. R. Register of Closed Passenger Stations and Goods Depots in England, Scotland and Wales, 1923–1962. *Padstow: C. R. Clinker*, February 1963. pp. viii, 91, plus loose errata sheet. Reproduced typescript. *See note 1.*
Supplement to Register . . . , 1923–1962. No. 1. *Padstow*, July, 1963. pp. ii, 11.
Supplement to Register . . . , 1923–1962. No. 2. *Padstow*, January, 1964. pp. i, 16.
—— Register . . . Vol. 2 (1900–1964). 2nd edn, *Padstow*, August, 1964. pp. viii, 131.
Supplement to Register . . . Vol. 2 (1900–1964). —— 2nd edn., No. 1. *Padstow*, January 1965. pp. 30. Title on cover.
Supplement to Register . . . Vol. 2 (1900–1964). —— 2nd edn., No. 2. *Padstow*, July 1965. pp. 21. Title on cover.
Supplement to Register . . . Vol. 2 (1900–1964). —— 2nd edn., No. 3. *Padstow*, January 1966. pp. 14. Title on cover.
—— Register . . . Vol. 1 (1830–1899). 1st edn., *Padstow*, June 1966. pp. [i], viii, 42.
Supplement to Register . . . Vol. 1 (1830–1899). 1st edn., and Vol. 2 (1900–1964). 2nd edn., No. 4. *Padstow*, July 1966. pp. 14. Title on cover.
Cumulative Supplement to Register . . . Vol. 1 (1830–1899). 1st edn., and Vol. 2 (1900–1964). 2nd edn., No. 5. *Padstow*, August, 1967. pp. 72. Title on cover. Printed.
Supplement to Register . . . Vol. 1 (1830–1899). 1st edn., and Vol. 2 (1900–1964). 2nd edn., No. 6. *Padstow*, July 1968. pp. 15. Title on cover.
Supplement to Register . . . Vol. 1. (1830–1899). 1st edn., and Vol. 2 (1900–1964). 2nd edn., No. 7. *Padstow*, July, 1969. pp. 10. Title on cover.
Supplement to Register . . . Vol. 1 (1830–1899). 1st edn., and Vol. 2 (1900–1964). 2nd edn., No. 8. *Padstow*, July, 1970. pp. 8. Title on cover.

CLINKER, C. R. and FIRTH, J. M. Clinker's Register . . . , (1830–1970). New edn. *Padstow*, August, 1971. pp. xii, 189. Dates on cover only.
Supplement to Clinker's Register . . . , 1830–1970. No. 1 by C. R. Clinker and J. M. Firth. *Padstow*, February 1972. pp. [i], 14. Title on cover.
Supplement to Clinker's Register . . . , 1830–1970. No. 2 by C. R. Clinker and J. M. Firth. *Padstow*, February, 1973. pp. [i], 8. Title on cover.
Supplement to Clinker's Register . . . , 1830–1970. No. 3. *Padstow*, February, 1975. pp. i, 8. Title on cover. *See note 2.*
Supplement to Clinker's Register . . . , 1830–1970. No. 4. *Padstow*, March, 1977. pp. 8. Title on cover. *See note 2.*

CLINKER, C. R. Clinker's Register . . . , 1830–1977. New edn. *Bristol: Avon Anglia*, October, 1978. pp. x, 181. Over 27,000 entries with (pp. 154–181) detailed notes. Printed.
Supplement to Clinker's Register . . . , 1830–1977. No. 1. *Bristol: Avon Anglia*, August, 1979. pp. 8. Reproduced typescript. Title on cover. *See note 2.*
Supplement to Clinker's Register . . . , 1830–1977. No. 2. *Weston-super-Mare: Avon Anglia*, November, 1981. pp. 10. Title on cover. *See note 2.*
Notes:
1. All issues have the words "Register of closed passenger stations and goods depots in England, Scotland and Wales" on title page. Format is quarto to 1970, A4 from 1971. Months of publication are included above, as there were several issues in some years. The Cumulative Supplement of 1967 and the New Edition of 1978 are printed. The other issues are in reproduced typescript with printed covers.
2. Without author(s), but the name of C. R. Clinker appears under Copyright notice. All issues of the Register and its Supplements up to and including the Supplement of 1977 are published by him. Thereafter the publisher is Avon-Anglia of Bristol (now of Weston-super-Mare). (Entry compiled by W. J. Skillern)

10862 HOYLE, H. Rolling stock management. (Proceedings of the British Railways (W.R.) London Lecture & Debating Society, 1964–65, no. 488). pp. 14, with discussion.
Author, 'Rolling Stock Manager, B.R.'.

10863 SINGH, J. Statistical aids to railway operation. *London: Asia Publishing House*, 1965. pp. 195, with tables, maps and mathematical workings.
A revised edition of the Indian Ministry of Information's Technical Paper no 330 (same title).
Statistical mathematics based on Indian railway working but applicable to railway operation in any country.

10864 NOCK, O. S. Single line railways: a handbook of management, engineering and operation, prepared by a panel of experts under the editorship of O. S. Nock . . . *Newton Abbot: David & Charles*, 1966. pp. 358, with 56 illus on 32 plates.

A text book grounded upon British practice and experience, produced by the United Kingdom Railway Advisory Service for the Economic Commission for Asia and the Far East.

10865 HAMMOND, R. Modern methods of railway operation. *London: F. Muller*, 1968. pp. x, 262, with 27 illus on 12 plates & 30 diagrams in text.

10866 BURROWS, R. Towards automated railways. British Rail Western (London) Lecture & Debating Society (Proceedings, 1969–70, no. 506). pp. 13, with 8 illus.
Author, Assistant Outdoor Machinery Engineer (Electrical), BR (WR).

10867 BALSILLIE, A. D. That was my line. *Ilfra-combe: Stockwell*, 1976. pp. 34, with illus.
The work of a railway commercial representative, Strathclyde area, 1920–1965. Includes instances of practical problems associated with excursion trains and exceptional loads *en route*.

10868 KING, M. A. An Album of Pre-Grouping Signal Boxes. *Sheffield: Turntable Publications*, 1976. pp. 44. Preface & 76 illus with descrs.

10869 CLINKER, C. R. Some curiosities of railways and railway working. (Great Western Railway (Bristol) Lecture & Debating Society, meeting on 18th December 1928, no. 96). *Bristol: Avon-Anglia*, [1977]. (Specialist Monographs & Reprints series). pp. 12.
A facsimile reprint.

G 2   FREIGHT TRAFFIC
Goods station management—Marshalling—Cartage
10870–10909

For cartage see also **G 4**

10870 BOWLES, H. L. Some considerations in the economical working of goods traffic. Great Western Railway (London) Lecture & Debating Society, meeting on Thursday November 30th 1905 (no. 5) [no. 19]. pp. 8.

10871 VELTOM, O. The working of parcels traffic. Great Western Railway (London) Debating Society, meeting on Friday March 3rd, 1905 (no. 12). pp. 6.
At Paddington, GWR.

10872 MARSHALL, W. Traffic statistics and freight train working. Great Western Railway (London) Lecture & Debating Society, meeting on Thursday, December 6th, 1906 [no. 31]. pp. 12, with 4 tables.
Author, 'N.E. Rly, Hull'.

10873 ROBERTS, T. Goods train working. Great Western Railway (London) Lecture & Debating Society, meeting on February 4th, 1907 [no. 36]. pp. 24, with 13 illus & diagrams.

10874 WEST, F. W. The theory and operation of a tranship depot, with special reference to Crewe station. Great Western Railway (London) Lecture & Debating Society, meeting on November 21st, 1907 [no. 43]. pp. 11, with discussion.
Author, 'L.N.W.R. Agent at Crewe'.

10875 HADLEY, E. S. The theory and practice of marshalling and shunting. Great Western Railway (London) Lecture & Debating Society, meeting on January 30th, 1908 [no. 47]. pp. 15, with 15 diagrams.

10876 SAUNDERS, J. J. A consideration of a definite system of prepayment of carriage charges on goods traffic, with alternatives. Great Western Railway (London) Lecture & Debating Society, meeting on January 14th, 1909 [no. 55]. pp. 6, with discussion.

10877 WILSON, W. F. Goods under mark. Great Western Railway (London) Lecture & Debating Society, meeting on March 11th, 1911 [no. 80]. pp. 5, with discussion.

10878 FORD, E. The management of a first class goods station. Great Western Railway (London) Lecture & Debating Society, meeting on March 27th, 1913 [no. 101]. pp. 22, with discussion.
A detailed account based on experience at Cardiff, presented in the form of a manual for goods agents.

10879 THURGOOD, W. The use of freight rolling stock. Great Western Railway (London) Lecture & Debating Society, meeting on January 8th, 1914 (no. 107). pp. 37–49, with discussion & 2 la. folded charts.
Based on North Eastern Railway practice.
—— [rev. edn]. GWR (London) Lecture & Debating Society, February 12th, 1920 [no. 120]. pp. 78–93, with 14 specimen forms & dimensioned drawings but without the 2 la. folded charts of the 1914 edn, and with no discussion recorded.
This extended and updated edition has additional matter on the systems of monitoring individual wagon movements recently introduced on the North Eastern Railway.

10880 BULKELEY, G. Labour-aiding appliances. Great Western Railway (London) Lecture & Debating Society, meeting on February 26th, 1920 [no. 121]. pp. 94–108, with 18 illus.
Mechanical lifting and transferring in railway work.

10881 MORRIS, A. A. Making the most of existing traffic facilities by special attention to working details. Great Western Railway (London) Lecture & Debating Society, meeting on November 11th, 1920 [no. 126]. pp. 16, with discussion & 15 diagrams & illus.

10882 O'DONOGHUE, D. The future of freight train operating. Great Western Railway (London) Lecture & Debating Society, meeting on February 24th, 1921 [no. 134]. pp. 13, with discussion & 13 illus & diagrams.

10883 LAMB, D. R. Economy in goods handling and traffic operation. Great Western Railway (London) Lecture & Debating Society, meeting on December 14th, 1922 (no. 154). pp. 18, with discussion, & 8 diagrams & illus.

10884 JENKINS, G. W. The organisation of a goods station. Great Western Railway (London) Lecture & Debating Society, meeting on 3rd December 1925 (no. 187). pp. 19, with discussion.
Based on experience gained at GWR goods stations in Birmingham and Cardiff.

10885 PAYNE, H. W. Wagons and their ways. Great Western Railway (London) Lecture & Debating Society, meeting on 16th December 1926 (no. 200). pp. 40, with discussion & 18 illus & diagrams.
Author, 'Chief Goods Manager's Office, Paddington'.

10886 LAMPITT, F. W. Getting and holding traffic. Great Western Railway (London) Lecture & Debating Society, meeting on 29th November, 1934, no. 287. pp. 18, with discussion & 1 illus.
Author, 'Commercial Assistant to the Chief Goods Manager'.

10887 JAMES, S. H. Three hundred years of transport: the story of Pickfords. (Proceedings of the Great Western Railway (London) Lecture & Debating Society, 1934–35, no. 292). pp. 15, with discussion & 13 illus.
Author, 'of Messrs. Pickfords, Ltd'.

10888 BLEE, D. Personnel and Goods Department problems. Great Western Railway (London) Lecture & Debating Society, meeting on 4th March 1937, no. 311. pp. 17, with discussion.

10889 BRITISH COUNCIL. They carry the goods. London: British Council, [1945]. (The British People: How they Live and Work series, 5). pp. 32, with 38 illus.
Illustrations, with running commentary, on the wartime transport of freight by rail, road and canal.

10890 HOLLINGSWORTH, T. H. Railway wagons: their supply and demand. (Proceedings of the Great Western Railway (London) Lecture & Debating Society, 1946–47, no. 339). pp. 15, with discussion.

10891 CORNISH, G. Zonal collection and delivery: its aims and achievements. (Proceedings of the Great Western Railway (London) Lecture & Debating Society, 1947–8, no. 346). pp. 20, with discussion & 7 diagrams & illus.
Author, 'Principal Assistant to the Chief Goods Manager'.

10892 BOLTON, H. The work of a District Goods Manager. (Proceedings of the British Railways (W.R.) London Lecture & Debating Society, 1948/49, no. 253). pp. 15, with discussion.
His work at Bristol (GWR).

10893 CLIFFORD, A. I. Freight marshalling yard operations. (Proceedings of the British Railways (W.R.) London Lecture & Debating Society, 1948–49, no. 354). pp. 15, with discussion.
Author, 'Office of the Operating Supt, W.R.'.

10894 GRUNDY, F. The modernisation of freight station working. (Proceedings of the British Railways (W.R.) London Lecture & Debating Society, 1950–51, no. 381). pp. 15, with discussion & 10 illus.

10895 BRITISH RAILWAYS. Cartage Hand Book, for the use of supervisors, goods and parcels motor drivers, road motor attendants and others employed on cartage operations. London: B.R., [1951]. sm. 8°. pp. 72.

10896 WILSON, H. V. Some aspects of freight and terminal working. Proceedings of the British Railways (W.R.) London Lecture & Debating Society, 1952–53, no. 396. pp. 18, with discussion & 5 illus.
Author, 'Head of Working Dept, Commercial Supt's Office, W.R.'.

10897 BRITISH RAILWAYS. Cross-London Rail Freight Working Party: final report. London: B.R., July 1953. pp. 140, with folded diagrams, gradient profiles & maps. LU(THC)

10898 TURNER, A. H. J. Freight rolling stock arrangements on British Railways. Proceedings of the British Railways (W.R.) London Lecture & Debating Society, 1953–54, no. 413. pp. 25, with discussion, 6 illus, 2 tables, a diagram & a specimen form.
Author, 'Assistant to Chief of Operating Services B.T.C.'.

10899 COLLECTION AND DELIVERY EXHIBITION [Marylebone (London), 1954]. Collection and delivery, past and present. London: International Railway Congress, 1954. pp. 29, with 11 illus.
A concise history of cartage, with descriptions of exhibits, some as separate leaflets in end pocket.

10900 PICKFORD, A. C. B. Fifty years of railway commercial development. (Proceedings of the British Railways (W.R.) London Lecture & Debating Society, 1954–55, no. 420). pp. 19, with discussion & 10 illus.
Author, 'Chief Commercial Manager, W.R.'.

10901 BRITISH RAILWAYS. LONDON MIDLAND REGION. Principal express freight train services. [London]: B.R. (LMR), [1956]. pp. 12, with folded map at end.

10902 HONDELINK, E. R. Railway transport of coal. Northwood: Great Central Railway Association, [1963]. pp. 2. Reproduced typescript.
Proposals for a more economic process of handling coal and other whole-load railway traffic without recourse to excessive reliance upon concentration depots and extensive and costly distribution by road.

10903 BRITISH RAILWAYS. A study of the relative true costs of rail and road freight transport over trunk routes. London: B.R., [1964]. pp. 41, with tables & diagrams. Text dated 'June 1964'.
A quest for information to formulate a basis for the implementation of the Beeching Report (1963) in respect of freight transport planning.

10904 BRITISH RAILWAYS. LONDON MIDLAND REGION. Freight Handbook: facilities and principal express freight train services. London: B.R. (LMR), 1964. pp. 60, with 35 illus.

10905 MINISTRY OF TRANSPORT. The transport of freight. London: H.M.S.O., 1967. (Cmnd 3470). pp. iii, 28.
Includes railways.

10906 SANDERSON, H. C. The future of railway freight traffic. Proceedings of the British Railways (W.R.) London Lecture & Debating Society, 1967–68, no. 498. pp. 15, with 7 diagrams.
Author, 'Divisional Manager, Bristol'.

10907 BRITISH RAILWAYS. WESTERN REGION. Margam marshalling yard, Port Talbot, South Wales. London: BR(WR), [196–?]. pp. 24, with 10 illus & folded plan.

10908 BRITISH RAILWAYS. Guide to Staff on Handling of Animals. London: B.R., 1973. sm. 8°. pp. 32, with line illus by 'Fougasse'.
On cover: 'Customers can complain, cattle can't. Please treat your animal passengers as kindly as you can.'

10909 WOODLEY, G. and WOOD, R. Shunter duties, 1977–78 edition. Inter-City Railway Society, [1977]. pp. [36], with 7 illus. Title on cover.
A five-column table of shunting activity of locomotives, including their stabling points.

G 3   PASSENGER TRAIN SERVICES

Special trains—Excursions—Pullman trains—Royal trains—Speed—High Speed Trains—Advanced Passenger Train—Curtailment of passenger train services—Passenger station management

10910–48

For social aspects of rail closures see **K 1**

Reference sources 10910–14

10910 BRANCH LINE SOCIETY. List of Passenger Train Services over Unusual Lines. Glasgow: the Society. Published annually. Reproduced typescript.
—— 11th edn. May 1971–May 1972, by R. Hamilton. 1971. pp. 14.
—— 12th edn, 1972–3, by R. Hamilton. 1972. pp. 13.
—— 13th edn, 1973–4, by R. Hamilton. 1973. pp. 12.
—— 14th edn, 1974–5, by R. Hamilton. 1974. pp. 15.
—— 15th edn, 1975–6, by R. Hamilton. 1975. pp. 20.
—— 16th edn, 1976–7, by R. Hamilton. 1976. pp. 21.
—— 17th edn, 1977–8, by R. Hamilton. 1977. pp. 21.
—— 18th edn, 1978–9, by R. Hamilton. 1978. pp. 22.

—— 19th edn, 1979–80, by R. Hamilton. 1979. pp. 22.
—— 20th edn, 1980–1, by R. Hamilton. 1980. pp. 24.
Supplementary notes are published in the Group's Branch Line News-Sheet. Supplements to the News-Sheet consisting of additional information and corrections are published separately as single sheets.

10911 GREVILLE, M. D. and SPENCE, J. Closed passenger lines of Great Britain, 1827–1947. rev. & enl. edn. Caterham: Railway & Canal Historical Society, 1974. sm. obl. format. pp. 64, with 8 maps.
First published in two parts: England & Wales (1955) and Scotland (1963). In this combined edition the coverage is extended from 3 September 1939 to 31 December 1947. 600 (approx.) sections of line are accounted for, with over 350 notes.

10912 LOMAX, E. Bradshaw the timetable man, *in* Antiquarian Book Monthly Review, vol. 2, nos 9 & 10 (issues 19 & 20). pt. 1, September 1975, pp. 2–10; pt. 2, October 1975, pp. 13–16, with portrait & 7 facsimile pages of timetables.
A bibliographical statement, with historical commentary, on all George Bradshaw's publications.

10913 HILL, N. J. and McDOUGALL, A. O. A Guide to Closed Railway Lines in Britain, 1948–75. *Branch Line Society*, 1977. tall 8°. pp. 115, xii. Reproduced typescript in printed cover.
—— Amendment List, no. 1 (for 1976 closures). 1977. bound with the main work (pp. 1–xii at end).
—— Amendment List, no. 2 (for 1977–78 closures).

10914 RAYNER, B. W. and CHAPTER, J. F. Southern Region unusual train services. [1st edn]. *Purley: Southern Electric Group*, June 1979. pp. 24, incl. covers.
Details of train workings 'difficult or impossible to identify from the public timetables'; variations in multiple-unit rolling stock; locomotive-hauled trains.
—— 2nd edn. Southern Region unusual train services, 1979. *Southern Electric Group*, October 1979. pp. 24, incl. covers.
—— 3rd edn. Southern Region unusual train services, 1980–81. *Southern Electric Group*, 1980. pp. 24, incl. covers.

10915 FOX, W. Station accounts. Great Western Railway (London) Lecture & Debating Society, Friday October 21st, 1904 [no. 2]. pp. 8.
Author, 'Audit Office, Paddington Station, GWR'.

10916 ENSER, J. W. The public and the luggage question. Great Western Railway (London) Lecture & Debating Society, meeting on November 30th, 1911 [no. 84]. pp. 13, with discussion.

10917 LEIGH, D. A princely path to Paris by the Golden Arrow . . . , illustrated by Christopher Clark. [*London: Sleeping Car Co.*, 1929?]. pp. 44, with 17 illus.
A travel brochure with noteworthy illustrations.

10918 ENSER, J. W. The management of an important passenger station. Great Western Railway (London) Lecture & Debating Society, meeting on 29th January, 1931 (no. 249). pp. 12, with discussion.
General observations based upon experience at Birmingham (Snow Hill) station, GWR.

10919 ALLEN, C. J. High speed by rail, *in* The Book of Speed (*Batsford*, 1934), pp. 115–24, with 11 illus.

10920 PEACOCK, H. J. The evolution of railway passenger train transport. Great Western Railway (London) Lecture & Debating Society, meeting on 10th January 1935 (no. 289). pp. 16, with discussion & 2 illus.
Author, 'Divisional Supt, Worcester'.

10921 RAILWAY CORRESPONDENCE & TRAVEL SOCIETY. The possibilities of regular interval train services on the British railways. *R.C. & T.S.*, 1944. (Railway Observer Supplement, no. 1 of 1944). pp. 12, with map & 10 timetables (conjectural).

10922 EDWARDS, L. The compilation of the passenger timetable. (Proceedings of the Great Western Railway (London) Lecture & Debating Society, 1947–8, no. 350). pp. 18, with discussion & 3 diagrams.
Author, 'Operating Assistant to the Supt. of the Line, W.R.'.

10923 POWELL, C. W. The provision and working of coaching stock. (Proceedings of the British Railways (W.R.) London Lecture & Debating Society, 1948–49, no. 358). pp. 14, with discussion.
Author, 'Divisional Supt, London'.

10924 GEDEN, W. T. The work of a large passenger station. (Proceedings of the British Railways (W.R.) London Lecture & Debating Society, 1949–50, no. 373). pp. 12, with discussion.
Author, Station Master, Paddington.

10925 MILLER, H. T. G. The development of passenger and parcels traffic. (Proceedings of the British Railways (W.R.) London Lecture & Debating Society, 1950–51, no. 377). pp. 15, with discussion & 15 diagrams.

10926 HILL, R. J. The working of special traffic by passenger train. (Proceedings of the British Railways (W.R.) London Lecture & Debating Society, 1951–52, no. 388). pp. 16, with discussion.
Author, 'Office of the Operating Supt, W.R.'.

10927 BRITISH RAILWAYS. Conditions upon which tickets, including season tickets, are issued: regulations and conditions applicable to passengers' luggage. *London: Railway Executive*, 1 May 1952. pp. 23.
—— another edn. Extracts from the Book of Regulations containing conditions of carriage of passengers and their luggage . . . *London: B.R.*, 1st July 1958. pp. 29.
—— another edn. Conditions of carriage of passengers and their luggage applicable from 1 December 1968. 1968. pp. 20.
—— another edn. August 1971. pp. 20.
—— another edn. December 1975. pp. 20.

10928 STÖCKL, F. Die zwölf besten Züge Europas. *Salzburg: Verlage des Verfassers*, 1956. pp. 271 & folded plate at end.
ch. 2 (pp. 21–31), The Elizabethan, London to Edinburgh, with 4 illus.
ch. 4 (pp. 45–66), Flèche d'Or: Golden Arrow,

Paris to London, with 8 illus & 6 dimensioned drawings.

ch. 7 (pp. 103–13), Night Ferry, Paris to London.

In the final chapter, 'Eine Reise in die Vergangenheit' the following British trains are selected: Queen of Scots Pullman, Royal Scot, Bristolian, Flying Scotsman, Berlin–London Express, Silver Jubilee, Coronation, and Coronation Scot.

10929 RESEARCH PROJECTS LTD. London–Norwich interval service project: final report, conclusions and recommendations, for Eastern Region headquarters, British Railways (with reports 1–8 and associated correspondence & papers, 1963–65). *London*, August 1963. 9 vols & a folder containing correspondence & papers.

The information gained from this research led eventually to a change of policy by BR with regard to the pricing of passenger fares, the system whereby fare scales were governed by mileage being abandoned in favour of one which took account of quality, competition and demand.

10930 SCOTTISH RAILFANS. Scottish steam passenger services. *Edinburgh: Scottish Railfans*, [1965]. obl. 8°. pp. 22. Reproduced typescript in printed covers.

Lists the steam-hauled trains currently available.

10931 BRITISH RAILWAYS. Ticket Examiners' Handbook. *London: B.R.*, September 1966. (B.R. 25952). pp. 109, with (pp. 89–104) illustrations of passes.

Issued to staff. Not published.

10932 BRITTON, C. P. Express passenger train headcodes. *Prestwich (Manchester): C. P. Britton.*

1970, 'effective from 4 May 1970'. [1970]. pp. 29. 1971, 'effective from 3 May 1971'. [1971]. pp. 22.

10933 GRIFFITHS, A. E. T. Traffic planning for Inter-City rail. *Westminster: Institution of Civil Engineers, Transportation Engineering Group*, 1970. pp. 5. Reproduced typescript. Not published.

Introductory address to an informal discussion, 10 December, 1970.

10934 NOCK, O. S. Rail, steam and speed. *London: Allen & Unwin*, 1970. pp. 163, with 62 illus on 32 plates.

Speed in British railway history.

10935 NOCK, O. S. Speed records on Britain's railways. *Newton Abbot: David & Charles*, 1971. pp. 207, with 43 illus on 16 plates.
—— *Pan Books*, 1972.

10936 SANDERSON, H. C. Passenger travel in the seventies. Proceedings of the British Rail (Western) London Lecture & Debating Society, no. 510, 11 February 1971. pp. 15, with 6 diagrams & 4 illus.

Author, 'Assistant General Manager, BR (WR)'.

Inter-city services and high-speed trains.

10937 COCKMAN, F. G. Discovering lost railways. *Aylesbury: Shire Publications*, 1973. (Discovering Series, 178). pp. 87, with 31 illus on 16 plates, 24 maps, & a bibliography (14 sources).
—— 2nd edn. *Shire Publications*, 1976. (Discovering Series, 178). pp. 88, with 31 illus, 23 maps, & a bibliography (14 sources).
—— 3rd edn. *Shire Publications*, 1980. (Discovering Series, 178). pp. 88, with 31 illus, 23 maps, but in place of the bibliography, an appendix: 'Preserved railways referred to in the text' (pp. 85–6).

10938 LOWE, S. R. Avoidable costs of local railway passenger services. Thesis, M. Phil., University of Leicester, 1973.

10939 BRITISH RAILWAYS. WESTERN REGION Rail 125. [*London*]: *B.R.(WR)*, 1977. pp. 24, with 22 illus (11 col.), 11 detailed diagrams (1 col.) & 2 maps. Title from cover. Text extends onto covers.

Issued to commemorate the inauguration of the 'Inter-City 125' train service on 4 October 1976, BR's new 'High Speed Train'.
—— new edn. Rail 125 in action. *B.R.(WR), in association with Avon-Anglia Publications*, 1979. obl. format. pp. 24, with 26 illus & 13 dimensioned drawings (incl. col. illus & col. drawing on covers) & a map.

10940 WATTS, P. High Speed Train, Bristol to York. *Gloucester: P. Watts*, [1977]. obl. format. pp. [8], with 6 illus.

An account of the first H.S.T. excursion.

10941 ALLEN, G. F. The fastest trains in the world. *London: Ian Allan*, 1978. la. 8°. pp. 160, with many illus.

ch. 6 (pp. 94–113), 'Britain's Inter-City spurts ahead', with 22 illus & a map.

The first two chapters are historical and include a general account of British railway speed achievements.

10942 BRITISH RAILWAYS. Inter-City 125 Review. *London: B.R.*, [1978]. la. 8°. pp. [16], with 38 illus (30 col.), incl. 7 portraits & a pictorial route chart. Intro by Peter Parker, Chairman, BR.

A brochure issued to publicise the introduction of the Inter-City 125 High Speed Train service onto the East Coast route from London to Aberdeen in 1978.

10943 CROUGHTON, G. R. Ones that Bradshaw missed. *Luton: Transport Ticket Society*, 1979. pp. 17, with facsimiles of 144 tickets. Reproduced typescript.

Presidential address, Leeds, 1979. Exceptional tickets for unadvertised and otherwise unusual railway journeys.

10944 KICHENSIDE, G. The restaurant car: a century of railway catering. *Newton Abbot: David & Charles*, 1979. pp. [44], with 60 illus, including specimen menus.

10945 RAILWAY DEVELOPMENT SOCIETY. Your local trains in the 80s. 2nd edn. *R.D.S.*, Oct. 1979. pp. 39, with 9 illus.
   The need to plan for a continuation of services of cross-country, rural and main-line stopping trains by replacing ageing d.m.u.'s (diesel multiple-unit trains).

10946 HOWARD, K. 1 H 80, compiled and edited by Ken Howard. *Gloucester: Peter Watts*, 1980. pp. 40.
   Lists of every currently available express passenger train. Excluded are electric and diesel multiple units, and mail and newspaper trains with no passenger accommodation.

10947 NOCK, O. S. Two miles a minute: the story behind the conception and operation of

Britain's High Speed and Advanced Passenger Trains. Foreword by Sir Peter Parker. *Cambridge: P. Stephens*, 1980. pp. 184, with 100 illus, 38 graphs and diagrams, 21 logs of runs, 2 maps & a humorous drawing; 3 appendices: 1, Bibliography (9 sources); 2, Production HST technical data; 3, Specification for APT-P.

10948 TILLER, R. BR 125 High Speed Train, by Robert Tiller; edited, with additional material by Michael Oakley; graphics by Bob Morris. *Truro: Bradford Barton; Sutton Coldfield: Diesel & Electric Group*, [1980]. pp. [32], with 22 illus, 3 tables (logs of runs), a dimensioned drawing & a map of 'High Speed' routes.

G 4   RAILWAY ROAD SERVICES (Omnibus services and freight cartage)
10949–53

For cartage see also **G 2**

10949 HEARN, S. G. How should railway companies avail themselves of their newly-acquired road powers? Great Western Railway (London) Lecture & Debating Society, meeting on 21st March 1929 (no. 231). pp. 15, with discussion.
   Author, 'Office of the Supt of the Line', GWR.

10950 HALLIDAY, G. S. The work of the Road Motor Engineer's Department. (Proceedings of the British Railways (W.R.) London Lecture & Debating Society, 1952–53, no. 402). pp. 18, with discussion, 8 illus & 2 charts.

10951 WILSON, G. Measuring productivity: a case study in transport. *Oxford: Pergamon Press*, 1968. (Productivity Progress Series). pp. 16, with 5 tables.
   A system devised for the Road Services Dept of British Railways.

10952 TURNBULL, G. L. Pickfords, 1750–1920: a study in the development of transportation. Thesis, Ph.D., University of Glasgow, 1972.
   The latter part of the work is largely concerned with the involvement of Pickfords in railway cartage.

10953 CUMMINGS, J. M. Railway motor buses and bus services in the British Isles, 1902–1933. *Oxford: Oxford Publishing Co.* la. 8°. 2 vols.
   vol. 1, [East and North East England and Scotland]. 1978. pp. 136, with frontis, 156 illus, 10 maps & 3 appendices (pp. 113–34): A, An adaptation of the Railways (Road Transport) Act, 1928; B, Routes; C, Vehicles.
   vol. 2, [West, South, South West and South East England, Wales]. 1908. pp. vi, 182, with frontis, 263 illus, 13 maps & 3 appendices as for vol. 1 (pp. 155–78).

G 5   RAILWAY WATER SERVICES
Railways in ports, harbours and docks—Shipping services owned and operated by railways—Train ferries—Boat trains—Inland waterway services
10954–75

10954 LAMBERT-GIBSON, G. Harbours and docks, with special reference to Fishguard Harbour works. Great Western Railway (London) Lecture & Debating Society, meeting on November 2nd, 1905 (no. 3) [no. 17]. pp. 7, with 9 illus.

10955 NICHOLLS, R. H. Should British railway companies establish their own Atlantic services? Great Western Railway (London) Lecture & Debating Society, meeting on Friday, March 17th, 1905 (no. 13). pp. 11.

10956 BULKELEY, G. Bulk-handling machinery at British and North American ports. Great Western Railway (London) Lecture & Debating Society, meeting on March 20th, 1924 (no. 171). pp. 28, with discussion & 24 illus.
   Mechanical appliances for rail/ship transfers.

10957 BULKELEY, G. Seaport equipment. Great Western Railway (London) Lecture & Debating Society, meeting on October 23rd,

1924 (no. 173). pp. 21, with discussion, 5 diagrams & a table.
Author, 'Dock Traffic Supt at Swansea, GWR'.
The importance of having modern and efficient railway facilities at docks.

10958 CARPMAEL, R. and MORGAN, H. W. The maintenance of waterways to docks and harbours from the points of view of the docks engineer and dock superintendent. Great Western Railway (London) Lecture & Debating Society, meeting on 19th November 1925 (no. 186). pp. 29, with discussion & 12 illus.
The South Wales docks and harbours of the GWR.

10959 CAMERON, D. E. Hydraulic power production on docks. Great Western Railway (London) Lecture & Debating Society, meeting on 15th December 1927 (no. 212). pp. 16, with discussion & 3 illus.
Author, 'Dock Mechanical Engineer, GWR, Port Talbot'.

10960 MISSENDEN, E. J. Southampton Docks: paper read to the Railway Students Association, 18th July 1936. Southampton: Walton, printer, [1936?] pp. 19.
Author was Docks & Marine Manager, Southern Rly, Southampton, 1933–6, and chairman, BR, 1947–51.

10961 CARPENTER, B. Port management and operations at Cardiff. Great Western Railway (London) Lecture & Debating Society, meeting on 17th March 1938, no. 322. pp. 14, with 9 illus.

10962 EDWARDS, R. H. Maintenance of civil engineering works at South Wales ports. (Great Western Railway (London) Lecture & Debating Society, 1946–7, no. 337). pp. 15, with discussion.

10963 BRITISH TRANSPORT COMMISSION. South Wales ports. Cardiff: Office of the Chief Docks Manager, 1948. pp. xxxviii, 170, with 90 illus.
The railway track layouts of Cardiff, Swansea, Newport, Barry, Port Talbot and Penarth are shown in detail in the Plan section, pp. [63–77].

10964 BEHREND, G. Grand European expresses: the story of Wagons-Lits. London: Allen & Unwin, 1962. pp. 258, with frontis, & 61 illus on 23 plates.
pp. 23–44, the Night Ferry, London (Victoria) to Paris.

10965 STEARN, W. A. and MOODY, B. The Hythe–Southampton Ferry, including Hythe Pier Railway. Southampton: Southern Counties Railway Society, 1962. pp. 16, with 1p. illus. Reproduced typescript.
—— 2nd edn. New Malden: Eltrac Publications, 1970. pp. 16, with 4 illus & a map.

10966 RANSOME-WALLIS, P. Train ferries of Western Europe. London: Ian Allan, 1968.

pp. ix, 289, with frontis, 240 illus, 20 line drawings, 6 maps (1 folded) & a bibliography (23 sources).
ch. 2 (pp. 41–100), Great Britain.

10967 CLEGG, W. P. and STYRING, J. S. British nationalised shipping, 1947–1968. Newton Abbot: David & Charles, 1969. pp. 304, with col. frontis & 175 illus.
Railway-owned and operated shipping services.

10968 McNEILL, D. B. Irish passenger steamship services. Newton Abbot: David & Charles.
Includes ships of railway companies.
vol. 1, North of Ireland. 1969. pp. 232, with 31 illus on 16 plates, 3 maps, bibliography (pp. 180–2), fleet lists (pp. 183–223), General Index and Steamships Index.
vol. 2, South of Ireland. 1971. pp. 240, with 34 illus on 17 plates, 2 maps, bibliography (pp. 176–8), fleet lists (pp. 179–228), General Index and Steamships Index.

10969 PATERSON, A. J. S. The golden years of the Clyde steamers, 1889–1914. Newton Abbot: David & Charles, 1969. pp. 296, with col. frontis, 37 illus on 24 plates, 13 line drawings, 10 appendices, incl. detailed fleet lists; bibliography (30+ sources), a general index and an index of vessels.
Includes much information on railway-owned vessels and services.

10970 BIRD, J. Seaports and seaport terminals. London: Hutchinson University Library, 1971. pp. 240, with 22 maps & diagrams.
Index has 21 page refs to railway approaches to ports.

10971 MacARTHUR, I. C. The Caledonian Steam Packet Company. Glasgow: Clyde River Steamboat Club, 1971. pp. xxiv, 290, with col. frontis, 137 illus on plates, 7 line drawings in text, 2 maps on end papers, lists (pp. 235–74), general index and ships index (pp. 275–90).
Includes railway-owned vessels.

10972 PATERSON, A. J. The Victorian Summer of the Clyde steamers, 1864–1888. Newton Abbot: David & Charles, 1972. pp. 260, with col. frontis, 25 illus on 15 plates, 20 drawings, 10 appendices, incl. detailed fleet lists; a bibliography (31 sources), a general index and an index of vessels.
Includes railway-owned vessels and services.

10973 ADAMS, G. Organization of the British port transport industry. London: National Ports Council, Oct. 1973. pp. 262.
Transport systems within ports, pp. 140–8; Transport systems linked with ports: rail and road, pp. 149–55.

10974 BRODIE, I. Steamers of the Forth. Newton Abbot: David & Charles, 1976. pp. 168, with illus & fleet lists.
ch. 4 (pp. 47–59), The railway ferries, with 4 illus on 2 plates. The North British Rly, the LNER, and BR.

10975 WREN, W. J. Ports of the Eastern Counties: the development of harbours on the coast of the Eastern Counties from Boston in Lincolnshire to Rochford in Essex.

Lavenham: T. Dalton, 1976. pp. 207, with many illus, diagrams & a bibliography (pp. 196–200).
Index has 52 page refs to railways, 51 of which are to individual lines.

G 6   RAILWAY AIR SERVICES
10976–77

Public Relations and Publicity, previously classed at **G 6**, *is now at* **G 9**

10976 WATERS, G. O. Commercial air transport. Great Western Railway (London) Lecture & Debating Society, meeting on 17th October 1935, no. 294. pp. 20, with discussion, 10 illus & a map.
Author, 'Commercial Assistant, Railway Air Services Ltd'.

10977 BALDWIN, N. C. Railway Air Services: British inland air posts. *Railway Philatelic Group*, [1979?]. pp. 7, with 2 illus, map & a chart.
Railway Air Services Ltd, 1934–1947. Mainly philatelic, but has some general information such as the dates of the opening of particular routes.

G 7   RAILWAY ANCILLARY SERVICES
Hotels—Catering (at stations and on trains)—Station shops and kiosks
10978–84

10978 MAXWELL, H. Life and times of the Right Honourable William Henry Smith, M.P. *Edinburgh & London: W. Blackwood*, 1893. 2 vols (pp. xiii, 360; xii, 374).
vol. 1: pp. 48–58, Railway bookstalls; pp. 72–4, Railway advertising; pp. 84–7, Railway novels.

10979 BUTTERWORTH, W. Railway bookstalls. *Manchester: Sherratt & Hughes*, 1901. pp. 4.
Reprinted from the *Manchester Quarterly*, January 1901.

10980 BRITISH TRANSPORT CATERING SERVICES. The hungry traveller. *London: B.T.C.S.*, [1955]. pp. [12], with 12 illus.
A publicity brochure.

10981 PORTMAN-DIXON, E. K. Catering and the railway passenger. (Proceedings of the British Railways (W.R.) London Lecture & Debating Society, 1955–56, no. 427). pp. 15, with discussion & 6 illus.
Author, 'Chief of Restaurant Cars and Refreshment Rooms, B.T. Hotels & Catering Services'.

10982 BRITISH TRANSPORT HOTELS. The chairman requests the pleasure . . . *London: British Transport Hotels*, [ca. 1958]. pp. 36, with 37 illus.
A publicity brochure for four hotels: Gleneagles, Perthshire; Turnberry, Ayrshire; North British, Edinburgh; Caledonian, Edinburgh.

10983 RUSSELL, G. N. Current trends in the development of railway property. (Proceedings of the British Railways (W.R.) London Lecture & Debating Society, 1963–64, no. 485).
Author, 'Chairman, Railway Sites, Ltd'. Non-operational properties (buildings and sites not required for railway purposes).

10984 BRITISH TRANSPORT HOTELS. 1879–1979: food and drink to us: 100 years of refreshment. *London: B.T.H.*, 1979. pp. 16, with 18 col. illus.
A brochure issued to celebrate the centenary of on-train catering.

G 8   RESEARCH (Operational and maintenance problems)—Soil analysis
10985–88

10985 HARVEY, S. C. The case for a research department in railway business. Great Western Railway (London) Lecture & Debating Society, meeting on 20th January 1938, no. 319. pp. 11, with discussion.
Author, 'General Manager's Office'.

10986 ROBINS, P. The work of a railway chemist.

Proceedings of the British Railways (W.R.) London Lecture & Debating Society, 1951–52, no. 386. pp. 16, with discussion, 7 illus, a chart & a table.
Author, 'Assistant Chief Chemist, Swindon'.

10987 BRITISH RAILWAYS. WESTERN REGION. The Soil Mechanics Laboratory. *London:*

B.R. (WR), [195–]. tall 8°. pp. 30, with 17 illus & 2 diagrams.

Investigating soil behaviour aspects of track bed, embankments, cuttings and structures; testing and assessing the suitability of new materials for railway use.

10988 JONES, S. The British Rail research programme. (British Railway Western (London) Lecture & Debating Society, Proceedings, 1970–71, no. 508). pp. 12, with discussion & 6 illus.

Author, Member of BR Board.

G 9   PUBLIC RELATIONS AND PUBLICITY
10989–98

For pictorial advertising (posters) see N

10989 MARSH, H. The railwayman and the public. Great Western Railway (London) Lecture & Debating Society, meeting on 22nd January 1925 (no. 178). pp. 14, with discussion.

10990 RICHARDS, D. Advertising, with special reference to railway publicity. Great Western Railway (London) Lecture & Debating Society, meeting on February 5th, 1925 (no. 179), pp. 20, with discussion & 8 illus.

10991 LONDON & NORTH EASTERN RLY. Billposting on the L.N.E.R. *London: L.N.E.R.*, [1926]. sm. 8°. pp. [12], with 8 illus.

A manual for billposters issued by the Advertising Manager's Office, Kings Cross Station, London, January 1926.   LU(THC)

10992 LOCK, C. S. and PICKFORD, A. C. B. Railway advertising: is it on right lines? Great Western Railway (London) Lecture & Debating Society, meeting on 24th January 1929 (no. 227). pp. 15, with discussion.

10993 ORTON, G. E. Railway publicity. Great Western Railway (London) Lecture & Debating Society, meeting on 18th October, 1934, no. 284. pp. 16, with discussion & 12 illus.

Author, 'Commercial Assistant to the Superintendent of the Line'.

10994 POTTER, B. S. New demands for transport: how they may be created and developed profitably by the Great Western Railway Company. Great Western Railway (London) Lecture & Debating Society,

meeting on 24th January 1935, no. 290. pp. 10, with discussion.

Author, 'Chief Goods Manager's Office'.

10995 LAYTON, F. H. and ROSEVEARE, E. D. Railway salesmanship: how can it be improved?; a discussion . . . Great Western Railway (London) Lecture & Debating Society, meeting on 18th March 1937, no. 312. pp. 11, with discussion.

10996 HARVEY, S. C. Selling transport in the new Railway Age. (Proceedings of the British Railways (W.R.) London Lecture & Debating Society, 1957–58, no. 447). pp. 11, with discussion.

10997 FENTON, E. W. A Portfolio of Railway Notices, 1825–1892; selected and edited by E. W. Fenton. *London: Holland Press*, 1964. Folio. 24 plates preceded by notes (pp. 5–16).

10998 WILSON, R. B. Go Great Western: a history of GWR publicity. *Newton Abbot: David & Charles*, 1970. pp. 198, with col. frontis, 76 illus (36 on plates & 40 in text), notes on sources & a bibliography (pp. 189–92).

A detailed and informative survey of the devices used by the GWR to encourage patronage: posters, travel brochures, the 32 editions of *Holiday Haunts* (1906–1947), W. G. Chapman's *For Boys of all Ages* series, films, souvenir pictorial luggage labels, GWR assorted biscuits and GWR whisky being examples of what the author describes as 'the GWR's skilful use of public sentiment'. A marked feature of the work is the listing in 5 & 6 columns, with notes, of the GWR's sale publications (pp. 178–82) and its 44 jig-saw puzzles, with notes on variants (pp. 183–5).

I

H RAILWAY LIFE AND LABOUR

Work, working conditions and social environment of railway employees, railway navvies and labourers—Pay, welfare, pensions & superannuation—Labour/management relationships—Labour questions and disputes—Trade unions and strikes—Staff training—Safety of employees—Medical services—Biographies and memoirs of railway life and of railway trade union personalities

10999–11136

For railways and politics generally see **K**
For memoirs of railwaymen associated with a particular railway see **L**
or **B 10**, *or with railways in a particular area,* **C 1 – C 7**

Historical   10999–11050
Contemporaneous   11051–11136

Historical

10999 BARNES, P. Railway life in South Essex: a story of fifty years. *Stratford: Stratford Express*, 1894. la. 8°. (Monthly Illustrated Supplements, June 9th and October 27th, 1894). pp. 12, 4.

11000 BRASSEY, T. Papers and addresses. *London: Longmans Green*.
vol. 5, Political and miscellaneous: from 1861 to 1894, arranged and edited by A. H. Loring. 1895. pp. ix, 328.
pp. 119–20, Speech on introducing a deputation of railway servants to the Home Secretary, 22 March 1878; pp. 120–3, Speech in the House of Commons on the second reading of the Employers' Liability for Injuries Bill, 10 April 1878. (Also p. 237).

11001 COLLISON, W. The Apostle of Free Labour: the life story of William Collison . . . , told by himself. *London: Hurst & Blackett*, 1913. pp. xvi, 336.
pp. 139–57, The Taff Vale Railway strike of 1900 and the Amalgamated Society of Railway Servants.
pp. 184–90, The Bristol Tramways strike, 1901, with 2 plates.

11002 BUSSY, J. F. M. From E.C. to P.C.: a biographical sketch of the Rt. Hon. J. H. Thomas, M.P., General Secretary of the National Union of Railwaymen, with a preface by . . . J. H. Thomas. *London: Co-operative Printing Society*, 1917. pp. 147, with portrait. Cover title: From Engine Cleaner to Privy Councillor.

11003 CHANNING, F. A. Memories of Midland politics, 1885–1910. *London: Constable*, 1918. pp. xx, 434, with plates.
Author was Liberal Party Member of Parliament for East Northamptonshire. For his comments on railway labour questions during this period, see the Index, p. 426.

11004 ASKWITH, G. R. Industrial problems and disputes. *London: J. Murray*, 1920. pp. x, 494.
Includes railway strikes.

11005 MILNE-BAILEY, W. Trade union documents, compiled and edited with an Introduction by W. Milne-Bailey. *London: G. Bell*, 1929. pp. xxvii, 552.
Author, 'Secretary of the Research and Economic Department of the Trades Union Congress'.
The texts of a selected 247 documents. In the Index there are ca. 50 page refs under 'Railway . . .', 'Transport . . .', 'Taff Vale Case', 'Osborne Case' and other headings embracing railway trade union developments.

11006 MAXWELL, H. Evening memories. *London: J. Maclehose*, 1932. pp. xiii, 366.
pp. 304–6, The Railway Association. The influence of David Lloyd George, as President of the Board of Trade, on the decision by The Railway Association to establish Conciliation Boards or Committees (1907).

11007 PHILLPOTT, H. R. S. The Rt. Hon. J. H. Thomas: impressions of a remarkable career. *London: Sampson Low, Marston & Co.*, [1932]. pp. vii, 214, with frontis & 13 plates (portraits & caricatures).

11008 FULLER, B. The life story of the Rt. Hon. J. H. Thomas: a statesman of the people. *London: S. Paul*, [1933]. pp. 252, with plates.

11009 RAILWAYS STAFF CONFERENCE. Summary of the Railway National Agreements and subsequent amendments, extensions and interpretations: rates of pay, hours and conditions of service, conciliation grades and other grades under conciliation conditions. *Westminster: R.S.C.*, January 1935. tall 8°. pp. 508. Not published.   LU(THC)

11010 THOMAS, J. H. My story. *London: Hutchinson*. 1937. pp. 312, with frontis & 22 plates (portraits).
J. H. Thomas, a Great Western engine-driver, was general secretary of the National Union of Railwaymen, 1917 to 1931, M.P. for Derby, 1910–1936, was made Privy Councillor in 1917 and held a succession of Cabinet posts untl 1936. 'A good and loyal man' (King George V).

11011 MARCHBANK, J. What trade unionism has done for railwaymen and for other transport workers: a glance at the past. *London: National Union of Railwaymen*, 1938. pp. 32, with 4 illus & 2 facsimiles.

At head of cover title: 'National Union of Railwaymen Silver Jubilee, 1938'.

11012 RAILWAY CLERKS ASSOCIATION. Behind the lines. *London: R.C.A.*, [1938]. pp. [16], with illus.

The R.C.A., its work and its personnel.

11013 RAILWAY CLERKS ASSOCIATION. Between two wars: the inspiring story of twenty-five years' trade union endeavour and achievement for women railway clerks. *Welwyn Garden City: R.C.A.*, November 1941. pp. 20.   LU(THC)

11014 CLARK, L. Alfred Williams: his life and work. *Bristol: W. George's Sons, via Blackwell*, 1945. pp. xi, 206.

Life on the shop floor at Swindon Works, GWR, 1891 (or 1892)–1914, and after.

11015 EVERSHED, A. G. The Southern Railway Servants' Orphanage in association with the Southern Railway Homes for Old People. [*Woking*]: *Board of Management of the S.R.S.O., in association with the S.R.H.O.P.*, [1947?]. pp. 15, with 16 illus.

11016 TYRREL, W. Early history of the Railway Convalescent Homes . . . , and a short account of their growth. *London: Railway Convalescent Homes*, [1950]. pp. 12. Title from cover. Text headed: 'To the members of the General Committee . . .' and dated at end, 'May 1947.'

11017 KNOWLES, K. G. J. C. Strikes: a study in industrial conflict, with special reference to British experience between 1911 and 1947. *Oxford: Blackwell*, 1952. pp. xiv, 330, with 18 graphs, 11 tables and many notes, some lengthy & detailed.

Railway strikes are findable from the Index under 'Strikes in various industries and services: transport: railways'.

11018 WILLIAMS, C. G. The process of negotiation in the railway industry under nationalization.

Thesis, M.A., University of Manchester, 1958–9.

11019 PRIBIĆEVIĆ, B. The Shop Stewards' Movement and Workers' Control, 1910–1922. *Oxford: Blackwell*, 1959. pp. xii, 179.

pp. 4–7, 'Workers' Control and the railwaymen', with 6 notes. A brief account of a subject treated in detail by the author in his D. Phil. thesis in 1957 (Ottley 3991).

11020 PEITCHINIS, S. G. The determination of the wages of railwaymen: a study of British experience, with a comparative study of Canadian, since 1914.

Thesis, Ph.D, University of London (L.S.E.), 1959–60.

11021 SAVILLE, J. Trade unions and free labour: the background to the Taff Vale decision, *in* Essays in Labour History, by Asa Briggs and John Saville. (*Macmillan*, 1960). pp. 317–50, with 116 notes.

—— rev edn. *Macmillan*, 1967. pp. 317–50, with 117 notes.

11022 BRIGGS, A. A study of the work of Seebohm Rowntree, 1871–1954. *London: Longmans*, 1961. (Social Thought & Social Action series). pp. x, 371.

pp. 248–53, Seebohm Rowntree's part in the settlement of the railway strike of September/October, 1919.

11023 MITCHELL, W. R. The 'Long Drag': a story of men under stress during the construction of the Settle–Carlisle line. *Settle: the author*, 1962. pp. 32, with line drawings & route chart.

The harsh conditions imposed by the Midland Rly Co. upon the men building the line; the 'Long Drag' being the steeply-graded section between Settle and Ais Gill.

11024 BLAXLAND, G. J. H. Thomas: a life for unity. *London: F. Muller*, 1964. pp. 303, with frontis & 30 illus on 16 plates.

Politics, trade unionism and the railwaymen seen through the life of 'Jimmy' Thomas, General Secretary of the National Union of Railwaymen, 1917 to 1931.

11025 COLEMAN, T. The railway navvies: a history of the men who made the railways. *London: Hutchinson*, 1965. pp. xvii, [19]–224, with frontis, 28 illus on 16 plates, 7 drawings & a map. 'Sources' (a select evaluative bibliographical essay), pp. 207–12; 'Selected bibliography', pp. 213–15 (43 sources).

—— 1st edn revised. *Penguin Books*, 1968. pp. 256, with plates, etc.

11026 LEA, J. T. The Great Western Railway Enginemen and Firemen's Mutual Assurance, Sick and Superannuation Society, 1865–1965: a centenary history. *Swindon: printed by Swindon Signcraft*, [1965]. pp. 28, with frontis, 2 illus & a list, 'Branches and their committee men' (1865–1965).

11027 RANDELL, A. R. Sixty years a fenman; edited by Enid Porter. *London: Routledge & Kegan Paul*, 1966. pp. ix, 126, with 13 illus on 8 plates.

ch. 13 (pp. 120–6). 'The End of the Line': memoirs of his life and work as a porter–signalman at Magdelen Road and Waldensea, 1918–1966. This chapter was enlarged & republished as *Fenland Railwayman* (1968).

11028 CUNNINGTON, P. and LUCAS, C. Occupational costume in England, from the eleventh century to 1914. *London: A. & C. Black*, 1967.

ch. 8, Transport. (Railways. pp. 215–22 (6 illus); cabbies and cads, bus and tram crews, pp. 222–31).

—— Reprint, with corrections, 1968.

11029   MELLORS, D. Folklore and traditions of the railway industry, with special reference to Doncaster. Thesis, M.A., University of Leeds, 1967.
The inherited popular traditions of the railway community: their social customs, attitudes, beliefs and sayings, based upon interviews in Doncaster.

11030   RANDELL, A. R. Fenland railwayman; edited by Enid Porter, designed and illustrated by Andrew Young. *London: Routledge & Kegan Paul*, 1968. sm. 8°. pp. 94, with 11 line drawings.
An extended version of chapter 13 of his *Sixty Years a Fenman* (1966). The author's life as a porter–signalman on the LNER at Magdelen Road and Waldensea, 1918–1966.

11031   MARTIN, R. Communism and the British trade unions, 1924–1933: a study of the National Minority Movement. *Oxford: Clarendon Press*, 1969. pp. xii, 209, with a bibliography (pp. 192–202).
The Railwaymen's Minority Movement and the Railway Vigilance Movement have 14 page refs in the Index.

11032   HUDSON, K. Working to rule: railway workshop rules; a study of industrial discipline. *Bath: Adams & Dart*, 1970. pp. 115, with 51 notes, many in detail.
A study of the development of the Rule Book since 1933, with many extracts.

11033   KINGSFORD, P. W. Victorian railwaymen: the emergence and growth of railway labour, 1830–1870. *London: Frank Cass*, 1970. pp. xvi, 192, with frontis, 4 plates, 3 maps, 47 tables & a 12-column list, "Railway companies' friendly societies in 1871" (pp. [194–8]), 161 notes & a bibliography (pp. 182–8).

11034   McLEOD, C. All change: railway industrial relations in the sixties . . . , Foreword by Ray Gunter, Minister of Labour, 1964–8. *London: Gower Press*, 1970. (Gower Press Special Study). pp. xviii, 222, with frontis, 7 illus, 4 graphs & 2 maps.

11035   NATIONAL UNION OF RAILWAYMEN. The railway servants: a century of railway trade unionism, 1871 to 1971; the Amalgamated Society of Railway Servants and its successor, The National Union of Railwaymen. *London: N.U.R.*, 1971. la. 8°. pp. 36, with 21 illus (11 col.) & 6 illus (5 col.) on covers.
The illustrations include portraits and group photographs.

11036   GRIGG, A. E. In railway service: the history of Bletchley branch of the National Union of Railwaymen. [*Bletchley: the author?*], 1972. la. 8°. pp. 219, with 85 illus (1 col.).
The workaday scene and its personalities at Bletchley, 1872–1972.

11037   ROBERTSON, G. A history of the Railway Clearing System Superannuation Fund Corporation, [by] G. Robertson, Secretary. *Darlington: the author*, December 1973. pp. [2], 16. Reproduced typescript; no covers.
LU(THC)

11038   MITCHELL, W. R. The Railway shanties: navvy life during the construction of the Settle–Carlisle line. *Settle: Settle & District Civic Society*, 1975. sm. 8°. pp. 16, with 11 illus (incl. cover illus) by W. Brocklebank.
Issued as a souvenir of an exhibition on shanty towns organised by the Settle–Carlisle Railway Centenary Committee of the Settle & District Civic Society, April 1975.

11039   BROOKE, D. Railway navvies in the Pennines, 1841–71. Journal of Transport History, new series vol. 3 (1975–6), pp. 41–53, with 3 tables & 33 notes.

11040   BEDALE, L. Station master: my lifetime's railway service in Yorkshire, by Len Bedale, as told to C. T. Goode. *Sheffield: Turntable Publications*, 1976. pp. 80, with 44 illus on 24 plates, 3 maps & 2 station plans.
Period, 1923–1970.

11041   MITCHELL, W. R. and MUSSETT, N. J. Seven years hard: building the Settle–Carlisle Railway; with visuals by W. Brocklebank. *Clapham (N. Yorks): Dalesman Books*, 1976. sm. 8°. pp. 64, with 13 illus on 8 plates, 2 maps (1 on 5 pp.), & a bibliography (15 sources).
A chronological 'on site' account, with particular emphasis on the problems, hardships and achievements of the 6,000 men involved.

11042   MANNING, R. Rosemary Manning's Book of Railways and Railwaymen, *Harmondsworth: Kestrel Books*, 1977. pp. 143, with many illus. Spine title: Railways and Railwaymen.
The railway environment expressed by railwaymen: a collection of extracts from the letters, memoirs and published writings of railwaymen, passengers and others, from George Stephenson to the present day.

11043   WOODLAND, C. The Taff Vale case: a guide to the ASRS records, compiled by Christine Woodland; edited by Richard Storey. *Coventry: University of Warwick Library*, 1978. (Occasional Publications, 3). pp. 28.

11044   BURTON, C. Behind the lines: the lighter side of railway life: (recollections of a G.W.R. goods agent), edited by Harold Parsons; illustrations by Richard S. Potts. *Birmingham: Barbryn Press*, 1979. pp. 48, with line illus.
Sixteen sketches drawn from the author's recollections of working life in GWR goods depots in the West Midlands (Hockley, Netherton, Blowers Green) and centred upon the environment of hut-based railwaymen. 'The hut was the answer to the problem of keeping the men close to their

work while at the same time enabling them to keep dry or to dry themselves out in wet weather . . . The smell was unmistakable: stale tobacco, bacon, damp clothes, and paraffin . . . Asleep in front of the stove would be one of the station cats . . .' (p. 6).

11045 SALTLEY WORKERS EDUCATIONAL ASSOCIATION. The railwaymen. *Saltley: Saltley WEA*, 1979. (Memories of Saltley, no. 1). pp. 8, with 2 illus, a map & a table.
Social aspects recalled by local residents.

11046 WESTWATER, T. A. The early life of T. A. Westwater: railway signalman, trade unionist and town councillor in County Durham. *Oxford: Ruskin College Library*, 1979. (Ruskin College Library Occasional Publication, 1). pp. 64. Introductory note by D. Horsfield.
T. A. Westwater was a signalman from 1902 to 1953. These memoirs were written in 1940 & 1941.

11047 WOODLAND, C. The Osborne Case papers and other records of the Amalgamated Society of Railway Servants, compiled by Christine Woodland; edited by Richard Storey. *Coventry: University of Warwick Library*, 1979. (Occasional Papers, 4). pp. 48.

11048 BENNETT, J. M. Random reflections of a roving railwayman. *Cupar, (Fife): J. & G. Innes*, [197–?]. pp. 56, with 8 illus on 4 plates, & a map.
Memoirs of a country station-master in Scotland. 1923–1969.

11049 GRIGG, A. E. Town of trains: Bletchley and the Oxbridge line. *Buckingham: Barracuda Books*, 1980. la. 8°. pp. 160, with 120 illus, 5 maps (one double-spread on end papers), 3 timetables & a signalling diagram of 1881. Foreword by Peter Parker, Preface by Sidney Weighell.
A detailed narrative. The author was a railwayman at Bletchley.

11050 McKENNA, F. The railway workers, 1840–1970. *London: Faber*, 1980. pp. 280, with 31 illus on 16 plates, 279 notes & a bibliography (10 sources). Foreword by Jack Simmons; Glossary, pp. 230–41.
A detailed and sensitive account of the working life and conditions of railwaymen from 1840 to the present day, written by a locomotiveman of 20 years' experience.

Contemporaneous

11051 BAILLIE, J. An impartial history of the town and county of Newcastle upon Tyne and its vicinity. *Newcastle: Vint & Anderson*, 1801. pp. 612.
pp. 483–4, list of the number of persons employed and dependent on the coal trade on the rivers Tyne and Wear in the year 1792. Includes waggon-smiths, waggon and waggon-way wrights, engine-men, brake-men, creasers, staithmen, and off-putters.

11052 HAND-BOOK Guide to Railway Situations, including the complete system of railway accounts and returns; to which are added valuable hints on commercial employments generally . . . *London: Cassell, Petter & Galpin*, [1861 or 2]. (Cassell's Elementary Handbooks). pp. 60.
Includes reproductions of GWR station accounts at Newnham, Gloucestershire, in full.

11053 FAYERS, T. Labour among the navvies. *London: Wertheim, Macintosh & Hunt; Kendal: J. Robinson*, [1862]. pp. vi, 160.
Missionary work in Westmorland.

11054 HOLYOAKE, G. J. Imitable features of the Railway Permanent Benefit Building Society, Euston. *London: McCorquodale*, 1864. pp. 8.
A paper read at York, September 26, 1864, in the Social Economy section at the Congress of the National Association for Promoting Social Science. The nature and aims of the R.P.B.B.S. simply explained.

11055 LEVI, L. Wages and earnings of the working classes, with some facts illustrative of their economic condition, drawn from authentic and official sources, in a report to Michael T. Bass. *London: J. Murray*, 1867. pp. lix, 140.
pp. 1–2, Letter from M. T. Bass dated 25 April 1866 asking L. Levi to undertake this work; pp. 27–9, 'Railways', and a paragraph on the weekly wages of various grades of railwaymen.
—— 2nd edn. *J. Murray*, 1885. pp. vii, 151.
pp. 81–3, 'Railways', with a table of weekly wages of various grades of railwaymen on seven railways.

11056 GARNETT, E. Little Rainbow: a story of navvy life, by Mrs C. Garnett [i.e. Mrs Charles (née Elizabeth) Garnett]. *London: Daldy, Isbister & Co.*, 1877. pp. 39.
The needs of children in navvy settlements. Not a railway one in this instance, but on pp. 37–9 are details of the establishment of the Navvy Mission and its sponsors.

11057 SUTHERST, T. Long hours and over-work on railways. *London: New Otto Printing Co.*, [1885]. pp. 16.
An address delivered before the Railway Servants Congress at Leicester, 7th October 1885.

11058 NATIONAL COUPLING CONTEST [Newcastle upon Tyne 1886]. Report of Committee appointed to arrange National Coupling Contest, held at Forth Station, Newcastle upon Tyne on Good Friday, April 23rd, 1886, with a brief history of the shunting pole and coupling hook. *Newcastle upon Tyne: printed by H. Nixon*, 1886. pp. 23.
A competition promoted to encourage speed and safety in coupling and to urge improvements in the design of couplings.

11059 NATIONAL COUPLING CONTEST [Burton-on-Trent, 1890]. National Coupling Contest held at Burton-on-Trent on Good Friday, April 4th, 1890: committee's report.

Burton-on-Trent: G. A. Bellamy, printer, [1890]. pp. 7.
A list of the prizewinners and their awards. The object, to couple and uncouple a train of wagons in the shortest possible time.

11060 KINNEAR, J. B. The railway strike: a speech . . . at a public meeting held in the Masonic Hall, Ladybank, on 10th January 1891. [*Edinburgh*, 1891?]. pp. 8.
Support for the strikers in their struggle for shorter hours of labour (10 hours per day).

11061 WEBB, S. The London programme. *London: Swan Sonnenschein*, 1891. pp. vii, 218.
pp. 73–85, 'London's tramways', with 2 tables.
The plight of grossly under-paid and over-worked tramwaymen in London. Urges the adoption of the eleven tramway companies by the London County Council.

11062 DAWSON, W. Selecting, training and disciplining railwaymen. Great Western Railway (London) Lecture & Debating Society, meeting on Friday, March 31st, 1905 [no. 14]. pp. 6.

11063 SAUNDERS, H. H. L. Railway education. Great Western Railway (London) Lecture & Debating Society, meeting on December 20th, 1906 [no. 32]. pp. 8.

11064 AMALGAMATED SOCIETY OF RAILWAY SERVANTS. The Railwaymen's Charter: a reply to its critics by Richard Bell, May 1907. *London: Co-operative Printing Society*, 1907. pp. 24.

11065 STOREY, T. Bonus and piece-work systems, and profit sharing. Great Western Railway (London) Lecture & Debating Society, meeting on October 17th, 1907 [no. 41]. pp. 12.
Drawn largely from North Eastern Rly practice.

11066 AMALGAMATED SOCIETY OF RAILWAY SERVANTS. Osborne *v.* the A.S.R.S. and others, November 1908. *London: the Society*, 1908. pp. 109.
The verbatim report.

11067 AMALGAMATED SOCIETY OF RAILWAY SERVANTS. Report giving a statement of the results of the Census of Wages, Hours of Labour etc., of men (in the grades referred to in the demands of the A.S.R.S.) employed on the railways of the United Kingdom. *London: Co-operative Printing Society*, 1908. pp. 136, with numerous diagrams to illustrate the statistics.

11068 LIVESEY, G. Co-partnership. Great Western Railway (London) Lecture & Debating Society, meeting on Thursday, March 12th 1908 [no. 48]. pp. 11, with discussion, and a specimen schedule of principles to be used as the basis of a scheme for co-partnership.

11069 POLE, F. J. C. The element of chance in a railway career: could it be minimised? Great Western Railway (London) Lecture & Debating Society, meeting on December 2nd, 1909 [no. 64]. pp. 9.

11070 OSBORNE, W. V. My case: the causes and effects of the Osborne judgement. *London: E. Nash*, 1910. pp. vi, 116.
Walter V. Osborne, as secretary to the Walthamstow branch of the Amalgamated Society of Railway Servants was opposed to a compulsory levy upon union members to support the Parliamentary Labour Party. He brought an action against the A.S.R.S. in 1907, lost it, and had to pay costs. An appeal to the House of Lords in 1909 reversed the judgement and furthermore made all expenditure by trade unions on political objectives illegal. This decision was, however, nullified by the Trade Union Act on 1913 which re-allowed political levies subject to certain safeguards.

11071 BIRAM, R. S. Interior daylight illumination of railway offices. Great Western Railway (London) Lecture & Debating Society, meeting on November 2nd, 1911 [no. 82]. pp. 9, with discussion.
Author, 'North Eastern Rly'.

11072 HARDIE, J. K. Killing no murder: the Government and the railway strike. What caused the recent railway strike? Who settled it? For what purpose were the troops called out? *Manchester: National Labour Press*, 1911. pp. 23.

11073 GLOVER, R. R. P. Conciliation and arbitration. Great Western Railway (London) Lecture & Debating Society, meeting on February 8th, 1912 [no. 88]. pp. 11, with discussion.

11074 LEUBUSCHER, C. Der Arbeitskampf der englischen Eisenbahner im Jahre 1911 . . . *München u. Leipzig: Duncker & Humblot*, 1913. (Staats- und Sozialwissenschaftliche Forschungen, 174). pp. x, 117, with 119 notes & a bibliography (49 sources).

11075 HARE, E. The commercial mind. Great Western Railway (London) Lecture & Debating Society, meeting on February 11th, 1914 [no. 109]. pp. 72–82.
Advice on principles addressed to young men in the early years of a career in the railway industry.

11076 JOINT CONFERENCE RE NEW CONCILIATION SCHEME. Meeting of joint executive committees of the National Union of Railwaymen and Amalgamated Society of Locomotive Engineers & Firemen, Unity House, Euston Road, [London], N.W., March 10th, 1914. [Proceedings]. [*London: the Conference*, 1914]. pp. 131.

11077 RAILWAY STRIKE COMMITTEE [Gloucester]. The railway strike: true facts. *Gloucester: the Committee*, 1919. pp. [4].

Published 1 October 1919 by the 'Railway Strike Committee, Labour Club and Institute, Gloucester'.

11078 ARTHURTON, A. W. Fatigue in railway work: to what extent can it be eliminated? Great Western Railway (London) Lecture & Debating Society meeting on January 1st, 1920 [no. 117]. pp. 41–52, with 5 diagrams.

11079 GLEASON, A. H. What the workers want: a study of British labor. London: Allen & Unwin, 1920. pp. vii, 518.
pp. 70–78, Railway labour within the context of post-war conditions generally, and following the railway strike of 1919.

11080 UNDERGROUND ELECTRIC RAILWAYS COMPANY OF LONDON. Typical examination papers for operating staff. London: the Company. [1920]. pp. [44]. Separate papers bound into a single volume with the above title printed on a label on the cover. Certificates of proficiency, to be signed by trainer and trainee, are inserted.
The papers are for motormen, conductors (these vary between individual lines), gatemen, signalmen, liftmen, ticket collectors, porters and booking clerks.   LU(THC)

11081 MUSCIO, B. and HADLEY, E. S. The scientific selection of employees: is it a practical scheme? Great Western Railway (London) Lecture & Debating Society, meeting on January 27th 1921 [no. 132]. pp. 15.
A debate, with discussion and vote.

11082 RAILWAY CLERKS ASSOCIATION. Schemes for the establishment of local departmental committees, sectional railway councils and railway councils; also, central and national wages boards . . . London: R.C.A., [1921]. pp. 23.

11083 GREAT WESTERN RLY. Railway councils: arrangements in connection with the election of employee representatives, May 1922. London: G.W.R., May 1922. (Circular 2814). pp. 46.
Copies were distributed to all staff affected by the Railway Councils Scheme.

11084 LONDON & NORTH WESTERN RLY. Scheme for establishment of local departmental committees, sectional railway councils and Railway Council. [London]: L.N.W.R, [1922]. pp. 100, with folded map.

11085 SAMWAYS, H., SPITTLE, G., and BUTLER, B. W. Esprit de corps and teamwork in railway service. Great Western Railway (London) Lecture & Debating Society, meeting on March 23rd, 1922 (no. 148). pp. 21, with discussion.

11086 BUTTON, F. S. The present need for industrial stability. Great Western Railway (London) Lecture & Debating Society,

meeting on February 1st, 1923 (no. 158). pp. 14, with discussion.
Includes references to the subject in terms of recent railway development. Author, 'Industrial Conciliation Board'.

11087 HIGGINSON, P. R. A suggested base for the discussion of one union for railway workers . . . , with a Foreword by G. D. H. Cole. [London]: Independent Labour Party Information Committee, [1924]. pp. 19.
'The strike of 1924 proves the desirability of unity of NUR, RCA & ASLEF.'

11088 LONDON MIDLAND & SCOTTISH RLY. Scheme for the establishment of local departmental committees, sectional railway councils and Railway Council. Euston Station (London): L.M.S.R., January 1924. pp. 96.   LU(THC)

11089 MILES, G. H. Can psychology help in railway work? Great Western Railway (London) Lecture & Debating Society, meeting on 5th March, 1925 (no. 181). pp. 14, with discussion.

11090 RAILWAY CLERKS ASSOCIATION. National agreements respecting rates of pay and conditions of service; also, negotiating machinery schemes. London: R.C.A., 1925. pp. 172 & addenda (6 pp.).
The full text of current agreements for clerical, administrative & supervisory grades, with related documents. Text printed on recto pages only, with 'amendments, additions etc.' occasionally printed on the facing pages.

11091 SPITTLE, G. H. The railwayman and citizenship. Great Western Railway (London) Lecture & Debating Society, meeting on 5th November, 1925 (no. 185). pp. 14, with discussion.
'A man voluntarily entering an industry which functions only by accepting obligations to the State automatically accepts his share of the responsibility by reason of his engagement'.

11092 RACKLEY, F. Equality of opportunity in the railway service. Great Western Railway (London) Lecture & Debating Society, meeting on 18th November, 1926 (no. 198). pp. 17, with discussion.

11093 RAILWAY COMPANIES ASSOCIATION. The eight-hour day and forty-eight hour week: working conditions on the railways of Belgium, France, Germany, Italy. London: R.C.A., December 1927. (Pamphlet, 2). pp. 22.
Issued as a supplementary pamphlet to no. 1 of June 1927 (Ottley 4147).

11094 HADLEY, E. S. Accident prevention for permanent-way men: presented by the Great Western Railway Company to each of their permanent-way employees. Hanwell (London): Institute of Accident Prevention. 1928. sm. 8°. pp. 62, with 75 illus.

11095 HAVERS, E. and BOWLES, H. G. Does promotion in commercial life depend unduly on seniority? Great Western Railway (London) Lecture & Debating Society, meeting on 29th November 1928 (no. 224). pp. 14, with discussion.
The problem generally, and within the GWR.

11096 LEVIEN, D. V. To what extent is it practicable and desirable to introduce co-partnership into the railway industry? Great Western Railway (London) Lecture & Debating Society, meeting on 29th March, 1928 (no. 220). pp. 15, with discussion.
Author, 'Secretary's Office, Paddington', General observations, and co-partnership proposals applied to the GWR.

11097 NATIONAL TRANSPORT WORKERS' MINORITY MOVEMENT. Danger ahead!: the railwaymen's conditions and their next struggle; an examination of the policy of the companies and the financial situation of the railways. London: N.T.W.M.M., 1928. pp. 16.

11098 PICK, F. Education and training in the transport service. [Birmingham]: Association for Education in Industry & Commerce, 1929. pp. 21.
Address by the Managing Director of the Underground Group of Companies, July 3rd, 1929, based on the facilities introduced on London Underground for weekly paid staff (the 'wages grades'), including tramwaymen.

11099 RAILWAYS STAFF CONFERENCE, 1929. Safety precautions for railway shopmen. London, June 1929. 8°. pp. 12.
A handbook for employees in railway foundries and workshops.

11100 'THAT the railway specialist is of more value to the Company than the all-round railwayman:' introduced by H. Marsh, P. F. Glendon, E. A. Lyons and D. Blee. Great Western Railway (London) Lecture & Debating Society, meeting on the 7th November 1929, no. 234. pp. 13, with discussion.

11101 LONDON, MIDLAND & SCOTTISH RLY. Prevention of accidents to men working on or about the permanent way. Euston Station [London]: LMS Rly, [192–]. pp. 53, with 66 illus.

11102 RAILWAYWORKERS' MINORITY MOVEMENT. November thirteenth!: what it means to railway workers; a fighting programme and policy against wage cuts and dismissals. London: R.M.M., 1930. pp. 15.
Anticipating a worsening of adversities following the termination of the National Agreement on November 13th.

11103 WATSON, L. A. and GODFREY, E. Vocational training of railway staff: is there need for extension? Great Western Railway (London) Lecture & Debating Society,

meeting on the 20th November 1930 (no. 245). pp. 9, with discussion.

11104 RAILWAYWORKERS' MINORITY MOVEMENT. Smashing thro' January 19th: what the National Wages Board will mean to railway workers and how to fight it. London: R.M.M., [Dec. 1930 or Jan. 1931]. pp. 15.
A call to support united opposition to wage cuts and other disadvantageous economies following the end of the National Agreement on November 13th, 1930.

11105 COMPETITIVE examination as a basis for promotion in the railway service: a discussion initiated by H. Sutton and J. Dunn, and C. A. M. Peaty and G. M. Smith. Great Western Railway (London) Lecture & Debating Society, meeting on 30th November 1933, no. 277. pp. 12, with discussion; 1 illus.

11106 The RAILWAY service from the young clerk's point of view: four short papers by J. L. Webster, F. H. Bye, F. G. Richens and B. Y. Williams. Great Western Railway (London) Lecture & Debating Society, meeting on 23rd March 1933, no. 273. pp. 6.

11107 SAINT MARGARET'S DEPOT COUNCIL OF ACTION [Edinburgh]. Rail crisis!: which policy; capitalist pooling and wage cuts, Labour's public control, or Forward to Workers' Control through the fight against dismissals and starvation standards? [Edinburgh, 1933?]. pp. 16.

11108 'THAT a man of outstanding merit must succeed in the railway service.' Great Western Railway (London) Lecture & Debating Society, meeting on 14th December 1933, no. 278. pp. 13, with discussion.
A debate between J. L. Webster & T. H. Hollingsworth and R. W. Walter & R. H. Eden.

11109 TRAMWAYMEN'S MILITANT COMMITTEE. All London Tramwaymen Call Note, no. 8. London: Tramway Militants, April 1933. pp. [8].
A satirical commentary on a variety of ills associated with tramwaymen's duties, but particularly on the call to speed up journey timings.

11110 NATIONAL UNION OF RAILWAYMEN. Report of Committee on Formation of One Transport Union. London: N.U.R., [1934]. pp. 12.
Includes a list of unions representing transport workers, exclusively or inclusively.

11111 RICHENS, F. G. and WHITTINGTON, R. H. That the present system of clerical positions has proved unsatisfactory both to the Company and the staff: a debate. Great Western Railway (London) Lecture & Debating Society, meeting on 1st November 1934, no. 285. pp. 8, with discussion.

11112 'THAT the cult of efficiency is a menace to the best traditions of our civilisation:' a debate initiated by O. H. Downing & L. P. Bonnet and R. F. Thurtle & F. M. Jacques. Great Western Railway (London) Lecture & Debating Society, meeting on 13th December 1934, no. 288. pp. 12, with discussion.

11113 DOWNTON, A. The London Transport scandal. *London: Communist Party, London District Committee*, June 1936. pp. 30.
Alleged discontent of the people of London with passenger transport services, and also among the Board's employees; suggestions for improvement.

11114 'THAT employees should be paid what their individual services are deemed to be worth:' a discussion initiated by W. G. Roberts, N. S. Taylor and A. M. Webb. Great Western Railway (London) Lecture & Debating Society, meeting on 19th March 1936, no. 302. pp. 7, with discussion.
Largely concerned with staff structure within the GWR.

11115 NATIONAL UNION OF RAILWAYMEN. Rates of pay and conditions of service of railway employees except shopmen. 4th edn. *London: N.U.R.*, March 1937. pp. 163.
—— 7th edn, *N.U.R.*, January 1942. pp. 195.

11116 ASSOCIATED SOCIETY OF LOCOMOTIVE ENGINEERS AND FIREMEN. [Rules.] Revised rules . . . *Hampstead: A.S.L.E.F.*, 1948. sm 8°. pp. 96.

11117 HUMPHRIES, C. A. Staff welfare on the railways. (Proceedings of the British Railways (W.R.) London Lecture & Debating Society, 1948–49, no. 359). pp. 19, with discussion & 12 illus.
Author, 'Chief Welfare Officer, W.R.'.

11118 ROPER, W. H. The contribution which is necessary from the railwayman towards an efficient and economical British Railways service. Proceedings of the British Railways (W.R.) Lecture & Debating Society, 1948–49, no. 363. pp. 15, with discussion.
Author, 'District Goods Manager's Office, Newport'.

11119 BRITISH RAILWAYS. Joint Statement to the staff of British Railways by the Railway Executive and the National Union of Railwaymen, the Associated Society of Locomotive Engineers and Firemen, the Railway Clerks' Association. What the Settlement means to you and the part you are asked to play. *London: BR*, March 1951. pp. 16.
Issued to all employees affected by the agreement of 23 February 1951. Broad increases in pay and a firm basis for future co-operation. The resolution at the end of the joint declaration by BR Executive and the three unions: 'Let us go forward TOGETHER to better times'.

11120 BRITISH RAILWAYS. British Railways staff savings banks. *London: B.R.*, [1952?]. pp. 12. Cover title: Railway savings banks, 1852–1952.

11121 BRITISH RAILWAYS. Prevention of accidents. [*London*]: *British Transport Commission*, 1954. sm. obl. format. pp. 24, with 10 illus. Cover title: Your personal safety; operating and motive power.
A practical guide for railwaymen.

11122 NEWNHAM, C. T. The Railway Medical Service. (Proceedings of the British Railways (W.R.) London Lecture & Debating Society, 1954–55, no. 416). pp. 16, with discussion & 8 illus.
Author, 'Regional Medical Officer, W.R.'.

11123 DUNBAR, A. R. Modernisation and men. (Proceedings of the British Railways (W.R.) London Lecture & Debating Society, 1959–60, no. 458). pp. 15, with discussion.
Author, 'Manpower Adviser, B.T.C.'.

11124 SPECIAL JOINT COMMITTEE ON MACHINERY OF NEGOTIATION FOR RAILWAY STAFF. Report of Railway Pay Committee of Inquiry, 2nd March 1960. *London: the Committee*, 1960. pp. 94, with 21 appendices (detailed tables).
On relativity of pay among railwaymen. Members of the Committee: C. W. Guillebaud, E. Bishop, H. A. Clegg; H. A. Whitson (Secretary).

11125 COOK, P. L. Railway workshops: the problems of contraction. *Cambridge: Cambridge University Press*, 1964. (University of Cambridge, Department of Applied Economics, Occasional Papers, 2). pp. viii, 92.
A study of the application by BR of its Main Workshop Plan (1962) to the problem of the 29 main railway workshops facing a decline in work load.

11126 MacAMHLAIGH, D. An Irish navvy: the diary of an exile . . . translated by Valentin Iremonger. *London: Routledge & Kegan Paul*, 1964. pp. ix, 182.
Translated from the Irish: *Dialann Deorai*.
ch. 5 (pp. 95–110), 'Laying rails'. Platelaying in the English Midlands, 1956: social background rather than working life.

11127 BONAVIA, M. R. Training for transport. (Proceedings of the British Railways (W.R.) London Lecture & Debating Society, 1964/65, no. 489). pp. 15, with discussion.
Author, 'Director of Education & Training, BR'.

11128 WEDDERBURN, D. Redundancy and the railwayman. *Cambridge: Cambridge University Press*, 1965. (Cambridge University, Department of Applied Economics, Occasional Paper, 4). pp. 239, with 58 tables, 14 diagrams & 201 notes.
A study of the effects of contraction and closure of railway workshops at Faverdale and Gorton.

11129 TRANSPORT SALARIED STAFFS ASSOCI-
ATION. A look at life in the T.S.S.A.
London: the Association, 1966. pp. 32.
—— another edn. 1974. pp. 24.   LU(THC)

11130 TRANSPORT SALARIED STAFFS ASSOCI-
ATION. Rates of pay and conditions of
service, British Railways salaried staffs,
April 1966. *London: the Association*, 1966.
pp. xviii, 211.

11131 BUCKTON, R. Locomotivemen's dispute:
why? *London: Associated Society of
Locomotive Engineers & Firemen*, December 1973. pp. 69.

11132 FERNEYHOUGH, F. On the railways. *London: Wayland*, 1973. (Choosing a Job
series). pp. 80, with 83 illus & 2 maps.

11133 BROOKS, D. Race and labour in London
Transport. *London: Oxford University
Press, for the Institute of Race Relations and
the Acton Society Trust*, 1975. pp. xxii, 389,
with 87 tables, 5 diagrams, questionnaire
and a bibliography (ca. 140 sources). Index,
pp. 381–9.

chaps. 7–10 (pp. 123–237), The Railway Operating Department.

11134 COX, S. Railwayworker; text by Sarah
Cox, photographs by Robert Golden. *Har-
mondsworth: Kestrel Books*, 1976. (People
Working series). la. 8°. pp. 32, with 62 illus.
A pictorial account of work-a-day tasks at
Paddington Station and Old Oak Common depot.

11135 EMPLOYMENT SERVICE AGENCY. CA-
REERS AND OCCUPATIONAL INFORMA-
TION CENTRE. Road and rail. [*London*]:
H.M.S.O., 1976. (Choice of Careers: new
series, 20). pp. 44, with illus.
pt. 2 (pp. 24–42), 'Do you want to work on the
railways?', with 13 illus.

11136 BOWICK, D. Man management and manpower productivity, *in* International Transport: The common problems. [Conference],
2, 3 & 4 October 1978, London, arranged by
the Chartered Institute of Transport and the
Financial Times Conference Organisation.
pp. 113–27, Principles of labour-management
relationship based upon railway operating experience.

K   RAILWAYS AND THE NATION

Railways within the framework of national life—The nationalized railways discussed—The Beeching reforms of 1963—Railways and politics—Railway policy—Railways and the future (Planning)—Inter-modal relationships—Integration of all forms of public transport

11137–11363

For actual parliamentary and governmental participation in railway affairs see **K 6**
For actual nationalization see **B 9**

Historical   11137–78
Contemporaneous   11179–11363

Historical

11137 POPE, S. A. The evolution of travel and the early history of the Great Western Railway. Great Western Railway (London) Lecture & Debating Society, meeting on February 25th, 1909 [no. 59]. pp. 21, with 33 illus.

11138 SEARLE, M. Railways *v.* turnpikes, *in his* Turnpikes and Toll Bars (*Hutchinson*, 1930), pp. 477–501.
A collection of reproduced extracts, 1829–1869.

11139 HUNT, B. C. The development of the business corporation in England, 1800–1867. *Cambridge (Mass.): Harvard University Press*, 1936. (Harvard Economic Studies, 52). pp. xii, 182.
ch. 5 (pp. 90–115), The Joint Stock Companies Registration and Regulation Act of 1844 and the railway boom, 1844–46.

11140 ROLT, L. T. C. The inland waterways of England. *London: Allen & Unwin*, 1950. pp. 221, with plates.
pp. 62–7, The influence of railways upon canal development.
—— 2nd edn. *Allen & Unwin*, 1979. pp. 221 (pp. 62–7).

11141 MOWAT, C. L. Britain between the wars, 1918–1940. *London: Methuen*, 1956 (the 1955 edn. reprinted with minor corrections). pp. ix, 694, with ca. 1700 notes & a 'bibliographical note' (pp. 659–64).
Index has 19 page refs to railways.
—— Reprint with 'additional bibliographical note' (pp. 665–7). *Methuen*, 1968 (reprinted 1972). pp. ix, 698.

11142 SYMONS, J. The General Strike: a historical portrait. *London: Cresset Press*, 1957. pp. xi, 259, with 16 illus on 8 plates, 2 appendices & a bibliography (60+ sources).
pp. 71–101, 'The wheels turn': the transport situation during the nine days of the strike.

11143 KELF-COHEN, R. Nationalisation in Britain: the end of a dogma. *London: Macmillan*, 1958. pp. x, 310, with 5 statistical tables & a bibliography (pp. 303–5), mostly of official sources.
ch. 4 (pp. 54–84), Transport.

11144 LABOUR PARTY. The nationalised industries: success story: air, transport, coal, electricity, gas, atomic power. *London: Labour Party*, 1958. (Labour Party Pamphlet). pp. 42.
pp. 20–6, Transport (Railways, pp. 20–3). Improved efficiency and economy as a result of nationalisation; present problems and future prospects.

11145 ROBSON, W. A. Nationalised industry and public ownership. *London: Allen & Unwin*, 1960. pp. 544.
Railways and the British Transport Commission are important elements in the work. The index and bibliography are both detailed and together occupy pp. 499–544.
—— 2nd edn. *Allen & Unwin*, 1962. pp. xxxiii, [11], 544.
This 2nd edition is substantially unchanged apart from the correction of a few literal inaccuracies, but in the new Introduction the author discusses a number of important matters of policy which have arisen since the publication of the first edition.

11146 TURTON, B. J. Geographical aspects of the railway industry. Thesis, Ph.D., University of Nottingham, 1960–61. 2 vols. (text; maps, graphs & tables).
The railway industry and urban development, and the railway towns (Crewe, Swindon, etc.)

11147 CHAMBERS, J. D. The workshop of the world: British economic history from 1820 to 1880. *London: Oxford University Press*, 1961. sm. 8°. pp. 239.
Railways, pp. 52–61, 161–2 *et passim*.
—— 2nd edn. *O.U.P.*, 1968. pp. ix, 165.
Railways, pp. 35–41, 108–9 *et passim*.

11148 ELLIOT, J. Railways in a changing world. (Proceedings of the British Railways (W.R.) London Lecture & Debating Society, 1961–2, no. 475). pp. 11, with discussion.
Author, ex-General Manager, Southern Rly. Chairman of London Transport Executive, etc., etc. Reminiscences, and current problems.

[267]

11149 DEANE, P. and COLE, W. A. British economic growth, 1688–1959: trends and structure. *Cambridge: Cambridge University Press*, 1962. (University of Cambridge Dept of Applied Economics. Monographs, 8). pp. xvi, 348, with 91 tables, map, 7 graphs (1 folded at end) & a bibliography (230 sources), 3 appendices & many notes.
Railways, pp. 229–34 *et passim*.
—— 2nd edn. *Cambridge University Press*, 1967. pp. xx, 350, with 92 tables, map, 7 graphs, bibliography (230 sources), 3 appendices and many notes.

11150 McBRIAR, A. M. Fabian Socialism and English politics, 1884–1918. *Cambridge: Cambridge University Press*, 1962. pp. x, 387.
ch. 8, Municipalization of tramways: the influence of the Fabians in the London County Council.
pp. 26, 191–2, 222–5 *et passim*: nationalisation of railways.

11151 BARRY, E. E. Nationalisation in British politics: the historical background. *London: Jonathan Cape*, 1965. pp. 397, with 1228 notes (many detailed).
Railways *passim*, but especially pp. 80–108, 'The railways and state purchase'; pp. 290–94, 'The London Passenger Transport Board'. This being a retrospective study, the actual nationalization of British railways is treated comparatively briefly, on pp. 375–6.

11152 HADFIELD, C. The Canal Age. *Newton Abbot: David & Charles*, 1968. pp. 233, with col. frontis, 32 illus on 16 plates, 33 illus & 14 maps in text, 4 appendices & a bibliography (108 sources).
Index has 6 page refs under 'Canals connected to horse tramroads' and 23 under 'Canals and railway building' and 'Canals and railways'.

11153 POLANYI, G. Contrasts in nationalised transport since 1947: a study of the conflict between co-ordination and competition as criteria for transport policy in Britain. *London: Institute of Economic Affairs*, 1968. (Background Memorandum, 2). la. 8°. pp. 54, with 4 tables.
Comparing the policies of BR and the Transport Holding Co. (road haulage and buses).

11154 SMITH, W. An historical introduction to the economic geography of Great Britain, with an Appreciation by M. J. Wise. *London: G. Bell*, 1968. (Bell's Advanced Economic Geographies). pp. xxxiii, 228, with 21 tables, 41 maps & diagrams and many notes.
Originally published as part 1 of his *An Economic Geography of Great Britain* (1949; 2nd edn, 1953) (Ottley 4749).
Railways: 18 page refs in Index.

11155 ALDCROFT, D. H. Innovation on the railways. pp. 12; 44 bibliogr. notes. (Reprinted from *Journal of Transport Economics & Policy*, vol. 3, no. 1, January 1969).
An examination of the factors responsible for the delay in the application of electric and diesel traction to main-line railways in Britain.

11156 KELF-COHEN, R. Twenty years of nationalisation: the British experience. *London: Macmillan*, 1969. pp. 339, with a bibliography (pp. 323–8).
pp. 60–98 *et passim*, Railways.

11157 ALDCROFT, D. H. The Inter-War economy: Britain, 1919–1939. *London: Batsford*, 1970. pp. 441, with an extensive bibliography, 43 tables & many bibliogr. notes.
Index has 66 page refs under 'Railways', 'Railways Act 1921', and 'Tramways'.

11158 HAWKE, G. R. Railways and economic growth in England and Wales, 1840–1970. *Oxford: Clarendon Press*, 1970. pp. xiv, 421, with 47 tables, diagrams & graphs, & over 1100 notes; bibliography, pp. 413–7 (company archives, Parliamentary Papers, secondary sources).
Produced from the author's thesis, *The Effects of the Railways on the Growth of the Economy of England and Wales, 1840–1870* (Oxford, D. Phil., 1968).

11159 PERKIN, H. The Age of the Railway. *London: Panther, and simultaneously by Routledge & Kegan Paul*, 1970. pp. 351, with 21 illus on 16 plates, map, chapter bibliographies (95 sources), 338 notes and a chronology of the development of transport generally, and of roads, waterways and railways from 1485 to 1969 (pp. 312–33).
The impact of railways upon the structure of social and industrial development in 19th century Britain.
—— Reprinted as a hardback edn. *Newton Abbot: David & Charles*, 1971. pp. 351, with 28 illus on 16 plates, 2 maps in text, bibliography (95 sources), 338 notes and a chronology.

11160 RICHARDSON, J. J. The formation of transport policy in Britain, 1950–1956. Thesis, Ph.D., University of Manchester, 1970/71.

11161 LUBENOW, W. C. The politics of government growth: early Victorian attitudes toward state intervention, 1833–1848. *Newton Abbot: David & Charles; Hamden (Conn.): Archon Books*, 1971.
ch. 4 (pp. 107–36), 'Private opportunities and public responsibilities: early Victorian railway legislation, 1840–1847', with 93 notes & a bibliography, for the whole work, of 287 sources.

11162 ALDCROFT, D. H. Railways and economic growth: a review article. Journal of Transport History, new series, vol. 1 (1971–2), pp. 238–49, with 28 bibliogr. notes.
On the book of that name by G. R. Hawke.

11163 HILLMAN, J. J. The parliamentary structuring of British road-rail freight co-ordination. *Evanston (Illinois): Northwestern University Transportation Center*, 1973. (Monographs, 2). pp. 302, with 429 notes, many extensive.

A detailed study of varying conditions of competition and co-operation, and of conflicting political ideologies, since 1918.

11164 KELF-COHEN, R. British nationalisation, 1945–1973. *London: Macmillan*, 1973. pp. xii, 288, with tables & a detailed bibliography (pp. 278–86).

A successor to this author's *Twenty Years of Nationalisation* (1969).

11165 SIMMONS, J. The power of the railway, *in* The Victorian City: images and realities, by H. J. Dyos and Michael Wolff (1973), pp. 277–310, with 24 illus on 16 plates & 130 notes.

11166 CHESTER, N. The nationalisation of British industry, 1945–51. *London: H.M.S.O.*, 1975. pp. xv, 1075.

Legislation and general policy: a study 'based almost entirely upon Cabinet and Department records and Parliamentary Debates'. Industries (coal, transport, iron & steel, etc.) are not discussed in turn, but considered comparatively within a series of thematic studies of the creation and administration of the whole system of nationalisation during this six-year period of post-war Labour government under Clem Atlee. The railway element is readily traceable via the Index (pp. 1061–75) under 'Railways' and 'Transport'.

11167 CHURCH, R. A. The great Victorian boom, 1850–1873, prepared for the Economic History Society by R. A. Church. *London: Macmillan*, 1975. (Studies in Economic & Social History series). pp. 95, with 20 notes & a bibliography (163 sources).

pp. 30–34, Railways, capitalism and growth.

11168 FULLERTON, B. The development of British transport networks. *London: Oxford University Press*, 1975. (Theory and Practice in Geography series). pp. iv, 60, with illus, maps and an evaluative bibliography (pp. 53–9).

ch. 3 (pp. 16–23), Railway development, 1830–50.

ch. 4 (pp. 24–9), The Railway Age, 1850–1920.

ch. 5 (pp. 30–8), Road transport expands, 1920–70.

ch. 7 (pp. 45–52), Towards integrated transport systems.

11169 EDMONDS, T. F. The location of passenger railway stations in British towns. Thesis, M.A., University of Hull, 1976.

11170 POTTER, S. Transport and new towns. *Milton Keynes: Open University, New Towns Study Unit*, 1976. 2 vols.

Vol. 1, The historical perspective: the development of transportation planning for new communities, 1898–1939. pp. iv, 63, with maps, diagrams, tables & 26 notes.

vol. 2, The transport assumptions underlying the design of Britain's new towns, 1946–1976. pp. [5], ix, 64–272, with illus, maps, plans & a bibliography (100+ sources).

11171 PORTEOUS, J. D. Canal ports: the urban achievement of the Canal Age. *London: Academic Press*, 1977. pp. xvii, 249.

pp. 157–89. 'The challenge of the railways, 1830–1918', with 2 maps, 3 tables & 67 notes.

11172 THRIFT, N. The diffusion of Greenwich Mean Time in Great Britain: an essay on a neglected aspect of social and economic history. *Leeds: University of Leeds, School of Geography*, May 1977. (Working Paper, 188). Reproduced typescript. pp. 12, with 2 maps.

The bringing of standard time (G.M.T.) to cities and towns via the railway guard's watch and the station clock (hence 'London Time' or 'Railway Time') in the 1840s.

11173 OKAYAY, T. Railway development and population change in nineteenth century East Anglia. Thesis, Ph. D., University of Bristol, 1979.

11174 CAIN, P. J. Private enterprise or public utility?: output, pricing and investment on English and Welsh railways, 1870–1914, *in* Journal of Transport History, 3rd series, vol. 1, no 1, September 1980, pp. 9–28, with 8 tables, a graph & 46 notes.

A study in the decline of profitability.

11175 GOURVISH, T. R. Railways and the British economy, 1830–1914, prepared for the Economic History Society by T. R. Gourvish. *London: Macmillan*, 1980. (Studies in Economic & Social History). pp. 70, with 6 tables, 16 notes & a bibliography (88 sources).

11176 MINISTRY OF TRANSPORT and BRITISH RAILWAYS. British Railways network for development, with foreword by the Ministry of Transport and the Chairman of British Railways Board. *London: Ministry of Transport and B.R.B.*, March 1967. A la. folded map illustrating 'the basic railway network which the Government and B.R.B. have decided should be retained and developed . . .' Produced in accord with Cmnd 3057.

11177 RAILWAY INVIGORATION SOCIETY. The Railway Invigoration Society: a brief bibliography for students of the transport crisis. *London: R.I.S.*, 1972. pp. 9.

A selection of 68 sources under facet headings addressed to economists and planners who may have been busy reading each other rather than the problem.

11178 DEPARTMENT OF THE ENVIRONMENT. LIBRARY. National Index of Traffic and Transportation Surveys. *London: D.o.E.*, October 1975. (Lib/Inf/21). pp. 98.

An index to the D.o.E.'s microfiche records of 1000 surveys undertaken by various organisations. Classified first by type of survey and sub-divided by geographical region or locality.

Individual surveys are not analysed in this publication: it is simply a key to the Department's resources.

Contemporaneous

11179 LITTLE, J. Practical observations on the improvement and management of mountain sheep and sheep farms; also, remarks on stock of various kinds. *Edinburgh: Macredie, Skelly & Muckersy; London: Longman, Hurst, Rees, Orme & Brown*, 1815. pp. iii, 198.

ch. 7 (pp. 128–47), Observations on the improvement of the country by means of railways. 'Were rail-ways formed throughout the country all the different classes of the community would derive as much benefit from them as either merchants or manufacturers'. Advocates feuing the land adjacent to railways.

11180 MONEY the representative of value, with considerations on the bank question, railway companies, savings banks, and the National Debt. *London: P. Richardson*, 1837. pp. 79.

pp. 50–7, on the economic advantage of railway financing by government.

11181 TEISSERENC, E. Études sur les voies de communication perfectionnées et sur les lois économiques de la production du transport suivies de tableaux statistiques sur les frais de navigation et d'une analyse raisonnée des comptes des principaux chemins de fer français, belges, anglais et allemands. *Paris: Librairie Scientifique-Industrielle de L. Mathias*, 1847. pp. 944, with la. folded statistical tables for France.

ch. 2 (pp. 16–63), Concurrence des canaux et des chemins de fer dans le Royaume-Uni. ch. 11 (pp. 469–89), De la transformation des canaux en railways. [Includes Britain.] Notes et pièces justificatives: note 27, page 302 (pp. 679–720). Examen raisonné des résultats de l'exploitation des chemins de fer français, belges, allemands et anglais: circulation, recette, dépense, calcul des prix de revient.

11182 LOCKE, J. A letter to the Right Hon. Lord John Russell, M.P. on the best mode of avoiding the evils of mixed gauge railways and the break of gauge. *London: J. Ridgway*, 1848. pp. 16, with folded map & tables.

Urging narrow (i.e. 'standard') gauge rather than mixed gauge for future railways.

11183 DODD, G. The food of London: a sketch of the chief varieties, sources of supply, probable quantities, modes of arrival, processes of manufacture, suspected adulteration, and machinery of distribution, of the food for a community of two millions and a half. *London: Longman, Brown, Green & Longmans*, 1856. pp. xii, 524.

Includes transport of food by rail.

11184 RAILWAYS, in a letter to the Right Honourable the President of the Board of Trade: a plan for the systematic reform of the railways of the United Kingdom by legislative enactment. 2nd edn. *London: Longman,* Green, Longman, Roberts & Green, 1865. pp. [4], 173, with tables.   NUC

11185 SANKEY, W. H. V. Railway reform: being the essence of a larger work which will appear shortly, containing apposite suggestions for adopting certain requisite measures with a view to ensure firstly, security of life and immunity from personal injury . . .; secondly, security of capital . . . *London: Effingham Wilson*, 1866. pp. 45.

11186 BOLAS, T. Equitable railway nationalisation: a problem of the near future, being primarily a reprint of the Railway Reform Leaflets, 1 to 8. *London: printed and published by Thomas Bolas at the Leaflet Press . . . Chiswick*, 1895. pp. [16]. (Railway Reform Pamphlets, 1–8).

'The sole guiding principle of railway management is big dividends to the shareholders, the misery of others [passengers] counting for nothing'.

11187 PALMER, J. E. How to cheapen inland transit. *Dublin: Hodges, Figgis & Co.*, 1896. pp. 12.

'Reprinted from the *New Ireland Review*, March 1896, and revised by the writer.' Wider and deeper canals would enable goods to be carried at far less cost than by rail.

11188 The NATIONALISATION of British railways. *London: Financial Review of Reviews*, [1907]. (Popular Financial Booklets, 32). pp. 16.

Reprinted from the November 1907 issue.

11189 BAZLEY, B. M. Should British railways be redistributed? Great Western Railway (London) Lecture & Debating Society, meeting on October 21st, 1909 [no. 61]. pp. 10, with discussion.

Proposed grouping with a central authority as an alternative to nationalization.

11190 BROWN, H. S. The future of railways. Great Western Railway (London) Lecture & Debating Society, meeting on November 3rd 1910 [no. 71]. p. 20.

Author, 'North Eastern Rly'.

11191 SHOWERS, F. W. Local government and taxation. Great Western Railway (London) Lecture & Debating Society, meeting on January 11th, 1912 [no. 86]. pp. 27, with discussion & 11 financial statements & diagrams.

'The G.W.R. . . . is the largest ratepayer in the Kingdom.'

11192 WHITE, O. J. Would regeneration of inland transportation by water be in the public interest? Great Western Railway (London) Lecture & Debating Society, meeting on January 22nd, 1914 [no. 108]. pp. 50–71, with map.

Railways preferred to canals.

11193 BASHAM, W. Is it likely that enterprise in road transport will prove a serious competitor to railways? Great Western Railway (London) Lecture & Debating Society, meeting on December 11th, 1919 [no. 116]. pp. 30–40.

11194 CHUBB, F. W. Prussian State Railway working, introducing the question 'Is a state-owned railway more efficient than one which is privately owned?'. Great Western Railway (London) Lecture & Debating Society, meeting on November 25th, 1920 [no. 127]. pp. 12, with discussions & 11 illus, & diagrams on 4 plates.

11195 GREAT WESTERN RLY. Nationalising the railways without paying for them. [London: G.W. Rly, 1920]. (Great Western Pamphlets). pp. 16.
Reprinted from the Railway Gazette, Dec. 10th, 1920. Amalgamation as an alternative to proposed nationalization.

11196 NATIONAL GUILDS LEAGUE. Workers' Control on the railways. London: the League, [1921?]. pp. 4.

11197 TEE, B. F. The menace of road transport. Great Western Railway (London) Lecture & Debating Society, meeting on November 24th, 1921 (no. 141). pp. 26, with discussion & 10 diagrams, maps & tables.

11198 MINISTRY OF TRANSPORT. Valuation for rating of amalgamated railways situated partly in England & Wales and partly in Scotland: report of the committee. London: HMSO, 1923. pp. 51. (Chairman: C. W. Hurcomb).

11199 WILKINSON, E. F. Passenger train working in relation to road motor competition. Great Western Railway (London) Lecture & Debating Society, meeting on 8th January, 1925 (no. 177). pp. 13, with discussion.
Author, 'L.N.E.R., Newcastle'.

11200 MINISTRY OF TRANSPORT. LONDON AND HOME COUNTIES TRAFFIC ADVISORY COMMITTEE. Omnibus competition with tramways. London: HMSO, 1926. pp. 16. (Chairman: Sir Henry P. Maybury).

11201 RAILWAY COMPANIES ASSOCIATION. Railways, road transport and local taxation. London: the Association, [1926]. pp. 14.
The unfair conditions under which increasing road transport competition is being allowed to develop. Railways pay 19% of their net revenue to local rates, thus subsidising their opponents by contributing towards the upkeep of roads.

11202 SHRAPNELL-SMITH, E. S. The future of road transport. Great Western Railway (London) Lecture & Debating Society, meeting on the 7th January 1926 (no. 189). pp. 19, with discussion & 4 tables.
Road-rail relationships.

11203 ARTHURTON, A. W. How can road transport competition be countered most effectively by the railways? Great Western Railway (London) Lecture & Debating Society meeting on 17th February 1927 (no. 204). pp. 20, with discussion.
Author, 'Railway Companies Association'.

11204 LEVIEN, D. V. Have British railways progressed sufficiently to meet the needs of present-day transport? Great Western Railway (London) Lecture & Debating Society, meeting on 17th March 1927 (no. 206). pp. 11.
Author, 'Secretary's Office, Paddington'. Suggested reforms.

11205 COMMERCIAL MOTOR USERS ASSOCIATION. London, Midland and Scottish Railway (Road Transport) Bill and similar bills: statement concerning points which arise in the public interest. London: the Association, [1928]. pp. [3]. Text dated 18 February 1928.
The threat to the road haulage industry by proposed legislation which would allow railways to extend their road feeder services to compete against road passenger and haulage undertakings.

11206 'THAT effective competition of rail against road transport is hampered by inequitable government control.' Great Western Railway (London) Lecture & Debating Society, meeting on 18th December 1930, no. 247. pp. 19, with discussion.
A debate between Messrs D. Blee, S. B. Taylor & H. G. Bowles (G.W.R.), and Messrs W. R. Lawrence, C. E. R. Sherrington, & P. L. E. Rawlins (Gray's Inn Debating Society).

11207 RAILWAYMEN'S MINORITY MOVEMENT. Railway nationalisation?: the argument in a nutshell. London: [R.M.M., 1931]. pp. 16. Title from cover.

11208 HAWKESWOOD, D. H. and MORRIS, W. R. Will the institution of tariffs by the British government increase the prosperity of home railways? Great Western Railway (London) Lecture & Debating Society, meeting on 15th December 1932 (no. 268). pp. 14, with discussion.
A debate.

11209 MUNICIPAL TRAMWAYS AND TRANSPORT ASSOCIATION. Private discussion on the Road Traffic Act, 1930, to be opened by John Barnard, A. H. Gledhill and A. R. Fearnley. London: the Association, 1932. pp. 12, with chart & 6 tables.
Discussion at annual conference of the Association, Eastbourne, June 22, 23 & 24, 1932. Financial problems of tramway undertakings resulting from growing competition with buses.

11210 'THAT a unified British railway system would be in the national interest.' Great Western Railway (London) Lecture & Debating Society, meeting on 17th November 1932, no. 266. pp. 15, with discussion.
A debate between N. J. L. Brodrick & M. D. Mills and P. W. Kingsford & H. G. Bowles.

11211 MORRISON, H. Socialisation of transport: the organisation of socialised industries, with particular reference to the London Passenger Transport Bill. *London: Constable*, 1933. pp. xi, 313.
Includes a chapter on the Salter Report (1932).

11212 HURCOMB, C. Progress in the coordination of transport in Great Britain: inaugural address delivered in London on October 14th, 1935. pp. 22.
Reprinted from the *Journal of the Institute of Transport*, November 1935. Period. since 1919.

11213 MIDDLETON, P. H. Railways of thirty nations: government *versus* private ownership. *New York: Prentice-Hall*, 1937. pp. xix, 328, with frontis & 63 illus. Summary, pp. 291–305; bibliography, pp. 309–12.
pp. 37–55, 'Great Britain'.
Government ownership examined, country by country, in order to determine whether or not the U.S.A. should also nationalize its railways.

11214 PILCHER, R. S. Road passenger transport: survey and development. *London: Pitman*, 1937. pp. xii, 393, with 33 illus.
Includes tramways, and the effect of suburban railway electrification on road passenger services.

11215 COMMUNIST PARTY. How to end muddle on the railways. *London: the Party*, 1944. pp. 16.

11216 COMMUNIST PARTY. Transport for the people: proposals for the post-war organisation of British transport services . . . *London: the Party*, [1944]. pp. 24.
The need for a nationalized transport system.

11217 ELLIOTT, H. Road transport: the new regime. (Proceedings of the British Railways (W.R.) London Lecture & Debating Society, 1948–49, no. 355). pp. 11, with discussion.
Author, 'Chief Officer (Freight), Road Transport Executive'.

11218 HURCOMB, C. Transport as an integrated public service. (Proceedings of the British Railways (W.R.) London Lecture & Debating Society, 1949–50, no. 364). pp. 12, with discussion.
Author, 'Chairman, B.T.C.'.

11219 'THAT a more efficient and economical system of transport in this country could be secured by the abolition of railways and the conversion of the tracks to motorways', proposed by K. Woodward and J. R. F. Melluish; opposed by F. G. Dean and W. H. Roper. Proceedings of the British Railways (W.R.) London Lecture & Debating Society, 1949–50, no. 372. pp. 16, with discussion.

11220 BRADY, R. A. Crisis in Britain: plans and achievements of the Labour Government. *Berkeley & Los Angeles: University of California Press; London: Cambridge University Press*, 1950.
ch. 6, pp. 236–83. National transport, with 140 notes (some detailed), chart, & a map.

11221 HOLLINGSWORTH, T. H. The changing pattern of railway transport. (Proceedings, British Railways (W.R.) London Lecture & Debating Society, 1951–52, no. 393). pp. 14, with discussion.
Author, 'Commercial Supt, Scottish Region'.

11222 MINISTRY OF TRANSPORT. Transport policy. *London: HMSO*, 1952. (Cmd 8538). pp. 4.

11223 MUNBY, D. L. The nationalised industries, *in* The British Economy in the Nineteen-Fifties, ed. by G. D. N. Worswick and P. H. Ady (1952), ch. 11 (pp. 378–428) with 87 notes, 3 tables & a bibliography (13 sources).
Includes transport.

11224 ROBSON, W. A. Problems of nationalised industry, edited by William A. Robson. *London: Allen & Unwin*, 1952. pp. 390, with a bibliography (pp. 369–80).
In the index there are 34 page refs to railways.

11225 TAIT, A. W. Costing road and rail traffic. Proceedings of the British Railways (W.R.) London Lecture & Debating Society, 1952–53, no. 395. pp. 15, with discussion.
Author, 'Director of Costings, B.T.C.'.

11226 CHAMBERS, S. P. The effect on the national economy of government policy in relation to nationalisation and the control of industry. (Proceedings of the British Railways (W.R.) London Lecture & Debating Society, 1953–54, no. 408). pp. 12, with discussion.
Author, 'Deputy Chairman, Imperial Chemical Industries, Ltd'.

11227 LENNOX-BOYD, A. T. The railways and the state. (Proceedings of the British Railways (W.R.) London Lecture & Debating Society, 1953–54, no. 405). pp. 13.
The complexities—and perplexities—of current transport problems informally presented by the Minister of Transport, with intermittent references to parliamentary influence and control over railways in the past.

11228 MINISTRY OF TRANSPORT AND CIVIL AVIATION. Railways Reorganisation Scheme. (The submission of the British Transport Commission to the . . . Minister of Transport and Civil Aviation: Reorganisation of Railways). *H.M.S.O.*, 1954. (Cmd 9191). pp. 22. Introduction by the Minister of Transport followed by the full text of the B.T.C.'s Scheme: pt. 1, Explanatory statement; pt. 2, The British Transport Commission (Organisation) Scheme, 1954.

11229 WATKINSON, H. The implications of the Railway Modernisation Plan. Proceedings of the British Railways (W.R.) London Lecture & Debating Society, 1956–57, no. 434. pp. 10, with discussion.

Author, 'Minister of Transport & Civil Aviation'.

11230 LABOUR PARTY. Public enterprise: Labour's review of the nationalised industries. *London: Labour Party*, June 1957. pp. 60.

pp. 16–21, Transport.

11231 POLITICAL AND ECONOMIC PLANNING. Paying for the railways. *London: P.E.P.*, 1958. (Planning, vol. 24, no. 429, 19 December 1958, pp. 279–307).

'The long drift of the railways into insolvency and the distortion of the national transport facilities that has accompanied it must not be allowed to continue. Above all, a subsidy without a policy must be avoided.'

11232 DENHOLM, B. Rail and road competition in Great Britain. *London: London School of Economics & Political Science*. 1959. pp. 115, with 56 detailed tables. Reproduced typescript in printed covers.

An essay submitted for the Rees Jeffreys Studentship for Research into Transport, 1958–59.

11233 NATIONAL UNION OF RAILWAYMEN. Planning transport for you. *London: N.U.R.*, [1959]. pp. 66, with 3 appendices.

Transport problems past & present, and proposals for reforms. Appendix C (pp. 61–6), 'What others said', consists of quotations by prominent persons relating to transport, from 1906 to 1956.

11234 POLITICAL AND ECONOMIC PLANNING. Growth in the British economy: a study of economic problems and policies in contemporary Britain. *London: P.E.P.; Allen & Unwin*, 1960. pp. xii, 256.

pp. 74 . . . 95 *et passim*, railways.

11235 WANSBROUGH-JONES, L. The way ahead. Proceedings of the British Railways (W.R.) London Lecture & Debating Society, 1960–61, no. 468. pp. 12, with discussion.

Author, 'Secretary General, B.T.C.'

11236 OWEN, W. The Transport Revolution in Europe. *Washington: Brookings Institution*, 1961. (Reprint, 53). pp. 279–311.

A reprint of ch. 9 of *Europe's Needs and Resources: trends and prospects in eighteen countries*, by J. F. Dewhurst and others, 1961.

pp. 284–91, 'Rail transport', with 7 tables.

Increasing volume of movement in the 1950s seen as both cause and effect of the expansion of European economies, technological advances, mounting trade and rising prosperity.

11237 RATTER, J. 'All change!'. (Proceedings of the British Railways (W.R.) London Lecture & Debating Society, 1961–62, no. 470. pp. 8, with discussion.

Author, 'Member, B.T.C.'.

The continual need to adapt railways to economic, social and technological changes.

11238 BAXTER, R. D. Railway extension and its results, *in* Essays in Economic History, vol. 3, 1962, ed. by E. M. Carus-Wilson, pp. 29–67, with tables.

Written in 1866. In his conclusion the future of railways is considered.

11239 LIBERAL PARTY. TRANSPORT COMMITTEE. Transport: a report submitted to the Liberal Party by a committee under the chairmanship of Arthur Holt, M.P. [*London: Liberal Publications Dept.*], September 1962. pp. 76.

Proposed reforms.

11240 NATIONAL UNION OF RAILWAYMEN. The future of British railways: is this what you want? [*London: N.U.R.*, 1962]. pp. 6, with 3 maps.

The maps depict the railway network in 1962 and as it might be if the Beeching Plan were to be carried out. 'Putting the need for a profit first means putting the needs of the people second.'

11241 KOLSEN, H. M. The economics and public control of road–rail competition, with special reference to Great Britain, United States and Australia. Thesis, Ph. D., University of London (L.S.E.), 1962–3.

11242 BRANCH LINE RE-INVIGORATION SOCIETY. Can bus replace train?: a commentary on railway-replacement omnibus services [by G. R. Croughton]. *Upminster: the Society*, August 1963. pp. 21. Reproduced typescript.

—— another edn, *B.L.R.S.*, 1977. pp. 24, with 6 point-to-point map diagrams & 16 notes. Appendix: Railway services which could be substituted by subsidised bus services.

A re-statement of the case for retaining railway services, based on the work of the same name by G. R. Croughton and published by the Society in 1963, with added comments on the continued policy of rail closures and allegedly inadequate alternative bus services.

11243 BRANCH LINE RE-INVIGORATION SOCIETY. Unprofitable lines?: a financial study of certain railway passenger services in Somerset, Dorset and Hampshire. *London: the Society*, October 1963. pp. 26, with diagrams & a map. Reproduced typescript.

The case against threatened closures by BR. The validity of revenue and cost figures supplied by BR to objectors is questioned.

11244 FERRIS, P. Beeching's revolt: inside story. *London: Observer* [newspaper], 1963. (Observer Week End Review, March 24, 1963). pp. 21 & 36.

—— How Beeching did it. *London: Observer*, 1963. (Observer Week End Review, March 31st, 1963). pp. 21 & 24.

11245 FOSTER, C. D. The transport problem. *London, Glasgow: Blackie*, 1963, pp. xii, 354, with 18 charts & diagrams, 5 tables & 218 notes.

An introduction to the principles of transport economics.
part 2 (pp. 69–161), 'The rail problem'.
—— 2nd edn, rev. *London: Croom Helm*, 1975. pp. 362, with 283 notes. pt. 2 (pp. 69–161).

11246 MINISTRY OF TRANSPORT. The transport needs of Great Britain in the next twenty years: report of a group under the chairmanship of Sir Robert Hall. *London: HMSO*, 1963. pp. 27, with 8 tables.

11247 MUNBY, D. L. Road and rail track costs. *Manchester: Manchester Statistical Society*, [1963]. pp. 41, with 9 tables, & notes.
A paper read to the Society on 14th November 1962.

11248 NATIONAL COUNCIL ON INLAND TRANSPORT. Rail closure procedure: preparing a case of objection. *London: N.C.I.T.*, [1963]. pp. 8, with specimen questionnaire.

11249 NATIONAL COUNCIL ON INLAND TRANSPORT. The road and rail crisis: correspondence between the Minister of Transport, Ernest Marples, and Lord Stonham, Chairman of the National Council on Inland Transport. *London: N.C.I.T.*, 1963. pp. 11.
Two letters dated February 1963 and extracts from a memorandum to the Prime Minister.

11250 RAILWAY DEVELOPMENT ASSOCIATION. Statement on 'Reshaping the British railways'. *London: R.D.A.*, 1963. pp. 6.

11251 TRANSPORT is everyone's problem. *London: Socialist Commentary Publications*, [1963]. pp. xli.
Reprinted from *Socialist Commentary*, April 1963.
Report of a group of transport experts, town-planners and economists on rail and road problems. (Hugh Cleggy, Denys L. Munby, Christopher Foster, Ernest Davies, Richard Edmonds, Malcolm McEwen, Betty Trevena and Peter Hall.)

11252 TRANSPORT USERS' CONSULTATIVE COMMITTEE. The Re-shaping of British Railways: T.U.C.C. procedure: notes of meeting held at the Great Western Royal Hotel, Paddington on Thursday 2nd May, 1963. pp. 10,4. Reproduced typescript.

11253 WILSON, H. The future of British transport. *London: Labour Party*, May [1963]. pp. 8.
Speech in the House of Commons as Leader of the Opposition during the debate of April 30th 1963 on the Beeching Report.

11254 MARGETTS, F. C. The benefits to be derived from a re-shaped railway system. (Proceedings of the British Railways (W.R.) London Lecture & Debating Society, 1963–64, no. 484). pp. 11, with discussion.
Author, 'Member of the B.R. Board'.

11255 DANIEL, A. W. T. The Beeching and Buchanan reports. *London: Railway Development Association*, 1964. la. 8°. pp. 4.
A talk to Weymouth Civic Society, January 16th, 1964.

11256 HAMMOND, R. Railways in the new air age. *London: London University Press*, 1964. pp. 154, with 53 illus, maps & diagrams.

11257 NATIONAL COUNCIL ON INLAND TRANSPORT. A future policy for Britain's transport. *London: N.C.I.T.*, [October 1964]. pp. 15, with 4 plates.

11258 ALLEN, C. J. The future of railways, *in* Journal of the Royal Society of Arts, vol. 113 (no. 5105, April 1965), pp. 334–51, with 6 illus & discussion.
A paper read to the Society on 3rd February 1965. Chairman, G. F. Fiennes, General Manager, BR (WR).
Modern developments in railway operation and technology in France, Germany, Italy, Japan & the U.S.A. and their value as indicators for planning on the railways of Britain.

11259 BRITISH RAILWAYS. The development of the major railway trunk routes. *London: B.R.*, February 1965. la. 8°. pp. 100, with 27 col. maps (contemporary and projected (1984)), 13 tables, and additional tables (some folded) and diagrams in appendices A, B, C & D.

11260 CALVERT, R. The future of Britain's railways. Foreword by Lord Stonham. *London: Allen & Unwin*, 1965. pp. 175, with 16 plates, 14 maps & diagrams & 3 tables in text.

11261 RADICE, J. Transport. *London: Fabian Society*, March 1965. (Young Fabian Pamphlet, 8). pp. 28.
An outline of basic 'Transport in Society' principles including suggested reforms for railways. A Socialist view.

11262 RAILWAY CONVERSION LEAGUE. No alternative: the case for transforming Britain's railways into motor roads; submitted to the Ministry of Transport, July 1965. *London: R.C.L.*, July 1965. pp. 48, with 15 illus & 2 maps.

11263 SHARP, C. The problem of transport. *London: Pergamon Press*, 1965. pp. 202, with 35 tables, 10 diagrams & a bibliography (37 sources).
A general survey, but with particular emphasis on passenger transport by road and rail in Britain. The main problem: to meet demands upon transport by the most economical means.

11264 TRADES UNION CONGRESS. Transport policy. *London: T.U.C.*, 1965. pp. 36.
'The range of considerations which must be taken into account in arriving at a coherent transport policy.'

11265 HUXLEY, G. L. The plight of the railways. *Belfast: the author*, October 1966. pp. 8.

A discussion of the proposals embodied in *Transport Policy* (Cmnd 3057). Professor Huxley writes as President of the Great Central Railway Association, and in the Appendix (p. 8) which is reprinted from the *Yorkshire Post* of 9 September 1966, he deplores the threatened closure of the Great Central Railway, calling this 'an exploitation of the ignorance of the public.'

11266 MINISTRY OF TRANSPORT. Transport policy. *London: HMSO*, [1966]. (Cmnd 3057). pp. iii, 36, with table.

11267 DANIEL, A. W. T. Transport in Great Britain today. *London: National Council on Inland Transport*, 1967. pp. 12, with 5 tables, 3 charts.

Author, Chairman of the N.C.I.T.

11268 ELLISON, A. P. The allocation of resources in the public transport sector: a case study of public passenger transport competition between air, rail and road over the London–Glasgow route, 1960–65. Thesis, M.A., University of Leicester, 1967.

11269 LABOUR PARTY. Action: transport. *London: Labour Party*, 1967. pp. 50.

Co-ordination and integration of public transport with planning for social as well as economic needs.

pp. 10–21, Railways.

11270 MINISTRY OF TRANSPORT. Public transport and traffic, by the Ministry of Transport, Scottish Development Department, Welsh Office. *London: HMSO*, 1967. (Cmnd 3481). pp. iii, 41.

Includes railways.

11271 MINISTRY OF TRANSPORT. Railway policy. *London: HMSO*, [1967]. (Cmnd 3439). pp. 69.

11272 WHITE Elephant and (Barbara) Castle: Government threat to transport. *London: Aims of Industry*, August [1967]. pp. [6].

Barbara Castle, Minister of Transport, 1965–1968.

11273 INTEGRATED transport: myth or necessity? Proceedings of the 9th Symposium, July 1968. *Cranfield: Cranfield Society*, 1968. pp. 101.

pp. 36–42, Transport system elements: rail, by A.E.T. Griffiths, Planning Director, BR.

11274 KOLSEN, H. M. The economics and control of road–rail competition: a critical study of theory and practice in the United States of America, Great Britain, and Australia. [*Sydney*]: *Sydney University Press*, 1968. pp. 182, with 196 notes.

A study of theories, aims and actual effects of various methods of trying to regulate road–rail competition.

ch. 8 (pp. 121–31), Regulation in Great Britain.

11275 SHERMAN, A. V. Everybody's business: the economic consequences of Mrs Barbara Castle. *London: Aims of Industry*. [1968]. pp. 16.

A critical analysis of Barbara Castle's Transport Bill (resulting in the Transport Act, 1968).

11276 STRUB, U. A. Reshaping British Railways. [*London*]: *Union Publications*, 1968. sm. 8°. pp. 22.

Proposed radical reforms, including the separating of fast and slow line traffics, with slow lines served by 'trainlets'—light trains travelling up to 40 mph at frequent intervals, with signals only at junctions. (Not to be confused with *The Reshaping of British Railways* by Richard Beeching, 1963 ('The Beeching Report').)

11277 WALKER, P. Transport policy. *London: Conservative Political Centre*, May 1968. (Outline series, 4). pp. 11.

11278 WALTERS, A. A. Integration in freight transport. *London: Institute of Economic Affairs*, 1968. (Research Monographs, 15). pp. 99, with 22 tables & 95 notes.

Concepts of road and rail integration since 1920.

11279 BONHAM-CARTER, J. Forward into the seventies. (Proceedings of the British Railways (W.R.) London Lecture & Debating Society, 1968/69, no. 499). pp. 9.

Author, 'General Manager, W.R'.

11280 DANIEL, A. W. T. and CALVERT, R. Electrify now! *London: National Council on Inland Transport*, November 1969. pp. 16, with 5 tables.

The case for further railway electrification, especially between Crewe and Glasgow.

11281 O'FLAHERTY, C. A. Passenger transport, present and future: an inaugural lecture. *Leeds: Leeds University Press*, 1969. pp. 76, with 15 illus on 12 plates, 15 diagrams, graphs & maps, & a bibliography (52 sources).

Includes monorail and other developments in laterally-controlled vehicles. The overall need for public and governmental co-operation in association with technological progress.

11282 PONSONBY, G. J. Transport policy: co-ordination through competition. *London: Institute of Economic Affairs*, 1969. (Hobart Paper, 49). pp. 66, with 4 tables, 45 notes & a bibliography (36 sources).

11283 RAILWAY CONVERSION LEAGUE. A survey of railway conversion in Great Britain and Northern Ireland. *London: R.C.L.*, 1969. pp. 7, with map & table.

Schemes completed and others proposed.

11284 BRITISH RAILWAYS BOARD. British Rail is travelling, 1970. *London: B.R.; Shepperton: Ian Allan*, [1970]. la. 8°. pp. 50, with many illus (mostly col.). Map inside cover.

A brochure publicising BR's plans following the passing of the *Transport Act, 1968*.

11285 LAWRENCE, R. L. E. The railways in the 1970s. pp. 14. Reproduced typescript.
Paper read to the Institute of Transport by the Chairman and General Manager, BR (LMR), 5th January 1970.

11286 RAILWAY CONVERSION LEAGUE. The conversion of railways into roads in the United Kingdom, 1970. London: R.C.L., [1970]. pp. 28, with 10 illus, map & a detailed table.
Conversions completed and others proposed, with comments and recommendations.

11287 REID, G. L. and ALLEN, K. Nationalized industries. Harmondsworth: Penguin Books, 1970. pp. 196.
ch. 5 (pp. 106–29), 'the railway industry'.

11288 SHARP, E. Transport planning: the men for the job; a report to the Ministry of Transport by Lady Sharp, January 1970. London: H.M.S.O., 1970. pp. v, 138, with illus.
The manpower needs of urban transport planning.

11289 WRIGLEY, D. and GEORGE, A. Transport. London: Liberal Publications Dept, [1970]. (Liberal Focus series, 4). pp. 14. Cover title: A realistic approach to Transport.

11290 McCULLAGH, P. S. Transport in modern Britain. London: Oxford University Press, 1971. (Changing World series). obl. format. pp. 64, with 41 illus, 57 line drawings, maps, plans, diagrams & graphs.
ch. 1 (pp. 5–18), The railways.
—— 2nd edn. Oxford U.P., 1975. (Changing World series). obl. format. pp. 64.

11291 SOUTH EAST JOINT PLANNING TEAM. Strategic plan for the South East: studies. London: H.M.S.O., for the Dept of the Environment.
vol. 3, Transportation. 1971. tall 8°. pp. xvii, 198, with 109 tables, 100 col. maps, graphs & diagrams.

11292 DEPARTMENT OF THE ENVIRONMENT. Transport and the environment. London: D.o.E., September 1972. pp. [8]. A printed folder, with 6 illus.
Contemporary transport planning objectives.

11293 KALLA-BISHOP, P. M. Future railways: an adventure in engineering. London: IPC Transport Press, for the Railway Magazine, 1972. pp. [4], 124, with frontis, 15 illus & 4 drawings: bibliography, p. 124. Cover title: Future railways and guided transport.

11294 TRANSPORT 2000. A Transport Manifesto: action now! London: Transport 2000, [1972?]. s. sh. pp. [2].
A summary of priorities for transport reform, including railways.

11295 BROMHEAD, P. A. The great white elephant at Maplin Sands: the neglect of comprehensive transport planning in government decision-making. London: Paul Elek, 1973. pp. 296, with 21 tables, many notes & a bibliography (94 sources).
Of the 17 chapters, 4 discuss railways, and the Channel Tunnel.

11296 CALVERT, R. Transport dis-integrated. London: R. Calvert, 1973. pp. vi, 144, with 69 tables & diagrams & 33 line illus.
Appended is a pamphlet: Improving London's Rail Transport, by R. Calvert: a reprint from British Engineer, November 1970. pp. 7.
A spirited and detailed statement of the case for railways and waterways as opposed to road transport in planning.

11297 CATON, M. P. L. and STANLEY, J. M. Railways in the seventies . . . , with a foreword by John Arlott. London: Railway Invigoration Society, 1973. pp. 24, with 6 illus.
The case for utilizing and developing rail transport.

11298 COMMITTEE FOR ENVIRONMENTAL CONSERVATION. Transport and the environment. London: the Committee, 1973. pp. [32]. la. 8°.
Railways, p. [16] et passim.

11299 COUNCIL FOR THE PROTECTION OF RURAL ENGLAND. Transport: co-ordination or chaos? London: the Council, [1973]. pp. 35. Title on cover only.
'We consider that this country is becoming dangerously over-dependent on roads and road transport'. pp. 19–22. Alternatives to roads: rail.

11300 GLADWIN, D. D. The canals of Britain, with illustrations by J. K. Ebblewhite. London: Batsford, 1973. pp. 254, with 58 illus on 32 plates.
ch. 8 (pp. 162–201), 'Outside influences' (railways, pp. 163, 172–80).

11301 HAMPSHIRE TECHNICAL RESEARCH INDUSTRIAL AND COMMERCIAL SERVICE. Urban transport innovations: a bibliography. Southampton: Southampton Central Library, 1973. pp. viii, 72.
800 sources (books, periodicals & reports, 1967–August 1972) relating to 44 modern forms of transport, tracked and otherwise, for urban and inter-urban communication.

11302 MARSH, R. The future of British Railways. London: Royal Society of Arts, 1973. (Journal of the R.S.A., vol. 120, Dec. 1971–Nov. 1972; Paper no. 5190, May 1972) pp. 370–81 (Discussion, pp. 378–81).
Richard William Marsh, Chairman of British Railways Board, 1971–6.

11303 BRUTON, M. J. The spirit and purpose of planning. London: Hutchinson, 1974. pp. 233.
ch. 7 (pp. 169–204), 'Transport planning', with 7 diagrams and a bibliography (48 sources).

11304 INDEPENDENT COMMISSION ON TRANS-
PORT. Changing directions: the report of
the Independent Commission on Transport.
London: Coronet Books, 1974. pp. 365,
with many tables & notes.
The threat to national well-being of increasing
transport problems, with an introduction by Hugh
Montefiore, Bishop of Kingston-on-Thames and
Chairman of the Commission. Executive Secret-
ary, Stephen Plowden.

11305 NATIONAL COUNCIL ON INLAND TRANS-
PORT. Energy crisis: account of speeches at
a public meeting (March 12th, 1974). *London: N.C.I.T.*, 1974. pp. 8. Reproduced
typescript.
Includes (p.5), 'The future of the railways'.

11306 RAILWAY CONVERSION LEAGUE. Railways into roads: what the League said in
1958 and what the experts are saying now.
London: R.C.L., 1974. pp. 4, with text
extending onto inside covers. Title from
cover.
'Everything has gone to prove how right the
League then was.'

11307 RAILWAY DEVELOPMENT SOCIETY.
Railfreight or Juggernaut? *London:
R.D.S.*, [ca. 1974]. pp. [4], with 5 illus.
'A double-track railway has 3 to 4 times the
carrying capacity of a 6-lane motorway but only
requires one third of the land space.'

11308 TRADES UNION CONGRESS. TRANSPORT
INDUSTRIES COMMITTEE. TUC statements on Transport: integration of transport; British Rail finance; urban transport.
London: T.U.C., 1974. pp. 31.
—— another edn. TUC statements on
Transport: integration of transport; urban
transport; civil aviation; airports policy;
rural transport and bus service licensing.
[*London: T.U.C.*, 1978?]. pp. 51.

11309 TRANSPORT 2000. British Rail, 1975–
2000. *London: Transport 2000*, [1974?]. pp.
8.
The environmental, social, energy conservation
and material resource arguments for the retention
and development of railways.

11310 TRANSPORT 2000. Policy statement. *London: Transport 2000*, [1974]. A printed
folder.
Of four stated aims, the second is: To pursue
the development and promotion of rail transport
within an integrated transport system.

11311 GWILLIAM, K. M. and MACKIE, P. J.
Economics and transport policy. *London:
Allen & Unwin*, 1975. pp. x, 390, with 37
tables & many bibliogr. notes.
An overall survey of current problems of inland
transport and considerations on the means whereby improved inter-modal efficiency might be
achieved.

11312 TRANSPORT 2000. An electrifying case.
London: Transport 2000, [1975]. pp. 8, with
map.

The urgent need for nation-wide electrification
of railways.

11313 TRANSPORT 2000. A transport policy for
today. *London: Transport 2000*, 1975. pp.
8. Title from cover.

11314 TRANSPORT 2000. Why we need the
railways more than ever before. (Blueprint
for British Rail). *London: Transport 2000*,
1975. pp. 13, with 7 tables & a graph.
'Contents' on inside of front cover.

11315 ADVISORY COUNCIL ON ENERGY CON-
SERVATION. TRANSPORT WORKING
GROUP. Passenger transport: short and
medium-term considerations. (T.W.G. Pap-
er, no. 2). *London: H.M.S.O., for Dept of
Energy*, 1976. (Energy Paper, no. 10). pp.
iv, 16.
Includes rail.

11316 ASSOCIATED SOCIETY OF LOCOMOTIVE
ENGINEERS AND FIREMEN. Transport for
the nation; ASLEF's reply to the Transport
Policy Consultation Document. *London:
ASLEF*, 1976. pp. v, Ill. Foreword by Ray
Buckton, General Secretary of ASLEF.
Compiled with the co-operation of the
Labour Research Department.
Detailed comments on the Ministry of Trans-
port's *Transport Policy: a consultation document*
(1976).

11317 BRITISH RAILWAYS. An opportunity for
change: comments on the government consultation document. [*London*]: *B.R.*, 1976.
pp. 14.
A summary of the BR Board's full report.
Transport policy: an opportunity for change
(1976).

11318 BRITISH RAILWAYS. Transport policy: an
opportunity for change: comments by British Railways Board on the government
consultation document (with summary).
London: B.R., [1976]. tall 8°. pp. 87.
Proposals offered as a basis for 'a major
reappraisal of the nation's approach to transport
policy in general and railways in particular'
(Richard Marsh, Chairman BR, in the Foreword).

11319 DEPARTMENT OF THE ENVIRONMENT.
Transport Policy: a consultation document.
London: H.M.S.O. 2 vols.
vol. 1, with a foreword by Anthony Crosland,
1976. pp. v, 98.
vol. 2, Technical papers 'intended to give more
detailed, technical background to the main consultative document', 1976. pp. v, 130, with illus.

11320 HALL, P. and SMITH, E. Better use of
railways. *Reading: University of Reading,
Dept of Geography*, 1976. (Reading Geographical Papers, 43). pp. 132.
'The main engineering and economic considerations affecting the conversion of a railway to a
road and the replacement of trains with buses and
lorries.' Five case studies are made within the
Eastern Region of BR.

11321 HERIOT WATT UNIVERSITY. DEPART-
MENT OF ECONOMICS. Comments on
Transport Policy: a consultation document
(1976), by Peter Clarke and Leslie Simpson.
Edinburgh: the Department, 1976. pp. 20.

11322 LIBERAL PARTY. The role of transport in
our society: the Liberal Party's response to
the Orange Paper 'Transport [Policy]: a
consultation document', July 1976. *London:
Liberal Party*, August 1976. pp. 4. Reproduced typescript.
Transport must be treated as an integral part of
the nation's economic structure, and planning
should be broadened and re-cast on that basis; the
views of the Liberal Party's Transport Panel
(chairman, Gavin MacPherson).

11323 LONDON TRANSPORT. Comments on
'Transport Policy: a consultation document'. *London: L.T.*, August 1976. pp.
[17]. Reproduced typescript.

11324 NASH, C. A. Public versus private transport. *London: Macmillan*, 1976. (Macmillan Studies in Economics). pp. 94, with a
bibliography (130 sources).
The economic & environmental characteristics
of public and of private transport modes, and the
potential for modifying modal split problems in
each main sector of the transport market.

11325 NATIONAL CONSUMER COUNCIL. Prior-
ity for passengers: comments . . . on transport policy. (Research: Jenny Potter). *London: N.C.C.*, August 1976. pp. 18. Reproduced typescript, no covers.
A report, for the Department of Prices and
Consumer Protection, of an enquiry made to 55
organisations and individuals who were invited to
comment on the Government's *Transport Policy:
a consultation document* (HMSO, 1976).

11326 NATIONAL COUNCIL ON INLAND TRANS-
PORT. Transport policy: an account of
speeches and discussion at a conference
held in the Council Chamber at the Castle,
Shrewsbury, on Friday 9th April 1976.
London: N.C.I.T., 1976. pp. [8].
Speakers: Eric Robinson (councillor, Shrop-
shire C.C.), Christopher Hall (Director of the
Council for the Protection of Rural England),
J. S. Gilks (Assistant Secretary, District Councils
Association), Gerard Fiennes (formerly General
Manager BR (WR) & BR (ER)).
The meeting was held in the week preceding the
publication of the Government's *Transport Policy:
a consultation document* (1976) and was concerned
generally with plans for transport, especially rural
transport, the current world-wide interest in rapid
transit and suburban railway construction, and the
provision of long-distance passenger and freight
train services.

11327 NATIONAL UNION OF RAILWAYMEN. A
policy for transport: submissions to the
Secretary of State for the Environment . . .
on the consultation document. *London:
[N.U.R.]*, 1976. pp. 52.
The case against further cuts in rail services, the
need for increased investment and in the volume
of freight transport by rail.

11328 POLITICAL AND ECONOMIC PLANNING
(P.E.P.). Transport Policy: a consultation
document: memorandum of comment from
Dr. Mayer Hillman and Anne Whalley.
London: PEP, 1976. pp. 13.

11329 RAILWAY CONVERSION LEAGUE. Transport Policy: comments by the Railway
Conversion League, Ltd, on the Government's consultation document published in
April 1976. *Chertsey: R.C.L.*, July 1976. pp.
20. Cover title: Conversion vindicated . . .

11330 RAILWAY DEVELOPMENT ASSOCIATION.
Transport: a policy for co-ordination. *The
Association*, and *Walsall Area Passenger
Action Group* and *West Midlands Action
Committee for Public Transport*, 1976. pp.
40.
Response to the Government's *Transport Poli-
cy: a consultation document* (1976).

11331 RAILWAY INVIGORATION SOCIETY. Transport Policy: a consultation document,
observations to the Secretary of State.
London: the Society, 1976. pp. 9.

11332 SCOTTISH ASSOCIATION FOR PUBLIC
TRANSPORT. The Green Paper on trans-
port policy: a critical review. *Glasgow: the
Association*, July 1976. (Study Papers, 7).
pp. 29.
Concerning the Dept of the Environment's
Transport Policy: a consultation document (1976).

11333 SCOTTISH ASSOCIATION FOR PUBLIC
TRANSPORT. The review of transport policy: a submission to Government. *Glasgow:
the Association*, February 1976. pp. 12, with
2 maps.

11334 SHARP, C. H. and JENNINGS, A. Transport and the environment. *Leicester: Leicester University Press*, 1976. pp. [viii], 229,
with 52 tables, 4 diagrams, & a bibliography
(185 sources).
A study of the social costs of road and rail
transport and the unwanted by-products produced
by transport services (pollution, congestion, noise,
etc.), and the economic and technical problems of
measures devised to lessen them.
ch. 9 (pp. 167–95), 'Railways and the environment'; also pp. 211–2, 'The road and rail solu-
tions'.

11335 SOUTH YORKSHIRE PASSENGER TRANS-
PORT EXECUTIVE. Observations on the
Government's Transport Policy consultation document. *Sheffield: the Executive*,
1976. pp. 14.

11336 TRANSPORT FOR SOCIETY [Conference,
London, 1975]. Transport for society: proceedings of the conference organized by the
Institution of Civil Engineers, 11–13
November, 1975. *London: I.C.E.*, 1976. la.
8°. pp. 175.
Railways and air transport are not considered in
detail in any of the fourteen papers and discussions.

11337 TRANSPORT 2000. Transport policy tomorrow: Transport 2000's views on the consultation document. *London: Transport 2000*, 1976. pp. 58.

11338 TYNESIDE ACTION COMMITTEE AGAINST THE CUTS. No public transport cuts!: a response to the Government's consultation document on Transport. *The Committee*, 1976. pp. 27.

11339 UNIVERSITY OF GLASGOW. DEPARTMENT OF SOCIAL AND ECONOMIC RESEARCH. Memorandum on the consultation document 'Transport Policy', by H. Gillender. *Glasgow: the Department*, 1976. pp. 40 & appendices.

11340 WHITE, P. R. Planning for public transport. *London: Hutchinson*, 1976. (Built Environment series). pp. 224, with 12 illus on 4 plates, 39 diagrams, tables & maps; bibliography (ca. 150 sources noted & discussed).
    A general, yet concise, survey of the national transport scene: organization & control, urban & rural problems; economic pressures set against the need for improvement and progress: inter-city railways and rapid-transit.

11341 BAGWELL, P. S. Transport: private privilege or public service? *London: Christian Socialist Movement*, [1977]. pp. 14.
    Includes railways. The case for an integrated public transport system.

11342 CENTRAL TRANSPORT CONSULTATIVE COMMITTEE. Report on the British Railways Board's proposals for the integration and co-ordination of some bus and rail services. *London: the Committee*, March 1977. pp. 7.
    Appendix: Integration and co-ordination of bus and train services: a proposal by the British Railways Board. pp. 2. Reproduced typescript.

11343 COOPER, J. C. and SPAVEN, D. L. Railways into busways won't go: a re-examination of two case studies. *London: Polytechnic of Central London, Transport Studies Group*, March 1977. (Discussion Paper, 6). pp. 53, with maps & tables. Reproduced typescript.
    The Crouch Valley line and the Colchester to Sudbury line (both on the Eastern Region of BR).

11344 DENNEY, M. London's waterways. *London: Batsford*, 1977. pp. 192, with 43 illus on 24 plates.
    Includes railway/canal relationships.

11345 DEPARTMENT OF TRANSPORT. The role of British Rail in public transport: the Government's response to the first report from the Select Committee on Nationalised Industries, Session 1976–77 (HC Paper 305). *London: HMSO*, 1977. (Cmnd 7038). pp. 41.

11346 DEPARTMENT OF TRANSPORT. Transport Policy (Department of Transport; Scottish Development Department; Welsh Office). *London: HMSO*, 1977. (Cmnd 6836). pp. vi, 76.

11347 FOWLER, N. The Right Track: a paper on Conservative transport policy, by Norman Fowler, M.P. *London: Conservative Political Centre*, September 1977. (Publication 612). pp. 39.
    pp. 10–13, Making sense of the railways.

11348 LAMBERT, C. M. Transport Policy: consultation document, 1976: responses to the Government's transport policy consultation document: a select list of material. *London: Department of the Environment*, 1977. (Dept. of the Environment Library. Bibliographies, no. 17D). tall 8°. pp. 27. Reproduced typescript in printed cover.
    Bibliographical descriptions of a selected 114 responses (as monographs or as periodical articles) from a wide range of organizations. Of these, monographs from bodies directly concerned with rail transport are incorporated into section K of this present work, but as for others, C. M. Lambert's generous summary notes appended to many entries will enable students of railway development in the 1970s to decide which are likely to be relevant to particular avenues of enquiry.

11349 MacPHERSON, G. Transport: its role in society. *London: Liberal Publication Department*, February 1977. (Study Paper, 5). tall 8°. pp. 5.

11350 NATIONAL COUNCIL ON INLAND TRANSPORT. Comments on the Transport Bill, 1977. *London: the Council*, [1977]. pp. 3. Reproduced typescript.
    County transport planning. General approval for the proposals.

11351 PASSENGER transport and the environment: the integration of public passenger transport with the urban environment; edited by Roy Cresswell. *London: Leonard Hill*, 1977. pp. xvi, 299, with 87 illus & diagrams, 27 tables & 83 notes.
    Proceedings of the conference, University of York, March 1976, organised by the Construction Industry Conference Centre in association with the Royal Institute of British Architects, Institution of Municipal Engineers, Royal Town Planning Institute, Institution of Highway Engineers, Society of Industrial Artists & Designers.
    Twelve papers, with discussions. Rail transport is not the subject of any particular paper but railways, rapid transit, underground railways and tramways are essential ingredients of the work as a whole.

11352 ADVISORY COUNCIL ON ENERGY CONSERVATION. TRANSPORT WORKING GROUP. Energy for transport: long-term possibilities. *London: H.M.S.O., for Dept. of Energy*, 1978. (T.W.G. Paper, no. 8) (Energy Paper, no. 26). pp. iv, 20.
    Energy for tracked vehicles considered, p.10.

11353 CRESSWELL, R. Rural transport and country planning, edited by Roy Cresswell. *Glasgow: L. Hill*, 1978.

Proceedings of the conference held at the University of Nottingham in March 1977. Railways: *passim* and pp. 139–47, 'Rural rail services' by P. A. Keen.

11354 LABOUR PARTY. Transport policy: statement by the National Executive Committee, June 1978. *London: Labour Party*, 1978. pp. 10. Text extends onto covers. Reproduced typescript.

11355 PARKER, P. Operational developments and interface: Rail, by Peter Parker, Chairman, British Railways Board, *in* International Transport: the common problems [conference], London, 2, 3, & 4 October 1978: Speakers' Papers. *London: Financial Times Conference Organisation*, 1978. pp. 65–73.

Railways and the integration of transport.

11356 SCOPE FOR THE USE OF CERTAIN OLD-ESTABLISHED URBAN TRANSPORT TECHNIQUES: TRAMS AND TROLLEY BUSES [Conference, Paris, 1977]. Report. *Paris: European Conference of Ministers of Transport*; London: [*H.M.S.O.*], 1978. (Round Table on Transport Economics, 38th). pp. 73, with illus.

Proposed re-introduction of tramways.

11357 SMITH, E. Better use of railways: comments and rejoinders, edited by Edward Smith. (Foreword by Peter Hall). *Reading: University of Reading, Department of Geography*, 1978. (Reading Geographical Papers, 63). pp. 89.

Detailed response to the body of 'far from unexpected' criticism directed against *Better Use of Railways* (Reading Geographical Papers, 43, 1976).

11358 THOMAS, R. Future transport. *London: Cassell*, 1978. (Future Environments in Britain series). pp. 64, with 75 illus (photos, diagrams, maps, plans & charts), & 6 tables; bibliography (32 sources & addresses).

A study manual. 'Fewer and more expensive rail services, congested roads and dearer petrol, neglected waterways and air services that only businessmen can afford to use—is this future fact or fiction?' (Preface).

ch. 4 (pp. 32–42), 'The Impermanent Way', with 8 illus, 6 diagrams, 4 maps, 2 tables & 4 bibliogr. refs (p.63).

11359 DALGLEISH, A. A solution to our transport problems. *Railway Conversion League*, [1979]. pp. [8], with 7 illus, maps, 2 tables, 14 notes.

Reprinted from the *Journal of the Institution of Highway Engineers*, October 1979. The case for converting railways into roads.

11360 KOMPFNER, P. Notes on light rail transit in Great Britain. *Crowthorne: Transport & Road Research Laboratory*, 1979. (T.R.R.L. Supplementary Report, 482). tall 8°. pp. 38, with illus, maps, drawings, tables & a bibliography (40 sources).

The present state and future prospects of light rail transit systems and the long-term economic advantage of LRT over buses, although it is thought that in towns, rail-less electric vehicles (battery or trolley) would be even better. The Blackpool tramway system and the Tyne & Wear Metro are described and commented upon.

11361 LINDSAY, J. The Trent & Mersey Canal. *Newton Abbot: David & Charles*, 1979. pp. 182, with 16 illus on 8 plates, & in text, 10 maps & plans, 233 notes.

ch. 5 (pp. 115–34), Railway competition. Index has entries for individual railways.

11362 NATIONAL COUNCIL ON INLAND TRANSPORT. Why the Sheffield–Woodhead–Manchester route should not be closed. *London: the Council*, Dec. 1979. pp. 6. Reproduced typescript.

The already electrified Woodhead route should not be closed while plans for a nation-wide extension of electrification are under consideration. Instead, it should be converted to 25,000 v. a-c and linked to the planned Bedford to Sheffield electrification.

11363 RAILWAY DEVELOPMENT SOCIETY. Railway electrification: why we need it NOW. *London: the Society*, [1980?]. la. 8°. pp. [4], with 6 illus.

K 1   RAILWAYS AND SOCIETY

Railways and the life of the people—Urban and suburban development—Commuting—Workmen's trains—Holiday areas and increased facilities for travel and recreation made possible by railways—Excursions—Sunday trains controversy (19th century)—Rail closures and the community

11364–11448

Historical   11364–82
Contemporaneous   11383–448

Historical

11364   PIMLOTT, J. A. R. The Englishman's holiday: a social history. *London: Faber*, 1947. pp. 318, with 37 illus on 24 plates & 17 in text, & an evaluative bibliography (pp. 284–301).
Index has 36 page refs under 'Railways'.

11365   ASHWORTH, W. The genesis of modern town planning . . . *London: Routledge & Kegan Paul*, 1954. pp. xii, 259.
pp. 147–52, the influence of railways on suburban development.

11366   BOVILL, E. W. The England of Nimrod and Surtees. *London: Oxford University Press*, 1959. pp. xii, 188, with col. frontis, 16 illus on 16 plates, & map.
In index, 11 page refs to railways in relation to fox-hunting, and to their effect upon stage coach travel.

11367   BRIGGS, A. Victorian cities. *London: Odhams Press*, 1963. pp. 416, with plates & a 'Bibliographical note' (pp. 395–409).
In index, 30 page refs to railways and tramways.

11368   STONE, R. The measurement of consumers' expenditure and behaviour in the United Kingdom, 1920–1938. *Cambridge: Cambridge University Press*, 1954–66. 2 vols. (Studies in the National Income & Expenditure of the United Kingdom, 1 & 2).
In vol. 2, 1966, ch. 6 (pp. 60–72), 'Public transportation', with 4 tables (railways and tramways, pp. 62–5).

11369   CALDER, A. The People's War: Britain, 1939–45. *London: Jonathan Cape*, 1969. pp. 656, with many notes, a detailed evaluative bibliography, and an index of 17 pp.
Social aspects of war-time Britain. Includes the evacuation of school children and the use of London Underground tube stations as shelters from air raids.

11370   GREGORY, S. Railways and life in Britain. *London: Ginn & Co.*, 1969. (Aspects of Social & Economic History series). obl. 8°. pp. 80, with 8 col. plates, & in text, 30 illus & 2 tables.
An informative introductory historical survey.

11371   KELLETT, J. R. The impact of railways on Victorian cities. *London: Routledge &*

Kegan Paul; Toronto: University of Toronto Press, 1969. (Studies in Social History series). pp. xxi, [v], 467, with 12 plates, 15 maps & plans, 4 appendices & 1404 notes. Index, pp. 441–67.
—— Reprinted as a paperback edn. with a different title: Railways and Victorian cities. *London: Routledge & Kegan Paul; Toronto: University of Toronto Press*, 1979. (Studies in Social History series). pp. xxi, [v], 467.

11372   MARGETSON, S. Leisure and pleasure in the nineteenth century. *London: Cassell*, 1969. pp. [viii], 228, with plates.
ch. 6 (pp. 76–89), Holidays and excursions.

11373   SPRING, D. English landowners and nineteenth century industrialism, *in* Land and Industry: the landed estate and the Industrial Revolution, edited by J. T. Ward and R. G. Wilson. *Newton Abbot: David & Charles*, 1971, ch. 1, pp. 16–62, with 176 notes.
There are 49 page refs to railways in the Index, 31 of which are to passages in chapter 1.

11374   SWINGLEHURST, E. The Romantic Journey: the story of Thomas Cook and Victorian travel. *London: Pica Editions*, 1974. 4to. pp. 208, with many illus.
ch. 1 (pp. 9–36), Thomas Cook and railways in Britain.

11375   FERNEYHOUGH, F. Steam trains down the line. *[Brighton]: R. Tyndall*, 1975. pp. 48, with 67 illus.
Among the illustrations are contemporary photographs, prints, sketches and press cartoons depicting social effects of railways in the 19th century. Coverage, British and foreign. An informative introductory work.

11376   HEPPLE, J. R. The influence of landowners' attitudes on railway alignment in nineteenth century England. Thesis, Ph.D., University of Hull, 1975.

11377   JONES, R. B. The Victorians: a century of achievement. *St Albans: Hart-Davis*, 1975. pp. vii, [i], 273, with 13 graphs & 4 maps.
ch. 4 (pp. 35–45), 'A new age in the development of transport'. The social impact of railways.

11378   THOMAS, D. St J. The country railway. *Newton Abbot: David & Charles*, 1976. pp.

160, with 129 illus, incl. frontis, maps & drawings.

The railway as an element in the development and well-being of rural life.

—— *Penguin Books*, 1979. pp. 192 (re-set in smaller format), with illus.

11379 THOMAS, R. Commuting flows & the growth of London's new towns, 1951–1971. *Milton Keynes: Open University, New Towns Study Unit*, April 1977. pp. 35, with 4 tables, 4 graphs & a bibliography inside back cover (15 sources).

11380 WALVIN, J. Beside the seaside: a social history of the popular seaside holiday. *London: Allen Lane*, 1978. pp. 176, with 26 illus on 16 plates & a bibliography (203 sources).

ch. 2 (pp. 34–51), 'The coming of the railways', with 20 bibliogr. notes; *et passim.*

11381 BARKER, T. Towards an historical classification of urban transport development since the later eighteenth century, *in* Journal of Transport History, 3rd series, vol. 1, no. 1, September 1980, pp. 75–90, with table & 44 notes.

A statistical survey of the growth and decline of road and rail transport in London, 1825 to 1977, from which a framework of constants is derived and formulated into a table (p. 77) which can be applied to other urban areas.

11382 GUILCHER, G. Trains de plaisir à l'époque victorienne, *in* Études Anglaises, vol. 33, no. 1, January–March 1980, pp. 55–63, with 27 notes & 1 illus.

The development of excursion train traffic in 19th century Britain.

Contemporaneous

11383 HOWITT, W. Visits to remarkable places . . . *London: Longman, Orme, Brown, Green & Longmans*, 1840.

pp. 197–231 (esp. pp. 203–4), Visit to Bolton Priory. 'Railways now make it possible to visit places which had before only been known through reading.'

11384 STOPPAGE of the mails on Sunday, from the Scotsman of Wednesday April 14, 1841. *[Glasgow: The Scotsman*, 1841]. pp. 3.

A reprint, with introduction, of a report by Mr Johnson of Kentucky to the Senate of the U.S.A. on 19 January, 1829, advocating Sunday trains.

The Introduction relates the subject to Britain: 'It appears to us [The Scotsman] to exhaust the question' and goes on to advise the Government 'to be jealous of the Judaizing, intolerant spirit which would force on a reluctant community the stoppage of mails on Sunday in order to minister to the Pharasaical spirit manifested by a small portion of the Scottish clergy and their creatures . . . We suspect the Government have already yielded too much to the demands of these zealots'.

11385 SUMMERLY, Felix [pseud. of Henry Cole]. Felix Summerly's Pleasure Excursions. *London: Railway Chronicle*, [1846].

A series of essays from the *Railway Chronicle* republished separately as guide-companions for day trippers from London.

Unlike the *Railway Chronicle Travelling Charts*, published at the same time, these guides have only incidental references to the railways serving the places described, but some of the writer's throw-away comments are not without interest for the railway historian: 'The South Western is the only railway out of London whose embankments are fringed by the heather', and of Guildford station: 'A very common-place, flat-faced brick edifice wanting altogether feature and expression, symmetry and beauty of form'.

The following descriptions are from the LU(THC) set:

[1]. Harrow, on the London and Birmingham Railway. pp. 4, with 7 illus (2 of the railway).

[2]. Shoreham, on the Brighton and Chichester railways. pp. 4, with 4 illus.

[3]. Croydon, on the Croydon, Brighton and South-Eastern railways. pp. 8, with 9 illus (1 of 'the Atmospheric Station-house at Dartmouth Arms').

[4]. Walton and Weybridge on the South-Western Railway. pp. 8, with 13 illus (2 of the railway).

[5]. Guildford, on the South-Western Railway. pp. 12, with 9 illus.

[6]. Panshanger, on the Eastern Counties Railway. pp. 8, with 5 illus (three of the ECR and one, a full page drawing: 'The terminus of the South-Eastern and Brighton railways at London Bridge').

[7]. Winchester, on the South-Western Railway. pp. 12, with 11 illus.

[8]. Reigate, on the Brighton and South-Eastern railways. pp. 8, with 10 illus (1 of the railway).

See also 11388.

11386 EDINBURGH & GLASGOW RLY. Report of the discussion at the general meeting of shareholders of the Edinburgh & Glasgow Railway Company held at Glasgow on 5th March 1847 in regard to the question of Sunday trains. *Glasgow*, 1847. Newspaper format. pp. 4 in double column.   LU(THC)

11387 RUNNING of railway trains on Sabbath: report of the proceedings of a great public meeting of the inhabitants of Edinburgh. *[Edinburgh]: printed at the 'Witness' office, by Miller and Fairly,* [1847]. pp. 15.

11388 SUMMERLY, Felix [pseud. of Henry Cole]. Felix Summerly's Pleasure Excursions as guides for making day's excursions on the Eastern Counties, South-Eastern, Brighton & South Coast, South-Western and London & North Western railways. [*London*]: *Railway Chronicle Office*, 1847. pp. [76], with 74 engravings.

See also 11385.

11389 SUNDAY trains on the Edinburgh and Glasgow Railway: reasons why we voted for the resumption of Sunday trains; respectfully dedicated to our brother shareholders. *Glasgow: Wm. Lang,* 1847. pp. 15.

11390 The SUNDAY trains question: report of the great public meeting in the City Hall on

Tuesday April 27, 1847; reprinted from the Glasgow Argus. [*Glasgow*]: *J. Clark, printer*, [1847]. pp. 16.

An 'uproarious convocation of five thousand people lasting four hours in which the proposers for a resumption of Sunday trains were subjected to a continued stream of abuse from the Anti-Sunday Trains party'.

11391 WORKING Men's Prize Essays in Defence of their Sabbath Rights: supplementary series, ed. by John Jordon. *London: Partridge & Oakey*, [1849]. pp. iv, 404.

The essays are in small print set in double column. Each is a version of the same theme, uses the same words and phrases and comes to the same conclusion without considering opposing views, thereby qualifying for a prize. The following essays include more than a passing reference to the evils of Sunday train travel:

'Labour's great charter', by David Maxwell, pp. 67–84 (pp. 80–83, Sunday trains).
'Hope amidst danger', by Benjamin Smith, pp. 139–50 (pp. 145–7, Sunday trains).
'The Sabbath, the working man's happy retreat', by W. S. Currie, pp. 151–62 (pp. 157–9, Sunday trains).
'The Sabbath: life's milestone to Eternity', by John Guile, pp. 161–84 (p. 179, Sunday trains).
'God's chartered right to Man', by W. Ross, pp. 397–404 (p. 398, Sunday trains).

11392 KING, D. The adaptation of the Sabbath to the temporal well-being of men, and more especially of the working-classes, with application of the argument to Sabbath railway travelling, *in* The Christian Sabbath considered in its various aspects by ministers of different denominations; with Preface by . . . W. Noel. *Edinburgh: Johnston & Hunter*, 1850. ch. 4, pp. 100–124.
—— People's edn. *London: Religious Tract Society*, 1856. (ch. 4, pp. 89–109).

11393 SYMINGTON, A. The sin and evil of Sabbath mails, *in* The Christian Sabbath considered in its various aspects by ministers of different denominations. *Edinburgh: Johnston & Hunter*, 1850. ch. 12, pp. 320–52.
—— People's edn. *London: Religious Tract Society*, 1856. ch. 12, pp. 278–305.

Condemnation, not of mail trains specifically, but of the overall process of collecting, sorting and delivering of mail on Sundays.

11394 GOULTY, J. N. An appeal to conscience and humanity, the self interest of railway proprietors and the consistency of professing Christians generally, occasioned by the awful collision at the Clayton tunnel. *Brighton: S. Miall; London: John Snow*, [1861].

The author is Rev. J. N. Goulty of Union Street Congregational Church, Brighton. The accident occurred on Sunday, August 25th. This pamphlet is cited in the *United Reformed Church Journal*, vol. 1 (1974), pp. 91–3.

11395 SABBATH observance on railroads vindicated and enforced in an appeal to directors and shareholders, from a clerical railroad proprietor. [*London*]: *Macintosh, printer*, [1861]. pp. 8.

Text ends: 'I am . . . your humble servant, A Clerical Railroad Proprietor, January 1, 1861'. On p. 1 of the BL copy is a pencilled inscription 'by Revd Garton Harvard [or Haward]'.

'Sabbath desecration is an element of moral and social weakness in the railroad' (p. 7 *fn*).

11396 INGRAM, T. D. Compensation to land and house owners; being a treatise on the law of the compensation for interests in lands, etc. payable by railway and other public companies, with an appendix of forms and statutes. *London: Butterworths*, 1864. pp. xii, 299.

11397 COX, R. The literature of the Sabbath question. *Edinburgh: Maclachlan & Stewart*, 1865. 2 vols.

In the index to vol. 2 there are 11 page refs to Sunday railways in books and pamphlets.

11398 GRITTON, J. An address to railway proprietors. [*London*]: *Lord's Day Observance Society*, [1878]. pp. [4].

John Gritton writes as Secretary of the L.D.O.S. and calls upon shareholders to protest to their railway directors against the running of Sunday trains.

11399 BASS, RATCLIFF & GRETTON LTD. Excursion to Great Yarmouth, Vauxhall Station, by the Midland and Great Eastern railways via Peterborough, on Friday June 16th, 1893. (Produced by William Walters, Traffic Manager). [*Burton-on-Trent*]: *Bass*, [1893]. Reprinted in original form by the Bass Museum, Burton-on-Trent, 1977. pp. 15.

11400 PEAKE, F. Sunday railway excursions: a letter addressed to the Conference of Railway Managers, November 1897, by the Committee of the Lord's Day Observance Society. *London: the Society*, 1901. pp. 9.

Railway companies asked not to encourage Sunday excursions, which are 'destructive to godliness, to righteousness and to soberness'.

11401 BASS, RATCLIFF & GRETTON LTD. Excursion to Liverpool and New Brighton by the Midland and Cheshire Lines railways via the Peak of Derbyshire on Friday July 15th, 1904. (Produced by William Walters, Traffic Manager). [*Burton-on-Trent*]: *Bass*, [1904]. Reprinted in original form by the Bass Museum, 1977. pp. 96, with 117 illus, 3 maps, 2 plans. Inserted is a folded memo headed 'Train arrangements' with an illus plan of the docks at Liverpool. pp. 54–60, The Liverpool Overhead Railway; pp. 61–4, The Mersey Railway, with map.

11402 LONDON & NORTH WESTERN RLY. List of Caterers, railway fares, places of interest for Sunday School parties, within easy access from Manchester. *Euston Stn (London): LNWR*, 1907. pp. 16, with 18 illus.

11403 BASS, RATCLIFF & GRETTON LTD. Excursion to Scarborough, Friday July 24th,

1914. (Produced by William Walters, Traffic Manager). *Burton-on-Trent: Bass*, 1914. Reprinted in original form by the Bass Museum, Burton-on-Trent, 1977. pp. 40, with 18 illus on 6 plates. Inserted is a folded memo headed 'Train arrangements'.

11404   DOWNTON, A. The London Transport scandal. *London: Communist Party, London District Committee*, June 1936. pp. 30.
Alleged discontent of the people of London with passenger transport services and also among the Board's employees; suggestions for improvement.

11405   CRUMP, N. Railways and the public. (Proceedings of the British Railways (W.R.) London Lecture & Debating Society, 1949–50, no. 371). pp. 12, with discussion. Author, 'City Editor, Sunday Times'.

11406   LICKORISH, L. J. and KERSHAW, A. G. The travel trade. *London: Practical Press*, 1958. pp. xi, 356.
Railways, pp. 32–3, 182–9 *et passim*.
A description of the contemporary travel industry and its economics, with briefer accounts of historical developments in chapter 2.

11407   TABER, T. T. Some information, observations and conclusions concerning the handling of London's half-million daily commuters by railroad in 1961: a study . . . *Morristown (New Jersey): Board of Public Transportation of Morris County*, 1962. pp. 57, with 33 illus & line drawings, 3 tables & 2 maps.

11408   CENTRAL TRANSPORT CONSULTATIVE COMMITTEE. Transport users consultative committees: handbook. 2nd edn. *London: the Committee*, 1963. pp. 21.

11409   HONDELINK, E. R. Stopping trains. *Northwood: Great Central Association*, November 1963. pp. 6. Reproduced typescript.
An appraisal of the policy of BR and the Ministry of Transport in regard to the curtailment of branch line and stopping train services. Examples are given of unpopular withdrawals and closures on the Great Central line which can be seen as preliminary tactics, to be followed by the closing of the line altogether. The views of the Transport Users Consultative Committee are considered.

11410   THOMAS, D. St J. The rural transport problem. *London: Routledge & Kegan Paul*, 1963. (Dartington Hall Studies in Rural Sociology). pp. xiv, 176, with 20 tables, 5 maps, & bibliogr. footnotes.
Includes railway bus services and branch line closures. The railway element is well represented, two of the nine chapters being wholly concerned with it. In the Index, page refs are not grouped under 'Railways', but an A–Z scan reveals 36.

11411   HONDELINK, E. R. Suburban passenger services: a paper on commuter traffic, showing the inadequate and misleading effect of

figures put forward by the railways authorities in support of closure proposals. *Northwood: Great Central Association*, [1964]. pp. [ii], 3. Reproduced typescript, no covers.
How local authorities can contest proposals for withdrawal of suburban and other stopping passenger train services. Urges more careful scrutiny into actual figures of earnings and operating costs, and into the operating pattern potential of the line in question. Preface by Peter R. J. Walker, chairman of the Great Central Association.

11412   NATIONAL COUNCIL ON INLAND TRANSPORT. A fair deal for rail passengers: correspondence between the Prime Minister, the Right Hon. Sir Alec Douglas Home, and Lord Stonham, chairman of the National Council on Inland Transport. *London: N.C.I.T.*, [1964]. pp. [8]. Reproduced typescript.
Two letters from Lord Stonham and a reply to the first from Sir Alec dated January 3rd, 1964. Lord Stonham questions BR's bases of assessment when a line closure is being considered and believes that there is often a wide discrepancy—as much as ten-fold has been known—between the figure arrived at by BR and the actual earnings generated by a feeder line being where it is. The Preston–Southport closure is cited as an example.

11413   RICHARDS, B. New movement in cities. *London: Studio Vista*, 1966. pp. 96, with 147 illus, diagrams & drawings.
Includes various forms of guided transport; historical & contemporary.

11414   EVANS, A. W. A study of inter-city travel between London, the West Midlands and the north west of England. Thesis presented for an official degree, University of Birmingham, September 1967.
Weekday passenger travel by road, rail and air before and after the introduction of electrified services between Manchester, Liverpool and London on 18th April 1966, showing an increase by rail of 52%.

11415   HUTCHINGS, K. Urban transport: public or private? *London: Fabian Society*, 1967. (Fabian Research Series, 261). pp. 24.
The problem in London, primarily.

11416   MINISTRY OF TRANSPORT. Report on the effects of closing three rail passenger services: the 'Marplan' survey. *London: Ministry of Transport*, 1967. pp. 16, [22], with 16 tables & 2 appendices. Reproduced typescript.
Three widely different passenger services: Hailsham to Eridge (Sussex); Bradford to Huddersfield via Mirfield; Dumfries to Stranraer.

11417   PUBLIC TRANSPORT ASSOCIATION INCORPORATED. Passenger transport authorities: memorandum to the Minister of Transport, July 1967. *London: the Association*, July 1967. pp. 17.
pp. 6–8, 'Suburban railways'. Issues raised by Cmnd 3057, *Transport Policy: a consultation document*, by the Ministry's written and oral

evidence to the Royal Commission on Local Government in England, and by the paper on the proposed structure and powers of passenger transport authorities, submitted by the Ministry to the P.T.A.I. on 22 June 1967.

The Association is concerned with the Minister of Transport's proposals for the control of bus/rail relationships by the proposed new passenger transport authorities for the major conurbations.

11418 WATERS, B. Get our cities moving. *London: Conservative Political Centre*, 1967. pp. 36, with frontis, illus, maps & diagrams.

Underground, surface and airborne transport in towns generally, and (pp. 25–34) in London.

11419 JENNINGS, P. The living village: a report on rural life in England and Wales, based on actual village scrapbooks. *London: Hodder & Stoughton*, 1968. pp. 252.

A selection from 2,600 Women's Institute scrapbooks, collected in 1965.

pp. 146–58, 'Transport'. Comments and extracts concerning the contribution once made by the railway station to village life, and the present situation in which the station is closed and the bus service sometimes reduced or withdrawn.

—— another edn. The living village: a picture of rural life drawn from village scrapbooks. *Harmondsworth: Penguin Books*, 1972. pp. 318 (pp. 183–99, 'Transport').

11420 THOMAS, R. Journeys to work. *London: Political & Economic Planning*, 1968. (P.E.P. Broadsheet, no. 504). pp. 335–419, with ca. 100 notes & 20 tables. Title from cover.

Much of the work relates to commuting in London.

11421 LOTT, C. H. The modern traveller: our customer? (Proceedings of the British Railways (W.R.) London Lecture & Debating Society, 1968–69, no. 501). pp. 11, with discussion.

Author, Project Manager (Passenger Studies), Western Region. The challenges of the Motor Age.

11422 RUBINSTEIN, D. and SPEAKMAN, C. Leisure, transport, and the countryside. [*London*]: *Fabian Society*, 1969. (Fabian Research Series, 277). pp. 27, with 9 tables.

The problem of increasing infestation of the countryside by private cars. The need for a national policy for traffic and transport, including special rail facilities for leisure and recreation.

11423 WARNES, A. M. The increase of journey-to-work and its consequences for the residential structure of towns, with special reference to Chorley, Lancashire. Thesis, Ph.D., University of Salford, 1969.

11424 APPLETON, J. H. Disused railways in the countryside of England and Wales: a report to the Countryside Commission. *London: H.M.S.O.*, 1970. la. 8°. pp. 82, with 15 maps & diagrams, 13 illus, 7 tables, 5 appendices.

Reform needed to ensure that disposal and re-use of ex-railway property is in the public interest. pp. 32–9, 'Disused railways and agriculture', by Richard J. Appleton.

11425 EDWARDS, R. P. A. The Branch Line: illustrated by Gareth Floyd. *London: Burke*, 1970. (The Changing Scene: Environmental Studies series). pp. [64], with 63 col. drawings.

A sociological study of the birth, life and closure of an imaginary branch line presented in a clear and evocative style for school use, with each of the 63 illustrations carefully related to the text.

11426 RURAL DISTRICT COUNCILS ASSOCIATION. Rural transport: what future now?: report of . . . one-day conference, 19 October 1971, and passengers' guide to the bus and train systems. *London: the Association*, 1971. pp. 40, with 12 illus (6 on covers).

The guide to passenger services includes the amounts of the current grants paid to rural rail services.

11427 BUCKMAN, J. C. The locational effects of a railway closure: a case study of the withdrawal of passenger services from the Steyning line in March 1966. Thesis, M.Sc., University of Bristol, 1972–3.

The Horsham to Shoreham line.

11428 HATCH, T. The recreational potential of a disused railway line. Thesis, Ph.D., University of Bradford, 1974.

11429 JARMAN, R. The railways of Dorset: their relevance to wildlife conservation. Thesis, M.Sc., University of London (U.C.L.), 1974.

11430 [MATTHEW.] ROBERT MATTHEW, JOHNSON-MARSHALL AND PARTNERS. Transport for countryside recreation: a report prepared for the Countryside Commission. *Cheltenham: Countryside Commission*, May 1974. tall 8°. pp. [ii], iii, 114.

pp. 25–38, a wide variety of tracked systems for conveying visitors in recreational areas is discussed, with 8 illus & 5 tables.

11431 BRENT, R. J. The Minister of Transport's social welfare function: a study of the closure factors behind railway closure decisions, 1963–1970. Thesis, Ph.D., University of Manchester, 1975.

11432 DAVIDSON, J. W. An examination of disused railways and their future. Thesis, M.Sc., University of London (U.C.L.), 1975.

11433 DEPARTMENT OF THE ENVIRONMENT. National Travel Survey, 1972–73: cross sectional analysis of passenger travel in Great Britain. *London: H.M.S.O.*, 1975. pp. v, 24.

11434 BRIGHTON LINE COMMUTERS' ASSOCIATION. The Brighton Plan: a reply to the

Government Green Paper on Transport Policy. *Brighton: the Association*, 1976. pp. 13.

11435 DARTINGTON AMENITY RESEARCH TRUST. Public transport for countryside recreation: a report of the Countryside Commission. [*Cheltenham*]: *Countryside Commission*; [*Dartington*]: *the Trust*, May 1976. (CCP series, 94) (Dart Publication, 21). la. 8°. pp. 52, with 14 maps, 12 illus, 5 diagrams, & a bibliography (36 sources).

11436 DEPARTMENT OF THE ENVIRONMENT. National Travel Survey, 1972–73: a comparison of 1965 and 1972–73 surveys. *London: H.M.S.O.*, 1976. pp. vii, 42. 25 detailed tables.

11437 POLYTECHNIC OF CENTRAL LONDON. TRANSPORT STUDIES GROUP. A survey and review of the Exeter–Barnstaple railway service, [by] S. R. Williams, P. R. White [and] P. Heels. *London: P.C.L.*, February 1976. tall 8°. pp. 62, with maps, tables & diagrams.
A survey carried out in June 1975. 'It is shown clearly that revenue generated over the inter-city network as a result of the line's existence is well in excess of the operating loss assigned to the route. This confirms views generally held since the time of the 'Beeching' period cuts, that the role of feeder traffic is often under-stated'.

11438 DAS, M. Travel to work in Britain: a selective review. *Crowthorne: Transport & Road Research Laboratory*, 1978. (Report LR 849). tall 8°. pp. 36, with 18 tables & 6 graphs; bibliography (37 sources).

11439 KEEN, P. A. Rural rail services, *in* Rural Transport and Country Planning, ed. by Roy Cresswell (1978). pp. 139–46.

11440 NOISE ADVISORY COUNCIL. Noise implications of the transfer of freight from road to rail: report by a working group of the Council. *London: H.M.S.O., for the Department of the Environment*, 1978. pp. 16, with 2 illus, 3 graphs, 2 tables.

11441 CENTRAL TRANSPORT CONSULTATIVE COMMITTEE. Rural railways: a report on British Rail's 'other provincial services'. *London: the Committee*, September 1979. pp. [20].
'The Report concerns that group of about 85 railway services known as Other Provincial Services (O.P.S.) which falls outside the London and South East, Inter-City and P.T.E. networks.'

11442 DEPARTMENT OF TRANSPORT. National Travel Survey: 1975–76 report, by Rocky Harris, Paul Standish, & others. *London: H.M.S.O., for the Government Statistical Office*, 1979. pp. xviii, 190, with 223 detailed tables & charts.
Designed to provide data on the travel patterns

of the population of Great Britain for use in transport planning. Railways and other transport modes are compared in each section of the survey.

11443 HAMER, M. and POTTER, S. Vital travel statistics: a basic analysis of how and why people travel. 1979 edition. *London: Transport 2000; Milton Keynes: Open University, New Towns Study Unit*, 1979. tall 8°. pp. 24, with 20 tables & 4 diagrams.
'A simple yet complete picture of how and why people travel and what the major influences are on their choice of transport' (Conclusions, p. 23).

11444 NEWBURY & DISTRICT RAILWAY PASSENGER ASSOCIATION. Passenger Survey Report. *Newbury: the Association*, 1979. tall 8°. pp. 24 (20 detailed tables & graphs and the questionnaire).
Object: to establish the pattern of travel on the Kennet Valley line in anticipation of the proposed introduction of a High Speed Train service to the West Country in May 1980. Survey carried out on Friday October 17th 1978, between 6.45am and 6.45pm.
The report is presented as a study document. It does not include an analysis, makes no observations and offers no recommendations.

11445 RAILWAY DEVELOPMENT SOCIETY. Guide for Rail Users' Groups. 2nd edn. *London: the Society*, 1979. pp. 12. Reproduced typescript.
'Why and how to set up rail user groups.'

11446 SOMERVILLE, C. Walking old railways. *Newton Abbot: David & Charles*, 1979. pp. 144, with 29 illus, 7 maps, & a directory with notes, of 151 converted lines, & a bibliography (30 sources).

11447 HILLMAN, M. and WHALLEY, A. The social consequences of rail closures. *London: Policy Studies Institute*, 1980. pp. vii, 137, with 55 tables, 1 general map & 10 area maps.
The general map shows the ten closed lines and related survey areas. The 10 area maps are for the following closed lines: Haltwhistle—Alston; Maiden Newton—Bridport; Paignton—Kingswear; Alton—Winchester; Exeter—Okehampton; Keswick—Carlisle; Cambridge—St Ives; Bangor—Caernarfon; Dundee—Newport-on-Tay (East); Edinburgh—Hawick—Carlisle.
A study of the social effects of the post-Beeching closures of the late 1960s and early 1970s.

11448 JONES, G. L. Railway walks: exploring disused railways. *London: Pierrot Publishing*, 1980. pp. 285, with 284 illus, 2 general maps & 20 of individual locations.
Appendix: A select list of disused railways in England and Wales now officially open to the public as paths (pp. 279–81); bibliography (26 sources).
Based on a survey of a selected 20 locations visited by the author. In part 4 (pp. 255–78) he presents a detailed proposal for a planned national network of preserved 'Greenways' (preserved railway trackways) for walkers, cyclists and horse-riders.

Travelling conditions—Accounts of journeys—Fear of tunnels
(19th century)—Classes of accommodation—Special facilities
for physically-handicapped passengers
11449–80

For workmen's trains see **K 1**

Historical   11449–58
Contemporaneous   11459–80

Historical

11449 RUTHERFORD, M. Mark Rutherford's Deliverance, being the second part of his autobiography; edited by his friend Reuben Shapcott. [various editions from 1885].
ch. 9: 'Holidays', in which he describes a return journey on an excursion train from Bexhill (Sussex coast) to London Bridge, L B & S C R, ca. 1860.

11450 MORRIS, M. C. F. Yorkshire reminiscences, with others, by M. C. F. Morris. *London: Humphrey Milford, Oxford U.P.*, 1922. pp. vii, 359.
ch. 2 (pp. 15–22), 'Railways'; p. 14, Travelling conditions in the 1850s; also *passim*, George Hudson.

11451 JONES, K. W. Great railway journeys of the world. *London: A. Redman*, 1964. pp. 192, with 43 illus on 24 plates.
pp. 167–75, 'London to Fort William and the Isles' (the *Aberdonian* via the East Coast).

11452 JONES, K. W. Exciting railway journeys of the world. *London: A. Redman*, 1967. pp. 192, with 24 plates, illus, maps on lining papers.
pp. 180–5, 'To the Delectable Duchy, past & present'. The journey from Paddington to Penzance.

11453 BRIGHTFIELD, M. F. Victorian England in its novels, 1840–1870; introduction by Gordon N. Ray; prefatory note by Bradford A. Booth. *Los Angeles: University of California Library*, 1968. 4 vols.
vol. 3, ch. 8, pp. 188–211: 'Railroad travel': extracts selected from imaginative literature illustrating a variety of effects which train travel has upon the passenger: discomforts of early carriages, the effects of speed and rapidly changing scenery, the tedium of rail journeys, crowded compartments, the confusion of a busy terminus, refreshment rooms, waiting at stations, accidents to trains, etc.

11454 JONES, K. W. Romantic railways. *London: Arlington Books*, 1971. pp. 208, with col. frontis & 67 illus.
Accounts of train journeys in many countries. In the British Isles, pp. 82–113.

11455 GOING by train, 1825–1975: 150 years of rail travel in Britain, including a guide to the National Railway Museum at York; editor, John Slater. *London: IPC Transport Press*, 1975. ('A Railway Magazine Special'). magazine format. pp. 60, with 46 illus (4 col.).

11456 BIGNELL, P. Taking the train: railway travel in Victorian times, by Philippa Bignell [Philippa Richardson]. *London: H.M.S.O., for the National Railway Museum, Science Museum*, 1978. sm. obl. 8°. pp. 32, with 48 illus (20 col.), 4 maps, & a bibliography (8 sources) on p. [3] of cover.

11457 UNWIN, P. Travelling by train in the Edwardian Age. *London: Allen & Unwin*, 1979. pp. 106, with 59 illus.
The Edwardian railway scene recalled.

11458 SCHIVELBUSCH, W. The railway journey: trains and travel in the 19th century, by Wolfgang Schivelbusch; translated from the German by Anselm Hollo; design by Brayton Harris. *Oxford: Blackwell*, 1980. pp. 213, with many illus & 400 notes.
Originally published as *Geschichte der Eisenbahnreise* (Munich, 1978).
A traveller's view of railways in various countries, including Britain.

Contemporaneous

11459 KENNEDY, [Miss]. Miss Kennedy's first trip on the railway from Manchester to Liverpool, and a visit to Liverpool docks, July 1833; from her diary of a journey from Carlsruhe, now in the Liverpool Record Office. *Wallasey: Lilac Tree Press*, 1963. pp. [6], with 3 wood engravings (one on cover) by Noel Parker. Cover title: 'An extract from Miss Kennedy's diary, July 1833'. An edition of six copies.
A note on the original MS reads: 'Journey to England from Carlsruhe with Mrs. Amelia Briggs to her marriage with John Kennedy, Secretary of Legation of Naples, 1834'.   LU(THC)

11460 RAILWAY tunnels. [*London*]: *printed by Wm. Clowes*, [1837]. pp. 3. Three reports. Text headed: 'Tunnels'.
[1], Report on the Primrose Hill tunnel on the London and Birmingham Railway, by Dr Paris, Dr Watson, Mr William Lawrence, Mr R. Phillips and Mr Lucas.
Dated 21st February 1837 and signed: John Ayrton Paris, Thomas Watson, William Lawrence, Richard Phillips, William Owen Lucas. Their visit was made during construction 'to

ascertain the probable effect of such tunnels upon the health and feelings of those who may traverse them'. Verdict: perfectly agreeable. Fear of tunnels 'futile and groundless'.

[2]. Reports on the tunnel on the Leeds and Selby Railway: report of Dr Davy and Dr Rothman. [Dr John Davy and Dr R. W. Rothman].

Dated 21 February 1837. 'We are of the opinion that it has no injurious influence on the health of the passengers.'

[3]. Dr Williamson's report. [Dr James Williamson].

Dated 19 February 1837. 'I conceive that the vapour, smoke and gaseous results of combustion can never exist in such proportions as materially to deteriorate the air.'   MCL

11461 REID, D. B. Report on the atmosphere of tunnels, founded on chemical analysis. *Edinburgh*: [*the author*?], 13 March 1837. p. 1.

A report based on his visit to the Leeds & Selby Rly tunnel in which he found the air 'not injurious to the health of passengers'.   MCL

11462 DERBY, E. H. Two months abroad; or, a trip to England, France, Baden, Prussia and Belgium in August 1843, by 'a railroad director of Massachusetts' [i.e. Elias Hasket Derby]. *Boston (Mass.): Reading & Co.*, 1844. pp. 64.

pp. 6–14, Liverpool—Birmingham—London; a call on Mr. Herapath; London Bridge Station; a rail trip to Brighton.

pp. 40–41, The G.W.R., Paddington to Steventon (the broad gauge criticised).

pp. 45–8, Birmingham & Derby Junction Rly; Derby Station and 'engine house' and three similar buildings; to York, Leeds, Manchester and Liverpool (Bury & Co.'s works).   LU(THC)

11463 HOLT, W., ANDERSON, H. D. and ARTHURTON, A. W. One, two or three classes for passenger traffic: which is most desirable? Great Western Railway (London) Lecture & Debating Society, meeting on Thursday October 19th, 1905 (no. 2) [no. 16]. pp. 10.

11464 POPE, S. A. The Cheap Trains Act, 1883, and its equitable interpretation as affecting the Government, the public and the English railways. Great Western Railway (London) Lecture & Debating Society, meeting on February 22nd, 1906 [no. 23]. pp. 12.

11465 SCOTT, W. J. The express of 1920: one class only. Great Western Railway (London) Lecture & Debating Society, meeting on December 16th, 1919 [no. 65]. pp. 6, with discussion.

11466 BULKELEY, G. and ROBINSON, E. Compartments in British railway passenger coaches: should they be abolished? Great Western Railway (London) Lecture & Debating Society, meeting on December 30th, 1920 [no. 129]. pp. 18, with 8 illus.

A debate, with discussion and vote.

11467 DE SALIS, H. R. Criticisms of railway travelling from the passenger's point of view. Great Western Railway (London) Lecture & Debating Society, meeting on March 31st, 1921 [no. 137]. pp. 10, with discussion.

11468 BIRCH, H. Railway fares reform. Great Western Railway (London) Lecture & Debating Society, meeting on 3rd January 1924 (no. 166). pp. 20, with discussion.

11469 BECKETT, A. W. Railways and the public. Great Western Railway (London) Lecture & Debating Society, meeting on 19th March 1925 (no. 182). pp. 16, with discussion.

Author from the 'Office of the Superintendent of the Line, Paddington'.

11470 MOUNT, G. N. A passenger's criticisms of British railways. Great Western Railway (London) Lecture & Debating Society, meeting on 22nd March 1934, no. 283. pp. 15.

11471 'THAT first class accommodation in trains be discontinued:' proposed by J. R. Turk and N. R. F. Geiger; opposed by H. L. Wilkinson and J. M. Leighton-Bailey. Proceedings of the Great Western Railway (London) Lecture & Debating Society, 1947–8, no. 345. pp. 20, with discussion.

11472 BRITISH RAILWAYS. EASTERN REGION. Passenger train facilities, Eastern Region, including list of enquiry offices, stations and ticket agencies. [*London*]: *B.R. (ER)*, 1954. pp. 64.

11473 BRITISH RAILWAYS. SOUTHERN REGION. Want to run a railway? *London: B.R. (SR)*, October 1962. pp. 43, with 21 illus, 4 map diagrams & a train occupation graph.

Published for the enlightenment of commuters and issued free as a spirited response to current criticisms about train delays: 'Perhaps you could run the Southern better than we do!'. The complex nature of running a high capacity network of services revealed in a counter-challenge of facts, statistics and comparisons.

11474 PHILLIPS, J. Travel facilities for the disabled [caption title]. [*London: London Transport Passengers Committee, 1971*]. pp. 3 & 5 pp. tables. Reproduced typescript.

A memorandum for wheel-chair passengers on London Underground.

11475 A GUIDE to London's Underground Stations for the handicapped person . . . produced by a group of physically-handicapped children from Cloudesley School in London . . . *London: Central Council for the Disabled*, [1973]. pp. 32, with map.

An alphabetical table in 6 columns and notes to facilitate interchanging.

11476 RICE, P. Queuing and stochastic aspects of urban railway capacity, with special reference to London Transport underground railways. Thesis, Ph.D., London (U.C.L.), December 1974.

An approach to the train frequency problem based on lineal variations in passenger waiting-time.

11477 CENTRAL COUNCIL FOR THE DISABLED. A Guide to British Rail for the physically-handicapped. *London: the Council*, 1975. pp. 160.

Access to platforms, buffets, toilets, etc, and the presence or otherwise of special facilities for disabled persons at stations and from car parks to station booking offices. Arranged alphabetically under stations.

A later edition was published by the Royal Association for Disability and Rehabilitation in 1979. *See* 11479.

11478 JOINT COMMITTEE ON MOBILITY FOR THE DISABLED. British Rail and disabled travellers. *Guildford: the Joint Committee*, June 1978. (no. 313). pp. 5. Reproduced typescript on headed notepaper; no covers.

Practical advice for the physically handicapped

on rail journeys, emphasising the willingness of BR to help if notification of a particular journey is given. BR's new Mark III carriages, modified for disabled passengers, and advice to those travelling in normal carriages (entraining, seat reservations, sleeping accommodation, toilets, etc.).

11479 ROYAL ASSOCIATION FOR DISABILITY AND REHABILITATION. A Guide to British Rail for the physically handicapped. revised 1979 edn. *London: the Association*, 1979. pp. 288.

Special facilities for disabled passengers at stations, hotels and on trains, listing specific facilities with precise locations at each of 403 stations on BR.

An earlier edition was published at the Central Council for the Disabled in 1975. *See* 11477.

11480 HOLLINGSWORTH, J. B. The Atlas of Train Travel. *London: Sidgwick & Jackson*, 1980. la. 8°. pp. 192 with many illus, some col.

An informal narrative and commentary on rail travel in many countries, including (pp. 21–37) Great Britain.

K 3   SAFETY IN TRANSIT
Accidents and their prevention
11481–11503

11481 REMARKS on the accident at the Euston Square terminus; with hints on the structure of the brick columns. *Pimlico* [*London*]: *J. Roberts*, 1848. pp. 31.

The date of the accident was 6 January 1848. GL

11482 ERICHSEN, J. E. On railway and other injuries of the nervous system. *London: Walton & Maberly*, 1866. pp. viii, 144.

Lectures to students, University College Hospital, London, Spring 1866.

11483 MORRIS, E. A practical treatise on shock after surgical operations and injuries, with especial reference to shock caused by railway accidents. *London: R. Hardwicke*, 1867. pp. vi,[i], 88.

pp. 43–67, shock from railway injuries.

11484 BROWN, J. The evils of the unlimited liability for accidents of masters and railway companies, especially since Lord Campbell's Act. *London: Butterworths*, 1870. pp. 34.

A paper read before the Social Science Association.

11485 The CARLISLE accident and the Vacuum Brake: opinions of the Press. [no imprint]. pp. 122.

Facsimile reprints of 18 press reports prefaced by a brief introduction and the verdict of the jury at the coroner's inquest on the collision at Carlisle on 4th March 1890. Appendix (pp. 99–120), 'Failures of the Vacuum Brake caused by ice and water, extracted from the Board of Trade Re-

turns, January 1886 to December 1889'. The Postscript (pp. 121–2) is directed against advocates of the Vacuum Brake and ends with the text of a circular issued by the LNWR to its locomotive foremen and enginemen on 7th July 1890 reminding them of the danger of ice formation in the Vacuum Brake apparatus and giving instructions to be followed before taking out a train so fitted in extremely cold weather. This Postscript, or, rather, the circular at its end, is signed 'F. W. Webb'.

The Preface says that interests of public safety prompted the publication of these press reports in 'handy pamphlet form', but implicit throughout is the impression that this accident provided an opportunity for opponents of the Vacuum Brake to try to destroy public confidence in that device.

At the Board of Trade enquiry the Inspecting Officer, Colonel Rich, found that the accident was caused not by ice in the train pipe but by the driver applying 'simple vacuum' instead of 'automatic vacuum' on an engine fitted with alternative brake operation controls.

For a commentary on the railway brake controversy at this time see *Red for Danger*, by L. T. C. Rolt, and *The Railways of Britain* by Jack Simmons (2nd edn, 1967), pp. 164–5.   LU(THC)

11486 BOWDEN, E. A. The safe working of a railway; its ideals and limitations. Great Western Railway (London) Lecture & Debating Society, meeting on Thursday, January 16th, 1908 [no. 46]. pp. 13, with discussion & 4 diagrams.

11487 JENKIN, F. C. J. C. The chief provisions of the law relating to railways and the safety of passengers and the public. Great Western Railway (London) Lecture & Debating Society, meeting on December 3rd, 1908 [no. 54]. pp. 16.

11488 ANDERSON, H. D. Railway accidents: some facts and figures. In what directions are further preventative measures possible? Great Western Railway (London) Lecture & Debating Society meeting on December 19th, 1912 (no. 94). pp. 19, with discussion, 13 tables & diagrams.

11489 WATSON, H. A. Prevention of railway accidents. Great Western Railway (London) Lecture & Debating Society, meeting on 19th February 1925. pp. 22, with 12 illus.

11490 LANGLEY, C. A. The history and work of the Railway Inspectorate. (Proceedings of the British Railways (W.R.) London Lecture & Debating Society, 1954–55, no. 419). pp. 12, with discussion.
Author, 'Inspecting Officer of Railways'.

11491 LANGLEY, C. A. Safety on the railways. (Proceedings of the British Railways (W.R.) London Lecture & Debating Society, 1964–65, no. 487). pp. 12, with discussion.
Author, Brigadier C. A. Langley, ex Chief Inspecting Officer, Ministry of Transport.

11492 NOCK, O. S. Historic railway disasters. London: Ian Allan, 1966. pp. ix, 170, with 55 illus on 32 plates, 15 diagrams in text.
—— 2nd edn. Ian Allan, 1969. pp. ix, 206, with 56 illus on 32 plates & 19 diagrams in text.

11493 HAMILTON, J. A. B. British railway accidents of the twentieth century. London: Allen & Unwin, 1967. pp. 180, with 32 illus on 16 plates.
27 accidents, from 1905 to 1962.

11494 SCHNEIDER, A. and MASE, A. Railway accidents of Great Britain and Europe: their causes and consequences; translated from the German by E. L. Dellow. Newton Abbot: David & Charles, 1968. pp. 334, with 16 illus on 8 plates, 16 diagrams, maps & a bibliography (12 sources).
First published as Katastrophen auf Schienen (Zürich, 1968).

11495 HAMILTON, J. A. B. Britain's greatest rail disaster: the Quintinshill blaze of 1915. London: Allen & Unwin, 1969. pp. 96, with 19 illus on 8 plates, 3 plans & a diagram.
Sometimes referred to as the 'Gretna accident'.

11496 THOMAS, J. Gretna: Britain's worst railway disaster, 1915. Newton Abbot: David & Charles, 1969. pp. 143, with 32 illus on 16 plates, 5 diagrams & a map.
Quintinshill, Caledonian Rly, May 22nd. Double collision & fire.

11497 SMITH, H. Personal injuries claims in Victorian Britain. Thesis, Ph.D., University of London (external), 1970.
Includes highways and railway accidents, chaps 3 & 4, Railways, with some statistics of accidents to passengers and to employees. The appendices contain a bibliography, Parliamentary Papers, and a list of Acts and cases at law.

11498 CURRIE, J. R. L. The runaway train: Armagh, 1889. Newton Abbot: David & Charles, 1971. pp. 148, with 26 illus on 16 plates, map, 3 diagrams, gradient profile & a plan.

11499 THOMAS, J. The Tay Bridge disaster: new light on the 1879 tragedy. Newton Abbot: David & Charles, 1972. pp. 208, with 24 illus on 12 plates & 26 in text, incl. facsimiles, documents & letters; bibliography (30 sources).

11500 PERKINS, J. The Tay Bridge disaster. Dundee: City of Dundee District Council, Museums & Art Galleries Dept, 1975. 4°. pp. [56], with 49 illus (photos, facsimiles, drawings).

11501 COOMBS, L. F. E. The Harrow railway disaster, 1952: twenty-five years on. Newton Abbot: David & Charles, 1977. pp. 164, with 13 illus on 8 plates, & in text, 4 maps, 5 plans, 3 appendices & a bibliography (40+ sources).

11502 BONNETT, H. The Grantham rail crash of 1906. Grantham: Bygone Grantham, 1978. pp. 40, with 24 illus, diagrams, & a col. plan of the accident, 19 September.

11503 TREVENA, A. Trains in trouble: railway accidents in pictures. Penryn: Atlantic Books, 1980. pp. [48]. Intro & 78 illus with historical notes.

Consignor aspects—The call for rates and charges reform—
Private sidings and private wagon ownership
11504–46

Reference source   11504
Historical   11505–15
Contemporaneous   11516–46

For rates and charges by railways see **F 1**

Reference source

11504   GRAY'S Practical Railway Distance Book,
shewing distances for goods traffic between
the principal ports, towns, exchange junctions and goods stations in England and
Wales. *Manchester: Gray's Railway Publishing Co.*, [1913]. pp. 23, [226]. 248 tables.
   Devised to enable traders to compute distances,
and thereby freight rates, between all stations of
moderate size or larger.

Historical

11505   TOOKE, T. and NEWMARCH, W.   A history
of prices . . . *London: Longman, Brown,
Green, Longmans & Roberts.*
   vol. 5, 1857, part 3, (pp. 348–90): On the
progress of railway construction . . . , 1843 to the
present time; the effects of the great railway
expenditure of 1845–50 and the operation of
railway transit on the supply and consumption,
and therefore on the prices, of commodities.

11506   PARNELL, W. S.   The commercial geography of the Great Western Railway. Great
Western Railway (London) Lecture & Debating Society, meeting on February 22nd,
1912 [no. 89]. pp. 19, with col. folded map.

11507   CLAPHAM, J. H.   An economic history of
modern Britain. *Cambridge: Cambridge
University Press.*
   vol. 2: Free Trade and steel, 1850–1886. 1932.
pp. xiii, 554, with 9 diagrams & maps, & many
notes. Railways, pp. 180–98 *et passim.*
   vol. 3: Machines and national rivalries, 1887–
1914, with an epilogue, 1914–1929. 1938. pp. xiv,
577, with 11 diagrams & many notes. Railways,
pp. 347–62 *et passim.*

11508   FRASER-STEPHEN, E.   Two centuries in
the London coal trade: the story of Char-
ringtons. *London: privately printed*, 1952.
pp. viii, [3], 157.
   ch. 16 (pp. 106–11), 'The Great Railway Rebates Case, 1901'.

11509   BROOKS, E.   Regional functions of the
mineral transport system in the South Wales
coalfield, 1830–1951. Thesis, Ph.D., St
John's College, University of Cambridge,
1957–8.

11510   BELL, G. E.   The railway as a factor in the
location of manufacturing industry in the
East Midlands. Thesis, Ph.D., University of
Nottingham, 1958–9.

11511   CAIN, P. J.   The railway rates problem and
combination amongst the railway companies of Great Britain, 1893–1913. Thesis,
B. Litt., University of Oxford, 1969.

11512   VAMPLEW, W.   The railways and the iron
industry: a study of their relationship in
Scotland, *in* Railways in the Victorian
Economy, ed. by M. C. Reed (1969), pp.
33–75, with 173 notes & sources, & 5 tables.

11513   THOMAS, J.   The rise of the Staffordshire
potteries. *Bath: Adams & Dart*, 1971. pp.
228, with plates.
   pp. 74–102, roads, canals and railways (pp.
95–102, railways, with a railway map of 1837
showing the Potteries as 'a railway desert').

11514   CAIN, P. J.   Traders versus railways: the
genesis of The Railway and Canal Traffic
Act of 1894, *in* Journal of Transport History, new series, vol. 2 (1973–4), pp. 65–84,
with 147 notes.

11515   LE GUILLOU, M.   Freight rates and their
influence on the Black Country iron trade in
a period of growing domestic and foreign
competition, 1850–1914, *in* Journal of
Transport History, new series, vol. 3 (1975–
6), pp. 108–18, with 32 notes.

Contemporaneous

11516   The RAILWAY considered with reference to
British commerce . . . *London: J. Rickerby,
printer*, [1844]. pp. 2, [1].   NUC

11517   REID, W.   The story of the truck; or, the
why and the wherefore of cattle diseases.
Edinburgh: A. Elliot, 1867. pp. 140, with
illus, incl. views of the interior of a proposed cattle-truck.
   Concerned with the care of cattle in transit by
rail.   N. KERR CAT. 224/308

11518   HUNTER, W. A.   The law relating to railway rates: a guide to farmers and traders.
London: Agricultural Press Co., 1881. pp.
39.
   Reprinted from the *Mark Lane Express.*

11519   HUNTER, W. A.   The Report of the Railway Rates Committee 1881–2, and future
railway legislation. *London: Railway &
Canal Traders' Association*, 1882. (Publication no. 1). pp. vii, 13.

A paper read at the Nottingham Congress of the National Association for the Promotion of Sciences, September 1882. Text headed: 'What action should be taken on the Report of the Select Committee on Railways (Rates and Fares) 1882?, by W. A. Hunter'.

Parliament should strengthen the authority of the Railway Commissioners so as to effectively control the charges made for goods transport by the railway monopoly, and to free canals from railway ownership so as to provide a competitive means of transit for slow and heavy traffic.

11520 BROWN, J. Railway rates and charges: a letter to the ironmasters . . . and others in the counties of Monmouth and Glamorgan: an exposé of the combined attack made by the railway companies for the purpose of raising their existing high charges. *Newport*, 1885. pp. 11.

11521 GREAT CENTRAL RLY. Great Central Railway: illustrated official album. [*London: G.C.R.*, ca. 1900]. obl. format. pp. 156, with many illus.

A high quality publicity production presenting the G.C.R.'s achievements and associating the railway and its route with trades and industries in its catchment area, and with places of historical and topographical interest through which the line passes.

11522 RENDELL, T. H. The functions of railways in relation to trade and commerce. Great Western Railway (London) Lecture & Debating Society, opening meeting, October 7th, 1904 [no. 1]. pp. 14.

11523 POTTER, F. Claims and compensation. Great Western Railway (London) Lecture & Debating Society, meeting on February 28th, 1907 [no. 37]. pp. 12.

11524 ARTHURTON, A. W. The part to be played by railways in the revival of British agriculture. Great Western Railway (London) Lecture & Debating Society, meeting on October 30th, 1913 [no. 103]. pp. 5–14, with discussion.

11525 JONES, C. M. J. The case for and against Common User of Wagons. Great Western Railway (London) Lecture & Debating Society, meeting on 1st November 1923 (no. 162). pp. 22, with discussion.

11526 RAILWAY siding agreements: model agreement for siding noted with legal decisions & amendments; extracts from railway traffic Acts . . . *Manchester: Gray's Railway Publishing Co.*, [between 1914 & 1923]. la. 8°. pp. 62. Reproduced typescript with a facsimile MS title-page.

'The object of this volume is to present, in the form of an agreement, the various obligations which the railways usually ask the trader to enter into in relation to siding accommodation.'

11527 MARSH, H. How can the railways foster a trade revival? Great Western Railway (Lon-

don) Lecture & Debating Society, meeting on October 21st, 1926 (no. 196). pp. 15, with discussion.

11528 LARKE, W. J. The iron and steel industry and its relation to railways. Great Western Railway (London) Lecture & Debating Society, meeting on 6th January 1927 (no. 201). pp. 13, with discussion.

Author, 'Director, National Federation of Iron & Steel Manufacturers'.

11529 BELL, R. The effect of trade fluctuations on rail transport: a paper read at a meeting of the Hull (LNER) Lecture & Debating Society, January 17th 1928. pp. 16.

Author, 'Assistant General Manager, L & NE Rly'. Examples are given from the NBR, the NER and the LNER.

11530 HOLLINGSWORTH, J. H. Is it desirable that private, as distinct from railway, ownership of railway wagons should be abolished . . . ? Great Western Railway (London) Lecture & Debating Society, meeting on the 13th March 1930 (no. 242). pp. 13, with discussion.

Author, 'Chief Goods Manager's Office'.

11531 ACWORTH, B. Coal in relation to transport and power. Great Western Railway (London) Lecture & Debating Society, meeting on 16th November 1933, no. 276. pp. 13, with discussion.

11532 HUGHES, J. J. The trader's view in regard to transport by rail and road. (Great Western Railway (London) Lecture & Debating Society, meeting on 31st October, 1935, no. 295). pp. 6, with discussion & 2 illus.

The Road & Rail Traffic Act, 1933.

11533 WESTCOTT, L. F. South Wales: a survey of its trade and resources, with special reference to transport. Great Western Railway (London) Lecture & Debating Society, meeting on 21st January 1937, no. 309. pp. 11, with discussion.

Author, 'Mineral Traffic Manager's Office, Paddington'.

11534 PHILLIPS, H. H. Coal as a transport problem. (Proceedings of the Great Western Railway (London) Lecture & Debating Society, 1946–47, no. 334). pp. 16, with discussion.

Author, 'Assistant to the Supt of the Line, Cardiff'.

11535 ASSOCIATION OF CHAMBERS OF COMMERCE. Transport Bill, 1947. *London: A.C.C.*, August 1947. pp. 6.

A report on the concessions secured by the Central Committee of Transport Users on behalf of traders.

11536 HAVERS, E. The coal industry and the Western Region. (Proceedings, British Railways (W.R.) London Lecture & Debat-

ing Society, 1951–52, no. 391). pp. 27, with discussion, 4 tables, 3 maps, 2 charts.
Author, 'Assistant to the Commercial Supt (Mineral)'.

11537 PIKE, J. R. The B.T.C. (Railway Merchandise) Charges Scheme. (Proceedings of the British Railways (W.R.) London Lecture & Debating Society, 1955–56, no. 428). pp. 12, with discussion.
Author, 'Chief Commercial Officer, British Railways Division (B.T.C.)'.

11538 CHAMBERLAIN, A. The railways and railwaymen as seen by industry. (Proceedings of the British Railways (W.R.) London Lecture & Debating Society, 1957–58, no. 440). pp. 10, with discussion.
Author, 'Member, Western Area Board of the B.T.C.'.

11539 GOODING, E. R. The distribution of bananas by railway. (Proceedings of the British Railways (W.R.) Lecture & Debating Society, 1958–59, no. 454). pp. 11, with discussion.
Author, 'Passenger & Traffic Manager, Elders & Fyffes Ltd'.

11540 KELLY, W. L. Coal transport in 1958. (Proceedings of the British Railways (W.R.) London Lecture & Debating Society, 1958–59, no. 452). pp. 14, with discussion & table.
Author, 'Assistant Marketing Director (Transport), National Coal Board'.

11541 KELLY, W. L. Coal distribution in Great Britain. (Proceedings of the British Railways (W.R.) London Lecture & Debating Society, 1963–64, no. 482). pp. 8, with discussion.
Author, 'Head of Transport Organisation of the National Coal Board'.

11542 GILBERTSON, A. G. Iron and steel transport. (Proceedings of the British Railways (W.R.) London Lecture & Debating Society, 1965–66, no. 490). pp. 15, with discussion & map.
Author, 'Member, W.R. Board'.

11543 AIMS OF INDUSTRY. Integration of freight transport: a survey of users' attitudes. London: Aims of Industry, [1968]. pp. 29.
'A survey of the attitude of industrialists and businessmen to the suggestion implicit in the White Paper The Transport of Freight that licensing procedure was to be used to steer as much freight as possible from road transport to the railways'.

11544 BAYLISS, B. T. and EDWARDS, S. L. Transport for industry . . . London: H.M.S.O., for the Ministry of Transport, 1968. pp. iv, 60, with 23 tables.
A study of the use made of transport by manufacturing industry. Includes railways.

11545 BAYLISS, B. T. and EDWARDS, S. L. Industrial demand for transport. London: H.M.S.O., for the Ministry of Transport, 1970. pp. 162, with 133 tables, 31 graphs & 2 maps.
'A study of the determinants of demand for transport, of transport facilities and the characteristics of consignments in manufacturing industry'.

11546 THOMPSON, P. A. The transport implications of British Steel Corporation's development plans. British Rail (Western) London Lecture & Debating Society Proceedings, 1970–71, no. 509. pp. 11, with discussion & 12 tables.
Author, Head of Transport, B.S.C. Transport of steel by road is more dependable than by rail. To avoid delays, BR must develop a system whereby the progress of individual consignments of steel can be closely monitored and controlled.

K 5   RAILWAYS AND THE MONEY MARKET
Investment—The 'Railway Mania' of 1844–7—George Hudson

11547–73

Reference sources   11547–48
Historical   11549–66
Contemporaneous   11567–73

Reference sources

11547 ENGLISH, H. A complete view of the joint stock companies formed during the years 1824 and 1825, being six hundred and twenty-four in number, shewing the amount of capital, number of shares, amount advanced, present value, amount liable to be called, fluctuations in price, names of bankers, solicitors, etc. with general summary and remarks and an appendix giving a list of companies formed antecedent to that period . . . London: Boossey & Sons, 1827. pp. 43, mostly tables.
Existing: Canal & rail road, etc. 20 companies (9-column list).
Abandoned: Rail Roads, 16 companies (7-column list).
Projected: Railroads, 15 companies (2-column list).

11548 SPACKMAN, W. F. Statistical Tables of the agriculture, shipping, colonies, manufactures, commerce and population of the

United Kingdom and its dependencies, brought down to the year 1843. *London: Longman*, [1843]. pp. 161.

pp. 149–50, Railways (3 columns: name, capital paid up, dividend per cent).

Historical

11549 JENKS, L. H. The migration of British capital to 1875. *New York & London: A. A. Knopf*, 1927. pp. xi, 442.

ch. 5 (pp. 126–57), 'The Railway Revolution: railways & contractors', with 71 notes, incl. evaluative bibliographical notes. The promotion and construction of foreign railways with British capital after 1845.

—— [2nd edn]. *London: Jonathan Cape*, 1938. (Bedford Series of Economic Handbooks). pp. x, 442.

—— re-issued by *T. Nelson, London*, 1963.

—— re-issued by *T. Nelson* (Nelson's University Paperbacks), 1971.

11550 MEREDITH, H. A. The drama of money making: tragedy and comedy of the London Stock Exchange. *London: Sampson, Low, Marston*, [1931]. pp. vi, 314.

pp. 82–96, The Railway King, George Hudson, 1840–1850; pp.97–103, The Railway Boom, 1845; pp. 104–11, The Overend Gurney crisis, 1866.

11551 KING, W. T. C. A history of the London discount market . . . , with an introduction by T. E. Gregory. *London: Routledge*, 1936. pp. xix, 355, with many notes & a bibliography (pp. 333–6).

pp. 129–33, 170–2, The Railway Mania.

11552 BRETHERTON, R. F., BURCHARDT, F. A. and RUTHERFORD, R. S. G. Public investment and the trade cycle in Great Britain. *Oxford: Clarendon Press*, 1941. pp. vii, 455, with 38 graphs & 62 tables.

Railways (inter-war years), *passim* & tables 35 to 50.

11553 GAYER, A. D., ROSTOW, W. W. and SCHWARTZ, A. J. The growth and fluctuation of the British economy, 1790–1850 . . . *Oxford: Clarendon Press*, 1953. 2 vols. (pp. xxxvi, 528; xii, 529–1028).

Investment in railways and railway construction, pp. 434–9 *et passim*.

11554 MATTHEWS, R. C. O. A study in trade cycle history: economic fluctuations in Great Britain, 1833–1842. *Cambridge: Cambridge University Press*, 1954. pp. xiv, 228, with 33 tables & 17 charts.

Railways, pp. 106–13, 120–6, 202–4 *et passim*; joint stock companies and the first railway investment mania, 1834–6, pp. 159–62.

11555 ALTHAUS, F. R. The Stock Exchange and the railways. (Proceedings of the British Railways (Western Region) London Lecture & Debating Society, 1954–55, no. 417). pp. 12, with discussion.

Author, Member of the Council of the Stock Exchange. A talk about the Stock Exchange and investment procedure generally, with some introductory paragraphs about investment in railways in the 19th century.

11556 WARD-PERKINS, C. N. The commercial crisis of 1847, *in* Essays in Economic History, ed. by E. M. Carus-Wilson (1962), vol. 3, pp. 263–79.

Discusses contributing factors, including distortions in financial structure following the Railway Mania due to consequential railway construction, with a chart showing the movement of railway shares against that of Consols, January 1845 to December 1848.

11557 BROADBRIDGE, S. The sources of railway share capital, *in* Railways in the Victorian Economy, ed. by M. C. Reed (1969), pp. 184–211, with 116 notes & 5 tables.

11558 REED, M. C. Railways and the growth of the capital market, *in* Railways in the Victorian Economy, ed. by M. C. Reed (1969), pp. 162–83, with 96 notes & 4 tables.

11559 BROADBRIDGE, S. Studies in railway expansion and the capital market in England, 1825–1873. *London: F. Cass*, 1970. pp. xv, 215, with 28 tables & 3 maps, 579 notes & a bibliography (234 sources).

pt. 1, The development and operation of the Lancashire & Yorkshire Railway network.

pt. 2, The early railway capital market.

11560 SUPPLE, B. The Royal Exchange Assurance: a history of British insurance, 1720–1970. *Cambridge: Cambridge University Press*, 1970. pp. xxii, 584.

pp. 224–30, Railway accident and passenger insurance; pp. 326 . . . 348, investment in railways.

11561 PEACOCK, A. J. and JOY, D. George Hudson of York. *Clapham (N. Yorks): Dalesman Books*, 1971. pp. 96, with 26 illus & map on 16 plates & a chronology (pp. 93–6).

11562 REED, M. C. Investment in railways in Britain, 1820–44. Thesis, D. Phil, University of Oxford, 1971. *See also* 11564.

11563 RICHARDS, E. The Leviathan of Wealth: the Sutherland fortune in the Industrial Revolution. *London: Routledge & Kegan Paul*, 1973. (Studies in Social History). pp. xx, 316, with 5 illus, 4 maps, 566 notes & a bibliography (330 sources). Foreword by S. G. Checkland.

pp. 37–148, The House of Sutherland and the coming of the railways.

The Stafford–Sutherland family as land-owners in the growing industrialisation of the Midlands and Lancashire in the first half of the 19th Century, and its involvement in canal and railway promotion. The Liverpool & Manchester Rly, the Grand Junction Rly, the Bridgewater Canal and the Birmingham & Liverpool Junction Canal figure prominently in this section as also does James Loch, the family's agent, as manager of an enormous and ever-changing collection of assets.

The scale of involvement is indicated by the family's financial support for the Liverpool & Manchester Rly venture in the 1820s, amounting to one-fifth of the total capital investment.

11564 REED, M. C. Investment in railways in Britain, 1820–1844: a study in the development of the capital market. *London: Oxford University Press*, 1975. pp. xiv, 315, with 47 tables, 2 maps, 3 diagrams, & over 700 notes and references.

The bibliography is extensive (pp. 290–304) and describes MSS, unpublished printed sources, Parliamentary Papers, periodical literature, & ca. 130 books, essays and theses. *See also* 11562.

11565 COTTRELL, P. L. Railway finance and the crisis of 1866: contractors' bills of exchange and the finance companies, *in* Journal of Transport History, new series, vol. 3 (1975–6). pp. 20–40, with 128 notes.

11566 MOUNTFIELD, D. The railway barons. *London: Osprey*, 1979. pp. 224, with 66 illus & a bibliography (65 sources).

In Britain and America. Includes chapters on the Railway Mania, George Hudson and Thomas Brassey.

Contemporaneous

11567 OBSERVATIONS upon the present railroad mania. *London: L. Booth*, 1845. pp. 23.

'The speculative and dangerous nature of the present mania.'

11568 BLACKHAM, J. and HICKEY, A. Advice to promoters, subscribers, scripholders and shareholders of joint-stock and railway companies, pointing out the rights and liabilities arising from signing parliamentary contracts, holding and transferring scrip letters of allotment and shares, etc., intended principally for the use of non-professional persons. *Dublin: A. Milliken*, 1846. pp. 42.

11569 WILSON, J. Capital, currency and banking, being a collection of a series of articles published in the Economist in 1845, on the principles of the Bank Act of 1844, and in 1847, on the recent monetarial and commercial currency. *London: The Office of the Economist*, 1847. pp. xxvi, 294.

Preface (pp. iii–xxvi): article 1, 'Railways, past, present and future', from the *Economist* of 4 October 1845; article 13 (pp. 146–6), 'Commerce and finance: our present state and future prospects' (the extent of railway investments and liabilities, the effects of railways on the capital of the country; the increase of imports caused by railway expenditure; the effect of railways in economising capital), from *The Economist*, 10 April, 1847.

—— 2nd edn. *London: D. M. Aird*, 1859. pp. xviii, 203, 100.

The Preface and Appendix are made to follow the text which is stated to be substantially the same as that of the first edition.

11570 PLAYFORD, F. Practical hints for investing money, with an explanation of the mode of transacting business on the Stock Exchange. *London: Smith, Elder & Co.*, 1855. pp. 144, with tables.

pp. 49–56, Railway investments.

—— 2nd edn. *Smith, Elder & Co.*, 1856. pp. xii, 145. (pp. 42–9).

—— 4th edn. *Virtue Bros*, 1865 (Weale's Rudimentary Series, 152). sm. 8°. pp. x, 110. (pp. 42–9).

—— 5th edn. *Virtue Bros*, 1865. (Weale's Rudimentary Series, 152). sm. 8°. pp. x, 110.

—— 6th edn. *Virtue Bros*, 1869. sm 8°. pp. x, 110.

11571 BOLTER, A. E. Stocks and shares in connection with railway management. Great Western Railway (London) Lecture & Debating Society, meeting on January 20th, 1905 (no. 8). pp. 8.

11572 BEAL, W. H. Banking in its railway connection, and the process of payment by cheque. Great Western Railway (London) Lecture & Debating Society, meeting on October 11th, 1906 (no. 27). pp. 7.

11573 BAKER, E. O. Banking and its aid to transport. (Proceedings of the British Railway (W.R.) London Lecture & Debating Society, 1956–57, no. 433). pp. 16, with discussion & 1 illus.

Governmental control and inspection, the regulation of railway promotion and the safeguarding of the public interest and the needs of rail users by the legislature and by government department supervision—The Railway Interest—Acts—Light Railway Orders—The Railway Passenger Duty (Travelling Tax)

11574–11625

Reference source   11574
Historical   11575–97
Contemporaneous   11598–625

Reference source

11574   ENGLISH Historical Documents, vol. XI, 1783–1832, ed. by A. Aspinall and E. A. Smith. *London: Eyre & Spottiswoode*, 1959. pp. 992.
no. 385 (pp. 544–5), 'Railways Acts passed by Parliament, 1801–1832', reprinted from *The Progress of the Nation*, by G. R. Porter, vol. 2 (1838), pp. 63–4.

Historical

11575   TRAVELLING TAX ABOLITION COMMITTEE. [A collection of 28 pamphlets & leaflets published by the T.T.A.C. from 1878 to 1890].   BL
Railway Passenger Duty was introduced in 1832 and revised in 1842. Exemption was made in 1843 for workmen's trains and in 1883 for 'parliamentary' trains. The earlier Stage Carriage Tax, for public road vehicles, was repealed in 1870.
With the rapid spread of untaxed urban tramways following the introduction of the Tramways Act, 1870, came growing resentment on the part of some railway capitalists who contended that a tramway is a railway and like railways should be taxed. In opposition to this some maintained that a tramway is a tramway, not a railway, when it uses a publicly-owned roadway, and is then exempt from tax. From 1880 this controversy is a prominent theme in pamphlets on railway reform and one of this Collection, possibly the last to be published by the T.T.A.C., epitomises the case fought by the Committee over its 20 years of existence and is described below (11611).
For an account of the Travelling Tax Abolition Committee see *The Railway Interest*, by Geoffrey Alderman (1973), pp. 89–90.

11576   HOLYOAKE, G. J.   History of the Travelling Tax. *London: printed by A. Bonner*, 1901. pp. 16.
'Reprinted from the *Co-operative Wholesale Society Annual of England & Scotland* for 1901.'

11577   POTTER, F.   The requirements of the Board of Trade. Great Western Railway (London) Debating Society, meeting on Friday, December 2nd, 1904 (no. 5). pp. 10.
Historical and contemporary.

11578   POTTER, F.   The Government in relation to the railways of the country. Great Western Railway (London) Lecture & Debating Society, meeting on Thursday February 11th, 1909 (no. 58). pp. 24.
Historical and contemporary.

11579   BASSETT, A. T.   Gladstone's speeches: descriptive index and bibliography. *London: Methuen*, 1916. pp. x, 667.
Railways: Index refers to 26 places in text.

11580   OFFICE OF THE PARLIAMENTARY COUNCIL.   Index to Statutory Definitions. *London: H.M.S.O.*, 1923. tall 8°. pp. 120.
A record of the use of terms in the wording of Acts of Parliament, 1830 to 1922. Includes 'Railways', 'Tramways', and many other terms which derive from these.
—— another edn. *H.M.S.O.*, 1936. pp. 301.
A revised edition extending the coverage to 1934.

11581   CHARLETON, H. C.   Parliament: the birthplace of the railways. Great Western Railway (London) Lecture & Debating Society [meeting on October 8th, 1925] (no. 183). pp. 2.
Reprinted from the *G.W.R. Magazine*, November 1925.

11582   ENGLISH Historical Documents, vol. XII, pt. 1, 1833–1874, ed. by G. M. Young and W. D. Handcock. *London: Eyre & Spottiswoode*, 1956. pp. xxiii, 1017.
no. 84 (pp. 219–20), 'Railway Returns, 1842–1874', *from* Statistical Abstracts.
no. 96 (pp. 248–50), 'Select Committee of 1844 on Railways'. Resolutions with regard to new railways, *from* Parly. Papers, 1844, XI, pp. 9–11.
no. 98 (pp. 257–9), Second Report of the Select Committee of 1846 on the Amalgamation of Railways and Canals, *from* Parly. Papers, 1846, XIII, pp. 95–96.
no. 101 (pp. 264–71), Select Committee of 1852–1853 on Railway and Canal Amalgamation, *from* Parly. Papers, 1852–3, XXXVIII, with evidence of Samuel Laing, Mark Huish, Charles Russell, E. E. P. Kelsey, John Hawkshaw, R. Baxter.
no. 109 (pp. 315–9), Select Committee of 1872 on Railway Amalgamation, *from* Parly. Papers, 1872, XVIII–XXIII.

11583   PARRIS, H. W.   The regulation of railways by the Government in Great Britain: the work of the Board of Trade and the Railway Commissioners, 1840–1867. Thesis, Ph.D., University of Leicester, 1960/61.

11584   MORGAN, E. V. and THOMAS, W. A.   The Stock Exchange: its history and functions. *London: Elek Books*, 1962. pp. 293.

pp. 100–12, 'Transport and public utilities', with 20 notes (railways & tramways, pp. 105–11).
—— 2nd edn. *Elek Books*, 1969. pp. 295.
pp. 105–11, railways & tramways.

11585 BURN, W. L. The age of equipoise: a study of the mid-Victorian generation. *London: Allen & Unwin*, 1964. pp. 340.
pp. 161–5, Laissez-faire *v.* regulation: Parliament and the railways.

11586 PARRIS, H.W. Government and the railways in nineteenth-century Britain. *London: Routledge & Kegan Paul; Toronto: Toronto University Press*, 1965. (Studies in Political History). pp. xii, 244, with 11 illus on 8 plates, a bibliography with notes (pp. 235–7), & 905 notes in the text.

11587 ROBERTS, G. K. The development of a railway interest and its relation to Parliament, 1830–1868. Thesis, Ph.D., University of London (L.S.E.), November 1965.

11588 BAGWELL, P. S. The railway interest: its organisation and influence, 1839–1914. In Journal of Transport History, vol. 7 (1965–6), pp. 65–86, with 97 notes.

11589 ALDERMAN, G. The railway interest, 1873–1913. Thesis, D.Phil., University of Oxford, 1969.
See also 11591.

11590 BOND, M. F. Guide to the Records of Parliament. *London: H.M.S.O.*, 1971. pp. x, 352.
Index (pp. 313–352) has 20 entries under 'Railways', 'Tramways', and 'Transport'. Valuable also as a guide to parliamentary procedure.

11591 ALDERMAN, G. The railway interest. *Leicester: Leicester University Press*, 1973. pp. 344, with 1320 notes & a bibliography, pp. 251–70 (over 500 sources).
The influence of railway director MPs in Parliament, 1830–1914, and of the railway companies as business concerns, upon the course of British party politics and upon the pattern of railway development.
Appendix (pp. 229–50), a series of 8-column statistical tables of party representation in the railway interest in the House of Commons and the House of Lords, 1868–1914, introduced by a note (pp. 229–31) on the interpretation of information on directors in contemporary published sources.
See also 11589.

11592 HILLMAN, J. J. The parliamentary structuring of British road-rail freight co-ordination. *Evanston (Illinois): Northwestern University Transportation Center*, 1973. (Monographs, 2). pp. 302, with 429 notes, many extensive.
A detailed study of varying conditions of competition and co-operation, and of conflicting political ideologies, since 1918.

11593 CAIN, P. J. Traders versus railways: the genesis of the Railway and Canal Traffic Act of 1894. In Journal of Transport His-

tory, new series, vol. 2, 1973–4, pp. 65–84, with 147 notes.

11594 BUTTON, K. J. The 1968 Transport Act and after. *Loughborough: University of Loughborough, Department of Economics*, April 1974. (Loughborough Papers on Recent Developments in Economic Policy & Thought, 6). pp. 22.
pp. 4–7, Railways; pp. 20–22, bibliography.

11595 TRACEY, D. B. The influence of Private Bill procedure upon the formation of the first railways between Liverpool and Manchester and London. Thesis, M.A., University of Manchester, 1974.

11596 CLINKER, C. R. Light Railway Orders: introductory notes on, and schedule of, Light Railway Orders confirmed by the Board of Trade and its successors under the terms of the Light Railway Acts of 1896, 1901, 1906, and 1912. *Bristol: Avon Anglia Publications*, 1977. (Reference Aid Series, 2). pp. 31.

11597 SWANN, B. and TURNBULL, M. Records of interest to social scientists, 1919 to 1939: employment and unemployment. *London: H.M.S.O.*, 1978. (Public Record Office Handbooks, 18). pp. v, 590.
Published with the co-operation of the Social Science Research Council.
pp. 102–05, Railways, (including the proposed Channel Tunnel), consisting of a summary of the government/railway relationships of this period which affected levels of manpower.

Contemporaneous

11598 RAILWAY Bills: some reasons against the Duke of Wellington's clause. [*London: Vacher & Son*, 1836]. pp. 2. Caption title, Railway Bills: reasons against the clause proposed by the Duke of Wellington.
The proposal is discussed by Henry Parris in his *Government and the Railways in Nineteenth-Century Britain* (1965), on pp. 21–2. NUC

11599 BURKE, J. St G. Remarks on the Standing Orders and Resolutions of the last session of Parliament relating to railways, with practical instructions for their observance, and some suggestions for their amendment, by a parliamentary agent [i.e. James St George Burke]. [*London*]: *J. Bigg*, 1837. pp. 168.

11600 BOARD OF TRADE. Reports of the Committee of the Board of Trade on the various railways projected and in progress, with an introductory preface and general index. *London: Simpkin*, 1845. pp. 126.

11601 PARLIAMENT. HOUSE OF COMMONS. The Standing Orders of the House of Commons relative to Private Bills as amended the 15th July 1847, with an abstract of the orders respecting Railway Bills arranged in the order of the proceedings thereon, and a

copious index. *Westminster: James Bigg & Son*, 1847. pp. 118, with specimen deposited plan & section with insets (folded) facing title-page.
Also published with *The House of Lords Standing Orders* in one volume as *The Standing Orders of Both Houses of Parliament* (1847).

11602 PARLIAMENT. HOUSE OF LORDS. The Standing Orders of the House of Lords relative to Private Bills as amended the 22nd of July 1847, with an abstract of the orders respecting Railway Bills arranged in order of the proceedings thereon, and a copious index. *Westminster: James Bigg & Son*, 1847. pp. 97, with specimen deposited plan & section with inset (folded) facing title-page.
Also published with *The House of Commons Standing Orders* in one volume as *The Standing Orders of Both Houses of Parliament* (1847).

11603 TRAVELLING TAX ABOLITION COMMIT- TEE. The Travelling Tax Abolition Committee to the people of the United Kingdom. *London*: [*the Committee*], January 1878. pp. 16.
General statement of the case for repeal of the railway passenger duty.

11604 TRAVELLING TAX ABOLITION COMMIT- TEE. Memorial to Sir Henry James, M.P., Her Majesty's Attorney-General, from the Travelling Tax Abolition Committee. *London: the Committee*, [1882]. pp. 8.
On the liability of tramways for railway passenger duty (5%).

11605 TRAVELLING TAX ABOLITION COMMIT- TEE. Railway passenger duty: the petition . . . to the House of Commons of Great Britain & Ireland in Parliament assembled, 9 April, 1883. [*London: the Committee*, 1883]. pp. 4.
Asking for railway passenger duty to be repealed.

11606 TRAVELLING TAX ABOLITION COMMIT- TEE. What is a tramway?: the petition of the Travelling Tax Abolition Committee, 30 April 1883 to the . . . House of Commons of Great Britain & Ireland in Parliament assembled. [*London: the Committee*, 1883]. pp. 2.

11607 TRAVELLING TAX ABOLITION COMMIT- TEE. The tramway imposture: meeting of The Association of Railway Shareholders, Manchester, 8 January 1884; extract from the speech of Lord A. S. Churchill [followed by a letter addressed to him by C. D. Collet, Secretary to the T.T.A.C. dated 5 April, 1884]. *London: the Committee*, [1884]. pp. 8, with 19 notes.
The central issue, 'Is a tramway a railway or a tramway?' is dealt with at length and in detail by C. D. Collet, who uses the Wantage Tramway and the Swansea & Mumbles Railway to illustrate his argument. A tramway is defined by him (p.5) as a railway which has grooved rails.

11608 TRAVELLING TAX ABOLITION COMMIT- TEE. The Railway and Canal Traffic Bill, 1886: a coercion Bill. Letter to the President of the Board of Trade. *London: the Committee*, 1886. pp. 8.
Passenger duty on railways—a 'pure robbery'.

11609 RAWLINGS, E. C. Railway and Canal Commission: a short digest in a popular form of the chief provisions of the Railway & Canal Traffic Act, 1888, for the use of merchants and traders by E. C. Rawlings, Solicitor of the Supreme Court. *London: Evison & Bridge*, 1888. pp. 21.

11610 TRAVELLING TAX ABOLITION COMMIT- TEE. The new taxes on locomotion: an analysis of their danger and a plea for their rejection. *London: the Committee*, 1888. pp. 8.
The 'Wheel Tax', i.e. the Trade Cart Tax: should it be applied to railways and tramways?

11611 TRAVELLING TAX ABOLITION COMMIT- TEE. Two memorials, to the Prime Minister and the Chancellor of the Exchequer, to which is prefixed a brief history of the railway passenger duty. *London: the Committee*, [1890]. pp. 12.
The railway passenger duty since 1842 and the case for its abolition: tramways are exempt, railways are not, yet how can the two be distinguished in legal terms? Also, the tax is on gross receipts, not on profits which for railways are small—the average dividend in 1888 being only 4.06%.   TCD; LU(THC)

11612 TRAVELLING TAX ABOLITION COMMIT- TEE. Address to the Right Hon. Sir Michael Hicks-Beach, M.P., President of the Board of Trade. *London: the Committee*, [1891]. pp. 4.

11613 TRAVELLING TAX ABOLITION COMMIT- TEE. The Board of Trade and the Board of Inland Revenue. *London: the Committee*, [1891]. pp. 8.

11614 BOARD OF TRADE. DEPARTMENTAL COMMITTEE ON RAILWAY AGREEMENTS AND AMALGAMATIONS, 1911. Report, Appendices & Minutes of Evidence. (Chairman, Russell Rea.) *London: H.M.S.O.*, 1911. (Cd 5631). pp. 49, 1023.
On the nature and terms of agreements between Government and railway companies, and between railway companies.

11615 GRAVESON, F. H. Parliamentary procedure in the promotion of Railway Bills. Great Western Railway (London) Lecture & Debating Society, meeting on November 19th, 1912 [no. 93]. pp. 6, with discussion.
Author, 'North Eastern Rly'.

11616 DAVIS, F. R. E. Are railway companies unduly handicapped by their statutory obligations? Great Western Railway (London) Lecture & Debating Society, meeting on December 18th, 1913 (no. 106). pp. 28–36, with discussion.

11617 PARLIAMENT. HOUSE OF COMMONS. Railways Bill: memorandum as to Road Transport clause. *Westminster: House of Commons*, 1921. pp. 4.
A circular to MPs. Railways should be allowed to develop their own road transport.

11618 GODFREY, E. The Railways Act, 1921: is it a failure? Great Western Railway (London) Lecture & Debating Society, meeting on December 4th 1924 (no. 176). pp. 17, with discussion.

11619 ADIE, K. S. Fair and just: sequel to The Scandal of the British Railways. *London: K. S. Adie*, October 1944. pp. 24.
The Railway Control Agreement, 1941. *See* 5457.

11620 HEALD, L. The relationship of the nationalised industries to the Legislature. (Proceedings of the British Railways (W.R.) London Lecture & Debating Society, 1952–53, no. 400). pp. 15, with discussion.
Author, the Attorney General.

11621 MINISTRY OF TRANSPORT. Re-organisation of the nationalised transport undertakings. *London: H.M.S.O.*, [1961]. (Cmnd 1248). pp. 14.

11622 AIMS OF INDUSTRY. White Elephant and (Barbara) Castle: Government threat to transport. *London: Aims of Industry*, August [1967]. pp. [6].
Barbara Castle was Minister of Transport from December 1965 to April 1968.

11623 MORRIS, J. Address [on the Government's new transport policies]. (Proceedings of the British Railways (W.R.) London Lecture & Debating Society, 1967–68, no. 497). pp. 11, with discussion.
Author, Parliamentary Secretary, Ministry of Transport.

11624 DANIEL, A. W. T. Transport Bill: a critical commentary. *London: National Council on Inland Transport*, February 1968. pp. 10.
Concerning H.C. Bill [43], 1966–7.

11625 DUNSTON, R. E. Transports of State. *London: Aims of Industry*, [1968]. pp. 14.
Comment on 'The Transport Bill now before Parliament . . . a Bill with repressive elements, and founded on bigotry rather than economics'.

K 7   RAILWAY LAW

Manuals and treatises on statute and case law relating to railways

11626–37

11626 JONES, T. I. J. Acts of Parliament concerning Wales, 1714–1901; compiled and edited by T. I. Jeffreys Jones. *Cardiff: University of Wales Press*, 1966. (Board of Celtic Studies, University of Wales History of Law series, 17). pp. xiii, 343.
pp. 81–167, 'Railways and early tramways' (726 Local & Personal Acts, 3 Public General Acts); pp. 168–70, 'Urban tramways' (23 Local & Personal Acts).

11627 SPEARMAN, G. An enquiry into the ancient and present state of the County Palatine of Durham. [no place, no publisher], 1729. pp. [iv], 128 & 4 pp. inserted.
On pp. 61, 73, 87–8, legal problems presented by wagonways.

11628 SIMON, H. A. The law relating to railway accidents, including an outline of the liabilities of railway companies as carriers generally. *London: V. & R. Stevens, Sons, & Haynes*, 1862. pp. xii, 100.

11629 BOWEN, J. E. The duties of a solicitor to a railway company. Great Western Railway (London) Lecture & Debating Society, meeting on Thursday, January 11th 1906 [no. 21]. pp. 15.

11630 WAGHORN, T. The law relating to railway traffic. *London: E. Wilson*, 1906. pp. xiii, 149.
From *The Law relating to Traffic on Railways and Canals*, by E. Boyle & T. Waghorn (3 vols. 1901).

11631 REVIEW of the Railways Act, 1921. pp. 60. Reproduced typescript. Text dated 'April 3rd, 1925'. Possibly not published.
Detailed explanatory notes on each section of the Act.   LU(THC)

11632 RAWLINGS, P. L. E. Some aspects of the law of carriage by railway. (Proceedings of the Great Western Railway (London) Lecture & Debating Society, 1931–32, no. 257). pp. 8, with discussion.
Author, 'Barrister-at-Law'.

11633 PLOWMAN, R. G. Some aspects of the law of carriage by railway. (Proceedings of the Great Western Railway (London) Lecture & Debating Society, 1947–48, no. 344). pp. 14, with discussion.
Author, 'Common Law Assistant to the Solicitor'.

11634 RIDLEY, J. The law of carriage of goods by land, sea and air. *London: Shaw & Sons*, 1957. pp. xlviii, 254.
—— 2nd edn, 1965. pp. xlviii, 226.

—— 3rd edn, 1971. pp. xlviii, 223.
—— 4th edn, edited by Geoffrey Whitehead, 1975. pp. 287.

11635 DAVIES, R. The Offices, Shops and Railway Premises Act, 1963. *London: Oyez
Publications*, 1965. pp. xliii, 299.
   An Act to ensure minimum standards of working conditions: commentary.

11636 POWELL-SMITH, V. Transport Act, 1968.

London: Butterworths, 1969. pp. vi, 290.
Index, pp. 271–90.
   The sections and schedules of the Act analysed
and explained in detail.

11637 BONNER, G. A. British transport law by
road and rail. *Newton Abbot: David &
Charles*, 1974. pp. xxv, 406.
   Includes tables of Statutes, Statutory Instru-
ments and cases at law, and in appendix, BR's
General Conditions of Carriage of Goods.

K 8   RAILWAYS AND CRIME

Offences against railways or committed upon railway property—Railway police

11638–54

11638 GREAT NORTHERN RLY. Report of the
proceedings of the trials of Leopold Redpath and Chas. James Comyns Kent for
forgery, at the Central Criminal Court on
Friday 16th January 1857, before Mr. Baron
Martin and Mr. Justice Willes. *London:
printed by Waterlow & Sons [for the G.N.
Rly*, 1857]. pp. 47.

11639 JENKIN, F. C. The preservation of law and
order on railways. Great Western Railway
(London) Lecture & Debating Society,
meeting on December 1st, 1910 [no. 73].
pp. 26.

11640 IRVING, H. B. The trial of Franz Müller,
edited by H. B. Irving. *Edinburgh & London: W. Hodge*, 1911. (Notable English
Trials series). pp. xlviii, 194, with frontis &
10 illus on plates.
   The murder of Thomas Briggs on the North
London Rly, 9th July 1864.

11641 ROWAN-HAMILTON, S. O. The trial of
John Alexander Dickman, edited by S. O.
Rowan-Hamilton. *Edinburgh & London:
W. Hodge*, 1914. (Notable English Trials
series). pp. viii, 208, with frontis & 5 illus.
   The murder of John Nisbet on the North
Eastern Rly, between Newcastle & Alnmouth, 18
March 1910.
   The Introduction includes a brief resumé of the
seven murders known to have been committed in
railway carriages in Britain.

11642 DILNOT, G. The trial of William Pierce,
James Burgess and William George Tester
within the Central Criminal Court, Old
Bailey, London, January 13th, 1857 and the
following day . . . [appended to] The Trial
of Jim the Penman, edited by George
Dilnot. *London: G. Bles*, 1930. pp. 125–
269, with 7 plates.
   The gold bullion robbery on the South Eastern
Rly between London Bridge and Boulogne on 15
May 1855.

11643 ADAM, H. L. Murder by persons unknown. *London: N. Collins, Sons & Co.*,
1931. pp. 286.

Three train mysteries (pp. 130–148):
   The Merstham Tunnel mystery [London Brigh-
ton & South Coast Rly, Sept. 1924].
   A Strange Weapon [London & S.W. Rly,
Feltham to Waterloo, Feb. 1897].
   The Starchfield Case [North London Rly, Jan.
1914].

11644 STEPHENS, G. The history and functions of
railway police. Great Western Railway
(London) Lecture & Debating Society,
meeting on 12th November 1936, no. 305.
pp. 12.
   Author, 'Chief of Police, G.W.R.'.

11645 RICHARDS, W. O. History and work of
the British Transport Commission Police.
(Proceedings of the British Railways
(W.R.) London Lecture & Debating Society, 1953–54, no. 406). pp. 19, with discussion.
   Author, 'Chief Officer [Police], B.T.C.'

11646 GAY, W. O. Communications and crime,
by William O. Gay, Chief Constable, British Transport Police. *Chichester: Barry
Rose*, [1974]. pp. 44, with 4 illus & a
bibliography (25 sources).
   Originally published in the *Police Journal*. The
origin and development of the British Transport
Police and the nature and extent of crime associated with public transport.

11647 CRICHTON, M. The Great Train Robbery.
London: Jonathan Cape, 1975. pp. 255.
   The gold bullion robbery on the S.E. Rly on
May 15th 1855: a conjectured narrative.

11648 MACKENZIE, C. The most wanted man:
the story of Ronald Biggs. *London: Hart-
Davis, MacGibbon*, 1975. pp. [vi], 295, with
26 illus on 16 plates.
   Relating to the 'Great Train Robbery', Ched-
dington, 8 August 1963.
   —— another edn. *Granada*, 1976. pp. 303,
with 14 illus on 8 plates. (reprinted, 1978).

11649 DELANO, A. Slip up: how Fleet Street
caught Ronnie Biggs and Scotland Yard lost
him: the story behind the scoop. *London:
Deutsch*, 1977. pp. 174.

Activity sequential to the Great Train Robbery of August 1963.

11650 READ, P. P. The train robbers. *London: W. H. Allen*, 1978. pp. xviii, 285, with 36 illus (portraits) on 16 plates, 3 maps & a bibliography (15 sources).
The Great Train Robbery, 1963.

11651 SELLWOOD, A. and SELLWOOD, M. The Victorian railway murders. *Newton Abbot: David & Charles*, 1979. pp. 160, with frontis & 20 illus.
Four cases: Franz Müller, North London Rly, 9 July, 1864; Percy Lefroy, L.B.S.C.R., 27 June, 1881; Elizabeth Camp (victim), L.S.W.R., 11 February, 1897; George H. Parker, L.S.W.R., 17 January, 1901.

11652 FEWTRELL, M. The train robbers, by ex-detective superintendent Malcolm Fewtrell . . . who investigated the Great Train Robbery. *London: A. Barker*, 1964. pp. 157, with 17 illus on 8 plates, incl. 13 portraits.

11653 GOSLING, J. and CRAIG, D. The Great Train Robbery. *London: W. H. Allen*, 1964. pp. 142, with frontis & 8 illus on 8 plates.
The Great Train Robbery, 1963.

11654 FORDHAM, P. The robbers' tale: the real story of the Great Train Robbery. *London: Hodder & Stoughton*, 1965. pp. 160.
The Great Train Robbery, 1963.
—— Reprinted (re-set), *Penguin Books*, 1968. pp. 205.

K 9   RAILWAYS AND THE POST OFFICE
Travelling post offices—The Post Office (London) Railway—Railway philately
11655–76

11655 HYDE, J. W. The Royal Mail: its curiosities and romance. *Edinburgh & London: W. Blackwood*, 1885. pp. 378.
ch. 10 (pp. 145–54), 'The Travelling Post Office', with 2 illus.
—— 2nd edn. *W. Blackwood*, 1885. pp. xi, 391.
—— 3rd edn. *Simpkin Marshall*, [1889]. pp. xvi, 306, 4. (pp. 116–23).

11656 LANE, F. Post Office transport arrangements. (Proceedings of the Great Western Railway (London) Lecture & Debating Society, 1931–32, no. 254). pp. 15, with discussion, 7 illus & a map of the Post Office (London) Railway.
Author, 'Secretary's Office, G.P.O.'.

11657 HAY, I. The Post Office went to war. *London: H.M.S.O.*, 1946. pp. 96, with 67 illus, & maps.
pp. 29–30, 'The Post Office Railway', with 3 illus.

11658 WATSON, J. Stamps and railways. *London: Faber*, 1960. pp. 142, with numerous illus of stamps on 16 plates.
World coverage.

11659 CORNISH, R. P. A List of Postage Stamps of the World associated with Railways. 2nd edn. *Altrincham: Railway Philatelic Group*, 1969. pp. 52, with illus. Reproduced typescript.
Previous edition, 1967.

11660 POTTER, D. The Talyllyn Railway stamps and postal history. [*Hale*]: *Railway Philatelic Group*, [1969]. pp. 24, with 10 illus (some composite).

11661 HART, C. A. The railway theme: a study of railways on stamps. *Railway Philatelic Group*, 1970. pp. 46, with illus.

11662 JACKSON, H. T. The railway letter posts of Great Britain. *Railway Philatelic Group*.
part 1, General history. 1968. pp. 51, with 7 illus (of railway letter stamps); pp. 48–51, List of railways and their successors known to have operated a railway letter service.
part 1, 2nd edn, 1970. pp. 58; 8 illus & list of railways.
No more published so far.

11663 ISLE OF MAN POST OFFICE AUTHORITY. Centenary of the Isle of Man steam railway. [*Douglas: Isle of Man P.O. Authority*, 1973].
Four commemorative stamps (2½p, 3p, 7½p, 9p) in a printed folder with historical notes.

11664 JERSEY POSTAL ADMINISTRATION. Centenary of the Jersey Eastern Railway. [*St Helier: the J.P.A.*, 1973]. Cover title: Jersey: centenary of the Eastern Railway, 1873.
Four commemorative stamps in a printed folder with historical notes.

11665 BRITISH POST OFFICE. Railways, 1825–1975: British Post Office mint stamps. *London: B.P.O.*, 1975. obl. format. pp. [16].
A booklet with four commemorative stamps (7p, 8p, 10p, 12p) in raised plastic mounts on cover. The text '150 years of railways in Britain' is by G. Freeman Allen & has 19 illus including two folded double-spread in colour: the GER 4-4-0 locomotive 'Claud Hamilton' of 1900, and a 4-6-2 of the LMS, 'Duchess of Montrose', 1938.

11666　GOODBODY, A. M. and HART, C. A. Railways on stamps. *Chippenham: Picton Publishing.*
　　vol. 2, Western Europe; part 4, France, Monaco, Great Britain, Italy. 1975. pp. 60. pp. 32–53, 'Great Britain, Isle of Man, Jersey', with illus.

11668　BOWMAN, R. Railway perfins of Great Britain. *Security Endorsement & Perfin Society of Great Britain*, 1976. la. 8°. pp. 73. Reproduced typescript in printed covers.
　　Examples with notes. Arranged under companies.

11669　ISLE OF MAN POST OFFICE AUTHORITY. Douglas horse trams centenary, 1876–1976. [*Douglas: Isle of Man P.O. Authority*, 1976].
　　Four commemorative stamps (5½p, 7p, 11p, 13p) in a printed folder with historical notes.

11670　POTTER, D. C. D. Great Britain railway letter stamps, 1957–1976: a handbook and catalogue, compiled by David Potter, edited by Peter Johnson. 3rd edn. *Leicester: Railway Philatelic Group*, 1976. pp. 36, with frontis & 31 illus, depicting 70 stamps, of the Bluebell Rly and of some narrow gauge railways in Wales.

11671　GOODBODY, A. M. An Introduction and Guide to the travelling post offices of Great Britain, edited by Peter Johnson. *Leicester: Railway Philatelic Group*, 1977. pp. 16, with 4 illus, map, & 21 T.P.O. post marks.

11672　HILL, N. The railway travelling post offices of Great Britain and Ireland, 1838–1975. *Batley: H. Hayes*, 1977. pp. 24.
　　An alphabetical list with notes.

11673　WILSON, H. S. T.P.O.: a history of the travelling post offices of Great Britain; edited by Peter Johnson. [*Altrincham*]: *Railway Philatelic Group.* 1st edn.
　　part 1, England; the 'Specials' and associated T.P.O.'s. 1971. pp. 76, with 10 illus & 205 facsimiles of handstamps.
　　part 2, England; South of the Midland T.P.O. 1975. pp. 76, with frontis, 14 illus, facsimiles of 418 handstamps, 5 timebills & a map.
　　part 3, Scotland and Ireland. 1977. pp. 78, with frontis, 15 illus, facsimiles of 436 handstamps, 2 timebills, 2 maps, 8 appendices, incl. a bibliography (8 sources), & a facsimile reproduction of a pamphlet: Remarks on the Post Office arrivals and departures to the north of Perth (Aberdeen, 1849).
　　—— 2nd edn. *Leicester: Railway Philatelic Group.*
　　part 1, England; the 'Specials' and associated T.P.O.'s. 1977. pp. 76, with frontis, 6 illus, facsimiles of 205 handstamps, map, & 7 appendices (historical documents).
　　—— 3rd edn. *Leicester: Railway Philatelic Group.*
　　part 1, England; the 'Specials' and associated T.P.O.'s. 1979. pp. 76, with frontis, 6 illus, facsimiles of 205 handstamps & 7 appendices.

11674　BAYLISS, D. A. The Post Office Railway, London. *Sheffield: Turntable Publications*, 1978. pp. 96, with 32 illus on 32 plates, 3 maps, 2 plans & a bibliography (31 sources).

11675　GOWEN, D. P. Railway station postmarks; edited by Peter Johnson. *Leicester: Railway Philatelic Group*, 1978. pp. 44, with 201 postmarks reproduced in text.

11676　BRITISH POST OFFICE. Liverpool and Manchester Railway, 1830: British Post Office mint stamps. *Edinburgh: B.P.O. Philatelic Bureau*, 1980.
　　A set of five commemorative 12p stamps, together forming a complete train, in a printed folder with historical notes.

K 10　RAILWAYS AND NATIONAL DEFENCE

The use of public railways for the movement of military personnel and equipment—Ambulance trains

11677–80

For military railways see **K 11**
For fears of invasion via the proposed Channel Tunnel see **C 8**

11677　LANCASHIRE & YORKSHIRE RLY. Exhibition of ambulance train constructed by the Lancashire & Yorkshire Railway to the order of the War Office for use on the Continent. *Hunt's Bank (Manchester): L. & Y. Rly*, Nov. 1917. obl. format. pp. 12, with col. frontis & 7 illus.

11678　GREAT CENTRAL RLY. U.S.63 ambulance train, constructed for the United States Army Medical Department at the Great Central Railway Company's carriage works, 1918. *London: G.C.R.*, [1918]. sm. obl. format. pp. 28, with 14 illus.

11679　CARTER, E. F. Railways in wartime. *London: F. Muller*, 1964. pp. 221, with 29 illus on 16 plates, 3 appendices & a bibliography (32 sources).
　　See review in *Railway World*, July 1964.

11680　PLUMRIDGE, J. H. Hospital ships and ambulance trains. *London: Seeley Service*, 1975. pp. 203, with 45 illus & a bibliography (ca. 140 sources).
　　A highly informative work with generous detail in text, appendices, bibliography and index.
　　Ambulance trains, chapters 7–14 (pp. 80–159).
　　The appendices are designated A to Q, and of these, G to Q are on ambulance trains.

Systems owned, operated and maintained by military or naval authorities
11681–92

11681 ROYAL ENGINEERS. Chronicles of the 20th Light Railway Train Crews Co., Royal Engineers, with the British Expeditionary Force, 1917–1919. *Bath: Coward & Gradwell*, [1919]. pp. 52, with 25 illus & a nominal roll of 3 officers & 252 men.

Western Front reminiscences by various members of the Company. The nominal roll gives the name of the railway company from which each member came.

11682 MILITARY Railways Rule Book, 1938. *London: H.M.S.O.*, 1939. sm. 8°. pp. 121.

11683 WAR OFFICE. Notes on military railway engineering. *London: War Office*, 2 vols.

pt 1, Survey. 1940. pp. vi, 126, with 20 tables & 25 diagrams (7 folded).

pt 2, Engineering. 1940. pp. 195, with 23 tables & 97 diagrams (64 folded).

11684 ROBBINS, M. 190 in Persia: some notes on wartime railway operation. *London: the author*, 1951, pp. 40, with 7 illus & a map on covers. Reproduced typescript in printed covers.

A narrative of the achievements of 190 Railway Operating Company, Royal Engineers in Persia, December 1941 to January 1943 when responsibility was transferred to the U.S. Army. Text written in 1943, supplemented by Introduction and appendices, including a list of War Department locomotives in Persia.

11685 BIRMINGHAM LOCOMOTIVE CLUB. British War Department locomotives, 1952–1960. *Birmingham: B.L.C., Industrial Locomotive Information Section*, 1960. (Pocket Book, WD). sm. 8°. pp. 20. Lists.

Compiled by G. P. Roberts from information mostly supplied by members.

11686 DAVIES, W. J. K. Light railways of the First World War: a history of tactical rail communications on the British fronts, 1914–18. *Newton Abbot: David & Charles*, 1967. pp. 196, with frontis, 58 illus on 24 plates, 35 maps & diagrams, 14 tables & a bibliography (22 sources).

Railways laid down and operated by the Royal Engineers Railway Operating Division.

11687 TOWNSEND, C. E. C. All rank and no file: a history of the Engineer and Railway Staff Corps, R.E., 1865–1965. *London: the Corps*, [1969]. pp. xi, 126, with col. frontis, 4 plates & 9 detailed lists.

—— 1980 Supplement, (1966–1980). *Purley: Engineer & Railway Staff Corps RE(TAVR)*, 1981. pp. vi, 24.

11688 WILLIAMS, G. Citizen soldiers of the Royal Engineers Transportation and Movements and the Royal Army Service Corps, 1859 to 1965 . . . *Longmoor: Institute of the Royal Corps of Transport*, [1969]. pp. [xii], 196, with 30 illus.

11689 BISHOP, D. and DAVIES, W. J. K. Railways and war before 1918. *London: Blandford Press*, 1972. pp. 154, with 156 col. drawings on 96 plates (pp. 7–102).

Includes military railways in the First World War, 1914–18.

11690 BISHOP, D. and DAVIES, W. J. K. Railways and war since 1917. *London: Blandford Press*, 1974. pp. 127, incl. 113 col. drawings on 80 plates.

11691 RONALD, D. W. and CARTER, R. J. The Longmoor Military Railway. *Newton Abbot: David & Charles*, 1974. pp. 255, with col. frontis & 30 illus on 16 plates, 24 maps, plans & diagrams & 13 tables.

11692 KALLA-BISHOP, P. M. Locomotives at war: army railway reminiscences of The Second World War. *Truro: Bradford Barton*, [1980]. pp. 151, with 16 illus on 8 plates. No maps or plans.

Depots in Gt. Britain: Martin Mill, Longmoor, Melbourne, the Shropshire & Montgomeryshire Rly, and military railways in Northern Ireland and at British bases abroad.

L   INDIVIDUAL RAILWAYS

The history and development of the network of 120 railway companies (the 'old companies' or 'pre-Grouping companies') which were amalgamated to form the LMS, LNER, GWR (new company) and the SR in 1923 (*see table in main work*, pp. 472–3), and their subsequent history as the 'Big Four' up to their nationalization in 1948 when, together with fifty-five smaller companies not included in the 1923 Grouping, 'British Railways' was formed (*see table in main work*, p. 474).

11693–12558

For British Railways see **B 10**
For rail transport in particular areas of the British Isles see **C 1 – C 7**
For Scottish railway companies see **C 2**

Reference sources   11693–5
Collective works   11696–8

Reference sources

11693   PEDDIE, R. A.   Railway history, *in* The Library World, vol. 45, no. 515 (December 1942), pp. 74–6.
A bibliography of 82 books and pamphlets on the history of individual British railway companies. A supplement, compiled by W. J. Skillern, was published in vol. 56, no. 657 (March 1955). *See* 11694.

11694   SKILLERN, W. J.   Railway history: a supplement to Peddie, *in* The Library World, vol. 56, no. 657 (March, 1955), pp. 139–43.
91 sources (histories of individual railways): a continuation to December 1954 of the listing by R. A. Peddie in. The December 1942 issue, with discovered earlier items. *See* 11693.

11695   ROUNDHOUSE [bookshop & publisher]. A Short List of some 19th Century Railway Guide Books, [compiled by Iris Doyle]. *Harrow-on-the-Hill: Roundhouse*, [Dec. 1980 or Jan 1981]. pp. 8. Reproduced typescript.
104 items.

Collective works

11696   [RAILWAY prospectuses and reports]. A collection of 65 railway company prospectuses, reports, statements, and MS letters, dated from 1825 to 1891 (46 having dates before 1850), with a typescript contents list, bound into a guard book. Title from spine, la. folio.   UL(GL)

11697   CASSERLEY, H. C.   Britain's joint lines. *London: Ian Allan*, 1968. pp. 224, with 220 illus.
A survey of the inter-relationships of 64 railway companies.

11698   HEAP, C. and VAN RIEMSDIJK, J.   The pre-Grouping railways: their development and individual characters. *London: H.M.S.O., for the Science Museum*.
part 1, North Eastern, Great Northern, L.&N.W., Great Western, Midland. 1972. pp. 75, with frontis & 39 illus (7 col.), 5 maps, facsimiles & 5 col. company coats of arms on cover.

part 2, L.&S.W., Great Eastern, Great Central, Lancashire & Yorkshire, S.E.&C., L.B.&S.C. 1980. pp. viii, 89, with frontis, 51 illus (7 col.), 6 maps, facsimiles & 6 col. company coats of arms on cover.

Brecon & Merthyr Rly

11699   PARRY, V. J.   Brecon & Merthyr Railway. [*Brecon*]: *the author*, 1970. pp. 84, with 9 illus, incl. maps & portraits.
Originally published as a series of essays in the Brecon & Radnor Express during 1969.
Pant to Brecon only. The building of the line from 1858 to 1872.

Caledonian Rly *See* **C 2 L**

Cambrian Rlys *See* **C 3 L**

Cheshire Lines Committee

11700   CHESHIRE LINES COMMITTEE. Rules and Regulations for the guidance of the officers and men in the service of the Cheshire Lines Committee. *Manchester: C.L.C.*, November 1883. pp. xiii, 199.
—— another edn. *Liverpool*, 1 January 1915. pp. 372, with First Supplementary Pamphlet, to come into operation January 1st 1917. pp. 8.   STOCKPORT PL

11701   EDWARDES, T. E.   New routes and old acres: the illustrated official guide of the Cheshire Lines Committee. *Liverpool: C.L.C.*, 1902. pp. 154, with 104 illus, 7 portraits, 3 facsimiles & 6 pictorial maps.
ch. 2 (pp. 7–16), 'The Cheshire Lines Committee': historical.

11702   CHESHIRE LINES COMMITTEE. Handbook of Stations, showing facilities for dealing with merchandise, mineral, live stock and passenger traffic. *Liverpool: C.L.C.*, 1927. pp. 44, with 2 maps (1 col.).
STOCKPORT PL

11703 SOUTHPORT & Cheshire Lines Extension Railway. *Norwich: Klofron*, 1977. pp. 24, with 4 maps, 4 timetables, 3 illus & a bibliography (26 sources).

Colne Valley Rly

11704 PORTWAY, C. The Colne Valley Railway, 1856–1923. *Halstead (Essex): Colne Valley Railway Preservation Society*, [197–?]. pp. [40], with 64 annotated illus, 10 station layout plans & a map inside front cover.
pp. 25–6, 'Locomotives of the Colne Valley Railway, 1861–1923', by J. Holbrook; p. 34, 'Colne Valley Preservation Society', by J. R. Hymas and R. G. Hymas.

Didcot, Newbury & Southampton Rly

11705 PANNELL, J. P. M. Old Southampton shores. *Newton Abbot: David & Charles*, 1967. pp. 196, with 27 illus on 16 plates, 21 illus in text.
pp. 122–33, 'Dockland'; pp. 134–49, 'Ghost railways': the Didcot, Newbury & Southampton Rly and other local lines now defunct.

11706 SANDS, T. B. The Didcot, Newbury and Southampton Railway. *Lingfield: Oakwood Press*, 1971. (Oakwood Library of Railway History, 28). pp. 50, with 16 illus on 8 plates, table, list, map, facsimile, gradient profile & a bibliography (30 sources).

Furness Rly

11707 RUSH, R. W. The Furness Railway, 1843–1923. *Lingfield: Oakwood Press*, 1973. (Oakwood Library of Railway History, 35). pp. 113, with 30 illus on 12 plates, 3 maps, 5 gradient profiles, 11 lists.
—— Supplement: Furness Railway locomotives and rolling stock. *Oakwood Press*, 1973. pp. 64. Intro, lists & 40 line drawings.

11708 SANKEY, R. and NORMAN, K. J. The Furness Railway: a photographic recollection. *Clapham (N. Yorks): Dalesman*, 1977. obl. format. pp. 80. Intro & 127 illus with descrs, & a map.

Glasgow & South Western Rly *See* C 2 L

Great Central Rly

11709 SKIDMORE, B. Sheffield, Ashton under Lyne and Manchester Railway: report of the present traffic on the different lines of road between Sheffield and Manchester, and an estimate of the increased and additional traffic which may be expected to pass upon the railway between those towns; taken from actual observation in the months of November, 1836 and February 1837, and founded on the opinion and experience of individuals living upon and engaged in business on the line and neighbourhood of the railway, presented to, and accepted by, committees of both Houses of Parliament, by B. Skidmore, commercial agent, Sheffield. [*Sheffield*, 1837]. pp. [4]. Fol.
UL(GL)

11710 GRINLING, C. H. The Dukeries, Sherwood Forest and the Lincolnshire sea-side. *London: J. S. Virtue, for the Lancashire, Derbyshire and East Coast Rly and the Great Northern Rly*, 1897. pp. ix, 99, with illus & fare tables.
A topographical guide issued upon the opening of the L.D.&E.C. line between Chesterfield and Lincoln. Cover title: Illustrated Guide to the Dukeries, Sherwood Forest and the sea coast.

11711 GREAT CENTRAL RLY. Great Central Railway: illustrated official album. [*London: G.C.R.*, ca. 1900]. obl. format. pp. 156, with many illus.
A high quality publicity publication presenting the G.C.'s achievements and associating the railway and its route with trades and industries in its catchment area, and with places of historical and topographical interest through which it passes.

11712 GREAT CENTRAL RLY. Plans of the extension line to London, extending from Annesley . . . to Quainton Road. [Nottingham to Leicester only] . . . [1901]. *Leicester: Main Line Steam Trust*, June 1976. Fol. pp. [32].
Seven original coloured sections photographically reduced, Loughborough to Leicester and to Nottingham Victoria Station. Limited edition of 250 copies.

11713 GREAT CENTRAL RLY. Timetables, July, August & September 1903. [Reprint]. *London: Ian Allan*, 1968. pp. viii, 6, 168, 2 folded plates, 7 col. maps.
A facsimile reprint.

11714 GREAT CENTRAL RLY. Travels at home; or, Scenes on the G.C.R. *London: G.C.R.*, [ca. 1900–1905?] pp. iv, 216, with many illus (topographical and G.C.R.).
Topographical essays by A. E. Johnson followed by 'M.S.L. to G.C.R.' by G. A. Sekon (pp. 107–26) and 'Where are we now?', a gazetteer of the G.C.R. (pp. 129–215).

11715 GREAT CENTRAL RLY. Higher Grade examination scheme: syllabus, regulations and examination papers, 1910. *Oxford: printed by Horace Hart at the University Press, for the G.C.R.*, [1910]. pp. [44].
Includes details of work courses to be spent in various departments over a period of four years, and reading lists. ·

11716 GREAT CENTRAL RLY. The magnet of commerce. [*Westminster: Knapp, Drewett &*

Sons, 1914]. obl. 16°, with plate, map & other illus.   NUC

11717 DOW, G. Great Central. *London: Loco-motive Publishing Co*.
vol. 3. Fay sets the pace, 1900–1922. 1965. pp. x, 437, with col. frontis, 4 col. plates, & in text, 317 illus, 5 maps, 4 gradient profiles, 3 plans, folded plate at end. Appendices 1–18 (pp. 354–426) contain a great amount of detail, mostly in tables, 100 diagrams of rolling stock & signals. Index (pp. 427–37), and an errata list for all three volumes.
See 11722.

11718 CUPIT, J. and TAYLOR, W. The Lancashire, Derbyshire & East Coast Railway. *Lingfield: Oakwood Press*, 1966. (Oakwood Library of Railway History, 19). pp. 42, with 12 illus & 2 gradient profiles on 8 plates, map & tables.

11719 RAILWAY CORRESPONDENCE & TRAVEL SOCIETY. Itinerary of the Great Central Rail Tour . . . , Saturday, 13th August 1966. *R.C. & T.S.*, [1966]. pp. [16], with map & 3 insets, detailed notes and a timetable of the tour. Written by E.N.T. Platt.
Waterloo—Neasden—Harrow-on-the-Hill—Aylesbury—Rugby Central—Nottingham Victoria—Mansfield Central—Killamarsh—Shireoaks—Rotherham Central—Wath—Penistone—Sheffield Victoria—Nottingham Victoria—High Wycombe—Marylebone.

11720 TUPLIN, W. A. Great Central Steam. *London: Allen & Unwin*, 1967. pp. 234, with frontis, 48 illus on 16 plates, 5 in text, & 3 tables (1 folded).

11721 D'ORLEY, A. A. The Humber ferries. *Leeds: Nidd Valley Narrow Gauge Railways*, 1969. pp. 74, with 25 illus, map & 12-column list of vessels.
Includes the ferry boats and services of the Manchester, Sheffield & Lincolnshire (later Great Central) Railway.

11722 DOW, G. Great Central Album: a pictorial supplement to 'Great Central'. *London: Ian Allan*, 1969. pp. 128. Col. frontis, intro, & 255 illus with descrs.
See 11717.

11723 FRANKS, D. L. South Yorkshire Railway. *Leeds: Turntable Enterprises*, 1971. (Minor Railways of Britain series). pp. 62, with 15 illus, 5 plans, map, chronology, lists & folded timetable.

11724 ROLT, L. T. C. The making of a railway, by L. T. C. Rolt; photographed by S. W. A. Newton. *London: H. Evelyn*, 1971. 4°. pp. 154. General introduction & 290 illus with descrs & introductions to each of the 12 sections; map, gradient profiles & diagrams.
The building of the Great Central Railway in the late 1890s. The photographs are from a collection of several hundred presented by

S. W. A. Newton to Leicester Museums in 1958 and subsequently deposited with Leicestershire Record Office.
The work was republished in 1980 by Godfrey Cave Associates.

11725 WALKER, C. Main line lament: the final years of the Great Central route to London. *Oxford: Oxford Publishing Co.*, 1973. la. obl. 8°. pp. [199], with 167 illus, map & gradient profile on end papers.

11726 HENTHORN, F. Letters and papers concerning the establishment of the Trent, Ancholme & Grimsby Railway, 1860–1862, edited by Frank Henthorn. *Lincoln: Lincoln Record Society*, 1975. pp. lv, 130, with frontis & 10 plates, incl. a map & 4 plans of the line.
A railway constructed upon the discovery of ironstone in the Scunthorpe area in 1859. Incorporated July 1861, dissolved July 1882, powers being vested in the Manchester, Sheffield & Lincolnshire Rly. Dr. Henthorn's Introduction (pp. ix–lv) is a detailed history of the formation of the railway, with many notes, wrought from study of the documents which make up the text.

11727 GRIMSBY—Immingham Electric Tramway, [compiled by] G. Parratt, M. J. Oaten, M. J. Phillipson. *Grimsby: Environmental Studies Curriculum Development Group*, 1976. (Resource Packs, 1). 25 photocopies.
A portfolio containing 25 sheets, reproduced from material in the Local History Collection, Grimsby Central Library, except for no. 21, 'Background information' and no. 22, 'Teachers' notes'.

11728 DOW, G. Great Central recalled. *Truro: Bradford Barton*, 1978. pp. 96. Frontis, intro, & 117 illus with descrs.

11729 DUTT, S. L. Enterprise misled: the struggle of the Manchester, Sheffield & Lincolnshire Railway to gain independent access to London, 1889–99. Thesis, M.A., University of Manchester, 1978.

11730 JOBY, R. S. The Great Central Railway in South Lancashire. *Norwich: Klofron*, [197–]. pp. 24, with 5 illus, 2 maps & a bibliography (27 sources).

Great Eastern Rly

11731 GREAT EASTERN RLY. OPERATING DEPARTMENT. Diagrammatic Map of System, drawn by B. C. Dix. [*Stratford: G.E.R.*, 1919]. a la. folded map, 3 ft 2 in. × 4 ft 9 in. Reprinted by the Great Eastern Railway Society, 1974.
The whole of the G.E.R. is shown in detail (stations, junctions, sidings, crossings, bridges, signals, signal boxes, etc.). For practical reasons, long cross-country stretches of line are much shortened.

11732 BECKETT, M. D. and DAVISON, A. P. Passenger stations & mileages, Great Eastern Railway, 1922. *Great Shelford: Midland & Great Northern Joint Railway Society, Norfolk and South Midland Groups*, 1973. pp. 10. Reproduced typescript.

Lists of stations on 62 passenger train routes with mileages from Liverpool St Stn, London, and 2 maps.

—— Errors and omissions noted by Alan J. Summers, 2 pp. reproduced typescript. [Published by the Great Eastern Railway Society, March 1981]. 55 amendments.

A new listing, based on the above work, has since been compiled by A. J. Summers and was published by the Great Eastern Railway Society in November 1980 as *Information Sheet* M130, with the title *Great Eastern Railway passenger stations and mileages at 31st December 1922*. This also has 61 routes & 2 maps and is on ten pages of reproduced typescript.

11733 TAYLOR, D. Public Record Office, Kew: list of documents in the 'Rail' section [relating to the Great Eastern Railway and its constituents, etc.]. *Great Eastern Railway Society*, August 1978. (Information Sheet, no M102). pp. [37]. An introduction and index followed by a photostat copy of entries in the P.R.O. 36 loose sheets.

11734 WILLIS, P. J. Great Eastern articles in the railway press; part 1, 1950–1975. *Great Eastern Railway Society*, March 1981. (Information Sheet, no. N.103). pp. 14. Reproduced typescript.

References to 227 articles and related correspondence in the *Railway Magazine, Railway World* and seven other periodicals.

11735 WALKER, J. Northern and Eastern Railway. Report to the Committee for Promoting a Railway from London to York, with a branch to Norwich, etc. *London: Knight*, 1835. pp. 20, with la. folded col. map.

The proposed branch was to have been from Cambridge, but only the main line from London to Cambridge was authorised in the Act of Incorporation of July 1836.

11736 EASTERN UNION RLY. Regulations for the clerks at the different stations. [*Ipswich*], [1846]. pp. [4]. Folio. Signed: 'James F. Saunders, Secretary', and dated, Ipswich Station, May 1846.

17 general rules and a further 7 in more detail concerning the procedure to be followed in the booking of passengers. Appended is a form to be completed and returned as an acknowledgement of having received the copy.

One of a collection of 23 Eastern Union Rly printed documents (reports, 1844–61) bound into a volume.   UL(GL)

11737 The REPORT of an accident on the Eastern Counties' Railway by which the engine-driver & fireman lost their lives. [n.d. but between 1842 & 1846]. pp. 8.

The date of the accident is not given but from the text it is evident that it occurred 'on Sunday the 28th ultimo', at about 12 o'clock 'in Springfield cutting, about one mile on the Witham side of Chelmsford'.

The pamphlet is addressed 'to the workmen employed in repairing the London and Birmingham Railway from London to Rugby, and the text begins 'Mr Jackson is induced to send the Report to impress upon the minds of his workmen how needful it is that the utmost caution and attention should be observed . . .'   MCL

11738 ANDREWS, W. S. Report to the directors and shareholders of the Lowestoft Railway and Harbour Company at the half-yearly meeting held at Lowestoft on the 1st March 1851, by W. S. Andrews, Harbour Master. *Lowestoft: printed by Oliver & Emerson*, [1851]. pp. 10.

Reporting a steady increase in trade and revenue (harbour dues) for the railway. The report includes an account of the work of the harbour and ends with the author's opinion on its prospects.   LU(THC)

11739 The DEVELOPMENT of railway goods traffic as exemplified at Lowestoft harbour; from the Artizan Journal for December 1851. *London: Office of the Artizan Journal*, 1851. pp. 7.

'A revival of prosperity to Lowestoft has been signally achieved by the Norfolk Railway and the harbour in connexion with it . . . A new town has arisen . . .'   LU(THC)

11740 TURNER, D. A Collection of handbills, playbills, reports of the Yarmouth & Norwich Railway Company . . . 1830–62. 9 vols.

vol. 6: A Collection of Handbills issued in Great Yarmouth during the years 1842, 1843 & 1844, including all those in reference to the opening of the Norwich & Yarmouth Railway on the first of May 1844.

vol. 5 also contains a few more N & Y Rly items, for 1840 & 1841.

The line became the Norfolk Rly in 1845 and was absorbed into the Eastern Counties Rly in 1848.   BL

11741 The GREAT Eastern Railway Company and Mr Bass and Sir E. Watkin: a short statement of the origin and subject of the present agitation. *London: printed by Waterlow & Sons*, 1876. pp. 15.

11742 NORTH, S. H. Oil fuel: its supply, composition and application. *London: C. Griffin*, 1905. pp. viii, 151.

ch. 9 (pp. 106–16), 'Oil fuel on locomotives', with folded plate & drawing of J. Holden's GER oil-burning locomotive.

—— 2nd edn., rev. & enl. by Edward Butler. *C. Griffin*, 1911. pp. xi, 238. (pp. 131–50), with 11 engineering drawings & folded plate of J. Holden's converted locomotive.

—— 3rd edn., by Edward Butler. *C. Griffin*, 1914. pp. xiv, 328. (pp. 198–228).

—— 4th edn., by Edward Butler. *C. Griffin*, 1921. pp. xvi, 310. (pp. 188–214).

11743 GREAT EASTERN RLY. Great Eastern Railway [carriage panel map]. *London: G.E.R.*, ca. 1910. [Reproduced by the Bulleid Society, 1978]. Size 6¾ in. × 25 in.

A coloured carriage panel map in 3 sections: centre section, a general map with illustrations in corners of a 4-4-0 locomotive, a railway bus, a steamship, and the G.E.R. coat of arms; on the left, a map of the G.E.R. suburban network; on the right, a map of the Broads district. The panel was a common feature of G.E.R. and L.N.E.R. carriage interiors for 30 years or so.

]1744   ROW, P. and ANDERSON, A. H. By forest and countryside: a guide to the residential localities on the Great Eastern Railway. 3rd edn. [*London*]: *Homeland Association, for the G.E.R.*, 1912. pp. 111, with plates.
Includes prices of season tickets to London.
—— 4th edn. 1913. pp. 107, with plates.
—— 5th edn. 1915. pp. 107, with plates.

11745   RAILWAY CORRESPONDENCE & TRAVEL SOCIETY. Itinerary of the Great Eastern Commemorative Steam Rail Tour . . . , Saturday, 31st March, 1962. *R.C. & T.S.*, [1962]. pp. 4, with 1 illus, map & schedule. Text by P. Proud.
London (Liverpool St)—Ipswich—Norwich—Dereham—Foulsham—Swaffham—Thetford—Ely—Cambridge—London (Liverpool St).

11746   GORDON, D. I. The East Anglian Railways Company: a study in railway and financial history. Thesis, Ph.D., University of Nottingham, 1964.

11747   PARKER, J. O. The Oxley Parker Papers: from the letters and diaries of an Essex family of land agents in the nineteenth century. *Colchester: Benham & Co.*, 1964. pp. ix, 300, with frontis & 4 plates.
ch. 12 (pp. 184–204), 'Railways'. An estate agent's work in connection with land settlement claims relating to railway construction in Essex (Eastern Counties Rly), 1837–1860.

11748   RAILWAY INVIGORATION SOCIETY. The East Suffolk Railway line: a historical outline. *Upminster: R.I.S.* 1965. pp. 11, with map. Reproduced typescript.

11749   EDWARDS, J. K. Communications and the economic development of Norwich, 1750–1850, *in* Journal of Transport History, vol. 7 (1965–6), pp. 96–108, with 82 notes.

11750   BODY, G. and EASTLEIGH, R. L. The East Anglian Railway. *Walthamstow: Trans-Rail Publications*, 1967. (Trans-Rail series, 3). pp. 30, with 4 illus on 2 plates, & in text, 1 line drawing & 2 maps, with 2 illus & a drawing on covers. Reproduced typescript.

11751   GORDON, D. I. The Eastern Counties. *Newton Abbot: David & Charles* 1968. (A Regional History of the Railways of Great Britain, 5). pp. 252, with frontis & 39 illus on 16 plates, 8 illus & 8 maps in text, folded map, & an evaluative bibliography (pp. 234–8, ca. 90 sources).
—— 2nd edn. *David & Charles*, 1977.
(Regional History of the Railways of Great Britain, 5). pp. 256, with frontis, 39 illus on 16 plates, 8 timetables, facsims, 8 maps, evaluative bibliography & a folded map.

11752   RILEY, R. C. Great Eastern Album. *London: Ian Allan*, 1968. pp. [112]. Intro (pp. 5–12), frontis & 228 illus with descrs.

11753   WALSH, B. D. J. The Stour Valley Railway. *Chappel: Stour Valley Railway Preservation Society*, 1971. pp. [iv], 26, with 20 illus on 10 plates, a map & a stock list.
—— 2nd edn. *S.V. Rly*, 1972. pp. 60, with 29 illus (incl. cover illus), a map, 6 track diagrams, gradient profile, stock list & facsimiles of tickets.
—— 3rd edn. *S.V. Rly*, 1978. pp. 44, with 32 illus (incl. cover illus), map, 6 track diagrams, gradient profile, etc.
The 3rd edition is produced in a larger format than were the 1st & 2nd editions.

11754   JOBSON, A. The old Great Eastern, *in his* Victorian Suffolk. *Robert Hale*, 1972. ch. 6 (pp. 72–80).

11755   LAWRENCE, E. W. Stour Valley Album: a Great Eastern Railway line. *Chappel: Stour Valley Railway Preservation Society*, 1973. pp. 46. 85 illus with descrs.

11756   BROWN, P. F. The fighting branch: The Wivenhoe to Brightlingsea railway line, 1866–1964: a history. *Brightlingsea: Scribe Publishing*, May 1975. pp. 68, with 7 illus & 5 maps.
The fight against closure in 1964.

11757   GREAT Eastern Railway, 1913. *Norwich: Klofron*, [1975]. obl. format. pp. 24, Intro, 21 illus, map, & timetables.

11758   JOBY, R. S. The East Norfolk Railway. *Norwich: Klofron*, [1975]. pp. 48, with 8 illus, 6 maps, 4 layout plans, 3 timetables & 2 graphs; chronology (1845–1969) & a bibliography (24 sources). Title on cover only. Index extends onto p. [3] of cover.
A detailed history set within the social & economic development of north east Norfolk.

11759   JOBY, R. S. The Ely & St Ives Railway. *Norwich: Klofron*, [1976]. pp. 20, with maps, layout diagrams, timetables & a bibliography. Title on cover only.

11760   JOBY, R. S. Rails across Breckland . . . [by R. S. Joby]. *Norwich: Klofron*, 1976. pp. 20, with 5 line illus & diagrams, 4 maps, timetables, chronology & a bibliography.
The Thetford & Watton, the Bury St Edmunds & Thetford, and the Watton & Swaffham railways.

11761   JOBY, R. S. Railways of north-western Norfolk . . . *Norwich: Klofron*, 1976. pp. 19, with map, timetables, station layout diagrams, 7 illus on covers.
The Wells & Fakenham, the Lynn & Hunstan-

ton, the West Norfolk Junction and the Hunstanton & West Norfolk railways.

11762 NORFOLK'S railways: no. 1 [Great Eastern Railway], pictures, timetables & maps, *Norwich: Klofron*, 1976. pp. 24. Intro, 25 illus, 2 maps & 7 timetables.

11763 PAYE, P. The Elsenham & Thaxted Light Railway. *Tarrant Hinton: Oakwood Press*, 1976. (Locomotion Papers, 96). pp. 31, with 16 illus on 8 plates, 3 station layout plans & a map.
Period, 1913–1952.

11764 JOBY, R. S. Felixstowe railway centenary, 1877–1977. *Norwich: Klofron*, 1977. pp. 24, with 8 illus, 2 maps, 6 layout diagrams, timetables, & a bibliography. Title on cover only.

11765 SWINDALE, D. L. Branch lines to Maldon. *Chappel: Stour Valley Railway Preservation Society*, [1977?]. pp. 64, with 21 illus, 9 layout plans & a map.
Witham—Maldon branch, to 1966, and Woodham Ferrers—Maldon branch, to 1935.

11766 DALLING, G. Enfield's 'Railway King': David Waddington and the great pew controversey. *Edmonton Hundred Historical Society*, 1978. (Occasional Papers, new series, 38). pp. 10, with 5 illus & 42 notes.
Mainly concerned with a local ecclesiastical controversy, but has also brief passages relating to his association with George Hudson, and his chairmanship of the Eastern Counties Rly, 1851–1856.

11767 QUAYLE, H. I. and BRADBURY, G. T. The Felixstowe Railway. *Tarrant Hinton: Oakwood Press*, 1978. (Oakwood Library of Railway History). pp. 52, with 24 illus on 12 plates, 9 layout plans, 2 maps, 2 plans, & gradient profiles.
The GER branch from Ipswich (Westerfield) and the railway system of the Felixstowe Dock & Rly Co.

11768 TURNER, P. By rail to Mildenhall: the story of the Cambridge to Mildenhall Railway. *Mildenhall: Mildenhall Museum Publications*, 1978. (Local History of the Mildenhall Area, 2). pp. iv, 36, with 24 illus on 12 plates, a map & a bibliography (17 sources).

11769 PAYE, P. The Buntingford branch. *Oxford: Oxford Publishing Co.*, 1980. pp. vii, 170, with 101 illus, 18 line drawings, 17 facsimiles, 16 layout plans, 13 timetables, 3 maps & a gradient profile, 6 appendices & a bibliography (30 sources).
The Ware, Hadham & Buntingford branch of the GER, 1863–1965.

11770 PAYE, P. The Mellis & Eye Railway. *Tarrant Hinton: Oakwood Press*, 1980. (Locomotion Papers, 123). pp. 35, with 8

illus on 4 plates, map, 2 station plans, 2 dimensioned drawings, a table of locomotive details & a bibliography (13 sources).

Great North of Scotland Rly
See C 2 L

Great Northern Rly

11771 GREAT NORTHERN RLY. Report of the proceedings of the trials of Leopald Redpath and Chas. James Comyns Kent for forgery, at the Central Criminal Court on Friday 16th January 1857, before Mr. Baron Martin and Mr. Justice Willes. *London: printed by Waterlow & Sons [for the G.N. Rly*, 1857]. pp. 47.

11772 LEECH, K. H. and BODDY, M. G. The Stirling Singles of the Great Northern Railway. *Dawlish: David & Charles; London: Macdonald*, 1965. pp. 160, with col. frontis, 138 illus, 33 line drawings & working drawings, tables & a chronology.

11773 BROWN, F. A. S. Great Northern locomotive engineers. *London: Allen & Unwin*.
vol. 1, 1846–1881. 1966. pp. 252, with frontis & 14 plates, 20 line drawings in text & 2 detailed tables.

11774 FRANKS, D. L. The Stamford & Essendine Railway: the Marquis of Exeter's railway. *Leeds: Turntable Enterprises*, 1971. (Minor Railways of Britain series). pp. 40, with 12 illus & track diagram.

11775 TUPLIN, W. A. Great Northern Steam. *London: Ian Allan*, 1971. pp. 208, with 62 illus on 32 plates, 13 diagrams & 5 detailed tables.

11776 WRIGHT, N. R. The railways of Boston: their origins and development. *Boston (Lincs): Richard Kay*, 1971. (History of Boston series, 4). pp. viii, 55, with 24 illus, maps & plans, 225 notes, & a list of Holland County Council 'Old Files' referred to in the text. Pages 54 & 55 are blank, headed 'Notes', and in the LU(THC) copy an errata slip is pasted onto p. 55.

11777 BROWN, F. A. S. From Stirling to Gresley, 1882–1922. *Oxford: Oxford Publishing Co.*, 1974. pp. 149, with 99 illus, incl. some dimensioned drawings.
Locomotives and rolling stock.

11778 HODGE, P. The Hertford Loop: the first hundred years of a local railway. *Southgate: Southgate Civic Trust*, 1976. pp. 32, with 6 illus & a map.

11779 WOODWARD, G. S. The Hatfield, Luton & Dunstable Railway, and on to Leighton Buzzard. *Tarrant Hinton: Oakwood Press*,

1977. (Oakwood Library of Railway History, 44). pp. 72, with 25 illus on 12 plates, 9 layout plans, 7 drawings, 4 timetables, 3 layout plans, & a map.

11780   YOUNG, J. N.   Great Northern suburban. *Newton Abbot: David & Charles*, 1977. pp. 168, with 19 illus on 8 plates, 3 maps, 2 layout plans, a chronology & a bibliography (43 sources).

11781   NOCK, O. S.   Great Northern, edited by O. S. Nock, *London: Ian Allan*, 1979. (Pre-Grouping Scene, 2). pp. 96, with illus.
Text, & a selection of illustrations from the Rixon Bucknall Collection, with descriptions by O. S. Nock.

11782   WHITAKER, A. and CRYER, B.   The Queensbury triangle, by Alan Whitaker, with an introduction and illustrations compiled by Bob Cryer. *Bradford: the author*, [1979]. pp. 40, with 24 illus (2 on covers), map, plan, chronology, a gradient table & a bibliography (14 sources).
An account of the history and operation of the spectacular three-way junction of GNR lines from Bradford, Halifax and Keighley, set into the hills and valleys of West Yorkshire.

11783   WROTTESLEY, A. J. F.   The Great Northern Railway, by A. J. F. Wrottesley, partly based on research by the late J. R. Whittle. *London: Batsford*.
vol. 1, Origin and development. 1979. pp. 256, with 36 illus on 24 plates, 7 maps, 2 appendices & a bibliography (90 sources).
vol. 2, Expansion and competition. 1979. pp. x, 201, with 36 illus on 24 plates, & in text, facsimiles, lists of locomotives & rolling stock, and of officers & officials, & 3 maps.
Period, 1868 to 1890.

11784   DAVIES, R.   Rails to the People's Palace. *Hornsey: Hornsey Historical Society*, 1980. (Occasional Papers 2). pp. 39, with 5 illus on 4 plates, cover illus, 2 maps, 2 timetables, gazetteer, drawing, 6 notes & a bibliography (7 sources).
The Finsbury Park to Alexandra Palace service, 1873–1953.

Great Northern and
London & North Western Joint Rly

11785   FRANKS, D. L.   Great Northern and London & North Western Joint Railway. *Leeds: Turntable Enterprises*, 1974. (Minor Railways of Britain series). pp. 71, with 12 illus, map, 4 station plans, & a list of openings & closures.

Great Western Rly

Reference sources

11786   GREAT WESTERN RLY.   Index to Great Western Railway Acts of Parliament and lines owned jointly or amalgamated therewith, compiled by E. Ford, General Manager's Office, Paddington Station. [*London: G.W.R.*], August 1905. pp. 288. Thumb-indexed, with numerous blank pages. Not published.

11787   SLINN, J. N.   The Great Western Railway: locomotives, carriages, vans, wagons, buildings and signals, 1835–1947. *Bromley: Historical Model Railway Society*, 1967. (Livery Register of the H.M.R.S., no. 2). pp. 46, with 24 illus on 8 plates & a plate of GWR colours, & in text, 12 pp. of diagrams. Foreword by F. W. Hawksworth, Chief Mechanical Engineer, G.W.R., 1941–1947. Cover title: A Livery Register of the Historical Model Railway Society, no. 2: the Great Western Railway.
—— a much enlarged edn; Great Western Way; a description of distinctive features of the Great Western railway, with particular reference to the liveries of locomotives, rolling stock, road vehicles, buildings, uniforms; an account of permanent way and signal practice and notes on the original liveries of the companies it absorbed. *Frome: Historical Model Railway Society*, 1978. pp. vi, 274, with 333 illus, 50 composite drawings, a colour panel chart, 10 appendices & a bibliography (23 sources).

11788   ROGERSON, I.   The Great Western Railway: a select reading list. *Cheltenham: Gloucestershire Technical Information Service*, 1971. pp. 16.
96 books and 2 periodicals currently in the stock of Gloucestershire County Technical Library, with brief annotations. Arranged under subject headings.

11789   PRYTHERCH, R. J.   The Great Western Railway and other services in the West Country and South Wales; a bibliography of British books published 1950–1969. *Leeds: Viaduct Press*. 1980. pp. [16].
120 books arranged in a single alphabetical sequence under authors.

General, historical and descriptive

11790 SCOTT, W. J. Some turning points in the history of the Great Western Railway. G.W.R. (London) Lecture & Debating Society, meeting on October 25th 1906 [no. 28]. pp. 10.

11791 PARNELL, W. S. The commercial geography of the Great Western Railway. Great Western Railway (London) Lecture & Debating Society, meeting on February 22nd, 1912 [no. 89]. pp. 19, with col. folded map.
An historical review of the spatial development of the GWR in relation to commerce, industry and travel.

11792 MARSH, H. The Great Western Railway as an index of national economic development throughout the century of its existence. Great Western Railway (London) Lecture & Debating Society, meeting on 23rd January 1936, no. 299. pp. 10, with discussion.

11793 THEN and now on the Western. *Swindon: Evening Advertiser*, 25 November 1958. (Railway Supplement). pp. 24, with many illus.

11794 BEHREND, G. Gone with regret. *Sidcup: Lambarde Press*, 1964. pp. 193, with 83 illus on 48 plates, 6 appendices & a bibliography (43+ sources). Maps on end papers.
An evocation of the GWR, period 1923–1947.
—— 2nd edn, revised. *St. Martin (Jersey): Jersey Artists*, 1966. pp. 203, with 113 illus on 64 plates, 6 appendices (detailed lists), & a bibliography (50+ sources).
—— 3rd edn, 'revised'. *London: N. Spearman, for Jersey Artists*, [1969]. pp. 204, with 136 illus. on 80 plates, 6 appendices & a bibliography (56+ sources). Map on end papers.

11795 NOCK, O. S. History of the Great Western Railway. vol. 3, 1923–1947. *London: Ian Allan*, 1967. pp. xii, 268, with 110 illus on 48 plates, 29 maps, layout plans, diagrams & numerous tables; 10 appendices.
A continuation of 'McDermot' from 1923 to 1947.
(The revision and republication of E. T. McDermot's *History of the Great Western Railway*, (1833 to 1921) was accomplished by C. R. Clinker in 1964. *See* 5958).

11796 ROCHE, T. W. E. More Great Westernry. *Bracknell: Town & Country Press*, 1969. pp. 92, with 69 illus, 2 maps & a stock list of the Great Western Society.
Essays on scenes and aspects of the GWR remembered, from the 1920s to the 1960s.

11797 ALLEN, C. J. Salute to the Great Western. *London: Ian Allan*, 1970. pp. 64, with 83 illus.

11798 PERRY, G. The Book of the Great Western, edited by George Perry, assisted by Graham Norton and Christopher Bushell; Introduction by Sir John Betjeman . . . *London: Sunday Times Magazine*, 1970. la. obl. format. pp. [96], chiefly illus (some col.), facsimiles (some col.), & portraits. Limited edition of 3000 numbered copies.
The work includes many facsimiles of GWR ephemera (documents, handbills, notices, maps & tickets), a prospectus of 1833, a press-out cardboard model with instruction leaflet in end pocket, and a reproduction of the GWR seal of 1835.

11799 NOCK, O. S. Milestones in G.W.R. history. (British Rail (W.R.) London Lecture & Debating Society, Proceedings, 1970–71, no. 512). pp. 9, with discussion.

11800 HARRIS, H. The Grand Western Canal, with . . . a foreword by Charles Hadfield. *Newton Abbot: David & Charles*, 1973. (Inland Waterways Histories). pp. 206, with col. frontis, 29 illus on 16 plates, & in text, 10 maps & illus, 70 notes; 8 appendices.
Railways: 23 page refs in index to the GWR and associated lines.

11801 DAVIS, B. L. and RIVERS, A. I. A Great Western Gallery. *Didcot: Great Western Society*, 1974. obl. 8°. pp. viii, 136, with 172 illus.
A portrayal of a variety of GWR activities from the 1880s to the 1970s.

11802 THOMAS, D. St J. The Great Way West: the history and romance of the Great Western Railway's route from Paddington to Penzance. *Newton Abbot: David & Charles*, 1975. pp. [96]. Text, pp. [3–17]; 100 illus with descrs, pp. [18–85]; route map, pp. [86–90]; bibliography (49 sources), a chronology & a gradient profile.
'A panorama of the line's history and scenery'.

11803 KINGDOM, A. R. The Great Western at the turn of the century. *Oxford: Oxford Publishing Co.*, 1976. obl. format. pp. 112. Intro, frontis & ca. 180 illus with descrs.

11804 BOOKER, F. The Great Western Railway: a new history. *Newton Abbot: David & Charles*, 1977. pp. 206, with 34 illus on 16 plates, 3 maps, and an evaluative bibliography, pp. 199–201 (ca. 50 sources).

11805 NOCK, O. S. Great Western in colour; illustrated by Clifford and Wendy Meadway. *Poole: Blandford Press*, 1978 (Great Railways of the World series). pp. 160, with 50 coloured, & numerous monochrome, illus, maps & diagrams.

11806 BICK, D. The Hereford & Gloucester Canal; with a contribution on the Gloucester–Ledbury Railway by John Norris. *Newent: the author*, 1979. pp. 80, with 31 illus, 4 plans, facsimiles, diagrams & tables.
The canal was owned by the West Midland Rly and was absorbed by the GWR in 1862.

11807 KINGDOM, A. The Newton Abbot 'blitz'.

Oxford: Oxford Publishing Co., 1979. pp. 32, with 22 illus & 2 station layout plans.

The air bombing of Newton Abbot Station, 20 August 1940.

11808 RUSSELL, J. H. Great Western Miscellany. *Oxford: Oxford Publishing Co.* la. 8°.
vol. 1, 1978. pp. 96 & 178 plates with descrs.
vol. 2, 1979. pp. 96 & plates 179–316 with descrs.

A 'family album of the G.W.R.': based on the life and environment of the Great Western generally, rather than its locomotives, from ca. 1920.

Contemporaneous general works

11809 GREAT WESTERN RLY. Great Western Railway between London and Bristol. *London: G.W.R.*, 1835. Foolscap. pp. 2.

A printed letter from 47 Parliament Street, London, dated 30th May 1835, circulated [to Members of Parliament?] prior to the second reading of the GWR's new Bill on Tuesday 2nd June. Object, to allay criticisms made against the original Bill for two sections of the line only, the present Bill being for the entire line, from London to Bristol.   LU(THC)

11810 GREAT WESTERN RLY. Reply to the case of the opponents of the Great Western Railway. *[London]: Savill, printer*, [1835]. pp. 10.

Refuting gross misrepresentation and misstatements by agents of the Southampton Railway (London & Southampton Rly, later London & South Western Rly) anxious to extend from Basingstoke to Bath in opposition to the GWR's line.

11811 DIRECT line of railway connecting South Wales, Gloucester, Cheltenham, Oxford, Tring and London. *Cheltenham: G. A. Williams* [& other booksellers], 1836. pp. 28.

Supporting the promotion of the Cheltenham, Oxford & London & Birmingham Union Rly in opposition to the Cheltenham & Great Western Union Rly.

11812 LETTER to the shareholders of the London & North Western and Great Western railways, by a well-wisher to both companies. *London: Pelham Richardson*, 1849. pp. 14.

A MS note in red ink on the half-title of the MCL copy: 'By T. [or J.] Cobb, Banbury'.

Advocates removal of competition between the LNWR and the GWR, the LNWR to have control of all lines north of Oxford; also, the abolition of Paddington station (London terminus of the GWR), the LNWR providing instead a junction for it near Wormwood Scrubs, with mixed gauge from there into Euston (London terminus of the LNWR) as in the original GWR Act of August 1835.

11813 GREAT WESTERN RLY. The new short & direct route to the West of England via Castle Cary & Langport, to be opened July 2nd, 1906. *Paddington Stn (London): G.W.R.*, June 1906. pp 12, with 7 illus & a map.

11814 ANTHONY, P. A. The new route to the West of England. Great Western Railway (London) Lecture & Debating Society meeting on January 17th, 1907 [no. 34]. pp. 11, with 9 illus.

A shortened route between Patney & Chirton via Castle Cary to Durston.

Broad gauge, and the Gauge Commission

11815 HINTS to the directors and shareholders of the Great Western Railway, with reference to the probable loss of traffic by adopting the broad gage, intended as a companion to the reports of Mr Wood and Mr Hawkshaw; to be submitted to the general meeting of the proprietors to be held on the 9th January, 1839. *London: printed for the author by R. Middleton*, 1838. pp. 7. Text signed at end: 'London, 24th December 1838. 'TRAFFIC'.'

11816 RYLEY, E. Letter to the shareholders in the Great Western Railway on the fitness of the width of gauge of that railway for the attainment of a high rate of speed and a maximum of profit. *London: J. Weale*, 1839. pp. 83.   MCL

11817 STEELE, A. K. Great Western Broad Gauge Album, compiled by A. K. Steele. *Oxford: Oxford Publishing Co.*, 1972. obl. format. pp. 80. Intro & 76 contemporary illus (photos) with descrs, & a map.

11818 CLINKER, C. R. New light on the gauge conversion. *Bristol: Avon Anglia*, 1978. pp. 28, with 11 illus, diagram, facsimile, layout plan, & 2 specimen timetables.

Biography

11819 GRAFTON, P. Men of the Great Western. *London: Allen & Unwin*, 1979. pp. 94, with 60 illus.

GWR railwaymen and their work, based on interviews and the author's own experience.

11820 CARPMAEL, R. Brunel: the first engineer of the Great Western Railway Company. Great Western Railway (London) Lecture & Debating Society, meeting on 20th October 1932. (Proceedings, session 1932–3, no. 264). pp. 23, with discussion and 13 illus.

Author, 'Chief Engineer' [GWR].

11821 QUARTERMAINE, A. I. K. Brunel: the man and his works. (Proceedings of the British Railways (W.R.) London Lecture and Debating Society, 1958–59, no. 456). pp. 15, with discussion & 8 illus.

Author, Chief Engineer, GWR and BR(WR), 1939–1951.

11822 ROLT, L. T. C. The story of Brunel; illustrated by Paul Sharp. *London: Methuen*, 1965. sm. 8°. pp. 124, with frontis & 10 line drawings. (pp. 119–24 are advertisements).

An informative introductory work.

11823 TAMES, R. Isambard Kingdom Brunel . . ., 1806–1859. *Princes Risborough: Shire*

Publications, 1972. (Lifelines series, 1). pp. 48, with 28 illus, chronology & brief bibliography.

11824 HAY, P. Brunel: his achievements in the transport revolution. *Reading: Osprey*, 1973. (The Great Innovation series). pp. ix, 134, with 33 illus on 24 plates, map, illus & a bibliography (19 sources).

11825 PUDNEY, J. Brunel and his world. *London: Thames & Hudson*, 1974. pp. 128, with 122 illus, chronology & a brief bibliography.

11826 PUGSLEY, A. The works of Isambard Kingdom Brunel: an engineering appreciation, edited by Sir Alfred Pugsley . . . *London: Institution of Civil Engineers; Bristol: University of Bristol*, 1976. pp. [viii], 222, with 45 illus, 46 notes & a bibliography (138 sources).
　　ch. 1 (pp. 5–23), I. K. Brunel, engineer, by R. A. Buchanan.
　　ch. 2 (pp. 25–68), Tunnels, by Sir Harold Harding.
　　ch. 4 (pp. 69–88), Railways, by O. S. Nock.
　　ch. 5 (pp. 89–106), Arch bridges, by J. B. B. Owen.
　　ch. 6 (pp. 107–62), Timber works, by L. G. Booth.
　　ch. 8 (pp. 163–82), Royal Albert Bridge, Saltash, by Sir Hubert Shirley-Smith.

11827 JENKINS, D. and JENKINS, H. Isambard Kingdom Brunel, engineer extraordinary. *Hove: Priory Press*, 1977. (Pioneers of Science & Discovery series). 4°. pp. 96, with 71 illus & a chronology.

11828 STANIER, W. George Jackson Churchward, Chief Mechanical Engineer, Great Western Railway: the man and his work. pp. 7. Reproduced typescript.
　　A Newcomen Society paper to be read at the Science Museum, London, 12 October 1955.

11829 ROGERS, H. C. B. G. J. Churchward: a locomotive biography. *London: Allen & Unwin*, 1975. pp. 216, with 59 illus on 16 plates, 11 diagrams & 325 notes.

11830 GOOCH, D. Memoirs & diary; transcribed from the original manuscript and edited, with an introduction and notes, by Roger Burdett Wilson. *Newton Abbot: David & Charles*, 1972. pp. xxiv, 386, with 15 illus on 8 plates, 311 notes and a biographical index (pp. 354–77).

11831 PARRIS, H. Sir Daniel Gooch: a biographical sketch, *in* Journal of Transport History, new series, vol. 3 (1975–6), pp. 203–16, with 61 notes.

Documents (published copies)

11832 HENDRY, R. P. Railway documents illustrated; editor R. Powell Hendry. *Rugby: Isle of Man Railway Society*.
　　vol. 2, Great Western Railway. 1977. pp. [18]. 46 photocopies.

Administration

11833 NICHOLLS, R. H. The work of a Divisional Superintendent's office. Great Western Railway (London) Lecture & Debating Society, meeting on April 5th, 1907 [no. 39]. pp. 18.
　　The London Division of the GWR.

11834 CHURCHILL, [Viscount]. Chairman's speech at the annual general meeting of the proprietors held at the Company's offices, Paddington Station on Thursday 23rd February 1922. *Paddington Station [London]: Great Western Rly*, March 1922. (Great Western Pamphlets, 8). pp. 16.
　　The main provisions of the Railways Act, 1921, and consequential arrangements within the GWR for its immediate future.

11835 GREAT WESTERN RLY. Concerning the mutual interests of the trader, the traveller and the Great Western Railway. *London: G.W.R.*, April 1923. pp. 24, with 5 illus & la. folded map. Cover title: Trade, travel, and the Great Western Railway.

11836 LEAN, J. F. The aim of education. Great Western Railway (London) Lecture & Debating Society, meeting on 17th January 1924 (no 167). pp. 19, with discussion.
　　Discussion includes references to educational standards among applicants and to classes for junior clerks.

11837 HOWARD, H. W. The Staff Department: its work and opportunities. Great Western Railway (London) Lecture & Debating Society, meeting on 16th February 1928. (no. 217). pp. 17, with discussion.
　　The GWR Staff Department.

11838 GREAT WESTERN RLY. Organisation: list of chief, divisional and district officers, limits of divisions and districts, etc. *Paddington Station (London): G.W.R.*, February 1930. (Circular, no 2955). pp. 40. 'Private'.
　　pp. 10–40, List of stations (13 columns).

11839 CARTWRIGHT, F. A. By what means can the Company effectively extend the scope of its earning powers? Great Western Railway (London) Lecture & Debating Society, meeting on 26th March 1931 (no. 253). pp. 14, with discussion.

11840 HOCKRIDGE, F. C. The work of the Surveyor's and Estate Department. Great Western Railway (London) Lecture & Debating Society, meeting on the 8th March 1934, no. 282, pp. 20, with discussion.

11841 POTTER, E. E. Should the Company's departmental system be modified? If so, how, and why? Great Western Railway (London) Lecture & Debating Society, meeting on 25th January 1934, no. 280. pp. 14, with discussion.

11842 RICHENS, F. G. and WHITTINGTON, R. H. That the present system of clerical positions has proved unsatisfactory both to the Company and the staff: a debate. Great Western Railway (London) Lecture & Debating Society, meeting on 1st November, 1934 no. 285. pp. 8, with discussion

11843 POTTER, B. S. New demands for transport: how they may be created and developed profitably by the Great Western Railway Company. Great Western Railway (London) Lecture & Debating Society, meeting on 24th January 1935, no. 290. pp. 10, with discussion.
Author, 'Chief Goods Manager's Office'.

11844 GREAT WESTERN RLY. Camping & rambling holidays. London: G.W.R., March 1939. pp. 63, with 7 illus & la. folded map. Foreword (pp. 3–11) by Harry Rowntree followed by a 'list of camping sites' accessible by the G.W.R. (pp. 15–47) and 'youth hostels in G.W.R. territory' (pp. 49–51).

11845 GREAT WESTERN RLY. Telephone Directory for Emergency Headquarters' Offices. [Aldermaston?]: G.W.R., June 1940. pp. 15.

11846 SMITH, M. G .R. Modernisation progress and developments in the Civil Engineering Department. Proceedings of the British Railways (W.R.) London Lecture & Debating Society, 1959–60, no. 460. pp. 16, with discussion & 8 illus.
Author, 'Chief Civil Engineer, W.R.'.

Publicity

11847 WILSON, R. B. Go Great Western: a history of GWR publicity. Newton Abbot: David & Charles, 1970. pp. 198, with col. frontis, 76 illus (36 on plates & 40 in text), notes on sources & a bibliography (pp. 189–92).
A detailed and informative survey of the devices used by the GWR to encourage patronage: posters, brochures, the 32 editions of Holiday Haunts (1906–1947), W. G. Chapman's For Boys of all Ages series, souvenir pictorial luggage labels, GWR assorted biscuits and GWR whisky being examples of what the author describes as 'the GWR's skilful use of public sentiment'. A marked feature of the work is the listing in 5 & 6 columns, with notes, of the GWR's sale publications (pp. 171–82) and its 44 jig-saw puzzles, with notes on variants (pp. 183–5).

Employees

11848 GREAT WESTERN RLY. Rules and regulations for the guidance of the officers and men, to come into operation on 1st January, 1905. London: Waterlow & Sons, printers [for the G.W.R.], 1904. [Re-published as a facsimile reprint by] Ian Allan, [1969]. pp. xxxvi, 7–161.

11849 SHARPE, W. S. The Great Western Railway Medical Department, by Dr. W. Salisbury Sharpe. G.W.R. (London) Lecture & Debating Society, meeting on 4th December 1930 (no. 246). pp. 8, with discussion.

11850 GREAT WESTERN RAILWAY SCOUT SOCIETY. Handbook of the Great Western Railway Scout Society. London: G.W.R., 1936. sm. 8°. pp. 16, with 1 illus & a map. Title from cover.
A Scouting support organisation founded by GWR staff in 1931.

11851 GREAT WESTERN RAILWAY (LONDON) MUSICAL SOCIETY. Great Western Railway Concert . . . at Queens Hall, 16th March, 1939. London: the Society, 1939. pp. 35.
Programme of a performance of Edward German's 'Tom Jones'.   LU(THC)

11852 LEA, J. T. The Great Western Railway Enginemen & Firemen's Mutual Assurance, Sick and Superannuation Society, 1865–1965; a centenary history. Swindon: printed by Swindon Signcraft, [1965]. pp. 28, with frontis, 2 illus & a list, 'Branches and their committee men', (1865–1965).

Operation of services

11853 SCOTT, W. J. Great Western train speeds, 1845–1905. Great Western Railway (London) Lecture & Debating Society, meeting on Thursday, October 5th, 1905 [no. 15]. pp. 9.

11854 ROBERTS, T. Goods train working. Great Western Railway (London) Lecture & Debating Society, meeting on February 14th, 1907 [no. 36]. pp. 24, with 13 illus & diagrams.

11855 SCOTT, W. J. Gradients and train loads: Paddington to Penzance. Great Western Railway (London) Lecture & Debating Society, meeting on October 17th, 1907 [no. 40]. pp. 8, with gradient profile.

11856 LAW, H. C. A day's work at Paddington goods station. Great Western Railway (London) Lecture & Debating Society, meeting on Thursday, March 26th, 1908 [no. 49]. pp. 21, with 8 diagrams, illus & chart.

11857 SCOTT, W. J. Suburban travel, particularly Great Western. Great Western Railway (London) Lecture & Debating Society, meeting on December 7th, 1911 [no. 85]. pp. 7.

11858 HOLBROOK, H. H. A day and a night at Paddington Station. Great Western Railway (London) Lecture & Debating Society, meeting on March 19th, 1914 [no. 112]. pp. 96–107.

11859 POTTER, F. R. Working of traffic to and from Paddington Station. Great Western Railway (London) Lecture & Debating Society, meeting on November 25th, 1922 (no. 152). pp. 24, with discussion & 14 illus.

11860 DAVISON, E. H. Geology of the Paddington—Penzance line and its relation to scenery and traffic. Great Western Railway (London) Lecture & Debating Society, meeting on 17th November 1927 (no. 210). pp. 11, with discussion & 8 illus.

11861 RAYNER-SMITH, C. Concerning Great Western passenger train special traffic. Great Western Railway (London) Lecture & Debating Society, meeting on 19th January 1928 (no. 214). pp. 35, with 17 illus, tables & diagrams, & discussion.
Author, 'Office of the Supt of the Line, G.W.R., Paddington'.

11862 POTTER, F. R. Features of railway operation. Great Western Railway (London) Lecture & Debating Society, meeting on the 2nd January 1930 (no. 237). pp. 28, with discussion, 14 illus, 4 tables, a diagram & a map.
Author, 'Operating Assistant to Supt of the Line.'

11863 GREEN, F. W. The working of Paddington passenger station. Great Western Railway (London) Lecture & Debating Society, meeting on the 7th January 1937, no. 308. pp. 20, with discussion, 12 illus & a diagram.

11864 ROBERTS, T. Factors in the working of passenger and freight traffic in the Newport Division. Great Western Railway (London) Lecture & Debating Society, meeting on 6th January 1938. no, 318. pp. 12, with discussion.
Author, 'Divisional Supt, Newport'.

11865 BROWN, A. V. R. Some aspects of the working in the Birmingham Traffic Division. (Proceedings of the Great Western Railway (London) Lecture & Debating Society, session 1947–8, no. 348). pp. 20, with discussion.

11866 GEDEN, W. T. The work of a large passenger station. (Proceedings of the British Railways (W.R.) London Lecture & Debating Society, 1949–50, no. 373). pp. 12, with discussion.
Author, 'Station Master, Paddington'.

Road services and cartage

11867 GREAT WESTERN RLY. Door to door by country cartage services: scales of charges. *Paddington Station (London): G.W.R.*, [ca. 1930]. pp. 8.
'List of stations from which cartage services operate.'

11868 PRAGNELL, A. J. Great Western Railway cartage activities. Great Western Railway

(London) Lecture & Debating Society, 1931–32, no. 263. pp. 26, with 19 illus & charts.
Author, 'Road Transport Dept'.

11869 GREAT WESTERN RLY. Country cartage services: list of villages served and scales of charges. *London: G.W.R.*, [March 1935]. pp. 65, with 6 illus & folded map. Cover title: Door to door by country cartage services: scales of charges & list of villages served.

11870 DENT, A. E. C. Road transport operation from the engineer's point of view. Great Western Railway (London) Lecture & Debating Society, meeting on 2nd March 1939, no 332. pp. 15.
The Road Transport Dept of the GWR.

11871 KELLEY, P. J. Road vehicles of the Great Western Railway. *Oxford: Oxford Publishing Co.*, 1973. pp. 128. 209 illus with descrs, & an introduction to each of the four sections.

The GWR in its catchment areas; branch lines and subsidiaries

11872 KRAUSE, I. Great Western Branch Line Album. *London: Ian Allan*, 1969. pp. 112, with frontis & 174 illus with descrs. Preface by Ian Krause; Introduction by B. J. Ashworth.
The work of various photographers, including B. J. Ashworth.

11873 BANNISTER, G. F. Great Western Steam off the beaten track. *Truro: Bradford Barton*, 1975. pp. 96. Intro & 116 illus with descrs.
Rural branch line scenes, 1950s.

11874 GAMMELL, C. J. Great Western branch lines, 1955–1965. *Oxford: Oxford Publishing Co.*, 1975. la. 8°. pp. [96]. Intro, frontis, 171 illus with descrs & area maps.

11875 WILLIAMS, C. L. Great Western branch line Steam. *Truro: Bradford Barton*.
vol. 1, 1976. pp. 96. 106 illus, with descrs. No text.
vol. 2, [1979]. pp. 96. 101 illus, with descrs. No text.

11876 PRICE, M. R. C. The Lambourn Valley Railway. *Lingfield: Oakwood Press*, 1964. (Locomotion Papers, 32). pp. 22, with frontis, 10 illus on 4 plates, 7 layout diagrams, a line drawing & a map.

11877 BRITISH RAILWAYS. WESTERN REGION. Lambourn Valley Railway Scrap-book, produced by British Rail Western on the occasion of the last trains on this line, Saturday 3 November, 1973. [*Reading*]: *B.R.* (WR), [1973]. Title from folder.
An historical essay (6 pp.) and 9 other separate items relating to the line (facsimiles of documents, photographs, station layout plans, and an intro-

duction by the compilers, Andrew Emmerson, Frank Dumbleton and Gordon Rushton), inserted in a folder.

11878   LINGARD, R.   The Woodstock branch. *Oxford: Oxford Publishing Co.*, 1973. pp. 60, with 55 illus, tables, diagrams & 2 line drawings.

11879   WELLS, M. and TILLEY, M.   Souvenir Brochure commemorating 100 years of the Marlow Donkey: published on the day of celebrations, Sunday July 15th, 1973 . . . ; history by Matthew Wells; description of route today by Michael Tilley. *Cookham: Marlow–Maidenhead Railway Passengers' Association*, 1973. pp. [21], with 20 illus & 2 maps.

11880   HOLDEN, J. S.   The Watlington branch. *Oxford: Oxford Publishing Co.*, 1974. pp. 120, with 71 illus, 6 maps, 7 line drawings, tables, diagrams, gradient profile.
        Watlington to Princes Risborough; also the GWR branch to Wallingford.

11881   PHILLIPS, D.   How the Great Western came to Berkshire: a railway history, 1833–1882. *Reading: Reading Libraries*, 1975. pp. 35, with 10 illus (engravings) & a timetable.

11882   WELLS, M.   First stop, Maidenhead. *Maidenhead: the author*, [1975?]. pp. 40, with 35 illus, 2 facsimiles & a map.
        A detailed history of the two stations at Maidenhead, GWR. 15 of the illustrations are pre-1900 drawings or photographs.

11883   LINGARD, R.   Princes Risborough—Thame—Oxford Railway. *Oxford: Oxford Publishing Co.*, 1979. la. 8°. pp. v, 130, with frontis & ca. 300 illus, facsimiles, maps, layout plans, dimensioned drawings & timetables.
        The western portion of the Wycombe Rly. estd. 1847 (GWR from 1867).

11884   VAUGHAN, A.   A history of the Faringdon branch and Uffington station. *Oxford: Oxford Publishing Co.*, 1979. pp. 184, with 62 illus, 8 layout plans, map, deposited plan & section, gradient profile, tables, 12 appendices & a note on sources used.

11885   PEARSE, M. and PEARSE, J.   The broad-gauge railway at Twyford. [*Twyford*]: *Twyford & Ruscombe Local History Society*, 1980. pp. 26, with 9 illus, 4 plans, a map (1835) & a timetable (1839).
        Appendix includes a list of Twyford station staff 1842–1898 and details of landowners from the Book of Reference (1835). The illustrations are drawings by Ron Durrant.

11886   HOLT Junction: the story of a village railway station . . . *Holt (Wiltshire): Holt Magazine*, 1966. pp. 36, with line drawings & maps. 'A Holt Magazine Supplement'.

11887   A LAST look at Holt Junction for Devizes branch. *Holt (Wiltshire): Holt Magazine*, 1967. pp. 32, with 20 illus & map. 'A Holt Magazine Supplement'.

11888   TANNER, G. H. J.   The Calne branch, by G. H. J. Tanner; research by Brian Lovelock, photographs by Donald Lovelock. *Oxford: Oxford Publishing Co.*, 1972. pp. 64, with 43 illus, 5 maps, 3 layout plans & a chronology.
        The GWR branch from Chippenham to Calne, 1863–1965.

11889   FENTON, D. M.   The Malmesbury Railway: to commemorate the centenary of its opening. 1877–1977. [*Tarrant Hinton*]: *Oakwood Press*, 1977. (Oakwood Library of Railway History, 41). pp. 57, with 23 illus on 12 plates, 2 maps, 4 plans & a brief bibliography.

11890   SMITH, T. M. and HEATHCLIFFE, G. S.   An illustrated history of the Highworth branch, originally the Swindon & Highworth Light Railway. *Upper Bucklebury: Wild Swan Publications*, 1979. la. 8°. pp. v, 90, with 94 illus, 10 layout plans, 2 maps, facsimiles & timetables, & 5 appendices.

11891   MOWAT, C. L.   The Golden Valley Railway: railway enterprise on the Welsh border in late Victorian times. *Cardiff: University of Wales Press*, 1964. pp. x, 121, with frontis, 10 plates (16 illus, map, timetable, gradient profile), folded map, & in 6 appendices, detailed tables of revenue & traffic; 244 notes.
        A generous work, in detail and in depth, set firmly into the social & economic pattern of the area served by the line.

11892   SMITH, D. J.   The Severn Valley Railway. *Bracknell: Town & Country Press, for the Severn Valley Railway Society*, 1968. pp. 60, with 26 illus, 7 layout plans, map, 2 timetables & a gradient profile.
        A history of the line and its revival (Bridgnorth to Hampton Loade) in 1967.
        —— 2nd edn. *Town & Country Press*, 1970. pp. 64, with 29 illus, 7 layout plans, map, 2 timetables & a gradient profile.

11893   WILLIAMS, J. N.   By rail to Wombourn: the history of the G.W.R. line from Oxley Junction to Kingswinford Junction. *Dudley: Uralia Press*, 1969. pp. 55, with illus, facsimiles & maps.
        —— 2nd edn. By rail to Wombourn: a new edition of the history of the G.W.R. line from Oxley Junction to Kingswinford Junction, with additional information, photographs and drawings. *Wolverhampton: Uralia Press*, 1977. pp. vi, 52, vi-xii, with 42 illus (2 on covers), 6 layout plans, 2 timetables, gradient profile, map, & a bibliography (5 sources).

11894 WILLIAMS, C. L. Great Western Steam through the Cotswolds . . . *Truro: Bradford Barton*, 1975. pp. 96. Intro & 103 illus with descrs.
> GWR locomotives & trains in BR(WR) days, 1950s–60s.

11895 MENSING, M. Great Western Steam in the Midlands. *Truro: Bradford Barton*, 1973. pp. 96. Intro & 105 illus with descrs.

11896 WALKER, C. Twixt Hatton and Harbury. *Oxford: Oxford Illustrated Press*, 1973, (Steam Railway series, 8). obl. 8°. pp. [64]. Intro & 59 illus with descrs.
> The GWR in the Warwick and Leamington Spa area, 1960s.

11897 JENKINS, S. C. The Witney and East Gloucestershire Railway: Fairford branch. *Tarrant Hinton: Oakwood Press*, 1975. (Locomotion Papers, 86). pp. 52, with 18 illus on 8 plates, map, 10 plans, 10 diagrams, 8 timetables.
> —— another edn. *Witney: the author*, 1975. pp. 32. A slightly shortened text, with map, plates and appendices omitted but with additional illustrations in the text.

11898 JENKINS, S. C. and QUAYLE, H. The Oxford, Worcester and Wolverhampton Railway: a history of the 'Cotswold line' and its branches from the 1840s to the present day. *Tarrant Hinton: Oakwood Press*, 1977. (Oakwood Library of Railway History, 40). pp. 128, with 27 illus on 12 plates, map, drawings, tables, timetables, gradient profiles, layout plans and a list of sources.

11899 RUSSELL, J. H. The Banbury and Cheltenham Railway, 1887–1962. *Oxford: Oxford Publishing Co.*, 1977. la. 4°. pp. 140, with frontis, 248 illus, 40 maps & layout plans and 19 engineering drawings of locomotives.

11900 GOODE, C. T. The North Warwickshire Railway. *Tarrant Hinton: Oakwood Press*, 1978. (Locomotion Papers, 114). pp. 46, with 17 illus on 8 plates, 10 track diagrams, gradient profile, & timetables.

11901 NEWTON, H. C. The Cornwall Railway: an address to the shareholders of the Cornwall Railway Company. *Plymouth*, 1877. pp. 12.

11902 CROMBLEHOLME, R., STUCKEY, D. and WHETMATH, C. F. D. The Culm Valley Light Railway (The Hemyock branch). *Teddington: Branch Line Handbooks; Stoke-on-Trent: West Country Publications*, 1964. (West Country Handbooks, 5). pp. 31, with 16 illus, 5 line drawings, map, 3 timetables & lists.

11903 ROCHE, T. W. E. Plymouth and Launceston. 2nd edn. *Teddington: Branch Line Handbooks*, 1965. (Branch Line Hand-books, 15). pp. 32, with 11 illus, 8 layout plans, 6 timetables & a map.
> A GWR branch.

11904 ROCHE, T. W. E. Go Great Western: reminiscences of the G.W.R. main line and branches in Devon. *Teddington: Branch Line Handbooks; Bracknell; West Country Handbooks*, 1966. (West Country Handbooks, 8). pp. 64, with 16 illus & a map.

11905 MINEHEAD AND DISTRICT ROUND TABLE. The Taunton to Minehead Railway: a short history and description of the line [compiled by members]. *Minehead: M. & D. Round Table*, [1970]. pp. 28, with 14 illus, incl. map.
> The West Somerset Rly.

> —— 2nd edn, May 1971. pp. 32; 14 illus & map.

11906 ANTHONY, G. H. The Tavistock, Launceston and Princetown railways. *Lingfield: Oakwood Press*, 1971. (Oakwood Library of Railway History, 29.) pp. 100 with 20 illus on 10 plates, 3 maps, 14 layout plans & a bibliography (20+ sources).
> The South Devon and Tavistock, Launceston & South Devon, and Princetown railways.

11907 LUCKING, J. H. The Great Western at Weymouth: a railway and shipping history. *Newton Abbot: David & Charles*, 1971. pp. 253, with frontis & 33 illus on 16 plates, 12 maps, plans, layout plans, & facsimiles; bibliography (40 sources), 161 notes & a register of ships in 8 tables.

11908 BUTT, B. and FAIRCLOUGH, T. Great Western Steam in Cornwall. *Truro: Bradford Barton*, 1972. pp. 96. Intro & 90 illus with descrs.

11909 FAIRCLOUGH, T. Great Western Steam in Devon. *Truro: Bradford Barton*, 1973. pp. 96. Intro & 94 illus, with descrs.
> Period, 1949–1960s.

11910 TOOP, R. E. Great Western Steam: south of the Severn. *Truro: Bradford Barton*, 1973. pp. 96. Intro & 101 illus with descrs.
> The GWR in Wiltshire & Somerset.

11911 FAIRCLOUGH, T. and WILLS, A. More Great Western Steam in Devon. *Truro: Bradford Barton*, 1974. pp. 96. Intro & 127 illus with descrs.

11912 KINGDOM, A. R. The Yealmpton branch (South Hams Light Railway). *Oxford: Oxford Publishing Co.*, 1974. pp. 136, with 85 illus, 20 maps, diagrams, facsimiles, operational documents, & timetables.

11913 GREAT Western Steam in the West Country, edited by '4588'. *Truro: Bradford Barton*, 1976. pp. 96. Intro, & 102 illus with descrs.
> Period, 1950s–1960s.

11914 JACKSON, B. L. and TATTERSHALL, M. J. The Bridport branch. *Oxford: Oxford Publishing Co.*, 1976. pp. 208, with 108 illus, maps (incl. O.S. map in page sections), layout plans, gradient profile, diagrams, facsims, a chronology & a bibliography (19 sources).
The GWR branch from Maiden Newton to West Bay.

11915 KINGDOM, A. R. The Ashburton branch and the Totnes Quay line. *Oxford: Oxford Publishing Co.*, 1977. pp. 152, with 78 illus, a map on 21 pages, tables, timetables, facsimiles, operations data & many diagrams, layout plans, a gradient profile & a bibliography (13 sources).

11916 MAGGS, C. G. The East Somerset Railway 1858–1972. *[Cranmore]: East Somerset Rly (1973) in association with Avon-Anglia*, 1977. obl. 8°. pp. 28, with 10 illus, 5 track diagrams & a map, 4 appendices & a bibliography (16 sources).

11917 WILLIAMS, K. and REYNOLDS, D. The Kingsbridge branch (The Primrose Line). *Oxford: Oxford Publishing Co.*, 1977. pp. viii, 248, with over 200 illus, 22 timetables, detailed map (pp. 218–39), gradient profile, & other tables; bibliography (37 sources).

11918 FARR, M. The Wrington Vale Light Railway, [by] Michael Farr, Colin G. Maggs, Robert Lovell, Charles Whetmath. *Bristol: Avon-Anglia*, 1978. pp. 28, with 10 illus, map, gradient profile & 5 layout plans.
A branch from Congresbury on the Cheddar Valley line, GWR, 1901–1963.

11919 WARNOCK, D. The Bristol & North Somerset Railway, 1863–1884. *Bristol: Temple Cloud Publications*, 1978. pp. 17, with 2 maps on inside front cover & a bibliography (12 sources) on inside back cover. Reproduced typescript. Title from cover.
Amalgamated into the GWR in 1884.

11920 KINGDOM, A. R. The Princetown branch. *Oxford: Oxford Publishing Co.*, 1979. pp. 159, with 160 illus, diagrams, maps (incl. O.S. map in paged sections), layout plans, facsimiles, timetables & a bibliography (13 sources).

11921 STANISTREET, J. A. and EDGE, S. J. Stations and buildings of the West Somerset Railway. *Taunton: West Somerset Railway Association*, 1979. obl. format. pp. 15, with 30 illus, 12 layout plans, 3 gradient profiles & a map.

11922 WARNOCK, D. W. and PARSONS, R. G. The Bristol & North Somerset Railway since 1884. *Bristol: Avon-Anglia*, 1979. la. 8°. pp. 28, with 10 illus, 9 layout plans, timetable & map. Imprint & bibliographical note on inside cover.

11923 CLINKER, C. R. The West Somerset Railway: a history in pictures, with an account by C. R. Clinker. *Dulverton: Exmoor Press*, 1980. (Microstudies series). pp. 64, with 84 illus, 15 notes, and a map & gradient profile inside covers.
The line was closed by BR in 1971 but a 20 mile stretch, from Minehead to Bishops Lidyeard was restored and re-opened by the West Somerset Rly Co. (1971) between 1976 and 1979 to provide a year-round daily passenger service (Sundays excepted).

11924 The TAFF Vale Railway and the Penarth Docks: their history, management and equipment. *Cardiff: [Taff Vale Rly Co?]*, 1908. pp. 32, with illus, incl. portraits, & 2 maps. Title from cover.
Reprinted from the *South Wales Coal Annual*, 1908. Presented to the representatives of the Chamber of Commerce of the United Kingdom at their meeting in Cardiff, September 1908.

11925 ROBERTS, C. The Great Western Railway in South Wales. Great Western Railway (London) Lecture and Debating Society, meeting on March 13th, 1913 [no 100]. pp. 15, with 12 maps, plans & illus.

11926 MORRIS, J. P. The North Pembrokeshire & Fishguard Railway, *Lingfield: Oakwood Press*, 1969. (Oakwood Library of Railway History, 24). pp. 40, with 16 illus on 8 plates, map, gradient profile, 9 layout plans & a chronology.

11927 RICKARD, S. Great Western Steam in South Wales. *Truro: Bradford Barton*, 1973. pp. 96. Intro & 101 illus with descrs.

11928 PADFIELD R. and BURGESS, B. The Teifi Valley Railway. *Haverfordwest: Laidlaw-Burgess*, 1974. pp. 64, with 68 illus.
From Aberystwyth to Carmarthen, with branches.

11929 RICKARD, S. More Great Western Steam in South Wales. *Truro: Bradford Barton*, 1974. pp. 96. Intro & 109 illus with descrs.

11930 WILLIAMS, C. L. Great Western Steam in Wales and the border counties. *Truro: Bradford Barton*, 1974. pp. 96. Intro & 117 illus with descrs.
Period, 1950s & 1960s.

11931 WILLIAMS, C. L. More Great Western Steam in Wales and the border counties. *Truro: Bradford Barton*, 1975. pp. 96. Intro & 107 illus with descrs.

11932 PRICE, M. R. C. The Whitland & Cardigan Railway. *Tarrant Hinton: Oakwood Press*, 1976. (Oakwood Library of Railway History, 39). pp. 72, with 21 illus on 8 plates, 13 layout plans & 2 maps.

11933 RICHARDS, S. Rhonnda & Swansea Bay Railway and South Wales Mineral Railway. *[Norwich]: Morgannwg*, [1976]. pp. 28, with

6 illus, 6 maps & a bibliography (20 sources). Title from cover.

11934 KENNEDY, R. Ebbw Vale Rambler: railtour, Sunday 18th September 1977. (Oxford—Swindon—Severn Tunnel—Newport Eastern and Western Valleys—Chepstow—Gloucester—Stroud—Swindon—Oxford). [Text by Rex Kennedy]. *Oxford: Oxford Publishing Co., in conjunction with the Railway Book Centre, Headington, Oxford*, 1977. pp. [27], with 28 illus, 6 small maps & 2 timetables.
A souvenir booklet.

11935 RICHARDS, S. and HARRIS, C. W. Alexandra (Newport & South Wales) Docks & Railway Company. *Norwich: Morgannwg*, [1977]. pp. 24, with 4 illus, 4 maps, plan & timetables; bibliography (15 sources). Title on cover only.

11936 RICHARDS, S. The Cardiff Railway. *Norwich: Morgannwg*, 1977. pp. 24, with 7 illus, 2 maps, 2 plans, timetables & a bibliography (16 sources). Title from cover. Reproduced typescript.

11937 RICHARDS, S. The Gwendraeth Valley Railway [and] the Burry Port & Gwendraeth Valley Railway. *Norwich: S. Richards*, 1977. pp. 24, with 7 illus, maps, timetables, a list of Acts & a bibliography (17 sources). Title from cover. Reproduced typescript.

11938 RICHARDS, S. The Llynvi & Ogmore Railway. [*Norwich*]: *Morgannwg*, 1977. pp. 24, with 5 illus, 4 maps, timetables & a bibliography (12 sources). Title from cover. Reproduced typescript.

11939 BOSLEY, P. B. The Manchester & Milford Railway, 1860–1906: the promotion, construction and operation of a Welsh rural railway line. Thesis, M.A., University of Wales (Lampeter), 1978.

11940 RICHARDS, S. The Monmouthshire Railway & Canal Company. [*Norwich*]: *Morgannwg*, [1978]. pp. 24, with 4 illus, 4 maps, 5 timetables & a bibliography (14 sources). Title from cover. Reproduced typescript in card covers.

11941 RICHARDS, S. The Vale of Neath Railway. [*Norwich*]: *Morgannwg*, [1978]. pp. 24, with 4 illus, 3 maps, 5 timetables & a bibliography (13 sources). Title from cover. Reproduced typescript.

11942 HOLDEN, J. S. The Manchester and Milford Railway. *Tarrant Hinton: Oakwood Press*, 1979. (Oakwood Library of Railway History, 50). pp. 152, with 26 illus on 12 plates, 13 layout plans, 7 maps, gradient profile, dimensioned drawings & tables.
The work is prefaced by 'A bibliographical note on the Oakwood Library series, for the benefit of present and future collectors'.

Locomotives and trains

11943 WHITEHURST, B. Great Western engines: names, numbers, types, classes: 1940 to preservation. *Oxford: Oxford Publishing Co.*, 1973. pp. [iv], 169. Intro (pp. 1–6), detailed tables (pp. 7–100), 32 illus on 16 plates & 47 engine diagrams (dimensioned drawings).
Compiled and produced as a companion to *Great Western Railway Engines (G.W.R. Engine Book)* published in successive editions by the GWR, 1922–1946. *See* 6150.

11944 RUSSELL, J. H. A Pictorial Record of Great Western Engines. *Oxford: Oxford Publishing Co.*
vol. 1, [The Gooch, Armstrong and Dean engines]. 1975. la. 8°. pp. 188. Intro & 523 illus & diagrams with detailed descrs & lists.
vol. 2, [The Churchward, Collett and Hawksworth engines]. 1975. la. 8°. pp. 244. Intro & 624 illus & line drawings with detailed descrs.

11945 FREEZER, C. J. Locomotives in outline: GWR. *Seaton: Peco*, 1977. la. obl. format. pp. 38, with 77 official GWR drawings (side and end elevations) accompanied by detailed historical notes and a list of named locomotives of all classes (pp. 35–8).
A collected edition of drawings first published in the *Railway Modeller* from 1958 to 1972, with revised text.

11946 RUSSELL, J. H. A Pictorial Record of Great Western Absorbed Engines. *Oxford: Oxford Publishing Co.*, 1978. la. obl. format. pp. 280, with 619 illus & dimensioned drawings, 14 maps & a complete stock list.
700 locomotives from the six constituent and twelve subsidiary companies of the re-formed GWR in 1923.

11947 BURROWS, G. H. Great Western Railway locomotives. Great Western Railway (London) Debating Society, meeting on December 16th, 1904 (no. 6). pp. 8, with diagrams.

11948 BURRIDGE, F. H. A. Nameplates of the G.W.R. locomotives. *Bournemouth: the author, Sydenham & Co.*, September 1947. sm. 8°. pp. 56, with lists, diagrams & 44 illus.

11949 CASSERLEY, H. C. and JOHNSTON, S. W. Locomotives at the Grouping: 4, Great Western Railway. *London: Ian Allan*, 1966. pp. 144, with 95 illus. Lists.

11950 RILEY, R. C. Great Western Album [no. 1]. *London: Ian Allan*, 1966. pp. 115. Intro (pp. 5–10), frontis, & 200 illus with descrs.
Period, since 1923.
——— no. 2. *Ian Allan*, 1970. pp. 112. Intro (pp. 5–10), frontis, & 218 illus with descrs.
Period, since 1923.

11951 EARLEY, M. W. The Great Western scene: an album of photographs by Maurice W. Earley. *Oxford: Oxford Publishing Co.*, 1970. obl. 8°. pp. 57. Preface & 95 illus with descrs.

11952 TUPLIN, W. A. Great Western Saints and Sinners. *London: Allen & Unwin*, 1971. pp. 200, with 46 illus on 15 plates (incl. frontis), 19 line drawings & 3 detailed tables in text.
An appraisal of some mechanical features of GWR locomotive design & performance, including some 'un-saintly features too rare to justify mention'. The author offers an alternative to the 'smooth, lush adoration' so common in books about locomotives.

11953 VAUGHAN, A. Great Western portrait: 1913–1921, compiled by Adrian Vaughan. *Oxford: Oxford Publishing Co.*, 1971. obl. format. pp. 59. Intro & 58 photographs from the collection of W. L. Kenning, with descriptions.

11954 BLENKINSOP, R. J. Shadows of the Great Western. *Oxford: Oxford Publishing Co.*, 1972. la. 8°. pp. [96]. Intro & 130 illus with descrs.

11955 NOCK, O. S. GWR Steam. *Newton Abbot: David & Charles*, 1972. pp. 239, with col. frontis, 74 illus on 32 plates, & many lists.

11956 STEELE, A. K. Great Western Broad Gauge Album, compiled by A. K. Steele. *Oxford: Oxford Publishing Co.*, 1972. obl. format. pp. 80. Intro & 76 contemporary illus (photos) with descrs, & a map.

11957 BLENKINSOP, R. J. Echoes of the Great Western. *Oxford: Oxford Publishing Co.*, 1973. la. 8°. pp. [96]. Intro & 119 illus with descrs.

11958 SEMMENS, P. W. B. Great Western Steam in close-up. *Truro: D. Bradford Barton*, 1973. pp. 96. Intro & 94 illus with descrs.
Photographs taken by the author.

11959 ALLEN, C. J. Titled trains of the Western. *London: Ian Allan*, 1974. pp. 96, with 86 illus.

11960 BLENKINSOP, R. J. Reflections of the Great Western. *Oxford: Oxford Publishing Co.*, 1974. la. 8°. pp. [96]. Intro & 122 illus with descrs.

11961 EARLEY, M. W. Truly the Great Western. *Oxford: Oxford Publishing Co.*, [1975]. 4°. pp. [96]. Preface & 138 illus with descrs.
Photographs by M. W. Earley. The preface includes technical (photographic) details.

11962 NOCK, O. S. Great Western. *London: Ian Allan*, 1975. (Pre-Grouping Railway Scene, 1). pp. 96, with 151 illus.
Text, and a selection of illustrations from the Rixon Bucknall Collection, with descriptions by O. S. Nock.

11963 TUPLIN, W. A. Great Western power. *London: Allen & Unwin*, 1975. pp. 215, with frontis, 39 illus on 14 plates & in text, 22 diagrams, graphs & gradient profiles, & 9 tables.

11964 WILLIAMS, C. L. Great Western Steam double-headed. *Truro: Bradford Barton*, 1975. pp. 96. Intro & 76 illus with descrs.

11965 BLENKINSOP, R. J. Silhouettes of the Great Western. *Oxford: Oxford Publishing*, 1976. la. 8°. pp. [96]. Intro & 121 illus. Photographed 1960–62.

11966 HARESNAPE, B. and SWAIN, A. Churchward locomotives: a pictorial history. *London: Ian Allan*, 1976. pp. 112, with 155 illus, 11 dimensioned drawings, 2 tables, 2 appendices & a short bibliography.

11967 JUDGE, C. W. The Great Western era: a collection of photographs compiled by Colin Judge. *Oxford: Oxford Publishing Co.*, 1976. pp. 90. Intro & 162 illus with captions, 4 facsimiles, 2pp of signal diagrams, a timetable (Banbury 1959) & a map. A limited edition of 1000 numbered copies, each signed by the compiler.

11968 MONTAGUE, K. Great Western. *Oxford: Oxford Publishing Co.*, 1976. (Pocket Railway Books, 2). pp. [64]. Intro & 112 illus with descrs.

11969 WILLIAMS, T. E. The last decade of Great Western main line Steam. *Truro: Bradford Barton*, 1976. pp. 96. Intro & 90 illus with descrs.
GWR locomotives in BR(WR) days, 1950s & 1960s.

11970 JEFFERSON, G. F. Great Western Pictorial: typical scenes of Great Western Railway steam locomotives in action before and after nationalisation. *Dorking: Railway Pictorial Publications*, [1977]. obl. format. pp. [48]. Intro & 52 illus with descrs.
The introduction includes a discussion on technical difficulties in photographing moving trains.

11971 WILLIAMS, C. L. Great Western Steam Miscellany, edited by C. L. Williams. *Truro: Bradford Barton*.
vol. 1, 1977. Intro & 98 illus with descrs.

11972 WILLIAMS, C. L. More Great Western Steam double-headed. *Truro: Bradford Barton*, 1977. pp. 96. Intro & 94 illus with descrs.

11973 COLLINS, L. M. Great Western Steam in action. *Truro: Bradford Barton*.
vol. [1], 1973. pp. 96. Intro & 97 illus with descrs.
vol. 2, 1974. pp. 96. Intro & 103 illus with descrs.
vol. 3, 1974. pp. 96. Intro & 96 illus with descrs.
vol. 4, 1975. pp. 96. Intro & 95 illus with descrs.
vol. 5, 1975. pp. 96. Intro & 96 illus with descrs.
vol. 6, 1977. pp. 96. Intro & 96 illus with descrs.
vol. 7, 1978. pp. 96. Intro & 97 illus with descrs.

11974 FAIRCLOUGH, T. and WILLS, A. Great Western Steam through the years: [vol. 1].

Truro: Bradford Barton, 1976. pp. 96. Intro & 107 illus with descrs.
—— vol. 2. *Bradford Barton*, 1978. pp. 96. Intro & 106 illus with descrs.

11975 HARESNAPE, B. Collett and Hawksworth locomotives: a pictorial history. *London: Ian Allan*, 1978. pp. 128, with 187 illus & descrs, 19 diagrams, many lists & a short bibliography.

11976 BLOOM, A. Locomotives of the Great Western Railway, written by Alan Bloom; compiled by David Williams. *Norwich: Jarrold*, 1979. (Jarrold Railway Series, 1). pp. [32], with 68 illus (51 col.) & a map.
Text & illus extend onto covers.

11977 ESAU, M. Spirit of Great Western. *Oxford: Oxford Publishing Co.*, [1980]. la. 8°. Intro (pp. [4–6]) & 204 illus with descrs.

11978 LEECH, K. H. The Great Western Railway 'Kings': commemorative brochure celebrating 35 years of 'top link' main line service. *Birmingham: Stephenson Locomotive Society*, 1962. pp. [8], with 12 illus (5 on covers) & a 4-column list. Title from cover.
Supplement, Journal of the S.L.S., November 1962.

11979 CASTLES and Kings: a pictorial tribute. *Hatch End: Roundhouse Books*, 1964. la. 8°. pp. [96]. Frontis, preface & 12 illus with descrs.

11980 LEECH, K. and HIGSON, M. F. Pendennis Castle. *Hatch End: Roundhouse Books*, 1965. pp. [28], with 29 illus & 6 logs of runs.
An account of the performance of this engine in the locomotive exchanges between the GWR and the LNER in 1925, its subsequent overhaul at Swindon and its acquisition by Michael Higson in 1964 for continued service and preservation.

11981 NOCK, O. S. The GWR Stars, Castles & Kings. *Newton Abbot: David & Charles*.
part 1, 1906–1930, 1967. pp. 160, with col. frontis, 153 illus, working drawings & many tables, including logs of runs.
part 2, 1930–1965, 1970. pp. 160, with frontis, 140 illus, working drawings & many tables, including logs of runs.

11982 NOCK, O. S. Engine 6000: the saga of a locomotive. *Newton Abbot: David & Charles*, 1972. pp. 108, with 29 illus on 16 plates.
The GWR locomotive *King George V*.

11983 COFFIN, R. O. Kings of the Great Western, 1927–1977. *Hereford: 6000 Locomotive Association*, 1977. pp. 104, with 150 illus with descrs, & a list of shed allocations.

11984 NOCK, O. S. Standard gauge Great Western 4-4-0s. *Newton Abbot: David & Charles*.
part 1, Inside-cylinder classes, 1894–1910. 1977. pp. 96, with frontis, 75 illus, 9 diagrams, tables, including logs of runs.

part 2, 'Counties' to the close, 1904–1961. 1978. pp. 96, with frontis & 67 illus, diagrams & many lists.

11985 NOCK, O. S. The GWR mixed-traffic 4-6-0 classes. *London: Ian Allan*, 1978. pp. 96, with 98 illus on 24 plates, 6 diagrams & a list.

11986 HOLDEN, B. and LEECH, K. H. Portraits of 'Kings': portraits of every Western Region 'King' class locomotive . . . , with footplate comments; with additional research & drawings by Richard S. Potts. *Ashbourne: Moorland Publishing Co., in association with Barbryn Press*, 1979. pp. [96], with 92 illus, 18 line drawings and 1 dimensioned drawing.

11987 WORCESTER LOCOMOTIVE SOCIETY. Pannier parade. 2nd edn. *Hereford: the Society*, [197?]. pp. [12], with 14 illus.
Produced to aid purchase of former GWR 0-6-0 pannier tank locomotive 5786.

11988 VEAL, C. and GOODMAN, J. Heavy freight: 28XX and 38XX consolidations of the Great Western. *Didcot: Great Western Society*, 1980. pp. 28, with 42 illus & a dimensioned drawing; 4 appendices, incl. two 8-column lists of the locomotives of the 2800 and the 2884 classes.

11989 ROCHE, T. W. E. Cornish Riviera Limited: a review of the life of a famous train. *Bracknell: Town & Country Press*, 1969. obl. format. pp. 24, with 10 illus & 2 tables.

11990 BODY, G. Riviera Express: the train and its route. [*London*]: *British Railways (Western Region) and Avon-Anglia*, 1979. pp. 32, with 20 illus, map (on title-page) & chronology, 1838–1979.
A booklet issued to commemorate the introduction of the Inter-City 125 high-speed trains onto the West of England main line, and 75 years of the Cornish Riviera express.

11991 NOCK, O. S. The Limited: the story of the Cornish Riviera Express. *London: Allen & Unwin*, 1979. pp. 95, with 61 illus.

11992 NASH, A. H. A day's work in the Swindon foundry. Great Western Railway (London) Lecture & Debating Society, meeting on January 12th, 1911 [no. 75]. pp. 11, with 14 illus & diagrams.

11993 GREAT WESTERN RAILWAY MECHANICS INSTITUTION, SWINDON. Centenary of the G.W.R. Mechanics Institution, Swindon, 1843–1943; souvenir and prospectus . . . with a general outline of its history by P. H. Phillips. *Swindon: the Institution*, 1943. pp. v, [9], with 8 illus.

11994 CLARK, K. Alfred Williams: his life and work. *Bristol: W. George's Sons, via Blackwell*, 1945. pp. xi, 206.

L.

Life on the shop floor at Swindon works, GWR, 1891 (or 1892)–1914, and after.

11995   COOK, K. J.   Locomotive maintenance problems. (Proceedings of the Great Western Railway (London) Lecture & Debating Society, session 1947–8 (no. 343).) pp. 20, with discussion, 6 illus, 2 tables, 2 charts.
Author, 'Works Assistant to the C.M.E.'.

11996   EVERSLEY, D. E. C.   The Great Western Railway Works, Swindon, in Victoria History of the Counties of England: Wiltshire, vol. 4, 1959. pp. 207–19, with 3 illus on 2 plates & 118 notes.

11997   MOUNTFORD, E.   Caerphilly works, 1901–1964. Hatch End: Roundhouse Books, 1965. pp. 132, with 100 illus, map, 2 layout plans, 7 detailed lists in appendices.
The building, rebuilding and repair of locomotives, carriages and wagons, by and for the Rhymney Rly (later GWR).

11998   HASWELL, E. G. F. and SHEPPERD, K.   Great Western shed diagrams (illustrated by Kaye Shepherd). Shepperton: Ian Allan, 1969. pp. 100, with intro, contents list & 96 layout plans.
'All the W.R. [i.e. ex-GWR] sheds are depicted, except a few minor ones.' The drawings, by Kay Shepperd are from free-hand work sketched on the spot by E. G. F. Haswell between 1950 & 1959.

11999   LYONS, E. T.   An Historical Survey of Great Western Engine Sheds, 1947. Oxford: Oxford Publishing Co., 1972. la. obl. format. pp. 284, with over 400 illus, layout plans & area maps with details of each shed and its locomotive allocation at the end of 1947. Produced with the co-operation of the Great Western Society.
—— 2nd edn. O.P.C., & G.W. Society, 1974. la. obl. format. pp. 284, with over 400 illus, etc.

12000   COOK, K. J.   Swindon Steam, 1921–1951. London: Ian Allan, 1974. pp. 174, with 67 illus on 32 plates, & in text, plan & diagrams.
The author's life at Swindon Works, the last ten years as Manager.

12001   THE GWR locomotive factory at Swindon. Swindon: S. Hurwitz, via Borough News, [1974]. pp. [16], with 12 illus (incl. 2 on covers).
A reprinting of an essay first published in the Illustrated Exhibitor & Magazine of Art, 1852, with the original line drawings reproduced.

12002   WILLIAMS, C. L.   Great Western Steam on shed. Truro: Bradford Barton, 1974. pp. 96. Intro & 113 illus with descrs.

12003   MORRISON, B.   Great Western Steam at Swindon Works. Truro: Bradford Barton, 1975. pp. 96. Intro & 101 illus with descrs.
Period, 1950s.

12004   WILLIAMS, C. L.   More Great Western. Steam on shed. Truro: Bradford Barton, 1976. pp. 96. Intro & 118 illus with descrs.

12005   NUTTY, E. J.   G.W.R. two-cylinder piston valve locomotives. 2nd edn. Swindon: the author, 1948. pp. 36, with 12 diagrams & a table.
—— [3rd edn, greatly enlarged]. Swindon: E. J. Nutty & Sons, [1977]. pp. 107, with 19 illus, 39 diagrams & tables.
A detailed exposition on the construction, characteristics and working of this type of locomotive, produced as a workshop guide for those engaged in their restoration, running and maintenance. Based on the author's life-long acquaintance with GWR locomotives at Swindon Works.

12006   LYONS, E. T. and MOUNTFORD, E. R.   Historical Survey of Great Western Engine Sheds, 1837–1947, including amalgamated companies. Oxford: Oxford Publishing Co., 1979. obl. format. pp. 216. Intro & 147 illus with detailed commentaries, 203 layout plans & line drawings, 11 maps & 2 lists.
There is also a detailed historical introduction to broad gauge sheds, pp. 3–12.

12007   SILTO, J.   The railway town: description of life and events in Swindon from 22 January 1901 to 11 November 1918. Swindon: J. Silto, 1980. tall 8°. pp. 84, with 38 illus (some composite) on 21 plates, & a bibliography (28 sources).
ch. 4 (pp. 54–60), Tramways and electricity; ch. 6 (pp. 73–80), Swindon Works, 1901–1918.

12008   CAMERON, A.   Work of a main-line engineman. (Proceedings of the Great Western Railway (London) Lecture & Debating Society, session 1946–7, no. 335). pp. 16, with discussion.
Author, 'Senior Loco. Running Inspector, Swindon'.

12009   GASSON, H.   Firing days: reminiscences of a Great Western fireman. Oxford: Oxford Publishing Co., 1973. pp. [6], 113, with 46 illus on 32 plates; map.
Centred upon Didcot locomotive depot in the 1940s.

12010   MORGAN, B. and MEYRICK, B.   Behind the steam. London: Hutchinson, 1973. pp. 222, with 19 illus on 12 plates.
Autobiography of a locomotiveman (GWR, 1916–1964) centred upon Neyland depot, Dyfed.

12011   DRAYTON, J.   On the footplate: memories of a GWR engineman. Truro: Bradford Barton, 1976. pp. 111, with frontis, 20 illus & a map.
Over 50 years on the GWR and BR(WR) from 1923, based mostly on Welsh depots. Illustrated by photographs, mainly by the author.

12012   GASSON, H.   Footplate days: more reminiscences of a Great Western fireman. Oxford: Oxford Publishing Co., 1976. pp. vi, 112, with 56 illus on 32 plates.

12013 'ASLEFT'. No steam without fire: memories of life on the footplate at Wolverhampton, Kidderminster and Newton Abbot, by 'Asleft'. *Wolverhampton: Uralia Press*, 1978. pp. 108, with 19 illus.

12014 GASSON, H. Nostalgic days: further reminiscences of a Great Western fireman. *Oxford: Oxford Publishing Co.*, 1980. pp. [4], 79, with 63 illus on 32 plates.
In chapter 4 the work and character of Driver Bert Edmonds is recalled.

12015 ELLIOTT, R. J. Preserved locomotives of the Great Western Railway. [*Buckfastleigh*]: *Dumbleton Hall Preservation Society*, 1977. (Preserved Locomotives, 1). sm. 8°. pp. 36, with 31 illus.
Details of 100 steam locomotives, a location list, and a further list of 54 awaiting scrapping, 7 of which are earmarked for adoption.

12016 WOOD, G. C. 6000: King George V: a chronology. *Oxford: Oxford Illustrated Press for the 6000 Locomotive Association*, May 1972. pp. [72], with 53 illus.
A history, produced as a guide for visitors to the locomotive preserved by H. P. Bulmer Ltd at Hereford.

12017 WOOD, G. C. Renaissance from rust: King George V (1968–1973). *Hereford: 6000 Locomotive Association; Oxford: Oxford Publishing Co.*, 1973. obl. 8°. pp. [64]. 61 illus with descrs.
Restoration of the GWR 4-6-0 locomotive by H. P. Bulmer Ltd, and its subsequent running career.

12018 HOUNSELL, G. R. Great Western Steam preserved. *Truro: Bradford Barton*, 1975. pp. 96. Intro & 110 illus with descrs.

12019 HARRIS, M. Great Western coaches: 1890–1954. *Newton Abbot: David & Charles*, 1966. la. 8°. pp. 160, with frontis & 106 illus; diagrams, lists (pp. 133–56), chronology, & a bibliography (20+ sources).
—— new edn. [2nd edn]. *David & Charles*, 1972. pp. 160, with frontis, 118 illus, chronology & bibliography.

12020 RUSSELL, J. H. A Pictorial Record of Great Western Wagons. *Oxford: Oxford Publishing Co.*, 1971. obl. format. pp. 138, with 261 illus, 54 diagrams, with 21 additional diagrams in appendices.
—— Great Western Wagons Appendix. *Oxford Publ. Co.*, 1974. pp. [4], 193. Intro & 338 illus & line drawings. (Re-issued, 1979).

12021 RUSSELL, J. H. A Pictorial Record of Great Western Coaches, including the brown vehicles. *Oxford: Oxford Publishing Co.*
part 1, 1838–1903. 1972. obl. format. pp. [4], 240. Intro & 237 illus, & 162 line drawings & a plan, with descrs & tables.

part 2, 1903–1948. 1973. obl. format. pp. [4], 273. Intro & 462 illus, & many supporting line drawings with detailed descrs & lists.

12022 A HISTORY of G.W.R. goods wagons, by A. G. Atkins, W. Beard, D. J. Hyde and R. Tourret. *Newton Abbot: David & Charles*.
vol. 1, General. 1975. pp. 95, with 52 illus, 10 diagrams, charts & dimensioned drawings, 9 tables (2 of which are detailed, table 7 being an 8 pp. index of GWR goods wagon diagrams in 8 columns, and table 9, a chronology).
vol. 2, Wagon types in detail. 1976. pp. 128, with 177 illus, many dimensioned drawings, a bibliography (24 sources) and an addendum to vol. 1.

12023 RUSSELL, J. H. Great Western Wagon Plans. *Oxford: Oxford Publishing Co.*, 1976. la. 8°. pp. xii, 137. Many hundreds of drawings, with index.
Reproduced from official plans and scale drawings made in the Swindon drawing office between 1892 and 1952.

12024 ALL about GWR iron minks, by J. H. Lewis, M. E. M. Lloyd, R. C. Metcalf [and] N. R. Miller. [*Birmingham*]: *Historical Model Railway Society*, 1980. la. 8°. pp. 56, with 42 illus, 25 tables, & 10 dimensioned drawings (composite).
'Mink'—the term used in the *GWR Telegraph Code Book* of 1892 to describe any type of covered goods wagon.

12025 GREAT WESTERN SOCIETY. Vintage train. *Didcot: the Society*, 1980. pp. 32, with 52 illus (5 col.).
An illustrated record of the Society's Vintage Train trips (restored carriages) between 1972 and the final one on 26 January 1980.

12026 IRWIN, S. R. Great Western two-coach close-coupled 'B' sets. 3rd edn. [*Newport*]: *Monmouthshire Railway Society*, Spring 1962. pp. 4. Reproduced typescript.
The first edition was published as a single sheet dated 'Winter 1958'. A second edition appeared in Summer 1959.

12027 MOUNTFORD, E. R. A Register of G.W.R. Absorbed Coaching Stock, 1922–3. *Tarrant Hinton: Oakwood Press*, 1978. pp. 77, with 51 illus on 16 plates & many detailed lists.

Stations and architecture

12028 LYONS, E. T. An Historical Survey of Great Western Engine Sheds, 1947. *Oxford: Oxford Publishing Co.*, 1972. la. obl. format. pp. 284, with over 400 illus, layout plans and area maps with details of each shed and its locomotive allocation at the end of 1947. Produced with the co-operation of the Great Western Society.
—— 2nd edn. *O.P.C. & G.W. Society*, 1974. la. obl. format. pp. 284, with over 400 illus, etc.

12029 CLINKER, C. R. Great Western Railway: a register of halts and platforms, 1903–1975. *Padstow: the author*, April 1975. la. 8°. pp. iii, 10. Historical introduction followed by a six-column list, notes, & a statistical analysis. Title on cover only.
—— [2nd edn], 1903–1979. *Avon Anglia*, 1979. (Reference Aids series, 5). pp. 14.
   pp. 1–3, Historical introduction; pp. 3–12, Register; pp. 12–14, Notes.

12030 CLARK, R. H. An Historical Survey of Selected Great Western Stations: layouts and illustrations. *Oxford: Oxford Publishing Co.* la. 8°.
   [vol. 1], 1976. pp. xii, 188. 243 illus with supporting layout plans and notes relating to 141 stations.
   vol. 2, 1979. pp. iv, 204. 214 illus with supporting layout plans and notes relating to 101 stations.
   Termini and large stations are excluded.

12031 KARAU, P. Great Western branch line termini. *Oxford: Oxford Publishing Co.* 4°.
   vol. 1, (Fairford, Lambourn, Tetbury, Wallingford, Watlington). 1977. pp. 124, with frontis, 173 illus, 6 maps, 12 layout plans, timetables and many scale drawings of buildings on plates, some folded.
   vol. 2, (Abbotsbury, Ashburton, Hemyock, Moretonhampstead, Princetown). 1978. pp. 128, with frontis, 207 illus, 6 maps, 12 layout plans & numerous line drawings (some folded) of buildings.

12032 VAUGHAN, A. Pictorial Record of Great Western Architecture. *Oxford: Oxford Publishing Co.*, 1977. 4°. pp. vi, 442, with intro (pp. 1–28), frontis, & 644 illus.
   A comprehensive selection of photographs, with some early engravings and supporting dimensioned drawings, of the whole range of GWR structures and (pp. 407–34) their appurtenances, from the earliest days to the 1940s. Each illustration is described, with informative supporting text and notes.

12033 HARRISON, D. Salute to Snow Hill: the rise and fall of Birmingham's Snow Hill railway station, 1852–1977. *Birmingham: Barbryn Press*, 1978. pp. 120, with 97 illus & 5 layout plans.

12034 LYONS, E. T. and MOUNTFORD, E. R. Historical Survey of Great Western Engine Sheds, 1837–1947, including amalgamated companies. *Oxford: Oxford Publishing Co.*, 1979. obl. format. pp. 216. Intro & 147 illus with detailed commentaries, 203 layout plans & line drawings, 11 maps & 2 lists. There is also a detailed historical introduction to broad gauge sheds, pp. 3–12.

Signals and automatic train control

12035 CROOK, G. H. The track circuit: its application to automatic signalling and its bearing upon Rule 55. Great Western Railway (London) Lecture & Debating Society, meeting on October 26th 1911 [no. 81]. pp. 18, with discussion & 11 illus.

12036 GREAT WESTERN RLY. Description and notes on the G.W.R. system of automatic train control. *London: G.W.R.*, July 1931. pp. 15, with 14 diagrams & illus (some folded). Cover title: Automatic train control.

12037 WESTINGHOUSE BRAKE AND SIGNAL COMPANY. Signalling concentration at Johnston station, G.W.R.: long-distance point operation by double wires. *London: the Company*, [1937]. pp. 3, with 6 illus & a track diagram.
   Reprinted from the *Railway Gazette*, October 29, 1937. The junction for Neyland on the Carmarthen to Milford Haven line.

12038 VAUGHAN, A. A Pictorial Record of Great Western Signalling. *Oxford: Oxford Publishing Co.*, 1973. 4°. pp. 160. Intro (pp. 7–31) & 200+ illus (photos & diagrams) with full descriptions and much accompanying detailed information on GWR equipment and operation in appendices A–K, with illustrations.

Docks and shipping services

12039 WILLIAMS, T. E. The Great Western Railway steamboat services. G.W.R. (London) Lecture & Debating Society, meeting on Friday February 10th, 1905 (no. 10). pp. 8.

12040 STRADLING, R. A. The Port of Bristol and its goods stations and depots. Great Western Railway (London) Lecture & Debating Society, meeting on November 12th, 1908 [no. 53]. pp. 15, with discussion, 8 maps, diagrams & illus.

12041 BROWN, F. The docks of the Great Western Railway. Great Western Railway (London) Lecture & Debating Society, meeting on January 18th 1923 (no. 156). pp. 32, with discussion, plans & illus.

12042 BOYLE, P. The Channel Islands service. Great Western Railway (London) Lecture & Debating Society, meeting on 21st January 1926 (no. 190). pp. 40, with discussion, summarised.
   The Weymouth maritime services of the GWR.

12043 BROWN, F. Great Western ports. Great Western Railway (London) Lecture & Debating Society, meeting on 18th October 1928 (no. 221). pp. 16, with discussion.
   Author: Chief Docks Manager, GWR.

12044 HOPPINS, D. G. The trade of the port of Cardiff. (Proceedings of the Great Western Railway (London) Lecture & Debating Society, 1947–48, no. 341). pp. 16, with discussion & 8 illus.
   Author, Dock Manager, Cardiff and Penarth.

Guides and timetables, and journeys described

12045 FREELING, A. The Windsor Railway Companion and guide to the castle and town . . .

London: G. Bell, 1840. pp. 18, 52, 18, with folded map of the G.W.R. (London to Reading).
The first section is entitled 'The Great Western Companion from London to Reading'.

12046   GREAT WESTERN RLY. Timetables of 1865. [*Paddington Station (London)*]: *G.W.R.*, 1865. [Facsimile reprint by] *Oxford Publishing Co.*, 1971. pp. 62.
[pp. 9–16] comprise a supplement: 'Programme of tourist arrangements for the season commencing June 1st and ending October 31st, 1865. First issue'.

12047   BRISTOL AND EXETER RLY. Timetables for January 1877. *Bristol: printed for the Company by I. Arrowsmith*, [1877]. Reprinted by E. G. Brown, Bristol, 1971, and re-issued by the Inter-City Railway Society in 1978. pp. 40, with map. Title on cover only. 'Contents' inside front cover.

12048   GREAT WESTERN RLY. Service Time Tables, printed for the use of the Company's servants. Bristol to Exeter, including the Weston-super-Mare loop line and the Portishead, Clevedon, Wells, Yeovil, Chard, Minehead, Barnstaple, Tiverton, Culm Valley, Crediton and Exe Valley branches. October 1886. [*Paddington: G.W.R.*, 1886]. Facsimile reprint with an historical introduction by Arthur B. Grandfield of Taunton inside front cover. Includes broad and 'narrow' gauge (i.e. standard gauge) train workings. *Bracknell: Town & Country Press*, [1971]. pp. 82.

12049   GREAT WESTERN RLY. Timetables of the Great Western Railway. [*London: G.W.R.*, 1902]. [Facsimile reprint by *Ian Allan*, 1967]. pp. 184, with 4 plates (maps).
The issue for the first quarter of 1902.

12050   RULE, H. J. The development of timetables on the Great Western Railway. Great Western Railway (London) Lecture & Debating Society, meeting on February 24th, 1910 [no. 68]. pp. 16, with 9 illus.

12051   SCOTT, W. J. The G.W.R. Penny Time-Book: as it is and as it might be. Great Western Railway (London) Lecture & Debating Society, meeting on January 26th 1911 [no. 77]. pp. 4.

12052   GREAT WESTERN RLY. Through the window: no 1, Paddington to Penzance, Cornish Riviera route. 300 miles of English country as seen from the G.W.R. trains. *Paddington Station (London): G.W.R.*, 1924. pp. 127, with a large-scale route map on the recto pages, descriptive text on the verso, 16 illus (drawings) & 2 maps: Paddington to Langport; Langport to Penzance. 'Compiled and produced for the G.W.R. Co. by Ed. J. Burrow & Co.'
—— another edn. Through the window: points of interest seen from the train by the

G.W.R. 'Cornish Riviera' route, Paddington—Penzance, including the Torquay, Newquay and Falmouth lines. *Paddington Station (London): G.W.R.*, 1939. pp. 64, with frontis, 2 maps: London to Langport, Langport to Penzance, and a large-scale route map on recto pages and descriptive text and illustrations (photographs) on facing pages.

12053   GREAT WESTERN RLY. Timetables: July 18th to September 11th, 1932. *London: G.W.R.*, 1932. [Facsimile reprint by] *Oxford Publishing Co.*, 1973. pp. [2], xii, 265, with 5 maps on folded sheet.

12054   GREAT WESTERN RLY. G.W.R. Service Timetable Appendices, 1945. Reprinted, *Truro: Bradford Barton*, 1977. pp. [200].
Appendices to working timetables for GWR Sections 1, 3–17, October 1st, 1945 until further notice.

12055   GREAT WESTERN RLY. Timetables, October 6th, 1947 and until further notice. [*London: G.W.R.*, 1947]. [Facsimile reprint published by *Oxford Publishing Co.*, 1976]. pp. 168, with folded map in pocket.

12056   MAGNER, G. Cornwall to Caithness, 1972 (Great Western railtour, May 19, 20, 21, 1972. Orcadian railtour [Crewe to Wick & Thurso and back], October 6, 7, 8, 1972). *Bromborough: Wirral Railway Circle*, 1973. pp. 48, with 10 illus & 4 lists.
A commemorative booklet of the two tours.

12057   HOLLAND, P. Illustrated rail route to the West of England, as seen from the train window, by Philip Holland; illustrated by Barry Craddock; managing editor, Kevin Hart. *London: Hart & Allen*, 1978. pp. [32], with 18 illus [photos], 23 vignettes, a page-by-page route map and a coloured general map of the GWR inside folded back cover.
Topographical, but with notes on the GWR and on the Kennet & Avon Canal.

Miscellaneous

12058   POTTER, F. Presidential address. Great Western Railway (London) Lecture and Debating Society, meeting on October 24th 1912 [no. 91]. pp. 9.
On the progress and achievements of the Society.

12059   LEVIEN, D. V. Great Western heirlooms. Great Western Railway (London) Lecture & Debating Society, meeting on February 9th 1922, no. 146. pp. 26, with discussion & 39 illus on 10 plates.
Relics and documents preserved at Paddington Station, London.

Great Western & Great Central Joint Rly

12060   JENKINS, S. C. The Great Western & Great Central Joint Railway. *Tarrant Hin-*

ton: Oakwood Press, 1978. (Oakwood Library of Railway History, 46). pp. 51, with 25 illus on 12 plates, 3 maps, 14 layout plans, gradient profile, 4 appendices (lists) & a bibliography (33+ sources).

Great Western and London & North Western Joint Rly

12061 PARTRIDGE, E. J. The route of the Shrewsbury & Hereford Railway described and illustrated . . . *Leominster: Edward J. Partridge*, [1860]. pp. vi, 64, [12], with notes & vignettes (topographical) & a folded map of the railway. [Reprinted by] *Shropshire County Library*, [1970].
A facsimile reprint with spiral binding.

Great Western & Midland Railways Joint Committee

12062 GREAT WESTERN AND MIDLAND RAILWAYS JOINT COMMITTEE. Severn & Wye Joint Lines, 1923. [Map]. *[Derby]: Midland Rly*, 1917. (Book no. 24, sheet 51A, 5th edn.) Republished by *Avon Anglia, Bristol*, 1977. (Official Railway Mileage Maps with Historical Notes, no. 1) as a printed folder, 8°, with detailed historical notes by C. R. Clinker on the reverse. Scale of map, 1 inch to ¾ mile.

Highland Rly *See* C 2 L

Hull & Barnsley Rly

12063 The HULL & Barnsley Railway. *Newton Abbot: David & Charles; Sheffield: Turntable Publications.*
vol. 1, edited by K. Hoole. *David & Charles,* 1972. pp. 331, with col. frontis, 31 illus on 16 plates, 18 maps, diagrams & gradient profiles.
Chapters by M. Edward Ingram & 12 others, incl. A. L. Barnett, A. G. H. Wannop, I. K. Watson, R. J. Pickering and R. C. Copeman.
vol. 2, edited by B. Hinchliffe. *Turntable Publications*, 1980. pp. 288, with 125 illus on 64 plates, 18 line drawings, plan, & folded map inside back cover, 317 notes, & 11 appendices, incl. Acts and a chronology.
The 19 chapters are by various authors, including B. Hinchliffe, K. Hoole, D. R. Smith & G. Y. Hemingway.

Lancashire & Yorkshire Rly

12064 COOK, R. A. Lancashire & Yorkshire Railway: historical maps. *Caterham: Railway & Canal Historical Society*, 1974. tall 8°. pp. 10, & 18 maps.
—— 2nd edn. *R. & C.H.S.*, 1976. pp. 20. Historical intro, table of constituent companies and Acts, followed by 18 maps.

12065 MANCHESTER & LEEDS RLY. Reply of the directors of the Manchester and Leeds Railway Company to the report of the directors of the Liverpool and Manchester Company at their last half-yearly meeting, on the subject of the proposed junction line through Manchester. *Manchester: Love & Barton, printers*, 1842. pp. 14, [3].   MCL

12066 MANCHESTER & LEEDS RLY. Report of the proceedings at a special meeting of the proprietors in the Manchester & Leeds Railway . . . respecting the extension line to Hunt's Bank and the guarantee to the Newcastle & Darlington Junction Railway Company. From the shorthand writer's notes. *Manchester: Love & Barton*, 1842. pp. xx, 3–34.

12067 MANCHESTER & LEEDS RLY. Statement of the Manchester and Leeds Railway Company in reference to the projected scheme of the Leeds and West Riding Junction Railways Company, and the connexion of that company with the Manchester and Leeds Railway Company; laid before the . . . Privy Council for Trade and Foreign Plantations. *Manchester: Love & Barton, printers*, 1845. pp. 20, with la. folded col. map & 10 tables. Dated January 9th, 1845.   MCL

12068 WILKINS, C. Wakefield, Pontefract and Goole Railway: reply of Mr. Wilkins as counsel on behalf of the promoters of the Bill, Wednesday, July 23, 1845; Lord Monteagle in the chair. *York: W. & J. Hargrove*, 1845. pp. 40. At head of title-page: 'House of Lords'.
A plea to pass the Bill for the projected railway.

12069 HAWKSHAW, J. Mr Hawlshaw's report on the rolling stock and permanent way, and the question of a reserve or equalising fund. *Manchester: Cave & Sever, printers*, 1850. pp. 12, [12], with 15 tables.
A report to the Lancashire & Yorkshire Rly.

12070 COWAN, C. A. The Holcombe Brook branch. *Kidderminster: Branch Line Society*, 1965. pp. 13, with 17 illus, map, 2 layout plans, gradient profile. Title on cover only.
Period, 1882–1963.

12071 LIVERIES of the Lancashire & Yorkshire Railway Company and its constituents, 1840–1921, including locomotive, carriage and wagon stock. *Colne (Lancs.): Vintage Carriages Trust, in co-operation with the Lancashire & Yorkshire Railway Society*, [1966]. obl. format. pp. [4], with illus on covers only.
An amplification of the chapter on the L. & Y. in *Britain's Railway Liveries*, by E. F. Carter (1952), 'with an attempt to remove ambiguities'.

12072 BULLEID, H. A. The Aspinall era. *London: Ian Allan*, 1967. pp. viii, 270, with 104 illus on 40 plates, & 68 in text.

12073 MARSHALL, J. The Lancashire & Yorkshire Railway. *Newton Abbot: David & Charles.*

A comprehensive & detailed history.

vol. 1, [The history of the main constituent railways]. 1969. pp. 288, with col. frontis, 38 illus on 20 plates, 11 maps, 5 text illus, 15 gradient profiles, 5 timetables, 295 notes.

vol. 2, [Extensions, additions, cut-off lines, widenings and improvements]. 1970. pp. 327, with col. frontis, 42 illus on 20 plates, 15 maps, 9 layout plans, 9 illus & diagrams, 31 gradient profiles, 189 notes & 8 detailed appendices incl. a chronology, list of Acts & table of dividends, 1832–1922.

vol. 3, [Locomotives & rolling stock]. 1972. pp. 293, with col. frontis, 75 illus on 24 plates, & in the text, 15; 164 notes & 8 appendices incl. detailed lists of locomotives (pp. 211–72).

12074 NOCK, O. S. The Lancashire & Yorkshire Railway: a concise history. *London: Ian Allan*, 1969. pp. 159, with col. frontis, 82 illus on 32 plates, 26 tables, 27 diagrams (incl. 10 layout plans) & 4 maps.

12075 BROADBRIDGE, S. The development and operation of the Lancashire and Yorkshire Railway network, *in his* Studies in Railway Expansion and the capital market in England, 1825–1873 (1970), pp. 3–76, with 10 tables & 212 notes.

12076 COATES, N. and WATERS, M. Lancashire & Yorkshire Album. *London: Ian Allan*, 1971. pp. 128. Col. frontis, intro, & 287 illus with descrs.

12077 FLETCHER, T. A. The Werneth incline: the first railway in Oldham, 1842–1963. *Manchester: the author*, [1972]. pp. 70. Reproduced typescript in printed cover.

A 3½ mile branch of the Manchester & Leeds Rly from Oldham Junction (later re-named Middleton Junction).

12078 TATTERSALL, W. D. The Bolton, Blackburn, Clitheroe & West Yorkshire Railway. *Lingfield: Oakwood Press*, 1973. (Oakwood Library of Railway History, 36). pp. 64, with 20 illus & a map on 8 plates, & diagrams in text.

12079 FORBES, N. N., FELTON, B. J. and RUSH, R. W. The electric lines of the Lancashire & Yorkshire Railway. *Sutton Coldfield: Electric Railway Society*, 1976. obl. format. pp. [46], with 71 illus on 21 plates, 29 line illus, & a map.

12080 MARSHALL, J. The Lancashire & Yorkshire Railway. [Album]. *Newton Abbot: David & Charles*, 1977. (Railway History in Pictures series). pp. 96. Intro (pp. 5–12, with 2 illus & 2 maps), frontis, & 131 illus with descrs.

A pictorial supplement to his 3-volume history of the same name (1969–72).

London & Blackwall Rly

12081 BODY, G. and EASTLEIGH, R. L. The London & Blackwall Railway. *Enfield: Trans-Rail Publications*, [1964]. pp. 31, with 8 illus & 4 maps.

London & North Eastern Rly

General, historical and descriptive 12082–85
Locomotives and trains 12086–12126
Signalling 12127

General, historical and descriptive

12082 EASTERN GROUP OF RAILWAYS. Eastern Group of Railways at your service. 2nd edn. [*London*]: *the Group*, [ca. 1922]. pp. 20, with folded map.

Publicity booklet issued by the nascent LNER.

12083 ALLEN, C. J. The London & North Eastern Railway. *London: Ian Allan*, 1966. pp. 228, with 144 illus on 40 plates, 12 tables, 18 logs of runs. Index, pp. 223–8.

Includes summary historical accounts of the constituent companies (pp. 16–33), and the LNER's maritime activities.

12084 ALLEN, G. F. Salute to the L.N.E.R. *London: Ian Allan*, 1977. pp. 100, with 136 illus (1 col.).

12085 THROWER, W. R. King's Cross in the twenties. *Tarrant Hinton: Oakwood Press*, 1978. (Locomotion Papers, 110). pp. 52, with 19 illus on 8 plates (pp. 23–30) & a facsimile.

The work issues directly from Dr Thrower's lifelong interest and acquaintance with the GNR and LNER through frequent journeyings between Hadley Woods and Kings Cross.

Locomotives and trains

12086 LONDON & NORTH EASTERN RLY. L.N.E.R. express passenger engine 4-6-2 Pacific type 4472 'Flying Scotsman', constructed in the Company's works at Doncaster 1922 to the designs of Mr. H. N. Gresley, Chief Mechanical Engineer, and exhibited at the British Empire Exhibition, Wembley, 1924. [*L.N.E.R.*, 1924. pp. 16]. tall 8°.

An engineering description of the locomotive, with 24 detailed working drawings, a gradient profile and a table recording 6 test runs made in June & July 1923 between Kings Cross and Doncaster.

The above description is from a photocopy of an original with covers missing. Presumably the work was produced for visitors to the Palace of Engineering in the Wembley exhibition where the locomotive was on display.   LU(THC)

12087 WILKINSON, W. London and North Eastern 4-6-2 (drawn by W. Wilkinson). *London: Locomotive Publishing Co.*, [192–?]. (Locomotive Charts Series).

A 12-section folded chart showing the interior of a Gresley Pacific locomotive.

12088 PEACHY, C. The non-stop run to Scotland, by engine-driver C. Peachy, *in* The Book of Speed (*Batsford*, 1934). pp. 125–31, with 7 illus.
The East Coast route on the 'Flying Scotsman'.

12089 BURRIDGE, F. H. A. Nameplates of the L.N.E.R. locomotives. *Bournemouth: the author via Sydenham & Co.*, June 1947. sm. 8°. pp. 56, with 61 illus & drawings, with notes.

12090 SPENCER, B. The development of L.N.E.R. locomotive design, 1923–1941. *London: Institution of Locomotive Engineers*, 1947. pp. 39, with 48 illus & diagrams, incl. 4 folded, & 8 on 8-page insert; 4 tables. No cover, no title-page. Title from head of text.
'Paper to be read before the Institution . . . on 19th March 1947, in London.'

12091 STEPHENSON LOCOMOTIVE SOCIETY. Golden Jubilee Tour, London & Doncaster, 23rd May 1959. *S.L.S.*, [1959]. pp. [8], with 2 illus & schedule.
Text: 'The Stephenson Locomotive Society', by J. S. Davies; 'Some notes on the G.N.R. and its early history', by J. G. Brown; 'The 'A4' locomotives in brief', by R. A. H. Weight; 'Driver W. Hoole', by Norman Harvey.

12092 RAILWAY CORRESPONDENCE & TRAVEL SOCIETY AND STEPHENSON LOCOMOTIVE SOCIETY JOINT TOURS COMMITTEE. Guide and notes to the Jubilee Requiem Railtour: London   (Kings   Cross)— Newcastle (Central) & back, Saturday, 24th October 1964 . . . *the Committee*, 1964. pp. [8], with 5 illus & a schedule. Notes by P. Proud, E. Neve, Harold Creamer and Bill Hoole.
'Commemorative special train handled by an ex-LNER A4 Pacific locomotive'.

12093 CASSERLEY, H. C. and JOHNSTON, S. W. Locomotives at the Grouping: vol. 2, London & North Eastern Railway. *London: Ian Allan*, 1966. pp. 128, with 89 illus. Lists.

12094 SEMMENS, P. W. B. Bill Hoole: engineman extraordinary. *London: Ian Allan*, 1966. pp. ix, 205, with frontis & 77 illus on 32 plates.
—— [1st edn. reprinted, with a new preface by the author]. *Ian Allan*, 1974. pp. xvii, 205; 32 plates.
1907–1912, Midland Rly; 1912–1959, GCR—LNER—BR.

12095 BLACK, E. The Pacifics of the L.N.E.R. *Skipton: Yorkshire Dales Society*, 1969. pp. 46, with 10 illus on 9 plates, 3 lists. Reproduced typescript in printed pictorial covers.

12096 FLYING Scotsman, [by] Alan Pegler, Cecil J. Allen, Trevor Bailey. *London: Ian Allan*, 1969. pp. [64], with 58 illus.
The history and re-introduction into service of the LNER Pacific locomotive 4472, 'Flying Scotsman'.
—— 2nd edn, enl., by Alan Pegler, Cecil J. Allen, Trevor Bailey, Harold Edmonson. *Ian Allan*, 1970. pp. 80, with 74 illus (3 col.) & 2 engineering drawings.
This edition includes an account of the American tour in 1969.
—— 3rd edn, by Alan Pegler, Cecil J. Allen, Trevor Bailey, Harold Edmonson, Brian Haresnape. *Ian Allan*, 1976. pp. 80, with 82 illus (7 col.) & 2 engineering drawings.

12097 FLYING Scotsman: The history of a famous engine in pictures, words and sounds. *Leeds: Turntable Enterprises*, 1969. obl. format. pp. [24], with 27 illus & 5 working drawings.
Published with a gramophone record in an envelope affixed to inside of back cover, of the *Flying Scotsman* on journeys made in October 1968.

12098 NOCK, O. S. L.N.E.R. Steam. *Newton Abbot: David & Charles*, 1969. pp. 292, with col. frontis & 72 illus on 32 plates & 77 logs of runs.
—— Re-issued as a paperback, *Pan Books*, 1971. pp. xii, 274, with 32 plates.

12099 STEPHENSON, B. LNER Album. *London: Ian Allan*.
vol. 1, [a general & varied selection, with some pre-Grouping 'absorbed' engines]. 1970. pp. 128. Intro, frontis & 108 illus with descrs.
vol. 2, [North Eastern and Scottish areas, including pre-Grouping locomotives]. 1970. pp. 112. Intro, frontis & 176 illus with descrs.
vol. 3, [a supplementary selection]. 1976. pp. 128. Intro, frontis & 198 illus with descrs.

12100 GRAFTON, P. Edward Thompson of the L.N.E.R. *Knaresborough: Kestrel Books*, 1971. pp. 139, with 68 illus on 32 plates & 5 appendices, incl. lists & diagrams.

12101 JUDGE, C. W. The L.N.E.R. era: a collection of photographs of locomotives. *Oxford: Oxford Publishing Co.*, 1971. pp. 89. Intro & 172 illus with captions, & an index. A limited edition of 1000 numbered copies, each signed by the compiler.

12102 CLAY, J. F. and CLIFFE, J. The LNER 2-8-2 and 2-6-2 classes. *London: Ian Allan*, 1973. pp. 111, with 65 illus on 32 plates, & a bibliography (22+ sources).

12103 EARLEY, M. W. The L.N.E.R. scene: an album of photographs by Maurice W. Earley, *Oxford: Oxford Publishing Co.*, 1973. pp. [62]. obl. format. Intro & 91 illus with descrs.

12104 HARRIS, M. Gresley's coaches: coaches built for G.N.R., E.C.J.S. and L.N.E.R., 1905–53. *Newton Abbot: David & Charles*, 1973. pp. 160, with frontis, 97 illus, a detailed 8-column table (pp. 130–54), a chronology & a bibliography.

12105 NOCK, O. S. The Gresley Pacifics. *Newton Abbot: David & Charles.*
    part 1, 1922–1935. 1973. pp. 144, with frontis, 105 illus, 33 diagrams, 2 graphs, logs of 50 runs, 2 gradient profiles & many tables.
    part 2, 1935–74. [1974]. pp. 144, with frontis, 126 illus, 5 diagrams, 3 graphs from speed recorders, including that of *Mallard*'s record-breaking run of July 3rd 1938, and logs of 48 runs.

12106 ARMSTRONG, J. L.N.E.R. locomotive development between 1911 and 1947, with a brief history of developments from 1850 to 1911. *Seaton: Peco*, 1974. pp. x, 93, with 98 illus & 31 diagrams; bibliography (31 sources).

12107 PREEDY, N. E. North Eastern Pacifics: a pictorial survey. *Truro: Bradford Barton*, 1974. pp. 96. Intro & 11 illus with descrs.
    Ex-LNER locomotives and trains at work on the East Coast route.

12108 CLAY, J. F. and CLIFFE, J. The LNER 4-6-0 classes. *London: Ian Allan*, 1975. pp. 149, with 91 illus on 40 plates; tables, & 15 dimensioned drawings & a bibliography (24+ sources).

12109 LYNCH, P. J. North Eastern Steam Locomotive Album. *Truro: Bradford Barton*, 1975. pp. 96. Intro & 111 illus with descrs.

12110 BELLWOOD, J. and JENKINSON, D. Gresley and Stanier: a centenary tribute. *London: H.M.S.O., for the National Railway Museum, York*, 1976. 4°. pp. vii, 99, with 142 illus, incl. 2 portraits as frontis; bibliography (p. 99).

12111 TATLOW, P. A Pictorial Record of LNER Wagons. *Oxford: Oxford Publishing*, 1976. la. 8°. pp. vi, 180, with 353 illus, 89 diagrams, detailed tables in 5 appendices & a bibliography (7 sources).

12112 ADAMS, J. and WHITEHOUSE, P. Eastern Steam in camera. *London: Ian Allan*, 1977. pp. 64. Intro & 90 illus with descrs.
    LNER locomotives in BR(ER) days, 1950's & 1960's.

12113 CASSERLEY, H. C. L.N.E.R. locomotives, 1923–1948. *Truro: Bradford Barton*, 1977. pp. 96. Intro & 106 illus with descrs.

12114 CASSERLEY, H. C. L.N.E.R. Steam, 1923–1948. *Truro: Bradford Barton*, 1977. 4°. pp. 96. Intro & 96 illus with descrs.

12115 CLAY, J. F. and CLIFFE, J. The LNER 2-6-0 classes. *London: Ian Allan*, 1978. pp. 80 with 51 illus on 24 plates, & in text, 20 tables (mostly logs of runs), 13 diagrams, 10 dimensioned drawings & a bibliography (20+ sources).

12116 MEACHER, C. LNER footplate memories: the story of twenty-five years on and off shed. *Truro: Bradford Barton*, 1978. pp. 150, with 22 illus, 2 maps & 2 plans.
    Centred upon Haymarket and St Margaret's locomotive depots, Edinburgh.

12117 MORRISON, B. The power of the A4s. *Oxford: Oxford Publishing Co.*, [1978]. 4°. pp. [112]. Intro & 218 illus (9 col.) with descrs.

12118 SELF, A. Streamlined expresses of the LNER, 1935–39, *in* Design history: fad or function? *London: Design Council*, 1978. pp. 17–23, with 10 illus & 35 notes.

12119 ELLIOTT, R. J. Preserved locomotives of the London, North Eastern Railway [sic], 1979. *Buckfastleigh: Dumbleton Hall Preservation Society*, 1979. (Preserved Locomotives, 4). pp. [32], with 38 illus.
    Details of 43 steam locomotives and a location list.

12120 GAMMELL, C. J. LNER branch lines, 1945–1965. *Oxford: Oxford Publishing Co.*, [1979]. la. 8°. pp. [96]. General intro, & 162 illus with descrs arranged into areas, each with a map and short introduction.

12121 LARKING, E. J. Memoirs of a railway engineer. *Bury St Edmunds: Mechanical Engineering Publications*, 1979. pp. [x], 212, with over 200 illus, working drawings, maps, diagrams & tables.
    52 years in railway service (1914–1965) with the Midland, LMS and BR(LMR). Steam locomotive design, building & maintenance, workshop training of apprentices and engineers.

12122 ROGERS, H. C. B. Thompson and Peppercorn: locomotive engineers. *London: Ian Allan*, 1979. pp. 160, with 155 illus.

12123 WHITELEY, J. S. and MORRISON, G. W. The LNER remembered. *Oxford: Oxford Publishing Co.*, 1979. la. 8°. pp. [112]. Intro & 270 illus with descrs.

12124 BLOOM, A. Locomotives of the London and North Eastern Railway, written by Alan Bloom; compiled by David Williams. *Norwich: Jarrold*, 1980. (Jarrold Railway Series, 4). pp. [32], with 64 illus (50 col.), & a map. Text & illus extend onto covers.

12125 KEELEY, R. Memories of LNER Steam. *London: Ian Allan*, 1980. pp. 110. Intro, 6 essays, & 160 illus with descrs.

12126 SEMMENS, P. W. B. North Eastern engineman: driver Syd Midgley and fifty years of Steam. *Truro: Bradford Barton*, 1980. pp. 119, with 23 illus on 16 plates (pp. 53–60, 77–84).
    Period, 1914–1963, NER—LNER—BR.

Signalling

12127 WESTINGHOUSE BRAKE AND SIGNAL COMPANY. Colour-light signalling on the Chingford branch, L.N.E.R. *London: the Company*, [1938]. pp. 7, with 18 illus, 2 track diagrams & a map.
Reprinted from the *Railway Gazette*, 29 April 1938.

London & North Western Rly

General, historical and descriptive 12128–12200
Locomotives and trains 12201–10

General, historical and descriptive

12128 BIRMINGHAM AND LIVERPOOL RAILWAY. [Report from the committee of management of the intended Birmingham & Liverpool Railway Company to the subscribers, on the failure to obtain parliamentary sanction for the Bill giving effect to their plans. Dated Sept. 23, 1825]. *Birmingham: T. Knott, printer*, [1825]. Fol. pp. 2.

12129 MEMOIR of the Right Honourable William Huskisson, with particulars of his lamented death. *Liverpool: Journal Office*, 1830. pp. 16. Text signed 'T.T.'.
pp. 9–11, his fatal accident.

12130 A BIOGRAPHICAL memoir of the Right Honourable William Huskisson, derived from authentic sources. *London: privately printed by J. L. Cox*, 1831. pp. iv, 275, with frontis (portrait).
p. 232 *et seq.*, his death at Parkside.

12131 CLAYTON, A. B. Views on the Liverpool and Manchester Railway, taken on the spot by Mr. A. B. Clayton, with a descriptive reference to each view. *Liverpool: J. Cannell*, [1831]. pp. [3], with 3 plates (lithographs of drawings). [*Newcastle upon Tyne: Frank Graham*, 1970]. obl. format.
A facsimile reprint with a new introduction by C. R. Clinker. A limited edition of 950 copies.

12132 AUSTIN, S. Lancashire illustrated, from drawings by S. Austin, J. Harwood, G. & C. Pye, etc., etc., with historical & topographical descriptions. *London: H. Fisher, Son, & Jackson*, 1831. la. 8°. pp. 104, with 100 engravings.
pp. 20–23, 'Entrance to the tunnel of the Liverpool & Manchester Railway, Edge Hill', with 1 engraving.
—— 2nd edn, 1832. pp. 112. (pp. 98–100).

12133 LECOUNT, P. Mr Lecount's 'General results of the traffic returns, etc. between London and Birmingham for one year; also, the expenses of travelling and carriage by the present means and by the railway'. *London: J. B. Nichols & Sons (printer)*, [1832]. pp. 16, with 4 tables.

12134 EXTRACTS from the Minutes of Evidence given before the Committee of the Lords on the London and Birmingham Railway Bill in June 1832, shewing the great advantage to landowners and the public of this mode of communication in general. *Bristol: printed by J. Chilcott*, 1833. pp. vii, 24. Signed: 'Bristol, 15th December 1833'.
Anonymous, but Foreword states that 'there are no good grounds for the formation of a railway between London and Birmingham which do not also support the proposed line between the Metropolis and Bristol'. The writer says that the *Extracts* (see 6423) can hardly fail to dissipate the prejudices entertained by some landowners against the Great Western Railway.

12135 DIRECT line of railway connecting South Wales, Gloucester, Cheltenham, Oxford, Tring and London. *Cheltenham: G. A. Williams [& other booksellers]*, 1836. pp. 28.
Supporting the promotion of the Cheltenham, Oxford & London & Birmingham Union Rly in opposition to the Cheltenham & Great Western Union Rly.

12136 A COMPENDIOUS history and description of the North Union Railway: comprising an introductory sketch, the prospective advantages of the railway, its statistics, a delineation of the operations which have marked its progress, a detailed reference to all the important features of the route, viz, the tunnels, viaducts, gradients, localities, etc; also, a list of the fares from Preston to Liverpool or Manchester and all the intermediate places. *Preston*, 1838. sm. 8°. pp. 42 & the fares list.

12137 LARMER, G. A description of the rival lines of railway between Carlisle and Lancaster, with the advantages of an inland line considered. *Carlisle: J. Steel, Journal Office*, 1839. pp. 11, with frontis (map). Caption title: Rival lines of railway between Carlisle & Lancaster. NUC

12138 VIGNOLES, C. Copy of Mr Vignoles' observations on Mr Stephenson's report to the Chester and Crewe railway directors. *Dublin: A. Thom*, 1839. pp. 4.
BLACK 5183

12139 COPY of the correspondence between the North Union and Lancaster & Preston railways on the subject of locomotive power and station accommodation. *Manchester: J. Gadsby*, [1841]. pp. 22.
BLACKWELL'S CAT. A 1051 (1976), 272

12140 COMPARATIVE lengths of new railway to be made by the Liverpool and Manchester Company and parties co-operating with them, to connect the several railways centering in Manchester, as the question now stands for the consideration of the Liverpool proprietors. s. sh. folded [1842?]. No imprint. MCL

12141 LONDON & BIRMINGHAM RLY. Timetable, corrected to 1st September 1842.

London: Smith & Ebbs, printers, [1842]. la. 8°. single sheet.

A reprint with no added imprint, published by *Avon Anglia* of Bristol (later of Weston-super-Mare) as no.2 in their *Historical Documents* series.

12142 CORRESPONDENCE between the Manchester and Birmingham Railway Company and the General Post Office with reference to the conveyance of the mails between Manchester and Crewe. [*Manchester & Birmingham Rly Co.*, 1843?]. pp. 36.

12143 COMMITTEE OF MR BOOTH'S TESTIMONIAL. Testimonial to Mr Henry Booth. *Liverpool:* [*L. & M. Rly*], 1846. pp. 23.

'A meeting chaired by Charles Lawrence held at the Clarendon Rooms, Liverpool on 31st March for the purpose of presenting Mr Henry Booth with some Testimonial for the valuable services rendered by him to the Liverpool & Manchester Rly and to the progress of railways generally during a period of twenty years.' The total amount subscribed was 3000 guineas. The text includes an exchange of letters between Charles Lawrence and Henry Booth and a list of subscriptions (pp. 11–23). The Committee formed for the purpose comprised the directors of the late Liverpool & Manchester Rly, those of the Grand Junction Rly, and nine individuals.   LU(THC)

12144 LETTER to the shareholders of the London and North Western and Great Western railways, by a well-wisher to both companies. *London: Pelham Richardson*, 1849. pp. 14. On half-title page of the MCL copy, a MS note in red ink: 'By T. [or J.] Cobb, Banbury'.

Advocates removal of competition between the LNWR and the GWR, the LNWR to have control of all the lines north of Oxford; also, the abolition of Paddington station (London terminus of the GWR), the LNWR providing a junction for it near Wormwood Scrubs, with mixed gauge from there into Euston (London terminus of the LNWR), as in the original GWR Act of August 1835.   MCL

12145 POOLE, B. A report to the directors of the London and North Western Railway Company on iron ore. *Newton: M'Corquodale & Co., printers*, 1850. pp. 8, with 11 tables.   MCL

12146 JUST in time: a tale of the L. & N.W.R., by a railway sleeper. *Montrose: printed at the Standard Office*, 1870. pp. 58, with illus.

Anecdotes, facetiae and satire.

12147 MEMOIR of Robert Benson Dockray. *London: printed by William Clowes & Son*, 1872. pp. 5.

Excerpt, *Annual Report of the Institution of Civil Engineers*, 1871–72.   LU(THC)

12148 PICTON, J. A. Memorials of Liverpool. *London: Longmans, Green*.

vol. 1, Historical. 1873. pp. 704. pp. 486–9, opening of the Liverpool & Manchester Railway.

12149 NICHOLSON, C. Cornelius Nicholson: a well-spent life; memoir of Cornelius Nichol-

son, with a selection of his lectures and letters. *Kendal: T. Wilson*, 1890. pp. 290, [3], with a facsimile letter of Sept. 17, 1843 from William Wordsworth and a facsimile poem from Mr. Hartley Coleridge.

pp. 17–88, 'The opening of the Lancaster & Carlisle Railway to Kendal': a detailed narrative with press reports & speeches.

pp. 119–39, 'The London and Glasgow Railway: the interests of Kendal considered (1837)'. (*See* 1150 or 6325).

12150 LONDON & NORTH WESTERN RLY. The Official Guide to the London and North Western Railway, the Royal Mail West Coast route between England, Scotland, Ireland and the Continent. New & rev. edn, illustrated. *London: Cassell*, 1892. pp. A–C, xiv, 434, 28, D–F, with folded map in pocket, 28 folded maps & town plans in text and numerous engravings.

12151 The STORY of Lancashire. *London: Edward Arnold*, [1897]. pp. 256.

ch. 42 (pp. 163–7), Lancashire's first railway.

ch. 44 (pp. 167–70), The draining of Chat Moss.

12152 LONDON & NORTH WESTERN RLY. The London & North Western Railway: the premier line of England. *London: L.N.W.R.*, October 1907 (2nd issue). sm. obl. format. pp. 64, with folded diagram & folded map. On cover: 'The London & North Western Railway Company of England sends greetings to the American voyagers and presents this little book of information'.

Mainly topographical.

12153 STEPHENSON, G. Copy of a report made by George Stephenson and letters written by his son, Robert Stephenson, in reference to the Liverpool and Manchester Railway, 1828–9. *London: London & North Western Rly*, 1908. pp. 15. Text in English & French.

The original letters were exhibited at the LNWR's stand in the Machinery Hall at the Franco–British Exhibition, London, 1908.

LU(THC)

12154 LONDON & NORTH WESTERN RLY. Comfort in railway travel in 1909. *London: Boswell Printing & Publishing Co.*, [1909]. pp. 20, with 21 illus.

Reprinted from the *Railway News*. A publicity brochure. Includes (pp. 12–20), the LNWR Irish steamboat services.

12155 LONDON & NORTH WESTERN RLY. Manchester and where to live. *London: LNWR*, [1910]. pp. 36, with 30 illus & a map.

STOCKPORT PL

12156 A HUNDRED years ago: the early history of the Liverpool & Manchester Railway. *Manchester: Fletcher Miller Ltd.*, [1930]. pp. 32, with 20 illus, 2 maps, 5 portraits, & 4 facsimiles.

Reprinted in the *Beyer Peacock Quarterly Review*, July 1930.

12157 FAY, C. R. Huskisson and his Age. *London: Longmans, Green*, 1951. pp. xv, 398.
pp. 1–30, 360, his accidental death at the opening of the Liverpool & Manchester Rly, 15 September 1830. *See also* 'Railway Age' in the index.

12158 CARLSON, R. E. The Liverpool—Manchester railway project, 1821–1831.
Thesis, Ph.D., University of Pittsburgh, 1955. *See also* 12168.

12159 ENGLISH Historical Documents, vol. XI, 1783–1832, edited by A. Aspinall and F. Anthony Smith. *London: Eyre & Spottiswoode*, 1959. pp. xxx, 992.
no. 385 (pp. 544–5): 'Railway Acts passed by Parliament, 1801–1832' from *The Progress of the Nation*, by G. R. Porter, vol. 2 (1838), pp. 63–4. A five-column listing of 48 railway companies.
no. 386 (pp. 546–8): 'Prospectus of the Liverpool and Manchester Railroad Company, 1824' from *History of . . . Liverpool*, by T. Baines (1852), pp. 601–3.
no. 387 (pp. 548–9): Thomas Creevey to Miss Ord, 14 Nov. 1829', from *The Creevey Papers*, ed. by Sir Herbert Maxwell, vol. 2, pp. 203–4. 'Today we had a lark of a very high order'; his ride on the Liverpool and Manchester Rly, at that time still under construction.
no. 387A (p. 549): 'The Quarterly Review on the projected Liverpool and Manchester Railway, March 1825' (pp. 361–2), an anti-railway view: '. . . but with all these assurances we should as soon expect the people of Woolwich to suffer themselves to be fired off upon one of Congreve's ricochet rockets as trust themselves to the mercy of such a machine going at such a rate'. [23 m.p.h.].

12160 DONAGHY, [Brother] Lewis. Operational history of the Liverpool and Manchester Railway, 1831–1845, by Brother Lewis Donaghy [i.e.Thomas J. Donaghy]. Thesis, Ph.D., University of Pittsburgh, 1960. *See also* 12177.

12161 SWANSEA RAILWAY CIRCLE. The Central Wales. *Swansea: the Circle*, [1964]. pp. 22, with 8 line drawings, a map and a plan. Reproduced typescript. Text extends onto covers.

12162 O'SHEA, M. J. The Buxton branch: a geographical study of the railway from Stockport to Buxton via Whaley Bridge. Thesis, M.A. (Honours, Geography), University of Aberdeen, 1965.

12163 DONAGHY, T. J. The Liverpool & Manchester Railway as an investment, *in* Journal of Transport History, vol. 7 (1965–6), pp. 225–33, with 28 notes.

12164 ROBBINS, M. From R. B. Dockray's diary, *in* Journal of Transport History, vol. 7 (1965–6), pp. 1–13, 109–19, 149–59, with 4 notes.
Extracts, with notes, of entries in three volumes, for 1850, 1853 and 1860, relating to Dockray's professional life with the LNWR, and to other current railway matters and personalities, and to permanent way and maintenance.

—— Publisher's note: 'The Dockray Diaries', *in* J.T.H., new series, vol. 3, no. 4 (Sept. 1976), p. 293.
The presentation in that year of the diaries, and a commonplace book made by R. B. Dockray, to Leicester University Library.

12165 JOY, D. Main line over Shap: the story of the Lancaster–Carlisle Railway. *Clapham (North Yorks): Dalesman Publishing Co.*, 1967. pp. 88, with 56 illus, map & a route chart.

12166 GOURVISH, T. R. British railway management in the nineteenth century, with special reference to the career of Captain Mark Huish, 1808–1867. Thesis, Ph.D., University of London, 1968.

12167 NOCK, O. S. North Western: saga of the Premier Line of Great Britain, 1846–1922. *London: Ian Allan*, 1968. pp. xii, 311, with 80 illus on 32 plates, 6 maps, 8 layout plans, 15 diagrams, many tables, a gradient profile & 6 appendices, including a list of all named LNWR locomotives.

12168 CARLSON, R. E. The Liverpool & Manchester Railway project, 1821–1831. *Newton Abbot: David & Charles*, 1969. pp. 292, with 28 illus & maps on 12 plates, map in text; also, text of documents and list of share values in appendices. Many bibliogr notes and a bibliography (pp. 246–64). Index (pp. 279–92).
See also 12158.

12169 REED, B. Crewe to Carlisle. *London: Ian Allan*, 1969. pp. 234, with 69 illus on 32 plates, 19 tables, 18 maps, layout plans & graphs, a bibliography (52 sources) & a list of Acts.
The history of the Crewe to Carlisle division of the West Coast route to Scotland, LNWR.

12170 WILLIAMS, J. H. The Crewe mechanics institutions, 1843–1913. Thesis, M. Ed., University of Manchester, 1969.

12171 GEESON, A. W. The development of elementary education in Crewe, 1840–1918. Thesis, M.Ed., University of Durham, 1970.
Includes a section on the LNWR schools.

12172 HUGHES, M. Stockport Viaduct, by Mrs M. Hughes. *Stockport: Stockport Municipal Museum*, June 1970. (Information Leaflet, 2). pp. 2, with timetable of 1840. Reproduced typescript.
—— rev. edn, by M. Hughes and V. Holland, Nov. 1970. (Information Leaflet, 2). pp. 4, with illus & timetable. Reproduced typescript.

12173 A PICTURE history of the Liverpool & Manchester Railway. *Liverpool: Scouse Press*, [1970 or 71].
A pack of reproductions from early prints,

maps, reports, etc, showing scenes on the L & M Rly during and after its construction, with notices, press comments, cartoons, etc.   MCL

12174 SMITH, D. J. Shrewsbury to Swansea: the story of the railway through Central Wales. *Bracknell: Town & Country Press*, 1971. pp. 111, with frontis, 30 illus, 9 layout plans, 6 gradient profiles, 4 timetables, 3 maps, lists & a chronology.
  The Central Wales Rly (LNWR).

12175 WESTERN, R. G. The Lowgill branch: a lost route to Scotland. *Lingfield: Oakwood Press*, 1971. (Locomotion Papers, 51). pp. 55, with 15 illus on 8 plates, 5 maps, chronology & a bibliography (15 sources).
  The Ingleton to Lowgill branch.

12176 BAUGHAN, P. E. The Chester & Holyhead Railway. *Newton Abbot: David & Charles*.
  vol. 1, [The main line up to 1880]. 1972. pp. 324, with col. frontis & 28 illus on 16 plates, & in text, 17 maps, drawings & facsims, a chronology, 248 notes and 3 lists.

12177 DONAGHY, T. J. Liverpool & Manchester Railway operations, 1831–1845. *Newton Abbot: David & Charles*, 1972. pp. 212, with 21 illus on 8 plates, 344 notes, a detailed and extensive bibliography (pp. 185–206) & 6 appendices. *See also* 12160.

12178 GOURVISH, T. R. Mark Huish and the London & North Western Railway: a study of management. *Leicester: Leicester University Press*, 1972. pp. 319, with 8 plates (portraits), 6 maps, 3 line illus, 63 tables (nos. 44–63 in Appendix 1), 819 notes, & a select bibliography (pp. 301–9) of ca. 170 sources.

12179 HARDMAN, D. B. Chat Moss and the Liverpool—Manchester Railway: a study in historical geography. *Manchester: Manchester Polytechnic, Dept of Education*, [1972?]. (Occasional Paper, 5). pp. 26, with map, 2 line illus & a bibliography (41 sources). Reproduced typescript.

12180 SCOTT, P. G. The Harrow & Stanmore Railway. *Stanmore: the author*, 1972. pp. 36, with 15 illus, 3 station layout plans & a map.
  Period, 1890–1964.

12181 SWANN, R. The Liverpool & Manchester Railway: transport developments and economic changes in the first half of the nineteenth century. Dissertation, B.Sc. (Hons) in Economics, University of Salford, 1972.

12182 WEBSTER, N. W. Britain's first trunk line: the Grand Junction Railway. *Bath: Adams & Dart*, 1972. pp. 196, with 49 illus (photos, maps, drawings, diagrams, facsimiles) & 127 notes.

12183 DIXON, F. The Manchester South Junction & Altrincham Railway. *Lingfield: Oakwood Press*, 1973. (Oakwood Library of Railway History, 34). pp. 88, with 41 illus on 20 plates, 3 timetables, 2 maps, 24 layout plans, a list of Acts with notes & 13 appendices.
  Period, 1845–1971.

12184 TRACEY, D. B. The influence of Private Bill procedure upon the formation of the first railways between Liverpool and Manchester and London.
  Thesis, M.A., University of Manchester, 1974.

12185 NELSON, J. LNWR portrayed: a survey of the design and construction methods of the Premier Line. *Seaton: Peco*, 1975. pp. 192, with 370 illus & dimensioned drawings & a bibliography (12 sources).
  An historical record of the physical features of the LNWR (civil engineering, architecture, design), presented as a reference source for modellers.

12186 SINGLETON, D. Liverpool and Manchester Railway: a mile by mile guide to the world's first 'modern' railway. *Clapham (N. Yorks): Dalesman*, 1975. pp. 96, with 27 illus, 9 layout plans, 2 maps & a bibliography (23 sources).

12187 WRIGHT, J. B. The Cromford and High Peak Railway in the nineteenth century: a technical and economic study. Dissertation, M.A., University of Leicester (Victorian Studies), 1975. With mounted photographs.

12188 HALSALL, D. A. The Chester and Holyhead Railway and its branches; a geographical perspective. Thesis, Ph.D., University of Liverpool, 1976.

12189 SIMPSON, B. The Banbury to Verney Junction branch. *Oxford: Oxford Publishing Co.*, 1978. pp. 168, with 108 illus incl. facsimiles, 2 maps, 2 layout plans, gradient profiles, diagrams, timetables, 2 folded pp. of plans & a bibliography (11 sources).
  A detailed historical coverage of the 21 mile Banbury branch of the Buckinghamshire Rly, 1850–1968.

12190 TALBOT, E. L. & N.W.R. Miscellany. [vol. 1]. *Oxford: Oxford Publishing Co.*, 1978. la. 8°. pp. [112]. Intro, map, & 218 illus with descrs.
  —— vol. 2. *Oxford Publishing Co.*, 1980. la. 8°. pp. [104]. Intro, map & 227 illus with descrs.
  Two albums of photographs, mostly of locomotives and trains, but also of carriages, wagons, road vehicles, signalling, and personnel (group photographs).

12191 THOMPSON, T. The Prestatyn & Dyserth Railway. *Prestatyn: North Clwyd Railway Association*, 1978. pp. 71, with 21 illus & 8 layout plans & tables, timetables, diagrams & a gradient profile; 81 notes.

A branch of the Chester & Holyhead Rly, 1869–1973, known as the Prestatyn & Cwm branch.

12192   PRATT, I. S.   By Rocket to Rainhill: a history to mark the 150th anniversary of the Liverpool and Manchester Railway; editor, Ian S. Pratt. [*Manchester*]: *I. S. Pratt*, 1979. tall 8°. pp. 64, with 42 illus, 2 facsimiles, a map, a brief chronology & a bibliography (11 sources).

Written by staff members of the History Department, Walkden High School, for young teenage readers. Most of the illustrations are from those traditionally associated with the early Railway Age but there are some modern photographs of historic L&M Rly sites and some noteworthy pencil drawings by Brian Worthington.

12193   BOOTH, H.   Henry Booth: inventor, partner in the Rocket and the father of railway management. *Ilfracombe: Stockwell*, 1980. pp. 232, with 11 illus on 8 plates & 24 line drawings, mostly of locomotives, 6 appendices & a bibliography (50+ sources). ·

Henry Booth (1788–1869), mechanical engineer, was secretary & treasurer to the Liverpool & Manchester Rly and joint secretary of the LNWR, 1846–1859.

12194   BRITISH RAIL. LONDON MIDLAND REGION.   Rocket 150: 150th anniversary of the Liverpool & Manchester Railway, 1830–1980. Official handbook. [*London*]: *B.R. (LMR)*; [*Bristol*]: *Avon–Anglia Publications*, 1980. pp. 84, with 91 illus (49 col.), 5 maps, 3 plans & a gradient profile. On covers, a col. picture of the *Rocket* at the Rainhill Trial, by Alan Fearnley.

A pictorial record of the foundation and early years of the L & M, its route, and (pp. 33–52) of the Cavalcade of Locomotives which was the central feature of the Rail 150 Celebrations in 1980, followed by 'The Railway today'.

12195   BURTON, A.   The Rainhill Story: the great locomotive trial. *London: British Broadcasting Corporation*, 1980. pp. 164, 12 illus (7 col.) & a bibliography (17 sources).

'Published to accompany the BBC-TV documentary *The Rainhill Story* and the coverage of British Rail's Rocket 150 celebrations, both produced by Martin L. Bell.'

12196   FERNEYHOUGH, F.   Liverpool & Manchester Railway, 1830–1980: foreword by Sir Peter Parker, chairman, British Railways Board. *London: Robert Hale*, 1980. pp. xii, 193, with 67 illus on 32 plates, 3 maps & a bibliography (43 sources).

12197   GREAT RAILWAY EXPOSITION [Manchester, 1980]. Souvenir Programme. *Manchester: Liverpool Road Celebrations Joint Advisory Committee, in association with Europress*, 1980. la. 8°. pp. 42. Intro by James Bingham, chairman of Greater Manchester Council and the Liverpool Road Celebrations Committee. 7 historical essays

(6 anonymous and 1 by Moira Rudolph) & many illus & adverts.

An exposition at Liverpool Road station to celebrate the 150th anniversary of the opening of the Liverpool & Manchester Rly.

12198   GREAVES, S.   The Liverpool and Manchester Railway: Newton's story. *Newton-le-Willows: Newton 150 Committee*, 1980. pp. 12, with 6 illus & 2 maps.

12199   THOMAS, R. H. G.   The Liverpool & Manchester Railway: foreword by Jack Simmons. *London: Batsford*, 1980. pp. 264, with 122 illus, incl. frontis & many other portraits, drawings, diagrams, facsimiles & maps; 299 notes.

The main text is followed by a chronology from 1845; appendix A is a list of guests at the opening ceremony and details of the train crews on that day; Appendix B is a detailed 6-column listing of the locomotives of the L & M up to the amalgamation of the line into the LNWR in 1846 (105 engines in all).

12200   YOUNG, C.   [A journey on the Liverpool and Manchester Railway]. *Manchester: Lancashire & Cheshire Antiquarian Society*, 1980. pp. 8.

Reprinted from the *Transactions of the L. & C.A.S.*, vol. 80 (1979).

A letter from Charles Young to his sister Jane in St Albans, written from the Isle of Man, August 6th, 1835, describing his journey from St Albans (pp. 2–4). Introduction (p. 1) by Tony Rees, and an informative commentary with 5 bibliogr. refs by 'V.I.T.' (V.I. Tomlinson).

Locomotives and trains

12201   MACLAREN, C.   Steam carriage experiments at Liverpool in 1829, *in his* Select Writings . . . (1869) vol. 2, pp. 49–58.

Reprinted from *The Scotsman*, 21 October 1829.

12202   'SIROCCO'.   Farewell to the L.N.W.R. locomotives: a brief history of the eight-coupled freight engines, by 'Sirocco'. *Morecambe: Lancaster Railway Circle*, 1964. pp. 10. Text extends onto cover (p. 10).

12203   SPINK, J. F.   Francis William Webb, Chief Mechanical Engineer, London & North Western Railway, 1871–1903: a survey of his life and work. Thesis, F.L.A., Library Association, 1964. pp. 4; 142.

An extensive bibliography on F.W.W., and a chronology.

12204   DORMAN, C. C.   North Western Album. *London: Ian Allan*, 1965. pp. 100, with 95 illus & descrs.

12205   NOCK, O. S.   The LNWR Precursor family: the Precursors, Georges, Princes, of the London & North Western Railway. *Newton Abbot: David & Charles*, 1966. pp. 160, with col. frontis, 158 illus, 19 diagrams & working drawings, & many tables.

12206 DORMAN, C. C. The London & North Western Railway. *London: Priory Press*, 1975. pp. 128. Frontis, foreword, & 103 illus, with descrs; chronology, list of locomotive classes, bibliography (10 sources).
> Arranged in 10 sections, each with an introduction. Foreword by L. T. C. Rolt.

12207 NOCK, O. S. LNWR locomotives of C. J. Bowen Cooke. *Truro: Bradford Barton*, 1977. pp. 112, with 47 illus, a dimensioned drawing & many graphs & logs of runs.

12208 ROBERTS, J. E. North Western engineman: recollections of 34 years on the footplate. *Clapham (N Yorks): Dalesman*, 1977. pp. 88, with 15 illus on 8 plates.
> Period, 1918–1952, LNWR & LMS.

12209 JENKINSON, D. An Illustrated History of LNWR Coaches, including West Coast joint stock. *Oxford: Oxford Publishing Co.*, 1978. la. 8°. pp. x, 190, with frontis, 237 illus, three 12-column tables (pp. 168–82) & a bibliography (38 sources).

12210 ROBERTS, J. E. Hazards of the footplate: L.N.W.R. to B.R. *[Carnforth]: the author*, [1980]. pp. 142, with 33 illus & a map.
> Observations on railway life in the North West of England, 1918–1967.

London & North Western and Lancashire & Yorkshire Joint Rly

12211 MOSS, I. P. Farewell to the summit: historical notes to accompany a visit to the Walton Summit branch of the Leeds and Liverpool Canal and the Lancaster Canal tramway, made by members and friends of the North Western Group on May 4th, 1968. *Chester: Railway & Canal Historical Society*, 1968. pp. [10], with 2 maps & 2 plans by W. J. Dean on folded plate at end, & a drawing on cover by Norman Wilkinson.
> The Preston and Walton Summit plateway.

12212 PARKER, N. The Preston & Longridge Railway. *Lingfield: Oakwood Press*, 1971. (Oakwood Library of Railway History, 30). pp. 47, with 9 illus on 4 plates, 9 line drawings, 3 maps, 2 layout plans, a table & a bibliography (6 sources).

London & South Western Rly

Reference source 12213
General, historical and descriptive 12214–39
Locomotives 12240–44

Reference source

12213 TAVENDER, L. LSWR and Southern. *Bromley: Historical Model Railway Society*, 1970. (HMRS Livery Register, 3). pp. 76, with 24 illus on 8 plates, 25 groups of line drawings, 4 tables, a page of 18 colour palettes & 496 notes.

General, historical and descriptive

12214 SHORT reasons shewing why the Southampton Railway can never answer. [1834]. s. sh.
> 18 reasons, and a list of engineers for and against the Bill: for, W. Giles, Mr Milne; against, George Stephenson, Robert Stephenson, Joseph Locke, Mr Brunel.
> Apparently motivated by supporters of the nascent GWR (1835).   UL(GL) & LU(THC)

12215 GREAT WESTERN RLY. Reply to the case of the opponents of the Great Western Railway. *[London]: Savill, printer*, [1835]. pp. 10.
> Refuting gross misrepresentation and misstatements by agents of the Southampton Railway (London & Southampton Rly, later the London & South Western Rly) anxious to extend from Basingstoke to Bath.

12216 LETTER addressed to the share holders in the London and Southampton Railway, by 'A Shareholder'. *Southampton: J. Wheeler*, 1836. pp. 14.
> Enthusiastic support for the proposed railway (opened throughout, May 1840).   MCL

12217 LETTER from the Chairman of the London and South Western Railway to the Rt Hon. the Lord de Mauley, Chairman of the Southampton and Dorchester Railway, 1845. pp. 14.
> —— Reply from Lord de Mauley . . . *Ringwood*, 1846. pp. 12.   N. KERR CAT. 224/297

12218 MOORSOM, W. S. London & South Western Railway. *London: Metchim & Burtt, printers*, [1853]. pp. 20.
> A letter to his 'fellow shareholders' concerning a document dated 19th October, 'published by Mr Snell's committee, replying to the chairman's circular of the 17th October'.   BLACK 7197

12219 MEASOM, G. The Official Illustrated Guide to the London and South-Western Railway, including the branch lines and continuations, and a distinct guide to the Isle of Wight . . . *London: H. G. Collins*, [1856]. pp. [12], 144, [2], 110, [20].
> The first railway in the Isle of Wight was opened in 1862.

12220 MEASOM, G. The Official Illustrated Guide to the London and South-Western, North and South Devon, Cornwall, and West Cornwall railways and the Isle of Wight . . . , embellished with 380 engravings, steel plate frontispiece and maps. *[London]: C. Griffin*, 1864. pp. lii, 145, vi, [3], 190, [2], 64, viii.
> The middle section (pp. vi, [3], 190) is a separate publication with its own title page: The Official Illustrated Guide to the Isle of Wight . . . by George Measom. *C. Griffin*, [1864], with illus & a folded map. This work is followed by advertisements (pp. 64, viii).

12221 LONDON & SOUTH WESTERN RLY.
Gradient Manual, 1887. *London: Waterlow
& Sons, printers, for the LSWR*, 1887. pp. ii,
80.
Gradient profiles for the whole system, prefaced
with an index.

12222 LONDON & SOUTH WESTERN RLY.
Working Time Tables of passenger & goods
trains from 1st June to 30th September
1909. *London: Waterlow & Sons, printers*,
[1909]. Reprinted by *Ian Allan*, 1969. pp.
irregular: ca. 690.

12223 LONDON & SOUTH WESTERN RLY. The
Official Guide to the London & South
Western Railway: the royal route to the
south and the west of England, the Channel
Islands, Europe and America; illustrated.
11th edn. *London: Cassell*, 1912. pp. A–C,
[20], viii, 424, D–F, with 26 folded maps &
town plans, many illus & maps in text.

12224 HAYTHORNTHWAITE, E. Railway Centenary Exhibition to commemorate the opening of the Salisbury and Yeovil Railway to
Sherborne, May 7th, 1860. (Historical notes
by E. Haythornthwaite). *Sherborne: Sherborne Historical Society*, 1960. pp. 11, with
2 plates & a map.   DORSET CO. LIB.

12225 WHETMATH, C. F. D. and FAULKNER,
D. The Bodmin and Wadebridge Railway.
*Teddington: Branch Line Handbooks; Mor-
den: Falcon Publishing Co.*, 1963. sm. 8°.
pp. 50, with 14 illus, 6 layout plans & a map.
—— 2nd edn. *Teddington: Branch Line
Handbooks; Bracknell: West Country
Handbooks*, 1967. pp. 63, with 31 illus, 6
layout plans, 4 timetables & 3 maps.
—— 3rd edn. *Bracknell: Town & Country
Press*, 1972. pp. 64, with 31 illus, 6 layout
plans, 4 timetables & 3 maps.

12226 NOCK, O. S. The London & South Western Railway. *London: Ian Allan*, [1965]. pp.
vi, 165, with col. frontis, 69 illus on 32
plates, 5 maps (1 folded), 4 line drawings, 2
layout plans of Waterloo Stn (1 folded),
many tables & a bibliography (10 sources).
—— Reprinted 1971, but with no frontis.

12227 RAILWAY CORRESPONDENCE & TRAVEL
SOCIETY. Itinerary of the Solent Rail
Tour . . . , Sunday, 20th March, 1966. *R.C.
& T.S.*, [1966]. pp. [8], with 1 illus, map, &
schedule. Text by J. R. Fairman.
Waterloo—Salisbury—Romsey—Southampton
Docks—Fawley—Southampton terminus—
Netley—Fareham—Gosport—Havant—
Guildford—Effingham Junction—Surbiton—
Waterloo.

12228 CHEESMAN, A. J. The Plymouth, Devonport & South Western Junction Railway.
Lingfield: Oakwood Press, 1967. (Oakwood
Library of Railway History, 20). pp. 30,
with 16 illus & 2 maps on 8 plates, & in text,
4 layout plans, gradient profile, chronology.

12229 KENDALL, H. G. The Plymouth & Dartmoor Railway and its fore-runners, by
H. G. Kendall, with additional research by
R. J. Sellick. *Lingfield: Oakwood Press*,
1968. (Oakwood Library of Railway History, 23). pp. 100, with 27 illus & maps on
16 plates, 2 diagrams, 1 facsimile, 34 notes
& a bibliography (45 sources).

12230 WILLIAMS, R. A. The London & South
Western Railway. *Newton Abbot: David &
Charles*.
vol. 1, The formative years. 1968. pp. 267, with
col. frontis, 26 illus on 16 plates, 13 maps, 12 line
drawings & a bibliography (13 sources). Index
(pp. 259–67).
vol. 2, Growth and consolidation. 1973. pp. 283,
with frontis, 28 illus on 16 plates, 11 maps, 7 line
drawings, 7 layout plans, lists of LSWR ships (pp.
344–57) & a bibliography (168 sources); index (pp.
366–83).
Vol. 2 continues the history of the LSWR up to
the turn of the century.

12231 COURSE, E. The Southampton & Netley
Railway. *Southampton: City of Southampton*, 1973. (Southampton Papers, 9).
pp. 79, with 10 illus & 5 maps on 8 plates, &
27 notes.

12232 LOCK, J. The centenary of the
Barnstaple—Ilfracombe line, 1874–1974.
[*Ilfracombe*]: *North Devon Railway Preservation Society*, [1974]. pp. 34, with 13
illus & a map. Title from cover. Text
headed: The Barnstaple—Ilfracombe Railway, by Jim Lock.

12233 COX, J. G. Castleman's Corkscrew: the
Southampton and Dorchester Railway,
1844–1848. *Southampton: City of Southampton*, 1975. (Southampton Papers, 10).
pp. 37, with 27 illus (incl. 6 maps) on 12
plates, timetable & 141 notes.

12234 BARKER, J. The Meyrick Park Halt.
*Bournemouth: Dorset County Council
Education Committee*, 1976. pp. 5, with
plan, timetable, a map, & 2 facsimiles inside
covers. Reproduced typescript in printed
covers.
A halt built for the Bournemouth—
Christchurch service, inaugurated in 1906 and
closed in 1920.
—— 2nd edn. *Bournemouth: Bournemouth
Local Studies Publications*, 1980. (Publication no. 648). pp. 12, with 3 maps, a
dimensioned drawing, a timetable & a
bibliography (7 sources). Reproduced typescript in printed covers.

12235 MAGGS, C. and PAYE, P. The Sidmouth,
Seaton and Lyme Regis branches. *Tarrant
Hinton: Oakwood Press*, 1977. (Locomotion Papers, 107). pp. 66, with 27 illus, 2
maps, 4 plans, a table & a bibliography (6
sources).
The Sidmouth Rly, the Seaton & Beer Rly, and
the Axminster & Lyme Regis Rly.

12236 MAGGS, C. G. The Barnstaple & Ilfracombe Railway. *Tarrant Hinton: Oakwood Press*, 1978. (Locomotion Papers, 111). pp. 50, with 28 illus on 12 plates, 4 plans, map, gradient profile, timetable & a bibliography (25 sources).

12237 MITCHELL, V. Route Map, London & South Western Railway: main lines, Waterloo to Exeter, Weymouth, Portsmouth. *Midhurst: Middleton Press*, 1978. pp. 36.
Based upon the 1 inch to 1 mile Ordnance Survey map, 4th edn, 1919–25. The route is reproduced in page-by-page sections and is accompanied by gradient profiles and a detailed commentary on noteworthy features and points of historical interest relating to the LSWR.

12238 FAIRCLOUGH, T. and WILLS, A. Bodmin and Wadebridge, 1834–1978. *Truro: Bradford Barton*, 1979. (Southern Branch Line Special series, 1). pp. 96, with frontis, preface, & 124 illus with descrs; map & plan.

12239 PAYE, P. The Lymington branch. *Tarrant Hinton: Oakwood Press*, 1979. (Locomotion Papers, 120). pp. 44, with 16 illus on 8 plates, 8 layout plans & a map.

Locomotives

12240 BRADLEY, D. L. Locomotives of the London & South Western Railway. *Solihull: Railway Correspondence & Travel Society*:
part 1, 1965. pp. 142, with 99 illus, 4 working drawings, many lists, 2 folded maps at end.
part 2, 1967. pp. 211, with frontis, 145 illus on 50 plates & many illus in text.

12241 CASSERLEY, H. C. London & South Western locomotives. Enlarged edn. *London: Ian Allan*, 1971. pp. 184, with 216 illus & descrs, & many detailed lists and notes.
This work incorporates *L.S.W.R. Locomotives: a survey, 1872–1923*, by F. Burtt (1949).

12242 QUAINTON RAILWAY SOCIETY. The centenary of the Beattie well tank [locomotive] at Quainton. *Quainton: the Society*, [1975]. pp. [28], incl covers, with 30 illus.
The ex-LSWR Beyer Peacock 2-4-0 tank locomotive (1874) no. 314.

12243 BRADLEY, D. L. London & South Western Railway Album. *London: Ian Allan*, 1976. pp. 96, with col. frontis, intro & 204 illus with descrs.

12244 BRADLEY, D. L. The Drummond Greyhounds of the LSWR. *Newton Abbot: David & Charles*, 1977. pp. 96, with 77 illus, 11 diagrams, tables, & a bibliography (27 sources).

London, Brighton & South Coast Rly

General, historical and descriptive

12245 BISHOP, J. G. A Peep into the Past: Brighton in the olden time, with glances at the present. *Brighton: the author, at the Brighton Herald Office*, 1880. la. 8°. pp. 390, with 28 illus.
pp. 249–67. 'The railway and its growth', with a detailed chronological table of the LBSCR's network, 1835–79, & 4 other tables.

12246 LONDON, BRIGHTON & SOUTH COAST RLY. 'Elevated Electric'. South London line elevated electric railway: electric trains between Victoria and London Bridge will commence running, 1st December 1909. [*London: L.B.S.C.R.*, 1909]. Republished as a facsimile reprint by the *Southern Electric Group*, 1979, with no additional imprint. A folded s. sh. timetable.

12247 LONDON, BRIGHTON & SOUTH COAST RLY. Time Tables, June to September 1912 and until further notice. *London: L.B.S.C.Rly*, 1912; *Shepperton: Ian Allan*, [1968]. pp. 168, [12], with 4 folded plates, illus, & 3 col. maps.
A facsimile reprint.

12248 RAILWAY CORRESPONDENCE & TRAVEL SOCIETY. The Kemp Town branch, by Derek W. Winkworth; itinerary of the Kemp Town Branch Special, 5th October, 1952. *R.C.T.S.*, [1952]. pp. 4, with 2 illus & a brief schedule.

12249 GILBERT, E. W. Brighton: old ocean's bauble. *London: Methuen*. 1954. pp. xvi, 275.
ch. 8 (pp. 132–52): 'The railway comes to Brighton', with 5 illus & 2 maps on 4 plates, & in text, 2 maps & 19 notes.

12250 FARRANT, J. H. Mid-Victorian Littlehampton: the railway and the cross-Channel steamers. *Littlehampton Urban District Council*, 1972. (Littlehampton Papers, 4). pp. 27, with 4 illus, 2 maps, 3 lists, 68 notes. Title from cover.

12251 GRAY, A. The railways of mid-Sussex. *Tarrant Hinton: Oakwood Press*, [1975]. (Oakwood Library of Railway History, 38). pp. 86, with 32 illus, 4 maps & 12 layout plans on 24 plates, 3 appendices & a brief bibliography.
Mainly 'a history of the LBSCR lines from Dorking and Three Bridges southwards to Midhurst, Shoreham and Bognor'.

12252 HODD, H. R. The Horsham–Guildford Direct Railway. *Tarrant Hinton: Oakwood Press*, 1975. (Locomotion Papers, 87). pp. 54, with 17 illus, 2 diagrams, 4 maps, 2 timetables & a bibliography (26 sources).

12253 GRAY, A. The London to Brighton line, 1841–1977. *Blandford Forum: Oakwood Press*, 1977. (Oakwood Library of Railway

History, 43). pp. 127, with 33 illus on 16 plates, 4 maps, 7 layout plans, 9 appendices & a bibliography (17+ sources).

12254 TURNER, J. H. The London, Brighton and South Coast Railway. *London: Batsford*.
  vol. 1, Origins and formation (1799–1846). 1977. pp. xv, 287, with 16 illus on 8 plates, 16 maps, 8 plans, 9 diagrams & line illus, 4 lists & 208 notes.
  vol. 2, Establishment and growth (1846–1869). 1978. pp. xv, 320, with 16 illus on 8 plates, 22 maps, 22 layout plans & diagrams, lists, & 184 notes.
  vol. 3, Completion and maturity (1870–1922). 1979. pp. xx, 283, with 32 illus on 16 plates, 26 maps & plans, & a comprehensive index to all 3 volumes (pp. 225–83).

12255 CLARK, P. The Chichester & Midhurst Railway. *Sheffield: Turntable Publications*, 1979. (Minor Railways of Britain series). pp. 72, with 34 illus, 6 facsims, 2 maps, 6 layout plans, gradient profile, 3 timetables, fare table, 2 statistical tables, a folded-drawing & a bibliography (52 sources).

12256 KIDNER, R. W. The Newhaven & Seaford branch, with additional notes by R. C. Riley. *Tarrant Hinton: Oakwood Press*, 1979. (Locomotion Papers, 117). pp. 32, with 32 illus on 16 plates, 8 maps & layout plans.

12257 PAYE, P. The Hayling Railway, with additional notes by R. C. Riley. *Tarrant Hinton: Oakwood Press*, 1979. (Oakwood Library of Railway History, 49). pp. 31, with 15 illus on 8 plates, 6 layout plans & a map.

12258 PALLANT, N. The Brighton to Portsmouth line. *Tisbury: Oakwood Press (Element Books)*, [1980]. (Locomotion Papers, 133). pp. 44, with 32 illus on 16 plates, 3 junction diagrams, 2 timetables, map, chron. list of stations & a bibliography (8 sources).

Locomotives

12259 BRADLEY, D. L. The locomotives of the London Brighton & South Coast Railway. *London: Railway Correspondence & Travel Society*.
  A detailed record with many lists & illustrations.
  part 1, 1969. pp. 179, with 143 illus on 72 plates.
  part 2, 1972. pp. 123, with frontis & 70 illus on 35 plates.
  part 3, 1974. pp. 156, with frontis & 112 illus on 56 plates.

12260 HAYLING Billy: the life story of the engine 'Newington'. *Lingfield: Oakwood Press, for Brickwoods Ltd*, [1967]. pp. 15, with 12 illus & map, & 2 illus on cover.

12261 RILEY, R. C. Brighton Line Album. *London: Ian Allan*, 1967. pp. 112. Intro, frontis & 200 illus with descrs.

12262 CORNWELL, H. J. C. William Stroudley, craftsman of Steam. *Newton Abbot: David & Charles*, 1968. pp. 263, with frontis, 34 illus on 16 plates, 34 drawings in text, 34 tables, bibliography (52 sources).

12263 PERRYMAN, A. C. The 'Brighton Baltics'. *Lingfield: Oakwood Press*, 1973. (Locomotion Papers, 64). pp. 65, with 19 illus on 8 plates, 14 diagrams & 11 tables.
  The class 'L' 4-6-4 tank locomotives of the LBSCR, introduced in 1914.

12264 NEWBURY, P. J. Carriage stock of the L.B. & S.C.R. *Tarrant Hinton: Oakwood Press*, 1976. pp. 80, with 31 illus on 12 plates, & 90 line drawings & many lists in text.

London, Midland & Scottish Rly

Reference source 12265
General, historical and descriptive 12266–73
Locomotives 12274–12313 (Reference sources 12274–78)
Rolling stock 12314–15
Signalling 12316–17

Reference source

12265 LONDON, MIDLAND & SCOTTISH RLY. Handbook of Statistics for 1913, & 1922–1926. *London: LMS*, 1927. pp. 240.
  —— Handbook of Statistics, 1930–31, years 1913 and 1923 to 1929. *LMS*, [1932?]
                                        LU(THC)
  —— Handbook of Statistics, years 1929, and 1933 to 1936. *LMS*, October 1937. pp. 288.
  Trade statistics (pp. 24–35); financial & statistical tables for the LMS (pp. 36–205); and for all British railways (pp. 207–76); Index (pp. 277–88).
                                        LU(THC)
  All marked 'Private & confidential'. An important source of information but one that was printed in limited numbers for staff use and consequently not commonly to be found in libraries. There will be, no doubt, editions other than the three described above.

General, historical and descriptive

12266 LONDON, MIDLAND & SCOTTISH RLY. LMS Guide to cheap fares and other facilities, 1938. *London: LMS Rly*, [1938]. pp. 32.
  Addressed to the travelling public. Inserted in the LU(THC) copy is a three-page printed Foreword by Ashton Davies, Chief Commercial Manager, addressed to LMS staff.

12267 LONDON, MIDLAND & SCOTTISH RLY. Progress and developments in the Chief Operating Manager's Department in the years prior to the War. *Watford: L.M.S. C.O.M.'s Office*, February 1940. tall 8°. pp. 82, iv, with folded plan & folded map. Foreword by T. W. Royle.
  'A picture of progress and development of railway operating policy adopted by the L.M.S. in recent years'. A record of achievement interrupted by the War, for use as a base from which further progress can be made when peace returns.

12268 JONES, J. H. Josiah Stamp: public servant: the life of the first Baron Stamp of Shortlands. *London: Pitman*, 1964. pp. x, 365, with 2 ports. on plates.

In index, 19 page refs under 'London, Midland & Scottish Rly'. 'Railways', 'South Eastern Rly' and 'London Passenger Transport Bill'. Lord Stamp was chairman of the LMS from 1926–1941.

12269 SMITHSON, A. and SMITHSON, P. The Euston Arch and the growth of the London Midland & Scottish Railway; foreword by Nikolaus Pevsner. *London: Thames & Hudson*, 1968. la. obl. format. pp. [72], with many illus, facsimiles & maps relating to the construction of Euston Station, its history, and its destruction in the 1960s.

A memorial to 'Old' Euston: a vigorous outcry against the senseless destruction of an outstanding monument to 19th century achievement and a protest also against the obduracy of an official decision made in the face of widespread contrary opinion. (see *Architectural Review*, April 1962, pp. 234–8).

12270 ELLIS, C. H. London, Midland & Scottish: a railway in retrospect. *London: Ian Allan*, 1970. pp. 224, with col. frontis, 80 illus on 24 plates, tables & notes.

Includes (pp. 205–12) 'The Irish enclave' [the Northern Counties Committee].

12271 LMS SOCIETY. The LMS Society Teach-In. *Chesterfield: the Society*, 1978. obl. format. pp. 85, with a map. Edited by M. Peascod.

A collection of detailed tables and memoranda concerning the organisation of the LMS, its locomotives, rolling stock, buildings, road vehicles, shipping, signalling, ancillary activities and equipment. Contributing author/members: D. P. Rowland, H. N. Twells, D. F. Tee, D. Jenkinson, F. W. Shuttleworth, T. W. Bourne, N. G. Coates, K. R. Morgan, V. R. Anderson, G. K. Fox, J. B. Hinchliffe, L. G. Warburton.

12272 LONDON, MIDLAND & SCOTTISH RLY. General Appendix to the Working Timetables (1937). [*London: LMS*, 1937]. Published as a reprint by P. H. Abell: Barnsley, [1979]. pp. ix, 96.

A facsimile reprint with an added cover.

12273 GRIGG, A. E. Town of trains: Bletchley and the Oxbridge line. *Buckingham: Barracuda Books*, 1980. la. 8°. pp. 160, with 120 illus, 5 maps (one double-spread on end papers), 3 timetables & a signalling diagram of 1881. Foreword by Peter Parker, preface by Sidney Weighell.

A detailed narrative. The author was a railwayman at Bletchley.

Locomotives

12274 CASSERLEY, H. C. and JOHNSTON, S. W. Locomotives at the Grouping: [vol. 3], London Midland and Scottish Railway. *London: Ian Allan*, 1966. pp. 192, with 126 illus on 32 plates. Lists.

12275 JENKINSON, D. and ESSERY, R. J. Locomotive liveries of the L.M.S. *London: Roundhouse Books and Ian Allan*, 1967. pp. xiv, 234, with frontis, 15 col. panels on 3 plates, 160 illus on 48 plates, 9 composite diagrams (insignia, lettering, numerals, etc.), 40 tables and many lists and notes.

12276 CASSERLEY, H. C. LMSR locomotives, 1923–48. *Truro: Bradford Barton*, 3 vols.

[vol. 1], 1975. pp. 96. Intro & 108 illus with descrs.

vol. 2, 1976. pp. 96. Intro & 101 illus with descrs.

vol. 3, 1976. pp. 96. Intro & 98 illus with descrs.

Each of these three volumes was published in both standard and limited editions. The limited editions were of 250 copies, signed, and bound in full cloth with the LMS insignia on the cover.

12277 ROWLEDGE, J. W. P. Engines of the L.M.S. built 1923–51. *Oxford: Oxford Publishing Co.*, 1975. pp. 108, with 86 illus on 39 plates.

The text consists of classified lists with 70 diagrams. 'The purpose of this book is to provide numerical and dimensional information to amplify the many books and albums published about LMSR locomotives.'

12278 ELLIOTT, R. J. Preserved locomotives of the London, Midland and Scottish Railway. [*Buckfastleigh*]: *Dumbleton Hall Preservation Society*, 1978. (Preserved Locomotives, 3). sm. 8°. pp. 32, with 31 illus.

Details of 78 steam locomotives, a location list, and a further list of 15 awaiting scrapping, of which 3 are earmarked for adoption.

12279 ROBINSON, E. E. The standard 3-cyl. 4-4-0 compound passenger class. *Egham: the author*, [1935]. (LMS Locomotives series: class book, 2). pp. 18, with 3 illus, 3 diagrams & a complete list (4-column).

12280 'SIROCCO'. Black Five, by 'Sirocco'. [*Lancaster*]: *Lancaster Railway Circle*, 1965. pp. 16, with 2 lists. Reproduced typescript.

The Stanier Class 5 4-6-0s.

12281 DUNN, J. M. Reflections on a railway career: from LNWR to BR. *London: Ian Allan*, 1966. pp. 184, with 55 illus on 32 plates.

Motive-power management, 1913–1958.

12282 DORMAN, C. C. L.M.S. Album. *London: Ian Allan*, 1967. pp. [115]. Frontis, foreword & 165 illus with descrs.

12283 HIGSON, M. LM Pacifics: a pictorial tribute [compiled by Michael Higson]. [*Hatch End*]: *Roundhouse Books*, 1967. la. 8°. pp. [120]. Intro, notes, a list of the 51 Pacific-type steam locomotives of the LMS and BR(LMR), 1933 to 1948, & 135 illus with descrs.

12284 DOHERTY, D. Royal Scots of the LMS, edited by Douglas Doherty. *London: Ian*

Allan, 1970. pp. 64, with 62 illus on 32 plates, 9 logs of runs, 3 dimensioned drawings & 3 lists.

Four essays, by E. S. Cox, W. A. Tuplin, John Powell, and Peter G. Johnson.

12285 HARESNAPE, B. Stanier locomotives: a pictorial history. *London: Ian Allan*, 1970. pp. 128, with frontis, 153 illus, 11 diagrams, & lists.

12286 ANDERSON, V. R., ESSERY, R. J. and JENKINSON, D. Portrait of the LMS. *Seaton: Peco Publications*, 1971. la. 8°. pp. 112, with col. frontis & 256 illus.

12287 CLAY, J. F. Jubilees of the LMS. *London: Ian Allan*, 1971. pp. 112, with 49 illus, & 2 diagrams.

12288 NOCK, O. S. LMS Steam. *Newton Abbot: David & Charles*, 1971. pp. 269, with col. frontis, 82 illus on 32 plates, 61 tables, 23 of which are logs of runs.

An analysis of the performance of steam-hauled trains on the LMS.

12289 ALLEN, C. J. Salute to the L.M.S. *London: Ian Allan*, 1972. pp. 84, with 113 illus (1 col.).

12290 CLAY, J. F. and CLIFFE, J. The Stanier 'Black Fives'. *London: Ian Allan*, 1972. pp. 96, with 5 illus on 24 plates, tables, a chronology & a bibliography (11 sources).

12291 EARLEY, M. W. The L.M.S. scene: an album of photographs by Maurice W. Earley. *Oxford: Oxford Publishing Co.*, 1972. obl. format. pp. 56. Intro & 77 illus with descrs.

12292 HARESNAPE, B. Fowler locomotives: a pictorial history. *London: Ian Allan*, 1972. pp. 128, with frontis, 152 illus with descrs, 18 diagrams, lists & a brief bibliography.

Midland Rly and LMSR.

12293 DOHERTY, D. The L.M.S. Duchesses. *Hemel Hempstead: Model & Allied Publications*, 1973. la. 8°. pp. vi, 89, with 58 illus, 11 diagrams (2 folded), 16 tables, 6 performance diagrams, a list and a log.

Contributors: E. A. Langridge, John Powell, Peter Johnson, W. A. Tuplin.

12294 HIGHET, C. All steamed up! *Oxford: Oxford Publishing Co.*, 1975. pp. [iv], 106, with 97 illus.

Recollections of a career in motive power management, Midland Rly, LMS Rly and BR, 1920–1964.

12295 MORRISON, B. London Midland steam locomotives: a pictorial survey of ex-LMSR locomotives in the 1950s. *Truro: Bradford Barton*.

vol. 1, 1975. pp. 96. Intro & 114 with descrs.
vol. 2, 1975. pp. 96. Intro & 96 illus with descrs.

12296 ROWLEDGE, J. W. P. Diesel locomotives of the L.M.S. *Tarrant Hinton: Oakwood Press*, 1975. (Locomotion Papers, 88). pp. 72, with 36 illus on 16 plates, 16 diagrams, 5 tables, lists.

12297 THORLEY, W. G. F. A breath of steam. *London: Ian Allan*.

vol. 1, [Apprenticeship and early years of railway service with the LMS, 1927–1941]. 1975. pp. 199, with 69 illus on 32 plates, 37 diagrams, 10 tables.

12298 ADAMS, J. and WHITEHOUSE, P. London Midland Steam in camera. *London: Ian Allan*, 1976. pp. 64. Intro & 83 illus with descrs.

LMS locomotives & trains south of the Scottish border, and on the Somerset & Dorset Rly, 1948–1968.

12299 BELLWOOD, J. and JENKINSON, D. Gresley and Stanier: a centenary tribute. *London: H.M.S.O., for the National Railway Museum, York*, 1976. 4°. pp. vii, 99, with 142 illus, incl. 2 portraits as frontis; bibliography (p. 99).

12300 CLAY, J. F. and CLIFFE, J. The West Coast Pacifics. *London: Ian Allan*, 1976. pp. 208, with 71 illus on 32 plates, tables, dimensioned drawings & a bibliography (30+ sources).

12301 JUDGE, C. LMS era. *Oxford: Oxford Publishing Co.*, 1969. pp. 64. Intro & 120 illus with descrs.

12302 PRINCESS ELIZABETH LOCOMOTIVE SOCIETY. The rebirth of a giant. *Haraton Ltd, for the Society*, [1976]. pp. [8], with 40 illus.

The adoption and restoration of the ex-LMS Pacific locomotive 6201, *Princess Elizabeth*.

12303 ROBERTS, J. E. North Western engineman: recollections of 34 years on the footplate. *Clapham (N. Yorks): Dalesman*, 1977. pp. 88, with 15 illus on 8 plates.

Period, 1918–1952, LNWR & LMS.

12304 ROWLEDGE, J. W. P. and REED, B. The Stanier 4-6-0s of the LMS: the Jubilees, class 5s and the BR Standard Class 5s. *Newton Abbot: David & Charles*, 1977. pp. 96 with 61 illus, 28 drawings and diagrams, & many detailed lists and tables.

12305 NOCK, O. S. The Royal Scots and Patriots of the LMS. *Newton Abbot: David & Charles*, 1978. pp. 96, with frontis & 50 illus, engineering drawings, logs of runs & gradient profiles.

12306 STANIER 8F LOCOMOTIVE SOCIETY. Stanier 8F 2-8-0: a study of the Stanier LMSR class 8F locomotive, edited by Keith Tyler, John Bond, Alan Wilkinson. [*Cheltenham?*]: *Stanier 8F Locomotive Society*,

[1978]. pp. 96. Intro, frontis & 120 illus, with descrs; bibliography (20 sources). Title on spine: The Stanier LMSR class 8F locomotive.

12307 BLOOM, A. Locomotives of the London, Midland and Scottish Railway, written by Alan Bloom; compiled by David Williams. *Norwich: Jarrold*, 1979. (Jarrold Railway Series, 3). pp. [32], with 66 illus (56 col.) & a map. Text & illus extend onto covers.

12308 CARTER, R. S. LMS turbine locomotive 6202. *Gloucester: Peter Watts*, 1979. la. obl. format. pp. 16, with 7 illus (2 on covers), 10 drawings (dimensions & arrangement details of drive mechanism), 4 performance graphs (Euston to Glasgow), and a record of mileage set against years of service (1935–1963).

12309 COOPER, W. D. and COOPER, D. S. L.M.S. days. *London: Ian Allan*, 1979. pp. [80]. Intro (pp. 5–7) & 155 illus with descrs.
     Photographs of locomotives and trains by W. D. and D. S. Cooper. Introduction discusses technicalities of train photography.

12310 JENKINSON, D. The power of the Duchesses . . . ; foreword by R. A. Riddles. *Oxford: Oxford Publishing Co.*, 1979. (Power Series). la. 8°. pp. [112]. Intro & 280 illus (20 col.) with descrs, short intermittent essays & a list (22 columns).

12311 WHITELEY, J. S. and MORRISON, G. W. The LMS remembered. *Oxford: Oxford Publishing Co.*, 1979. la. 8°. pp. [112]. Intro & 271 illus with descrs.

12312 GAMMELL, C. J. LMS branch lines, 1945–65. *Oxford: Oxford Publishing Co.*, [1980]. la. 8°. pp. [96]. Intro, frontis & 160 illus, a map & a bibliography (13 sources).

12313 HOPE, S. G. Reflections of the London, Midland & Scottish Railway. *Macclesfield: the author*, 1980. pp. 30, with 11 illus.
     Reminiscences and observations of a retired railwayman, LNWR—LMS—BR(LMR), 1914–1957.

Rolling stock

12314 ESSERY, R. J. and JENKINSON, D. L. The L.M.S. coach, 1923–1957. *London: Ian Allan*, 1969. 4°. pp. 134, with frontis (4 illus), 204 illus (4 col.) on 49 plates, & in text, 23 composite line drawings and 31 detailed tables.
     —— enl. & rev. edn. An Illustrated History of L.M.S. Coaches, 1923–1957. *Oxford: Oxford Publishing Co.*, 1977. la. 8°. pp. viii, 218, with 238 illus, 51 line drawings, 31 tables & 16 colour panels of various LMS carriage liveries (pp. v–vi).

12315 ESSERY, R. J. and MORGAN, K. R. The L.M.S. wagon. *Newton Abbot: David &*

Charles, 1977. pp. 128, with 101 illus, 37 dimensioned drawings, many detailed lists, & specimens of lettering.

Signalling

12316 LONDON MIDLAND & SCOTTISH RLY. Description of automatic train control, Gas Factory Junction to Shoeburyness. L.T. & S. Section. *Euston (London): L.M.S. Rly*, 1947. pp. 12, with 4 illus & 2 folded diagrams.

12317 WARBURTON, L. G. A Pictorial Record of L.M.S. Signals; standard semaphore signals and signal boxes of the L.M.S. . . . , with the signal box section by V. R. Anderson. *Headington: Oxford Publishing Co.*, 1972. 4°. pp. iv, 58. 76 illus & 46 diagrams with descrs, often lengthy.

Maryport & Carlisle Rly

12318 'AMICUS'. A report of the case: Irving, a contractor *v.* the Maryport and Carlisle Railway Company, referred from the Carlisle Assizes to R. B. Armstrong, Q.C., and heard at Carlisle on the 7th of September 1841 and the following four days. *London: Whittaker*, [1841]. pp. viii, 76.
     The Introduction (pp. v–viii) is signed 'Amicus, Cumberland, December 1841'.

12319 MARYPORT & CARLISLE RLY. Report of the Committee of Investigation of the Maryport & Carlisle Railway appointed by resolution of the general meeting held at Maryport on the 4th September, 1850. *Carlisle: James Steel, printer, Journal Office*, 1850. pp. 4 with financial tables.
     'A worse state of things never was brought to light than this report . . .' (*Herapath's Railway & Commercial Journal*, 23 November, 1850). The matter is described at some length in *The Maryport & Carlisle Railway*, by Jack Simmons (1947), pp. 11–15, with bibliographical notes.

Mersey Rly

12320 METROPOLITAN-VICKERS ELECTRICAL COMPANY. The Mersey Railway electrification: new equipments, by C. Corbridge. *Trafford Park: Metropolitan-Vickers*, [1924]. pp. 12, with 11 illus, map, gradient profile & diagram.

12321 PARKIN, G. W. The Mersey Railway. *Lingfield: Oakwood Press*, [1965]. (Oakwood Library of Railway History, 18). pp. 64, with 12 illus & 2 diagrams on 6 plates, & in text, 2 maps, a financial table (1899–1939) & 3 diagrams.

12322 CULL, J. E. and PRIGMORE, B. J. Mersey Railway electric stock; drawings by G. Redmayne Hosking. *London: P. R. Davis*, 1968. (Signal Transport Papers, 5). pp. 47, with 41 illus on 16 plates, 4 diagrams, 4 layout plans, gradient profile, & 7 appendices.

Metropolitan Rly

12323 The METROPOLITAN Railway: a fifteen per cent paying line. *London: Adams & Francis*, 1868. pp. 52, with a table of passengers carried, 1863–1867.
Assurance to shareholders that the Metropolitan will be able to pay dividends of 15% against the present 7% when the new extensions and the junction with the Metropolitan District Rly at Brompton are opened.

12324 ELLIS, L. Guide to the Metropolitan Railway extension to Harrow, Pinner, Northwood, Rickmansworth, Chenies and Chesham. [*London: Metropolitan Rly?*, 1889 or 1890]. pp. 80, with 20 illus (drawings).
Topographical & archaeological, with only incidental references to Met. Rly. facilities.

12325 METROPOLITAN RLY. Country homes in Metro-Land: the official residential guide of the Metropolitan Railway. [*London*]: *Met. Rly.*, 1915. pp. 72, with 51 illus (12 col.) & la. folded map.
Loosely inserted is a handbill, *Rambles in the Chiltern Country*, 2nd series, Sept–Oct 1915, arranged by the Selborne Society.
Issued periodically, the above issue being described as vol. 1, no. 2, October–December 1915 (on front cover only).

12326 METROPOLITAN RAILWAY WAR SERVICE CORPS. [Programmes of sports meetings, president's addresses and reports of sections, 1916–1919].
Contents: Programme of sports meetings, 16th September 1916. pp. 15.
President's address and reports of sections, 8th February 1917. pp. 32.
Programme of sports meeting, 28th July 1917. pp. 15.
President's address and reports of sections, 14th February 1918. pp. 40.
Programme of sports meeting, 27th July 1918. pp. 34.
Two specimen letters sent with parcels to employees on war service, and three Christmas greeting cards.
A group photograph is mounted as a frontispiece.   LU(THC)

12327 METROPOLITAN RLY. Metroland. *London: Met. Rly*, 1919–1932.
Successive editions of an illustrated publicity booklet designed to encourage settlement in the area served by the Metropolitan Rly beyond Harrow for the most part, the Chilterns and the Vale of Aylesbury in Buckinghamshire.

12328 METROPOLITAN RLY. Instructions to lift attendants and lift machinery men. [*London: Met. Rly*], July 1932. pp. 12. Title from cover.   LU(THC)

12329 ASSOCIATED ELECTRICAL INDUSTRIES. The electrification of the Metropolitan Railway. *London: London Underground Railway Society*, 1965. pp. iii, 32, with 15 illus on 4 plates, & diagrams in text.
A reprint of a pamphlet originally published in 1923.

12330 LEE, C. E. The Metropolitan Line. *Westminster: London Transport*, 1972. pp. 32, with 38 illus on frontis & 16 plates, & 2 maps.

12331 EDMONDS, A. History of the Metropolitan District Railway Company to June 1908 . . . , prepared for publication, with preface, notes and an epilogue, by Charles E. Lee. *London: London Transport Executive*, 1973. tall 8°. pp. vii, 250; index.
A limited edition in facsimile of the typescript of a work written by Alexander Edmonds in 1922, with 19 notes by C. E. Lee.

12332 JONES, K. The Wotton Tramway (Brill branch). *Lingfield: Oakwood Press*, 1974. (Locomotion Papers, 75). pp. 60, with 25 illus on 12 plates, 4 maps, 13 layout plans, 6 line drawings, 2 diagrams, 3 tables & a bibliography (14 sources).
Opened 1871, closed 1935.

12333 EDWARDS D. and PIGRAM, R. Metro memories: an armchair odyssey through the countryside served by the Metropolitan Railway. *Tunbridge Wells: Midas Books*, 1977. 4°. pp. 128, with frontis & 155 illus; map on end papers.

12334 CASSERLEY, H. C. The later years of Metropolitan Steam. *Truro: Bradford Barton*, [1979]. pp. 96. Intro & 103 illus with descrs.

12335 EDWARDS, D. and PIGRAM, R. The romance of Metroland: a further armchair odyssey through the countryside served by the old Metropolitan Railway. *Speldhurst: Midas Books*, 1979. pp. 128, with 173 illus, incl. maps & facsims; map on end papers.

Midland Rly

Reference source

12336 DOW, G. Midland style: a livery and decor register of the Midland Railway, its absorbed lines and its joint lines, to the end of 1922 . . . , with a contribution on Midland coaching stock by R. E. Lacy. *Bromley: Historical Model Railway Society*, 1975. pp. vi, 192, with 256 illus (photos, line drawings & diagrams), & 4 appendices, incl. a set of 14 colours.

General, historical and descriptive

12337 ALLEN, R. The North Midland Railway Guide, illustrated with twelve views of stations and a map of the line. *Nottingham: R. Allen; Leicester: E. Allen*, 1842. [*Leeds: Turntable Enterprises*, 1973]. pp. 32, with 12 illus & folded map.
A facsimile reproduction with an introduction by O. Carter. 'The engravings by Samuel Russell were not included in the original work and are reproduced from negatives.'

12338 MIDLAND RLY. GENERAL MANAGER'S OFFICE, DERBY. Orders, nos. 1–315. *Derby: Midland Rly*, 1853–1880.
A collection of single-sheet printed orders circulated to station masters, arranged in numerical order and bound into a volume. The orders relate to recurrent administrative an operational matters which need to be clarified. Each is numbered and dated, with its subject usually set out in bold type as a heading, and with 'James Allport, General Manager' as a printed signature. A footnote carries the instruction: 'Keep this Order, affix it in your Order Book, and acknowledge receipt of it on annexed Form'.
A MS note on the fly-leaf of the volume reads: 'These orders were collected by me from a quantity of apparent waste-paper, and bound at my expense. J. O. Manton'.
A wide variety of topics is covered by the orders. A few examples: Soliciting of passengers for contributions towards staff Christmas dinners; Workmen travelling with passes not allowed in 1st or 2nd class compartments; Stationmasters not to take lodgers; Loading round timber; Dogs to have chains; Dogs to be pre-paid; Cattle by passenger trains; Engine-drivers whistling unnecessarily; Paid ons; Walking passes; Smoking [not allowed at stations or in carriages] (orders 110 of December 1858 and 222 of December 1866); Smoking allowed, 'smoking carriages having now been provided' (no. 289, October 1868); Exhibition of fare tables for the information of passengers; Porters' outstandings to be reduced. LU(THC)

12339 MIDLAND RLY. Rules and Regulations for the guidance of the officers and men in the service of the Midland Railway Company, June 1871. *London, Derby: Bemrose* [re-published by] *Brontë-Hill Publications, Haworth*, 1972. pp. 209.
A facsimile reprint.

12340 THOMSON, J. R. Guide to the district of Craven and the Settle & Carlisle Railway. 2nd edn. *London: Simpkin & Marshall*, 1879. pp. 134.
ch. 10 (pp. 79–92) 'The Settle & Carlisle Railway' with 2 lists of viaducts and tunnels. A commentary on the history of the line and its features, described 'to a traveller'.

12341 MIDLAND RAILWAY FRIENDLY SOCIETY. Rules of the Midland Railway Friendly Society. *Derby: the Society*, 1917. pp. 87.

12342 BRITISH RAILWAYS. EASTERN REGION. London, Tilbury & Southend Railway Centenary, 1856–1956. *London: B.R.(ER)*, 1956. A printed folder (6 pp.) with illus.
p. [3]. A concise history of the line.

12343 ELLIS, C. H. The Midland Railway in pictures. *London: Ian Allan*, [195–]. pp. 32.
Illustrations from this author's *The Midland Railway*.

12344 MITCHELL, W. R. The 'Long Drag': a story of men under stress during the construction of the Settle–Carlisle line. *Settle: the author*, 1962. pp. 32, with line drawings & a route chart.
The harsh conditions imposed by the Midland Rly Co. upon the men building the line; the 'Long Drag' being the steeply graded section between Settle and Ais Gill.

12345 FROST, K. A. The Romford–Upminster branch. *London: P. R. Davis*, 1964. (Signal Transport Papers, 1). pp. 56, with 18 illus, map, gradient profile & 3 timetables (pp. 34–43, 49–50).

12346 BARNES, E. G. The rise of the Midland Railway, 1844–1874. *London: Allen & Unwin*, 1966. pp. 317, with 22 illus on 16 plates, & in text, 44 line illus, maps, plans & timetables.

12347 BAUGHAN, P. E. North of Leeds: the Leeds–Settle–Carlisle line and its branches. *Hatch End: Roundhouse Books*, 1966. pp. 506, with frontis, 60 illus on 40 plates, 4 maps, & a bibliography (56 sources); pp. 422–60, 24 appendices, incl. detailed tables & a chronology.
Period, to 1923.

12348 MITCHELL, W. R. and JOY, D. Settle–Carlisle Railway: the Midland's record-breaking route to Scotland. *Clapham (N. Yorks.): Dalesman Publishing Co.*, 1966. pp. 88, with 51 illus, 2 line drawings & a route chart in 4 sections.
—— rev. edn [2nd edn], *Dalesman*, 1969. pp. 96, with 57 illus, route chart & a bibliography (14 sources).
—— new edn [3rd edn], *Dalesman*, 1973. pp. 96, with frontis, 60 illus, map, route chart, bibliography (16 sources).
—— rev. edn [4th edn], *Dalesman*, 1976. pp. 96 with 73 illus [not seen].
—— 5th edn, *Dalesman*, 1979. pp. 96, with 46 illus on 32 plates, map & line drawings in text.

12349 ROUNTHWAITE, T. E. The Midland Railway London extension, 1868–1968, (by T. E. Rounthwaite). *Flitwick: Midland Railway London Extension Centenary Celebration Association*, [1968]. pp. 47, with 44 illus, timetable & 2 maps inside covers.
Introduction & 9 essays on particular aspects by various writers.

12350 BARNES, E. G. The Midland main line, 1875–1922. *London: Allen & Unwin*, 1969. pp. 280, with 19 illus on 12 plates, 3 maps & a diagram.

12351 MAGGS, C. G. The Bristol & Gloucester

Railway, and Avon & Gloucestershire Railway. *Lingfield: Oakwood Press*, 1969. (Oakwood Library of Railway History, 26). pp. 66, with 12 illus on 8 plates, 5 maps, 2 plans & a diagram.

12352 DUNSTAN, J. The origins of the Sheffield and Chesterfield Railway. *Dore (Sheffield): Dore Village Society*, 1970. (Occasional Publications, 2). pp. 32, with 2 plans, map, & many notes.

12353 PARR, R. B. Burton and Ashby Light Railway. *Crich: Tramway Museum Society*, 1970. pp. 28, with 19 illus; map & illus on covers. Cover title: An English country tramway.

12354 JENKINSON, D. Rails in the Fells: a railway case study . . . with a foreword by the Right Rev. Eric Treacy, Lord Bishop of Wakefield. *Seaton: Peco Publications*, 1973. pp. [xii], 157, with frontis, 167 illus, 42 maps, drawings & diagrams & 28 tables: bibliography (pp. 154–5).
 'An account of the origins, characteristics and contribution of a railway [the Settle & Carlisle] to the landscape; together with an attempt to evaluate its past and present influence on the area through which it passes'.
 —— 2nd edn. *Peco*, 1980. pp. xii, 157, with frontis, 167 illus, 42 maps, drawings & diagrams, & 28 tables; bibliography (29+ sources).

12355 MITCHELL, W. R. The railway shanties: navvy life during the construction of the Settle–Carlisle line. *Settle: Settle & District Civic Society*, 1975. sm. 8°. pp. 16, with 11 illus, (incl. cover illus) by W. Brocklebank.
 Issued as a souvenir of an exhibition on shanty towns organised by the Settle–Carlisle Railway Centenary Committee of the Settle & District Civic Society, April 1975.

12356 CASSERLEY, H. C. The Lickey Incline. *Tarrant Hinton: Oakwood Press*, 1976. (Locomotion Papers, 91). pp. 34, with 32 illus on 16 plates & a map.

12357 JENKINSON, D. Settle–Carlisle Railway Centenary, 1876–1976. *[London]: British Rail*, 1976. obl. format. pp. 16, with 47 illus (22 col.), gradient profile & 3 col. illus & map on covers.
 A commemorative brochure produced jointly by BR and the National Railway Museum, York.

12358 MITCHELL, W. R. and MUSSETT, N. J. Seven years hard: building the Settle–Carlisle Railway; with visuals by W. Brocklebank. *Clapham (N. Yorks.): Dalesman Books*, 1976. sm. 8°. pp. 64, with 13 illus on 8 plates, 2 maps (1 on 5 pp.), & a bibliography (15 sources).
 A chronological 'on site' account, with particular emphasis on the problems, hardships & achievements of the 6,000 men involved.

12359 PALMER, J. The Midland line to London. *Chesterfield: Grayson Publications*, 1976.

pp. 52, with 29 illus & a map & table inside covers. Text extends to pp. 2 & 3 of covers.
 A running commentary on features of historical, topographical and railway interest which may be seen from the train between Matlock/Derby/Nottingham and London.

12360 SMITH, S. and COX, I. The Settle & Carlisle Railway Map; notes by Stuart Smith and Ian Cox. *Derby: I & G Prints*, 1976. la. folded map, scale, ca. 2 miles to 1 inch, with a summary history, notes, distance table, gradient profile, & details of tunnels & viaducts.

12361 CANNON, J. and CANNON, H. The Nicky Line: the story of the Hemel Hempstead and Harpenden Railway. *Chesham: Barracuda Books*, 1977. pp. 120, with frontis, 74 illus, 8 facsims, 3 maps, a gradient profile and a chronology; 101 notes.

12362 RADFORD, J. B. and SMITH, S. W. The Midland Railway: a pictorial history, edited by J. B. Radford and S. W. Smith for the Midland Railway Trust. *Truro: Bradford Barton* [1978]. pp. 96. Historical intro & 111 illus with descrs.
 The photographs are mostly from official Midland Rly prints.

12363 BLUHM, R. K. Didsbury's railway: a commemoration of the opening of Didsbury Station in January 1880 [edited by R. K. Bluhm]. *[Didsbury]: Didsbury Civic Society*, 1980. pp. 31, with 7 illus & a map.

Locomotives

12364 TEE, D. F. The Midland Compounds. *Southampton: Railway Correspondence & Travel Society*, 1962. pp. 24, with 28 illus & 1 col. illus (mounted), & lists.

12365 NOCK, O. S. The Midland Compounds. *Dawlish: David & Charles; London: Macdonald*, 1964. pp. 160, with col. frontis, 160 illus, 15 diagrams & many tables & graphs.

12366 CASSERLEY, H. C. and DORMAN, C. C. Midland Album. *London: Ian Allan*, 1967. pp. 112. Intro & 245 illus with descrs.

12367 RADFORD, J. B. Derby Works and Midland locomotives: the story of the works, its men, and the locomotives they built. *London: Ian Allan*, 1971. pp. 239, with 105 illus on 48 plates, plan of works, 6 line drawings of locomotives, 4 appendices including 3 very detailed lists of locomotive & boiler construction; brief bibliography.
 Period, 1839–1967.

12368 TUPLIN, W. A. Midland Steam. *Newton Abbot: David & Charles*, 1973. pp. 260, with 46 illus on 16 plates, & in text, 19 maps, diagrams, line drawings & gradient profiles, & 4 tables (table 1 being a chronology).

12369 RADFORD, J. B. A century of progress: centenary brochure of the Derby Carriage and Wagon Works; introduction by P. Gray, Works Manager. *Derby: British Rail Engineering*, [1976]. pp. 56, with 87 illus & a plan.

12370 RADFORD, J. B. Midland Railway Centre locomotives and rolling stock. *Butterley Station, Ripley: Midland Railway Trust*, 1977. pp. 32, with 29 illus & 4 stock lists.

12371 SUMMERSON, S. The history of 1708 and the Midland open cab 0-6-0 tanks. [*Luton*]: 1708 Locomotive Preservation Trust, 1979. pp. 16, with 5 illus (1 col. on cover).
An outline history of the Midland Rly's 0-6-0 tank engines and an account of the rescue and restoration of one of them—the sole survivor of a total of 350.

Rolling stock

12372 ESSERY, R. J. An Illustrated History of Midland Wagons. *Oxford: Oxford Publishing Co.*, 1980. 4°. 2 vols. (pp. [vi], 178; [vi], 169), with 462 illus, 140 diagrams & 141 tables of details of individual wagons.
Appendix 1, Passenger and Goods Stock Telegraphic Code, MR; Appendix 2, Midland Railway Company's Lot List, 1877–1923 (5 column) (pp. 152–69).

Timetables (reprints)

12373 MIDLAND RLY. Timetable, Bristol and Birmingham branch, February 1852. [Reprint]. [*Bristol: Avon Anglia*, 197–?]. (Historic Document series, 3). 4°. s. sh.
A facsimile reprint with no additional imprint.

12374 MANCHESTER, BUXTON, MATLOCK & MIDLANDS JUNCTION RLY. [Timetable] June 1st 1852 and until further notice. *Derby: printed by Wm Bemrose & Son*, [1852]. Republished as a facsimile reprint by the *Arkwright Society*, 1975. s. sh.

12375 MIDLAND RLY. Time tables . . . July, August & September, 1903. [Reprint]. *Shepperton: Ian Allan*, [1968]. pp. xviii, 184, 49, with 9 folded col. maps.
Includes the Midland's programme of tourist ticket arrangements, Season 1903.

Midland & Great Northern Joint Rly

12376 WATLING, J. Midland & Great Northern Joint Railway: diagrammatic map. [*Chelmsford*]: *Great Eastern Railway Society*, 1975. Folded map, 2'2" × 3'3".
A map of the whole of the M & GNJ Rly, drawn by John Watling. Everything except the full length representation of featureless cross-country stretches is shown: stations, junctions, crossings & sidings (the layout of each is reproduced in detail), and the location of signals, signal boxes, bridges, turntables, etc. Correct to closures of 28 February 1959.

12377 CLARK, R. H. A short history of the Midland & Great Northern Joint Railway. *Norwich: Goose & Son*, 1967. 4°. pp. [xiii], 210, with 111 illus, incl. line drawings, maps & plans, 5 stock lists, a chronology & a bibliography (50 sources); pp. 207–10, a la. folded diagrammatic map, drawn by J. Watling & dated 20.11.63.

12378 WROTTESLEY, A. J. F. The Midland & Great Northern Joint Railway. *Newton Abbot: David & Charles*, 1970. pp. 221, with col. frontis, 33 illus on 16 plates, 11 line drawings, 8 maps & plans, 6 appendices & a bibliography (36 sources).

12379 MARRIOTT, W. Forty years of a Norfolk railway; edited by C. Beckett. *Sheringham: Midland & Great Northern Joint Railway Society Publications*, 1974. (Publication, 1). pp. 32, with frontis & 13 illus on 8 plates.
An autobiography originally published in the *Norfolk Chronicle*, 1921. Author was Engineer & Traffic Manager of the M & GN, 1893–1924.

12380 CLARK, R. H. Scenes from the Midland & Great Northern Joint Railway. *Buxton: Moorland Publishing Co.*, 1978. pp. 112, with frontis (map), historical intro, 161 illus, & 13 working drawings of locomotives.

12381 BECKETT, M. D. and HEMNELL, P. R. M & GN in focus. *Norwich & King's Lynn: Becknell Books*, 1980. pp. 64. Historical intro, 106 illus with descrs, & a map.

Midland & North Eastern Joint Rly

12382 FRANKS, D. L. Swinton & Knottingley Railway. *Clapham (N. Yorks): Dalesman Books*, 1979. pp. 70, with 24 illus on 16 plates & 1 map.
The Midland & North Eastern Joint Rly.

Midland & South Western Junction Rly

12383 MIDLAND & SOUTH WESTERN JUNCTION RLY. Time tables, July 12, 1915, until further notice. [Reprint]. *Swindon: M & S.W.J. Rly*, 1915. [*Oxford*]: Oxford Publishing Co., 1975. pp. 36.
A facsimile reprint. Includes fare tables.

12384 RAILWAY CORRESPONDENCE & TRAVEL SOCIETY. Itinerary of the Midland & South Western Junction Railway Tour . . . , Sunday, 10th September, 1961. *R.C. & T.S.*, [1961]. pp. 4, with map & schedule. Notes by C. H. A. Townley.
Swindon—Savernake—Cheltenham Spa—Gloucester South Junction—Swindon.

12385 MAGGS, C. G. The Midland & South Western Junction Railway. *Newton Abbot: David & Charles*, 1967. pp. 160, with col. frontis, 49 illus on 24 plates, 16 maps, facsimiles, gradient profile, 131 notes, 5 appendices, & a bibliography (33 sources). Period, 1871–1964.

—— rev. edn. *David & Charles*, 1980. pp. 160, with 49 illus on 24 plates, etc.

Neath & Brecon Rly

12386 RICHARDS, S. and HARRIS, C. Neath & Brecon Railway. *Norwich: S. Richards*, 1977. pp. 24, with 4 illus, 4 maps, timetables & a bibliography (12 sources). Title from cover. Reproduced typescript.

Norfolk & Suffolk Joint Railways Committee

12387 The NORFOLK & Suffolk Joint Railways Committee. *Norwich: Klofron*, [1975]. pp. 56, with 18 illus on 8 plates, 5 timetables, 4 maps, 3 station layout plans, a gradient profile, chronology with page refs, & a bibliography (22 sources). Title from cover. Reproduced typescript. Text extends onto p. [3] of printed cover.

    Two copies in LU(THC) are apparently identical apart from slight differences in the order in which the plates are arranged, but on the cover of one the author is given as H. Ellesdon and on the other as R. S. Joby.

North & South Western Junction Rly

12388 COURSE, E. A. Itinerary of the Hammersmith and Chiswick Branch Rail Tour, Saturday, 10th November, 1956. *Railway Correspondence & Travel Society*, [1956]. pp. [2], with journey schedule.

    A branch from the North & South Western Junction Rly (Willesden Junction, LNWR to near Kew, LSWR), at South Acton.

North British Rly *See* C 2 L

North Eastern Rly

Reference source 12389
General, historical and descriptive 12390–12430
Locomotives 12431–40 (Reference source, 12431)

Reference source

12389 NORTH EASTERN RLY. Index of North Eastern Railway Acts, 1854–1914. *York: Delittle, Fenwick & Co., for the N.E.R.* 2 vols.

    part 1, Works. 1905. pp. xlii, 245 & 26 ruled blank pages for addenda. Preface (pp. v–x) by A. Kaye Butterworth, general manager, NER, 1906–21.

    part 2, Subjects. 1908. pp. 201 & 24 ruled blank pages.

—— Index of North Eastern Railway Acts, 1905–1911. 2 vols.

    part 1, Works. 1912. pp. 65 & 3 blank pages.

    part 2, Subjects. 1912. pp. 30 & 2 blank pages.

—— Index of North Eastern Railway Acts, 1913 & 1914. 1 vol.

    part 1, Works; part 2, Subjects. 1914. pp. 37; 19.   LU(THC)

General, historical and descriptive

12390 DARLINGTON PUBLIC LIBRARY. Stockton & Darlington Railway. *Darlington: Darlington P.L., Local History Dept*, November 1972. (Local History Guides, 3). pp.19. A bibliography (100 sources); letters, documents, printed & published material, timetables, posters and maps.

12391 COOK, R. A. and HOOLE, K. North Eastern Railway: historical maps. *Caterham: Railway & Canal Historical Society*, 1975. pp. 19 & 31 maps, with insets.

    pp. 5–12, Historical introduction to the N.E. Rly, by Ken Hoole; pp. 13–19, constituent companies of the N.E.R., with details of the principal Acts.

12392 The WHITBY and Pickering Railway: an impartial examination of the estimates published relative to that undertaking, by 'A Looker On'. *Malton: printed by G. Barnby*, 1834. pp. 17.   NUC

12393 MARTIN, W. The follies of the day; or, the effects of a gold chain, with observations on the unnecessary expenses of the North Shields Railway . . . *Newcastle: [the author]*, [1839]. pp. 8.

    Criticising the decision to use wood to construct viaducts for the Newcastle & North Shields Rly.

12394 BRANDLING, R. W. Extension line to the Brandling Junction Railway through the town of Newcastle upon Tyne and part of the county of Northumberland to Fisher Lane. *Low Gosforth: the author*, 1844. pp. 3.

    A printed letter to encourage support for his plan, addressed 'To the Public', & dated Nov. 22nd 1844.

12395 TURNBULL, G. An account of the drops used for the shipment of coals at Middlesboro'-on-Tees . . . (Excerpt, Minutes of Proceedings of the Institution of Civil Engineers, 1846). pp. 8 & 3 folded plates: 1, a plan of the approach to the staiths through the town; 2 & 3, diagrams of the drops.

    The Stockton & Darlington Rly, Middlesbrough branch, and the Docks branch railway.

12396 WILDRIDGE, T. T. Handbook to the Hull & Withernsea Railway. *Hull: C. H. Barnwell*, 1884. pp. 152, with illus.

    Topographical. Contains no railway information.

12397 BROOKE, D. The origins and development of four constituent lines of the North Eastern Railway, 1824–1854. Thesis, M.A., University of Hull, 1961–2.

The Leeds & Selby, the York & North Midland, the Hull & Selby and the Great North of England railways.

12398   HARTLEY, K. E. The Cawood, Wistow & Selby Light Railway. *London: Trans-Rail Publications*, 1968. (Trans-Hist series, 4). pp. 48, with 19 illus (7 on covers), 2 maps, layout plans, drawings and timetables. Reproduced typescript in printed covers.
—— another edn. *Timetable Enterprises*, 1973. (Minor Railways of Britain series). pp. 40, with 15 illus, map, 3 layout plans, 6 composite diagrams.

12399   JOY, D. Whitby and Pickering Railway. *Clapham (North Yorks.): Dalesman Publishing Co.*, 1969. pp. 80, with 47 illus, 3 maps (on 6 pp.), & an evaluative bibliography (pp. 74–5).
Published in collaboration with the North Yorkshire Moors Railway Preservation Society.
—— 2nd edn. *Dalesman*, 1971. pp. 80, with 50 illus, 3 maps (on 6 pp.), bibliography (pp. 75–6).
—— 3rd edn. *Dalesman*, 1973. pp. 80, with 48 illus, 3 maps (on 6 pp.), bibliography (pp. 75–6).

12400   WHITTLE, G. G. J. The historical geography of the Newcastle and Carlisle Railway system up to 1914. Thesis, M.A., Queen's University, Belfast, 1969. With 39 mounted photographs (34 col.).

12401   HENNESSEY, R. A. S. The electric railway that never was: York—Newcastle, 1919. *Newcastle upon Tyne: Oriel Press*, 1970. pp. 32, with 6 illus, 17 diagrams & line drawings, & a map.

12402   BROOKE, D. The North Eastern Railway, 1854–80, with special reference to the forces of amalgamation and competition. Thesis, Ph.D., University of Leeds, 1971.

12403   BROOKE, D. The struggle between Hull and the North Eastern Railway, 1854–80, in Journal of Transport History, new series, vol. 1 (1971–2), pp. 220–37, with 69 notes.

12404   IRVING, R. J. An economic history of the North Eastern Railway Company, 1870 to 1914. Thesis, Ph.D., University of Birmingham, 1972.

12405   CARLTON, I. C. The Brandling Junction Railway. *Gateshead: Gateshead Public Library*, 1973. (Local History Project, 1).
A portfolio containing a handbook and 17 facsimile documents, maps & illustrations dated from 1835 to 1845, and the 18-page prospectus of 1835 (Ottley 7079). The handbook (12 pages) contains a history of the line and a description with comments on each of the items in the portfolio.

12406   HARDY, G. The Londonderry Railway; edited and introduced by Charles E. Lee.

Norwich: Goose & Son, 1973. pp. 115, with frontis & 23 illus on 12 plates, & 39 notes.
pp. 9–19, Introduction, with 19 notes. The railway from Seaham to Sunderland, projected and largely constructed by C. W. Stewart, 3rd Marquis of Londonderry. The author was with the railway from 1855 to 1900 (manager from 1883–1900), in which year the line was acquired by the N.E. Rly.

12407   HAYES, R. H. and RUTTER, J. G. Rosedale mines & railway. *Scarborough: Scarborough & District Archaeological Society*, 1973. pp. 23, with map, 2 tables, 13 notes. Reproduced typescript.
Offprint (revised) from the *Transactions of the S. & D.A.S.*, vol. 2, no. 11, 1968.
—— [2nd edn], *Scarborough & District Archaeological Society*, 1974. (Research Report, 9). pp. 32, with 17 illus, on 16 plates, map, 6 track plans, 4 tables, incl. chronology, 22 notes.
The North Eastern Railway's Rosedale and Rosedale East branches for the transport of ironstone, 1861–1926.

12408   HOOLE, K. The Stainmore Railway. *Clapham (North Yorkshire): Dalesman Publishing Co.*, 1973. pp. 128, with 51 illus, 6 layout plans, 3 diagrams, 3 facsims, 2 maps, 2 gradient profiles, 10 appendices.
The South Durham & Lancashire Union Rly.

12409   HOOLE, K. North Eastern Album. *London: Ian Allan*, 1974. pp. 112. Intro, col. frontis, map, & 188 illus, incl. facsims, with descrs.

12410   HOOLE, K. Stockton & Darlington Railway: anniversary celebrations of the World's first steam-worked public railway. *Clapham (North Yorkshire): Dalesman*, 1974. pp. 95, with 56 illus & a bibliography (25 sources).
The celebrations of 1875, 1881, 1925 and 1948.

12411   ABLEY, R. S. The Byers Green branch of the Clarence Railway. *Durham City: Durham County Local History Society*, 1975. pp. 46, with 11 maps & 2 gradient profiles.

12412   DARLINGTON S & D 150 COMMITTEE. 150th anniversary. Stockton and Darlington Railway. [*Darlington*]: *the Committee*, [1975]. la. 4°.
Portfolio containing 11 reproductions of documents, maps, notices and prints, with explanatory notes by A. Suddes and K. Taylor.

12413   DURHAM COUNTY COUNCIL. Stockton & Darlington Railway. 1825–1975: access to the historic sites. [*Durham*]: *the Council*. [1975]. A sm. folded route map.

12414   DURHAM JOINT CURRICULUM STUDY GROUP. Stockton & Darlington Railway: a collection of material to celebrate the 150th anniversary of the opening of the Stockton & Darlington Railway. *Newcastle upon Tyne: Frank Graham*, [1975].

A portfolio containing 30 separate items and an explanatory handbook of 24 pp. Photocopies of documents, maps, illustrations, timetables, a chronology, 6 coloured plates, and *Railway People*, a booklet with biographies of George Stephenson, Timothy Hackworth, Edward Pease, Jonathan Backhouse, Thomas Meynell, compiled by P. Daniels, D. Hewitt, D. J. Cowey and G. Flynn (pp. 40, with 22 illus).

12415 HOLMES, P. J. The Stockton & Darlington Railway, 1825–1975. *Ayr: First Avenue Publishing Co.*, [1975]. pp. viii, 194, with frontis, 40 illus on 16 plates, 15 line drawings, 8 maps, diagrams, lists, tables & a bibliography (15 sources).

12416 HOOLE, K. The Stockton & Darlington Railway. *Newton Abbot: David & Charles*, 1975. (Railway History in Pictures series). pp. 96. Intro (pp. 9–16) & 106 illus incl. facsims & map, with descrs.

12417 McDOUGALL, C. A. The Stockton & Darlington Railway, 1821–1863. *Durham: Durham County Council*, 1975. (Local History Publications, 9). pp. iv, 56, with 17 line illus (map, diagrams, facsimiles), & a bibliography (19 sources).

12418 MOORSOM, N. The Stockton & Darlington Railway: the foundation of Middlesbrough: compiled from original sources. *Middlesbrough: J. G. Peckston*, [1975]. pp. v, 198, with 7 illus on 4 plates, map, 1 illus, chronology, & a bibliography (18 sources).

12419 NATIONAL BENZOLE COMPANY. The 150th anniversary of the Stockton & Darlington Railway, the world's first passenger steam railway. *London: National Benzole*, [1975]. pp. 6, [6]. A printed folder with 16 line illus. No text.

12420 NORTHERN ECHO [newspaper]. [Railway Jubilee Celebrations in Darlington, 1875]. *Darlington: Northern Echo*, 1975. (Great Events in History Series, 2). pp. 4.
A reprint of issue no. 1785, Tuesday September 28, 1875 relating to the Railway Jubilee Celebrations at North Road locomotive works, Darlington, the previous day.

12421 SEMMENS, P. W. B. Exploring the Stockton & Darlington Railway. *Newcastle upon Tyne: Frank Graham*, 1975. pp. 72, with 33 illus on 16 plates, 5 maps and a pictorial cover by R. Embleton.

12422 COTTRELL, P. L. and OTTLEY, G. The beginnings of the Stockton & Darlington Railway: people and documents, 1813–25: a celebratory note, in Journal of Transport History, new series vol 3 (1975–6), pp. 86–93, with table & 24 notes.

12423 GOODE, C. T. The Goole and Selby Railway. *Tarrant Hinton: Oakwood Press*, 1976. (Locomotion Papers, 100). pp. 42, with 16 illus on 8 plates, 2 maps, 10 layout plans, & timetables.

12424 IRVING, R. J. The North Eastern Railway Company, 1870–1914: an economic history. [*Leicester*]: *Leicester University Press*, 1976. pp. 320, with 68 tables, 7 graphs, map, 14 detailed appendices, 968 notes & a bibliography (200+ sources).

12425 HOOLE, K. The story of North Road Station Railway Museum, Darlington. *Darlington: the Museum*, 1977. pp. 11, with 5 illus.

12426 LIDSTER, J. R. The Scarborough & Whitby Railway: a photographic & historical survey. *Nelson: Hendon Publishing Co.*, 1977. obl. format. pp. 44, with 56 illus, 2 maps, layout plan, diagrams & a gradient profile.
No separate text, but the Introduction and lengthy descriptions to many of the illustrations provide much information. Period, 1885–1965.

12427 HOOLE, K. North Eastern branch lines since 1925. *London: Ian Allan*, 1978. pp. 128, with 166 annotated illus & 8 appendices.

12428 HOOLE, K. Railways in the North Eastern landscape. *Hassocks: Branch Line (Harvester Press)*, 1978. pp. 70, with 90 illus.

12429 HOOLE, K. The North East Railway Book. *Newton Abbot: David & Charles*, 1979. pp. 96, with 30 illus.
The North Eastern Rly, and the London & North Eastern Railway in that area.

12430 WHITTLE, G. The Newcastle & Carlisle Railway. *Newton Abbot: David & Charles*, 1979. pp. 208, with 32 illus on 16 plates, 3 plans, 2 gradient profiles & a map; 7 appendices, incl. passenger traffic statistics, timetables, rules & lists.

Locomotives

12431 HOOLE, K. North Eastern Railway locomotive stock as at 31.12.20; prepared by K. Hoole. *Knaresborough: Nidd Valley Narrow Gauge Railways*, [1969]. pp. [34]. Reproduced typescript in printed cover.
Numerical 10-column lists showing the building date and withdrawal date of every N.E.R. locomotive in stock at the end of 1920, together with the shed to which it was allocated at that time.

12432 HOOLE, K. North Eastern Atlantics. *Hatch End: Roundhouse Books*, 1965. pp. 64, with 29 illus on 16 plates & ca. 30 detailed tables & lists.

12433 HOOLE, K. North Road locomotive works, Darlington, 1863–1966. *Hatch End: Roundhouse Books*, 1967. pp. xiv, 102, with 92 illus on 48 plates, 2 plans of the works, 2 diagrams, lists.

12434 HOOLE, K. North Eastern Railway buses, lorries & autocars. *Knaresborough: Nidd Valley Narrow Gauge Railways*, 1969. pp. 79, with 37 illus on 20 plates, 5 drawings; lists & timetables.

12435 HOOLE, K. and MALLON, J. North Eastern Railway: diagrams of snow ploughs. *Knaresborough: Nidd Valley Narrow Gauge Railways, for the N.E.R. Association*, 1969. pp. 24, with 8 illus & 12 diagrams.

12436 TUPLIN, W. A. North Eastern Steam. *London: Allen & Unwin*, 1970. pp. 215, with 51 illus on frontis & 14 plates, & 6 tables.

12437 HOOLE, K. North Eastern locomotive sheds. *Newton Abbot: David & Charles*, 1972. pp. 263, with 18 illus.

12438 HOOLE, K. North Eastern stations: a photographic collection compiled by K. Hoole. *Clapham (North Yorkshire): Dalesman Publishing Co.*, 1978. obl. format. Intro (pp. 5–8) & 96 illus with descrs.

12439 HOOLE, K. The 4-4-0 classes of the North Eastern Railway. *London: Ian Allan*, 1979. pp. 112, with 138 illus & descrs.

12440 SEMMENS, P. W. B. North Eastern engineman: driver Syd Midgley and fifty years of Steam. *Truro: Bradford Barton*, 1980. pp. 119, with 23 illus on 16 plates (pp. 53–60, 77–84).
Period, 1914–1963, NER—LNER—BR.

North London Rly

12441 NORTH London Railway: a pictorial record. *London: H.M.S.O.*, 1979. obl. format. pp. xix, 62. Frontis, 7 illus, bibliography (16 sources), map with 4 layout plans as insets, and an introduction (pp. vii–xvi) by C. P. Atkins and T. J. Edgington, followed by 56 illus with descrs (pp. 1–62).
The title-page is headed: National Railway Museum, York; Science Museum, London.

12442 CONNOR, J. E. All stations to Poplar: a brief history & description. *London: THAP Publishing (Tower Hamlets Arts Project)*, 1980. pp. 56, with 29 illus & map.
The Broad Street to Poplar line of the ex-North London Rly.

North Staffordshire Rly

12443 A SHORT letter to the shareholders of the North Staffordshire Railway Company on the proposed terms of union between that company and the London and North Western Company recommended by Mr Hope and Mr Stephenson, by a Shareholder. *London: Piper Brothers & Co.*, 1852. pp. 7.
MCL.

12444 MOORES, G. The Official Holiday Guide to the North Staffordshire Railway. 2nd edn. *Manchester: N. S. Rly*, 1891. pp. 171, with 38 illus.
Topographical, with 2 pp. on the railway.

12445 DOW, G. North Staffordshire Album. *London: Ian Allan*, 1970. pp. 112. Intro, map, & 247 illus with descrs.
Period, 1846–1922.

12446 CHRISTIANSEN, R. and MILLER, R. W. The North Staffordshire Railway. *Newton Abbot: David & Charles*, 1971. pp. 333, with col. frontis, 32 illus on 16 plates, 30 in text (8 maps, 11 diagrs, specimen time-tables), 5 detailed appendices; 79 notes & a bibliography (24 sources).

12447 KEYS, R. The Churnet Valley Railway, by R. Keys and the North Staffordshire Railway Society. *Buxton: Moorland Publishing Co.*, 1974. pp. 84, with frontis (map), 103 illus on 48 plates, & a map.
Period, 1849–1964.

12448 BAKER, A. C. The Cheadle Railway: a history of the Cheadle (Staffordshire) Railway, the Foxfield Colliery Railway, and adjoining industrial railways and their locomotives; maps and drawings by T. D. Allen Civil. *Tarrant Hinton: Oakwood Press*, 1979. (Oakwood Library of Railway History, 47). pp. 76, with 34 illus on 16 plates. map, 5 layout plans, a gradient profile and 7 appendices, including Acts.
A 4-mile branch of the North Staffordshire (later LMS) Rly.

12449 JEUDA B. The Leek, Caldon & Waterhouses Railway. *Cheddleton: North Staffordshire Railway Co. (1978)*, 1980. (North Staffordshire Railway Monograph, 1). pp. 80, with 53 illus, facsimiles & dimensioned drawings on 32 plates (pp. 25–56), map, gradient profile, 10 layout plans & 16+ tables.
A detailed account of the N.S.R.'s branch from Leek to the limestone quarries at Caldon Low and to the terminus of the Leek & Manifold Valley Light Railway at Waterhouses (1895 to the present day).

Port Talbot Railway & Docks

12450 RICHARDS, S. Port Talbot Railway. *Norwich: Morgannwg*, 1977. pp. 24, with 5 illus, 4 maps, timetables & a bibliography (15 sources). Title from cover. Reproduced typescript.

Portpatrick & Wigtownshire Joint Rly *See* C 2 L

Somerset & Dorset Rly

12451 DORSET CENTRAL RLY. Wimborne to Poole extension. Poole. Resolutions of public meeting held at the Town Hall February 22nd 1860, for railway extension from Wimborne to Poole, with copy of the petition to the House of Commons. [Caption title] *Poole: Lankester, printer*, [1860]. pp. 4. No title-page.   BLACKWELLS CAT. A1051/129

12452   ATTHILL, R. The Somerset & Dorset Railway, with contributions on locomotives, etc. by O. S. Nock. *Newton Abbot: David & Charles*, 1967. pp. 200, with col. frontis, 56 illus on 24 plates, & in text, 19 illus (maps, facsimiles, gradient profiles, layout plans, 6 appendices, bibliography (20+ sources).
—— rev. edn. *Pan Books*, 1970. pp. 236, with 28 illus on 16 plates, tables.

12453   STEPHENSON LOCOMOTIVE SOCIETY. MIDLAND AREA. Farewell to the former Somerset and Dorset Joint Railway: photographic souvenir in connection with last passenger train on the Bath—Templecombe—Bournemouth section, Sunday 6th March, 1966. *Handsworth: S.L.S., Midland Area*, 1967. pp. 16, incl. covers. 28 illus with descrs.

12454   ATTHILL, R. The Picture History of the Somerset & Dorset Railway. *Newton Abbot: David & Charles*, 1970. pp. 112, with col. frontis, intro, & 145 illus with descrs.

12455   MILTON, D. The Somerset & Dorset 2-8-0s. *Somerset & Dorset Railway Circle*, [1972]. pp. [29], with 6 illus, 2 tables & a bibliography (9 sources).
—— 2nd edn. *Washford: Somerset & Dorset Railway Museum Trust*, 1980. pp. 28, with 11 illus, 2 tables & a bibliography (7+ sources).

12456   SMITH, P. W. Mendips engineman, with photographs by Ivo Peters. *Oxford: Oxford Publishing Co.*, 1972. pp. viii, 79, with 58 illus on 32 plates & a map.
Memoirs, Somerset & Dorset Joint Rly, 1954–1962.

12457   BRADLEY, D. L. and MILTON, D. Somerset & Dorset Locomotive History. *Newton Abbot: David & Charles*, 1973. pp. 218, with 39 illus on 16 plates & many tables.

12458   MAGGS, C. G. Highbridge in its heyday. *Lingfield: Oakwood Press*, 1973. (Locomotion Papers, 69). pp. 50, with 48 illus on 24 plates, & 8 layout plans of S. & D.J. Rly loco depots.
Largely based upon the recollections of 'S.F.R.' who spent his working life at Highbridge works and at Bath locomotive depot, from 1910 to 1960.
The illustrations are mostly of locomotives and rolling stock.

12459   PETERS, I. The Somerset & Dorset: an English cross-country railway. *Oxford: Oxford Publishing Co.*, 1974. la. 8°. pp. [128]. Intro & 235 illus with descrs.

12460   RICHARDSON, G. A. Steam on the Somerset & Dorset. *Truro: Bradford Barton*, 1975. pp. 96. Intro & 95 illus with descrs. Period, 1960s.

12461   PETERS, I. Jinty: the story of a small tank engine on the Somerset and Dorset Railway. *Washford: Somerset & Dorset Railway Museum Trust*, [1976]. pp. 32, with 30 illus.

12462   SMITH, P. Footplate over the Mendips. *Oxford: Oxford Publishing Co*, 1978. pp. vi, 138, with 73 illus on 40 plates, map (frontis) & tables.
Memoirs of the Somerset & Dorset Joint Rly: a sequel to this author's *Mendips Engineman* (1972).

12463   JUDGE, C. W. and POTTS, C. R. An historical survey of the Somerset and Dorset Railway: track layouts and illustrations. *Oxford: Oxford Publishing Co.*, 1979. la. 8°. pp. 135. Intro, frontis & 231 illus (mostly of stations) with layout plans and historical notes.

12464   SOMERSET AND DORSET JOINT RLY. Working Time Book from 4th October 1920, and Working Time Book, passenger and milk trains, from 14th September, 1931. *Oxford: Oxford Publishing Co.*, 1979. pp. 52, 20.
A facsimile reprint of the two working timetables reproduced in a period-style cover with a combined title.

12465   STICKLEY, F. E. Somerset & Dorset engineman. *Tarrant Hinton: Oakwood Press*, 1979. (Locomotion Papers, 118). pp. 51, with 21 illus on 12 plates & 4 drawings.
An autobiographical account of life on the S & D, with photographs by Ivo Peters.

South Eastern & Chatham Railway Companies Managing Committee

General, historical and descriptive 12466–84
Locomotives 12485–87

General, historical and descriptive

12466   LANDMANN, G. T. Observations on the Greenwich Railway, in a letter addressed to the subscribers, by an inhabitant of Greenwich [Col. G. T. Landmann]. *London: James Ridgway*, 1833. pp. 36.
The copy in Greenwich Local History Centre has an inscription in MS: 'by "the Inhabitant of Greenwich, Colonel Landmann, Esquire"'.

12467   WHITTOCK, N. The modern picture of London, Westminster and the Metropolitan boroughs . . . *London: G. Virtue*, 1836. pp. 550–2, The London & Greenwich Rly.

12468   SOUTH EASTERN RLY. [Timetable]. London and Dover Railway, open to Folkestone, seven miles from Dover. [*London: S.E. Rly*, 1843]. *Republished as a facsimile*

reprint by the Isle of Wight Rly Co., ca. 1973. s. sh, with no added imprint, but at foot of page: 'Reproduced by Robert Vale, Printer, Ltd, Ryde, I. Wight'.
A timetable with, on the reverse, 'features of interest'.

12469 HILTON, J. The Canterbury & Whitstable Railway. *Hadlow (Kent): the author*, [1966]. pp. [8], with 2 illus & a map.

12470 KIDNER, R. W. The Dartford Loop line. 1866–1966. *Lingfield: Oakwood Press*, 1966. (Locomotion Papers, 34). pp. 23, with 11 illus on 4 plates, 2 maps, 4 plans, 6 drawings.

12471 MAXTED, I. The Canterbury & Whitstable Railway. *Lingfield: Oakwood Press*, 1970. (Oakwood Library of Railway History, 27). pp. 35, with 16 illus on 8 plates, lists, & a bibliography (22 sources).

12472 KIDNER, R. W. The Oxted line. [*Lingfield*]: *Oakwood Press*, 1972. (Locomotion Papers, 58). pp. 40, with 32 illus on 8 plates, 3 maps, & 3 layout plans.
The Croydon, Oxted & East Grinstead Rly and other lines serving Oxted.

12473 THOMAS, R. H. G. London's first railway: the London & Greenwich. *London: Batsford*, 1972. pp. 270, with 39 illus on 16 plates, 21 illus in text (maps, plans & drawings), 295 notes & a bibliography of 20 sources additional to those already mentioned in the text.
Period, 1824–1923.

12474 GOULD, D. Westerham Valley Railway. *Lingfield: Oakwood Press*, 1974. (Locomotion Papers, 72). pp. 40, with 19 illus, map, 4 station layout plans, 5 timetables.

12475 KIDNER, R. W. The Reading to Tonbridge line. *Lingfield: Oakwood Press*, 1974. (Locomotion Papers, 79). pp. 70, with 36 illus on 16 plates, 2 maps, 6 layout plans, & a working timetable.

12476 SMITH, C. L. W. The romance of Faversham's own railway, *in his* Stories of Faversham. *Faversham: the author*, 1974. ch. 57, pp. 472–96, with 3 illus.

12477 FORWOOD, M. J. The Elham Valley Railway. *London: Phillimore*, 1975. pp. vi, 88, with 24 illus on 12 plates, 13 maps, plans, gradient profiles, facsimiles.

12478 KIDNER, R. W. Southern Railway branch lines in the thirties. *Tarrant Hinton: Oakwood Press*, 1976. (Locomotion Papers, 93). pp. 72, with 44 illus on 20 plates.

12479 DEVEREUX, C. M. Railways to Sevenoaks. *Tarrant Hinton: Oakwood Press*, 1977. (Locomotion Papers, 102). pp. 60,

with 24 illus on 12 plates, map, gradient profile, timetable & 12 layout plans.
The main line (from 1864) of the S.E. Rly, and the L.C. & D. Rly branch from Swanley Junction to Sevenoaks 'Bat & Ball'.

12480 KIDNER, R. W. The North Kent line. *Tarrant Hinton: Oakwood Press*, 1977. (Locomotion Papers, 103). pp. 62, with 26 illus on 12 plates, map, 10 layout plans, 30 notes.
Period, 1824 to the present.

12481 HILTON, J. A history of the South Eastern & Chatham Railway. *Hadlow (Kent): the author via J. Hannon & Co., Oxford*.
vol. 1, from 1812–1845. [1978]. pp. 52, with 6 illus, 2 maps & a timetable. Title on cover only.
The origin and early years of the South Eastern Rly.
vol. 2, from 1845–1855. [1979]. pp. 53–92, with 6 illus, diagrams, maps & a timetable. The South Eastern Rly and the emergence of the East Kent Rly in 1853 (later to become the London, Chatham & Dover Rly).

12482 OWEN, N. The Tattenham Corner branch. *Tarrant Hinton: Oakwood Press*, 1978. (Locomotion Papers, 108). pp. 32, with 15 illus on 8 plates, map, 8 layout plans, gradient plan & timetable.
Period, 1897 to the present.

12483 ELLIS, P. The 150th anniversary of the opening of the Canterbury & Whitstable Railway: a pioneer line and the area it served. [*London*]: *British Railways, Southern Region; Weston-super-Mare: Avon-Anglia*. April 1980. pp. 32, with 21 illus (incl. 4 col. reproductions of paintings), 7 facsimiles & a map. Foreword by Peter Parker, chairman, BR.

12484 RATCLIFFE, R. L. The Canterbury and Whitstable Railway, 1830–1980: a pictorial survey. *London: Locomotive Club of Great Britain*, 1980. pp. 24, with 31 illus & 2 maps (1 on cover and 1, a route map in 4 sections between pp. 6 & 14), and 2 plans of the termini; bibliography (7 sources).

Locomotives

12485 BRADLEY, D. L. The locomotives of the South Eastern Railway. *Railway Correspondence & Travel Society*, 1963. pp. 125, with frontis (map), 64 illus on 26 plates, 8 line drawings, lists.

12486 GOULD, D. Carriage stock of the S.E. & C.R. *Tarrant Hinton: Oakwood Press*, 1976. pp. 152, with 36 illus on 12 plates, and numerous diagrams & detailed tables. Reproduced from typescript.

12487 KIDNER, R. W. Service stock of the Southern Railway, its constituents and B.R. Southern Region. *Tarrant Hinton: Oakwood Press*, 1980. (Locomotion Papers, 124). pp. 66; with 105 illus on 36 plates (pp.

17–52), 2 drawings & 2 lists of vehicles, 1927–1970 (pp. 61–66).

Southern Railway

Reference sources 12488–89
General, historical and descriptive 12490–98
Locomotives and trains 12499–12552 (Reference sources 12499–12500)
Electrification 12553–55
Timetables (reprints) 12556–57

For the Southern Rly in the Isle of Wight see also **C 5**

Reference sources

12488 TAVENDER, L. LSWR and Southern. *Bromley: Historical Model Railway Society*, 1970. (HMRS Livery Register, 3). pp. 76, with 24 illus on 8 plates, 25 groups of line drawings, 4 tables, a page of 18 colour palettes & 496 notes.

12489 PRYER, G. A. A Pictorial Record of Southern Signals. *Oxford: Oxford Publishing Co.*, 1977. la. 8°. pp. 200, with 220 illus & 51 diagrams & drawings.

General, historical and descriptive

12490 SOUTHERN RLY. The passing scene: an account of what is seen from the train on the route from London to Portsmouth and the Isle of Wight. *London: Southern Rly*, [1938?] pp. 24, with 9 illus; 2 maps on covers.
Topographical.

12491 SOUTHERN RAILWAY SERVANTS' ORPHANAGE. Notes on the Southern Railway Servants' Orphanage [and] Notes on the Southern Railway Homes for Old People, by A. G. Evershead, Secretary-Superintendent of the Board of Management of the S.R.S.O., in association with the S.R.H.O.P. *Woking: The Board of Management*, [ca. 1950]. pp. 15, with 16 illus.

12492 ROCHE, T. W. E. The Withered Arm: reminiscences of the Southern lines west of Exeter. *Teddington: Branch Line Handbooks; Bracknell: West Country Handbooks*, 1967. pp. 69, with frontis, 31 illus, a map & a layout plan.
—— new edn. *Bracknell: Forge Books*, 1977. pp. 76, with 37 illus, a map & a layout plan.

12493 SYMES, R. and COLE, D. Railway architecture of the South East. *Reading: Osprey*, 1972. (Railway Architecture Series). pp. 128. Intro (pp. 7–15), & 42 drawings with commentaries.
Pen drawings of a selected 42 stations and other railway structures and detail on the Southern Rly in Kent, Surrey, Sussex & Hampshire, each with an historical & descriptive note. The introduction provides a general historical commentary and the work is an objective (not imaginative) encapsulation of what is judged to be noteworthy (significant, striking or characteristic) in 19th century railway architecture in this area.

12494 KLAPPER, C. F. Sir Herbert Walker's Southern Railway. *London: Ian Allan*, 1973. pp. 295, with 66 illus on 32 plates, map & 3 layout plans.
Sir Herbert Walker was general manager of the LSWR, 1912–1922, and of the Southern Rly, 1923–37.

12495 ALLEN, C. J. Salute to the Southern. *London: Ian Allan*, 1974. pp. 100, with 127 illus (1 col.).

12496 GAMMELL, C. J. Southern branch lines, 1955–1965. *Oxford: Oxford Publishing Co.*, 1976. 4°. pp. [96]. Intro, frontis & 166 illus with descrs, 7 maps, bibliography (11 sources) & a list of closure dates of lines.

12497 JACKMAN, M. The Bricklayers Arms branch and loco shed. *Tarrant Hinton: Oakwood Press*, 1980. (Locomotion Papers, 125). pp. 43, with 13 illus, 4 layout plans, a table of locomotive head-codes & a bibliography (6 sources).
Period—from its formation by the SER & the London & Croydon Rly in 1843, to 1979.

12498 REEVE, G. and HAWKINS, C. Branch lines of the Southern Railway. *Upper Bucklebury: Wild Swan Publications*.
vol. 1, [The Crowhurst, Sidley & Bexhill Rly; the Bordon Light Rly: the Hayling Rly; the Swanage Rly]. 1980. la. 8°. pp. viii, 136, with 222 illus, 28 composite drawings of structures (stations, bridges, etc.), 15 station layout plans with signalling diagrams, 5 maps & 4 timetables.

Locomotives and trains

12499 BRADLEY, D. L. Locomotives of the Southern Railway. *London: Railway Correspondence & Travel Society*.
part 1, The Maunsell Lord Nelsons, Schools, Qs, Zs, etc. 1975. pp. 86, with frontis & 90 illus & dimensioned drawings on 50 plates: many lists in text.
part 2, [The Merchant Navy class; the West Country and Battle of Britain classes]. 1976. pp. 109, with frontis & 100 illus on 56 plates, & lists in text.

12500 FAIRCLOUGH, T. and WILLS, A. Southern steam locomotive survey. *Truro: Bradford Barton*.
vol. 1, Early Maunsell classes. 1976. pp. 96. Intro & 108 illus, with descrs.
vol. 2, Later Maunsell classes. 1976. pp. 96. Intro & 104 illus, with descrs.
vol. 3, Bulleid 'Merchant Navy' Pacifics, 1976. pp. 96. Intro & 108 illus, with descrs.
vol. 4, Bulleid Light Pacifics. 1976. pp. 96. Intro & 102 illus, with descrs.
vol. 5, Urie classes. 1977. pp. 96. Intro & 103 illus, with descrs.
vol. 6, Drummond classes. 1977. pp. 96. Intro & 106 illus, with descrs.
vol. 7, Adams classes. 1978. pp. 96. Intro & 112 illus, with descrs.

vol. 8, Wainwright classes. 1979. pp. 96. Intro & 106 illus, with descrs.

12501 BURRIDGE, F. H. A. Streamlining the Southern Railway: special edition. *Boscombe: F, H. A. Burridge*, 1945. sm. 8°. pp. [8], with drawings (incl. 3 folded & mounted). Reproduced from manuscript.
The Merchant Navy and West Country classes.

12502 BURRIDGE, F. H. A. Southern Locomotive Spotting Chart: a complete list of all the named locomotives of the Southern Railway Co. [*London*]: *Ian Allan*, [1947]. A la. folded table.
Locomotives arranged under classes with 'place first seen' and date columns.

12503 MACK, L. A. Southern loco-hauled corridor stock. *Twickenham: the author*, Autumn 1959. pp. 26. Reproduced typescript, paper covers.

12504 CASSERLEY, H. C. and JOHNSTON, S. W. Locomotives at the Grouping: no. 1, Southern Railway. *London: Ian Allan*, [1965]. pp. 60, with 91 illus on 24 plates. Lists.

12505 NOCK, O. S. Southern Steam. *Newton Abbot: David & Charles*, 1966. pp. 200, with col. frontis, 61 illus on 33 plates, logs of 55 runs and other tables, 2 appendices (lists of locomotives).
—— *Pan Books*, 1972. sm. 8°. pp. xii, 210; 31 illus on 16 plates.

12506 RANSOME-WALLIS, P. Southern Album. *London: Ian Allan*, 1968. pp. 128, Intro (pp. 7–12), frontis & 219 illus with descrs.
Mostly steam locomotives at work, but includes Southern Rly electric traction, ships and docks.

12507 HASENSON, A. The Golden Arrow: a history and contemporary illustrated account. *London: Howard Baker*, 1970. pp. 208, with 32 illus on 16 plates, 25 maps & diagrams, and a list of passenger vessels of the railway-owned Dover—Folkestone fleet, 1923 to date.
pp. 121–84: a selection of timetables; pp. 185–95, a chronology; pp. 197–200, a bibliography (96 sources).

12508 JUDGE, C. W. The Southern era: a collection of photographs of locomotives. *Oxford: Oxford Publishing Co.*, 1972. pp. 96. Intro & 166 illus with captions & an index. A limited edition of 1000 numbered copies, each signed by the compiler. 'The fourth & last in the series.'

12509 OWEN, N. The Brighton Belle. 2nd edn. *Southern Electric Group*, June 1972. pp. 27, with 7 illus, map & gradient profile. Preface by Alan Melville.

12510 PERRYMAN, A. C. Life at Brighton locomotive works, 1928–1936. *Lingfield: Oakwood Press*, [1972]. (Locomotion Papers, 54). pp. 67, with 20 illus on 8 plates, & a plan.

12511 CREER, S. Southern Steam: south and east. *Truro: Bradford Barton*, 1973. pp. 96. Intro & 91 illus with descrs.
Southern Rly locomotives in BR(SR) days (1950s and 1960s).

12512 EARLEY, M. W. The Southern scene: an album of photographs by Maurice W. Earley. *Oxford: Oxford Publishing Co.*, 1973. obl. 8°. pp. [64]. Intro & 93 illus with descrs.
Southern Rly; period, 1920s to 1960s.

12513 FAIRCLOUGH, T. and WILLS, A. Southern Steam in the West Country. *Truro: Bradford Barton*, 1973. pp. 96. Intro & 105 illus with descrs.
Scenes on the former LSWR lines of the Southern Rly in BR(SR) days.

12514 SOUTH EASTERN STEAM CENTRE. Welcome to the South Eastern Steam Centre. *Ashford: the Centre*, 1973. pp. 4 & paper cover.
Locomotives and rolling stock of the SE & CR and Southern Rly. A guide; includes a stocklist.

12515 TOWNROE, S. C. The Arthurs, Nelsons and Schools of the Southern. *Shepperton: Ian Allan*, 1973. pp. 103, with 81 illus on 40 plates, diagrams, lists & a bibliography (13 sources).
A more detailed version of the author's two pamphlets: *Book of the Schools Class* (1947), and *King Arthurs and Lord Nelsons of the Southern Railway* (1949).

12516 CREER, S. More Southern Steam: south and east. *Truro: Bradford Barton*, 1974. pp. 96. Intro & 97 illus with descrs.
Southern Railway locomotives in BR(SR) days, 1950s–1960s.

12517 CROSS, D. Southern Steam from lineside. *Truro: Bradford Barton*, 1974. pp. 96. Intro & 97 illus with descrs.

12518 DAVEY, R. My life on the footplate. *Beer: Peco*, 1974. pp. 56, with 30 illus, 2 maps, gradient profile, layout plan. Imprint on p. [2] of cover.
Period 1918 (S.E.C.R. at Slades Green depot) to 1966 (Southern Region of B.R.).

12519 FAIRCLOUGH, T. and WILLS, A. Southern Steam in action. *Truro: Bradford Barton*.
Southern Railway trains in BR(SR) days, 1950s–1960s.
vol. 1, 1974. pp. 96. Intro & 100 illus with descrs.
vol. 2, 1975. pp. 96. Intro & 105 illus with descrs.
vol. 3, 1976. pp. 96. Intro & 110 illus with descrs.
vol. 4, 1977. pp. 96. Intro & 99 illus with descrs.

12520 FAIRCLOUGH, T. and WILLS, A. Southern Steam south and west. *Truro: Bradford Barton*, 1974. pp. 96. Intro & 110 illus with descrs.
>   Scenes on the old LSWR lines out of Waterloo in BR(SR) days (1960s).

12521 KIDNER, R. W. Notes on Southern Railway rolling stock . . . , drawings by David Gould. *Lingfield: Oakwood Press*, 1974. (Locomotion Papers, 74). pp. 59, with 38 illus on plates, 38 line drawings, & detailed lists. Cover title: Southern Railway rolling stock.
>   Steam-hauled carriages, service vehicles and coach sets of the 1920s & 1930s.

12522 WINKWORTH, D. W. Bulleid's Pacifics. *London: Allen & Unwin*, 1974. pp. 264, with 32 illus on 16 plates, 97 performance tables, 3 appendices (tables of locomotive data) & a bibliography (19 sources).

12523 FAIRCLOUGH, T. and WILLS, A. More Southern Steam on shed. *Truro: Bradford Barton*, 1975. pp. 96. Intro & 121 illus with descrs.

12524 FAIRCLOUGH, T. and WILLS, A. Southern Steam on shed. *Truro: Bradford Barton*, 1975. pp. 96. Intro & 130 illus with descrs.

12525 PERRYMAN, A. C. Steam on the Brighton line: a pictorial survey. *Truro: Bradford Barton*, 1975. Intro & 172 illus with descrs, from photographs in the collection of Maurice Joly.

12526 CASSERLEY, H. C. Recollections of the Southern between the wars. *Truro: Bradford Barton*, 1976. pp. 96. Intro & 122 illus with descrs.

12527 FAIRCLOUGH, T. and WILLS, A. Southern branch line Steam. *Truro: Bradford Barton*.
>   vol. 1, 1976. pp. 96. Intro, & 110 illus with descrs.
>   vol. 2, 1977. pp. 96. Intro, & 102 illus with descrs.
>   Period, 1950s–1960s.

12528 JACKMAN, M. Thirty years at Bricklayers Arms: Southern Steam from the footplate. *Newton Abbot: David & Charles*, 1976. pp. 152, with 15 illus on 8 plates, 2 maps, 2 layout plans.

12529 NOCK, O. S. The Southern King Arthur family. *Newton Abbot: David & Charles*, 1976. pp. 96, with frontis, 85 illus, 18 diagrams, tables & logs of runs.

12530 ROWLEDGE, J. W. P. The Maunsell Moguls. *Tarrant Hinton: Oakwood Press*, 1976. (Locomotion Papers, 99). pp. 64, with 18 illus & 4 diagrams on 12 plates, 15 diagrams & 5 detailed tables in text.

12531 SMITH, J. L. Southern Steam, 1923–1939. *Truro: Bradford Barton*, 1976. (Southern Steam series). pp. 96. Intro & 110 illus with descrs.

12532 ADAMS, J. and WHITEHOUSE, P. Southern Steam in camera. *London: Ian Allan*, 1977. pp. 64. Intro & 96 illus with descrs.

12533 BULLEID, H. A. V. Bulleid of the Southern. *London: Ian Allan*, 1977. pp. 229, with 100 illus on 48 plates, tables, 54 diagrams & 9 appendices (pp. 187–221); bibliography (21 sources).

12534 FAIRCLOUGH, T. and WILLS, A. Southern Steam double-headed. *Truro: Bradford Barton*, 1977. pp. 96. Intro & 99 illus with descrs.
>   Southern Region of BR, 1950s & 1960s.

12535 HARESNAPE, B. Bulleid locomotives: a pictorial history. *London: Ian Allan*, 1977. pp. 112, with 138 illus, lists, diagrams & a short bibliography.

12536 HARESNAPE, B. Maunsell locomotives: a pictorial history. *London: Ian Allan*, 1977. pp. 128, with 166 illus, 21 dimensioned drawings, lists & a brief bibliography.

12537 SOUTHERN trains. *London: Ian Allan*, [1977]. pp. 80. Intro & 125 illus with descrs.
>   Steam-hauled and electric trains.

12538 WILLIAMS, A. Southern Electric Album. *London: Ian Allan*, 1977. pp. 96. Intro & 133 illus with descrs.
>   The first and last pages of the text are pasted down as endpapers.
>   The Southern Rly, and BR(SR) to 1970.

12539 FAIRCLOUGH, T. and WILLS, A. Southern Steam in works: Brighton, Ashford, Eastleigh. *Truro: Bradford Barton*, 1978. pp. 96, with 104 illus.

12540 FAIRCLOUGH, T. and WILLS, A. Southern Steam through the years. *Truro: Bradford Barton*, 1978. pp. 96. Intro & 104 illus with descrs.

12541 GOULD, D. Maunsell's S.R. steam passenger stock, 1923–1939. *Tarrant Hinton: Oakwood Press*, 1978. pp. 100, with 26 illus on 12 plates & many lists & diagrams.

12542 FAIRCLOUGH, T. and WILLS, A. Southern Steam in close-up. *Truro: Bradford Barton*, [1979]. pp. 96. Intro & 107 illus.

12543 HAWKINS, C. and REEVE, G. Historical survey of Southern sheds. *Oxford: Oxford Publishing Co.*, 1979. obl. format. pp. 156. Intro & map (pp. 1–4), & 190 illus with detailed commentaries and 115 layout plans & line drawings.

12544 PALLANT, N. Hither Green motive power depot. *Tarrant Hinton: Oakwood Press*,

1979. (Locomotion Papers, 119). pp. 50, with 17 illus on 8 plates, 3 tables, 3 allocation lists, map, plan & a bibliography (16 sources).

12545 RANSOME-WALLIS, P. Roaming the Southern rails. *London: Ian Allan*, 1979. la. 8°. pp. 128. Intro, by Eric Treacy, 264 illus with descrs, & an intro to each of the 8 sections; 2 maps on end papers.
Photographs by the author.

12546 BLOOM, A. Locomotives of the Southern Railway, written by Alan Bloom; compiled by David Williams. *Norwich: Jarrold*, 1980. (Jarrold Railway Series, 2). pp. [32], with 65 illus (53 col.), & a map. Text & illus extend onto covers.

12547 EVANS, J. Man of the Southern: Jim Evans looks back; edited by Peter Grafton. *London: Allen & Unwin*, 1980. pp. 102, with 59 illus & commentaries.
Memoirs of a locomotiveman, 1944 to his driving of the last steam-hauled train out of Waterloo Station, 6 July 1967.

12548 GOULD, D. Bulleid's S.R. steam passenger stock. [*Tarrant Hinton*]: *Oakwood Press*, 1980. pp. 80, with 23 illus, 23 dimensioned drawings & some detailed tables (pp. 65–80).

12549 RATCLIFFE, A. R. L. Bygone South Eastern Steam, compiled from the collection of A. R. L. Ratcliffe. *Chatham: John Hallewell*.
vol. 1, [Locomotives]. 1980. obl. format. pp. 57. Intro, map, & 52 illus (2 on covers) with descrs, & a 9-column list of details at end.
Photographs of locomotives & trains of the SER, SECR, Southern Rly & BR (SR).

12550 ROGERS, H. C. B. Bulleid Pacifics at work. *London: Ian Allan*, 1980. la. 8°. pp. 128, with over 200 illus, line drawings & diagrams, & a list of all the Bulleid Pacifics (pp. 124–6).

12551 WHITELEY, J. S. and MORRISON, G. W. The Southern remembered. *Oxford: Oxford Publishing Co.*, 1980. pp. [112]. Intro & 270 illus with descrs.

12552 WINKWORTH, D. W. Maunsell's Nelsons. *London: Allen & Unwin*, 1980. pp. 123, with 61 illus & dimensioned drawings, 18 logs of runs, & as appendix, 'Construction, modification and withdrawal dates' of the 16 locomotives of the Lord Nelson class.

Electrification

12553 ELECTRIC railway traction: Southern Railway electrification extension to Eastbourne and Hastings. *London: Railway Gazette*, 1935. pp. viii, 24, ix–xv, with many illus, diagrams & tables.
Supplement, *Railway Gazette*, June 28, 1935.

12554 SOUTHERN Railway electrification extension: Rochester, Chatham, Gillingham and Maidstone. *London: Railway Gazette*, 1939. (Electric Railway Traction Supplement, June 30, 1939). pp. 57–76, with illus, maps & diagrams.
pp. 58–9, 'The Medway group of lines', by Charles E. Lee.

12555 BAILEY, M. Switchover on the Southern. [*London*]: *The Times*, 1947. (Southern Electrification Supplement, 10 July 1947). pp. VIII.

Timetables (reprints)

12556 SOUTHERN RLY. WESTERN DIVISION. Working Timetables of Passenger & Freight Trains from 17th July 1932 and until further notice. *Waterloo Station (London): S. Rly*, 1932. [Republished as a facsimile reprint by] *Oxford Publishing Co.*, [1978]. pp. A–D, 1–79, E–Y.

12557 SOUTHERN RLY. WESTERN SECTION. Working Timetable Appendices, Western Section, 1934. *London: S. Rly*, 1934. [Republished as a facsimile reprint by] *Bradford Barton*, 1978. pp. 163.

West London Rly and the West London Extension Rly

12558 BORLEY, H. V. and KIDNER, R. W. The West London Railway and the W.L.E.R. *Lingfield: Oakwood Press*, 1969. (Oakwood Library of Railway History, 22). pp. 32, with 13 illus on 6 plates, 2 maps & 3 layout plans.

12559 JENKINSON, D. and ESSERY, R. J. Locomotive liveries of the LMS. *London: Roundhouse Books and Ian Allan*, 1967. pp. xiv, 234, with frontis, 15 col. panels on 3 plates, 160 illus on 48 plates & 9 composite diagrams (insignia, lettering, numerals, etc.), 40 tables and many lists and notes.

12560 SLINN, J. N. The Great Western Railway: locomotives, carriages, vans, wagons, buildings and signals, 1835–1947. *Bromley: Historical Model Railway Society*, 1967. (Livery Register of the H.M.R.S., no. 2). pp. 46, with 24 illus on 8 plates & a plate of GWR colours, & in text, 12 pp. of diagrams. Foreword by F. N. Hawksworth, Chief Mechanical Engineer, GWR, 1941–1947. Cover title: A Livery Register of the Historical Model Railway Society, no. 2: the Great Western Railway . . .

——— a much enlarged edn. Great Western Way: a description of distinctive features of the Great Western Railway, with particular reference to the liveries of locomotives, rolling stock, road vehicles, buildings, uniforms; an account of permanent way and signalling practice and notes on the original liveries of the companies it absorbed. *Frome: Historical Model Railway Society*, 1978. pp. vi, 274, with 333 illus, 50 composite drawings, a colour panel chart, 10 appendices & a bibliography (23 sources).

12561 TAVENDER, L. LSWR and Southern. *Bromley: Historical Model Railway Society*, 1970. (HMRS Livery Register, 3). pp. 76, with 24 illus on 8 plates, 25 groups of line drawings, 4 tables, a page of 18 colour palettes & 496 notes.

12562 DOW, G. Railway heraldry and other insignia. *Newton Abbot: David & Charles*, 1973. pp. 269, with 81 armorial devices in colour on 24 plates, and 110 in monochrome in text.
British and Irish railways.

12563 DOW, G. Midland style: a livery and decor register of the Midland Railway, its absorbed lines and its joint lines, to the end of 1922 . . . , with a contribution on Midland coaching stock by R. E. Lacy. *Bromley: Historical Model Railway Society*, 1975. pp. vi, 192, with 256 illus (photos, line drawings & diagrams), & 4 appendices, incl. a set of 14 colours.

12564 DYER, M. A history of British Railways diesel and electric locomotive liveries; edited by Michael Oakley; photographed by C. Bush . . . [*et al.*]. *Sutton Coldfield: Diesel & Electric Group*, 1979. magazine format. pp. 32, with 55 illus (13 col., incl. 5 on covers).
——— rev. edn. *D.&E. Group*, 1980. pp. 24 incl. covers, with 55 illus (13 col.). Photos supplied by C. Baker & 21 others.

Paintings, poster art and drawings

12565–91

12565 CONWAY, M. The elevation of poster art: an appreciation by Sir Martin Conway. *London: Eyre & Spottiswoode, for the London, Midland & Scottish Rly Co.*, [1925]. obl. format. pp. 10, & 18 col. plates of LMS posters. Cover title: Posters by Royal Academicians and other eminent artists.

The artists whose work is reproduced are: Maurice Grieffenhagen, Julius Olsson, Algernon Talmage, Arnesby Brown, Richard Jack, Stanhope Forbes, Norman Wilkinson (3), Sir David Murray, Sir William Orpen, D. Y. Cameron, G. Clausen, Cayley Robinson, L. Campbell Taylor, George Henry, Adrian Stokes, and Sir Bertram Mackennal.

12566 DESIGN in Modern Life and Industry: the year book of the Design & Industries Association, 1924–25, with an introduction by John Gloag. *London: Ernest Benn*, 1925. la. 8°. pp. 148, with 126 plates, incl. 20 of contemporary underground railway, tramway and railway design features, including posters.

12567 LEIGH, D. A Princely Path to Paris by the Golden Arrow . . . , illustrated by Christopher Clark. [*London: Sleeping Car Co.*, 1929?]. pp. 44, with 17 illus.

A travel brochure with noteworthy illustrations.

12568 TRUSSLER, D. J. Early buses and trams. *London: Hugh Evelyn*, 1964. la. obl. format. pp. [48]. Preface & 10 col. plates, each interleaved with a commentary and details.

Five buses and five tramcars are depicted and described; three of the tramcars are British, two are foreign.

12569 CADFRYN-ROBERTS, J. Coaches and trains, edited and introduced by John Cadfryn-Roberts. *London: Ariel Press*, 1965. (Golden Ariels, 7). pp. 12, & 20 col. plates, incl. 8 early railway prints.

12570 ELLIS, C. H. The splendour of Steam; with a foreword by Peter Allen. *London: Allen & Unwin*, 1965. obl. 8°. pp. 132, with col. frontis, 15 col. plates & 43 drawings.

Mostly British locomotives and trains.

12571 ELLIS, C. H. The engines that passed. *London: Allen & Unwin*, 1968. la. 8°. pp. 133, with col. frontis, 3 col. plates, 48 illus & 11 vignettes, all drawn by C. H. Ellis.

Steam locomotives, mostly British, but with some European examples.

12572 ELLIS, C. H. King Steam: selected railway paintings and drawings by C. Hamilton Ellis; edited and introduced by George Perry; captions by C. Hamilton Ellis. *London: Sunday Times Magazine*, 1971. la. obl.

8°. pp. 79, with 12 full-page col. illus, 17 full-page illus in monochrome, & 16 smaller illus in groups of 2 or 3, all of trains, British and foreign. A limited edition of 3000 copies.

12573 GAGE, J. Turner: 'Rain, Steam and Speed'. *London: Allen Lane*, 1972. (Art in Context series). pp. 99, with 51 monochrome illus & a folded col. plate of the painting at end.

A detailed study of the allegorical painting by J. M. W. Turner of a train crossing Maidenhead Bridge, GWR, in 1844, and upon the wider theme of the impact of railways upon the work of artists and writers, with contemporary quotations and (ch. 8, pp. 77–84), 'Wordsworth and the Morning Post', on the poet's opposition to the construction of the Kendal & Windermere Rly in that year.

12574 LE FLEMING, H. M. International locomotives, from the collection of paintings by the late H. M. Le Fleming; with descriptive material by A. E. Durrant; edited by J. B. Snell. *London: Institution of Mechanical Engineers*, 1972. obl. format. pp. 192, with 92 whole-page col. illus.

38 of the illustrations are of British railway locomotives. The Introduction is a biographical account of H. M. Le Fleming by R. Le Fleming.

12575 MAY, John, and MAY, Jennifer. Commemorative pottery, 1780–1900: a guide for collectors. *London: Heinemann*, 1972. pp. [viii], 180, with 250 illus.

ch. 5 (159–67), 'A note on railways', with 6 illus, and 2 on pp. 169–170.

12576 SYMES, R. and COLE, D. Railway architecture of the South East. *Reading; Osprey*, 1972. (Railway Architecture Series). pp. 128. Intro (pp. 7–15) & 42 drawings with commentaries.

Pen drawings of a selected 42 stations and other railway structures and detail on the Southern Rly in Kent, Surrey, Sussex & Hampshire, each with an historical & descriptive note. The Introduction provides a general historical commentary and the work is an objective (not imaginative) encapsulation of what is judged to be noteworthy (significant, striking, or characteristic) in 19th century railway architecture in this area.

12577 HEIRON, G. The majesty of British Steam: paintings by George Heiron; introduction by O. S. Nock. *London: Ian Allan*, 1973. la. obl. format. pp. [103]. Intro [3 pp.] & 48 col. plates, with descrs. by O. S. Nock on facing pages.

Locomotives with trains in the British railway environment, 1900–1951.

12578 SYMES, R. and COLE, D. Railway architecture of Greater London. *Reading: Osprey*, 1973. pp. 128. Intro (pp. 7–15) &

120 drawings of 62 stations and other structures, with commentaries.

A companion work to *Railway Architecture of the South East* (1972) by the same author/artists. The Introduction, like that of the former work is an historical commentary. Both works achieve more than photographs in conveying style and character.

12579 DARBY, M. Early railway prints from the collection of Mr and Mrs M. G. Powell, described, with an introduction, by Michael Darby. *London: H.M.S.O.*, 1974. obl. format. pp. [x], 73.

An exhibition of 37 prints in the Dept. of Prints & Drawings, Victoria & Albert Museum. The prints are reproduced in monochrome, accompanying notes providing background historical information to each picture.

The collection of Arthur Underwood, comprising over 200 prints, latterly the property of Mr & Mrs Powell, from which the selection was made, was sold by Phillips in 1977 (*See* 12587).

12580 HILL, J. The Railway Picture Book: paintings by Jack Hill; described by O. S. Nock. *London: A.&C. Black*, 1975. la. obl. format. pp. [40] & [16] leaves of plates.

The 16 paintings were originally reproduced in smaller format in some of the books of O. S. Nock's series *Railways of the World*. Five are of British railway scenes.

12581 SHEPHERD, D. The man who loves giants: an artist among elephants and engines; David Shepherd's autobiography. *Cape Town, London: Purnell*, 1975. pp. 164.

pp. 84–102, 'Steam-age love affair'. David Shepherd's paintings of railway locomotives, with 19 illus.

12582 TRIBUTE to British Steam. *Shepperton: Ian Allan*, [1975]. la. 8°. pp. [60]. 85 col. illus (paintings & photographs).

Paintings chiefly by George Heiron; photographs chiefly by Peter Williams.

12583 LONDON TRANSPORT. London Transport posters [presented, with an historical commentary and notes by] Michael F. Levey, with an introduction by Roy Strong. *London: Phaidon Press, and London Transport*, 1976. la. 8°. pp. [16], 80.

80 illustrations (64 in col.) being reproductions of L.T. and earlier (i.e. pre-1933) posters. A different work with the same title was published by London Transport in 1963 (*See* 756 or 7457).

12584 SHACKLETON, J. T. The golden age of the railway poster. *London: New English Library*, 1976. la. 8°. pp. 128, with 148 illus (116 col.) & illus on end papers.

12585 CUNEO, T. The Mouse and its Master: the life and work of Terence Cuneo. (Foreword by Prince Philip, Duke of Edinburgh: preface by 'E.H.') *London: New Cavendish Books*, 1977. (Grand Format series.) la. obl. format. pp. 244.

Includes biographical background to his railway poster work and his subsequent railway environment paintings. In the section 'Fire, water, steel and labour' there are 60 reproductions of railway scenes (pp. 157–86), 41 of which are in colour.

12586 ELLIS, C. H. Railway art; edited by Susan Hyman. *London: Ash & Grant*. 1977. pp. 144, with col. frontis & 180 illus (45 col.).

12587 PHILLIPS, SON AND NEALE. Fine early railway prints, to be sold by auction on Monday November 7th, 1977 . . . Sale no. 21,471. *London: Phillips*, [1977]. pp. 46, with 62 illus on 31 plates, with descrs.

The collection of Arthur Underwood, comprising over 200 prints of railway scenes, 1830–1865. A selection of 37 was loaned to the Victoria & Albert Museum, London, in 1974 where they were exhibited as 'Early Railway Prints' (*See* 12579).

12588 SCHOFIELD, R. and MARTIN, J. The Story of Merddin Emrys and the Festiniog Railway. *Cheam: Travel About Books*, 1977. sm. 8°. pp. [16], with 20 col. drawings.

An exquisite presentation of the history of the Festiniog Rly: pictures by Roy Schofield, story by Joe Martin.

12589 WESTON, D. The Weston Collection. *London: New Cavendish Books*, 1977. obl. format. pp. [52], consisting of 24 groups of paintings in colour by David Weston, with descriptions.

Descriptive catalogue of a travelling exhibition of paintings depicting the history of the British steam locomotive.

12590 FEARNLEY, A. and TREACY, E. Steam in the North: an enthusiast's guide, featuring the paintings of Alan Fearnley and the photographs of Eric Treacy. *Clapham (N. Yorks): Dalesman*, 1978. sm. obl. format. pp. 40, with 12 paintings (2 on covers) & 9 photographs; text on facing pages; introduction by David Joy.

12591 REES, G. Early railway prints: a social history of the railways from 1825 to 1850. *Oxford: Phaidon*, 1980. obl. 8°. pp. 128. Intro (pp. 9–26), bibliography (17 sources), & 95 plates (31 col.), each with details and historical commentary by Gareth Rees.

O THE RAILWAY IN LITERATURE
(Belles-lettres)
12592–12715

Arranged alphabetically by author within each section

Reference sources 12592–93
Selections 12594–95
Autobiography and memoirs 12596–99
Essays 12600–7
Fiction:
   (a) General 12608–27
   (b) Novels of adventure, crime and detection 12628–72
      (Reference source, 12628)
Verse 12673–12715 (Anthologies 12673–75)
Individual works and collections of individual authors 12676–12715

Reference sources

12592 PEART, D. A. Literature and the Railway in the nineteenth and twentieth centuries: a thesis for the degree of Master of Arts in the School of English Language and Literature, University of Liverpool. 1964. pp. 306.
> Section A (pp. 2–65): 'Books on railways as such': a commentary on 125 works.
> ch. 1, The railway guide book
> ch. 2, General books relating to the early days of railways
> ch. 3, Some of the biographical material relating to the early days of railways
> ch. 4, Later general books about railways
> ch. 5, Locomotive books
> ch. 6, Some important railway histories
> ch. 7, Allen, Nock and Ellis: the most influential modern writers on railways proper
> Section B (pp. 66–294): 'The Railway in English Literature': an analytical survey of 224 books and poems.
> ch. 8, Dickens and the Railway
> ch. 9, Railways in the nineteenth century novel and short story
> ch. 10, Railways in the twentieth century novel and short story
> ch. 11, Railways in the detective story
> ch. 12, Carlyle and Ruskin
> ch. 13, Some railway essayists
> ch. 14, Nineteenth century magazines
> ch. 15, Poems celebrating or deploring the coming of the Railway
> ch. 16, Poems about the Train
> ch. 17, The railway scene in poetry
> ch. 18, Railway love poems
> ch. 19, Poems on underground railways
> ch. 20, John Betjeman's railway poems
> ch. 21, Railwaymen's verse
> The index entries are under author and title arranged chronologically within a framework of subject headings.

12593 SCOWCROFT, P. L. Railways and detective fiction, *in* Journal of the Railway and Canal Historical Society, vol. 23, no. 3 (November 1977), pp. 87–93, with 34 notes.
—— An addendum, *in* J.R.C.H.S., vol. 25, no. 1 (March 1979), pp. 32–5, with 11 notes.
—— Railways and detective fiction: further observations *in* J.R.C.H.S., vol. 27, no. 3 (November 1981), pp. 16–18, with 10 notes.

Selections

12594 BRIGHTFIELD, M. F. Victorian England in its novels, 1840–1870; introduction by Gordon N. Ray; prefatory notes by Bradford A. Booth. *Los Angeles: University of California Library*, 1968. 4 vols.
> vol. 3, ch. 8, pp. 188–211: 'Railroad travel': extracts selected from imaginative literature illustrating a variety of effects which train travel has upon the passenger: discomforts of early carriages, the effects of speed and rapidly changing scenery, the tedium of rail journeys, crowded compartments, the confusion of a busy terminus, refreshment rooms, waiting at stations, accidents to trains, etc.

12595 ROLT, L. T. C. Best railway stories, edited, with an Introduction, by L. T. C. Rolt. *London: Faber*, 1969. pp. 256.
> The Signalman, by Charles Dickens.
> [The Fracas at Paddington], by Anthony Trollope, *from his* The Small House at Allington (1864).
> .007, by Rudyard Kipling
> The Bruce-Partington Plans, by A. Conan Doyle
> The Story Teller, by 'Saki'
> Pipes in Arcady, by 'Q'
> Poisson d'Avril, by E. O. Somerville & Martin Ross
> 5.27 to Dundee, by A. J. Cronin
> Death of a Train, by Freeman Wills Crofts
> The Garside Fell Disaster, by L. T. C. Rolt
> The Trains, by Robert Aickman
> Ninety-Eight Up, by John Masters
> The Strike, by Raymond Williams
> Last Journey, by Leo Tolstoy
> The Yellow Mail Story, by Frank H. Spearman
> Mrs Union Station, by Doug Welch

Autobiography and memoirs

12596 DEWES, S. 'The Hadleigh Express'. ch.2 of his A Suffolk Childhood. *London: Hutchinson*, 1959.
> Hadleigh to Bentley, G.E.R., 1916 or 1917. A childhood footplate ride recalled.

12597 HUGHES, M. V. A London Child of the Seventies. *Oxford: Oxford University Press*, 1934. pp. 173.

ch. 9 (pp. 85–91) 'A long railway journey'. Paddington to Camborne, Cornwall, by GWR, 9 am to 9 pm, and on pp. 321–8 in ch: 11, Camborne to Aberdovey in 1888, an account of a derailment at Glandovey Junction (now Dovey Junction) observed when en route from Aberdovey to Machynlleth, and a trip on the Corris Rly.
—— Re-issued as part one of the trilogy: *A London Family, 1870—1900* (O.U.P., 1946). pp. viii, 594 (pp. 1–141).

12598 KILVERT, F. Kilvert's Diary: selections from the diary of the Rev. Francis Kilvert, 1 January 1870—13 March 1879: chosen, edited and introduced by William Plomer. *London: Cape*, 1938–40. 3 vols.
—— new edn, 1960; reprinted with index, 1961.
Includes 44 entries relating to railways, mostly the GWR, in Radnorshire and Herefordshire.
—— abridged edn in 1 vol., 1944; reprinted 1947, 1950 & 1956.

12599 KIRKUP, J. The Only Child: an autobiography of infancy. *London: Collins*, 1957. pp. 192, with frontis (portrait).
pp. 60–3: tram journeys in South Shields, 1920s (also on pp. 114–5); pp. 168–70: a ride on the 'scenic railway'.

Essays

12600 BETJEMAN, J. Metro-land: a script for television, written and narrated by John Betjeman, *in* The Best of Betjeman, selected by John Guest. *London: John Murray*, 1978. pp. 215–36.
A slightly abbreviated version.

12601 CARLYLE, T. Hudson's statue (no. 7 of his Latter-Day Pamphlets). *London: Chapman & Hall*, 1850.
A discourse on the proposal to erect a public statue of George Hudson (1800–1871). 'Foolish railway people gave him two millions and thought it not enough without a statue, to boot!' (In, e.g., the *Centenary Edition of the Collected Works*, 1896–9, this essay is on pp. 254–92).

12602 KNOX, R. A. A Ramble in Barsetshire, *in his* Essays in Satire (*London: Sheed & Ward*, 1928). ch. 6, pp. 179–98.
A geographical interpretation of Anthony Trollope's *Barsetshire*, with a map showing conjectured roads and railways.

12603 MORTON, H. V. The Engine Driver, *in his* The Spell of London (*Methuen*, 1926), pp. 149–52.
A footplate ride through the night, and thoughts on the romance, comedy or pathos which accompanies each passenger journeying in the train.

12604 MORTON, H. V. From Bow to Ealing, *in his* The Heart of London (*Methuen*, 1925), pp. 133–6.
A journey in the motorman's cab of an underground train on the District Line.

12605 MORTON, H. V. The Last Tube, *in his* The Spell of London (*Methuen*, 1926), pp. 209–13.
Observations on home-going passengers, Northern Line, London Underground.

12606 MORTON, H. V. When the Tubes Stop, *in his* The Nights of London (*Methuen*, 1926), pp. 11–15.
Night life on London Underground: the maintenance workers.

12607 SALA, G. A. Twice Round the Clock; or, the hours of the day and night in London. *London: W. McConnell*, [1859]. pp. xii, 392. Reprinted, with an added Introduction by Philip Collins (pp. 7–22). *Leicester: Leicester University Press*, 1971. (Victorian Library Series).
pp. 41–65, 'Seven o'clock a.m.: a parliamentary train', including pp. 59–65, a social commentary from observing waiting passengers at Euston Station. 'What a motley assemblage of men, women and children . . . , yet all marked with the homogeneous penny-a-mile stamp of poverty.'

Fiction: (a) General

12608 ANDERSON, J. R. L. A Sprig of Sea Lavender: a novel. *Gollancz*, 1978. pp. [324].

12609 BARNUM, F. C. 'An incident of English railway travel', *in her* A Shocking Example and other sketches. *Philadelphia: J. B. Lippincott*, 1889. pp. 224–39.
An encounter on a train journey.

12610 BRIDGES, T. C. Driver Dick, the hero of the line. *London: G. Newnes*, [1916]. (Newnes Adventure Library, no. 6). pp. 128.

12611 CARROLL, L. Through the Looking Glass. *London: Macmillan*, 1872. pp. 224.
In ch. 3, The train journey episode, beginning: '"Tickets, please!" said the Guard'.

12612 ETON, R. The Faithful Years. *London: Nicholson & Watson*, 1939. pp. 376.
Country life and local railway affairs in the late 19th century and up to the 1930s.

12613 FARRIMOND, J. The Unending Track: a novel. *London: Harrap*, 1970. pp. 237.
Centred upon the life of a navvy engaged in building the Liverpool & Manchester Rly in the late 1820s. The battle to overcome Chat Moss is a feature of the story.

12614 HAMMOND, B. Chums of the Footplate. *London: G. Newnes*, [1919]. (Newnes Adventure Library, 58). pp. 64.

12615 LEAHCIMRAC, J. John Ingram; or, railway life behind the curtain, by J. Leahcimrac [i.e. J. Carmichael]. *Glasgow: W. & R. Holmes; London: Simpkin, Marshall*, 1889. pp. 192.
A moral tale set in the Glasgow area and centred upon the 'hard and down-trodden condition' of railwaymen of that day.

12616 MACDONALD, M. The Rich are with You

Always. *London: Hodder & Stoughton*, 1977. pp. 483.

A sequel to his *World from Rough Stones* (1974), continuing the saga of the railway navvy John Stevenson who became a contractor. The story now moves forward through the Railway Mania period (mid 1840's) and includes references to George Hudson.

12617 MACDONALD, M. World from Rough Stones. *Hodder & Stoughton*, 1974. pp. 567.

A novel built around the events and personalities surrounding the construction of the Summit Tunnel, Littleborough, on the Manchester & Leeds Rly, 1839–41.

12618 POPE, R. The Model-Railway Men; illustrated by Gareth Floyd. *London: Macdonald*, 1970. pp. 95.

A tale about model railway enthusiasts.

12619 POPE, R. The Model-Railway Men take over . . . ; illustrated by Gareth Floyd. *London: Macdonald*, 1971. pp. 95.

12620 ROLT, L. T. C. The Garside Fell Disaster, *in his* Sleep No More: twelve stories of the supernatural. *London: Constable*, 1948. pp. 83–93.

Also published in *Best Railway Stories*, ed. by L. T. C. Rolt (*Faber*, 1969), and in *Crime on the Lines*, ed. by Bryan Morgan (*Routledge*, 1975).

12621 ROWLANDS, A. God's Wonderful Railway. *London: British Broadcasting Corporation*.

[pt. 1], Permanent Way. 1980. pp. 111, with 14 chapter-heading silhouettes & a map.

[pt. 2], Clear Ahead. 1980. pp. 103, with 14 chapter-heading silhouettes & a map.

The story of a railway family on the Severn Valley line (GWR), 1858–1862. Adapted from the BBC TV series *God's Wonderful Railway*. An appendix 'Railway signalling' explains the historical development of working trains through sections of a line. Illustrator, Jo Worth.

12622 SURTEES, R. Handley Cross; or, the Spa Hunt: a sporting tale. *London: H. Colburn*, 1843. 3 vols.

In vol. 1, on pp. 155–64, a description of the arrival of a train, the setting-down of passengers, including Mr & Mrs Jorrocks and their daughter Belinda, and the departure of the train.

12623 TROLLOPE, A. The Prime Minister. *London: Chapman & Hall*, 1876. 4 vols.

ch. 60: 'Tenway Junction'. The environment of Willesden Junction, LNWR.

12624 TURNER, P. Steam on the line; illustrated by Trevor Ridley. *London: Oxford University Press*, 1968. pp. 162.

A novel for older children, set in the North of England, about a narrow-gauge railway, with some features akin to the Festiniog Rly in North Wales. Period, mid 19th century.

12625 UPWARD, E. The Railway Accident, and other stories. *London: Heinemann*, 1969. pp. xxx, 222. Introduction (pp. vii–xxx) by W. H. Sellers.

p. 142, 'The Railway Accident'. Mental and moral disorientation before and after two imaginary catastrophes. W. H. Sellers's Introduction includes a commentary on this story.

12626 WELLS, H. G. War of the Worlds. *London: Heinemann*, 1898. pp. viii, 304.

In ch. 14, local train services to Woking and Weybridge, LSWR, are disturbed by invaders from Mars.

12627 WOOD, H. Johnny Ludlow, by Mrs. Henry Wood [Ellen Wood]. *London: Richard Bentley*, 1874. 3 vols.

vol. 1, ch. 6 (pp. 156–91), 'Lease, the pointsman'.

An accident caused by overwork and long hours of duty.

vol. 1, ch. 8 (pp. 229–60), 'Going through the tunnel'.

A previously extinguished carriage light enables a pickpocket & accomplice to use an excited lap-dog to cause confusion in a tunnel, LBSCR.

Fiction: (b) Novels of adventure, crime and detection

12628 SCOWCROFT, P. L. Railways and detective fiction, *in* Journal of the Railway & Canal Historical Society, vol. 23, no. 3 (November 1977), pp. 87–93, with 34 notes.

—— An addendum *in J.R.C.H.S.*, vol. 25, no. 1 (March 1979), pp. 32–5, with 11 notes.

—— Railways and detective fiction: further observations, *in J.R.C.H.S.*, vol. 27, no. 3 (November 1981), pp. 16, 18, with 10 notes.

12629 MORGAN, B. Crime on the Lines: an anthology of mystery short stories with a railway setting, edited by Bryan Morgan; illustrated by Robin Wiggins. *London: Routledge & Kegan Paul*, 1975. pp. xiv, 173, with 12 illus.

12 stories preceded by an introduction and bibliographical notes (pp. vii–xiv):

1, The Signalman, by Charles Dickens
2, How he cut his Stick, by M. McD. Bodkin
3, The Adventure of the Bruce-Partington Plans, by A. Conan Doyle
4, The Case of Oscar Brodski, by R. Austin Freeman
5, Sir Gilbert Murrell's Picture, by V. L. Whitechurch
6, The Eighth Lamp, by Roy Vickers
7, The Mystery of the Sleeping-Car Express, by Freeman Wills-Crofts
8, Crime on the Footplate, by Freeman Wills-Crofts
9, Beware of the Trains, by Edmund Crispin
10, The Very Silent Traveller, by Paul Tabori
11, Mr. Duckworth's Night Out, by Michael Gilbert
12, The Garside Fell Disaster, by L. T. C. Rolt

12630 BODKIN, M. M. How He Cut his Stick. *In* Crime on the Lines, ed. by Bryan Morgan (1975). pp. 13–21.

12631 BROCK, L. The Slip Carriage Mystery. *London: Collins*, [1928]. (Colonel Gore's Cases, 4). pp. 304.

12632 BURTON, M. Death in the Tunnel. *London: Collins*, [1936]. pp. 252.

12633 CARR, J. D. The Case of the constant Suicides. *London: Hamish Hamilton*, 1941. pp. 287.
On a Euston to Glasgow express, period, 1940–41.

12634 CARR, J. D. Scandal at High Chimneys. *London: Hamish Hamilton*, 1959. pp. 235.
Set in 1867 and featuring Paddington Station and the characters depicted in W. P. Frith's famous painting of 1862.

12635 CHRISTIE, A. At Bertram's Hotel. *London: Collins*, [1965]. pp. 255.
ch. 8 is virtually a re-play of the 'Great Train Robbery' of 1963, the train in the story being, however, not the Glasgow to Euston T.P.O. but the Irish Mail.

12636 CHRISTIE, A. 4.50 from Paddington. *London: Collins*, 1957. pp. 256.

12637 CHRISTIE, A. The Plymouth Express, *in her* Poirot's Early Cases. *London: Collins*, 1974. pp. 253.

12638 COLE, G. D. H. and COLE, M. A Lesson in Crime and other stories. *London: Collins*, [1933]. pp. 284.

12639 CONAN DOYLE, A. The Man with the Watches, *in his* Tales of Terror and Mystery. *London: John Murray*, [1922]. pp. 310.
Setting, on an express train from Euston to Manchester, LNWR.

12640 CREASEY, J. Murder on the Line. *London: Hodder & Stroughton*, 1960. pp. 188.

12641 CRISPIN, E. Beware of the Trains: sixteen stories by Edmund Crispin. *London: Gollancz*, 1953. pp. 192.
pp. 9–20: 'Beware of the Trains': revised version of a story first published in the London *Evening Standard*. After bringing his train to halt at a station the motorman disappears.

12642 CRISPIN, E. The Case of the Gilded Fly. *London: Gollancz*, 1944. pp. 158.
The railway interest is confined to the Prologue and the Epilogue and concerns the GWR.

12643 CRISPIN, E. Holy Disorders. *London: Gollancz*, 1945. pp. 175.
Includes a description of Paddington in wartime and of war-time conditions for railway passengers.

12644 CROFTS, F. W. The Pit Prop Syndicate. *London: W. Collins*, [1922]. pp. 304.

12645 CROSS, T. Footplate Luck: stories of railway adventure at home and abroad . . . ; illustrated by E. S. Hodgson. *London: Blackie*, [1922]. pp. 256, with 6 plates.
14 short stories.

12646 CROSS, T. Railway Adventure: adapted from stories by T. Cross. *London & Glasgow: Blackie*, 1935. (Blackie's Graded Story Readers). pp. 96.
From stories in his collection entitled *Footplate Luck*.

12647 CROSS, T. Railway Yarns: railway adventure at home and abroad. *London & Glasgow: Blackie*, [1936]. pp. 190.
Ten short stories originally published in his *Footplate Luck*.

12648 DRAKE, M. The Ocean Sleuth. *London: Methuen*, 1915. pp. 311.
pp. 158–73, 200–26, crime involving the stopping of a train in Parson's Tunnel, Dawlish, and a visit to the scene by investigators.

12649 FARJEON, J. J. The 5.18 Mystery. *London: Collins*, 1929. pp. 256.
Involuntary involvement in a planned crime on the 5.18 Liverpool St (London) to Cromer train.

12650 FLETCHER, J. S. The Charing Cross Mystery. *London: Herbert Jenkins*, 1923. pp. 312.

12651 FREEMAN, R. A. The Stolen Ingots, *in his* Dr. Thorndyke's Casebook. *London: Hodder & Stoughton*, 1923. pp. 317.

12652 FREEMAN, R. A. When Rogues Fall Out. *London: Hodder & Stoughton*, 1932. pp. 320.
A murder in Greenhithe tunnel, SECR.

12653 GASH, J. Spend Game. *London: Collins*, 1980. pp. 204.
The first train on the opening day of a new railway in East Anglia in 1847 is halted by a tunnel landslip. A mystery story, with two early railway enthusiasts appearing briefly half-way through.

12654 GILBERT, M. Mr. Duckworth's Night Out. *London: Routledge*, 1975.
Also in *Crime on the Lines*, ed. by Bryan Morgan (1975). pp. 151–65. First published in *Argosy*, 1959.

12655 The GREAT Railway Mystery. *London: G. Newnes*, [1919]. (Tubby Haig, Detective series, no. 59 of the Bulldog Library). pp. 49.

12656 HASTINGS, M. Cork on The Telly. *London: M. Joseph*, 1966. pp. 232.
A theft from a BBC studio leads to events on a sleeping-car express to the North West.

12657 HINCKS, C. M. Danger Signals. *London: G. Newnes*, [1920]. (Newnes Adventure Library, no. 72). pp. 96.
A signal-box drama.

12658 HOLT, H. The Midnight Mail: a mystery novel. *London: Harrap*, 1931. pp. 283.

12659 KING, F. Death on the 8.45, *in A Century of Detective Stories*, ed. by G. K. Chesterton (1975). pp. 183–200.

12660 ORCZY, E. [Baroness Orczy]. The Old Man in the Corner. *London: Greening & Co.*, 1909. pp. 340.
ch. 10, The Mysterious Death on the Underground Railway (Metropolitan Rly).

12661 PHILLPOTTS, E. My Adventure in the Flying Scotsman: a romance of the London and North Western Railway shares. *London: J. Hogg*, 1888. pp. 63.
An early railway 'detective' story, culminating in a journey from Euston to Carlisle on the 'Flying Scotsman'—a popular name for the West Coast sleeping car express of the LNWR in the 1880s. *See* O. S. Nock's *Railway Reminiscences of the Interwar Years* (1980), p. 57.

12662 PIRATES of the Line. *London: G. Newnes*, [1919]. (Joe Pickford Library, no. 74). pp. 64. On cover, and as running headline on verso pages: 'Joe Pickford, the Fleet Street Sleuth'.
Crime on the 'Great West Counties Rly' solved by Joe Pickford and his assistant, 'Click'.

12663 RHODE, J. Death on the Boat Train. *London: Collins*, 1940. pp. 252.

12664 RHODE, J. The Elusive Bullet, *in* Great Short Stories of Detection, Mystery and Horror, ed. by Dorothy L. Sayers. 2nd series. *London: Victor Gollancz*, 1931. pp. 329–43.
Crime on the London, Tilbury & Southend line (LMS), between Rainham and Purfleet.

12665 RHODE, J. Tragedy on the Line. *London: Collins*, 1931. (A Crime Club Novel). pp. 252.

12666 'SAPPER'. The Mystery of the Slip Coach, *in his* Ronald Standish. *London: Hodder & Stoughton*, 1933, pp. 163–89.

12667 SAYERS, D. L. The Documents in the Case. *New York: Brewer & Warren*, 1930. pp. 304. (*London: Gollancz*, 1935. pp. 285).
The railway incidence in this story is brief but the locality is clearly defined and in some detail: to Newton Abbot on the Moretonhampstead branch, GWR.

12668 SAYERS, D. L. The Five Red Herrings. *London: Gollancz*, 1931. pp. 351.
A Lord Peter Wimsey story with important railway connotations (LMS, Galloway, late 1920s).

12669 SAYERS, D. L. One Too Many, *from* Hangman's Holiday [short stories]. *London: Gollancz*, 1933. pp. 288.

12670 SINSTADT, G. Whisper in a Lonely Place. *London: John Long*, 1966. pp. 184.

12671 VAUGHAN, M. The Discretion of Dominick Ayres. *London: Martin, Secker & Warburg*, 1976. pp. 243.

12672 WHITECHURCH, V. L. The Adventures of Captain Ivan Koravitch. *Edinburgh & London: W. Blackwood*, 1925. pp. vi, 307.
One of the adventures concerns a train journey to Hastings featuring, in particular, Bo-Peep Junction.

Verse: anthologies

12673 WARBURG, J. The Industrial Muse: the Industrial Revolution in English poetry: an anthology compiled, with introduction and comment, by Jeremy Warburg and decorated by Roy Morgan. *London: London University Press*, 1958. pp. xxxv, 174, with 204 notes & a bibliography (17 sources).
Of the 77 examples selected (1754–1954), 30 or more are derived from the railway environment or refer to some aspect of it. The Introduction (pp. xvii–xxxv) is noteworthy and the notes generous. Furthermore, each poem or extract is introduced by a commentary on writer and subject, thus enabling it to be experienced more readily within the contemporary setting.

12674 HOPKINS, K. The poetry of railways: an anthology selected and introduced by Kenneth Hopkins. *London: L. Frewin*, 1966. pp. 271, with an index of authors & titles and of first lines.

12675 CARR, S. The poetry of railways, edited by Samuel Carr. *London: Batsford*, 1978. pp. 88, with frontis, 4 col. plates & 29 illus in text.
Intro & 53 poems, popular ballads and an extract from *Dombey & Son* (Charles Dickens). American and British authors, and one Japanese.

Verse: individual works and collections of single authors

12676 ABSE, D. After a Departure, *in his* Poems: Golders Green. *London: Hutchinson*, 1962, on pp. 48–9.
'Intimate god of stations . . .'

12677 ABSE, D. Not Adlestrop, *in his* Collected Poems, 1948–1976. *London: Hutchinson*, 1977, on p. 106.
'Not Adlestrop, no—besides, the name hardly matters. Nor did I languish in June heat . . .'

12678 ABSE, D. Shunters, *in his* Poems: Golders Green. *London: Hutchinson*, 1962, on p. 20.
'The colour of grief, and thoroughly tame . . .'

12679 ANDERSON, A. A Song of Labour and other poems. *Dundee: Advertiser Office*, 1873. pp. vii, 200.
Includes: A Song of Labour; The Engine; On the Engine Again; On the Engine in the Night-Time.

12680 ARMSTRONG, M. D. After the Journey, *in his* The Buzzards and other poems. *London: Martin Secker*, 1921, on pp. 26–7.
'Between red firelight and yellow lamplight seated . . .'

12681 BETJEMAN, J. Dilton Marsh Halt, *in his* A Nip in the Air. *London: John Murray*, 1974, on pp. 38–9.

'Was it worth keeping the Halt open | We thought as we looked at the sky . . .'

12682 BETJEMAN, J. Great Central Railway: Sheffield Victoria to Banbury. [Poem] *in his* High and Low. *London: John Murray*, 1966, on pp. 22–4.
'"Unmitigated England" came swinging down the line . . .'

12683 BRANDLING and Ridley, *in* Rhymes of the Northern Bards: being a collection of old and new songs and poems peculiar to the counties of Newcastle upon Tyne, Northumberland and Durham, edited by John Bell junior. *Newcastle: J. Bell via M. Angus & Son*, 1812. pp. 328, on p. 300.
'Brandling for ever and Ridley for aye . . .'

12684 BROWN, A. L. J. Railway ditties. [*Saltley*]: *the author*, [between 1892 & 1923]. sm. 8°. pp. 15. Title from cover. No Introduction.
Seven sets of verses on work-a-day aspects of railway life, partly associated with Saltley locomotive depot and ending with 'A driver's lament on the abolition of the Broad Gauge'. The name on the cover, assumed to be that of the author, but which could be that of the compiler of these verses, is given as 'Arthur Leoline Jenkyn Brown, B.A., LL.B.'.

12685 BROWNING, R. 'A tune was born in my head last week | Out of the thump-thump and the shriek-shriek | Of the train . . .' lines 249–59 of his poem Christmas Eve and Easter Day (1850), 1040 lines. *In* Robert Browning: the poems, ed. by John Pettigrew, vol. 1. *Harmondsworth: Penguin*, 1981. on p. 469.

12686 CASWELL, A. S. and ROCHE, T. W. E. Through Western Windows: verses of the G.W.R., with drawings by D. J. Smith. *Bracknell: Town & Country Press*, 1969. pp. 39, with 12 drawings. 28 poems.

12687 CHURCH, R. S.R., *in his* Mood without Measure, (a group of poems in free verse). *London: Faber*, 1927. Reprinted *in his* Collected Poems. *London: J. M. Dent*, 1948, on p. 88.

12688 COLERIDGE, M. The Train, *in* The Collected Poems of Mary Coleridge, edited with an introduction by Theresa Whistler. *London: Rupert Hart-Davis*, 1954. no. 158, on p. 180.
'A green eye—and a red—in the dark . . .'

12689 The COLLIER'S Rant. *In* The Northumberland Garland; or, Newcastle Nightingale: a matchless collection of famous songs, [collected and edited by J. Ritson]. *Newcastle: Elliot*, 1793. sm. 8°.
pp. 67–8: Song 13, The Collier's Rant.
Second verse begins: 'As me and my marrow was putting the tram . . .'.

12690 CORNFORD, F. Figures on the Platform, *in* her Collected Poems. *London: Cresset Press*, 1954, on pp. 97–8.

'Travelling at night no man has any home Beyond the station's melancholy dome . . .'

12691 DAVIDSON, J. Brockenhurst Station, *in* The Poems of John Davidson, edited by Andrew Turnbull, vol. 2. *Edinburgh & London: Scottish Academic Press*, 1973. (Association for Scottish Literary Studies, Publication no. 3). no. 212, on pp. 474–6. Notes on p. 529.
'Early on Easter Monday . . .' An uncompleted poem.

12692 DAVIDSON, J. Rail and Road, *in* The Poems of John Davidson, edited by Andrew Turnbull, vol. 1. *Edinburgh & London: Scottish Academic Press*, 1973. (Association for Scottish Literary Studies, Publication no. 2). no. 134, on pp. 181–4, 133 lines, beginning:
'March Many-Weathers, bluff and affable . . .'

12693 DAVIDSON, J. Railway Stations, *in* The Poems of John Davidson, edited by Andrew Turnbull, vol. 2. *Edinburgh & London: Scottish Academic Press*, 1973. (Association for Scottish Literary Studies, Publication no. 3). no. 176, on pp. 434–43. Notes & commentary on pp. 524–5.
Two poems: London Bridge (106 lines), 'Much tolerance and genial strength of mind . . .'; Liverpool Street (342 lines), 'Through crystal roofs the sunlight fell . . .'

12694 DAVIDSON, J. Song of a Train, *in his* Ballads and Songs. *John Lane the Bodley Head*, 1894, on pp. 103–6.
'A monster taught | To come to hand | Amain . . .'

12695 DAVIDSON, J. Southampton West, *in* The Poems of John Davidson, edited by Andrew Turnbull, vol. 2. *Edinburgh & London: Scottish Academic Press*, 1973. (Association for Scottish Literary Studies, Publication no. 3). no. 211, on pp. 473–4. Notes on p. 529.
'I sauntered in the station a while . . .' An uncompleted poem.

12696 DURRELL, L. Night Express, *in his* Collected Poems, 1931–1974, edited by James A. Brigham. rev. edn. *London: Faber*, 1980, on pp. 250–1.
'Night falls. The dark expresses . . .'

12697 HARDAKER, J. The Aeropteron; or, Steam Carriage: a poem. *Keighley: printed for the author by R. Aked, and sold in London by William Crofts*, 1830. sm. 8°. pp. 24.
In 35 stanzas, beginning:
'I sing of scenes which science in its pride
Inspir'd with genius to the world reveals
The iron pave, where *Aeroptera* glide
Like *Phaeton's Chariot* with its flaming wheels.'
A footnote explains the term 'Aeropteron' as a Greek compound derived from 'air' and 'wing'.
The poem is an exultation of railways and the Frontispiece is a drawing of the *Rocket* and carriage *Queen Adelaide* of the Liverpool & Manchester Rly (1830).

12698 HENLEY, W. E. We Flash across the Level
(no. XXI of his Echoes, 1872–89), *in his*
Poems, vol. 1 *David Nutt*, 1908, on p. 145.
'We flash across the level . . .'

12699 KNOX, E. V. The Everlasting Percy; or,
Mr John Masefield on the Railway Centenary, *in his* Poems of Impudence by 'EVOE'
[E. V. Knox]. *London: T. Fisher Unwin*,
1926.
'I used to be a fearful lad | The things I did were
downright bad | . . . For several years I was so
wicked | I used to go without a ticket . . .'

12700 LARKIN, P. Whitsun Weddings. [Title
poem in his collection, The Whitsun Wed-
dings]. *London: Faber*, 1964, pp. 21–3.
'That Whitsun, I was late getting away . . .' A
train journey through Lincolnshire to London.

12701 LEWIS, C. D. Transitional Poem. *London:
Hogarth Press*, 1929. (Hogarth Living
Poets, 9).
no. 20 (pp. 42–3): 'How often, watching the
windy boughs . . .'.

12702 MAXWELL, H. A Railway Rubaiyyat.
Cambridge: Golden Head Press, 1968. pp.
54.
Verses (quatrains) 'to evoke the lost magic of
the steam engine upon the railways'.

12703 MONRO, H. Journey, *in his* Collected
Poems, edited by Alido Monro. *London:
Duckworth*, 1970, on pp. 116–9.
'How many times I nearly miss the train . . .'

12704 PLOMER, W. The Last Train, *in his* Taste
and Remember. *London: Jonathan Cape*,
1966, on pp. 25–6.
'Suddenly awake at two . . .' Thoughts on
hearing the last train before closure of a line.

12705 ROSSETTI, D. G. A Trip to Paris and
Belgium, *in* The Poems of Dante Gabriel
Rossetti, edited by William H. Rossetti.
London: Ellis & Elvey, 1895, on pp. 255–
60.
part 1: London to Folkestone:
'A constant keeping-past of shaken trees . . .'

12706 ROUSE, A. L. Oxford Station, *in his* The
Road to Oxford. *London: Jonathan Cape*,
1978.
'See that man standing on the platform | Hat in
hand, west wind in his hair . . .'

12707 SELVER, P. New Cross: suburban landscape [1943] *in* The Train, compiled by
Roger Green. *London: Oxford University
Press*, 1982.
'Pallid with heat, a stark metallic sky | Is looped
above the siding . . .

12708 SINKINSON, W. N. Flying Scotsman: railway poems; preface by Eric Treacy.

Knaresborough: Niddersdale Press, 1970.
pp. 40.
45 poems.

12709 SINKINSON, W. N. See How They Run:
railway rhymes by Walter Nugent Sinkinson, with preface by General Sir Brian H.
Robertson [Chairman, British Transport
Commission, 1953–1961]. *Mirfield: printed
by Leslie Brook*, [1961]. pp. [48].
Verses under 55 titles on a variety of workaday
themes, by a railwayman.

12710 SMYTHE, J. The Peoples Road: poems by
Joe Smythe, with illustrations by Derek
Jones. [*Manchester: National Union of Rail-
waymen*, 1980]. pp. 64, with 9 illus & 3
portraits (pencil drawings). Introduction by
Sidney Weighell, General Secretary of the
N.U.R., inside front cover.
'Specially commissioned by the NUR for the
Great Railway Exposition, Manchester 1980.'

12711 STEWART, G. Poem IV: 'At main line
junctions where such journeys have beginning . . .', *in* The Terrible Rain: The War
poets, 1939 to 1945; an anthology selected
and arranged, with introduction and notes,
by Brian Gardner. *London: Methuen*, 1966,
on pp. 149–50.

12712 THOMAS, E. Adlestrop, *in* Golden Jour-
ney: poems for young people, compiled by
Louise Bogan and William Jay Smith. *Chi-
cago: Reilly & Smith*, [1965] *London: Evans
Bros*, 1967.
'Yes, I remember Adlestrop . . .'

12713 THWAITE, A. Sunday Afternoons, *in his*
The Owl in the Tree: poems, *London:
Oxford University Press*, 1963.
'On Sunday afternoons | In winter, snow in the
air . . .'

12714 The WAGGONER, *in* Rhymes of the Northern Bards, being a collection of old and new
songs and poems peculiar to the counties of
Newcastle upon Tyne, Northumberland and
Durham; edited by John Bell junior. *Newcastle: J. Bell via M. Angus & Son*, 1812. pp.
328, on p. 300.
'Saw ye owt o'ma lad, gannin doon the waggon-
way? . . .'

12715 WILSON, T. The Pitman's Pay and other
poems . . . with a memoir of the author.
Gateshead: W. Douglas, 1843. pp. xxxvi,
168.
First published in *Mitchell's Magazine*, 1826–30.
A long dialect poem on mining conditions in the
Tyneside area. On pp. 26–32, the labour of
'putting trams' before the introduction of iron
plate-rails is described; pp. 101–07, 'The Opening
of the Newcastle & Carlisle Railway'—'Lass, lay
me out maw Sunday claes, te-morn's to be the day
o' days, Th' railroad's gaun te oppen . . .'
——— another edn. *London: Routledge*,
1872. pp. xx–iv, 232. (pp. 36–44 and pp.
117–26).

P   HUMOUR, HUMOROUS DRAWING AND SATIRE

Anecdotes—Allegory—Curiosa—Doggerel—Satire—Cartoons—Sound recordings—
Songs—Miscellanea

12716–74

Reference sources   12716–17
Collections and selections   12718–25
Individual works   12726–74

Reference sources

12716 SILVESTER, R. Official railway postcards of the British Isles. *Chippenham: Picton Publishing.*
part 1: London and North Western Railway. 1978. pp. 104, with 144 illus.
96 sets delineated, with captions & notes.

12717 PALM, J. Railways on record, compiled by Jim Palm. *Weston-super-Mare: Avon Anglia*, 1980. pp. 128.
A discography: British railway sounds recorded (commercially) since the 1950s on 184 records. The work is blessed with seven alternative presentations of its information, according to approach:
1, Records alphabetically by title; 2, Records by prefix and number; 3, Steam locomotive by name; 4, Steam locomotives numerically; 5, Diesels; 6, Narrow-gauge; 7, Geographical list; 8, Manufacturers' addresses. Appendix, additions up to February 1980.

Collections and selections

12718 [SONGS. Railway songs and pianoforte solos.] A collection of 19th century songs and pianoforte solos with railway themes, ca. 1830–1906, all published in London; bound into a single volume.
1, Railways now are all the go with steam, steam, steam, by W. E. K. [ca. 1830?]
2, The Railway Quadrille, by T. Hallwood; a piano duet [ca. 1840?]
3, De Railroad Overture, adapted for the pianoforte by J. J. Haite. [?]
4, The Railroad Quadrille, for the pianoforte, by G. Redler. [after 1846]
5, The Railroad Galop, by Jos. Gung'l. [?]
6, The Railway Guard, by John Stamford. [ca. 1855?]
7, Paris in 10½ hours: galop, by H. Weist Hill. [after 1875]
8, The Railway Porter, written by Worton David; composed by Maurice Scott. 1906
9, The Tuppenny Tube, written by Edgar Bateman; composed by Henry E. Pether. 1900. [Central London Line]
10, A Trip to Blackpool: descriptive pianoforte solo, by Felix Godard. [c. 1900]
11, We Do Travel on Our Line!, written & composed by Mills and Castling. 1902
12, The 11.69 Express, composed by William S. Robinson; written & performed by Ronald Bagnall. 1906   LU(THC)

12719 McLAGAN, W. Steam Lines: railway poems from the steam age on, collected by William McLagan. *Gartocharn: Famedram*, [1973]. pp. [77].

51 railway poems, rhymes and pieces of doggerel, collected from engine drivers, firemen, guards and engine shed staff on the Scottish railways, with aspects of life at Polmadie engine sheds, Glasgow, often the chosen theme.

12720 RAILWAYS in song. *London: E.F.D.S. Publications*, 1973. (Sounds Like Folk series, 2), sm. 8°. pp. 28, with 8 illus (vignettes).
Twelve songs with music (melody line only), traditional and modern.

12721 POVEY, R. O. T. The Bedside Book of Railway History. *Clapham (N. Yorks): Dalesman*, 1974. pp. 72, with 3 illus, 3 maps & 3 diagrams.
A collection of entertaining facts, anecdotes and singular occasions, grouped regionally, with a Miscellany section at end. The sources of the extracts are not given.

12722 BAYNES, Ken and BAYNES, Kate. The Railway Cartoon Book. *Newton Abbot: David & Charles*, 1976. pp. 96. Intro, & reproductions of 126 cartoons with added captions.

12723 EMETT, R. The Early Morning Milk Train: the cream of Emett railway drawings. *London: J. Murray*, 1976. la. 8°. pp. [110].
150 drawings from his previously published works.

12724 RAVEN, J. Victoria's Inferno: songs of the old mills, mines, manufactories, canals and railways, edited by Jon Raven. *Wolverhampton: Broadside*, 1978. pp. 192.
A collection of 18th and 19th century industrial songs with a bibliography (32 main sources, 14 locations of broadside collections, & a further list of 100 books which include industrial songs as a subject, national and regional, and 4 records).
pp. 8–11, Introduction, 'The nature of industrial song'. The text is in 5 chapters: 19th century industry; the canals & railways; the mines; the mills; the manufactories. Each chapter is introduced by a commentary.
pp. 22–56, 'The canals and railways'. Commentary, pp. 22–27; 16 songs with music (melody line only) of which 8 are on railways. Also, on pp. 70–71, 'The Collier's Rant' (1793).

12725 MIDDLEMASS, T. King Edward's railways: contemporary impressions from the Railway Magazine. *Theydon Bois: Steamchest Publications*, 1979. pp. 96, with 16 illus on 8 plates. Title from cover.
Piquant extracts, arranged by subject, 1901–1910.

Individual works

12726 MARTIN, W. The Flash of Forked Lightning from the Dark Thunder Cloud! *Newcastle: printed by Wm. Fordyce*, 1834. pp. 8.
Includes proposals for railway extension in the Newcastle area (p.4). Claims to be the 'Inventor of Rail-Ways' (p.6) and urges punishment for engineers for not fixing an alarm bell to every carriage.

12727 MARTIN, W. The Thunder Storm of Dreadful Forked Lightning: God's judgment against all false teachers, that cause the people to err, and those that are led by them are destroyed, according to God's Word; including an account of the railway phenomenon, the wonder of the world! *Newcastle upon Tyne: [the author]*, 1837. pp. 40.
pp. 3–5, 'The railway phenomenon, the wonder of the world'. A recital of wild denunciations and claims, in which the author reveals that he is the true inventor of 'metallic railways laid on stone blocks'—the 'Martinian Railway'. He condemns 'Stevenson' (George Stephenson) as neither mechanic nor genius.

12728 MARTIN, W. The Follies of the Day; or, the effects of a gold chain, with observations on the unnecessary expenses of the North Shields Railway and other remarks of importance. *Newcastle: printed by Pattison & Ross*, 1839. pp. 8.
Concerning his proposed timber viaducts for the Newcastle & North Shields Rly.

12729 MARTIN, W. The Martinian Bridge triumphant . . . likewise an improvement in the shape of locomotive engines. *Newcastle*, [1841]. pp. 4.

12730 MARTIN, W. To the engineers and directors of railways: a revolution in colleges and mechanics produced by the philosopher's discovery of the perpetual motion in 1807 . . . I invented metallic railways in 1796 . . . *Newcastle*, [1841]. pp. 4.

12731 MARTIN, W. Invention of metallic railways, being a refutation of a paragraph on the subject which appeared in the newspapers. *Newcastle*, [1842]. pp. 4.

12732 MARTIN, W. On railway gates, etc., etc. *Newcastle*, [1842]. pp. 4.

12733 MARTIN, W. The philosopher, with the eye of a hawk, exposing traitors for imposing upon poor ingenious men. *[Newcastle upon Tyne*, 1843]. pp. 2.
On the alleged pirating of his invention of a gate for the Brandling Junction Railway Co.

12734 MARTIN, W. A letter to the Queen and Government. *Newcastle on Tyne*, [1846]. s. sh.
On the advantages of the broad gauge.

12735 MARTIN, W. To the conductors of railways and the gentlemen of Newcastle upon Tyne. *Newcastle upon Tyne*, [1846]. s. sh.

12736 MARTIN, W. To the Honourable the Lords and Commons of Great Britain and Ireland in Parliament assembled . . . *[Newcastle upon Tyne*, 1846]. s. sh.
A petition in favour of the broad gauge, dated 5th March 1846.

12737 A RAILWAY adventure that Mr Larkins encountered with the lady of Captn Coleraine, showing the power of platonic love. *London: Ackermann*, [1846]. 19 leaves, folded accordion-wise. Title page pasted onto stiff paper upper cover.
20 humorous drawings, hand-coloured, each with text beneath, depicting a romantic encounter on a train journey from London to Brighton. Captions to the first two illustrations: At the London Bridge Station, Mr Lionel Larkins first encounters the brilliant glances of the lady who, with thrilling effect, works the Electric Telegraph of Love. Having entered the same carriage and mutually developed the power of Love's Electricity, they converse; she talks of the delights of a walk on the Esplanade!'   NUC

12738 CHAMBERS, R. The 'Innocent Railway', *in* Select Writings of Robert Chambers, *Edinburgh*, 1847. vol. 1, pp. 397–402.
The Edinburgh & Dalkeith Rly's horse-drawn trains, a delight; trains on other railways hauled by steam locomotives, an abomination. A journey described at length. 'Readers, if ever you want to dispel the blues or put rout to the megrims . . . take a forenoon trip by the "Innocent Railway".'

12739 FARRER, H. L. The navvies: no. 1, Harry Johnson; a tale (no. 2, Frank Meade; a tale). *London: W. J. Cleaver*, 1847. sm. 8°. pp. 94.
Two works in one (pp. 1–34; 35–86) and an Appendix (pp. 87–94), 'Report of a trial for murder in a fight by railway laborers' [*sic*], from *The Times* of 9th August.

12740 DOYLE, R. and LEIGH, P. Manners and customs of ye Englyshe, drawn from ye quick by Richard Doyle . . . *[London]*: *Bradbury & Evans*, [1849]. obl. 8°. 2 vols.
Illustrations (humorous line drawings) of various activities, with commentaries. Two railway scenes are portrayed: 'A Raylwaye Meetynge', and 'A Raylwaye Statyon, showynge ye Travellers refreshynge themselves' (at Swindon).
—— new edn; rev. & extended, *Bradbury, Agnew & Co.*, 1876. obl. 8°.
—— another edn; *T. Foulis*, 1911.

12741 HUNT, L. Readings for railways; or, anecdotes and other short stories, reflections, maxims, characteristics, passages of wit, humour and poetry, etc., together with points of information on matters of general interest collected in the course of his own reading, by Leigh Hunt. *London: C. Gilpin*, [1849]. pp. 136.
132 short pieces of which only the 2nd, 3rd, 4th & 5th have to do with railway travel. These include a description of means of a communication between passengers and drivers by electrical contact from buttons in every compartment to the whistle on the engine. Also an essay on the transmission of money by railway, by Mr. Chubb,

and a paper read to the British Association by Mr. Scott Russell on the effects of railway velocity on sound.

12742 RAILWAY literature, *in* Dublin University Magazine, vol. 34, no. 201, September 1849. pp. 280–91.

A critical essay on some examples of railway bookstall reading 'which itinerent vendors persist in poking through the carriage windows into the face of the traveller', with extracts. Some lengthy passages are reprinted from the novels of James Hannay, and some shorter excerpts from the humorous sketches of Horace Mayhew.

12743 ROBSON, J. P. Songs of the bards of the Tyne; or, a choice selection of original songs chiefly in the Newcastle dialect . . . , edited by J. P. Robson. *Newcastle: P. France*, 1849. pp. 552.

Includes 'The changes on the Tyne' with verses about the changeover from horse to locomotive and the spread of railways (pp. 214–8).

12744 FAYERS, T. A Navvy's dying words; or, lessons from the death-bed of a railway workman. 2nd edn. *London: Wertheim, Macintosh & Hunt; Kendal: J. Robinson*, 1861. pp. 52.

12745 MACFARLANE, J. The Railway, in six lectures. *Edinburgh: Paton & Ritchie*, 1863. sm. 8°. pp. 111.

Religious allegory.

12746 HOGG, N. [pseudonym for Henry Baird]. A turrabul ride bee Rayl, *in his* A New Series of Poems in the Devonshire Dialect . . . 4th edn. *London: J. R. Smith*, 1866. pp. 16–20.

'Yu've yer'd a Janny Gulpin's ride . . .'
From Teignmouth to Starcross on the South Devon Rly. Glossary, pp. 78–80.

—— 5th edn. *Torquay: A. Iredale*, 1888. pp. 16–20.

12747 JUST in time!: a tale of the L. & N.W.R.; by a Railway Sleeper. *Montrose: printed at the Standard Office*, 1870. pp. 58, with illus.

Anecdotes, facetiae, satire, etc., on the LNWR.
NUC

12748 JAMES, R. The Railway Calamity on the River Tay, Scotland: a descriptive poem. *Portsmouth: R. James*, [1880?] (R.J. Political Tracts series). sm. 8°. pp. [4].

12749 SPRING, E. H. Outline history of the Gloucester branch of the Railway Mission, with especial reference to Miss Hollis and Mr H. Waters. *Gloucester: Smart, printer*, [1891]. pp. 20.

The writer addresses his words to 'My Railway Friends' and is mainly concerned with a point by point denunciation of Miss Hollis and Mr Waters whom he accuses of having attempted to oust him from his position as Superintendent.

12750 WYKES, F. H. The wreck of the Manchester express at Wellingborough, 8.10 pm, Sept. 2nd, 1898. s. sh. with 1 illus (photo).

Verses. 'All right? Yes! Let her go!'

12751 MILLAR, H. R. Dreamland Express, written and illustrated by H. R. Millar. *London: Humphrey Milford, Oxford University Press*, [1927]. la. obl. format. pp. 94, with col. title-page, 14 col. illus and many more in monochrome.

A dream-train on a world-wide journey. Juvenile.

12752 CLARKE, T. E. B. The Titfield Thunderbolt: Ealing's first technicolour comedy . . . ; a Michael Balcon production. [*London*]: *General Film Distributors*, [1952]. pp. [16], with 24 illus.

A souvenir brochure with details on the making of the film, including the use of the Liverpool & Manchester locomotive '*Lion*', built in 1838.

12753 JENNINGS, P. Dieselisation, *in his* Model Oddlies (1956), pp. 51–3.

12754 JENNINGS, P. NUR + ASLEF = FUNERALS, *in his* Model Oddlies (1956), pp. 47–50.

12755 SNELL, J. B. Jennie; illustrated by G. K. Sewell. *London: Nelson*, 1958. pp. 176, with 22 drawings.

A story about a fictional Welsh narrow gauge line—the Gwernol Valley Rly—and its locomotives. For older children or young enthusiasts.

12756 JENNINGS, P. Bala likely! *in his* Idly Oddly (1959), pp. 95–7.

12757 JENNINGS, P. Very Great Eastern, *in his* Idly Oddly (1959), pp. 92–4.

12758 JENNINGS, P. The Dining-Car Mystery, *in his* Oodles of Oddlies (1963), pp. 98–101.

The 'other-worldliness' of train catering.

12759 JENNINGS, P. Les Ferryboatings, *in his* Oodles of Oddlies (1963), pp. 92–5.

12760 MILLS, W. 4ft 8½ and all that!: for maniacs only. *London: Ian Allan*, 1964. pp. 64, with 61 humorous drawings.

A light-hearted railway history, written & illustrated by W. Mills and 'in fairness to everyone else' dedicated to himself.

12761 ROLT, L. T. C. Alec's Adventures in Railwayland. *London: Ian Allan*, 1964. pp. 46, with 13 drawings.

A satire on current railway policy. The Prime Minister, 1963–4, was Sir Alec Douglas-Home.

12762 JENNINGS, P. Abroad: the last train to St Petersburg, *in his* I was Joking of course (1968), pp. 56–61.

Whimsical observations on timetables.

12763 JENNINGS, P. And East is Anglia, *in his* I was Joking of course (1968), pp. 81–4.

On the 'mystery' of Liverpool Street Station, London.

12764 JENNINGS, P. Pass along *whose* car? *in his* I was Joking of course (1968), pp. 77–80.

Station car park regulations.

12765 SMULLEN, I. Taken for a ride: a distressing account of the misfortunes and misbehaviour of the early British railway traveller. *London: H. Jenkins*, 1968. pp. 192, with 36 line drawings.

Satirical commentaries on reported incidents.

12766 WYNKYN DE WORDE SOCIETY and NEWCASTLE IMPRINT CLUB. Printers' trains. *Wylam: Allenholme Press, for the Wynkyn de Worde Society and the Newcastle Imprint Club*, 1969. sm. obl. 8°. pp. 31.

A fine quality presentation of blocks used by printers in the early days of railway publicity (ca. 1839–1850) as ornaments for prospectuses, handbills, posters, etc. and for book decoration. Designed by J. J. Nesbit, hand-set by Peter Isaac, text by William Fenton and James Mosley; Introduction by Kenneth Day.

Contents: 'Railway origins of the printers' trains', by William Fenton; 'Making the printers' trains', by James Mosley.

MANCHESTER POLYTECHNIC LIBRARY

12767 PEARSON, M. S. W. Hold tight! *Thurnby: the author*, [196–?]. obl. format. pp. [24].

24 humorous drawings of imaginary tramway scenes—and predicaments! Sold to support the preservation endeavours of the Tramway Museum at Crich.

12768 JENNINGS, P. Meet me under the Unmanned Halt Clock, *in his* It's an Odd Thing, But . . . (1971), pp. 53–6.

12769 JENNINGS, P. The Neck Strine from Platform 2, *in his* It's an Odd Thing, But . . . (1971), pp. 60–63.

Musings on the symbolism of station names in Western Australia and in Britain.

12770 SPENCE, K. M. Season ticket: travellers' tales from the urban subtopia. (Illustrations by 'Baker'). *London: Macdonald & Jane's*, 1973. pp. [5], 106, with 27 humorous drawings.

Whimsical essays on commuting.

12771 WATTS, D. G. Railway Rivals: book one. *Milford Haven: the author*, 1973. pp. 29.

A booklet issued as a supplement to a geographical games kit for school use to illustrate the interplay of physical, economic and human factors which account for the resultant pattern of railway networks. The areas chosen are: South Wales; London to Liverpool; Western U.S.A.; New York to Chicago. Each of these areas is the subject of a chapter outlining the historical background, to enable players to construct their lines upon what they decide are the best available geographic, economic and social considerations.

12772 JENNINGS, P. Train to Yesterday; illustrated by Patricia Casey. *London: Harrap*, 1974. pp. 72.

'As they follow the old line, the children undergo a time-slip to a Victorian railway scene . . .'

12773 MIDDLEMASS, T. Locomotive nicknames. *Theydon Bois: Steamchest Publications*, [1978]. pp. 64, with 21 illus on 12 plates. Title from cover.

'Aberdares' to 'Yorkies', with historical notes.

12774 GOODWYN, A. M. and TOWNSEND, A. The Unofficial Guide to the Isle of Man Railways: an incredible compendium of Manx railway cartoons. *Douglas: Manx Electric Rly*, 1980. obl. format. pp. [64]. Intro & 68 humorous drawings with captions, & 3 pages of verse.

Q APPRECIATION OF RAILWAYS

The appeal of railways and locomotives—Railway aesthetics—
Railway enthusiast societies—Rail tour reminiscences

12775–12804

Note: In the three preceding Classes, **N**, **O** and **P**, are many items in
which railway appreciation is implicit. **Q** is for works which *express* it.

The following sub-divisions, **Q 1**, **Q 2** and **Q 3** are for works in which
the appeal of railways and locomotives is expressed in three different ways

12775 LEICESTER RAILWAY SOCIETY. L.R.S., 1961. [*Leicester: the Society*, 1961]. pp. 12, with 17 illus.
Issued to commemorate 21 years of progress.

12776 ALLEN, C. J. Two million miles of train travel: the autobiography of Cecil J. Allen. *London: Ian Allan*, 1965. pp. 232, with frontis (portrait) & 99 illus on 32 plates.
Includes two chapters on his publications as journalist and author (ch. 19, pp. 161–73, & ch. 20, pp. 174–80).

12777 HOBDEY, L. M., SUMMER, M. W. and WOOLISCROFT, J. J. Locomotive Nameplate Register, 1964–65. [*Buxton*?]: [*L. M. Hobdey*?], 1965. sm. 8°. pp. 51.
A directory of current owners (individuals and corporate bodies) grouped under the names of the railways for which the nameplates were made.

12778 SCOTTISH RAILFANS. Scottish steam passenger services. *Edinburgh: Scottish Railfans*, [1965]. obl. 8°. pp. 22. Reproduced typescript.
Tables of all advertised steam-hauled passenger train services, with classes of locomotive and parent depots.

12779 LOCOMOTIVE CLUB OF GREAT BRITAIN. RAIL TOURS COMMITTEE. The first hundred: rail tours, 1953–1967. (Memories of a hundred Club rail tours, 1953–1967), compiled and produced by C. R. Firminger for and on behalf of the Locomotive Club of Great Britain. *London: L.C.G.B.*, [1967]. pp. 36, with 33 illus.
'Based on a list supplied by H. W. Gandy.'

12780 PUDNEY, J. The Golden Age of Steam. *London: Hamilton*, 1967. la. 8°. pp. 187, with many illus.
Includes railways.

12781 MAXWELL, H. A Railway Rubaiyyat. *Cambridge: Golden Head Press*, 1968. pp. 54.
Verses (quatrains) 'to evoke the lost magic of the steam engine upon the railways'.

12782 STEPHENSON, B. and RUSSELL, P. Specials in steam. *London: Ian Allan*, 1968. pp. [127]. Intro, frontis & 229 illus with descrs.
A selection of photographs taken on rail tours organised by enthusiast societies.

12783 STEPHENSON LOCOMOTIVE SOCIETY. MIDLAND AREA. Commemorative Photographic Souvenir in connection with Farewell to Steam special trains, Sunday 4th August, 1968. *Handsworth: S.L.S.*, 1968. pp. 32, with 53 illus & 1 col. plate.

12784 JENNINGS, P. Just a few lines: Guinness trains of thought, by Paul Jennings, with photographs by Graham Finlayson and maps by Denzil Reeves. *London: Guinness Superlatives*, 1969. la. 8°, with col. frontis, 103 illus. (40 col.) & 4 maps.
A commentary on the past and present of four closed rural lines: Colne Valley, Whitby to Scarborough, Oxford to Fairford and Neath to Brecon, with accounts of interviews with past railwaymen and elderly residents, and photographs of present day scenes of dereliction and decay.

12785 OXFORD UNIVERSITY RAILWAY SOCIETY. A Commemorative Journal, 1931–1972. *Oxford: the Society*, [1972]. tall 8°. pp. 24, with 27 illus & map.
Essays by members & past members. List of secretaries, 1931–72, on back cover.

12786 RATCLIFFE, R. L. The LCGB returns to steam. *Rochester: Locomotive Club of Great Britain*, [1972]. pp. 12, with 13 illus, 2 dimensioned drawings & 2 tables: 1, Routes authorised by B.R. for use by steam-hauled trains, and 2, Preserved locomotives accepted for use by B.R. on these routes.
A resumé of the rail tours of the LCGB since 1967 and commemorating its return to steam-haulage with the *Welsh Borderer*, 14th October 1972.
A sequel to the Club's *The First Hundred: rail tours, 1953–67* (1967).

12787 SIMPSON, B. S. T. Just in time! *Bracknell: Town & Country Press*, 1972. pp. 159, with frontis, 95 illus, 6 maps & 6 diagrams.
Reminiscences of steam railways in Great Britain, Switzerland, North America, South Africa, Australia and New Zealand.
pp. 11–38, Great Britain, mostly light and narrow gauge lines.

12788 WIRRAL RAILWAY CIRCLE. Hebridean Express . . . September 1971: commemorative booklet. *Bromborough: the Circle*, 1972. pp. 24, with 4 illus & an itinerary.
Text by David Joy and Chris Bakalarski

A 34-hour trip from Crewe to Kyle to Lochalsh & back by 480 passengers in a 17-coach train.

12789 HUME, J. R. and DUCKHAM, B. F. Steam entertainment. *Newton Abbot: David & Charles*, 1974. pp. 96, with 123 illus.
Locomotives, ships, fairground organs and traction engines. pp. 42–96, 'Railways: the appeal of Steam', with 70 illus.

12790 JENNINGS, P. The English Difference; words . . . by Paul Jennings; illustrations & design . . . by John Gorham. *Aurelia Enterprises*, 1974. la. 8°. pp. 144.
pp. 120–1, The Second Steam Age, with 10 illus. A commentary on the British love of Steam.

12791 MONTAGUE K. and BECKETT, M. Railtour: a day out with a difference. *Sheringham: Midland & Great Northern Joint Railway Society Publications*, 1974. (Publication, 2). pp. [33], with 23 illus.
An account of 21 tours to various preserved lines arranged & conducted by the North Norfolk Rly, 1971–1974.

12792 RATCLIFFE, R. L. and NEWCOMBE, R. 25 years of enthusiasm: being the story of the first 25 years of the Locomotive Club of Great Britain, 1949–1974. *Bexleyheath: L.C.G.B.*, [1974]. pp. 40, with 50 illus.

12793 BUTCHER, A. R. Specials in action. *Truro: Bradford Barton*, 1975. pp. 96. Intro & 103 illus with descrs.
Steam-hauled train runs ('specials') for railway enthusiasts, 1958–1968.

12794 BODY, G. Railways for pleasure. *Newton Abbot: David & Charles*, 1976. pp. 125, with 40 illus.
A survey of various manifestations of railway appreciation.

12795 LAWRANCE, F. W. J. The Bath Railway Society: a brief history: [*Bath*]: *the author*, 1976. pp. 56, with 16 illus.
Author was chairman, 1961–70.

12796 RAILTOUR in colour. *Shepperton: Ian Allan*, 1976. pp. [64]. Intro & 84 col. illus, with descrs.
Scenes on BR, on rail-tours, and on preserved lines.

12797 TAYLORSON, K. The fun we had!: an inside look at the railway enthusiast hobby; compiled and edited by K. Taylorson. *London: Phoenix Publications*, 1976. pp. 130, with 21 illus on 16 plates.

26 essays by 19 authors writing on various aspects of railway appreciation, including the photographic. The Introduction and commentaries to some of the essays are by K. Taylorson.

12798 WALKER, C. Happy Return!: the Rail 150 Steam Cavalcade. *Southam: Pendyke Publications*, 1976. pp. [146]. Intro, list of 35 locomotives taking part, & 140 illus.
The environment of the Cavalcade captured in photographs, with locomotives the central theme.

12799 EATWELL, D. and COOPER-SMITH, J. H. Return to Steam: steam tours on British Rail from 1969. *London: Batsford*, 1978. pp. 120. Intro & 164 illus with descrs.

12800 HOLDEN, B. The best of 'Steam Scene': twenty-five articles based on programmes broadcast on B.B.C. Radio Birmingham between February 1974–April 1977 (written by programme presenter Bryan Holden; edited by Harold Parsons). *Birmingham: Barbryn Press*, 1978. pp. 128, with 55 illus.
'Illustrating various aspects of, mainly, steam traction and subsequent preservation, recalled by drivers, firemen, signalmen, railway artists, photographers and others, as originally broadcast.'

12801 STEAM for pleasure, by P. B. Whitehouse, J. B. Snell, J. B. Hollingsworth. *London: Routledge & Kegan Paul*, 1978. la. 8°. pp. 240, with over 200 illus (some col.), & location maps.
The live steam railway revival throughout the world.
pp. 140–83, 'Britain and Ireland'.

12802 DERRY, R. W. Richard Derry's Railway Diary, 1971–1974. *Camberley: Steam & Diesel Publications*, 1979. pp. 116, with 34 illus.
Random jottings of a railway enthusiast.

12803 VAUGHAN, J. A. M. Railtour Pictorial: a pictorial survey of the first 25 Railway Pictorial Publications railtours from October 1976 to November 1978. *Dorking: Railway Pictorial Publications*, 1979. pp. [64]. Intro & 115 illus with descrs.

12804 BULL, K. and COGAN, J. Five years of Steam on Britain's main lines: from Shildon 1975 to Rainhill 1980. *Oadby: Leander Locomotive Ltd*, [1980]. pp. [64]. Intro (inside front cover), & 98 illus with descrs & 2 col. illus on covers. Title from cover.
Photographs of 'steam specials' on British Rail.

For the restoration and preservation of railway material generally see **E 3–E 16**
For steam locomotive restoration and preservation generally see **E 8c**

Reference sources 12805–15, but note also that among the works that follow
(12816–76) are many surveys of preservation activity which may be found
useful as additional sources of reference

12805   RAILWAY Enthusiasts' Handbook, edited
by Geoffrey Body. *Newton Abbot: David &*
Charles. With illustrations, lists & tables.
Published biennially.
    A comprehensive handbook to all preservation
activity and industrial railways.
    —— [no. 1], 1967. pp. 160.
    —— [no. 2], 1968–69 edn. pp. 155, [5].
    —— [no. 3], 1969–70 edn. 1969. pp. 157.
    —— [no. 4], 1970–71 edn. 1970. pp. 176,
xvi.
    —— [no. 5], 1972–3 edn. Railway & Steam
Enthusiasts' Handbook. 1972. pp. 176, xvi.
    —— [no. 6], 1974. pp. 172, xvi.
    —— [no. 7], ed. by Geoffrey Body and Ian
G. Body. *Bristol: Avon Anglia*, 1977. pp.
120, xiii.

12806   LEITHEAD, R. H. British Locomotive Preservation and Light Railway Stocklist. *Not-*
tingham: the compiler, 1969. pp. 43, with 14
plates.
    —— 1970 edn. [1970]. pp. ii, 72, with illus.
    —— 1971 edn. R. H. Leithead's Stockbook
of Light railways, miniature railways, preserved locomotives and tramcars. *Notting-*
ham: the compiler, 1971. pp. 88, with illus.

12807   LIGHT Railways Timetables & Guide,
edited by Geoffrey Body. *Newton Abbot:*
David & Charles.
    An illustrated handbook.
    —— 1969 edn. 1969. pp. [xvi], 1–8, [xvi],
9–16 [xvi].
    —— 1970 edn. 1970. pp. [xx], 1–8, [xvi],
9–16, [xx].
    —— 1971 edn. 1971. pp. 36, xvi.
    —— 1972 edn. 1972. pp. [18], 46.
        continued as:
Light Railway & vintage Transport Guide.
David & Charles, 1973. pp. 30, & 42 pp.
adverts.
    —— 1974 edn. *David & Charles*, 1974. pp.
[xx], 1–16, [xvi], 17–35, [xvii].
    —— 1975 edn.
        continued as:
Light Railways, Steamers and Historic
Transport, edited by Geoffrey Body. *Bris-*
tol: Avon Anglia, 1976. pp. 76.
        continued as:
Light Railways, Steamers, Aircraft and
Industrial Preservation, edited by Geoffrey
Body and Ian G. Body. *Avon Anglia*, 1977.
pp. 68.
    —— 1978 edn. *Avon Anglia*, 1978. pp. 72.
        continued as:
Light Railways, Canals, Steamers and In-

dustrial Preservation, edited by Geoffrey
Body. *Avon Anglia*, 1979. pp. 72.

12808   SIMMONS, J. Transport museums in Britain
and Western Europe. *London: Allen &*
Unwin, 1970. pp. 300, with 133 illus on 64
plates.
    A companion guide to 34 museums of public
transport by road and rail.

12809   NABARRO, G. Steam nostalgia: locomotive and railway preservation in Great Britain. *London: Routledge & Kegan Paul*,
1972. pp. xv, 270, with col. frontis, 158 illus
on 80 plates, 40 tables, 15 maps, lists of
preserved   locomotives,   preservation
societies, and a bibliography (59 sources).
    A comprehensive survey of organised preserva-
tion.

12810   GUIDE   Book   of   Railway   Museums,
Europe, 1974; editor, Béla Czére. (Prepared by Eduardo Alfonso of the International Railway Union). *Budapest: Interna-*
tional Association of Transport Museums,
1976. pp. 464.
    pp. 183–304: Great Britain.

12811   HOLLINGSWORTH, B. Steam into the
seventies. *London: New English Library*,
1976. la. 8°. pp. 192, with 235 illus (87 col.),
2 general maps & a bibliography (56
sources).
    A record of steam railway preservation and
re-operation. One map shows the location of 98
'live steam clubs'; the other is for 105 steam
railways, pleasure lines, depots and museums and
has a gazetteer (pp. 176–85) giving a summary
description of each, with length of line, gauge, and
number of locomotives.

12812   TIP, Handbook, 77/78: transport & industrial preservation: a guide to what, where &
when; edited, produced & published by
Derek Baines. 2nd edn. *Crawley*, 1977. pp.
139, with 22 illus on 12 plates.
    An alphabetical arrangement with subject and
geographical indexes. Subject Index has 97 entries
under individual railways and tramways.

12813   AWDRY, W. and COOK, C. A. Guide to
the Steam Railways of Great Britain. *Lon-*
don: Pelham Books, 1979. pp. 240, with
frontis, 22 col. illus on 8 plates, & in text,
133 illus & 55 maps & plans. Gazetteer, pp.
221–38. General map on endpapers.
    60 preserved & re-opened lengths of railway
described, wtih historical background, and 68
lesser steam centres, museums & miniature rail-

ways. The 8 chapters, for regions of Britain, are by Reg Palk, Bertram Vigor, Eric Buck, Edgar Jones, John Ransom, John Hume.

12814   RAILWAYS restored. *Shepperton: Ian Allan and the Association of Railway Preservation Societies*, 1980. pp. 96, with 66 illus (9 col.), map, list of preservation societies and time-tables for services of member preserved lines. *In progress as annual revisions.*
Initially issued as *Forum*, by the Railway Preservation Society in Spring 1962. A second edition appeared in the Summer as *Railway Forum*, edited by Terence Kirtland and published by the Association of Railway Preservation Societies. The work was first produced for general publication in 1968:
—— [2nd] edn. Railway Forum: official A.R.P.S. stock list, compiled by John True. *Haraton Ltd*, [1968]. pp. 58, with illus.
—— 3rd edn. A.R.P.S. Year Book and Stock List, compiled by Roger Crombleholme. *Haraton Ltd*, [1970]. pp. 90. Cover title, Railway Forum.
—— 4th edn. A.R.P.S. Year Book & Steam Preservation Guide, 1971, compiled by Roger Crombleholme. *Haraton Ltd*, [1971]. pp. 88. Index extends onto p. [3] of cover. 185 locations. Cover title: Railway Forum.
—— 5th edn. Steam '72: the official A.R.P.S. Year Book & Steam Guide. *Haraton*, 1972. pp. [140]. 274 locations.
—— [6th] edn. Steam '73: the official A.R.P.S Year Book & Steam Guide. *Haraton*, 1973. pp. [188]. 326 locations.
—— [7th] edn. Steam '74 . . . pp. 114. 330 locations.
—— [8th] edn. Steam '75 . . . pp. [134]. 511 locations.
—— [9th] edn. Steam '76 . . . pp. [160]. 512 locations.
—— [10th] edn. Steam '77 . . . pp. [160]. 514 locations.

12815   STEAM: a complete enthusiasts' handbook to railway preservation activities and minor railways in the British Isles, edited by Roger Crombleholme and Terry Kirtland. *London: Allen & Unwin*, 1980. (Steam Past series). pp. [205], with numerous stock lists & 50 illus. Foreword by William McAlpine. *In progress as annual revisions.*
Previously published as *Steam Year Book*.
A definitive and comprehensive work of reference referred to in the Introduction as the 'Steam Freaks' Bible'. This edition provides detailed summary information—including stock lists—of 512 preservation activity centres (museums, re-opened lines, locomotive preservation societies, narrow-gauge railways, miniature railways, pier railways, tramways and mineral wagonways). Electric and diesel traction are included and the coverage extends to activity *directed towards* the preservation or operation of a particular line or locomotive or item of rolling stock, such as the Alderney Railway Society, and includes at least one centre (entry 509) where the stock has been reduced to dereliction by vandals.
The work is a compendium of all guides and stocklists associated with rail transport in the

British Isles, to which have been added descriptions of minor preservation activity by individuals or small groups who do not necessarily provide public access.

12816   GREAT EXHIBITION OF THE WORKS OF INDUSTRY OF ALL NATIONS. 1851. Official Descriptive and Illustrated Catalogue, in three volumes. *London: Spicer Bros; W. Clowes*, 1851.
vol. 1, pp. 236–52. paras. 488–757: Railway machinery, including locomotives.

12817   IMPERIAL INSTITUTE. Official Catalogue of the Exhibition of Railway Appliances & Inventions during the period of the International Railway Congress, 1895. [*London: Imperial Institute*, 1895]. pp. 66, with folded plan. No illustrations.
90 exhibits described.

12818   BRITISH TRANSPORT COMMISSION. Souvenir Booklet to commemorate the opening of the Great Western Railway Museum, Swindon, 22 June 1962. [*London: B.T.C.*, 1962]. sm. 8°. pp. [12], with 17 illus.

12819   LEEDS CITY MUSEUM. 150 years of steam locomotives, 1812–1962: exhibition, Leeds City Museum, September 15th–22nd, 1962. [*Leeds: the Museum*, 1962]. pp. 8 (incl. cover). Reproduced typescript, printed cover.
Date on cover altered in MS from '22nd' to '29th'.

12820   LONDON TRANSPORT. Underground Centenary: display of rolling stock at Neasden depot, Saturday May 25 and Sunday May 26, 1963. [*London: Bayard Press, for London Transport*, 1963]. pp. [8], with 11 illus. Title on cover.
Illustrations of the eleven exhibits, with notes.

12821   DOWTY RAILWAY PRESERVATION SOCIETY. Catalogue of Exhibits. rev. edn. [*Ashchurch*]: *the Society*, [1967]. pp. 16. Reproduced typescript. Compiled by Ken Vincent.
—— 1971 edn, by 'R.A.R.'.
—— 1974 edn, by 'R.H.W.'. pp. 32.
—— 1978 edn, by 'R.A.R.'. pp. 32.
The guide was first published in 1964; editor, Ken Vincent. 2nd edn, 1965, edited by R. A. Rainbow. All editions before 1978 have duplicated or photocopied pages but the 1974 edn has a litho cover of the same design as that of 1978. The 1974 edn is in A4 format. (Information supplied by the Society).

12822   YIELDINGTREE RAILWAY MUSEUM TRUST. [Guide]. *Bleedon & Uphill Station: the Trust*, [1967]. pp. [16], with 27 illus & cover illus.
Founded in 1961 when a collection of 3000 items of railway equipment were acquired from R.W.F. Smallman.

12823   KICHENSIDE, G. and RILEY, R. C. Still in

steam. *London: Ian Allan*, 1969. pp. 64, with 5 col. illus on 4 plates & 86 in text.
Locomotives preserved and restored to working order.
—— [2nd edn] by L. E. Cornwell. *Ian Allan*, 1978. pp. 80, with 109 illus & 3 diagrams.

12824 MORGAN, B. Railway relics. *London: Ian Allan*, 1969. pp. 128, with 101 illus on 40 plates.

12825 BRITISH TRANSPORT HISTORICAL RECORDS. Railway records: basic sources of information. [*London: B.T.H.R.*], 1970. pp. 5. Reproduced typescript.
A guide to BTHR sources 'relating to the conception, construction and operation of a railway.'

12826 CONSULTATIVE PANEL FOR THE PRESERVATION OF BRITISH TRANSPORT RELICS. [A booklet describing the foundation of the Panel in 1958, its constitution and its achievements, with details of the work of the six sub-committees. Dated September 1970]. obl. 8°. pp. 24. Reproduced typescript.

12827 BRESSINGHAM STEAM MUSEUM. [Guides]. Bressingham: gardens, steam railways and engines . . . *Norwich: Jarrold*, 1971. sm. 8°. pp. 24, with 9 col. illus, map & 2 col. illus on covers. Text by Alan Bloom.
Stocklist of locomotives, pp. 21–4. Cover title: The Bressingham Book.
—— 6th edn. Bressingham Gardens and Live Steam Museum. *Jarrold*, 1976. pp. 32, with 34 illus (32 col., of which 14 are duplicated on covers). Text by Alan Bloom.

12828 DINTING RAILWAY CENTRE. [Guides]. The Dinting Railway Centre: an illustrated guide; compiled by J. R. Hillier. *Dinting: the Centre*, [1971]. pp. 16, with 12 illus (10 col.), map, plan & 2 col. illus on covers.
—— another edn. An illustrated Guide to the Dinting Railway Centre. [1976]. pp. [16], with 16 illus (10 col.), map & 3 illus (2 col.) on covers.
—— another edn. The Dinting Story (1968–1978), compiled by T. E. Cozens & designed by H. Parrish. [1978]. pp. [12], with 25 illus (monochrome), chronology, & 2 illus on covers.

12829 SMITH, D. J. Discovering railwayana. *Tring: Shire Publications*, 1971. sm. 8°. pp. 64, with 12 illus on 8 plates, & drawings in text; bibliography on p. 61.
From Armbands, Badges, and Buttons . . . to Whistles, and York Museum.

12830 STANDING COMMISSION ON MUSEUMS AND GALLERIES. The preservation of technological material: report and recommendations. *London: H.M.S.O.*, 1971. pp. v, 47.
'To consider the problem presented by the preservation of historical technological relics and records . . .' Includes railway relics, structures and archives.

12831 YORKSHIRE railways. *Leeds: Yorkshire Post Newspapers*, 1971. newspaper format. pp. 24, with many illus (some col.).
Railway preservation in Yorkshire.

12832 JOY, D. Steamtown: the Carnforth Live Steam Museum; a visitor's guide. *Clapham (N. Yorks): Dalesman*, 1972. sm. 8°. pp. 40, with 24 illus; map & illus on covers.

12833 STANDARD Gauge Standard. *Birmingham: Colourviews Ltd*, 1972. newspaper format. pp. [24], with 38 illus (4 col.), 6 maps (1 col.), 3 timetables & 1 col. facsimile.
Details of six preserved and re-opened lengths of standard-gauge railway.

12834 BIRMINGHAM RAILWAY MUSEUM. Official Guide to Exhibits . . . , compiled by A. H. Bryan Holden. *Birmingham: Standard Gauge Steam Trust*, [1973?]. pp. 18, with 13 illus.
'The Tyseley Locomotive Collection', with stocklist & notes by C. M. Whitehouse; 'Tyseley in the days of steam', by P. B. Whitehouse; and 'Engine preparation', by R. S. Potts.
—— Souvenir Guide. *Birmingham Railway Museum*. [1974?]. obl. format. pp. 19 (incl. covers), with 16 illus (2 col.).

12835 BRITAIN'S small railways. *St. Ives (Cambs.): Balfour Publications*, 1973. pp. 96, with 31 col. illus & 14 maps.
Accounts of fourteen preserved steam lines, standard and narrow gauge, with stock lists, and a summary of ten others.

12836 LONDON TRANSPORT. The London Transport Collection of Historical Relics at Syon Park. *Syon Park: L.T.*, 1973. pp. 8. Reproduced typescript.
A descriptive list of the exhibits, for visitors.

12837 RANSOM, P. J. G. Railways revived: an account of the preserved steam railways. *London: Faber*, 1973. pp. 183, with 30 illus on 16 plates, 15 maps, a graph, 3 appendices & a bibliography (50+ sources). Foreword by L. T. C. Rolt.
The graph shows the growth of traffic on six preserved lines, 1951–1971.

12838 RATCLIFFE R. L. and NEWCOMBE, R. 25 years of enthusiasm: being the story of the first 25 years of the Locomotive Club of Great Britain, 1949–1974. *Bexleyheath: L.C.G.B.*, [1974]. pp. 40, with 50 illus.
Includes an account of the Ken Nunn Collection of Railway Photographs, the Club's rail tours, and its preservation activities.

12839 WILLIAMS, P. Britain's railway museums. *London: Ian Allan*, 1974. pp. 176, with 48 col. illus on 16 plates & 281 monochrome illus in text.

12840 DINTING RAILWAY CENTRE. 2 Jubilees. *Dinting: the Centre*, [1975]. pp. 16 (incl. covers), with 5 illus & a list of all Jubilee class locomotives.

The two ex-LMS 4-6-0 locomotives: 'Bahamas' (5596) and 'Leander' (5690).

12841 GREAT WESTERN SOCIETY. [Guidebooks]. Didcot. *Didcot: the Society*, [1975]. sm. obl. format. pp. 36, incl. covers, with 38 illus (18 col.) & a plan. Includes a stock list and membership application forms (pp. I–IV in centre).

—— another edn. [1977]. pp. 36 & pp. I–IV.

—— another edn. Didcot Railway Centre, 1979. pp. 32, with 34 illus (24 col.) & a plan. (Stocklist, pp. 27–30).

12842 NATIONAL RAILWAY MUSEUM. [Guide]. National Railway Museum. (Text by John Coiley, Keeper). *Norwich: Jarrold*, 1975. la. 8°. pp. [16], with 41 illus (24 col.) by Richard Tilbrook.

—— [1976 edn]. Text by J. Coiley. *Jarrold*, [1976]. la. 8°. pp. [16], with 38 illus (28 col.).

—— [1978 edn]. Text by J. Coiley. *N.R.M. & Jarrold*, [1978]. la. 8°. pp. [36], with 65 illus (47 col.).

12843 SCOTTISH RAILWAY PRESERVATION SOCIETY. Guide and Stocklist. 2nd edn. *Edinburgh: The Society*, 1975. pp. [32], with 32 illus; & 3 illus (2 col.), on covers. Foreword by John Thomas.

12844 SIMMONDS, J. Scottish railways. *St. Ives (Cornwall): J. Pike*, 1975. (Viewing Scotland series). pp. 32, with 12 illus of locomotives & a map.

An introductory history and lists of preserved lines, societies & museums.

12845 STEAMTOWN Railway Museum. *Norwich: Jarrold & Sons*, 1975. pp. 16, with 22 illus (11 col.), plan, route map. A guidebook.

—— 2nd edn. *Jarrold*, 1977. pp. 16, with 24 illus (13 col.), plan & stock list.

12846 STOCKTON AND DARLINGTON RAILWAY 150 CELEBRATIONS JOINT COMMITTEE. Rail 150 Exhibition. Grand Steam Cavalcade (souvenir guide); editor, Alan Bowman. *Darlington: Exhibition Administration*, [1975]. pp. 80, with 96 illus (50 col.).

Illustrations, with historical commentaries and accounts of various aspects of preparations for the Exhibition by Viscount Downe, P. W. B. Semmens, K. W. Ashberry, Maurice Burns, Michael Wheeler, George Hinchliffe, M. G. Satow, K. Hoole and Alan Batty.

12847 WHITEHOUSE, P. B. Railway relics and regalia; general editor, P. B. Whitehouse. *London: Hamlyn, for 'Country Life'*, 1975. la. 8°. pp. 176, with over 200 illus & maps (many col.); bibliography (29 sources).

Tickets & passes, timetables, station lamps, cast iron and enamel signs & notices, maps, signals & signalling equipment, luggage labels, posters & handbills, cutlery, china & glass, carriage panels, heraldry, nameplates, number plates, shed plates, works plates, clocks & watches.

12848 BRITISH TOURIST AUTHORITY. Steam in Britain: a map guide to some of the many small railways operating steam-hauled passenger trains, and to the live museums where visitors can inspect locomotives in steam. 2nd edn. *London: B.T.A.*, 1976. A folded map with 42 col. illus, and on reverse, a gazetteer giving details of 42 locations.

12849 DINTING RAILWAY CENTRE. Stock List: a brief history of the exhibits normally to be seen at the Dinting Railway Centre, Glossop, Derbyshire. *Stockport: Bahamas Locomotive Society*, [1976]. pp. 6, with 12 illus. Reproduced typescript within printed cover.

12850 LONDON TRANSPORT. The London Transport Collection, Syon Park, Brentford, Middlesex. [*London: L.T.*, 1976]: obl. format. pp. [24]. with 64 illus (62 col.), & a diagram.

Includes tramcars and locomotives.

12851 NATIONAL RAILWAY MUSEUM. Preserved locomotives and rolling stock in the National Railway Museum, York, [described by] John van Riemsdijk and David Jenkinson. [*London*]: HMSO. (N.R.M. Selections).

no. 1: Great Northern Railway locomotives no. 990 and no. 251, [1976]. pp. [8], with 4 illus & 6 mechanical drawings.

H. A. Ivatt's 4-4-2 locomotive of 1898 and his large-boilered version of 1902.

no. 2: South Eastern and Chatham Railway no. 737; Pullman car 'Topaz'. [1976]. pp. [8], with 2 illus & 4 mechanical drawings.

The Wainwright & Surtees 4-4-0 locomotive of 1901, and a British-built Pullman car of 1913.

no. 3: London, Brighton and South Coast Railway locomotives no. 214, 'Gladstone' and no. 82, 'Boxhill'. [1976]. pp. [8], with 4 illus & 3 mechanical drawings.

The sole surviving example of a British 0-4-2 tender locomotive (the LBSC's class B, 1902), and one of the class A 'Terriers', built in 1880.

no. 4: North Eastern Railway locomotive no. 1621; Great Eastern Railway locomotive no. 490. [1976]. pp. [8], with 8 illus & 3 mechanical drawings.

One of Wilson Worsdell's class M1 4-4-0 engines of 1892, and a G.E.R. 'Intermediate' of 1895.

no. 5: Great Northern Railway 4-2-2 express locomotive no. 1; Grand Junction Railway 2-2-2 no. 49, 'Columbine'. [1976]. pp. [8], with 5 illus & 7 mechanical drawings.

no. 6: Midland Compound no. 1000; Midland 6-wheel composite coach. [1976]. pp. [8], with 7 illus & 3 mechanical drawings.

12852 RAIL Museum and historic York. *York: Yorkshire Evening Press*, [1976]. obl. 8°. pp. 52, with 81 illus (63 col.).

A guide to the recently opened National Railway Museum, with essays by Vivian Brooks, John Potts and Ronald Willis; edited by John White.

12853   ASSOCIATION OF RAILWAY PRESERVA-
TION SOCIETIES. Introducing the Associa-
tion of Railway Preservation Societies, Ltd.
Whitkirk (Leeds): A.R.P.S., [1977]. pp. 4.

12854   BURTON, A. Industrial archaeological sites
of Britain: photographs by Clive Cooke.
London: Weidenfeld & Nicolson, 1977. pp.
160, with 57 illus.
Includes railway museums and preservation.

12855   CAMPBELL, J. E. Railway preservation in
North and Mid Wales, edited by J. E.
Campbell. *Published by Cambrian Railways, Corris Railway Society, Foxcote Man-
or Society, Glyn Valley Tramway Group,
and Rheilffordd Llyn Tegid Cyf (Bala Lake
Rly, Ltd)*, 1977. pp. 32, with 14 illus; map
on cover.

12856   HEDGES, M. Full steam ahead!: a guide to
Britain's little railways. [*Birmingham:
Evening Mail*, 1977]. (Evening Mail
Special). newspaper format. pp. 20, with 49
illus.
Preserved and re-opened lines of standard
gauge and narrow gauge.
—— Steam '78: a guide to Britain's little
railways. [*Birmingham*]: *Evening Mail*, May
1978. (Evening Mail Special). newspaper
format. pp. 23, with 34 illus (6 col.), a col.
map & 2 portraits.

12857   NIXON, I. A. Steam around Britain in the
seventies. *Truro: Bradford Barton*, 1977.
pp. 96. Intro & 97 illus with descrs.
Steam-hauled trains on preserved lines.

12858   TURNER, K. Discovering trams and tramways. *Aylesbury: Shire Publications*, 1977.
(Discovering Series, 231). pp. 64, with 28
illus on 16 plates & a brief evaluative
bibliography (10+ sources).
A stock guide to tramcar preservation on
working tramways and in museums in Britain.

12859   HEAVYSIDE, G. T. Steaming into the
eighties: the standard gauge railway preservation scene. *Newton Abbot: David &
Charles*, 1978. pp. [96]. Text, pp. 5–11,
60–2, & p. 38, by G. M. Kichenside; 138
illus, with descrs, & a map showing locations of preserved lines.

12860   MACKAY, J. Railway antiques. *London:
Ward Lock*, 1978. la. 8°. pp. 136, with ca.
200 illus (many composite, some col.),
bibliography (20+ sources).
Parts and accessories, uniforms, tickets, timetables & guides, philately, numismatics, souve-
nirs, models, ephemera.

12861   MARTIN, B. P. Tramways in Britain. *Sale:
Brennan Publications*, 1978. pp. 32, with 23
illus.
Descriptions of tramways currently in operation, tramcars preserved, closures of tramway

systems, and societies for the history, preservation
and operation of tramways.

12862   RAILWAY PRESERVATION SYMPOSIUM
[London, November 1978]. Proceedings of
the Railway Preservation Symposium held
at the Institution of Civil Engineers . . . ,
London, on Tuesday, 28th November 1978.
*York: Friends of the National Railway
Museum*, 1978. pp. 46, with 29 illus. Intro-
duction by W. O. Skeat.
The papers, reprinted in full, are by John
Bellwood, Nigel Trotter, A. G. W. Garroway,
David H. Ward, Peter Allen and M. G. Satow. In
his Introduction W. O. Skeat provides a summary
of the discussions.

12863   STEAMPORT TRANSPORT MUSEUM. History and Guide to Exhibits (compiled by
N. R. Nutter). *Southport: Steamport Southport Ltd*, [1978]. pp. 16, with 15 illus (3 on
covers) & a map.

12864   WHITEHOUSE, P. B., SNELL, J. B. and
HOLLINGSWORTH, J. B. Steam for pleasure. *London: Routledge & Kegan Paul*,
1978. la. 8°. pp. 240, with many illus, maps
& a bibliography (30 sources).
A world-wide survey of restored and re-opened
stretches of line, and of live steam museums.
Great Britain and Ireland, pp. 140–83, with 49
illus (5 col.), 3 maps, & a 4-column list.

12865   BURY TRANSPORT MUSEUM. Guide &
Stockbook. 2nd edn, compiled by Charles
Cooke. *Bury: East Lancashire Railway
Preservation Society*, [1979]. pp. 26, with 20
illus, incl. cover illus.

12866   GARRATT, C. D. A Popular Guide to the
preserved steam railways of Britain. *Poole:
Blandford Press*, 1979. pp. 192, with 40 col.
illus on 32 plates, & in text, 45 illus & 10
area maps.
Passenger-carrying railways, 'live steam'
museums, and museums & collections with static
exhibits.

12867   MIDLAND RAILWAY CENTRE. Site
Guide. *Butterley Station, Ripley: the Centre*,
[1979]. A printed 6-page folder with an inset
folder, 'Introducing the Midland Railway
Centre.'

12868   NATIONAL RAILWAY MUSEUM. Stage-
coach to Supertrain: the story of Britain's
railways; a guide to help you look at the
Long Gallery of the National Railway
Museum. *York: N.R.M.*, 1979. pp. 48, with
100 illus, & 60 col. illus on folded covers.
Text by Dick Hanson.
The folding pictorial covers open to form a wall
chart depicting 60 drawings in colour of British
steam locomotives and carriages of all periods.
The guide is designed as a companion for young
visitors, and consists of illustrations relating to the
exhibits, with questions based upon the information accompanying each item on display.

12869   SPENCE, J. Surviving steam railways; illustrated from colour photographs by Anthony

J. Lambert. *London: Batsford*, 1979. pp. [64], with col. frontis, 29 col. illus & a 4-page map.

12870 TREVENA, N. Steam exposure: photography on Britain's preserved railways. *Penryn: Atlantic Books*, 1979. obl. format. pp. [88], with text [pp. 4–14], & 142 illus with descrs.

12871 COCKMAN, F. G. Discovering preserved railways. *Princes Risborough: Shire Publications*, 1980. (Discovering series, 253). sm. 8°. pp. 80, with 30 illus on 16 plates (pp. 33–48), & 36 route maps.
36 re-opened stretches of line described, a list of 38 railway centres & museums, & a brief bibliography.

12872 CONWY VALLEY RAILWAY MUSEUM. Souvenir Booklet, incorporating 'A brief history of Britain's railways' by Alan Maund. *Betwys-y-Coed: the Museum*, 1980. pp. [20], incl. covers, wtih 26 illus (15 col.) & a plan. Title from cover.
A museum of British railway locomotives & rolling stock, with special emphasis on the standard and narrow-gauge railways of North Wales.

12873 EATWELL, D. and COOPER-SMITH, J. H. Live Steam: locomotives and lines today. *London: Batsford*, 1980. pp. 120. Intro & 160 illus with descrs.
Preserved lines and their locomotives.

12874 JONES, K. W. Railways for pleasure: the complete guide to steam and scenic lines in Great Britain and Ireland. *Guildford: Lutterworth Press*, 1980. pp. 160, with col. t. p. & 200 illus (34 col.), 1 general map & 7 col. pictorial maps of geographical regions & 36 smaller maps of individual lines.

12875 PRICE, J. H. A Source Book of Trams. *London: Ward Lock*, 1980. sm. obl. format. pp. 151, with 118 illus & lists of 22 tramways and 16 tramway museums in the British Isles (including 12 cliff railways, and transport museums with tramway exhibits).

12876 RAILWAY PRESERVATION CONVENTION [Manchester, August–September 1980.] Railway Preservation Convention at University of Manchester Institute of Science & Technology, 13 September, 1980. [Papers]. *[Manchester: the Convention*, 1980]. pp. [100]. Reproduced typescript. Title from cover, which is headed 'The Great Railway Exposition, August 2nd to September 14th, 1980'.
Resumés of papers read at the Convention. Chairman of morning session, John Coiley; chairman of afternoon session, Trevor Anderson. Papers by Christopher Forrest, Richard Greenwood, Don Cowen, George Hinchliffe, Michael Satow, A. Jarvis, Clive B. Luhrs, Dai Woodham, Peter Manisty, Barry Wright, Ian McCubbin, Jack Boston, John Stockley, Geoffrey Hare, and the guest of honour, Dame Margaret Weston.

Q 2   MODEL RAILWAY ENGINEERING
12877–97
Railway engineering reduced in scale, yet retaining essential features of full-scale practice and prototype. Small-scale indoor model railways are excluded

For passenger-carrying railways run for pleasure on gauges of 3ft 6in or less
see **D 2** and **D 6**

12877 CHRISTIE, MANSON & WOODS. Catalogue of Fine Historical Steam Engine Models and ship models, railway relics, locomotive name plates, etc. . . . which will be sold at auction . . . Wednesday August 2, 1967. *London: the firm*, [1967]. pp. 95, with 33 plates (16 of model steam locomotives).

12878 CHRISTIE, MANSON & WOODS. Catalogue of Fine Historical Steam Engine Models and ship models, railway relics, locomotive name plates, etc. . . . which will be sold at auction . . . on Wednesday June 5, 1968. *London: the firm*, [1968]. pp. 108, with 38 plates (20 of model steam locomotives).

12879 'L.B.S.C.' Simple model locomotive building, introducing L.B.S.C.'s 'Tich'; edited by Martin Evans. *Hemel Hempstead: Model & Allied Publications*, 1968. pp. 268, with 51 illus on 28 plates & numerous dimensioned drawings.

12880 CHRISTIE, MANSON & WOODS. Catalogue of Fine Historical Steam Engine Models and ship models, railway relics, locomotive name plates, etc. . . . which will be sold at auction . . . on Wednesday May, 7 1969. *London: the firm*, [1969]. pp. 86, with 46 illus on plates (26 of model steam locomotives).

12881 'L.B.S.C.' Betty the Mongoliper, by 'L.B.S.C.': a 2-6-2 outside cylinder locomotive in 3½in. gauge to the proposed N2 Southern class of 1934. *Hemel Hempstead: Model & Allied Publications*, [1969]. pp. [47], with illus.

12882 'L.B.S.C.' Mona: a simple 0-6-2 tank engine. *Hemel Hempstead: Model & Allied Publications*, [1969]. (Specialist Booklets, 3). pp. [77], with 11 illus & numerous dimensioned drawings.
An inside-cylinder model locomotive in 3½in. gauge. Based on an LCDR design.

12883 'L.B.S.C.' Speedy Great Western 0-6-0 tank engine: a powerful 0-6-0 in 5in. gauge, by 'L.B.S.C.' *Hemel Hempstead: Model & Allied Publications*, [1969]. (Specialist Booklets, 6). pp. [60], with 2 illus and many dimensioned drawings.
—— [2nd edn]. *Watford: Model & Allied Publications*, 1978. (Specialist Booklets, 6). pp. 63, with 2 illus & many dimensioned drawings.

12884 MINNS, J. E. Model railway engines. *London: Weidenfeld & Nicolson*, 1969. pp. 120, with 121 illus (24 col.).
Live steam model railway locomotives of all gauges, from 1797 to the present; Europe, America and the Far East.
—— another edn. *Octopus Books*, 1973. pp. 97, with 121 illus (33 col.).

12885 CHRISTIE, MANSON & WOODS. Catalogue of Fine Historical Steam Engine Models and ship models, railway relics, locomotive name plates, etc. . . . which will be sold at auction . . . on Wednesday July 29, 1970. *London: the firm*, [1970]. pp. 88, with 32 plates (10 of model steam locomotives).

12886 EVANS, M. Outdoor model railways. *Hemel Hempstead: Model & Allied Publications*, 1970. pp. 96, with 116 illus on 62 plates, & 68 drawings in text.
Track and lineside construction for gauges from 'O' (i.e. 1¼ inch) to 15 inch gauge.

12887 'L.B.S.C.' Princess Marina: L.M.S. 2-6-0 Mogul class locomotive in 3½in gauge. *Hemel Hempstead: Model & Allied Publications*, [1970]. (Specialist Booklets, 5). pp. 35, with 3 illus & many dimensioned drawings.
From a series which first appeared in the periodical *Mechanics*.

12888 EVANS, M. Rob Roy: how to build a simple 3½in. gauge 0-6-0 tank locomotive based on the dockyard engines of the old Caledonian Railway. *Hemel Hempstead: Model & Allied Publications*, 1972. pp. 112, with 25 illus on 16 plates & many dimensioned drawings in text.

12889 JACKSON-STEVENS, E. Scale model electric tramcars and how to model them, with drawings by Eric Thornton. *Newton Abbot: David & Charles*, 1972. pp. 196, with col. frontis, 34 illus on plates & 53 drawings in text.

12890 DOW, G. World locomotive models. *Bath: Adams & Dart*, 1973. 4°. pp. 168, with 16 col. plates & 258 illus in text.
Steam, electric and diesel model locomotives of 40 countries, largely from museums, but also from manufacturers and private owners. Arranged chronologically by year of prototype, 1804–1960.

12891 ADAMS, J. H. L. and WHITEHOUSE, P. B. Model and miniature railways. *London: Hamlyn; New English Library*, 1976, magazine format. pp. 512. Profusely illustrated. Issued serially.

12892 CROMAR WHITE LTD. Garden & estate railways. *London: the firm*, [1977]. pp. 18, incl. cover, with 30 illus.
A sales brochure: locomotives, rolling stock, track, and signalling equipment for gauges from 3½ inch to 10¼ inch.

12893 NEALE, D. Railways in the garden. *Seaton: Peco*, 1978. pp. 72, with 24 illus (6 col.) & a layout plan.

12894 CLARKSONS OF YORK. [Catalogue]. *York: Clarkson*, [1979]. pp. [76], with numerous illus & specifications.
Model locomotives, 3½ inch, 5 inch & 7¼ inch gauges.

12895 EVANS, M. Workshop chatter: a bedside book for model engineers. *Watford: Model & Allied Publications*, 1979. pp. 128, with many illus.
Includes model steam locomotives, and a chapter 'on personalities' (pp. 98–118), being impressions, with portraits, of Percival Marshall, Henry Greenly, A. J. Campbell, L. Lawrence ('L.B.S.C.'), Edgar T. Westbury, John Neville Maskelyne and K. N. Harris.

12896 HAMMOND, P. An introduction to tramway modelling. *London: Tramway & Light Railway Society*, 1979. pp. 80, with 40 groups of dimensioned drawings, 12 illus (photos) & a la. folded sheet of working diagrams, on both sides.
A manual for the construction of a ¾ inch scale Preston type 4-wheeled open-top tramcar of the 1900-1910 period.

12897 EVANS, M. and 'L.B.S.C.' 'Evening Star'. *Watford: Model & Allied Publications*, 1980. pp. 224, with many illus & diagrams.
A manual for the construction of a 3½ inch gauge model of the BR 2-10-0 locomotive.

Q 3   RAILWAY PHOTOGRAPHY, CINEMATOGRAPHY AND FILMS

12898–12907

12898 TRANSPORT AND TRAVEL FILM LIBRARY (BRITISH TRANSPORT FILM LIBRARY). [Catalogues]. 1952–. *In progress* as revised annual or biennial editions.

16mm sound films available on loan to institutions, societies, clubs and groups. All aspects of transport and travel are represented and the films are produced mainly as publicity venues by British

Railways, London Transport and various other transport undertakings, the Festiniog Railway, and other preserved lines and tourist bodies.

12899 COOPER, H. The experiences of a railway photographer. Great Western Railway (London) Lecture & Debating Society, meeting on November 5th, 1908 [no. 52]. pp. 10, with 6 illus.
Work undertaken for the GWR.

12900 THOMPSON, C. J. The Photographic Section of the Chief Civil Engineer's Office. Proceedings of the British Railways (W.R.) London Lecture & Debating Society, 1956–57, no. 432. pp. 14, with discussion & 7 illus.
Author, Chief Photographer, Chief Civil Engineer's Office, Western Region.

12901 ANSTEY, E. The work of the B.T.C. Film Unit. (Proceedings of the British Railways (W.R.) London Lecture & Debating Society, 1960–61, no. 466). pp. 12, with discussion.
Author, Chief Officer (Films), British Transport Commission.

12902 EARLEY, M. W. A generation in railway photography, in Main Line Album, by P. B. Whitehouse (1964), pp. 6–15.

12903 WALKER, C. Tribute to Steam: an exhibition of railway photographs by Colin Walker. Leicester: Leicester Museums, 1967. pp. [24], with intro & descriptions of 145 exhibited photographs, with 6 reproduced as illustrations.

12904 HUNTLEY, J. Railways in the cinema. London: Ian Allan, 1969. pp. 168, with 100 illus on 64 plates.
A survey of films (documentary, fiction, publicity, educational) in which the railway is an essential element, with an alphabetical list of details of ca. 700 made since 1895 (pp. 111–68). Some films are described in considerable detail and notes on the making of them are given.

12905 CASSERLEY, H. C. H. C. Casserley. Newton Abbot: David & Charles, 1972. (Famous Railway Photographers series). 4°. pp. 96. Intros (pp. 5–10, 93–5) & 84 photographs with descriptive commentaries.
Period, pre-1939.

12906 CROSS, D. Derek Cross. Newton Abbot: David & Charles, 1975. (Famous Railway Photographers series). 4°. pp. [96]. Intro [pp. 5–8] & 87 illus with descrs.

12907 MORRISON, B. The Steam Cameramen, compiled by Brian Morrison for the Railway Photographic Society. Oxford: Oxford Publishing Co., 1980. la. 8°. pp. [240], with 412 illus. Foreword by Maurice W. Earley; Introduction by Brian Morrison. A limited edition of 2,000 copies, each issued in a slip case.
A record of the work of 58 members of the R.P.S., 1922–1976, consisting of a selected 6 photographs from each, with a portrait and a brief biographical note.

Q 4   ILLUSTRATIONS

Closed. (See 16 and note on p. 20)

Sources and methods—Bibliography—Railway historians and writers—Railway-book publishing—Glossaries—Dictionaries

12908–37

12908 POTTER, F. Presidential address. Great Western Railway (London) Lecture & Debating Society, meeting on October 24th, 1912 [no. 91]. pp. 9.
On the progress and achievements of the G.W.R. (London) Lecture & Debating Society.

12909 POLE, F. J. C. The Debating Society's quarter-centenary. Great Western Railway (London) Lecture & Debating Society, meeting on 3rd October 1929 (no. 232). pp. 8.

12910 RAILWAY GAZETTE. One hundred years of railway publishing: a brief history of the Railway Gazette and its incorporated journals: Herapath's Railway Journal, the Railway Times, the Railway Engineer, etc. in Railway Gazette, vol. 62 (January–June 1935), pp. 849–53, with a genealogical chart.

12911 BRITISH RAILWAYS. SCOTTISH REGION. Instructions for the preservation or destruction of records and correspondence. Glasgow: B.R.(Sc.R.), September 1957. pp. 55.
Policy derived from consultation between BR Departmental Committees, the BTC Archivist and the Public Record Office.

12912 BUREAU INTERNATIONAL DE DOCUMENTATION DES CHEMINS DE FER. Chemins de fer: glossaire des termes ferroviaires, français, anglais, allemand, espagnol, italien, suédois. Amsterdam: Elsevier Publishing Co., 1960. (Collection Glossaria Interpretum, 31). pp. 413.
The range of terms (ca. 2500) is not confined to railway equipment but includes operation, personnel, and workaday expressions such as 'setting back' and 'six-foot way', and some more venturesome phrases such as 'rush of passengers' and 'ease of breathing' (air in tunnels).

12913 KELLETT, J. R. Urban and transport history from legal records: an example from Glasgow solicitors' papers, in Journal of Transport History, vol. 6 (1963–4). pp. 222–40, with 2 maps & 68 notes.
The Stobcross extension of the North British Rly is used as an example.

12914 SHEPPARD, H. Dictionary of Railway Slang. Ilminster: Dillington House College for Adult Education, [1965]. pp. 11.
The Introduction is dated 'October 1965' but at the end of the text are the words 'Printed by the Somerset County Gazette, Castle Green, Taunton, 1951.'
Compiled from examples given by railwaymen attending courses at the College.

12915 FOWKES, E. H. The records of the Railway Clearing House, in Journal of Transport History, vol. 7, 1965–6. (Sources of Transport History). pp. 141–8, with 30 notes.

12916 [ALLAN.] IAN ALLAN LIMITED. Twenty-five years, 1942–1967. [Shepperton]: Ian Allan Ltd, [1967]. sm. 8°. pp. [32], with 30 illus.

12917 ROBBINS, M. Points and Signals: a railway historian at work. London: Allen & Unwin, 1967. pp. 256, with 8 illus on 4 plates, & 10 maps.
Reprinted essays by M. Robbins on various aspects of British railway history; also (pp. 18–31), 'The railway historian's craft', on the elements regarded as essential to the study and presentation of the subject.

12918 ROGERSON, I. L.T.C. Rolt: books and monographs, compiled by Ian Rogerson. Cheltenham: Gloucestershire Technical Information Service, 1968. pp. 18.
Includes his books on railways.

12919 CLINKER, C. R. Railway history: a handlist of the principal sources of original material, with notes and guidance on its use. Padstow: C. R. Clinker, 1969. pp. 16. Reproduced typescript in card cover.
A revised and much enlarged version of a 'tentative guide' produced for limited circulation in 1959 (Ottley 7894).
—— rev. & expanded edn. Railway history Sources: a handlist of the principal sources of original material, with notes and guidance on its use. Bristol: Avon-Anglia, 1976. (Reference Aid Series, 1). pp. 20.
The value of the work is out of all proportion to its modest size. In three sections:
1, Summary of Sources; Parliamentary material, Government Departmental records, official railway material, local records, printed books, newspapers, periodicals, guides (annual), timetables, maps (railway), maps (Ordnance Survey).
2, Notes and Information; Acts of Parliament, reports of Government Inspectors, official railway material, the Hand-Book of Stations (R.C.H.), printed books (contemporary), printed books (non-contemporary), newspapers, Bradshaw's Manual, timetables, official railway maps, railway junction diagrams, Ordnance Survey maps and plans.
3, Appendix: articles [on sources] in The Journal of Transport History (12 papers).

12920 KELLETT, J. R. Writing on Victorian railways: an essay in nostalgia, in Victorian Studies, vol. 13, no. 1, Sept. 1969, pp. 90–6.

12921 RAY, J. A history of the railways. *London: Heinemann Educational*, 1969. pp. [8], 77, with 66 illus, incl. 2 maps; bibliography (97 sources).
Written to encourage young readers (ages 11–18) who want to know more about railway history. A guide to sources, research method, and presentation.

12922 BOND, M. F. Guide to the Records of Parliament. *London: H.M.S.O.*, 1971. pp. x, 352.
Index (pp. 313–352) has 20 entries under Railways, Tramways, and Transport. Valuable also as a guide to parliamentary procedure.

12923 SWANN, B. and TURNBULL, M. Records of interest to social scientists, 1919 to 1939: Introduction. *London: H.M.S.O.*, 1971. (Public Record Office Handbooks, 14). pp. viii, 282.
'Published with the co-operation of the Social Sciences Research Council'.
pp. 97–108, 'Ministry of Transport (MT)': a calendar of the records available for study at the P.R.O., preceded by a summary history of the Department.

12924 MOWAT, C. L. The heyday of the British railway system: vanishing evidence and the historian's task, *in* Journal of Transport History, new series, vol. 1 (1971–2), pp. 1–17, with 36 notes.

12925 ROGERS, A. This was their world: approaches to local history. *London: B.B.C.*, 1972. pp. xiii, 284, with 50 illus & 29 tables, diagrams, graphs, maps, plans & facsimiles.
ch. 6 (pp. 109–32). 'Transport and communication', with 43 notes. Railways, pp. 116–24 *et passim*.

12926 OTTLEY, G. Railway history: a guide to sixty-one collections in libraries and archives in Great Britain. *London: Library Association, Reference, Special & Information Section*, 1973. (Subject Guides to Library Resources, 1). pp. 80, with frontis (map) & 12 notes.
The map shows the approximate relative sizes of railway history resources in the collections described in the Guide.
The Introduction (pp. 9–12) is followed by a note on the subject of access to libraries and archives (pp. 13–14).
As an Appendix (pp. 74–5): 'Railway history in local record offices'.
Each of the 61 collections is introduced by tabulated information (location, opening times, terms of admission, services etc.) followed by a prose description incorporating bibliographical information and notes.

12927 STEPHENS, W. B. Sources for English local history. *Manchester: Manchester University Press*, 1973. pp. x, 260, with many notes.
pp. 56, 99–104, Railways; p. 104, Tramways.

12928 RICHARDSON, J. The Local Historian's

Encyclopaedia. [*London*]: *Historical Publications*, 1974. pp. 312.
Section K, part 2 (pp. 183–97), 'Railways': a list of 'most of the railways' with dates of incorporation, opening, later amalgamation, and changes of name.
Some important lines, e.g. the Great Central, the Great Eastern, the South Eastern & Chatham and the London & South Western, are omitted, and of the Big Four only the Southern is included. Alternative sources for this kind of information: *Bradshaw's Railway Manual* (1863 to 1923), *Index to Local & Personal Acts* (1949) and C. R. Clinker's *Register of Closed Passenger Stations and Goods Depots* (latest edn. 1978, & two supplements; no. 1, 1979, & no. 2, 1981).

12929 DIXON, D. Jack Simmons: a bibliography of his published writings, *in* Journal of Transport History, new series, vol. 3 (1975–6), pp. 145–58.
266 publications. Of 83 on transport subjects 65 are on railway history.

12930 DYOS, H. J. Jack Simmons: an appreciation, *in* Journal of Transport History, new series, vol. 3 (1975–6), pp. 133–44, with portrait.
Published on the retirement of Professor Simmons from the Chair of History, University of Leicester.

12931 HADFIELD, C. Register of Research Interests, November 1976; edited, and an index compiled, by Charles Hadfield. *Caterham: Railway & Canal Historical Society*, [1976]. pp. 20. Reproduced typescript. No covers.
An alphabetical list of members of the R. & C.H.S. who consented to the publication of information on their past & present research interests; with a subject index.

12932 O'BRIEN, P. The new economic history of the railways. *London: Croom Helm*, 1977. pp. 121, with 7 tables, 2 diagrams & a bibliography (75 sources).
An appraisal of current trends in economic theory and quantitative analysis as applied to the railway history of America, Russia, Britain and Italy, based largely upon the researches of A. Fishlow, R. Fogel, G. Hawke, J. Metzer and S. Fenoaltea.

12933 PUBLIC RECORD OFFICE. The British Transport Historical Records Collection: a provisional guide. *London: P.R.O.*, 1977. pp. [i], 13. Reproduced typescript, paper covers. Title from cover.
The general arrangement of the records as they existed before being taken over by the P.R.O. in January 1969 (Scottish records excepted), with new coded references to accord with existing P.R.O. practice.

12934 RAILWAY AND CANAL HISTORICAL SOCIETY. Location of research material: a guide to the R.C.H.S. card index. *Caterham: the Society*, 1977. pp. [12].
Study material in local and county libraries, English and Welsh record offices, and in the libraries of some 70 universities, learned societies

and local archives, arranged alphabetically by the names of undertakings in four sections: Railways, Tramroads, Canals, and Miscellaneous. Published primarily for the use of members of the R. & C.H.S.

12935 PUBLIC RECORD OFFICE. British Transport Historical Records: finding aids and key to former record groups. [*Kew*]: *P.R.O.*, 1978. pp. 15. Reproduced typescript.

12936 [ALLAN.] IAN ALLAN LIMITED. Steaming into the eighties. *Shepperton: Ian Allan*

Ltd, [1979]. pp. 20, with 27 illus.
A history of the firm's progress.

12937 BARKER, T. Towards an historical classification of urban transport development since the later eighteenth century, *in* Journal of Transport History, 3rd series, vol. 1, no. 1, September 1980, pp. 75–90, with table & 44 notes.
A statistical survey of the growth and decline of road & rail transport in London, 1825 to 1977, from which a framework of constants is derived and formulated into a table (p. 77) which may be applied to other urban areas.

S   STATISTICS (General), STATISTICAL SOURCES AND METHOD

12938–46

12938 DEWSNUP, E. R. The necessity of care in the interpretation of railway statistics used comparatively. *London: Railway Gazette*, 1910. pp. 24.
Reprinted from the *Railway Gazette* of 3 June 1910.

12939 RAPER, C. L. Railway transportation: a history of its economics and of its relation to the state. *New York, London: Putnam, 1912.*
Based on *Railroad Transportation: its history and its laws*, by A. T. Hadley, 1885.
pp. 14–60, 'Railway transportation in Great Britain'. International comparisons, with statistics, are frequently made throughout the text.

12940 SMALLPIECE, B. The use of statistics in the measurement of efficiency in Transport. Proceedings of the British Railways (W.R.) London Lecture & Debating Society, 1949–50, no. 367. pp. 15, with discussion.
Author, 'Director of Costs & Statistics, B.T.C.'.

12941 MITCHELL, B. R. Abstract of British Historical Statistics, by B. R. Mitchell, with the collaboration of Phyllis Deane. *Cambridge: Cambridge University Press*, 1962. pp. xiv, 513.
Railways, pp. 225–9 *et passim*. Tramways, p 230.
—— Second Abstract . . . , by B. R. Mitchell and H. C. Jones. *Cambridge University Press*, 1971. pp. ix, 227.
Railways, pp. 104, 145, 157; Tramcars in use, p. 106.

12942 BALINT, M. L.M.R. Survey, Watford Line: information on tabulations. [*Lon-*

don]: *Greater London Council, Dept. of Highways & Transportation*, December 1968. (Memoranda, 127). Reproduced typescript.
A list of tabulations prepared for the use of London Midland Region. The Survey is described and the interpretation of data discussed.

12943 BALINT, M. Reliability of railway postal questionnaires. *London: Greater London Council, Dept. of Highways & Transportation, Transportation Branch*, August 1968. (Research Memoranda, 89). pp. 14. Reproduced typescript.
The merits of different survey methods and the comparative value of resulting responses, with recommended outline for future survey procedure.

12944 HARVEY, J. M. Sources of statistics. *London: C. Bingley*, 1969. pp. 100.
ch. 10 (pp. 83–94), 'Transport and communications'. (Railways, pp. 84–5).
—— 2nd edn. *C. Bingley*, 1971. pp. 126.
Railways, pp. 94–6.

12945 CENTRAL STATISTICAL OFFICE. Guide to Official Statistics. *HMSO*.
no. 1, 1976. Railways, section 8.2, pp. 243–5; bibliography, pp. 363–87.
no. 2, 1978. Railways, section 8.2, pp. 255–7; bibliography, pp. 358–82.
no. 3, 1980. Railways, section 8.2, pp. 281–4; bibliography, pp. 401–28.

12946 MUNBY, D. L. Inland transport statistics: Great Britain, 1900–1970, by D. L. Munby; edited and completed by A. H. Watson. *Oxford: Clarendon Press*.
vol. 1: Railways, public road passenger transport. London's transport. 1978. la. 8°. pp. xii, 693.

T   ATLASES AND GAZETTEERS

12947–56

Reference sources   12947–49

For dictionaries and glossaries previously classed here, see **R**

12947 HARLEY, J. B. The Historian's Guide to Ordnance Survey Maps. *London: National Council for Social Service, for the Standing Conference for Local History,* 1964. pp. 51, with 4 plates (maps) & 14 maps in text.
Reprinted, with added material, from the *Amateur Historian* (1962–3), with a chapter on the period maps of the O.S. by C. W. Phillips.
In checking for the existence of railways in any area it is important to bear in mind that revisions were not undertaken simultaneously over the whole country. The building of a railway could lead to a revised printing, especially in regions of rapid industrial and urban expansion, and many lines constructed before 1850 did not appear on O.S. maps until the 1860s.

12948 HARLEY, J. B. Maps for the local historian: a guide to the British sources. *London: National Council of Social Service, for the Standing Conference for Local History,* 1972. pp. 86, with 8 plates (maps), 7 maps in text & a bibliography (174 sources) consisting of references to works not already mentioned in the text.
Reprinted, with minor corrections, from a series of essays in the *Local Historian,* 1967–9. pp. 48–50, 'Railway maps'.

12949 HARLEY, J. B. Ordnance Survey maps: a descriptive manual. *Southampton: Ordnance Survey,* 1975. 4°. pp. xv, 200, with 40 plates (some col.), notes & a select bibliography (172 sources).
A guide to what the user is likely to find (or not find) in a particular map series. Railways are included in the index to each chapter (i.e. each series) and in the General Index there are 15 page references to railways in the text.

12950 HALL, S. A Travelling County Atlas with all the coach and rail roads accurately laid down and coloured, and carefully corrected to the present time. *London: Chapman & Hall,* 1842. Title-page & 46 col. maps (42 in double-opening & 4 on 4-page foldings).
—— another issue, *Chapman & Hall,* 1845. 46 maps.
—— another edn. A Travelling Atlas of the English Counties . . . *Chapman & Hall,* [1860]. 46 maps.
—— another edn. A Travelling Atlas of the English Counties . . . *Chapman & Hall,* [1873]. 46 maps.

12951 RAILWAY and Telegraphic Atlas of England and Wales. *London,* [1857?].
Forty 2-page maps of English counties and two of Wales, marking and naming all railways, stations and tunnels, projected lines, extent of telegraph, and some mineral lines. Scales vary from 1¼ miles to 1 inch (Rutland) to 5¼ miles to 1 inch (Yorkshire). 8 maps are dated Jan 1, 1855, 2 are dated 1857; the rest are undated.

12952 MAP of the railways proposed by the Bills of the Session of 1863 in the Metropolis & its vicinity. *London: London Topographical Society,* 1973. (Publication 116). Scale: 2 inches to 1 mile.
A facsimile of the map in the General Report of the Board of Trade on the Railway and Canal Bills of Session 1863 (H.C. Papers 1863, vol. LXII).

12953 BAXTER, B. Stone blocks and iron rails. *Newton Abbot: David & Charles,* 1966. (Industrial Archaeology of the British Isles series). pp. 272, with 41 illus on 17 plates, 4 line drawings in text, & 203 bibliogr. notes.
Gazetteer of wagonways & tramroads, pp. 143–236; Bibliography (384 sources), pp. 237–55; Index, pp. 264–72; Addenda, pp. 259–60.

12954 BRITISH Rail Atlas. *London: Ian Allan,* 1967. pp. 85. Cover title: Sectional Maps of British Railways. Scale: 8 miles to 1 inch.
An atlas and gazetteer of BR in the late Spring of 1966, with some subsequent major closures and alterations. Distinctive colours for BR Regions; closed lines in yellow.

12955 COSSONS, N. The BP Book of Industrial Archaeology. *Newton Abbot: David & Charles,* 1975. pp. 496, with 103 illus & 31 line drawings, a gazetteer of sites (pp. 428–50), list of museums (pp. 451–7), list of organisations (pp. 458–75), & a bibliography (pp. 476–88). Index (pp. 489–96).
Railways, pp. 366–99 *et passim.*

12956 BAKER, S. K. Rail Atlas of Britain, 1977; [maps, drawn by Paul Karaul]. *Oxford: Oxford Publishing,* 1977. pp. [5], 82, [26].
The current network, including light railways and preserved sections of line.
—— 2nd edn. *O.P.C.,* 1978. pp. iii, 107 (pp. 1–82, maps; pp. 83–107, indexes).
—— 3rd edn. *O.P.C.,* 1980. pp. iii, 115 (pp. 1–88, maps; pp. 89–115, indexes).

()

P

()

R

SMITH, John H. Cooper-. *See* COOPER-SMITH, John H.

SMITH, John L. *Rails to Tenterden* 8853
Southern Steam, 1923–1939 12531

SMITH, M.G.R. *Modernisation progress and developments in the Civil Engineering Department* 11846

SMITH, M.K. *West Somerset Railway Stock List, 1980* 8518

Smith, M.K. 8518

SMITH, P.G. *Opinion survey of the Yorkshire Dales rail service in 1975* 9318

SMITH, Peter W. *Footplate over the Mendips* 12462
Mendips engineman 12456

SMITH, R.H. *The practical working of locomotives* 10550

SMITH, Robert Gillen *Ad hoc governments* 8152 8604

SMITH, Roger T. *The electrification of the Hammersmith and City Railway* 10301
How British railways strike a new recruit 10729

SMITH, Simon Rocksborough *Summer Saturdays in the West* 8383

SMITH, Stuart William *The Midland Railway: a pictorial history* 12362
The Settle & Carlisle Railway Map 12360

SMITH, T.M. *An Illustrated History of the Highworth Branch* 11890

SMITH, Vincent Powell-. *See* POWELL-SMITH, Vincent

SMITH, W.A.C. *Rails around Glasgow* 9467

[Smith.] W.H. Smith & Son 10978

SMITH, Wilfred *An historical introduction to the economic geography of Great Britain* 11154

SMITH, William, [1940–] *The Cleobury Mortimer and Ditton Priors Light Railway* 8946

SMITH, William Henry 10978

SMITHSON, Alison *The Euston Arch and the growth of the London Midland & Scottish Railway* 8751 12269

SMITHSON, Peter *The Euston Arch and the growth of the London Midland & Scottish Railway* 8751 12269

SMULLEN, Ivor *Taken for a ride* 12765

SMYTHE, Joe *The Peoples' Road* 12710

Snaefell Mountain Rly 1906* 9915 9917

Snaefell Mountain Railway, 1895–1970 1906* 9915

SNELL, John Bernard *Britain's railways under steam* 7997
Early railways 10177
Jennie 12755
Land transportation by rail 10182
Mechanical engineering: railways 10370
Railways: mechanical engineering 10370
Steam for pleasure 12801 12864

Snell, John Bernard 12574

SNELLGROVE, Lawrence Ernest *From 'Rocket' to railcar* 7995

Snow Hill Station, Birmingham 8959 10918 12033

Snow ploughs: North Eastern Rly 12435

Snowdon Mountain Rly 7198* 9743–4
bibliography 9744
chronology 9744

Snowdon Mountain Railway (P. Ransome-Wallis) 7198*

Snowdon Mountain Railway (K. Turner) 9744

Snowdon Mountain Railway Travelogue 9743

Soar, Phil 8039

Social consequences of rail closures 11447

Social Science Association 11484

Socialisation of transport (H. Morrison) 11211

Socialism and the railways **K** (11137 . . . 11363) 8667

Socialist Commentary Publications 11251

SOCIÉTÉ D'ÉTUDES TECHNIQUES ET ÉCONOMIQUES *Channel Tunnel: traffic and revenue study* 9953

Société Française du Tunnel sous la Manche 9963

'SOCRATES' [pseud. of Alfred Oliver] *Elementary principles of the electric locomotive* 10616
The propulsive principles of the steam locomotive 10554

Soil analysis 10289 10987

Soil Mechanics Laboratory (B.R. (WR)) 10289 10987

Solent Rail Tour, 1966 12227

Solicitor's work [railway solicitor]: Great Western Rly 11629

Solution to our transport problems (A.Dalgleish) 11359

Some aspects of freight and terminal working 10896

Some aspects of my Connemara (P.J. Kennelly) 9827

Some aspects of railway economics (H.R. Griffiths) 10721

Some aspects of route selection for canals, railways and roads in the West Midlands 8921

Some aspects of the commercial development of British railways 10710

Some aspects of the law of carriage by railway (P.L.E. Rawlings) 11632

Some aspects of the law of carriage by railway (R.G. Plowman) 11633

Some aspects of the working in the Birmingham Traffic Division 11865

Some chapters in the history of Denby 9031

Some considerations in the economical working of goods traffic 10870

Some curiosities of railways and railway working 10869

Some facts about British railways 7953

Some features of the steam locomotive (H.G. Johnson) 10414

Some important aspects of railway traffic operation 10846

Some information, observations and conclusions concerning the handling of London's half million daily commuters by railroad in 1961 8784 11407

Some notes towards a Bibliographical History of the Stockton & Darlington and other railways, 1770–1926 7955

Some possible ways of railway organization 10730

Some present-day methods of construction and maintenance 10283

Some principles and practices of railway operation 10855

Some recent improvements in electric signalling and electric signalling apparatus 10685

Some tramway pioneers, known and unknown 10017

Some turning points in the history of the Great Western Railway 11790

Some views in the workshops (Peckett & Sons) 10100

Somerset: rail transport 8507–23
closed lines 8438
mineral railways 8509 8521–3 8543

Somerset & Dorset (the): an English cross-country railway 12459

Somerset & Dorset engineman (F.E. Stickley) 12465

Somerset and Dorset Farewell Rail Tour, 1966 8452

Somerset & Dorset locomotive history (D.L. Bradley & D. Milton) 12457

SOMERSET & DORSET RLY *Working Time Book from 4th October 1920, and Working Time Book, passenger and milk trains, from 14th September 1931* [Reprint] 12464

Somerset & Dorset Rly 12451–65 8531 12298
bibliography 12452
locomotives 12457 12460–1
Radstock area 8512
rolling stock 12458

Somerset & Dorset Railway (R. Atthill) 12452

Somerset & Dorset Railway Museum Trust 8512 12461

Sonnet

On the Completion of a Railway Bibliography

OTTLEY! Thy signal falls, the green lamp shines!
England had need of thee: too long no pen
Industrious essay'd the task, while men
Wander'd benighted in that maze of lines
Proliferate. Though now the rail declines
(By suspect interest hemm'd), and ne'er again
Such mighty splendours various meet our ken,
Still in thy work stand forth the great designs.

Directors, navvies, engines (and what oil
Hath match'd the power and poetry of steam?)
And all that human and metallic toil—
These here compound thy loving labour's theme.
Vandals the Doric Arch to dust have sent
Be then thy book our Railways' monument.

C. CORNEY

D 5 UNUSUAL FORMS OF RAILWAY AND LOCOMOTION

D 6 MINIATURE RAILWAYS

E RAILWAY ENGINEERING (Civil and Mechanical) Archaeology of railways

    E 1 BIOGRAPHIES OF RAILWAY CIVIL AND CIVIL/MECHANICAL ENGINEERS

    E 2 RAILWAY CIVIL ENGINEERING (General)

    E 3 PERMANENT WAY

    E 4 ELECTRIC RAILWAY ENGINEERING Electrification—Underground electric railways

    E 5 ARCHITECTURE AND DESIGN Bridges, viaducts, stations, tunnel entrances, etc—Archaeology of railway structures

    E 6 RAILWAY MECHANICAL ENGINEERING (General)

    E 7 LOCOMOTIVES

    E 8 STEAM LOCOMOTIVES

    E 9 – 10 ELECTRIC AND DIESEL LOCOMOTIVES

    E 9 ELECTRIC LOCOMOTIVES AND TRAINS

    E 10 DIESEL, DIESEL-ELECTRIC, AND OTHER SELF-GENERATING TYPES OF LOCOMOTIVE AND TRAIN

    E 11 ROLLING STOCK (Carriages and wagons)

    E 12 CARRIAGES

    E 13 WAGONS

    E 14 BRAKES

    E 15 SAFETY ENGINEERING Signals and signalling

    E 16 OTHER RAILWAY EQUIPMENT

F RAILWAY ADMINISTRATION Organization, finance and management, commercial aspects

    F 1 RATES, CHARGES, FARES, TOLLS AND TICKETS

    F 2 INTER-RAILWAY RELATIONS Competition—Co-operation and amalgamation—Gauge controversy

    F 3 CLEARING HOUSE SYSTEM

G RAILWAY OPERATION

    G 1 OPERATION OF RAILWAY SERVICES Train control—Station and goods depot management—Closures

    G 2 FREIGHT TRAFFIC Marshalling—Cartage

    G 3 PASSENGER TRAIN SERVICES

    G 4 RAILWAY ROAD SERVICES Omnibus and freight

    G 5 RAILWAY WATER SERVICES Docks and harbours—Train ferries and boat trains

    G 6 RAILWAY AIR SERVICES

    G 7 ANCILLARY SERVICES Hotels and catering—Station kiosks and bookstalls—Camping coaches

    G 8 RESEARCH (operational and maintenance)

    G 9 PUBLIC RELATIONS AND PUBLICITY

H RAILWAY LIFE AND LABOUR Work and working conditions—Trade unions—Strikes—Staff welfare—Memoirs of railway life

K RAILWAYS AND THE NATION Railways within the framework of national life—Railway policy—Integration of transport modes—Planning—Railways and politics

    K 1 RAILWAYS AND SOCIETY Railways and the life of the people—Urban and suburban development—Commuting—Increased facilities for travel—Holidays and tourism—Objections to Sunday trains (19th century)—Social aspects of rail closures